THIS BIBLE BELONGS TO

THE FAMILY REGISTER

of_____

MARRIAGES

BIRTHS

_____

_____

_____

_____

_____

_____

_____

_____

_____

_____

_____

_____

_____

_____

BIRTHS

DEATHS

TANAKH תנ״ך

THE HOLY SCRIPTURES

The New JPS Translation
According to the Traditional Hebrew Text

TORAH	תורה
NEVI'IM	נביאים
KETHUVIM	כתובים

TANAKH תנ"ך
THE HOLY SCRIPTURES

The New JPS Translation
According to the Traditional Hebrew Text

THE JEWISH PUBLICATION SOCIETY
Philadelphia · Jerusalem

Library of Congress Cataloging in Publication Data

Bible. O.T. English. 1985.
  Tanakh, a new translation of the Holy Scriptures
according to the traditional Hebrew text.

  I. Jewish Publication Society.
II. Title.
BS896.A1P45   1985   221.5'2   85-10006
ISBN 0-8276-0252-9 (cloth)
     0-8276-0264-2 (leatherette)

25   24   23   22   21   20

19   18   17   16   15   14

13   12   11

Contents

For weekly Sabbath readings, see page ix.

NEVI'IM THE PROPHETS

KETHUVIM THE WRITINGS

Table of Scriptural Readings

TORAH		NEVI'IM

Weekly Sabbath Readings

GENESIS

בראשית	1.1-6.8	Isaiah 42.5-43.10 (42.5-21)[a]
נח	6.9-11.32	Isaiah 54.1-55.5 (54.1-10)
לך לך	12.1-17.27	Isaiah 40.27-41.16
וירא	18.1-22.24	II Kings 4.1-37 (4.1-23)
חיי שרה	23.1-25.18	I Kings 1.1-31
תולדת	25.19-28.9	Malachi 1.1-2.7
ויצא	28.10-32.3	Hosea 12.13-14.10; 14.7 or Micah 7.18 (11.7-12.12)
וישלח	32.4-36.43	Hosea 11.7-12.12 (Obadiah 1.1-21)
וישב	37.1-40.23	Amos 2.6-3.8
מקץ	41.1-44.17	I Kings 3.15-4.1
ויגש	44.18-47.27	Ezekiel 37.15-28
ויחי	47.28-50.26	I Kings 2.1-12

EXODUS

שמות	1.1-6.1	Isaiah 27.6-28.13; 29.22, 23 (Jeremiah 1.1-2.3)
וארא	6.2-9.35	Ezekiel 28.25-29.21
בא	10.1-13.16	Jeremiah 46.13-28
בשלח	13.17-17.16	Judges 4.4-5.31 (5.1-31)
יתרו	18.1-20.26	Isaiah 6.1-7.6; 9.5, 6 (6.1-13)
משפטים	21.1-24.18	Jeremiah 34.8-22; 33.25, 26
תרומה	25.1-27.19	I Kings 5.26-6.13
תצוה	27.20-30.10	Ezekiel 43.10-27
כי תשא	30.11-34.35	I Kings 18.1-39 (18.20-39)
ויקהל	35.1-38.20	I Kings 7.40-50 (7.13-26)
פקודי	38.21-40.38	I Kings 7.51-8.21 (7.40-50)

[a] *Parentheses indicate Sephardi ritual.*

TORAH		NEVI'IM

LEVITICUS

ויקרא	1.1-5.26	Isaiah 43.21-44.23
צו	6.1-8.36	Jeremiah 7.21-8.3; 9.22, 23
שמיני	9.1-11.47	II Samuel 6.1-7.17 (6.1-19)
תזריע	12.1-13.59	II Kings 4.42-5.19
מצרע	14.1-15.33	II Kings 7.3-20
אחרי מות	16.1-18.30	Ezekiel 22.1-19 (22.1-16)
קדשים	19.1-20.27	Amos 9.7-15 (Ezekiel 20.2-20)
אמר	21.1-24.23	Ezekiel 44.15-31
בהר סיני	25.1-26.2	Jeremiah 32.6-27
בחקתי	26.3-27.34	Jeremiah 16.19-17.14

NUMBERS

במדבר	1.1-4.20	Hosea 2.1-22
נשא	4.21-7.89	Judges 13.2-25
בהעלתך	8.1-12.16	Zechariah 2.14-4.7
שלח לך	13.1-15.41	Joshua 2.1-24
קרח	16.1-18.32	I Samuel 11.14-12.22
חקת	19.1-22.1	Judges 11.1-33
בלק	22.2-25.9	Micah 5.6-6.8
פינחס	25.10-30.1	I Kings 18.46-19.21
מטות	30.2-32.42	Jeremiah 1.1-2.3
מסעי	33.1-36.13	Jeremiah 2.4-28; 3.4 (2.4-28; 4.1, 2)

DEUTERONOMY

דברים	1.1-3.22	Isaiah 1.1-27
ואתחנן	3.23-7.11	Isaiah 40.1-26
עקב	7.12-11.25	Isaiah 49.14-51.3
ראה	11.26-16.17	Isaiah 54.11-55.5
שפטים	16.18-21.9	Isaiah 51.12-52.12
כי תצא	21.10-25.19	Isaiah 54.1-10
כי תבוא	26.1-29.8	Isaiah 60.1-22
נצבים	29.9-30.20	Isaiah 61.10-63.9
וילך	31.1-30	Isaiah 55.6-56.8
האזינו	32.1-52	II Samuel 22.1-51
וזאת הברכה	33.1-34.12	Joshua 1.1-18 (1.1-9)

	TORAH	NEVI'IM

Readings for Special Sabbaths

	TORAH	NEVI'IM
Sabbath coinciding with Rosh Hodesh	Weekly portion and Numbers 28.9-15	Isaiah 66.1-24
Sabbath immediately preceding Rosh Hodesh	Weekly portion	I Samuel 20.18-42
Shekalim	Weekly portion and Exodus 30.11-16	II Kings 12.1-17 (11.17-12.17)
Zakhor	Weekly portion and Deuteronomy 25.17-19	I Samuel 15.2-34 (15.1-34)
Parah	Weekly portion and Numbers 19.1-22	Ezekiel 36.16-38 (36.16-36)
Ha-Hodesh	Weekly portion and Exodus 12.1-20	Ezekiel 45.16-46.18 (45.18-46.15)
Ha-Gadol	Weekly portion	Malachi 3.4-24
First Sabbath Hanukkah	Weekly portion and Numbers 7.1-11 plus the verses relating to the prince (*nasi*) of the day corresponding to the day of Hanukkah	Zechariah 2.14-4.7
Second Sabbath Hanukkah	Weekly portion and Hanukkah portions as above	I Kings 7.40-50

	TORAH	NEVI'IM

Readings for the Days of Awe

Rosh Ha-Shanah

First Day	Genesis 21.1-34; Numbers 29.1-6	I Samuel 1.1-2.10
Second Day	Genesis 22.1-24; Numbers 29.1-6	Jeremiah 31.1-19
Sabbath Shuvah	Weekly portion	Hosea 14.2-10; Micah 7.18-20, or Hosea 14.2-10; Joel 2.15-17 (Hosea 14.2-10; Micah 7.18-20)

Yom Kippur

Morning	Leviticus 16.1-34; Numbers 29.7-11	Isaiah 57.14-58.14
Afternoon	Leviticus 18.1-30	Jonah 1.1-4.11; Micah 7.18-20

Readings for the Festivals

Sukkoth (Tabernacles)

First Day	Leviticus 22.26-23.44; Numbers 29.12-16	Zechariah 14.1-21
Second Day	Leviticus 22.26-23.44; Numbers 29.12-16	I Kings 8.2-21
Sabbath during the Middle Days	Exodus 33.12-34.26; Daily portion from Numbers 29	Ezekiel 38.18-39.16
Eighth Day	Deuteronomy 14.22-16.17; Numbers 29.35-30.1	I Kings 8.54-66
Simhat Torah	Deuteronomy 33.1-34.12; Genesis 1.1-2.3; Numbers 29.35-30.1	Joshua 1.1-18 (1.1-9)

	TORAH	NEVI'IM
Pesah (Passover)		
First Day	Exodus 12.21-51; Numbers 28.16-25	Joshua 3.5-7; 5.2-6.1; 6.27 (5.2-6.1)
Second Day	Leviticus 22.26-23.44; Numbers 28.16-25	II Kings 23.1-9; 21-25
Sabbath during the Middle Days	Exodus 33.12-34.26; Numbers 28.19-25	Ezekiel 36.37-37.14 (37.1-14)
Seventh Day	Exodus 13.17-15.26; Numbers 28.19-25	II Samuel 22.1-51
Eighth Day	Deuteronomy 15.19-16.17; Numbers 28.19-25	Isaiah 10.32-12.6
Shavuoth (Pentecost)		
First Day	Exodus 19.1-20.23; Numbers 28.26-31	Ezekiel 1.1-28; 3.12
Second Day	Deuteronomy 15.19-16.17[a] Numbers 28.26-31	Habakkuk 3.1-19 (2.20-3.19)

Readings on Weekday Occasions

Purim	Exodus 17.8-16	
Ninth of Av		
Morning	Deuteronomy 4.25-40	Jeremiah 8.13-9.23
Afternoon	Exodus 32.11-14; 34.1-10	Isaiah 55.6-56.8 (Hosea 14.2-10; Micah 7.18-20)
Public Fast Days	Exodus 32.11-14; 34.1-10	Isaiah 55.6-56.8 (none)

[a] *On Sabbath, 14.22-16.17*

Readings of the Five Megilloth

The Song of Songs	Sabbath during Pesah (Passover)
Ruth	Shavuoth (Pentecost)
Lamentations	Ninth of Av
Ecclesiastes	Sabbath during Sukkoth (Tabernacles)
Esther	Purim

Preface

This translation of *Tanakh,* the Holy Scriptures, produced by the Jewish Publication Society, was made directly from the traditional Hebrew text into the idiom of modern English. It represents the collaboration of academic scholars with rabbis from the three largest branches of organized Jewish religious life in America. Begun in 1955, the ongoing translation was published in three main stages: *The Torah* in 1962, *The Prophets (Nevi'im)* in 1978, and *The Writings (Kethuvim)* in 1982. These three volumes, with revisions, are now brought together in a complete English *Tanakh (Torah-Nevi'im-Kethuvim),* the latest link in the chain of Jewish Bible translations.

On the History of Bible Translation

Bible translation began about 2,200 years ago, in the third century B.C.E., as the large Jewish population of Alexandria, Egypt, came under the influence of Hellenism. When the Greek language replaced Hebrew and Aramaic as their vernacular, and the Torah in its Hebrew original was no longer commonly understood, a translation into Greek was made for the Jewish community of Alexandria. This translation came to be known as the Septuagint, Latin for "seventy," because of the legend that the committee of translators numbered seventy-two, six elders from each of the twelve tribes of Israel.

In the last few centuries B.C.E., the Jews who lived to the north and east of Judea also found the Hebrew Bible difficult to understand, for their spoken language had become largely Aramaic. Translations into Aramaic, first of the Torah and then of the rest of the Bible, became known as the Targums.

The Septuagint and the Targums are not only the oldest translations of the Bible but also the most influential. Down to our own day, virtually every Christian translation has followed the methods of the Jewish translators who created the Septuagint, and generally followed their renderings of the Hebrew as well. The Christian translators also were influenced by the interpretation of the Hebrew text set forth in the Targums (much of it in oral form at the time) and by the writings of the Jewish philosopher-interpreter Philo of Alexandria (died about 45 C.E.).

The forerunners and leaders of the Renaissance and the Reformation (fourteenth-fifteenth centuries), and especially Martin Luther and William Tyndale (sixteenth century), made use of Latin translations of the classic Jewish commentators Rashi, Ibn Ezra, and Kimhi (eleventh-thirteenth centuries), whose works were imbued with the direct knowledge of the Targums. Luther was greatly indebted to Nicholas of Lyre (1270–1349), who had adopted Rashi's exegesis for his Latin Bible commentary. Rashi's influence on all authorized and most unofficial English translations of the Hebrew Bible becomes evident when Tyndale's dependence on Luther is considered. Tyndale is central to many subsequent English translations: the King James Version of 1611, the (British) Revised Version of 1881–1885, the American Standard Version of 1901, and especially the Revised Standard Version of 1952.

Alongside the close, literal method of Bible translation, the earliest Jewish translators were also influenced by the widely held view that, along with the Written Law *(torah she-biktav),* God had given Moses on Mount Sinai an Oral Law *(torah she-be'al peh)* as well; so that to comprehend God's Torah fully and correctly, it was essential to make use of both. Thus, when a translation of the Hebrew Bible into the Judeo-Arabic vernacular was deemed necessary for Jewry in Moslem countries toward the end of the first millennium, the noted philologian, philosopher, and community leader Saadia Gaon (882–942) produced a version that incorporated traditional Jewish interpretation but was not based on word-for-word translation; at the same time, it was a model of clarity and stylistic elegance. The present version is in the spirit of Saadia.

With the growth of Christianity in the first century, the Church adopted the Septuagint as its Bible, and the Septuagint was translated into the languages of the various Christian communities. As Greek began to give way to Latin in the Roman Empire, it was only a matter of time before a Latin translation of Scripture became the recognized Bible of the Church. The Church father Jerome (c. 340–420) produced the official Latin version. Drawing on Jewish tradition and consulting Jewish teachers, he achieved what came to be known as the Vulgate, the Bible in the language of the common people. The Vulgate, the Bible of European Christianity until the Reformation, is clearly the most significant Bible translation after the Septuagint.

With the rise of Protestantism in Europe, scholars within this movement set themselves the task of making the Bible available in the various vernaculars of the time. By 1526 the first parts of two notable translations began to appear: Martin Luther's in German and William Tyndale's in English. The latter, by way of several subsequent revisions, became the King James Version of 1611. The more modern English versions—such as *The Holy Scriptures* by the American rabbi Isaac Leeser (1855), the (British) Revised Version (1881–1885), the American Standard Version (1901), the Jewish Publication Society's *The Holy Scriptures* (1917), and the (American) Revised Standard Version (1952)—made extensive use of the King James.

On the Making of the New Translation

After World War II, when the Jewish Publication Society began to consider a new edition of the Bible, the idea of a modest revision of the 1917 translation met with resistance, and the concept of a completely new translation gradually took hold. The proposed translation would reproduce the Hebrew idiomatically and reflect contemporary scholarship, thus laying emphasis upon intelligibility and correctness. It would make critical use of the early rabbinic and medieval Jewish commentators, grammarians, and philologians and would rely on the traditional Hebrew text, avoiding emendations. The need for this new translation was the focus of the Jewish Publication Society's annual meeting in 1953. Later that year the Society announced its intention to proceed with the project, and in 1955 the committee of translators began their task.

Harry M. Orlinsky, Professor of Bible at Hebrew Union College–Jewish Institute of Religion (New York), was asked to serve as editor-in-chief for the new translation, along with H. L. Ginsberg, Professor of Bible at the Jewish Theological Seminary, and Ephraim A. Speiser, Professor of Semitic and Oriental Languages at the University of Pennsylvania, as fellow editors. Associated with them were three rabbis: Max Arzt, Bernard J. Bamberger, and Harry Freedman, representing the Conservative, Reform, and Orthodox branches of organized Jewish religious life. Solomon Grayzel, editor of the Jewish Publication Society, served as secretary of the committee.

The committee profited much from the work of previous translators; the present rendering, however, is essentially a new translation. A few of its characteristics may be noted. The committee undertook to follow faithfully the traditional Hebrew text, but there were certain points at which footnotes appeared necessary: (1) where the committee had to admit that it did not understand a word or passage; (2) where an alternative rendering was possible; (3) where an old rendering, no longer retained, was so well known that it would very likely be missed, in which case the traditional translation was given in the name of "Others" (usually referring to the Society's version of 1917); (4) where the understanding of a passage could be facilitated by reference to another passage elsewhere in the Bible; and (5) where important textual variants are to be found in some of the ancient manuscripts or versions of the Bible.

The translators avoided obsolete words and phrases and, whenever possible, rendered Hebrew idioms by means of their normal English equivalents. For the second person singular, the modern "you" was used instead of the archaic "thou," even when referring to the Deity ("You"). A further obvious difference between this translation and most of the older ones is in the rendering of the Hebrew particle *waw*, which is usually translated "and." Biblical Hebrew demanded the frequent use of the *waw*, but in that style it had the force not only of "and" but also of "however," "but," "yet," "when," and any number of other such words and particles, or none at all that can be translated into English. Always to render it as "and" is to misrepresent the Hebrew rather than be faithful to it. Consequently, the committee translated the particle as the sense required, or left it untranslated.

The chapter and verse divisions found in the printed Bible are indispensable as a system of precise reference, but they do not always coincide with the organic divisions of the text. The chapter divisions, whose origin is neither ancient nor Jewish but medieval Christian, sometimes join or separate the wrong paragraphs, sentences, or even parts of sentences. The verse divisions, though considerably older and of Jewish origin, sometimes join together parts of different sentences or separate from each other parts of the same sentence. The translation of Saadia Gaon often does not correspond to our chapter divisions, which did not exist in his day. More noteworthy is the readiness with which he joined separate verses of the Hebrew text (whose authority he did not question) into single sentences when the sense required it. Thus, in joining Genesis 7.24 and 8.1 into a single sentence, or combining the last part of 1 Kings 6.38 with 7.1, the present translation is following the example of Saadia. The attentive reader will discover other instances in which the translators have followed what they considered to be the logical units of meaning even when they did not coincide with the conventional chapters and verses. The latter, however, are marked and numbered throughout.

The preface to the first edition of *The Torah* was dated September 25, 1962, Erev Rosh Ha-Shanah 5723. A second edition, incorporating some changes by the translators, came out five years later. The committee also produced translations of *The Five Megilloth and Jonah* (1969), *Isaiah* (1973), and *Jeremiah* (1974). The latter two books and Jonah were incorporated, with some corrections and revisions, into the complete translation of *The Prophets (Nevi'im)*. For this volume, which was published in 1978, Professor Ginsberg served as editor, in association with Professor Orlinsky. Whereas Professor Orlinsky had initially prepared a draft translation of the entire Torah, individual members of the committee undertook to prepare a draft of an entire prophetic book or part of a book; but, as in translating the Torah, everyone had an opportunity to criticize the draft and to offer detailed suggestions at periodic committee sessions, which were presided over by Rabbi Bamberger. Differences of opinion were settled by majority vote.

In preparing the translation of *The Prophets*, the translators faced a recurring problem that deserves special mention. The prophetic books contain many passages whose meaning is uncertain. Thus, in order to provide an intelligible rendering, modern scholars have resorted to emending the Hebrew text. Some of these emendations derive from the ancient translators, especially of the Septuagint and the Targums, who had before them a Hebrew text that sometimes differed from today's traditional text. Where these ancient versions provide no help, some scholars have made conjectural emendations of their own. Many modern English versions contain translations of emended texts, sometimes without citing any departure from the traditional Hebrew text.

Like the translation of *The Torah*, the present translation of the prophetic books adheres strictly to the traditional Hebrew text; but where the text remains obscure and an alteration provides marked clarification, a footnote is offered with a rendering of the suggested emendation. If the emendation is based on one or two ancient versions, they are mentioned by name; if more than two versions agree, they are summed up as "ancient versions." Conjectural emendations are introduced by "Emendation yields." Sometimes, however, it was deemed sufficient to offer only a change of vowels, and such modifications are indicated by "Change of vocalization yields." In all cases, the emendation is given in a footnote, which may be readily disregarded by those who reject it on either scholarly or religious grounds. The only exceptions involve such changes in grammatical form as those, say, from second person to third or from singular to plural. In such rare instances, the change is incorporated in the text, and the traditional Hebrew is translated in a footnote.

The committee of translators for *The Writings (Kethuvim)*, the third part of the Hebrew Bible, was set up by the Jewish Publication Society in 1966. It consisted of Moshe Greenberg, now Professor of Bible at the Hebrew University, Jonas C. Greenfield, now Professor of Semitic Languages at the Hebrew University, and Nahum M. Sarna, Professor of Biblical Studies at Brandeis University, in association with Rabbis Saul Leeman, Martin S. Rozenberg, and David Shapiro of the Conservative, Reform, and Orthodox movements. Chaim Potok, then editor of the Society, served as secretary of the committee.

The present English rendering of *Kethuvim*, like *Torah* and *Nevi'im*, is based on the traditional Hebrew text—its consonants, vowels, and syntactical divisions—although the traditional accentuation occasionally has been replaced by an alternative construction. Following the approach of the original committee, the entire gamut of biblical interpretation, ancient and modern, Jewish and non-Jewish, has been consulted, and, whenever possible, the results of modern study of the languages and cultures of the ancient Near East have been brought to bear on the biblical text. In choosing between alternatives, however, just as antiquity was not in itself a disqualification, so modernity was not in itself a recommendation. Divergences of the present translation from recent renderings reflect the committee's judgment that certain innovations, though interesting, are too speculative for adoption in the present state of knowledge. The as yet imperfect understanding of the language of the Bible, or what appears to be some disorder in the Hebrew text, makes sure translation of many passages impossible. This uncertainty in *Kethuvim* is indicated in a note; and, where the Hebrew text permits, alternative renderings have been offered. However, emendations of the text of *Kethuvim*—except for the five *Megilloth*—were not proposed, and notes were kept to a minimum.

Some passages in *Kethuvim* are identical or very similar to passages in *Torah* and *Nevi'im*. The rendering of these passages in *Kethuvim* generally follows the wording in the earlier books; on occasion, however, owing to various considerations, divergences in style and translation will be found.

For example, in the presentation of the poetry of the Psalms, it was deemed fitting, because of their liturgical use, to indicate the thought units through appropriate indentation. The text of *Kethuvim* frequently presented the translators with extraordinary difficulties, for it is hardly possible to convey in English the fullness of the Hebrew, with its ambiguities, its overtones, and the richness that it carries from centuries of use. Still, it was their goal to transmit something of the directness, the simplicity, and the uniquely Israelite expressions of piety that are so essential to the sublimity of the Hebrew Bible.

The committee's translation of *The Psalms* appeared in 1973; of *The Book of Job*, in 1980. The two were incorporated, with revisions, into the complete translations of *The Writings (Kethuvim)*, which appeared in 1982.

For this one-volume edition of *Tanakh*, the translation of *The Torah*, first published twenty years earlier, has undergone more revision than the more recent publications of *The Prophets* and *The Writings*. A number of the changes had already been projected in *Notes on the New Translation of the Torah*, edited by Harry M. Orlinsky and published by the Society in 1969. Subsequent research on the text has led to further revisions in the translations of *Torah* and some revisions in *Nevi'im* as well.

Ephraim Speiser, of the original committee, died in June 1965. Max Arzt, also an active member of the original committee, died in 1975, when the work of translating the prophetic books was almost complete. Since the appearance of *The Prophets* and *The Writings*, Bernard J. Bamberger, Solomon Grayzel, and Harry Freedman have also passed on. Their memory, and their scholarship, will be for a blessing.

The Jewish Publication Society joins the members of the committees of translators in the hope that the results of our labors will find favor with God and man.

The Jewish Publication Society
September 15, 1985

ערב ראש השנה תשמ"ו

Glossary for the Footnotes

Akkadian	An ancient Semitic language spoken in Mesopotamia; its chief dialects were Babylonian and Assyrian.
Aquila	A second-century convert to Judaism who made a literal translation of the Bible into Greek.
Berakhot	One of the treatises of the Mishnah and the Talmud.
Ibn Ezra	Rabbi Abraham ibn Ezra, a Bible commentator and grammarian who lived in Spain in the twelfth century.
Kethib	The way a word, usually unvocalized, is written in the Bible; see *qere*.
Kimhi	Rabbi David Kimhi (Radak), a Bible commentator and grammarian who lived in Southern France in the late twelfth and early thirteenth centuries.
Masorah	The text of the Bible as transmitted, with vowel signs and accents.
Mishnah	The code of Jewish law prepared by Rabbi Judah ha-Nasi about 200 C.E. The word is usually followed by the name of the relevant treatise.
Peshitta	A translation of the Bible into Syriac, parts of which are said to have been made in the first century C.E.
Qere	The way the Masorah requires a word to be read, especially when it diverges from the *kethib*.
Qumran	The site of the caves where Bible manuscripts were found in 1949/50. The manuscripts are identified by such symbols as 4QSam^a (for manuscript a of Samuel, found in the fourth cave of Qumran); 1QIs^a (for manuscript a of Isaiah found in the first cave of Qumran).

Rashbam	Rabbi Shmuel ben Meir, a grandson of Rashi, who commented on the Torah.
Rashi	Rabbi Shlomo Yitzhaki, the best-known Jewish commentator on the Bible. He lived in France at the end of the eleventh century.
Saadia	A *gaon,* i.e., a head of a Babylonian talmudic academy, in the early part of the tenth century. His works include the famous translation of the Bible into Arabic.
Septuagint	The oldest Jewish translation of the Bible, into Greek. The Torah translation dates from the third century B.C.E; other books of the Bible were translated somewhat later.
Syriac	See *Peshitta.*
Targum	A Jewish translation of the Bible into Aramaic, a language once widely spoken in Western Asia, of which Syriac was a later development.
Ugaritic	A language of inscriptions found at Ras Shamra, on the Syrian coast, in the second millennium B.C.E. Both the language and its literature have shed much light on the Hebrew Bible.
Vulgate	The Latin translation of the Bible made by the Church father Jerome about the year 400 C.E. It became the official Bible of the Roman Catholic Church.

Abbreviations and Terms

Cf.	A reference to another version, or to a cognate language, that justifies the translation adopted.
Heb.	The Hebrew word or phrase in transliteration, especially when necessary to point out a pun, homonym, or the like. *Heb.* is also used to indicate the literal wording for which a superior rendering was employed; see Genesis 46.23, note d, or 49.9, note a. An example of a somewhat different type may be seen at Exodus 21.22, note e.
I.e.	An explanation, to avoid adding words to the text, in order to clarify the translation; see Exodus 22.29, note j.
Lit.	For the literal translation of a word or phrase that was given an idiomatic or somewhat free translation in the text; see Genesis 30.27, note j, and 30.38, k; or 43.21, note b, and 43.34, note c; or Deuteronomy 18.1, note a (where the Hebrew and English cannot agree in number).
Meaning of Heb. uncertain	Where the translation represents the best that the committee could achieve with an elusive or difficult text. In some cases the text may be unintelligible because of corruption.
Moved up	Where clarity required the shifting of a word or phrase within a verse or from one verse to another; see Genesis 10.14, note d.
Or	Indicates an alternative reading that the committee found almost as acceptable as the one adopted for the text.

Others   Indicates a well-known traditional translation, especially if it was used in the older (1917) JPS version, that the committee does not find acceptable even as an alternative reading.

See   Frequently used in place of *cf.,* but usually intended to begin a note attached to another passage in the Bible.

TANAKH תנ"ך

THE HOLY SCRIPTURES

The New JPS Translation
According to the Traditional Hebrew Text

תורה

TORAH

THE FIVE BOOKS OF MOSES

GENESIS

1 When God began to create[a] heaven and earth—[2]the earth being unformed and void, with darkness over the surface of the deep and a wind from[b] God sweeping over the water—[3] God said, "Let there be light"; and there was light. [4]God saw that the light was good, and God separated the light from the darkness. [5]God called the light Day, and the darkness He called Night. And there was evening and there was morning, a first day.[c]

[6]God said, "Let there be an expanse in the midst of the water, that it may separate water from water." [7]God made the expanse, and it separated the water which was below the expanse from the water which was above the expanse. And it was so. [8]God called the expanse Sky. And there was evening and there was morning, a second day.

[9]God said, "Let the water below the sky be gathered into one area, that the dry land may appear." And it was so. [10]God called the dry land Earth, and the gathering of waters He called Seas. And God saw that this was good. [11]And God said, "Let the earth sprout vegetation: seed-bearing plants, fruit trees of every kind on earth that bear fruit with the seed in it." And it was so. [12]The earth brought forth vegetation: seed-bearing plants of every kind, and trees of every kind bearing fruit with the seed in it. And God saw that this was good. [13]And there was evening and there was morning, a third day.

[14]God said, "Let there be lights in the expanse of the sky to separate day from night; they shall serve as signs for the set times—the days and the years; [15]and they shall serve as lights in the expanse of the sky to shine upon the earth." And it was so. [16]God made the two great lights, the greater light to dominate the day and the lesser light to dominate the night, and the stars. [17]And God set them in the expanse of the sky to shine upon the earth, [18]to dominate the day and the night, and to separate light from darkness. And God saw that this was good. [19]And there was evening and there was morning, a fourth day.

[a] Others "In the beginning God created."
[b] Others "the spirit of."
[c] Others "one day."

²⁰God said, "Let the waters bring forth swarms of living creatures, and birds that fly above the earth across the expanse of the sky." ²¹God created the great sea monsters, and all the living creatures of every kind that creep, which the waters brought forth in swarms, and all the winged birds of every kind. And God saw that this was good. ²²God blessed them, saying, "Be fertile and increase, fill the waters in the seas, and let the birds increase on the earth." ²³And there was evening and there was morning, a fifth day.

²⁴God said, "Let the earth bring forth every kind of living creature: cattle, creeping things, and wild beasts of every kind." And it was so. ²⁵God made wild beasts of every kind and cattle of every kind, and all kinds of creeping things of the earth. And God saw that this was good. ²⁶And God said, "Let us make man in our image, after our likeness. They shall rule the fish of the sea, the birds of the sky, the cattle, the whole earth, and all the creeping things that creep on earth." ²⁷And God created man in His image, in the image of God He created him; male and female He created them. ²⁸God blessed them and God said to them, "Be fertile and increase, fill the earth and master it; and rule the fish of the sea, the birds of the sky, and all the living things that creep on earth."

²⁹God said, "See, I give you every seed-bearing plant that is upon all the earth, and every tree that has seed-bearing fruit; they shall be yours for food. ³⁰And to all the animals on land, to all the birds of the sky, and to everything that creeps on earth, in which there is the breath of life, [I give] all the green plants for food." And it was so. ³¹And God saw all that He had made, and found it very good. And there was evening and there was morning, the sixth day.

2 The heaven and the earth were finished, and all their array. ²On the seventh day God finished the work that He had been doing, and He ceased^a on the seventh day from all the work that He had done. ³And God blessed the seventh day and declared it holy, because on it God ceased from all the work of creation that He had done. ⁴Such is the story of heaven and earth when they were created.

When the LORD God made earth and heaven—⁵when no shrub of the field was yet on earth and no grasses of the field had yet sprouted, because

ª *Or "rested."*

the LORD God had not sent rain upon the earth and there was no man to till the soil, 6but a flow would well up from the ground and water the whole surface of the earth—7the LORD God formed manb from the dust of the earth.c He blew into his nostrils the breath of life, and man became a living being.

8The LORD God planted a garden in Eden, in the east, and placed there the man whom He had formed. 9And from the ground the LORD God caused to grow every tree that was pleasing to the sight and good for food, with the tree of life in the middle of the garden, and the tree of knowledge of good and bad.

10A river issues from Eden to water the garden, and it then divides and becomes four branches. 11The name of the first is Pishon, the one that winds through the whole land of Havilah, where the gold is. (12The gold of that land is good; bdellium is there, and lapis lazuli.d) 13The name of the second river is Gihon, the one that winds through the whole land of Cush. 14The name of the third river is Tigris, the one that flows east of Asshur. And the fourth river is the Euphrates.

15The LORD God took the man and placed him in the garden of Eden, to till it and tend it. 16And the LORD God commanded the man, saying, "Of every tree of the garden you are free to eat; 17but as for the tree of knowledge of good and bad, you must not eat of it; for as soon as you eat of it, you shall die."

18The LORD God said, "It is not good for man to be alone; I will make a fitting helper for him." 19And the LORD God formed out of the earth all the wild beasts and all the birds of the sky, and brought them to the man to see what he would call them; and whatever the man called each living creature, that would be its name. 20And the man gave names to all the cattle and to the birds of the sky and to all the wild beasts; but for Adam no fitting helper was found. 21So the LORD God cast a deep sleep upon the man; and, while he slept, He took one of his ribs and closed up the flesh at that spot. 22And the LORD God fashioned the rib that He had taken from the man into a woman; and He brought her to the man. 23Then the man said,

> "This one at last
> Is bone of my bones
> And flesh of my flesh.
> This one shall be called Woman,e
> For from manf was she taken."

b *Heb.* 'adam.
c *Heb.* 'adamah.
d *Others "onyx"; meaning of Heb.* shoham *uncertain.*
e *Heb.* 'ishshah.
f *Heb.* 'ish.

24Hence a man leaves his father and mother and clings to his wife, so that they become one flesh.

25The two of them were naked,g the man and his wife, yet they felt no shame. **3** 1Now the serpent was the shrewdest of all the wild beasts that the LORD God had made. He said to the woman, "Did God really say: You shall not eat of any tree of the garden?" 2The woman replied to the serpent, "We may eat of the fruit of the other trees of the garden. 3It is only about fruit of the tree in the middle of the garden that God said: 'You shall not eat of it or touch it, lest you die.'" 4And the serpent said to the woman, "You are not going to die, 5but God knows that as soon as you eat of it your eyes will be opened and you will be like a-divine beings who know-a good and bad." 6When the woman saw that the tree was good for eating and a delight to the eyes, and that the tree was desirable as a source of wisdom, she took of its fruit and ate. She also gave some to her husband, and he ate. 7Then the eyes of both of them were opened and they perceived that they were naked; and they sewed together fig leaves and made themselves loincloths.

8They heard the sound of the LORD God moving about in the garden at the breezy time of day; and the man and his wife hid from the LORD God among the trees of the garden. 9The LORD God called out to the man and said to him, "Where are you?" 10He replied, "I heard the sound of You in the garden, and I was afraid because I was naked, so I hid." 11Then He asked, "Who told you that you were naked? Did you eat of the tree from which I had forbidden you to eat?" 12The man said, "The woman You put at my side—she gave me of the tree, and I ate." 13And the LORD God said to the woman, "What is this you have done!" The woman replied, "The serpent duped me, and I ate." 14Then the LORD God said to the serpent,

> "Because you did this,
> More cursed shall you be
> Than all cattle
> And all the wild beasts:
> On your belly shall you crawl
> And dirt shall you eat
> All the days of your life.
> 15I will put enmity
> Between you and the woman,

g Heb. 'arummim, play on 'arum "shrewd" in 3.1.

a-a Others "God, who knows."

And between your offspring and hers;
They shall strike at your head,
And you shall strike at their heel."

16And to the woman He said,
"I will make most severe
Your pangs in childbearing;
In pain shall you bear children.
Yet your urge shall be for your husband,
And he shall rule over you."

17To Adam He said, "Because you did as your wife said and ate of the tree about which I commanded you, 'You shall not eat of it,'
Cursed be the ground because of you;
By toil shall you eat of it
All the days of your life:
18Thorns and thistles shall it sprout for you.
But your food shall be the grasses of the field;
19By the sweat of your brow
Shall you get bread to eat,
Until you return to the ground—
For from it you were taken.
For dust you are,
And to dust you shall return."

20The man named his wife Eve,b because she was the mother of all the living.c 21And the LORD God made garments of skins for Adam and his wife, and clothed them.

22And the LORD God said, "Now that the man has become like one of us, knowing good and bad, what if he should stretch out his hand and take also from the tree of life and eat, and live forever!" 23So the LORD God banished him from the garden of Eden, to till the soil from which he was taken. 24He drove the man out, and stationed east of the garden of Eden the cherubim and the fiery ever-turning sword, to guard the way to the tree of life.

4 Now the man knewa his wife Eve, and she conceived and bore Cain, saying, "I have gainedb a male child with the help of the LORD." 2She then bore his brother Abel. Abel became a keeper of sheep, and Cain

b *Heb.* hawwah.
c *Heb.* hay.

a *Heb.* yada', *often in a sexual sense.*
b *Heb.* qanithi, *connected with "Cain."*

became a tiller of the soil. ³In the course of time, Cain brought an offering to the LORD from the fruit of the soil; ⁴and Abel, for his part, brought the choicest of the firstlings of his flock. The LORD paid heed to Abel and his offering, ⁵but to Cain and his offering He paid no heed. Cain was much distressed and his face fell. ⁶And the LORD said to Cain,

"Why are you distressed,
And why is your face fallen?
^{7c}Surely, if you do right,
There is uplift.
But if you do not do right
Sin couches at the door;
Its urge is toward you,
Yet you can be its master."

⁸Cain said to his brother Abel^d . . . and when they were in the field, Cain set upon his brother Abel and killed him. ⁹The LORD said to Cain, "Where is your brother Abel?" And he said, "I do not know. Am I my brother's keeper?" ¹⁰Then He said, "What have you done? Hark, your brother's blood cries out to Me from the ground! ¹¹Therefore, you shall be more cursed than the ground,^e which opened its mouth to receive your brother's blood from your hand. ¹²If you till the soil, it shall no longer yield its strength to you. You shall become a ceaseless wanderer on earth."

¹³Cain said to the LORD, "My punishment is too great to bear! ¹⁴Since You have banished me this day from the soil, and I must avoid Your presence and become a restless wanderer on earth—anyone who meets me may kill me!" ¹⁵The LORD said to him, "I promise, if anyone kills Cain, sevenfold vengeance shall be taken on him." And the LORD put a mark on Cain, lest anyone who met him should kill him. ¹⁶Cain left the presence of the LORD and settled in the land of Nod, east of Eden.

¹⁷Cain knew his wife, and she conceived and bore Enoch. And he then founded a city, and named the city after his son Enoch. ¹⁸To Enoch was born Irad, and Irad begot Mehujael, and Mehujael^f begot Methusael, and Methusael begot Lamech. ¹⁹ Lamech took to himself two wives: the name of the one was Adah, and the name of the other was Zillah. ²⁰Adah bore Jabal; he was the ancestor of those who dwell in tents and amidst herds. ²¹And the name of his brother was Jubal; he was the ancestor of all who play the lyre and the pipe. ²²As for Zillah, she bore Tubal-cain, who forged

---

^c *Meaning of verse uncertain.*
^d *Ancient versions, including the Targum, read "Come, let us go out into the field."*
^e *See 3.17.*
^f *Heb.* Meḥijael.

all implements of copper and iron. And the sister of Tubal-cain was Naa-mah.

²³And Lamech said to his wives,

"Adah and Zillah, hear my voice;
O wives of Lamech, give ear to my speech.
I have slain a man for wounding me,
And a lad for bruising me.
²⁴If Cain is avenged sevenfold,
Then Lamech seventy-sevenfold."

²⁵Adam knew his wife again, and she bore a son and named him Seth, meaning, "God has ᵍ⁻provided me with⁻ᵍ another offspring in place of Abel," for Cain had killed him. ²⁶And to Seth, in turn, a son was born, and he named him Enosh. It was then that men began to invoke the LORD by name.

5 This is the record of Adam's line.—When God created man, He made him in the likeness of God; ²male and female He created them. And when they were created, He blessed them and called them Man.—³When Adam had lived 130 years, he begot a son in his likeness after his image, and he named him Seth. ⁴After the birth of Seth, Adam lived 800 years and begot sons and daughters. ⁵All the days that Adam lived came to 930 years; then he died.

⁶When Seth had lived 105 years, he begot Enosh. ⁷After the birth of Enosh, Seth lived 807 years and begot sons and daughters. ⁸All the days of Seth came to 912 years; then he died.

⁹When Enosh had lived 90 years, he begot Kenan. ¹⁰After the birth of Kenan, Enosh lived 815 years and begot sons and daughters. ¹¹All the days of Enosh came to 905 years; then he died.

¹²When Kenan had lived 70 years, he begot Mahalalel. ¹³After the birth of Mahalalel, Kenan lived 840 years and begot sons and daughters. ¹⁴All the days of Kenan came to 910 years; then he died.

¹⁵When Mahalalel had lived 65 years, he begot Jared. ¹⁶After the birth of Jared, Mahalalel lived 830 years and begot sons and daughters. ¹⁷All the days of Mahalalel came to 895 years; then he died.

¹⁸When Jared had lived 162 years, he begot Enoch. ¹⁹After the birth

ᵍ⁻ᵍ Or "established for me"; Heb. shath, connected with "Seth."

of Enoch, Jared lived 800 years and begot sons and daughters. 20All the days of Jared came to 962 years; then he died.

21When Enoch had lived 65 years, he begot Methuselah. 22After the birth of Methuselah, Enoch walked with God 300 years; and he begot sons and daughters. 23All the days of Enoch came to 365 years. 24Enoch walked with God; then he was no more, for God took him.

25When Methuselah had lived 187 years, he begot Lamech. 26After the birth of Lamech, Methuselah lived 782 years and begot sons and daughters. 27All the days of Methuselah came to 969 years; then he died.

28When Lamech had lived 182 years, he begot a son. 29And he named him Noah, saying, "This one will provide us reliefa from our work and from the toil of our hands, out of the very soil which the LORD placed under a curse." 30After the birth of Noah, Lamech lived 595 years and begot sons and daughters. 31All the days of Lamech came to 777 years; then he died.

32When Noah had lived 500 years, Noah begot Shem, Ham, and Japheth.

6 When men began to increase on earth and daughters were born to them, 2the divine beingsa saw how beautiful the daughters of men were and took wives from among those that pleased them.—3The LORD said, "My breath shall not abideb in man forever, since he too is flesh; let the days allowed him be one hundred and twenty years."—4It was then, and later too, that the Nephilim appeared on earth—when the divine beings cohabited with the daughters of men, who bore them offspring. They were the heroes of old, the men of renown.

5The LORD saw how great was man's wickedness on earth, and how every plan devised by his mind was nothing but evil all the time. 6And the LORD regretted that He had made man on earth, and His heart was saddened. 7The LORD said, "I will blot out from the earth the men whom I created—men together with beasts, creeping things, and birds of the sky; for I regret that I made them." 8But Noah found favor with the LORD.

---

a *Connecting Noah with Heb.* niḥam *"to comfort"; cf. 9.20 ff.*

a *Others "the sons of God."*
b *Meaning of Heb. uncertain.*

נֹחַ

⁹This is the line of Noah.—Noah was a righteous man; he was blameless in his age; Noah walked with God.—¹⁰Noah begot three sons: Shem, Ham, and Japheth.

¹¹The earth became corrupt before God; the earth was filled with lawlessness. ¹²When God saw how corrupt the earth was, for all flesh had corrupted its ways on earth, ¹³God said to Noah, "I have decided to put an end to all flesh, for the earth is filled with lawlessness because of them: I am about to destroy them with the earth. ¹⁴Make yourself an ark of gopher wood; make it an ark with compartments, and cover it inside and out with pitch. ¹⁵This is how you shall make it: the length of the ark shall be three hundred cubits, its width fifty cubits, and its height thirty cubits. ¹⁶Make an opening for daylight in the ark, and ᶜ⁻terminate it within a cubit of the top.⁻ᶜ Put the entrance to the ark in its side; make it with bottom, second, and third decks.

¹⁷"For My part, I am about to bring the Flood—waters upon the earth—to destroy all flesh under the sky in which there is breath of life; everything on earth shall perish. ¹⁸But I will establish My covenant with you, and you shall enter the ark, with your sons, your wife, and your sons' wives. ¹⁹And of all that lives, of all flesh, you shall take two of each into the ark to keep alive with you; they shall be male and female. ²⁰From birds of every kind, cattle of every kind, every kind of creeping thing on earth, two of each shall come to you to stay alive. ²¹For your part, take of everything that is eaten and store it away, to serve as food for you and for them." ²²Noah did so; just as God commanded him, so he did.

7 Then the LORD said to Noah, "Go into the ark, with all your household, for you alone have I found righteous before Me in this generation. ²Of every clean animal you shall take seven pairs, males and their mates, and of every animal that is not clean, two, a male and its mate; ³of the birds of the sky also, seven pairs, male and female, to keep seed alive upon all the earth. ⁴For in seven days' time I will make it rain upon the earth, forty days and forty nights, and I will blot out from the earth all existence that I created." ⁵And Noah did just as the LORD commanded him.

⁶Noah was six hundred years old when the Flood came, waters upon

ᶜ⁻ᶜ *Meaning of Heb. uncertain.*

the earth. [7]Noah, with his sons, his wife, and his sons' wives, went into the ark because of the waters of the Flood. [8]Of the clean animals, of the animals that are not clean, of the birds, and of everything that creeps on the ground, [9]two of each, male and female, came to Noah into the ark, as God had commanded Noah. [10]And on the seventh day the waters of the Flood came upon the earth.

[11]In the six hundredth year of Noah's life, in the second month, on the seventeenth day of the month, on that day

All the fountains of the great deep burst apart,
And the floodgates of the sky broke open.

([12]The rain fell on the earth forty days and forty nights.) [13]That same day Noah and Noah's sons, Shem, Ham, and Japheth, went into the ark, with Noah's wife and the three wives of his sons—[14]they and all beasts of every kind, all cattle of every kind, all creatures of every kind that creep on the earth, and all birds of every kind, every bird, every winged thing. [15]They came to Noah into the ark, two each of all flesh in which there was breath of life. [16]Thus they that entered comprised male and female of all flesh, as God had commanded him. And the LORD shut him in.

[17]The Flood continued forty days on the earth, and the waters increased and raised the ark so that it rose above the earth. [18]The waters swelled and increased greatly upon the earth, and the ark drifted upon the waters. [19]When the waters had swelled much more upon the earth, all the highest mountains everywhere under the sky were covered. [20]Fifteen cubits higher did the waters swell, as the mountains were covered. [21]And all flesh that stirred on earth perished—birds, cattle, beasts, and all the things that swarmed upon the earth, and all mankind. [22]All in whose nostrils was the merest breath of life, all that was on dry land, died. [23]All existence on earth was blotted out—man, cattle, creeping things, and birds of the sky; they were blotted out from the earth. Only Noah was left, and those with him in the ark.

[24]And when the waters had swelled on the earth one hundred and fifty **8** days, [1]God remembered Noah and all the beasts and all the cattle that were with him in the ark, and God caused a wind to blow across the earth, and the waters subsided. [2]The fountains of the deep and the floodgates of the sky were stopped up, and the rain from the sky was held back; [3]the waters then receded steadily from the earth. At the end of one hundred and fifty days the waters diminished, [4]so that in the seventh

month, on the seventeenth day of the month, the ark came to rest on the mountains of Ararat. 5The waters went on diminishing until the tenth month; in the tenth month, on the first of the month, the tops of the mountains became visible.

6At the end of forty days, Noah opened the window of the ark that he had made 7and sent out the raven; it went to and fro until the waters had dried up from the earth. 8Then he sent out the dove to see whether the waters had decreased from the surface of the ground. 9But the dove could not find a resting place for its foot, and returned to him to the ark, for there was water over all the earth. So putting out his hand, he took it into the ark with him. 10He waited another seven days, and again sent out the dove from the ark. 11The dove came back to him toward evening, and there in its bill was a plucked-off olive leaf! Then Noah knew that the waters had decreased on the earth. 12He waited still another seven days and sent the dove forth; and it did not return to him any more.

13In the six hundred and first year, in the first month, on the first of the month, the waters began to dry from the earth; and when Noah removed the covering of the ark, he saw that the surface of the ground was drying. 14And in the second month, on the twenty-seventh day of the month, the earth was dry.

15God spoke to Noah, saying, 16"Come out of the ark, together with your wife, your sons, and your sons' wives. 17Bring out with you every living thing of all flesh that is with you: birds, animals, and everything that creeps on earth; and let them swarm on the earth and be fertile and increase on earth." 18So Noah came out, together with his sons, his wife, and his sons' wives. 19Every animal, every creeping thing, and every bird, everything that stirs on earth came out of the ark by families.

20Then Noah built an altar to the LORD and, taking of every clean animal and of every clean bird, he offered burnt offerings on the altar. 21The LORD smelled the pleasing odor, and the LORD said to Himself: "Never again will I doom the earth because of man, since the devisings of man's mind are evil from his youth; nor will I ever again destroy every living being, as I have done.

22So long as the earth endures,
Seedtime and harvest,
Cold and heat,
Summer and winter,
Day and night
Shall not cease."

9 God blessed Noah and his sons, and said to them, "Be fertile and increase, and fill the earth. ²The fear and the dread of you shall be upon all the beasts of the earth and upon all the birds of the sky—everything with which the earth is astir—and upon all the fish of the sea; they are given into your hand. ³Every creature that lives shall be yours to eat; as with the green grasses, I give you all these. ⁴You must not, however, eat flesh with its life-blood in it. ⁵But for your own life-blood I will require a reckoning: I will require it of every beast; of man, too, will I require a reckoning for human life, of every man for that of his fellow man!

⁶Whoever sheds the blood of man,
By man shall his blood be shed;
For in His image
Did God make man.

⁷Be fertile, then, and increase; abound on the earth and increase on it."

⁸And God said to Noah and to his sons with him, ⁹"I now establish My covenant with you and your offspring to come, ¹⁰and with every living thing that is with you—birds, cattle, and every wild beast as well—all that have come out of the ark, every living thing on earth. ¹¹I will maintain My covenant with you: never again shall all flesh be cut off by the waters of a flood, and never again shall there be a flood to destroy the earth."

¹²God further said, "This is the sign that I set for the covenant between Me and you, and every living creature with you, for all ages to come. ¹³I have set My bow in the clouds, and it shall serve as a sign of the covenant between Me and the earth. ¹⁴When I bring clouds over the earth, and the bow appears in the clouds, ¹⁵I will remember My covenant between Me and you and every living creature among all flesh, so that the waters shall never again become a flood to destroy all flesh. ¹⁶When the bow is in the clouds, I will see it and remember the everlasting covenant between God and all living creatures, all flesh that is on earth. ¹⁷That," God said to Noah, "shall be the sign of the covenant that I have established between Me and all flesh that is on earth."

¹⁸The sons of Noah who came out of the ark were Shem, Ham, and Japheth—Ham being the father of Canaan. ¹⁹These three were the sons of Noah, and from these the whole world branched out.

²⁰Noah, the tiller of the soil, was the first to plant a vineyard. ²¹He drank of the wine and became drunk, and he uncovered himself within

his tent. 22Ham, the father of Canaan, saw his father's nakedness and told his two brothers outside. 23But Shem and Japheth took a cloth, placed it against both their backs and, walking backward, they covered their father's nakedness; their faces were turned the other way, so that they did not see their father's nakedness. 24When Noah woke up from his wine and learned what his youngest son had done to him, 25he said,

"Cursed be Canaan;
The lowest of slaves
Shall he be to his brothers."

26And he said,

"Blessed be the LORD,
The God of Shem;
Let Canaan be a slave to them.
27May God enlargea Japheth,
And let him dwell in the tents of Shem;
And let Canaan be a slave to them."

28Noah lived after the Flood 350 years. 29And all the days of Noah came to 950 years; then he died.

10

These are the lines of Shem, Ham, and Japheth, the sons of Noah: sons were born to them after the Flood.

2The descendants of Japheth: Gomer, Magog, Madai, Javan, Tubal, Meshech, and Tiras. 3The descendants of Gomer: Ashkenaz, Riphath, and Togarmah. 4The descendants of Javan: Elishah and Tarshish, the Kittim and the Dodanim.a 5From these the maritime nations branched out. [These are the descendants of Japheth]b by their lands—each with its language—their clans and their nations.

6The descendants of Ham: Cush, Mizraim, Put, and Canaan. 7The descendants of Cush: Seba, Havilah, Sabtah, Raamah, and Sabteca. The descendants of Raamah: Sheba and Dedan.

8Cush also begot Nimrod, who was the first man of might on earth. 9He was a mighty hunter by the grace of the LORD; hence the saying, "Like Nimrod a mighty hunter by the grace of the LORD." 10The mainstays of his kingdom were Babylon, Erech, Accad, and Calnehc in the land of Shinar. 11From that land Asshur went forth and built Nineveh, Rehoboth-ir, Calah, 12and Resen between Nineveh and Calah, that is the great city.

---

a *Heb.* yapht, *play on Heb.* yepheth *"Japheth."*

a *Septuagint and 1 Chron. 1.7 "Rodanim."*
b *Cf. vv. 20 and 31.*
c *Heb.* we-khalneh, *better vocalized* we-khullanah *"all of them being."*

13And Mizraim begot the Ludim, the Anamim, the Lehabim, the Naphtuhim, 14the Pathrusim, the Casluhim, and the Caphtorim,d whence the Philistines came forth.

15Canaan begot Sidon, his first-born, and Heth; 16and the Jebusites, the Amorites, the Girgashites, 17the Hivites, the Arkites, the Sinites, 18the Arvadites, the Zemarites, and the Hamathites. Afterward the clans of the Canaanites spread out. (19The [original] Canaanite territory extended from Sidon as far as Gerar, near Gaza, and as far as Sodom, Gomorrah, Admah, and Zeboiim, near Lasha.) 20These are the descendants of Ham, according to their clans and languages, by their lands and nations.

21Sons were also born to Shem, ancestor of all the descendants of Eber and older brother of Japheth. 22The descendants of Shem: Elam, Asshur, Arpachshad, Lud, and Aram. 23The descendants of Aram: Uz, Hul, Gether, and Mash. 24Arpachshad begot Shelah, and Shelah begot Eber. 25Two sons were born to Eber: the name of the first was Peleg, for in his days the earth was divided;e and the name of his brother was Joktan. 26Joktan begot Almodad, Sheleph, Hazarmaveth, Jerah, 27Hadoram, Uzal, Diklah, 28Obal, Abimael, Sheba, 29Ophir, Havilah, and Jobab; all these were the descendants of Joktan. 30Their settlements extended from Mesha as far as Sephar, the hill country to the east. 31These are the descendants of Shem according to their clans and languages, by their lands, according to their nations.

32These are the groupings of Noah's descendants, according to their origins, by their nations; and from these the nations branched out over the earth after the Flood.

11 Everyone on earth had the same language and the same words. 2And as they migrated from the east, they came upon a valley in the land of Shinar and settled there. 3They said to one another, "Come, let us make bricks and burn them hard."—Brick served them as stone, and bitumen served them as mortar.—4And they said, "Come, let us build us a city, and a tower with its top in the sky, to make a name for ourselves; else we shall be scattered all over the world." 5The LORD came down to look at the city and tower that man had built, 6and the LORD said, "If, as one people with one language for all, this is how they have begun to act, then

d I.e., the Cretans; moved up for the sake of clarity; cf. Amos 9.7.
e Heb. niphlegah, play on "Peleg."

nothing that they may propose to do will be out of their reach. ⁷Let us, then, go down and confound their speech there, so that they shall not understand one another's speech." ⁸Thus the LORD scattered them from there over the face of the whole earth; and they stopped building the city. ⁹That is why it was called Babel,ᵃ because there the LORD confoundedᵇ the speech of the whole earth; and from there the LORD scattered them over the face of the whole earth.

¹⁰This is the line of Shem. Shem was 100 years old when he begot Arpachshad, two years after the Flood. ¹¹After the birth ofᶜ Arpachshad, Shem lived 500 years and begot sons and daughters.

¹²When Arpachshad had lived 35 years, he begot Shelah. ¹³After the birth of Shelah, Arpachshad lived 403 years and begot sons and daughters.

¹⁴When Shelah had lived 30 years, he begot Eber. ¹⁵After the birth of Eber, Shelah lived 403 years and begot sons and daughters.

¹⁶When Eber had lived 34 years, he begot Peleg. ¹⁷After the birth of Peleg, Eber lived 430 years and begot sons and daughters.

¹⁸When Peleg had lived 30 years, he begot Reu. ¹⁹After the birth of Reu, Peleg lived 209 years and begot sons and daughters.

²⁰When Reu had lived 32 years, he begot Serug. ²¹After the birth of Serug, Reu lived 207 years and begot sons and daughters.

²²When Serug had lived 30 years, he begot Nahor. ²³After the birth of Nahor, Serug lived 200 years and begot sons and daughters.

²⁴When Nahor had lived 29 years, he begot Terah. ²⁵After the birth of Terah, Nahor lived 119 years and begot sons and daughters.

²⁶When Terah had lived 70 years, he begot Abram, Nahor, and Haran. ²⁷Now this is the line of Terah: Terah begot Abram, Nahor, and Haran; and Haran begot Lot. ²⁸Haran died in the lifetime of his father Terah, in his native land, Ur of the Chaldeans. ²⁹Abram and Nahor took to themselves wives, the name of Abram's wife being Sarai and that of Nahor's wife Milcah, the daughter of Haran, the father of Milcah and Iscah. ³⁰Now Sarai was barren, she had no child.

³¹Terah took his son Abram, his grandson Lot the son of Haran, and his daughter-in-law Sarai, the wife of his son Abram, and they set out together from Ur of the Chaldeans for the land of Canaan; but when they had come as far as Haran, they settled there. ³²The days of Terah came to 205 years; and Terah died in Haran.

ᵃ I.e., "Babylon."
ᵇ Heb. balal "confound," play on "Babel."
ᶜ Lit. "After he begot," and so throughout.

לך לך

12 The LORD said to Abram, "Go forth from your native land and from your father's house to the land that I will show you.

²I will make of you a great nation,
And I will bless you;
I will make your name great,
And you shall be a blessing.[a]
³I will bless those who bless you
And curse him that curses you;
And all the families of the earth
Shall bless themselves by you."

⁴Abram went forth as the LORD had commanded him, and Lot went with him. Abram was seventy-five years old when he left Haran. ⁵Abram took his wife Sarai and his brother's son Lot, and all the wealth that they had amassed, and the persons that they had acquired in Haran; and they set out for the land of Canaan. When they arrived in the land of Canaan, ⁶Abram passed through the land as far as the site of Shechem, at the terebinth of Moreh. The Canaanites were then in the land.

⁷The LORD appeared to Abram and said, "I will assign this land to your offspring." And he built an altar there to the LORD who had appeared to him. ⁸From there he moved on to the hill country east of Bethel and pitched his tent, with Bethel on the west and Ai on the east; and he built there an altar to the LORD and invoked the LORD by name. ⁹Then Abram journeyed by stages toward the Negeb.

¹⁰There was a famine in the land, and Abram went down to Egypt to sojourn there, for the famine was severe in the land. ¹¹As he was about to enter Egypt, he said to his wife Sarai, "I know[b] what a beautiful woman you are. ¹²If the Egyptians see you, and think, 'She is his wife,' they will kill me and let you live. ¹³Please say that you are my sister, that it may go well with me because of you, and that I may remain alive thanks to you."

¹⁴When Abram entered Egypt, the Egyptians saw how very beautiful the woman was. ¹⁵Pharaoh's courtiers saw her and praised her to Pharaoh, and the woman was taken into Pharaoh's palace. ¹⁶And because of her, it went well with Abram; he acquired sheep, oxen, asses, male and female slaves, she-asses, and camels.

---

a *I.e., a standard by which blessing is invoked; cf. v. 3 end.*
b *Or "You"; cf. the second person feminine form -ti in Judg. 5.7; Jer. 2.20; Mic. 4.13, etc.*

[17]But the Lord afflicted Pharaoh and his household with mighty plagues on account of Sarai, the wife of Abram. [18]Pharaoh sent for Abram and said, "What is this you have done to me! Why did you not tell me that she was your wife? [19]Why did you say, 'She is my sister,' so that I took her as my wife? Now, here is your wife; take her and begone!" [20]And Pharaoh put men in charge of him, and they sent him off with his wife and all that he possessed.

13

From Egypt, Abram went up into the Negeb, with his wife and all that he possessed, together with Lot. [2]Now Abram was very rich in cattle, silver, and gold. [3]And he proceeded by stages from the Negeb as far as Bethel, to the place where his tent had been formerly, between Bethel and Ai, [4]the site of the altar that he had built there at first; and there Abram invoked the Lord by name.

[5]Lot, who went with Abram, also had flocks and herds and tents, [6]so that the land could not support them staying together; for their possessions were so great that they could not remain together. [7]And there was quarreling between the herdsmen of Abram's cattle and those of Lot's cattle.—The Canaanites and Perizzites were then dwelling in the land.—[8]Abram said to Lot, "Let there be no strife between you and me, between my herdsmen and yours, for we are kinsmen. [9]Is not the whole land before you? Let us separate:[a] if you go north, I will go south; and if you go south, I will go north." [10]Lot looked about him and saw how well watered was the whole plain of the Jordan, all of it—this was before the Lord had destroyed Sodom and Gomorrah—all the way to Zoar, like the garden of the Lord, like the land of Egypt. [11]So Lot chose for himself the whole plain of the Jordan, and Lot journeyed eastward. Thus they parted from each other; [12]Abram remained in the land of Canaan, while Lot settled in the cities of the Plain, pitching his tents near Sodom. [13]Now the inhabitants of Sodom were very wicked sinners against the Lord.

[14]And the Lord said to Abram, after Lot had parted from him, "Raise your eyes and look out from where you are, to the north and south, to the east and west, [15]for I give all the land that you see to you and your offspring forever. [16]I will make your offspring as the dust of the earth, so that if one can count the dust of the earth, then your offspring too can be counted. [17]Up, walk about the land, through its length and its breadth,

---

a Lit. "Please separate from me."

for I give it to you." [18]And Abram moved his tent, and came to dwell at the terebinths of Mamre, which are in Hebron; and he built an altar there to the LORD.

14

Now, when King Amraphel of Shinar, King Arioch of Ellasar, King Chedorlaomer of Elam, and King Tidal of Goiim [2]made war on King Bera of Sodom, King Birsha of Gomorrah, King Shinab of Admah, King Shemeber of Zeboiim, and the king of Bela, which is Zoar, [3]all the latter joined forces at the Valley of Siddim, now the Dead Sea.[a] [4]Twelve years they served Chedorlaomer, and in the thirteenth year they rebelled. [5]In the fourteenth year Chedorlaomer and the kings who were with him came and defeated the Rephaim at Ashteroth-karnaim, the Zuzim at Ham, the Emim at Shaveh-kiriathaim, [6]and the Horites in their hill country of Seir as far as El-paran, which is by the wilderness. [7]On their way back they came to En-mishpat, which is Kadesh, and subdued all the territory of the Amalekites, and also the Amorites who dwelt in Hazazon-tamar. [8]Then the king of Sodom, the king of Gomorrah, the king of Admah, the king of Zeboiim, and the king of Bela, which is Zoar, went forth and engaged them in battle in the Valley of Siddim: [9]King Chedorlaomer of Elam, King Tidal of Goiim, King Amraphel of Shinar, and King Arioch of Ellasar—four kings against those five.

[10]Now the Valley of Siddim was dotted with bitumen pits; and the kings of Sodom and Gomorrah, in their flight, threw themselves into them, while the rest escaped to the hill country. [11][The invaders] seized all the wealth of Sodom and Gomorrah and all their provisions, and went their way. [12]They also took Lot, the son of Abram's brother, and his possessions, and departed; for he had settled in Sodom.

[13]A fugitive brought the news to Abram the Hebrew, who was dwelling at the terebinths of Mamre the Amorite, kinsman of Eshkol and Aner, these being Abram's allies. [14]When Abram heard that his kinsman had been taken captive, he mustered his retainers,[b] born into his household, numbering three hundred and eighteen, and went in pursuit as far as Dan. [15]At night, he and his servants deployed against them and defeated them; and he pursued them as far as Hobah, which is north of Damascus. [16]He brought back all the possessions; he also brought back his kinsman Lot and his possessions, and the women and the rest of the people.

[17]When he returned from defeating Chedorlaomer and the kings with

---

[a] Heb. "Salt Sea."
[b] Meaning of Heb. hanikh uncertain.

him, the king of Sodom came out to meet him in the Valley of Shaveh, which is the Valley of the King. ¹⁸And King Melchizedek of Salem brought out bread and wine; he was a priest of God Most High.^c ¹⁹He blessed him, saying,

> "Blessed be Abram of God Most High,
> Creator of heaven and earth.
> ²⁰And blessed be God Most High,
> Who has delivered your foes into your hand."

And [Abram] gave him a tenth of everything.

²¹Then the king of Sodom said to Abram, "Give me the persons, and take the possessions for yourself." ²²But Abram said to the king of Sodom, "I swear^d to the LORD, God Most High, Creator of heaven and earth: ²³I will not take so much as a thread or a sandal strap of what is yours; you shall not say, 'It is I who made Abram rich.' ²⁴For me, nothing but what my servants have used up; as for the share of the men who went with me—Aner, Eshkol, and Mamre—let them take their share."

15

Some time later, the word of the LORD came to Abram in a vision. He said,

> "Fear not, Abram,
> I am a shield to you;
> Your reward shall be very great."

²But Abram said, "O Lord GOD, what can You give me, seeing that I shall die childless, ^{a-}and the one in charge of my household is Dammesek Eliezer!"^{-a} ³Abram said further, "Since You have granted me no offspring, my steward will be my heir." ⁴The word of the LORD came to him in reply, "That one shall not be your heir; none but your very own issue shall be your heir." ⁵He took him outside and said, "Look toward heaven and count the stars, if you are able to count them." And He added, "So shall your offspring be." ⁶And because he put his trust in the LORD, He reckoned it to his merit.

⁷Then He said to him, "I am the LORD who brought you out from Ur of the Chaldeans to assign this land to you as a possession." ⁸And he said, "O Lord GOD, how shall I know that I am to possess it?" ⁹He answered, "Bring Me a three-year-old heifer, a three-year-old she-goat, a three-year-old ram, a turtledove, and a young bird." ¹⁰He brought Him all these and cut them in two, placing each half opposite the other; but he did not

---

^c *Heb.* El 'Elyon.
^d *Lit. "lift up my hand."*

^{a-a}*Meaning of. Heb. uncertain.*

cut up the bird. 11Birds of prey came down upon the carcasses, and Abram drove them away. 12As the sun was about to set, a deep sleep fell upon Abram, and a great dark dread descended upon him. 13And He said to Abram, "Know well that your offspring shall be strangers in a land not theirs, and they shall be enslaved and oppressed four hundred years; 14but I will execute judgment on the nation they shall serve, and in the end they shall go free with great wealth. 15As for you,

You shall go to your fathers in peace;
You shall be buried at a ripe old age.

16And they shall return here in the fourth generation, for the iniquity of the Amorites is not yet complete."

17When the sun set and it was very dark, there appeared a smoking oven, and a flaming torch which passed between those pieces. 18On that day the LORD made a covenant with Abram, saying, "To your offspring I assign this land, from the river of Egypt to the great river, the river Euphrates: 19the Kenites, the Kenizzites, the Kadmonites, 20the Hittites, the Perizzites, the Rephaim, 21the Amorites, the Canaanites, the Girgashites, and the Jebusites."

16

Sarai, Abram's wife, had borne him no children. She had an Egyptian maidservant whose name was Hagar. 2And Sarai said to Abram, "Look, the LORD has kept me from bearing. Consort with my maid; perhaps I shall have a sona through her." And Abram heeded Sarai's request. 3So Sarai, Abram's wife, took her maid, Hagar the Egyptian— after Abram had dwelt in the land of Canaan ten years—and gave her to her husband Abram as concubine. 4He cohabited with Hagar and she conceived; and when she saw that she had conceived, her mistress was lowered in her esteem. 5And Sarai said to Abram, "The wrong done me is your fault! I myself put my maid in your bosom; now that she sees that she is pregnant, I am lowered in her esteem. The LORD decide between you and me!" 6Abram said to Sarai, "Your maid is in your hands. Deal with her as you think right." Then Sarai treated her harshly, and she ran away from her.

7An angel of the LORD found her by a spring of water in the wilderness, the spring on the road to Shur, 8and said, "Hagar, slave of Sarai, where have you come from, and where are you going?" And she said, "I am running away from my mistress Sarai."

---

a Lit. "be built up," play on ben "son" and banah "build up."

⁹And the angel of the LORD said to her, "Go back to your mistress, and submit to her harsh treatment." ¹⁰And the angel of the LORD said to her,

"I will greatly increase your offspring,
And they shall be too many to count."

¹¹The angel of the LORD said to her further,

"Behold, you are with child
And shall bear a son;
You shall call him Ishmael,ᵇ
For the LORD has paid heed to your suffering.
¹²He shall be a wild ass of a man;
His hand against everyone,
And everyone's hand against him;
He shall dwell alongside of all his kinsmen."

¹³And she called the LORD who spoke to her, "You Are El-roi,"ᶜ by which she meant, ᵈ-"Have I not gone on seeing after He saw me!"-ᵈ ¹⁴Therefore the well was called Beer-lahai-roi;ᵉ it is between Kadesh and Bered.— ¹⁵Hagar bore a son to Abram, and Abram gave the son that Hagar bore him the name Ishmael. ¹⁶Abram was eighty-six years old when Hagar bore Ishmael to Abram.

17

When Abram was ninety-nine years old, the LORD appeared to Abram and said to him, "I am El Shaddai.ᵃ Walk in My ways and be blameless. ²I will establish My covenant between Me and you, and I will make you exceedingly numerous."

³Abram threw himself on his face; and God spoke to him further, ⁴"As for Me, this is My covenant with you: You shall be the father of a multitude of nations. ⁵And you shall no longer be called Abram, but your name shall be Abraham,ᵇ for I make you the father of a multitude of nations. ⁶I will make you exceedingly fertile, and make nations of you; and kings shall come forth from you. ⁷I will maintain My covenant between Me and you, and your offspring to come, as an everlasting covenant throughout the ages, to be God to you and to your offspring to come. ⁸I assign the land you sojourn in to you and your offspring to come, all the land of Canaan, as an everlasting holding. I will be their God."

⁹God further said to Abraham, "As for you, you and your offspring to come throughout the ages shall keep My covenant. ¹⁰Such shall be the

---

ᵇ I.e., "God heeds."
ᶜ Apparently "God of Seeing."
ᵈ⁻ᵈ Meaning of Heb. uncertain.
ᵉ Apparently "the Well of the Living One Who sees me."

ᵃ Traditionally rendered "God Almighty."
ᵇ Understood as "father of a multitude."

covenant between Me and you and your offspring to follow which you shall keep: every male among you shall be circumcised. [11]You shall circumcise the flesh of your foreskin, and that shall be the sign of the covenant between Me and you. [12]And throughout the generations, every male among you shall be circumcised at the age of eight days. As for the homeborn slave and the one bought from an outsider who is not of your offspring, [13]they must be circumcised, homeborn and purchased alike. Thus shall My covenant be marked in your flesh as an everlasting pact. [14]And if any male who is uncircumcised fails to circumcise the flesh of his foreskin, that person shall be cut off from his kin; he has broken My covenant."

[15]And God said to Abraham, "As for your wife Sarai, you shall not call her Sarai, but her name shall be Sarah.[c] [16]I will bless her; indeed, I will give you a son by her. I will bless her so that she shall give rise to nations; rulers of peoples shall issue from her." [17]Abraham threw himself on his face and laughed, as he said to himself, "Can a child be born to a man a hundred years old, or can Sarah bear a child at ninety?" [18]And Abraham said to God, "O that Ishmael might live by Your favor!" [19]God said, "Nevertheless, Sarah your wife shall bear you a son, and you shall name him Isaac;[d] and I will maintain My covenant with him as an everlasting covenant for his offspring to come. [20]As for Ishmael, I have heeded you.[e] I hereby bless him. I will make him fertile and exceedingly numerous. He shall be the father of twelve chieftains, and I will make of him a great nation. [21]But My covenant I will maintain with Isaac, whom Sarah shall bear to you at this season next year." [22]And when He was done speaking with him, God was gone from Abraham.

[23]Then Abraham took his son Ishmael, and all his homeborn slaves and all those he had bought, every male in Abraham's household, and he circumcised the flesh of their foreskins on that very day, as God had spoken to him. [24]Abraham was ninety-nine years old when he circumcised the flesh of his foreskin, [25]and his son Ishmael was thirteen years old when he was circumcised in the flesh of his foreskin. [26]Thus Abraham and his son Ishmael were circumcised on that very day; [27]and all his household, his homeborn slaves and those that had been bought from outsiders, were circumcised with him.

[c] *I.e., "princess."*
[d] *Heb.* Yiṣḥaq, *from* ṣaḥaq, *"laugh."*
[e] *Heb.* shema'tikha, *play on "Ishmael."*

18

וירא

The LORD appeared to him by the terebinths of Mamre; he was sitting at the entrance of the tent as the day grew hot. ²Looking up, he saw three men standing near him. As soon as he saw them, he ran from the entrance of the tent to greet them and, bowing to the ground, ³he said, "My lords,ᵃ if it please you, do not go on past your servant. ⁴Let a little water be brought; bathe your feet and recline under the tree. ⁵And let me fetch a morsel of bread that you may refresh yourselves; then go on—seeing that you have come your servant's way." They replied, "Do as you have said."

Abraham hastened into the tent to Sarah, and said, "Quick, three *seahs* of choice flour! Knead and make cakes!" ⁷Then Abraham ran to the herd, took a calf, tender and choice, and gave it to a servant-boy, who hastened to prepare it. ⁸He took curds and milk and the calf that had been prepared and set these before them; and he waited on them under the tree as they ate.

⁹They said to him, "Where is your wife Sarah?" And he replied, "There, in the tent." ¹⁰Then one said, "I will return to you next year,ᵇ and your wife Sarah shall have a son!" Sarah was listening at the entrance of the tent, which was behind him. ¹¹Now Abraham and Sarah were old, advanced in years; Sarah had stopped having the periods of women. ¹²And Sarah laughed to herself, saying, "Now that I am withered, am I to have enjoyment—with my husband so old?" ¹³Then the LORD said to Abraham, "Why did Sarah laugh, saying, 'Shall I in truth bear a child, old as I am?' ¹⁴Is anything too wondrous for the LORD? I will return to you at the same season next year, and Sarah shall have a son." ¹⁵Sarah lied, saying, "I did not laugh," for she was frightened. But He replied, "You did laugh."

¹⁶The men set out from there and looked down toward Sodom, Abraham walking with them to see them off. ¹⁷Now the LORD had said, "Shall I hide from Abraham what I am about to do, ¹⁸since Abraham is to become a great and populous nation and all the nations of the earth are to bless themselves by him? ¹⁹For I have singled him out, that he may instruct his children and his posterity to keep the way of the LORD by doing what is just and right, in order that the LORD may bring about for Abraham what He has promised him." ²⁰Then the LORD said, "The outrage of Sodom and Gomorrah is so great, and their sin so grave! ²¹I will

---

ᵃ *Or "My Lord."*
ᵇ *Cf. Gen. 17.21; 2 Kings 4.16–17.*

go down to see whether they have acted altogether according to the outcry that has reached Me; if not, I will take note."

²²The men went on from there to Sodom, while Abraham remained standing before the LORD. ²³Abraham came forward and said, "Will You sweep away the innocent along with the guilty? ²⁴What if there should be fifty innocent within the city; will You then wipe out the place and not forgive it for the sake of the innocent fifty who are in it? ²⁵Far be it from You to do such a thing, to bring death upon the innocent as well as the guilty, so that innocent and guilty fare alike. Far be it from You! Shall not the Judge of all the earth deal justly?" ²⁶And the LORD answered, "If I find within the city of Sodom fifty innocent ones, I will forgive the whole place for their sake." ²⁷Abraham spoke up, saying, "Here I venture to speak to my Lord, I who am but dust and ashes: ²⁸What if the fifty innocent should lack five? Will You destroy the whole city for want of the five?" And He answered, "I will not destroy if I find forty-five there." ²⁹But he spoke to Him again, and said, "What if forty should be found there?" And He answered, "I will not do it, for the sake of the forty." ³⁰And he said, "Let not my Lord be angry if I go on: What if thirty should be found there?" And He answered, "I will not do it if I find thirty there." ³¹And he said, "I venture again to speak to my Lord: What if twenty should be found there?" And He answered, "I will not destroy, for the sake of the twenty." ³²And he said, "Let not my Lord be angry if I speak but this last time: What if ten should be found there?" And He answered, "I will not destroy, for the sake of the ten."

³³When the LORD had finished speaking to Abraham, He departed; and Abraham returned to his place.

19 The two angels arrived in Sodom in the evening, as Lot was sitting in the gate of Sodom. When Lot saw them, he rose to greet them and, bowing low with his face to the ground, ²he said, "Please, my lords, turn aside to your servant's house to spend the night, and bathe your feet; then you may be on your way early." But they said, "No, we will spend the night in the square." ³But he urged them strongly, so they turned his way and entered his house. He prepared a feast for them and baked unleavened bread, and they ate.

⁴They had not yet lain down, when the townspeople, the men of Sodom, young and old—all the people to the last man—gathered about the house. ⁵And they shouted to Lot and said to him, "Where are the men who

came to you tonight? Bring them out to us, that we may be intimate with them." [6]So Lot went out to them to the entrance, shut the door behind him, [7]and said, "I beg you, my friends, do not commit such a wrong. [8]Look, I have two daughters who have not known a man. Let me bring them out to you, and you may do to them as you please; but do not do anything to these men, since they have come under the shelter of my roof." [9]But they said, "Stand back! The fellow," they said, "came here as an alien, and already he acts the ruler! Now we will deal worse with you than with them." And they pressed hard against the person of Lot, and moved forward to break the door. [10]But the men stretched out their hands and pulled Lot into the house with them, and shut the door. [11]And the people who were at the entrance of the house, young and old, were struck with blinding light, so that they were helpless to find the entrance.

[12]Then the men said to Lot, "Whom else have you here? Sons-in-law, your sons and daughters, or anyone else that you have in the city—bring them out of the place. [13]For we are about to destroy this place; because the outcry against them before the LORD has become so great that the LORD has sent us to destroy it." [14]So Lot went out and spoke to his sons-in-law, who had married his daughters, and said, "Up, get out of this place, for the LORD is about to destroy the city." But he seemed to his sons-in-law as one who jests.

[15]As dawn broke, the angels urged Lot on, saying, "Up, take your wife and your two remaining daughters, lest you be swept away because of the iniquity of the city." [16]Still he delayed. So the men seized his hand, and the hands of his wife and his two daughters—in the LORD's mercy on him—and brought him out and left him outside the city. [17]When they had brought them outside, one said, "Flee for your life! Do not look behind you, nor stop anywhere in the Plain; flee to the hills, lest you be swept away." [18]But Lot said to them, "Oh no, my lord! [19]You have been so gracious to your servant, and have already shown me so much kindness in order to save my life; but I cannot flee to the hills, lest the disaster overtake me and I die. [20]Look, that town there is near enough to flee to; it is such a little place! Let me flee there—it is such a little place—and let my life be saved." [21]He replied, "Very well, I will grant you this favor too, and I will not annihilate the town of which you have spoken. [22]Hurry, flee there, for I cannot do anything until you arrive there." Hence the town came to be called Zoar.[a]

[23]As the sun rose upon the earth and Lot entered Zoar, [24]the LORD rained upon Sodom and Gomorrah sulfurous fire from the LORD out of

---

[a] Connected with miṣʿar "a little place," v. 20.

heaven. 25He annihilated those cities and the entire Plain, and all the inhabitants of the cities and the vegetation of the ground. 26Lot'sᵇ wife looked back,ᶜ and she thereupon turned into a pillar of salt.

27Next morning, Abraham hurried to the place where he had stood before the LORD, 28and, looking down toward Sodom and Gomorrah and all the land of the Plain, he saw the smoke of the land rising like the smoke of a kiln.

29Thus it was that, when God destroyed the cities of the Plain and annihilated the cities where Lot dwelt, God was mindful of Abraham and removed Lot from the midst of the upheaval.

30Lot went up from Zoar and settled in the hill country with his two daughters, for he was afraid to dwell in Zoar; and he and his two daughters lived in a cave. 31And the older one said to the younger, "Our father is old, and there is not a man on earth to consort with us in the way of all the world. 32Come, let us make our father drink wine, and let us lie with him, that we may maintain life through our father." 33That night they made their father drink wine, and the older one went in and lay with her father; he did not know when she lay down or when she rose. 34The next day the older one said to the younger, "See, I lay with Father last night; let us make him drink wine tonight also, and you go and lie with him, that we may maintain life through our father." 35That night also they made their father drink wine, and the younger one went and lay with him; he did not know when she lay down or when she rose.

36Thus the two daughters of Lot came to be with child by their father. 37The older one bore a son and named him Moab;ᵈ he is the father of the Moabites of today. 38And the younger also bore a son, and she called him Ben-ammi;ᵉ he is the father of the Ammonites of today.

20 Abraham journeyed from there to the region of the Negeb and settled between Kadesh and Shur. While he was sojourning in Gerar, 2Abraham said of Sarah his wife, "She is my sister." So King Abimelech of Gerar had Sarah brought to him. 3But God came to Abimelech in a dream by night and said to him, "You are to die because of the woman that you have taken, for she is a married woman." 4Now Abimelech had not approached her. He said, "O Lord, will You slay people even though innocent? 5He himself said to me, 'She is my sister!' And she also said, 'He is my brother.' When I did this, my heart was blameless and my hands

ᵇ Lit. "His."
ᶜ Lit. "behind him."
ᵈ As though me-'ab "from (my) father."
ᵉ As though "son of my (paternal) kindred."

were clean." 6And God said to him in the dream, "I knew that you did this with a blameless heart, and so I kept you from sinning against Me. That was why I did not let you touch her. 7Therefore, restore the man's wife—since he is a prophet, he will intercede for you—to save your life. If you fail to restore her, know that you shall die, you and all that are yours."

8Early next morning, Abimelech called his servants and told them all that had happened; and the men were greatly frightened. 9Then Abimelech summoned Abraham and said to him, "What have you done to us? What wrong have I done that you should bring so great a guilt upon me and my kingdom? You have done to me things that ought not to be done. 10What, then," Abimelech demanded of Abraham, "was your purpose in doing this thing?" 11"I thought," said Abraham, "surely there is no fear of God in this place, and they will kill me because of my wife. 12And besides, she is in truth my sister, my father's daughter though not my mother's; and she became my wife. 13So when God made me wander from my father's house, I said to her, 'Let this be the kindness that you shall do me: whatever place we come to, say there of me: He is my brother.'"

14Abimelech took sheep and oxen, and male and female slaves, and gave them to Abraham; and he restored his wife Sarah to him. 15And Abimelech said, "Here, my land is before you; settle wherever you please." 16And to Sarah he said, "I herewith give your brother a thousand pieces of silver; this will serve you as vindicationa before all who are with you, and you are cleared before everyone." 17Abraham then prayed to God, and God healed Abimelech and his wife and his slave girls, so that they bore children; 18for the LORD had closed fast every womb of the household of Abimelech because of Sarah, the wife of Abraham.

21 The LORD took note of Sarah as He had promised, and the LORD did for Sarah as He had spoken. 2Sarah conceived and bore a son to Abraham in his old age, at the set time of which God had spoken. 3Abraham gave his newborn son, whom Sarah had borne him, the name of Isaac. 4And when his son Isaac was eight days old, Abraham circumcised him, as God had commanded him. 5Now Abraham was a hundred years old when his son Isaac was born to him. 6Sarah said, "God has brought me laughter; everyone who hears will laugh witha me." 7And she added,

a Lit. "a covering of the eyes"; meaning of latter half of verse uncertain.
a Lit. "for."

"Who would have said to Abraham
That Sarah would suckle children!
Yet I have borne a son in his old age."

8The child grew up and was weaned, and Abraham held a great feast on the day that Isaac was weaned.

9Sarah saw the son whom Hagar the Egyptian had borne to Abraham playing. 10She said to Abraham, "Cast out that slave-woman and her son, for the son of that slave shall not share in the inheritance with my son Isaac." 11The matter distressed Abraham greatly, for it concerned a son of his. 12But God said to Abraham, "Do not be distressed over the boy or your slave; whatever Sarah tells you, do as she says, for it is through Isaac that offspring shall be continuedb for you. 13As for the son of the slave-woman, I will make a nation of him, too, for he is your seed."

14Early next morning Abraham took some bread and a skin of water, and gave them to Hagar. He placed them over her shoulder, together with the child, and sent her away. And she wandered about in the wilderness of Beer-sheba. 15When the water was gone from the skin, she left the child under one of the bushes, 16and went and sat down at a distance, a bowshot away; for she thought, "Let me not look on as the child dies." And sitting thus afar, she burst into tears.

17God heard the cry of the boy, and an angel of God called to Hagar from heaven and said to her, "What troubles you, Hagar? Fear not, for God has heeded the cry of the boy where he is. 18Come, lift up the boy and hold him by the hand, for I will make a great nation of him." 19Then God opened her eyes and she saw a well of water. She went and filled the skin with water, and let the boy drink. 20God was with the boy and he grew up; he dwelt in the wilderness and became a bowman. 21He lived in the wilderness of Paran; and his mother got a wife for him from the land of Egypt.

22At that time Abimelech and Phicol, chief of his troops, said to Abraham, "God is with you in everything that you do. 23Therefore swear to me here by God that you will not deal falsely with me or with my kith and kin, but will deal with me and with the land in which you have sojourned as loyally as I have dealt with you." 24And Abraham said, "I swear it."

25Then Abraham reproached Abimelech for the well of water which the servants of Abimelech had seized. 26But Abimelech said, "I do not know

b Lit. "called."

who did this; you did not tell me, nor have I heard of it until today." ²⁷Abraham took sheep and oxen and gave them to Abimelech, and the two of them made a pact. ²⁸Abraham then set seven ewes of the flock by themselves, ²⁹and Abimelech said to Abraham, "What mean these seven ewes which you have set apart?" ³⁰He replied, "You are to accept these seven ewes from me as proof that I dug this well." ³¹Hence that place was called Beer-sheba,ᶜ for there the two of them swore an oath. ³²When they had concluded the pact at Beer-sheba, Abimelech and Phicol, chief of his troops, departed and returned to the land of the Philistines. ³³[Abraham] planted a tamarisk at Beer-sheba, and invoked there the name of the LORD, the Everlasting God. ³⁴And Abraham resided in the land of the Philistines a long time.

22 Some time afterward, God put Abraham to the test. He said to him, "Abraham," and he answered, "Here I am." ²And He said, "Take your son, your favored one, Isaac, whom you love, and go to the land of Moriah, and offer him there as a burnt offering on one of the heights that I will point out to you." ³So early next morning, Abraham saddled his ass and took with him two of his servants and his son Isaac. He split the wood for the burnt offering, and he set out for the place of which God had told him. ⁴On the third day Abraham looked up and saw the place from afar. ⁵Then Abraham said to his servants, "You stay here with the ass. The boy and I will go up there; we will worship and we will return to you."

⁶Abraham took the wood for the burnt offering and put it on his son Isaac. He himself took the firestoneᵃ and the knife; and the two walked off together. ⁷Then Isaac said to his father Abraham, "Father!" And he answered, "Yes, my son." And he said, "Here are the firestone and the wood; but where is the sheep for the burnt offering?" ⁸And Abraham said, "God will see to the sheep for His burnt offering, my son." And the two of them walked on together.

⁹They arrived at the place of which God had told him. Abraham built an altar there; he laid out the wood; he bound his son Isaac; he laid him on the altar, on top of the wood. ¹⁰And Abraham picked up the knife to slay his son. ¹¹Then an angel of the LORD called to him from heaven: "Abraham! Abraham!" And he answered, "Here I am." ¹²And he said, "Do not raise your hand against the boy, or do anything to him. For now

ᶜ I.e., "well of seven" or "well of oath."

ᵃ Lit. "fire."

I know that you fear God, since you have not withheld your son, your favored one, from Me." [13]When Abraham looked up, his eye fell upon a[b] ram, caught in the thicket by its horns. So Abraham went and took the ram and offered it up as a burnt offering in place of his son. [14]And Abraham named that site Adonai-yireh,[c] whence the present saying, "On the mount of the LORD there is vision."[d]

[15]The angel of the LORD called to Abraham a second time from heaven, [16]and said, "By Myself I swear, the LORD declares: Because you have done this and have not withheld your son, your favored one, [17]I will bestow My blessing upon you and make your descendants as numerous as the stars of heaven and the sands on the seashore; and your descendants shall seize the gates of their foes. [18]All the nations of the earth shall bless themselves by your descendants, because you have obeyed My command." [19]Abraham then returned to his servants, and they departed together for Beer-sheba; and Abraham stayed in Beer-sheba.

[20]Some time later, Abraham was told, "Milcah too has borne children to your brother Nahor: [21]Uz the first-born, and Buz his brother, and Kemuel the father of Aram; [22]and Chesed, Hazo, Pildash, Jidlaph, and Bethuel"—[23]Bethuel being the father of Rebekah. These eight Milcah bore to Nahor, Abraham's brother. [24]And his concubine, whose name was Reumah, also bore children: Tebah, Gaham, Tahash, and Maacah.

חיי שרה

23 Sarah's lifetime—the span of Sarah's life—came to one hundred and twenty-seven years. [2]Sarah died in Kiriath-arba—now Hebron—in the land of Canaan; and Abraham proceeded to mourn for Sarah and to bewail her. [3]Then Abraham rose from beside his dead, and spoke to the Hittites, saying, [4]"I am a resident alien among you; sell me a burial site among you, that I may remove my dead for burial." [5]And the Hittites replied to Abraham, saying to him, [6]"Hear us, my lord: you are the elect of God among us. Bury your dead in the choicest of our burial places; none of us will withhold his burial place from you for burying your dead." [7]Thereupon Abraham bowed low to the people of the land, the Hittites, [8]and he said to them, "If it is your wish that I remove my dead for burial, you must agree to intercede for me with Ephron son of Zohar. [9]Let him

---

b Reading 'eḥad *with many Heb. mss. and ancient versions; text* 'aḥar *"after."*
c I.e., *"the Lord will see"; cf. v. 8.*
d *Heb.* Behar Adonai yera'eh.

sell me the cave of Machpelah that he owns, which is at the edge of his land. Let him sell it to me, at the full price, for a burial site in your midst."

[10]Ephron was present among the Hittites; so Ephron the Hittite answered Abraham in the hearing of the Hittites, all who entered the gate of his town,[a] saying, [11]"No, my lord, hear me: I give you the field and I give you the cave that is in it; I give it to you in the presence of my people. Bury your dead." [12]Then Abraham bowed low before the people of the land, [13]and spoke to Ephron in the hearing of the people of the land, saying, "If only you would hear me out! Let me pay the price of the land; accept it from me, that I may bury my dead there." [14]And Ephron replied to Abraham, saying to him, [15]"My lord, do hear me! A piece of land worth four hundred shekels of silver—what is that between you and me? Go and bury your dead." [16]Abraham accepted Ephron's terms. Abraham paid out to Ephron the money that he had named in the hearing of the Hittites—four hundred shekels of silver at the going merchants' rate.

[17]So Ephron's land in Machpelah, near Mamre—the field with its cave and all the trees anywhere within the confines of that field—passed [18]to Abraham as his possession, in the presence of the Hittites, of all who entered the gate of his town.[a] [19]And then Abraham buried his wife Sarah in the cave of the field of Machpelah, facing Mamre—now Hebron—in the land of Canaan. [20]Thus the field with its cave passed from the Hittites to Abraham, as a burial site.

24 Abraham was now old, advanced in years, and the LORD had blessed Abraham in all things. [2]And Abraham said to the senior servant of his household, who had charge of all that he owned, "Put your hand under my thigh [3]and I will make you swear by the LORD, the God of heaven and the God of the earth, that you will not take a wife for my son from the daughters of the Canaanites among whom I dwell, [4]but will go to the land of my birth and get a wife for my son Isaac." [5]And the servant said to him, "What if the woman does not consent to follow me to this land, shall I then take your son back to the land from which you came?" [6]Abraham answered him, "On no account must you take my son back there! [7]The LORD, the God of heaven, who took me from my father's house and from my native land, who promised me on oath, saying, 'I will

---

[a] I.e., all his fellow townsmen.

assign this land to your offspring'—He will send His angel before you, and you will get a wife for my son from there. 8And if the woman does not consent to follow you, you shall then be clear of this oath to me; but do not take my son back there." 9So the servant put his hand under the thigh of his master Abraham and swore to him as bidden.a

10Then the servant took ten of his master's camels and set out, taking with him all the bounty of his master; and he made his way to Aram-naharaim, to the city of Nahor. 11He made the camels kneel down by the well outside the city, at evening time, the time when women come out to draw water. 12And he said, "O LORD, God of my master Abraham, grant me good fortune this day, and deal graciously with my master Abraham: 13Here I stand by the spring as the daughters of the townsmen come out to draw water; 14let the maiden to whom I say, 'Please, lower your jar that I may drink,' and who replies, 'Drink, and I will also water your camels'—let her be the one whom You have decreed for Your servant Isaac. Thereby shall I know that You have dealt graciously with my master."

15He had scarcely finished speaking, when Rebekah, who was born to Bethuel, the son of Milcah the wife of Abraham's brother Nahor, came out with her jar on her shoulder. 16The maiden was very beautiful, a virgin whom no man had known. She went down to the spring, filled her jar, and came up. 17The servant ran toward her and said, "Please, let me sip a little water from your jar." 18"Drink, my lord," she said, and she quickly lowered her jar upon her hand and let him drink. 19When she had let him drink his fill, she said, "I will also draw for your camels, until they finish drinking." 20Quickly emptying her jar into the trough, she ran back to the well to draw, and she drew for all his camels.

21The man, meanwhile, stood gazing at her, silently wondering whether the LORD had made his errand successful or not. 22When the camels had finished drinking, the man took a gold nose-ring weighing a half-shekel,b and two gold bands for her arms, ten shekels in weight. 23"Pray tell me," he said, "whose daughter are you? Is there room in your father's house for us to spend the night?" 24She replied, "I am the daughter of Bethuel the son of Milcah, whom she bore to Nahor." 25And she went on, "There is plenty of strawc and feed at home, and also room to spend the night." 26The man bowed low in homage to the LORD 27and said, "Blessed be the LORD, the God of my master Abraham, who has not withheld His

---

a Lit. "about this matter."
b Heb. beqaʻ.
c Heb. teben, shredded straw, which in the East is mixed with feed; cf. v. 32.

steadfast faithfulness from my master. For I have been guided on my errand by the LORD, to the house of my master's kinsmen.'"

28The maiden ran and told all this to her mother's household. 29Now Rebekah had a brother whose name was Laban. Laban ran out to the man at the spring—30when he saw the nose-ring and the bands on his sister's arms, and when he heard his sister Rebekah say, "Thus the man spoke to me." He went up to the man, who was still standing beside the camels at the spring. 31"Come in, O blessed of the LORD," he said, "why do you remain outside, when I have made ready the house and a place for the camels?" 32So the man entered the house, and the camels were unloaded. The camels were given straw and feed, and water was brought to bathe his feet and the feet of the men with him. 33But when food was set before him, he said, "I will not eat until I have told my tale." He said, "Speak, then."

34"I am Abraham's servant," he began. 35"The LORD has greatly blessed my master, and he has become rich: He has given him sheep and cattle, silver and gold, male and female slaves, camels and asses. 36And Sarah, my master's wife, bore my master a son in her old age, and he has assigned to him everything he owns. 37Now my master made me swear, saying, 'You shall not get a wife for my son from the daughters of the Canaanites in whose land I dwell; 38but you shall go to my father's house, to my kindred, and get a wife for my son.' 39And I said to my master, 'What if the woman does not follow me?' 40He replied to me, 'The LORD, whose ways I have followed, will send His angel with you and make your errand successful; and you will get a wife for my son from my kindred, from my father's house. 41Thus only shall you be freed from my adjuration: if, when you come to my kindred, they refuse you—only then shall you be freed from my adjuration.'

42"I came today to the spring, and I said: O LORD, God of my master Abraham, if You would indeed grant success to the errand on which I am engaged! 43As I stand by the spring of water, let the young woman who comes out to draw and to whom I say, 'Please, let me drink a little water from your jar,' 44and who answers, 'You may drink, and I will also draw for your camels'—let her be the wife whom the LORD has decreed for my master's son.' 45I had scarcely finished praying in my heart, when Rebekah came out with her jar on her shoulder, and went down to the spring and drew. And I said to her, 'Please give me a drink.' 46She quickly lowered her jar and said, 'Drink, and I will also water your camels.' So I drank, and she also watered the camels. ⁴⁷I inquired of her, 'Whose daughter are you?' And she said, 'The daughter of Bethuel, son of Nahor, whom Milcah bore to him.' And I put the ring on her nose and the bands on her arms. ⁴⁸Then I bowed low in homage to the LORD and blessed the LORD, the God of my master Abraham, who led me on the right way to get the daughter of my master's brother for his son. ⁴⁹And now, if you mean to treat my master with true kindness, tell me; and if not, tell me also, that I may turn right or left."

⁵⁰Then Laban and Bethuel answered, "The matter was decreed by the LORD; we cannot speak to you bad or good. ⁵¹Here is Rebekah before you; take her and go, and let her be a wife to your master's son, as the LORD has spoken." ⁵²When Abraham's servant heard their words, he bowed low to the ground before the LORD. ⁵³The servant brought out objects of silver and gold, and garments, and gave them to Rebekah; and he gave presents to her brother and her mother. ⁵⁴Then he and the men with him ate and drank, and they spent the night. When they arose next morning, he said, "Give me leave to go to my master." ⁵⁵But her brother and her mother said, "Let the maiden remain with us ᵈ-some ten days;-ᵈ then you may go." ⁵⁶He said to them, "Do not delay me, now that the LORD has made my errand successful. Give me leave that I may go to my master." ⁵⁷And they said, "Let us call the girl and ask for her reply." ⁵⁸They called Rebekah and said to her, "Will you go with this man?" And she said, "I will." ⁵⁹So they sent off their sister Rebekah and her nurse along with Abraham's servant and his men. ⁶⁰And they blessed Rebekah and said to her,

> "O sister!
> May you grow
> Into thousands of myriads;
> May your offspring seize
> The gates of their foes."

⁶¹Then Rebekah and her maids arose, mounted the camels, and followed the man. So the servant took Rebekah and went his way.

⁶²Isaac had just come back from the vicinity of Beer-lahai-roi, for he was settled in the region of the Negeb. ⁶³And Isaac went out walkingᵉ in the field toward evening and, looking up, he saw camels approaching. ⁶⁴Raising her eyes, Rebekah saw Isaac. She alighted from the camel ⁶⁵and said to the servant, "Who is that man walking in the field toward us?"

ᵈ-ᵈ Lit. "days or ten."
ᵉ Others "to meditate"; meaning of Heb. uncertain.

And the servant said, "That is my master." So she took her veil and covered herself. 66The servant told Isaac all the things that he had done. 67Isaac then brought her into the tent of his mother Sarah, and he took Rebekah as his wife. Isaac loved her, and thus found comfort after his mother's death.

25
Abraham took another wife, whose name was Keturah. 2She bore him Zimran, Jokshan, Medan, Midian, Ishbak, and Shuah. 3Jokshan begot Sheba and Dedan. The descendants of Dedan were the Asshurim, the Letushim, and the Leummim. 4The descendants of Midian were Ephah, Epher, Enoch,a Abida, and Eldaah. All these were descendants of Keturah. 5Abraham willed all that he owned to Isaac; 6but to Abraham's sons by concubines Abraham gave gifts while he was still living, and he sent them away from his son Isaac eastward, to the land of the East.

7This was the total span of Abraham's life: one hundred and seventy-five years. 8And Abraham breathed his last, dying at a good ripe age, old and contented; and he was gathered to his kin. 9His sons Isaac and Ishmael buried him in the cave of Machpelah, in the field of Ephron son of Zohar the Hittite, facing Mamre, 10the field that Abraham had bought from the Hittites; there Abraham was buried, and Sarah his wife. 11After the death of Abraham, God blessed his son Isaac. And Isaac settled near Beer-lahai-roi.

12This is the line of Ishmael, Abraham's son, whom Hagar the Egyptian, Sarah's slave, bore to Abraham. 13These are the names of the sons of Ishmael, by their names, in the order of their birth: Nebaioth, the first-born of Ishmael, Kedar, Adbeel, Mibsam, 14Mishma, Dumah, Massa, 15Hadad, Tema, Jetur, Naphish, and Kedmah. 16These are the sons of Ishmael and these are their names by their villages and by their encampments: twelve chieftains of as many tribes.—17These were the years of the life of Ishmael: one hundred and thirty-seven years; then he breathed his last and died, and was gathered to his kin.—18They dwelt from Havilah, by Shur, which is close to Egypt, all the way to Asshur; they camped alongside all their kinsmen.

תולדת

19This is the story of Isaac, son of Abraham. Abraham begot Isaac. 20Isaac was forty years old when he took to wife Rebekah, daughter of

a Or "Hanoch."

Bethuel the Aramean of Paddan-aram, sister of Laban the Aramean. ²¹Isaac pleaded with the LORD on behalf of his wife, because she was barren; and the LORD responded to his plea, and his wife Rebekah conceived. ²²But the children struggled in her womb, and she said, "If so, why do I exist?"ᵇ She went to inquire of the LORD, ²³and the LORD answered her,

"Two nations are in your womb,
Two separate peoples shall issue from your body;
One people shall be mightier than the other,
And the older shall serve the younger."

²⁴When her time to give birth was at hand, there were twins in her womb. ²⁵The first one emerged red, like a hairy mantle all over; so they named him Esau.ᶜ ²⁶Then his brother emerged, holding on to the heel of Esau; so they named him Jacob.ᵈ Isaac was sixty years old when they were born.

²⁷When the boys grew up, Esau became a skillful hunter, a man of the outdoors; but Jacob was a mild man who stayed in camp. ²⁸Isaac favored Esau because ᵉ⁻he had a taste for game;⁻ᵉ but Rebekah favored Jacob. ²⁹Once when Jacob was cooking a stew, Esau came in from the open, famished. ³⁰And Esau said to Jacob, "Give me some of that red stuff to gulp down, for I am famished"—which is why he was named Edom.ᶠ ³¹Jacob said, "First sell me your birthright." ³²And Esau said, "I am at the point of death, so of what use is my birthright to me?" ³³But Jacob said, "Swear to me first." So he swore to him, and sold his birthright to Jacob. ³⁴Jacob then gave Esau bread and lentil stew; he ate and drank, and he rose and went away. Thus did Esau spurn the birthright.

26 There was a famine in the land—aside from the previous famine that had occurred in the days of Abraham—and Isaac went to Abimelech, king of the Philistines, in Gerar. ²The LORD had appeared to him and said, "Do not go down to Egypt; stay in the land which I point out to you. ³Reside in this land, and I will be with you and bless you; I will assign all these lands to you and to your heirs, fulfilling the oath that I swore to your father Abraham. ⁴I will make your heirs as numerous as the stars of heaven, and assign to your heirs all these lands, so that all the nations of the earth shall bless themselves by your heirs—⁵inasmuch as Abraham obeyed Me and kept My charge: My commandments, My laws, and My teachings."

⁶So Isaac stayed in Gerar. ⁷When the men of the place asked him about

---

ᵇ *Meaning of Heb. uncertain.*
ᶜ *Synonym of "Seir," play on Heb.* seʿar *"hair."*
ᵈ *Play on Heb.* ʿaqeb *"heel."*
ᵉ⁻ᵉ *Lit. "game was in his mouth."*
ᶠ *Play on Heb.* ʾadom *"red."*

his wife, he said, "She is my sister," for he was afraid to say "my wife," thinking, "The men of the place might kill me on account of Rebekah, for she is beautiful." ⁸When some time had passed, Abimelech king of the Philistines, looking out of the window, saw Isaac fondling his wife Rebekah. ⁹Abimelech sent for Isaac and said, "So she is your wife! Why then did you say: 'She is my sister?'" Isaac said to him, "Because I thought I might lose my life on account of her." ¹⁰Abimelech said, "What have you done to us! One of the people might have lain with your wife, and you would have brought guilt upon us." ¹¹Abimelech then charged all the people, saying, "Anyone who molests this man or his wife shall be put to death."

¹²Isaac sowed in that land and reaped a hundredfold the same year. The LORD blessed him, ¹³and the man grew richer and richer until he was very wealthy: ¹⁴he acquired flocks and herds, and a large household, so that the Philistines envied him. ¹⁵And the Philistines stopped up all the wells which his father's servants had dug in the days of his father Abraham, filling them with earth. ¹⁶And Abimelech said to Isaac, "Go away from us, for you have become far too big for us."

¹⁷So Isaac departed from there and encamped in the wadi of Gerar, where he settled. ¹⁸Isaac dug anew the wells which had been dug in the days of his father Abraham and which the Philistines had stopped up after Abraham's death; and he gave them the same names that his father had given them. ¹⁹But when Isaac's servants, digging in the wadi, found there a well of spring water, ²⁰the herdsmen of Gerar quarreled with Isaac's herdsmen, saying, "The water is ours." He named that well Esek,ᵃ because they contended with him. ²¹And when they dug another well, they disputed over that one also; so he named it Sitnah.ᵇ ²²He moved from there and dug yet another well, and they did not quarrel over it; so he called it Rehoboth, saying, "Now at last the LORD has granted us ample spaceᶜ to increase in the land."

²³From there he went up to Beer-sheba. ²⁴That night the LORD appeared to him and said, "I am the God of your father Abraham. Fear not, for I am with you, and I will bless you and increase your offspring for the sake of My servant Abraham." ²⁵So he built an altar there and invoked the LORD by name. Isaac pitched his tent there and his servants started digging a well. ²⁶And Abimelech came to him from Gerar, with Ahuzzath his councilor and Phicol chief of his troops. ²⁷Isaac said to them, "Why have you come to me, seeing that you have been hostile to me and have

ᵃ *I.e., "contention."*
ᵇ *I.e., "harassment."*
ᶜ *Heb.* hirhib, *connected with "Rehoboth."*

driven me away from you?" 28And they said, "We now see plainly that the LORD has been with you, and we thought: Let there be a sworn treaty between our two parties, between you and us. Let us make a pact with you 29that you will not do us harm, just as we have not molested you but have always dealt kindly with you and sent you away in peace. From now on, be you blessed of the LORD!" 30Then he made for them a feast, and they ate and drank.

31Early in the morning, they exchanged oaths. Isaac then bade them farewell, and they departed from him in peace. 32That same day Isaac's servants came and told him about the well they had dug, and said to him, "We have found water!" 33He named it Shibah;d therefore the name of the city is Beer-sheba to this day.

34When Esau was forty years old, he took to wife Judith daughter of Beeri the Hittite, and Basemath daughter of Elon the Hittite; 35and they were a source of bitterness to Isaac and Rebekah.

27 When Isaac was old and his eyes were too dim to see, he called his older son Esau and said to him, "My son." He answered, "Here I am." 2And he said, "I am old now, and I do not know how soon I may die. 3Take your gear, your quiver and bow, and go out into the open and hunt me some game. 4Then prepare a dish for me such as I like, and bring it to me to eat, so that I may give you my innermost blessing before I die."

5Rebekah had been listening as Isaac spoke to his son Esau. When Esau had gone out into the open to hunt game to bring home, 6Rebekah said to her son Jacob, "I overheard your father speaking to your brother Esau, saying, 7'Bring me some game and prepare a dish for me to eat, that I may bless you, with the LORD's approval, before I die.' 8Now, my son, listen carefully as I instruct you. 9Go to the flock and fetch me two choice kids, and I will make of them a dish for your father, such as he likes. 10Then take it to your father to eat, in order that he may bless you before he dies." 11Jacob answered his mother Rebekah, "But my brother Esau is a hairy man and I am smooth-skinned. 12If my father touches me, I shall appear to him as a trickster and bring upon myself a curse, not a blessing." 13But his mother said to him, "Your curse, my son, be upon me! Just do as I say and go fetch them for me."

14He got them and brought them to his mother, and his mother pre-

---

d As though "oath."

pared a dish such as his father liked. ¹⁵Rebekah then took the best clothes of her older son Esau, which were there in the house, and had her younger son Jacob put them on; ¹⁶and she covered his hands and the hairless part of his neck with the skins of the kids. ¹⁷Then she put in the hands of her son Jacob the dish and the bread that she had prepared.

¹⁸He went to his father and said, "Father." And he said, "Yes, which of my sons are you?" ¹⁹Jacob said to his father, "I am Esau, your first-born; I have done as you told me. Pray sit up and eat of my game, that you may give me your innermost blessing." ²⁰Isaac said to his son, "How did you succeed so quickly, my son?" And he said, "Because the LORD your God granted me good fortune." ²¹Isaac said to Jacob, "Come closer that I may feel you, my son—whether you are really my son Esau or not." ²²So Jacob drew close to his father Isaac, who felt him and wondered. "The voice is the voice of Jacob, yet the hands are the hands of Esau." ²³He did not recognize him, because his hands were hairy like those of his brother Esau; and so he blessed him.

²⁴He asked, "Are you really my son Esau?" And when he said, "I am," ²⁵he said, "Serve me and let me eat of my son's game that I may give you my innermost blessing." So he served him and he ate, and he brought him wine and he drank. ²⁶Then his father Isaac said to him, "Come close and kiss me, my son"; ²⁷and he went up and kissed him. And he smelled his clothes and he blessed him, saying, "Ah, the smell of my son is like the smell of the fields that the LORD has blessed.

²⁸"May God give you
Of the dew of heaven and the fat of the earth,
Abundance of new grain and wine.
²⁹Let peoples serve you,
And nations bow to you;
Be master over your brothers,
And let your mother's sons bow to you.
Cursed be they who curse you,
Blessed they who bless you."

³⁰No sooner had Jacob left the presence of his father Isaac—after Isaac had finished blessing Jacob—than his brother Esau came back from his hunt. ³¹He too prepared a dish and brought it to his father. And he said to his father, "Let my father sit up and eat of his son's game, so that you may give me your innermost blessing." ³²His father Isaac said to him, "Who are you?" And he said, "I am your son, Esau, your first-born!" ³³Isaac was seized with very violent trembling. "Who was it then," he

demanded, "that hunted game and brought it to me? Moreover, I ate of it before you came, and I blessed him; now he must remain blessed!" ³⁴When Esau heard his father's words, he burst into wild and bitter sobbing, and said to his father, "Bless me too, Father!" ³⁵But he answered, "Your brother came with guile and took away your blessing." ³⁶[Esau] said, "Was he, then, named Jacob that he might supplant me[a] these two times? First he took away my birthright and now he has taken away my blessing!" And he added, "Have you not reserved a blessing for me?" ³⁷Isaac answered, saying to Esau, "But I have made him master over you: I have given him all his brothers for servants, and sustained him with grain and wine. What, then, can I still do for you, my son?" ³⁸And Esau said to his father, "Have you but one blessing, Father? Bless me too, Father!" And Esau wept aloud. ³⁹And his father Isaac answered, saying to him,

"See, your abode shall [b]enjoy the fat of the earth
And[b] the dew of heaven above.
⁴⁰Yet by your sword you shall live,
And you shall serve your brother;
But when you grow restive,
You shall break his yoke from your neck."

⁴¹Now Esau harbored a grudge against Jacob because of the blessing which his father had given him, and Esau said to himself, "Let but the mourning period of my father come, and I will kill my brother Jacob." ⁴²When the words of her older son Esau were reported to Rebekah, she sent for her younger son Jacob and said to him, "Your brother Esau is consoling himself by planning to kill you. ⁴³Now, my son, listen to me. Flee at once to Haran, to my brother Laban. ⁴⁴Stay with him a while, until your brother's fury subsides—⁴⁵until your brother's anger against you subsides—and he forgets what you have done to him. Then I will fetch you from there. Let me not lose you both in one day!"

⁴⁶Rebekah said to Isaac, "I am disgusted with my life because of the Hittite women. If Jacob marries a Hittite woman like these, from among **28** the native women, what good will life be to me?" ¹So Isaac sent for Jacob and blessed him. He instructed him, saying, "You shall not take a wife from among the Canaanite women. ²Up, go to Paddan-aram, to the house of Bethuel, your mother's father, and take a wife there from among the daughters of Laban, your mother's brother. ³May El Shaddai[a] bless you, make you fertile and numerous, so that you become

---

ᵃ Heb. 'aqab, connected with "Jacob."
ᵇ⁻ᵇ Others "be away from the fat of the earth and from."

ᵃ See note at 17.1.

an assembly of peoples. 4May He grant the blessing of Abraham to you and your offspring, that you may possess the land where you are sojourning, which God assigned to Abraham."

5Then Isaac sent Jacob off, and he went to Paddan-aram, to Laban the son of Bethuel the Aramean, the brother of Rebekah, mother of Jacob and Esau.

6When Esau saw that Isaac had blessed Jacob and sent him off to Paddan-aram to take a wife from there, charging him, as he blessed him, "You shall not take a wife from among the Canaanite women," 7and that Jacob had obeyed his father and mother and gone to Paddan-aram, 8Esau realized that the Canaanite women displeased his father Isaac. 9So Esau went to Ishmael and took to wife, in addition to the wives he had, Mahalath the daughter of Ishmael son of Abraham, sister of Nebaioth.

ויצא

10Jacob left Beer-sheba, and set out for Haran. 11He came upon a certain place and stopped there for the night, for the sun had set. Taking one of the stones of that place, he put it under his head and lay down in that place. 12He had a dream; a stairwayb was set on the ground and its top reached to the sky, and angels of God were going up and down on it. 13And the LORD was standing beside him and He said, "I am the LORD, the God of your father Abraham and the God of Isaac: the ground on which you are lying I will assign to you and to your offspring. 14Your descendants shall be as the dust of the earth; you shall spread out to the west and to the east, to the north and to the south. All the families of the earth shall bless themselves by you and your descendants. 15Remember, I am with you: I will protect you wherever you go and will bring you back to this land. I will not leave you until I have done what I have promised you."

16Jacob awoke from his sleep and said, "Surely the LORD is present in this place, and I did not know it!" 17Shaken, he said, "How awesome is this place! This is none other than the abode of God, and that is the gateway to heaven." 18Early in the morning, Jacob took the stone that he had put under his head and set it up as a pillar and poured oil on the top of it. 19He named that site Bethel;c but previously the name of the city had been Luz.

20Jacob then made a vow, saying, "If God remains with me, if He

b Or "ramp"; others "ladder."
c I.e., "house of God."

43

protects me on this journey that I am making, and gives me bread to eat and clothing to wear, 21and if I return safe to my father's house—the LORD shall be my God. 22And this stone, which I have set up as a pillar, shall be God's abode; and of all that You give me, I will set aside a tithe for You."

29 Jacob ᵃ⁻resumed his journey⁻ᵃ and came to the land of the Easterners. 2There before his eyes was a well in the open. Three flocks of sheep were lying there beside it, for the flocks were watered from that well. The stone on the mouth of the well was large. 3When all the flocks were gathered there, the stone would be rolled from the mouth of the well and the sheep watered; then the stone would be put back in its place on the mouth of the well.

4Jacob said to them, "My friends, where are you from?" And they said, "We are from Haran." 5He said to them, "Do you know Laban the son of Nahor?" And they said, "Yes, we do." 6He continued, "Is he well?" They answered, "Yes, he is; and there is his daughter Rachel, coming with the flock." 7He said, "It is still broad daylight, too early to round up the animals; water the flock and take them to pasture." 8But they said, "We cannot, until all the flocks are rounded up; then the stone is rolled off the mouth of the well and we water the sheep."

9While he was still speaking with them, Rachel came with her father's flock; for she was a shepherdess. 10And when Jacob saw Rachel, the daughter of his uncleᵇ Laban, and the flock of his uncle Laban, Jacob went up and rolled the stone off the mouth of the well, and watered the flock of his uncle Laban. 11Then Jacob kissed Rachel, and broke into tears. 12Jacob told Rachel that he was her father's kinsman, that he was Rebekah's son; and she ran and told her father. 13On hearing the news of his sister's son Jacob, Laban ran to greet him; he embraced him and kissed him, and took him into his house. He told Laban all that had happened, 14and Laban said to him, "You are truly my bone and flesh."

When he had stayed with him a month's time, 15Laban said to Jacob, "Just because you are a kinsman, should you serve me for nothing? Tell me, what shall your wages be?" 16Now Laban had two daughters; the name of the older one was Leah, and the name of the younger was Rachel. 17Leah had weak eyes; Rachel was shapely and beautiful. 18Jacob loved

ᵃ⁻ᵃ Lit. "lifted up his feet."
ᵇ Lit. "his mother's brother."

Rachel; so he answered, "I will serve you seven years for your younger daughter Rachel." [19]Laban said, "Better that I give her to you than that I should give her to an outsider. Stay with me." [20]So Jacob served seven years for Rachel and they seemed to him but a few days because of his love for her.

[21]Then Jacob said to Laban, "Give me my wife, for my time is fulfilled, that I may cohabit with her." [22]And Laban gathered all the people of the place and made a feast. [23]When evening came, he took his daughter Leah and brought her to him; and he cohabited with her.—[24]Laban had given his maidservant Zilpah to his daughter Leah as her maid.—[25]When morning came, there was Leah! So he said to Laban, "What is this you have done to me? I was in your service for Rachel! Why did you deceive me?" [26]Laban said, "It is not the practice in our place to marry off the younger before the older. [27]Wait until the bridal week of this one is over and we will give you that one too, provided you serve me another seven years." [28]Jacob did so; he waited out the bridal week of the one, and then he gave him his daughter Rachel as wife.—[29]Laban had given his maidservant Bilhah to his daughter Rachel as her maid.—[30]And Jacob cohabited with Rachel also; indeed, he loved Rachel more than Leah. And he served him another seven years.

[31]The LORD saw that Leah was unloved and he opened her womb; but Rachel was barren. [32]Leah conceived and bore a son, and named him Reuben;[c] for she declared, "It means: 'The LORD has seen[d] my affliction'; it also means: 'Now my husband will love me.'"[e] [33]She conceived again and bore a son, and declared, "This is because the LORD heard[f] that I was unloved and has given me this one also"; so she named him Simeon. [34]Again she conceived and bore a son and declared, "This time my husband will become attached[g] to me, for I have borne him three sons." Therefore he was named Levi. [35]She conceived again and bore a son, and declared, "This time I will praise[h] the LORD." Therefore she named him Judah. Then she stopped bearing.

30

When Rachel saw that she had borne Jacob no children, she became envious of her sister; and Rachel said to Jacob, "Give me children, or I shall die." [2]Jacob was incensed at Rachel, and said, "Can I take the place of God, who has denied you fruit of the womb?" [3]She said, "Here

---

[c] Understood as "See a son."
[d] Heb. ra'ah, connected with the first part of "Reuben."
[e] Heb. ye'ehabani, connected with the last part of "Reuben."
[f] Heb. shama', connected with "Simeon."
[g] Heb. yillaweh, connected with "Levi."
[h] Heb. 'odeh, connected with "Judah."

is my maid Bilhah. Consort with her, that she may bear on my knees and that through her I too may have children." [4]So she gave him her maid Bilhah as concubine, and Jacob cohabited with her. [5]Bilhah conceived and bore Jacob a son. [6]And Rachel said, "God has vindicated me;[a] indeed, He has heeded my plea and given me a son." Therefore she named him Dan. [7]Rachel's maid Bilhah conceived again and bore Jacob a second son. [8]And Rachel said, [b-]"A fateful contest I waged[-b] with my sister; yes, and I have prevailed." So she named him Naphtali.

[9]When Leah saw that she had stopped bearing, she took her maid Zilpah and gave her to Jacob as concubine. [10]And when Leah's maid Zilpah bore Jacob a son, [11]Leah said, "What luck!"[c] So she named him Gad. [12]When Leah's maid Zilpah bore Jacob a second son, [13]Leah declared, "What fortune!"[d] meaning, "Women will deem me fortunate." So she named him Asher.

[14]Once, at the time of the wheat harvest, Reuben came upon some mandrakes in the field and brought them to his mother Leah. Rachel said to Leah, "Please give me some of your son's mandrakes." [15]But she said to her, "Was it not enough for you to take away my husband, that you would also take my son's mandrakes?" Rachel replied, "I promise, he shall lie with you tonight, in return for your son's mandrakes." [16]When Jacob came home from the field in the evening, Leah went out to meet him and said, "You are to sleep with me, for I have hired you with my son's mandrakes." And he lay with her that night. [17]God heeded Leah, and she conceived and bore him a fifth son. [18]And Leah said, "God has given me my reward[e] for having given my maid to my husband." So she named him Issachar. [19]When Leah conceived again and bore Jacob a sixth son, [20]Leah said, "God has given me a choice gift;[f] this time my husband will exalt me,[g] for I have borne him six sons." So she named him Zebulun. [21]Last, she bore him a daughter, and named her Dinah.

[22]Now God remembered Rachel; God heeded her and opened her womb. [23]She conceived and bore a son, and said, "God has taken away[h] my disgrace." [24]So she named him Joseph, which is to say, "May the LORD add[i] another son for me."

[25]After Rachel had borne Joseph, Jacob said to Laban, "Give me leave to go back to my own homeland. [26]Give me my wives and my children, for whom I have served you, that I may go; for well you know what

---

[a] *Heb.* dananni, *connected with "Dan."*
[b-b] *Heb.* naphtule . . . naphtalti, *connected with "Naphtali." Lit. "A contest of God . . ."*
[c] Kethib begad; *the* qere *reads* ba gad *"luck has come"; connected with "Gad."*
[d] *Heb.* be'oshri, *connected with "Asher."*
[e] *Heb.* sekhari, *connected with "Issachar."*
[f] *Heb.* zebadani . . . zebed.
[g] *Heb.* yizbeleni; *others "will dwell with me."*
[h] *Heb.* 'asaph.
[i] *Heb.* yoseph.

services I have rendered you." ²⁷But Laban said to him, "If you will indulge me,ʲ I have learned by divination that the LORD has blessed me on your account." ²⁸And he continued, "Name the wages due from me, and I will pay you." ²⁹But he said, "You know well how I have served you and how your livestock has fared with me. ³⁰For the little you had before I came has grown to much, since the LORD has blessed you wherever I turned. And now, when shall I make provision for my own household?" ³¹He said, "What shall I pay you?" And Jacob said, "Pay me nothing! If you will do this thing for me, I will again pasture and keep your flocks: ³²let me pass through your whole flock today, removing from there every speckled and spotted animal—every dark-colored sheep and every spotted and speckled goat. Such shall be my wages. ³³In the future when you go over my wages, let my honesty toward you testify for me: if there are among my goats any that are not speckled or spotted or any sheep that are not dark-colored, they got there by theft." ³⁴And Laban said, "Very well, let it be as you say."

³⁵But that same day he removed the streaked and spotted he-goats and all the speckled and spotted she-goats—every one that had white on it—and all the dark-colored sheep, and left them in the charge of his sons. ³⁶And he put a distance of three days' journey between himself and Jacob, while Jacob was pasturing the rest of Laban's flock.

³⁷Jacob then got fresh shoots of poplar, and of almond and plane, and peeled white stripes in them, laying bare the white of the shoots. ³⁸The rods that he had peeled he set up in front of the goatsᵏ in the troughs, the water receptacles, that the goats came to drink from. Their mating occurred when they came to drink, ³⁹and since the goats mated by the rods, the goats brought forth streaked, speckled, and spotted young. ⁴⁰But Jacob dealt separately with the sheep; he made these animals face the streaked or wholly dark-colored animals in Laban's flock. And so he produced special flocks for himself, which he did not put with Laban's flocks. ⁴¹Moreover, when the sturdierˡ animals were mating, Jacob would place the rods in the troughs, in full view of the animals, so that they mated by the rods; ⁴²but with the feeblerᵐ animals he would not place them there. Thus the feeble onesᵐ went to Laban and the sturdy to Jacob. ⁴³So the man grew exceedingly prosperous, and came to own large flocks, maidservants and menservants, camels and asses.

ʲ Lit. "If I have found favor in your eyes."
ᵏ Lit. "flocks."
ˡ Or "early-breeding."
ᵐ Or "late-breeding."

31

Now he heard the things that Laban's sons were saying: "Jacob has taken all that was our father's, and from that which was our father's he has built up all this wealth." ²Jacob also saw that Laban's manner toward him was not as it had been in the past. ³Then the LORD said to Jacob, "Return to the land of your fathers where you were born, and I will be with you." ⁴Jacob had Rachel and Leah called to the field, where his flock was, ⁵and said to them, "I see that your father's manner toward me is not as it has been in the past. But the God of my father has been with me. ⁶As you know, I have served your father with all my might; ⁷but your father has cheated me, changing my wages time and again.ᵃ God, however, would not let him do me harm. ⁸If he said thus, 'The speckled shall be your wages,' then all the flocks would drop speckled young; and if he said thus, 'The streaked shall be your wages,' then all the flocks would drop streaked young. ⁹God has taken away your father's livestock and given it to me.

¹⁰"Once, at the mating time of the flocks, ᵇ⁻I had a dream in which I saw⁻ᵇ that the he-goats mating with the flock were streaked, speckled, and mottled. ¹¹And in the dream an angel of God said to me, 'Jacob!' 'Here,' I answered. ¹²And he said, 'Note well that all the he-goats which are mating with the flock are streaked, speckled, and mottled; for I have noted all that Laban has been doing to you. ¹³I am the God of Beth-el, where you anointed a pillar and where you made a vow to Me. Now, arise and leave this land and return to your native land.'"

¹⁴Then Rachel and Leah answered him, saying, "Have we still a share in the inheritance of our father's house? ¹⁵Surely, he regards us as outsiders, now that he has sold us and has used up our purchase price. ¹⁶Truly, all the wealth that God has taken away from our father belongs to us and to our children. Now then, do just as God has told you."

¹⁷Thereupon Jacob put his children and wives on camels; ¹⁸and he drove off all his livestock and all the wealth that he had amassed, the livestock in his possession that he had acquired in Paddan-aram, to go to his father Isaac in the land of Canaan.

¹⁹Meanwhile Laban had gone to shear his sheep, and Rachel stole her father's household idols. ²⁰Jacob ᶜ⁻kept Laban the Aramean in the dark,⁻ᶜ not telling him that he was fleeing, ²¹and fled with all that he had. Soon he was across the Euphrates and heading toward the hill country of Gilead.

ᵃ Lit. "ten times."
ᵇ⁻ᵇ Lit. "I raised my eyes and saw in a dream, behold."
ᶜ⁻ᶜ Lit. "stole the mind of Laban the Aramean"; similarly in v. 26.

²²On the third day, Laban was told that Jacob had fled. ²³So he took his kinsmen with him and pursued him a distance of seven days, catching up with him in the hill country of Gilead. ²⁴But God appeared to Laban the Aramean in a dream by night and said to him, "Beware of attempting anything with Jacob, good or bad."

²⁵Laban overtook Jacob. Jacob had pitched his tent on the Height, and Laban with his kinsmen encamped in the hill country of Gilead. ²⁶And Laban said to Jacob, "What did you mean by keeping me in the dark and carrying off my daughters like captives of the sword? ²⁷Why did you flee in secrecy and mislead me and not tell me? I would have sent you off with festive music, with timbrel and lyre. ²⁸You did not even let me kiss my sons and daughters good-by! It was a foolish thing for you to do. ²⁹I have it in my power to do you harm; but the God of your father said to me last night, 'Beware of attempting anything with Jacob, good or bad.' ³⁰Very well, you had to leave because you were longing for your father's house; but why did you steal my gods?"

³¹Jacob answered Laban, saying, "I was afraid because I thought you would take your daughters from me by force. ³²But anyone with whom you find your gods shall not remain alive! In the presence of our kinsmen, point out what I have of yours and take it." Jacob, of course, did not know that Rachel had stolen them.

³³So Laban went into Jacob's tent and Leah's tent and the tents of the two maidservants; but he did not find them. Leaving Leah's tent, he entered Rachel's tent. ³⁴Rachel, meanwhile, had taken the idols and placed them in the camel cushion and sat on them; and Laban rummaged through the tent without finding them. ³⁵For she said to her father, "Let not my lord take it amiss that I cannot rise before you, for the period of women is upon me." Thus he searched, but could not find the household idols.

³⁶Now Jacob became incensed and took up his grievance with Laban. Jacob spoke up and said to Laban, "What is my crime, what is my guilt that you should pursue me? ³⁷You rummaged through all my things; what have you found of all your household objects? Set it here, before my kinsmen and yours, and let them decide between us two.

³⁸"These twenty years I have spent in your service, your ewes and she-goats never miscarried, nor did I feast on rams from your flock. ³⁹That which was torn by beasts I never brought to you; I myself made good the loss; you exacted it of me, whether snatched by day or snatched by night. ⁴⁰Often,^d scorching heat ravaged me by day and frost by night;

---

^d Lit. "I was."

and sleep fled from my eyes. [41]Of the twenty years that I spent in your household, I served you fourteen years for your two daughters, and six years for your flocks; and you changed my wages time and again.[c] [42]Had not the God of my father, the God of Abraham and the Fear[f] of Isaac, been with me, you would have sent me away empty-handed. But God took notice of my plight and the toil of my hands, and He gave judgment last night."

[43]Then Laban spoke up and said to Jacob, "The daughters are my daughters, the children are my children, and the flocks are my flocks; all that you see is mine. Yet what can I do now about my daughters or the children they have borne? [44]Come, then, let us make a pact, you and I, that there may be a witness between you and me." [45]Thereupon Jacob took a stone and set it up as a pillar. [46]And Jacob said to his kinsmen, "Gather stones." So they took stones and made a mound; and they partook of a meal there by the mound. [47]Laban named it Yegar-sahadutha,[g] but Jacob named it Gal-ed.[h] And Laban declared, "This mound is a witness between you and me this day." That is why it was named Gal-ed; [49]and [it was called] Mizpah, because he said, "May the LORD watch[i] between you and me, when we are out of sight of each other. [50]If you ill-treat my daughters or take other wives besides my daughters—though no one else be about, remember, God Himself will be witness between you and me."

[51]And Laban said to Jacob, "Here is this mound and here the pillar which I have set up between you and me: [52]this mound shall be witness and this pillar shall be witness that I am not to cross to you past this mound, and that you are not to cross to me past this mound and this pillar, with hostile intent. [53]May the God of Abraham and the god of Nahor"—their ancestral deities—"judge between us." And Jacob swore by the Fear[f] of his father Isaac. [54]Jacob then offered up a sacrifice on the Height, and invited his kinsmen to partake of the meal. After the meal, they spent the night on the Height.

32

Early in the morning, Laban kissed his sons and daughters and bade them good-by; then Laban left on his journey homeward. [2]Jacob went on his way, and angels of God encountered him. [3]When he saw

---

[c] Lit. "ten times."
[f] Meaning of Heb. paḥad uncertain.
[g] Aramaic for "the mound (or, stone-heap) of witness."
[h] Heb. for "the mound (or, stone-heap) of witness," reflecting the name Gilead, v. 23.
[i] Heb. yiseph, associated with Mizpah.

them, Jacob said, "This is God's camp." So he named that place Maha-naim.ᵃ

וישלח

⁴Jacob sent messengers ahead to his brother Esau in the land of Seir, the country of Edom, ⁵and instructed them as follows, ᵇ⁻"Thus shall you say, 'To my lord Esau, thus says your servant Jacob:⁻ᵇ I stayed with Laban and remained until now; ⁶I have acquired cattle, asses, sheep, and male and female slaves; and I send this message to my lord in the hope of gaining your favor.' " ⁷The messengers returned to Jacob, saying, "We came to your brother Esau; he himself is coming to meet you, and there are four hundred men with him." ⁸Jacob was greatly frightened; in his anxiety, he divided the people with him, and the flocks and herds and camels, into two camps, ⁹thinking, "If Esau comes to the one camp and attacks it, the other camp may yet escape."

¹⁰Then Jacob said, "O God of my father Abraham and God of my father Isaac, O LORD, who said to me, 'Return to your native land and I will deal bountifully with you'! ¹¹I am unworthy of all the kindness that You have so steadfastly shown Your servant: with my staff alone I crossed this Jordan, and now I have become two camps. ¹²Deliver me, I pray, from the hand of my brother, from the hand of Esau; else, I fear, he may come and strike me down, mothers and children alike. ¹³Yet You have said, 'I will deal bountifully with you and make your offspring as the sands of the sea, which are too numerous to count.' "

¹⁴After spending the night there, he selected from what was at hand these presents for his brother Esau: ¹⁵200 she-goats and 20 he-goats; 200 ewes and 20 rams; ¹⁶30 milch camels with their colts; 40 cows and 10 bulls; 20 she-asses and 10 he-asses. ¹⁷These he put in the charge of his servants, drove by drove, and he told his servants, "Go on ahead, and keep a distance between droves." ¹⁸He instructed the one in front as follows, "When my brother Esau meets you and asks you, 'Whose man are you? Where are you going? And whose [animals] are these ahead of you?' ¹⁹you shall answer, 'Your servant Jacob's; they are a gift sent to my lord Esau; and [Jacob] himself is right behind us.' " ²⁰He gave similar instructions to the second one, and the third, and all the others who followed the droves, namely, "Thus and so shall you say to Esau when you reach him. ²¹And you shall add, 'And your servant Jacob himself is

---

ᵃ *Connected with Heb.* maḥaneh, "camp."
ᵇ⁻ᵇ *Or "Thus you shall say to my lord Esau, 'Thus says your servant Jacob,' . . ."*

right behind us.' " For he reasoned, "If I propitiate him with presents in advance, and then face him, perhaps he will show me favor." 22And so the gift went on ahead, while he remained in camp that night.

23That same night he arose, and taking his two wives, his two maid-servants, and his eleven children, he crossed the ford of the Jabbok. 24After taking them across the stream, he sent across all his possessions. 25Jacob was left alone. And a man wrestled with him until the break of dawn. 26When he saw that he had not prevailed against him, he wrenched Jacob's hip at its socket, so that the socket of his hip was strained as he wrestled with him. 27Then he said, "Let me go, for dawn is breaking." But he answered, "I will not let you go, unless you bless me." 28Said the other, "What is your name?" He replied, "Jacob." 29Said he, "Your name shall no longer be Jacob, but Israel, for you have striven^c with ^{d-}beings divine and human,^{-d} and have prevailed." 30Jacob asked, "Pray tell me your name." But he said, "You must not ask my name!" And he took leave of him there. 31So Jacob named the place Peniel,^e meaning, "I have seen a divine being face to face, yet my life has been preserved." 32The sun rose upon him as he passed Penuel, limping on his hip. 33That is why the children of Israel to this day do not eat the thigh muscle that is on the socket of the hip, since Jacob's hip socket was wrenched at the thigh muscle.

33 Looking up, Jacob saw Esau coming, accompanied by four hundred men. He divided the children among Leah, Rachel, and the two maids, 2putting the maids and their children first, Leah and her children next, and Rachel and Joseph last. 3He himself went on ahead and bowed low to the ground seven times until he was near his brother. 4Esau ran to greet him. He embraced him and, falling on his neck, he kissed him; and they wept. 5Looking about, he saw the women and the children. "Who," he asked, "are these with you?" He answered, "The children with whom God has favored your servant." 6Then the maids, with their children, came forward and bowed low; 7next Leah, with her children, came forward and bowed low; and last, Joseph and Rachel came forward and bowed low; 8And he asked, "What do you mean by all this company which I have met?" He answered, "To gain my lord's favor." 9Esau said, "I have enough, my brother; let what you have remain yours." 10But Jacob said, "No, I pray you; if you would do me this favor, accept from me this gift; for to see your face is like seeing the face of God, and you have received

---

^c *Heb.* saritha, *connected with first part of "Israel."*
^{d-d} *Or* "God (Elohim, *connected with second part of 'Israel') and men."*
^e *Understood as "face of God."*

me favorably. [11]Please accept my present which has been brought to you, for God has favored me and I have plenty." And when he urged him, he accepted.

[12]And [Esau] said, "Let us start on our journey, and I will proceed at your pace." [13]But he said to him, "My lord knows that the children are frail and that the flocks and herds, which are nursing, are a care to me; if they are driven hard a single day, all the flocks will die. [14]Let my lord go on ahead of his servant, while I travel slowly, at the pace of the cattle before me and at the pace of the children, until I come to my lord in Seir."

[15]Then Esau said, "Let me assign to you some of the men who are with me." But he said, "Oh no, my lord is too kind to me!" [16]So Esau started back that day on his way to Seir. [17]But Jacob journeyed on to Succoth, and built a house for himself and made stalls for his cattle; that is why the place was called Succoth.[a]

[18]Jacob arrived safe in the city of Shechem which is in the land of Canaan—having come thus from Paddan-aram—and he encamped before the city. [19]The parcel of land where he pitched his tent he purchased from the children of Hamor, Shechem's father, for a hundred *kesitahs*.[b] [20]He set up an altar there, and called it El-elohe-yisrael.[c]

34

Now Dinah, the daughter whom Leah had borne to Jacob, went out to visit the daughters of the land. [2]Shechem son of Hamor the Hivite, chief of the country, saw her, and took her and lay with her by force. [3]Being strongly drawn to Dinah daughter of Jacob, and in love with the maiden, he spoke to the maiden tenderly. [4]So Shechem said to his father Hamor, "Get me this girl as a wife."

[5]Jacob heard that he had defiled his daughter Dinah; but since his sons were in the field with his cattle, Jacob kept silent until they came home. [6]Then Shechem's father Hamor came out to Jacob to speak to him. [7]Meanwhile Jacob's sons, having heard the news, came in from the field. The men were distressed and very angry, because he had committed an outrage in Israel by lying with Jacob's daughter—a thing not to be done.

[8]And Hamor spoke with them, saying, "My son Shechem longs for your daughter. Please give her to him in marriage. [9]Intermarry with us: give your daughters to us, and take our daughters for yourselves: [10]You

a *Meaning "stalls," "huts," "booths."*
b *Heb.* qesitah, *a unit of unknown value.*
c *"El, God of Israel."*

will dwell among us, and the land will be open before you; settle, move about, and acquire holdings in it." ¹¹Then Shechem said to her father and brothers, "Do me this favor, and I will pay whatever you tell me. ¹²Ask of me a bride-price ever so high, as well as gifts, and I will pay what you tell me; only give me the maiden for a wife."

¹³Jacob's sons answered Shechem and his father Hamor—speaking with guile because he had defiled their sister Dinah—¹⁴and said to them, "We cannot do this thing, to give our sister to a man who is uncircumcised, for that is a disgrace among us. ¹⁵Only on this condition will we agree with you; that you will become like us in that every male among you is circumcised. ¹⁶Then we will give our daughters to you and take your daughters to ourselves; and we will dwell among you and become as one kindred. ¹⁷But if you will not listen to us and become circumcised, we will take our daughter and go."

¹⁸Their words pleased Hamor and Hamor's son Shechem. ¹⁹And the youth lost no time in doing the thing, for he wanted Jacob's daughter. Now he was the most respected in his father's house. ²⁰So Hamor and his son Shechem went to the ᵃ-public place-ᵃ of their town and spoke to their fellow townsmen, saying, ²¹"These people are our friends; let them settle in the land and move about in it, for the land is large enough for them; we will take their daughters to ourselves as wives and give our daughters to them. ²²But only on this condition will the men agree with us to dwell among us and be as one kindred: that all our males become circumcised as they are circumcised. ²³Their cattle and substance and all their beasts will be ours, if we only agree to their terms, so that they will settle among us." ²⁴All ᵇ-who went out of the gate of his town-ᵇ heeded Hamor and his son Shechem, and all males, ᵇ-all those who went out of the gate of his town,-ᵇ were circumcised.

²⁵On the third day, when they were in pain, Simeon and Levi, two of Jacob's sons, brothers of Dinah, took each his sword, came upon the city unmolested, and slew all the males. ²⁶They put Hamor and his son Shechem to the sword, took Dinah out of Shechem's house, and went away. ²⁷The other sons of Jacob came upon the slain and plundered the town, because their sister had been defiled. ²⁸They seized their flocks and herds and asses, all that was inside the town and outside; ²⁹all their wealth, all their children, and their wives, all that was in the houses, they took as captives and booty.

ᵃ⁻ᵃ Lit. "gate."
ᵇ⁻ᵇ I.e., all his fellow townsmen.

[30]Jacob said to Simeon and Levi, "You have brought trouble on me, making me odious among the inhabitants of the land, the Canaanites and the Perizzites; my men are few in number, so that if they unite against me and attack me, I and my house will be destroyed." [31]But they answered, "Should our sister be treated like a whore?"

35

God said to Jacob, "Arise, go up to Bethel and remain there; and build an altar there to the God who appeared to you when you were fleeing from your brother Esau." [2]So Jacob said to his household and to all who were with him, "Rid yourselves of the alien gods in your midst, purify yourselves, and change your clothes. [3]Come, let us go up to Bethel, and I will build an altar there to the God who answered me when I was in distress and who has been with me wherever I have gone." [4]They gave to Jacob all the alien gods that they had, and the rings that were in their ears, and Jacob buried them under the terebinth that was near Shechem. [5]As they set out, a terror from God fell on the cities round about, so that they did not pursue the sons of Jacob.

[6]Thus Jacob came to Luz—that is, Bethel—in the land of Canaan, he and all the people who were with him. [7]There he built an altar and named the site El-bethel,[a] for it was there that God had revealed Himself to him when he was fleeing from his brother.

[8]Deborah, Rebekah's nurse, died, and was buried under the oak below Bethel; so it was named Allon-bacuth.[b]

[9]God appeared again to Jacob on his arrival from Paddan-aram, and He blessed him. [10]God said to him,

"You whose name is Jacob,
You shall be called Jacob no more,
But Israel shall be your name."

Thus He named him Israel.

[11]And God said to him,

"I am El Shaddai.[c]
Be fertile and increase;
A nation, yea an assembly of nations,
Shall descend from you.
Kings shall issue from your loins.

[12]The land that I assigned to Abraham and Isaac

---

[a] "The God of Bethel."
[b] Understood as "the oak of the weeping."
[c] Cf. 17.1.

I assign to you;
And to your offspring to come
Will I assign the land."

¹³God parted from him at the spot where He had spoken to him; ¹⁴and Jacob set up a pillar at the site where He had spoken to him, a pillar of stone, and he offered a libation on it and poured oil upon it. ¹⁵Jacob gave the site, where God had spoken to him, the name of Bethel.

¹⁶They set out from Bethel; but when they were still some distance short of Ephrath, Rachel was in childbirth, and she had hard labor. ¹⁷When her labor was at its hardest, the midwife said to her, "Have no fear, for it is another boy for you." ¹⁸But as she breathed her last—for she was dying—she named him Ben-oni;ᵈ but his father called him Benjamin.ᵉ Thus Rachel died. She was buried on the road to Ephrath—now Bethlehem. ²⁰Over her grave Jacob set up a pillar; it is the pillar at Rachel's grave to this day. ²¹Israel journeyed on, and pitched his tent beyond Migdal-eder.

²²While Israel stayed in that land, Reuben went and lay with Bilhah, his father's concubine; and Israel found out.

Now the sons of Jacob were twelve in number. ²³The sons of Leah: Reuben—Jacob's first-born—Simeon, Levi, Judah, Issachar, and Zebulun. ²⁴The sons of Rachel: Joseph and Benjamin. ²⁵The sons of Bilhah, Rachel's maid: Dan and Naphtali. ²⁶And the sons of Zilpah, Leah's maid: Gad and Asher. These are the sons of Jacob who were born to him in Paddan-aram.

²⁷And Jacob came to his father Isaac at Mamre, at Kiriath-arba—now Hebron—where Abraham and Isaac had sojourned. ²⁸Isaac was a hundred and eighty years old ²⁹when he breathed his last and died. Heᶠ was gathered to his kin in ripe old age; and he was buried by his sons Esau and Jacob.

36 This is the line of Esau—that is, Edom.

²Esau took his wives from among the Canaanite women—Adah daughter of Elon the Hittite, and Oholibamah daughter of Anah daughter of Zibeon the Hiviteᵃ—³and also Basemath daughter of Ishmael and sister of Nebaioth. ⁴Adah bore to Esau Eliphaz; Basemath bore Reuel; ⁵and

---

ᵈ Understood as "son of my suffering (or, strength)."
ᵉ I.e., "son of the right hand," or "son of the south."
ᶠ Lit. "Isaac."

ᵃ Cf. v. 20, "Horite."

Oholibamah bore Jeush, Jalam, and Korah. Those were the sons of Esau, who were born to him in the land of Canaan.

⁶Esau took his wives, his sons and daughters, and all the members of his household, his cattle and all his livestock, and all the property that he had acquired in the land of Canaan, and went to another land because of his brother Jacob. ⁷For their possessions were too many for them to dwell together, and the land where they sojourned could not support them because of their livestock. ⁸So Esau settled in the hill country of Seir—Esau being Edom.

⁹This, then, is the line of Esau, the ancestor of the Edomites, in the hill country of Seir.

¹⁰These are the names of Esau's sons: Eliphaz, the son of Esau's wife Adah; Reuel, the son of Esau's wife Basemath. ¹¹The sons of Eliphaz were Teman, Omar, Zepho, Gatam, and Kenaz. ¹²Timna was a concubine of Esau's son Eliphaz; she bore Amalek to Eliphaz. Those were the descendants of Esau's wife Adah. ¹³And these were the sons of Reuel: Nahath, Zerah, Shammah, and Mizzah. Those were the descendants of Esau's wife Basemath. ¹⁴And these were the sons of Esau's wife Oholibamah, daughter of Anah daughter of Zibeon: she bore to Esau Jeush, Jalam, and Korah.

¹⁵These are the clans of the children of Esau. The descendants of Esau's first-born Eliphaz: the clans Teman, Omar, Zepho, Kenaz, ¹⁶Korah, Gatam, and Amalek; these are the clans of Eliphaz in the land of Edom. Those are the descendants of Adah. ¹⁷And these are the descendants of Esau's son Reuel: the clans Nahath, Zerah, Shammah, and Mizzah; these are the clans of Reuel in the land of Edom. Those are the descendants of Esau's wife Basemath. ¹⁸And these are the descendants of Esau's wife Oholibamah: the clans Jeush, Jalam, and Korah; these are the clans of Esau's wife Oholibamah, the daughter of Anah. ¹⁹Those were the sons of Esau—that is, Edom—and those are their clans.

²⁰These were the sons of Seir the Horite, who were settled in the land: Lotan, Shobal, Zibeon, Anah, ²¹Dishon, Ezer, and Dishan. Those are the clans of the Horites, the descendants of Seir, in the land of Edom.

²²The sons of Lotan were Hori and Hemam; and Lotan's sister was Timna. ²³The sons of Shobal were these: Alvan, Manahath, Ebal, Shepho, and Onam. ²⁴The sons of Zibeon were these: Aiah[b] and Anah—that was the Anah who discovered the hot springs[c] in the wilderness while pasturing the asses of his father Zibeon. ²⁵The children of Anah were these:

ᵇ *Heb. "and Aiah."*
ᶜ *Meaning of Heb.* yemim *uncertain.*

57

Dishon and Anah's daughter Oholibamah. ²⁶The sons of Dishon[d] were these: Hemdan, Eshban, Ithran, and Cheran. ²⁷The sons of Ezer were these: Bilhan, Zaavan, and Akan. ²⁸And the sons of Dishan were these: Uz and Aran.

²⁹These are the clans of the Horites: the clans Lotan, Shobal, Zibeon, Anah, ³⁰Dishon, Ezer, and Dishan. Those are the clans of the Horites, clan by clan, in the land of Seir.

³¹These are the kings who reigned in the land of Edom before any king reigned over the Israelites. ³²Bela son of Beor reigned in Edom, and the name of his city was Dinhabah. ³³When Bela died, Jobab son of Zerah, from Bozrah, succeeded him as king. ³⁴When Jobab died, Husham of the land of the Temanites succeeded him as king. ³⁵When Husham died, Hadad son of Bedad, who defeated the Midianites in the country of Moab, succeeded him as king; the name of his city was Avith. ³⁶When Hadad died, Samlah of Masrekah succeeded him as king. ³⁷When Samlah died, Saul[e] of Rehoboth-on-the-river succeeded him as king. ³⁸When Saul died, Baal-hanan son of Achbor succeeded him as king. ³⁹And when Baal-hanan son of Achbor died, Hadar succeeded him as king; the name of his city was Pau, and his wife's name was Mehetabel daughter of Matred daughter of Me-zahab.

⁴⁰These are the names of the clans of Esau, each with its families and locality, name by name: the clans Timna, Alvah, Jetheth, ⁴¹Oholibamah, Elah, Pinon, ⁴²Kenaz, Teman, Mibzar, ⁴³Magdiel, and Iram. Those are the clans of Edom—that is, of Esau, father of the Edomites—by their settlements in the land which they hold.

וישב

37

Now Jacob was settled in the land where his father had sojourned, the land of Canaan. ²This, then, is the line of Jacob:

At seventeen years of age, Joseph tended the flocks with his brothers, as a helper to the sons of his father's wives Bilhah and Zilpah. And Joseph brought bad reports of them to their father. ³Now Israel loved Joseph best of all his sons, for he was the child of his old age; and he had made him an ornamented tunic.[a] ⁴And when his brothers saw that their father loved him more than any of his brothers, they hated him so that they could not speak a friendly word to him.

d *Heb.* Dishan; *but cf. vv. 21, 25, 28, and 30, and 1 Chron. 1.41.*
e *Or "Shaul."*

a *Or "a coat of many colors"; meaning of Heb. uncertain.*

⁵Once Joseph had a dream which he told to his brothers; and they hated him even more. ⁶He said to them, "Hear this dream which I have dreamed: ⁷There we were binding sheaves in the field, when suddenly my sheaf stood up and remained upright; then your sheaves gathered around and bowed low to my sheaf." ⁸His brothers answered, "Do you mean to reign over us? Do you mean to rule over us?" And they hated him even more for his talk about his dreams.

⁹He dreamed another dream and told it to his brothers, saying, "Look, I have had another dream: And this time, the sun, the moon, and eleven stars were bowing down to me." ¹⁰And when he told it to his father and brothers, his father berated him. "What," he said to him, "is this dream you have dreamed? Are we to come, I and your mother and your brothers, and bow low to you to the ground? ¹¹So his brothers were wrought up at him, and his father kept the matter in mind.

¹²One time, when his brothers had gone to pasture their father's flock at Shechem, ¹³Israel said to Joseph, "Your brothers are pasturing at Shechem. Come, I will send you to them." He answered, "I am ready." ¹⁴And he said to him, "Go and see how your brothers are and how the flocks are faring, and bring me back word." So he sent him from the valley of Hebron.

When he reached Shechem, ¹⁵a man came upon him wandering in the fields. The man asked him, "What are you looking for?" ¹⁶He answered, "I am looking for my brothers. Could you tell me where they are pasturing?" ¹⁷The man said, "They have gone from here, for I heard them say: Let us go to Dothan." So Joseph followed his brothers and found them at Dothan.

¹⁸They saw him from afar, and before he came close to them they conspired to kill him. ¹⁹They said to one another, "Here comes that dreamer! ²⁰Come now, let us kill him and throw him into one of the pits; and we can say, 'A savage beast devoured him.' We shall see what comes of his dreams!" ²¹But when Reuben heard it, he tried to save him from them. He said, "Let us not take his life." ²²And Reuben went on, "Shed no blood! Cast him into that pit out in the wilderness, but do not touch him yourselves"—intending to save him from them and restore him to his father. ²³When Joseph came up to his brothers, they stripped Joseph of his tunic, the ornamented tunic that he was wearing, ²⁴and took him and cast him into the pit. The pit was empty; there was no water in it.

²⁵Then they sat down to a meal. Looking up, they saw a caravan of

Ishmaelites coming from Gilead, their camels bearing gum, balm, and ladanum to be taken to Egypt. 26Then Judah said to his brothers, "What do we gain by killing our brother and covering up his blood? 27Come, let us sell him to the Ishmaelites, but let us not do away with him ourselves. After all, he is our brother, our own flesh." His brothers agreed. 28When Midianite traders passed by, they pulled Joseph up out of the pit. They sold Joseph for twenty pieces of silver to the Ishmaelites, who brought Joseph to Egypt.

29When Reuben returned to the pit and saw that Joseph was not in the pit, he rent his clothes. 30Returning to his brothers, he said, "The boy is gone! Now, what am I to do?" 31Then they took Joseph's tunic, slaughtered a kid, and dipped the tunic in the blood. 32They had the ornamented tunic taken to their father, and they said, "We found this. Please examine it; is it your son's tunic or not?" 33He recognized it, and said, "My son's tunic! A savage beast devoured him! Joseph was torn by a beast!" 34Jacob rent his clothes, put sackcloth on his loins, and observed mourning for his son many days. 35All his sons and daughters sought to comfort him; but he refused to be comforted, saying, "No, I will go down mourning to my son in Sheol." Thus his father bewailed him.

36The Midianites,b meanwhile, sold him in Egypt to Potiphar, a courtier of Pharaoh and his chief steward.

38

About that time Judah left his brothers and camped near a certain Adullamite whose name was Hirah. 2There Judah saw the daughter of a certain Canaanite whose name was Shua, and he married her and cohabited with her. 3She conceived and bore a son, and he named him Er. 4She conceived again and bore a son, and named him Onan. 5Once again she bore a son, and named him Shelah; he was at Chezib when she bore him.

6Judah got a wife for Er his first-born; her name was Tamar. 7But Er, Judah's first-born, was displeasing to the LORD, and the LORD took his life. 8Then Judah said to Onan, "Join with your brother's wife and do your duty by her as a brother-in-law,a and provide offspring for your brother." 9But Onan, knowing that the seed would not count as his, let it go to wasteb whenever he joined with his brother's wife, so as not to provide offspring for his brother. 10What he did was displeasing to the LORD, and He took his life also. 11Then Judah said to his daughter-in-law Tamar, "Stay as a widow in your father's house until my son Shelah

b Heb. "Medanites."

a Cf. Deut. 25.5.
b Lit. "spoil on the ground."

grows up"—for he thought, "He too might die like his brothers." So Tamar went to live in her father's house.

[12]A long time afterward, Shua's daughter, the wife of Judah, died. When [c]his period of mourning was over,[c] Judah went up to Timnah to his sheepshearers, together with his friend Hirah the Adullamite. [13]And Tamar was told, "Your father-in-law is coming up to Timnah for the sheepshearing." [14]So she took off her widow's garb, covered her face with a veil, and, wrapping herself up, sat down at the entrance to Enaim,[d] which is on the road to Timnah; for she saw that Shelah was grown up, yet she had not been given to him as wife. [15]When Judah saw her, he took her for a harlot; for she had covered her face. [16]So he turned aside to her by the road and said, "Here, let me sleep with you"—for he did not know that she was his daughter-in-law. "What," she asked, "will you pay for sleeping with me?" [17]He replied, "I will send a kid from my flock." But she said, "You must leave a pledge until you have sent it." [18]And he said, "What pledge shall I give you?" She replied, "Your seal and cord, and the staff which you carry." So he gave them to her and slept with her, and she conceived by him. [19]Then she went on her way. She took off her veil and again put on her widow's garb.

[20]Judah sent the kid by his friend the Adullamite, to redeem the pledge from the woman; but he could not find her. [21]He inquired of the people of that town, "Where is the cult prostitute, the one at Enaim, by the road?" But they said, "There has been no prostitute here." [22]So he returned to Judah and said, "I could not find her; moreover, the townspeople said: There has been no prostitute here." [23]Judah said, "Let her keep them, lest we become a laughingstock. I did send her this kid, but you did not find her."

[24]About three months later, Judah was told, "Your daughter-in-law Tamar has played the harlot; in fact, she is with child by harlotry." "Bring her out," said Judah, "and let her be burned." [25]As she was being brought out, she sent this message to her father-in-law, "I am with child by the man to whom these belong." And she added, "Examine these: whose seal and cord and staff are these?" [26]Judah recognized them, and said, "She is more in the right than I, inasmuch as I did not give her to my son Shelah." And he was not intimate with her again.

[27]When the time came for her to give birth, there were twins in her womb! [28]While she was in labor, one of them put out his hand, and the midwife tied a crimson thread on that hand, to signify: This one came

[c-c] Lit. "he was comforted."
[d] Cf. Enam, Josh. 15.34. Others "in an open place" or "at the crossroad."

out first. 29But just then he drew back his hand, and out came his brother; and she said, "What a breach^e you have made for yourself!" So he was named Perez. 30Afterward his brother came out, on whose hand was the crimson thread; he was named Zerah.^f

39 When Joseph was taken down to Egypt, a certain Egyptian, Potiphar, a courtier of Pharaoh and his chief steward, bought him from the Ishmaelites who had brought him there. 2The LORD was with Joseph, and he was a successful man; and he stayed in the house of his Egyptian master. 3And when his master saw that the LORD was with him and that the LORD lent success to everything he undertook, 4he took a liking to Joseph. He made him his personal attendant and put him in charge of his household, placing in his hands all that he owned. 5And from the time that the Egyptian put him in charge of his household and of all that he owned, the LORD blessed his house for Joseph's sake, so that the blessing of the LORD was upon everything that he owned, in the house and outside. 6He left all that he had in Joseph's hands and, with him there, he paid attention to nothing save the food that he ate. Now Joseph was well built and handsome.

7After a time, his master's wife cast her eyes upon Joseph and said, "Lie with me." 8But he refused. He said to his master's wife, "Look, with me here, my master gives no thought to anything in this house, and all that he owns he has placed in my hands. 9He wields no more authority in this house than I, and he has withheld nothing from me except yourself, since you are his wife. How then could I do this most wicked thing, and sin before God?" 10And much as she coaxed Joseph day after day, he did not yield to her request to lie beside her, to be with her.

11One such day, he came into the house to do his work. None of the household being there inside, 12she caught hold of him by his garment and said, "Lie with me!" But he left his garment in her hand and got away and fled outside. 13When she saw that he had left it in her hand and had fled outside, 14she called out to her servants and said to them, "Look, he had to bring us a Hebrew to dally with us! This one came to lie with me; but I screamed loud. 15And when he heard me screaming at the top of my voice, he left his garment with me and got away and fled outside." 16She kept his garment beside her, until his master came home. 17Then she told him the same story, saying, "The Hebrew slave whom you brought

---

e *Heb.* peres.
f *I.e., "brightness," perhaps alluding to the crimson thread.*

into our house came to me to dally with me; 18but when I screamed at the top of my voice, he left his garment with me and fled outside."

19When his master heard the story that his wife told him, namely, "Thus and so your slave did to me," he was furious. 20So Joseph's master had him put in prison, where the king's prisoners were confined. But even while he was there in prison, 21the LORD was with Joseph: He extended kindness to him and disposed the chief jailer favorably toward him. 22The chief jailer put in Joseph's charge all the prisoners who were in that prison, and he was the one to carry out everything that was done there. 23The chief jailer did not supervise anything that was in Joseph'sª charge, because the LORD was with him, and whatever he did the LORD made successful.

40 Some time later, the cupbearer and the baker of the king of Egypt gave offense to their lord the king of Egypt. 2Pharaoh was angry with his two courtiers, the chief cupbearer and the chief baker, 3and put them in custody, in the house of the chief steward, in the same prison house where Joseph was confined. 4The chief steward assigned Joseph to them, and he attended them.

When they had been in custody for some time, 5both of them—the cupbearer and the baker of the king of Egypt, who were confined in the prison—dreamed in the same night, each his own dream and each dream with its own meaning. 6When Joseph came to them in the morning, he saw that they were distraught. 7He asked Pharaoh's courtiers, who were with him in custody in his master's house, saying, "Why do you appear downcast today?" 8And they said to him, "We had dreams, and there is no one to interpret them." So Joseph said to them, "Surely God can interpret! Tell me [your dreams]."

9Then the chief cupbearer told his dream to Joseph. He said to him, "In my dream, there was a vine in front of me. 10On the vine were three branches. It had barely budded, when out came its blossoms and its clusters ripened into grapes. 11Pharaoh's cup was in my hand, and I took the grapes, pressed them into Pharaoh's cup, and placed the cup in Pharaoh's hand." 12Joseph said to him, "This is its interpretation: The three branches are three days. 13In three days Pharaoh will pardon youª and restore you to your post; you will place Pharaoh's cup in his hand, as was your custom formerly when you were his cupbearer. 14But think of me when all is well with you again, and do me the kindness of mentioning me to Pharaoh,

---

ª Lit. "his."

ª Lit. "lift up your head."

so as to free me from this place. 15For in truth, I was kidnapped from the land of the Hebrews; nor have I done anything here that they should have put me in the dungeon."

16When the chief baker saw how favorably he had interpreted, he said to Joseph, "In my dream, similarly, there were three openwork basketsb on my head. 17In the uppermost basket were all kinds of food for Pharaoh that a baker prepares; and the birds were eating it out of the basket above my head." 18Joseph answered, "This is its interpretation: The three baskets are three days. 19In three days Pharaoh will lift off your head and impale you upon a pole; and the birds will pick off your flesh."

20On the third day—his birthday—Pharaoh made a banquet for all his officials, and he singled outc his chief cupbearer and his chief baker from among his officials. 21He restored the chief cupbearer to his cupbearing, and he placed the cup in Pharaoh's hand; 22but the chief baker he impaled—just as Joseph had interpreted to them.

23Yet the chief cupbearer did not think of Joseph; he forgot him.

מקץ

41 After two years' time, Pharaoh dreamed that he was standing by the Nile, 2when out of the Nile there came up seven cows, handsome and sturdy, and they grazed in the reed grass. 3But presently, seven other cows came up from the Nile close behind them, ugly and gaunt, and stood beside the cows on the bank of the Nile; 4and the ugly gaunt cows ate up the seven handsome sturdy cows. And Pharaoh awoke.

5He fell asleep and dreamed a second time: Seven ears of grain, solid and healthy, grew on a single stalk. 6But close behind them sprouted seven ears, thin and scorched by the east wind. 7And the thin ears swallowed up the seven solid and full ears. Then Pharaoh awoke: it was a dream!

8Next morning, his spirit was agitated, and he sent for all the magicians of Egypt, and all its wise men; and Pharaoh told them his dreams, but none could interpret them for Pharaoh.

9The chief cupbearer then spoke up and said to Pharaoh, "I must make mention today of my offenses. 10Once Pharaoh was angry with his servants, and placed me in custody in the house of the chief steward, together with the chief baker. 11We had dreams the same night, he and I, each of us a dream with a meaning of its own. 12A Hebrew youth was there with

b Others "baskets with white bread" or "white baskets"; meaning of Heb. hori uncertain.
c Lit. "lifted the head of."

us, a servant of the chief steward; and when we told him our dreams, he interpreted them for us, telling each of the meaning of his dream. ¹³And as he interpreted for us, so it came to pass: I was restored to my post, and the other was impaled."

¹⁴Thereupon Pharaoh sent for Joseph, and he was rushed from the dungeon. He had his hair cut and changed his clothes, and he appeared before Pharaoh. ¹⁵And Pharaoh said to Joseph, "I have had a dream, but no one can interpret it. Now I have heard it said of you that for you to hear a dream is to tell its meaning." ¹⁶Joseph answered Pharaoh, saying, "Not I! God will see to Pharaoh's welfare."

¹⁷Then Pharaoh said to Joseph, "In my dream, I was standing on the bank of the Nile, ¹⁸when out of the Nile came up seven sturdy and well-formed cows and grazed in the reed grass. ¹⁹Presently there followed them seven other cows, scrawny, ill-formed, and emaciated—never had I seen their likes for ugliness in all the land of Egypt! ²⁰And the seven lean and ugly cows ate up the first seven cows, the sturdy ones; ²¹but when they had consumed them, one could not tell that they had consumed them, for they looked just as bad as before. And I awoke. ²²In my other dream, I saw seven ears of grain, full and healthy, growing on a single stalk; ²³but right behind them sprouted seven ears, shriveled, thin, and scorched by the east wind. ²⁴And the thin ears swallowed the seven healthy ears. I have told my magicians, but none has an explanation for me."

²⁵And Joseph said to Pharaoh, "Pharaoh's dreams are one and the same: God has told Pharaoh what He is about to do. ²⁶The seven healthy cows are seven years, and the seven healthy ears are seven years; it is the same dream. ²⁷The seven lean and ugly cows that followed are seven years, as are also the seven empty ears scorched by the east wind; they are seven years of famine. ²⁸It is just as I have told Pharaoh: God has revealed to Pharaoh what He is about to do. ²⁹Immediately ahead are seven years of great abundance in all the land of Egypt. ³⁰After them will come seven years of famine, and all the abundance in the land of Egypt will be forgotten. As the land is ravaged by famine, ³¹no trace of the abundance will be left in the land because of the famine thereafter, for it will be very severe. ³²As for Pharaoh having had the same dream twice, it means that the matter has been determined by God, and that God will soon carry it out.

³³"Accordingly, let Pharaoh find a man of discernment and wisdom, and set him over the land of Egypt. ³⁴And let Pharaoh take steps to

appoint overseers over the land, and organize[a] the land of Egypt in the seven years of plenty. [35]Let all the food of these good years that are coming be gathered, and let the grain be collected under Pharaoh's authority as food to be stored in the cities. [36]Let that food be a reserve for the land for the seven years of famine which will come upon the land of Egypt, so that the land may not perish in the famine."

[37]The plan pleased Pharaoh and all his courtiers. [38]And Pharaoh said to his courtiers, "Could we find another like him, a man in whom is the spirit of God?" [39]So Pharaoh said to Joseph, "Since God has made all this known to you, there is none so discerning and wise as you. [40]You shall be in charge of my court, and by your command shall all my people be directed;[b] only with respect to the throne shall I be superior to you." [41]Pharaoh further said to Joseph, "See, I put you in charge of all the land of Egypt." [42]And removing his signet ring from his hand, Pharaoh put it on Joseph's hand; and he had him dressed in robes of fine linen, and put a gold chain about his neck. [43]He had him ride in the chariot of his second-in-command, and they cried before him, "Abrek!"[c] Thus he placed him over all the land of Egypt.

[44]Pharaoh said to Joseph, "I am Pharaoh; yet without you, no one shall lift up hand or foot in all the land of Egypt." [45]Pharaoh then gave Joseph the name Zaphenath-paneah;[d] and he gave him for a wife Asenath daughter of Poti-phera, priest of On. Thus Joseph emerged in charge of the land of Egypt.—[46]Joseph was thirty years old when he entered the service of Pharaoh king of Egypt.—Leaving Pharaoh's presence, Joseph traveled through all the land of Egypt.

[47]During the seven years of plenty, the land produced in abundance. [48]And he gathered all the grain of [e-the seven years that the land of Egypt was enjoying,-e] and stored the grain in the cities; he put in each city the grain of the fields around it. [49]So Joseph collected produce in very large quantity, like the sands of the sea, until he ceased to measure it, for it could not be measured.

[50]Before the years of famine came, Joseph became the father of two sons, whom Asenath daughter of Poti-phera, priest of On, bore to him. [51]Joseph named the first-born Manasseh, meaning, "God has made me forget[f] completely my hardship and my parental home." [52]And the second he named Ephraim, meaning, "God has made me fertile[g] in the land of my affliction."

---

[a] Others "take a fifth part of"; meaning of Heb. uncertain.
[b] Others "order themselves" or "pay homage"; meaning of Heb. yishshaq uncertain.
[c] Others "Bow the knee," as though from Heb. barakh "to kneel"; perhaps from an Egyptian word of unknown meaning.
[d] Egyptian for "God speaks; he lives," or "creator of life."
[e-e] Lit. "the seven years that were in the land of Egypt."
[f] Heb. nashshani, connected with "Manasseh" (Menashsheh).
[g] Heb. hiprani, connected with "Ephraim."

53The seven years of abundance that the land of Egypt enjoyed came to an end, 54and the seven years of famine set in, just as Joseph had foretold. There was famine in all lands, but throughout the land of Egypt there was bread. 55And when all the land of Egypt felt the hunger, the people cried out to Pharaoh for bread; and Pharaoh said to all the Egyptians, "Go to Joseph; whatever he tells you, you shall do."—56Accordingly, when the famine became severe in the land of Egypt, Joseph laid open all that was within, and rationed out grain to the Egyptians. The famine, however, spread over the whole world. 57So all the world came to Joseph in Egypt to procure rations, for the famine had become severe throughout the world.

42 When Jacob saw that there were food rations to be had in Egypt, he[a] said to his sons, "Why do you keep looking at one another? 2Now I hear," he went on, "that there are rations to be had in Egypt. Go down and procure rations for us there, that we may live and not die." 3So ten of Joseph's brothers went down to get grain rations in Egypt; 4for Jacob did not send Joseph's brother Benjamin with his brothers, since he feared that he might meet with disaster. 5Thus the sons of Israel were among those who came to procure rations, for the famine extended to the land of Canaan.

6Now Joseph was the vizier of the land; it was he who dispensed rations to all the people of the land. And Joseph's brothers came and bowed low to him, with their faces to the ground. 7When Joseph saw his brothers, he recognized them; but he acted like a stranger toward them and spoke harshly to them. He asked them, "Where do you come from?" And they said, "From the land of Canaan, to procure food." 8For though Joseph recognized his brothers, they did not recognize him. 9Recalling the dreams that he had dreamed about them, Joseph said to them, "You are spies, you have come to see the land in its nakedness." 10But they said to him, "No, my lord! Truly, your servants have come to procure food. 11We are all of us sons of the same man; we are honest men; your servants have never been spies!" 12And he said to them, "No, you have come to see the land in its nakedness!" 13And they replied, "We your servants were twelve brothers, sons of a certain man in the land of Canaan; the youngest,

a Lit. "Jacob."

however, is now with our father, and one is no more." 14But Joseph said to them, "It is just as I have told you: You are spies! 15By this you shall be put to the test: unless your youngest brother comes here, by Pharaoh, you shall not depart from this place! 16Let one of you go and bring your brother, while the rest of you remain confined, that your words may be put to the test whether there is truth in you. Else, by Pharaoh, you are nothing but spies!" 17And he confined them in the guardhouse for three days.

18On the third day Joseph said to them, "Do this and you shall live, for I am a God-fearing man. 19If you are honest men, let one of you brothers be held in your place of detention, while the rest of you go and take home rations for your starving households; 20but you must bring me your youngest brother, that your words may be verified and that you may not die." And they did accordingly. 21They said to one another, "Alas, we are being punished on account of our brother, because we looked on at his anguish, yet paid no heed as he pleaded with us. That is why this distress has come upon us." 22Then Reuben spoke up and said to them, "Did I not tell you, 'Do no wrong to the boy'? But you paid no heed. Now comes the reckoning for his blood." 23They did not know that Joseph understood, for there was an interpreter between him and them. 24He turned away from them and wept. But he came back to them and spoke to them; and he took Simeon from among them and had him bound before their eyes. 25Then Joseph gave orders to fill their bags with grain, return each one's money to his sack, and give them provisions for the journey; and this was done for them. 26So they loaded their asses with the rations and departed from there.

27As one of them was opening his sack to give feed to his ass at the night encampment, he saw his money right there at the mouth of his bag. 28And he said to his brothers, "My money has been returned! It is here in my bag!" Their hearts sank; and, trembling, they turned to one another, saying, "What is this that God has done to us?"

29When they came to their father Jacob in the land of Canaan, they told him all that had befallen them, saying, 30"The man who is lord of the land spoke harshly to us and accused us of spying on the land. 31We said to him, 'We are honest men; we have never been spies! 32There were twelve of us brothers, sons by the same father; but one is no more, and the youngest is now with our father in the land of Canaan.' 33But the man who is lord of the land said to us, 'By this I shall know that you are honest men: leave one of your brothers with me, and take something for your starving households and be off. 34And bring your youngest brother to me, that I may know that you are not spies but honest men. I will then restore your brother to you, and you shall be free to move about in the land.' "

35As they were emptying their sacks, there, in each one's sack, was his money-bag! When they and their father saw their money-bags, they were dismayed. 36Their father Jacob said to them, "It is always me that you bereave: Joseph is no more and Simeon is no more, and now you would take away Benjamin. These things always happen to me!" 37Then Reuben said to his father, "You may kill my two sons if I do not bring him back to you. Put him in my care, and I will return him to you." 38But he said, "My son must not go down with you, for his brother is dead and he alone is left. If he meets with disaster on the journey you are taking, you will send my white head down to Sheol in grief."

43 But the famine in the land was severe. 2And when they had eaten up the rations which they had brought from Egypt, their father said to them, "Go again and procure some food for us." 3But Judah said to him, "The man warned us, a-'Do not let me see your faces-a unless your brother is with you.' 4If you will let our brother go with us, we will go down and procure food for you; 5but if you will not let him go, we will not go down, for the man said to us, a-'Do not let me see your faces-a unless your brother is with you.' " 6And Israel said, "Why did you serve me so ill as to tell the man that you had another brother?" 7They replied, "But the man kept asking about us and our family, saying, 'Is your father still living? Have you another brother?' And we answered him accordingly. How were we to know that he would say, 'Bring your brother here'?"

8Then Judah said to his father Israel, "Send the boy in my care, and let us be on our way, that we may live and not die—you and we and our children. 9I myself will be surety for him; you may hold me responsible: if I do not bring him back to you and set him before you, I shall stand guilty before you forever. 10For we could have been there and back twice if we had not dawdled."

11Then their father Israel said to them, "If it must be so, do this: take some of the choice products of the land in your baggage, and carry them down as a gift for the man—some balm and some honey, gum, ladanum,

---

a-a Lit. "Do not see my face."

pistachio nuts, and almonds. 12And take with you double the money, carrying back with you the money that was replaced in the mouths of your bags; perhaps it was a mistake. 13Take your brother too; and go back at once to the man. 14And may El Shaddai dispose the man to mercy toward you, that he may release to you your other brother, as well as Benjamin. As for me, if I am to be bereaved, I shall be bereaved."

15So the men took that gift, and they took with them double the money, as well as Benjamin. They made their way down to Egypt, where they presented themselves to Joseph. 16When Joseph saw Benjamin with them, he said to his house steward, "Take the men into the house; slaughter and prepare an animal, for the men will dine with me at noon." 17The man did as Joseph said, and he brought the men into Joseph's house. 18But the men were frightened at being brought into Joseph's house. "It must be," they thought, "because of the money replaced in our bags the first time that we have been brought inside, as a pretext to attack us and seize us as slaves, with our pack animals." 19So they went up to Joseph's house steward and spoke to him at the entrance of the house. 20"If you please, my lord," they said, "we came down once before to procure food. 21But when we arrived at the night encampment and opened our bags, there was each one's money in the mouth of his bag, our money in full.b So we have brought it back with us. 22And we have brought down with us other money to procure food. We do not know who put the money in our bags." 23He replied, "All is well with you; do not be afraid. Your God, the God of your father, must have put treasure in your bags for you. I got your payment." And he brought out Simeon to them.

24Then the man brought the men into Joseph's house; he gave them water to bathe their feet, and he provided feed for their asses. 25They laid out their gifts to await Joseph's arrival at noon, for they had heard that they were to dine there.

26When Joseph came home, they presented to him the gifts that they had brought with them into the house, bowing low before him to the ground. 27He greeted them, and he said, "How is your aged father of whom you spoke? Is he still in good health?" 28They replied, "It is well with your servant our father; he is still in good health." And they bowed and made obeisance.

29Looking about, he saw his brother Benjamin, his mother's son, and asked, "Is this your youngest brother of whom you spoke to me?" And he went on, "May God be gracious to you, my boy." 30With that, Joseph

b Lit. "by its weight."

hurried out, for he was overcome with feeling toward his brother and was on the verge of tears; he went into a room and wept there. ³¹Then he washed his face, reappeared, and—now in control of himself—gave the order, "Serve the meal." ³²They served him by himself, and them by themselves, and the Egyptians who ate with him by themselves; for the Egyptians could not dine with the Hebrews, since that would be abhorrent to the Egyptians. ³³As they were seated by his direction, from the oldest in the order of his seniority to the youngest in the order of his youth, the men looked at one another in astonishment. ³⁴Portions were served them from his table; but Benjamin's portion was several^c times that of anyone else. And they drank their fill with him.

44
Then he instructed his house steward as follows, "Fill the men's bags with food, as much as they can carry, and put each one's money in the mouth of his bag. ²Put my silver goblet in the mouth of the bag of the youngest one, together with his money for the rations." And he did as Joseph told him.

³With the first light of morning, the men were sent off with their pack animals. ⁴They had just left the city and had not gone far, when Joseph said to his steward, "Up, go after the men! And when you overtake them, say to them, 'Why did you repay good with evil? ⁵It is the very one from which my master drinks and which he uses for divination. It was a wicked thing for you to do!' "

⁶He overtook them and spoke those words to them. ⁷And they said to him, "Why does my lord say such things? Far be it from your servants to do anything of the kind! ⁸Here we brought back to you from the land of Canaan the money that we found in the mouths of our bags. How then could we have stolen any silver or gold from your master's house! ⁹Whichever of your servants it is found with shall die; the rest of us, moreover, shall become slaves to my lord." ¹⁰He replied, "Although what you are proposing is right, only the one with whom it is found shall be my slave; but the rest of you shall go free."

¹¹So each one hastened to lower his bag to the ground, and each one opened his bag. ¹²He searched, beginning with the oldest and ending with the youngest; and the goblet turned up in Benjamin's bag. ¹³At this they rent their clothes. Each reloaded his pack animal, and they returned to the city.

^c Lit. "five."

14When Judah and his brothers reentered the house of Joseph, who was still there, they threw themselves on the ground before him. 15Joseph said to them, "What is this deed that you have done? Do you not know that a man like me practices divination?" 16Judah replied, "What can we say to my lord? How can we plead, how can we prove our innocence? God has uncovered the crime of your servants. Here we are, then, slaves of my lord, the rest of us as much as he in whose possession the goblet was found." 17But he replied, "Far be it from me to act thus! Only he in whose possession the goblet was found shall be my slave; the rest of you go back in peace to your father."

ויגש

18Then Judah went up to him and said, "Please, my lord, let your servant appeal to my lord, and do not be impatient with your servant, you who are the equal of Pharaoh. 19My lord asked his servants, 'Have you a father or another brother?' 20We told my lord, 'We have an old father, and there is a child of his old age, the youngest; his full brother is dead, so that he alone is left of his mother, and his father dotes on him.' 21Then you said to your servants, 'Bring him down to me, that I may set eyes on him.' 22We said to my lord, 'The boy cannot leave his father; if he were to leave him, his father would die.' 23But you said to your servants, 'Unless your youngest brother comes down with you, do not let me see your faces.' 24When we came back to your servant my father, we reported my lord's words to him.

25"Later our father said, 'Go back and procure some food for us.' 26We answered, 'We cannot go down; only if our youngest brother is with us can we go down, for we may not a-show our faces to the man-a unless our youngest brother is with us.' 27Your servant my father said to us, 'As you know, my wife bore me two sons. 28But one is gone from me, and I said: Alas, he was torn by a beast! And I have not seen him since. 29If you take this one from me, too, and he meets with disaster, you will send my white head down to Sheol in sorrow.'

30"Now, if I come to your servant my father and the boy is not with us—since his own life is so bound up with his—31when he sees that the boy is not with us, he will die, and your servants will send the white head of your servant our father down to Sheol in grief. 32Now your servant has pledged himself for the boy to my father, saying, 'If I do not bring him back to you, I shall stand guilty before my father forever.' 33Therefore,

---

a-a Lit. "see the man's face."

please let your servant remain as a slave to my lord instead of the boy, and let the boy go back with his brothers. 34For how can I go back to my father unless the boy is with me? Let me not be witness to the woe that would overtake my father!"

45 Joseph could no longer control himself before all his attendants, and he cried out, "Have everyone withdraw from me!" So there was no one else about when Joseph made himself known to his brothers. 2His sobs were so loud that the Egyptians could hear, and so the news reached Pharaoh's palace.

3Joseph said to his brothers, "I am Joseph. Is my father still well?" But his brothers could not answer him, so dumfounded were they on account of him.

4Then Joseph said to his brothers, "Come forward to me." And when they came forward, he said, "I am your brother Joseph, he whom you sold into Egypt. 5Now, do not be distressed or reproach yourselves because you sold me hither; it was to save life that God sent me ahead of you. 6It is now two years that there has been famine in the land, and there are still five years to come in which there shall be no yield from tilling. 7God has sent me ahead of you to ensure your survival on earth, and to save your lives in an extraordinary deliverance. 8So, it was not you who sent me here, but God; and He has made me a father to Pharaoh, lord of all his household, and ruler over the whole land of Egypt.

9"Now, hurry back to my father and say to him: Thus says your son Joseph, 'God has made me lord of all Egypt; come down to me without delay. 10You will dwell in the region of Goshen, where you will be near me—you and your children and your grandchildren, your flocks and herds, and all that is yours. 11There I will provide for you—for there are yet five years of famine to come—that you and your household and all that is yours may not suffer want.' 12You can see for yourselves, and my brother Benjamin for himself, that it is indeed I who am speaking to you. 13And you must tell my father everything about my high station in Egypt and all that you have seen; and bring my father here with all speed."

14With that he embraceda his brother Benjamin around the neck and wept, and Benjamin wept on his neck. 15He kissed all his brothers and wept upon them; only then were his brothers able to talk to him.

16The news reached Pharaoh's palace: "Joseph's brothers have come."

---

a Lit. "fell on."

Pharaoh and his courtiers were pleased. [17]And Pharaoh said to Joseph, "Say to your brothers, 'Do as follows: load up your beasts and go at once to the land of Canaan. [18]Take your father and your households and come to me; I will give you the best of the land of Egypt and you shall live off the fat of the land.' [19]And you are bidden [to add], 'Do as follows: take from the land of Egypt wagons for your children and your wives, and bring your father here. [20]And never mind your belongings, for the best of all the land of Egypt shall be yours.' "

[21]The sons of Israel did so; Joseph gave them wagons as Pharaoh had commanded, and he supplied them with provisions for the journey. [22]To each of them, moreover, he gave a change of clothing; but to Benjamin he gave three hundred pieces of silver and several[b] changes of clothing. [23]And to his father he sent the following: ten he-asses laden with the best things of Egypt, and ten she-asses laden with grain, bread, and provisions for his father on the journey. [24]As he sent his brothers off on their way, he told them, "Do not be quarrelsome on the way."

[25]They went up from Egypt and came to their father Jacob in the land of Canaan. [26]And they told him, "Joseph is still alive; yes, he is ruler over the whole land of Egypt." His heart went numb, for he did not believe them. [27]But when they recounted all that Joseph had said to them, and when he saw the wagons that Joseph had sent to transport him, the spirit of their father Jacob revived. [28]"Enough!" said Israel. "My son Joseph is still alive! I must go and see him before I die."

46
So Israel set out with all that was his, and he came to Beer-sheba, where he offered sacrifices to the God of his father Isaac. [2]God called to Israel in a vision by night: "Jacob! Jacob!" He answered, "Here." [3]And He said, "I am God, the God of your father. Fear not to go down to Egypt, for I will make you there into a great nation. [4]I Myself will go down with you to Egypt, and I Myself will also bring you back; and Joseph's hand shall close your eyes."

[5]So Jacob set out from Beer-sheba. The sons of Israel put their father Jacob and their children and their wives in the wagons that Pharaoh had sent to transport him; [6]and they took along their livestock and the wealth that they had amassed in the land of Canaan. Thus Jacob and all his

b *Lit. "five"; cf. 43.34.*

offspring with him came to Egypt: [7]he brought with him to Egypt his sons and grandsons, his daughters and granddaughters—all his offspring.

[8]These are the names of the Israelites, Jacob and his descendants, who came to Egypt.

Jacob's first-born Reuben; [9]Reuben's sons: Enoch,[a] Pallu, Hezron, and Carmi. [10]Simeon's sons: Jemuel, Jamin, Ohad, Jachin, Zohar, and Saul[b] the son of a Canaanite woman. [11]Levi's sons: Gershon, Kohath, and Merari. [12]Judah's sons: Er, Onan, Shelah, Perez, and Zerah—but Er and Onan had died in the land of Canaan; and Perez's sons were Hezron and Hamul. [13]Issachar's sons: Tola, Puvah, Iob, and Shimron. [14]Zebulun's sons: Sered, Elon, and Jahleel. [15]Those were the sons whom Leah bore to Jacob in Paddan-aram, in addition to his daughter Dinah. Persons in all, male and female: 33.[c]

[16]Gad's sons: Ziphion, Haggi, Shuni, Ezbon, Eri, Arodi, and Areli. [17]Asher's sons: Imnah, Ishvah, Ishvi, and Beriah, and their sister Serah. Beriah's sons: Heber and Malchiel. [18]These were the descendants of Zilpah, whom Laban had given to his daughter Leah. These she bore to Jacob—16 persons.

[19]The sons of Jacob's wife Rachel were Joseph and Benjamin. [20]To Joseph were born in the land of Egypt Manasseh and Ephraim, whom Asenath daughter of Poti-phera priest of On bore to him. [21]Benjamin's sons: Bela, Becher, Ashbel, Gera, Naaman, Ehi, Rosh, Muppim, Huppim, and Ard. [22]These were the descendants of Rachel who were born to Jacob—14 persons in all.

[23]Dan's son:[d] Hushim. [24]Naphtali's sons: Jahzeel, Guni, Jezer, and Shillem. [25]These were the descendants of Bilhah, whom Laban had given to his daughter Rachel. These she bore to Jacob—7 persons in all.

[26]All the persons belonging to Jacob who came to Egypt[e]—his own issue, aside from the wives of Jacob's sons—all these persons numbered 66. [27]And Joseph's sons who were born to him in Egypt were two in number. Thus the total of Jacob's household who came to Egypt was seventy persons.[f]

[28]He had sent Judah ahead of him to Joseph, to point the way before him to Goshen. So when they came to the region of Goshen, [29]Joseph ordered[g] his chariot and went to Goshen to meet his father Israel; he

[a] Or "Hanoch."
[b] Or "Shaul."
[c] Including Jacob.
[d] Heb. "sons."
[e] Not including Joseph and Joseph's two sons.
[f] Including Jacob and Joseph.
[g] Lit. "hitched."

presented himself to him and, embracing him around the neck, he wept on his neck a good while. ³⁰Then Israel said to Joseph, "Now I can die, having seen for myself that you are still alive."

³¹Then Joseph said to his brothers and to his father's household, "I will go up and tell the news to Pharaoh, and say to him, 'My brothers and my father's household, who were in the land of Canaan, have come to me. ³²The men are shepherds; they have always been breeders of livestock, and they have brought with them their flocks and herds and all that is theirs.' ³³So when Pharaoh summons you and asks, 'What is your occupation?' ³⁴you shall answer, 'Your servants have been breeders of livestock from the start until now, both we and our fathers'—so that you may stay in the region of Goshen. For all shepherds are abhorrent to Egyptians."

47 Then Joseph came and reported to Pharaoh, saying, "My father and my brothers, with their flocks and herds and all that is theirs, have come from the land of Canaan and are now in the region of Goshen." ²And selecting a fewᵃ of his brothers, he presented them to Pharaoh. ³Pharaoh said to his brothers, "What is your occupation?" They answered Pharaoh, "We your servants are shepherds, as were also our fathers. ⁴We have come," they told Pharaoh, "to sojourn in this land, for there is no pasture for your servants' flocks, the famine being severe in the land of Canaan. Pray, then, let your servants stay in the region of Goshen." ⁵Then Pharaoh said to Joseph, "As regards your father and your brothers who have come to you, ⁶the land of Egypt is open before you: settle your father and your brothers in the best part of the land; let them stay in the region of Goshen. And if you know any capable men among them, put them in charge of my livestock."

⁷Joseph then brought his father Jacob and presented him to Pharaoh; and Jacob greeted Pharaoh. ⁸Pharaoh asked Jacob, "How many are the years of your life?" ⁹And Jacob answered Pharaoh, "The years of my sojourn [on earth] are one hundred and thirty. Few and hard have been the years of my life, nor do they come up to the life spans of my fathers during their sojourns." ¹⁰Then Jacob bade Pharaoh farewell, and left Pharaoh's presence.

¹¹So Joseph settled his father and his brothers, giving them holdings in the choicest part of the land of Egypt, in the region of Rameses, as

___
ᵃ Lit. "five."

Pharaoh had commanded. [12]Joseph sustained his father, and his brothers, and all his father's household with bread, down to the little ones.

[13]Now there was no bread in all the world, for the famine was very severe; both the land of Egypt and the land of Canaan languished because of the famine. [14]Joseph gathered in all the money that was to be found in the land of Egypt and in the land of Canaan, as payment for the rations that were being procured, and Joseph brought the money into Pharaoh's palace. [15]And when the money gave out in the land of Egypt and in the land of Canaan, all the Egyptians came to Joseph and said, "Give us bread, lest we die before your very eyes; for the money is gone!" [16]And Joseph said, "Bring your livestock, and I will sell to you against your livestock, if the money is gone." [17]So they brought their livestock to Joseph, and Joseph gave them bread in exchange for the horses, for the stocks of sheep and cattle, and the asses; thus he provided them with bread that year in exchange for all their livestock. [18]And when that year was ended, they came to him the next year and said to him, "We cannot hide from my lord that, with all the money and animal stocks consigned to my lord, nothing is left at my lord's disposal save our persons and our farmland. [19]Let us not perish before your eyes, both we and our land. Take us and our land in exchange for bread, and we with our land will be serfs to Pharaoh; provide the seed, that we may live and not die, and that the land may not become a waste."

[20]So Joseph gained possession of all the farm land of Egypt for Pharaoh, every Egyptian having sold his field because the famine was too much for them; thus the land passed over to Pharaoh. [21]And he removed the population town by town,[b] from one end of Egypt's border to the other. [22]Only the land of the priests he did not take over, for the priests had an allotment from Pharaoh, and they lived off the allotment which Pharaoh had made to them; therefore they did not sell their land.

[23]Then Joseph said to the people, "Whereas I have this day acquired you and your land for Pharaoh, here is seed for you to sow the land. [24]And when harvest comes, you shall give one-fifth to Pharaoh, and four-fifths shall be yours as seed for the fields and as food for you and those in your households, and as nourishment for your children." [25]And they said, "You have saved our lives! We are grateful to my lord, and we shall be serfs to Pharaoh." [26]And Joseph made it into a land law in Egypt,

b *Meaning of Heb. uncertain.*

which is still valid, that a fifth should be Pharaoh's; only the land of the priests did not become Pharaoh's.

27Thus Israel settled in the country of Egypt, in the region of Goshen; they acquired holdings in it, and were fertile and increased greatly.

ויחי

28Jacob lived seventeen years in the land of Egypt, so that the span of Jacob's life came to one hundred and forty-seven years. 29And when the time approached for Israel to die, he summoned his son Joseph and said to him, "Do me this favor, place your hand under my thigh as a pledge of your steadfast loyalty: please do not bury me in Egypt. 30When I lie down with my fathers, take me up from Egypt and bury me in their burial-place." He replied, "I will do as you have spoken." 31And he said, "Swear to me." And he swore to him. Then Israel bowed at the head of the bed.

48 Some time afterward, Joseph was told, "Your father is ill." So he took with him his two sons, Manasseh and Ephraim. 2When Jacob was told, "Your son Joseph has come to see you," Israel summoned his strength and sat up in bed.

3And Jacob said to Joseph, "El Shaddai appeared to me at Luz in the land of Canaan, and He blessed me, 4and said to me, 'I will make you fertile and numerous, making of you a community of peoples; and I will assign this land to your offspring to come for an everlasting possession.' 5Now, your two sons, who were born to you in the land of Egypt before I came to you in Egypt, shall be mine; Ephraim and Manasseh shall be mine no less than Reuben and Simeon. 6But progeny born to you after them shall be yours; they shall be recorded insteada of their brothers in their inheritance. 7I [do this because], when I was returning from Paddan, Rachel died, to my sorrow, while I was journeying in the land of Canaan, when still some distance short of Ephrath; and I buried her there on the road to Ephrath"—now Bethlehem.

8Noticing Joseph's sons, Israel asked, "Who are these?" 9And Joseph said to his father, "They are my sons, whom God has given me here." "Bring them up to me," he said, "that I may bless them." 10Now Israel's

___

a Lit. "under the name."

eyes were dim with age; he could not see. So [Joseph] brought them close to him, and he kissed them and embraced them. [11]And Israel said to Joseph, "I never expected to see you again, and here God has let me see your children as well."

[12]Joseph then removed them from his knees, and bowed low with his face to the ground. [13]Joseph took the two of them, Ephraim with his right hand—to Israel's left—and Manasseh with his left hand—to Israel's right—and brought them close to him. [14]But Israel stretched out his right hand and laid it on Ephraim's head, though he was the younger, and his left hand on Manasseh's head—thus crossing his hands—although Manasseh was the first-born. [15]And he blessed Joseph, saying,

"The God in whose ways my fathers Abraham and Isaac walked,
The God who has been my shepherd from my birth to this
  day—
[16]The Angel who has redeemed me from all harm—
Bless the lads.
In them may my name be recalled,
And the names of my fathers Abraham and Isaac,
And may they be teeming multitudes upon the earth."

[17]When Joseph saw that his father was placing his right hand on Ephraim's head, he thought it wrong; so he took hold of his father's hand to move it from Ephraim's head to Manasseh's. [18]"Not so, Father," Joseph said to his father, "for the other is the first-born; place your right hand on his head." [19]But his father objected, saying, "I know, my son, I know. He too shall become a people, and he too shall be great. Yet his younger brother shall be greater than he, and his offspring shall be plentiful enough for nations." [20]So he blessed them that day, saying, "By you shall Israel invoke blessings, saying: God make you like Ephraim and Manasseh." Thus he put Ephraim before Manasseh.

[21]Then Israel said to Joseph, "I am about to die; but God will be with you and bring you back to the land of your fathers. [22]And now, I assign to you one portion[b] more than to your brothers, which I wrested from the Amorites with my sword and bow."

49 And Jacob called his sons and said, "Come together that I may tell you what is to befall you in days to come.

---

[b] *Meaning of Heb.* shekhem *uncertain; others "mountain slope."*

²Assemble and hearken, O sons of Jacob;
Hearken to Israel your father:

³Reuben, you are my first-born,
My might and first fruit of my vigor,
Exceeding in rank
And exceeding in honor.
⁴Unstable as water, you shall excel no longer;
For when you mounted your father's bed,
You brought disgrace—my couch he mounted!

⁵Simeon and Levi are a pair;
Their weapons are tools of lawlessness.
⁶Let not my person be included in their council,
Let not my being be counted in their assembly.
For when angry they slay men,
And when pleased they maim oxen.
⁷Cursed be their anger so fierce,
And their wrath so relentless.
I will divide them in Jacob,
Scatter them in Israel.

⁸You, O Judah, your brothers shall praise;
Your hand shall be on the nape of your foes;
Your father's sons shall bow low to you.
⁹Judah is a lion's whelp;
On prey, my son, have you grown.
He crouches, lies down like a lion,
Like ᵃ-the king of beasts-ᵃ—who dare rouse him?
¹⁰The scepter shall not depart from Judah,
Nor the ruler's staff from between his feet;
So that tribute shall come to himᵇ
And the homage of peoples be his.

¹¹He tethers his ass to a vine,
His ass's foal to a choice vine;
He washes his garment in wine,
His robe in blood of grapes.
12 ᶜ-His eyes are darker than wine;
His teeth are whiter than milk.-ᶜ

ᵃ⁻ᵃ *Heb.* labi, *another word for "lion."*
ᵇ *Shiloh, understood as* shai loh *"tribute to him," following Midrash; cf. Isa. 18.7. Meaning of Heb. uncertain; lit. "Until he comes to Shiloh."*
ᶜ⁻ᶜ *Or "His eyes are dark from wine,*
    And his teeth are white from milk."

¹³Zebulun shall dwell by the seashore;
He shall be a haven for ships,
And his flank shall rest on Sidon.

¹⁴Issachar is a strong-boned ass,
Crouching among the sheepfolds.
¹⁵When he saw how good was security,
And how pleasant was the country,
He bent his shoulder to the burden,
And became a toiling serf.

¹⁶Dan shall govern his people,
As one of the tribes of Israel.
¹⁷Dan shall be a serpent by the road,
A viper by the path,
That bites the horse's heels
So that his rider is thrown backward.

¹⁸I wait for Your deliverance, O LORD!

¹⁹Gad shall be raided by raiders,
But he shall raid at their heels.

²⁰Asher's bread shall be rich,
And he shall yield royal dainties.

²¹Naphtali is a hind let loose,
Which yields lovely fawns.

²² d-Joseph is a wild ass,
A wild ass by a spring
—Wild colts on a hillside.-d

²³Archers bitterly assailed him;
They shot at him and harried him.
²⁴Yet his bow stayed taut,
And his arms^e were made firm
By the hands of the Mighty One of Jacob—
There, the Shepherd, the Rock of Israel—
²⁵The God of your father who helps you,
And Shaddai who blesses you
With blessings of heaven above,

d-d Others "Joseph is a fruitful bough,
   A fruitful bough by a spring,
   Its branches run over a wall."
e Heb. "the arms of his hands."

Blessings of the deep that couches below,
Blessings of the breast and womb.
26 f-The blessings of your father
Surpass the blessings of my ancestors,
To the utmost bounds of the eternal hills.-f
May they rest on the head of Joseph,
On the brow of the elect of his brothers.

27Benjamin is a ravenous wolf;
In the morning he consumes the foe,g
And in the evening he divides the spoil."

28All these were the tribes of Israel, twelve in number, and this is what their father said to them as he bade them farewell, addressing to each a parting word appropriate to him.

29Then he instructed them, saying to them, "I am about to be gathered to my kin. Bury me with my fathers in the cave which is in the field of Ephron the Hittite, 30the cave which is in the field of Machpelah, facing Mamre, in the land of Canaan, the field that Abraham bought from Ephron the Hittite for a burial site—31there Abraham and his wife Sarah were buried; there Isaac and his wife Rebekah were buried; and there I buried Leah—32the field and the cave in it, bought from the Hittites." 33When Jacob finished his instructions to his sons, he drew his feet into the bed and, breathing his last, he was gathered to his people.

50 Joseph flung himself upon his father's face and wept over him and kissed him. 2Then Joseph ordered the physicians in his service to embalm his father, and the physicians embalmed Israel. 3It required forty days, for such is the full period of embalming. The Egyptians bewailed him seventy days; 4and when the wailing period was over, Joseph spoke to Pharaoh's court, saying, "Do me this favor, and lay this appeal before Pharaoh: 5'My father made me swear, saying, "I am about to die. Be sure to bury me in the grave which I made ready for myself in the land of Canaan." Now, therefore, let me go up and bury my father; then I shall return.' " 6And Pharaoh said, "Go up and bury your father, as he made you promise on oath."

f-f Meaning of Heb. uncertain.
g Meaning of Heb. uncertain; others "booty."

7So Joseph went up to bury his father; and with him went up all the officials of Pharaoh, the senior members of his court, and all of Egypt's dignitaries, 8together with all of Joseph's household, his brothers, and his father's household; only their children, their flocks, and their herds were left in the region of Goshen. 9Chariots, too, and horsemen went up with him; it was a very large troop.

10When they came to Gorenª ha-Atad, which is beyond the Jordan, they held there a very great and solemn lamentation; and he observed a mourning period of seven days for his father. 11And when the Canaanite inhabitants of the land saw the mourning at Goren ha-Atad, they said, "This is a solemn mourning on the part of the Egyptians." That is why it was named Abel-mizraim,ᵇ which is beyond the Jordan. 12Thus his sons did for him as he had instructed them. 13His sons carried him to the land of Canaan, and buried him in the cave of the field of Machpelah, the field near Mamre, which Abraham had bought for a burial site from Ephron the Hittite. 14After burying his father, Joseph returned to Egypt, he and his brothers and all who had gone up with him to bury his father.

15When Joseph's brothers saw that their father was dead, they said, "What if Joseph still bears a grudge against us and pays us back for all the wrong that we did him!" 16So they sent this message to Joseph, "Before his death your father left this instruction: 17So shall you say to Joseph, 'Forgive, I urge you, the offense and guilt of your brothers who treated you so harshly.' Therefore, please forgive the offense of the servants of the God of your father." And Joseph was in tears as they spoke to him.

18His brothers went to him themselves, flung themselves before him, and said, "We are prepared to be your slaves." 19But Joseph said to them, "Have no fear! Am I a substitute for God? 20Besides, although you intended me harm, God intended it for good, so as to bring about the present result—the survival of many people. 21And so, fear not. I will sustain you and your children." Thus he reassured them, speaking kindly to them.

22So Joseph and his father's household remained in Egypt. Joseph lived one hundred and ten years. 23Joseph lived to see children of the third generation of Ephraim; the children of Machir son of Manasseh were

ª Or "the threshing floor of."
ᵇ Interpreted as "the mourning of the Egyptians."

likewise born upon Joseph's knees. ²⁴At length, Joseph said to his brothers, "I am about to die. God will surely take notice of you and bring you up from this land to the land that He promised on oath to Abraham, to Isaac, and to Jacob." ²⁵So Joseph made the sons of Israel swear, saying, "When God has taken notice of you, you shall carry up my bones from here."

²⁶Joseph died at the age of one hundred and ten years; and he was embalmed and placed in a coffin in Egypt.

חזק

EXODUS

1 These are the names of the sons of Israel who came to Egypt with Jacob, each coming with his household: [2]Reuben, Simeon, Levi, and Judah; [3]Issachar, Zebulun, and Benjamin; [4]Dan and Naphtali, Gad and Asher. [5]The total number of persons that were of Jacob's issue came to seventy, Joseph being already in Egypt. [6]Joseph died, and all his brothers, and all that generation. [7]But the Israelites were fertile and prolific; they multiplied and increased very greatly, so that the land was filled with them.

[8]A new king arose over Egypt who did not know Joseph. [9]And he said to his people, "Look, the Israelite people are much too numerous for us. [10]Let us deal shrewdly with them, so that they may not increase; otherwise in the event of war they may join our enemies in fighting against us and a-rise from the ground."-a [11]So they set taskmasters over them to oppress them with forced labor; and they built garrison cities[b] for Pharaoh: Pithom and Raamses. [12]But the more they were oppressed, the more they increased and spread out, so that the [Egyptians] came to dread the Israelites.

[13]The Egyptians ruthlessly imposed upon the Israelites [14c-]the various labors that they made them perform. Ruthlessly-[c] they made life bitter for them with harsh labor at mortar and bricks and with all sorts of tasks in the field.

[15]The king of Egypt spoke to the Hebrew midwives, one of whom was named Shiphrah and the other Puah, [16]saying, "When you deliver the Hebrew women, look at the birthstool:[d] if it is a boy, kill him; if it is a girl, let her live." [17]The midwives, fearing God, did not do as the king of Egypt had told them; they let the boys live. [18]So the king of Egypt summoned the midwives and said to them, "Why have you done this thing, letting the boys live?" [19]The midwives said to Pharaoh, "Because the Hebrew women are not like the Egyptian women: they are vigorous. Before the midwife can come to them, they have given birth." [20]And God

---

a-a *Meaning perhaps from their wretched condition, cf. Hos. 2.2; or "gain ascendancy over the country." Others "get them up out of the land."*
b *Others "store cities."*
c-c *Brought up from the end of the verse for clarity.*
d *More exactly, the brick or stone supports used by Egyptian women during childbirth.*

dealt well with the midwives; and the people multiplied and increased greatly. 21And because the midwives feared God, He established households^c for them. 22Then Pharaoh charged all his people, saying, "Every boy that is born you shall throw into the Nile, but let every girl live."

2 A certain man of the house of Levi went and married a Levite woman. 2The woman conceived and bore a son; and when she saw how beautiful he was, she hid him for three months. 3When she could hide him no longer, she got a wicker basket for him and caulked it with bitumen and pitch. She put the child into it and placed it among the reeds by the bank of the Nile. 4And his sister stationed herself at a distance, to learn what would befall him.

5The daughter of Pharaoh came down to bathe in the Nile, while her maidens walked along the Nile. She spied the basket among the reeds and sent her slave girl to fetch it. 6When she opened it, she saw that it was a child, a boy crying. She took pity on it and said, "This must be a Hebrew child." 7Then his sister said to Pharaoh's daughter, "Shall I go and get you a Hebrew nurse to suckle the child for you?" 8And Pharaoh's daughter answered, "Yes." So the girl went and called the child's mother. 9And Pharaoh's daughter said to her, "Take this child and nurse it for me, and I will pay your wages." So the woman took the child and nursed it. 10When the child grew up, she brought him to Pharaoh's daughter, who made him her son. She named him Moses,^a explaining, "I drew him out of the water."

11Some time after that, when Moses had grown up, he went out to his kinsfolk and witnessed their labors. He saw an Egyptian beating a Hebrew, one of his kinsmen. 12He turned this way and that and, seeing no one about, he struck down the Egyptian and hid him in the sand 13When he went out the next day, he found two Hebrews fighting; so he said to the offender, "Why do you strike your fellow?" 14He retorted, "Who made you chief and ruler over us? Do you mean to kill me as you killed the Egyptian?" Moses was frightened, and thought: Then the matter is known! 15When Pharaoh learned of the matter, he sought to kill Moses; but Moses fled from Pharaoh. He arrived^b in the land of Midian, and sat down beside a well.

---

^c Meaning of Heb. batim uncertain.

^a Heb. Mosheh from Egyptian for "born of"; here associated with mashah "draw out."
^b Lit. "sat" or "settled."

16Now the priest of Midian had seven daughters. They came to draw water, and filled the troughs to water their father's flock; 17but shepherds came and drove them off. Moses rose to their defense, and he watered their flock. 18When they returned to their father Reuel, he said, "How is it that you have come back so soon today?" 19They answered, "An Egyptian rescued us from the shepherds; he even drew water for us and watered the flock." 20He said to his daughters, "Where is he then? Why did you leave the man? Ask him in to break bread." 21Moses consented to stay with the man, and he gave Moses his daughter Zipporah as wife. 22She bore a son whom he named Gershom,c for he said, "I have been a stranger in a foreign land."

23A long time after that, the king of Egypt died. The Israelites were groaning under the bondage and cried out; and their cry for help from the bondage rose up to God. 24God heard their moaning, and God remembered His covenant with Abraham and Isaac and Jacob. 25God looked upon the Israelites, and God took notice of them.

3 Now Moses, tending the flock of his father-in-law Jethro, the priest of Midian, drove the flock into the wilderness, and came to Horeb, the mountain of God. 2An angel of the LORD appeared to him in a blazing fire out of a bush. He gazed, and there was a bush all aflame, yet the bush was not consumed. 3Moses said, "I must turn aside to look at this marvelous sight; why doesn't the bush burn up?" 4When the LORD saw that he had turned aside to look, God called to him out of the bush: "Moses! Moses!" He answered, "Here I am." 5And He said, "Do not come closer. Remove your sandals from your feet, for the place on which you stand is holy ground. 6I am," He said, "the God of your father, the God of Abraham, the God of Isaac, and the God of Jacob." And Moses hid his face, for he was afraid to look at God.

7And the LORD continued, "I have marked well the plight of My people in Egypt and have heeded their outcry because of their taskmasters; yes, I am mindful of their sufferings. 8I have come down to rescue them from the Egyptians and to bring them out of that land to a good and spacious land, a land flowing with milk and honey, the region of the Canaanites, the Hittites, the Amorites, the Perizzites, the Hivites, and the Jebusites.

c *Associated with* ger sham, *"a stranger there."*

9Now the cry of the Israelites has reached Me; moreover, I have seen how the Egyptians oppress them. 10Come, therefore, I will send you to Pharaoh, and you shall free My people, the Israelites, from Egypt."

11But Moses said to God, "Who am I that I should go to Pharaoh and free the Israelites from Egypt?" 12And He said, "I will be with you; that shall be your sign that it was I who sent you. And when you have freed the people from Egypt, you shall worship God at this mountain."

13Moses said to God, "When I come to the Israelites and say to them 'The God of your fathers has sent me to you,' and they ask me, 'What is His name?' what shall I say to them?" 14And God said to Moses, "Ehyeh-Asher-Ehyeh."a He continued, "Thus shall you say to the Israelites, 'Ehyehb sent me to you.' " 15And God said further to Moses, "Thus shall you speak to the Israelites: The LORD,c the God of your fathers, the God of Abraham, the God of Isaac, and the God of Jacob, has sent me to you:

This shall be My name forever,
This My appellation for all eternity.

16"Go and assemble the elders of Israel and say to them: the LORD, the God of your fathers, the God of Abraham, Isaac, and Jacob, has appeared to me and said, 'I have taken note of you and of what is being done to you in Egypt, 17and I have declared: I will take you out of the misery of Egypt to the land of the Canaanites, the Hittites, the Amorites, the Perizzites, the Hivites, and the Jebusites, to a land flowing with milk and honey.' 18They will listen to you; then you shall go with the elders of Israel to the king of Egypt and you shall say to him, 'The LORD, the God of the Hebrews, manifested Himself to us. Now therefore, let us go a distance of three days into the wilderness to sacrifice to the LORD our God.' 19Yet I know that the king of Egypt will let you go only because of a greater might. 20So I will stretch out My hand and smite Egypt with various wonders which I will work upon them; after that he shall let you go. 21And I will dispose the Egyptians favorably toward this people, so that when you go, you will not go away empty-handed. 22Each woman shall borrow from her neighbor and the lodger in her house objects of silver and gold, and clothing, and you shall put these on your sons and daughters, thus stripping the Egyptians."

4 But Moses spoke up and said, "What if they do not believe me and do not listen to me, but say: The LORD did not appear to you?" 2The

---

a *Meaning of Heb. uncertain; variously translated: "I Am That I Am"; "I Am Who I Am"; "I Will Be What I Will Be"; etc.*
b *Others "I Am" or "I Will Be."*
c *The name YHWH (traditionally read Adonai "the LORD") is here associated with the root hayah "to be."*

LORD said to him, "What is that in your hand?" And he replied, "A rod." [3]He said, "Cast it on the ground." He cast it on the ground and it became a snake; and Moses recoiled from it. [4]Then the LORD said to Moses, "Put out your hand and grasp it by the tail"—he put out his hand and seized it, and it became a rod in his hand—[5]"that they may believe that the LORD, the God of their fathers, the God of Abraham, the God of Isaac, and the God of Jacob, did appear to you."

[6]The LORD said to him further, "Put your hand into your bosom." He put his hand into his bosom; and when he took it out, his hand was encrusted with snowy scales![a] [7]And He said, "Put your hand back into your bosom."—He put his hand back into his bosom; and when he took it out of his bosom, there it was again like the rest of his body.—[8]"And if they do not believe you or pay heed to the first sign, they will believe the second. [9]And if they are not convinced by both these signs and still do not heed you, take some water from the Nile and pour it on the dry ground, and it—the water that you take from the Nile—will turn to blood on the dry ground."

[10]But Moses said to the LORD, "Please, O Lord, I have never been a man of words, either in times past or now that You have spoken to Your servant; I am slow of speech and slow of tongue." [11]And the LORD said to him, "Who gives man speech? Who makes him dumb or deaf, seeing or blind? Is it not I, the LORD? [12]Now go, and I will be with you as you speak and will instruct you what to say." [13]But he said, "Please, O Lord, make someone else Your agent."[b] [14]The LORD became angry with Moses, and He said, "There is your brother Aaron the Levite. He, I know, speaks readily. Even now he is setting out to meet you, and he will be happy to see you. [15]You shall speak to him and put the words in his mouth—I will be with you and with him as you speak, and tell both of you what to do—[16]and he shall speak for you to the people. Thus he shall serve as your spokesman, with you playing the role of God[c] to him, [17]And take with you this rod, with which you shall perform the signs."

[18]Moses went back to his father-in-law Jether[d] and said to him, "Let me go back to my kinsmen in Egypt and see how they are faring."[e] And Jethro said to Moses, "Go in peace."

[19]The LORD said to Moses in Midian, "Go back to Egypt, for all the men who sought to kill you are dead." [20]So Moses took his wife and sons, mounted them on an ass, and went back to the land of Egypt; and Moses took the rod of God with him.

---

[a] Cf. Lev. 13.2–3.
[b] Lit. "send through whomever You will send."
[c] Cf. 7.1.
[d] I.e., Jethro.
[e] Lit. "whether they are still alive."

21And the LORD said to Moses, "When you return to Egypt, see that you perform before Pharaoh all the marvels that I have put within your power. I, however, will stiffen his heart so that he will not let the people go. 22Then you shall say to Pharaoh, 'Thus says the LORD: Israel is My first-born son. 23I have said to you, "Let My son go, that he may worship Me," yet you refuse to let him go. Now I will slay your first-born son.' "

24At a night encampment on the way, the LORD encountered him and sought to kill him. 25 fSo Zipporah took a flint and cut off her son's foreskin, and touched his legs with it, saying, "You are truly a bridegroom of blood to me!" 26And when He let him alone, she added, "A bridegroom of blood because of the circumcision."

27The LORD said to Aaron, "Go to meet Moses in the wilderness." He went and met him at the mountain of God, and he kissed him. 28Moses told Aaron about all the things that the LORD had committed to him and all the signs about which He had instructed him. 29Then Moses and Aaron went and assembled all the elders of the Israelites. 30Aaron repeated all the words that the LORD had spoken to Moses, and he performed the signs in the sight of the people, 31and the people were convinced. When they heard that the LORD had taken note of the Israelites and that He had seen their plight, they bowed low in homage.

5 Afterward Moses and Aaron went and said to Pharaoh, "Thus says the LORD, the God of Israel: Let My people go that they may celebrate a festival for Me in the wilderness." 2But Pharaoh said, "Who is the LORD that I should heed Him and let Israel go? I do not know the LORD, nor will I let Israel go." 3They answered, "The God of the Hebrews has manifested Himself to us. Let us go, we pray, a distance of three days into the wilderness to sacrifice to the LORD our God, lest He strike us with pestilence or sword." 4But the king of Egypt said to them, "Moses and Aaron, why do you distract the people from their tasks? Get to your labors!" 5And Pharaoh continued, a-"The people of the land are already so numerous,-a and you would have them cease from their labors!"b

6That same day Pharaoh charged the taskmasters and foremen of the people, saying, 7"You shall no longer provide the people with straw for

---

f Meaning of vv. 25–26 uncertain.

a-a Samaritan "Even now they are more numerous than the people of the land," i.e., than the native population (cf. Gen. 23.7).

b See 1.5–11.

making bricks as heretofore; let them go and gather straw for themselves. [8]But impose upon them the same quota of bricks as they have been making heretofore; do not reduce it, for they are shirkers; that is why they cry, 'Let us go and sacrifice to our God!' [9]Let heavier work be laid upon the men; let them keep at it and not pay attention to deceitful promises."

[10]So the taskmasters and foremen of the people went out and said to the people, "Thus says Pharaoh: I will not give you any straw. [11]You must go and get the straw yourselves wherever you can find it; but there shall be no decrease whatever in your work." [12]Then the people scattered throughout the land of Egypt to gather stubble for straw. [13]And the taskmasters pressed them, saying, "You must complete the same work assignment each day as when you had straw." [14]And the foremen of the Israelites, whom Pharaoh's taskmasters had set over them, were beaten. "Why," they were asked, "did you not complete the prescribed amount of bricks, either yesterday or today, as you did before?"

[15]Then the foremen of the Israelites came to Pharaoh and cried: "Why do you deal thus with your servants? [16]No straw is issued to your servants, yet they demand of us: Make bricks! Thus your servants are being beaten, when the fault is with your own people." [17]He replied, "You are shirkers, shirkers! That is why you say, 'Let us go and sacrifice to the LORD.' [18]Be off now to your work! No straw shall be issued to you, but you must produce your quota of bricks!"

[19]Now the foremen of the Israelites found themselves in trouble because of the order, "You must not reduce your daily quantity of bricks." [20]As they left Pharaoh's presence, they came upon Moses and Aaron standing in their path, [21]and they said to them, "May the LORD look upon you and punish you for making us loathsome to Pharaoh and his courtiers— putting a sword in their hands to slay us." [22]Then Moses returned to the LORD and said, "O Lord, why did You bring harm upon this people? Why did You send me? [23]Ever since I came to Pharaoh to speak in Your name, he has dealt worse with this people; and still You have not delivered Your people."

6 Then the LORD said to Moses, "You shall soon see what I will do to Pharaoh: he shall let them go because of a greater might; indeed, because of a greater might he shall drive them from his land."

וארא

2God spoke to Moses and said to him, "I am the LORD. 3I appeared to Abraham, Isaac, and Jacob as El Shaddai, but I did not make Myself known to them by My name יהוה.ᵃ 4I also established My covenant with them, to give them the land of Canaan, the land in which they lived as sojourners. 5I have now heard the moaning of the Israelites because the Egyptians are holding them in bondage, and I have remembered My covenant. 6Say, therefore, to the Israelite people: I am the LORD. I will free you from the labors of the Egyptians and deliver you from their bondage. I will redeem you with an outstretched arm and through extraordinary chastisements. 7And I will take you to be My people, and I will be your God. And you shall know that I, the LORD, am your God who freed you from the labors of the Egyptians. 8I will bring you into the land which I sworeᵇ to give to Abraham, Isaac, and Jacob, and I will give it to you for a possession, I the LORD." 9But when Moses told this to the Israelites, they would not listen to Moses, their spirits crushed by cruel bondage.

10The LORD spoke to Moses, saying, 11"Go and tell Pharaoh king of Egypt to let the Israelites depart from his land." 12But Moses appealed to the LORD, saying, "The Israelites would not listen to me; how then should Pharaoh heed me, a man of impeded speech!" 13So the LORD spoke to both Moses and Aaron in regard to the Israelites and Pharaoh king of Egypt, instructing them to deliver the Israelites from the land of Egypt.

14The following are the heads of their respective clans.

The sons of Reuben, Israel's first-born: Enochᶜ and Pallu, Hezron and Carmi; those are the families of Reuben. 15The sons of Simeon: Jemuel, Jamin, Ohad, Jachin, Zohar, and Saulᵈ the son of a Canaanite woman; those are the families of Simeon. 16These are the names of Levi's sons by their lineage: Gershon, Kohath, and Merari; and the span of Levi's life was 137 years. 17The sons of Gershon: Libni and Shimei, by their families. 18The sons of Kohath: Amram, Izhar, Hebron, and Uzziel; and the span of Kohath's life was 133 years. 19The sons of Merari: Mahli and Mushi. These are the families of the Levites by their lineage.

20Amram took to wife his father's sister Jochebed, and she bore him Aaron and Moses; and the span of Amram's life was 137 years. 21The sons of Izhar: Korah, Nepheg, and Zichri. 22The sons of Uzziel: Mishael,

ᵃ This divine name is traditionally not pronounced; instead, Adonai, "(the) LORD," is regularly substituted for it.
ᵇ Lit. "raised My hand."
ᶜ Or "Hanoch"; cf. on Gen. 46.9.
ᵈ Or "Shaul"; cf. on Gen. 46.10.

Elzaphan, and Sithri. 23Aaron took to wife Elisheba, daughter of Amminadab and sister of Nahshon, and she bore him Nadab and Abihu, Eleazar and Ithamar. 24The sons of Korah: Assir, Elkanah, and Abiasaph. Those are the families of the Korahites. 25And Aaron's son Eleazar took to wife one of Putiel's daughters, and she bore him Phinehas. Those are the heads of the fathers' houses of the Levites by their families.

26It is the same Aaron and Moses to whom the LORD said, "Bring forth the Israelites from the land of Egypt, troop by troop." 27It was they who spoke to Pharaoh king of Egypt to free the Israelites from the Egyptians; these are the same Moses and Aaron. 28For when the LORD spoke to Moses in the land of Egypt 29and the LORD said to Moses, "I am the LORD; speak to Pharaoh king of Egypt all that I will tell you," 30Moses appealed to the LORD, saying, "See, I am of impeded speech; how then should Pharaoh heed me!"

7 The LORD replied to Moses, "See, I place you in the role of God to Pharaoh, with your brother Aaron as your prophet.ᵃ 2You shall repeat all that I command you, and your brother Aaron shall speak to Pharaoh to let the Israelites depart from his land. 3But I will harden Pharaoh's heart, that I may multiply My signs and marvels in the land of Egypt. 4When Pharaoh does not heed you, I will lay My hand upon Egypt and deliver My ranks, My people the Israelites, from the land of Egypt with extraordinary chastisements. 5And the Egyptians shall know that I am the LORD, when I stretch out My hand over Egypt and bring out the Israelites from their midst." 6This Moses and Aaron did; as the LORD commanded them, so they did. 7Moses was eighty years old and Aaron eighty-three, when they made their demand on Pharaoh.

8The LORD said to Moses and Aaron, 9"When Pharaoh speaks to you and says, 'Produce your marvel,' you shall say to Aaron, 'Take your rod and cast it down before Pharaoh.' It shall turn into a serpent." 10So Moses and Aaron came before Pharaoh and did just as the LORD had commanded: Aaron cast down his rod in the presence of Pharaoh and his courtiers, and it turned into a serpent. 11Then Pharaoh, for his part, summoned the wise men and the sorcerers; and the Egyptian magicians, in turn, did the same with their spells; 12each cast down his rod, and they turned into serpents. But Aaron's rod swallowed their rods. 13Yet Pharaoh's heart stiffened and he did not heed them, as the LORD had said.

ᵃ Cf. 4.16.

¹⁴And the LORD said to Moses, "Pharaoh is stubborn; he refuses to let the people go. ¹⁵Go to Pharaoh in the morning, as he is coming out to the water, and station yourself before him at the edge of the Nile, taking with you the rod that turned into a snake. ¹⁶And say to him, 'The LORD, the God of the Hebrews, sent me to you to say, "Let My people go that they may worship Me in the wilderness." But you have paid no heed until now. ¹⁷Thus says the LORD, "By this you shall know that I am the LORD." See, I shall strike the water in the Nile with the rod that is in my hand, and it will be turned into blood; ¹⁸and the fish in the Nile will die. The Nile will stink so that the Egyptians will find it impossible to drink the water of the Nile.' "

¹⁹And the LORD said to Moses, "Say to Aaron: Take your rod and hold out your arm over the waters of Egypt—its rivers, its canals, its ponds, all its bodies of water—that they may turn to blood; there shall be blood throughout the land of Egypt, even in vessels of wood and stone." ²⁰Moses and Aaron did just as the LORD commanded: he lifted up the rod and struck the water in the Nile in the sight of Pharaoh and his courtiers, and all the water in the Nile was turned into blood ²¹and the fish in the Nile died. The Nile stank so that the Egyptians could not drink water from the Nile; and there was blood throughout the land of Egypt. ²²But when the Egyptian magicians did the same with their spells, Pharaoh's heart stiffened and he did not heed them—as the LORD had spoken. ²³Pharaoh turned and went into his palace, paying no regard even to this. ²⁴And all the Egyptians had to dig round about the Nile for drinking water, because they could not drink the water of the Nile.

²⁵When seven days had passed after the LORD struck the Nile, ²⁶the LORD said to Moses, "Go to Pharaoh and say to him, 'Thus says the LORD: Let My people go that they may worship Me. ²⁷If you refuse to let them go, then I will plague your whole country with frogs. ²⁸The Nile shall swarm with frogs, and they shall come up and enter your palace, your bedchamber and your bed, the houses of your courtiers and your people, and your ovens and your kneading bowls. ²⁹The frogs shall come up on you and on your people and on all your courtiers.' "

8 And the LORD said to Moses, "Say to Aaron: Hold out your arm with the rod over the rivers, the canals, and the ponds, and bring up the frogs on the land of Egypt." ²Aaron held out his arm over the waters of

Egypt, and the frogs came up and covered the land of Egypt. ³But the magicians did the same with their spells, and brought frogs upon the land of Egypt.

⁴Then Pharaoh summoned Moses and Aaron and said, "Plead with the LORD to remove the frogs from me and my people, and I will let the people go to sacrifice to the LORD." ⁵And Moses said to Pharaoh, "You may have this triumph over me: for what time shall I plead in behalf of you and your courtiers and your people, that the frogs be cut off from you and your houses, to remain only in the Nile?" ⁶"For tomorrow," he replied. And [Moses] said, "As you say—that you may know that there is none like the LORD our God; ⁷the frogs shall retreat from you and your courtiers and your people; they shall remain only in the Nile." ⁸Then Moses and Aaron left Pharaoh's presence, and Moses cried out to the LORD in the matter of the frogs which He had inflicted upon Pharaoh. ⁹And the LORD did as Moses asked; the frogs died out in the houses, the courtyards, and the fields. ¹⁰And they piled them up in heaps, till the land stank. ¹¹But when Pharaoh saw that there was relief, he became stubborn and would not heed them, as the LORD had spoken.

¹²Then the LORD said to Moses, "Say to Aaron: Hold out your rod and strike the dust of the earth, and it shall turn to lice throughout the land of Egypt." ¹³And they did so. Aaron held out his arm with the rod and struck the dust of the earth, and vermin came upon man and beast; all the dust of the earth turned to lice throughout the land of Egypt. ¹⁴The magicians did the like with their spells to produce lice, but they could not. The vermin remained upon man and beast; ¹⁵and the magicians said to Pharaoh, "This is the finger of God!" But Pharaoh's heart stiffened and he would not heed them, as the LORD had spoken.

¹⁶And the LORD said to Moses, "Early in the morning present yourself to Pharaoh, as he is coming out to the water, and say to him, 'Thus says the LORD: Let My people go that they may worship Me. ¹⁷For if you do not let My people go, I will let loose ᵃ⁻swarms of insects⁻ᵃ against you and your courtiers and your people and your houses; the houses of the Egyptians, and the very ground they stand on, shall be filled with swarms of insects. ¹⁸But on that day I will set apart the region of Goshen, where My people dwell, so that no swarms of insects shall be there, that you may know that I the LORD am in the midst of the land. ¹⁹And I will make a distinctionᵇ between My people and your people. Tomorrow this sign shall come to pass.' " ²⁰And the LORD did so. Heavy swarms of

---

ᵃ⁻ᵃ *Others "wild beasts."*
ᵇ *Meaning of* peduth *uncertain.*

insects invaded Pharaoh's palace and the houses of his courtiers; throughout the country of Egypt the land was ruined because of the swarms of insects.

21Then Pharaoh summoned Moses and Aaron and said, "Go and sacrifice to your God within the land." 22But Moses replied, "It would not be right to do this, for what we sacrifice to the LORD our God is untouchable to the Egyptians. If we sacrifice that which is untouchable to the Egyptians before their very eyes, will they not stone us! 23So we must go a distance of three days into the wilderness and sacrifice to the LORD our God as He may command us." 24Pharaoh said, "I will let you go to sacrifice to the LORD your God in the wilderness; but do not go very far. Plead, then, for me." 25And Moses said, "When I leave your presence, I will plead with the LORD that the swarms of insects depart tomorrow from Pharaoh and his courtiers and his people; but let not Pharaoh again act deceitfully, not letting the people go to sacrifice to the LORD."

26So Moses left Pharaoh's presence and pleaded with the LORD. 27And the LORD did as Moses asked: He removed the swarms of insects from Pharaoh, from his courtiers, and from his people; not one remained. 28But Pharaoh became stubborn this time also, and would not let the people go.

9 The LORD said to Moses, "Go to Pharaoh and say to him, 'Thus says the LORD, the God of the Hebrews: Let My people go to worship Me. 2For if you refuse to let them go, and continue to hold them, 3then the hand of the LORD will strike your livestock in the fields—the horses, the asses, the camels, the cattle, and the sheep—with a very severe pestilence. 4But the LORD will make a distinction between the livestock of Israel and the livestock of the Egyptians, so that nothing shall die of all that belongs to the Israelites. 5The LORD has fixed the time: tomorrow the LORD will do this thing in the land.'" 6And the LORD did so the next day: all the livestock of the Egyptians died, but of the livestock of the Israelites not a beast died. 7When Pharaoh inquired, he found that not a head of the livestock of Israel had died; yet Pharaoh remained stubborn, and he would not let the people go.

8Then the LORD said to Moses and Aaron, "Each of you take handfuls of soot from the kiln, and let Moses throw it toward the sky in the sight of Pharaoh. 9It shall become a fine dust all over the land of Egypt, and cause an inflammation breaking out in boils on man and beast throughout the land of Egypt." ¹⁰So they took soot of the kiln and appeared before Pharaoh; Moses threw it toward the sky, and it caused an inflammation breaking out in boils on man and beast. ¹¹The magicians were unable to confront Moses because of the inflammation, for the inflammation afflicted the magicians as well as all the other Egyptians. ¹²But the LORD stiffened the heart of Pharaoh, and he would not heed them, just as the LORD had told Moses.

¹³The LORD said to Moses, "Early in the morning present yourself to Pharaoh and say to him, 'Thus says the LORD, the God of the Hebrews: Let My people go to worship Me. ¹⁴For this time I will send all My plagues upon your person, and your courtiers, and your people, in order that you may know that there is none like Me in all the world. ¹⁵I could have stretched forth My hand and stricken you and your people with pestilence, and you would have been effaced from the earth. ¹⁶Nevertheless I have spared you for this purpose: in order to show you My power, and in order that My fame may resound throughout the world. ¹⁷Yet you continue to thwartᵃ My people, and do not let them go! ¹⁸This time tomorrow I will rain down a very heavy hail, such as has not been in Egypt from the day it was founded until now. ¹⁹Therefore, order your livestock and everything you have in the open brought under shelter; every man and beast that is found outside, not having been brought indoors, shall perish when the hail comes down upon them!' " ²⁰Those among Pharaoh's courtiers who feared the LORD's word brought their slaves and livestock indoors to safety; ²¹but those who paid no regard to the word of the LORD left their slaves and livestock in the open.

²²The LORD said to Moses, "Hold out your arm toward the sky that hail may fall on all the land of Egypt, upon man and beast and all the grasses of the field in the land of Egypt." ²³So Moses held out his rod toward the sky, and the LORD sent thunder and hail, and fire streamed down to the ground, as the LORD rained down hail upon the land of Egypt. ²⁴The hail was very heavy—fire flashing in the midst of the hail—such as had not fallen on the land of Egypt since it had become a nation. ²⁵Throughout the land of Egypt the hail struck down all that were in the open, both man and beast; the hail also struck down all the grasses of the field and shattered all the trees of the field. ²⁶Only in the region of Goshen, where the Israelites were, there was no hail.

²⁷Thereupon Pharaoh sent for Moses and Aaron and said to them, "I

ᵃ *Others "exalt yourself over."*

stand guilty this time. The LORD is in the right, and I and my people are in the wrong. 28Plead with the LORD that there may be an end of God's thunder and of hail. I will let you go; you need stay no longer." 29Moses said to him, "As I go out of the city, I shall spread out my hands to the LORD; the thunder will cease and the hail will fall no more, so that you may know that the earth is the LORD's. 30But I know that you and your courtiers do not yet fear the LORD God."—31Now the flax and barley were ruined, for the barley was in the ear and the flax was in bud; 32but the wheat and the emmer^b were not hurt, for they ripen late.—33Leaving Pharaoh, Moses went outside the city and spread out his hands to the LORD: the thunder and the hail ceased, and no rain came pouring down upon the earth. 34But when Pharaoh saw that the rain and the hail and the thunder had ceased, he became stubborn and reverted to his guilty ways, as did his courtiers. 35So Pharaoh's heart stiffened and he would not let the Israelites go, just as the LORD had foretold through Moses.

בא

10 Then the LORD said to Moses, "Go to Pharaoh. For I have hardened his heart and the hearts of his courtiers, in order that I may display these My signs among them, 2and that you may recount in the hearing of your sons and of your sons' sons how I made a mockery of the Egyptians and how I displayed My signs among them—in order that you may know that I am the LORD." 3So Moses and Aaron went to Pharaoh and said to him, "Thus says the LORD, the God of the Hebrews, 'How long will you refuse to humble yourself before Me? Let My people go that they may worship Me. 4For if you refuse to let My people go, tomorrow I will bring locusts on your territory. 5They shall cover the surface of the land, so that no one will be able to see the land. They shall devour the surviving remnant that was left to you after the hail; and they shall eat away all your trees that grow in the field. 6Moreover, they shall fill your palaces and the houses of all your courtiers and of all the Egyptians— something that neither your fathers nor fathers' fathers have seen from the day they appeared on earth to this day.' " With that he turned and left Pharaoh's presence.

7Pharaoh's courtiers said to him, "How long shall this one be a snare to us? Let the men go to worship the LORD their God! Are you not yet

b *A kind of wheat.*

aware that Egypt is lost?" 8So Moses and Aaron were brought back to Pharaoh and he said to them, "Go, worship the LORD your God! Who are the ones to go?" 9Moses replied, "We will all go, young and old: we will go with our sons and daughters, our flocks and herds; for we must observe the LORD's festival." 10But he said to them, "The LORD be with you the same as I mean to let your children go with you! Clearly, you are bent on mischief. 11No! You menfolk go and worship the LORD, since that is what you want." And they were expelled from Pharaoh's presence.

12Then the LORD said to Moses, "Hold out your arm over the land of Egypt for the locusts, that they may come upon the land of Egypt and eat up all the grasses in the land, whatever the hail has left." 13So Moses held out his rod over the land of Egypt, and the LORD drove an east wind over the land all that day and all night; and when morning came, the east wind had brought the locusts. 14Locusts invaded all the land of Egypt and settled within all the territory of Egypt in a thick mass; never before had there been so many, nor will there ever be so many again. 15They hid all the land from view, and the land was darkened; and they ate up all the grasses of the field and all the fruit of the trees which the hail had left, so that nothing green was left, of tree or grass of the field, in all the land of Egypt.

16Pharaoh hurriedly summoned Moses and Aaron and said, "I stand guilty before the LORD your God and before you. 17Forgive my offense just this once, and plead with the LORD your God that He but remove this death from me." 18So he left Pharaoh's presence and pleaded with the LORD. 19The LORD caused a shift to a very strong west wind, which lifted the locusts and hurled them into the Sea of Reeds;ª not a single locust remained in all the territory of Egypt. 20But the LORD stiffened Pharaoh's heart, and he would not let the Israelites go.

21Then the LORD said to Moses, "Hold out your arm toward the sky that there may be darkness upon the land of Egypt, a darkness that can be touched." 22Moses held out his arm toward the sky and thick darkness descended upon all the land of Egypt for three days. 23People could not see one another, and for three days no one could get up from where he was; but all the Israelites enjoyed light in their dwellings.

24Pharaoh then summoned Moses and said, "Go, worship the LORD! Only your flocks and your herds shall be left behind; even your children may go with you." 25But Moses said, "You yourself must provide us with sacrifices and burnt offerings to offer up to the LORD our God; 26our

---

ª *Traditionally, but incorrectly, "Red Sea."*

own livestock, too, shall go along with us—not a hoof shall remain behind: for we must select from it for the worship of the LORD our God; and we shall not know with what we are to worship the LORD until we arrive there." 27But the LORD stiffened Pharaoh's heart and he would not agree to let them go. 28Pharaoh said to him, "Be gone from me! Take care not to see me again, for the moment you look upon my face you shall die." 29And Moses replied, "You have spoken rightly. I shall not see your face again!"

11 And the LORD said to Moses, "I will bring but one more plague upon Pharaoh and upon Egypt; after that he shall let you go from here; indeed, when he lets you go, he will drive you out of here one and all. 2Tell the people to borrow, each man from his neighbor and each woman from hers, objects of silver and gold." 3The LORD disposed the Egyptians favorably toward the people. Moreover, Moses himself was much esteemed in the land of Egypt, among Pharaoh's courtiers and among the people.

4Moses said, "Thus says the LORD: Toward midnight I will go forth among the Egyptians, 5and every first-born in the land of Egypt shall die, from the first-born of Pharaoh who sits on his throne to the first-born of the slave girl who is behind the millstones; and all the first-born of the cattle. 6And there shall be a loud cry in all the land of Egypt, such as has never been or will ever be again; 7but not a dog shall snarla at any of the Israelites, at man or beast—in order that you may know that the LORD makes a distinction between Egypt and Israel. 8Then all these courtiers of yours shall come down to me and bow low to me, saying, 'Depart, you and all the people who follow you!' After that I will depart." And he left Pharaoh's presence in hot anger.

9Now the LORD had said to Moses, "Pharaoh will not heed you, in order that My marvels may be multiplied in the land of Egypt." 10Moses and Aaron had performed all these marvels before Pharaoh, but the LORD had stiffened the heart of Pharaoh so that he would not let the Israelites go from his land.

12 The LORD said to Moses and Aaron in the land of Egypt: 2This month shall mark for you the beginning of the months; it shall be the

---

a Others "move (or whet) his tongue."

first of the months of the year for you. ³Speak to the whole community of Israel and say that on the tenth of this month each of them shall take a lamb^a to a family, a lamb to a household. ⁴But if the household is too small for a lamb, let him share one with a neighbor who dwells nearby, in proportion to the number of persons: you shall contribute for the lamb according to what each household will eat. ⁵Your lamb shall be without blemish, a yearling male; you may take it from the sheep or from the goats. ⁶You shall keep watch over it until the fourteenth day of this month; and all the assembled congregation of the Israelites shall slaughter it at twilight. ⁷They shall take some of the blood and put it on the two door-posts and the lintel of the houses in which they are to eat it. ⁸They shall eat the flesh that same night; they shall eat it roasted over the fire, with unleavened bread and with bitter herbs. ⁹Do not eat any of it raw, or cooked in any way with water, but roasted—head, legs, and entrails—over the fire. ¹⁰You shall not leave any of it over until morning; if any of it is left until morning, you shall burn it.

¹¹This is how you shall eat it: your loins girded, your sandals on your feet, and your staff in your hand; and you shall eat it hurriedly: it is a passover offering^b to the LORD. ¹²For that night I will go through the land of Egypt and strike down every first-born in the land of Egypt, both man and beast; and I will mete out punishments to all the gods of Egypt, I the LORD. ¹³And the blood on the houses where you are staying shall be a sign for you: when I see the blood I will pass over you, so that no plague will destroy you when I strike the land of Egypt.

¹⁴This day shall be to you one of remembrance: you shall celebrate it as a festival to the LORD throughout the ages; you shall celebrate it as an institution for all time. ¹⁵Seven days you shall eat unleavened bread; on the very first day you shall remove leaven from your houses, for whoever eats leavened bread from the first day to the seventh day, that person shall be cut off from Israel.

¹⁶You shall celebrate a sacred occasion on the first day, and a sacred occasion on the seventh day; no work at all shall be done on them; only what every person is to eat, that alone may be prepared for you. ¹⁷You shall observe the [Feast of] Unleavened Bread, for on this very day I brought your ranks out of the land of Egypt; you shall observe this day throughout the ages as an institution for all time. ¹⁸In the first month, from the fourteenth day of the month at evening, you shall eat unleavened bread until the twenty-first day of the month at evening. ¹⁹No leaven shall

---

^a Or "kid." Heb. seh *means either "sheep" or "goat"; cf. v. 5.*
^b Or *"protective offering"; Heb.* pesaḥ.

be found in your houses for seven days. For whoever eats what is leavened, that person shall be cut off from the community of Israel, whether he is a stranger or a citizen of the country. 20You shall eat nothing leavened; in all your settlements you shall eat unleavened bread.

21Moses then summoned all the elders of Israel and said to them, "Go, pick out lambs for your families, and slaughter the passover offering. 22Take a bunch of hyssop, dip it in the blood that is in the basin, and apply some of the blood that is in the basin to the lintel and to the two doorposts. None of you shall go outside the door of his house until morning. 23For when the LORD goes through to smite the Egyptians, He will see the blood on the lintel and the two doorposts, and the LORD will pass over^c the door and not let the Destroyer enter and smite your home.

24"You shall observe this as an institution for all time, for you and for your descendants. 25And when you enter the land that the LORD will give you, as He has promised, you shall observe this rite. 26And when your children ask you, 'What do you mean by this rite?' 27you shall say, 'It is the passover sacrifice to the LORD, because He passed over the houses of the Israelites in Egypt when He smote the Egyptians, but saved our houses.' "

The people then bowed low in homage. 28And the Israelites went and did so; just as the LORD had commanded Moses and Aaron, so they did.

29In the middle of the night the LORD struck down all the first-born in the land of Egypt, from the first-born of Pharaoh who sat on the throne to the first-born of the captive who was in the dungeon, and all the first-born of the cattle. 30And Pharaoh arose in the night, with all his courtiers and all the Egyptians—because there was a loud cry in Egypt; for there was no house where there was not someone dead. 31He summoned Moses and Aaron in the night and said, "Up, depart from among my people, you and the Israelites with you! Go, worship the LORD as you said! 32Take also your flocks and your herds, as you said, and begone! And may you bring a blessing upon me also!"

33The Egyptians urged the people on, impatient to have them leave the country, for they said, "We shall all be dead." 34So the people took their dough before it was leavened, their kneading bowls wrapped in their cloaks upon their shoulders. 35The Israelites had done Moses' bidding and borrowed from the Egyptians objects of silver and gold, and clothing.

c *Or "protect"; cf. v. 11, note b.*

³⁶And the LORD had disposed the Egyptians favorably toward the people, and they let them have their request; thus they stripped the Egyptians.

³⁷The Israelites journeyed from Rameses to Succoth, about six hundred thousand men on foot, aside from children. ³⁸Moreover, a mixed multitude went up with them, and very much livestock, both flocks and herds. ³⁹And they baked unleavened cakes of the dough that they had taken out of Egypt, for it was not leavened, since they had been driven out of Egypt and could not delay; nor had they prepared any provisions for themselves.

⁴⁰The length of time that the Israelites lived in Egypt was four hundred and thirty years; ⁴¹at the end of the four hundred and thirtieth year, to the very day, all the ranks of the LORD departed from the land of Egypt. ⁴²That was for the LORD a night of vigil to bring them out of the land of Egypt; that same night is the LORD's, one of vigil for all the children of Israel throughout the ages.

⁴³The LORD said to Moses and Aaron: This is the law of the passover offering: No foreigner shall eat of it. ⁴⁴But any slave a man has bought may eat of it once he has been circumcised. ⁴⁵No bound or hired laborer shall eat of it. ⁴⁶It shall be eaten in one house: you shall not take any of the flesh outside the house; nor shall you break a bone of it. ⁴⁷The whole community of Israel shall offer it. ⁴⁸If a stranger who dwells with you would offer the passover to the LORD, all his males must be circumcised; then he shall be admitted to offer it; he shall then be as a citizen of the country. But no uncircumcised person may eat of it. ⁴⁹There shall be one law for the citizen and for the stranger who dwells among you.

⁵⁰And all the Israelites did so; as the LORD had commanded Moses and Aaron, so they did.

⁵¹That very day the LORD freed the Israelites from the land of Egypt, troop by troop.

13

The LORD spoke further to Moses, saying, ²"Consecrate to Me every first-born; man and beast, the first issue of every womb among the Israelites is Mine."

³And Moses said to the people,

"Remember this day, on which you went free from Egypt, the house of bondage, how the LORD freed you from it with a mighty hand: no leavened bread shall be eaten. ⁴You go free on this day, in the month[a] of Abib. ⁵So, when the LORD has brought you into the land of the Canaanites, the Hittites, the Amorites, the Hivites, and the Jebusites, which He swore to your fathers to give you, a land flowing with milk and honey, you shall observe in this month the following practice:

⁶"Seven days you shall eat unleavened bread, and on the seventh day there shall be a festival of the LORD. ⁷Throughout the seven days unleavened bread shall be eaten; no leavened bread shall be found with you, and no leaven shall be found in all your territory. ⁸And you shall explain to your son on that day, 'It is because of what the LORD did for me when I went free from Egypt.'

⁹"And this shall serve you as a sign on your hand and as a reminder on your forehead[b]—in order that the Teaching of the LORD may be in your mouth—that with a mighty hand the LORD freed you from Egypt. ¹⁰You shall keep this institution at its set time from year to year.

¹¹"And when the LORD has brought you into the land of the Canaanites, as He swore to you and to your fathers, and has given it to you, ¹²you shall set apart for the LORD every first issue of the womb: every male firstling that your cattle drop shall be the LORD's. ¹³But every firstling ass you shall redeem with a sheep; if you do not redeem it, you must break its neck. And you must redeem every first-born male among your children. ¹⁴And when, in time to come, your son asks you, saying, 'What does this mean?' you shall say to him, 'It was with a mighty hand that the LORD brought us out from Egypt, the house of bondage. ¹⁵When Pharaoh stubbornly refused to let us go, the LORD slew every first-born in the land of Egypt, the first-born of both man and beast. Therefore I sacrifice to the LORD every first male issue of the womb, but redeem every first-born among my sons.'

¹⁶"And so it shall be as a sign upon your hand and as a symbol[c] on your forehead that with a mighty hand the LORD freed us from Egypt."

בשלח

¹⁷Now when Pharaoh let the people go, God did not lead them by way of the land of the Philistines, although it was nearer; for God said, "The people may have a change of heart when they see war, and return to

---

a Or "on the new moon."
b Lit. "between your eyes."
c Others "frontlet."

Egypt." [18]So God led the people roundabout, by way of the wilderness at the Sea of Reeds.

Now the Israelites went up armed[d] out of the land of Egypt. [19]And Moses took with him the bones of Joseph, who had exacted an oath from the children of Israel, saying, "God will be sure to take notice of you: then you shall carry up my bones from here with you."

[20]They set out from Succoth, and encamped at Etham, at the edge of the wilderness. [21]The LORD went before them in a pillar of cloud by day, to guide them along the way, and in a pillar of fire by night, to give them light, that they might travel day and night. [22]The pillar of cloud by day and the pillar of fire by night did not depart from before the people.

14

The LORD said to Moses: [2]Tell the Israelites to turn back and encamp before Pi-hahiroth, between Migdol and the sea, before Baal-zephon; you shall encamp facing it, by the sea. [3]Pharaoh will say of the Israelites, "They are astray in the land; the wilderness has closed in on them." [4]Then I will stiffen Pharaoh's heart and he will pursue them, that I may gain glory through Pharaoh and all his host; and the Egyptians shall know that I am the LORD.

And they did so.

[5]When the king of Egypt was told that the people had fled, Pharaoh and his courtiers had a change of heart about the people and said, "What is this we have done, releasing Israel from our service?" [6]He ordered[a] his chariot and took his men with him; [7]he took six hundred of his picked chariots, and the rest of the chariots of Egypt, with officers[b] in all of them. [8]The LORD stiffened the heart of Pharaoh king of Egypt, and he gave chase to the Israelites. As the Israelites were departing defiantly,[c] [9]the Egyptians gave chase to them, and all the chariot horses of Pharoah, his horsemen, and his warriors overtook them encamped by the sea, near Pi-hahiroth, before Baal-zephon.

[10]As Pharaoh drew near, the Israelites caught sight of the Egyptians advancing upon them. Greatly frightened, the Israelites cried out to the LORD. [11]And they said to Moses, "Was it for want of graves in Egypt that you brought us to die in the wilderness? What have you done to us, taking us out of Egypt? [12]Is this not the very thing we told you in Egypt, saying, 'Let us be, and we will serve the Egyptians, for it is better for us

---

[d] *Meaning of Heb.* hamushim *uncertain.*

[a] *See on Gen. 46.29.*
[b] *Heb.* shalish; *originally "third man on royal chariot"; hence "adjutant," "officer."*
[c] *Lit. "with upraised hand."*

to serve the Egyptians than to die in the wilderness'?" [13]But Moses said to the people, "Have no fear! Stand by, and witness the deliverance which the LORD will work for you today; for the Egyptians whom you see today you will never see again. [14]The LORD will battle for you; you hold your peace!"

[15]Then the LORD said to Moses, "Why do you cry out to Me? Tell the Israelites to go forward. [16]And you lift up your rod and hold out your arm over the sea and split it, so that the Israelites may march into the sea on dry ground. [17]And I will stiffen the hearts of the Egyptians so that they go in after them; and I will gain glory through Pharaoh and all his warriors, his chariots and his horsemen. [18]Let the Egyptians know that I am LORD, when I gain glory through Pharaoh, his chariots, and his horsemen."

[19]The angel of God, who had been going ahead of the Israelite army, now moved and followed behind them; and the pillar of cloud shifted from in front of them and took up a place behind them, [20]and it came between the army of the Egyptians and the army of Israel. Thus there was the cloud with the darkness, and it cast a spell[d] upon the night, so that the one could not come near the other all through the night.

[21]Then Moses held out his arm over the sea and the LORD drove back the sea with a strong east wind all that night, and turned the sea into dry ground. The waters were split, [22]and the Israelites went into the sea on dry ground, the waters forming a wall for them on their right and on their left. [23]The Egyptians came in pursuit after them into the sea, all of Pharaoh's horses, chariots, and horsemen. [24]At the morning watch, the LORD looked down upon the Egyptian army from a pillar of fire and cloud, and threw the Egyptian army into panic. [25]He locked[e] the wheels of their chariots so that they moved forward with difficulty. And the Egyptians said, "Let us flee from the Israelites, for the LORD is fighting for them against Egypt."

[26]Then the LORD said to Moses, "Hold out your arm over the sea, that the waters may come back upon the Egyptians and upon their chariots and upon their horsemen." [27]Moses held out his arm over the sea, and at daybreak the sea returned to its normal state, and the Egyptians fled at its approach. But the LORD hurled the Egyptians into the sea. [28]The waters turned back and covered the chariots and the horsemen—Pharaoh's entire army that followed them into the sea; not one of them remained.

[d] From root 'rr, "cast a spell" or "curse." Others "and it lit up."
[e] From root 'sr, with several ancient versions. Others "took off."

²⁹But the Israelites had marched through the sea on dry ground, the waters forming a wall for them on their right and on their left.

³⁰Thus the LORD delivered Israel that day from the Egyptians. Israel saw the Egyptians dead on the shore of the sea. ³¹And when Israel saw the wondrous power which the LORD had wielded against the Egyptians, the people feared the LORD; they had faith in the LORD and His servant Moses.

15

Then Moses and the Israelites sang this song to the LORD. They said:

> I will sing to the LORD, for He has triumphed gloriously;
> Horse and driver He has hurled into the sea.
> ²The LORDᵃ is my strength and might;ᵇ
> He is become my deliverance.
> This is my God and I will enshrineᶜ Him;
> The God of my father, and I will exalt Him.
> ³The LORD, the Warrior—
> LORD is His name!
> ⁴Pharaoh's chariots and his army
> He has cast into the sea;
> And the pick of his officers
> Are drowned in the Sea of Reeds.
> ⁵The deeps covered them;
> They went down into the depths like a stone.
> ⁶Your right hand, O LORD, glorious in power,
> Your right hand, O LORD, shatters the foe!
> ⁷In Your great triumph You break Your opponents;
> You send forth Your fury, it consumes them like straw.
> ⁸At the blast of Your nostrils the waters piled up,
> The floods stood straight like a wall;
> The deeps froze in the heart of the sea.
> ⁹The foe said,
> "I will pursue, I will overtake,
> I will divide the spoil;
> My desire shall have its fill of them.

ᵃ *Heb.* Yah.
ᵇ *Others "song."*
ᶜ *Others "glorify."*

I will bare my sword—
My hand shall subdue them."
10You made Your wind blow, the sea covered them;
They sank like lead in the majestic waters.

11Who is like You, O LORD, among the celestials;[d]
Who is like You, majestic in holiness,
Awesome in splendor, working wonders!
12You put out Your right hand,
The earth swallowed them.
13In Your love You lead the people You redeemed;
In Your strength You guide them to Your holy abode.
14The peoples hear, they tremble;
Agony grips the dwellers in Philistia.
15Now are the clans of Edom dismayed;
The tribes of Moab—trembling grips them;
All the dwellers in Canaan are aghast.
16Terror and dread descend upon them;
Through the might of Your arm they are still as stone—
Till Your people cross over, O LORD,
Till Your people cross whom You have ransomed.

17You will bring them and plant them in Your own mountain,
The place You made to dwell in, O LORD,
The sanctuary, O LORD, which Your hands established.
18The LORD will reign for ever and ever!

19For the horses of Pharaoh, with his chariots and horsemen, went into the sea; and the LORD turned back on them the waters of the sea; but the Israelites marched on dry ground in the midst of the sea.

20Then Miriam the prophetess, Aaron's sister, took a timbrel in her hand, and all the women went out after her in dance with timbrels. 21And Miriam chanted for them:

Sing to the LORD, for He has triumphed gloriously;
Horse and driver He has hurled into the sea.

d Others "mighty."

22Then Moses caused Israel to set out from the Sea of Reeds. They went on into the wilderness of Shur; they traveled three days in the wilderness and found no water. 23They came to Marah, but they could not drink the water of Marah because it was bitter; that is why it was named Marah.c 24And the people grumbled against Moses, saying, "What shall we drink?" 25So he cried out to the LORD, and the LORD showed him a piece of wood; he threw it into the water and the water became sweet.

There He made for them a fixed rule, and there He put them to the test. 26He said, "If you will heed the LORD your God diligently, doing what is upright in His sight, giving ear to His commandments and keeping all His laws, then I will not bring upon you any of the diseases that I brought upon the Egyptians, for I the LORD am your healer."

27And they came to Elim, where there were twelve springs of water and seventy palm trees; and they encamped there beside the water.

16 Setting out from Elim, the whole Israelite community came to the wilderness of Sin, which is between Elim and Sinai, on the fifteenth day of the second month after their departure from the land of Egypt. 2In the wilderness, the whole Israelite community grumbled against Moses and Aaron. 3The Israelites said to them, "If only we had died by the hand of the LORD in the land of Egypt, when we sat by the fleshpots, when we ate our fill of bread! For you have brought us out into this wilderness to starve this whole congregation to death."

4And the LORD said to Moses, "I will rain down bread for you from the sky, and the people shall go out and gather each day that day's portion—that I may thus test them, to see whether they will follow My instructions or not. 5But on the sixth day, when they apportion what they have brought in, it shall prove to be double the amount they gather each day." 6So Moses and Aaron said to all the Israelites, "By evening you shall know it was the LORD who brought you out from the land of Egypt; 7and in the morning you shall behold the Presencea of the LORD, because He has heard your grumblings against the LORD. For who are we that you should grumble against us? 8Since it is the LORD," Moses continued, "who will give you flesh to eat in the evening and bread in the morning

c *I.e., "bitter."*

a *Others "glory."*

to the full, because the LORD has heard the grumblings you utter against Him, what is our part? Your grumbling is not against us, but against the LORD!"

⁹Then Moses said to Aaron, "Say to the whole Israelite community: Advance toward the LORD, for He has heard your grumbling." ¹⁰And as Aaron spoke to the whole Israelite community, they turned toward the wilderness, and there, in a cloud, appeared the Presence of the LORD.

¹¹The LORD spoke to Moses: ¹²"I have heard the grumbling of the Israelites. Speak to them and say: By evening you shall eat flesh, and in the morning you shall have your fill of bread; and you shall know that I the LORD am your God."

¹³In the evening quail appeared and covered the camp; in the morning there was a fall of dew about the camp. ¹⁴When the fall of dew lifted, there, over the surface of the wilderness, lay a fine and flaky substance, as fine as frost on the ground. ¹⁵When the Israelites saw it, they said to one another, "What is it?"ᵇ—for they did not know what it was. And Moses said to them, "That is the bread which the LORD has given you to eat. This is what the LORD has commanded: Gather as much of it as each of you requires to eat, an *omer* to a person for as many of you as there are; each of you shall fetch for those in his tent."

¹⁷The Israelites did so, some gathering much, some little. ¹⁸But when they measured it by the *omer,* he who had gathered much had no excess, and he who had gathered little had no deficiency: they had gathered as much as they needed to eat. ¹⁹And Moses said to them, "Let no one leave any of it over until morning." ²⁰But they paid no attention to Moses; some of them left of it until morning, and it became infested with maggots and stank. And Moses was angry with them.

²¹So they gathered it every morning, each as much as he needed to eat; for when the sun grew hot, it would melt. ²²On the sixth day they gathered double the amount of food, two *omer*s for each; and when all the chieftains of the community came and told Moses, ²³he said to them, "This is what the LORD meant: Tomorrow is a day of rest, a holy sabbath of the LORD. Bake what you would bake and boil what you would boil; and all that is left put aside to be kept until morning." ²⁴So they put it aside until morning, as Moses had ordered; and it did not turn foul, and there were no maggots in it. ²⁵Then Moses said, "Eat it today, for today is a sabbath of the LORD; you will not find it today on the plain. ²⁶Six

ᵇ *Heb.* man hu; *others "It is manna."*

days you shall gather it; on the seventh day, the sabbath, there will be none."

27Yet some of the people went out on the seventh day to gather, but they found nothing. 28And the LORD said to Moses, "How long will you men refuse to obey My commandments and My teachings? 29Mark that the LORD has given you the sabbath; therefore He gives you two days' food on the sixth day. Let everyone remain where he is: let no one leave his place on the seventh day." 30So the people remained inactive on the seventh day.

31The house of Israel named it manna;c it was like coriander seed, white, and it tasted like wafersd in honey. 32Moses said, "This is what the LORD has commanded: Let one *omer* of it be kept throughout the ages, in order that they may see the bread that I fed you in the wilderness when I brought you out from the land of Egypt." 33And Moses said to Aaron, "Take a jar, put one *omer* of manna in it, and place it before the LORD, to be kept throughout the ages." 34As the LORD had commanded Moses, Aaron placed it before the Pact,e to be kept. 35And the Israelites ate manna forty years, until they came to a settled land; they ate the manna until they came to the border of the land of Canaan. 36The *omer* is a tenth of an *ephah*.

17 From the wilderness of Sin the whole Israelite community continued by stages as the LORD would command. They encamped at Rephidim, and there was no water for the people to drink. 2The people quarreled with Moses. "Give us water to drink," they said; and Moses replied to them, "Why do you quarrel with me? Why do you try the LORD?" 3But the people thirsted there for water; and the people grumbled against Moses and said, "Why did you bring us up from Egypt, to kill us and our children and livestock with thirst?" 4Moses cried out to the LORD, saying, "What shall I do with this people? Before long they will be stoning me!" 5Then the LORD said to Moses, "Pass before the people; take with you some of the elders of Israel, and take along the rod with which you struck the Nile, and set out. 6I will be standing there before you on the rock at Horeb. Strike the rock and water will issue from it, and the people will drink." And Moses did so in the sight of the elders of Israel. 7The place was named Massaha and Meribah,b because the Israelites quarreled

c *Heb.* man.
d *Meaning of Heb.* ṣappiḥith *uncertain.*
e *Others "Testimony."*

a *I.e., "Trial."*
b *I.e., "Quarrel."*

and because they tried the LORD, saying, "Is the LORD present among us or not?"

8Amalek came and fought with Israel at Rephidim. 9Moses said to Joshua, "Pick some men for us, and go out and do battle with Amalek. Tomorrow I will station myself on the top of the hill, with the rod of God in my hand." 10Joshua did as Moses told him and fought with Amalek, while Moses, Aaron, and Hur went up to the top of the hill. 11Then, whenever Moses held up his hand, Israel prevailed; but whenever he let down his hand, Amalek prevailed. 12But Moses' hands grew heavy; so they took a stone and put it under him and he sat on it, while Aaron and Hur, one on each side, supported his hands; thus his hands remained steady until the sun set. 13And Joshua overwhelmed the people of Amalekc with the sword.

14Then the LORD said to Moses, "Inscribe this in a document as a reminder, and read it aloud to Joshua: I will utterly blot out the memory of Amalek from under heaven!" 15And Moses built an altar and named it Adonai-nissi.d 16He said, "It means, 'Hand upon the thronee of the LORD!' The LORD will be at war with Amalek throughout the ages."

יתרו

18 Jethro priest of Midian, Moses' father-in-law, heard all that God had done for Moses and for Israel His people, how the LORD had brought Israel out from Egypt. 2So Jethro, Moses' father-in-law, took Zipporah, Moses' wife, after she had been sent home, 3and her two sons—of whom one was named Gershom, that is to say, "I have been a strangera in a foreign land"; 4and the other was named Eliezer,b meaning, "The God of my father was my help, and He delivered me from the sword of Pharaoh." 5Jethro, Moses' father-in-law, brought Moses' sons and wife to him in the wilderness, where he was encamped at the mountain of God. 6He sent word to Moses, "I, your father-in-law Jethro, am coming to you, with your wife and her two sons." 7Moses went out to meet his father-in-law; he bowed low and kissed him; each asked after the other's welfare, and they went into the tent.

8Moses then recounted to his father-in-law everything that the LORD had done to Pharaoh and to the Egyptians for Israel's sake, all the hard-

c Lit. "Amalek and his people."
d I.e., "The LORD is my banner."
e Meaning of Heb. kes uncertain.

a Heb. ger.
b Lit. "(My) God is help."

ships that had befallen them on the way, and how the LORD had delivered them. [9]And Jethro rejoiced over all the kindness that the LORD had shown Israel when He delivered them from the Egyptians. [10]"Blessed be the LORD," Jethro said, "who delivered you from the Egyptians and from Pharaoh, and who delivered the people from under the hand of the Egyptians. [11]Now I know that the LORD is greater than all gods, [c]yes, by the result of their very schemes against [the people]."[-c] [12]And Jethro, Moses' father-in-law, brought a burnt offering and sacrifices for God; and Aaron came with all the elders of Israel to partake of the meal before God with Moses' father-in-law.

[13]Next day, Moses sat as magistrate among the people, while the people stood about Moses from morning until evening. [14]But when Moses' father-in-law saw how much he had to do for the people, he said, "What is this thing that you are doing to the people? Why do you act[d] alone, while all the people stand about you from morning until evening?" [15]Moses replied to his father-in-law, "It is because the people come to me to inquire of God. [16]When they have a dispute, it comes before me, and I decide between one person and another, and I make known the laws and teachings of God."

[17]But Moses' father-in-law said to him, "The thing you are doing is not right; [18]you will surely wear yourself out, and these people as well. For the task is too heavy for you; you cannot do it alone. [19]Now listen to me. I will give you counsel, and God be with you! You represent the people before God: you bring the disputes before God, [20]and enjoin upon them the laws and the teachings, and make known to them the way they are to go and the practices they are to follow. [21]You shall also seek out from among all the people capable men who fear God, trustworthy men who spurn ill-gotten gain. Set these over them as chiefs of thousands, hundreds, fifties, and tens, and [22]let them judge the people at all times. Have them bring every major dispute to you, but let them decide every minor dispute themselves. Make it easier for yourself by letting them share the burden with you. [23]If you do this—and God so commands you—you will be able to bear up; and all these people too will go home unwearied."

[24]Moses heeded his father-in-law and did just as he had said. [25]Moses chose capable men out of all Israel, and appointed them heads over the people—chiefs of thousands, hundreds, fifties, and tens; [26]and they judged the people at all times: the difficult matters they would bring to Moses,

[c-c] *Meaning of Heb. uncertain.*
[d] *Lit. "sit" as magistrate; cf. v. 13.*

and all the minor matters they would decide themselves. ²⁷Then Moses bade his father-in-law farewell, and he went his way to his own land.

19 On the third new moon after the Israelites had gone forth from the land of Egypt, on that very day, they entered the wilderness of Sinai. ²Having journeyed from Rephidim, they entered the wilderness of Sinai and encamped in the wilderness. Israel encamped there in front of the mountain, ³and Moses went up to God. The LORD called to him from the mountain, saying, "Thus shall you say to the house of Jacob and declare to the children of Israel: ⁴'You have seen what I did to the Egyptians, how I bore you on eagles' wings and brought you to Me. ⁵Now then, if you will obey Me faithfully and keep My covenant, you shall be My treasured possession among all the peoples. Indeed, all the earth is Mine, ⁶but you shall be to Me a kingdom of priests and a holy nation.' These are the words that you shall speak to the children of Israel."

⁷Moses came and summoned the elders of the people and put before them all that the LORD had commanded him. ⁸All the people answered as one, saying, "All that the LORD has spoken we will do!" And Moses brought back the people's words to the LORD. ⁹And the LORD said to Moses, "I will come to you in a thick cloud, in order that the people may hear when I speak with you and so trust you ever after." Then Moses reported the people's words to the LORD, ¹⁰and the LORD said to Moses, "Go to the people and warn them to stay pure^a today and tomorrow. Let them wash their clothes. ¹¹Let them be ready for the third day; for on the third day the LORD will come down, in the sight of all the people, on Mount Sinai. ¹²You shall set bounds for the people round about, saying, 'Beware of going up the mountain or touching the border of it. Whoever touches the mountain shall be put to death: ¹³no hand shall touch him, but he shall be either stoned or shot; beast or man, he shall not live.' When the ram's horn ^{b-}sounds a long blast,^{-b} they may go up on the mountain."

¹⁴Moses came down from the mountain to the people and warned the people to stay pure, and they washed their clothes. ¹⁵And he said to the people, "Be ready for the third day: do not go near a woman."

¹⁶On the third day, as morning dawned, there was thunder, and light-

---

^a *Cf. v. 15.*
^{b-b} *Meaning of Heb. uncertain.*

ning, and a dense cloud upon the mountain, and a very loud blast of the horn; and all the people who were in the camp trembled. ¹⁷Moses led the people out of the camp toward God, and they took their places at the foot of the mountain.

¹⁸Now Mount Sinai was all in smoke, for the LORD had come down upon it in fire; the smoke rose like the smoke of a kiln, and the whole mountain^c trembled violently. ¹⁹The blare of the horn grew louder and louder. As Moses spoke, God answered him in thunder. ²⁰The LORD came down upon Mount Sinai, on the top of the mountain, and the LORD called Moses to the top of the mountain and Moses went up. ²¹The LORD said to Moses, "Go down, warn the people not to break through to the LORD to gaze, lest many of them perish. ²²The priests also, who come near the LORD, must stay pure, lest the LORD break out against them." ²³But Moses said to the LORD, "The people cannot come up to Mount Sinai, for You warned us saying, 'Set bounds about the mountain and sanctify it.'" ²⁴So the LORD said to him, "Go down, and come back together with Aaron; but let not the priests or the people break through to come up to the LORD, lest He break out against them." ²⁵And Moses went down to the people and spoke to them.

20 God spoke all these words,ᵃ saying:

²I the LORD am your God who brought you out of the land of Egypt, the house of bondage: ³You shall have no other gods besides Me.

⁴You shall not make for yourself a sculptured image, or any likeness of what is in the heavens above, or on the earth below, or in the waters under the earth. ⁵You shall not bow down to them or serve them. For I the LORD your God am an impassioned God, visiting the guilt of the parents upon the children, upon the third and upon the fourth generations of those who reject Me, ⁶but showing kindness to the thousandth generation of those who love Me and keep My commandments.

⁷You shall not ᵇ⁻swear falsely by⁻ᵇ the name of the LORD your God; for the LORD will not clear one who swears falsely by His name.

⁸Remember the sabbath day and keep it holy. ⁹Six days you shall labor and do all your work, ¹⁰but the seventh day is a sabbath of the LORD your God: you shall not do any work—you, your son or daughter, your male or female slave, or your cattle, or the stranger who is within your settlements. ¹¹For in six days the LORD made heaven and earth and sea,

---

ᶜ *Some Hebrew manuscripts and the Greek read "all the people"; cf. v. 16.*

ᵃ *Tradition varies as to the division of the Commandments in vv. 2–14, and as to the numbering of the verses from 13 on.*

ᵇ⁻ᵇ *Others "take in vain."*

and all that is in them, and He rested on the seventh day; therefore the LORD blessed the sabbath day and hallowed it.

12Honor your father and your mother, that you may long endure on the land that the LORD your God is assigning to you.

13You shall not murder.

You shall not commit adultery.

You shall not steal.

You shall not bear false witness against your neighbor.

14You shall not covet your neighbor's house: you shall not covet your neighbor's wife, or his male or female slave, or his ox or his ass, or anything that is your neighbor's.

15All the people witnessed the thunder and lightning, the blare of the horn and the mountain smoking; and when the people saw it, they fell back and stood at a distance. 16"You speak to us," they said to Moses, "and we will obey; but let not God speak to us, lest we die." 17Moses answered the people, "Be not afraid; for God has come only in order to test you, and in order that the fear of Him may be ever with you, so that you do not go astray." 18So the people remained at a distance, while Moses approached the thick cloud where God was.

19The LORD said to Moses:

Thus shall you say to the Israelites: You yourselves saw that I spoke to you from the very heavens: 20With Me, therefore, you shall not make any gods of silver, nor shall you make for yourselves any gods of gold. 21Make for Me an altar of earth and sacrifice on it your burnt offerings and your sacrifices of well-being,c your sheep and your oxen; in every place where I cause My name to be mentioned I will come to you and bless you. 22And if you make for Me an altar of stones, do not build it of hewn stones; for by wielding your tool upon them you have profaned them. 23Do not ascend My altar by steps, that your nakedness may not be exposed upon it.

c Others "peace-offering." Meaning of shelamin uncertain.

21

These are the rules that you shall set before them:

[2]When you acquire a Hebrew slave, he shall serve six years; in the seventh year he shall go free, without payment. [3]If he came single, he shall leave single; if he had a wife, his wife shall leave with him. [4]If his master gave him a wife, and she has borne him children, the wife and her children shall belong to the master, and he shall leave alone. [5]But if the slave declares, "I love my master, and my wife and children: I do not wish to go free," [6]his master shall take him before God.[a] He shall be brought to the door or the doorpost, and his master shall pierce his ear with an awl; and he shall then remain his slave for life.

[7]When a man sells his daughter as a slave, she shall not be freed as male slaves are. [8]If she proves to be displeasing to her master, who designated her for himself, he must let her be redeemed; he shall not have the right to sell her to outsiders, since he broke faith with her. [9]And if he designated her for his son, he shall deal with her as is the practice with free maidens. [10]If he marries another, he must not withhold from this one her food, her clothing, or her conjugal rights.[b] [11]If he fails her in these three ways, she shall go free, without payment.

[12]He who fatally strikes a man shall be put to death. [13]If he did not do it by design, but it came about by an act of God, I will assign you a place to which he can flee.

[14]When a man schemes against another and kills him treacherously, you shall take him from My very altar to be put to death.

[15]He who strikes his father or his mother shall be put to death.

[16]He who kidnaps a man—whether he has sold him or is still holding him—shall be put to death.

[17]He who insults[c] his father or his mother shall be put to death.

[18]When men quarrel and one strikes the other with stone or fist, and he does not die but has to take to his bed—[19]if he then gets up and walks outdoors upon his staff, the assailant shall go unpunished, except that he must pay for his idleness and his cure.

[20]When a man strikes his slave, male or female, with a rod, and he dies there and then,[d] he must be avenged. [21]But if he survives a day or two, he is not to be avenged, since he is the other's property.

[a] Others "to the judges."
[b] Or "ointments."
[c] Or "reviles."
[d] Lit. "under his hand."

22When men fight, and one of them pushes a pregnant woman and a miscarriage results, but no other damage ensues, the one responsible[c] shall be fined according as the woman's husband may exact from him, the payment to be based on reckoning.[f] 23But if other damage ensues, the penalty shall be life for life, 24eye for eye, tooth for tooth, hand for hand, foot for foot, 25burn for burn, wound for wound, bruise for bruise.

26When a man strikes the eye of his slave, male or female, and destroys it, he shall let him go free on account of his eye. 27If he knocks out the tooth of his slave, male or female, he shall let him go free on account of his tooth.

28When an ox gores a man or a woman to death, the ox shall be stoned and its flesh shall not be eaten, but the owner of the ox is not to be punished. 29If, however, that ox has been in the habit of goring, and its owner, though warned, has failed to guard it, and it kills a man or a woman—the ox shall be stoned and its owner, too, shall be put to death. 30If ransom is laid upon him, he must pay whatever is laid upon him to redeem his life. 31So, too, if it gores a minor, male or female, [the owner] shall be dealt with according to the same rule. 32But if the ox gores a slave, male or female, he shall pay thirty shekels of silver to the master, and the ox shall be stoned.

33When a man opens a pit, or digs a pit and does not cover it, and an ox or an ass falls into it, 34the one responsible for the pit must make restitution; he shall pay the price to the owner, but shall keep the dead animal.

35When a man's ox injures his neighbor's ox and it dies, they shall sell the live ox and divide its price; they shall also divide the dead animal. 36If, however, it is known that the ox was in the habit of goring, and its owner has failed to guard it, he must restore ox for ox, but shall keep the dead animal.

37gWhen a man steals an ox or a sheep, and slaughters it or sells it, he

22 shall pay five oxen for the ox, and four sheep for the sheep.—1If the thief is seized while tunneling,[a] and he is beaten to death, there is no bloodguilt in his case. 2If the sun has risen on him, there is bloodguilt in that case.—He[b] must make restitution; if he lacks the means, he shall be sold for his theft. 3But if what he stole—whether ox or ass or sheep—is found alive in his possession, he shall pay double.

4When a man lets his livestock loose to graze in another's land, and so

---

c Heb. "he."
f Others "as the judges determine."
g This constitutes chap. 22.1 in some editions.

a I.e, under a wall for housebreaking.
b I.e, the thief of 21.37.

allows a field or a vineyard to be grazed bare, he must make restitution for the impairment^c of that field or vineyard.

⁵When a fire is started and spreads to thorns, so that stacked, standing, or growing^d grain is consumed, he who started the fire must make restitution.

⁶When a man gives money or goods to another for safekeeping, and they are stolen from the man's house—if the thief is caught, he shall pay double; ⁷if the thief is not caught, the owner of the house shall depose before God^e that he has not laid hands on the other's property. ⁸In all charges of misappropriation—pertaining to an ox, an ass, a sheep, a garment, or any other loss, whereof one party alleges, "This is it"—the case of both parties shall come before God: he whom God declares guilty shall pay double to the other.

⁹When a man gives to another an ass, an ox, a sheep or any other animal to guard, and it dies or is injured or is carried off, with no witness about, ¹⁰an oath before the LORD shall decide between the two of them that the one has not laid hands on the property of the other; the owner must acquiesce, and no restitution shall be made. ¹¹But if [the animal] was stolen from him, he shall make restitution to its owner. ¹²If it was torn by beasts, he shall bring it as evidence; he need not replace what has been torn by beasts.

¹³When a man borrows [an animal] from another and it dies or is injured, its owner not being with it, he must make restitution. ¹⁴If its owner was with it, no restitution need be made; but if it was hired, he is entitled to the hire.

¹⁵If a man seduces a virgin for whom the bride-price has not been paid,^f and lies with her, he must make her his wife by payment of a bride-price. ¹⁶If her father refuses to give her to him, he must still weigh out silver in accordance with the bride-price for virgins.

¹⁷You shall not tolerate^g a sorceress.

¹⁸Whoever lies with a beast shall be put to death.

¹⁹Whoever sacrifices to a god other than the LORD alone shall be proscribed.^h

²⁰You shall not wrong a stranger or oppress him, for you were strangers in the land of Egypt.

²¹You shall not ill-treat any widow or orphan. ²²If you do mistreat them, I will heed their outcry as soon as they cry out to Me, ²³and My

---

^c Lit. "excellence."
^d Lit. "field."
^e See note on 21.6.
^f So that she is unmarried; cf. Deut. 20.7; 22.23 ff.
^g Lit. "let live."
^h See Lev. 27.29.

anger shall blaze forth and I will put you to the sword, and your own wives shall become widows and your children orphans.

24If you lend money to My people, to the poor among you, do not act toward them as a creditor; exact no interest from them. 25If you take your neighbor's garment in pledge, you must return it to him before the sun sets; 26it is his only clothing, the sole covering for his skin. In what else shall he sleep? Therefore, if he cries out to Me, I will pay heed, for I am compassionate.

27You shall not revile God, nor put a curse upon a chieftain among your people.

28You shall not i-put off the skimming of the first yield of your vats.-i You shall give Me the first-born among your sons. 29You shall do the same with your cattle and your flocks: seven days itj shall remain with its mother; on the eighth day you shall give it to Me.

30You shall be holy people to Me: you must not eat flesh torn by beasts in the field; you shall cast it to the dogs.

23 You must not carry false rumors; you shall not join hands with the guilty to act as a malicious witness: 2You shall neither side with the mightya to do wrong—you shall not give perverse testimony in a dispute so as to pervert it in favor of the mightya—3nor shall you show deference to a poor man in his dispute.

4When you encounter your enemy's ox or ass wandering, you must take it back to him.

5When you see the ass of your enemy lying under its burden and would refrain from raisingb it, you must nevertheless raise it with him.

6You shall not subvert the rights of your needy in their disputes. 7Keep far from a false charge; do not bring death on those who are innocent and in the right, for I will not acquit the wrongdoer. 8Do not take bribes, for bribes blind the clear-sighted and upset the pleas of those who are in the right.

9You shall not oppress a stranger, for you know the feelings of the stranger, having yourselves been strangers in the land of Egypt.

10Six years you shall sow your land and gather in its yield; 11but in the seventh you shall let it rest and lie fallow. Let the needy among your people eat of it, and what they leave let the wild beasts eat. You shall do the same with your vineyards and your olive groves.

---

i-i *Meaning of Heb. uncertain.*
i *I.e., the male first-born.*

a *Others "multitude."*
b *For this use of the verb 'zb, cf. Neh. 3.8, 34. For the whole verse see Deut. 22.4.*

¹²Six days you shall do your work, but on the seventh day you shall cease from labor, in order that your ox and your ass may rest, and that your bondman and the stranger may be refreshed.

¹³Be on guard concerning all that I have told you. Make no mention of the names of other gods; they shall not be heard on your lips.

¹⁴Three times a year you shall hold a festival for Me: ¹⁵You shall observe the Feast of Unleavened Bread—eating unleavened bread for seven days as I have commanded you—at the set time in the monthᶜ of Abib, for in it you went forth from Egypt; and none shall appear before Me empty-handed; ¹⁶and the Feast of the Harvest, of the first fruits of your work, of what you sow in the field; and the Feast of Ingathering at the end of the year, when you gather in the results of your work from the field. ¹⁷Three times a year all your males shall appear before the Sovereign, the LORD.

¹⁸You shall not offer the blood of My sacrifice with anything leavened; and the fat of My festal offering shall not be left lying until morning.

¹⁹The choice first fruits of your soil you shall bring to the house of the LORD your God.

You shall not boil a kid in its mother's milk.

²⁰I am sending an angel before you to guard you on the way and to bring you to the place that I have made ready. ²¹Pay heed to him and obey him. Do not defy him, for he will not pardon your offenses, since My Name is in him; ²²but if you obey him and do all that I say, I will be an enemy to your enemies and a foe to your foes.

²³When My angel goes before you and brings you to the Amorites, the Hittites, the Perizzites, the Canaanites, the Hivites, and the Jebusites, and I annihilate them, ²⁴you shall not bow down to their gods in worship or follow their practices, but shall tear them down and smash their pillars to bits. ²⁵You shall serve the LORD your God, and He will bless your bread and your water. And I will remove sickness from your midst. ²⁶No woman in your land shall miscarry or be barren. I will let you enjoy the full count of your days.

²⁷I will send forth My terror before you, and I will throw into panic all the people among whom you come, and I will make all your enemies turn tailᵈ before you. ²⁸I will send a plagueᵉ ahead of you, and it shall drive out before you the Hivites, the Canaanites, and the Hittites. ²⁹I will not drive them out before you in a single year, lest the land become desolate and the wild beasts multiply to your hurt. ³⁰I will drive them out

---

ᶜ *See note at 13.4.*
ᵈ *Lit. "back."*
ᵉ *Others "hornet"; meaning of Heb. uncertain.*

before you little by little, until you have increased and possess the land. ³¹I will set your borders from the Sea of Reeds to the Sea of Philistia, and from the wilderness to the Euphrates; for I will deliver the inhabitants of the land into your hands, and you will drive them out before you. ³²You shall make no covenant with them and their gods. ³³They shall not remain in your land, lest they cause you to sin against Me; for you will serve their gods—and it will prove a snare to you.

24 Then He said to Moses, "Come up to the LORD, with Aaron, Nadab and Abihu, and seventy elders of Israel, and bow low from afar. ²Moses alone shall come near the LORD; but the others shall not come near, nor shall the people come up with him."

³Moses went and repeated to the people all the commands of the LORD and all the rules; and all the people answered with one voice, saying, "All the things that the LORD has commanded we will do!" ⁴Moses then wrote down all the commands of the LORD.

Early in the morning, he set up an altar at the foot of the mountain, with twelve pillars for the twelve tribes of Israel. ⁵He designated some young men among the Israelites, and they offered burnt offerings and sacrificed bulls as offerings of well-being to the LORD. ⁶Moses took one part of the blood and put it in basins, and the other part of the blood he dashed against the altar. ⁷Then he took the record of the covenant and read it aloud to the people. And they said, "All that the LORD has spoken ᵃ⁻we will faithfully do!"⁻ᵃ ⁸Moses took the blood and dashed it on the people and said, "This is the blood of the covenant that the LORD now makes with you concerning all these commands."

⁹Then Moses and Aaron, Nadab and Abihu, and seventy elders of Israel ascended; ¹⁰and they saw the God of Israel: under His feet there was the likeness of a pavement of sapphire, like the very sky for purity. ¹¹Yet He did not raise His hand against the leadersᵇ of the Israelites; they beheld God, and they ate and drank.

¹²The LORD said to Moses, "Come up to Me on the mountain and wait there, and I will give you the stone tablets with the teachings and commandments which I have inscribed to instruct them." ¹³So Moses and his attendant Joshua arose, and Moses ascended the mountain of God.

ᵃ⁻ᵃ *Lit. "we will do and obey."*
ᵇ *Meaning of Heb. 'aṣilim uncertain.*

¹⁴To the elders he had said, "Wait here for us until we return to you. You have Aaron and Hur with you; let anyone who has a legal matter approach them."

¹⁵When Moses had ascended the mountain, the cloud covered the mountain. ¹⁶The Presence of the LORD abode on Mount Sinai, and the cloud hid it for six days. On the seventh day He called to Moses from the midst of the cloud. ¹⁷Now the Presence of the LORD appeared in the sight of the Israelites as a consuming fire on the top of the mountain. ¹⁸Moses went inside the cloud and ascended the mountain; and Moses remained on the mountain forty days and forty nights.

25 תרומה

The LORD spoke to Moses, saying: ²Tell the Israelite people to bring Me gifts; you shall accept gifts for Me from every person whose heart so moves him. ³And these are the gifts that you shall accept from them: gold, silver, and copper; ⁴blue, purple, and crimson yarns, fine linen, goats' hair; ⁵tanned ram skins,ᵃ dolphinᵇ skins, and acacia wood; ⁶oil for lighting, spices for the anointing oil and for the aromatic incense; ⁷lapis lazuliᶜ and other stones for setting, for the ephod and for the breastpiece. ⁸And let them make Me a sanctuary that I may dwell among them. ⁹Exactly as I show you—the pattern of the Tabernacle and the pattern of all its furnishings—so shall you make it.

¹⁰They shall make an ark of acacia wood, two and a half cubits long, a cubit and a half wide, and a cubit and a half high. ¹¹Overlay it with pure gold—overlay it inside and out—and make upon it a gold molding round about. ¹²Cast four gold rings for it, to be attached to its four feet, two rings on one of its side walls and two on the other. ¹³Make poles of acacia wood and overlay them with gold; ¹⁴then insert the poles into the rings on the side walls of the ark, for carrying the ark. ¹⁵The poles shall remain in the rings of the ark: they shall not be removed from it. ¹⁶And deposit in the Ark [the tablets of] the Pact which I will give you.

¹⁷You shall make a cover of pure gold, two and a half cubits long and a cubit and a half wide. ¹⁸Make two cherubim of gold—make them of hammered work—at the two ends of the cover. ¹⁹Make one cherub at one

---

ᵃ Others "rams' skins dyed red."
ᵇ Or "dugong"; meaning of Hebrew taḥash uncertain.
ᶜ Cf. Gen. 2.12 and note.

end and the other cherub at the other end; of one piece with the cover shall you make the cherubim at its two ends. ²⁰The cherubim shall have their wings spread out above, shielding the cover with their wings. They shall confront each other, the faces of the cherubim being turned toward the cover. ²¹Place the cover on top of the Ark, after depositing inside the Ark the Pact that I will give you. ²²There I will meet with you, and I will impart to you—from above the cover, from between the two cherubim that are on top of the Ark of the Pact—all that I will command you concerning the Israelite people.

²³You shall make a table of acacia wood, two cubits long, one cubit wide, and a cubit and a half high. ²⁴Overlay it with pure gold, and make a gold molding around it. ²⁵Make a rim of a hand's breadth around it, and make a gold molding for its rim round about. ²⁶Make four gold rings for it, and attach the rings to the four corners at its four legs. ²⁷The rings shall be next to the rim, as holders for poles to carry the table. ²⁸Make the poles of acacia wood, and overlay them with gold; by these the table shall be carried. ²⁹Make its bowls, ladles, jars and jugs with which to offer libations; make them of pure gold. ³⁰And on the table you shall set the bread of display, to be before Me always.

³¹You shall make a lampstand of pure gold; the lampstand shall be made of hammered work; its base and its shaft, its cups, calyxes, and petals shall be of one piece. ³²Six branches shall issue from its sides; three branches from one side of the lampstand and three branches from the other side of the lampstand. ³³On one branch there shall be three cups shaped like almond-blossoms, each with calyx and petals, and on the next branch there shall be three cups shaped like almond-blossoms, each with calyx and petals; so for all six branches issuing from the lampstand. ³⁴And on the lampstand itself there shall be four cups shaped like almond-blossoms, each with calyx and petals: ³⁵a calyx, of one piece with it, under a pair of branches; and a calyx, of one piece with it, under the second pair of branches, and a calyx, of one piece with it, under the last pair of branches; so for all six branches issuing from the lampstand. ³⁶Their calyxes and their stems shall be of one piece with it, the whole of it a single hammered piece of pure gold. ³⁷Make its seven lamps—the lamps shall be so mounted as to give the light on its front side—³⁸and its tongs and fire pans of pure gold. ³⁹It shall be made, with all these furnishings, out of a talent of pure gold. ⁴⁰Note well, and follow the patterns for them that are being shown you on the mountain.

26

As for the tabernacle,[a] make it of ten strips of cloth; make these of fine twisted linen, of blue, purple, and crimson yarns, with a design of cherubim worked into them. [2]The length of each cloth shall be twenty-eight cubits, and the width of each cloth shall be four cubits, all the cloths to have the same measurements. [3]Five of the cloths shall be joined to one another, and the other five cloths shall be joined to one another. [4]Make loops of blue wool on the edge of the outermost cloth of the one set; and do likewise on the edge of the outermost cloth of the other set: [5]make fifty loops on the one cloth, and fifty loops on the edge of the end cloth of the other set, the loops to be opposite one another. [6]And make fifty gold clasps, and couple the cloths to one another with the clasps, so that the tabernacle becomes one whole.

[7]You shall then make cloths of goats' hair for a tent over the tabernacle; make the cloths eleven in number. [8]The length of each cloth shall be thirty cubits, and the width of each cloth shall be four cubits, the eleven cloths to have the same measurements. [9]Join five of the cloths by themselves, and the other six cloths by themselves; and fold over the sixth cloth at the front of the tent. [10]Make fifty loops on the edge of the outermost cloth of the one set, and fifty loops on the edge of the cloth of the other set. [11]Make fifty copper clasps, and fit the clasps into the loops, and couple the tent together so that it becomes one whole. [12]As for the overlapping excess of the cloths of the tent, the extra half-cloth shall overlap the back of the tabernacle, [13]while the extra cubit at either end of each length of tent cloth shall hang down to the bottom of the two sides of the Tabernacle and cover it. [14]And make for the tent a covering of tanned ram skins, and a covering of dolphin skins above.

[15]You shall make the planks for the Tabernacle of acacia wood, upright. [16]The length of each plank shall be ten cubits and the width of each plank a cubit and a half. [17]Each plank shall have two tenons, parallel[b] to each other; do the same with all the planks of the Tabernacle. [18]Of the planks of the Tabernacle, make twenty planks on the south[c] side: [19]making forty silver sockets under the twenty planks, two sockets under the one plank for its two tenons and two sockets under each following plank for its two tenons; [20]and for the other side wall of the Tabernacle, on the north side, twenty planks, [21]with their forty silver sockets, two sockets under the one plank and two sockets under each following plank. [22]And for the rear of the Tabernacle, to the west, make six planks; [23]and make two planks for

---

[a] *Here the lowest of the covers of the Tabernacle.*
[b] *Meaning of Heb.* meshullaboth *uncertain.*
[c] *Heb. uses two terms for "south."*

the corners of the Tabernacle at the rear. 24 d-They shall match at the bottom, and terminate alike at the top inside one ring;-d thus shall it be with both of them: they shall form the two corners. 25Thus there shall be eight planks with their sockets of silver: sixteen sockets, two sockets under the first plank, and two sockets under each of the other planks.

26You shall make bars of acacia wood: five for the planks of the one side wall of the Tabernacle, 27five bars for the planks of the other side wall of the Tabernacle, and five bars for the planks of the wall of the Tabernacle at the rear to the west. 28The center bar halfway up the planks shall run from end to end. 29Overlay the planks with gold, and make their rings of gold, as holders for the bars; and overlay the bars with gold. 30Then set up the Tabernacle according to the manner of it that you were shown on the mountain.

31You shall make a curtain of blue, purple, and crimson yarns, and fine twisted linen; it shall have a design of cherubim worked into it. 32Hang it upon four posts of acacia wood overlaid with gold and having hooks of gold, [set] in four sockets of silver. 33Hang the curtain under the clasps, and carry the Ark of the Pact there, behind the curtain, so that the curtain shall serve you as a partition between the Holy and the Holy of Holies. 34Place the cover upon the Ark of the Pact in the Holy of Holies. 35Place the table outside the curtain, and the lampstand by the south wall of the Tabernacle opposite the table, which is to be placed by the north wall.

36You shall make a screen for the entrance of the Tent, of blue, purple, and crimson yarns, and fine twisted linen, done in embroidery. 37Make five posts of acacia wood for the screen and overlay them with gold—their hooks being of gold—and cast for them five sockets of copper.

27 You shall make the altar of acacia wood, five cubits long and five cubits wide—the altar is to be square—and three cubits high. 2Make its horns on the four corners, the horns to be of one piece with it; and overlay it with copper. 3Make the pails for removing its ashes, as well as its scrapers, basins, flesh hooks, and fire pans—make all its utensils of copper. 4Make for it a grating of meshwork in copper; and on the mesh make four copper rings at its four corners. 5Set the mesh below, under the ledge

d-d Meaning of Heb. uncertain.

of the altar, so that it extends to the middle of the altar. ⁶And make poles for the altar, poles of acacia wood, and overlay them with copper. ⁷The poles shall be inserted into the rings, so that the poles remain on the two sides of the altar when it is carried. ⁸Make it hollow, of boards. As you were shown on the mountain, so shall they be made.

⁹You shall make the enclosure of the Tabernacle:

On the south side,^a a hundred cubits of hangings of fine twisted linen for the length of the enclosure on that side—¹⁰with its twenty posts and their twenty sockets of copper, the hooks and bands of the posts to be of silver.

¹¹Again a hundred cubits of hangings for its length along the north side—with its twenty posts and their twenty sockets of copper, the hooks and bands of the posts to be of silver.

¹²For the width of the enclosure, on the west side, fifty cubits of hangings, with their ten posts and their ten sockets.

¹³For the width of the enclosure on the front, or east side, fifty cubits: ¹⁴fifteen cubits of hangings on the one flank, with their three posts and their three sockets; ¹⁵fifteen cubits of hangings on the other flank, with their three posts and their three sockets; ¹⁶and for the gate of the enclosure, a screen of twenty cubits, of blue, purple, and crimson yarns, and fine twisted linen, done in embroidery, with their four posts and their four sockets.

¹⁷All the posts round the enclosure shall be banded with silver and their hooks shall be of silver; their sockets shall be of copper.

¹⁸The length of the enclosure shall be a hundred cubits, and the width fifty throughout; and the height five cubits—[with hangings] of fine twisted linen. The sockets shall be of copper: ¹⁹all the utensils of the Tabernacle,^b for all its service, as well as all its pegs and all the pegs of the court, shall be of copper.

תצוה

²⁰You shall further instruct the Israelites to bring you clear oil of beaten olives for lighting, for kindling lamps regularly. ²¹Aaron and his sons shall set them up in the Tent of Meeting, outside the curtain which is over [the Ark of] the Pact, [to burn] from evening to morning before the LORD. It shall be a due from the Israelites for all time, throughout the ages.

^a *Cf. note at 26.18.*
^b *I.e., of the Tabernacle enclosure; the furnishings inside were of gold.*

28

You shall bring forward your brother Aaron, with his sons, from among the Israelites, to serve Me as priests: Aaron, Nadab and Abihu, Eleazar and Ithamar, the sons of Aaron. 2Make sacral vestments for your brother Aaron, for dignity and adornment. 3Next you shall instruct all who are a-skillful, whom I have endowed with the gift of skill,-a to make Aaron's vestments, for consecrating him to serve Me as priest. 4These are the vestments they are to make: a breastpiece, an ephod, a robe, a fringedb tunic, a headdress, and a sash. They shall make those sacral vestments for your brother Aaron and his sons, for priestly service to Me; 5they, therefore, shall receive the gold, the blue, purple, and crimson yarns, and the fine linen.

6They shall make the ephod of gold, of blue, purple, and crimson yarns, and of fine twisted linen, worked into designs. 7It shall have two shoulder-pieces attached; they shall be attached at its two ends. 8And the decorated band that is upon it shall be made like it, of one piece with it: of gold, of blue, purple, and crimson yarns, and of fine twisted linen. 9Then take two lazuli stones and engrave on them the names of the sons of Israel: 10six of their names on the one stone, and the names of the remaining six on the other stone, in the order of their birth. 11On the two stones you shall make seal engravings—the work of a lapidary—of the names of the sons of Israel. Having bordered them with frames of gold, 12attach the two stones to the shoulder-pieces of the ephod, as stones for remembrance of the Israelite people, whose names Aaron shall carry upon his two shoulder-pieces for remembrance before the LORD.

13Then make frames of gold 14and two chains of pure gold; braid these like corded work, and fasten the corded chains to the frames.

15You shall make a breastpiece of decision,c worked into a design; make it in the style of the ephod: make it of gold, of blue, purple, and crimson yarns, and of fine twisted linen. 16It shall be square and doubled, a span in length and a span in width. 17Set in it mounted stones, in four rows of stones. The first row shall be a row of dcarnelian, chrysolite, and emerald; 18the second row: a turquoise, a sapphire, and an amethyst; 19the third row: a jacinth, an agate, and a crystal; 20and the fourth row: a beryl, a lapis lazuli, and a jasper. They shall be framed with gold in their mountings. 21The stones shall correspond [in number] to the names of the sons of Israel: twelve, corresponding to their names. They shall be engraved like seals, each with its name, for the twelve tribes.

a-a Lit. "wise of heart, whom I have filled with a spirit of wisdom."
b Others "checkered."
c See v. 30 below; others "judgment."
d The identity of several of these twelve stones is uncertain.

²²On the breastpiece make braided chains of corded work in pure gold. ²³Make two rings of gold on the breastpiece, and fasten the two rings at the two ends of the breastpiece, ²⁴attaching the two golden cords to the two rings at the ends of the breastpiece. ²⁵Then fasten the two ends of the cords to the two frames, which you shall attach to the shoulder-pieces of the ephod, at the front. ²⁶Make two rings of gold and attach them to the two ends of the breastpiece, at its inner edge, which faces the ephod. ²⁷And make two other rings of gold and fasten them on the front of the ephod, low on the two shoulder-pieces, close to its seam above the decorated band. ²⁸The breastpiece shall be held in place by a cord of blue from its rings to the rings of the ephod, so that the breastpiece rests on the decorated band and does not come loose from the ephod. ²⁹Aaron shall carry the names of the sons of Israel on the breastpiece of decision over his heart, when he enters the sanctuary, for remembrance before the LORD at all times. ³⁰Inside the breastpiece of decision you shall place the Urim and Thummim,ᵉ so that they are over Aaron's heart when he comes before the LORD. Thus Aaron shall carry the instrument of decision for the Israelites over his heart before the LORD at all times.

³¹You shall make the robe of the ephod of pure blue.ᶠ ³²The opening for the head shall be in the middle of it; the opening shall have a binding of woven work round about—it shall be like the opening of a coat of mail—so that it does not tear. ³³On its hem make pomegranates of blue, purple, and crimson yarns, all around the hem, with bells of gold between them all around: ³⁴a golden bell and a pomegranate, a golden bell and a pomegranate, all around the hem of the robe. ³⁵Aaron shall wear it while officiating, so that the sound of it is heard when he comes into the sanctuary before the LORD and when he goes out—that he may not die.

³⁶You shall make a frontlet of pure gold and engrave on it the seal inscription: "Holy to the LORD." ³⁷Suspend it on a cord of blue, so that it may remain on the headdress; it shall remain on the front of the headdress. ³⁸It shall be on Aaron's forehead, that Aaron may take away any sin arising from the holy things that the Israelites consecrate, from any of their sacred donations; it shall be on his forehead at all times, to win acceptance for them before the LORD.

³⁹You shall make the fringed tunic of fine linen.

You shall make the headdress of fine linen.

You shall make the sash of embroidered work.

⁴⁰And for Aaron's sons also you shall make tunics, and make sashes for

---

ᵉ *Meaning of these two words uncertain. They designate a kind of oracle; cf. Num. 27.21.*
ᶠ *Others "all of blue."*

them, and make turbans for them, for dignity and adornment. [41]Put these on your brother Aaron and on his sons as well; anoint them, and ordain them[g] and consecrate them to serve Me as priests.

[42]You shall also make for them linen breeches to cover their nakedness; they shall extend from the hips to the thighs. [43]They shall be worn by Aaron and his sons when they enter the Tent of Meeting or when they approach the altar to officiate in the sanctuary, so that they do not incur punishment and die. It shall be a law for all time for him and for his offspring to come.

29 This is what you shall do to them in consecrating them to serve Me as priests: Take a young bull of the herd and two rams without blemish; [2]also unleavened bread, unleavened cakes with oil mixed in, and unleavened wafers spread with oil—make these of choice wheat flour. [3]Place these in one basket and present them in the basket, along with the bull and the two rams. [4]Lead Aaron and his sons up to the entrance of the Tent of Meeting, and wash them with water. [5]Then take the vestments, and clothe Aaron with the tunic, the robe of the ephod, the ephod, and the breastpiece, and gird him with the decorated band of the ephod. [6]Put the headdress on his head, and place the holy diadem upon the headdress. [7]Take the anointing oil and pour it on his head and anoint him. [8]Then bring his sons forward; clothe them with tunics [9]and wind turbans upon them. And gird both Aaron and his sons with sashes. And so they shall have priesthood as their right for all time.

You shall then ordain Aaron and his sons. [10]Lead the bull up to the front of the Tent of Meeting, and let Aaron and his sons lay their hands upon the head of the bull. [11]Slaughter the bull before the LORD, at the entrance of the Tent of Meeting, [12]and take some of the bull's blood and put it on the horns of the altar with your finger; then pour out the rest of the blood at the base of the altar. [13]Take all the fat that covers the entrails, the protuberance on the liver, and the two kidneys with the fat on them, and turn them into smoke upon the altar. [14]The rest of the flesh of the bull, its hide, and its dung shall be put to the fire outside the camp; it is a sin offering.

[15]Next take the one ram, and let Aaron and his sons lay their hands upon the ram's head. [16]Slaughter the ram, and take its blood and dash it against all sides of the altar. [17]Cut up the ram into sections, wash its

g Lit. "and fill their hands."

entrails and legs, and put them with its quarters and its head. [18]Turn all of the ram into smoke upon the altar. It is a burnt offering to the LORD, a pleasing odor, an offering by fire to the LORD.

[19]Then take the other ram, and let Aaron and his sons lay their hands upon the ram's head. [20]Slaughter the ram, and take some of its blood and put it on the ridge[a] of Aaron's right ear and on the ridges of his sons' right ears, and on the thumbs of their right hands, and on the big toes of their right feet; and dash the rest of the blood against every side of the altar round about. [21]Take some of the blood that is on the altar and some of the anointing oil and sprinkle upon Aaron and his vestments, and also upon his sons and his sons' vestments. Thus shall he and his vestments be holy, as well as his sons and his sons' vestments.

[22]You shall take from the ram the fat parts—the broad tail, the fat that covers the entrails, the protuberance on the liver, the two kidneys with the fat on them—and the right thigh; for this is a ram of ordination. [23]Add one flat loaf of bread, one cake of oil bread, and one wafer, from the basket of unleavened bread that is before the LORD. [24]Place all these on the palms of Aaron and his sons, and offer them as an elevation offering before the LORD. [25]Take them from their hands and turn them into smoke upon the altar with the burnt offering, as a pleasing odor before the LORD; it is an offering by fire to the LORD.

[26]Then take the breast of Aaron's ram of ordination and offer it as an elevation offering before the LORD; it shall be your portion. [27]You shall consecrate the breast that was offered as an elevation offering and the thigh that was offered as a gift offering from the ram of ordination—from that which was Aaron's and from that which was his sons'—[28]and those parts shall be a due for all time from the Israelites to Aaron and his descendants. For they are a gift; and so shall they be a gift from the Israelites, their gift to the LORD out of their sacrifices of well-being.

[29]The sacral vestments of Aaron shall pass on to his sons after him, for them to be anointed and ordained in. [30]He among his sons who becomes priest in his stead, who enters the Tent of Meeting to officiate within the sanctuary, shall wear them seven days.

[31]You shall take the ram of ordination and boil its flesh in the sacred precinct; [32]and Aaron and his sons shall eat the flesh of the ram, and the bread that is in the basket, at the entrance of the Tent of Meeting. [33]These things shall be eaten only by those for whom expiation was made with them when they were ordained and consecrated; they may not be eaten

---

[a] Or "lobe."

by a layman, for they are holy. ³⁴And if any of the flesh of ordination, or any of the bread, is left until morning, you shall put what is left to the fire; it shall not be eaten, for it is holy.

³⁵Thus you shall do to Aaron and his sons, just as I have commanded you. You shall ordain them through seven days, ³⁶and each day you shall prepare a bull as a sin offering for expiation; you shall purge the altar by performing purification upon it, and you shall anoint it to consecrate it. ³⁷Seven days you shall perform purification for the altar to consecrate it, and the altar shall become most holy; whatever touches the altar shall become consecrated.

³⁸Now this is what you shall offer upon the altar: two yearling lambs each day, regularly. ³⁹You shall offer the one lamb in the morning, and you shall offer the other lamb at twilight. ⁴⁰There shall be a tenth of a measure of choice flour with a quarter of a *hin* of beaten oil mixed in, and a libation of a quarter *hin* of wine for one lamb; ⁴¹and you shall offer the other lamb at twilight, repeating with it the meal offering of the morning with its libation—an offering by fire for a pleasing odor to the LORD, ⁴²a regular burnt offering throughout the generations, at the entrance of the Tent of Meeting before the LORD.

For there I will meet with you, and there I will speak with you, ⁴³and there I will meet with the Israelites, and it shall be sanctified by My Presence. ⁴⁴I will sanctify the Tent of Meeting and the altar, and I will consecrate Aaron and his sons to serve Me as priests. ⁴⁵I will abide among the Israelites, and I will be their God. ⁴⁶And they shall know that I the LORD am their God, who brought them out from the land of Egypt that I might abide among them, I the LORD their God.

30 You shall make an altar for burning incense; make it of acacia wood. ²It shall be a cubit long and a cubit wide—it shall be square—and two cubits high, its horns of one piece with it. ³Overlay it with pure gold: its top, its sides round about, and its horns; and make a gold molding for it round about. ⁴And make two gold rings for it under its molding; make them on its two side walls, on oppositeᵃ sides. They shall serve as holders for poles with which to carry it. ⁵Make the poles of acacia wood, and overlay them with gold.

⁶Place it in front of the curtain that is over the Ark of the Pact—in front of the cover that is over the Pact—where I will meet with you. ⁷On it Aaron shall burn aromatic incense: he shall burn it every morning when

ᵃ *Lit. "its two."*

he tends the lamps, [8]and Aaron shall burn it at twilight when he lights the lamps—a regular incense offering before the LORD throughout the ages. [9]You shall not offer alien incense on it, or a burnt offering or a meal offering; neither shall you pour a libation on it. [10]Once a year Aaron shall perform purification upon its horns with blood of the sin offering of purification; purification shall be performed upon it once a year throughout the ages. It is most holy to the LORD.

כי תשא

[11]The LORD spoke to Moses, saying: [12]When you take a census of the Israelite people according to their enrollment, each shall pay the LORD a ransom for himself on being enrolled, that no plague may come upon them through their being enrolled. [13]This is what everyone who is entered in the records shall pay: a half-shekel by the sanctuary weight—twenty *gerah*s to the shekel—a half-shekel as an offering to the LORD. [14]Everyone who is entered in the records, from the age of twenty years up, shall give the LORD's offering: [15]the rich shall not pay more and the poor shall not pay less than half a shekel when giving the LORD's offering as expiation for your persons. [16]You shall take the expiation money from the Israelites and assign it to the service of the Tent of Meeting; it shall serve the Israelites as a reminder before the LORD, as expiation for your persons.

[17]The LORD spoke to Moses, saying: [18]Make a laver of copper and a stand of copper for it, for washing; and place it between the Tent of Meeting and the altar. Put water in it, [19]and let Aaron and his sons wash their hands and feet [in water drawn] from it. [20]When they enter the Tent of Meeting they shall wash with water, that they may not die; or when they approach the altar to serve, to turn into smoke an offering by fire to the LORD, [21]they shall wash their hands and feet, that they may not die. It shall be a law for all time for them—for him and his offspring—throughout the ages.

[22]The LORD spoke to Moses, saying: [23]Next take choice spices: five hundred weight of solidified[b] myrrh, half as much—two hundred and fifty—of fragrant cinnamon, two hundred and fifty of aromatic cane, [24]five hundred—by the sanctuary weight—of cassia, and a *hin* of olive oil. [25]Make of this a sacred anointing oil, a compound of ingredients expertly blended, to serve as sacred anointing oil. [26]With it anoint the Tent of Meeting, the

---

b *Others "flowing."*

Ark of the Pact, 27the table and all its utensils, the lampstand and all its fittings, the altar of incense, 28the altar of burnt offering and all its utensils, and the laver and its stand. 29Thus you shall consecrate them so that they may be most holy; whatever touches them shall be consecrated. 30You shall also anoint Aaron and his sons, consecrating them to serve Me as priests.

31And speak to the Israelite people, as follows: This shall be an anointing oil sacred to Me throughout the ages. 32It must not be rubbed on any person's body, and you must not make anything like it in the same proportions; it is sacred, to be held sacred by you. 33Whoever compounds its like, or puts any of it on a layman, shall be cut off from his kin.

34And the LORD said to Moses: Take the herbs stacte, onycha, and galbanum—these herbs together with pure frankincense; let there be an equal part of each. 35Make them into incense, a compound expertly blended, refined, pure, sacred. 36Beat some of it into powder, and put some before the Pact in the Tent of Meeting, where I will meet with you; it shall be most holy to you. 37But when you make this incense, you must not make any in the same proportions for yourselves; it shall be held by you sacred to the LORD. Whoever makes any like it, to smell of it, shall be cut off from his kin.

31

The LORD spoke to Moses: 2See, I have singled out by name Bezalel son of Uri son of Hur, of the tribe of Judah. 3I have endowed him with a divine spirit of skill, ability, and knowledge in every kind of craft; 4to make designs for work in gold, silver, and copper, 5to cut stones for setting and to carve wood—to work in every kind of craft. 6Moreover, I have assigned to him Oholiab son of Ahisamach, of the tribe of Dan; and I have also granted skill to all who are skillful, that they may make everything that I have commanded you: 7the Tent of Meeting, the Ark for the Pact and the cover upon it, and all the furnishings of the Tent; 8the table and its utensils, the pure lampstanda and all its fittings, and the altar of incense; 9the altar of burnt offering and all its utensils, and the laver and its stand; 10the serviceb vestments, the sacral vestments of Aaron the priest and the vestments of his sons, for their service as priests; 11as well as the anointing oil and the aromatic incense for the sanctuary. Just as I have commanded you, they shall do.

12And the LORD said to Moses: 13Speak to the Israelite people and say:

a Or "lampstand of pure gold."
b Others "plaited."

Nevertheless, you must keep My sabbaths, for this is a sign between Me and you throughout the ages, that you may know that I the LORD have consecrated you. [14]You shall keep the sabbath, for it is holy for you. He who profanes it shall be put to death: whoever does work on it, that person shall be cut off from among his kin. [15]Six days may work be done, but on the seventh day there shall be a sabbath of complete rest, holy to the LORD; whoever does work on the sabbath day shall be put to death. [16]The Israelite people shall keep the sabbath, observing the sabbath throughout the ages as a covenant for all time: [17]it shall be a sign for all time between Me and the people of Israel. For in six days the LORD made heaven and earth, and on the seventh day He ceased from work and was refreshed.

[18]When He finished speaking with him on Mount Sinai, He gave Moses the two tablets of the Pact, stone tablets inscribed with the finger of God.

32 When the people saw that Moses was so long in coming down from the mountain, the people gathered against Aaron and said to him, "Come, make us a god who shall go before us, for that man Moses, who brought us from the land of Egypt—we do not know what has happened to him." [2]Aaron said to them, "Take off the gold rings that are on the ears of your wives, your sons, and your daughters, and bring them to me." [3]And all the people took off the gold rings that were in their ears and brought them to Aaron. [4]This he took from them and [a-]cast in a mold,[-a] and made it into a molten calf. And they exclaimed, [b-]"This is your god,[-b] O Israel, who brought you out of the land of Egypt!" [5]When Aaron saw this, he built an altar before it; and Aaron announced: "Tomorrow shall be a festival of the LORD!" [6]Early next day, the people offered up burnt offerings and brought sacrifices of well-being; they sat down to eat and drink, and then rose to dance.

[7]The LORD spoke to Moses, "Hurry down, for your people, whom you brought out of the land of Egypt, have acted basely. [8]They have been quick to turn aside from the way that I enjoined upon them. They have made themselves a molten calf and bowed low to it and sacrificed to it, saying: 'This is your god, O Israel, who brought you out of the land of Egypt!'"

[9]The LORD further said to Moses, "I see that this is a stiffnecked people.

a-a Cf. Zech. 11.13 (beth hayyoṣer, *"foundry"*); others *"fashioned it with a graving tool."*
b-b Others *"These are your gods."*

¹⁰Now, let Me be, that My anger may blaze forth against them and that I may destroy them, and make of you a great nation." ¹¹But Moses implored the LORD his God, saying, "Let not Your anger, O Lord, blaze forth against Your people, whom You delivered from the land of Egypt with great power and with a mighty hand. ¹²Let not the Egyptians say, 'It was with evil intent that He delivered them, only to kill them off in the mountains and annihilate them from the face of the earth.' Turn from Your blazing anger, and renounce the plan to punish Your people. ¹³Remember Your servants, Abraham, Isaac, and Israel, how You swore to them by Your Self and said to them: I will make your offspring as numerous as the stars of heaven, and I will give to your offspring this whole land of which I spoke, to possess forever." ¹⁴And the LORD renounced the punishment He had planned to bring upon His people.

¹⁵Thereupon Moses turned and went down from the mountain bearing the two tablets of the Pact, tablets inscribed on both their surfaces: they were inscribed on the one side and on the other. ¹⁶The tablets were God's work, and the writing was God's writing, incised upon the tablets. ¹⁷When Joshua heard the sound of the people in its boisterousness, he said to Moses, "There is a cry of war in the camp." ¹⁸But he answered,

"It is not the sound of the tune of triumph,
Or the sound of the tune of defeat;
It is the sound of song that I hear!"

¹⁹As soon as Moses came near the camp and saw the calf and the dancing, he became enraged; and he hurled the tablets from his hands and shattered them at the foot of the mountain. ²⁰He took the calf that they had made and burned it; he ground it to powder and strewed it upon the water and so made the Israelites drink it.

²¹Moses said to Aaron, "What did this people do to you that you have brought such great sin upon them?" ²²Aaron said, "Let not my lord be enraged. You know that this people is bent on evil. ²³They said to me, 'Make us a god to lead us; for that man Moses, who brought us from the land of Egypt—we do not know what has happened to him.' ²⁴So I said to them, 'Whoever has gold, take it off!' They gave it to me and I hurled it into the fire and out came this calf!"

²⁵Moses saw that the people were out of control—since Aaron had let them get out of control—so that they were a menaceᶜ to any who might oppose them. ²⁶Moses stood up in the gate of the camp and said, "Whoever is for the LORD, come here!" And all the Levites rallied to him. ²⁷He said

ᶜ Others "an object of derision."

to them, "Thus says the LORD, the God of Israel: Each of you put sword on thigh, go back and forth from gate to gate throughout the camp, and slay brother, neighbor, and kin." 28The Levites did as Moses had bidden; and some three thousand of the people fell that day. 29And Moses said, "Dedicate yourselvesd to the LORD this day—for each of you has been against son and brother—that He may bestow a blessing upon you today."

30The next day Moses said to the people, "You have been guilty of a great sin. Yet I will now go up to the LORD; perhaps I may win forgiveness for your sin." 31Moses went back to the LORD and said, "Alas, this people is guilty of a great sin in making for themselves a god of gold. 32Now, if You will forgive their sin [well and good]; but if not, erase me from the record which You have written!" 33But the LORD said to Moses, "He who has sinned against Me, him only will I erase from My record. 34Go now, lead the people where I told you. See, My angel shall go before you. But when I make an accounting, I will bring them to account for their sins."

35Then the LORD sent a plague upon the people, e-for what they did with the calf that Aaron made.-e

33 Then the LORD said to Moses, "Set out from here, you and the people that you have brought up from the land of Egypt, to the land of which I swore to Abraham, Isaac, and Jacob, saying, 'To your offspring will I give it'—2I will send an angel before you, and I will drive out the Canaanites, the Amorites, the Hittites, the Perizzites, the Hivites, and the Jebusites—3a land flowing with milk and honey. But I will not go in your midst, since you are a stiffnecked people, lest I destroy you on the way."

4When the people heard this harsh word, they went into mourning, and none put on his finery.

5The LORD said to Moses, "Say to the Israelite people, 'You are a stiffnecked people. If I were to go in your midst for one moment, I would destroy you. Now, then, leave off your finery, and I will consider what to do to you.'" 6So the Israelites remained stripped of the finery from Mount Horeb on.

7Now Moses would take the Tent and pitch it outside the camp, at some distance from the camp. It was called the Tent of Meeting, and whoever sought the LORD would go out to the Tent of Meeting that was

---

d Lit. "fill your hands."
e-e Meaning of Heb. uncertain.

outside the camp. [8]Whenever Moses went out to the Tent, all the people would rise and stand, each at the entrance of his tent, and gaze after Moses until he had entered the Tent. [9]And when Moses entered the Tent, the pillar of cloud would descend and stand at the entrance of the Tent, while He spoke with Moses. [10]When all the people saw the pillar of cloud poised at the entrance of the Tent, all the people would rise and bow low, each at the entrance of his tent. [11]The LORD would speak to Moses face to face, as one man speaks to another. And he would then return to the camp; but his attendant, Joshua son of Nun, a youth, would not stir out of the Tent.

[12]Moses said to the LORD, "See, You say to me, 'Lead this people forward,' but You have not made known to me whom You will send with me. Further, You have said, 'I have singled you out by name, and you have, indeed, gained My favor.' [13]Now, if I have truly gained Your favor, pray let me know Your ways, that I may know You and continue in Your favor. Consider, too, that this nation is Your people." [14]And He said, [a-]"I will go in the lead and will[-a] lighten your burden." [15]And he said to Him, "Unless You go in the lead, do not make us leave this place. [16]For how shall it be known that Your people have gained Your favor unless You go with us, so that we may be distinguished, Your people and I, from every people on the face of the earth?"

[17]And the LORD said to Moses, "I will also do this thing that you have asked; for you have truly gained My favor and I have singled you out by name." [18]He said, "Oh, let me behold Your Presence!" [19]And He answered, "I will make all My goodness pass before you, and I will proclaim before you the name LORD, [b-]and the grace that I grant and the compassion that I show.[-b] [20]But," He said, "you cannot see My face, for man may not see Me and live." [21]And the LORD said, "See, there is a place near Me. Station yourself on the rock [22]and, as My Presence passes by, I will put you in a cleft of the rock and shield you with My hand until I have passed by. [23]Then I will take My hand away and you will see My back; but My face must not be seen."

34
The LORD said to Moses: "Carve two tablets of stone like the first, and I will inscribe upon the tablets the words that were on the first tablets, which you shattered. [2]Be ready by morning, and in the morning

---

[a-a] Lit. "My face will go and I will."
[b-b] Lit. "and I will grant the grace that I will grant and show the compassion that I will show."

come up to Mount Sinai and present yourself there to Me, on the top of the mountain. ³No one else shall come up with you, and no one else shall be seen anywhere on the mountain; neither shall the flocks and the herds graze at the foot of this mountain."

⁴So Moses carved two tablets of stone, like the first, and early in the morning he went up on Mount Sinai, as the LORD had commanded him, taking the two stone tablets with him. ⁵The LORD came down in a cloud; He stood with him there, and proclaimed the name LORD. ⁶The LORD passed before him ªˉand proclaimed: "The LORD! the LORD!ˉª a God compassionate and gracious, slow to anger, abounding in kindness and faithfulness, ⁷extending kindness to the thousandth generation, forgiving iniquity, transgression, and sin; yet He does not remit all punishment, but visits the iniquity of parents upon children and children's children, upon the third and fourth generations."

⁸Moses hastened to bow low to the ground in homage, ⁹and said, "If I have gained Your favor, O Lord, pray, let the Lord go in our midst, even though this is a stiffnecked people. Pardon our iniquity and our sin, and take us for Your own!"

¹⁰He said: I hereby make a covenant. Before all your people I will work such wonders as have not been wrought on all the earth or in any nation; and all the people ᵇˉwho are with youˉᵇ shall see how awesome are the LORD's deeds which I will perform for you. ¹¹Mark well what I command you this day. I will drive out before you the Amorites, the Canaanites, the Hittites, the Perizzites, the Hivites, and the Jebusites. ¹²Beware of making a covenant with the inhabitants of the land against which you are advancing, lest they be a snare in your midst. ¹³No, you must tear down their altars, smash their pillars, and cut down their sacred posts; ¹⁴for you must not worship any other god, because the LORD, whose name is Impassioned, is an impassioned God. ¹⁵You must not make a covenant with the inhabitants of the land, for they will lust after their gods and sacrifice to their gods and invite you, and you will eat of their sacrifices. ¹⁶And when you take wives from among their daughters for your sons, their daughters will lust after their gods and will cause your sons to lust after their gods.

¹⁷You shall not make molten gods for yourselves.

¹⁸You shall observe the Feast of Unleavened Bread—eating unleavened bread for seven days, as I have commanded you—at the set time of the monthᶜ of Abib, for in the month of Abib you went forth from Egypt.

ᵃˉᵃ Or "and the Lord proclaimed: The LORD! a God compassionate," etc.; cf. Num. 14.17–18.
ᵇˉᵇ Lit. "in whose midst you are."
ᶜ See note at 13.4.

¹⁹Every first issue of the womb is Mine, from all your livestock that drop a male^d as firstling, whether cattle or sheep. ²⁰But the firstling of an ass you shall redeem with a sheep; if you do not redeem it, you must break its neck. And you must redeem every first-born among your sons.

None shall appear before Me empty-handed.

²¹Six days you shall work, but on the seventh day you shall cease from labor; you shall cease from labor even at plowing time and harvest time.

²²You shall observe the Feast of Weeks, of the first fruits of the wheat harvest; and the Feast of Ingathering at the turn of the year. ²³Three times a year all your males shall appear before the Sovereign LORD, the God of Israel. ²⁴I will drive out nations from your path and enlarge your territory; no one will covet your land when you go up to appear before the LORD your God three times a year.

²⁵You shall not offer the blood of My sacrifice with anything leavened; and the sacrifice of the Feast of Passover shall not be left lying until morning.

²⁶The choice first fruits of your soil you shall bring to the house of the LORD your God.

You shall not boil a kid in its mother's milk.

²⁷And the LORD said to Moses: Write down these commandments, for in accordance with these commandments I make a covenant with you and with Israel.

²⁸And he was there with the LORD forty days and forty nights; he ate no bread and drank no water; and he wrote down on the tablets the terms of the covenant, the Ten Commandments.

²⁹So Moses came down from Mount Sinai. And as Moses came down from the mountain bearing the two tablets of the Pact, Moses was not aware that the skin of his face was radiant, since he had spoken with Him. ³⁰Aaron and all the Israelites saw that the skin of Moses' face was radiant; and they shrank from coming near him. ³¹But Moses called to them, and Aaron and all the chieftains in the assembly returned to him, and Moses spoke to them. ³²Afterward all the Israelites came near, and he instructed them concerning all that the LORD had imparted to him on Mount Sinai. ³³And when Moses had finished speaking with them, he put a veil over his face.

³⁴Whenever Moses went in before the LORD to speak with Him, he would leave the veil off until he came out; and when he came out and

^d *Heb.* tizzakhar, *form uncertain.*

told the Israelites what he had been commanded, 35the Israelites would see how radiant the skin of Moses' face was. Moses would then put the veil back over his face until he went in to speak with Him.

35 ויקהל

Moses then convoked the whole Israelite community and said to them:

These are the things that the LORD has commanded you to do: 2On six days work may be done, but on the seventh day you shall have a sabbath of complete rest, holy to the LORD; whoever does any work on it shall be put to death. 3You shall kindle no fire throughout your settlements on the sabbath day.

4Moses said further to the whole community of Israelites:

This is what the LORD has commanded: 5Take from among you gifts to the LORD; everyone whose heart so moves him shall bring them—gifts for the LORD: gold, silver, and copper; 6ablue, purple, and crimson yarns, fine linen, and goats' hair; 7tanned ram skins, dolphin skins, and acacia wood; 8oil for lighting, spices for the anointing oil and for the aromatic incense; 9lapis lazuli and other stones for setting, for the ephod and the breastpiece.

10And let all among you who are skilled come and make all that the LORD has commanded: 11the Tabernacle, its tent and its covering, its clasps and its planks, its bars, its posts, and its sockets; 12the ark and its poles, the cover, and the curtain for the screen; 13the table, and its poles and all its utensils; and the bread of display; 14the lampstand for lighting, its furnishings and its lamps, and the oil for lighting; 15the altar of incense and its poles; the anointing oil and the aromatic incense; and the entrance screen for the entrance of the Tabernacle; 16the altar of burnt offering, its copper grating, its poles, and all its furnishings; the laver and its stand; 17the hangings of the enclosure, its posts and its sockets, and the screen for the gate of the court; 18the pegs for the Tabernacle, the pegs for the enclosure, and their cords; 19the service vestments for officiating in the sanctuary, the sacral vestments of Aaron the priest and the vestments of his sons for priestly service.

20So the whole community of the Israelites left Moses' presence. 21And everyone who excelled in ability and everyone whose spirit moved him

---

a See 25.4 ff. and the notes there.

came, bringing to the LORD his offering for the work of the Tent of Meeting and for all its service and for the sacral vestments. 22Men and women, all whose hearts moved them, all who would make an elevation offering of gold to the LORD, came bringing brooches, earrings, rings, and pendants[b]—gold objects of all kinds. 23And everyone who had in his possession blue, purple, and crimson yarns, fine linen, goats' hair, tanned ram skins, and dolphin skins, brought them; 24everyone who would make gifts of silver or copper brought them as gifts for the LORD; and everyone who had in his possession acacia wood for any work of the service brought that. 25And all the skilled women spun with their own hands, and brought what they had spun, in blue, purple, and crimson yarns, and in fine linen. 26And all the women who excelled in that skill spun the goats' hair. 27And the chieftains brought lapis lazuli and other stones for setting, for the ephod and for the breastpiece; 28and spices and oil for lighting, for the anointing oil, and for the aromatic incense. 29Thus the Israelites, all the men and women whose hearts moved them to bring anything for the work that the LORD, through Moses, had commanded to be done, brought it as a freewill offering to the LORD.

30And Moses said to the Israelites: See, the LORD has singled out by name Bezalel, son of Uri son of Hur, of the tribe of Judah. 31He has endowed him with a divine spirit of skill, ability, and knowledge in every kind of craft 32and [c-has inspired him-c] to make designs for work in gold, silver, and copper, 33to cut stones for setting and to carve wood—to work in every kind of designer's craft—34and to give directions. He and Oholiab son of Ahisamach of the tribe of Dan 35have been endowed with the skill to do any work—of the carver, the designer, the embroiderer in blue, **36** purple, crimson yarns, and in fine linen, and of the weaver—as workers in all crafts and as makers of designs. 1Let, then, Bezalel and Oholiab and all the skilled persons whom the LORD has endowed with skill and ability to perform expertly all the tasks connected with the service of the sanctuary carry out all that the LORD has commanded.

2Moses then called Bezalel and Oholiab, and every skilled person whom the LORD had endowed with skill, everyone who excelled in ability, to undertake the task and carry it out. 3They took over from Moses all the gifts that the Israelites had brought, to carry out the tasks connected with the service of the sanctuary. But when these continued to bring freewill offerings to him morning after morning, 4all the artisans who were en-

b *Meaning of Heb.* kumaz *uncertain.*
c-c *Moved up from v. 34 for clarity.*

gaged in the tasks of the sanctuary came, each from the task upon which he was engaged, 5and said to Moses, "The people are bringing more than is needed for the tasks entailed in the work that the LORD has commanded to be done." 6Moses thereupon had this proclamation made throughout the camp: "Let no man or woman make further effort toward gifts for the sanctuary!" So the people stopped bringing: 7their efforts had been more than enough for all the tasks to be done.

8Then all the skilled among those engaged in the work made the tabernacle of ten strips of cloth, which they made of fine twisted linen, blue, purple, and crimson yarns; into these they worked a design of cherubim. 9The length of each cloth was twenty-eight cubits, and the width of each cloth was four cubits, all cloths having the same measurements. 10They joined five of the cloths to one another, and they joined the other five cloths to one another. 11They made loops of blue wool on the edge of the outermost cloth of the one set, and did the same on the edge of the outermost cloth of the other set: 12they made fifty loops on the one cloth, and they made fifty loops on the edge of the end cloth of the other set, the loops being opposite one another. 13And they made fifty gold clasps and coupled the unitsa to one another with the clasps, so that the tabernacle became one whole.

14They made cloths of goats' hair for a tent over the tabernacle; they made the cloths eleven in number. 15The length of each cloth was thirty cubits, and the width of each cloth was four cubits, the eleven cloths having the same measurements. 16They joined five of the cloths by themselves, and the other six cloths by themselves. 17They made fifty loops on the edge of the outermost cloth of the one set, and they made fifty loops on the edge of the end cloth of the other set. 18They made fifty copper clasps to couple the tent together so that it might become one whole. 19And they made a covering of tanned ram skins for the tent, and a covering of dolphin skins above.

20They made the planks for the Tabernacle of acacia wood, upright. 21The length of each plank was ten cubits, the width of each plank a cubit and a half. 22Each plank had two tenons, parallelb to each other; they did the same with all the planks of the Tabernacle. 23Of the planks of the Tabernacle, they made twenty planks for the south side,c 24making forty silver sockets under the twenty planks, two sockets under one plank for

a Lit. "strip of cloth," here used collectively.
b See note at 26.17.
c See note at 26.18.

its two tenons and two sockets under each following plank for its two tenons; 25and for the other side wall of the Tabernacle, the north side, twenty planks, 26with their forty silver sockets, two sockets under one plank and two sockets under each following plank. 27And for the rear of the Tabernacle, to the west, they made six planks; 28and they made two planks for the corners of the Tabernacle at the rear. 29d-They matched at the bottom, but terminated as one at the top into one ring;-d they did so with both of them at the two corners. 30Thus there were eight planks with their sockets of silver: sixteen sockets, two under each plank.

31They made bars of acacia wood, five for the planks of the one side wall of the Tabernacle, 32five bars for the planks of the other side wall of the Tabernacle, and five bars for the planks of the wall of the Tabernacle at the rear, to the west; 33they made the center bar to run, halfway up the planks, from end to end. 34They overlaid the planks with gold, and made their rings of gold, as holders for the bars; and they overlaid the bars with gold.

35They made the curtain of blue, purple, and crimson yarns, and fine twisted linen, working into it a design of cherubim. 36They made for it four posts of acacia wood and overlaid them with gold, with their hooks of gold; and they cast for them four silver sockets.

37They made the screen for the entrance of the Tent, of blue, purple, and crimson yarns, and fine twisted linen, done in embroidery; 38and five posts for it with their hooks. They overlaid their tops and their bands with gold; but the five sockets were of copper.

37

Bezalel made the ark of acacia wood, two and a half cubits long, a cubit and a half wide, and a cubit and a half high. 2He overlaid it with pure gold, inside and out; and he made a gold molding for it round about. 3He cast four gold rings for it, for its four feet: two rings on one of its side walls and two rings on the other. 4He made poles of acacia wood, overlaid them with gold, 5and inserted the poles into the rings on the side walls of the ark for carrying the ark.

6He made a cover of pure gold, two and a half cubits long and a cubit and a half wide. 7He made two cherubim of gold; he made them of hammered work, at the two ends of the cover: 8one cherub at one end and the other cherub at the other end; he made the cherubim of one piece

d-d *See note at 26.24.*

with the cover, at its two ends. 9The cherubim had their wings spread out above, shielding the cover with their wings. They faced each other; the faces of the cherubim were turned toward the cover.

10He made the table of acacia wood, two cubits long, one cubit wide, and a cubit and a half high; 11he overlaid it with pure gold and made a gold molding around it. 12He made a rim of a hand's breadth around it and made a gold molding for its rim round about. 13He cast four gold rings for it and attached the rings to the four corners at its four legs. 14The rings were next to the rim, as holders for the poles to carry the table. 15He made the poles of acacia wood for carrying the table, and overlaid them with gold. 16The utensils that were to be upon the table— its bowls, ladles, jugs, and jars with which to offer libations—he made of pure gold.

17He made the lampstand of pure gold. He made the lampstand—its base and its shaft—of hammered work; its cups, calyxes, and petals were of one piece with it. 18Six branches issued from its sides: three branches from one side of the lampstand, and three branches from the other side of the lampstand. 19There were three cups shaped like almond-blossoms, each with calyx and petals, on one branch; and there were three cups shaped like almond-blossoms, each with calyx and petals, on the next branch; so for all six branches issuing from the lampstand. 20On the lamp- stand itself there were four cups shaped like almond-blossoms, each with calyx and petals: 21a calyx, of one piece with it, under a pair of branches; and a calyx, of one piece with it, under the second pair of branches; and a calyx, of one piece with it, under the last pair of branches; so for all six branches issuing from it. 22Their calyxes and their stems were of one piece with it, the whole of it a single hammered piece of pure gold. 23He made its seven lamps, its tongs, and its fire pans of pure gold. 24He made it and all its furnishings out of a talent of pure gold.

25He made the incense altar of acacia wood, a cubit long and a cubit wide—square—and two cubits high; its horns were of one piece with it. 26He overlaid it with pure gold: its top, its sides round about, and its horns; and he made a gold molding for it round about. 27He made two gold rings for it under its molding, on its two walls—on opposite sides— as holders for the poles with which to carry it. 28He made the poles of acacia wood, and overlaid them with gold. 29He prepared the sacred anointing oil and the pure aromatic incense, expertly blended.

38

He made the altar for burnt offering of acacia wood, five cubits long and five cubits wide—square—and three cubits high. [2]He made horns for it on its four corners, the horns being of one piece with it; and he overlaid it with copper. [3]He made all the utensils of the altar—the pails, the scrapers, the basins, the flesh hooks, and the fire pans; he made all these utensils of copper. [4]He made for the altar a grating of meshwork in copper, extending below, under its ledge, to its middle. [5]He cast four rings, at the four corners of the copper grating, as holders for the poles. [6]He made the poles of acacia wood and overlaid them with copper; [7]and he inserted the poles into the rings on the side walls of the altar, to carry it by them. He made it hollow, of boards.

[8]He made the laver of copper and its stand of copper, from the mirrors of the women who performed tasks[a] at the entrance of the Tent of Meeting.

[9]He made the enclosure:

On the south[b] side, a hundred cubits of hangings of fine twisted linen for the enclosure—[10]with their twenty posts and their twenty sockets of copper, the hooks and bands of the posts being silver.

[11]On the north side, a hundred cubits—with their twenty posts and their twenty sockets of copper, the hooks and bands of the posts being silver.

[12]On the west side, fifty cubits of hangings—with their ten posts and their ten sockets, the hooks and bands of the posts being silver.

[13]And on the front side, to the east, fifty cubits: [14]fifteen cubits of hangings on the one flank, with their three posts and their three sockets, [15]and fifteen cubits of hangings on the other flank—on each side of the gate of the enclosure[c]—with their three posts and their three sockets.

[16]All the hangings around the enclosure were of fine twisted linen. [17]The sockets for the posts were of copper, the hooks and bands of the posts were of silver, the overlay of their tops was of silver; all the posts of the enclosure were banded with silver.—[18]The screen of the gate of the enclosure, done in embroidery, was of blue, purple, and crimson yarns, and fine twisted linen. It was twenty cubits long. [d-]Its height—or width—was five cubits, like that of[-d] the hangings of the enclosure. [19]The posts were four; their four sockets were of copper, their hooks of silver; and the overlay of their tops was of silver, as were also their bands.—[20]All

[a] *Meaning of Heb. uncertain.*
[b] *Cf. note at 26.18.*
[c] *Which accounts for the remaining 20 cubits; cf. v. 18.*
[d-d] *Meaning of Heb. uncertain.*

the pegs of the Tabernacle and of the enclosure round about were of copper.

פקודי

²¹These are the records of the Tabernacle, the Tabernacle of the Pact, which were drawn up at Moses' bidding—the work of the Levites under the direction of Ithamar son of Aaron the priest. ²²Now Bezalel, son of Uri son of Hur, of the tribe of Judah, had made all that the LORD had commanded Moses; ²³at his side was Oholiab son of Ahisamach, of the tribe of Dan, carver and designer, and embroiderer in blue, purple, and crimson yarns and in fine linen.

²⁴All the gold that was used for the work, in all the work of the sanctuary—the elevation offering of gold—came to 29 talents^c and 730 shekels by the sanctuary weight. ²⁵The silver of those of the community who were recorded came to 100 talents and 1,775 shekels by the sanctuary weight: ²⁶a half-shekel^f a head, half a shekel by the sanctuary weight, for each one who was entered in the records, from the age of twenty years up, 603,550 men. ²⁷The 100 talents of silver were for casting the sockets of the sanctuary and the sockets for the curtain, 100 sockets to the 100 talents, a talent a socket. ²⁸And of the 1,775 shekels he made hooks for the posts, overlay for their tops, and bands around them.

²⁹The copper from the elevation offering came to 70 talents and 2,400 shekels. ³⁰Of it he made the sockets for the entrance of the Tent of Meeting; the copper altar and its copper grating and all the utensils of the altar; ³¹the sockets of the enclosure round about and the sockets of the gate of the enclosure; and all the pegs of the Tabernacle and all the pegs of the enclosure round about.

39

Of the blue, purple, and crimson yarns they also^a made the service vestments for officiating in the sanctuary; they made Aaron's sacral vestments—as the LORD had commanded Moses.

²The ephod was made^b of gold, blue, purple, and crimson yarns, and fine twisted linen. ³They hammered out sheets of gold and cut threads to be worked into designs among the blue, the purple, and the crimson yarns, and the fine linen. ⁴They made for it attaching shoulder-pieces; they were attached at its two ends. ⁵The decorated band that was upon it was made

---

ᶜ *A talent here equals 3,000 shekels.*
ᶠ *Heb.* beqaʿ.

ᵃ *See 36.8.*
ᵇ *Here and elsewhere in this chapter the singular active verb (lit. "he made") is used impersonally.*

like it, of one piece with it; of gold, blue, purple, and crimson yarns, and fine twisted linen—as the LORD had commanded Moses.

6They bordered the lazuli stones with frames of gold, engraved with seal engravings of the names of the sons of Israel. 7They were set on the shoulder-pieces of the ephod, as stones of remembrance for the Israelites—as the LORD had commanded Moses.

8The breastpiece was made in the style of the ephod: of gold, blue, purple, and crimson yarns, and fine twisted linen. 9It was square; they made the breastpiece doubled—a span in length and a span in width, doubled. 10They set in it four rows of stones. The first row was a row of ᶜcarnelian, chrysolite, and emerald; 11the second row: a turquoise, a sapphire, and an amethyst; 12the third row: a jacinth, an agate, and a crystal; 13and the fourth row: a beryl, a lapis lazuli, and a jasper. They were encircled in their mountings with frames of gold. 14The stones corresponded [in number] to the names of the sons of Israel: twelve, corresponding to their names; engraved like seals, each with its name, for the twelve tribes.

15On the breastpiece they made braided chains of corded work in pure gold. 16They made two frames of gold and two rings of gold, and fastened the two rings at the two ends of the breastpiece, 17attaching the two golden cords to the two rings at the ends of the breastpiece. 18They then fastened the two ends of the cords to the two frames, attaching them to the shoulder-pieces of the ephod, at the front. 19They made two rings of gold and attached them to the two ends of the breastpiece, at its inner edge, which faced the ephod. 20They made two other rings of gold and fastened them on the front of the ephod, low on the two shoulder-pieces, close to its seam above the decorated band. 21The breastpiece was held in place by a cord of blue from its rings to the rings of the ephod, so that the breastpiece rested on the decorated band and did not come loose from the ephod—as the LORD had commanded Moses.

22The robe for the ephod was made of woven work, of pure blue.ᵈ 23The opening of the robe, in the middle of it, was like the opening of a coat of mail, with a binding around the opening, so that it would not tear. 24On the hem of the robe they made pomegranates of blue, purple, and crimson yarns, twisted. 25They also made bells of pure gold, and attached the bells between the pomegranates, all around the hem of the robe, between the pomegranates: 26a bell and a pomegranate, a bell and

ᶜ See note at 28.17.
ᵈ See note at 28.31.

a pomegranate, all around the hem of the robe for officiating in—as the LORD had commanded Moses.

27They made the tunics of fine linen, of woven work, for Aaron and his sons; 28and the headdress of fine linen, and the decorated turbans of fine linen, and the linen breeches of fine twisted linen; 29and sashes of fine twisted linen, blue, purple, and crimson yarns, done in embroidery— as the LORD had commanded Moses.

30They made the frontlet for the holy diadem of pure gold, and incised upon it the seal inscription: "Holy to the LORD." 31They attached to it a cord of blue to fix it upon the headdress above—as the LORD had commanded Moses.

32Thus was completed all the work of the Tabernacle of the Tent of Meeting. The Israelites did so; just as the LORD had commanded Moses, so they did. 33Then they brought the Tabernacle to Moses, with the Tent and all its furnishings: its clasps, its planks, its bars, its posts, and its sockets; 34the covering of tanned ram skins, the covering of dolphin skins, and the curtain for the screen; 35the Ark of the Pact and its poles, and the cover; 36the table and all its utensils, and the bread of display; 37the pure lampstand,c its lamps—lamps in due order—and all its fittings, and the oil for lighting; 38the altar of gold, the oil for anointing, the aromatic incense, and the screen for the entrance of the Tent; 39the copper altar with its copper grating, its poles and all its utensils, and the laver and its stand; 40the hangings of the enclosure, its posts and its sockets, the screen for the gate of the enclosure, its cords and its pegs—all the furnishings for the service of the Tabernacle, the Tent of Meeting; 41the service vestments for officiating in the sanctuary, the sacral vestments of Aaron the priest, and the vestments of his sons for priestly service. 42Just as the LORD had commanded Moses, so the Israelites had done all the work. 43And when Moses saw that they had performed all the tasks—as the LORD had commanded, so they had done—Moses blessed them.

40 And the LORD spoke to Moses, saying:

2On the first day of the first month you shall set up the Tabernacle of the Tent of Meeting. 3Place there the Ark of the Pact, and screen off the

c *See note at 31.8.*

ark with the curtain. 4Bring in the table and lay out its due setting; bring in the lampstand and light its lamps; 5and place the gold altar of incense before the Ark of the Pact. Then put up the screen for the entrance of the Tabernacle.

6You shall place the altar of burnt offering before the entrance of the Tabernacle of the Tent of Meeting. 7Place the laver between the Tent of Meeting and the altar, and put water in it. 8Set up the enclosure round about, and put in place the screen for the gate of the enclosure.

9You shall take the anointing oil and anoint the Tabernacle and all that is in it to consecrate it and all its furnishings, so that it shall be holy. 10Then anoint the altar of burnt offering and all its utensils to consecrate the altar, so that the altar shall be most holy. 11And anoint the laver and its stand to consecrate it.

12You shall bring Aaron and his sons forward to the entrance of the Tent of Meeting and wash them with the water. 13Put the sacral vestments on Aaron, and anoint him and consecrate him, that he may serve Me as priest. 14Then bring his sons forward, put tunics on them, 15and anoint them as you have anointed their father, that they may serve Me as priests. This their anointing shall serve them for everlasting priesthood throughout the ages.

16This Moses did; just as the LORD had commanded him, so he did.

17In the first month of the second year, on the first of the month, the Tabernacle was set up. 18Moses set up the Tabernacle, placing its sockets, setting up its planks, inserting its bars, and erecting its posts. 19He spread the tent over the Tabernacle, placing the covering of the tent on top of it—just as the LORD had commanded Moses.

20He took the Pact and placed it in the ark; he fixed the poles to the ark, placed the cover on top of the ark, 21and brought the ark inside the Tabernacle. Then he put up the curtain for screening, and screened off the Ark of the Pact—just as the LORD had commanded Moses.

22He placed the table in the Tent of Meeting, outside the curtain, on the north side of the Tabernacle. 23Upon it he laid out the setting of bread before the LORD—as the LORD had commanded Moses. 24He placed the lampstand in the Tent of Meeting opposite the table, on the south side of the Tabernacle. 25And he lit the lamps before the LORD—as the LORD had commanded Moses. 26He placed the altar of gold in the Tent of

Meeting, before the curtain. ²⁷On it he burned aromatic incense—as the LORD had commanded Moses.

²⁸Then he put up the screen for the entrance of the Tabernacle. ²⁹At the entrance of the Tabernacle of the Tent of Meeting he placed the altar of burnt offering. On it he offered up the burnt offering and the meal offering—as the LORD had commanded Moses. ³⁰He placed the laver between the Tent of Meeting and the altar, and put water in it for washing. ³¹From it Moses and Aaron and his sons would wash their hands and feet; ³²they washed when they entered the Tent of Meeting and when they approached the altar—as the LORD had commanded Moses. ³³And he set up the enclosure around the Tabernacle and the altar, and put up the screen for the gate of the enclosure.

When Moses had finished the work, ³⁴the cloud covered the Tent of Meeting, and the Presence of the LORD filled the Tabernacle. ³⁵Moses could not enter the Tent of Meeting, because the cloud had settled upon it and the Presence of the LORD filled the Tabernacle. ³⁶When the cloud lifted from the Tabernacle, the Israelites would set out, on their various journeys; ³⁷but if the cloud did not lift, they would not set out until such time as it did lift. ³⁸For over the Tabernacle a cloud of the LORD rested by day, and fire would appear in itᵃ by night, in the view of all the house of Israel throughout their journeys.

חזק

ᵃ I.e., in the cloud.

LEVITICUS

1 The LORD called to Moses and spoke to him from the Tent of Meeting, saying: ²Speak to the Israelite people, and say to them:

When any of you presents an offering of cattle to the LORD, ᵃ⁻he shall choose his⁻ᵃ offering from the herd or from the flock.

³If his offering is a burnt offering from the herd, he shall make his offering a male without blemish. He shall bring it to the entrance of the Tent of Meeting, for acceptance in his behalf before the LORD. ⁴He shall lay his hand upon the head of the burnt offering, that it may be acceptable in his behalf, in expiation for him. ⁵The bull shall be slaughtered before the LORD; and Aaron's sons, the priests, shall offer the blood, dashing the blood against all sides of the altar which is at the entrance of the Tent of Meeting. ⁶The burnt offering shall be flayed and cut up into sections. ⁷The sons of Aaron the priest shall put fire on the altar and lay out wood upon the fire; ⁸and Aaron's sons, the priests, shall lay out the sections, with the head and the suet, on the wood that is on the fire upon the altar. ⁹Its entrails and legs shall be washed with water, and the priest shall turn the whole into smoke on the altar as a burnt offering, an offering by fire of pleasing odor to the LORD.

¹⁰If his offering for a burnt offering is from the flock, of sheep or of goats, he shall make his offering a male without blemish. ¹¹It shall be slaughtered before the LORD on the north side of the altar, and Aaron's sons, the priests, shall dash its blood against all sides of the altar. ¹²When it has been cut up into sections, the priest shall lay them out, with the head and the suet, on the wood that is on the fire upon the altar. ¹³The entrails and the legs shall be washed with water; the priest shall offer up and turn the whole into smoke on the altar. It is a burnt offering, an offering by fire, of pleasing odor to the LORD.

¹⁴If his offering to the LORD is a burnt offering of birds, he shall choose his offering from turtledoves or pigeons. ¹⁵The priest shall bring it to the

ᵃ⁻ᵃ Lit. "you shall offer your."

altar, pinch off its head, and turn it into smoke on the altar; and its blood shall be drained out against the side of the altar. ¹⁶He shall remove its crop with its contents,ᵇ and cast it into the place of the ashes, at the east side of the altar. ¹⁷The priest shall tear it open by its wings, without severing it, and turn it into smoke on the altar, upon the wood that is on the fire. It is a burnt offering, an offering by fire, of pleasing odor to the LORD.

2 When a person presents an offering of meal to the LORD, his offering shall be of choice flour; he shall pour oil upon it, lay frankincense on it, ²and present it to Aaron's sons, the priests. The priest shall scoop out of it a handful of its choice flour and oil, as well as all of its frankincense; and this token portion he shall turn into smoke on the altar, as an offering by fire, of pleasing odor to the LORD. ³And the remainder of the meal offering shall be for Aaron and his sons, a most holy portion from the LORD's offerings by fire.

⁴When you present an offering of meal baked in the oven, [it shall be of] choice flour: unleavened cakes with oil mixed in, or unleavened wafers spread with oil.

⁵If your offering is a meal offering on a griddle, it shall be of choice flour with oil mixed in, unleavened. ⁶Break it into bits and pour oil on it; it is a meal offering.

⁷If your offering is a meal offering in a pan, it shall be made of choice flour in oil.

⁸When you present to the LORD a meal offering that is made in any of these ways, it shall be brought to the priest who shall take it up to the altar. ⁹The priest shall remove the token portion from the meal offering and turn it into smoke on the altar as an offering by fire, of pleasing odor to the LORD. ¹⁰And the remainder of the meal offering shall be for Aaron and his sons, a most holy portion from the LORD's offerings by fire.

¹¹No meal offering that you offer to the LORD shall be made with leaven, for no leaven or honey may be turned into smoke as an offering by fire to the LORD. ¹²You may bring them to the LORD as an offering of choice products;ᵃ but they shall not be offered up on the altar for a pleasing odor. ¹³You shall season your every offering of meal with salt; you shall not omit from your meal offering the salt of your covenant with God; with all your offerings you must offer salt.

ᵇ Others "feathers."
ᵃ Exact meaning of Heb. uncertain.

¹⁴If you bring a meal offering of first fruits to the LORD, you shall bring new ears parched with fire, grits of the fresh grain, as your meal offering of first fruits. ¹⁵You shall add oil to it and lay frankincense on it; it is a meal offering. ¹⁶And the priest shall turn a token portion of it into smoke: some of the grits and oil, with all of the frankincense, as an offering by fire to the LORD.

3 If his offering is a sacrifice of well-being^a—

If he offers of the herd, whether a male or a female, he shall bring before the LORD one without blemish. ²He shall lay his hand upon the head of his offering and slaughter it at the entrance of the Tent of Meeting; and Aaron's sons, the priests, shall dash the blood against all sides of the altar. ³He shall then present from the sacrifice of well-being, as an offering by fire to the LORD, the fat that covers the entrails and all the fat that is about the entrails; ⁴the two kidneys and the fat that is on them, that is at the loins; and the protuberance on the liver, which he shall remove with the kidneys. ⁵Aaron's sons shall turn these into smoke on the altar, with the burnt offering which is upon the wood that is on the fire, as an offering by fire, of pleasing odor to the LORD.

⁶And if his offering for a sacrifice of well-being to the LORD is from the flock, whether a male or a female, he shall offer one without blemish. ⁷If he presents a sheep as his offering, he shall bring it before the LORD ⁸and lay his hand upon the head of his offering. It shall be slaughtered before the Tent of Meeting, and Aaron's sons shall dash its blood against all sides of the altar. ⁹He shall then present, as an offering by fire to the LORD, the fat from the sacrifice of well-being: the whole broad tail, which shall be removed close to the backbone; the fat that covers the entrails and all the fat that is about the entrails; ¹⁰the two kidneys and the fat that is on them, that is at the loins; and the protuberance on the liver, which he shall remove with the kidneys. ¹¹The priest shall turn these into smoke on the altar as food, an offering by fire to the LORD.

¹²And if his offering is a goat, he shall bring it before the LORD ¹³and lay his hand upon its head. It shall be slaughtered before the Tent of Meeting, and Aaron's sons shall dash its blood against all sides of the altar. ¹⁴He shall then present as his offering from it, as an offering by fire to the LORD, the fat that covers the entrails and all the fat that is about the entrails; ¹⁵the two kidneys and the fat that is on them, that is at the

---

^a Others "peace offering." Exact meaning of shelamim uncertain.

loins; and the protuberance on the liver, which he shall remove with the kidneys. [16]The priest shall turn these into smoke on the altar as food, an offering by fire, of pleasing odor.

All fat is the LORD's. [17]It is a law for all time throughout the ages, in all your settlements: you must not eat any fat or any blood.

4 The LORD spoke to Moses, saying: [2]Speak to the Israelite people thus:

When a person unwittingly incurs guilt in regard to any of the LORD's commandments about things not to be done, and does one of them—

[3]If it is the anointed priest who has incurred guilt, so that blame falls upon the people, he shall offer for the sin of which he is guilty a bull of the herd without blemish as a sin offering[a] to the LORD. [4]He shall bring the bull to the entrance of the Tent of Meeting, before the Lord, and lay his hand upon the head of the bull. The bull shall be slaughtered before the LORD, [5]and the anointed priest shall take some of the bull's blood and bring it into the Tent of Meeting. [6]The priest shall dip his finger in the blood, and sprinkle of the blood seven times before the LORD, in front of the curtain of the Shrine. [7]The priest shall put some of the blood on the horns of the altar of aromatic incense, which is in the Tent of Meeting, before the LORD; and all the rest of the bull's blood he shall pour out at the base of the altar of burnt offering, which is at the entrance of the Tent of Meeting. [8]He shall remove all the fat from the bull of sin offering: the fat that covers the entrails and all the fat that is about the entrails; [9]the two kidneys and the fat that is on them, that is at the loins; and the protuberance on the liver, which he shall remove with the kidneys—[10]just as it is removed from the ox of the sacrifice of well-being. The priest shall turn them into smoke on the altar of burnt offering. [11]But the hide of the bull, and all its flesh, as well as its head and legs, its entrails and its dung—[12]all the rest of the bull—he shall carry to a clean place outside the camp, to the ash heap, and burn it up in a wood fire; it shall be burned on the ash heap.

[13]If it is the whole community of Israel that has erred and the matter escapes the notice of the congregation, so that they do any of the things which by the LORD's commandments ought not to be done, and they realize their guilt—[14]when the sin through which they incurred guilt becomes known, the congregation shall offer a bull of the herd as a sin

[a] *So traditionally; more precisely "offering of purgation."*

offering, and bring it before the Tent of Meeting. ¹⁵The elders of the community shall lay their hands upon the head of the bull before the LORD, and the bull shall be slaughtered before the LORD. ¹⁶The anointed priest shall bring some of the blood of the bull into the Tent of Meeting, ¹⁷and the priest shall dip his finger in the blood and sprinkle of it seven times before the LORD, in front of the curtain. ¹⁸Some of the blood he shall put on the horns of the altar which is before the LORD in the Tent of Meeting, and all the rest of the blood he shall pour out at the base of the altar of burnt offering, which is at the entrance of the Tent of Meeting. ¹⁹He shall remove all its fat from it and turn it into smoke on the altar. ²⁰He shall do with this bull just as is done with the [priest's] bull of sin offering; he shall do the same with it. Thus the priest shall make expiation for them, and they shall be forgiven. ²¹He shall carry the bull outside the camp and burn it as he burned the first bull; it is the sin offering of the congregation.

²²In case it is a chieftain who incurs guilt by doing unwittingly any of the things which by the commandment of the LORD his God ought not to be done, and he realizes his guilt—²³or the sin of which he is guilty is brought to his knowledge—he shall bring as his offering a male goat without blemish. ²⁴He shall lay his hand upon the goat's head, and it shall be slaughtered at the spot where the burnt offering is slaughtered^b before the LORD; it is a sin offering. ²⁵The priest shall take with his finger some of the blood of the sin offering and put it on the horns of the altar of burnt offering; and the rest of its blood he shall pour out at the base of the altar of burnt offering. ²⁶All its fat he shall turn into smoke on the altar, like the fat of the sacrifice of well-being. Thus the priest shall make expiation on his behalf for his sin, and he shall be forgiven.

²⁷If any person from among the populace^c unwittingly incurs guilt by doing any of the things which by the LORD's commandments ought not to be done, and he realizes his guilt—²⁸or the sin of which he is guilty is brought to his knowledge—he shall bring a female goat without blemish as his offering for the sin of which he is guilty. ²⁹He shall lay his hand upon the head of the sin offering, and the sin offering shall be slaughtered at the place of the burnt offering. ³⁰The priest shall take with his finger some of its blood and put it on the horns of the altar of burnt offering; and all the rest of its blood he shall pour out at the base of the altar. ³¹He shall remove all its fat, just as the fat is removed from the sacrifice of well-being; and the priest shall turn it into smoke on the altar, for a pleasing

^b Cf. 1.11.
^c Lit. "people of the country."

odor to the LORD. Thus the priest shall make expiation for him, and he shall be forgiven.

³²If the offering he brings as a sin offering is a sheep, he shall bring a female without blemish. ³³He shall lay his hand upon the head of the sin offering, and it shall be slaughtered as a sin offering at the spot where the burnt offering is slaughtered. ³⁴The priest shall take with his finger some of the blood of the sin offering and put it on the horns of the altar of burnt offering, and all the rest of its blood he shall pour out at the base of the altar. ³⁵And all its fat he shall remove just as the fat of the sheep of the sacrifice of well-being is removed; and this the priest shall turn into smoke on the altar, over the LORD's offering by fire. Thus the priest shall make expiation on his behalf for the sin of which he is guilty, and he shall be forgiven.

5 If a person incurs guilt—

When he has heard a public imprecationᵃ and—although able to testify as one who has either seen or learned of the matter—he does not give information, so that he is subject to punishment;

²Or when a person touches any unclean thing—be it the carcass of an unclean beast or the carcass of unclean cattle or the carcass of an unclean creeping thing—and the fact has escaped him, and then, being unclean, he realizes his guilt;

³Or when he touches human uncleanness—any such uncleanness whereby one becomes unclean—and, though he has known it, the fact has escaped him, but later he realizes his guilt;

⁴Or when a person uttersᵇ an oath to bad or good purpose—whatever a man may utter in an oath—and, though he has known it, the fact has escaped him, but later he realizes his guilt in any of these matters—

⁵when he realizes his guilt in any of these matters, he shall confess that wherein he has sinned. ⁶And he shall bring as his penalty to the LORD, for the sin of which he is guilty, a female from the flock, sheep or goat, as a sin offering; and the priest shall make expiation on his behalf for his sin.

⁷But if his means do not suffice for a sheep, he shall bring to the LORD, as his penalty for that of which he is guilty, two turtledoves or two

---

ᵃ Namely, against one who withholds testimony.
ᵇ Lit. "utters with his lips."

pigeons, one for a sin offering and the other for a burnt offering. [8]He shall bring them to the priest, who shall offer first the one for the sin offering, pinching its head at the nape without severing it. [9]He shall sprinkle some of the blood of the sin offering on the side of the altar, and what remains of the blood shall be drained out at the base of the altar; it is a sin offering. [10]And the second he shall prepare as a burnt offering, according to regulation. Thus the priest shall make expiation on his behalf for the sin of which he is guilty, and he shall be forgiven.

[11]And if his means do not suffice for two turtledoves or two pigeons, he shall bring as his offering for that of which he is guilty a tenth of an *ephah* of choice flour for a sin offering; he shall not add oil to it or lay frankincense on it, for it is a sin offering. [12]He shall bring it to the priest, and the priest shall scoop out of it a handful as a token portion of it and turn it into smoke on the altar, with the LORD's offerings by fire; it is a sin offering. [13]Thus the priest shall make expiation on his behalf for whichever of these sins he is guilty, and he shall be forgiven. It shall belong to the priest, like the meal offering.

[14]And the LORD spoke to Moses, saying: [15]When a person commits a trespass, being unwittingly remiss about any of the LORD's sacred things, he shall bring as his penalty to the LORD a ram without blemish from the flock, convertible into payment in silver by the sanctuary weight, as a guilt offering. [16]He shall make restitution for that wherein he was remiss about the sacred things, and he shall add a fifth part to it and give it to the priest. The priest shall make expiation on his behalf with the ram of the guilt offering, and he shall be forgiven.

[17]And when a person, without knowing it, sins in regard to any of the LORD's commandments about things not to be done, and then realizes his guilt, he shall be subject to punishment. [18]He shall bring to the priest a ram without blemish from the flock, or the equivalent,[c] as a guilt offering. The priest shall make expiation on his behalf for the error that he committed unwittingly, and he shall be forgiven. [19]It is a guilt offering; he has incurred guilt before the LORD.

[20]The LORD spoke to Moses, saying: [21]When a person sins and commits a trespass against the LORD by dealing deceitfully with his fellow in the matter of a deposit or a pledge,[d] or through robbery, or by defrauding his fellow, [22]or by finding something lost and lying about it; if he swears falsely regarding any one of the various things that one may do and sin

---

[c] *I.e., in currency; cf. v. 15.*
[d] *Meaning of Heb. uncertain.*

thereby—23when one has thus sinned and, realizing his guilt, would restore that which he got through robbery or fraud, or the deposit that was entrusted to him, or the lost thing that he found, 24or anything else about which he swore falsely, he shall repay the principal amount and add a fifth part to it. He shall pay it to its owner when he realizes his guilt. 25Then he shall bring to the priest, as his penalty to the LORD, a ram without blemish from the flock, or the equivalent,c as a guilt offering. 26The priest shall make expiation on his behalf before the LORD, and he shall be forgiven for whatever he may have done to draw blame thereby.

צו

6 The LORD spoke to Moses, saying: 2Command Aaron and his sons thus:

This is the ritual of the burnt offering: The burnt offering itself shall remain where it is burned upon the altar all night until morning, while the fire on the altar is kept going on it. 3The priest shall dress in linen raiment, with linen breeches next to his body; and he shall take up the ashes to which the fire has reduced the burnt offering on the altar and place them beside the altar. 4He shall then take off his vestments and put on other vestments, and carry the ashes outside the camp to a clean place. 5The fire on the altar shall be kept burning, not to go out: every morning the priest shall feed wood to it, lay out the burnt offering on it, and turn into smoke the fat parts of the offerings of well-being. 6A perpetual fire shall be kept burning on the altar, not to go out.

7And this is the ritual of the meal offering: Aaron's sons shall present it before the LORD, in front of the altar. 8A handful of the choice flour and oil of the meal offering shall be taken from it, with all the frankincense that is on the meal offering, and this token portion shall be turned into smoke on the altar as a pleasing odor to the LORD. 9What is left of it shall be eaten by Aaron and his sons; it shall be eaten as unleavened cakes, in the sacred precinct; they shall eat it in the enclosure of the Tent of Meeting. 10It shall not be baked with leaven; I have given it as their portion from My offerings by fire; it is most holy, like the sin offering and the guilt offering. 11Only the males among Aaron's descendants may eat of it, as their due for all time throughout the ages from the LORD's offerings by fire. Anything that touches these shall become holy.

c I.e., in currency; cf. v. 15.

¹²The LORD spoke to Moses, saying: ¹³This is the offering that Aaron and his sons shall offer to the LORD on the occasion of hisᵃ anointment: a tenth of an *ephah* of choice flour as a regular meal offering, half of it in the morning and half of it in the evening, ¹⁴shall be prepared with oil on a griddle. You shall bring it well soaked, and offer it as a meal offering of baked slices,ᵇ of pleasing odor to the LORD. ¹⁵And so shall the priest, anointed from among his sons to succeed him, prepare it; it is the LORD's— a law for all time—to be turned entirely into smoke. ¹⁶So, too, every meal offering of a priest shall be a whole offering: it shall not be eaten.

¹⁷The LORD spoke to Moses, saying: ¹⁸Speak to Aaron and his sons thus: This is the ritual of the sin offering: the sin offering shall be slaughtered before the LORD, at the spotᶜ where the burnt offering is slaughtered: it is most holy. ¹⁹The priest who offers it as a sin offering shall eat of it; it shall be eaten in the sacred precinct, in the enclosure of the Tent of Meeting. ²⁰Anything that touches its flesh shall become holy; and if any of its blood is spattered upon a garment, you shall wash the bespattered part in the sacred precinct. ²¹An earthen vessel in which it was boiled shall be broken; if it was boiled in a copper vessel, [the vessel] shall be scoured and rinsed with water. ²²Only the males in the priestly line may eat of it: it is most holy. ²³But no sin offering may be eaten from which any blood is brought into the Tent of Meeting for expiation in the sanctuary; any such shall be consumed in fire.

7 This is the ritual of the guilt offering: it is most holy. ²The guilt offering shall be slaughtered at the spot where the burnt offering is slaughtered, and the blood shall be dashed on all sides of the altar. ³All its fat shall be offered: the broad tail; the fat that covers the entrails; ⁴the two kidneys and the fat that is on them at the loins; and the protuberance on the liver, which shall be removed with the kidneys. ⁵The priest shall turn them into smoke on the altar as an offering by fire to the LORD; it is a guilt offering. ⁶Only the males in the priestly line may eat of it; it shall be eaten in the sacred precinct: it is most holy.

⁷The guilt offering is like the sin offering. The same rule applies to both: it shall belong to the priest who makes expiation thereby. ⁸So, too, the priest who offers a man's burnt offering shall keep the skin of the

ᵃ Or "their."
ᵇ Meaning of Heb. tuphine uncertain.
ᶜ Cf. 1.11.

burnt offering that he offered. 9Further, any meal offering that is baked in an oven, and any that is prepared in a pan or on a griddle, shall belong to the priest who offers it. 10But every other meal offering, with oil mixed in or dry, shall go to the sons of Aaron all alike.

11This is the ritual of the sacrifice of well-being that one may offer to the LORD:

12If he offers it for thanksgiving, he shall offer together with the sacrifice of thanksgiving unleavened cakes with oil mixed in, unleavened wafers spread with oil, and cakes of choice flour with oil mixed in, well soaked. 13This offering, with cakes of leavened bread added, he shall offer along with his thanksgiving sacrifice of well-being. 14Out of this he shall offer one of each kinda as a gift to the LORD; it shall go to the priest who dashes the blood of the offering of well-being. 15And the flesh of his thanksgiving sacrifice of well-being shall be eaten on the day that it is offered; none of it shall be set aside until morning.

16If, however, the sacrifice he offers is a votive or a freewill offering, it shall be eaten on the day that he offers his sacrifice, and what is left of it shall be eaten on the morrow. 17What is then left of the flesh of the sacrifice shall be consumed in fire on the third day. 18If any of the flesh of his sacrifice of well-being is eaten on the third day, it shall not be acceptable; it shall not count for him who offered it. It is an offensive thing, and the person who eats of it shall bear his guilt.

19Flesh that touches anything unclean shall not be eaten; it shall be consumed in fire. As for other flesh, only he who is clean may eat such flesh. 20But the person who, in a state of uncleanness, eats flesh from the LORD's sacrifices of well-being, that person shall be cut off from his kin. 21When a person touches anything unclean, be it human uncleanness or an unclean animal or any unclean creature,b and eats flesh from the LORD's sacrifices of well-being, that person shall be cut off from his kin.

22And the LORD spoke to Moses, saying: 23Speak to the Israelite people thus: You shall eat no fatc of ox or sheep or goat. 24Fat from animals that died or were torn by beasts may be put to any use, but you must not eat it. 25If anyone eats the fat of animals from which offerings by fire may be made to the LORD, the person who eats it shall be cut off from his kin. 26And you must not consume any blood, either of bird or of animal, in

---

a Lit. "offering."
b Heb. sheqeṣ, lit. "abomination"; several mss. and ancient versions read sheres "swarming things."
c I.e., hard, coarse fat (suet); cf. 3.3–5.

any of your settlements. [27]Anyone who eats blood shall be cut off from his kin.

[28]And the LORD spoke to Moses, saying: [29]Speak to the Israelite people thus: The offering to the LORD from a sacrifice of well-being must be presented by him who offers his sacrifice of well-being to the LORD: [30]his own hands shall present the LORD's offerings by fire. He shall present the fat with the breast, the breast to be elevated as an elevation offering before the LORD; [31]the priest shall turn the fat into smoke on the altar, and the breast shall go to Aaron and his sons. [32]And the right thigh from your sacrifices of well-being you shall present to the priest as a gift; [33]he from among Aaron's sons who offers the blood and the fat of the offering of well-being shall get the right thigh as his portion. [34]For I have taken the breast of elevation offering and the thigh of gift offering from the Israelites, from their sacrifices of well-being, and given them to Aaron the priest and to his sons as their due from the Israelites for all time.

[35]Those shall be the perquisites[d] of Aaron and the perquisites of his sons from the LORD's offerings by fire, once they have been inducted[e] to serve the LORD as priests; [36]these the LORD commanded to be given them, once they had been anointed, as a due from the Israelites for all time throughout the ages.

[37]Such are the rituals of the burnt offering, the meal offering, the sin offering, the guilt offering, the offering of ordination, and the sacrifice of well-being, [38]with which the LORD charged Moses on Mount Sinai, when He commanded that the Israelites present their offerings to the LORD, in the wilderness of Sinai.

8 The LORD spoke to Moses, saying: [2]Take Aaron along with his sons, and the vestments, the anointing oil, the bull of sin offering, the two rams, and the basket of unleavened bread; [3]and assemble the whole community at the entrance of the Tent of Meeting. [4]Moses did as the LORD commanded him. And when the community was assembled at the entrance of the Tent of Meeting, [5]Moses said to the community, "This is what the LORD has commanded to be done."

[d] Lit. "anointment," i.e., accruing from anointment.
[e] Lit. "brought forward."

⁶Then Moses brought Aaron and his sons forward and washed them with water. ⁷He put the tunic on him, girded him with the sash, clothed him with the robe, and put the ephod on him, girding him with the decorated band with which he tied it to him. ⁸He put the breastpiece on him, and put into the breastpiece the Urim and Thummim.ᵃ ⁹And he set the headdress on his head; and on the headdress, in front, he put the gold frontlet, the holy diadem—as the LORD had commanded Moses.

¹⁰Moses took the anointing oil and anointed the Tabernacle and all that was in it, thus consecrating them. ¹¹He sprinkled some of it on the altar seven times, anointing the altar, all its utensils, and the laver with its stand, to consecrate them. ¹²He poured some of the anointing oil upon Aaron's head and anointed him, to consecrate him. ¹³Moses then brought Aaron's sons forward, clothed them in tunics, girded them with sashes, and wound turbans upon them, as the LORD had commanded Moses.

¹⁴He led forward the bull of sin offering. Aaron and his sons laid their hands upon the head of the bull of sin offering, ¹⁵and it was slaughtered. Moses took the blood and with his finger put some on each of the horns of the altar, cleansing the altar; then he poured out the blood at the base of the altar. Thus he consecrated it in order to make expiation upon it.

¹⁶Moses then took all the fat that was about the entrails, and the protuberance of the liver, and the two kidneys and their fat, and turned them into smoke on the altar. ¹⁷The rest of the bull, its hide, its flesh, and its dung, he put to the fire outside the camp—as the LORD had commanded Moses.

¹⁸Then he brought forward the ram of burnt offering. Aaron and his sons laid their hands upon the ram's head, ¹⁹and it was slaughtered. Moses dashed the blood against all sides of the altar. ²⁰The ram was cut up into sections and Moses turned the head, the sections, and the suet into smoke on the altar; ²¹Moses washed the entrails and the legs with water and turned all of the ram into smoke. That was a burnt offering for a pleasing odor, an offering by fire to the LORD—as the LORD had commanded Moses.

²²He brought forward the second ram, the ram of ordination. Aaron and his sons laid their hands upon the ram's head, ²³and it was slaughtered. Moses took some of its blood and put it on the ridgeᵇ of Aaron's right ear, and on the thumb of his right hand, and on the big toe of his right foot. ²⁴Moses then brought forward the sons of Aaron, and put some of the blood on the ridges of their right ears, and on the thumbs

ᵃ See note on Exod. 28.30.
ᵇ Or "lobe."

of their right hands, and on the big toes of their right feet; and the rest of the blood Moses dashed against every side of the altar. ²⁵He took the fat—the broad tail, all the fat about the entrails, the protuberance of the liver, and the two kidneys and their fat—and the right thigh. ²⁶From the basket of unleavened bread that was before the LORD, he took one cake of unleavened bread, one cake of oil bread, and one wafer, and placed them on the fat parts and on the right thigh. ²⁷He placed all these on the palms of Aaron and on the palms of his sons, and elevated them as an elevation offering before the LORD. ²⁸Then Moses took them from their hands and turned them into smoke on the altar with the burnt offering. This was an ordination offering for a pleasing odor; it was an offering by fire to the LORD. ²⁹Moses took the breast and elevated it as an elevation offering before the LORD; it was Moses' portion of the ram of ordination—as the LORD had commanded Moses.

³⁰And Moses took some of the anointing oil and some of the blood that was on the altar and sprinkled it upon Aaron and upon his vestments, and also upon his sons and upon their vestments. Thus he consecrated Aaron and his vestments, and also his sons and their vestments.

³¹Moses said to Aaron and his sons: Boil the flesh at the entrance of the Tent of Meeting and eat it there with the bread that is in the basket of ordination—as I commanded:ᶜ Aaron and his sons shall eat it; ³²and what is left over of the flesh and the bread you shall consume in fire. ³³You shall not go outside the entrance of the Tent of Meeting for seven days, until the day that your period of ordination is completed. For your ordination will require seven days. ³⁴Everything done today, the LORD has commanded to be done [seven days], to make expiation for you. ³⁵You shall remain at the entrance of the Tent of Meeting day and night for seven days, keeping the LORD's charge—that you may not die—for so I have been commanded.

³⁶And Aaron and his sons did all the things that the LORD had commanded through Moses.

9

שמיני

On the eighth day Moses called Aaron and his sons, and the elders of Israel. ²He said to Aaron: "Take a calf of the herd for a sin offering and a ram for a burnt offering, without blemish, and bring them before the LORD. ³And speak to the Israelites, saying: Take a he-goat for a sin

---

ᶜ Or, vocalizing suwwethi, "I have been commanded"; cf. below, v. 35 and 10.13.

offering; a calf and a lamb, yearlings without blemish, for a burnt offering; [4]and an ox and a ram for an offering of well-being to sacrifice before the LORD; and a meal offering with oil mixed in. For today the LORD will appear to you."

[5]They brought to the front of the Tent of Meeting the things that Moses had commanded, and the whole community came forward and stood before the LORD. [6]Moses said: "This is what the LORD has commanded that you do, that the Presence of the LORD may appear to you." [7]Then Moses said to Aaron: "Come forward to the altar and sacrifice your sin offering and your burnt offering, making expiation for yourself and for the people; and sacrifice the people's offering and make expiation for them, as the LORD has commanded."

[8]Aaron came forward to the altar and slaughtered his calf of sin offering. [9]Aaron's sons brought the blood to him; he dipped his finger in the blood and put it on the horns of the altar; and he poured out the rest of the blood at the base of the altar. [10]The fat, the kidneys, and the protuberance of the liver from the sin offering he turned into smoke on the altar—as the LORD had commanded Moses; [11]and the flesh and the skin were consumed in fire outside the camp. [12]Then he slaughtered the burnt offering. Aaron's sons passed the blood to him, and he dashed it against all sides of the altar. [13]They passed the burnt offering to him in sections, as well as the head, and he turned it into smoke on the altar. [14]He washed the entrails and the legs, and turned them into smoke on the altar with the burnt offering.

[15]Next he brought forward the people's offering. He took the goat for the people's sin offering, and slaughtered it, and presented it as a sin offering like the previous one. [16]He brought forward the burnt offering and sacrificed it according to regulation. [17]He then brought forward the meal offering and, taking a handful of it, he turned it into smoke on the altar—in addition to the burnt offering of the morning.[a] [18]He slaughtered the ox and the ram, the people's sacrifice of well-being. Aaron's sons passed the blood to him—which he dashed against every side of the altar— [19]and the fat parts of the ox and the ram: the broad tail, the covering [fat], the kidneys, and the protuberances of the livers. [20]They laid these fat parts over the breasts; and Aaron[b] turned the fat parts into smoke on the altar, [21]and elevated the breasts and the right thighs as an elevation offering before the LORD—as Moses had commanded.

a *See Exod. 29.38–46.*
b *This word moved up from v. 21 for clarity.*

²²Aaron lifted his hands toward the people and blessed them; and he stepped down after offering the sin offering, the burnt offering, and the offering of well-being. ²³Moses and Aaron then went inside the Tent of Meeting. When they came out, they blessed the people; and the Presence of the Lord appeared to all the people. ²⁴Fire came forth from before the LORD and consumed the burnt offering and the fat parts on the altar. And all the people saw, and shouted, and fell on their faces.

10

Now Aaron's sons Nadab and Abihu each took his fire pan, put fire in it, and laid incense on it; and they offered before the LORD alien fire, which He had not enjoined upon them. ²And fire came forth from the LORD and consumed them; thus they died ᵃ⁻at the instance of⁻ᵃ the LORD. ³Then Moses said to Aaron, "This is what the LORD meant when He said:

Through those near to Me I show Myself holy,
And gain glory before all the people."
And Aaron was silent.

⁴Moses called Mishael and Elzaphan, sons of Uzziel the uncle of Aaron, and said to them, "Come forward and carry your kinsmen away from the front of the sanctuary to a place outside the camp." ⁵They came forward and carried them out of the camp by their tunics, as Moses had ordered. ⁶And Moses said to Aaron and to his sons Eleazar and Ithamar, "Do not ᵇ⁻bare your heads⁻ᵇ and do not rend your clothes, lest you die and anger strike the whole community. But your kinsmen, all the house of Israel, shall bewail the burning that the LORD has wrought. ⁷And so do not go outside the entrance of the Tent of Meeting, lest you die, for the LORD's anointing oil is upon you." And they did as Moses had bidden.

⁸And the LORD spoke to Aaron, saying: ⁹Drink no wine or other intoxicant, you or your sons, when you enter the Tent of Meeting, that you may not die. This is a law for all time throughout the ages, ¹⁰for you must distinguish between the sacred and the profane, and between the unclean and the clean; ¹¹and you must teach the Israelites all the laws which the LORD has imparted to them through Moses.

¹²Moses spoke to Aaron and to his remaining sons, Eleazar and Itha-

ᵃ⁻ᵃ Others "before."
ᵇ⁻ᵇ Or "dishevel your hair."

mar: Take the meal offering that is left over from the LORD's offerings by fire and eat it unleavened beside the altar, for it is most holy. [13]You shall eat it in the sacred precinct, inasmuch as it is your due, and that of your children, from the LORD's offerings by fire; for so I have been commanded. [14]But the breast of elevation offering and the thigh of gift offering you, and your sons and daughters with you, may eat in any clean place, for they have been assigned as a due to you and your children from the Israelites' sacrifices of well-being. [15]Together with the fat of fire offering, they must present the thigh of gift offering and the breast of elevation offering, which are to be elevated as an elevation offering before the LORD, and which are to be your due and that of your children with you for all time—as the LORD has commanded.

[16]Then Moses inquired about the goat of sin offering, and it had already been burned! He was angry with Eleazar and Ithamar, Aaron's remaining sons, and said, [17]"Why did you not eat the sin offering in the sacred area? For it is most holy, and He has given it to you to remove the guilt of the community and to make expiation for them before the LORD. [18]Since its blood was not brought inside the sanctuary,[c] you should certainly have eaten it in the sanctuary, as I commanded." [19]And Aaron spoke to Moses, "See, this day they brought their sin offering and their burnt offering before the LORD, and such things have befallen me! Had I eaten sin offering today, would the LORD have approved?" [20]And when Moses heard this, he approved.

11 The LORD spoke to Moses and Aaron, saying to them: [2]Speak to the Israelite people thus:

These are the creatures that you may eat from among all the land animals: [3]any animal that has true hoofs, with clefts through the hoofs, and that chews[a] the cud—such you may eat. [4]The following, however, of those that either chew the cud or have true hoofs, you shall not eat: the camel—although it chews the cud, it has no true hoofs: it is unclean for you; [5]the daman—although it chews the cud, it has no true hoofs: it is unclean for you; [6]the hare—although it chews the cud, it has no true hoofs: it is unclean for you; [7]and the swine—although it has true hoofs, with the hoofs cleft through, it does not chew the cud: it is unclean for you. [8]You

---

[c] As is done in the case of the most solemn offerings; see 4.3–21; 16.11–17.

[a] Lit. "brings up."

shall not eat of their flesh or touch their carcasses; they are unclean for you.

⁹These you may eat of all that live in water: anything in water, whether in the seas or in the streams, that has fins and scales—these you may eat. ¹⁰But anything in the seas or in the streams that has no fins and scales, among all the swarming things of the water and among all the other living creatures that are in the water—they are an abomination for you ¹¹and an abomination for you they shall remain: you shall not eat of their flesh and you shall abominate their carcasses. ¹²Everything in water that has no fins and scales shall be an abomination for you.

¹³The following^b you shall abominate among the birds—they shall not be eaten, they are an abomination: the eagle, the vulture, and the black vulture; ¹⁴the kite, falcons of every variety; ¹⁵all varieties of raven; ¹⁶the ostrich, the nighthawk, the sea gull; hawks of every variety; ¹⁷the little owl, the cormorant, and the great owl; ¹⁸the white owl, the pelican, and the bustard; ¹⁹the stork; herons of every variety; the hoopoe, and the bat.

²⁰All winged swarming things that walk on fours shall be an abomination for you. ²¹But these you may eat among all the winged swarming things that walk on fours: all that have, above their feet, jointed legs to leap with on the ground—²²of these you may eat the following:^b locusts of every variety; all varieties of bald locust; crickets of every variety; and all varieties of grasshopper. ²³But all other winged swarming things that have four legs shall be an abomination for you.

²⁴And the following shall make you unclean—whoever touches their carcasses shall be unclean until evening, ²⁵and whoever carries the carcasses of any of them shall wash his clothes and be unclean until evening—²⁶every animal that has true hoofs but without clefts through the hoofs, or that does not chew the cud. They are unclean for you; whoever touches them shall be unclean. ²⁷Also all animals that walk on paws, among those that walk on fours, are unclean for you; whoever touches their carcasses shall be unclean until evening. ²⁸And anyone who carries their carcasses shall wash his clothes and remain unclean until evening. They are unclean for you.

²⁹The following^b shall be unclean for you from among the things that swarm on the earth: the mole, the mouse, and great lizards of every variety; ³⁰the gecko, the land crocodile, the lizard, the sand lizard, and the chameleon. ³¹Those are for you the unclean among all the swarming

---

^b *A number of these cannot be identified with certainty.*

things; whoever touches them when they are dead shall be unclean until evening. ³²And anything on which one of them falls when dead shall be unclean: be it any article of wood, or a cloth, or a skin, or a sack—any such article that can be put to use shall be dipped in water, and it shall remain unclean until evening; then it shall be clean. ³³And if any of those falls into an earthen vessel, everything inside it shall be unclean and [the vessel] itself you shall break. ³⁴As to any food that may be eaten, it shall become unclean if it came in contact with water;^c as to any liquid that may be drunk, it shall become unclean if it was inside any vessel.^d ³⁵Everything on which the carcass of any of them falls shall be unclean: an oven or stove shall be smashed. They are unclean and unclean they shall remain for you. ³⁶However, a spring or cistern in which water is collected shall be clean, but whoever touches such a carcass in it shall be unclean. ³⁷If such a carcass falls upon seed grain that is to be sown, it is clean; ³⁸but if water is put on the seed and any part of a carcass falls upon it, it shall be unclean for you.

³⁹If an animal that you may eat has died, anyone who touches its carcass shall be unclean until evening; ⁴⁰anyone who eats of its carcass shall wash his clothes and remain unclean until evening; and anyone who carries its carcass shall wash his clothes and remain unclean until evening.

⁴¹All the things that swarm upon the earth are an abomination; they shall not be eaten. ⁴²You shall not eat, among all things that swarm upon the earth, anything that crawls on its belly, or anything that walks on fours, or anything that has many legs; for they are an abomination. ⁴³You shall not draw abomination upon yourselves through anything that swarms; you shall not make yourselves unclean therewith and thus become unclean. ⁴⁴For I the LORD am your God: you shall sanctify yourselves and be holy, for I am holy. You shall not make yourselves unclean through any swarming thing that moves upon the earth. ⁴⁵For I the LORD am He who brought you up from the land of Egypt to be your God: you shall be holy, for I am holy.

⁴⁶These are the instructions concerning animals, birds, all living creatures that move in water, and all creatures that swarm on earth, ⁴⁷for distinguishing between the unclean and the clean, between the living things that may be eaten and the living things that may not be eaten.

---

^c *I.e., if the food then came in contact with the carcass of any animal named in vv. 29–30.*
^d *I.e., a vessel that had become contaminated by such contact.*

תזריע

12 The LORD spoke to Moses, saying: [2]Speak to the Israelite people thus: When a woman at childbirth[a] bears a male, she shall be unclean seven days; she shall be unclean as at the time of her menstrual infirmity.— [3]On the eighth day the flesh of his foreskin shall be circumcised.—[4]She shall remain in a state of blood purification[b] for thirty-three days: she shall not touch any consecrated thing, nor enter the sanctuary until her period of purification is completed. [5]If she bears a female, she shall be unclean two weeks as during her menstruation, and she shall remain in a state of blood purification[b] for sixty-six days.

[6]On the completion of her period of purification, for either son or daughter, she shall bring to the priest, at the entrance of the Tent of Meeting, a lamb in its first year for a burnt offering, and a pigeon or a turtledove for a sin offering.[c] [7]He shall offer it before the LORD and make expiation on her behalf; she shall then be clean from her flow of blood. Such are the rituals concerning her who bears a child, male or female. [8]If, however, her means do not suffice for a sheep, she shall take two turtle-doves or two pigeons, one for a burnt offering and the other for a sin offering. The priest shall make expiation on her behalf, and she shall be clean.

13 The LORD spoke to Moses and Aaron, saying:
[2]When a person has on the skin of his body a swelling, a rash, or a discoloration, and it develops into a scaly affection on the skin of his body, it shall be reported[a] to Aaron the priest or to one of his sons, the priests. [3]The priest shall examine the affection on the skin of his body: if hair in the affected patch has turned white and the affection appears to be deeper than the skin of his body, it is a leprous affection;[b] when the priest sees it, he shall pronounce him unclean. [4]But if it is a white discoloration on the skin of his body which does not appear to be deeper than the skin and the hair in it has not turned white, the priest shall isolate the affected person for seven days. [5]On the seventh day the priest shall examine him, and if the affection has remained unchanged in color and the disease has not spread on the skin, the priest shall isolate him for

---

a *Heb. tazria', lit. "brings forth seed."*
b *Meaning of Heb. uncertain.*
c *See note at 4.3.*

a *Or "he shall be brought."*
b *Heb. ṣara'ath is used for a variety of diseases. Where a human being is declared unclean by reason of ṣara'ath, the traditional translation "leprosy" has been retained without regard to modern medical terminology.*

another seven days. [6]On the seventh day the priest shall examine him again: if the affection has faded and has not spread on the skin, the priest shall pronounce him clean. It is a rash; he shall wash his clothes, and he shall be clean. [7]But if the rash should spread on the skin after he has presented himself to the priest and been pronounced clean, he shall present himself again to the priest. [8]And if the priest sees that the rash has spread on the skin, the priest shall pronounce him unclean; it is leprosy.

[9]When a person has a scaly affection, it shall be reported[c] to the priest. [10]If the priest finds on the skin a white swelling which has turned some hair white, with [d-]a patch of undiscolored flesh[-d] in the swelling, [11]it is chronic leprosy on the skin of his body, and the priest shall pronounce him unclean; he need not isolate him, for he is unclean. [12]If the eruption spreads out over the skin so that it covers all the skin of the affected person from head to foot, wherever the priest can see—[13]if the priest sees that the eruption has covered the whole body—he shall pronounce the affected person clean; he is clean, for he has turned all white. [14]But as soon as undiscolored flesh appears in it, he shall be unclean; [15]when the priest sees the undiscolored flesh, he shall pronounce him unclean. The undiscolored flesh is unclean; it is leprosy. [16]But if the undiscolored flesh again turns white, he shall come to the priest, [17]and the priest shall examine him: if the affection has turned white, the priest shall pronounce the affected person clean; he is clean.

[18]When an inflammation appears on the skin of one's body and it heals, [19]and a white swelling or a white discoloration streaked with red develops where the inflammation was, he shall present himself to the priest. [20]If the priest finds that it appears lower than the rest of the skin and that the hair in it has turned white, the priest shall pronounce him unclean; it is a leprous affection that has broken out in the inflammation. [21]But if the priest finds that there is no white hair in it and it is not lower than the rest of the skin, and it is faded, the priest shall isolate him for seven days. [22]If it should spread in the skin, the priest shall pronounce him unclean; it is an affection. [23]But if the discoloration remains stationary, not having spread, it is the scar of the inflammation; the priest shall pronounce him clean.

[24]When the skin of one's body sustains a burn by fire, and the patch from the burn is a discoloration, either white streaked with red, or white, [25]the priest shall examine it. If some hair has turned white in the discoloration, which itself appears to go deeper than the skin, it is leprosy that has broken out in the burn. The priest shall pronounce him unclean; it is

[c] *See note a at 12.2.*
[d-d] *Others "quick raw flesh."*

a leprous affection. 26But if the priest finds that there is no white hair in the discoloration, and that it is not lower than the rest of the skin, and it is faded, the priest shall isolate him for seven days. 27On the seventh day the priest shall examine him: if it has spread in the skin, the priest shall pronounce him unclean; it is a leprous affection. 28But if the discoloration has remained stationary, not having spread on the skin, and it is faded, it is the swelling from the burn. The priest shall pronounce him clean, for it is the scar of the burn.

29If a man or a woman has an affection on the head or in the beard, 30the priest shall examine the affection. If it appears to go deeper than the skin and there is thin yellow hair in it, the priest shall pronounce him unclean; it is a scall, a scaly eruption in the hair or beard. 31But if the priest finds that the scall affection does not appear to go deeper than the skin, yet there is no black hair in it, the priest shall isolate the person with the scall affection for seven days. 32On the seventh day the priest shall examine the affection. If the scall has not spread and no yellow hair has appeared in it, and the scall does not appear to go deeper than the skin, 33the person with the scall shall shave himself, but without shaving the scall; the priest shall isolate him for another seven days. 34On the seventh day the priest shall examine the scall. If the scall has not spread on the skin, and does not appear to go deeper than the skin, the priest shall pronounce him clean; he shall wash his clothes, and he shall be clean. 35If, however, the scall should spread on the skin after he has been pronounced clean, 36the priest shall examine him. If the scall has spread on the skin, the priest need not look for yellow hair: he is unclean. 37But if the scall has remained unchanged in color, and black hair has grown in it, the scall is healed; he is clean. The priest shall pronounce him clean.

38If a man or a woman has the skin of the body streaked with white discolorations, 39and the priest sees that the discolorations on the skin of the body are of a dull white, it is a tetter broken out on the skin; he is clean.

40If a man loses the hair of his head and becomes bald, he is clean. 41If he loses the hair on the front part of his head and becomes bald at the forehead, he is clean. 42But if a white affection streaked with red appears on the bald part in the front or at the back of the head, it is a scaly eruption that is spreading over the bald part in the front or at the back of the head. 43The priest shall examine him: if the swollen affection on the bald part in the front or at the back of his head is white streaked with red, like the leprosy of body skin in appearance, 44the man is leprous; he is unclean. The priest shall pronounce him unclean; he has the affection on his head.

[45]As for the person with a leprous affection, his clothes shall be rent,
his head shall be left bare,[e] and he shall cover over his upper lip; and he
shall call out, "Unclean! Unclean!" [46]He shall be unclean as long as the
disease is on him. Being unclean, he shall dwell apart; his dwelling shall
be outside the camp.

[47]When an eruptive affection occurs in a cloth of wool or linen fabric,
[48]in the warp or in the woof of the linen or the wool, or in a skin or in
anything made of skin; [49]if the affection in the cloth or the skin, in the
warp or the woof, or in any article of skin, is streaky green[f] or red, it is
an eruptive affection. It shall be shown to the priest; [50]and the priest,
after examining the affection, shall isolate the affected article for seven
days. [51]On the seventh day he shall examine the affection: if the affection
has spread in the cloth—whether in the warp or the woof, or in the skin,
for whatever purpose the skin may be used—the affection is a malignant
eruption; it is unclean. [52]The cloth—whether warp or woof in wool or
linen, or any article of skin—in which the affection is found, shall be
burned, for it is a malignant eruption; it shall be consumed in fire. [53]But
if the priest sees that the affection in the cloth—whether in warp or in
woof, or in any article of skin—has not spread, [54]the priest shall order
the affected article washed, and he shall isolate it for another seven days.
[55]And if, after the affected article has been washed, the priest sees that
the affection has not changed color and that it has not spread, it is unclean.
It shall be consumed in fire; it is a fret,[g] whether on its inner side or on
its outer side. [56]But if the priest sees that the affected part, after it has
been washed, is faded, he shall tear it out from the cloth or skin, whether
in the warp or in the woof; [57]and if it occurs again in the cloth—whether
in warp or in woof—or in any article of skin, it is a wild growth; the
affected article shall be consumed in fire. [58]If, however, the affection dis-
appears from the cloth—warp or woof—or from any article of skin that
has been washed, it shall be washed again, and it shall be clean.

[59]Such is the procedure for eruptive affections of cloth, woolen or linen,
in warp or in woof, or of any article of skin, for pronouncing it clean or
unclean.

[e] *See note at 10.6.*
[f] *Or "yellow."*
[g] *Meaning of Heb.* pehetheth *uncertain.*

מצרע

14 The LORD spoke to Moses, saying: [2]This shall be the ritual for a leper at the time that he is to be cleansed.

When it has been reported[a] to the priest, [3]the priest shall go outside the camp. If the priest sees that the leper has been healed of his scaly affection, [4]the priest shall order two live clean birds, cedar wood, crimson stuff, and hyssop to be brought for him who is to be cleansed. [5]The priest shall order one of the birds slaughtered over fresh water in an earthen vessel; [6]and he shall take the live bird, along with the cedar wood, the crimson stuff, and the hyssop, and dip them together with the live bird in the blood of the bird that was slaughtered over the fresh water. [7]He shall then sprinkle it seven times on him who is to be cleansed of the eruption and cleanse him; and he shall set the live bird free in the open country. [8]The one to be cleansed shall wash his clothes, shave off all his hair, and bathe in water; then he shall be clean. After that he may enter the camp, but he must remain outside his tent seven days. [9]On the seventh day he shall shave off all his hair—of head, beard, and eyebrows. When he has shaved off all his hair, he shall wash his clothes and bathe his body in water; then he shall be clean. [10]On the eighth day he shall take two male lambs without blemish, one ewe lamb in its first year without blemish, three-tenths of a measure of choice flour with oil mixed in for a meal offering, and one *log* of oil. [11]These shall be presented before the LORD, with the man to be cleansed, at the entrance of the Tent of Meeting, by the priest who performs the cleansing.

[12]The priest shall take one of the male lambs and offer it with the *log* of oil as a guilt offering, and he shall elevate them as an elevation offering before the LORD. [13]The lamb shall be slaughtered at the spot in the sacred area where the sin offering and the burnt offering are slaughtered.[b] For the guilt offering, like the sin offering, goes to the priest; it is most holy. [14]The priest shall take some of the blood of the guilt offering, and the priest shall put it on the ridge of the right ear of him who is being cleansed, and on the thumb of his right hand, and on the big toe of his right foot. [15]The priest shall then take some of the *log* of oil and pour it into the palm of his own left hand. [16]And the priest shall dip his right finger in the oil that is in the palm of his left hand and sprinkle some of the oil with his finger seven times before the LORD. [17]Some of the oil

---

[a] *Cf. note a at 13.2.*
[b] *See 1.11; 4.23.*

left in his palm shall be put by the priest on the ridge of the right ear of the one being cleansed, on the thumb of his right hand, and on the big toe of his right foot—over the blood of the guilt offering. ¹⁸The rest of the oil in his palm the priest shall put on the head of the one being cleansed. Thus the priest shall make expiation for him before the LORD. ¹⁹The priest shall then offer the sin offering and make expiation for the one being cleansed of his uncleanness. Last, the burnt offering shall be slaughtered, ²⁰and the priest shall offer the burnt offering and the meal offering on the altar, and the priest shall make expiation for him. Then he shall be clean.

²¹If, however, he is poor and his means are insufficient, he shall take one male lamb for a guilt offering, to be elevated in expiation for him, one-tenth of a measure of choice flour with oil mixed in for a meal offering, and a *log* of oil; ²²and two turtledoves or two pigeons, depending on his means, the one to be the sin offering and the other the burnt offering. ²³On the eighth day of his cleansing he shall bring them to the priest at the entrance of the Tent of Meeting, before the LORD. ²⁴The priest shall take the lamb of guilt offering and the *log* of oil, and elevate them as an elevation offering before the LORD. ²⁵When the lamb of guilt offering has been slaughtered, the priest shall take some of the blood of the guilt offering and put it on the ridge of the right ear of the one being cleansed, on the thumb of his right hand, and on the big toe of his right foot. ²⁶The priest shall then pour some of the oil into the palm of his own left hand, ²⁷and with the finger of his right hand the priest shall sprinkle some of the oil that is in the palm of his left hand seven times before the LORD. ²⁸Some of the oil in his palm shall be put by the priest on the ridge of the right ear of the one being cleansed, on the thumb of his right hand, and on the big toe of his right foot, over the same places as the blood of the guilt offering; ²⁹and what is left of the oil in his palm the priest shall put on the head of the one being cleansed, to make expiation for him before the LORD. ³⁰He shall then offer one of the turtledoves or pigeons, depending on his means—³¹whichever he can afford—the one as a sin offering and the other as a burnt offering, together with the meal offering. Thus the priest shall make expiation before the LORD for the one being cleansed. ³²Such is the ritual for him who has a scaly affection and whose means for his cleansing are limited.

³³The LORD spoke to Moses and Aaron, saying:

³⁴When you enter the land of Canaan that I give you as a possession,

and I inflict an eruptive plague upon a house in the land you possess, [35]the owner of the house shall come and tell the priest, saying, "Something like a plague has appeared upon my house." [36]The priest shall order the house cleared before the priest enters to examine the plague, so that nothing in the house may become unclean; after that the priest shall enter to examine the house. [37]If, when he examines the plague, the plague in the walls of the house is found to consist of greenish[c] or reddish streaks[d] that appear to go deep into the wall, [38]the priest shall come out of the house to the entrance of the house, and close up the house for seven days. [39]On the seventh day the priest shall return. If he sees that the plague has spread on the walls of the house, [40]the priest shall order the stones with the plague in them to be pulled out and cast outside the city into an unclean place. [41]The house shall be scraped inside all around, and the coating[e] that is scraped off shall be dumped outside the city in an unclean place. [42]They shall take other stones and replace those stones with them, and take other coating and plaster the house.

[43]If the plague again breaks out in the house, after the stones have been pulled out and after the house has been scraped and replastered, [44]the priest shall come to examine: if the plague has spread in the house, it is a malignant eruption in the house; it is unclean. [45]The house shall be torn down—its stones and timber and all the coating on the house—and taken to an unclean place outside the city.

[46]Whoever enters the house while it is closed up shall be unclean until evening. [47]Whoever sleeps in the house must wash his clothes, and whoever eats in the house must wash his clothes.

[48]If, however, the priest comes and sees that the plague has not spread in the house after the house was replastered, the priest shall pronounce the house clean, for the plague has healed. [49]To purge the house, he shall take two birds, cedar wood, crimson stuff, and hyssop. [50]He shall slaughter the one bird over fresh water in an earthen vessel. [51]He shall take the cedar wood, the hyssop, the crimson stuff, and the live bird, and dip them in the blood of the slaughtered bird and the fresh water, and sprinkle on the house seven times. [52]Having purged the house with the blood of the bird, the fresh water, the live bird, the cedar wood, the hyssop, and the crimson stuff, [53]he shall set the live bird free outside the city in the open country. Thus he shall make expiation for the house, and it shall be clean.

[54]Such is the ritual for every eruptive affection—for scalls, [55]for an

---

[c] Or "yellowish."
[d] Meaning of Heb. sheqaʿaruroth uncertain.
[e] Lit. "dust," "mud."

eruption on a cloth or a house, ⁵⁶for swellings, for rashes, or for discolorations—⁵⁷to determine when they are unclean and when they are clean. Such is the ritual concerning eruptions.

15

The LORD spoke to Moses and Aaron, saying: ²Speak to the Israelite people and say to them:

When any man has a discharge issuing from his member,ᵃ he is unclean. ³The uncleanness from his discharge shall mean the following—whether his member runs with the discharge or is stopped up so that there is no discharge, his uncleanness means this: ⁴Any bedding on which the one with the discharge lies shall be unclean, and every object on which he sits shall be unclean. ⁵Anyone who touches his bedding shall wash his clothes, bathe in water, and remain unclean until evening. ⁶Whoever sits on an object on which the one with the discharge has sat shall wash his clothes, bathe in water, and remain unclean until evening. ⁷Whoever touches the body of the one with the discharge shall wash his clothes, bathe in water, and remain unclean until evening. ⁸If one with a discharge spits on one who is clean, the latter shall wash his clothes, bathe in water, and remain unclean until evening. ⁹Any means for riding that one with a discharge has mounted shall be unclean; ¹⁰whoever touches anything that was under him shall be unclean until evening; and whoever carries such things shall wash his clothes, bathe in water, and remain unclean until evening. ¹¹If one with a discharge, without having rinsed his hands in water, touches another person, that person shall wash his clothes, bathe in water, and remain unclean until evening. ¹²An earthen vessel that one with a discharge touches shall be broken; and any wooden implement shall be rinsed with water.

¹³When one with a discharge becomes clean of his discharge, he shall count off seven days for his cleansing, wash his clothes, and bathe his body in fresh water; then he shall be clean. ¹⁴On the eighth day he shall take two turtledoves or two pigeons and come before the LORD at the entrance of the Tent of Meeting and give them to the priest. ¹⁵The priest shall offer them, the one as a sin offering and the other as a burnt offering. Thus the priest shall make expiation on his behalf, for his discharge, before the LORD.

ᵃ Lit. "flesh."

16When a man has an emission of semen, he shall bathe his whole body in water and remain unclean until evening. 17All cloth or leather on which semen falls shall be washed in water and remain unclean until evening. 18And if a man has carnal relations with a woman, they shall bathe in water and remain unclean until evening.

19When a woman has a discharge, her discharge being blood from her body, she shall remain in her impurity seven days; whoever touches her shall be unclean until evening. 20Anything that she lies on during her impurity shall be unclean; and anything that she sits on shall be unclean. 21Anyone who touches her bedding shall wash his clothes, bathe in water, and remain unclean until evening; 22and anyone who touches any object on which she has sat shall wash his clothes, bathe in water, and remain unclean until evening. 23Be it the bedding or be it the object on which she has sat, on touching it he shall be unclean until evening. 24And if a man lies with her, her impurity is communicated to him; he shall be unclean seven days, and any bedding on which he lies shall become unclean.

25When a woman has had a discharge of blood for many days, not at the time of her impurity, or when she has a discharge beyond her period of impurity, she shall be unclean, as though at the time of her impurity, as long as her discharge lasts. 26Any bedding on which she lies while her discharge lasts shall be for her like bedding during her impurity; and any object on which she sits shall become unclean, as it does during her impurity: 27whoever touches them shall be unclean; he shall wash his clothes, bathe in water, and remain unclean until evening.

28When she becomes clean of her discharge, she shall count off seven days, and after that she shall be clean. 29On the eighth day she shall take two turtledoves or two pigeons, and bring them to the priest at the entrance of the Tent of Meeting. 30The priest shall offer the one as a sin offering and the other as a burnt offering; and the priest shall make expiation on her behalf, for her unclean discharge, before the LORD.

31You shall put the Israelites on guard against their uncleanness, lest they die through their uncleanness by defiling My Tabernacle which is among them.

32Such is the ritual concerning him who has a discharge: concerning him who has an emission of semen and becomes unclean thereby, 33and concerning her who is in menstrual infirmity, and concerning anyone, male or female, who has a discharge, and concerning a man who lies with an unclean woman.

16

אחרי מות

The LORD spoke to Moses after the death of the two sons of Aaron who died when they drew too close to the presence of the LORD. 2The LORD said to Moses:

Tell your brother Aaron that he is not to come at will[a] into the Shrine behind the curtain, in front of the cover that is upon the ark, lest he die; for I appear in the cloud over the cover. 3Thus only shall Aaron enter the Shrine: with a bull of the herd for a sin offering and a ram for a burnt offering.—4He shall be dressed in a sacral linen tunic, with linen breeches next to his flesh, and be girt with a linen sash, and he shall wear a linen turban. They are sacral vestments; he shall bathe his body in water and then put them on.—5And from the Israelite community he shall take two he-goats for a sin offering and a ram for a burnt offering.

6Aaron is to offer his own bull of sin offering, to make expiation for himself and for his household. 7Aaron[b] shall take the two he-goats and let them stand before the LORD at the entrance of the Tent of Meeting; 8and he shall place lots upon the two goats, one marked for the LORD and the other marked for Azazel. 9Aaron shall bring forward the goat designated by lot for the LORD, which he is to offer as a sin offering; 10while the goat designated by lot for Azazel shall be left standing alive before the LORD, to make expiation with it and to send it off to the wilderness for Azazel.

11Aaron shall then offer his bull of sin offering, to make expiation for himself and his household. He shall slaughter his bull of sin offering, 12and he shall take a panful of glowing coals scooped from the altar before the LORD, and two handfuls of finely ground aromatic incense, and bring this behind the curtain. 13He shall put the incense on the fire before the LORD, so that the cloud from the incense screens the cover that is over [the Ark of] the Pact, lest he die. 14He shall take some of the blood of the bull and sprinkle it with his finger over the cover on the east side; and in front of the cover he shall sprinkle some of the blood with his finger seven times. 15He shall then slaughter the people's goat of sin offering, bring its blood behind the curtain, and do with its blood as he

---

a Lit. "at any time."
b Moved up from v. 8 for clarity.

has done with the blood of the bull: he shall sprinkle it over the cover and in front of the cover.

¹⁶Thus he shall purge the Shrine of the uncleanness and transgression of the Israelites, whatever their sins; and he shall do the same for the Tent of Meeting, which abides with them in the midst of their uncleanness. ¹⁷When he goes in to make expiation in the Shrine, nobody else shall be in the Tent of Meeting until he comes out.

When he has made expiation for himself and his household, and for the whole congregation of Israel, ¹⁸he shall go out to the altar that is before the LORD and purge it: he shall take some of the blood of the bull and of the goat and apply it to each of the horns of the altar; ¹⁹and the rest of the blood he shall sprinkle on it with his finger seven times. Thus he shall cleanse it of the uncleanness of the Israelites and consecrate it.

²⁰When he has finished purging the Shrine, the Tent of Meeting, and the altar, the live goat shall be brought forward. ²¹Aaron shall lay both his hands upon the head of the live goat and confess over it all the iniquities and transgressions of the Israelites, whatever their sins, putting them on the head of the goat; and it shall be sent off to the wilderness through a designated^c man. ²²Thus the goat shall carry on it all their iniquities to an inaccessible region; and the goat shall be set free in the wilderness.

²³And Aaron shall go into the Tent of Meeting, take off the linen vestments that he put on when he entered the Shrine, and leave them there. ²⁴He shall bathe his body in water in the holy precinct and put on his vestments; then he shall come out and offer his burnt offering and the burnt offering of the people, making expiation for himself and for the people. ²⁵The fat of the sin offering he shall turn into smoke on the altar.

²⁶He who set the Azazel-goat free shall wash his clothes and bathe his body in water; after that he may reenter the camp.

²⁷The bull of sin offering and the goat of sin offering whose blood was brought in to purge the Shrine shall be taken outside the camp; and their hides, flesh, and dung shall be consumed in fire. ²⁸He who burned them shall wash his clothes and bathe his body in water; after that he may re-enter the camp.

²⁹And this shall be to you a law for all time: In the seventh month, on the tenth day of the month, you shall practice self-denial; and you shall do no manner of work, neither the citizen nor the alien who resides among you. ³⁰For on this day atonement shall be made for you to cleanse you of all your sins; you shall be clean before the LORD. ³¹It shall be a sabbath

---

^c *Meaning of Heb.* ʿitti *uncertain.*

of complete rest for you, and you shall practice self-denial; it is a law for all time. ³²The priest who has been anointed and ordained to serve as priest in place of his father shall make expiation. He shall put on the linen vestments, the sacral vestments. ³³He shall purge the innermost Shrine; he shall purge the Tent of Meeting and the altar; and he shall make expiation for the priests and for all the people of the congregation.

³⁴This shall be to you a law for all time: to make atonement for the Israelites for all their sins once a year.

And Moses did as the LORD had commanded him.

17 The LORD spoke to Moses, saying:

²Speak to Aaron and his sons and to all the Israelite people and say to them:

This is what the LORD has commanded: ³if anyone of the house of Israel slaughters an ox or sheep or goat in the camp, or does so outside the camp, ⁴and does not bring it to the entrance of the Tent of Meeting to present it as an offering to the LORD, before the LORD's Tabernacle, bloodguilt shall be imputed to that man: he has shed blood; that man shall be cut off from among his people. ⁵This is in order that the Israelites may bring the sacrifices which they have been making in the open—that they may bring them before the LORD, to the priest, at the entrance of the Tent of Meeting, and offer them as sacrifices of well-being to the LORD; ⁶that the priest may dash the blood against the altar of the LORD at the entrance of the Tent of Meeting, and turn the fat into smoke as a pleasing odor to the LORD; ⁷and that they may offer their sacrifices no more to the goat-demons after whom they stray. This shall be to them a law for all time, throughout the ages.

⁸Say to them further: If anyone of the house of Israel or of the strangers who reside among them offers a burnt offering or a sacrifice, ⁹and does not bring it to the entrance of the Tent of Meeting to offer it to the LORD, that person shall be cut off from his people.

¹⁰And if anyone of the house of Israel or of the strangers who reside among them partakes of any blood, I will set My face against the person who partakes of the blood, and I will cut him off from among his kin. ¹¹For the life of the flesh is in the blood, and I have assigned it to you for making expiation for your lives upon the altar; it is the blood, as life, that effects expiation. ¹²Therefore I say to the Israelite people: No person

among you shall partake of blood, nor shall the stranger who resides among you partake of blood.

¹³And if any Israelite or any stranger who resides among them hunts down an animal or a bird that may be eaten, he shall pour out its blood and cover it with earth. ¹⁴For the life of all flesh—its blood is its life. Therefore I say to the Israelite people: You shall not partake of the blood of any flesh, for the life of all flesh is its blood. Anyone who partakes of it shall be cut off.

¹⁵Any person, whether citizen or stranger, who eats what has died or has been torn by beasts shall wash his clothes, bathe in water, and remain unclean until evening; then he shall be clean. ¹⁶But if he does not wash [his clothes] and bathe his body, he shall bear his guilt.

18 The LORD spoke to Moses, saying: ²Speak to the Israelite people and say to them:

I the LORD am your God. ³You shall not copy the practices of the land of Egypt where you dwelt, or of the land of Canaan to which I am taking you; nor shall you follow their laws. ⁴My rules alone shall you observe, and faithfully follow My laws: I the LORD am your God.

⁵You shall keep My laws and My rules, by the pursuit of which man shall live: I am the LORD.

⁶None of you shall come near anyone of his own flesh to uncover nakedness: I am the LORD.

⁷ᵃ⁻Your father's nakedness, that is, the nakedness of your mother, you shall not uncover; she is your mother—you shall not uncover her nakedness.

⁸Do not uncover the nakedness of your father's wife;⁻ᵃ it is the nakedness of your father.

⁹The nakedness of your sister—your father's daughter or your mother's, whether born into the household or outside—do not uncover their nakedness.

¹⁰The nakedness of your son's daughter, or of your daughter's daughter—do not uncover their nakedness; for their nakedness is yours.ᵇ

¹¹The nakedness of your father's wife's daughter, who has born into your father's household—she is your sister; do not uncover her nakedness.

¹²Do not uncover the nakedness of your father's sister; she is your father's flesh.

ᵃ⁻ᵃ *A man and his wife are one flesh (Gen. 2.24), even if he should die or divorce her.*
ᵇ *Meaning uncertain.*

¹³Do not uncover the nakedness of your mother's sister; for she is your mother's flesh.

¹⁴Do not uncover the nakedness of your father's brother: do not approach his wife; she is your aunt.

¹⁵Do not uncover the nakedness of your daughter-in-law: she is your son's wife; you shall not uncover her nakedness.

¹⁶ᵃ⁻Do not uncover the nakedness of your brother's wife; it is the nakedness of your brother.⁻ᵃ

¹⁷Do not uncover the nakedness of a woman and her daughter; nor shall you marry her son's daughter or her daughter's daughter and uncover her nakedness: they are kindred; it is depravity.

¹⁸Do not marry a woman as a rival to her sister and uncover her nakedness in the other's lifetime.

¹⁹Do not come near a woman during her period of uncleanness to uncover her nakedness.

²⁰Do not have carnal relations with your neighbor's wife and defile yourself with her.

²¹Do not allow any of your offspring to be offered up to Molech, and do not profane the name of your God: I am the LORD.

²²Do not lie with a male as one lies with a woman; it is an abhorrence.

²³Do not have carnal relations with any beast and defile yourself thereby; and let no woman lend herself to a beast to mate with it; it is perversion.

²⁴Do not defile yourselves in any of those ways, for it is by such that the nations that I am casting out before you defiled themselves. ²⁵Thus the land became defiled; and I called it to account for its iniquity, and the land spewed out its inhabitants. ²⁶But you must keep My laws and My rules, and you must not do any of those abhorrent things, neither the citizen nor the stranger who resides among you; ²⁷for all those abhorrent things were done by the people who were in the land before you, and the land became defiled. ²⁸So let not the land spew you out for defiling it, as it spewed out the nation that came before you. ²⁹All who do any of those abhorrent things—such persons shall be cut off from their people. ³⁰You shall keep My charge not to engage in any of the abhorrent practices that were carried on before you, and you shall not defile yourselves through them: I the LORD am your God.

19

קדשים

The LORD spoke to Moses, saying: ²Speak to the whole Israelite community and say to them:

You shall be holy, for I, the LORD your God, am holy.

³You shall each revere his mother and his father, and keep My sabbaths: I the LORD am your God.

⁴Do not turn to idols or make molten gods for yourselves: I the LORD am your God.

⁵When you sacrifice an offering of well-being to the LORD, sacrifice it so that it may be accepted on your behalf. ⁶It shall be eaten on the day you sacrifice it, or on the day following; but what is left by the third day must be consumed in fire. ⁷If it should be eaten on the third day, it is an offensive thing, it will not be acceptable. ⁸And he who eats of it shall bear his guilt, for he has profaned what is sacred to the LORD; that person shall be cut off from his kin.

⁹When you reap the harvest of your land, you shall not reap all the way to the edges of your field, or gather the gleanings of your harvest. ¹⁰You shall not pick your vineyard bare, or gather the fallen fruit of your vineyard; you shall leave them for the poor and the stranger: I the LORD am your God.

¹¹You shall not steal; you shall not deal deceitfully or falsely with one another. ¹²You shall not swear falsely by My name, profaning the name of your God: I am the LORD.

¹³You shall not defraud your fellow. You shall not commit robbery. The wages of a laborer shall not remain with you until morning.

¹⁴You shall not insult the deaf, or place a stumbling block before the blind. You shall fear your God: I am the LORD.

¹⁵You shall not render an unfair decision: do not favor the poor or show deference to the rich; judge your kinsman fairly. ¹⁶Do not ᵃ⁻deal basely with⁻ᵃ your countrymen. Do not ᵇ⁻profit by⁻ᵇ the blood of your fellow: I am the LORD.

¹⁷You shall not hate your kinsfolk in your heart. Reprove your kinsman butᶜ incur no guilt because of him. ¹⁸You shall not take vengeance or bear a grudge against your countrymen. Love your fellow as yourself: I am the LORD.

¹⁹You shall observe My laws.

ᵃ⁻ᵃ Others "go about as a talebearer among"; meaning of Heb. uncertain.
ᵇ⁻ᵇ Lit. "stand upon"; precise meaning of Heb. phrase uncertain.
ᶜ Exact force of we- uncertain.

You shall not let your cattle mate with a different kind; you shall not sow your field with two kinds of seed; you shall not put on cloth from a mixture of two kinds of material.

20If a man has carnal relations with a woman who is a slave and has been designated for another man, but has not been redeemed or given her freedom, there shall be an indemnity; they shall not, however, be put to death, since she has not been freed. 21But he must bring to the entrance of the Tent of Meeting, as his guilt offering to the LORD, a ram of guilt offering. 22With the ram of guilt offering the priest shall make expiation for him before the LORD for the sin that he committed; and the sin that he committed will be forgiven him.

23When you enter the land and plant any tree for food, you shall regard its fruit as forbidden.d Three years it shall be forbiddend for you, not to be eaten. 24In the fourth year all its fruit shall be set aside for jubilation before the LORD; 25and only in the fifth year may you use its fruit—that its yield to you may be increased: I the LORD am your God.

26You shall not eat anything with its blood. You shall not practice divination or soothsaying. 27You shall not round off the side-growth on your head, or destroy the side-growth of your beard. 28You shall not make gashes in your flesh for the dead, or incise any marks on yourselves: I am the LORD.

29Do not degrade your daughter and make her a harlot, lest the land fall into harlotry and the land be filled with depravity. 30You shall keep My sabbaths and venerate My sanctuary: I am the LORD.

31Do not turn to ghosts and do not inquire of familiar spirits, to be defiled by them: I the LORD am your God.

32You shall rise before the aged and show deference to the old; you shall fear your God: I am the LORD.

33When a stranger resides with you in your land, you shall not wrong him. 34The stranger who resides with you shall be to you as one of your citizens; you shall love him as yourself, for you were strangers in the land of Egypt: I the LORD am your God.

35You shall not falsify measures of length, weight, or capacity. 36You shall have an honest balance, honest weights, an honest *ephah*, and an honest *hin*.

I the LORD am your God who freed you from the land of Egypt. 37You shall faithfully observe all My laws and all My rules: I am the LORD.

d *Heb. root* 'rl, *commonly "to be uncircumcised."*

20

And the LORD spoke to Moses: ²Say further to the Israelite people:

Anyone among the Israelites, or among the strangers residing in Israel, who gives any of his offspring to Molech, shall be put to death; the people of the land shall pelt him with stones. ³And I will set My face against that man and will cut him off from among his people, because he gave of his offspring to Molech and so defiled My sanctuary and profaned My holy name. ⁴And if the people of the land should shut their eyes to that man when he gives of his offspring to Molech, and should not put him to death, ⁵I Myself will set My face against that man and his kin, and will cut off from among their people both him and all who follow him in going astray after Molech. ⁶And if any person turns to ghosts and familiar spirits and goes astray after them, I will set My face against that person and cut him off from among his people.

⁷You shall sanctify yourselves and be holy, for I the LORD am your God. ⁸You shall faithfully observe My laws: I the LORD make you holy.

⁹If anyone insults his father or his mother, he shall be put to death; he has insulted his father and his mother—his bloodguilt is upon him.

¹⁰If a man commits adultery with a married woman, committing adultery with another man's wife, the adulterer and the adulteress shall be put to death. ¹¹If a man lies with his father's wife, it is the nakedness of his father that he has uncovered; the two shall be put to death—their bloodguilt is upon them. ¹²If a man lies with his daughter-in-law, both of them shall be put to death; they have committed incest—their bloodguilt is upon them. ¹³If a man lies with a male as one lies with a woman, the two of them have done an abhorrent thing; they shall be put to death—their bloodguilt is upon them. ¹⁴If a man marries a woman and her mother, it is depravity; both he and they shall be put to the fire, that there be no depravity among you. ¹⁵If a man has carnal relations with a beast, he shall be put to death; and you shall kill the beast. ¹⁶If a woman approaches any beast to mate with it, you shall kill the woman and the beast; they shall be put to death—their bloodguilt is upon them.

¹⁷If a man marries his sister, the daughter of either his father or his mother, so that he sees her nakedness and she sees his nakedness, it is a disgrace; they shall be excommunicatedᵃ in the sight of their kinsfolk. He has uncovered the nakedness of his sister, he shall bear his guilt. ¹⁸If a man lies with a woman in her infirmity and uncovers her nakedness, he

---

ᵃ Lit. "cut off."

has laid bare her flow and she has exposed her blood flow; both of them shall be cut off from among their people. ¹⁹You shall not uncover the nakedness of your mother's sister or of your father's sister, for that is laying bare one's own flesh; they shall bear their guilt. ²⁰If a man lies with his uncle's wife, it is his uncle's nakedness that he has uncovered. They shall bear their guilt: they shall die childless. ²¹If a man marries the wife of his brother, it is indecency. It is the nakedness of his brother that he has uncovered; they shall remain childless.

²²You shall faithfully observe all My laws and all My regulations, lest the land to which I bring you to settle in spew you out. ²³You shall not follow the practices of the nation that I am driving out before you. For it is because they did all these things that I abhorred them ²⁴and said to you: You shall possess their land, for I will give it to you to possess, a land flowing with milk and honey. I the LORD am your God who has set you apart from other peoples. ²⁵So you shall set apart the clean beast from the unclean, the unclean bird from the clean. You shall not draw abomination upon yourselves through beast or bird or anything with which the ground is alive, which I have set apart for you to treat as unclean. ²⁶You shall be holy to Me, for I the LORD am holy, and I have set you apart from other peoples to be Mine.

²⁷A man or a woman who has a ghost or a familiar spirit shall be put to death; they shall be pelted with stones—their bloodguilt shall be upon them.

אמר

21 The LORD said to Moses: Speak to the priests, the sons of Aaron, and say to them:

None shall defile himself for any [dead] person among his kin, ²except for the relatives that are closest to him: his mother, his father, his son, his daughter, and his brother; ³also for a virgin sister, close to him because she has not married, for her he may defile himself. ⁴But he shall not defile himself ᵃ‑as a kinsman by marriage,‑ᵃ and so profane himself.

⁵They shall not shave smooth any part of their heads, or cut the side-growth of their beards, or make gashes in their flesh. ⁶They shall be holy to their God and not profane the name of their God; for they offer the LORD's offerings by fire, the food of their God, and so must be holy.

⁷They shall not marry a woman defiled by harlotry, nor shall they marry

ᵃ‑ᵃ Lit. "as a husband among his kin"; meaning uncertain.

one divorced from her husband. For they are holy to their God ⁸and you must treat them as holy, since they offer the food of your God; they shall be holy to you, for I the LORD who sanctify you am holy.

⁹When the daughter of a priest defiles herself through harlotry, it is her father whom she defiles; she shall be put to the fire.

¹⁰The priest who is exalted above his fellows, on whose head the anointing oil has been poured and who has been ordained to wear the vestments, shall not bare his head[b] or rend his vestments. ¹¹He shall not go in where there is any dead body; he shall not defile himself even for his father or mother. ¹²He shall not go outside the sanctuary and profane the sanctuary of his God, for upon him is the distinction of the anointing oil of his God, Mine the LORD's. ¹³He may marry only a woman who is a virgin. ¹⁴A widow, or a divorced woman, or one who is degraded by harlotry—such he may not marry. Only a virgin of his own kin may he take to wife—¹⁵that he may not profane his offspring among his kin, for I the LORD have sanctified him.

¹⁶The LORD spoke further to Moses: ¹⁷Speak to Aaron and say: No man of your offspring throughout the ages who has a defect shall be qualified to offer the food of his God. ¹⁸No one at all who has a defect shall be qualified: no man who is blind, or lame, or [c-]has a limb too short or too long;[-c] ¹⁹no man who has a broken leg or a broken arm; ²⁰or who is a hunchback, or a dwarf, or who has a growth in his eye, or who has a boil-scar, or scurvy, or crushed testes. ²¹No man among the offspring of Aaron the priest who has a defect shall be qualified to offer the LORD's offering by fire; having a defect, he shall not be qualified to offer the food of his God. ²²He may eat of the food of his God, of the most holy as well as of the holy; ²³but he shall not enter behind the curtain or come near the altar, for he has a defect. He shall not profane these places sacred to Me, for I the LORD have sanctified them.

²⁴Thus Moses spoke to Aaron and his sons and to all the Israelites.

22 The LORD spoke to Moses, saying: ²Instruct Aaron and his sons to be scrupulous about the sacred donations that the Israelite people consecrate to Me, lest they profane My holy name, Mine the LORD's. ³Say to them:

Throughout the ages, if any man among your offspring, while in a state of uncleanness, partakes of any sacred donation that the Israelite people

---

b See note at 10.6.
c-c Or "mutilated or has a limb too long."

may consecrate to the LORD, that person shall be cut off from before Me: I am the LORD. ⁴No man of Aaron's offspring who has an eruption or a discharge[a] shall eat of the sacred donations until he is clean. If one touches anything made unclean by a corpse, or if a man has an emission of semen, ⁵or if a man touches any swarming thing by which he is made unclean or any human being by whom he is made unclean—whatever his uncleanness—⁶the person who touches such shall be unclean until evening and shall not eat of the sacred donations unless he has washed his body in water. ⁷As soon as the sun sets, he shall be clean; and afterward he may eat of the sacred donations, for they are his food. ⁸He shall not eat anything that died or was torn by beasts, thereby becoming unclean: I am the LORD. ⁹They shall keep My charge, lest they incur guilt thereby and die for it, having committed profanation: I the LORD consecrate them.

¹⁰No lay person shall eat of the sacred donations. No bound or hired laborer of a priest shall eat of the sacred donations; ¹¹but a person who is a priest's property by purchase may eat of them; and those that are born into his household may eat of his food. ¹²If a priest's daughter marries a layman, she may not eat of the sacred gifts; ¹³but if the priest's daughter is widowed or divorced and without offspring, and is back in her father's house as in her youth, she may eat of her father's food. No lay person may eat of it: ¹⁴but if a man eats of a sacred donation unwittingly, he shall pay the priest for the sacred donation, adding one-fifth of its value. ¹⁵But [the priests] must not allow the Israelites to profane the sacred donations that they set aside for the LORD, ¹⁶or to incur guilt requiring a penalty payment, by eating such sacred donations: for it is I the LORD who make them sacred.

¹⁷The LORD spoke to Moses, saying: ¹⁸Speak to Aaron and his sons, and to all the Israelite people, and say to them:

When any man of the house of Israel or of the strangers in Israel presents a burnt offering as his offering for any of the votive or any of the freewill offerings that they offer to the LORD, ¹⁹it must, to be acceptable in your favor, be a male without blemish, from cattle or sheep or goats. ²⁰You shall not offer any that has a defect, for it will not be accepted in your favor.

²¹And when a man offers, from the herd or the flock, a sacrifice of well-being to the LORD for an explicit[b] vow or as a freewill offering, it must, to be acceptable, be without blemish; there must be no defect in it. ²²Anything blind, or injured, or maimed, or with a wen, boil-scar, or

---

a See chapters 13 and 15.
b Or "unspecified" or "extraordinary"; meaning of Heb. lephalle uncertain.

scurvy—such you shall not offer to the Lord; you shall not put any of them on the altar as offerings by fire to the Lord. 23You may, however, present as a freewill offering an ox or a sheep with a limb extended or contracted; but it will not be accepted for a vow. 24You shall not offer to the Lord anything [with its testes] bruised or crushed or torn or cut. You shall have no such practices[c] in your own land, 25nor shall you accept such [animals] from a foreigner for offering as food for your God, for they are mutilated, they have a defect; they shall not be accepted in your favor.

26The Lord spoke to Moses, saying: 27When an ox or a sheep or a goat is born, it shall stay seven days with its mother, and from the eighth day on it shall be acceptable as an offering by fire to the Lord. 28However, no animal from the herd or from the flock shall be slaughtered on the same day with its young.

29When you sacrifice a thanksgiving offering to the Lord, sacrifice it so that it may be acceptable in your favor. 30It shall be eaten on the same day; you shall not leave any of it until morning: I am the Lord.

31You shall faithfully observe My commandments: I am the Lord. 32You shall not profane My holy name, that I may be sanctified in the midst of the Israelite people—I the Lord who sanctify you, 33I who brought you out of the land of Egypt to be your God, I the Lord.

23

The Lord spoke to Moses, saying: 2Speak to the Israelite people and say to them:

These are My fixed times, the fixed times of the Lord, which you shall proclaim as sacred occasions.

3On six days work may be done, but on the seventh day there shall be a sabbath of complete rest, a sacred occasion. You shall do no work; it shall be a sabbath of the Lord throughout your settlements.

4These are the set times of the Lord, the sacred occasions, which you shall celebrate each at its appointed time: 5In the first month, on the fourteenth day of the month, at twilight, there shall be a passover offering to the Lord, 6and on the fifteenth day of that month the Lord's Feast of Unleavened Bread. You shall eat unleavened bread for seven days. 7On the first day you shall celebrate a sacred occasion: you shall not work at your occupations. 8Seven days you shall make offerings by fire to the

---

c *I.e., mutilations.*

LORD. The seventh day shall be a sacred occasion: you shall not work at your occupations.

9The LORD spoke to Moses, saying: 10Speak to the Israelite people and say to them:

When you enter the land that I am giving to you and you reap its harvest, you shall bring the first sheaf of your harvest to the priest. 11He shall elevate the sheaf before the LORD for acceptance in your behalf; the priest shall elevate it on the day after the sabbath. 12On the day that you elevate the sheaf, you shall offer as a burnt offering to the LORD a lamb of the first year without blemish. 13The meal offering with it shall be two-tenths of a measure of choice flour with oil mixed in, an offering by fire of pleasing odor to the LORD; and the libation with it shall be of wine, a quarter of a *hin*. 14Until that very day, until you have brought the offering of your God, you shall eat no bread or parched grain or fresh ears;a it is a law for all time throughout the ages in all your settlements.

15And from the day on which you bring the sheaf of elevation offering—the day after the sabbath—you shall count off seven weeks. They must be complete: 16you must count until the day after the seventh week—fifty days; then you shall bring an offering of new grain to the LORD. 17You shall bring from your settlements two loaves of bread as an elevation offering; each shall be made of two-tenths of a measure of choice flour, baked after leavening, as first fruits to the LORD. 18With the bread you shall present, as burnt offerings to the LORD, seven yearling lambs without blemish, one bull of the herd, and two rams, with their meal offerings and libations, an offering by fire of pleasing odor to the LORD. 19You shall also offer one he-goat as a sin offering and two yearling lambs as a sacrifice of well-being. 20The priest shall elevate these—the two lambsb—together with the bread of first fruits as an elevation offering before the LORD; they shall be holy to the LORD, for the priest. 21On that same day you shall hold a celebration; it shall be a sacred occasion for you; you shall not work at your occupations. This is a law for all time in all your settlements, throughout the ages.

22And when you reap the harvest of your land, you shall not reap all the way to the edges of your field, or gather the gleanings of your harvest; you shall leave them for the poor and the stranger: I the LORD am your God.

---

a *I.e., of the new crop.*
b *Meaning of Heb. uncertain.*

²³The LORD spoke to Moses, saying: ²⁴Speak to the Israelite people thus: In the seventh month, on the first day of the month, you shall observe complete rest, a sacred occasion commemorated with loud blasts. ²⁵You shall not work at your occupations; and you shall bring an offering by fire to the LORD.

²⁶The LORD spoke to Moses, saying: ²⁷Mark, the tenth day of this seventh month is the Day of Atonement. It shall be a sacred occasion for you: you shall practice self-denial, and you shall bring an offering by fire to the LORD; ²⁸you shall do no work throughout that day. For it is a Day of Atonement, on which expiation is made on your behalf before the LORD your God. ²⁹Indeed, any person who does not practice self-denial throughout that day shall be cut off from his kin; ³⁰and whoever does any work throughout that day, I will cause that person to perish from among his people. ³¹Do no work whatever; it is a law for all time, throughout the ages in all your settlements. ³²It shall be a sabbath of complete rest for you, and you shall practice self-denial; on the ninth day of the month at evening, from evening to evening, you shall observe this your sabbath.

³³The LORD spoke to Moses, saying: ³⁴Say to the Israelite people:
On the fifteenth day of this seventh month there shall be the Feast of Booths[c] to the LORD, [to last] seven days. ³⁵The first day shall be a sacred occasion: you shall not work at your occupations; ³⁶seven days you shall bring offerings by fire to the LORD. On the eighth day you shall observe a sacred occasion and bring an offering by fire to the LORD; it is a solemn gathering:[d] you shall not work at your occupations.

³⁷Those are the set times of the LORD that you shall celebrate as sacred occasions, bringing offerings by fire to the LORD—burnt offerings, meal offerings, sacrifices, and libations, on each day what is proper to it— ³⁸apart from the sabbaths of the LORD, and apart from your gifts and from all your votive offerings and from all your freewill offerings that you give to the LORD.

³⁹Mark, on the fifteenth day of the seventh month, when you have gathered in the yield of your land, you shall observe the festival of the LORD [to last] seven days: a complete rest on the first day, and a complete

c *Others "Tabernacles."*
d *Precise meaning of Heb. ʿaṣereth uncertain.*

rest on the eighth day. ⁴⁰On the first day you shall take the product of *hadar*ᶜ trees, branches of palm trees, boughs of leafyᶠ trees, and willows of the brook, and you shall rejoice before the LORD your God seven days. ⁴¹You shall observe it as a festival of the LORD for seven days in the year; you shall observe it in the seventh month as a law for all time, throughout the ages. ⁴²You shall live in booths seven days; all citizens in Israel shall live in booths, ⁴³in order that future generations may know that I made the Israelite people live in booths when I brought them out of the land of Egypt, I the LORD your God.

⁴⁴So Moses declared to the Israelites the set times of the LORD.

24

The LORD spoke to Moses, saying:

²Command the Israelite people to bring you clear oil of beaten olives for lighting, for kindling lamps regularly. ³Aaron shall set them up in the Tent of Meeting outside the curtain of the Pact [to burn] from evening to morning before the LORD regularly; it is a law for all time throughout the ages. ⁴He shall set up the lamps on the pureᵃ lampstand before the LORD [to burn] regularly.

⁵You shall take choice flour and bake of it twelve loaves, two-tenths of a measure for each loaf. ⁶Place them on the pureᵃ table before the LORD in two rows, six to a row. ⁷With each row you shall place pure frankincense, which is to be a token offeringᵇ for the bread, as an offering by fire to the LORD. ⁸He shall arrange them before the LORD regularly every sabbath day—it is a commitment for all time on the part of the Israelites. ⁹They shall belong to Aaron and his sons, who shall eat them in the sacred precinct; for they are his as most holy things from the LORD's offerings by fire, a due for all time.

¹⁰There came out among the Israelites one whose mother was Israelite and whose father was Egyptian. And a fight broke out in the camp between that half-Israeliteᶜ and a certain Israelite. ¹¹The son of the Israelite woman pronounced the Name in blasphemy, and he was brought to Moses—now his mother's name was Shelomith daughter of Dibri of the tribe of Dan—¹²and he was placed in custody, until the decision of the LORD should be made clear to them.

ᶜ Others "goodly"; exact meaning of Heb. hadar uncertain. Traditionally the product is understood as "citron."
ᶠ Meaning of Heb. aboth uncertain.

ᵃ See note at Exod. 31.8.
ᵇ See Lev. 2.2.
ᶜ Lit. "the son of an Israelite woman."

[13]And the LORD spoke to Moses, saying: [14]Take the blasphemer outside the camp; and let all who were within hearing lay their hands upon his head, and let the whole community stone him.

[15]And to the Israelite people speak thus: Anyone who blasphemes his God shall bear his guilt; [16]if he also pronounces the name LORD, he shall be put to death. The whole community shall stone him; stranger or citizen, if he has thus pronounced the Name, he shall be put to death.

[17]If anyone kills any human being, he shall be put to death. [18]One who kills a beast shall make restitution for it: life for life. [19]If anyone maims his fellow, as he has done so shall it be done to him: [20]fracture for fracture, eye for eye, tooth for tooth. The injury he inflicted on another shall be inflicted on him. [21]One who kills a beast shall make restitution for it; but one who kills a human being shall be put to death. [22]You shall have one standard for stranger and citizen alike: for I the LORD am your God.

[23]Moses spoke thus to the Israelites. And they took the blasphemer outside the camp and pelted him with stones. The Israelites did as the LORD had commanded Moses.

25

בהר סיני

The LORD spoke to Moses on Mount Sinai: [2]Speak to the Israelite people and say to them:

When you enter the land that I assign to you, the land shall observe a sabbath of the LORD. [3]Six years you may sow your field and six years you may prune your vineyard and gather in the yield. [4]But in the seventh year the land shall have a sabbath of complete rest, a sabbath of the LORD: you shall not sow your field or prune your vineyard. [5]You shall not reap the aftergrowth of your harvest or gather the grapes of your untrimmed vines; it shall be a year of complete rest for the land. [6]But you may eat whatever the land during its sabbath will produce—you, your male and female slaves, the hired and bound laborers who live with you, [7]and your cattle and the beasts in your land may eat all its yield.

[8]You shall count off seven weeks of years—seven times seven years—so that the period of seven weeks of years gives you a total of forty-nine years. [9]Then you shall sound the horn loud; in the seventh month, on the tenth day of the month—the Day of Atonement—you shall have the

horn sounded throughout your land [10]and you shall hallow the fiftieth year. You shall proclaim release[a] throughout the land for all its inhabitants. It shall be a jubilee[b] for you: each of you shall return to his holding and each of you shall return to his family. [11]That fiftieth year shall be a jubilee for you: you shall not sow, neither shall you reap the aftergrowth or harvest the untrimmed vines, [12]for it is a jubilee. It shall be holy to you: you may only eat the growth direct from the field.

[13]In this year of jubilee, each of you shall return to his holding. [14]When you sell property to your neighbor,[c] or buy any from your neighbor, you shall not wrong one another. [15]In buying from your neighbor, you shall deduct only for the number of years since the jubilee; and in selling to you, he shall charge you only for the remaining crop years: [16]the more such years, the higher the price you pay; the fewer such years, the lower the price; for what he is selling you is a number of harvests. [17]Do not wrong one another, but fear your God; for I the LORD am your God.

[18]You shall observe My laws and faithfully keep My rules, that you may live upon the land in security; [19]the land shall yield its fruit and you shall eat your fill, and you shall live upon it in security. [20]And should you ask, "What are we to eat in the seventh year, if we may neither sow nor gather in our crops?" [21]I will ordain My blessing for you in the sixth year, so that it shall yield a crop sufficient for three years. [22]When you sow in the eighth year, you will still be eating old grain of that crop; you will be eating the old until the ninth year, until its crops come in.

[23]But the land must not be sold beyond reclaim, for the land is Mine; you are but strangers resident with Me. [24]Throughout the land that you hold, you must provide for the redemption of the land.

[25]If your kinsman is in straits and has to sell part of his holding, his nearest redeemer[d] shall come and redeem what his kinsman has sold. [26]If a man has no one to redeem for him, but prospers and acquires enough to redeem with, [27]he shall compute the years since its sale, refund the difference to the man to whom he sold it, and return to his holding. [28]If he lacks sufficient means to recover it, what he sold shall remain with the purchaser until the jubilee; in the jubilee year it shall be released, and he shall return to his holding.

[29]If a man sells a dwelling house in a walled city, it may be redeemed until a year has elapsed since its sale; the redemption period shall be a year. [30]If it is not redeemed before a full year has elapsed, the house in the walled city shall pass to the purchaser beyond reclaim throughout the

---

a Others "liberty."
b Heb. yobel, "ram" or "ram's horn."
c I.e., fellow Israelite; see v. 46.
d I.e., the closest relative able to redeem the land.

ages; it shall not be released in the jubilee. ³¹But houses in villages that have no encircling walls shall be classed as open country: they may be redeemed, and they shall be released through the jubilee. ³²As for the cities of the Levites, the houses in the cities they hold—the Levites shall forever have the right of redemption. ³³ᵉSuch property as may be redeemed from the Levites—houses sold in a city they hold—shall be released through the jubilee; for the houses in the cities of the Levites are their holding among the Israelites. ³⁴But the unenclosed land about their cities cannot be sold, for that is their holding for all time.

³⁵If your kinsman, being in straits, comes under your authority, and you hold him as though a resident alien, let him live by your side: ³⁶do not exact from him advance or accrued interest,ᶠ but fear your God. Let him live by your side as your kinsman. ³⁷Do not lend him your money at advance interest, or give him your food at accrued interest. ³⁸I the LORD am your God, who brought you out of the land of Egypt, to give you the land of Canaan, to be your God.

³⁹If your kinsman under you continues in straits and must give himself over to you, do not subject him to the treatment of a slave. ⁴⁰He shall remain with you as a hired or bound laborer; he shall serve with you only until the jubilee year. ⁴¹Then he and his children with him shall be free of your authority; he shall go back to his family and return to his ancestral holding.—⁴²For they are My servants, whom I freed from the land of Egypt; they may not give themselves over into servitude.—⁴³You shall not rule over him ruthlessly; you shall fear your God. ⁴⁴Such male and female slaves as you may have—it is from the nations round about you that you may acquire male and female slaves. ⁴⁵You may also buy them from among the children of aliens resident among you, or from their families that are among you, whom they begot in your land. These shall become your property: ⁴⁶you may keep them as a possession for your children after you, for them to inherit as property for all time. Such you may treat as slaves. But as for your Israelite kinsmen, no one shall rule ruthlessly over the other.

⁴⁷If a resident alien among you has prospered, and your kinsman being in straits, comes under his authority and gives himself over to the resident alien among you, or to an offshoot of an alien's family, ⁴⁸he shall have the right of redemption even after he has given himself over. One of his kinsmen shall redeem him, ⁴⁹or his uncle or his uncle's son shall redeem him, or anyone of his family who is of his own flesh shall redeem him;

ᵉ *Meaning of first half of verse uncertain.*
ᶠ *I.e., interest deducted in advance, or interest added at the time of repayment.*

or, if he prospers, he may redeem himself. 50He shall compute with his purchaser the total from the year he gave himself over to him until the jubilee year; the price of his sale shall be applied to the number of years, as though it were for a term as a hired laborer under the other's authority. 51If many years remain, he shall pay back for his redemption in proportion to his purchase price; 52and if few years remain until the jubilee year, he shall so compute: he shall make payment for his redemption according to the years involved. 53He shall be under his authority as a laborer hired by the year; he shall not rule ruthlessly over him in your sight. 54If he has not been redeemed in any of those ways, he and his children with him shall go free in the jubilee year. 55For it is to Me that the Israelites are servants: they are My servants, whom I freed from the land of Egypt, I the LORD your God.

26 You shall not make idols for yourselves, or set up for yourselves carved images or pillars, or place figureda stones in your land to worship upon, for I the LORD am your God. 2You shall keep My sabbaths and venerate My sanctuary, Mine, the LORD's.

בחקתי

3If you follow My laws and faithfully observe My commandments, 4I will grant your rains in their season, so that the earth shall yield its produce and the trees of the field their fruit. 5Your threshing shall overtake the vintage, and your vintage shall overtake the sowing; you shall eat your fill of bread and dwell securely in your land.

6I will grant peace in the land, and you shall lie down untroubled by anyone; I will give the land respite from vicious beasts, and no sword shall cross your land. 7You shall give chase to your enemies, and they shall fall before you by the sword. 8Five of you shall give chase to a hundred, and a hundred of you shall give chase to ten thousand; your enemies shall fall before you by the sword.

9I will look with favor upon you, and make you fertile and multiply you; and I will maintain My covenant with you. 10You shall eat old grain long stored, and you shall have to clear out the old to make room for the new.

11I will establish My abode in your midst, and I will not spurn you. 12I will be ever present in your midst: I will be your God, and you shall

---

a *Meaning of Heb.* maskith *uncertain.*

be My people. ¹³I the LORD am your God who brought you out from the land of the Egyptians to be their slaves no more, who broke the bars of your yoke and made you walk erect.

¹⁴But if you do not obey Me and do not observe all these commandments, ¹⁵if you reject My laws and spurn My rules, so that you do not observe all My commandments and you break My covenant, ¹⁶I in turn will do this to you: I will wreak misery upon you—ᵇconsumption and fever, which cause the eyes to pine and the body to languish; you shall sow your seed to no purpose, for your enemies shall eat it. ¹⁷I will set My face against you: you shall be routed by your enemies, and your foes shall dominate you. You shall flee though none pursues.

¹⁸And if, for all that, you do not obey Me, I will go on to discipline you sevenfold for your sins, ¹⁹and I will break your proud glory. I will make your skies like iron and your earth like copper, ²⁰so that your strength shall be spent to no purpose. Your land shall not yield its produce, nor shall the trees of the land yield their fruit.

²¹And if you remain hostile toward Me and refuse to obey Me, I will go on smiting you sevenfold for your sins. ²²I will loose wild beasts against you, and they shall bereave you of your children and wipe out your cattle. They shall decimate you, and your roads shall be deserted.

²³And if these things fail to discipline you for Me, and you remain hostile to Me, ²⁴I too will remain hostile to you: I in turn will smite you sevenfold for your sins. ²⁵I will bring a sword against you to wreak vengeance for the covenant; and if you withdraw into your cities, I will send pestilence among you, and you shall be delivered into enemy hands. ²⁶When I break your staff of bread, ten women shall bake your bread in a single oven; they shall dole out your bread by weight, and though you eat, you shall not be satisfied.

²⁷But if, despite this, you disobey Me and remain hostile to Me, ²⁸I will act against you in wrathful hostility; I, for My part, will discipline you sevenfold for your sins. ²⁹You shall eat the flesh of your sons and the flesh of your daughters. ³⁰I will destroy your cult places and cut down your incense stands, and I will heap your carcasses upon your lifeless fetishes.

I will spurn you. ³¹I will lay your cities in ruin and make your sanctuaries desolate, and I will not savor your pleasing odors. ³²I will make the land desolate, so that your enemies who settle in it shall be appalled

ᵇ *Precise nature of these ills is uncertain.*

by it. 33And you I will scatter among the nations, and I will unsheath the sword against you. Your land shall become a desolation and your cities a ruin.

34Then shall the land make up for its sabbath years throughout the time that it is desolate and you are in the land of your enemies; then shall the land rest and make up for its sabbath years. 35Throughout the time that it is desolate, it shall observe the rest that it did not observe in your sabbath years while you were dwelling upon it. 36As for those of you who survive, I will cast a faintness into their hearts in the land of their enemies. The sound of a driven leaf shall put them to flight. Fleeing as though from the sword, they shall fall though none pursues. 37With no one pursuing, they shall stumble over one another as before the sword. You shall not be able to stand your ground before your enemies, 38but shall perish among the nations; and the land of your enemies shall consume you.

39Those of you who survive shall be heartsick over their iniquity in the land of your enemies; more, they shall be heartsick over the iniquities of their fathers; 40and they shall confess their iniquity and the iniquity of their fathers, in that they trespassed against Me, yea, were hostile to Me. 41When I, in turn, have been hostile to them and have removed them into the land of their enemies, then at last shall their obdurate^c heart humble itself, and they shall atone for their iniquity. 42Then will I remember My covenant with Jacob; I will remember also My covenant with Isaac, and also My covenant with Abraham; and I will remember the land.

43For the land shall be forsaken of them, making up for its sabbath years by being desolate of them, while they atone for their iniquity; for the abundant reason that they rejected My rules and spurned My laws. 44Yet, even then, when they are in the land of their enemies, I will not reject them or spurn them so as to destroy them, annulling My covenant with them: for I the LORD am their God. 45I will remember in their favor the covenant with the ancients, whom I freed from the land of Egypt in the sight of the nations to be their God: I, the LORD.

46These are the laws, rules, and instructions that the LORD established, through Moses on Mount Sinai, between Himself and the Israelite people.

27 The LORD spoke to Moses, saying:

2Speak to the Israelite people and say to them: When anyone explicitly^a

---

c Others "uncircumcised"; lit. "blocked."

a Cf. note at Lev. 22.21.

vows to the LORD the equivalent for a human being, [3]the following scale shall apply: If it is a male from twenty to sixty years of age, the equivalent is fifty shekels of silver by the sanctuary weight; [4]if it is a female, the equivalent is thirty shekels. [5]If the age is from five years to twenty years, the equivalent is twenty shekels for a male and ten shekels for a female. [6]If the age is from one month to five years, the equivalent for a male is five shekels of silver, and the equivalent for a female is three shekels of silver. [7]If the age is sixty years or over, the equivalent is fifteen shekels in the case of a male and ten shekels for a female. [8]But if one cannot afford the equivalent, he shall be presented before the priest, and the priest shall assess him; the priest shall assess him according to what the vower can afford.

[9]If [the vow concerns] any animal that may be brought as an offering to the LORD, any such that may be given to the LORD shall be holy. [10]One may not exchange or substitute another for it, either good for bad, or bad for good; if one does substitute one animal for another, the thing vowed and its substitute shall both be holy. [11]If [the vow concerns] any unclean animal that may not be brought as an offering to the LORD, the animal shall be presented before the priest, [12]and the priest shall assess it. Whether [b-]high or low,[-b] whatever assessment is set by the priest shall stand; [13]and if he wishes to redeem it, he must add one-fifth to its assessment.

[14]If anyone consecrates his house to the LORD, the priest shall assess it. Whether [b-]high or low,[-b] as the priest assesses it, so it shall stand; [15]and if he who has consecrated his house wishes to redeem it, he must add one-fifth to the sum at which it was assessed, and it shall be his.

[16]If anyone consecrates to the LORD any land that he holds, its assessment shall be in accordance with its seed requirement: fifty shekels of silver to a *homer* of barley seed. [17]If he consecrates his land as of the jubilee year, its assessment stands. [18]But if he consecrates his land after the jubilee, the priest shall compute the price according to the years that are left until the jubilee year, and its assessment shall be so reduced; [19]and if he who consecrated the land wishes to redeem it, he must add one-fifth to the sum at which it was assessed, and it shall pass to him. [20]But if he does not redeem the land, and the land is sold to another, it shall no longer be redeemable: [21]when it is released in the jubilee, the land shall be holy to the LORD, as land proscribed; it becomes the priest's holding.

[22]If he consecrates to the LORD land that he purchased, which is not

b-b *Lit. "good or bad."*

land of his holding, 23the priest shall compute for him the proportionate assessment up to the jubilee year, and he shall pay the assessment as of that day, a sacred donation to the LORD. 24In the jubilee year the land shall revert to him from whom it was bought, whose holding the land is. 25All assessments shall be by the sanctuary weight, the shekel being twenty gerahs.

26A firstling of animals, however, which—as a firstling—is the LORD's, cannot be consecrated by anybody; whether ox or sheep, it is the LORD's. 27But if it is of unclean animals, it may be ransomed as its assessment, with one-fifth added; if it is not redeemed, it shall be sold at its assessment.

28But of all that anyone owns, be it man or beast or land of his holding, nothing that he has proscribed for the LORD may be sold or redeemed; every proscribed thing is totally consecrated to the LORD. 29No human being who has been proscribed can be ransomed: he shall be put to death.

30All tithes from the land, whether seed from the ground or fruit from the tree, are the LORD's; they are holy to the LORD. 31If anyone wishes to redeem any of his tithes, he must add one-fifth to them. 32All tithes of the herd or flock—of all that passes under the shepherd's staff, every tenth one—shall be holy to the LORD. 33He must not look out for good as against bad, or make substitution for it. If he does make substitution for it, then it and its substitute shall both be holy: it cannot be redeemed.

34These are the commandments that the LORD gave Moses for the Israelite people on Mount Sinai.

חזק

NUMBERS

1 On the first day of the second month, in the second year following the exodus from the land of Egypt, the LORD spoke to Moses in the wilderness of Sinai, in the Tent of Meeting, saying:

2Take a census of the whole Israelite community by the clans of a-its ancestral houses,-a listing the names, every male, head by head. 3You and Aaron shall record them by their groups, from the age of twenty years up, all those in Israel who are able to bear arms. 4Associated with you shall be a man from each tribe, each one the head of his ancestral house.

5These are the names of the men who shall assist you:

From Reuben, Elizur son of Shedeur.

6From Simeon, Shelumiel son of Zurishaddai.

7From Judah, Nahshon son of Amminadab.

8From Issachar, Nethanel son of Zuar.

9From Zebulun, Eliab son of Helon.

10From the sons of Joseph:

from Ephraim, Elishama son of Ammihud;

from Manasseh, Gamaliel son of Pedahzur.

11From Benjamin, Abidan son of Gideoni.

12From Dan, Ahiezer son of Ammishaddai.

13From Asher, Pagiel son of Ochran.

14From Gad, Eliasaph son of Deuel.

15From Naphtali, Ahira son of Enan.

16Those are the elected of the assembly, the chieftains of their ancestral tribes: they are the heads of the contingents of Israel.

17So Moses and Aaron took those men, who were designated by name, 18and on the first day of the second month they convoked the whole community, who were registered by the clans of their ancestral houses—the names of those aged twenty years and over being listed head by head.

---

a-a I.e., of its tribes.

¹⁹As the LORD had commanded Moses, so he recorded them in the wilderness of Sinai.

²⁰They totaled as follows:

The descendants of Reuben, Israel's first-born, the registration of the clans of their ancestral house, as listed by name, head by head, all males aged twenty years and over, all who were able to bear arms—²¹those enrolled from the tribe of Reuben: 46,500.

²²Of the descendants of Simeon, the registration of the clans of their ancestral house, their enrollment as listed by name, head by head, all males aged twenty years and over, all who were able to bear arms—²³those enrolled from the tribe of Simeon: 59,300.

²⁴Of the descendants of Gad, the registration of the clans of their ancestral house, as listed by name, aged twenty years and over, all who were able to bear arms—²⁵those enrolled from the tribe of Gad: 45,650.

²⁶Of the descendants of Judah, the registration of the clans of their ancestral house, as listed by name, aged twenty years and over, all who were able to bear arms—²⁷those enrolled from the tribe of Judah: 74,600.

²⁸Of the descendants of Issachar, the registration of the clans of their ancestral house, as listed by name, aged twenty years and over, all who were able to bear arms—²⁹those enrolled from the tribe of Issachar: 54,400.

³⁰Of the descendants of Zebulun, the registration of the clans of their ancestral house, as listed by name, aged twenty years and over, all who were able to bear arms—³¹those enrolled from the tribe of Zebulun: 57,400.

³²Of the descendants of Joseph:

Of the descendants of Ephraim, the registration of the clans of their ancestral house, as listed by name, aged twenty years and over, all who were able to bear arms—³³those enrolled from the tribe of Ephraim: 40,500.

³⁴Of the descendants of Manasseh, the registration of the clans of their ancestral house, as listed by name, aged twenty years and over, all who were able to bear arms—³⁵those enrolled from the tribe of Manasseh: 32,200.

³⁶Of the descendants of Benjamin, the registration of the clans of their ancestral house, as listed by name, aged twenty years and over, all who were able to bear arms—³⁷those enrolled from the tribe of Benjamin: 35,400.

³⁸Of the descendants of Dan, the registration of the clans of their an-

cestral house, as listed by name, aged twenty years and over, all who were able to bear arms—³⁹those enrolled from the tribe of Dan: 62,700.

⁴⁰Of the descendants of Asher, the registration of the clans of their ancestral house, as listed by name, aged twenty years and over, all who were able to bear arms—⁴¹those enrolled from the tribe of Asher: 41,500.

⁴²[Of] the descendants of Naphtali, the registration of the clans of their ancestral house as listed by name, aged twenty years and over, all who were able to bear arms—⁴³those enrolled from the tribe of Naphtali: 53,400.

⁴⁴Those are the enrollments recorded by Moses and Aaron and by the chieftains of Israel, who were twelve in number, one man to each ancestral house. ⁴⁵All the Israelites, aged twenty years and over, enrolled by ancestral houses, all those in Israel who were able to bear arms—⁴⁶all who were enrolled came to 603,550.

⁴⁷The Levites, however, were not recorded among them by their ancestral tribe. ⁴⁸For the LORD had spoken to Moses, saying: ⁴⁹Do not on any account enroll the tribe of Levi or take a census of them with the Israelites. ⁵⁰You shall put the Levites in charge of the Tabernacle of the Pact, all its furnishings, and everything that pertains to it: they shall carry the Tabernacle and all its furnishings, and they shall tend it; and they shall camp around the Tabernacle. ⁵¹When the Tabernacle is to set out, the Levites shall take it down, and when the Tabernacle is to be pitched, the Levites shall set it up; any outsider who encroaches shall be put to death. ⁵²The Israelites shall encamp troop by troop, each man with his division and each under his standard. ⁵³The Levites, however, shall camp around the Tabernacle of the Pact, that wrath may not strike the Israelite community; the Levites shall stand guard around the Tabernacle of the Pact.

⁵⁴The Israelites did accordingly; just as the LORD had commanded Moses, so they did.

2 The LORD spoke to Moses and Aaron, saying: ²The Israelites shall camp each with his standard, under the banners of their ancestral house; they shall camp around the Tent of Meeting at a distance.

³Camped on the front, or east side: the standard of the division of Judah, troop by troop.

Chieftain of the Judites: Nahshon son of Amminadab. ⁴His troop, as enrolled: 74,600.

⁵Camping next to it:

The tribe of Issachar.

Chieftain of the Issacharites: Nethanel son of Zuar. ⁶His troop, as enrolled: 54,400.

⁷The tribe of Zebulun.

Chieftain of the Zebulunites: Eliab son of Helon. ⁸His troop, as enrolled: 57,400.

⁹The total enrolled in the division of Judah: 186,400, for all troops. These shall march first.

¹⁰On the south: the standard of the division of Reuben, troop by troop. Chieftain of the Reubenites: Elizur son of Shedeur. ¹¹His troop, as enrolled: 46,500.

¹²Camping next to it:

The tribe of Simeon.

Chieftain of the Simeonites: Shelumiel son of Zurishaddai.

¹³His troop, as enrolled: 59,300.

¹⁴And the tribe of Gad.

Chieftain of the Gadites: Eliasaph son of Reuel. ¹⁵His troop, as enrolled: 45,650.

¹⁶The total enrolled in the division of Reuben: 151,450, for all troops. These shall march second.

¹⁷Then, midway between the divisions, the Tent of Meeting, the division of the Levites, shall move. As they camp, so they shall march, each in position, by their standards.

¹⁸On the west: the standard of the division of Ephraim, troop by troop. Chieftain of the Ephraimites: Elishama son of Ammihud. ¹⁹His troop, as enrolled: 40,500.

²⁰Next to it:

The tribe of Manasseh.

Chieftain of the Manassites: Gamaliel son of Pedahzur. ²¹His troop, as enrolled: 32,200.

²²And the tribe of Benjamin.

Chieftain of the Benjaminites: Abidan son of Gideoni. ²³His troop, as enrolled: 35,400.

²⁴The total enrolled in the division of Ephraim: 108,100 for all troops. These shall march third.

²⁵On the north: the standard of the division of Dan, troop by troop. Chieftain of the Danites: Ahiezer son of Ammishaddai. ²⁶His troop, as enrolled: 62,700.
²⁷Camping next to it:
The tribe of Asher.
Chieftain of the Asherites: Pagiel son of Ochran. ²⁸His troop, as enrolled: 41,500.
²⁹And the tribe of Naphtali.
Chieftain of the Naphtalites: Ahira son of Enan. ³⁰His troop, as enrolled: 53,400.

³¹The total enrolled in the division of Dan: 157,600. These shall march last, by their standards.

³²Those are the enrollments of the Israelites by ancestral houses. The total enrolled in the divisions, for all troops: 603,550. ³³The Levites, however, were not recorded among the Israelites, as the LORD had commanded Moses.

³⁴The Israelites did accordingly; just as the LORD had commanded Moses, so they camped by their standards, and so they marched, each with his clan according to his ancestral house.

3

This is the line of Aaron and Moses at the time that the LORD spoke with Moses on Mount Sinai. ²These were the names of Aaron's sons: Nadab, the first-born, and Abihu, Eleazar and Ithamar; ³those were the names of Aaron's sons, the anointed priests who were ordained for priesthood. ⁴But Nadab and Abihu died a-by the will of-a the LORD, when they offered alien fire before the LORD in the wilderness of Sinai; and they left no sons. So it was Eleazar and Ithamar who served as priests in the lifetime of their father Aaron.

⁵The LORD spoke to Moses, saying: ⁶Advance the tribe of Levi and place them in attendance upon Aaron the priest to serve him. ⁷They shall perform duties for him and for the whole community before the Tent of Meeting, doing the work of the Tabernacle. ⁸They shall take charge of all the furnishings of the Tent of Meeting—a duty on behalf of the Israelites—doing the work of the Tabernacle. ⁹You shall assign the Levites to Aaron and to his sons: they are formally assigned to him from among the

a-a Others "before."

Israelites. [10]You shall make Aaron and his sons responsible for observing their priestly duties; and any outsider who encroaches shall be put to death.

[11]The LORD spoke to Moses, saying: [12]I hereby take the Levites from among the Israelites in place of all the first-born, the first issue of the womb among the Israelites: the Levites shall be Mine. [13]For every first-born is Mine: at the time that I smote every first-born in the land of Egypt, I consecrated every first-born in Israel, man and beast, to Myself, to be Mine, the LORD's.

[14]The LORD spoke to Moses in the wilderness of Sinai, saying: [15]Record the Levites by ancestral house and by clan; record every male among them from the age of one month up. [16]So Moses recorded them at the command of the LORD, as he was bidden. [17]These were the sons of Levi by name: Gershon, Kohath, and Merari. [18]These were the names of the sons of Gershon by clan: Libni and Shimei. [19]The sons of Kohath by clan: Amram and Izhar, Hebron and Uzziel. [20]The sons of Merari by clan: Mahli and Mushi.

These were the clans of the Levites within their ancestral houses:

[21]To Gershon belonged the clan of the Libnites and the clan of the Shimeites; those were the clans of the Gershonites. [22]The recorded entries of all their males from the age of one month up, as recorded, came to 7,500. [23]The clans of the Gershonites were to camp behind the Tabernacle, to the west. [24]The chieftain of the ancestral house of the Gershonites was Eliasaph son of Lael. [25]The duties of the Gershonites in the Tent of Meeting comprised: the tabernacle,[b] the tent, its covering, and the screen for the entrance of the Tent of Meeting; [26]the hangings of the enclosure, the screen for the entrance of the enclosure which surrounds the Tabernacle, the cords thereof, and the altar—all the service connected with these.

[27]To Kohath belonged the clan of the Amramites, the clan of the Izharites, the clan of the Hebronites, and the clan of the Uzzielites; those were the clans of the Kohathites. [28]All the listed males from the age of one month up came to 8,600, attending to the duties of the sanctuary. [29]The clans of the Kohathites were to camp along the south side of the Tabernacle. [30]The chieftain of the ancestral house of the Kohathite clans was Elizaphan son of Uzziel. [31]Their duties comprised: the ark, the table, the lampstand, the altars, and the sacred utensils that were used with them, and the screen[c]—all the service connected with these. [32]The head chieftain

b *See note on Exod. 26.1.*
c *I.e., the screening curtain; cf. 4–5.*

of the Levites was Eleazar son of Aaron the priest, in charge of those attending to the duties of the sanctuary.

³³To Merari belonged the clan of the Mahlites and the clan of the Mushites; those were the clans of Merari. ³⁴The recorded entries of all their males from the age of one month up came to 6,200. ³⁵The chieftain of the ancestral house of the clans of Merari was Zuriel son of Abihail. They were to camp along the north side of the Tabernacle. ³⁶The assigned duties of the Merarites comprised: the planks of the Tabernacle, its bars, posts, and sockets, and all its furnishings—all the service connected with these; ³⁷also the posts around the enclosure and their sockets, pegs, and cords.

³⁸Those who were to camp before the Tabernacle, in front—before the Tent of Meeting, on the east—were Moses and Aaron and his sons, attending to the duties of the sanctuary, as a duty on behalf of the Israelites; and any outsider who encroached was to be put to death. ³⁹All the Levites who were recorded, whom at the LORD's command Moses and Aaron recorded by their clans, all the males from the age of one month up, came to 22,000.

⁴⁰The LORD said to Moses: Record every first-born male of the Israelite people from the age of one month up, and make a list of their names; ⁴¹and take the Levites for Me, the LORD, in place of every first-born among the Israelite people, and the cattle of the Levites in place of every first-born among the cattle of the Israelites. ⁴²So Moses recorded all the first-born among the Israelites, as the LORD had commanded him. ⁴³All the first-born males as listed by name, recorded from the age of one month up, came to 22,273.

⁴⁴The LORD spoke to Moses, saying: ⁴⁵Take the Levites in place of all the first-born among the Israelite people, and the cattle of the Levites in place of their cattle; and the Levites shall be Mine, the LORD's. ⁴⁶And as the redemption price of the 273 Israelite first-born over and above the number of the Levites, ⁴⁷take five shekels per head—take this by the sanctuary weight, twenty *gerahs* to the shekel—⁴⁸and give the money to Aaron and his sons as the redemption price for those who are in excess. ⁴⁹So Moses took the redemption money from those over and above the ones redeemed by the Levites; ⁵⁰he took the money from the first-born of the Israelites, 1,365 sanctuary shekels. ⁵¹And Moses gave the redemption money to Aaron and his sons at the LORD's bidding, as the LORD had commanded Moses.

4 The LORD spoke to Moses and Aaron, saying:

2Take a [separate] census of the Kohathites among the Levites, by the clans of their ancestral house, 3from the age of thirty years up to the age of fifty, all who are subject to service, to perform tasks for the Tent of Meeting. 4This is the responsibility of the Kohathites in the Tent of Meeting: the most sacred objects.

5At the breaking of camp, Aaron and his sons shall go in and take down the screening curtain and cover the Ark of the Pact with it. 6They shall lay a covering of dolphinª skin over it and spread a cloth of pure blue on top; and they shall put its poles in place.

7Over the table of display they shall spread a blue cloth; they shall place upon it the bowls, the ladles, the jars, and the libation jugs; and the regular bread shall rest upon it. 8They shall spread over these a crimson cloth which they shall cover with a covering of dolphin skin; and they shall put the poles in place.

9Then they shall take a blue cloth and cover the lampstand for lighting, with its lamps, its tongs, and its fire pans, as well as all the oil vessels that are used in its service. 10They shall put it and all its furnishings into a covering of dolphin skin, which they shall then place on a carrying frame.

11Next they shall spread a blue cloth over the altar of gold and cover it with a covering of dolphin skin; and they shall put its poles in place. 12They shall take all the service vessels with which the service in the sanctuary is performed, put them into a blue cloth and cover them with a covering of dolphin skin, which they shall then place on a carrying frame. 13They shall remove the ashes from the [copper] altar and spread a purple cloth over it. 14Upon it they shall place all the vessels that are used in its service: the fire pans, the flesh hooks, the scrapers, and the basins—all the vessels of the altar—and over it they shall spread a covering of dolphin skin; and they shall put its poles in place.

15 ªWhen Aaron and his sons have finished covering the sacred objects and all the furnishings of the sacred objects at the breaking of camp, only then shall the Kohathites come and lift them, so that they do not come in contact with the sacred objects and die. These things in the Tent of Meeting shall be the porterage of the Kohathites.

16Responsibility shall rest with Eleazar son of Aaron the priest for the

___

ª *See note at Ex. 25:4*

lighting oil, the aromatic incense, the regular meal offering, and the anointing oil—responsibility for the whole Tabernacle and for everything conse-crated that is in it or in its vessels.

¹⁷The LORD spoke to Moses and Aaron, saying: ¹⁸Do not let the group of Kohathite clans be cut off from the Levites. ¹⁹Do this with them, that they may live and not die when they approach the most sacred objects: let Aaron and his sons go in and assign each of them to his duties and to his porterage. ²⁰But let not [the Kohathites] go inside and ᵇ‑witness the dismantling of the sanctuary,‑ᵇ lest they die.

נשא

²¹The LORD spoke to Moses: ²²Take a census of the Gershonites also, by their ancestral house and by their clans. ²³Record them from the age of thirty years up to the age of fifty, all who are subject to service in the performance of tasks for the Tent of Meeting. ²⁴These are the duties of the Gershonite clans as to labor and porterage: ²⁵they shall carry the cloths of the Tabernacle, the Tent of Meeting with its covering, the covering of dolphin skin that is on top of it, and the screen for the entrance of the Tent of Meeting; ²⁶the hangings of the enclosure, the screen at the en-trance of the gate of the enclosure that surrounds the Tabernacle, the cords thereof, and the altar, and all their service equipment and all their accessories; and they shall perform the service. ²⁷All the duties of the Gershonites, all their porterage and all their service, shall be performed on orders from Aaron and his sons; you shall make them responsible for attending to all their porterage. ²⁸Those are the duties of the Gershonite clans for the Tent of Meeting; they shall attend to them under the direc-tion of Ithamar son of Aaron the priest.

²⁹As for the Merarites, you shall record them by the clans of their ancestral house; ³⁰you shall record them from the age of thirty years up to the age of fifty, all who are subject to service in the performance of the duties for the Tent of Meeting. ³¹These are their porterage tasks in con-nection with their various duties for the Tent of Meeting: the planks, the bars, the posts, and the sockets of the Tabernacle; ³²the posts around the enclosure and their sockets, pegs, and cords—all these furnishings and their service: you shall list by name the objects that are their porterage tasks. ³³Those are the duties of the Merarite clans, pertaining to their various duties in the Tent of Meeting under the direction of Ithamar son of Aaron the priest.

ᵇ‑ᵇ Others "look at the sacred objects even for a moment."

34So Moses, Aaron, and the chieftains of the community recorded the Kohathites by the clans of their ancestral house, 35from the age of thirty years up to the age of fifty, all who were subject to service for work relating to the Tent of Meeting. 36Those recorded by their clans came to 2,750. 37That was the enrollment of the Kohathite clans, all those who performed duties relating to the Tent of Meeting, whom Moses and Aaron recorded at the command of the LORD through Moses.

38The Gershonites who were recorded by the clans of their ancestral house, 39from the age of thirty years up to the age of fifty, all who were subject to service for work relating to the Tent of Meeting—40those recorded by the clans of their ancestral house came to 2,630. 41That was the enrollment of the Gershonite clans, all those performing duties relating to the Tent of Meeting whom Moses and Aaron recorded at the command of the LORD.

42The enrollment of the Merarite clans by the clans of their ancestral house, 43from the age of thirty years up to the age of fifty, all who were subject to service for work relating to the Tent of Meeting—44those recorded by their clans came to 3,200. 45That was the enrollment of the Merarite clans which Moses and Aaron recorded at the command of the LORD through Moses.

46All the Levites whom Moses, Aaron, and the chieftains of Israel recorded by the clans of their ancestral houses, 47from the age of thirty years up to the age of fifty, all who were subject to duties of service and porterage relating to the Tent of Meeting—48those recorded came to 8,580. 49Each one was given responsibility for his service and porterage at the command of the LORD through Moses, and each was recorded as the LORD had commanded Moses.

5 The LORD spoke to Moses, saying: 2Instruct the Israelites to remove from camp anyone with an a-eruption or a discharge-a and anyone defiled by a corpse. 3Remove male and female alike; put them outside the camp so that they do not defile the camp of those in whose midst I dwell.

4The Israelites did so, putting them outside the camp; as the LORD had spoken to Moses, so the Israelites did.

5The LORD spoke to Moses, saying: 6Speak to the Israelites: When a man or woman commits any wrong toward a fellow man, thus breaking

a-a See Lev. 13, 15.

faith with the LORD, and that person realizes his guilt, 7he shall confess the wrong that he has done. He shall make restitution in the principal amount and add one-fifth to it, giving it to him whom he has wronged. 8If the man has no kinsman[b] to whom restitution can be made, the amount repaid shall go to the LORD for the priest—in addition to the ram of expiation with which expiation is made on his behalf.[c] 9So, too, any gift among the sacred donations that the Israelites offer shall be the priest's. 10And each shall retain his sacred donations: each priest shall keep what is given to him.

11The LORD spoke to Moses, saying: 12Speak to the Israelite people and say to them:

If any man's wife has gone astray and broken faith with him 13in that a man has had carnal relations with her unbeknown to her husband, and she keeps secret the fact that she has defiled herself without being forced, and there is no witness against her—14but a fit of jealousy comes over him and he is wrought up about the wife who has defiled herself; or if a fit of jealousy comes over one and he is wrought up about his wife although she has not defiled herself—15the man shall bring his wife to the priest. And he shall bring as an offering for her one-tenth of an *ephah* of barley flour. No oil shall be poured upon it and no frankincense shall be laid on it, for it is a meal offering of jealousy, a meal offering of remembrance which recalls wrongdoing.

16The priest shall bring her forward and have her stand before the LORD. 17The priest shall take sacral water in an earthen vessel and, taking some of the earth that is on the floor of the Tabernacle, the priest shall put it into the water. 18After he has made the woman stand before the LORD, the priest shall bare the woman's head[d] and place upon her hands the meal offering of remembrance, which is a meal offering of jealousy. And in the priest's hands shall be the water of bitterness [e]that induces the spell.[e] 19The priest shall adjure the woman, saying to her, "If no man has lain with you, if you have not gone astray in defilement while married to your husband, be immune to harm from this water of bitterness that induces the spell. 20But if you have gone astray while married to your husband and have defiled yourself, if a man other than your husband has had carnal relations with you"—21here the priest shall administer the curse of adjuration to the woman, as the priest goes on to say to the woman—

b Lit. "redeemer."
c Cf. Lev. 5.15 f.
d See note at Lev. 10.6.
e-e Meaning of Heb. uncertain.

"may the LORD make you a curse and an imprecation among your people, as the LORD causes your thigh to sag and your belly to distend;ᶜ ²²may this water that induces the spell enter your body, causing the belly to distend and the thigh to sag." And the woman shall say, "Amen, amen!"

²³The priest shall put these curses down in writing and rub it off into the water of bitterness. ²⁴He is to make the woman drink the water of bitterness that induces the spell, so that the spell-inducing water may enter into her to bring on bitterness. ²⁵Then the priest shall take from the woman's hand the meal offering of jealousy, elevate the meal offering before the LORD, and present it on the altar. ²⁶The priest shall scoop out of the meal offering a token part of it and turn it into smoke on the altar. Last, he shall make the woman drink the water.

²⁷Once he has made her drink the water—if she has defiled herself by breaking faith with her husband, the spell-inducing water shall enter into her to bring on bitterness, so that her belly shall distend and her thigh shall sag; and the woman shall become a curse among her people. ²⁸But if the woman has not defiled herself and is pure, she shall be unharmed and able to retain seed.

²⁹This is the ritual in cases of jealousy, when a woman goes astray while married to her husband and defiles herself, ³⁰or when a fit of jealousy comes over a man and he is wrought up over his wife: the woman shall be made to stand before the LORD and the priest shall carry out all this ritual with her. ³¹The man shall be clear of guilt; but that woman shall suffer for her guilt.

6 The LORD spoke to Moses, saying: ²Speak to the Israelites and say to them: If anyone, man or woman, explicitlyᵃ utters a nazirite's vow, to set himself apart for the LORD, ³he shall abstain from wine and any other intoxicant; he shall not drink vinegar of wine or of any other intoxicant, neither shall he drink anything in which grapes have been steeped, nor eat grapes fresh or dried. ⁴Throughout his term as nazirite, he may not eat anything that is obtained from the grapevine, even seeds or skin.ᵇ

⁵Throughout the term of his vow as nazirite, no razor shall touch his head; it shall remain consecrated until the completion of his term as nazirite of the LORD, the hair of his head being left to grow untrimmed.

ᵃ See note at Lev. 22.21.
ᵇ Meaning of ḥarṣannim and zag uncertain.

⁶Throughout the term that he has set apart for the LORD, he shall not go in where there is a dead person. ⁷Even if his father or mother, or his brother or sister should die, he must not defile himself for them, since ᶜ-hair set apart for his God-ᶜ is upon his head: ⁸throughout his term as nazirite he is consecrated to the LORD.

⁹If a person dies suddenly near him,ᵈ defiling his consecrated hair, he shall shave his head on the day he becomes clean; he shall shave it on the seventh day. ¹⁰On the eighth day he shall bring two turtledoves or two pigeons to the priest, at the entrance of the Tent of Meeting. ¹¹The priest shall offer one as a sin offering and the other as a burnt offering, and make expiation on his behalf for the guilt that he incurred through the corpse. That same day he shall reconsecrate his head ¹²and rededicate to the LORD his term as nazirite; and he shall bring a lamb in its first year as a penalty offering. The previous period shall be void, since his consecrated hair was defiled.

¹³This is the ritual for the nazirite: On the day that his term as nazirite is completed, heᵉ shall be brought to the entrance of the Tent of Meeting. ¹⁴As his offering to the LORD he shall present: one male lamb in its first year, without blemish, for a burnt offering; one ewe lamb in its first year, without blemish, for a sin offering; one ram without blemish for an offering of well-being; ¹⁵a basket of unleavened cakes of choice flour with oil mixed in, and unleavened wafers spread with oil; and the proper meal offerings and libations.

¹⁶The priest shall present them before the LORD and offer the sin offering and the burnt offering. ¹⁷He shall offer the ram as a sacrifice of well-being to the LORD, together with the basket of unleavened cakes; the priest shall also offer the meal offerings and the libations. ¹⁸The nazirite shall then shave his consecrated hair, at the entrance of the Tent of Meeting, and take the locks of his consecrated hair and put them on the fire that is under the sacrifice of well-being.

¹⁹The priest shall take the shoulder of the ram when it has been boiled, one unleavened cake from the basket, and one unleavened wafer, and place them on the hands of the nazirite after he has shaved his consecrated hair. ²⁰The priest shall elevate them as an elevation offering before the LORD; and this shall be a sacred donation for the priest, in addition to the breast of the elevation offering and the thigh of gift offering. After that the nazirite may drink wine.

ᶜ⁻ᶜ *Others "his consecration unto God."*
ᵈ *Cf. Num. 19.14–16.*
ᵉ *Or "it," i.e., the consecrated hair; cf. v. 19.*

21Such is the obligation of a nazirite; except that he who vows an offering to the LORD of what he can afford, beyond his nazirite requirements, must do exactly according to the vow that he has made beyond his obligation as a nazirite.

22The LORD spoke to Moses: 23Speak to Aaron and his sons: Thus shall you bless the people of Israel. Say to them:
24The LORD bless you and protect you!
25The LORD f-deal kindly and graciously with you!-f
26The LORD g-bestow His favor-g upon you and grant you peace!h
27Thus they shall link My name with the people of Israel, and I will bless them.

7 On the day that Moses finished setting up the Tabernacle, he anointed and consecrated it and all its furnishings, as well as the altar and its utensils. When he had anointed and consecrated them, 2the chieftains of Israel, the heads of ancestral houses, namely, the chieftains of the tribes, those who were in charge of enrollment, drew neara 3and brought their offering before the LORD: six draught carts and twelve oxen, a cart for every two chieftains and an ox for each one.

When they had brought them before the Tabernacle, 4the LORD said to Moses: 5Accept these from them for use in the service of the Tent of Meeting, and give them to the Levites according to their respective services.

6Moses took the carts and the oxen and gave them to the Levites. 7Two carts and four oxen he gave to the Gershonites, as required for their service, 8and four carts and eight oxen he gave to the Merarites, as required for their service—under the direction of Ithamar son of Aaron the priest. 9But to the Kohathites he did not give any; since theirs was the service of the [most] sacred objects, their porterage was by shoulder.

10The chieftains also brought the dedication offering for the altar upon its being anointed. As the chieftains were presenting their offerings before the altar, 11the LORD said to Moses: Let them present their offerings for the dedication of the altar, one chieftain each day.

12The one who presented his offering on the first day was Nahshon son of Amminadab of the tribe of Judah. 13His offering: one silver bowl weighing 130 shekels and one silver basin of 70 shekels by the sanctuary weight, both filled with choice flour with oil mixed in, for a meal offering;

f-f Others "make His face to shine upon thee and be gracious to thee."
g-g Others "lift up His countenance."
h Or "friendship."

a Cf. Exod. 14.10.

[14] one gold ladle of 10 shekels, filled with incense; [15] one bull of the herd, one ram, and one lamb in its first year, for a burnt offering; [16] one goat for a sin offering; [17] and for his sacrifice of well-being: two oxen, five rams, five he-goats, and five yearling lambs. That was the offering of Nahshon son of Amminadab.

[18] On the second day, Nethanel son of Zuar, chieftain of Issachar, made his offering. [19] He presented as his offering: one silver bowl weighing 130 shekels and one silver basin of 70 shekels by the sanctuary weight, both filled with choice flour with oil mixed in, for a meal offering; [20] one gold ladle of 10 shekels, filled with incense; [21] one bull of the herd, one ram, and one lamb in its first year, for a burnt offering; [22] one goat for a sin offering; [23] and for his sacrifice of well-being: two oxen, five rams, five he-goats, and five yearling lambs. That was the offering of Nethanel son of Zuar.

[24] On the third day, it was the chieftain of the Zebulunites, Eliab son of Helon. [25] His offering: one silver bowl weighing 130 shekels and one silver basin of 70 shekels by the sanctuary weight, both filled with choice flour with oil mixed in, for a meal offering; [26] one gold ladle of 10 shekels, filled with incense; [27] one bull of the herd, one ram, and one lamb in its first year, for a burnt offering; [28] one goat for a sin offering; [29] and for his sacrifice of well-being: two oxen, five rams, five he-goats, and five yearling lambs. That was the offering of Eliab son of Helon.

[30] On the fourth day, it was the chieftain of the Reubenites, Elizur son of Shedeur. [31] His offering: one silver bowl weighing 130 shekels and one silver basin of 70 shekels by the sanctuary weight, both filled with choice flour with oil mixed in, for a meal offering; [32] one gold ladle of 10 shekels, filled with incense; [33] one bull of the herd, one ram, and one lamb in its first year, for a burnt offering; [34] one goat for a sin offering; [35] and for his sacrifice of well-being: two oxen, five rams, five he-goats, and five yearling lambs. That was the offering of Elizur son of Shedeur.

[36] On the fifth day, it was the chieftain of the Simeonites, Shelumiel son of Zurishaddai. [37] His offering: one silver bowl weighing 130 shekels and one silver basin of 70 shekels by the sanctuary weight, both filled with choice flour with oil mixed in, for a meal offering; [38] one gold ladle of 10 shekels, filled with incense; [39] one bull of the herd, one ram, and one lamb in its first year, for a burnt offering; [40] one goat for a sin offering; [41] and for his sacrifice of well-being: two oxen, five rams, five he-goats, and five yearling lambs. That was the offering of Shelumiel son of Zurishaddai.

⁴²On the sixth day, it was the chieftain of the Gadites, Eliasaph son of Deuel. ⁴³His offering: one silver bowl weighing 130 shekels and one silver basin of 70 shekels by the sanctuary weight, both filled with choice flour with oil mixed in, for a meal offering; ⁴⁴one gold ladle of 10 shekels, filled with incense; ⁴⁵one bull of the herd, one ram, and one lamb in its first year, for a burnt offering; ⁴⁶one goat for a sin offering; ⁴⁷and for his sacrifice of well-being: two oxen, five rams, five he-goats, and five yearling lambs. That was the offering of Eliasaph son of Deuel.

⁴⁸On the seventh day, it was the chieftain of the Ephraimites, Elishama son of Ammihud. ⁴⁹His offering: one silver bowl weighing 130 shekels and one silver basin of 70 shekels by the sanctuary weight, both filled with choice flour with oil mixed in, for a meal offering; ⁵⁰one gold ladle of 10 shekels, filled with incense; ⁵¹one bull of the herd, one ram, and one lamb in its first year, for a burnt offering; ⁵²one goat for a sin offering; ⁵³and for his sacrifice of well-being: two oxen, five rams, five he-goats, and five yearling lambs. That was the offering of Elishama son of Ammihud.

⁵⁴On the eighth day, it was the chieftain of the Manassites, Gamaliel son of Pedahzur. ⁵⁵His offering: one silver bowl weighing 130 shekels and one silver basin of 70 shekels by the sanctuary weight, both filled with choice flour with oil mixed in, for a meal offering; ⁵⁶ one gold ladle of 10 shekels, filled with incense; ⁵⁷one bull of the herd, one ram, and one lamb in its first year, for a burnt offering; ⁵⁸one goat for a sin offering; ⁵⁹and for his sacrifice of well-being: two oxen, five rams, five he-goats, and five yearling lambs. That was the offering of Gamaliel son of Pedahzur.

⁶⁰On the ninth day, it was the chieftain of the Benjaminites, Abidan son of Gideoni. ⁶¹His offering: one silver bowl weighing 130 shekels and one silver basin of 70 shekels by the sanctuary weight, both filled with choice flour with oil mixed in, for a meal offering; ⁶²one gold ladle of 10 shekels, filled with incense; ⁶³one bull of the herd, one ram, and one lamb in its first year, for a burnt offering; ⁶⁴one goat for a sin offering; ⁶⁵and for his sacrifice of well-being: two oxen, five rams, five he-goats, and five yearling lambs. That was the offering of Abidan son of Gideoni.

⁶⁶On the tenth day, it was the chieftain of the Danites, Ahiezer son of Ammishaddai. ⁶⁷His offering: one silver bowl weighing 130 shekels and one silver basin of 70 shekels by the sanctuary weight, both filled with choice flour with oil mixed in, for a meal offering; ⁶⁸one gold ladle of 10

shekels, filled with incense; [69]one bull of the herd, one ram, and one lamb in its first year, for a burnt offering; [70]one goat for a sin offering; [71]and for his sacrifice of well-being: two oxen, five rams, five he-goats, and five yearling lambs. That was the offering of Ahiezer son of Ammishaddai.

[72]On the eleventh day, it was the chieftain of the Asherites, Pagiel son of Ochran. [73]His offering: one silver bowl weighing 130 shekels and one silver basin of 70 shekels by the sanctuary weight, both filled with choice flour with oil mixed in, for a meal offering; [74]one gold ladle of 10 shekels, filled with incense; [75]one bull of the herd, one ram, and one lamb in its first year, for a burnt offering; [76]one goat for a sin offering; [77]and for his sacrifice of well-being: two oxen, five rams, five he-goats, and five yearling lambs. That was the offering of Pagiel son of Ochran.

[78]On the twelfth day, it was the chieftain of the Naphtalites, Ahira son of Enan. [79]His offering: one silver bowl weighing 130 shekels and one silver basin of 70 shekels by the sanctuary weight, both filled with choice flour with oil mixed in, for a meal offering; [80]one gold ladle of 10 shekels, filled with incense; [81]one bull of the herd, one ram, and one lamb in its first year, for a burnt offering; [82]one goat for a sin offering; [83]and for his sacrifice of well-being: two oxen, five rams, five he-goats, and five yearling lambs. That was the offering of Ahira son of Enan.

[84]This was the dedication offering for the altar from the chieftains of Israel upon its being anointed: silver bowls, 12; silver basins, 12; gold ladles, 12. [85]Silver per bowl, 130; per basin, 70. Total silver of vessels, 2,400 sanctuary shekels. [86]The 12 gold ladles filled with incense—10 sanctuary shekels per ladle—total gold of the ladles, 120.

[87]Total of herd animals for burnt offerings, 12 bulls; of rams, 12; of yearling lambs, 12—with their proper meal offerings; of goats for sin offerings, 12. [88]Total of herd animals for sacrifices of well-being, 24 bulls; of rams, 60; of he-goats, 60; of yearling lambs, 60. That was the dedication offering for the altar after its anointing.

[89]When Moses went into the Tent of Meeting to speak with Him, he would hear the Voice addressing him from above the cover that was on top of the Ark of the Pact between the two cherubim; thus He spoke to him.

בהעלתך

8 The LORD spoke to Moses, saying: [2]Speak to Aaron and say to him, "When you mount[a] the lamps, let the seven lamps give light at the front of the lampstand." [3]Aaron did so; he mounted the lamps at the front of the lampstand, as the LORD had commanded Moses.—[4]Now this is how the lampstand was made: it was hammered work of gold, hammered from base to petal. According to the pattern that the LORD had shown Moses, so was the lampstand made.

[5]The LORD spoke to Moses, saying: [6]Take the Levites from among the Israelites and cleanse them. [7]This is what you shall do to them to cleanse them: sprinkle on them water of purification, and let them go over their whole body with a razor, and wash their clothes; thus they shall be cleansed. [8]Let them take a bull of the herd, and with it a meal offering of choice flour with oil mixed in, and you take a second bull of the herd for a sin offering. [9]You shall bring the Levites forward before the Tent of Meeting. Assemble the whole Israelite community, [10]and bring the Levites forward before the LORD. Let the Israelites lay their hands upon the Levites, [11]and let Aaron designate[b] the Levites before the LORD as an elevation offering from the Israelites, that they may perform the service of the LORD. [12]The Levites shall now lay their hands upon the heads of the bulls; one shall be offered to the LORD as a sin offering and the other as a burnt offering, to make expiation for the Levites.

[13]You shall place the Levites in attendance upon Aaron and his sons, and designate them as an elevation offering to the LORD. [14]Thus you shall set the Levites apart from the Israelites, and the Levites shall be Mine. [15]Thereafter the Levites shall be qualified for the service of the Tent of Meeting, once you have cleansed them and designated them as an elevation offering. [16]For they are formally assigned to Me from among the Israelites: I have taken them for Myself in place of all the first issue of the womb, of all the first-born of the Israelites. [17]For every first-born among the Israelites, man as well as beast, is Mine; I consecrated them to Myself at the time that I smote every first-born in the land of Egypt. [18]Now I take the Levites instead of every first-born of the Israelites; [19]and from among the Israelites I formally assign the Levites to Aaron and his sons, to perform the service for the Israelites in the Tent of Meeting and to

[a] Cf. Exod. 25.37.
[b] Lit. "elevate."

make expiation for the Israelites, so that no plague may afflict the Israelites c-for coming-c too near the sanctuary.

20Moses, Aaron, and the whole Israelite community did with the Levites accordingly; just as the LORD had commanded Moses in regard to the Levites, so the Israelites did with them. 21The Levites purified themselves and washed their clothes; and Aaron designated them as an elevation offering before the LORD, and Aaron made expiation for them to cleanse them. 22Thereafter the Levites were qualified to perform their service in the Tent of Meeting, under Aaron and his sons. As the LORD had commanded Moses in regard to the Levites, so they did to them.

23The LORD spoke to Moses, saying: 24This is the rule for the Levites. From twenty-five years of age up they shall participate in the work force in the service of the Tent of Meeting; 25but at the age of fifty they shall retire from the work force and shall serve no more. 26They may assist their brother Levites at the Tent of Meeting by standing guard, but they shall perform no labor. Thus you shall deal with the Levites in regard to their duties.

9 The LORD spoke to Moses in the wilderness of Sinai, on the first new moon of the second year following the exodus from the land of Egypt, saying: 2Let the Israelite people offer the passover sacrifice at its set time: 3you shall offer it on the fourteenth day of this month, at twilight, at its set time; you shall offer it in accordance with all its rules and rites.

4Moses instructed the Israelites to offer the passover sacrifice; 5and they offered the passover sacrifice in the first month, on the fourteenth day of the month, at twilight, in the wilderness of Sinai. Just as the LORD had commanded Moses, so the Israelites did.

6But there were some men who were unclean by reason of a corpse and could not offer the passover sacrifice on that day. Appearing that same day before Moses and Aaron, 7those men said to them,a "Unclean though we are by reason of a corpse, why must we be debarred from presenting the LORD's offering at its set time with the rest of the Israelites?" 8Moses said to them, "Stand by, and let me hear what instructions the LORD gives about you."

9And the LORD spoke to Moses, saying: 10Speak to the Israelite people, saying: When any of you or of your posterity who are defiled by a corpse

c-c Lit. "when the Israelites come."

a Lit. "him."

or are on a long journey would offer a passover sacrifice to the LORD, [11]they shall offer it in the second month, on the fourteenth day of the month, at twilight. They shall eat it with unleavened bread and bitter herbs, [12]and they shall not leave any of it over until morning. They shall not break a bone of it. They shall offer it in strict accord with the law of the passover sacrifice. [13]But if a man who is clean and not on a journey refrains from offering the passover sacrifice, that person shall be cut off from his kin, for he did not present the LORD's offering at its set time; that man shall bear his guilt.

[14]And when a stranger who resides with you would offer a passover sacrifice to the LORD, he must offer it in accordance with the rules and rites of the passover sacrifice. There shall be one law for you, whether stranger or citizen of the country.

[15]On the day that the Tabernacle was set up, the cloud covered the Tabernacle, the Tent of the Pact; and in the evening it rested over the Tabernacle in the likeness of fire until morning. [16]It was always so: the cloud covered it, appearing as fire by night. [17]And whenever the cloud lifted from the Tent, the Israelites would set out accordingly; and at the spot where the cloud settled, there the Israelites would make camp. [18]At a command of the LORD the Israelites broke camp, and at a command of the LORD they made camp: they remained encamped as long as the cloud stayed over the Tabernacle. [19]When the cloud lingered over the Tabernacle many days, the Israelites observed the LORD's mandate and did not journey on. [20]At such times as the cloud rested over the Tabernacle for but a few days, they remained encamped at a command of the LORD, and broke camp at a command of the LORD. [21]And at such times as the cloud stayed from evening until morning, they broke camp as soon as the cloud lifted in the morning. Day or night, whenever the cloud lifted, they would break camp. [22]Whether it was two days or a month or a year—however long the cloud lingered over the Tabernacle—the Israelites remained encamped and did not set out; only when it lifted did they break camp. [23]On a sign from the LORD they made camp and on a sign from the LORD they broke camp; they observed the LORD's mandate at the LORD's bidding through Moses.

10

The LORD spoke to Moses, saying: [2]Have two silver trumpets made; make them of hammered work. They shall serve you to summon the community and to set the divisions in motion. ³When both are blown in long blasts,ᵃ the whole community shall assemble before you at the entrance of the Tent of Meeting; ⁴and if only one is blown, the chieftains, heads of Israel's contingents, shall assemble before you. ⁵But when you sound short blasts,ᵃ the divisions encamped on the east shall move forward; ⁶and when you sound short blasts a second time, those encamped on the south shall move forward. Thus short blasts shall be blown for setting them in motion, ⁷while to convoke the congregation you shall blow long blasts, not short ones. ⁸The trumpets shall be blown by Aaron's sons, the priests; they shall be for you an institution for all time throughout the ages.

9 ᵃ-When you are at war-ᵃ in your land against an aggressor who attacks you, you shall sound short blasts on the trumpets, that you may be remembered before the LORD your God and be delivered from your enemies. ¹⁰And on your joyous occasions—your fixed festivals and new moon days—you shall sound the trumpets over your burnt offerings and your sacrifices of well-being. They shall be a reminder of you before your God: I, the LORD, am your God.

¹¹In the second year, on the twentieth day of the second month, the cloud lifted from the Tabernacle of the Pact ¹²and the Israelites set out on their journeys from the wilderness of Sinai. The cloud came to rest in the wilderness of Paran.

¹³When the march was to begin, at the LORD's command through Moses, ¹⁴the first standard to set out, troop by troop, was the division of Judah. In command of its troops was Nahshon son of Amminadab; ¹⁵in command of the tribal troop of Issachar, Nethanel son of Zuar; ¹⁶and in command of the tribal troop of Zebulun, Eliab son of Helon.

¹⁷Then the Tabernacle would be taken apart; and the Gershonites and the Merarites, who carried the Tabernacle, would set out.

¹⁸The next standard to set out, troop by troop, was the division of Reuben. In command of its troop was Elizur son of Shedeur; ¹⁹in command of the tribal troop of Simeon, Shelumiel son of Zurishaddai; ²⁰and in command of the tribal troop of Gad, Eliasaph son of Deuel.

²¹Then the Kohathites, who carried the sacred objects, would set out; and by the time they arrived, the Tabernacle would be set up again.

²²The next standard to set out, troop by troop, was the division of Ephraim. In command of its troop was Elishama son of Ammihud; ²³in command of the tribal troop of Manasseh, Gamaliel son of Pedahzur;

ᵃ *Meaning of Heb. uncertain.*

²⁴and in command of the tribal troop of Benjamin, Abidan son of Gideoni.

²⁵Then, as the rear guard of all the divisions, the standard of the division of Dan would set out, troop by troop. In command of its troop was Ahiezer son of Ammishaddai; ²⁶in command of the tribal troop of Asher, Pagiel son of Ochran; ²⁷and in command of the tribal troop of Naphtali, Ahira son of Enan.

²⁸Such was the order of march of the Israelites, as they marched troop by troop.

²⁹Moses said to Hobab son of Reuel the Midianite, Moses' father-in-law, "We are setting out for the place of which the LORD has said, 'I will give it to you.' Come with us and we will be generous with you; for the LORD has promised to be generous to Israel."

³⁰"I will not go," he replied to him, "but will return to my native land."
³¹He said, "Please do not leave us, inasmuch as you know where we should camp in the wilderness and can be our guide.ᵇ So if you come with us, we will extend to you the same bounty that the LORD grants us."

³³They marched from the mountain of the LORD a distance of three days. The Ark of the Covenant of the LORD traveled in front of them on that three days' journey to seek out a resting place for them; ³⁴and the LORD's cloud kept above them by day, as they moved on from camp.
³⁵When the Ark was to set out, Moses would say:
    Advance, O LORD!
    May Your enemies be scattered,
    And may Your foes flee before You!
³⁶And when it halted, he would say:
    ᶜReturn, O LORD,
    You who are Israel's myriads of thousands!ᶜ

11 The people took to complaining bitterly before the LORD. The LORD heard and was incensed: a fire of the LORD broke out against them, ravaging the outskirts of the camp. ²The people cried out to Moses. Moses prayed to the LORD, and the fire died down. ³That place was named Taberah,ᵃ because a fire of the LORD had broken out against them.

ᵇ *Lit. "eyes."*
ᶜ⁻ᶜ *Others "Return, O LORD, unto the*
  ten thousands of the families of Israel!"

ᵃ *From root b'r, "to burn."*

⁴The riffraff in their midst felt a gluttonous craving; and then the Israelites wept and said, "If only we had meat to eat! ⁵We remember the fish that we used to eat free in Egypt, the cucumbers, the melons, the leeks, the onions, and the garlic. ⁶Now our gullets are shriveled. There is nothing at all! Nothing but this manna to look to!"

⁷Now the manna was like coriander seed, and in color it was like bdellium. ⁸The people would go about and gather it, grind it between millstones or pound it in a mortar, boil it in a pot, and make it into cakes. It tasted like rich cream.ᵇ ⁹When the dew fell on the camp at night, the manna would fall upon it.

¹⁰Moses heard the people weeping, every clan apart, each person at the entrance of his tent. The LORD was very angry, and Moses was distressed. ¹¹And Moses said to the LORD, "Why have You dealt ill with Your servant, and why have I not enjoyed Your favor, that You have laid the burden of all this people upon me? ¹²Did I conceive all this people, did I bear them, that You should say to me, 'Carry them in your bosom as a nurse carries an infant,' to the land that You have promised on oath to their fathers? ¹³Where am I to get meat to give to all this people, when they whine before me and say, 'Give us meat to eat!' ¹⁴I cannot carry all this people by myself, for it is too much for me. ¹⁵If You would deal thus with me, kill me rather, I beg You, and let me see no more of my wretchedness!"

¹⁶Then the LORD said to Moses, "Gather for Me seventy of Israel's elders of whom you have experience as elders and officers of the people, and bring them to the Tent of Meeting and let them take their place there with you. ¹⁷I will come down and speak with you there, and I will draw upon the spirit that is on you and put it upon them; they shall share the burden of the people with you, and you shall not bear it alone. ¹⁸And say to the people: ᶜ⁻Purify yourselves⁻ᶜ for tomorrow and you shall eat meat, for you have kept whining before the LORD and saying, 'If only we had meat to eat! Indeed, we were better off in Egypt!' The LORD will give you meat and you shall eat. ¹⁹You shall eat not one day, not two, not even five days or ten or twenty, ²⁰but a whole month, until it comes out of your nostrils and becomes loathsome to you. For you have rejected the LORD who is among you, by whining before Him and saying, 'Oh, why did we ever leave Egypt!' "

ᵇ Lit. "cream of oil (or, fat)."
ᶜ⁻ᶜ I.e., as for a sacrificial meal.

21But Moses said, "The people d-who are with me-d number six hundred thousand men; yet You say, 'I will give them enough meat to eat for a whole month.' 22Could enough flocks and herds be slaughtered to suffice them? Or could all the fish of the sea be gathered for them to suffice them?" 23And the LORD answered Moses, e-"Is there a limit to the LORD's power?-e You shall soon see whether what I have said happens to you or not!"

24Moses went out and reported the words of the LORD to the people. He gathered seventy of the people's elders and stationed them around the Tent. 25Then the LORD came down in a cloud and spoke to him; He drew upon the spirit that was on him and put it upon the seventy elders. And when the spirit rested upon them, they f-spoke in ecstasy,-f but did not continue.

26Two men, one named Eldad and the other Medad, had remained in camp; yet the spirit rested upon them—they were among those recorded, but they had not gone out to the Tent—and they f-spoke in ecstasy-f in the camp. 27A youth ran out and told Moses, saying, "Eldad and Medad are acting the prophet in the camp!" 28And Joshua son of Nun, Moses' attendant from his youth, spoke up and said, "My lord Moses, restrain them!" 29But Moses said to him, "Are you wrought up on my account? Would that all the LORD's people were prophets, that the LORD put His spirit upon them!" 30Moses then reentered the camp together with the elders of Israel.

31A wind from the LORD started up, swept quail from the sea and strewed them over the camp, about a day's journey on this side and about a day's journey on that side, all around the camp, and some two cubits deep on the ground. 32The people set to gathering quail all that day and night and all the next day—even he who gathered least had ten *homers*— and they spread them out all around the camp. 33The meat was still between their teeth, nor yet chewed,g when the anger of the LORD blazed forth against the people and the LORD struck the people with a very severe plague. 34That place was named Kibroth-hattaavah,h because the people who had the craving were buried there.

35Then the people set out from Kibroth-hattaavah for Hazeroth.

d-d *Lit. "in whose midst I am."*
e-e *Lit. "Is the Lord's hand too short?"*
f-f *Others "prophesied."*
g *Meaning of Heb.* yikkareth *uncertain.*
h *I.e., "the graves of craving."*

12

When they were in Hazeroth, [1]Miriam and Aaron spoke against Moses because of the Cushite woman he had married: "He married a Cushite woman!"

[2]They said, "Has the LORD spoken only through Moses? Has He not spoken through us as well?" The LORD heard it. [3]Now Moses was a very humble man, more so than any other man on earth. [4]Suddenly the LORD called to Moses, Aaron, and Miriam, "Come out, you three, to the Tent of Meeting." So the three of them went out. [5]The LORD came down in a pillar of cloud, stopped at the entrance of the Tent, and called out, "Aaron and Miriam!" The two of them came forward; [6]and He said, "Hear these My words: [a-]When a prophet of the LORD arises among you, I[-a] make Myself known to him in a vision, I speak with him in a dream. [7]Not so with My servant Moses; he is trusted throughout My household. [8]With him I speak mouth to mouth, plainly and not in riddles, and he beholds the likeness of the LORD. How then did you not shrink from speaking against My servant Moses!" [9]Still incensed with them, the LORD departed.

[10]As the cloud withdrew from the Tent, there was Miriam stricken with snow-white scales![b] When Aaron turned toward Miriam, he saw that she was stricken with scales. [11]And Aaron said to Moses, "O my lord, account not to us the sin which we committed in our folly. [12]Let her not be as one dead, who emerges from his mother's womb with half his flesh eaten away." [13]So Moses cried out to the LORD, saying, "O God, pray heal her!"

[14]But the LORD said to Moses, "If her father spat in her face, would she not bear her shame for seven days? Let her be shut out of camp for seven days, and then let her be readmitted." [15]So Miriam was shut out of camp seven days; and the people did not march on until Miriam was readmitted. [16]After that the people set out from Hazeroth and encamped in the wilderness of Paran.

13

שלח לך

The LORD spoke to Moses, saying, [2]"Send men to scout the land of Canaan, which I am giving to the Israelite people; send one man from each of their ancestral tribes, each one a chieftain among them." [3]So

---

[a-a] Meaning of Heb. uncertain. Others "If there be a prophet among you, I the LORD."
[b] Cf. Lev. 13.2–3.

Moses, by the LORD's command, sent them out from the wilderness of Paran, all the men being leaders of the Israelites. 4And these were their names:

From the tribe of Reuben, Shammua son of Zaccur.

5From the tribe of Simeon, Shaphat son of Hori.

6From the tribe of Judah, Caleb son of Jephunneh.

7From the tribe of Issachar, Igal son of Joseph.

8From the tribe of Ephraim, Hosea[a] son of Nun.

9From the tribe of Benjamin, Palti son of Rafu.

10From the tribe of Zebulun, Gaddiel son of Sodi.

11From the tribe of Joseph, namely, the tribe of Manasseh, Gaddi son of Susi.

12From the tribe of Dan, Ammiel son of Gemalli.

13From the tribe of Asher, Sethur son of Michael.

14From the tribe of Naphtali, Nahbi son of Vophsi.

15From the tribe of Gad, Geuel son of Machi.

16Those were the names of the men whom Moses sent to scout the land; but Moses changed the name of Hosea[a] son of Nun to Joshua.

17When Moses sent them to scout the land of Canaan, he said to them, "Go up there into the Negeb and on into the hill country, 18and see what kind of country it is. Are the people who dwell in it strong or weak, few or many? 19Is the country in which they dwell good or bad? Are the towns they live in open or fortified? 20Is the soil rich or poor? Is it wooded or not? And take pains to bring back some of the fruit of the land."— Now it happened to be the season of the first ripe grapes.

21They went up and scouted the land, from the wilderness of Zin to Rehob, at Lebo-hamath.[b] 22They went up into the Negeb and came to Hebron, where lived Ahiman, Sheshai, and Talmai, the Anakites.—Now Hebron was founded seven years before Zoan of Egypt.—23They reached the wadi Eshcol, and there they cut down a branch with a single cluster of grapes—it had to be borne on a carrying frame by two of them—and some pomegranates and figs. 24That place was named the wadi Eshcol[c] because of the cluster that the Israelites cut down there.

25At the end of forty days they returned from scouting the land. 26They went straight to Moses and Aaron and the whole Israelite community at Kadesh in the wilderness of Paran, and they made their report to them and to the whole community, as they showed them the fruit of the land. 27This is what they told him: "We came to the land you sent us to; it

a Or "Hoshea."
b Others "the entrance to Hamath."
c I.e., "cluster."

does indeed flow with milk and honey, and this is its fruit. ²⁸However, the people who inhabit the country are powerful, and the cities are fortified and very large; moreover, we saw the Anakites there. ²⁹Amalekites dwell in the Negeb region; Hittites, Jebusites, and Amorites inhabit the hill country; and Canaanites dwell by the Sea and along the Jordan."

³⁰Caleb hushed the people before Moses and said, "Let us by all means go up, and we shall gain possession of it, for we shall surely overcome it."

³¹But the men who had gone up with him said, "We cannot attack that people, for it is stronger than we." ³²Thus they spread calumnies among the Israelites about the land they had scouted, saying, "The country that we traversed and scouted is one that devours its settlers. All the people that we saw in it are men of great size; ³³we saw the Nephilim[d] there— the Anakites are part of the Nephilim—and we looked like grasshoppers to ourselves, and so we must have looked to them."

14 The whole community broke into loud cries, and the people wept that night. ²All the Israelites railed against Moses and Aaron. "If only we had died in the land of Egypt," the whole community shouted at them, "or if only we might die in this wilderness! ³Why is the LORD taking us to that land to fall by the sword? Our wives and children will be carried off! It would be better for us to go back to Egypt!" ⁴And they said to one another, "Let us [a-head back for-a] Egypt."

⁵Then Moses and Aaron fell on their faces before all the assembled congregation of the Israelites. ⁶And Joshua son of Nun and Caleb son of Jephunneh, of those who had scouted the land, rent their clothes ⁷and exhorted the whole Israelite community: "The land that we traversed and scouted is an exceedingly good land. ⁸If the LORD is pleased with us, He will bring us into that land, a land that flows with milk and honey, and give it to us; ⁹only you must not rebel against the LORD. Have no fear then of the people of the country, for they are our prey:[b] their protection has departed from them, but the LORD is with us. Have no fear of them!" ¹⁰As the whole community threatened to pelt them with stones, the Presence of the LORD appeared in the Tent of Meeting to all the Israelites.

¹¹And the LORD said to Moses, "How long will this people spurn Me, and how long will they have no faith in Me despite all the signs that I have performed in their midst? ¹²I will strike them with pestilence and

---

^d See Gen. 6.4.

^{a-a} Lit. "set the head and return to"; cf. Neh. 9.17. Others "Let us make a captain and return to."

^b Lit. "food (or, bread)."

disown them, and I will make of you a nation far more numerous than they!" 13But Moses said to the LORD, "When the Egyptians, from whose midst You brought up this people in Your might, hear the news, 14they will tell it to the inhabitants of that land. Now they have heard that You, O LORD, are in the midst of this people; that You, O LORD, appear in plain sight when Your cloud rests over them and when You go before them in a pillar of cloud by day and in a pillar of fire by night. 15If then You slay this people to a man, the nations who have heard Your fame will say, 16'It must be because the LORD was powerless to bring that people into the land He had promised them on oath that He slaughtered them in the wilderness.' 17Therefore, I pray, let my Lord's forbearance be great, as You have declared, saying,ᶜ 18'The LORD! slow to anger and abounding in kindness; forgiving iniquity and transgression; yet not re-mitting all punishment, but visiting the iniquity of fathers upon children, upon the third and fourth generations.' 19Pardon, I pray, the iniquity of this people according to Your great kindness, as You have forgiven this people ever since Egypt."

20And the LORD said, "I pardon, as you have asked. 21Nevertheless, as I live and as the LORD's Presence fills the whole world, 22none of the men who have seen My Presence and the signs that I have performed in Egypt and in the wilderness, and who have tried Me these manyᵈ times and have disobeyed Me, 23shall see the land that I promised on oath to their fathers; none of those who spurn Me shall see it. 24But My servant Caleb, because he was imbued with a different spirit and remained loyal to Me—him will I bring into the land that he entered, and his offspring shall hold it as a possession. 25Now the Amalekites and the Canaanites occupy the valleys. Start out, then, tomorrow and march into the wilder-ness by way of the Sea of Reeds."ᵉ

26The LORD spoke further to Moses and Aaron, 27"How much longer shall that wicked community keep muttering against Me? Very well, I have heeded the incessant muttering of the Israelites against Me. 28Say to them: 'As I live,' says the LORD, 'I will do to you just as you have urged Me. 29In this very wilderness shall your carcasses drop. Of all of you who were recorded in your various lists from the age of twenty years up, you who have muttered against Me, 30not one shall enter the land in which I sworeᶠ to settle you—save Caleb son of Jephunneh and Joshua son of Nun. 31Your children who, you said, would be carried off—these will I

ᶜ Cf. Exod. 34.6–7.
ᵈ Lit. "ten"; cf. note at Gen. 31.41.
ᵉ See note at Exod. 10.19.
ᶠ Lit. "raised My hand."

allow to enter; they shall know the land that you have rejected. ³²But your carcasses shall drop in this wilderness, ³³while your children roam the wilderness for forty years, suffering for your faithlessness, until the last of your carcasses is down in the wilderness. ³⁴You shall bear your punishment for forty years, corresponding to the number of days—forty days—that you scouted the land: a year for each day. Thus you shall know what it means to thwart Me. ³⁵I the LORD have spoken: Thus will I do to all that wicked band that has banded together against Me: in this very wilderness they shall die to the last man.' "

³⁶As for the men whom Moses sent to scout the land, those who came back and caused the whole community to mutter against him by spreading calumnies about the land—³⁷those who spread such calumnies about the land died of plague, by the will of the LORD. ³⁸Of those men who had gone to scout the land, only Joshua son of Nun and Caleb son of Je-phunneh survived.

³⁹When Moses repeated these words to all the Israelites, the people were overcome by grief. ⁴⁰Early next morning they set out toward the crest of the hill country, saying, "We are prepared to go up to the place that the LORD has spoken of, for we were wrong." ⁴¹But Moses said, "Why do you transgress the LORD's command? This will not succeed. ⁴²Do not go up, lest you be routed by your enemies, for the LORD is not in your midst. ⁴³For the Amalekites and the Canaanites will be there to face you, and you will fall by the sword, inasmuch as you have turned from following the LORD and the LORD will not be with you."

⁴⁴Yet defiantlyᵍ they marched toward the crest of the hill country, though neither the LORD's Ark of the Covenant nor Moses stirred from the camp. ⁴⁵And the Amalekites and the Canaanites who dwelt in that hill country came down and dealt them a shattering blow at Hormah.

15

The LORD spoke to Moses, saying: ²Speak to the Israelite people and say to them:

When you enter the land that I am giving you to settle in, ³and would present an offering by fire to the LORD from the herd or from the flock, be it burnt offering or sacrifice, in fulfillment of a vow explicitly uttered,ᵃ or as a freewill offering, or at your fixed occasions, producing an odor pleasing to the LORD:

ᵍ *Meaning of Heb. uncertain.*
ᵃ *See note at Lev. 22.21.*

⁴The person who presents the offering to the LORD shall bring as a meal offering: a tenth of a measure of choice flour with a quarter of a *hin* of oil mixed in. ⁵You shall also offer, with the burnt offering or the sacrifice, a quarter of a *hin* of wine as a libation for each sheep.

⁶In the case of a ram, you shall present as a meal offering: two-tenths of a measure of choice flour with a third of a *hin* of oil mixed in; ⁷and a third of a *hin* of wine as a libation—as an offering of pleasing odor to the LORD.

⁸And if it is an animal from the herd that you offer to the LORD as a burnt offering or as a sacrifice, in fulfillment of a vow explicitly uttered or as an offering of well-being, ⁹there shall be offered a meal offering along with the animal: three-tenths of a measure of choice flour with half a *hin* of oil mixed in; ¹⁰and as libation you shall offer half a *hin* of wine— these being offerings by fire of pleasing odor to the LORD.

¹¹Thus shall be done with each ox, with each ram, and with any sheep or goat, ¹²as many as you offer; you shall do thus with each one, as many as there are. ¹³Every citizen, when presenting an offering by fire of pleasing odor to the LORD, shall do so with them.

¹⁴And when, throughout the ages, a stranger who has taken up residence with you, or one who lives among you, would present an offering by fire of pleasing odor to the LORD—as you do, so ᵇ⁻shall it be done by ¹⁵the rest of the congregation.⁻ᵇ There shall be one law for you and for the resident stranger; it shall be a law for all time throughout the ages. You and the stranger shall be alike before the LORD; ¹⁶the same ritual and the same rule shall apply to you and to the stranger who resides among you.

¹⁷The LORD spoke to Moses, saying: ¹⁸Speak to the Israelite people and say to them:

When you enter the land to which I am taking you ¹⁹and you eat of the bread of the land, you shall set some aside as a gift to the LORD: ²⁰as the first yield of your baking,ᶜ you shall set aside a loaf as a gift; you shall set it aside as a gift like the gift from the threshing floor. ²¹You shall make a gift to the LORD from the first yield of your baking, throughout the ages.

²²If you unwittingly fail to observe any one of the commandments that the LORD has declared to Moses ²³—anything that the LORD has enjoined

---

ᵇ⁻ᵇ *Meaning of Heb. uncertain.*
ᶜ *Meaning of Heb.* ʿarisah *uncertain.*

upon you through Moses—from the day that the LORD gave the commandment and on through the ages:

²⁴If this was done unwittingly, through the inadvertence of the community, the whole community shall present one bull of the herd as a burnt
offering of pleasing odor to the LORD, with its proper meal offering and
libation, and one he-goat as a sin offering. ²⁵The priest shall make expiation for the whole Israelite community and they shall be forgiven; for it
was an error, and for their error they have brought their offering, an
offering by fire to the LORD and their sin offering before the LORD.
²⁶The whole Israelite community and the stranger residing among them
shall be forgiven, for it happened to the entire people through error.

²⁷In case it is an individual who has sinned unwittingly, he shall offer
a she-goat in its first year as a sin offering. ²⁸The priest shall make expiation before the LORD on behalf of the person who erred, for he sinned
unwittingly, making such expiation for him that he may be forgiven. ²⁹For
the citizen among the Israelites and for the stranger who resides among
them—you shall have one ritual for anyone who acts in error.

³⁰But the person, be he citizen or stranger, who acts defiantly*d* reviles
the LORD; that person shall be cut off from among his people. ³¹Because
he has spurned the word of the LORD and violated His commandment,
that person shall be cut off—he bears his guilt.

³²Once, when the Israelites were in the wilderness, they came upon a
man gathering wood on the sabbath day. ³³Those who found him as he
was gathering wood brought him before Moses, Aaron, and the whole
community. ³⁴He was placed in custody, for it had not been specified
what should be done to him. ³⁵Then the LORD said to Moses, "The man
shall be put to death: the whole community shall pelt him with stones
outside the camp." ³⁶So the whole community took him outside the camp
and stoned him to death—as the LORD had commanded Moses.

³⁷The LORD said to Moses as follows: ³⁸Speak to the Israelite people
and instruct them to make for themselves fringes on the corners of their
garments throughout the ages; let them attach a cord of blue to the fringe
at each corner. ³⁹That shall be your fringe; look at it and recall all the
commandments of the LORD and observe them, so that you do not follow
your heart and eyes in your lustful urge. ⁴⁰Thus you shall be reminded to

---

d *Lit. "with upraised hand."*

observe all My commandments and to be holy to your God. 41I the LORD am your God, who brought you out of the land of Egypt to be your God: I, the LORD your God.

קרח

16 Now Korah, son of Izhar son of Kohath son of Levi, a-betook himself,-a along with Dathan and Abiram sons of Eliab, b-and On son of Peleth—descendants of Reuben-b—2to rise up against Moses, together with two hundred and fifty Israelites, chieftains of the community, chosen in the assembly, men of repute. 3They combined against Moses and Aaron and said to them, "You have gone too far! For all the community are holy, all of them, and the LORD is in their midst. Why then do you raise yourselves above the LORD's congregation?"

4When Moses heard this, he fell on his face.c 5Then he spoke to Korah and all his company, saying, "Come morning, the LORD will make known who is His and who is holy, and will grant him access to Himself; He will grant access to the one He has chosen. 6Do this: You, Korah and all yourd band, take fire pans, 7and tomorrow put fire in them and lay incense on them before the LORD. Then the man whom the LORD chooses, he shall be the holy one. You have gone too far, sons of Levi!"

8Moses said further to Korah, "Hear me, sons of Levi. 9Is it not enough for you that the God of Israel has set you apart from the community of Israel and given you access to Him, to perform the duties of the LORD's Tabernacle and to minister to the community and serve them? 10Now that He has advanced you and all your fellow Levites with you, do you seek the priesthood too? 11Truly, it is against the LORD that you and all your company have banded together. For who is Aaron that you should rail against him?"

12Moses sent for Dathan and Abiram, sons of Eliab; but they said, "We will not come! 13Is it not enough that you brought us from a land flowing with milk and honey to have us die in the wilderness, that you would also lord it over us? 14 e-Even if you had-e brought us to a land flowing with milk and honey, and given us possession of fields and vineyards, should you gouge out those men's eyes?f We will not come!" 15Moses was much

---

a-a *Lit. "took"; meaning of Heb. uncertain.*
b-b *According to Num. 26.5, 8–9, Eliab was son of Pallu, son of Reuben.*
c *Perhaps in the sense of "his face fell."*
d *Lit. "his."*
e-e *Lit. "You have not even."*
f *"Those men's" is a euphemism for "our"; cf. 1 Sam 29.4. Gouging out the eyes was punishment for runaway slaves and rebellious vassals; cf. 2 Kings 25.4–7; Jer. 39.4–7, 52.7–11.*

aggrieved and he said to the LORD, "Pay no regard to their oblation. I have not taken the ass of any one of them, nor have I wronged any one of them."

16And Moses said to Korah, "Tomorrow, you and all your company appear before the LORD, you and they and Aaron. 17Each of you take his fire pan and lay incense on it, and each of you bring his fire pan before the LORD, two hundred and fifty fire pans; you and Aaron also [bring] your fire pans." 18Each of them took his fire pan, put fire in it, laid incense on it, and took his place at the entrance of the Tent of Meeting, as did Moses and Aaron. 19Korah gathered the whole community against them at the entrance of the Tent of Meeting.

Then the Presence of the LORD appeared to the whole community, 20and the LORD spoke to Moses and Aaron, saying, 21"Stand back from this community that I may annihilate them in an instant!" 22But they fell on their faces and said, "O God, Source^g of the breath of all flesh! When one man sins, will You be wrathful with the whole community?"

23The LORD spoke to Moses, saying, 24"Speak to the community and say: Withdraw from about the abodes of Korah, Dathan, and Abiram."

25Moses rose and went to Dathan and Abiram, the elders of Israel following him. 26He addressed the community, saying, "Move away from the tents of these wicked men and touch nothing that belongs to them, lest you be wiped out for all their sins." 27So they withdrew from about the abodes of Korah, Dathan, and Abiram.

Now Dathan and Abiram had come out and they stood at the entrance of their tents, with their wives, their children, and their little ones. 28And Moses said, "By this you shall know that it was the LORD who sent me to do all these things; that they are not of my own devising: 29if these men die as all men do, if their lot be the common fate of all mankind, it was not the LORD who sent me. 30But if the LORD brings about something unheard-of, so that the ground opens its mouth and swallows them up with all that belongs to them, and they go down alive into Sheol, you shall know that these men have spurned the LORD." 31Scarcely had he finished speaking all these words when the ground under them burst asunder, 32and the earth opened its mouth and swallowed them up with their households, all Korah's people and all their possessions. 33They went down alive into Sheol, with all that belonged to them; the earth closed

_____

g Lit. "God."

over them and they vanished from the midst of the congregation. 34All Israel around them fled at their shrieks, for they said, "The earth might swallow us!"

35And a fire went forth from the LORD and consumed the two hundred and fifty men offering the incense.

17 The LORD spoke to Moses, saying: 2Order Eleazar son of Aaron the priest to remove the fire pans—for they have become sacred—from among the charred remains; and scatter the coals abroad. 3 a[Remove] the fire pans of those who have sinned at the cost of their lives, and let them be made into hammered sheets as plating for the altar—for once they have been used for offering to the LORD, they have become sacred— and let them serve as a warning to the people of Israel. 4Eleazar the priest took the copper fire pans which had been used for offering by those who died in the fire; and they were hammered into plating for the altar, 5as the LORD had ordered him through Moses. It was to be a reminder to the Israelites, so that no outsider—one not of Aaron's offspring—should presume to offer incense before the LORD and suffer the fate of Korah and his band.

6Next day the whole Israelite community railed against Moses and Aaron, saying, "You two have brought death upon the LORD's people!" 7But as the community gathered against them, Moses and Aaron turned toward the Tent of Meeting; the cloud had covered it and the Presence of the LORD appeared.

8When Moses and Aaron reached the Tent of Meeting, 9the LORD spoke to Moses, saying, 10"Remove yourselves from this community, that I may annihilate them in an instant." They fell on their faces. 11Then Moses said to Aaron, "Take the fire pan, and put on it fire from the altar. Add incense and take it quickly to the community and make expiation for them. For wrath has gone forth from the LORD: the plague has begun!" 12Aaron took it, as Moses had ordered, and ran to the midst of the congregation, where the plague had begun among the people. He put on the incense and made expiation for the people; 13he stood between the dead and the living until the plague was checked. 14Those who died of the plague came to fourteen thousand and seven hundred, aside from those

a *Meaning of parts of verse uncertain.*

who died on account of Korah. ¹⁵Aaron then returned to Moses at the entrance of the Tent of Meeting, since the plague was checked.

¹⁶The LORD spoke to Moses, saying: ¹⁷Speak to the Israelite people and take from them—from the chieftains of their ancestral housesᵇ—one staff for each chieftain of an ancestral house: twelve staffs in all. Inscribe each man's name on his staff, ¹⁸there being one staff for each head of an ancestral house; also inscribe Aaron's name on the staff of Levi. ¹⁹Deposit them in the Tent of Meeting before the Pact, where I meet with you. ²⁰The staff of the man whom I choose shall sprout, and I will ridᶜ Myself of the incessant mutterings of the Israelites against you.

²¹Moses spoke thus to the Israelites. Their chieftains gave him a staff for each chieftain of an ancestral house, twelve staffs in all; among these staffs was that of Aaron. ²²Moses deposited the staffs before the LORD, in the Tent of the Pact. ²³The next day Moses entered the Tent of the Pact, and there the staff of Aaron of the house of Levi had sprouted: it had brought forth sprouts, produced blossoms, and borne almonds. ²⁴Moses then brought out all the staffs from before the LORD to all the Israelites; each identified and recovered his staff.

²⁵The LORD said to Moses, "Put Aaron's staff back before the Pact, to be kept as a lesson to rebels, so that their mutterings against Me may cease, lest they die." ²⁶This Moses did; just as the LORD had commanded him, so he did.

²⁷But the Israelites said to Moses, "Lo, we perish! We are lost, all of us lost! ²⁸Everyone who so much as ventures near the LORD's Tabernacle must die. Alas, we are doomed to perish!"

18 The LORD said to Aaron: You and your sons and the ancestral house under your charge shall bear any guilt connected with the sanctuary; you and your sons alone shall bear any guilt connected with your priesthood. ²You shall also associate with yourself your kinsmen the tribe of Levi, your ancestral tribe, to be attached to you and to minister to you, while you and your sons under your charge are before the Tent of the Pact.ᵃ ³They shall discharge their duties to you and to the Tent as a whole, but they must not have any contact with the furnishings of the Shrine or with the altar, lest both they and you die. ⁴They shall be attached to you

ᵇ I.e., of their tribes.
ᶜ Meaning of Heb. wahashikkothi uncertain.

ᵃ Meaning of latter part of verse uncertain.

and discharge the duties of the Tent of Meeting, all the service of the Tent; but no outsider shall intrude upon you 5as you discharge the duties connected with the Shrine and the altar, that wrath may not again strike the Israelites.

6I hereby take your fellow Levites from among the Israelites; they are assigned to you in dedication to the LORD, to do the work of the Tent of Meeting; 7while you and your sons shall be careful to perform your priestly duties in everything pertaining to the altar and to what is behind the curtain. I make your priesthood a service of dedication; any outsider who encroaches shall be put to death.

8The LORD spoke further to Aaron: I hereby give you charge of My gifts, all the sacred donations of the Israelites; I grant them to you and to your sons as a perquisite,b a due for all time. 9This shall be yours from the most holy sacrifices, c-the offerings by fire:-c every such offering that they render to Me as most holy sacrifices, namely, every meal offering, sin offering, and guilt offering of theirs, shall belong to you and your sons. 10You shall partake of them as most sacred donations: only males may eat them; you shall treat them as consecrated.d

11This, too, shall be yours: the gift offeringse of their contributions, all the elevation offerings of the Israelites, I give to you, to your sons, and to the daughters that are with you, as a due for all time; everyone of your household who is clean may eat it.

12All the best of the new oil, wine, and grain—the choice parts that they present to the LORD—I give to you. 13The first fruits of everything in their land, that they bring to the LORD, shall be yours; everyone of your household who is clean may eat them. 14Everything that has been proscribed in Israelf shall be yours. 15The first issue of the womb of every being, man or beast, that is offered to the LORD, shall be yours; but you shall have the first-born of man redeemed, and you shall also have the firstling of unclean animals redeemed. 16Take as their redemption price,g from the age of one month up, the money equivalent of five shekels by the sanctuary weight, which is twenty gerahs. 17But the firstlings of cattle, sheep, or goats may not be redeemed; they are consecrated. You shall dash their blood against the altar, and turn their fat into smoke as an offering by fire for a pleasing odor to the LORD. 18But their meat shall be yours: it shall be yours like the breast of elevation offering and like the right thigh.

b See note at Lev. 7.35.
c-c Meaning of Heb. uncertain; lit. "from the fire."
d Or "they are consecrated for your use."
e Cf. Lev. 7.29 ff.
f See Lev. 27.28.
g I.e., for human first-born; cf. Num. 3.44 ff. For animals see Exod. 34.19 f.

¹⁹All the sacred gifts that the Israelites set aside for the LORD I give to you, to your sons, and to the daughters that are with you, as a due for all time. It shall be an everlasting covenant of salt[h] before the LORD for you and for your offspring as well. ²⁰And the LORD said to Aaron: You shall, however, have no territorial share among them or own any portion in their midst; I am your portion and your share among the Israelites.

²¹And to the Levites I hereby give all the tithes in Israel as their share in return for the services that they perform, the services of the Tent of Meeting. ²²Henceforth, Israelites shall not trespass on the Tent of Meeting, and thus incur guilt and die: ²³only Levites shall perform the services of the Tent of Meeting; others[i] would incur guilt. It is the law for all time throughout the ages. But they shall have no territorial share among the Israelites; ²⁴for it is the tithes set aside by the Israelites as a gift to the LORD that I give to the Levites as their share. Therefore I have said concerning them: They shall have no territorial share among the Israelites.

²⁵The LORD spoke to Moses, saying: ²⁶Speak to the Levites and say to them: When you receive from the Israelites their tithes, which I have assigned to you as your share, you shall set aside from them one-tenth of the tithe as a gift to the LORD. ²⁷This shall be accounted to you as your gift. As with the new grain from the threshing floor or the flow from the vat, ²⁸so shall you on your part set aside a gift for the LORD from all the tithes that you receive from the Israelites; and from them you shall bring the gift for the LORD to Aaron the priest. ²⁹You shall set aside all gifts due to the LORD from everything that is donated to you, from each thing its best portion, the part thereof that is to be consecrated.

³⁰Say to them further: When you have removed the best part from it, you Levites may consider it the same as the yield of threshing floor or vat. ³¹You and your households may eat it anywhere, for it is your recompense for your services in the Tent of Meeting. ³²You will incur no guilt through it, once you have removed the best part from it; but you must not profane the sacred donations of the Israelites, lest you die.

19

חקת

The LORD spoke to Moses and Aaron, saying: ²This is the ritual law that the LORD has commanded:

---

h *See Lev. 2.13.*
i *Lit. "they."*

Instruct the Israelite people to bring you a red cow without blemish, in which there is no defect and on which no yoke has been laid. ³You shall give it to Eleazar the priest. It shall be taken outside the camp and slaughtered in his presence. ⁴Eleazar the priest shall take some of its blood with his finger and sprinkle it seven times toward the front of the Tent of Meeting. ⁵The cow shall be burned in his sight—its hide, flesh, and blood shall be burned, its dung included—⁶and the priest shall take cedar wood, hyssop, and crimson stuff, and throw them into the fire consuming the cow. ⁷The priest shall wash his garments and bathe his body in water; after that the priest may reenter the camp, but he shall be unclean until evening. ⁸He who performed the burning shall also wash his garments in water, bathe his body in water, and be unclean until evening. ⁹A man who is clean shall gather up the ashes of the cow and deposit them outside the camp in a clean place, to be kept for water of lustrationᵃ for the Israelite community. It is for cleansing. ¹⁰He who gathers up the ashes of the cow shall also wash his clothes and be unclean until evening.

This shall be a permanent law for the Israelites and for the strangers who reside among you.

¹¹He who touches the corpse of any human being shall be unclean for seven days. ¹²He shall cleanse himself with itᵇ on the third day and on the seventh day, and then be clean; if he fails to cleanse himself on the third and seventh days, he shall not be clean. ¹³Whoever touches a corpse, the body of a person who has died, and does not cleanse himself, defiles the LORD's Tabernacle; that person shall be cut off from Israel. Since the water of lustration was not dashed on him, he remains unclean; his uncleanness is still upon him.

¹⁴This is the ritual: When a person dies in a tent, whoever enters the tent and whoever is in the tent shall be unclean seven days; ¹⁵and every open vessel, with no lid fastened down, shall be unclean. ¹⁶And in the open, anyone who touches a person who was killedᶜ or who died naturally, or human bone, or a grave, shall be unclean seven days. ¹⁷Some of the ashesᵈ from the fire of cleansing shall be taken for the unclean person, and fresh water shall be added to them in a vessel. ¹⁸A person who is clean shall take hyssop, dip it in the water, and sprinkle on the tent and on all the vessels and people who were there, or on him who touched the bones or the person who was killed or died naturally or the grave. ¹⁹The clean person shall sprinkle it upon the unclean person on the third day and on the seventh day, thus cleansing him by the seventh day. Heᵉ shall

---

ᵃ Lit. "water for impurity."
ᵇ I.e., the ashes, as in v. 9.
ᶜ Lit. "slain by the sword."
ᵈ Lit. "earth" or "dust."
ᵉ I.e., the person being cleansed.

then wash his clothes and bathe in water, and at nightfall he shall be clean. 20If anyone who has become unclean fails to cleanse himself, that person shall be cut off from the congregation, for he has defiled the LORD's sanctuary. The water of lustration was not dashed on him: he is unclean.

21That shall be for them a law for all time. Further, he who sprinkled the water of lustration shall wash his clothes; and whoever touches the water of lustration shall be unclean until evening. 22Whatever that unclean person touches shall be unclean; and the person who touches him shall be unclean until evening.

20 The Israelites arrived in a body at the wilderness of Zin on the first new moon,a and the people stayed at Kadesh. Miriam died there and was buried there.

2The community was without water, and they joined against Moses and Aaron. 3The people quarreled with Moses, saying, "If only we had perished when our brothers perished at the instance of the LORD! 4Why have you brought the LORD's congregation into this wilderness for us and our beasts to die there? 5Why did you make us leave Egypt to bring us to this wretched place, a place with no grain or figs or vines or pomegranates? There is not even water to drink!"

6Moses and Aaron came away from the congregation to the entrance of the Tent of Meeting, and fell on their faces. The Presence of the LORD appeared to them, 7and the LORD spoke to Moses, saying, 8"You and your brother Aaron take the rod and assemble the community, and before their very eyes order the rock to yield its water. Thus you shall produce water for them from the rock and provide drink for the congregation and their beasts."

9Moses took the rod from before the LORD, as He had commanded him. 10Moses and Aaron assembled the congregation in front of the rock; and he said to them, "Listen, you rebels, shall we get water for you out of this rock?" 11And Moses raised his hand and struck the rock twice with his rod. Out came copious water, and the community and their beasts drank.

12But the LORD said to Moses and Aaron, "Because you did not trust Me enough to affirm My sanctity in the sight of the Israelite people, therefore you shall not lead this congregation into the land that I have given them." 13Those are the Waters of Meribahb—meaning that the

---

a Of the fortieth year; cf. Num. 33.36–38.
b I.e., "Quarrel"; cf. Exod. 17.7 and note b there.

Israelites quarrelled with the LORD—through which He affirmed His sanctity.

¹⁴From Kadesh, Moses sent messengers to the king of Edom: "Thus says your brother Israel: You know all the hardships that have befallen us; ¹⁵that our ancestors went down to Egypt, that we dwelt in Egypt a long time, and that the Egyptians dealt harshly with us and our ancestors. ¹⁶We cried to the LORD and He heard our plea, and He sent a messengerᶜ who freed us from Egypt. Now we are in Kadesh, the town on the border of your territory. ¹⁷Allow us, then, to cross your country. We will not pass through fields or vineyards, and we will not drink water from wells. We will follow the king's highway, turning off neither to the right nor to the left until we have crossed your territory."

¹⁸But Edom answered him, "You shall not pass through us, else we will go out against you with the sword." ¹⁹"We will keep to the beaten track," the Israelites said to them, "and if we or our cattle drink your water, we will pay for it. We ask only for passage on foot—it is but a small matter." ²⁰But they replied, "You shall not pass through!" And Edom went out against them in heavy force, strongly armed. ²¹So Edom would not let Israel cross their territory, and Israel turned away from them.

²²Setting out from Kadesh, the Israelites arrived in a body at Mount Hor. ²³At Mount Hor, on the boundary of the land of Edom, the LORD said to Moses and Aaron, ²⁴"Let Aaron be gathered to his kin: he is not to enter the land that I have assigned to the Israelite people, because you disobeyed my command about the waters of Meribah. ²⁵Take Aaron and his son Eleazar and bring them up on Mount Hor. ²⁶Strip Aaron of his vestments and put them on his son Eleazar. There Aaron shall be gathered ᵈ⁻unto the dead."⁻ᵈ

²⁷Moses did as the LORD had commanded. They ascended Mount Hor in the sight of the whole community. ²⁸Moses stripped Aaron of his vestments and put them on his son Eleazar, and Aaron died there on the summit of the mountain. When Moses and Eleazar came down from the mountain, ²⁹the whole community knew that Aaron had breathed his last. All the house of Israel bewailed Aaron thirty days.

ᶜ Or "angel."
ᵈ⁻ᵈ Lit. "and die."

21

When the Canaanite, king of Arad, who dwelt in the Negeb, learned that Israel was coming by the way of Atharim,[a] he engaged Israel in battle and took some of them captive. [2]Then Israel made a vow to the LORD and said, "If You deliver this people into our hand, we will proscribe[b] their towns." [3]The LORD heeded Israel's plea and delivered up the Canaanites; and they and their cities were proscribed. So that place was named Hormah.[c]

[4]They set out from Mount Hor by way of the Sea of Reeds[d] to skirt the land of Edom. But the people grew restive on the journey, [5]and the people spoke against God and against Moses, "Why did you make us leave Egypt to die in the wilderness? There is no bread and no water, and we have come to loathe this miserable food." [6]The LORD sent seraph[e] serpents against the people. They bit the people and many of the Israelites died. [7]The people came to Moses and said, "We sinned by speaking against the LORD and against you. Intercede with the LORD to take away the serpents from us!" And Moses interceded for the people. [8]Then the LORD said to Moses, "Make a seraph[e] figure and mount it on a standard. And if anyone who is bitten looks at it, he shall recover." [9]Moses made a copper serpent and mounted it on a standard; and when anyone was bitten by a serpent, he would look at the copper serpent and recover.

[10]The Israelites marched on and encamped at Oboth. [11]They set out from Oboth and encamped at Iye-abarim, in the wilderness bordering on Moab to the east. [12]From there they set out and encamped at the wadi Zered. [13]From there they set out and encamped beyond the Arnon, that is, in the wilderness that extends from the territory of the Amorites. For the Arnon is the boundary of Moab, between Moab and the Amorites. [14]Therefore the Book of the Wars of the LORD speaks of [f]". . . Waheb in Suphah, and the wadis: the Arnon [15]with its tributary wadis, stretched along the settled country of Ar, hugging the territory of Moab . . ."

[16]And from there to Beer,[g] which is the well where the LORD said to Moses, "Assemble the people that I may give them water." [17]Then Israel sang this song:

---

a Meaning of Heb. ha-'atharim uncertain. Targum and other ancient versions render "the way [taken by] the scouts."
b I.e., utterly destroy, reserving no booty except what is deposited in the Sanctuary; see Josh. 6.24.
c Connected with ḥeḥerim "to proscribe."
d See Exod. 10.19 note.
e Cf. Isa. 14.29; 30.6. Others "fiery"; exact meaning of Heb. saraph uncertain.
f The quotation that follows is a fragment; text and meaning are uncertain.
g Lit. "well."

Spring up, O well—sing to it—
[18]The well which the chieftains dug,
Which the nobles of the people started
With maces, with their own staffs.

And from Midbar[h] to Mattanah, [19]and from Mattanah to Nahaliel, and from Nahaliel to Bamoth, [20]and from Bamoth to the valley that is in the country of Moab, at the peak of Pisgah, overlooking the wasteland.[i]

[21]Israel now sent messengers to Sihon king of the Amorites, saying, [22]"Let me pass through your country. We will not turn off into fields or vineyards, and we will not drink water from wells. We will follow the king's highway until we have crossed your territory." [23]But Sihon would not let Israel pass through his territory. Sihon gathered all his people and went out against Israel in the wilderness. He came to Jahaz and engaged Israel in battle. [24]But Israel put them to the sword, and took possession of their land, from the Arnon to the Jabbok, as far as [Az] of the Ammonites, for Az[j] marked the boundary of the Ammonites. [25]Israel took all those towns. And Israel settled in all the towns of the Amorites, in Heshbon and all its dependencies.

[26]Now Heshbon was the city of Sihon king of the Amorites, who had fought against a former king of Moab and taken all his land from him as far as the Arnon. [27]Therefore the bards would recite:

[k]"Come to Heshbon; firmly built
And well founded is Sihon's city.
[28]For fire went forth from Heshbon,
Flame from Sihon's city,
Consuming Ar of Moab,
The lords of Bamoth[l] by the Arnon.
[29]Woe to you, O Moab!
You are undone, O people of Chemosh!
His sons are rendered fugitive
And his daughters captive
By an Amorite king, Sihon."
[30] [m]Yet we have cast them down utterly,

---

h *Septuagint "the well"* (= Beer); *cf. v. 16.*
i *Or "Jeshimon."*
j *Septuagint "Jazer," cf. v. 32. Others "for the boundary of the Ammonites was strong."*
k *The meaning of several parts of this ancient poem is no longer certain.*
l *Cf. vv. 19 and 20 and Num. 22.21.*
m *Meaning of verse uncertain. Alternatively:*
"*Their dominion is at an end*
From Heshbon to Dibon
And from Nashim to Nophah,
Which is hard by Medeba."

Heshbon along with Dibon;
We have wrought desolation at Nophah,
Which is hard by Medeba.

³¹So Israel occupied the land of the Amorites. ³²Then Moses sent to spy out Jazer, and they captured its dependencies and dispossessed the Amorites who were there.

³³They marched on and went up the road to Bashan, and King Og of Bashan, with all his people, came out to Edrei to engage them in battle. ³⁴But the LORD said to Moses, "Do not fear him, for I give him and all his people and his land into your hand. You shall do to him as you did to Sihon king of the Amorites who dwelt in Heshbon." ³⁵They defeated **22** him and his sons and all his people, until no remnant was left him; and they took possession of his country. ¹The Israelites then marched on and encamped in the steppes of Moab, across the Jordan from Jericho.

בלק

²Balak son of Zippor saw all that Israel had done to the Amorites.

³Moab was alarmed because that people was so numerous. Moab dreaded the Israelites, ⁴and Moab said to the elders of Midian, "Now this horde will lick clean all that is about us as an ox licks up the grass of the field."

Balak son of Zippor, who was king of Moab at that time, ⁵sent messengers to Balaam son of Beor in Pethor, which is by the Euphrates,ᵃ in the land of his kinsfolk, to invite him, saying, "There is a people that came out of Egypt; it hides the earth from view, and it is settled next to me. ⁶Come then, put a curse upon this people for me, since they are too numerous for me; perhaps I can thus defeat them and drive them out of the land. For I know that he whom you bless is blessed indeed, and he whom you curse is cursed."

⁷The elders of Moab and the elders of Midian, ᵇ-versed in divination,-ᵇ set out. They came to Balaam and gave him Balak's message. ⁸He said to them, "Spend the night here, and I shall reply to you as the LORD may instruct me." So the Moabite dignitaries stayed with Balaam.

ᵃ Lit. "the River."
ᵇ⁻ᵇ Lit. "with divination in their power (hand)."

⁹God came to Balaam and said, "What do these people want of you?" ¹⁰Balaam said to God, "Balak son of Zippor, king of Moab, sent me this message: ¹¹Here is a people that came out from Egypt and hides the earth from view. Come now and curse them for me; perhaps I can engage them in battle and drive them off." ¹²But God said to Balaam, "Do not go with them. You must not curse that people, for they are blessed."

¹³Balaam arose in the morning and said to Balak's dignitaries, "Go back to your own country, for the LORD will not let me go with you." ¹⁴The Moabite dignitaries left, and they came to Balak and said, "Balaam refused to come with us."

¹⁵Then Balak sent other dignitaries, more numerous and distinguished than the first. ¹⁶They came to Balaam and said to him, "Thus says Balak son of Zippor: Please do not refuse to come to me. ¹⁷I will reward you richly and I will do anything you ask of me. Only come and damn this people for me." ¹⁸Balaam replied to Balak's officials, "Though Balak were to give me his house full of silver and gold, I could not do anything, big or little, contrary to the command of the LORD my God. ¹⁹So you, too, stay here overnight, and let me find out what else the LORD may say to me." ²⁰That night God came to Balaam and said to him, "If these men have come to invite you, you may go with them. But whatever I command you, that you shall do."

²¹When he arose in the morning, Balaam saddled his ass and departed with the Moabite dignitaries. ²²But God was incensed at his going; so an angel of the LORD placed himself in his way as an adversary.

He was riding on his she-ass, with his two servants alongside, ²³when the ass caught sight of the angel of the LORD standing in the way, with his drawn sword in his hand. The ass swerved from the road and went into the fields; and Balaam beat the ass to turn her back onto the road. ²⁴The angel of the LORD then stationed himself in a lane between the vineyards, with a fence on either side. ²⁵The ass, seeing the angel of the LORD, pressed herself against the wall and squeezed Balaam's foot against the wall; so he beat her again. ²⁶Once more the angel of the LORD moved forward and stationed himself on a spot so narrow that there was no room to swerve right or left. ²⁷When the ass now saw the angel of the LORD, she lay down under Balaam; and Balaam was furious and beat the ass with his stick.

²⁸Then the LORD opened the ass's mouth, and she said to Balaam, "What have I done to you that you have beaten me these three times?"

²⁹Balaam said to the ass, "You have made a mockery of me! If I had a sword with me, I'd kill you." ³⁰The ass said to Balaam, "Look, I am the ass that you have been riding all along until this day! Have I been in the habit of doing thus to you?" And he answered, "No."

³¹Then the LORD uncovered Balaam's eyes, and he saw the angel of the LORD standing in the way, his drawn sword in his hand; thereupon he bowed c⁻right down to the ground.⁻c ³²The angel of the LORD said to him, "Why have you beaten your ass these three times? It is I who came out as an adversary, for the errand is obnoxiousd to me. ³³And when the ass saw me, she shied away because of me those three times. If she had not shied away from me, you are the one I should have killed, while sparing her." ³⁴Balaam said to the angel of the LORD, "I erred because I did not know that you were standing in my way. If you still disapprove, I will turn back." ³⁵But the angel of the LORD said to Balaam, "Go with the men. But you must say nothing except what I tell you." So Balaam went on with Balak's dignitaries.

³⁶When Balak heard that Balaam was coming, he went out to meet him at Ir-moab, which is on the Arnon border, at its farthest point. ³⁷Balak said to Balaam, "When I first sent to invite you, why didn't you come to me? Am I really unable to reward you?" ³⁸But Balaam said to Balak, "And now that I have come to you, have I the power to speak freely? I can utter only the word that God puts into my mouth."

³⁹Balaam went with Balak and they came to Kiriath-huzoth. ⁴⁰Balak sacrificed oxen and sheep, and had them served to Balaam and the dignitaries with him. ⁴¹In the morning Balak took Balaam up to Bamoth-baal. From there he could see a portion of the people.

23

Balaam said to Balak, "Build me seven altars here and have seven bulls and seven rams ready here for me." ²Balak did as Balaam directed; and Balak and Balaam offered up a bull and a ram on each altar. ³Then Balaam said to Balak, "Stay here beside your offerings while I am gone. Perhaps the LORD will grant me a manifestation, and whatever He reveals to me I will tell you." And he went off alone.a

⁴God manifested Himself to Balaam, who said to Him, "I have set up the seven altars and offered up a bull and a ram on each altar." ⁵And the LORD put a word in Balaam's mouth and said, "Return to Balak and speak thus."

c⁻c *Lit. "and prostrated himself to his nostrils."*
d *Precise meaning of Heb. uncertain.*

a *Others "to a bare height"; exact meaning of Heb. shephi uncertain.*

⁶So he returned to him and found him standing beside his offerings, and all the Moabite dignitaries with him. ⁷He took up his theme, and said:

> From Aram has Balak brought me,
> Moab's king from the hills of the East:
> Come, curse me Jacob,
> Come, tell Israel's doom!
> ⁸How can I damn whom God[b] has not damned,
> How doom when the LORD has not doomed?
> ⁹As I see them from the mountain tops,
> Gaze on them from the heights,
> There is a people that dwells apart,
> Not reckoned among the nations,
> ¹⁰Who can count the dust[c] of Jacob,
> Number[d] the dust-cloud of Israel?
> May I die the death of the upright,[e]
> May my fate be like theirs!

¹¹Then Balak said to Balaam, "What have you done to me? Here I brought you to damn my enemies, and instead you have blessed them!" ¹²He replied, "I can only repeat faithfully what the LORD puts in my mouth." ¹³Then Balak said to him, "Come with me to another place from which you can see them—you will see only a portion of them; you will not see all of them—and damn them for me from there." ¹⁴With that, he took him to Sedehzophim,[f] on the summit of Pisgah. He built seven altars and offered a bull and a ram on each altar. ¹⁵And [Balaam] said to Balak, "Stay here beside your offerings, while I seek a manifestation yonder."

¹⁶The LORD manifested Himself to Balaam and put a word in his mouth, saying, "Return to Balak and speak thus." ¹⁷He went to him and found him standing beside his offerings, and the Moabite dignitaries with him. Balak asked him, "What did the LORD say?" ¹⁸And he took up his theme, and said:

> Up, Balak, attend,
> Give ear unto me, son of Zippor!
> ¹⁹God is not man to be capricious,
> Or mortal to change His mind.

---

b *Heb.* El, *as often in these poems.*
c *Cf. Gen. 13.16.*
d *Lit. "and the number of."*
e *Heb.* yesharim, *a play on* yeshurun (*Jeshurun in Deut. 32.15*), *a name for Israel.*
f *Or "Lookout Point."*

Would He speak and not act,
Promise and not fulfill?
20My message was to bless:
When He blesses, I cannot reverse it.
21No harm is in sight for Jacob,
No woe in view for Israel.
The LORD their God is with them,
And their King's acclaim in their midst.
22God who freed them from Egypt
Is for them like the hornsg of the wild ox.
23Lo, there is no augury in Jacob,
No divining in Israel:h
Jacob is told at once,
Yea Israel, what God has planned.i
24Lo, a people that rises like a lion,
Leaps up like the j-king of beasts,-j
Rests not till it has feasted on prey
And drunk the blood of the slain.

25Thereupon Balak said to Balaam, "Don't curse them and don't bless them!" 26In reply, Balaam said to Balak, "But I told you: Whatever the LORD says, that I must do." 27Then Balak said to Balaam, "Come now, I will take you to another place. Perhaps God will deem it right that you damn them for me there." 28Balak took Balaam to the peak of Peor, which overlooks the wasteland.k 29Balaam said to Balak, "Build me here seven altars, and have seven bulls and seven rams ready for me here." 30Balak did as Balaam said: he offered up a bull and a ram on each altar.

24 Now Balaam, seeing that it pleased the LORD to bless Israel, did not, as on previous occasions, go in search of omens, but turned his face toward the wilderness. 2As Balaam looked up and saw Israel encamped tribe by tribe, the spirit of God came upon him. 3Taking up his theme, he said:

aWord of Balaam son of Beor,
Word of the man whose eye is true,b

g Lit. "eminences," used figuratively.
h Cf. Deut. 18.10–15.
i Or, "Else would it be told to Jacob,/Yea to Israel, what God has planned."
j-j Heb. 'ari, another term for "lion."
k Cf. note on 21.20.

a Some of the poetic portions of this chapter are unclear.
b Others "whose eye is (or, eyes are) open"; meaning of Heb. uncertain.

4Word of him who hears God's speech,
Who beholds visions from the Almighty,
Prostrate, but with eyes unveiled:
5How fair are your tents, O Jacob,
Your dwellings, O Israel!
6Like palm-groves that stretch out,
Like gardens beside a river,
Like aloes planted by the LORD,
Like cedars beside the water;
7Their boughs drip with moisture,
Their rootsᶜ have abundant water.
Their king shall rise above Agag,
Their kingdom shall be exalted.
8God who freed them from Egypt
Is for them like the hornsᵈ of the wild ox.
They shall devour enemy nations,
Crush their bones,
And smash their arrows.
9They crouch, they lie down like a lion,
Like the king of beasts;ᵉ who dare rouse them?
Blessed are they who bless you,
Accursed they who curse you!

10Enraged at Balaam, Balak struck his hands together. "I called you," Balak said to Balaam, "to damn my enemies, and instead you have blessed them these three times! 11Back with you at once to your own place! I was going to reward you richly, but the LORD has denied you the reward." 12Balaam replied to Balak, "But I even told the messengers you sent to me, 13'Though Balak were to give me his house full of silver and gold, I could not of my own accord do anything good or bad contrary to the LORD's command. What the LORD says, that I must say.' 14And now, as I go back to my people, let me inform you of what this people will do to your people in days to come." 15He took up his theme, and said:

Word of Balaam son of Beor,
Word of the man whose eye is true,ᵇ
16Word of him who hears God's speech,
Who obtains knowledge from the Most High,

ᶜ Lit. "and its seed."
ᵈ See note at 23.22.
ᵉ Heb. labi, another word for "lion"; cf. note at 23.24.

And beholds visions from the Almighty,
Prostrate, but with eyes unveiled:
[17]What I see for them is not yet,
What I behold will not be soon:
A star rises from Jacob,
A scepter comes forth from Israel;
It smashes the brow of Moab,
The foundation of[f] all children of Seth.
[18]Edom becomes a possession,
Yea, Seir a possession of its enemies;
But Israel is triumphant.
[19]A victor issues from Jacob
To wipe out what is left of Ir.

[20]He saw Amalek and, taking up his theme, he said:
A leading nation is Amalek;
But its fate is to perish forever.

[21]He saw the Kenites and, taking up his theme, he said:
Though your abode be secure,
And your nest be set among cliffs,
[22]Yet shall Kain[g] be consumed,
When Asshur takes you captive.

[23]He took up his theme and said:
Alas, who can survive except God has willed it!
[24]Ships come from the quarter of Kittim;
They subject Asshur, subject Eber.
They, too, shall perish forever.

[25]Then Balaam set out on his journey back home; and Balak also went his way.

25 While Israel was staying at Shittim, the people [a-]profaned themselves by whoring[-a] with the Moabite women, [2]who invited the people to the sacrifices for their god. The people partook of them and worshiped that god. [3]Thus Israel attached itself to Baal-peor, and the LORD was incensed with Israel. [4]The LORD said to Moses, "Take all the ringleaders[b] and have them publicly[c] impaled before the LORD, so that the LORD's

[f] Samaritan "the pate of," cf. Jer. 48.45; others "breaks down."
[g] I.e., the Kenites.

[a-a] Others "began to commit harlotry."
[b] Lit. "heads of the people."
[c] Others "in face of the sun."

wrath may turn away from Israel." 5So Moses said to Israel's officials, "Each of you slay those of his men who attached themselves to Baal-peor."

6Just then one of the Israelites came and brought a Midianite woman over to his companions, in the sight of Moses and of the whole Israelite community who were weeping at the entrance of the Tent of Meeting. 7When Phinehas, son of Eleazar son of Aaron the priest, saw this, he left the assembly and, taking a spear in his hand, 8he followed the Israelite into the chamber and stabbed both of them, the Israelite and the woman, through the belly. Then the plague against the Israelites was checked. 9Those who died of the plague numbered twenty-four thousand.

פינחס

10The LORD spoke to Moses, saying, 11"Phinehas, son of Eleazar son of Aaron the priest, has turned back My wrath from the Israelites by displaying among them his passion for Me, so that I did not wipe out the Israelite people in My passion. 12Say, therefore, 'I grant him My pact of friendship. 13It shall be for him and his descendants after him a pact of priesthood for all time, because he took impassioned action for his God, thus making expiation for the Israelites.'"

14The name of the Israelite who was killed, the one who was killed with the Midianite woman, was Zimri son of Salu, chieftain of a Simeonite ancestral house. 15The name of the Midianite woman who was killed was Cozbi daughter of Zur; he was the tribal head of an ancestral house in Midian.

16The LORD spoke to Moses, saying, 17"Assail the Midianites and defeat them—18for they assailed you by the trickery they practiced against you—because of the affair of Peor and because of the affair of their kinswoman Cozbi, daughter of the Midianite chieftain, who was killed at the time of the plague on account of Peor."

26 19When the plague was over, 1the LORD said to Moses and to Eleazar son of Aaron the priest, 2"Take a census of the whole Israelite community from the age of twenty years up, by their ancestral houses, all Israelites able to bear arms." 3 aSo Moses and Eleazar the priest, on the steppes of Moab, at the Jordan near Jericho, gave instructions about them, namely, 4those from twenty years up, as the LORD had commanded Moses.

a Meaning of parts of vv. 3 and 4 uncertain.

The descendants of the Israelites who came out of the land of Egypt were:

⁵Reuben, Israel's first-born. Descendants of Reuben: [Of] Enoch,ᵇ the clan of the Enochites; of Pallu, the clan of the Palluites; ⁶of Hezron, the clan of the Hezronites; of Carmi, the clan of the Carmites. ⁷Those are the clans of the Reubenites. The persons enrolled came to 43,730.

⁸ ᶜ⁻Born to⁻ᶜ Pallu: Eliab. ⁹The sons of Eliab were Nemuel, and Dathan and Abiram. These are the same Dathan and Abiram, chosen in the assembly, who agitated against Moses and Aaron as part of Korah's band when they agitated against the LORD. ¹⁰Whereupon the earth opened its mouth and swallowed them up with Korah—when that band died, when the fire consumed the two hundred and fifty men—and they became an example. ¹¹The sons of Korah, however, did not die.

¹²Descendants of Simeon by their clans: Of Nemuel, the clan of the Nemuelites; of Jamin, the clan of the Jaminites; of Jachin, the clan of the Jachinites; ¹³of Zerah, the clan of the Zerahites; of Saul,ᵈ the clan of the Saulites. ¹⁴Those are the clans of the Simeonites; [persons enrolled:] 22,200.

¹⁵Descendants of Gad by their clans: Of Zephon, the clan of the Zephonites; of Haggi, the clan of the Haggites; of Shuni, the clan of the Shunites; ¹⁶of Ozni, the clan of the Oznites; of Eri, the clan of the Erites; ¹⁷of Arod, the clan of the Arodites; of Areli, the clan of the Arelites. ¹⁸Those are the clans of Gad's descendants; persons enrolled: 40,500.

¹⁹ ᶜ⁻Born to⁻ᶜ Judah: Er and Onan. Er and Onan died in the land of Canaan.

²⁰Descendants of Judah by their clans: Of Shelah, the clan of the Shelanites; of Perez, the clan of the Perezites; of Zerah, the clan of the Zerahites. ²¹Descendants of Perez: of Hezron, the clan of the Hezronites; of Hamul, the clan of the Hamulites. ²²Those are the clans of Judah; persons enrolled: 76,500.

²³Descendants of Issachar by their clans: [Of] Tola, the clan of the Tolaites; of Puvah, the clan of the Punites; ²⁴of Jashub, the clan of the Jashubites; of Shimron, the clan of the Shimronites. ²⁵Those are the clans of Issachar; persons enrolled: 64,300.

²⁶Descendants of Zebulun by their clans: Of Sered, the clan of the Seredites; of Elon, the clan of the Elonites; of Jahleel, the clan of the Jahleelites. ²⁷Those are the clans of the Zebulunites; persons enrolled: 60,500.

²⁸The sons of Joseph were Manasseh and Ephraim—by their clans.

ᵇ Or "Hanoch."
ᶜ⁻ᶜ Or "descendants of."
ᵈ Or "Shaul."

²⁹Descendants of Manasseh: Of Machir, the clan of the Machirites.—Machir begot Gilead.—Of Gilead, the clan of the Gileadites. ³⁰These were the descendants of Gilead: [Of] Iezer, the clan of the Iezerites; of Helek, the clan of the Helekites; ³¹[of] Asriel, the clan of the Asrielites; [of] Shechem, the clan of the Shechemites; ³²[of] Shemida, the clan of the Shemidaites; [of] Hepher, the clan of the Hepherites. ³³—Now Zelophehad son of Hepher had no sons, only daughters. The names of Zelophehad's daughters were Mahlah, Noah, Hoglah, Milcah, and Tirzah.—³⁴Those are the clans of Manasseh; persons enrolled: 52,700.

³⁵These are the descendants of Ephraim by their clans: Of Shuthelah, the clan of the Shuthelahites; of Becher, the clan of the Becherites; of Tahan, the clan of the Tahanites. ³⁶These are the descendants of Shuthelah: Of Eran, the clan of the Eranites. ³⁷Those are the clans of Ephraim's descendants; persons enrolled: 32,500.

Those are the descendants of Joseph by their clans.

³⁸The descendants of Benjamin by their clans: Of Bela, the clan of the Belaites; of Ashbel, the clan of the Ashbelites; of Ahiram, the clan of the Ahiramites; ³⁹of Shephupham, the clan of the Shuphamites; of Hupham, the clan of the Huphamites. ⁴⁰The sons of Bela were Ard and Naaman: [Of Ard,] the clan of the Ardites; of Naaman, the clan of the Naamanites. ⁴¹Those are the descendants of Benjamin by their clans; persons enrolled: 45,600.

⁴²These are the descendants of Dan by their clans: Of Shuham, the clan of the Shuhamites. Those are the clans of Dan,ᶜ by their clans. ⁴³All the clans of the Shuhamites; persons enrolled: 64,400.

⁴⁴Descendants of Asher by their clans: Of Imnah, the clan of the Imnites; of Ishvi, the clan of the Ishvites; of Beriah, the clan of the Beriites. ⁴⁵Of the descendants of Beriah: Of Heber, the clan of the Heberites; of Malchiel, the clan of the Malchielites. ⁴⁶—The name of Asher's daughter was Serah.—⁴⁷These are the clans of Asher's descendants; persons enrolled: 53,400.

⁴⁸Descendants of Naphtali by their clans: Of Jahzeel, the clan of the Jahzeelites; of Guni, the clan of the Gunites; ⁴⁹of Jezer, the clan of the Jezerites; of Shillem, the clan of the Shillemites. ⁵⁰Those are the clans of the Naphtalites, clan by clan; persons enrolled: 45,400.

⁵¹This is the enrollment of the Israelites: 601,730.

⁵²The LORD spoke to Moses, saying, ⁵³"Among these shall the land be apportioned as shares, according to the listed names: ⁵⁴with larger groups

---

ᶜ *Meaning of parts of vv. 42 and 43 uncertain.*

increase the share, with smaller groups reduce the share. Each is to be assigned its share according to its enrollment. ⁵⁵The land, moreover, is to be apportioned by lot; and the allotment shall be made according to the listings of their ancestral tribes. ⁵⁶Each portion shall be assigned by lot, whether for larger or smaller groups."

⁵⁷This is the enrollment of the Levites by their clans: Of Gershon, the clan of the Gershonites; of Kohath, the clan of the Kohathites; of Merari, the clan of the Merarites. ⁵⁸These are the clans of Levi: The clan of the Libnites, the clan of the Hebronites, the clan of the Mahlites, the clan of the Mushites, the clan of the Korahites.—Kohath begot Amram. ⁵⁹The name of Amram's wife was Jochebed daughter of Levi, who was born to Levi in Egypt; she bore to Amram Aaron and Moses and their sister Miriam. ⁶⁰To Aaron were born Nadab and Abihu, Eleazar and Ithamar. ⁶¹Nadab and Abihu died when they offered alien fire before the LORD.— ⁶²Their enrollment of 23,000 comprised all males from a month up. They were not part of the regular enrollment of the Israelites, since no share was assigned to them among the Israelites.

⁶³These are the persons enrolled by Moses and Eleazar the priest who registered the Israelites on the steppes of Moab, at the Jordan near Jericho. ⁶⁴Among these there was not one of those enrolled by Moses and Aaron the priest when they recorded the Israelites in the wilderness of Sinai. ⁶⁵For the LORD had said of them, "They shall die in the wilderness." Not one of them survived, except Caleb son of Jephunneh and Joshua son of Nun.

27 The daughters of Zelophehad, of Manassite family—son of Hepher son of Gilead son of Machir son of Manasseh son of Joseph—came forward. The names of the daughters were Mahlah, Noah, Hoglah, Milcah, and Tirzah. ²They stood before Moses, Eleazar the priest, the chieftains, and the whole assembly, at the entrance of the Tent of Meeting, and they said, ³"Our father died in the wilderness. He was not one of the faction, Korah's faction, which banded together against the LORD, but died for his own sin; and he has left no sons. ⁴Let not our father's name be lost to his clan just because he had no son! Give us a holding among our father's kinsmen!"

⁵Moses brought their case before the LORD.

⁶And the LORD said to Moses, ⁷"The plea of Zelophehad's daughters is just: you should give them a hereditary holding among their father's kinsmen; transfer their father's share to them.

⁸"Further, speak to the Israelite people as follows: 'If a man dies without leaving a son, you shall transfer his property to his daughter. ⁹If he has no daughter, you shall assign his property to his brothers. ¹⁰If he has no brothers, you shall assign his property to his father's brothers. ¹¹If his father had no brothers, you shall assign his property to his nearest relative in his own clan, and he shall inherit it.' This shall be the law of procedure for the Israelites, in accordance with the LORD's command to Moses."

¹²The LORD said to Moses, "Ascend these heights of Abarim and view the land that I have given to the Israelite people. ¹³When you have seen it, you too shall be gathered to your kin, just as your brother Aaron was. ¹⁴For, in the wilderness of Zin, when the community was contentious, you disobeyed My command to uphold My sanctity in their sight by means of the water." Those are the Waters of Meribath-kadesh,ᵃ in the wilderness of Zin.

¹⁵Moses spoke to the LORD, saying, ¹⁶"Let the LORD, Source of the breath of all flesh, appoint someone over the community ¹⁷ ᵇ⁻who shall go out before them and come in before them, and who shall take them out and bring them in,⁻ᵇ so that the LORD's community may not be like sheep that have no shepherd." ¹⁸And the LORD answered Moses, "Single out Joshua son of Nun, an inspired man, and lay your hand upon him. ¹⁹Have him stand before Eleazar the priest and before the whole community, and commission him in their sight. ²⁰Invest him with some of your authority, so that the whole Israelite community may obey. ²¹But he shall present himself to Eleazar the priest, who shall on his behalf seek the decision of the Urim before the LORD. By such instruction they shall go out and by such instruction they shall come in, he and all the Israelites, the whole community."

²²Moses did as the LORD commanded him. He took Joshua and had him stand before Eleazar the priest and before the whole community. ²³He laid his hands upon him and commissioned him—as the LORD had spoken through Moses.

ᵃ *See note at 20.13.*
ᵇ⁻ᵇ *I.e., who shall lead them in all matters and whom they shall follow in all matters.*

28

The LORD spoke to Moses, saying: ²Command the Israelite people and say to them: Be punctilious in presenting to Me at stated times ᵃ·the offerings of food due Me,·ᵃ as offerings by fire of pleasing odor to Me.

³Say to them: These are the offerings by fire that you are to present to the LORD:

As a regular burnt offering every day, two yearling lambs without blemish. ⁴You shall offer one lamb in the morning, and the other lamb you shall offer at twilight. ⁵And as a meal offering, there shall be a tenth of an *ephah* of choice flour with a quarter of a *hin* of beaten oil mixed in ⁶—the regular burnt offering instituted at Mount Sinaiᵇ—an offering by fire of pleasing odor to the LORD.

⁷The libation with it shall be a quarter of a *hin* for each lamb, to be poured in the sacred precinct as an offering of fermented drinkᶜ to the LORD. ⁸The other lamb you shall offer at twilight, preparing the same meal offering and libation as in the morning—an offering by fire of pleasing odor to the LORD.

⁹On the sabbath day: two yearling lambs without blemish, together with two-tenths of a measureᵈ of choice flour with oil mixed in as a meal offering, and with the proper libation—¹⁰a burnt offering for every sabbath, in addition to the regular burnt offering and its libation.

¹¹On your new moons you shall present a burnt offering to the LORD: two bulls of the herd, one ram, and seven yearling lambs, without blemish. ¹²As meal offering for each bull: three-tenths of a measure of choice flour with oil mixed in. As meal offering for each ram: two-tenths of a measure of choice flour with oil mixed in. ¹³As meal offering for each lamb: a tenth of a measure of fine flour with oil mixed in. Such shall be the burnt offering of pleasing odor, an offering by fire to the LORD. ¹⁴Their libations shall be: half a *hin* of wine for a bull, a third of a *hin* for a ram, and a quarter of a *hin* for a lamb. That shall be the monthly burnt offering for each new moon of the year. ¹⁵And there shall be one goat as a sin offering to the LORD, to be offered in addition to the regular burnt offering and its libation.

¹⁶In the first month, on the fourteenth day of the month, there shall be a passover sacrifice to the LORD, ¹⁷and on the fifteenth day of that

---

ᵃ⁻ᵃ Lit. "My offering, My food."
ᵇ Exod. 29.38–41.
ᶜ I.e., wine.
ᵈ I.e., of an ephah.

month a festival. Unleavened bread shall be eaten for seven days. [18]The first day shall be a sacred occasion: you shall not work at your occupations. [19]You shall present an offering by fire, a burnt offering, to the LORD: two bulls of the herd, one ram, and seven yearling lambs—[e-]see that they are-[e] without blemish. [20]The meal offering with them shall be of choice flour with oil mixed in: prepare three-tenths of a measure for a bull, two-tenths for a ram; [21]and for each of the seven lambs prepare one-tenth of a measure. [22]And there shall be one goat for a sin offering, to make expiation in your behalf. [23]You shall present these in addition to the morning portion of the regular burnt offering. [24]You shall offer the like daily for seven days as food, an offering by fire of pleasing odor to the LORD; they shall be offered, with their libations, in addition to the regular burnt offering. [25]And the seventh day shall be a sacred occasion for you: you shall not work at your occupations.

[26]On the day of the first fruits, your Feast of Weeks, when you bring an offering of new grain to the LORD, you shall observe a sacred occasion: you shall not work at your occupations. [27]You shall present a burnt offering of pleasing odor to the LORD: two bulls of the herd, one ram, seven yearling lambs. [28]The meal offering with them shall be of choice flour with oil mixed in, three-tenths of a measure for a bull, two-tenths for a ram, [29]and one-tenth for each of the seven lambs. [30]And there shall be one goat for expiation in your behalf. [31]You shall present them—[e-]see that they are-[e] without blemish—with their libations, in addition to the regular burnt offering and its meal offering.

29 In the seventh month, on the first day of the month, you shall observe a sacred occasion: you shall not work at your occupations. You shall observe it as [a-]a day when the horn is sounded.-[a] [2]You shall present a burnt offering of pleasing odor to the LORD: one bull of the herd, one ram, and seven yearling lambs, without blemish. [3]The meal offering with them—choice flour with oil mixed in—shall be: three-tenths of a measure for a bull, two-tenths for a ram, [4]and one-tenth for each of the seven lambs. [5]And there shall be one goat for a sin offering, to make expiation in your behalf—[6]in addition to the burnt offering of the new moon with its meal offering and the regular burnt offering with its meal offering, each with its libation as prescribed, offerings by fire of pleasing odor to the LORD.

e-e *Lit. "they shall be to you."*
a-a *Or "a day of festivity."*

⁷On the tenth day of the same seventh month you shall observe a sacred occasion when you shall practice self-denial. You shall do no work. ⁸You shall present to the LORD a burnt offering of pleasing odor: one bull of the herd, one ram, seven yearling lambs; see that they areᵇ without blemish. ⁹The meal offering with them—of choice flour with oil mixed in—shall be: three-tenths of a measure for a bull, two-tenths for the one ram, ¹⁰one-tenth for each of the seven lambs. ¹¹And there shall be one goat for a sin offering, in addition to the sin offering of expiation and the regular burnt offering with its meal offering, each with its libation.

¹²On the fifteenth day of the seventh month, you shall observe a sacred occasion: you shall not work at your occupations.—Seven days you shall observe a festival of the LORD.—¹³You shall present a burnt offering, an offering by fire of pleasing odor to the LORD: Thirteen bulls of the herd, two rams, fourteen yearling lambs; they shall be without blemish. ¹⁴The meal offerings with them—of choice flour with oil mixed in—shall be: three-tenths of a measure for each of the thirteen bulls, two-tenths for each of the two rams, ¹⁵and one-tenth for each of the fourteen lambs. ¹⁶And there shall be one goat for a sin offering—in addition to the regular burnt offering, its meal offering and libation.

¹⁷Second day: Twelve bulls of the herd, two rams, fourteen yearling lambs, without blemish; ¹⁸the meal offerings and libations for the bulls, rams, and lambs, in the quantities prescribed; ¹⁹and one goat for a sin offering—in addition to the regular burnt offering, its meal offering and libations.

²⁰Third day: Eleven bulls, two rams, fourteen yearling lambs, without blemish; ²¹the meal offerings and libations for the bulls, rams, and lambs, in the quantities prescribed; ²²and one goat for a sin offering—in addition to the regular burnt offering, its meal offering and libation.

²³Fourth day: Ten bulls, two rams, fourteen yearling lambs, without blemish; ²⁴the meal offerings and libations for the bulls, rams, and lambs, in the quantities prescribed; ²⁵and one goat for a sin offering—in addition to the regular burnt offering, its meal offering and libation.

²⁶Fifth day: Nine bulls, two rams, fourteen yearling lambs, without blemish; ²⁷the meal offerings and libations for the bulls, rams, and lambs, in the quantities prescribed; ²⁸and one goat for a sin offering—in addition to the regular burnt offering, its meal offering and libation.

²⁹Sixth day: Eight bulls, two rams, fourteen yearling lambs, without blemish; ³⁰the meal offerings and libations for the bulls, rams, and lambs,

ᵇ See note at 28.19.

in the quantities prescribed; [31]and one goat for a sin offering—in addition to the regular burnt offering, its meal offering and libations.

[32]Seventh day: Seven bulls, two rams, fourteen yearling lambs, without blemish; [33]the meal offerings and libations for the bulls, rams, and lambs, in the quantities prescribed; [34]and one goat for a sin offering—in addition to the regular burnt offering, its meal offering and libation.

[35]On the eighth day you shall hold a solemn gathering;[c] you shall not work at your occupations. [36]You shall present a burnt offering, an offering by fire of pleasing odor to the LORD; one bull, one ram, seven yearling lambs, without blemish; [37]the meal offerings and libations for the bull, the ram, and the lambs, in the quantities prescribed; [38]and one goat for a sin offering—in addition to the regular burnt offering, its meal offering and libation.

[39]All these you shall offer to the LORD at the stated times, in addition to your votive and freewill offerings, be they burnt offerings, meal offerings, libations, or offerings of well-being. [1]So Moses spoke to the Israelites just as the Lord had commanded Moses.

30

מטות

[2]Moses spoke to the heads of the Israelite tribes, saying: This is what the LORD has commanded:

[3]If a man makes a vow to the LORD or takes an oath imposing an obligation[a] on himself, he shall not break his pledge; he must carry out all that has [b-]crossed his lips.[-b]

[4]If a woman makes a vow to the LORD or assumes an obligation while still in her father's household by reason of her youth, [5]and her father learns of her vow or her self-imposed obligation and offers no objection, all her vows shall stand and every self-imposed obligation shall stand. [6]But if her father restrains her on the day he finds out, none of her vows or self-imposed obligations shall stand; and the LORD will forgive her, since her father restrained her.

[7]If she should marry while her vow or the commitment[c] to which she bound herself is still in force, [8]and her husband learns of it and offers no objection on the day he finds out, her vows shall stand and her self-imposed obligations shall stand. [9]But if her husband restrains her on the day that he learns of it, he thereby annuls her vow which was in force or the commitment[c] to which she bound herself; and the LORD will forgive her. [10]—The vow of a widow or of a divorced woman, however, whatever

---

[c] *See note at Lev. 23.36.*

[a] *Or "a prohibition."*
[b-b] *Lit. "come out of his mouth."*
[c] *Lit. "utterance of her lips."*

she has imposed on herself, shall be binding upon her.—11So, too, if, while in her husband's household, she makes a vow or imposes an obligation on herself by oath, 12and her husband learns of it, yet offers no objection—thus failing to restrain her—all her vows shall stand and all her self-imposed obligations shall stand. 13But if her husband does annul them on the day he finds out, then nothing that has crossed her lips shall stand, whether vows or self-imposed obligations. Her husband has annulled them, and the LORD will forgive her. 14Every vow and every sworn obligation of self-denial may be upheld by her husband or annulled by her husband. 15If her husband offers no objection from that day to the next, he has upheld all the vows or obligations she has assumed: he has upheld them by offering no objection on the day he found out. 16But if he annuls them after [the day] he finds out, he shall bear her guilt.

17Those are the laws that the LORD enjoined upon Moses between a man and his wife, and as between a father and his daughter while in her father's household by reason of her youth.

31 The LORD spoke to Moses, saying, 2"Avenge the Israelite people on the Midianites; then you shall be gathered to your kin."

3Moses spoke to the people, saying, "Let men be picked out from among you for a campaign, and let them fall upon Midian to wreak the LORD's vengeance on Midian. 4You shall dispatch on the campaign a thousand from every one of the tribes of Israel."

5So a thousand from each tribe were furnished from the divisions of Israel, twelve thousand picked for the campaign. 6Moses dispatched them on the campaign, a thousand from each tribe, with Phinehas son of Eleazar serving as a priest on the campaign, equipped with the sacred utensilsa and the trumpets for sounding the blasts. 7They took the field against Midian, as the LORD had commanded Moses, and slew every male. 8Along with their other victims, they slew the kings of Midian: Evi, Rekem, Zur, Hur, and Reba, the five kings of Midian. They also put Balaam son of Beor to the sword.

9The Israelites took the women and children of the Midianites captive, and seized as booty all their beasts, all their herds, and all their wealth. 10And they destroyed by fire all the towns in which they were settled, and their encampments. 11They gathered all the spoil and all the booty, man and beast, 12and they brought the captives, the booty, and the spoil to

a *Perhaps the Urim; cf. 27.21.*

Moses, Eleazar the priest, and the whole Israelite community, at the camp in the steppes of Moab, at the Jordan near Jericho.

13Moses, Eleazar the priest, and all the chieftains of the community came out to meet them outside the camp. 14Moses became angry with the commanders of the army, the officers of thousands and the officers of hundreds, who had come back from the military campaign. 15Moses said to them, "You have spared every female! 16Yet they are the very ones who, at the bidding of Balaam, inducedᵇ the Israelites to trespass against the LORD in the matter of Peor, so that the LORD's community was struck by the plague. 17Now, therefore, slay every male among the children, and slay also every woman who has known a man carnally; 18but spare every young woman who has not had carnal relations with a man.

19"You shall then stay outside the camp seven days; every one among you or among your captives who has slain a person or touched a corpse shall cleanse himself on the third and seventh days. 20You shall also cleanse every cloth, every article of skin, everything made of goats' hair, and every object of wood."

21Eleazar the priest said to the troops who had taken part in the fighting, "This is the ritual law that the LORD has enjoined upon Moses: 22Gold and silver, copper, iron, tin, and lead23—any article that can withstand fire—these you shall pass through fire and they shall be clean, except that they must be cleansed with water of lustration; and anything that cannot withstand fire you must pass through water. 24On the seventh day you shall wash your clothes and be clean, and after that you may enter the camp."

25The LORD said to Moses: 26"You and Eleazar the priest and the family heads of the community take an inventory of the booty that was captured, man and beast, 27and divide the booty equally between the combatants who engaged in the campaign and the rest of the community. 28You shall exact a levy for the LORD: in the case of the warriors who engaged in the campaign, one item in five hundred, of persons, oxen, asses, and sheep, 29shall be taken from their half-share and given to Eleazar the priest as a contribution to the LORD; 30and from the half-share of the other Israelites you shall withhold one in every fifty human beings as well as cattle, asses, and sheep—all the animals—and give them to the Levites, who attend to the duties of the LORD's Tabernacle."

31Moses and Eleazar the priest did as the LORD commanded Moses. 32The amount of booty, other than the spoil that the troops had plun-

ᵇ Meaning of Heb. hayu . . . limsor uncertain.

dered, came to 675,000 sheep, 3372,000 head of cattle, 3461,000 asses, 35and a total of 32,000 human beings, namely, the women who had not had carnal relations.

36Thus, the half-share of those who had engaged in the campaign [was as follows]: The number of sheep was 337,500, 37and the LORD's levy from the sheep was 675; 38the cattle came to 36,000, from which the LORD's levy was 72; 39the asses came to 30,500, from which the LORD's levy was 61. 40And the number of human beings was 16,000, from which the LORD's levy was 32. 41Moses gave the contributions levied for the LORD to Eleazar the priest, as the LORD had commanded Moses.

42As for the half-share of the other Israelites, which Moses withdrew from the men who had taken the field, 43that half-share of the community consisted of 337,500 sheep, 4436,000 head of cattle, 4530,500 asses, 46and 16,000 human beings. 47From this half-share of the Israelites, Moses withheld one in every fifty humans and animals; and he gave them to the Levites, who attended to the duties of the LORD's Tabernacle, as the LORD had commanded Moses.

48The commanders of the troop divisions, the officers of thousands and the officers of hundreds, approached Moses. 49They said to Moses, "Your servants have made a check of the warriors in our charge, and not one of us is missing. 50So we have brought as an offering to the LORD such articles of gold as each of us came upon: armlets, bracelets, signet rings, earrings, and pendants,c that expiation may be made for our persons before the LORD." 51Moses and Eleazar the priest accepted the gold from them, all kinds of wrought articles. 52All the gold that was offered by the officers of thousands and the officers of hundreds as a contribution to the LORD came to 16,750 shekels. 53—But in the ranks, everyone kept his booty for himself.—54So Moses and Eleazar the priest accepted the gold from the officers of thousands and the officers of hundreds and brought it to the Tent of Meeting, as a reminder in behalf of the Israelites before the LORD.

32

The Reubenites and the Gadites owned cattle in very great numbers. Noting that the lands of Jazer and Gilead were a region suitable for cattle, 2the Gadites and the Reubenites came to Moses, Eleazar the priest, and the chieftains of the community, and said, 3"Ataroth, Dibon, Jazer, Nimrah, Heshbon, Elealeh, Sebam, Nebo, and Beon—4the land that the

c See note at Exod. 35.22.

LORD has conquered for the community of Israel is cattle country, and your servants have cattle. 5It would be a favor to us," they continued, "if this land were given to your servants as a holding; do not move us across the Jordan."

6Moses replied to the Gadites and the Reubenites, "Are your brothers to go to war while you stay here? 7Why will you turn the minds of the Israelites from crossing into the land that the LORD has given them? 8That is what your fathers did when I sent them from Kadesh-barnea to survey the land. 9After going up to the wadi Eshcol and surveying the land, they turned the minds of the Israelites from invading the land that the LORD had given them. 10Thereupon the LORD was incensed and He swore, 11'None of the men from twenty years up who came out of Egypt shall see the land that I promised on oath to Abraham, Isaac, and Jacob, for they did not remain loyal to Me—12none except Caleb son of Jephunneh the Kenizzite and Joshua son of Nun, for they remained loyal to the LORD.' 13The LORD was incensed at Israel, and for forty years He made them wander in the wilderness, until the whole generation that had provoked the LORD's displeasure was gone. 14And now you, a breed of sinful men, have replaced your fathers, to add still further to the LORD's wrath against Israel. 15If you turn away from Him and He abandons them once more in the wilderness, you will bring calamity upon all this people."

16Then they stepped up to him and said, "We will build here sheepfolds for our flocks and towns for our children. 17And we will hastena as shock-troops in the van of the Israelites until we have established them in their home, while our children stay in the fortified towns because of the inhabitants of the land. 18We will not return to our homes until every one of the Israelites is in possession of his portion. 19But we will not have a share with them in the territory beyond the Jordan, for we have received our share on the east side of the Jordan."

20Moses said to them, "If you do this, if you go to battle as shock-troops, at the instance of the LORD, 21and every shock-fighter among you crosses the Jordan, at the instance of the LORD, until He has dispossessed His enemies before Him, 22and the land has been subdued, at the instance of the LORD, and then you return—you shall be clear before the LORD and before Israel; and this land shall be your holding under the LORD. 23But if you do not do so, you will have sinned against the LORD; and know that your sin will overtake you. 24Build towns for your children and sheepfolds for your flocks, but do what you have promised."

---

a Meaning of Heb. hushim uncertain.

25The Gadites and the Reubenites answered Moses, "Your servants will do as my lord commands. 26Our children, our wives, our flocks, and all our other livestock will stay behindb in the towns of Gilead; 27while your servants, all those recruited for war, cross over, at the instance of the LORD, to engage in battle—as my lord orders."

28Then Moses gave instructions concerning them to Eleazar the priest, Joshua son of Nun, and the family heads of the Israelite tribes. 29Moses said to them, "If every shock-fighter among the Gadites and the Reubenites crosses the Jordan with you to do battle, at the instance of the LORD, and the land is subdued before you, you shall give them the land of Gilead as a holding. 30But if they do not cross over with you as shock-troops, they shall receive holdings among you in the land of Canaan."

31The Gadites and the Reubenites said in reply, "Whatever the LORD has spoken concerning your servants, that we will do. 32We ourselves will cross over as shock-troops, at the instance of the LORD, into the land of Canaan; and we shall keep our hereditary holding across the Jordan."c

33So Moses assigned to them—to the Gadites, the Reubenites, and the half-tribe of Manasseh son of Joseph—the kingdom of Sihon king of the Amorites and the kingdom of King Og of Bashan, the land with its various cities and the territories of their surrounding towns. 34The Gadites rebuilt Dibon, Ataroth, Aroer, 35Atroth-shophan, Jazer, Jogbehah, 36Beth-nimrah, and Beth-haran as fortified towns or as enclosures for flocks. 37The Reubenites rebuilt Heshbon, Elealeh, Kiriathaim, 38Nebo, Baal-meon—some names being changed—and Sibmah; they gave [their own] names to towns that they rebuilt.d 39The descendants of Machir son of Manasseh went to Gilead and captured it, dispossessing the Amorites who were there; 40so Moses gave Gilead to Machir son of Manasseh, and he settled there. 41Jair son of Manasseh went and captured e-their villages,-e which he renamed Havvoth-jair.f 42And Nobah went and captured Kenath and its dependencies, renaming it Nobah after himself.

33 מסעי

These were the marches of the Israelites who started out from the land of Egypt, troop by troop, in the charge of Moses and Aaron. 2Moses recorded the starting points of their various marches as directed by the LORD. Their marches, by starting points, were as follows:

b Lit. "there."
c I.e., in Transjordan.
d Cf. vv. 41, 42.
e-e Or "the villages of Ham"; cf. Gen. 14.5.
f I.e., "the villages of Jair."

³They set out from Rameses in the first month, on the fifteenth day of the first month. It was on the morrow of the passover offering that the Israelites started out defiantly,ᵃ in plain view of all the Egyptians. ⁴The Egyptians meanwhile were burying those among them whom the LORD had struck down, every first-born—whereby the LORD executed judgment on their gods.

⁵The Israelites set out from Rameses and encamped at Succoth. ⁶They set out from Succoth and encamped at Etham, which is on the edge of the wilderness. ⁷They set out from Etham and turned about toward Pi-hahiroth, which faces Baal-zephon, and they encamped before Migdol. ⁸They set out from Peneᵇ-hahiroth and passed through the sea into the wilderness; and they made a three-days' journey in the wilderness of Etham and encamped at Marah. ⁹They set out from Marah and came to Elim. There were twelve springs in Elim and seventy palm trees, so they encamped there. ¹⁰They set out from Elim and encamped by the Sea of Reeds.ᶜ ¹¹They set out from the Sea of Reeds and encamped in the wilderness of Sin. ¹²They set out from the wilderness of Sin and encamped at Dophkah. ¹³They set out from Dophkah and encamped at Alush. ¹⁴They set out from Alush and encamped at Rephidim; it was there that the people had no water to drink. ¹⁵They set out from Rephidim and encamped in the wilderness of Sinai. ¹⁶They set out from the wilderness of Sinai and encamped at Kibroth-hattaavah. ¹⁷They set out from Kibroth-hattaavah and encamped at Hazeroth. ¹⁸They set out from Hazeroth and encamped at Rithmah. ¹⁹They set out from Rithmah and encamped at Rimmon-perez. ²⁰They set out from Rimmon-perez and encamped at Libnah. ²¹They set out from Libnah and encamped at Rissah. ²²They set out from Rissah and encamped at Kehelath. ²³They set out from Kehelath and encamped at Mount Shepher. ²⁴They set out from Mount Shepher and encamped at Haradah. ²⁵They set out from Haradah and encamped at Makheloth. ²⁶They set out from Makheloth and encamped at Tahath. ²⁷They set out from Tahath and encamped at Terah. ²⁸They set out from Terah and encamped at Mithkah. ²⁹They set out from Mithkah and encamped at Hashmonah. ³⁰They set out from Hashmonah and encamped at Moseroth. ³¹They set out from Moseroth and encamped at Bene-jaakan. ³²They set out from Bene-jaakan and encamped at Hor-haggidgad. ³³They set out from Hor-haggidgad and encamped at Jotbath. ³⁴They set out from Jotbath and encamped at Abronah. ³⁵They set out from Abronah and encamped at Ezion-geber. ³⁶They set out from Ezion-geber and en-

ᵃ See note at Exod. 14.8.
ᵇ Many Hebrew manuscripts and ancient versions read "Pi."
ᶜ See note at Exod. 10.19.

camped in the wilderness of Zin, that is, Kadesh. ³⁷They set out from Kadesh and encamped at Mount Hor, on the edge of the land of Edom.

³⁸Aaron the priest ascended Mount Hor at the command of the LORD and died there, in the fortieth year after the Israelites had left the land of Egypt, on the first day of the fifth month. ³⁹Aaron was a hundred and twenty-three years old when he died on Mount Hor. ⁴⁰And the Canaanite, king of Arad, who dwelt in the Negeb, in the land of Canaan, learned of the coming of the Israelites.ᵈ

⁴¹They set out from Mount Hor and encamped at Zalmonah. ⁴²They set out from Zalmonah and encamped at Punon. ⁴³They set out from Punon and encamped at Oboth. ⁴⁴They set out from Oboth and encamped at Iye-abarim, in the territory of Moab. ⁴⁵They set out from Iyim and encamped at Dibon-gad. ⁴⁶They set out from Dibon-gad and encamped at Almon-diblathaim. ⁴⁷They set out from Almon-diblathaim and encamped in the hills of Abarim, before Nebo. ⁴⁸They set out from the hills of Abarim and encamped in the steppes of Moab, at the Jordan near Jericho; ⁴⁹they encamped by the Jordan from Beth-jeshimoth as far as Abel-shittim, in the steppes of Moab.

⁵⁰In the steppes of Moab, at the Jordan near Jericho, the LORD spoke to Moses, saying: ⁵¹Speak to the Israelite people and say to them: When you cross the Jordan into the land of Canaan, ⁵²you shall dispossess all the inhabitants of the land; you shall destroy all their figuredᵉ objects; you shall destroy all their molten images, and you shall demolish all their cult places. ⁵³And you shall take possession of the land and settle in it, for I have assigned the land to you to possess. ⁵⁴You shall apportion the land among yourselves by lot, clan by clan: with larger groups increase the share, with smaller groups reduce the share. Wherever the lot falls for anyone, that shall be his. You shall have your portions according to your ancestral tribes. ⁵⁵But if you do not dispossess the inhabitants of the land, those whom you allow to remain shall be stings in your eyes and thorns in your sides, and they shall harass you in the land in which you live; ⁵⁶so that I will do to you what I planned to do to them.

34

The LORD spoke to Moses, saying: ²Instruct the Israelite people and say to them: When you enter the land of Canaan, this is the land that

ᵈ *See 21.1–3.*
ᵉ *See note at Lev. 26.1.*

shall fall to you as your portion, the land of Canaan with its various boundaries:

³Your southern sector shall extend from the wilderness of Zin alongside Edom. Your southern boundary shall start on the east from the tip of the Dead Sea. ⁴Your boundary shall then turn to pass south of the ascent of Akrabbim and continue to Zin, and its limits shall be south of Kadesh-barnea, reaching Hazar-addar and continuing to Azmon. ⁵From Azmon the boundary shall turn toward the Wadi of Egypt and terminate at the Sea.ᵃ

⁶For the western boundary you shall have the coast of the Great Sea;ᵃ that shall serve as your western boundary.

⁷This shall be your northern boundary: Draw a line from the Great Sea to Mount Hor; ⁸from Mount Hor draw a line to Lebo-hamath,ᵇ and let the boundary reach Zedad. ⁹The boundary shall then run to Ziphron and terminate at Hazar-enan. That shall be your northern boundary.

¹⁰For your eastern boundary you shall draw a line from Hazar-enan to Shepham. ¹¹From Shepham the boundary shall descend to Riblah on the east side of Ain; from there the boundary shall continue downward and abut on the eastern slopes of the Sea of Chinnereth.ᶜ ¹²The boundary shall then descend along the Jordan and terminate at the Dead Sea.

That shall be your land as defined by its boundaries on all sides.

¹³Moses instructed the Israelites, saying: This is the land you are to receive by lot as your hereditary portion, which the LORD has commanded to be given to the nine and a half tribes. ¹⁴For the Reubenite tribe by its ancestral houses, the Gadite tribe by its ancestral houses, and the half-tribe of Manasseh have already received their portions: ¹⁵those two and a half tribes have received their portions across the Jordan, opposite Jericho, on the east, the orient side.

¹⁶The LORD spoke to Moses, saying: ¹⁷These are the names of the men through whom the land shall be apportioned for you: Eleazar the priest and Joshua son of Nun. ¹⁸And you shall also take a chieftain from each tribe through whom the land shall be apportioned. ¹⁹These are the names of the men: from the tribe of Judah: Caleb son of Jephunneh. ²⁰From the Simeonite tribe: Samuelᵈ son of Ammihud. ²¹From the tribe of Benjamin: Elidad son of Chislon. ²²From the Danite tribe: a chieftain, Bukki son of Jogli. ²³For the descendants of Joseph: from the Manassite tribe: a chieftain, Hanniel son of Ephod; ²⁴and from the Ephraimite tribe: a

ᵃ I.e., the Mediterranean Sea.
ᵇ See note at 13.21.
ᶜ I.e., the Sea (or Lake) of Galilee.
ᵈ Or "Shemuel."

chieftain, Kemuel son of Shiphtan. 25From the Zebulunite tribe: a chieftain, Elizaphan son of Parnach. 26From the Issacharite tribe: a chieftain, Paltiel son of Azzan. 27From the Asherite tribe: a chieftain, Ahihud son of Shelomi. 28From the Naphtalite tribe: a chieftain, Pedahel son of Ammihud.

29It was these whom the LORD designated to allot portions to the Israelites in the land of Canaan.

35 The LORD spoke to Moses in the steppes of Moab at the Jordan near Jericho, saying: 2Instruct the Israelite people to assign, out of the holdings apportioned to them, towns for the Levites to dwell in; you shall also assign to the Levites pasture land around their towns. 3The towns shall be theirs to dwell in, and the pasture shall be for the cattle they own and all their other beasts. 4The town pasture that you are to assign to the Levites shall extend a thousand cubits outside the town wall all around. 5You shall measure off two thousand cubits outside the town on the east side, two thousand on the south side, two thousand on the west side, and two thousand on the north side, with the town in the center. That shall be the pasture for their towns.

6The towns that you assign to the Levites shall comprise the six cities of refuge that you are to designate for a manslayer to flee to, to which you shall add forty-two towns. 7Thus the total of the towns that you assign to the Levites shall be forty-eight towns, with their pasture. 8In assigning towns from the holdings of the Israelites, take more from the larger groups and less from the smaller, so that each assigns towns to the Levites in proportion to the share it receives.

9The LORD spoke further to Moses: 10Speak to the Israelite people and say to them: When you cross the Jordan into the land of Canaan, 11you shall provide yourselves with places to serve you as cities of refuge to which a manslayer who has killed a person unintentionally may flee. 12The cities shall serve you as a refuge from the avenger,a so that the manslayer may not die unless he has stood trial before the assembly.

13The towns that you thus assign shall be six cities of refuge in all. 14Three cities shall be designated beyond the Jordan, and the other three shall be designated in the land of Canaan: they shall serve as cities of refuge. 15These six cities shall serve the Israelites and the resident aliens

---

a Lit. "redeemer," i.e., next of kin; cf. note at Lev. 25.25.

269

among them for refuge, so that anyone who kills a person unintentionally may flee there.

¹⁶Anyone, however, who strikes another with an iron object so that death results is a murderer; the murderer must be put to death. ¹⁷If he struck him with a stone tool[b] that could cause death, and death resulted, he is a murderer; the murderer must be put to death. ¹⁸Similarly, if the object with which he struck him was a wooden tool[b] that could cause death, and death resulted, he is a murderer; the murderer must be put to death. ¹⁹The blood-avenger himself shall put the murderer to death; it is he who shall put him to death upon encounter. ²⁰So, too, if he pushed him in hate or hurled something at him on purpose and death resulted, ²¹or if he struck him with his hand in enmity and death resulted, the assailant shall be put to death; he is a murderer. The blood-avenger shall put the murderer to death upon encounter.

²²But if he pushed him without malice aforethought or hurled any object at him unintentionally, ²³or inadvertently[c] dropped upon him any deadly object of stone, and death resulted—though he was not an enemy of his and did not seek his harm—²⁴in such cases the assembly shall decide between the slayer and the blood-avenger. ²⁵The assembly shall protect the manslayer from the blood-avenger, and the assembly shall restore him to the city of refuge to which he fled, and there he shall remain until the death of the high priest who was anointed with the sacred oil. ²⁶But if the manslayer ever goes outside the limits of the city of refuge to which he has fled,²⁷and the blood-avenger comes upon him outside the limits of his city of refuge, and the blood-avenger kills the manslayer, there is no bloodguilt on his account. ²⁸For he must remain inside his city of refuge until the death of the high priest; after the death of the high priest, the manslayer may return to his land holding.

²⁹Such shall be your law of procedure throughout the ages in all your settlements.

³⁰If anyone kills a person, the manslayer may be executed only on the evidence of witnesses; the testimony of a single witness against a person shall not suffice for a sentence of death. ³¹You may not accept a ransom for the life of a murderer who is guilty of a capital crime; he must be put to death. ³²Nor may you accept ransom in lieu of flight to a city of refuge, enabling one to return to live on his land before the death of the priest. ³³You shall not pollute the land in which you live; for blood pollutes the land, and the land can have no expiation for blood that is shed on it,

b *Lit. "of the hand."*
c *Lit. "without seeing."*

except by the blood of him who shed it. 34You shall not defile the land in which you live, in which I Myself abide, for I the LORD abide among the Israelite people.

36 The family heads in the clan of the descendants of Gilead son of Machir son of Manasseh, one of the Josephite clans, came forward and appealed to Moses and the chieftains, family heads[a] of the Israelites. 2They said, "The LORD commanded my lord to assign the land to the Israelites as shares by lot, and my lord was further commanded by the LORD to assign the share of our kinsman Zelophehad to his daughters. 3Now, if they marry persons from another Israelite tribe, their share will be cut off from our ancestral portion and be added to the portion of the tribe into which they marry; thus our allotted portion will be diminished. 4And even when the Israelites observe the jubilee, their share will be added to that of the tribe into which they marry, and their share will be cut off from the ancestral portion of our tribe."

5So Moses, at the LORD's bidding, instructed the Israelites, saying: "The plea of the Josephite tribe is just. 6This is what the LORD has commanded concerning the daughters of Zelophehad: They may marry anyone they wish, provided they marry into a clan of their father's tribe. 7No inheritance of the Israelites may pass over from one tribe to another, but the Israelites must remain bound each to the ancestral portion of his tribe. 8Every daughter among the Israelite tribes who inherits a share must marry someone from a clan of her father's tribe, in order that every Israelite may keep his ancestral share. 9Thus no inheritance shall pass over from one tribe to another, but the Israelite tribes shall remain bound each to its portion."

10The daughters of Zelophehad did as the LORD had commanded Moses: 11Mahlah, Tirzah, Hoglah, Milcah, and Noah, Zelophehad's daughters, were married to sons of their uncles, 12marrying into clans of descendants of Manasseh son of Joseph; and so their share remained in the tribe of their father's clan.

13These are the commandments and regulations that the LORD enjoined upon the Israelites, through Moses, on the steppes of Moab, at the Jordan near Jericho.

חזק

---

a I.e., tribal heads.

DEUTERONOMY

1 These are the words that Moses addressed to all Israel on the other side of the Jordan.—[a]Through the wilderness, in the Arabah near Suph, between Paran and Tophel, Laban, Hazeroth, and Di-zahab, [2]it is eleven days from Horeb to Kadesh-barnea by the Mount Seir route.—[3]It was in the fortieth year, on the first day of the eleventh month, that Moses addressed the Israelites in accordance with the instructions that the LORD had given him for them, [4]after he had defeated Sihon king of the Amorites, who dwelt in Heshbon, and King Og of Bashan, who dwelt at Ashtaroth [and[b]] Edrei. [5]On the other side of the Jordan, in the land of Moab, Moses undertook to expound this Teaching. He said:

[6]The LORD our God spoke to us at Horeb, saying: You have stayed long enough at this mountain. [7]Start out and make your way to the hill country of the Amorites and to all their neighbors in the Arabah, the hill country, the Shephelah,[c] the Negeb, the seacoast, the land of the Canaanites,[d] and the Lebanon, as far as the Great River, the river Euphrates. [8]See, I place the land at your disposal. Go, take possession of the land that the LORD swore to your fathers, Abraham, Isaac, and Jacob, to assign to them and to their heirs after them.

[9]Thereupon I said to you, "I cannot bear the burden of you by myself. [10]The LORD your God has multiplied you until you are today as numerous as the stars in the sky.—[11]May the LORD, the God of your fathers, increase your numbers a thousandfold, and bless you as He promised you.—[12]How can I bear unaided the trouble of you, and the burden, and the bickering! [13]Pick from each of your tribes men who are wise, discerning, and experienced, and I will appoint them as your heads." [14]You answered me and said, "What you propose to do is good." [15]So I took your tribal leaders, wise and experienced men, and appointed them heads over you: chiefs of thousands, chiefs of hundreds, chiefs of fifties, and chiefs of tens, and officials for your tribes. [16]I charged your magistrates at that time as

[a] *The rest of this verse and v. 2 are unclear; cf. v. 19 and Num. 33.16–36.*
[b] *Cf. Josh. 12.4; 13.12, 31.*
[c] *Others "Lowland."*
[d] *I.e., Phoenicia.*

follows, "Hear out your fellow men, and decide justly between any man and a fellow Israelite or a stranger. [17] You shall not be partial in judgment: hear out low and high alike. Fear no man, for judgment is God's. And any matter that is too difficult for you, you shall bring to me and I will hear it." [18] Thus I instructed you, at that time, about the various things that you should do.

[19] We set out from Horeb and traveled the great and terrible wilderness that you saw, along the road to the hill country of the Amorites, as the LORD our God had commanded us. When we reached Kadesh-barnea, [20] I said to you, "You have come to the hill country of the Amorites which the LORD our God is giving to us. [21] See, the LORD your God has placed the land at your disposal. Go up, take possession, as the LORD, the God of your fathers, promised you. Fear not and be not dismayed."

[22] Then all of you came to me and said, "Let us send men ahead to reconnoiter the land for us and bring back word on the route we shall follow and the cities we shall come to." [23] I approved of the plan, and so I selected twelve of your men, one from each tribe. [24] They made for the hill country, came to the wadi Eshcol, and spied it out. [25] They took some of the fruit of the land with them and brought it down to us. And they gave us this report: "It is a good land that the LORD our God is giving to us."

[26] Yet you refused to go up, and flouted the command of the LORD your God. [27] You sulked[c] in your tents and said, "It is because the LORD hates us that He brought us out of the land of Egypt, to hand us over to the Amorites to wipe us out. [28] [f-]What kind of place[-f] are we going to? Our kinsmen have taken the heart out of us, saying, 'We saw there a people stronger and taller than we, large cities with walls sky-high, and even Anakites.' "

[29] I said to you, "Have no dread or fear of them. [30] None other than the LORD your God, who goes before you, will fight for you, just as He did for you in Egypt before your very eyes, [31] and in the wilderness, where you saw how the LORD your God carried you, as a man carries his son, all the way that you traveled until you came to this place. [32] Yet for all that, you have no faith in the LORD your God, [33] who goes before you on your journeys—to scout the place where you are to encamp—in fire by night and in cloud by day, in order to guide you on the route you are to follow."

[34] When the LORD heard your loud complaint, He was angry. He vowed:

---

[c] *Precise meaning of Heb. uncertain.*
[f-f] *Lit. "Where."*

³⁵Not one of these men, this evil generation, shall see the good land that I swore to give to your fathers—³⁶none except Caleb son of Jephunneh; he shall see it, and to him and his descendants will I give the land on which he set foot, because he remained loyal to the LORD.

³⁷Because of you the LORD was incensed with me too, and He said: You shall not enter it either. ³⁸Joshua son of Nun, who attends you, he shall enter it. Imbue him with strength, for he shall allot it to Israel. ³⁹Moreover, your little ones who you said would be carried off, your children who do not yet know good from bad, they shall enter it; to them will I give it and they shall possess it. ⁴⁰As for you, turn about and march into the wilderness by the way of the Sea of Reeds.

⁴¹You replied to me, saying, "We stand guilty before the LORD. We will go up now and fight, just as the LORD our God commanded us." And you all girded yourselves with war gear and recklesslyᵍ started for the hill country. ⁴²But the LORD said to me, "Warn them: Do not go up and do not fight, since I am not in your midst; else you will be routed by your enemies." ⁴³I spoke to you, but you would not listen; you flouted the LORD's command and willfully marched into the hill country. ⁴⁴Then the Amorites who lived in those hills came out against you like so many bees and chased you, and they crushed you at Hormah in Seir. ⁴⁵Again you wept before the LORD; but the LORD would not heed your cry or give ear to you.

2 ⁴⁶Thus, after you had remained at Kadesh ʰ⁻all that long time,⁻ʰ ¹we marched back into the wilderness by the way of the Sea of Reeds, as the LORD had spoken to me, and skirted the hill country of Seir a long time.

²Then the LORD said to me: ³You have been skirting this hill country long enough; now turn north. ⁴And charge the people as follows: You will be passing through the territory of your kinsmen, the descendants of Esau, who live in Seir. Though they will be afraid of you, be very careful ⁵not to provoke them. For I will not give you of their land so much as a foot can tread on; I have given the hill country of Seir as a possession to Esau. ⁶ ᵃ⁻What food you eat you shall obtain from them for money; even the water you drink you shall procure from them for money.⁻ᵃ ⁷Indeed, the LORD your God has blessed you in all your undertakings. He has watched over your wanderings through this great wilderness; the LORD

ᵍ Meaning of Heb. uncertain.
ʰ⁻ʰ Lit. "many days, like the days that you remained."

ᵃ⁻ᵃ Or "You may obtain food from them to eat for money; and you may also procure water from them to drink for money."

your God has been with you these past forty years: you have lacked nothing.

8We then moved on, away from our kinsmen, the descendants of Esau, who live in Seir, away from the road of the Arabah, away from Elath and Ezion-geber; and we marched on in the direction of the wilderness of Moab. 9And the LORD said to me: Do not harass the Moabites or provoke them to war. For I will not give you any of their land as a possession; I have assigned Ar as a possession to the descendants of Lot.—

10It was formerly inhabited by the Emim, a people great and numerous, and as tall as the Anakites. 11Like the Anakites, they are counted as Rephaim; but the Moabites call them Emim. 12Similarly, Seir was formerly inhabited by the Horites; but the descendants of Esau dispossessed them, wiping them out and settling in their place, just as Israel did in the land they were to possess, which the LORD had given to them.—

13Up now! Cross the wadi Zered!

So we crossed the wadi Zered. 14The time that we spent in travel from Kadesh-barnea until we crossed the wadi Zered was thirty-eight years, until that whole generation of warriors had perished from the camp, as the LORD had sworn concerning them. 15Indeed, the hand of the LORD struck them, to root them out from the camp to the last man.

16When all the warriors among the people had died off, 17the LORD spoke to me, saying: 18You are now passing through the territory of Moab, through Ar. 19You will then be close to the Ammonites; do not harass them or start a fight with them. For I will not give any part of the land of the Ammonites to you as a possession; I have assigned it as a possession to the descendants of Lot.—

20It, too, is counted as Rephaim country. It was formerly inhabited by Rephaim, whom the Ammonites call Zamzummim, 21a people great and numerous and as tall as the Anakites. The LORD wiped them out, so that [the Ammonites] dispossessed them and settled in their place, 22as He did for the descendants of Esau who live in Seir, when He wiped out the Horites before them, so that they dispossessed them and settled in their place, as is still the case.b 23So, too, with the Avvim who dwelt in villages in the vicinity of Gaza: the Caphtorim, who came from Crete,c wiped them out and settled in their place.—

24Up! Set out across the wadi Arnon! See, I give into your power Sihon the Amorite, king of Heshbon, and his land. Begin the occupation: engage

b Lit. "until this day."
c Heb. "Caphtor."

him in battle. [25]This day I begin to put the dread and fear of you upon the peoples everywhere under heaven, so that they shall tremble and quake because of you whenever they hear you mentioned.

[26]Then I sent messengers from the wilderness of Kedemoth to King Sihon of Heshbon with an offer of peace, as follows, [27]"Let me pass through your country. I will keep strictly to the highway, turning off neither to the right nor to the left. [28]What food I eat you will supply for money, and what water I drink you will furnish for money; just let me pass through[d]—[29]as the descendants of Esau who dwell in Seir did for me, and the Moabites who dwell in Ar—that I may cross the Jordan into the land that the LORD our God is giving us."

[30]But King Sihon of Heshbon refused to let us pass through, because the LORD had stiffened his will and hardened his heart in order to deliver him into your power—as is now the case. [31]And the LORD said to me: See, I begin by placing Sihon and his land at your disposal. Begin the occupation; take possession of his land.

[32]Sihon with all his men took the field against us at Jahaz, [33]and the LORD our God delivered him to us and we defeated him and his sons and all his men. [34]At that time we captured all his towns, and we doomed[e] every town—men, women, and children—leaving no survivor. [35]We retained as booty only the cattle and the spoil of the cities that we captured. [36]From Aroer on the edge of the Arnon valley, including the town[f] in the valley itself, to Gilead, not a city was too mighty for us; the LORD our God delivered everything to us. [37]But you did not encroach upon the land of the Ammonites, all along the wadi Jabbok and the towns of the hill country, just as the LORD our God had commanded.

3 We made our way up the road toward Bashan, and King Og of Bashan with all his men took the field against us at Edrei. [2]But the LORD said to me: Do not fear him, for I am delivering him and all his men and his country into your power, and you will do to him as you did to Sihon king of the Amorites, who lived in Heshbon.

[3]So the LORD our God also delivered into our power King Og of Bashan, with all his men, and we dealt them such a blow that no survivor was left. [4]At that time we captured all his towns; there was not a town that we did not take from them: sixty towns, the whole district of Argob,

---

[d] Lit. "with my feet."

[e] I.e., placed under ḥerem, which meant the annihilation of the population. Cf. note b at Num. 21.2; Josh. 6.24.

[f] Meaning of Heb. uncertain.

the kingdom of Og in Bashan ⁵—all those towns were fortified with high walls, gates,ᵃ and bars—apart from a great number of unwalled towns. ⁶We doomed them as we had done in the case of King Sihon of Heshbon; we doomed every town—men, women, and children—⁷and retained as booty all the cattle and the spoil of the towns.

⁸Thus we seized, at that time, from the two Amorite kings, the country beyond the Jordan, from the wadi Arnon to Mount Hermon—⁹Sidonians called Hermon Sirion, and the Amorites call it Senir—¹⁰all the towns of the Tableland and the whole of Gilead and Bashan as far as Salcahᵇ and Edrei, the towns of Og's kingdom in Bashan. ¹¹Only King Og of Bashan was left of the remaining Rephaim. His bedstead, an iron bedstead, is now in Rabbah of the Ammonites; it is nine cubits long and four cubits wide, by ᶜ⁻the standard cubit!⁻ᶜ

12 ᵈAnd this is the land which we apportioned at that time: The part from Aroer along the wadi Arnon, with part of the hill country of Gilead and its towns, I assigned to the Reubenites and the Gadites. ¹³The rest of Gilead, and all of Bashan under Og's rule—the whole Argob district, all that part of Bashan which is called Rephaim country—I assigned to the half-tribe of Manasseh. ¹⁴Jair son of Manasseh received the whole Argob district (that is, Bashan) as far as the boundary of the Geshurites and the Maacathites, and named it after himself: Havvoth-jairᵉ—as is still the case. ¹⁵To Machir I assigned Gilead. ¹⁶And to the Reubenites and the Gadites I assigned the part from Gilead down to the wadi Arnon, the middle of the wadi being the boundary, and up to the wadi Jabbok, the boundary of the Ammonites.

17 ᶠ[We also seized] the Arabah, from the foot of the slopes of Pisgah on the east, to the edge of the Jordan, and from Chinnereth down to the sea of the Arabah, the Dead Sea.

¹⁸At that time I charged you,ᵍ saying, "The LORD your God has given you this country to possess. You must go as shock-troops, warriors all, at the head of your Israelite kinsmen. ¹⁹Only your wives, children, and livestock—I know that you have much livestock—shall be left in the towns I have assigned to you, ²⁰until the LORD has granted your kinsmen a haven such as you have, and they too have taken possession of the land that the LORD your God is assigning them, beyond the Jordan. Then you may return each to the homestead that I have assigned to him."

ᵃ I.e., two-leaf doors.
ᵇ Others "Salecah" or "Salchah."
ᶜ⁻ᶜ Lit. "by a man's forearm."
ᵈ Vv. 12–13 proceed from south to north; vv. 14–16 from north to south.
ᵉ I.e., "villages of Jair."
ᶠ Continuing vv. 8–10; cf. 4.47–49.
ᵍ I.e., the two and a half tribes.

21I also charged Joshua at that time, saying, "You have seen with your own eyes all that the LORD your God has done to these two kings; so shall the LORD do to all the kingdoms into which you shall cross over. 22Do not fear them, for it is the LORD your God who will battle for you."

ואתחנן

23I pleaded with the LORD at that time, saying, 24"O Lord GOD, You who let Your servant see the first works of Your greatness and Your mighty hand, You whose powerful deeds no god in heaven or on earth can equal! 25Let me, I pray, cross over and see the good land on the other side of the Jordan, that good hill country, and the Lebanon." 26But the LORD was wrathful with me on your account and would not listen to me. The LORD said to me, "Enough! Never speak to Me of this matter again! 27Go up to the summit of Pisgah and gaze about, to the west, the north, the south, and the east. Look at it well, for you shall not go across yonder Jordan. 28Give Joshua his instructions, and imbue him with strength and courage, for he shall go across at the head of this people, and he shall allot to them the land that you may only see."

29Meanwhile we stayed on in the valley near Beth-peor.

4 And now, O Israel, give heed to the laws and rules that I am in-structing you to observe, so that you may live to enter and occupy the land that the LORD, the God of your fathers, is giving you. 2You shall not add anything to what I command you or take anything away from it, but keep the commandments of the LORD your God that I enjoin upon you. 3You saw with your own eyes what the LORD did in the matter of Baal-peor, that the LORD your God wiped out from among you every person who followed Baal-peor; 4while you, who held fast to the LORD your God, are all alive today.

5See, I have imparted to you laws and rules, as the LORD my God has commanded me, for you to abide by in the land that you are about to enter and occupy. 6Observe them faithfully, for that will be proof of your wisdom and discernment to other peoples, who on hearing of all these laws will say, "Surely, that great nation is a wise and discerning people." 7For what great nation is there that has a god so close at hand as is the

LORD our God whenever we call upon Him? ⁸Or what great nation has laws and rules as perfect as all this Teaching that I set before you this day?

⁹But take utmost care and watch yourselves scrupulously, so that you do not forget the things that you saw with your own eyes and so that they do not fade from your mind as long as you live. And make them known to your children and to your children's children: ¹⁰The day you stood before the LORD your God at Horeb, when the LORD said to Me, "Gather the people to Me that I may let them hear My words, in order that they may learn to revere Me as long as they live on earth, and may so teach their children." ¹¹You came forward and stood at the foot of the mountain. The mountain was ablaze with flames to the very skies, dark with densest clouds. ¹²The LORD spoke to you out of the fire; you heard the sound of words but perceived no shape—nothing but a voice. ¹³He declared to you the covenant that He commanded you to observe, the Ten Commandments; and He inscribed them on two tablets of stone. ¹⁴At the same time the LORD commanded me to impart to you laws and rules for you to observe in the land that you are about to cross into and occupy.

¹⁵For your own sake, therefore, be most careful—since you saw no shape when the LORD your God spoke to you at Horeb out of the fire—¹⁶not to act wickedly and make for yourselves a sculptured image in any likeness whatever: the form of a man or a woman, ¹⁷the form of any beast on earth, the form of any winged bird that flies in the sky, ¹⁸the form of anything that creeps on the ground, the form of any fish that is in the waters below the earth. ¹⁹And when you look up to the sky and behold the sun and the moon and the stars, the whole heavenly host, you must not be lured into bowing down to them or serving them. These the LORD your God allotted to other peoples everywhere under heaven; ²⁰but you the LORD took and brought out of Egypt, that iron blast furnace, to be His very own people, as is now the case.

²¹Now the LORD was angry with me on your account and swore that I should not cross the Jordan and enter the good land that the LORD your God is assigning you as a heritage. ²²For I must die in this land; I shall not cross the Jordan. But you will cross and take possession of that good land. ²³Take care, then, not to forget the covenant that the LORD your God concluded with you, and not to make for yourselves a sculptured image in any likeness, against which the LORD your God has en-

joined you. [24]For the LORD your God is a consuming fire, an impassioned God.

[25]When you have begotten children and children's children and are long established in the land, should you act wickedly and make for yourselves a sculptured image in any likeness, causing the LORD your God displeasure and vexation, [26]I call heaven and earth this day to witness against you that you shall soon perish from the land that you are crossing the Jordan to possess; you shall not long endure in it, but shall be utterly wiped out. [27]The LORD will scatter you among the peoples, and only a scant few of you shall be left among the nations to which the LORD will drive you. [28]There you will serve man-made gods of wood and stone, that cannot see or hear or eat or smell.

[29]But if you search there for the LORD your God, you will find Him, if only you seek Him with all your heart and soul—[30]when you are in distress because all these things have befallen you and, in the end, return to the LORD your God and obey Him. [31]For the LORD your God is a compassionate God: He will not fail you nor will He let you perish; He will not forget the covenant which He made on oath with your fathers.

[32]You have but to inquire about bygone ages that came before you, ever since God created man on earth, from one end of heaven to the other: has anything as grand as this ever happened, or has its like ever been known? [33]Has any people heard the voice of a god speaking out of a fire, as you have, and survived? [34]Or has any god ventured to go and take for himself one nation from the midst of another by prodigious acts, by signs and portents, by war, by a mighty hand and an outstretched arm and awesome power, as the LORD your God did for you in Egypt before your very eyes? [35] [a-]It has been clearly demonstrated to you[-a] that the LORD alone is God; there is none beside Him. [36]From the heavens He let you hear His voice to discipline you; on earth He let you see His great fire; and from amidst that fire you heard His words. [37]And because He loved your fathers, He chose their heirs after them; He Himself,[b] in His great might, led you out of Egypt, [38]to drive from your path nations greater and more populous than you, to take you into their land and assign it to you as a heritage, as is still the case. [39]Know therefore this day and keep in mind that the LORD alone is God in heaven above and on earth below; there is no other. [40]Observe His laws and commandments, which I enjoin upon you this day, that it may go well with you and your children after

a-a Lit. "You have been shown to know."
b Lit. "With His face (or Presence)"; cf. note at Exod. 33.14.

you, and that you may long remain in the land that the LORD your God is assigning to you for all time.

⁴¹Then Moses set aside three cities on the east side of the Jordan ⁴²to which a manslayer could escape, one who unwittingly slew a fellow man without having been hostile to him in the past; he could flee to one of these cities and live: ⁴³Bezer, in the wilderness in the Tableland, belonging to the Reubenites; Ramoth, in Gilead, belonging to the Gadites; and Golan, in Bashan, belonging to the Manassites.

⁴⁴This is the Teaching that Moses set before the Israelites: ⁴⁵these are the decrees, laws, and rules that Moses addressed to the people of Israel, after they had left Egypt, ⁴⁶beyond the Jordan, in the valley at Beth-peor, in the land of King Sihon of the Amorites, who dwelt in Heshbon, whom Moses and the Israelites defeated after they had left Egypt. ⁴⁷They had taken possession of his country and that of King Og of Bashan—the two kings of the Amorites—which were on the east side of the Jordan ⁴⁸from Aroer on the banks of the wadi Arnon, as far as Mount Sion,ᶜ that is, Hermon; ⁴⁹also the whole Arabah on the east side of the Jordan, as far as the Sea of the Arabah, at the foot of the slopes of Pisgah.

5

Moses summoned all the Israelites and said to them: Hear, O Israel, the laws and rules that I proclaim to you this day! Study them and observe them faithfully!

²The LORD our God made a covenant with us at Horeb. ³It was not with our fathers that the LORD made this covenant, but with us, the living, every one of us who is here today. ⁴Face to face the LORD spoke to you on the mountain out of the fire—⁵I stood between the LORD and you at that time to convey the LORD's words to you, for you were afraid of the fire and did not go up the mountain—saying:

6 ᵃI the LORD am your God who brought you out of the land of Egypt, the house of bondage: ⁷You shall have no other gods beside Me.

⁸You shall not make for yourself a sculptured image, any likeness of what is in the heavens above, or on the earth below, or in the waters below the earth. ⁹You shall not bow down to them or serve them. For I the LORD your God am an impassioned God, visiting the guilt of the parents upon the children, upon the third and upon the fourth generations

---

ᶜ *Cf. "Sirion," 3.9.*

ᵃ *Tradition varies as to the divisions of the Commandments in vv. 6–18 and the numbering of the verses. Cf. Exod. 20, note a.*

of those who reject Me, [10]but showing kindness to the thousandth generation of those who love Me and keep My commandments.

[11]You shall not swear falsely by the name of the LORD your God; for the LORD will not clear one who swears falsely by His name.

[12]Observe the sabbath day and keep it holy, as the LORD your God has commanded you. [13]Six days you shall labor and do all your work, [14]but the seventh day is a sabbath of the LORD your God; you shall not do any work—you, your son or your daughter, your male or female slave, your ox or your ass, or any of your cattle, or the stranger in your settlements, so that your male and female slave may rest as you do. [15]Remember that you were a slave in the land of Egypt and the LORD your God freed you from there with a mighty hand and an outstretched arm; therefore the LORD your God has commanded you to observe the sabbath day.

[16]Honor your father and your mother, as the LORD your God has commanded you, that you may long endure, and that you may fare well, in the land that the LORD your God is assigning to you.

[17]You shall not murder.

You shall not commit adultery.

You shall not steal.

You shall not bear false witness against your neighbor.

[18]You shall not covet your neighbor's wife. You shall not crave your neighbor's house, or his field, or his male or female slave, or his ox, or his ass, or anything that is your neighbor's.

[19]The LORD spoke those words—those and no more—to your whole congregation at the mountain, with a mighty voice out of the fire and the dense clouds. He inscribed them on two tablets of stone, which He gave to me. [20]When you heard the voice out of the darkness, while the mountain was ablaze with fire, you came up to me, all your tribal heads and elders, [21]and said, "The LORD our God has just shown us His majestic Presence, and we have heard His voice out of the fire; we have seen this day that man may live though God has spoken to him. [22]Let us not die, then, for this fearsome fire will consume us; if we hear the voice of the LORD our God any longer, we shall die. [23]For what mortal ever heard the voice of the living God speak out of the fire, as we did, and lived? [24]You go closer and hear all that the LORD our God says, and then you tell us everything that the LORD our God tells you, and we will willingly do it."

25The LORD heard the plea that you made to me, and the LORD said to me, "I have heard the plea that this people made to you; they did well to speak thus. 26May they always be of such mind, to revere Me and follow all My commandments, that it may go well with them and with their children forever! 27Go, say to them, 'Return to your tents.' 28But you remain here with Me, and I will give you the whole Instruction— the laws and the rules—that you shall impart to them, for them to observe in the land that I am giving them to possess."

29Be careful, then, to do as the LORD your God has commanded you. Do not turn aside to the right or to the left: 30follow only the path that the LORD your God has enjoined upon you, so that you may thrive and that it may go well with you, and that you may long endure in the land you are to possess.

6 And this is the Instruction—the laws and the rules—that the LORD your God has commanded [me] to impart to you, to be observed in the land that you are about to cross into and occupy, 2so that you, your children, and your children's children may revere the LORD your God and follow, as long as you live, all His laws and commandments that I enjoin upon you, to the end that you may long endure. 3Obey, O Israel, willingly and faithfully, that it may go well with you and that you may increase greatly [in] a-a land flowing with milk and honey,-a as the LORD, the God of your fathers, spoke to you.

4Hear, O Israel! The LORD is our God, the LORD alone.b 5You shall love the LORD your God with all your heart and with all your soul and with all your might. 6Take to heart these instructions with which I charge you this day. 7Impress them upon your children. Recite them when you stay at home and when you are away, when you lie down and when you get up. 8Bind them as a sign on your hand and let them serve as a symbolc on your forehead;d 9inscribe them on the doorposts of your house and on your gates.

10When the LORD your God brings you into the land that He swore to your fathers, Abraham, Isaac, and Jacob, to assign to you—great and flourishing cities that you did not build, 11houses full of all good things that you did not fill, hewn cisterns that you did not hew, vineyards and olive groves that you did not plant—and you eat your fill, 12take heed that you do not forget the LORD who freed you from the land of Egypt,

---

a-a *According to Ibn Ezra, this phrase connects with the end of v. 1.*
b *Cf. Rashbam and Ibn Ezra; see Zech. 14.9. Others "The LORD our God, the LORD is one."*
c *Others "frontlet"; cf. Exod. 13.16.*
d *Lit. "between your eyes"; cf. Exod. 13.9.*

the house of bondage. [13]Revere only the LORD your God and worship Him alone, and swear only by His name. [14]Do not follow other gods, any gods of the peoples about you [15]—for the LORD your God in your midst is an impassioned God—lest the anger of the LORD your God blaze forth against you and He wipe you off the face of the earth.

[16]Do not try the LORD your God, as you did at Massah.[e] [17]Be sure to keep the commandments, decrees, and laws that the LORD your God has enjoined upon you. [18]Do what is right and good in the sight of the LORD, that it may go well with you and that you may be able to possess the good land that the LORD your God promised on oath to your fathers, [19]and that all your enemies may be driven out before you, as the LORD has spoken.

[20]When, in time to come, your children ask you, "What mean the decrees, laws, and rules that the LORD our God has enjoined upon you?"[f] [21]you shall say to your children, "We were slaves to Pharaoh in Egypt and the LORD freed us from Egypt with a mighty hand. [22]The LORD wrought before our eyes marvelous and destructive signs and portents in Egypt, against Pharaoh and all his household; [23]and us He freed from there, that He might take us and give us the land that He had promised on oath to our fathers. [24]Then the LORD commanded us to observe all these laws, to revere the LORD our God, for our lasting good and for our survival, as is now the case. [25]It will be therefore to our merit before the LORD our God to observe faithfully this whole Instruction, as He has commanded us."

7 When the LORD your God brings you to the land that you are about to enter and possess, and He dislodges many nations before you—the Hittites, Girgashites, Amorites, Canaanites, Perizzites, Hivites, and Jebusites, seven nations much larger than you—[2]and the LORD your God delivers them to you and you defeat them, you must doom them to destruction: grant them no terms and give them no quarter. [3]You shall not intermarry with them: do not give your daughters to their sons or take their daughters for your sons. [4]For they will turn your children away from Me to worship other gods, and the LORD's anger will blaze forth against you and He will promptly wipe you out. [5]Instead, this is what you shall do to them: you shall tear down their altars, smash their pillars, cut down their sacred posts, and consign their images to the fire.

---

[e] Cf. Exod. 17.1–7.
[f] Septuagint and rabbinic quotations read "us."

⁶For you are a people consecrated to the LORD your God: of all the peoples on earth the LORD your God chose you to be His treasured people. ⁷It is not because you are the most numerous of peoples that the LORD set His heart on you and chose you—indeed, you are the smallest of peoples; ⁸but it was because the LORD favored you and kept the oath He made to your fathers that the LORD freed you with a mighty hand and rescued you from the house of bondage, from the power of Pharaoh king of Egypt.

⁹Know, therefore, that only the LORD your God is God, the steadfast God who keeps His covenant faithfully to the thousandth generation of those who love Him and keep His commandments, ¹⁰but who instantly requites with destruction those who reject Him—never slow with those who reject Him, but requiting them instantly. ¹¹Therefore, observe faithfully the Instruction—the laws and the rules—with which I charge you today.

עקב

¹²And if you do obey these rules and observe them carefully, the LORD your God will maintain faithfully for you the covenant that He made on oath with your fathers: ¹³He will favor you and bless you and multiply you; He will bless the issue of your womb and the produce of your soil, your new grain and wine and oil, the calving of your herd and the lambing of your flock, in the land that He swore to your fathers to assign to you. ¹⁴You shall be blessed above all other peoples: there shall be no sterile male or female among you or among your livestock. ¹⁵The LORD will ward off from you all sickness; He will not bring upon you any of the dreadful diseases of Egypt, about which you know, but will inflict them upon all your enemies.

¹⁶You shall destroy all the peoples that the LORD your God delivers to you, showing them no pity. And you shall not worship their gods, for that would be a snare to you. ¹⁷Should you say to yourselves, "These nations are more numerous than we; how can we dispossess them?" ¹⁸You need have no fear of them. You have but to bear in mind what the LORD your God did to Pharaoh and all the Egyptians: ¹⁹the wondrous acts that you saw with your own eyes, the signs and the portents, the mighty hand, and the outstretched arm by which the LORD your God liberated you. Thus will the LORD your God do to all the peoples you now fear. ²⁰The LORD your God will also send a plague[a] against them, until those who

---

[a] Others "hornet"; meaning of Heb. uncertain. Cf. note at Exod. 23.28.

are left in hiding perish before you. ²¹Do not stand in dread of them, for the LORD your God is in your midst, a great and awesome God.

²²The LORD your God will dislodge those peoples before you little by little; you will not be able to put an end to them at once, else the wild beasts would multiply to your hurt. ²³The LORD your God will deliver them up to you, throwing them into utter panic until they are wiped out. ²⁴He will deliver their kings into your hand, and you shall obliterate their name from under the heavens; no man shall stand up to you, until you have wiped them out.

²⁵You shall consign the images of their gods to the fire; you shall not covet the silver and gold on them and keep it for yourselves, lest you be ensnared thereby; for that is abhorrent to the LORD your God. ²⁶You must not bring an abhorrent thing into your house, or you will be proscribed like it; you must reject it as abominable and abhorrent, for it is proscribed.

8 You shall faithfully observe all the Instruction that I enjoin upon you today, that you may thrive and increase and be able to possess the land that the LORD promised on oath to your fathers.

²Remember the long way that the LORD your God has made you travel in the wilderness these past forty years, that He might test you by hardships to learn what was in your hearts: whether you would keep His commandments or not. ³He subjected you to the hardship of hunger and then gave you manna to eat, which neither you nor your fathers had ever known, in order to teach you that man does not live on bread alone, but that man may live on anything that the LORD decrees. ⁴The clothes upon you did not wear out, nor did your feet swell these forty years. ⁵Bear in mind that the LORD your God disciplines you just as a man disciplines his son. ⁶Therefore keep the commandments of the LORD your God: walk in His ways and revere Him.

⁷For the LORD your God is bringing you into a good land, a land with streams and springs and fountains issuing from plain and hill; ⁸a land of wheat and barley, of vines, figs, and pomegranates, a land of olive trees and honey; ⁹a land where you may eat food without stint, where you will lack nothing; a land whose rocks are iron and from whose hills you can mine copper. ¹⁰When you have eaten your fill, give thanks to the LORD your God for the good land which He has given you.

[11]Take care lest you forget the LORD your God and fail to keep His commandments, His rules, and His laws, which I enjoin upon you today. [12]When you have eaten your fill, and have built fine houses to live in, [13]and your herds and flocks have multiplied, and your silver and gold have increased, and everything you own has prospered, [14]beware lest[a] your heart grow haughty and you forget the LORD your God—who freed you from the land of Egypt, the house of bondage; [15]who led you through the great and terrible wilderness with its *seraph*[b] serpents and scorpions, a parched land with no water in it, who brought forth water for you from the flinty rock; [16]who fed you in the wilderness with manna, which your fathers had never known, in order to test you by hardships only to benefit you in the end—[17]and you say to yourselves, "My own power and the might of my own hand have won this wealth for me." [18]Remember that it is the LORD your God who gives you the power to get wealth, in fulfillment of the covenant that He made on oath with your fathers, as is still the case.

[19]If you do forget the LORD your God and follow other gods to serve them or bow down to them, I warn you this day that you shall certainly perish; [20]like the nations that the LORD will cause to perish before you, so shall you perish—because you did not heed the LORD your God.

9 Hear, O Israel! You are about to cross the Jordan to go in and dispossess nations greater and more populous than you: great cities with walls sky-high; [2]a people great and tall, the Anakites, of whom you have knowledge; for you have heard it said, "Who can stand up to the children of Anak?" [3]Know then this day that none other than the LORD your God is crossing at your head, a devouring fire; it is He who will wipe them out. He will subdue them before you, that you may quickly dispossess and destroy them, as the LORD promised you. [4]And when the LORD your God has thrust them from your path, say not to yourselves, "The LORD has enabled us to possess this land because of our virtues"; it is rather because of the wickedness of those nations that the LORD is dispossessing them before you. [5]It is not because of your virtues and your rectitude that you will be able to possess their country; but it is because of their wickedness that the LORD your God is dispossessing those nations before

---

[a] Heb. pen *moved down from v. 12 for clarity.*
[b] See note at Num. 21.6.

you, and in order to fulfill the oath that the LORD made to your fathers, Abraham, Isaac, and Jacob.

⁶Know, then, that it is not for any virtue of yours that the LORD your God is giving you this good land to possess; for you are a stiffnecked people. ⁷Remember, never forget, how you provoked the LORD your God to anger in the wilderness: from the day that you left the land of Egypt until you reached this place, you have continued defiant toward the LORD.

⁸At Horeb you so provoked the LORD that the LORD was angry enough with you to have destroyed you. ⁹I had ascended the mountain to receive the tablets of stone, the Tablets of the Covenant that the LORD had made with you, and I stayed on the mountain forty days and forty nights, eating no bread and drinking no water. ¹⁰And the LORD gave me the two tablets of stone inscribed by the finger of God, with the exact words that the LORD had addressed to you on the mountain out of the fire on the day of the Assembly.

¹¹At the end of those forty days and forty nights, the LORD gave me the two tablets of stone, the Tablets of the Covenant. ¹²And the LORD said to me, "Hurry, go down from here at once, for the people whom you brought out of Egypt have acted wickedly; they have been quick to stray from the path that I enjoined upon them; they have made themselves a molten image." ¹³The LORD further said to me, "I see that this is a stiffnecked people. ¹⁴Let Me alone and I will destroy them and blot out their name from under heaven, and I will make you a nation far more numerous than they."

¹⁵I started down the mountain, a mountain ablaze with fire, the two Tablets of the Covenant in my two hands. ¹⁶I saw how you had sinned against the LORD your God: you had made yourselves a molten calf; you had been quick to stray from the path that the LORD had enjoined upon you. ¹⁷Thereupon I gripped the two tablets and flung them away with both my hands, smashing them before your eyes. ¹⁸I threw myself down before the LORD—eating no bread and drinking no water forty days and forty nights, as before—because of the great wrong you had committed, doing what displeased the LORD and vexing Him. ¹⁹For I was in dread of the LORD's fierce anger against you, which moved Him to wipe you out. And that time, too, the LORD gave heed to me.—²⁰Moreover, the LORD was angry enough with Aaron to have destroyed him; so I also interceded for Aaron at that time.—²¹As for that sinful thing you had made, the calf, I took it and put it to the fire; I broke it to bits and ground

it thoroughly until it was fine as dust, and I threw its dust into the brook that comes down from the mountain.

22Again you provoked the LORD at Taberah, and at Massah, and at Kibroth-hattaavah.

23And when the LORD sent you on from Kadesh-barnea, saying, "Go up and take possession of the land that I am giving you," you flouted the command of the LORD your God; you did not put your trust in Him and did not obey Him.

24As long as I have known you, you have been defiant toward the LORD.

25When I lay prostrate before the LORD ᵃ⁻those forty days and forty nights,⁻ᵃ because the LORD was determined to destroy you, 26I prayed to the LORD and said, "O Lord God, do not annihilate Your very own people, whom You redeemed in Your majesty and whom You freed from Egypt with a mighty hand. 27Give thought to Your servants, Abraham, Isaac, and Jacob, and pay no heed to the stubbornness of this people, its wickedness, and its sinfulness. 28Else the country from which You freed us will say, 'It was because the LORD was powerless to bring them into the land that He had promised them, and because He rejected them, that He brought them out to have them die in the wilderness.' 29Yet they are Your very own people, whom You freed with Your great might and Your outstretched arm."

10 Thereupon the LORD said to me, "Carve out two tablets of stone like the first, and come up to Me on the mountain; and make an ark of wood. 2I will inscribe on the tablets the commandments that were on the first tablets that you smashed, and you shall deposit them in the ark."

3I made an ark of acacia wood and carved out two tablets of stone like the first; I took the two tablets with me and went up the mountain. 4The LORD inscribed on the tablets the same text as on the first, the Ten Commandments that He addressed to you on the mountain out of the fire on the day of the Assembly; and the LORD gave them to me. 5Then I left and went down from the mountain, and I deposited the tablets in the ark that I had made, where they still are, as the LORD had commanded me.

6From Beeroth-bene-jaakanᵃ the Israelites marched to Moserah. Aaron

---

ᵃ⁻ᵃ Lit. "the forty days and forty nights that I lay prostrate."
ᵃ Lit. "wells of Bene-jaakan"; cf. Num. 33.31–32.

died there and was buried there; and his son Eleazar became priest in his stead. [7]From there they marched to Gudgod,[b] and from Gudgod to Jotbath, a region of running brooks.

[8]At that time the LORD set apart the tribe of Levi to carry the Ark of the LORD's Covenant, to stand in attendance upon the LORD, and to bless in His name, as is still the case. [9]That is why the Levites have received no hereditary portion along with their kinsmen: the LORD is their portion, as the LORD your God spoke concerning them.

[10]I had stayed on the mountain, as I did the first time, forty days and forty nights; and the LORD heeded me once again: the LORD agreed not to destroy you. [11]And the LORD said to me, "Up, resume the march at the head of the people, that they may go in and possess the land that I swore to their fathers to give them."

[12]And now, O Israel, what does the LORD your God demand of you? Only this: to revere the LORD your God, to walk only in His paths, to love Him, and to serve the LORD your God with all your heart and soul, [13]keeping the LORD's commandments and laws, which I enjoin upon you today, for your good. [14]Mark, the heavens [c]to their uttermost reaches[-c] belong to the LORD your God, the earth and all that is on it! [15]Yet it was to your fathers that the LORD was drawn in His love for them, so that He chose you, their lineal descendants, from among all peoples—as is now the case. [16]Cut away, therefore, the thickening about your hearts and stiffen your necks no more. [17]For the LORD your God is [d-]God supreme and Lord supreme,[-d] the great, the mighty, and the awesome God, who shows no favor and takes no bribe, [18]but upholds the cause of the fatherless and the widow, and befriends the stranger, providing him with food and clothing.—[19]You too must befriend the stranger, for you were strangers in the land of Egypt.

[20]You must revere the LORD your God: only Him shall you worship, to Him shall you hold fast, and by His name shall you swear. [21]He is your glory and He is your God, who wrought for you those marvelous, awesome deeds that you saw with your own eyes. [22]Your ancestors went down to Egypt seventy persons in all; and now the LORD your God has made you as numerous as the stars of heaven.

[b] "Hor-haggidgad" in Num. 33.32–33.
[c-c] Lit. "and the heaven of heavens."
[d-d] Lit. "the God of gods and the Lord of lords."

11 Love, therefore, the LORD your God, and always keep His charge, His laws, His rules, and His commandments. [2] ªTake thought this day that it was not your children, who neither experienced nor witnessed the lesson of the LORD your God— His majesty, His mighty hand, His outstretched arm; [3]the signs and the deeds that He performed in Egypt against Pharaoh king of Egypt and all his land; [4]what He did to Egypt's army, its horses and chariots; how the LORD rolled back upon them the waters of the Sea of Reeds when they were pursuing you, thus destroying them ᵇ⁻once and for all;⁻ᵇ [5]what He did for you in the wilderness before you arrived in this place; [6]and what He did to Dathan and Abiram, sons of Eliab son of Reuben, when the earth opened her mouth and swallowed them, along with their households, their tents, and every living thing in their train, from amidst all Israel— [7]but that it was you who saw with your own eyes all the marvelous deeds that the LORD performed.

[8]Keep, therefore, all the Instruction that I enjoin upon you today, so that you may have the strength to enter and take possession of the land that you are about to cross into and possess, [9]and that you may long endure upon the soil that the LORD swore to your fathers to assign to them and to their heirs, a land flowing with milk and honey.

[10]For the land that you are about to enter and possess is not like the land of Egypt from which you have come. There the grain you sowed had to be watered by your own labors,ᶜ like a vegetable garden; [11]but the land you are about to cross into and possess, a land of hills and valleys, soaks up its water from the rains of heaven. [12]It is a land which the LORD your God looks after, on which the LORD your God always keeps His eye, from year's beginning to year's end.

[13]If, then, you obey the commandments that I enjoin upon you this day, loving the LORD your God and serving Him with all your heart and soul, [14]Iᵈ will grant the rain for your land in season, the early rain and the late. You shall gather in your new grain and wine and oil—[15]Iᵈ will also provide grass in the fields for your cattle—and thus you shall eat your fill. [16]Take care not to be lured away to serve other gods and bow to them. [17]For the LORD's anger will flare up against you, and He will shut

---

ª *Syntax of Heb. uncertain.*
ᵇ⁻ᵇ *Lit. "to this day."*
ᶜ *Lit. "by your foot."*
ᵈ *I.e., the LORD; Samaritan reads "He."*

up the skies so that there will be no rain and the ground will not yield its produce; and you will soon perish from the good land that the LORD is assigning to you.

¹⁸Therefore impress these My words upon your ᵉ‑very heart:‑ᵉ bind them as a sign on your hand and let them serve as a ᶠ‑symbol on your forehead,‑ᶠ ¹⁹and teach them to your children—reciting them when you stay at home and when you are away, when you lie down and when you get up; ²⁰and inscribe them on the doorposts of your house and on your gates—²¹to the end that you and your children may endure, in the land that the LORD swore to your fathers to assign to them, as long as there is a heaven over the earth.

²²If, then, you faithfully keep all this Instruction that I command you, loving the LORD your God, walking in all His ways, and holding fast to Him, ²³the LORD will dislodge before you all these nations: you will dispossess nations greater and more numerous than you. ²⁴Every spot on which your foot treads shall be yours; your territory shall extend from the wilderness to the Lebanon and from the River—the Euphrates—to the Western⁸ Sea. ²⁵No man shall stand up to you: the LORD your God will put the dread and the fear of you over the whole land in which you set foot, as He promised you.

ראה

²⁶See, this day I set before you blessing and curse: ²⁷blessing, if you obey the commandments of the LORD your God that I enjoin upon you this day; ²⁸and curse, if you do not obey the commandments of the LORD your God, but turn away from the path that I enjoin upon you this day and follow other gods, ʰ‑whom you have not experienced.‑ʰ ²⁹When the LORD your God brings you into the land that you are about to enter and possess, you shall pronounce the blessing at Mount Gerizim and the curse at Mount Ebal.—³⁰Both are on the other side of the Jordan, beyond the west road that is in the land of the Canaanites who dwell in the Arabah—near Gilgal, by the terebinths of Moreh.

³¹For you are about to cross the Jordan to enter and possess the land that the LORD your God is assigning to you. When you have occupied it and are settled in it, ³²take care to observe all the laws and rules that I have set before you this day.

ᵉ‑ᵉ Lit. "heart and self."
ᶠ‑ᶠ See notes on 6.8.
⁸ I.e., Mediterranean.
ʰ‑ʰ I.e., who have not proved themselves to you; cf. Hos. 13.4.

12 These are the laws and rules that you must carefully observe in the land that the LORD, God of your fathers, is giving you to possess, as long as you live on earth.

²You must destroy all the sites at which the nations you are to dispossess worshiped their gods, whether on lofty mountains and on hills or under any luxuriant tree. ³Tear down their altars, smash their pillars, put their sacred posts to the fire, and cut down the images of their gods, obliterating their name from that site.

⁴Do not worship the LORD your God in like manner, ⁵but look only to the site that the LORD your God will choose amidst all your tribes as His habitation, to establish His name there. There you are to go, ⁶and there you are to bring your burnt offerings and other sacrifices, your tithes and contributions,ᵃ your votive and freewill offerings, and the firstlings of your herds and flocks. ⁷Together with your households, you shall feast there before the LORD your God, happy in all the undertakings in which the LORD your God has blessed you.

⁸You shall not act at all as we now act here, every man as he pleases, ⁹because you have not yet come to the allotted haven that the LORD your God is giving you. ¹⁰When you cross the Jordan and settle in the land that the LORD your God is allotting to you, and He grants you safety from all your enemies around you and you live in security, ¹¹then you must bring everything that I command you to the site where the LORD your God will choose to establish His name: your burnt offerings and other sacrifices, your tithes and contributions,ᵃ and all the choice votive offerings that you vow to the LORD. ¹²And you shall rejoice before the LORD your God with your sons and daughters and with your male and female slaves, along with the Levite in your settlements, for he has no territorial allotment among you.

¹³Take care not to sacrifice your burnt offerings in any place you like, ¹⁴but only in the place that the LORD will choose in one of your tribal territories. There you shall sacrifice your burnt offerings and there you shall observe all that I enjoin upon you. ¹⁵But whenever you desire, you may slaughter and eat meat in any of your settlements, according to the blessing that the LORD your God has granted you. The unclean and the clean alike may partake of it, as of the gazelle and the deer.ᵇ ¹⁶But you must not partake of the blood; you shall pour it out on the ground like water.

ᵃ Lit. "the contribution(s) of your hands."
ᵇ I.e., animals that may be eaten (cf. 14.5; Lev. 11.1 ff.), but not specified (Lev. 1.1 ff.).

¹⁷You may not partake in your settlements of the tithes of your new grain or wine or oil, or of the firstlings of your herds and flocks, or of any of the votive offerings that you vow, or of your freewill offerings, or of your contributions.^a ¹⁸These you must consume before the LORD your God in the place that the LORD your God will choose—you and your sons and your daughters, your male and female slaves, and the Levite in your settlements—happy before the LORD your God in all your undertakings. ¹⁹Be sure not to neglect the Levite as long as you live in your land.

²⁰When the LORD enlarges your territory, as He has promised you, and you say, "I shall eat some meat," for you have the urge to eat meat, you may eat meat whenever you wish. ²¹If the place where the LORD has chosen to establish His name is too far from you, you may slaughter any of the cattle or sheep that the LORD gives you, as I have instructed you; and you may eat to your heart's content in your settlements. ²²Eat it, however, as the gazelle and the deer are eaten: the unclean may eat it together with the clean. ²³But make sure that you do not partake of the blood; for the blood is the life, and you must not consume the life with the flesh. ²⁴You must not partake of it; you must pour it out on the ground like water: ²⁵you must not partake of it, in order that it may go well with you and with your descendants to come, for you will be doing what is right in the sight of the LORD.

²⁶But such sacred and votive donations as you may have ^{c-}shall be taken by you^{-c} to the site that the LORD will choose. ²⁷You shall offer your burnt offerings, both the flesh and the blood, on the altar of the LORD your God; and of your other sacrifices, the blood shall be poured out on the altar of the LORD your God, and you shall eat the flesh.

²⁸Be careful to heed all these commandments that I enjoin upon you; thus it will go well with you and with your descendants after you forever, for you will be doing what is good and right in the sight of the LORD your God.

²⁹When the LORD your God has cut down before you the nations that you are about to enter and dispossess, and you have dispossessed them and settled in their land, ³⁰beware of being lured into their ways after they have been wiped out before you! Do not inquire about their gods, saying, "How did those nations worship their gods? I too will follow those practices." ³¹You shall not act thus toward the LORD your God,

c-c *Lit. "you shall pick up and come."*

for they perform for their gods every abhorrent act that the LORD detests;
13 they even offer up their sons and daughters in fire to their gods.
¹Be careful to observe only that which I enjoin upon you: neither
add to it nor take away from it.

²If there appears among you a prophet or a dream-diviner and he gives
you a sign or a portent, ³saying, "Let us follow and worship another
god"—whom you have not experiencedᵃ—even if the sign or portent that
he named to you comes true, ⁴do not heed the words of that prophet or
that dream-diviner. For the LORD your God is testing you to see whether
you really love the LORD your God with all your heart and soul. ⁵Follow
none but the LORD your God, and revere none but Him; observe His
commandments alone, and heed only His orders; worship none but Him,
and hold fast to Him. ⁶As for that prophet or dream-diviner, he shall be
put to death; for he urged disloyalty to the LORD your God—who freed
you from the land of Egypt and who redeemed you from the house of
bondage—to make you stray from the path that the LORD your God
commanded you to follow. Thus you will sweep out evil from your midst.

⁷If your brother, ᵇyour own mother's son,ᵇ or your son or daughter,
or the wife of your bosom, or your ᶜclosest friendᶜ entices you in secret,
saying, "Come let us worship other gods"—whom neither you nor your
fathers have experiencedᵃ—⁸from among the gods of the peoples around
you, either near to you or distant, anywhere from one end of the earth
to the other: ⁹do not assent or give heed to him. Show him no pity or
compassion, and do not shield him; ¹⁰but take his life. Let your hand be
the first against him to put him to death, and the hand of the rest of the
people thereafter. ¹¹Stone him to death, for he sought to make you stray
from the LORD your God, who brought you out of the land of Egypt,
out of the house of bondage. ¹²Thus all Israel will hear and be afraid, and
such evil things will not be done again in your midst.

¹³If you hear it said, of one of the towns that the LORD your God is
giving you to dwell in, ¹⁴that some scoundrels from among you have gone
and subverted the inhabitants of their town, saying, "Come let us worship
other gods"—whom you have not experienced—¹⁵you shall investigate
and inquire and interrogate thoroughly. If it is true, the fact is established—that abhorrent thing was perpetrated in your midst—¹⁶put the
inhabitants of that town to the sword and put its cattle to the sword.
Doom it and all that is in it to destruction: ¹⁷gather all its spoil into the
open square, and burn the town and all its spoil as a holocaust to the

---

ᵃ *See note on 11.28.*
ᵇ⁻ᵇ *Samaritan reads, "the son of your father or the son of your mother."*
ᶜ⁻ᶜ *Lit. "your friend who is as yourself."*

LORD your God. And it shall remain an everlasting ruin, never to be rebuilt. [18]Let nothing that has been doomed stick to your hand, in order that the LORD may turn from His blazing anger and show you compassion, and in His compassion increase you as He promised your fathers on oath—[19]for you will be heeding the LORD your God, obeying all His commandments that I enjoin upon you this day, doing what is right in the sight of the LORD your God.

14 You are children of the LORD your God. You shall not gash yourselves or shave the front of your heads because of the dead. [2]For you are a people consecrated to the LORD your God: the LORD your God chose you from among all other peoples on earth to be His treasured people.

[3]You shall not eat anything abhorrent. [4]These are the animals that you may eat: the ox, the sheep, and the goat; [5a]the deer, the gazelle, the roebuck, the wild goat, the ibex, the antelope, the mountain sheep, [6]and any other animal that has true hoofs which are cleft in two and brings up the cud—such you may eat. [7]But the following, which do bring up the cud or have true hoofs which are cleft through, you may not eat: the camel, the hare, and the daman—for although they bring up the cud, they have no true hoofs—they are unclean for you; [8]also the swine—for although it has true hoofs, it does not bring up the cud—is unclean for you. You shall not eat of their flesh or touch their carcasses.

[9]These you may eat of all that live in water: you may eat anything that has fins and scales. [10]But you may not eat anything that has no fins and scales: it is unclean for you.

[11]You may eat any clean bird. [12]The following you may not eat: [a]the eagle, the vulture, and the black vulture; [13]the kite, the falcon, and the buzzard of any variety; [14]every variety of raven; [15]the ostrich, the nighthawk, the sea gull, and the hawk of any variety; [16]the little owl, the great owl, and the white owl; [17]the pelican, the bustard, and the cormorant; [18]the stork, any variety of heron, the hoopoe, and the bat.

[19]All winged swarming things are unclean for you: they may not be eaten. [20]You may eat only clean winged creatures.

[21]You shall not eat anything that has died a natural death; give it to the stranger in your community to eat, or you may sell it to a foreigner. For you are a people consecrated to the LORD your God.

[a] *A number of these creatures cannot be identified with certainty.*

You shall not boil a kid in its mother's milk.

²²You shall set aside every year a tenth part of all the yield of your sowing that is brought from the field. ²³You shall consume the tithes of your new grain and wine and oil, and the firstlings of your herds and flocks, in the presence of the LORD your God, in the place where He will choose to establish His name, so that you may learn to revere the LORD your God forever. ²⁴Should the distance be too great for you, should you be unable to transport them, because the place where the LORD your God has chosen to establish His name is far from you and because the LORD your God has blessed you,ᵇ ²⁵you may convert them into money. Wrap up the money and take it with you to the place that the LORD your God has chosen, ²⁶and spend the money on anything you want—cattle, sheep, wine, or other intoxicant, or anything you may desire. And you shall feast there, in the presence of the LORD your God, and rejoice with your household.

²⁷But do not neglect the Levite in your community, for he has no hereditary portion as you have. ²⁸ ᶜ⁻Every third year⁻ᶜ you shall bring out the full tithe of your yield of that year, but leave it within your settlements. ²⁹Then the Levite, who has no hereditary portion as you have, and the stranger, the fatherless, and the widow in your settlements shall come and eat their fill, so that the LORD your God may bless you in all the enterprises you undertake.

15

ᵃ⁻Every seventh year⁻ᵃ you shall practice remission of debts. ²This shall be the nature of the remission: every creditor shall remit the due that he claims from his fellow; he shall not dun his fellow or kinsman, for the remission proclaimed is of the LORD. ³You may dun the foreigner; but you must remit whatever is due you from your kinsmen.

⁴There shall be no needy among you—since the LORD your God will bless you in the land that the LORD your God is giving you as a hereditary portion—⁵if only you heed the LORD your God and take care to keep all this Instruction that I enjoin upon you this day. ⁶For the LORD your God will bless you as He has promised you: you will extend loans to many nations, but require none yourself; you will dominate many nations, but they will not dominate you.

ᵇ *I.e., with abundant crops.*
ᶜ⁻ᶜ *Lit. "After a period of three years"; cf. Deut. 26.12.*

ᵃ⁻ᵃ *Cf. 14.28.*

⁷If, however, there is a needy person among you, one of your kinsmen in any of your settlements in the land that the LORD your God is giving you, do not harden your heart and shut your hand against your needy kinsman. ⁸Rather, you must open your hand and lend him sufficient for whatever he needs. ⁹Beware lest you harbor the base thought, "The seventh year, the year of remission, is approaching," so that you are mean to your needy kinsman and give him nothing. He will cry out to the LORD against you, and you will incur guilt. ¹⁰Give to him readily and have no regrets when you do so, for in return the LORD your God will bless you in all your efforts and in all your undertakings. ¹¹For there will never cease to be needy ones in your land, which is why I command you: open your hand to the poor and needy kinsman in your land.

¹²If a fellow Hebrew, man or woman, is sold to you, he shall serve you six years, and in the seventh year you shall set him free. ¹³When you set him free, do not let him go empty-handed: ¹⁴Furnish him out of the flock, threshing floor, and vat, with which the LORD your God has blessed you. ¹⁵Bear in mind that you were slaves in the land of Egypt and the LORD your God redeemed you; therefore I enjoin this commandment upon you today.

¹⁶But should he say to you, "I do not want to leave you"—for he loves you and your household and is happy with you—¹⁷you shall take an awl and put it through his ear into the door, and he shall become your slave in perpetuity. Do the same with your female slave. ¹⁸When you do set him free, do not feel aggrieved; for in the six years he has given you double the service of a hired man. Moreover, the LORD your God will bless you in all you do.

¹⁹You shall consecrate to the LORD your God all male firstlings that are born in your herd and in your flock: you must not work your firstling ox or shear your firstling sheep. ²⁰You and your household shall eat it annually before the LORD your God in the place that the LORD will choose. ²¹But if it has a defect, lameness or blindness, any serious defect, you shall not sacrifice it to the LORD your God. ²²Eat it in your settlements, the unclean among you no less than the clean, just like the gazelle and the deer. ²³Only you must not partake of its blood; you shall pour it out on the ground like water.

16 Observe the month[a] of Abib and offer a passover sacrifice to the LORD your God, for it was in the month[a] of Abib, at night, that the LORD your God freed you from Egypt. [2]You shall slaughter the passover sacrifice for the LORD your God, from the flock and the herd, in the place where the LORD will choose to establish His name. [3]You shall not eat anything leavened with it; for seven days thereafter[b] you shall eat unleavened bread, bread of distress—for you departed from the land of Egypt hurriedly—so that you may remember the day of your departure from the land of Egypt as long as you live. [4]For seven days no leaven shall be found with you in all your territory, and none of the flesh of what you slaughter on the evening of the first day shall be left until morning.

[5]You are not permitted to slaughter the passover sacrifice in any of the settlements that the LORD your God is giving you; [6]but at the place where the LORD your God will choose to establish His name, there alone shall you slaughter the passover sacrifice, in the evening, at sundown, the time of day when you departed from Egypt. [7]You shall cook and eat it at the place that the LORD your God will choose; and in the morning you may start back on your journey home. [8]After eating unleavened bread six days, you shall hold a solemn gathering[c] for the LORD your God on the seventh day: you shall do no work.

[9]You shall count off seven weeks; start to count the seven weeks when the sickle is first put to the standing grain. [10]Then you shall observe the Feast of Weeks for the LORD your God, offering your freewill contribution according as the LORD your God has blessed you. [11]You shall rejoice before the LORD your God with your son and daughter, your male and female slave, the Levite in your communities, and the stranger, the fatherless, and the widow in your midst, at the place where the LORD your God will choose to establish His name. [12]Bear in mind that you were slaves in Egypt, and take care to obey these laws.

[13]After the ingathering from your threshing floor and your vat, you shall hold the Feast of Booths for seven days. [14]You shall rejoice in your festival, with your son and daughter, your male and female slave, the Levite, the stranger, the fatherless, and the widow in your communities. [15]You shall hold a festival for the LORD your God seven days, in the place that the LORD will choose; for the LORD your God will bless all[d] your crops and all your undertakings, and you shall have nothing but joy.

a *Cf. Exod. 13.4; 23.15; 34.18.*
b *Lit. "upon it."*
c *See note at Lev. 23.36.*
d *Lit. "you in all."*

16Three times a year—on the Feast of Unleavened Bread, on the Feast of Weeks, and on the Feast of Booths—all your males shall appear before the LORD your God in the place that He will choose. They shall not appear before the LORD empty-handed, 17but each with his own gift, according to the blessing that the LORD your God has bestowed upon you.

שפטים

18You shall appoint magistrates and officials for your tribes, in all the settlements that the LORD your God is giving you, and they shall govern the people with due justice. 19You shall not judge unfairly: you shall show no partiality; you shall not take bribes, for bribes blind the eyes of the discerning and upset the plea of the just. 20Justice, justice shall you pursue, that you may thrive and occupy the land that the LORD your God is giving you.

21You shall not set up a sacred post—any kind of pole beside the altar of the LORD your God that you may make—22or erect a stone pillar; for such the LORD your God detests.

17 You shall not sacrifice to the LORD your God an ox or a sheep that has any defect of a serious kind, for that is abhorrent to the LORD your God.

2If there is found among you, in one of the settlements that the LORD your God is giving you, a man or woman who has affronted the LORD your God and transgressed His covenant—3turning to the worship of other gods and bowing down to them, to the sun or the moon or any of the heavenly host, something I never commanded—4and you have been informed or have learned of it, then you shall make a thorough inquiry. If it is true, the fact is established, that abhorrent thing was perpetrated in Israel, 5you shall take the man or the woman who did that wicked thing out to the public place, and you shall stone them, man or woman, to death.—6A person shall be put to death only on the testimony of two or morea witnesses; he must not be put to death on the testimony of a single witness.—7Let the hands of the witnesses be the first against him

a Lit. "three."

to put him to death, and the hands of the rest of the people thereafter. Thus you will sweep out evil from your midst.

8If a case is too baffling for you to decide, be it a controversy over homicide, civil law, or assault—matters of dispute in your courts—you shall promptly repair to the place that the LORD your God will have chosen, 9and appear before the levitical priests, or the magistrate in charge at the time, and present your problem. When they have announced to you the verdict in the case, 10you shall carry out the verdict that is announced to you from that place that the LORD chose, observing scrupulously all their instructions to you. 11You shall act in accordance with the instructions given you and the ruling handed down to you; you must not deviate from the verdict that they announce to you either to the right or to the left. 12Should a man act presumptuously and disregard the priest charged with serving there the LORD your God, or the magistrate, that man shall die. Thus you will sweep out evil from Israel: 13all the people will hear and be afraid and will not act presumptuously again.

14If, after you have entered the land that the LORD your God has assigned to you, and taken possession of it and settled in it, you decide, "I will set a king over me, as do all the nations about me," 15you shall be free to set a king over yourself, one chosen by the LORD your God. Be sure to set as king over yourself one of your own people; you must not set a foreigner over you, one who is not your kinsman. 16Moreover, he shall not keep many horses or send people back to Egypt to add to his horses, since the LORD has warned you, "You must not go back that way again." 17And he shall not have many wives, lest his heart go astray; nor shall he amass silver and gold to excess.

18When he is seated on his royal throne, he shall have a copy of this Teaching written for him on a scroll by[b] the levitical priests. 19Let it remain with him and let him read in it all his life, so that he may learn to revere the LORD his God, to observe faithfully every word of this Teaching as well as these laws. 20Thus he will not act haughtily toward his fellows or deviate from the Instruction to the right or to the left, to the end that he and his descendants may reign long in the midst of Israel.

18
The levitical priests, the whole tribe of Levi, shall have no territorial portion with Israel. They shall live only off the LORD's offerings by fire

b *Nuance of Heb.* milliphne *uncertain.*

as their[a] portion, [2]and shall have no portion among their brother tribes: the LORD is their portion, as He promised them.

[3]This then shall be the priests' due from the people: Everyone who offers a sacrifice, whether an ox or a sheep, must give the shoulder, the cheeks, and the stomach to the priest. [4]You shall also give him the first fruits of your new grain and wine and oil, and the first shearing of your sheep. [5]For the LORD your God has chosen him and his descendants, out of all your tribes, to be in attendance for service in the name of the LORD for all time.

[6]If a Levite would go, from any of the settlements throughout Israel where he has been residing, to the place that the LORD has chosen, he may do so whenever he pleases. [7]He may serve in the name of the LORD his God like all his fellow Levites who are there in attendance before the LORD. [8]They shall receive equal shares of the dues, [b-]without regard to personal gifts or patrimonies.[-b]

[9]When you enter the land that the LORD your God is giving you, you shall not learn to imitate the abhorrent practices of those nations. [10]Let no one be found among you who consigns his son or daughter to the fire, or who is an augur, a soothsayer, a diviner, a sorcerer, [11]one who casts spells, or one who consults ghosts or familiar spirits, or one who inquires of the dead. [12]For anyone who does such things is abhorrent to the LORD, and it is because of these abhorrent things that the LORD your God is dispossessing them before you. [13]You must be wholehearted with the LORD your God. [14]Those nations that you are about to dispossess do indeed resort to soothsayers and augurs; to you, however, the LORD your God has not assigned the like.

[15]The LORD your God will raise up for you a prophet from among your own people, like myself; him you shall heed. [16]This is just what you asked of the LORD your God at Horeb, on the day of the Assembly, saying, "Let me not hear the voice of the LORD my God any longer or see this wondrous fire any more, lest I die." [17]Whereupon the LORD said to me, "They have done well in speaking thus. [18]I will raise up a prophet for them from among their own people, like yourself: I will put My words in his mouth and he will speak to them all that I command him; [19]and if anybody fails to heed the words he speaks in My name, I myself will call

---

[a] Lit. "its," i.e. the tribe's.
[b-b] Meaning of Heb. uncertain.

him to account. [20]But any prophet who presumes to speak in My name an oracle that I did not command him to utter, or who speaks in the name of other gods—that prophet shall die." [21]And should you ask yourselves, "How can we know that the oracle was not spoken by the LORD?"— [22]if the prophet speaks in the name of the LORD and the oracle does not come true, that oracle was not spoken by the LORD; the prophet has uttered it presumptuously: do not stand in dread of him.

19 When the LORD your God has cut down the nations whose land the LORD your God is assigning to you, and you have dispossessed them and settled in their towns and homes, [2]you shall set aside three cities in the land that the LORD your God is giving you to possess. [3]You shall survey the distances, and divide into three parts the territory of the country that the LORD your God has allotted to you, so that any manslayer may have a place to flee to. [4]—Now this is the case of the manslayer who may flee there and live: one who has killed another unwittingly, without having been his enemy in the past. [5]For instance, a man goes with his neighbor into a grove to cut wood; as his hand swings the ax to cut down a tree, the ax-head flies off the handle and strikes the other so that he dies. That man shall flee to one of these cities and live.—[6]Otherwise, when the distance is great, the blood-avenger, pursuing the manslayer in hot anger, may overtake him and kill him; yet he did not incur the death penalty, since he had never been the other's enemy. [7]That is why I command you: set aside three cities.

[8]And when the LORD your God enlarges your territory, as He swore to your fathers, and gives you all the land that He promised to give your fathers—[9]if you faithfully observe all this Instruction that I enjoin upon you this day, to love the LORD your God and to walk in His ways at all times—then you shall add three more towns to those three. [10]Thus blood of the innocent will not be shed, bringing bloodguilt upon you in the land that the LORD your God is allotting to you.

[11]If, however, a person who is the enemy of another lies in wait for him and sets upon him and strikes him a fatal blow and then flees to one of these towns, [12]the elders of his town shall have him brought back from there and shall hand him over to the blood-avenger to be put to death; [13]you must show him no pity. Thus you will purge Israel of the blood of the innocent,[a] and it will go well with you.

[a] Cf. Num. 35.33–34.

¹⁴You shall not move your countryman's landmarks, set up by previous generations, in the property that will be allotted to you in the land that the LORD your God is giving you to possess.

¹⁵A single witness may not validate against a person any guilt or blame for any offense that may be committed; a case can be valid only on the testimony of two witnesses or more.ᵇ ¹⁶If a man appears against another to testify maliciously and gives false testimony against him, ¹⁷the two parties to the dispute shall appear before the LORD, before the priests or magistrates in authority at the time, ¹⁸and the magistrates shall make a thorough investigation. If the man who testified is a false witness, if he has testified falsely against his fellow, ¹⁹you shall do to him as he schemed to do to his fellow. Thus you will sweep out evil from your midst; ²⁰others will hear and be afraid, and such evil things will not again be done in your midst. ²¹Nor must you show pity: life for life, eye for eye, tooth for tooth, hand for hand, foot for foot.

20 When you take the field against your enemies, and see horses and chariots—forces larger than yours—have no fear of them, for the LORD your God, who brought you from the land of Egypt, is with you. ²Before you join battle, the priest shall come forward and address the troops. ³He shall say to them, "Hear, O Israel! You are about to join battle with your enemy. Let not your courage falter. Do not be in fear, or in panic, or in dread of them. ⁴For it is the LORD your God who marches with you to do battle for you against your enemy, to bring you victory."

⁵Then the officials shall address the troops, as follows: "Is there anyone who has built a new house but has not dedicated it? Let him go back to his home, lest he die in battle and another dedicate it. ⁶Is there anyone who has planted a vineyard but has never harvested it? Let him go back to his home, lest he die in battle and another harvest it. ⁷Is there anyone who has paid the bride-price for a wife,ᵃ but who has not yet married her? Let him go back to his home, lest he die in battle and another marry her." ⁸The officials shall go on addressing the troops and say, "Is there anyone afraid and disheartened? Let him go back to his home, lest the courage of his comrades flag like his." ⁹When the officials have finished addressing the troops, army commanders shall assume command of the troops.

ᵇ *See note at 17.6.*

ᵃ *Thereby making her his wife legally, even though the marriage has not yet taken place.*

¹⁰When you approach a town to attack it, you shall ᵇ⁻offer it terms of peace.·ᵇ ¹¹If it responds peaceably and lets you in, all the people present there shall serve you at forced labor. ¹²If it does not surrender to you, but would join battle with you, you shall lay siege to it; ¹³and when the LORD your God delivers it into your hand, you shall put all its males to the sword. ¹⁴You may, however, take as your booty the women, the children, the livestock, and everything in the town—all its spoil—and enjoy the use of the spoil of your enemy, which the LORD your God gives you.

¹⁵Thus you shall deal with all towns that lie very far from you, towns that do not belong to nations hereabout. ¹⁶In the towns of the latter peoples, however, which the LORD your God is giving you as a heritage, you shall not let a soul remain alive. ¹⁷No, you must proscribeᶜ them— the Hittites and the Amorites, the Canaanites and the Perizzites, the Hivites and the Jebusites—as the LORD your God has commanded you, ¹⁸lest they lead you into doing all the abhorrent things that they have done for their gods and you stand guilty before the LORD your God.

¹⁹When in your war against a city you have to besiege it a long time in order to capture it, you must not destroy its trees, wielding the ax against them. You may eat of them, but you must not cut them down. Are trees of the field human to withdraw before you into the besieged city? ²⁰Only trees that you know do not yield food may be destroyed; you may cut them down for constructing siegeworks against the city that is waging war on you, until it has been reduced.

21

If, in the land that the LORD your God is assigning you to possess, someone slain is found lying in the open, the identity of the slayer not being known, ²your elders and magistrates shall go out and measure the distances from the corpse to the nearby towns. ³The elders of the town nearest to the corpse shall then take a heifer which has never been worked, which has never pulled in a yoke; ⁴and the elders of that town shall bring the heifer down to an everflowing wadi, which is not tilled or sown. There, in the wadi, they shall break the heifer's neck. ⁵The priests, sons of Levi, shall come forward; for the LORD your God has chosen them to minister to Him and to pronounce blessing in the name of the LORD, and every lawsuit and case of assaultᵃ is subject to their ruling. ⁶Then all the elders of the town nearest to the corpse shall wash their hands over

ᵇ⁻ᵇ Or, "call on it to surrender."
ᶜ See Lev. 27.29.

ᵃ Cf. 17.8. Or "skin affection"; cf. 24.8.

the heifer whose neck was broken in the wadi. [7]And they shall make this declaration: "Our hands did not shed this blood, nor did our eyes see it done. [8]Absolve, O LORD, Your people Israel whom You redeemed, and do not let guilt for the blood of the innocent remain among Your people Israel." And they will be absolved of bloodguilt. [9]Thus you will remove from your midst guilt for the blood of the innocent, for you will be doing what is right in the sight of the LORD.

כי תצא

[10]When you take the field against your enemies, and the LORD your God delivers them into your power and you take some of them captive, [11]and you see among the captives a beautiful woman and you desire her and would take her to wife, [12]you shall bring her into your house, and she shall trim her hair, pare her nails, [13]and discard her captive's garb. She shall spend a month's time in your house lamenting her father and mother; after that you may come to her and possess her, and she shall be your wife. [14]Then, should you no longer want her, you must release her outright. You must not sell her for money: since you had your will of her, you must not enslave her.

[15]If a man has two wives, one loved and the other unloved, and both the loved and the unloved have borne him sons, but the first-born is the son of the unloved one—[16]when he wills his property to his sons, he may not treat as first-born the son of the loved one in disregard of the son of the unloved one who is older. [17]Instead, he must accept the first-born, the son of the unloved one, and allot to him a double portion[b] of all he possesses; since he is the first fruit of his vigor, the birthright is his due.

[18]If a man has a wayward and defiant son, who does not heed his father or mother and does not obey them even after they discipline him, [19]his father and mother shall take hold of him and bring him out to the elders of his town at the public place of his community. [20]They shall say to the elders of his town, "This son of ours is disloyal and defiant; he does not heed us. He is a glutton and a drunkard." [21]Thereupon the men of his town shall stone him to death. Thus you will sweep out evil from your midst: all Israel will hear and be afraid.

[22]If a man is guilty of a capital offense and is put to death, and you impale him on a stake, [23]you must not let his corpse remain on the stake

---

[b] Lit. *two-thirds.*

overnight, but must bury him the same day. For an impaled body is an affront to God: you shall not defile the land that the LORD your God is giving you to possess.

22 If you see your fellow's ox or sheep gone astray, do not ignore it; you must take it back to your fellow. 2If your fellow does not live near you or you do not know who he is, you shall bring it home and it shall remain with you until your fellow claims it; then you shall give it back to him. 3You shall do the same with his ass; you shall do the same with his garment; and so too shall you do with anything that your fellow loses and you find: you must not remain indifferent.

4If you see your fellow's ass or ox fallen on the road, do not ignore it; you must help him raise it.

5A woman must not put on man's apparel, nor shall a man wear woman's clothing; for whoever does these things is abhorrent to the LORD your God.

6If, along the road, you chance upon a bird's nest, in any tree or on the ground, with fledglings or eggs and the mother sitting over the fledglings or on the eggs, do not take the mother together with her young. 7Let the mother go, and take only the young, in order that you may fare well and have a long life.

8When you build a new house, you shall make a parapet for your roof, so that you do not bring bloodguilt on your house if anyone should fall from it.

9You shall not sow your vineyard with a second kind of seed, else the crop—from the seed you have sown—and the yield of the vineyard may not be used. 10You shall not plow with an ox and an ass together. 11You shall not wear cloth combining wool and linen.

12You shall make tassels on the four corners of the garment with which you cover yourself.

13A man marries a woman and cohabits with her. Then he takes an aversion to her 14and makes up charges against her and defames her, saying, "I married this woman; but when I approached her, I found that she was not a virgin." 15In such a case, the girl's father and mother shall produce the evidence of the girl's virginity before the elders of the town at the gate. 16And the girl's father shall say to the elders, "I gave this man my daughter to wife, but he has taken an aversion to her; 17so he has made up charges, saying, 'I did not find your daughter a virgin.' But here is the evidence of my daughter's virginity!'" And they shall spread out the cloth before the elders of the town. [18]The elders of that town shall then take the man and flog him, [19]and they shall fine him a hundred [shekels of] silver and give it to the girl's father; for the man has defamed a virgin in Israel. Moreover, she shall remain his wife; he shall never have the right to divorce her.

[20]But if the charge proves true, the girl was found not to have been a virgin, [21]then the girl shall be brought out to the entrance of her father's house, and the men of her town shall stone her to death; for she did a shameful thing in Israel, committing fornication while under her father's authority. Thus you will sweep away evil from your midst.

[22]If a man is found lying with another man's wife, both of them—the man and the woman with whom he lay—shall die. Thus you will sweep away evil from Israel.

[23]In the case of a virgin who is [a-]engaged to a man[-a]—if a man comes upon her in town and lies with her, [24]you shall take the two of them out to the gate of that town and stone them to death: the girl because she did not cry for help in the town, and the man because he violated another man's wife. Thus you will sweep away evil from your midst. [25]But if the man comes upon the engaged girl in the open country, and the man lies with her by force, only the man who lay with her shall die, [26]but you shall do nothing to the girl. The girl did not incur the death penalty, for this case is like that of a man attacking another and murdering him. [27]He came upon her in the open; though the engaged girl cried for help, there was no one to save her.

[28]If a man comes upon a virgin who is not engaged and he seizes her and lies with her, and they are discovered, [29]the man who lay with her shall pay the girl's father fifty [shekels of] silver, and she shall be his wife. Because he has violated her, he can never have the right to divorce her.

23

No man shall marry his father's former wife, so as [a-]to remove his father's garment.[-a]

[2]No one whose testes are crushed or whose member is cut off shall be admitted into the congregation of the LORD.

[3]No one misbegotten[b] shall be admitted into the congregation of the

---

[a-a] *I.e., for whom a bride-price had been paid; see 20.7.*

[a-a] *I.e., lay claim to what his father had possessed. Cf. Lev. 18.8, 20.11; Ezek. 16.8; Ruth 3.9.*

[b] *Meaning of Heb.* mamzer *uncertain; in Jewish law, the offspring of adultery or incest between Jews.*

LORD; none of his descendants, even in the tenth generation, shall be admitted into the congregation of the LORD.

⁴No Ammonite or Moabite shall be admitted into the congregation of the LORD; none of their descendants, even in the tenth generation, shall ever be admitted into the congregation of the LORD, ⁵because they did not meet you with food and water on your journey after you left Egypt, and because they hired Balaam son of Beor, from Pethor of Aram-naharaim, to curse you.—⁶But the LORD your God refused to heed Balaam; instead, the LORD your God turned the curse into a blessing for you, for the LORD your God loves you.—⁷You shall never concern yourself with their welfare or benefit as long as you live.

⁸You shall not abhor an Edomite, for he is your kinsman. You shall not abhor an Egyptian, for you were a stranger in his land. ⁹Children born to them may be admitted into the congregation of the LORD in the third generation.ᶜ

¹⁰When you go out as a troop against your enemies, be on your guard against anything untoward. ¹¹If anyone among you has been rendered unclean by a nocturnal emission, he must leave the camp, and he must not reenter the camp. ¹²Toward evening he shall bathe in water, and at sundown he may reenter the camp. ¹³Further, there shall be an area for you outside the camp, where you may relieve yourself. ¹⁴With your gear you shall have a spike, and when you have squatted you shall dig a hole with it and cover up your excrement. ¹⁵Since the LORD your God moves about in your camp to protect you and to deliver your enemies to you, let your camp be holy; let Him not find anything unseemly among you and turn away from you.

¹⁶You shall not turn over to his master a slave who seeks refuge with you from his master. ¹⁷He shall live with you in any place he may choose among the settlements in your midst, wherever he pleases; you must not ill-treat him.

¹⁸No Israelite woman shall be a cult prostitute, nor shall any Israelite man be a cult prostitute. ¹⁹You shall not bring the fee of a whore or the pay of a dogᵈ into the house of the LORD your God in fulfillment of any vow, for both are abhorrent to the LORD your God.

²⁰You shall not deduct interest from loans to your countrymen, whether in money or food or anything else that can be deducted as interest; ²¹but you may deduct interest from loans to foreigners. Do not deduct interest

---

ᶜ I.e., of residence in Israel's territory.
ᵈ I.e., a male prostitute.

from loans to your countrymen, so that the LORD your God may bless you in all your undertakings in the land that you are about to enter and possess.

²²When you make a vow to the LORD your God, do not put off fulfilling it, for the LORD your God will require it of you, and you will have incurred guilt; ²³whereas you incur no guilt if you refrain from vowing. ²⁴You must fulfill what has crossed your lips and perform what you have voluntarily vowed to the LORD your God, having made the promise with your own mouth.

²⁵When you enter another man's vineyard, you may eat as many grapes as you want, until you are full, but you must not put any in your vessel. ²⁶When you enter another man's field of standing grain, you may pluck ears with your hand; but you must not put a sickle to your neighbor's grain.

24

A man takes a wife and possesses her. She fails to please him because he finds something obnoxious about her, and he writes her a bill of divorcement, hands it to her, and sends her away from his house; ²she leaves his household and becomes the wife of another man; ³then this latter man rejects her, writes her a bill of divorcement, hands it to her, and sends her away from his house; or the man who married her last dies. ⁴Then the first husband who divorced her shall not take her to wife again, since she has been defiledª—for that would be abhorrent to the LORD. You must not bring sin upon the land that the LORD your God is giving you as a heritage.

⁵When a man has taken a bride, he shall not go out with the army or be assigned to it for any purpose; he shall be exempt one year for the sake of his household, to give happiness to the woman he has married.

⁶A handmill or an upper millstone shall not be taken in pawn, for that would be taking someone's life in pawn.

⁷If a man is found to have kidnapped a fellow Israelite, enslaving him or selling him, that kidnapper shall die; thus you will sweep out evil from your midst.

⁸In cases of a skin affectionᵇ be most careful to do exactly as the levitical priests instruct you. Take care to do as I have commanded them. ⁹Remember what the LORD your God did to Miriam on the journey after you left Egypt.ᶜ

ª I.e., disqualified for him.
ᵇ Cf. Lev. 13.1 ff.
ᶜ See Num. 12.10 ff.

10When you make a loan of any sort to your countryman, you must not enter his house to seize his pledge. 11You must remain outside, while the man to whom you made the loan brings the pledge out to you. 12If he is a needy man, you shall not go to sleep in his pledge; 13you must return the pledge to him at sundown, that he may sleep in his cloth and bless you; and it will be to your merit before the LORD your God.

14You shall not abuse a needy and destitute laborer, whether a fellow countryman or a stranger in one of the communities of your land. 15You must pay him his wages on the same day, before the sun sets, for he is needy and urgently depends on it; else he will cry to the LORD against you and you will incur guilt.

16Parents shall not be put to death for children, nor children be put to death for parents: a person shall be put to death only for his own crime.

17You shall not subvert the rights of the stranger or the fatherless; you shall not take a widow's garment in pawn. 18Remember that you were a slave in Egypt and that the LORD your God redeemed you from there; therefore do I enjoin you to observe this commandment.

19When you reap the harvest in your field and overlook a sheaf in the field, do not turn back to get it; it shall go to the stranger, the fatherless, and the widow—in order that the LORD your God may bless you in all your undertakings.

20When you beat down the fruit of your olive trees, do not go over them again; that shall go to the stranger, the fatherless, and the widow. 21When you gather the grapes of your vineyard, do not pick it over again; that shall go to the stranger, the fatherless, and the widow. 22Always remember that you were a slave in the land of Egypt; therefore do I enjoin you to observe this commandment.

25 When there is a dispute between men and they go to law, and a decision is rendered declaring the one in the right and the other in the wrong—2if the guilty one is to be flogged, the magistrate shall have him lie down and be given lashes in his presence, by count, as his guilt warrants. 3He may be given up to forty lashes, but not more, lest being flogged further, to excess, your brother be degraded before your eyes.

4You shall not muzzle an ox while it is threshing.

5When brothers dwell together and one of them dies and leaves no son, the wife of the deceased shall not be married to a stranger, outside the family. Her husband's brother shall unite with her: he shall take her as his wife and perform the levir's duty. 6The first son that she bears shall be accounted to the dead brother, that his name may not be blotted out in Israel. 7But if the man does not want to marry his brother's widow, his brother's widow shall appear before the elders in the gate and declare, "My husband's brother refuses to establish a name in Israel for his brother; he will not perform the duty of a levir." 8The elders of his town shall then summon him and talk to him. If he insists, saying, "I do not want to marry her," 9his brother's widow shall go up to him in the presence of the elders, pull the sandal off his foot, spit in his face, and make this declaration: Thus shall be done to the man who will not build up his brother's house! 10And he shall go in Israel by the name of "the family of the unsandaled one."

11If two men get into a fight with each other, and the wife of one comes up to save her husband from his antagonist and puts out her hand and seizes him by his genitals, 12you shall cut off her hand; show no pity.

13You shall not have in your pouch alternate weights, larger and smaller. 14You shall not have in your house alternate measures, a larger and a smaller. 15You must have completely honest weights and completely honest measures, if you are to endure long on the soil that the LORD your God is giving you. 16For everyone who does those things, everyone who deals dishonestly, is abhorrent to the LORD your God.

17Remember what Amalek did to you on your journey, after you left Egypt—18how, undeterred by fear of God, he surprised you on the march, when you were famished and weary, and cut down all the stragglers in your rear. 19Therefore, when the LORD your God grants you safety from all your enemies around you, in the land that the LORD your God is giving you as a hereditary portion, you shall blot out the memory of Amalek from under heaven. Do not forget!

כי תבוא

26 When you enter the land that the LORD your God is giving you as a heritage, and you possess it and settle in it, 2you shall take some of every first fruit of the soil, which you harvest from the land that the LORD your God is giving you, put it in a basket and go to the place where the LORD your God will choose to establish His name. ³You shall go to the priest in charge at that time and say to him, "I acknowledge this day before the LORD your God that I have entered the land that the LORD swore to our fathers to assign us."

⁴The priest shall take the basket from your hand and set it down in front of the altar of the LORD your God.

⁵You shall then recite as follows before the LORD your God: "My father was a fugitive Aramean. He went down to Egypt with meager numbers and sojourned there; but there he became a great and very populous nation. ⁶The Egyptians dealt harshly with us and oppressed us; they imposed heavy labor upon us. ⁷We cried to the LORD, the God of our fathers, and the LORD heard our plea and saw our plight, our misery, and our oppression. ⁸The LORD freed us from Egypt by a mighty hand, by an outstretched arm and awesome power, and by signs and portents. ⁹He brought us to this place and gave us this land, a land flowing with milk and honey. ¹⁰Wherefore I now bring the first fruits of the soil which You, O LORD, have given me."

You shall leave itᵃ before the LORD your God and bow low before the LORD your God. ¹¹And you shall enjoy, together with the Levite and the stranger in your midst, all the bounty that the LORD your God has bestowed upon you and your household.

¹²When you have set aside in full the tenth part of your yield—in the third year, the year of the titheᵇ—and have given it to the Levite, the stranger, the fatherless, and the widow, that they may eat their fill in your settlements, ¹³you shall declare before the LORD your God: "I have cleared out the consecrated portion from the house; and I have given it to the Levite, the stranger, the fatherless, and the widow, just as You commanded me; I have neither transgressed nor neglected any of Your commandments: ¹⁴ᶜI have not eaten of it while in mourning, I have not cleared out any of it while I was unclean, and I have not deposited any of it with the dead.ᵈ I have obeyed the LORD my God; I have done just as You commanded me. ¹⁵Look down from Your holy abode, from heaven, and bless Your people Israel and the soil You have given us, a land flowing with milk and honey, as You swore to our fathers."

¹⁶The LORD your God commands you this day to observe these laws and rules; observe them faithfully with all your heart and soul. ¹⁷You have affirmedᵉ this day that the LORD is your God, that you will walk in His

---

ᵃ I.e., the basket of v. 4.
ᵇ See Deut. 14.28–29.
ᶜ Meaning of first part of verse uncertain.
ᵈ No part of the tithe may be left as food for the dead.
ᵉ Exact nuance of Heb. uncertain.

ways, that you will observe His laws and commandments and rules, and that you will obey Him. [18]And the LORD has affirmed[c] this day that you are, as He promised you, His treasured people who shall observe all His commandments, [19]and that He will set you, in fame and renown and glory, high above all the nations that He has made; and that you shall be, as He promised, a holy people to the LORD your God.

27 Moses and the elders of Israel charged the people, saying: Observe all the Instruction that I enjoin upon you this day. [2] [a]As soon as you have crossed the Jordan into the land that the LORD your God is giving you, you shall set up large stones. Coat them with plaster [3]and inscribe upon them all the words of this Teaching. When you cross over to enter the land that the LORD your God is giving you, a land flowing with milk and honey, as the LORD, the God of your fathers, promised you—[4]upon crossing the Jordan, you shall set up these stones, about which I charge you this day, on Mount Ebal, and coat them with plaster. [5]There, too, you shall build an altar to the LORD your God, an altar of stones. Do not wield an iron tool over them; [6]you must build the altar of the LORD your God of unhewn[b] stones. You shall offer on it burnt offerings to the LORD your God, [7]and you shall sacrifice there offerings of well-being and eat them, rejoicing before the LORD your God. [8]And on those stones you shall inscribe every word of this Teaching most distinctly.

[9]Moses and the levitical priests spoke to all Israel, saying: Silence! Hear, O Israel! Today you have become the people of the LORD your God: [10]Heed the LORD your God and observe His commandments and His laws, which I enjoin upon you this day.

[11]Thereupon Moses charged the people, saying: [12c]After you have crossed the Jordan, the following shall stand on Mount Gerizim when the blessing for the people is spoken: Simeon, Levi, Judah, Issachar, Joseph, and Benjamin. [13]And for the curse, the following shall stand on Mount Ebal: Reuben, Gad, Asher, Zebulun, Dan, and Naphthali. [14]The Levites shall then proclaim in a loud voice to all the people of Israel:

[15]Cursed be anyone who makes a sculptured or molten image, abhorred by the LORD, a craftsman's handiwork, and sets it up in secret.—And all the people shall respond, Amen.

[16]Cursed be he who insults his father or mother.—And all the people shall say, Amen.

---

[a] *Construction of vv. 2–4 uncertain.*
[b] *Lit. "whole."*
[c] *Construction of vv. 12–13 uncertain.*

¹⁷Cursed be he who moves his fellow countryman's landmark.—And all the people shall say, Amen.

¹⁸Cursed be he who misdirects a blind person on his way.—And all the people shall say, Amen.

¹⁹Cursed be he who subverts the rights of the stranger, the fatherless, and the widow.—And all the people shall say, Amen.

²⁰Cursed be he who lies with his father's wife, for he has removed his father's garment.ᵈ—And all the people shall say, Amen.

²¹Cursed be he who lies with any beast.—And all the people shall say, Amen.

²²Cursed be he who lies with his sister, whether daughter of his father or of his mother.—And all the people shall say, Amen.

²³Cursed be he who lies with his mother-in-law.—And all the people shall say, Amen.

²⁴Cursed be he who strikes down his fellow countryman in secret.—And all the people shall say, Amen.

²⁵Cursed be he who accepts a bribe ᵉ⁻in the case of the murder of⁻ᵉ an innocent person.—And all the people shall say, Amen.

²⁶Cursed be he who will not uphold the terms of this Teaching and observe them.—And all the people shall say, Amen.

28 Now, if you obey the LORD your God, to observe faithfully all His commandments which I enjoin upon you this day, the LORD your God will set you high above all the nations of the earth. ²All these blessings shall come upon you and take effect, if you will but heed the word of the LORD your God:

³Blessed shall you be in the city and blessed shall you be in the country.

⁴Blessed shall be the issue of your womb, the produce of your soil, and the offspring of your cattle, the calving of your herd and the lambing of your flock.

⁵Blessed shall be your basket and your kneading bowl.

⁶Blessed shall you be in your comings and blessed shall you be in your goings.

⁷The LORD will put to rout before you the enemies who attack you; they will march out against you by a single road, but flee from you by manyᵃ roads. ⁸The LORD will ordain blessings for you upon your barns and upon all your undertakings: He will bless you in the land that the

---

ᵈ *See note at 23.1.*

ᵉ⁻ᵉ *I.e., to acquit the murderer; others "to slay."*

ᵃ *Lit. "seven."*

LORD your God is giving you. 9The LORD will establish you as His holy people, as He swore to you, if you keep the commandments of the LORD your God and walk in His ways. 10And all the peoples of the earth shall see that the LORD's name is proclaimed over you,[b] and they shall stand in fear of you. 11The LORD will give you abounding prosperity in the issue of your womb, the offspring of your cattle, and the produce of your soil in the land that the LORD swore to your fathers to assign to you. 12The LORD will open for you His bounteous store, the heavens, to provide rain for your land in season and to bless all your undertakings. You will be creditor to many nations, but debtor to none.

13The LORD will make you the head, not the tail; you will always be at the top and never at the bottom—if only you obey and faithfully observe the commandments of the LORD your God that I enjoin upon you this day, 14and do not deviate to the right or to the left from any of the commandments that I enjoin upon you this day and turn to the worship of other gods.

15But if you do not obey the LORD your God to observe faithfully all His commandments and laws which I enjoin upon you this day, all these curses shall come upon you and take effect:

16Cursed shall you be in the city and cursed shall you be in the country.

17Cursed shall be your basket and your kneading bowl.

18Cursed shall be the issue of your womb and the produce of your soil, the calving of your herd and the lambing of your flock.

19Cursed shall you be in your comings and cursed shall you be in your goings.

20The LORD will let loose against you calamity, panic, and frustration in all the enterprises you undertake, so that you shall soon be utterly wiped out because of your evildoing in forsaking Me. 21The LORD will make pestilence cling to you, until He has put an end to you in the land that you are entering to possess. 22The LORD will strike you with [c]consumption, fever, and inflammation, with scorching heat and drought, with blight and mildew; they shall hound you until you perish. 23The skies above your head shall be copper and the earth under you iron. 24The LORD will make the rain of your land dust, and sand shall drop on you from the sky, until you are wiped out.

25The LORD will put you to rout before your enemies; you shall march

[b] I.e., the LORD recognizes you as His own; cf. Isa. 4.1.
[c] Exact nature of these afflictions uncertain.

out against them by a single road, but flee from them by many[a] roads; and you shall become a horror to all the kingdoms of the earth. [26]Your carcasses shall become food for all the birds of the sky and all the beasts of the earth, with none to frighten them off.

[27]The LORD will strike you with the Egyptian inflammation,[d] with hemorrhoids, boil-scars, and itch, from which you shall never recover.

[28]The LORD will strike you with madness, blindness, and dismay.[e] [29]You shall grope at noon as a blind man gropes in the dark; you shall not prosper in your ventures, but shall be constantly abused and robbed, with none to give help.

[30]If you pay the bride-price for a wife, another man shall enjoy her. If you build a house, you shall not live in it. If you plant a vineyard, you shall not harvest it.[f] [31]Your ox shall be slaughtered before your eyes, but you shall not eat of it; your ass shall be seized in front of you, and it shall not be returned to you; your flock shall be delivered to your enemies, with none to help you. [32]Your sons and daughters shall be delivered to another people, while you look on; and your eyes shall strain for them constantly, but you shall be helpless. [33]A people you do not know shall eat up the produce of your soil and all your gains; you shall be abused and downtrodden continually, [34]until you are driven mad by what your eyes behold. [35]The LORD will afflict you at the knees and thighs with a severe inflammation, from which you shall never recover—from the sole of your foot to the crown of your head.

[36]The LORD will drive you, and the king you have set over you, to a nation unknown to you or your fathers, where you shall serve other gods, of wood and stone. [37]You shall be a consternation, a proverb, and a byword among all the peoples to which the LORD will drive you.

[38]Though you take much seed out to the field, you shall gather in little, for the locust shall consume it. [39]Though you plant vineyards and till them, you shall have no wine to drink or store, for the worm shall devour them. [40]Though you have olive trees throughout your territory, you shall have no oil for anointment, for your olives shall drop off. [41]Though you beget sons and daughters, they shall not remain with you, for they shall go into captivity. [42]The cricket shall take over all the trees and produce of your land.

[43]The stranger in your midst shall rise above you higher and higher, while you sink lower and lower: [44]he shall be your creditor, but you shall not be his; he shall be the head and you the tail.

---

[d] *See Exod. 9.9–10.*
[e] Lit. *"numbness of heart."*
[f] *Cf. 20.6.*

⁴⁵All these curses shall befall you; they shall pursue you and overtake you, until you are wiped out, because you did not heed the LORD your God and keep the commandments and laws that He enjoined upon you. ⁴⁶They shall serve as signs and proofs against you and your offspring for all time. ⁴⁷Because you would not serve the LORD your God in joy and gladness over the abundance of everything, ⁴⁸you shall have to serve—in hunger and thirst, naked and lacking everything—the enemies whom the LORD will let loose against you. He will put an iron yoke upon your neck until He has wiped you out.

⁴⁹The LORD will bring a nation against you from afar, from the end of the earth, which will swoop down like the eagle—a nation whose language you do not understand, ⁵⁰a ruthless nation, that will show the old no regard and the young no mercy. ⁵¹It shall devour the offspring of your cattle and the produce of your soil, until you have been wiped out, leaving you nothing of new grain, wine, or oil, of the calving of your herds and the lambing of your flocks, until it has brought you to ruin. ⁵²It shall shut you up in all your towns throughout your land until every mighty, towering wall in which you trust has come down. And when you are shut up in all your towns throughout your land that the LORD your God has assigned to you, ⁵³you shall eat your own issue, the flesh of your sons and daughters that the LORD your God has assigned to you, because of the desperate straits to which your enemy shall reduce you. ⁵⁴He who is most tender and fastidious among you shall be too mean to his brother and the wife of his bosom and the children he has spared ⁵⁵to share with any of them the flesh of the children that he eats, because he has nothing else left as a result of the desperate straits to which your enemy shall reduce you in all your towns. ⁵⁶And she who is most tender and dainty among you, so tender and dainty that she would never venture to set a foot on the ground, shall begrudge the husband of her bosom, and her son and her daughter, ⁵⁷the afterbirth that issues from between her legs and the babies she bears; she shall eat them secretly, because of utter want, in the desperate straits to which your enemy shall reduce you in your towns.

⁵⁸If you fail to observe faithfully all the terms of this Teaching that are written in this book, to reverence this honored and awesome Name, the LORD your God, ⁵⁹the LORD will inflict extraordinary plagues upon you and your offspring, strange and lasting plagues, malignant and chronic diseases. ⁶⁰He will bring back upon you all the sicknesses of Egypt that

you dreaded so, and they shall cling to you. ⁶¹Moreover, the LORD will bring upon you all the other diseases and plagues that are not mentioned in this book of Teaching, until you are wiped out. ⁶²You shall be left a scant few, after having been as numerous as the stars in the skies, because you did not heed the command of the LORD your God. ⁶³And as the LORD once delighted in making you prosperous and many, so will the LORD now delight in causing you to perish and in wiping you out; you shall be torn from the land that you are about to enter and possess.

⁶⁴The LORD will scatter you among all the peoples from one end of the earth to the other, and there you shall serve other gods, wood and stone, whom neither you nor your ancestors have experienced.ᵍ ⁶⁵Yet even among those nations you shall find no peace, nor shall your foot find a place to rest. The LORD will give you there an anguished heart and eyes that pine and a despondent spirit. ⁶⁶The life you face shall be precarious; you shall be in terror, night and day, with no assurance of survival. ⁶⁷In the morning you shall say, "If only it were evening!" and in the evening you shall say, "If only it were morning!"—because of what your heart shall dread and your eyes shall see. ⁶⁸The LORD will send you back to Egypt in galleys, by a route which I told you you should not see again. There you shall offer yourselves for sale to your enemies as male and female slaves, but none will buy.

⁶⁹These are the terms of the covenant which the LORD commanded Moses to conclude with the Israelites in the land of Moab, in addition to the covenant which He had made with them at Horeb.

29 Moses summoned all Israel and said to them:

You have seen all that the LORD did before your very eyes in the land of Egypt, to Pharaoh and to all his courtiers and to his whole country: ²the wondrous feats that you saw with your own eyes, those prodigious signs and marvels. ³Yet to this day the LORD has not given you a mind to understand or eyes to see or ears to hear.

⁴I led you through the wilderness forty years; the clothes on your back did not wear out, nor did the sandals on your feet; ⁵you had no bread to eat and no wine or other intoxicant to drink—that you might know that I the LORD am your God.

⁶When you reached this place, King Sihon of Heshbon and King Og

---

ᵍ *See note at 11.28.*

of Bashan came out to engage us in battle, but we defeated them. ⁷We took their land and gave it to the Reubenites, the Gadites, and the half-tribe of Manasseh as their heritage. ⁸Therefore observe faithfully all the terms of this covenant, that you may succeed in all that you undertake.

נצבים

⁹You stand this day, all of you, before the LORD your God—your tribal heads, your elders and your officials, all the men of Israel, ¹⁰your children, your wives, even the stranger within your camp, from woodchopper to waterdrawer—¹¹to enter into the covenant of the LORD your God, which the LORD your God is concluding with you this day, with its sanctions;ª ¹²to the end that He may establish you this day as His people and be your God, as He promised you and as He swore to your fathers, Abraham, Isaac, and Jacob. ¹³I make this covenant, with its sanctions, not with you alone, ¹⁴but both with those who are standing here with us this day before the LORD our God and with those who are not with us here this day.

¹⁵Well you know that we dwelt in the land of Egypt and that we passed through the midst of various other nations through which you passed; ¹⁶and you have seen the detestable things and the fetishes of wood and stone, silver and gold, that they keep. ¹⁷Perchance there is among you some man or woman, or some clan or tribe, whose heart is even now turning away from the LORD our God to go and worship the gods of those nations—perchance there is among you a stock sprouting poison weed and wormwood. ¹⁸When such a one hears the words of these sanctions, he may fancy himself immune, thinking, "I shall be safe, though I follow my own willful heart"—to the utter ruin of moist and dry alike.ᵇ ¹⁹The LORD will never forgive him; rather will the LORD's anger and passion rage against that man, till every sanction recorded in this book comes down upon him, and the LORD blots out his name from under heaven.

²⁰The LORD will single themᶜ out from all the tribes of Israel for misfortune, in accordance with all the sanctions of the covenant recorded in this book of Teaching. ²¹And later generations will ask—the children who succeed you, and foreigners who come from distant lands and see the plagues and diseases that the LORD has inflicted upon that land, ²²all its soil devastated by sulfur and salt, beyond sowing and producing, no grass growing in it, just like the upheaval of Sodom and Gomorrah, Admah and Zeboiim, which the LORD overthrew in His fierce anger—²³all nations will ask, "Why did the LORD do thus to this land? Wherefore

---

ª I.e., the curses that violations of the covenant will entail.
ᵇ I.e., everything.
ᶜ I.e., clan or tribe, v. 17.

that awful wrath?" [24]They will be told, "Because they forsook the covenant that the LORD, God of their fathers, made with them when He freed them from the land of Egypt; [25]they turned to the service of other gods and worshiped them, gods whom they had not experienced[d] and whom He had not allotted[e] to them. [26]So the LORD was incensed at that land and brought upon it all the curses recorded in this book. [27]The LORD uprooted them from their soil in anger, fury, and great wrath, and cast them into another land, as is still the case."

[28]Concealed acts concern the LORD our God; but with overt acts, it is for us and our children ever to apply all the provisions of this Teaching.

30 When all these things befall you—the blessing and the curse that I have set before you—and you take them to heart amidst the various nations to which the LORD your God has banished you, [2]and you return to the LORD your God, and you and your children heed His command with all your heart and soul, just as I enjoin upon you this day, [3]then the LORD your God will restore your fortunes[a] and take you back in love. He will bring you together again from all the peoples where the LORD your God has scattered you. [4]Even if your outcasts are at the ends of the world,[b] from there the LORD your God will gather you, from there He will fetch you. [5]And the LORD your God will bring you to the land that your fathers possessed, and you shall possess it; and He will make you more prosperous and more numerous than your fathers.

[6]Then the LORD your God will open up[c] your heart and the hearts of your offspring to love the LORD your God with all your heart and soul, in order that you may live. [7]The LORD your God will inflict all those curses upon the enemies and foes who persecuted you. [8]You, however, will again heed the LORD and obey all His commandments that I enjoin upon you this day. [9]And the LORD your God will grant you abounding prosperity in all your undertakings, in the issue of your womb, the off-spring of your cattle, and the produce of your soil. For the LORD will again delight in your well-being, as He did in that of your fathers, [10]since you will be heeding the LORD your God and keeping His commandments and laws that are recorded in this book of the Teaching—once you return to the LORD your God with all your heart and soul.

[11]Surely, this Instruction which I enjoin upon you this day is not too

d *See note at 11.28.*
e *See 4.19–20.*

a *Others "captivity."*
b *Lit. "sky."*
c *Others "circumcise."*

baffling for you, nor is it beyond reach. ¹²It is not in the heavens, that you should say, "Who among us can go up to the heavens and get it for us and impart it to us, that we may observe it?" ¹³Neither is it beyond the sea, that you should say, "Who among us can cross to the other side of the sea and get it for us and impart it to us, that we may observe it?" ¹⁴No, the thing is very close to you, in your mouth and in your heart, to observe it.

¹⁵See, I set before you this day life and prosperity, death and adversity. ¹⁶For[d] I command you this day, to love the LORD your God, to walk in His ways, and to keep His commandments, His laws, and His rules, that you may thrive and increase, and that the LORD your God may bless you in the land that you are about to enter and possess. ¹⁷But if your heart turns away and you give no heed, and are lured into the worship and service of other gods, ¹⁸I declare to you this day that you shall certainly perish; you shall not long endure on the soil that you are crossing the Jordan to enter and possess. ¹⁹I call heaven and earth to witness against you this day: I have put before you life and death, blessing and curse. Choose life—if you and your offspring would live—²⁰by loving the LORD your God, heeding His commands, and holding fast to Him. For thereby you shall have life and shall long endure upon the soil that the LORD swore to your ancestors, Abraham, Isaac, and Jacob, to give to them.

31

וַיֵּלֶךְ

[a-]Moses went and spoke[-a] these things to all Israel. ²He said to them:

I am now one hundred and twenty years old, I can no longer [b-]be active.[-b] Moreover, the LORD has said to me, "You shall not go across yonder Jordan." ³The LORD your God Himself will cross over before you; and He Himself will wipe out those nations from your path and you shall dispossess them.—Joshua is the one who shall cross before you, as the LORD has spoken.—⁴The LORD will do to them as He did to Sihon and Og, kings of the Amorites, and to their countries, when He wiped them out. ⁵The LORD will deliver them up to you, and you shall deal with them in full accordance with the Instruction that I have enjoined upon you. ⁶Be strong and resolute, be not in fear or in dread of them;

---

d *Septuagint reads "If you obey the commandments of the* LORD *your God, which."*

a-a *An ancient Heb. ms. and the Septuagint read: "When Moses had finished speaking . . ."; cf. 29.1.*

b-b *Lit. "come and go."*

for the LORD your God Himself marches with you: He will not fail you or forsake you.

7Then Moses called Joshua and said to him in the sight of all Israel: "Be strong and resolute, for it is you who shall go with this people into the land that the LORD swore to their fathers to give them, and it is you who shall apportion it to them. 8And the LORD Himself will go before you. He will be with you; He will not fail you or forsake you. Fear not and be not dismayed!"

9Moses wrote down this Teaching and gave it to the priests, sons of Levi, who carried the Ark of the LORD's Covenant, and to all the elders of Israel.

10And Moses instructed them as follows: Every seventh year,c the year set for remission, at the Feast of Booths, 11when all Israel comes to appear before the LORD your God in the place that He will choose, you shall read this Teaching aloud in the presence of all Israel. 12Gather the people—men, women, children, and the strangers in your communities—that they may hear and so learn to revere the LORD your God and to observe faithfully every word of this Teaching. 13Their children, too, who have not had the experience, shall hear and learn to revere the LORD your God as long as they live in the land that you are about to cross the Jordan to possess.

14The LORD said to Moses: The time is drawing near for you to die. Call Joshua and present yourselves in the Tent of Meeting, that I may instruct him. Moses and Joshua went and presented themselves in the Tent of Meeting. 15The LORD appeared in the Tent, in a pillar of cloud, the pillar of cloud having come to rest at the entrance of the tent.

16The LORD said to Moses: You are soon to lie with your fathers. This people will thereupon go astray after the alien gods in their midst, in the land that they are about to enter; they will forsake Me and break My covenant that I made with them. 17Then My anger will flare up against them, and I will abandon them and hide My countenance from them. They shall be ready prey; and many evils and troubles shall befall them. And they shall say on that day, "Surely it is because our God is not in our midst that these evils have befallen us." 18Yet I will keep My countenance hidden on that day, because of all the evil they have done in turning to other gods. 19Therefore, write down this poem and teach it to the people of Israel; put it in their mouths, in order that this poem

c See note at 15.1.

may be My witness against the people of Israel. ²⁰When I bring them into the land flowing with milk and honey that I promised on oath to their fathers, and they eat their fill and grow fat and turn to other gods and serve them, spurning Me and breaking My covenant, ²¹and the many evils and troubles befall them—then this poem shall confront them as a witness, since it will never be lost from the mouth of their offspring. For I know what plans they are devising even now, before I bring them into the land that I promised on oath.

²²That day, Moses wrote down this poem and taught it to the Israelites.

²³And He charged Joshua son of Nun: "Be strong and resolute: for you shall bring the Israelites into the land that I promised them on oath, and I will be with you."

²⁴When Moses had put down in writing the words of this Teaching to the very end, ²⁵Moses charged the Levites who carried the Ark of the Covenant of the LORD, saying: ²⁶Take this book of Teaching and place it beside the Ark of the Covenant of the LORD your God, and let it remain there as a witness against you. ²⁷Well I know how defiant and stiffnecked you are: even now, while I am still alive in your midst, you have been defiant toward the LORD; how much more, then, when I am dead! ²⁸Gather to me all the elders of your tribes and your officials, that I may speak all these words to them and that I may call heaven and earth to witness against them. ²⁹For I know that, when I am dead, you will act wickedly and turn away from the path that I enjoined upon you, and that in time to come misfortune will befall you for having done evil in the sight of the LORD and vexed Him by your deeds.

³⁰Then Moses recited the words of this poem to the very end, in the hearing of the whole congregation of Israel:

32
האזינו

Give ear, O heavens, let me speak;
  Let the earth hear the words I utter!
²May my discourse come down as the rain,
  My speech distill as the dew,
  Like showers on young growth,
  Like droplets on the grass.ᵃ
³For the name of the LORD I proclaim;
  Give glory to our God!

ᵃ *I.e., may my words be received eagerly; cf. Job 29.22–23.*

4The Rock!—His deeds are perfect,
Yea, all His ways are just;
A faithful God, never false,
True and upright is He.
5 bChildren unworthy of Him—
That crooked, perverse generation—
Their baseness has played Him false.
6Do you thus requite the LORD,
O dull and witless people?
Is not He the Father who created you,
Fashioned you and made you endure!

7Remember the days of old,
Consider the years of ages past;
Ask your father, he will inform you,
Your elders, they will tell you:
8When the Most High gave nations their homes
And set the divisions of man,
He fixed the boundaries of peoples
In relation to Israel's numbers.
9For the LORD's portion is His people,
Jacob His own allotment.

10He found him in a desert region,
In an empty howling waste.
He engirded him, watched over him,
Guarded him as the pupil of His eye.
11Like an eagle who rouses his nestlings,
Gliding down to his young,
So did He spread His wings and take him,
Bear him along on His pinions;
12The LORD alone did guide him,
No alien god at His side.

13He set him atop the highlands,
To feast on the yield of the earth;
He fed him honey from the crag,
And oil from the flinty rock,
14Curd of kine and milk of flocks;

b *Meaning of Heb. uncertain.*

326

With the best^c of lambs,
And rams of Bashan, and he-goats;
With the ^{d-}very finest^{-d} wheat—
And foaming grape-blood was your drink.

¹⁵So Jeshurun grew fat and kicked—
You grew fat and gross and coarse^e—
He forsook the God who made him
And spurned the Rock of his support.
¹⁶They incensed Him with alien things,
Vexed Him with abominations.
¹⁷They sacrificed to demons, no-gods,
Gods they had never known,
New ones, who came but lately,
^{f-} Who stirred not your fathers' fears.^{-f}
¹⁸You neglected the Rock that begot you,
Forgot the God who brought you forth.

¹⁹The LORD saw and was vexed
And spurned His sons and His daughters.
²⁰He said:
I will hide My countenance from them,
And see how they fare in the end.
For they are a treacherous breed,
Children with no loyalty in them.
²¹They incensed Me with no-gods,
Vexed Me with their futilities;^g
I'll incense them with a no-folk,
Vex them with a nation of fools.
²²For a fire has flared in My wrath
And burned to the bottom of Sheol,
Has consumed the earth and its increase,
Eaten down to the base of the hills.
²³I will sweep^e misfortunes on them,
Use up My arrows on them:
²⁴Wasting famine, ravaging plague,
Deadly pestilence, and fanged beasts
Will I let loose against them,
With venomous creepers in dust.

---

^c Lit. "fat."
^{d-d} "kidney fat of."
^e Meaning of Heb. uncertain.
^{f-f} Meaning of Heb. uncertain. Arabic sha'ara suggests the rendering "Whom your fathers did not know."
^g I.e., idols.

²⁵The sword shall deal death without,
As shall the terror within,
To youth and maiden alike,
The suckling as well as the aged.
²⁶ h-I might have reduced them to naught,-h
Made their memory cease among men,
²⁷But for fear of the taunts of the foe,
Their enemies who might misjudge
And say, "Our own hand has prevailed;
None of this was wrought by the LORD!"
²⁸ iFor they are a folk void of sense,
Lacking in all discernment.
²⁹Were they wise, they would think upon this,
Gain insight into their future:
³⁰"How could one have routed a thousand,
Or two put ten thousand to flight,
Unless their Rock had sold them,
The LORD had given them up?"
³¹For their rock is not like our Rock,
j-In our enemies' ownk estimation.-j

³²Ah! The vine for them is from Sodom,
From the vineyards of Gomorrah;
The grapes for them are poison,
A bitter growth their clusters.
³³Their wine is the venom of asps,
The pitiless poison of vipers.
³⁴Lo, I have it all put away,
Sealed up in My storehouses,
³⁵To be My vengeance and recompense,
At the time that their foot falters.
Yea, their day of disaster is near,
And destiny rushes upon them.

³⁶For the LORD will vindicate His people
l-And take revenge for-l His servants,
When He sees that their might is gone,
And neither bond nor free is left.
³⁷He will say: Where are their gods,

h-h *Lit. "I said, I will reduce . . .*"; *meaning of Heb.* 'aph'ehem *uncertain.*
i *Here, apparently, Moses is the speaker; God resumes in v. 32.*
j-j *I.e., as everyone must admit.*
k *For Heb.* pelilim *see Exod. 21.22; cf. Gen. 48.11.*
l-l *Cf. Isa. 1.24. Others "and repent Himself concerning."*

The rock in whom they sought refuge,
[38]Who ate the fat of their offerings
And drank their libation wine?
Let them rise up to your help,
And let them be a shield unto you!
[39]See, then, that I, I am He;
There is no god beside Me.
I deal death and give life;
I wounded and I will heal:
None can deliver from My hand.
[40]Lo, I raise My hand to heaven
And say: As I live forever,
[41]When I whet My flashing blade
And My hand lays hold on judgment,
Vengeance will I wreak on My foes,
Will I deal to those who reject Me.
[42]I will make My arrows drunk with blood—
As My sword devours flesh—
Blood of the slain and the captive
From the long-haired enemy chiefs.

[43]O nations, acclaim His people!
For He'll avenge the blood of His servants,
Wreak vengeance on His foes,
And cleanse the land of His people.[m]

[44]Moses came, together with Hosea son of Nun, and recited all the words of this poem in the hearing of the people.

[45]And when Moses finished reciting all these words to all Israel, [46]he said to them: Take to heart all the words with which I have warned you this day. Enjoin them upon your children, that they may observe faithfully all the terms of this Teaching. [47]For this is not a trifling thing for you: it is your very life; through it you shall long endure on the land that you are to possess upon crossing the Jordan.

[48]That very day the LORD spoke to Moses: [49]Ascend these heights of Abarim to Mount Nebo, which is in the land of Moab facing Jericho, and view the land of Canaan, which I am giving the Israelites as their holding. [50]You shall die on the mountain that you are about to ascend, and shall be gathered to your kin, as your brother Aaron died on Mount

---

[m] Cf. Num. 35.33. Meaning of Heb. uncertain; Ugaritic 'udm't "tears" suggests the rendering "And wipe away His people's tears." Cf. Isa. 25.8.

Hor and was gathered to his kin; 51for you both broke faith with Me among the Israelite people, at the waters of Meribath-kadesh in the wilderness of Zin, by failing to uphold My sanctity among the Israelite people. 52You may view the land from a distance, but you shall not enter it—the land that I am giving to the Israelite people.

וזאת הברכה

33 This is the blessing with which Moses, the man of God, bade the Israelites farewell before he died. 2He said:

The LORD came from Sinai;
He shone upon them from Seir;
He appeared from Mount Paran,
And approached from Ribeboth-kodesh,a
Lightning flashing at them from His right.b
3 cLover, indeed, of the people,
Their hallowed are all in Your hand.
They followed in Your steps,
Accepting Your pronouncements,
4When Moses charged us with the Teaching
As the heritage of the congregation of Jacob.
5Then He became King in Jeshurun,
When the heads of the people assembled,
The tribes of Israel together.

6May Reuben live and not die,
Though few be his numbers.

7And this he said of Judah:
Hear, O LORD the voice of Judah
And restore him to his people.
d-Though his own hands strive for him,-d
Help him against his foes.

8And of Levi he said:
Let Your Thummim and Urim
Be with Your faithful one,

---

a *Cf. Meribath-kadesh, 32.51.*
b *Meaning of Heb. mimino 'eshdath uncertain, perhaps a place name.*
c *The meaning of vv. 3–5 is uncertain. An alternative rendering, with v. 3 apostrophizing Moses, is:* 3Then were, O lover of the people,/All His worshipers in your care;/They followed your lead,/ Accepted your precepts./4Moses charged us with the Teaching/As the heritage of the congregation of Jacob./5Thus was he king in Jeshurun . . . .
d-d *Better (vocalizing rab with pathaḥ) "Make his hands strong for him." Cf. rabbeh, Judg. 9.29.*

Whom You tested at Massah,
Challenged at the waters of Meribah;
⁹Who said of his father and mother,
"I consider them not."
His brothers he disregarded,
Ignored his own children.
Your precepts alone they observed,
And kept Your covenant.
¹⁰They shall teach Your laws to Jacob
And Your instructions to Israel.
ᵉ⁻They shall offer You incense to savor⁻ᵉ
And whole-offerings on Your altar.
¹¹Bless, O LORD, his substance,
And favor his undertakings.
Smite the loins of his foes;
Let his enemies rise no more.

¹²Of Benjamin he said:
Beloved of the LORD,
He rests securely beside Him;
Ever does He protect him,
ᶠ⁻As he rests between His shoulders.⁻ᶠ

¹³And of Joseph he said:
Blessed of the LORD be his land
With the bounty of dewᵍ from heaven,
And of the deep that couches below;
¹⁴With the bounteous yield of the sun,
And the bounteous crop of the moons;
¹⁵With the best from the ancient mountains,
And the bounty of hills immemorial;
¹⁶With the bounty of earth and its fullness,
And the favor of the Presenceʰ in the Bush.
May these rest on the head of Joseph,
On the crown of the elect of his brothers.
¹⁷Like a firstling bull in his majesty,

ᵉ⁻ᵉ *Lit. "They shall place incense in Your nostril."*
ᶠ⁻ᶠ *Or "He dwells amid his slopes."*
ᵍ *Targum Onkelos and two Hebrew manuscripts read: "With the bounty of heaven above"* (me'al for mittal, *cf. Gen. 49.25*).
ʰ *Lit. "Dweller"; cf. Exod. 3.1 ff.*

He has horns like the horns of the wild-ox;
With them he gores the peoples,
The ends of the earth one and all.
These[i] are the myriads of Ephraim,
Those[j] are the thousands of Manasseh.

18And of Zebulun he said:
Rejoice, O Zebulun, on your journeys,
And Issachar, in your tents.
19They invite their kin to the mountain,
Where they offer sacrifices of success.
For they draw from the riches of the sea
And the hidden hoards of the sand.

20And of Gad he said:
Blessed be He who enlarges Gad!
Poised is he like a lion
To tear off arm and scalp.
21 k-He chose for himself the best,
For there is the portion of the revered chieftain,
Where the heads of the people come.
He executed the LORD's judgments
And His decisions for Israel.-k

22And of Dan he said:
Dan is a lion's whelp
That leaps forth from Bashan.

23And of Naphtali he said:
O Naphtali, sated with favor
And full of the LORD's blessing,
Take possession on the west and south.

24And of Asher he said:
Most blessed of sons be Asher;
May he be the favorite of his brothers,
May he dip his foot in oil.
25 lMay your doorbolts be iron and copper,
And your security last all your days.

---

i *I.e., the one horn.*
j *I.e., the other horn.*
k-k *Meaning of Heb. uncertain; cf. vv. 3–5 (with note c) above, and* saphun *"esteemed" in post-biblical Heb.*
l *Meaning of Heb. uncertain.*

²⁶O Jeshurun, there is none like God,
Riding through the heavens to help you,
Through the skies in His majesty.
²⁷ ¹The ancient God is a refuge,
A support are the arms everlasting.
He drove out the enemy before you
By His command: Destroy!
²⁸Thus Israel dwells in safety,
Untroubled is Jacob's abode,ᵐ
In a land of grain and wine,
Under heavens dripping dew.
²⁹O happy Israel! Who is like you,
A people delivered by the LORD,
Your protecting Shield, your Sword triumphant!
Your enemies shall come cringing before you,
And you shall tread on their backs.

34 Moses went up from the steppes of Moab to Mount Nebo, to the summit of Pisgah, opposite Jericho, and the LORD showed him the whole land: Gilead as far as Dan; ²all Naphtali; the land of Ephraim and Manasseh; the whole land of Judah as far as the Westernᵃ Sea; ³the Negeb; and the Plain—the Valley of Jericho, the city of palm trees—as far as Zoar. ⁴And the LORD said to him, "This is the land of which I swore to Abraham, Isaac, and Jacob, 'I will assign it to your offspring.' I have let you see it with your own eyes, but you shall not cross there."

⁵So Moses the servant of the LORD died there, in the land of Moab, at the command of the LORD. ⁶He buried him in the valley in the land of Moab, near Beth-peor; and no one knows his burial place to this day. ⁷Moses was a hundred and twenty years old when he died; his eyes were undimmed and his vigor unabated. ⁸And the Israelites bewailed Moses in the steppes of Moab for thirty days.

The period of wailing and mourning for Moses came to an end. ⁹Now Joshua son of Nun was filled with the spirit of wisdom because Moses had laid his hands upon him; and the Israelites heeded him, doing as the LORD had commanded Moses.

ᵐ Others "fountain."

ᵃ I.e., Mediterranean; cf. note at 11.24.

¹⁰Never again did there arise in Israel a prophet like Moses—whom the LORD singled out, face to face, ¹¹for the various signs and portents that the LORD sent him to display in the land of Egypt, against Pharaoh and all his courtiers and his whole country, ¹²and for all the great might and awesome power that Moses displayed before all Israel.

חזק חזק ונתחזק

נביאים

NEVI'IM

THE PROPHETS

JOSHUA	יהושע
JUDGES	שופטים
I SAMUEL	שמואל א
II SAMUEL	שמואל ב
I KINGS	מלכים א
II KINGS	מלכים ב
ISAIAH	ישעיה
JEREMIAH	ירמיה
EZEKIEL	יחזקאל

The Twelve Minor Prophets

HOSEA	הושע
JOEL	יואל
AMOS	עמוס
OBADIAH	עבדיה
JONAH	יונה
MICAH	מיכה
NAHUM	נחום
HABAKKUK	חבקוק
ZEPHANIAH	צפניה
HAGGAI	חגי
ZECHARIAH	זכריה
MALACHI	מלאכי

JOSHUA

1 After the death of Moses the servant of the LORD, the LORD said to Joshua son of Nun, Moses' attendant:

²"My servant Moses is dead. Prepare to cross the Jordan, together with all this people, into the land that I am giving to the Israelites. ³Every spot on which your foot treads I give to you, as I promised Moses. ⁴Your territory shall extend from the wilderness and the Lebanon to the Great River, the River Euphrates [on the east]—the whole Hittite country— and up to the Mediterraneanᵃ Sea on the west. ⁵No one shall be able to resist you as long as you live. As I was with Moses, so I will be with you; I will not fail you or forsake you.

⁶"Be strong and resolute, for you shall apportion to this people the land that I swore to their fathers to assign to them. ⁷But you must be very strong and resolute to observe faithfully all the Teaching that My servant Moses enjoined upon you. Do not deviate from it to the right or to the left, that you may be successful wherever you go. ⁸Let not this Book of the Teaching cease from your lips, but recite it day and night, so that you may observe faithfully all that is written in it. Only then will you prosper in your undertakings and only then will you be successful.

⁹"I charge you: Be strong and resolute; do not be terrified or dismayed, for the LORD your God is with you wherever you go."

¹⁰Joshua thereupon gave orders to the officials of the people: ¹¹"Go through the camp and charge the people thus: Get provisions ready, for in three days' time you are to cross the Jordan, in order to enter and possess the land that the LORD your God is giving you as a possession."

¹²Then Joshua said to the Reubenites, the Gadites, and the half-tribe of Manasseh, ¹³"Remember what Moses the servant of the LORD enjoined upon you, when he said: 'The LORD your God is granting you a haven; He has assigned this territory to you.' ¹⁴Let your wives, children, and

---

ᵃ *Heb. "Great."*

livestock remain in the land that Moses assigned to you b-on this side of-b the Jordan; but every one of your fighting men shall go across armed^c in the van of your kinsmen. And you shall assist them ¹⁵until the LORD has given your kinsmen a haven, such as you have, and they too have gained possession of the land that the LORD your God has assigned to them. Then you may return to the land on the east side of the Jordan, which Moses the servant of the LORD assigned to you as your possession, and you may possess it."

¹⁶They answered Joshua, "We will do everything you have commanded us and we will go wherever you send us. ¹⁷We will obey you just as we obeyed Moses; let but the LORD your God be with you as He was with Moses! ¹⁸Any man who flouts your commands and does not obey every order you give him shall be put to death. Only be strong and resolute!"

2 Joshua son of Nun secretly sent two spies from Shittim, saying, "Go, reconnoiter the region of Jericho." So they set out, and they came to the house of a harlot named Rahab and lodged there. ²The king of Jericho was told, "Some men have come here tonight, Israelites, to spy out the country." ³The king of Jericho thereupon sent orders to Rahab: "Produce the men who came to you and entered your house, for they have come to spy out the whole country." ⁴The woman, however, had taken the two men and hidden them. "It is true," she said, "the men did come to me, but I didn't know where they were from. ⁵And at dark, when the gate was about to be closed, the men left; and I don't know where the men went. Quick, go after them, for you can overtake them."—⁶Now she had taken them up to the roof and hidden them under some stalks of flax which she had lying on the roof.—⁷So the men pursued them in the direction of the Jordan down to the fords; and no sooner had the pursuers gone out than the gate was shut behind them.

⁸ᵃ⁻The spies⁻ᵃ had not yet gone to sleep when she came up to them on the roof. ⁹She said to the men, "I know that the LORD has given the country to you, because dread of you has fallen upon us, and all the inhabitants of the land are quaking before you. ¹⁰For we have heard how the LORD dried up the waters of the Sea of Reeds for you when you left Egypt, and what you did to Sihon and Og, the two Amorite kings across the Jordan, whom you doomed.ᵇ ¹¹When we heard about it, we lost heart, and no man had any more spirit left because of you; for the LORD your

---

b-b Lit. "across."
c Meaning of Heb. uncertain.

a-a Heb. "They."
b I.e., placed under herem, which meant the annihilation of the inhabitants. Cf. Deut. 2.34 ff.

God is the only God in heaven above and on earth below. 12Now, since I have shown loyalty to you, swear to me by the LORD that you in turn will show loyalty to my family. Provide me with a reliable sign 13that you will spare the lives of my father and mother, my brothers and sisters, and all who belong to them, and save us from death." 14The men answered her, "Our persons are pledged for yours, even to death! If you do not disclose this mission of ours, we will show you true loyalty when the LORD gives us the land."

15She let them down by a rope through the window—for her dwelling was at the outer side of the city wall and she lived in the actual wall. 16She said to them, "Make for the hills, so that the pursuers may not come upon you. Stay there in hiding three days, until the pursuers return; then go your way."

17But the men warned her, "We will be released from this oath which you have made us take 18[unless,] when we invade the country, you tie this length of crimson cord to the window through which you let us down. Bring your father, your mother, your brothers, and all your family together in your house; 19and if anyone ventures outside the doors of your house, his blood will be on his head, and we shall be clear. But if a hand is laid on anyone who remains in the house with you, his blood shall be on our heads. 20And if you disclose this mission of ours, we shall likewise be released from the oath which you made us take." 21She replied, "Let it be as you say."

She sent them on their way, and they left; and she tied the crimson cord to the window.

22They went straight to the hills and stayed there three days, until the pursuers turned back. And so the pursuers, searching all along the road, did not find them.

23Then the two men came down again from the hills and crossed over. They came to Joshua son of Nun and reported to him all that had happened to them. 24They said to Joshua, "The LORD has delivered the whole land into our power; in fact, all the inhabitants of the land are quaking before us."

3

Early next morning, Joshua and all the Israelites set out from Shittim and marched to the Jordan. They did not cross immediately, but spent the night there. 2Three days later, the officials went through the camp

³and charged the people as follows: "When you see the Ark of the Covenant of the LORD your God being borne by the levitical priests, you shall move forward. Follow it—⁴but keep a distance of some two thousand cubits from it, never coming any closer to it—so that you may know by what route to march, since it is a road you have not traveled before." ⁵And Joshua said to the people, "Purify yourselves,ᵃ for tomorrow the LORD will perform wonders in your midst."

⁶Then Joshua ordered the priests, "Take up the Ark of the Covenant and advance to the head of the people." And they took up the Ark of the Covenant and marched at the head of the people.

⁷The LORD said to Joshua, "This day, for the first time, I will exalt you in the sight of all Israel, so that they shall know that I will be with you as I was with Moses. ⁸For your part, command the priests who carry the Ark of the Covenant as follows: When you reach the edge of the waters of the Jordan, make a halt in the Jordan."

⁹And Joshua said to the Israelites, "Come closer and listen to the words of the LORD your God. ¹⁰By this," Joshua continued, "you shall know that a living God is among you, and that He will dispossess for you the Canaanites, Hittites, Hivites, Perizzites, Girgashites, Amorites, and Jebusites: ¹¹the Ark of the Covenant of the Sovereign of all the earth is advancing before you into the Jordan. ¹²Now select twelve men from the tribes of Israel, one man from each tribe. ¹³When the feet of the priests bearing the Ark of the LORD, the Sovereign of all the earth, come to rest in the waters of the Jordan, the waters of the Jordan—the water coming from upstream—will be cut off and will stand in a single heap."

¹⁴When the people set out from their encampment to cross the Jordan, the priests bearing the Ark of the Covenant were at the head of the people. ¹⁵Now the Jordan keeps flowing over its entire bed throughout the harvest season. But as soon as the bearers of the Ark reached the Jordan, and the feet of the priests bearing the Ark dipped into the water at its edge, ¹⁶the waters coming down from upstream piled up in a single heap a great way off, atᵇ Adam, the town next to Zarethan; and those flowing away downstream to the Sea of the Arabah (the Dead Sea) ran out completely. So the people crossed near Jericho. ¹⁷The priests who bore the Ark of the LORD's Covenant stood on dry land exactly in the middle of the Jordan, while all Israel crossed over on dry land, until the entire nation had finished crossing the Jordan.

ᵃ *See Exod. 19.10, 15.*
ᵇ *So* kethib; qere *"from."*

4 When the entire nation had finished crossing the Jordan, the LORD said to Joshua, 2"Select twelve men from among the people, one from each tribe, 3and instruct them as follows: Pick up twelve stones from the spot exactly in the middle of the Jordan, where the priests' feet are standing; take them along with you and deposit them in the place where you will spend the night."

4Joshua summoned the twelve men whom he had designated among the Israelites, one from each tribe; 5and Joshua said to them, "Walk up to the Ark of the LORD your God, in the middle of the Jordan, and each of you lift a stone onto his shoulder—corresponding to the number of the tribes of Israel. 6This shall serve as a symbol among you: in time to come, when your children ask, 'What is the meaning of these stones for you?' 7you shall tell them, 'The waters of the Jordan were cut off because of the Ark of the LORD's Covenant; when it passed through the Jordan, the waters of the Jordan were cut off.' And so these stones shall serve the people of Israel as a memorial for all time."

8The Israelites did as Joshua ordered. They picked up twelve stones, corresponding to the number of the tribes of Israel, from the middle of the Jordan—as the LORD had charged Joshua—and they took them along with them to their night encampment and deposited them there.

9Joshua also set up twelve stones in the middle of the Jordan, at the spot where the feet of the priests bearing the Ark of the Covenant had stood; and they have remained there to this day.

10The priests who bore the Ark remained standing in the middle of the Jordan until all the instructions that the LORD had ordered Joshua to convey to the people had been carried out. And so the people speedily crossed over, a-just as Moses had assured Joshua in his charge to him.-a 11And when all the people finished crossing, the Ark of the LORD and the priests advanced to the head of the people.

12The Reubenites, the Gadites, and the half-tribe of Manasseh went across armedb in the van of the Israelites, as Moses had charged them.c 13About forty thousand shock troops went across, at the instance of the LORD, to the steppes of Jericho for battle.

14On that day the LORD exalted Joshua in the sight of all Israel, so that they revered him all his days as they had revered Moses.

15The LORD said to Joshua, 16"Command the priests who bear the Ark

---

a-a *Connection of clause uncertain; cf. Deut. 31.7–8.*
b *Meaning of Heb. uncertain.*
c *See Num. 32.20–22.*

of the Pact to come up out of the Jordan." ¹⁷So Joshua commanded the priests, "Come up out of the Jordan." ¹⁸As soon as the priests who bore the Ark of the LORD's Covenant came up out of the Jordan, and the feet of the priests stepped onto the dry ground, the waters of the Jordan resumed their course, flowing over its entire bed as before.

¹⁹The people came up from the Jordan on the tenth day of the first month, and encamped at Gilgal on the eastern border of Jericho. ²⁰And Joshua set up in Gilgal the twelve stones they had taken from the Jordan. ²¹He charged the Israelites as follows: "In time to come, when your children ask their fathers, 'What is the meaning of those stones?' ²²tell your children: 'Here the Israelites crossed the Jordan on dry land.' ²³For the LORD your God dried up the waters of the Jordan before you until you crossed, just as the LORD your God did to the Sea of Reeds, which He dried up before us until we crossed. ²⁴Thus all the peoples of the earth shall know how mighty is the hand of the LORD, and you shall fear the LORD your God always."

5 When all the kings of the Amorites on the western side of the Jordan, and all the kings of the Canaanites near the Sea, heard how the LORD had dried up the waters of the Jordan for the sake of the Israelites until they crossed over, they lost heart, and no spirit was left in them because of the Israelites.

²At that time the LORD said to Joshua, "Make flint knives and proceed with a second circumcision of the Israelites." ³So Joshua had flint knives made, and the Israelites were circumcised at Gibeath-haaraloth.ᵃ

⁴This is the reason why Joshua had the circumcision performed: All the people who had come out of Egypt, all the males of military age, had died during the desert wanderings after leaving Egypt. ⁵Now, whereas all the people who came out of Egypt had been circumcised, none of the people born after the exodus, during the desert wanderings, had been circumcised. ⁶For the Israelites had traveled in the wilderness forty years, until the entire nation—the men of military age who had left Egypt—had perished; because they had not obeyed the LORD, and the LORD had sworn never to let them see the land that the LORD had sworn to their fathers to assign to us, a land flowing with milk and honey. ⁷But He had raised up their sons in their stead; and it was these that Joshua circum-

ᵃ I.e., "the Hill of Foreskins."

cised, for they were uncircumcised, not having been circumcised on the way. ⁸After the circumcising of the whole nation was completed, they remained where they were, in the camp, until they recovered.

⁹And the LORD said to Joshua, "Today I have rolled away from you the disgrace of Egypt."ᵇ So that place was called Gilgal,ᶜ as it still is.

¹⁰Encamped at Gilgal, in the steppes of Jericho, the Israelites offered the passover sacrifice on the fourteenth day of the month, toward evening.

¹¹On the day after the passover offering, on that very day, they ate of the produce of the country, unleavened bread and parched grain. ¹²On that same day,ᵈ when they ate of the produce of the land, the manna ceased. The Israelites got no more manna; that year they ate of the yield of the land of Canaan.

¹³Once, when Joshua was near Jericho, he looked up and saw a man standing before him, drawn sword in hand. Joshua went up to him and asked him, "Are you one of us or of our enemies?" ¹⁴He replied, "No, I am captain of the LORD's host. Now I have come!" Joshua threw himself face down to the ground and, prostrating himself, said to him, "What does my lord command his servant?" ¹⁵The captain of the LORD's host answered Joshua, "Remove your sandals from your feet, for the place where you stand is holy." And Joshua did so.

6 Now Jericho was shut up tight because of the Israelites; no one could leave or enter.

²The LORD said to Joshua, "See, I will deliver Jericho and her king [and her] warriors into your hands. ³Let all your troops march around the city and complete one circuit of the city. Do this six days, ⁴with seven priests carrying seven ram's horns preceding the Ark. On the seventh day, march around the city seven times, with the priests blowing the horns. ⁵And when a long blast is sounded on the horn—as soon as you hear that sound of the horn—all the people shall give a mighty shout. Thereupon the city wall will collapse, and the people shall advance, every man straight ahead."

⁶Joshua son of Nun summoned the priests and said to them, "Take up the Ark of the Covenant, and let seven priests carrying seven ram's horns precede the Ark of the LORD." ⁷And he instructed the people, "Go forward, march around the city, with the vanguard marching in front of the

---

ᵇ *I.e., of the Egyptian bondage.*
ᶜ *Interpreted as "rolling."*
ᵈ *Lit. "on the day after."*

Ark of the LORD." [8]When Joshua had instructed the people, the seven priests carrying seven ram's horns advanced before the LORD, blowing their horns; and the Ark of the LORD's Covenant followed them. [9]The vanguard marched in front of the priests who were blowing the horns, and the rear guard marched behind the Ark, with the horns sounding all the time. [10]But Joshua's orders to the rest of the people were, "Do not shout, do not let your voices be heard, and do not let a sound issue from your lips until the moment that I command you, 'Shout!' Then you shall shout."

[11]So he had the Ark of the LORD go around the city and complete one circuit; then they returned to camp and spent the night in camp. [12]Joshua rose early the next day; and the priests took up the Ark of the LORD, [13]while the seven priests bearing the seven ram's horns marched in front of the Ark of the LORD, blowing the horns as they marched. The vanguard marched in front of them, and the rear guard marched behind the Ark of the LORD, with the horns sounding all the time. [14]And so they marched around the city once on the second day and returned to the camp. They did this six days.

[15]On the seventh day, they rose at daybreak and marched around the city, in the same manner, seven times; that was the only day that they marched around the city seven times. [16]On the seventh round, as the priests blew the horns, Joshua commanded the people, "Shout! For the LORD has given you the city. [17]The city and everything in it are to be proscribed for the LORD; only Rahab the harlot is to be spared, and all who are with her in the house, because she hid the messengers we sent. [18]But you must beware of that which is proscribed, or else you will be proscribed:[a] if you take anything from that which is proscribed, you will cause the camp of Israel to be proscribed; you will bring calamity upon it. [19]All the silver and gold and objects of copper and iron are consecrated to the LORD; they must go into the treasury of the LORD."

[20]So the people shouted when the horns were sounded. When the people heard the sound of the horns, the people raised a mighty shout and the wall collapsed. The people rushed into the city, every man straight in front of him, and they captured the city. [21]They exterminated everything in the city with the sword: man and woman, young and old, ox and sheep and ass. [22]But Joshua bade the two men who had spied out the land, "Go into the harlot's house and bring out the woman and all that belong to her, as you swore to her." [23]So the young spies went in

---

[a] I.e., be put to death; cf. Lev. 27.28–29.

and brought out Rahab, her father and her mother, her brothers and all that belonged to her—they brought out her whole family and left them outside the camp of Israel. ²⁴They burned down the city and everything in it. But the silver and gold and the objects of copper and iron were deposited in the treasury of the House of the LORD. ²⁵Only Rahab the harlot and her father's family were spared by Joshua, along with all that belonged to her, and she dwelt among the Israelites—as is still the case. For she had hidden the messengers that Joshua sent to spy out Jericho.

²⁶At that time Joshua pronounced this oath: "Cursed of the LORD be the man who shall undertake to fortify this city of Jericho: he shall lay its foundations at the cost of his first-born, and set up its gates at the cost of his youngest."

²⁷The LORD was with Joshua, and his fame spread throughout the land.

7 The Israelites, however, violated the proscription: Achan son of Carmi son of Zabdi son of Zerah, of the tribe of Judah, took of that which was proscribed, and the LORD was incensed with the Israelites.

²Joshua sent men from Jericho to Ai, which lies close to Beth-aven—east of Bethel—with orders to go up and spy out the country. So the men went up and spied out Ai. ³They returned to Joshua and reported to him, "Not all the troops need go up. Let two or three thousand men go and attack Ai; do not trouble all the troops to go up there, for [the people] there are few." ⁴So about three thousand of the troops marched up there; but they were routed by the men of Ai. ⁵The men of Ai killed about thirty-six of them, pursuing them outside the gate as far as Shebarim, and cutting them down along the descent. And the heart of the troops ᵃ⁻sank in utter dismay.⁻ᵃ

⁶Joshua thereupon rent his clothes. He and the elders of Israel lay until evening with their faces to the ground in front of the Ark of the LORD; and they strewed earth on their heads. ⁷"Ah, Lord GOD!" cried Joshua. "Why did You lead this people across the Jordan only to deliver us into the hands of the Amorites, to be destroyed by them? If only we had been content to remain on the other side of the Jordan! ⁸O Lord, what can I say after Israel has turned tail before its enemies? ⁹When the Canaanites and all the inhabitants of the land hear of this, they will turn upon us and

---

ᵃ⁻ᵃ Lit. "melted and turned to water."

wipe out our very name from the earth. And what will You do about Your great name?"

¹⁰But the LORD answered Joshua: "Arise! Why do you lie prostrate? ¹¹Israel has sinned! They have broken the covenant by which I bound them. They have taken of the proscribed and put it in their vessels; they have stolen; they have broken faith! ¹²Therefore, the Israelites will not be able to hold their ground against their enemies; they will have to turn tail before their enemies, for they have become proscribed. I will not be with you any more unless you root out from among you what is proscribed. ¹³Go and purify the people. Order them: Purify yourselves for tomorrow. For thus says the LORD, the God of Israel: Something proscribed is in your midst, O Israel, and you will not be able to stand up to your enemies until you have purged the proscribed from among you. ¹⁴Tomorrow morning you shall present yourselves by tribes. Whichever tribe the LORD indicatesᵇ shall come forward by clans; the clan that the LORD indicates shall come forward by ancestral houses, and the ancestral house that the LORD indicates shall come forward man by man. ¹⁵Then he who is ᶜ-indicated for proscription,⁻ᶜ and all that is his, shall be put to the fire, because he broke the Covenant of the LORD and because he committed an outrage in Israel."

¹⁶Early next morning, Joshua had Israel come forward by tribes; and the tribe of Judah was indicated. ¹⁷He then had the clans of Judah come forward, and the clan of Zerah was indicated. Then he had the clan of Zerah come forward by ᵈ-ancestral houses,⁻ᵈ and Zabdi was indicated. ¹⁸Finally he had his ancestral house come forward man by man, and Achan son of Carmi, son of Zabdi, son of Zerah, of the tribe of Judah, was indicated.

¹⁹Then Joshua said to Achan, "My son, pay honor to the LORD, the God of Israel, and make confession to Him. Tell me what you have done; do not hold anything back from me." ²⁰Achan answered Joshua, "It is true, I have sinned against the LORD, the God of Israel. This is what I did: ²¹I saw among the spoil a fine Shinar mantle, two hundred shekels of silver, and a wedge of gold weighing fifty shekels, and I coveted them and took them. They are buried in the ground in my tent, with the silver under it."ᵉ

²²Joshua sent messengers, who hurried to the tent; and there itᵉ was, buried in his tent, with the silver underneath. ²³They took them from the tent and brought them to Joshua and all the Israelites, and displayedᶠ them

---

ᵇ Lit. "catches."
ᶜ⁻ᶜ Or "caught in the net."
ᵈ⁻ᵈ So some Heb. mss. and some ancient versions; most mss. and editions have "men."
ᵉ I.e., the mantle.
ᶠ Meaning of Heb. uncertain.

before the LORD. 24Then Joshua, and all Israel with him, took Achan son of Zerah—and the silver, the mantle, and the wedge of gold—his sons and daughters, and his ox, his ass, and his flock, and his tent, and all his belongings, and brought them up to the Valley of Achor. 25And Joshua said, "What calamity you have brought upon us! The LORD will bring calamity upon you this day." And all Israel pelted him with stones. They put them to the fire and stoned them. 26They raised a huge mound of stones over him, which is still there. Then the anger of the LORD subsided. That is why that place was named the Valley of Achor*g*—as is still the case.

8 The LORD said to Joshua, "Do not be frightened or dismayed. Take all the fighting troops with you, go and march against Ai. See, I will deliver the king of Ai, his people, his city, and his land into your hands. 2You shall treat Ai and her king as you treated Jericho and her king; however, you may take the spoil and the cattle as booty for yourselves. Now set an ambush against the city behind it."

3So Joshua and all the fighting troops prepared for the march on Ai. Joshua chose thirty thousand men, valiant warriors, and sent them ahead by night. 4He instructed them as follows: "Mind, you are to lie in ambush behind the city; don't stay too far from the city, and all of you be on the alert. 5I and all the troops with me will approach the city; and when they come out against us, as they did the first time, we will flee from them. 6They will come rushing after us until we have drawn them away from the city. They will think, 'They are fleeing from us the same as last time'; but while we are fleeing before them, 7you will dash out from your ambush and seize the city, and the LORD your God will deliver it into your hands. 8And when you take the city, set it on fire. Do as the LORD has commanded. Mind, I have given you your orders."

9Joshua then sent them off, and they proceeded to the ambush; they took up a position between Ai and Bethel—west of Ai—while Joshua spent the night with the rest of the troops.

10Early in the morning, Joshua mustered the troops; then he and the elders of Israel marched upon Ai at the head of the troops. 11All the fighting force that was with him advanced near the city and encamped to the north of Ai, with a hollow between them and Ai. —12He selected about five thousand men and stationed them as an ambush between Bethel and Ai, west of the city. 13Thus the main body of the army was disposed

---

g *Connected with* 'akhar *"to bring calamity upon"; cf. v. 25.*

on the north of the city, but the far end of it was on the west. (This was after Joshua had a-spent the night-a in the valley.b) —14When the king of Ai saw them, he and all his people, the inhabitants of the city, rushed out in the early morning to the c-meeting place,-c facing the Arabah, to engage the Israelites in battle; for he was unaware that a force was lying in ambush behind the city. 15Joshua and all Israel fled in the direction of the wilderness, as though routed by them. 16All the troops in the city gathered to pursue them; pursuing Joshua, they were drawn out of the city. 17Not a man was left in Ai or in Bethel who did not go out after Israel; they left the city open while they pursued Israel.

18The LORD then said to Joshua, "Hold out the javelin in your hand toward Ai, for I will deliver it into your hands." So Joshua held out the javelin in his hand toward the city. 19As soon as he held out his hand, the ambush came rushing out of their station. They entered the city and captured it; and they swiftly set fire to the city. 20The men of Ai looked back and saw the smoke of the city rising to the sky; they had no room for flight in any direction.

The people who had been fleeing to the wilderness now became the pursuers. 21For when Joshua and all Israel saw that the ambush had captured the city, and that smoke was rising from the city, they turned around and attacked the men of Ai. 22Now the other [Israelites] were coming out of the city against them, so that they were between two bodies of Israelites, one on each side of them. They were slaughtered, so that no one escaped or got away. 23The king of Ai was taken alive and brought to Joshua.

24When Israel had killed all the inhabitants of Ai who had pursued them into the open wilderness, and all of them, to the last man, had fallen by the sword, all the Israelites turned back to Ai and put it to the sword.

25The total of those who fell that day, men and women, the entire population of Ai, came to twelve thousand.

26Joshua did not draw back the hand with which he held out his javelin until all the inhabitants of Ai had been exterminated. 27However, the Israelites took the cattle and the spoil of the city as their booty, in accordance with the instructions that the LORD had given to Joshua.

28Then Joshua burned down Ai, and turned it into a mound of ruins for all time, a desolation to this day. 29And the king of Ai was impaled on a stake until the evening. At sunset, Joshua had the corpse taken down

---

a-a So with some mss. (cf. v. 9); most mss. and editions read "marched."
b Syriac reads "with the troops"; cf. v. 9.
c-c Emendation yields "descent"; cf. 7.5.

from the stake and it was left lying at the entrance to the city gate. They raised a great heap of stones over it, which is there to this day.

30At that time Joshua built an altar to the LORD, the God of Israel, on Mount Ebal, 31as Moses, the servant of the LORD, had commanded the Israelites—as is written in the Book of the Teaching of Mosesd—an altar of unhewn stone upon which no iron had been wielded. They offered on it burnt offerings to the LORD, and brought sacrifices of well-being. 32And there, on the stones, he inscribed a copy of the Teaching that Moses had written for the Israelites. 33All Israel—stranger and citizen alike—with their elders, officials, and magistrates, stood on either side of the Ark, facing the levitical priests who carried the Ark of the LORD's Covenant. Half of them faced Mount Gerizim and half of them faced Mount Ebal, as Moses the servant of the LORD had commanded them of old, in order to bless the people of Israel. 34After that, he read all the words of the Teaching, the blessing and the curse, just as is written in the Book of the Teaching.e 35There was not a word of all that Moses had commanded that Joshua failed to read in the presence of the entire assembly of Israel, including the women and children and the strangers who accompanied them.

9 When all the kings a-west of-a the Jordan—in the hill country, in the Shephelah, and along the entire coast of the Mediterranean Sea up to the vicinity of Lebanon, the [land of the] Hittites, Amorites, Canaanites, Perizzites, Hivites, and Jebusites—learned of this, 2they gathered with one accord to fight against Joshua and Israel.

3But when the inhabitants of Gibeon learned how Joshua had treated Jericho and Ai, 4they for their part resorted to cunning. They set out b-in disguise:-b they took worn-out sacks for their asses, and worn-out waterskins that were cracked and patched; 5they had worn-out, patched sandals on their feet, and threadbare clothes on their bodies; and all the bread they took as provision was dry and crumbly. 6And so they went to Joshua in the camp at Gilgal and said to him and to the men of Israel, "We come from a distant land; we propose that you make a pact with us." 7The men of Israel replied to the Hivites, "But perhaps you live among us; how then can we make a pact with you?"c

d See Deut. 27.3–8.
e See Deut. 27.11–28.68.

a-a Lit. "across."
b-b Meaning of Heb. uncertain.
c Cf. Deut. 7.2.

⁸They said to Joshua, "We will be your subjects." But Joshua asked them, "Who are you and where do you come from?" ⁹They replied, "Your servants have come from a very distant country, because of the fame of the LORD your God. For we heard the report of Him: of all that He did in Egypt, ¹⁰and of all that He did to the two Amorite kings on the other side of the Jordan, King Sihon of Heshbon and King Og of Bashan who lived in Ashtaroth. ¹¹So our elders and all the inhabitants of our country instructed us as follows, 'Take along provisions for a trip, and go to them and say: We will be your subjects; come make a pact with us.' ¹²This bread of ours, which we took from our houses as provision, was still hot when we set out to come to you; and see how dry and crumbly it has become. ¹³These wineskins were new when we filled them, and see how they have cracked. These clothes and sandals of ours are worn out from the very long journey." ¹⁴The men ᵇ⁻took [their word] because of⁻ᵇ their provisions, and did not inquire of the LORD. ¹⁵Joshua established friendship with them; he made a pact with them to spare their lives, and the chieftains of the community gave them their oath.

¹⁶But when three days had passed after they made this pact with them, they learned that they were neighbors, living among them. ¹⁷So the Israelites set out, and on the third day they came to their towns; these towns were Gibeon, Chephirah, Beeroth, and Kiriath-jearim. ¹⁸But the Israelites did not attack them, since the chieftains of the community had sworn to them by the LORD, the God of Israel. The whole community muttered against the chieftains, ¹⁹but all the chieftains answered the whole community, "We swore to them by the LORD, the God of Israel; therefore we cannot touch them. ²⁰This is what we will do to them: We will spare their lives, so that there may be no wrath against us because of the oath that we swore to them." ²¹And the chieftains declared concerning them, "They shall live!" And they became hewers of wood and drawers of water for the whole community, as the chieftains had decreed concerning them.

²²Joshua summoned them and spoke to them thus: "Why did you deceive us and tell us you lived very far from us, when in fact you live among us? ²³Therefore, be accursed! Never shall your descendants cease to be slaves, hewers of wood and drawers of water for the House of my God." ²⁴But they replied to Joshua, "You see, your servants had heard that the LORD your God had promised His servant Moses to give you the whole land and to wipe out all the inhabitants of the country on your account; so we were in great fear for our lives on your account. That is why we

did this thing. ²⁵And now we are at your mercy; do with us what you consider right and proper." ²⁶And he did so; he saved them from being killed by the Israelites. ²⁷That day Joshua made them hewers of wood and drawers of water—as they still are—for the community and for the altar of the LORD, in the place that He would choose.

10 When King Adoni-zedek of Jerusalem learned that Joshua had captured Ai and proscribed it, treating Ai and its king as he had treated Jericho and its king, and that, moreover, the people of Gibeon had come to terms with Israel and remained among them, 2 ᵃ⁻he was⁻ᵃ very frightened. For Gibeon was a large city, like one of the royal cities—in fact, larger than Ai—and all its men were warriors. ³So King Adoni-zedek of Jerusalem sent this message to King Hoham of Hebron, King Piram of Jarmuth, King Japhia of Lachish, and King Debir of Eglon: ⁴"Come up and help me defeat Gibeon; for it has come to terms with Joshua and the Israelites."

⁵The five Amorite kings—the king of Jerusalem, the king of Hebron, the king of Jarmuth, the king of Lachish, and the king of Eglon, with all their armies—joined forces and marched on Gibeon, and encamped against it and attacked it. ⁶The people of Gibeon thereupon sent this message to Joshua in the camp at Gilgal: "Do not fail your servants; come up quickly and aid us and deliver us, for all the Amorite kings of the hill country have gathered against us." ⁷So Joshua marched up from Gilgal with his whole fighting force, all the trained warriors.

⁸The LORD said to Joshua, "Do not be afraid of them, for I will deliver them into your hands; not one of them shall withstand you." ⁹Joshua took them by surprise, marching all night from Gilgal. ¹⁰The LORD threw them into a panic before Israel: [Joshua] inflicted a crushing defeat on them at Gibeon, pursued them in the direction of the Beth-horon ascent, and harried them all the way to Azekah and Makkedah. ¹¹While they were fleeing before Israel down the descent from Beth-horon, the LORD hurled huge stones on them from the sky, all the way to Azekah, and they perished; more perished from the hailstones than were killed by the Israelite weapons.

¹²On that occasion, when the LORD routed the Amorites before the Israelites, Joshua addressed the LORD; he said in the presence of the Israelites:

ᵃ⁻ᵃ *Heb. "they were."*

"Stand still, O sun, at Gibeon,
O moon, in the Valley of Aijalon!"

13And the sun stood still
And the moon halted,
While a nation wreaked judgment on its foes

—as is written in the Book of Jashar.b Thus the sun halted in midheaven, and did not press on to set, for a whole day; 14for the LORD fought for Israel. Neither before nor since has there ever been such a day, when the LORD acted on words spoken by a man. 15Then Joshua together with all Israel returned to the camp at Gilgal.

16Meanwhile, those five kings fled and hid in a cave at Makkedah. 17When it was reported to Joshua that the five kings had been found hiding in a cave at Makkedah, 18Joshua ordered, "Roll large stones up against the mouth of the cave, and post men over it to keep guard over them. 19But as for the rest of you, don't stop, but press on the heels of your enemies and harass them from the rear. Don't let them reach their towns, for the LORD your God has delivered them into your hands." 20When Joshua and the Israelites had finished dealing them a deadly blow, they were wiped out, except for some fugitives who escaped into the fortified towns. 21The whole army returned in safety to Joshua in the camp at Makkedah; no one so much as snarledc at the Israelites. 22And now Joshua ordered, "Open the mouth of the cave, and bring those five kings out of the cave to me." 23This was done. Those five kings—the king of Jerusalem, the king of Hebron, the king of Jarmuth, the king of Lachish, and the king of Eglon—were brought out to him from the cave. 24And when the kings were brought out to Joshua, Joshua summoned all the men of Israel and ordered the army officers who had accompanied him, "Come forward and place your feet on the necks of these kings." They came forward and placed their feet on their necks. 25Joshua said to them, "Do not be frightened or dismayed; be firm and resolute. For this is what the LORD is going to do to all the enemies with whom you are at war." 26After that, Joshua had them put to death and impaled on five stakes, and they remained impaled on the stakes until evening. 27At sunset Joshua ordered them taken down from the poles and thrown into the cave in which they had hidden. Large stones were placed over the mouth of the cave, [and there they are] to this very day.

28At that time Joshua captured Makkedah and put it and its king to the sword, proscribing itd and every person in it and leaving none that

b *Presumably a collection of war songs.*
c *Cf. Exod. 11.7.*
d *So several mss.; most mss. and the editions read "them."*

escaped. And he treated the king of Makkedah as he had treated the king of Jericho.

²⁹From Makkedah, Joshua proceeded with all Israel to Libnah, and he attacked it. ³⁰The LORD delivered it and its king into the hands of Israel; they put it and all the people in it to the sword, letting none escape. And he treated its king as he had treated the king of Jericho.

³¹From Libnah, Joshua proceeded with all Israel to Lachish; he encamped against it and attacked it. ³²The LORD delivered Lachish into the hands of Israel. They captured it on the second day and put it and all the people in it to the sword, just as they had done to Libnah.

³³At that time King Horam of Gezer marched to the help of Lachish; but Joshua defeated him and his army, letting none of them escape.

³⁴From Lachish, Joshua proceeded with all Israel to Eglon; they encamped against it and attacked it. ³⁵They captured it on the same day and put it to the sword, proscribing all the people that were in it, as they had done to Lachish.

³⁶From Eglon, Joshua marched with all Israel to Hebron and attacked it. ³⁷They captured it and put it, its king, and all its towns, and all the people that were in it, to the sword. He let none escape, proscribing it and all the people in it, just as he had done in the case of Eglon.

³⁸Joshua and all Israel with him then turned back to Debir and attacked it. ³⁹He captured it and its king and all its towns. They put them to the sword and proscribed all the people in it. They let none escape; just as they had done to Hebron, and as they had done to Libnah and its king, so they did to Debir and its king.

⁴⁰Thus Joshua conquered the whole country:^c the hill country, the Negeb, the Shephelah, and the slopes, with all their kings; he let none escape, but proscribed everything that breathed—as the LORD, the God of Israel, had commanded. ⁴¹Joshua conquered them from Kadesh-barnea to Gaza, all the land of Goshen, and up to Gibeon. ⁴²All those kings and their lands were conquered by Joshua at a single stroke, for the LORD, the God of Israel, fought for Israel. ⁴³Then Joshua, with all Israel, returned to the camp at Gilgal.

11 When the news reached King Jabin of Hazor, he sent messages to King Jobab of Madon, to the king of Shimron, to the king of Achshaph, ²and to the other kings in the north—in the hill country, in the Arabah

---

^c I.e., the whole southern part of Canaan.

south of Chinnereth, in the lowlands, and in the district[a] of Dor on the west; [3]to the Canaanites in the east and in the west; to the Amorites, Hittites, Perizzites, and Jebusites in the hill country; and to the Hivites at the foot of Hermon, in the land of Mizpah. [4]They took the field with all their armies—an enormous host, as numerous as the sands on the seashore—and a vast multitude of horses and chariots. [5]All these kings joined forces; they came and encamped together at the Waters of Merom to give battle to Israel.

[6]But the LORD said to Joshua, "Do not be afraid of them; tomorrow at this time I will have them all lying slain before Israel. You shall hamstring their horses and burn their chariots." [7]So Joshua, with all his fighting men, came upon them suddenly at the Waters of Merom, and pounced upon them. [8]The LORD delivered them into the hands of Israel, and they defeated them and pursued them all the way to Great Sidon [b-]and Misrephothmaim,[-b] and all the way to the Valley of Mizpeh[c] on the east; they crushed them, letting none escape. [9]And Joshua dealt with them as the LORD had ordered him; he hamstrung their horses and burned their chariots.

[10]Joshua then turned back and captured Hazor and put her king to the sword.—Hazor was formerly the head of all those kingdoms.— [11]They proscribed and put to the sword every person in it. Not a soul survived, and Hazor itself was burned down. [12]Joshua captured all those royal cities and their kings. He put them to the sword; he proscribed them in accordance with the charge of Moses, the servant of the LORD. [13]However, all those towns that are still standing on their mounds were not burned down by Israel; it was Hazor alone that Joshua burned down. [14]The Israelites kept all the spoil and cattle of the rest of those cities as booty. But they cut down their populations with the sword until they exterminated them; they did not spare a soul. [15]Just as the LORD had commanded His servant Moses, so Moses had charged Joshua, and so Joshua did; he left nothing undone of all that the LORD had commanded Moses.

[16]Joshua conquered the whole of this region: the hill country [of Judah], the Negeb, the whole land of Goshen, the Shephelah, the Arabah, and the hill country and coastal plain of Israel—[17][everything] from Mount Halak, which ascends to Seir, all the way to Baal-gad in [d-]the Valley of the Lebanon[-d] at the foot of Mount Hermon; and he captured all the kings there and executed them.

[18]Joshua waged war with all those kings over a long period. [19]Apart

---

[a] Meaning of Heb. uncertain.
[b-b] Change of vocalization yields "and Misrephoth on the west."
[c] Apparently identical with Mizpah in v. 3.
[d-d] I.e., the valley between the Lebanon and Anti-Lebanon ranges.

from the Hivites who dwelt in Gibeon, not a single city made terms with the Israelites; all were taken in battle. [20]For it was the LORD's doing to stiffen their hearts to give battle to Israel, in order that they might be proscribed without quarter and wiped out, as the LORD had commanded Moses.

[21]At that time, Joshua went and wiped out the Anakites from the hill country, from Hebron, Debir, and Anab, from the entire hill country of Judah, and from the entire hill country of Israel; Joshua proscribed them and their towns. [22]No Anakites remained in the land of the Israelites; but some remained in Gaza, Gath, and Ashdod.

[23]Thus Joshua conquered the whole country, just as the LORD had promised Moses; and Joshua assigned it to Israel to share according to their tribal divisions. And the land had rest from war.

12 The following are the local kings whom the Israelites defeated and whose territories they took possession of:

East of the Jordan, from the Wadi Arnon to Mount Hermon, including the eastern half of the Arabah:[a] [2a]King Sihon of the Amorites, who resided in Heshbon and ruled over part of Gilead—from Aroer on the bank of the Wadi Arnon and the wadi proper up to the Wadi Jabbok [and] the border of the Ammonites— [3]and over the eastern Arabah up to the Sea of Chinnereth and, southward by way of Beth-jeshimoth at the foot of the slopes of Pisgah on the east, down to the Sea of the Arabah, that is, the Dead Sea. [4]Also the territory of King Og of Bashan—one of the last of the Rephaim—who resided in Ashtaroth and in Edrei [5]and ruled over Mount Hermon, Salcah, and all of Bashan up to the border of the Geshurites and the Maacathites, as also over part of Gilead [down to] the border of King Sihon of Heshbon. [6]These were vanquished by Moses, the servant of the LORD, and the Israelites; and Moses, the servant of the LORD, assigned [b]that territory[b] as a possession to the Reubenites, the Gadites, and the half-tribe of Manasseh.

[7]And the following are the local kings whom Joshua and the Israelites defeated on the west side of the Jordan—from Baal-gad in the Valley of the Lebanon to Mount Halak, which ascends to Seir—which Joshua assigned as a possession to the tribal divisions of Israel: [8]in the hill country, in the lowlands, in the Arabah, in the slopes,[c] in the wilderness, and in

---

[a] Meaning of vv. 2 and 3 uncertain.
[b-b] Lit. "it."
[c] I.e., the slopes of Pisgah; cf. 13.20.

the Negeb—[in the land of] the Hittites, the Amorites, the Canaanites, the Perizzites, the Hivites, and the Jebusites. 9They were:

the king of Jericho	1
the king of Ai, near Bethel,	1
10the king of Jerusalem	1
the king of Hebron	1
11the king of Jarmuth	1
the king of Lachish	1
12the king of Eglon	1
the king of Gezer	1
13the king of Debir	1
the king of Geder	1
14the king of Hormah	1
the king of Arad	1
15the king of Libnah	1
the king of Adullam	1
16the king of Makkedah	1
the king of Bethel	1
17the king of Tappuah	1
the king of Hepher	1
18the king of Aphek	1
the king of Sharon	1
19the king of Madon	1
the king of Hazor	1
20the king of Shimron-meron	1
the king of Achshaph	1
21the king of Taanach	1
the king of Megiddo	1
22the king of Kedesh	1
the king of Jokneam in the Carmel	1
23the king of Dor in the districtd of Dor	1
the king of Goiim in Gilgal	1
24the king of Tirzah	1
Total number of kings	31.

13

Joshua was now old, advanced in years. The LORD said to him, "You have grown old, you are advanced in years; and very much of the

---

d Meaning of Heb. uncertain.

land still remains to be taken possession of. ²This is the territory that remains: all the districts of the Philistines and all [those of] the Geshurites, ³from the Shihor, which is close to Egypt, to the territory of Ekron on the north, are accounted Canaanite, namely, those of the five lords of the Philistines—the Gazites, the Ashdodites, the Ashkelonites, the Gittites, and the Ekronites—and those of the Avvim ⁴on the south; further, all the Canaanite country from Mearah of the Sidonians to Aphek at the Amorite border ⁵and the land of the Gebalites, with the whole [Valley of the] Lebanon, from Baal-gad at the foot of Mount Hermon to Lebo-hamath on the east, ⁶with all the inhabitants of the hill country from the [Valley of the] Lebanon to ªᐧMisrephoth-maim,ᐧª namely, all the Sidonians. I Myself will dispossess ᵇᐧthose nationsᐧᵇ for the Israelites; you have only to apportion ᶜᐧtheir landsᐧᶜ by lot among Israel, as I have commanded you. ⁷Therefore, divide this territory into hereditary portions for the nine tribes and the half-tribe of Manasseh."

⁸Now the Reubenites and the Gadites, along with ᶜᐧthe other half-tribe,ᐧᶜ had already received the shares which Moses assigned to them on the east side of the Jordan—as assigned to them by Moses the servant of the LORD: ⁹from Aroer on the edge of the Wadi Arnon and the town in the middle of the wadi, the entire Tableland [from] Medeba to Dibon, ¹⁰embracing all the towns of King Sihon of the Amorites, who had reigned in Heshbon, up to the border of the Ammonites; ¹¹further, Gilead, the territories of the Geshurites and the Maacathites, and all of Mount Hermon, and the whole of Bashan up to Salcah—¹²the entire kingdom of Og, who had reigned over Bashan at Ashtaroth and at Edrei. (He was the last of the remaining Rephaim.) These were defeated and dispossessed by Moses; ¹³but the Israelites failed to dispossess the Geshurites and the Maacathites, and Geshur and Maacath remain among Israel to this day. ¹⁴No hereditary portion, however, was assigned to the tribe of Levi, their portion being the fire offerings of the LORD, the God of Israel, as He spoke concerning them.ᵈ

¹⁵And so Moses assigned [the following] to the tribe of the Reubenites, for their various clans, ¹⁶and it became theirs: The territory from Aroer, on the edge of the Wadi Arnon and the town in the middle of the wadi, up to Medeba—the entire Tableland—¹⁷Heshbon and all its towns in the Tableland: Dibon, Bamoth-baal, Beth-baal-meon, ¹⁸Jahaz, Kedemoth, Mephaath, ¹⁹Kiriathaim, Sibmah, and Zereth-shahar ᶜᐧin the hill of the valley,ᐧᶜ ²⁰Beth-peor, the slopes of Pisgah, and Beth-jeshimoth— ²¹all the

---

ᵃ⁻ᵃ *See note on 11.8.*
ᵇ⁻ᵇ *Lit. "them."*
ᶜ⁻ᶜ *Lit. "it."*
ᵈ *See Deut. 18.1.*
ᵉ⁻ᵉ *Emendation yields "in the hill country; and in the Valley. . . ."*

towns of the Tableland and the entire kingdom of Sihon, the king of the Amorites, who had reigned in Heshbon. (For Moses defeated him and the Midianite chiefs Evi, Rekem, Zur, Hur, and Reba, who had dwelt in the land as princes of Sihon. 22Together with the others that they slew, the Israelites put Balaam son of Beor, the augur, to the sword.) 23The boundary of the Reubenites was the edge of the Jordan. That was the portion of the Reubenites for their various clans—those towns with their villages.

24To the tribe of Gad, for the various Gadite clans, Moses assigned [the following], 25and it became their territory: Jazer, all the towns of Gilead, part of the country of the Ammonites up to Aroer, which is close to Rabbah, 26and from Heshbon to Ramath-mizpeh and Betonim, and from Mahanaim to the border of Lidbir;f 27and in the Valley, Beth-haram, Beth-nimrah, Succoth, and Zaphon—the rest of the kingdom of Sihon, the king of Heshbon—down to the edge of the Jordan and up to the tip of the Sea of Chinnereth on the east side of the Jordan. 28That was the portion of the Gadites, for their various clans—those towns with their villages.

29And to the half-tribe of Manasseh Moses assigned [the following], so that it went to the half-tribe of Manasseh, for its various clans, 30and became their territory: Mahanaim,g all of Bashan, the entire kingdom of Og, king of Bashan, and all of Havvoth-jairh in Bashan, sixty towns; 31and part of Gilead, and Ashtaroth and Edrei, the royal cities of Og in Bashan, were assigned to the descendants of Machir son of Manasseh—to a part of the descendants of Machir—for their various clans.

32Those, then, were the portions that Moses assigned in the steppes of Moab, on the east side of the Jordan. 33But no portion was assigned by Moses to the tribe of Levi; the LORD, the God of Israel, is their portion, as He spoke concerning them.d

14 And these are the allotments of the Israelites in the land of Canaan, that were apportioned to them by the priest Eleazar, by Joshua son of Nun, and by the heads of the ancestral houses of the Israelite tribes, 2the portions that fell to them by lot, as the LORD had commanded through Moses for the nine and a half tribes. 3For the portion of the other two and a half tribes had been assigned to them by Moses on the other side of the Jordan. He had not assigned any portion among them to the

f *Change of vocalization yields "Lo-debar"; cf. 2 Sam. 9.4, 5; 17.27.*
g *Lit. "from Mahanaim."*
h *See note on Num. 32.41.*

Levites; ⁴for whereas the descendants of Joseph constituted two tribes, Manasseh and Ephraim, the Levites were assigned no share in the land, but only some towns to live in, with the pastures for their livestock and cattle. ⁵Just as the LORD had commanded Moses, so the Israelites did when they apportioned the land.

⁶The Judites approached Joshua at Gilgal, and Caleb son of Jephunneh the Kenizzite said to him: "You know what instructions the LORD gave at Kadesh-barnea to Moses, the man of God, concerning you and me. ⁷I was forty years old when Moses the servant of the LORD sent me from Kadesh-barnea to spy out the land, and I gave him a forthright report. ⁸While my companions who went up with me took the heart out of the people, I was loyal to the LORD my God. ⁹On that day, Moses promised on oath, 'The land on which your foot trod shall be a portion for you and your descendants forever, because you were loyal to the LORD my God.' ¹⁰Now the LORD has preserved me, as He promised. It is forty-five years since the LORD made this promise to Moses, when Israel was journeying through the wilderness; and here I am today, eighty-five years old. ¹¹I am still as strong today as on the day that Moses sent me; my strength is the same now as it was then, for battle and for activity.ᵃ ¹²So assign to me this hill country as the LORD promised on that day. Though you too heard on that day that Anakites are there and great fortified cities, if only the LORD is with me, I will dispossess them, as the LORD promised."

¹³So Joshua blessed Caleb son of Jephunneh and assigned Hebron to him as his portion. ¹⁴Thus Hebron became the portion of Caleb son of Jephunneh the Kenizzite, as it still is, because he was loyal to the LORD, the God of Israel. —¹⁵The name of Hebron was formerly Kiriath-arba: [Arba] was the great man among the Anakites.

And the land had rest from war.

15

The portion that fell by lot to the various clans of the tribe of Judah lay farthest south, down to the border of Edom, which is the Wilderness of Zin. ²Their southern boundary began from the tip of the Dead Sea, from the tongue that projects southward. ³It proceeded to the south of the Ascent of Akrabbim, passed on to Zin, ascended to the south of Kadesh-barnea, passed on to Hezron, ascended to Addar, and made a turn to Karka. ⁴From there it passed on to Azmon and proceeded to the

ᵃ Lit. "and to go out and come in."

Wadi of Egypt; and the boundary ran on to the Sea. That shall be your southern boundary.

5The boundary on the east was the Dead Sea up to the mouth of the Jordan. On the northern side, the boundary began at the tongue of the Sea at the mouth of the Jordan. 6The boundary ascended to Beth-hoglah and passed north of Beth-arabah; then the boundary ascended to the Stone of Bohan son of Reuben. 7The boundary ascended a-from the Valley of Achor to Debir and turned north-a to Gilgal,b facing the Ascent of Adummim which is south of the wadi; from there the boundary continued to the waters of En-shemesh and ran on to En-rogel. 8Then the boundary ascended into the Valley of Ben-hinnom, along the southern flank of the Jebusites—that is, Jerusalem. The boundary then ran up to the top of the hill which flanks the Valley of Hinnom on the west, at the northern end of the Valley of Rephaim. 9From that hilltop the boundary curved to the fountain of the Waters of Nephtoah and ran on to the towns of Mount Ephron; then the boundary curved to Baalah—that is, Kiriath-jearim. 10From Baalah the boundary turned westward to Mount Seir,c passed north of the slope of Mount Jearim—that is, Chesalon—descended to Beth-shemesh, and passed on to Timnah. 11The boundary then proceeded to the northern flank of Ekron; the boundary curved to Shikkeron, passed on to Mount Baalah, and proceeded to Jabneel; and the boundary ran on to the Sea. 12And the western boundary was the edge of the Mediterranean Sea. Those were the boundaries of the various clans of the Judites on all sides.

13In accordance with the LORD's command to Joshua, Caleb son of Jephunneh was given a portion among the Judites, namely, Kiriath-arba—that is, Hebron. ([Arba] was the father of Anak.) 14Caleb dislodged from there the three Anakites: Sheshai, Ahiman, and Talmai, descendants of Anak. 15From there he marched against the inhabitants of Debir—the name of Debir was formerly Kiriath-sepher— 16and Caleb announced, "I will give my daughter Achsah in marriage to the man who attacks and captures Kiriath-sepher." 17His kinsman Othniel the Kenizzited captured it; and Caleb gave him his daughter Achsah in marriage.

18e-When she came [to him], she induced him-e to ask her father for some property. She dismounted from her donkey, and Caleb asked her,

---

a-a Meaning of Heb. uncertain.
b Apparently identical with Geliloth, 18.17.
c Not the Seir of Edom.
d Cf. 14.6, 14.
e-e Meaning of Heb. uncertain. Some Greek mss. read "he induced her"; cf. Judg. 1.14.

"What is the matter?" [19]She replied, "Give me a present; for you have given me away as Negeb-land;[f] so give me springs of water." And he gave her Upper and Lower Gulloth.[g]

[20]This was the portion of the tribe of the Judites by their clans:

[21]The towns at the far end of the tribe of Judah, near the border of Edom, in the Negeb, were: Kabzeel, Eder, Jagur, [22]Kinah, Dimonah, Adadah, [23]Kedesh, Hazor, Ithnan, [24]Ziph, Telem, Bealoth, [25]Hazor-hadattah, Kerioth-hezron—that is, Hazor—[26]Amam, Shema, Moladah, [27]Hazar-gaddah, Heshmon, Beth-pelet, [28]Hazar-shual, Beer-sheba, Biziothiah, [29]Baalah, Iim, Ezem, [30]Eltolad, Chesil, Hormah, [31]Ziklag, Madmannah, Sansannah, [32h-]Lebaoth, Shilhim,[-h] Ain and Rimmon.[i] Total: 29[j] towns, with their villages.

[33]In the Lowland: Eshtaol, Zorah, Ashnah, [34]Zanoah, En-gannim, Tappuah, Enam, [35]Jarmuth, Adullam, Socoh, Azekah, [36]Shaaraim, Adithaim, Gederah, and Gederothaim—14[k] towns, with their villages.

[37]Zenan, Hadashah, Migdal-gad, [38]Dilan, Mizpeh, Joktheel, [39]Lachish, Bozkath, Eglon, [40]Cabbon, Lahmas, Chithlish, [41]Gederoth, Beth-dagon, Naamah, and Makkedah: 16 towns, with their villages.

[42]Libnah, Ether, Ashan, [43]Iphtah, Ashnah, Nezib, [44]Keilah, Achzib, and Mareshah: 9 towns, with their villages.

[45]Ekron, with its dependencies and villages. [46]From Ekron westward, all the towns in the vicinity of Ashdod, with their villages—[47]Ashdod, its dependencies and its villages—Gaza, its dependencies and its villages, all the way to the Wadi of Egypt and the edge of the Mediterranean Sea.

[48]And in the hill country: Shamir, Jattir, Socoh, [49]Dannah, Kiriathsannah[l]—that is, Debir—[50]Anab, Eshtemoh, Anim, [51]Goshen, Holon, and Giloh: 11 towns, with their villages.

[52]Arab, Dumah, Eshan, [53]Janum, Beth-tappuah, Aphekah, [54]Humtah, Kiriath-arba—that is, Hebron—and Zior: 9 towns, with their villages.

[55]Maon, Carmel, Ziph, Juttah, [56]Jezreel, Jokdeam, Zanoah, [57]Kain, Gibeah, and Timnah: 10 towns, with their villages.

[58]Halhul, Beth-zur, Gedor, [59]Maarath, Beth-anoth, and Eltekon: 6 towns, with their villages.[m]

[60]Kiriath-baal—that is, Kiriath-jearim—and Rabbah: 2 towns, with their villages.

[f] I.e., as a dry land, that is, without a dowry.
[g] I.e., "springs."
[h-h] Cf. below 19.6.
[i] Cf. Ain, Rimmon, 19.7 below, and 1 Chron. 4.32; En-rimmon, Neh. 11.29.
[j] The number is uncertain. Some of the same towns are listed under Simeon, cf. 19.1–9; so Rashi.
[k] The number is uncertain. Tappuah and Enam may have been one place; so Rashi on basis of 17.7.
[l] Emendation yields "Kiriath-sepher"; cf. Septuagint.
[m] Septuagint adds: Tekoa, Ephrathah—that is, Bethlehem—Peor, Etam, Kulon, Tatam, Sores, Karem, Gallim, Bether, and Manach—11 towns, with their villages.

[61]In the wilderness: Beth-arabah, Middin, Secacah, [62]Nibshan, Ir-me-lah,[n] and En-gedi: 6 towns, with their villages.

[63]But the Judites could not dispossess the Jebusites, the inhabitants of Jerusalem; so the Judites dwell with the Jebusites in Jerusalem to this day.

16

The portion that fell by lot to the Josephites ran from the Jordan at Jericho—from the waters of Jericho east of the wilderness. From Jericho it ascended through the hill country to Bethel. [2]From Bethel it ran to Luz and passed on to the territory of the Archites at Ataroth, [3]descended westward to the territory of the Japhletites as far as the border of Lower Beth-horon and Gezer, and ran on to the Sea. [4]Thus the Josephites—that is, Manasseh and Ephraim—received their portion.

[5]The territory of the Ephraimites, by their clans, was as follows: The boundary of their portion ran from Atroth-addar on the east to Upper Beth-horon, [6]and the boundary ran on to the Sea. And on the north, the boundary proceeded from Michmethath to the east of Taanath-shiloh and passed beyond it up to the east of Janoah; [7]from Janoah it descended to Ataroth and Naarath, touched on Jericho, and ran on to the Jordan. [8]Westward, the boundary proceeded from Tappuah to the Wadi Kanah and ran on to the Sea. This was the portion of the tribe of the Ephraimites, by their clans, [9]together with the towns marked off[a] for the Ephraimites within the territory of the Manassites—all those towns with their villages. [10]However, they failed to dispossess the Canaanites who dwelt in Gezer; so the Canaanites remained in the midst of Ephraim, as is still the case. But they had to perform forced labor.

17

And this is the portion that fell by lot to the tribe of Manasseh— for he was Joseph's first-born. Since Machir, the first-born of Manasseh and the father of Gilead, was a valiant warrior, Gilead and Bashan were assigned to him. [2]And now assignments were made to the remaining Manassites, by their clans: the descendants of Abiezer, Helek, Asriel, Shechem, Hepher, and Shemida. Those were the male descendants of Manasseh son of Joseph, by their clans.

[3a]Now Zelophehad son of Hepher son of Gilead son of Machir son of Manasseh had no sons, but only daughters. The names of his daughters were Mahlah, Noah, Hoglah, Milcah, and Tirzah. [4]They appeared before

---

[n] *Or "the City of Salt."*

[a] *Meaning of Heb. uncertain.*

[a] *Cf. Num. 27.1–11.*

the priest Eleazer, Joshua son of Nun, and the chieftains, saying: "The LORD commanded Moses to grant us a portion among our male kinsmen." So, in accordance with the LORD's instructions, they were granted a portion among their father's kinsmen. ⁵Ten districts fell to Manasseh, apart from the lands of Gilead and Bashan, which are across the Jordan. ⁶Manasseh's daughters inherited a portion in these together with his sons, while the land of Gilead was assigned to the rest of Manasseh's descendants.

⁷The boundary of Manasseh ran from Asher to Michmethath, which lies near Shechem. The boundary continued to the right, toward the inhabitants of En-tappuah. —⁸The region of Tappuah belonged to Manasseh; but Tappuah, on the border of Manasseh, belonged to the Ephraimites.—⁹Then the boundary descended to the Wadi Kanah. Those towns to the south of the wadi belonged to Ephraim as an enclave among the towns of Manasseh. The boundary of Manasseh lay north of the wadi and ran on to the Sea. ¹⁰What lay to the south belonged to Ephraim, and what lay to the north belonged to Manasseh, with the Sea as its boundary. [This territory] was contiguous with Asher on the north and with Issachar on the east. ¹¹Within Issachar and Asher, Manasseh possessed Beth-shean and its dependencies, Ibleam and its dependencies, the inhabitants of Dor and its dependencies, the inhabitants of En-dor and its dependencies, the inhabitants of Taanach and its dependencies, and the inhabitants of Megiddo and its dependencies: ᵇ⁻these constituted three regions.⁻ᵇ

¹²The Manassites could not dispossess [the inhabitants of] these towns, and the Canaanites stubbornly remained in this region. ¹³When the Israelites became stronger, they imposed tribute on the Canaanites; but they did not dispossess them.

¹⁴The Josephites complained to Joshua, saying, "Why have you assigned as our portion a single allotment and a single district, seeing that we are a numerous people whom the LORD has blessed so greatly?" ¹⁵"If you are a numerous people," Joshua answered them, "go up to the forest country and clear an area for yourselves there, in the territory of the Perizzites and the Rephaim, seeing that you are cramped in the hill country of Ephraim." ¹⁶"The hill country is not enough for us," the Josephites replied, "and all the Canaanites who live in the valley area have iron chariots, both those in Beth-shean and its dependencies and those in the Valley of Jezreel." ¹⁷But Joshua declared to the House of Joseph, to

ᵇ⁻ᵇ *Meaning of Heb. uncertain.*

Ephraim and Manasseh, "You are indeed a numerous people, possessed of great strength; you shall not have one allotment only. [18]The hill country shall be yours as well; true, it is forest land, but you will clear it and possess it to its farthest limits. And you shall also dispossess the Canaanites, even though they have iron chariots and even though they are strong."

18

The whole community of the Israelite people assembled at Shiloh, and set up the Tent of Meeting there. The land was now under their control; [2]but there remained seven tribes of the Israelites which had not yet received their portions. [3]So Joshua said to the Israelites, "How long will you be slack about going and taking possession of the land which the LORD, the God of your fathers, has assigned to you? [4]Appoint three men of each tribe; I will send them out to go through the country and write down a description of it for purposes of apportionment, and then come back to me. [5]They shall divide it into seven parts—Judah shall remain by its territory in the south, and the house of Joseph shall remain by its territory in the north.—[6]When you have written down the description of the land in seven parts, bring it here to me. Then I will cast lots for you here before the LORD our God. [7]For the Levites have no share among you, since the priesthood of the LORD is their portion; and Gad and Reuben and the half-tribe of Manasseh have received the portions which were assigned to them by Moses the servant of the LORD, on the eastern side of the Jordan."

[8]The men set out on their journeys. Joshua ordered the men who were leaving to write down a description of the land—"Go, traverse the country and write down a description of it. Then return to me, and I will cast lots for you here at Shiloh before the LORD."

[9]So the men went and traversed the land; they described it in a document, town by town, in seven parts, and they returned to Joshua in the camp at Shiloh. [10]Joshua cast lots for them at Shiloh before the LORD, and there Joshua apportioned the land among the Israelites according to their divisions.

[11]The lot of the tribe of the Benjaminites, by their clans, came out first. The territory which fell to their lot lay between the Judites and the Josephites. [12]The boundary on their northern rim began at the Jordan; the boundary ascended to the northern flank of Jericho, ascended westward into the hill country and ran on to the Wilderness of Beth-aven. [13]From

there the boundary passed on southward to Luz, to the flank of Luz—that is, Bethel; then the boundary descended to Atroth-addar [and] to the hill south of Lower Beth-horon. 14The boundary now turned and curved onto the western rim; and the boundary ran southward from the hill on the south side of Beth-horon till it ended at Kiriath-baal—that is, Kiriath-jearim—a town of the Judites. That was the western rim. 15The southern rim: From the outskirts of Kiriath-jearim, the boundary passed westwarda and ran on to the fountain of the Waters of Nephtoah. 16Then the boundary descended to the foot of the hill by the Valley of Ben-hinnom at the northern end of the Valley of Rephaim; then it ran down the Valley of Hinnom along the southern flank of the Jebusites to En-rogel. 17Curving northward, it ran on to En-shemesh and ran on to Gel-iloth, facing the Ascent of Adummim, and descended to the Stone of Bohan son of Reuben. 18It continued northward to the edge of the Arabah and descended into the Arabah. 19The boundary passed on to the northern flank of Beth-hoglah, and the boundary ended at the northern tongue of the Dead Sea, at the southern end of the Jordan. That was the southern boundary. 20On their eastern rim, finally, the Jordan was their boundary. That was the portion of the Benjaminites, by their clans, according to its boundaries on all sides.

21And the towns of the tribe of the Benjaminites, by its clans, were: Jericho, Beth-hoglah, Emek-keziz, 22Beth-arabah, Zemaraim, Bethel, 23Avvim, Parah, Ophrah, 24Chephar-ammonah, Ophni, and Geba—12 towns, with their villages. 25Also Gibeon, Ramah, Beeroth, 26Mizpeh, Chephirah, Mozah, 27Rekem, Irpeel, Taralah, 28Zela, Eleph, and Jebusb—that is, Jerusalem—Gibeath [and] Kiriath:c 14 towns, with their villages. That was the portion of the Benjaminites, by their clans.

19

The second lot fell to Simeon. The portion of the tribe of the Simeonites, by their clans, lay inside the portion of the Judites. 2Their portion comprised: Beer-sheba—or Sheba—Moladah, 3Hazar-shual, Balah, Ezem, 4Eltolad, Bethul,a Hormah, 5Ziklag, Beth-marcaboth, Hazarsu-sah, 6b-Beth-lebaoth, and Sharuhen-b—13 towns, with their villages. 7Ain, Rimmon, Ether, and Ashan: 4 towns, with their villages—8together with all the villages in the vicinity of those towns, down to Baalath-beer [and] Ramath-negeb. That was the portion of the tribe of the Simeonites, by their clans. 9The portion of the Simeonites was part of the territory of

---

a Emendation yields "eastward."
b Heb. "the Jebusite."
c Emendation yields "and Kiriath-jearim."

a 15.30 reads "Chesil."
b-b 15.32 reads "Shilhim."

the Judites; since the share of the Judites was larger than they needed, the Simeonites received a portion inside their portion.

10 The third lot emerged for the Zebulunites, by their clans. The boundary of their portion: Starting at Sarid, 11 their boundary[c] ascended westward to Maralah, touching Dabbesheth and touching the wadi alongside Jokneam. 12 And it also ran from Sarid along the eastern side, where the sun rises, past the territory of Chisloth-tabor and on to Daberath and ascended to Japhia. 13 From there it ran [back] to the east, toward the sunrise, to Gath-hepher, to Eth-kazin, and on to Rimmon, where it curved to Neah. 14 Then it turned—that is, the boundary on the north—to Hannathon. Its extreme limits[d] were the Valley of Iphtah-el, 15 Kattath, Nahalal, Shimron, Idalah, and Bethlehem: 12 towns, with their villages. 16 That was the portion of the Zebulunites by their clans—those towns, with their villages.

17 The fourth lot fell to Issachar, the Issacharites by their clans. 18 Their territory comprised: Jezreel, Chesulloth, Shunem, 19 Hapharaim, Shion, Anaharath, 20 Rabbith, Kishion, Ebez, 21 Remeth, En-gannim, En-haddah, and Beth-pazzez. 22 The boundary touched Tabor, Shahazimah, and Beth-shemesh; and their boundary ran to the Jordan: 16 towns, with their villages. 23 That was the portion of the tribe of the Issacharites, by their clans—the towns with their villages.

24 The fifth lot fell to the tribe of the Asherites, by their clans. 25 Their boundary[c] ran along Helkath, Hali, Beten, Achshaph, 26 Allammelech, Amad, and Mishal; and it touched Carmel on the west, and Shihor-libnath. 27 It also ran[e] along the east side to Beth-dagon, and touched Zebulun and the Valley of Iphtah-el to the north, [as also] Beth-emek and Neiel; [f-]then it ran to Cabul on the north,[-f] 28 Ebron,[g] Rehob, Hammon, and Kanah, up to Great Sidon. 29 The boundary turned to Ramah and on to the fortified city of Tyre; then the boundary turned to Hosah [f-]and it ran on westward to Mehebel,[-f] Achzib, 30 Ummah, Aphek, and Rehob: 22 towns, with their villages. 31 That was the portion of the tribe of the Asherites, by their clans—those towns, with their villages.

32 The sixth lot fell to the Naphtalites, the Naphtalites by their clans. 33[h] Their boundary ran from Heleph, Elon-bezaanannim, Adami-nekeb, and Jabneel to Lakkum, and it ended at the Jordan. 34 The boundary then turned westward to Aznoth-tabor and ran from there to Hukok. It touched Zebulun on the south, and it touched Asher on the west, and Judah at the Jordan on the east. 35 Its fortified towns were Ziddim, Zer, Hammath,

---

c *I.e., the southern one.*

d *I.e., the northwest corner, opposite the starting point, Sarid.*

e *I.e., from Helkath, v. 25.*

f-f *Meaning of Heb. uncertain.*

g *Some Heb. mss., as well as Josh. 21.30 and 1 Chron. 6.59, read "Abdon."*

h *The geography of vv. 33–35 is unclear in part.*

Rakkath, Chinnereth, ³⁶Adamah, Ramah, Hazor, ³⁷Kedesh, Edrei, En-hazor, ³⁸Iron, Migdal-el, Horem, Beth-anath, and Beth-shemesh: 19 towns, with their villages. ³⁹That was the portion of the tribe of the Naphtalites, by their clans—the towns, with their villages.

⁴⁰The seventh lot fell to the tribe of the Danites, by their clans. ⁴¹Their allotted territory comprised: Zorah, Eshtaol, Ir-shemesh, ⁴²Shaalabbin, Aijalon, Ithlah, ⁴³Elon, Timnah, Ekron, ⁴⁴Eltekeh, Gibbethon, Baalath, ⁴⁵Jehud, Bene-berak, Gath-rimmon, ⁴⁶Me-jarkon, and Rakkon, at the bor-der near Joppa. ⁴⁷But the territory of the Danites slipped from their grasp. So the Danites migrated and made war on Leshem.ⁱ They captured it and put it to the sword; they took possession of it and settled in it. And they changed the name of Leshem to Dan, after their ancestor Dan. ⁴⁸That was the portion of the tribe of the Danites, by their clans—those towns, with their villages.

⁴⁹When they had finished allotting the land by its boundaries, the Is-raelites gave a portion in their midst to Joshua son of Nun. ⁵⁰At the command of the LORD they gave him the town that he asked for, Tim-nath-serah in the hill country of Ephraim; he fortified the town and settled in it.

⁵¹These are the portions assigned by lot to the tribes of Israel by the priest Eleazar, Joshua son of Nun, and the heads of the ancestral houses, before the LORD at Shiloh, at the entrance of the Tent of Meeting.

20

When they had finished dividing the land, ¹the LORD said to Joshua: ²"Speak to the Israelites: Designate the cities of refuge—about which I commanded you through Moses—³to which a manslayer who kills a person by mistake, unintentionally, may flee. They shall serve you as a refuge from the blood avenger. ⁴He shall flee to one of those cities, present himself at the entrance to the city gate, and plead his case before the elders of that city; and they shall admit him into the city and give him a place in which to live among them. ⁵Should the blood avenger pursue him, they shall not hand the manslayer over to him, since he killed the other person without intent and had not been his enemy in the past. ⁶He shall live in that city until he can stand trial before the assembly, [and remain there] until the death of the high priest who is in office at that time. Thereafter, the manslayer may go back to his home in his own town, to the town from which he fled."

ⁱ *Called Laish in Judg. 18.7 ff.*

7So they set aside Kedesh in the hill country of Naphtali in Galilee, Shechem in the hill country of Ephraim, and Kiriath-arba—that is, Hebron—in the hill country of Judah. 8And across the Jordan, east of Jericho, they assigned Bezer in the wilderness, in the Tableland, from the tribe of Reuben; Ramoth in Gilead from the tribe of Gad; and Golan in Bashan from the tribe of Manasseh. 9Those were the towns designated[a] for all the Israelites and for aliens residing among them, to which anyone who killed a person unintentionally might flee, and not die by the hand of the blood avenger before standing trial by the assembly.

21 The heads of the ancestral houses of the Levites approached the priest Eleazer, Joshua son of Nun, and the heads of the ancestral houses of the Israelite tribes, 2and spoke to them at Shiloh in the land of Canaan, as follows: "The LORD commanded through Moses that we be given towns to live in, along with their pastures for our livestock." 3So the Israelites, in accordance with the LORD's command, assigned to the Levites, out of their own portions, the following towns with their pastures:

4The [first] lot among the Levites fell to the Kohathite clans. To the descendants of the priest Aaron, there fell by lot 13 towns from the tribe of Judah, the tribe of Simeon, and the tribe of Benjamin; 5and to the remaining Kohathites [there fell] by lot 10 towns from the clans of the tribe of Ephraim, the tribe of Dan, and the half-tribe of Manasseh.

6To the Gershonites [there fell] by lot 13 towns from the clans of the tribe of Issachar, the tribe of Asher, the tribe of Naphtali, and the half-tribe of Manasseh in Bashan.

7[And] to the Merarites, by their clans—12 towns from the tribe of Reuben, the tribe of Gad, and the tribe of Zebulun. 8The Israelites assigned those towns with their pastures by lot to the Levites—as the LORD had commanded through Moses.

9From the tribe of the Judites and the tribe of the Simeonites were assigned the following towns, which will be listed by name; 10they went to the descendants of Aaron among the Kohathite clans of the Levites, for the first lot had fallen to them. 11To them were assigned in the hill country of Judah Kiriath-arba—that is, Hebron—together with the pastures around it. [Arba was] the father of the Anokites.[a] 12They gave the fields and the villages of the town to Caleb son of Jephunneh as his

---

a *Meaning of Heb. uncertain.*

a *Elsewhere Anakites; cf. Num. 13.22; Deut. 9.2.*

holding. 13But to the descendants of Aaron the priest they assigned Hebron—the city of refuge for manslayers—together with its pastures, Libnah with its pastures, 14Jattir with its pastures, Eshtemoa with its pastures, 15Holon with its pastures, Debir with its pastures, 16Ain with its pastures, Juttah with its pastures, and Beth-shemesh with its pastures—9 towns from those two tribes. 17And from the tribe of Benjamin: Gibeon with its pastures, Geba with its pastures, 18Anathoth with its pastures, and Almon with its pastures—4 towns. 19All the towns of the descendants of the priest Aaron, 13 towns with their pastures.

20bAs for the other clans of the Kohathites, the remaining Levites descended from Kohath, the towns in their lot were: From the tribe of Ephraim 21they were given, in the hill country of Ephraim, Shechem—the city of refuge for manslayers—with its pastures, Gezer with its pastures, 22Kibzaim with its pastures, and Beth-horon with its pastures—4 towns. 23From the tribe of Dan, Elteke with its pastures, Gibbethon with its pastures, 24Aijalon with its pastures, and Gath-rimmon with its pastures—4 towns. 25And from the half-tribe of Manasseh, Taanach with its pastures, and Gath-rimmon with its pastures—2 towns. 26All the towns for the remaining clans of the Kohathites came to 10, with their pastures.

27To the Gershonites of the levitical clans: From the half-tribe of Manasseh, Golan in Bashan—the city of refuge for manslayers—with its pastures, and Beeshterah with its pastures—2 towns. 28From the tribe of Issachar: Kishion with its pastures, Dobrath with its pastures, 29Jarmuth with its pastures, and En-gannim with its pastures—4 towns. 30From the tribe of Asher: Mishal with its pastures, Abdon with its pastures, 31Helkath with its pastures, and Rehob with its pastures—4 towns. 32From the tribe of Naphtali, Kedesh in Galilee—the city of refuge for manslayers—with its pastures, Hammoth-dor with its pastures, and Kartan with its pastures—3 towns. 33All the towns of the Gershonites, by their clans, came to 13 towns, with their pastures.

34To the remaining Levites, the clans of the Merarites: From the tribe of Zebulun, Jokneam with its pastures, Kartah with its pastures, 35Dimnah with its pastures, and Nahalal with its pastures—4 towns.c 36From the tribe of Gad, Ramoth in Gilead—the city of refuge for manslayers—with its pastures, Mahanaim with its pastures, 37Heshbon with its pastures, and Jazer with its pastures—4 towns in all. 38All the towns which went by lot to the Merarites, by their clans—the rest of the levitical clans—came to 12 towns. 39All the towns of the Levites within the holdings of

b *Explicating v. 5.*
c *Some mss. and editions add the following (cf. 1 Chron. 6.63–64): "And from the tribe of Reuben: Bezer with its pastures, Jahaz with its pastures, Kedemoth with its pastures, and Mephaath with its pastures—4 towns."*

the Israelites came to 48 towns, with their pastures. [40d]Thus those towns were assigned, every town with its surrounding pasture; and so it was with all those towns.

[41]The LORD gave to Israel the whole country which He had sworn to their fathers that He would assign to them; they took possession of it and settled in it. [42]The LORD gave them rest on all sides, just as He had promised to their fathers on oath. Not one man of all their enemies withstood them; the LORD delivered all their enemies into their hands. [43]Not one of the good things which the LORD had promised to the House of Israel was lacking. Everything was fulfilled.

22 Then Joshua summoned the Reubenites, the Gadites, and the half-tribe of Manasseh, [2]and said to them, "You have observed all that Moses the servant of the LORD commanded you, and have obeyed me in everything that I commanded you. [3]You have not forsaken your kinsmen through the long years down to this day, but have faithfully observed the Instruction of the LORD your God. [4]Now the LORD your God has given your kinsmen rest, as He promised them. Therefore turn and go to your homes, to the land of your holdings beyond the Jordan that Moses the servant of the LORD assigned to you. [5]But be very careful to fulfill the Instruction and the Teaching that Moses the servant of the LORD enjoined upon you, to love the LORD your God and to walk in all His ways, and to keep His commandments and hold fast to Him, and to serve Him with all your heart and soul." [6]Then Joshua blessed them and dismissed them, and they went to their homes.

[7]To the one half-tribe of Manasseh Moses had assigned territory in Bashan, and to the other Joshua assigned [territory] on the west side of the Jordan, with their kinsmen.[a]

Furthermore, when Joshua sent them[b] off to their homes, he blessed them [8]and said to them, "Return to your homes with great wealth—with very much livestock, with silver and gold, with copper and iron, and with a great quantity of clothing. Share the spoil of your enemies with your kinsmen." [9]So the Reubenites, the Gadites, and the half-tribe of Manasseh left the Israelites at Shiloh, in the land of Canaan, and made their way back to the land of Gilead, the land of their own holding, which they had acquired by the command of the LORD through Moses. [10]When they came to the region of the Jordan in the land of Canaan, the Reubenites

d *Meaning of verse uncertain.*

a *I.e., the other nine tribes.*
b *I.e., the two and a half tribes.*

and the Gadites and the half-tribe of Manasseh built an altar there by the Jordan, a great conspicuous altar.

11A report reached the Israelites: "The Reubenites, the Gadites, and the half-tribe of Manasseh have built an altar opposite the land of Canaan, in the region of the Jordan, across from the Israelites." 12When the Israelites heard this, the whole community of the Israelites assembled at Shiloh to make war on them. 13But [first] the Israelites sent the priest Phinehas son of Eleazar to the Reubenites, the Gadites, and the half-tribe of Manasseh in the land of Gilead, 14accompanied by ten chieftains, one chieftain from each ancestral house of each of the tribes of Israel; they were every one of them heads of ancestral houses of the contingents of Israel. 15When they came to the Reubenites, the Gadites, and the half-tribe of Manasseh in the land of Gilead, they spoke to them as follows:

16"Thus said the whole community of the LORD: What is this treachery that you have committed this day against the God of Israel, turning away from the LORD, building yourselves an altar and rebelling this day against the LORD! 17Is the sin of Peor, which brought a plague upon the community of the LORD, such a small thing to us? We have not cleansed ourselves from it to this very day; 18and now you would turn away from the LORD! If you rebel against the LORD today, tomorrow He will be angry with the whole community of Israel. 19If it is because the land of your holding is unclean, cross over into the land of the LORD's own holding, where the Tabernacle of the LORD abides, and acquire holdings among us. But do not rebel against the LORD, and do not rebel against us by building for yourselves an altar other than the altar of the LORD our God. 20When Achan son of Zerah violated the proscription, anger struck the whole community of Israel; he was not the only one who perished for that sin."

21The Reubenites, the Gadites, and the half-tribe of Manasseh replied to the heads of the contingents of Israel: They said, 22"God, the LORD God! God, the LORD God! He knows, and Israel too shall know! If we acted in rebellion or in treachery against the LORD, do not vindicate us this day! 23If we built an altar to turn away from the LORD, if it was to offer burnt offerings or meal offerings upon it, or to present sacrifices of well-being upon it, may the LORD Himself demand [a reckoning]. 24We did this thing only out of our concern that, in time to come, your children might say to our children, 'What have you to do with the LORD, the God of Israel? 25The LORD has made the Jordan a boundary between you and us, O Reubenites and Gadites; you have no share in the LORD!' Thus your children might prevent our children from worshiping the LORD. 26So we decided to provide [a witness] for ourselves by building an altar—not for burnt offerings or [other] sacrifices, 27but as a witness between you and us, and between the generations to come—that we may perform the service of the LORD before Him^c with our burnt offerings, our sacrifices, and our offerings of well-being; and that your children should not say to our children in time to come, 'You have no share in the LORD.' 28We reasoned: should they speak thus to us and to our children in time to come, we would reply, 'See the replica of the LORD's altar,^c which our fathers made—not for burnt offerings or sacrifices, but as a witness between you and us.' 29Far be it from us to rebel against the LORD, or to turn away this day from the LORD and build an altar for burnt offerings, meal offerings, and sacrifices other than the altar of the LORD our God which stands before His Tabernacle."

30When the priest Phinehas and the chieftains of the community—the heads of the contingents of Israel—who were with him heard the explanation given by the Reubenites, the Gadites, and the Manassites, they approved. 31The priest Phinehas son of Eleazar said to the Reubenites, the Gadites, and the Manassites, "Now we know that the LORD is in our midst, since you have not committed such treachery against the LORD. You have indeed saved the Israelites from punishment by the LORD."

32Then the priest Phinehas son of Eleazar and the chieftains returned from the Reubenites and the Gadites in the land of Gilead to the Israelites in the land of Canaan, and gave them their report. 33The Israelites were pleased, and the Israelites praised God; and they spoke no more of going to war against them, to ravage the land in which the Reubenites and Gadites dwelt.

34The Reubenites and the Gadites named the altar ["Witness"], meaning, "It is a witness between us and them that the LORD is [our] God."

23 Much later, after the LORD had given Israel rest from all the enemies around them, and when Joshua was old and well advanced in years, 2Joshua summoned all Israel, their elders and commanders, their magistrates and officials, and said to them: "I have grown old and am advanced in years. 3You have seen all that the LORD your God has done to all those nations on your account, for it was the LORD your God who

---

^c *I.e., at Shiloh.*

fought for you. 4See, I have allotted to you, by your tribes, [the territory of] these nations that still remain, and that of all the nations that I have destroyed, from the Jordan to the Mediterranean Sea in the west. 5The LORD your God Himself will thrust them out on your account and drive them out to make way for you, and you shall possess their land as the LORD your God promised you.

6"But be most resolute to observe faithfully all that is written in the Book of the Teaching of Moses, without ever deviating from it to the right or to the left, 7and without intermingling with these nations that are left among you. Do not utter the names of their gods or swear by them; do not serve them or bow down to them. 8But hold fast to the LORD your God as you have done to this day.

9"The LORD has driven out great, powerful nations on your account, and not a man has withstood you to this day. 10A single man of you would put a thousand to flight, for the LORD your God Himself has been fighting for you, as He promised you. 11For your own sakes, therefore, be most mindful to love the LORD your God. 12For should you turn away and attach yourselves to the remnant of those nations—to those that are left among you—and intermarry with them, you joining them and they joining you, 13know for certain that the LORD your God will not continue to drive these nations out before you; they shall become a snare and a trap for you, a scourge to your sides and thorns in your eyes, until you perish from this good land that the LORD your God has given you.

14"I am now going the way of all the earth. Acknowledge with all your heart and soul that not one of the good things that the LORD your God promised you has failed to happen; they have all come true for you, not a single one has failed. 15But just as every good thing that the LORD your God promised you has been fulfilled for you, so the LORD can bring upon you every evil thing until He has wiped you off this good land that the LORD your God has given you. 16If you break the covenant that the LORD your God enjoined upon you, and go and serve other gods and bow down to them, then the LORD's anger will burn against you, and you shall quickly perish from the good land that He has given you."

24 Joshua assembled all the tribes of Israel at Schechem. He summoned Israel's elders and commanders, magistrates and officers; and they presented themselves before God. 2Then Joshua said to all the people,

"Thus said the LORD, the God of Israel: In olden times, your forefathers—Terah, father of Abraham and father of Nahor—lived beyond the Euphrates and worshiped other gods. ³But I took your father Abraham from beyond the Euphrates and led him through the whole land of Canaan and multiplied his offspring. I gave him Isaac, ⁴and to Isaac I gave Jacob and Esau. I gave Esau the hill country of Seir as his possession, while Jacob and his children went down to Egypt.

⁵"Then I sent Moses and Aaron, and I plagued Egypt with [the wonders] that I wrought in their midst, after which I freed you—⁶I freed your fathers—from Egypt, and you came to the Sea. But the Egyptians pursued your fathers to the Sea of Reeds with chariots and horsemen. ⁷They cried out to the LORD, and He put darkness between you and the Egyptians; then He brought the Sea upon them, and it covered them. Your own eyes saw what I did to the Egyptians.

"After you had lived a long time in the wilderness, ⁸I brought you to the land of the Amorites who lived beyond the Jordan. They gave battle to you, but I delivered them into your hands; I annihilated them for you, and you took possession of their land. ⁹Thereupon Balak son of Zippor, the king of Moab, made ready to attack Israel. He sent for Balaam son of Beor to curse you, ¹⁰but I refused to listen to Balaam; he had to bless you, and thus I saved you from him.

¹¹"Then you crossed the Jordan and you came to Jericho. The citizens of Jericho and the Amorites, Perizzites, Canaanites, Hittites, Girgashites, Hivites, and Jebusites fought you, but I delivered them into your hands. ¹²I sent a plagueᵃ ahead of you, and it drove them out before you—[just like] the two Amorite kings—not by your sword or by your bow. ¹³I have given you a land for which you did not labor and towns which you did not build, and you have settled in them; you are enjoying vineyards and olive groves which you did not plant.

¹⁴"Now, therefore, revere the LORD and serve Him with undivided loyalty; put away the gods that your forefathers served beyond the Euphrates and in Egypt, and serve the LORD. ¹⁵Or, if you are loath to serve the LORD, choose this day which ones you are going to serve—the gods that your forefathers served beyond the Euphrates, or those of the Amorites in whose land you are settled; but I and my household will serve the LORD."

¹⁶In reply, the people declared, "Far be it from us to forsake the LORD and serve other gods! ¹⁷For it was the LORD our God who brought us

---

ᵃ *See note at Exod. 23.28.*

and our fathers up from the land of Egypt, the house of bondage, and who wrought those wondrous signs before our very eyes, and guarded us all along the way that we traveled and among all the peoples through whose midst we passed. ¹⁸And then the LORD drove out before us all the peoples—the Amorites—that inhabited the country. We too will serve the LORD, for He is our God."

¹⁹Joshua, however, said to the people, "You will not be able to serve the LORD, for He is a holy God. He is a jealous God; He will not forgive your transgressions and your sins. ²⁰If you forsake the LORD and serve alien gods, He will turn and deal harshly with you and make an end of you, after having been gracious to you." ²¹But the people replied to Joshua, "No, we will serve the LORD!" ²²Thereupon Joshua said to the people, "You are witnesses against yourselves that you have by your own act chosen to serve the LORD." "Yes, we are!" they responded. ²³"Then put away the alien gods that you have among you and direct your hearts to the LORD, the God of Israel." ²⁴And the people declared to Joshua, "We will serve none but the LORD our God, and we will obey none but Him."

²⁵On that day at Shechem, Joshua made a covenant for the people and he made a fixed rule for them. ²⁶Joshua recorded all this in a book of divine instruction. He took a great stone and set it up at the foot of the oak in the sacred precinct of the LORD; ²⁷and Joshua said to all the people, "See, this very stone shall be a witness against us, for it heard all the words that the LORD spoke to us; it shall be a witness against you, lest you break faith with your God." ²⁸Joshua then dismissed the people to their allotted portions.

²⁹After these events, Joshua son of Nun, the servant of the LORD, died at the age of one hundred and ten years. ³⁰They buried him on his own property, at Timnath-serah in the hill country of Ephraim, north of Mount Gaash. ³¹Israel served the LORD during the lifetime of Joshua and the lifetime of the elders who lived on after Joshua, and who had experienced all the deeds that the LORD had wrought for Israel.

³²The bones of Joseph, which the Israelites had brought up from Egypt, were buried at Shechem, in the piece of ground which Jacob had bought for a hundred *kesitahs*[b] from the children of Hamor, Shechem's father, and which had become a heritage of the Josephites.

³³Eleazar son of Aaron also died, and they buried him on the hill of his son Phinehas, which had been assigned to him in the hill country of Ephraim.

b *See note at Gen. 33.19.*

שׁוֹפְטִים

JUDGES*

1 After the death of Joshua, the Israelites inquired of the LORD, "Which of us shall be the first to go up against the Canaanites and attack them?" ²The LORD replied, "Let [the tribe of] Judah go up. I now deliver the land into their hands." ³Judah then said to their brother-tribe Simeon, "Come up with us to our allotted territory and let us attack the Canaanites, and then we will go with you to your allotted territory." So Simeon joined them.

⁴When Judah advanced, the LORD delivered the Canaanites and the Perizzites into their hands, and they defeated ten thousand of them at Bezek. ⁵At Bezek, they encountered Adoni-bezek, engaged him in battle, and defeated the Canaanites and the Perizzites. ⁶Adoni-bezek fled, but they pursued him and captured him; and they cut off his thumbs and his big toes. ⁷And Adoni-bezek said, "Seventy kings, with thumbs and big toes cut off, used to pick up scraps under my table; as I have done, so God has requited me." They brought him to Jerusalem and he died there.

⁸The Judites attacked Jerusalem and captured it; they put it to the sword and set the city on fire. ⁹After that the Judites went down to attack the Canaanites who inhabited the hill country, the Negeb, and the Shephelah.

¹⁰The Judites marched against the Canaanites who dwelt in Hebron, and they defeated Sheshai, Ahiman, and Talmai. (The name of Hebron was formerly Kiriath-arba.) ¹¹From there they marched against the inhabitants of Debir (the name of Debir was formerly Kiriath-sepher). ¹²And Caleb announced, "I will give my daughter Achsah in marriage to the man who attacks and captures Kiriath-sepher." ¹³His younger kinsman, Othniel the Kenizzite,ᵃ captured it; and Caleb gave him his daughter Achsah in marriage. ¹⁴ᵇ⁻When she came [to him], she induced him to ask her father for some property. She dismounted from her donkey, and Caleb asked her, "What is the matter?" ¹⁵She replied, "Give me a present, for

---

* This is the traditional rendering of *shophetim*, which, however, in the text is rendered "chieftains." The corresponding verb *shaphaṭ* is usually translated not "judged" but "ruled" or "led."

ᵃ Cf. Josh. 14.6, 14.
ᵇ⁻ᵇ Cf. Josh. 15.18–19 and notes.

you have given me away as Negeb-land; give me springs of water." And Caleb gave her Upper and Lower Gulloth.-b

16The descendants of the Kenite, the father-in-law of Moses, went up with the Judites from the City of Palms to the wilderness of Judah; and they went and settled among the peoplec in the Negeb of Arad. 17And Judah with its brother-tribe Simeon went on and defeated the Canaanites who dwelt in Zephath. They proscribed it, and so the town was named Hormah.d 18And Judah capturede Gaza and its territory, Ashkelon and its territory, and Ekron and its territory.

19The LORD was with Judah, so that they took possession of the hill country; but they were not able to dispossess the inhabitants of the plain, for they had iron chariots. 20They gave Hebron to Caleb, as Moses had promised; and he drove the three Anakites out of there. 21The Benjamin-ites did not dispossess the Jebusite inhabitants of Jerusalem; so the Jebusites have dwelt with the Benjaminites in Jerusalem to this day.

22The House of Joseph, for their part, advanced against Bethel, and the LORD was with them. 23While the House of Joseph were scouting at Bethel (the name of the town was formerly Luz), 24their patrolsf saw a man leaving the town. They said to him, "Just show us how to get into the town, and we will treat you kindly." 25He showed them how to get into the town; they put the town to the sword, but they let the man and all his relatives go free. 26The man went to the Hittite country. He founded a city and named it Luz, and that has been its name to this day.

27Manasseh did not dispossess [the inhabitants of] Beth-shean and its dependencies, or [of] Taanach and its dependencies, or the inhabitants of Dor and its dependencies, or the inhabitants of Ibleam and its de-pendencies, or the inhabitants of Megiddo and its dependencies. The Canaanites persisted in dwelling in this region. 28And when Israel gained the upper hand, they subjected the Canaanites to forced labor; but they did not dispossess them. 29Nor did Ephraim dispossess the Canaanites who inhabited Gezer; so the Canaanites dwelt in their midst at Gezer.

30Zebulun did not dispossess the inhabitants of Kitron or the inhab-itants of Nahalol; so the Canaanites dwelt in their midst, but they were subjected to forced labor. 31Asher did not dispossess the inhabitants of Acco or the inhabitants of Sidon, Ahlab, Achzib, Helbah, Aphik, and Rehob. 32So the Asherites dwelt in the midst of the Canaanites, the in-

c *Meaning of Heb. uncertain. Emendation yields "Amalekites"; cf. 1 Sam. 15.6.*
d *I.e., "Proscribed." Cf. notes at Num. 21.2–3.*
e *Septuagint reads "But Judah did not capture Gaza. . . ." Gaza is in the coastal plain referred to in v. 19.*
f *Lit. "watchmen."*

habitants of the land, for they did not dispossess them. ³³Naphtali did not dispossess the inhabitants of Beth-shemesh or the inhabitants of Beth-anath. But they settled in the midst of the Canaanite inhabitants of the land, and the inhabitants of Beth-shemesh and Beth-anath had to perform forced labor for them.

³⁴The Amorites pressed the Danites into the hill country; they would not let them come down to the plain. ³⁵The Amorites also persisted in dwelling in Har-heres, in Aijalon, and in Shaalbim. But the hand of the House of Joseph bore heavily on them and they had to perform forced labor. ³⁶The territory of the Amorites^g extended from the Ascent of Ak-rabbim—from Sela—onward.

2 An angel of the LORD came up from Gilgal to Bochim and said, "I brought you up from Egypt and I took you into the land which I had promised on oath to your fathers. And I said, 'I will never break My covenant with you. ²And you, for your part, must make no covenant with the inhabitants of this land; you must tear down their altars.' But you have not obeyed Me—look what you have done! ³Therefore, I have re-solved not to drive them out before you; they shall become your oppres-sors,^a and their gods shall be a snare to you." ⁴As the angel of the LORD spoke these words to all the Israelites, the people broke into weeping. ⁵So they named that place Bochim,^b and they offered sacrifices there to the LORD.

⁶When Joshua dismissed the people, the Israelites went to their allotted territories and took possession of the land. ⁷The people served the LORD during the lifetime of Joshua and the lifetime of the older people who lived on after Joshua and who had witnessed all the marvelous deeds that the LORD had wrought for Israel. ⁸Joshua son of Nun, the servant of the LORD, died at the age of one hundred and ten years, ⁹and was buried on his own property, at Timnath-heres^c in the hill country of Ephraim, north of Mount Gaash. ¹⁰And all that generation were likewise gathered to their fathers.

Another generation arose after them, which had not experienced [the deliverance of] the LORD or the deeds that He had wrought for Israel. ¹¹And the Israelites did what was offensive to the LORD. They worshiped

---

g *Some Septuagint mss. read "Edomites."*

a *So Targum and other ancient versions. Meaning of Heb. uncertain.*

b *I.e., "weepers."*

c *Some mss. read "Timnath-serah"; cf. Josh. 24.30.*

the Baalim 12and forsook the LORD, the God of their fathers, who had brought them out of the land of Egypt. They followed other gods, from among the gods of the peoples around them, and bowed down to them; they provoked the LORD. 13They forsook the LORD and worshiped Baal and the Ashtaroth.d 14Then the LORD was incensed at Israel, and He handed them over to foese who plundered them. He surrendered them to their enemies on all sides, and they could no longer hold their own against their enemies. 15In all their campaigns, the hand of the LORD was against them to their undoing, as the LORD had declared and as the LORD had sworn to them; and they were in great distress. 16Then the LORD raised up chieftains who delivered them from those who plundered them. 17But they did not heed their chieftains either; they went astray after other gods and bowed down to them. They were quick to turn aside from the way their fathers had followed in obedience to the commandments of the LORD; they did not do right. 18When the LORD raised up chieftains for them, the LORD would be with the chieftain and would save them from their enemies during the chieftain's lifetime; for the LORD would be moved to pity by their moanings because of those who oppressed and crushed them. 19But when the chieftain died, they would again act basely, even more than f-the preceding generation-f—following other gods, worshiping them, and bowing down to them; they omitted none of their practices and stubborn ways.

20Then the LORD became incensed against Israel, and He said, "Since that nation has transgressed the covenant that I enjoined upon their fathers and has not obeyed Me, 21I for My part will no longer drive out before them any of the nations that Joshua left when he died." 22For it was in order to test Israel by them—[to see] whether or not they would faithfully walk in the ways of the LORD, as their fathers had done—23that the LORD had left those nations, instead of driving them out at once, and had not delivered them into the hands of Joshua.

3 aThese are the nations that the LORD left so that He might test by them all the Israelites who had not known any of the wars of Canaan, 2so that succeeding generations of Israelites might be made to experience war—but only those who had not known the b-former wars:-b 3the five principalitiesc of the Philistines and all the Canaanites, Sidonians, and

---

d Canaanite female deities.
e Lit. "plunderers."
f-f Lit. "their fathers."

a The sentence structure of vv. 1–2 is uncertain.
b-b Lit. "them formerly."
c Lit. "lords."

Hivites who inhabited the hill country of the Lebanon from Mount Baal-hermon to Lebo-hamath.ᵈ ⁴These served as a means of testing Israel, to learn whether they would obey the commandments which the LORD had enjoined upon their fathers through Moses.

⁵The Israelites settled among the Canaanites, Hittites, Amorites, Perizzites, Hivites, and Jebusites; ⁶they took their daughters to wife and gave their own daughters to their sons, and they worshiped their gods. ⁷The Israelites did what was offensive to the LORD; they ignored the LORD their God and worshiped the Baalim and the Asheroth. ⁸The LORD became incensed at Israel and surrendered them to King Cushan-rishathaim of Aram-naharaim; and the Israelites were subject to Cushan-rishathaim for eight years. ⁹The Israelites cried out to the LORD, and the LORD raised a champion for the Israelites to deliver them: Othniel the Kenizzite, a younger kinsman of Caleb. ¹⁰The spirit of the LORD descended upon him and he became Israel's chieftain. He went out to war, and the LORD delivered King Cushan-rishathaim of Aram into his hands. He prevailed over Cushan-rishathaim, ¹¹and the land had peace for forty years.

When Othniel the Kenizzite died, ¹²the Israelites again did what was offensive to the LORD. And because they did what was offensive to the LORD, the LORD let King Eglon of Moab prevail over Israel. ¹³[Eglon] brought the Ammonites and the Amalekites together under his command, and went and defeated Israel and occupied the City of Palms. ¹⁴The Israelites were subject to King Eglon of Moab for eighteen years.

¹⁵Then the Israelites cried out to the LORD, and the LORD raised up a champion for them: the Benjaminite Ehud son of Gera, a left-handed man. It happened that the Israelites sent tribute to King Eglon of Moab through him. ¹⁶So Ehud made for himself a two-edged dagger, a *gomed* in length, which he girded on his right side under his cloak. ¹⁷He presented the tribute to King Eglon of Moab. Now Eglon was a very stout man. ¹⁸When [Ehud] had finished presenting the tribute, he dismissed the people who had conveyed the tribute. ¹⁹But he himself returned from Pesilim, near Gilgal, and said, "Your Majesty, I have a secret message for you." [Eglon] thereupon commanded, "Silence!" So all those in attendance left his presence; ²⁰and when Ehud approached him, he was sitting alone in his cool upper chamber. Ehud said, "I have a message for you from God"; whereupon he rose from his seat. ²¹Reaching with his left hand, Ehud drew the dagger from his right side and drove it into [Eglon's]ᵉ

ᵈ *See note at Num. 13.21.*
ᵉ *Heb. "his."*

belly. 22The fat closed over the blade and the hilt went in after the blade—for he did not pull the dagger out of his belly—and the filth[f] came out.

23Stepping out into the vestibule,[f] Ehud shut the doors of the upper chamber on him and locked them. 24After he left, the courtiers returned. When they saw that the doors of the upper chamber were locked, they thought, "He must be relieving himself in the cool chamber." 25They waited a long time; and when he did not open the doors of the chamber, they took the key and opened them—and there their master was lying dead on the floor! 26But Ehud had made good his escape while they delayed; he had passed Pesilim and escaped to Seirah. 27When he got there, he had the ram's horn sounded through the hill country of Ephraim, and all the Israelites descended with him from the hill country; and he took the lead. 28"Follow me closely," he said, "for the LORD has delivered your enemies, the Moabites, into your hands." They followed him down and seized the fords of the Jordan against the Moabites; they let no one cross. 29On that occasion they slew about 10,000 Moabites; they were all robust and brave men, yet not one of them escaped. 30On that day, Moab submitted to Israel; and the land was tranquil for eighty years.

31After him came Shamgar [g]son of Anath,[g] who slew six hundred Philistines with an oxgoad. He too was a champion of Israel.

4 The Israelites again did what was offensive to the LORD—Ehud now being dead. 2And the LORD surrendered them to King Jabin of Canaan, who reigned in Hazor. His army commander was Sisera, whose base was Harosheth-goiim. 3The Israelites cried out to the LORD; for he had nine hundred iron chariots, and he had oppressed Israel ruthlessly for twenty years.

4Deborah, wife of Lappidoth, was a prophetess; she led Israel at that time. 5She used to sit under the Palm of Deborah, between Ramah and Bethel in the hill country of Ephraim, and the Israelites would come to her for decisions.

6She summoned Barak son of Abinoam, of Kedesh in Naphtali, and said to him, "The LORD, the God of Israel, has commanded: Go, march up to Mount Tabor, and take with you ten thousand men of Naphtali and Zebulun. 7And I will draw Sisera, Jabin's army commander, with his chariots and his troops, toward you up to the Wadi Kishon; and I will deliver him into your hands." 8But Barak said to her, "If you will go with

f Meaning of Heb. uncertain.
g-g Or "the Beth-anathite."

me, I will go; if not, I will not go." 9"Very well, I will go with you," she answered. "However, there will be no glory for you in the course you are taking, for then the LORD will deliver Sisera into the hands of a woman." So Deborah went with Barak to Kedesh. 10Barak then mustered Zebulun and Naphtali at Kedesh; ten thousand men marched up a-after him;-a and Deborah also went up with him.

11Now Heber the Kenite had separated b-from the other Kenites,-b descendants of Hobab, father-in-law of Moses, and had pitched his tent at Elon-bezaanannim, which is near Kedesh.

12Sisera was informed that Barak son of Abinoam had gone up to Mount Tabor. 13So Sisera ordered all his chariots—nine hundred iron chariots—and all the troops he had to move from Harosheth-goiim to the Wadi Kishon. 14Then Deborah said to Barak, "Up! This is the day on which the LORD will deliver Sisera into your hands: the LORD is marching before you." Barak charged down Mount Tabor, followed by the ten thousand men, 15and the LORD threw Sisera and all his chariots and army into a panic c-before the onslaught of Barak.-c Sisera leaped from his chariot and fled on foot 16as Barak pursued the chariots and the soldiers as far as Harosheth-goiim. All of Sisera's soldiers fell by the sword; not a man was left.

17Sisera, meanwhile, had fled on foot to the tent of Jael, wife of Heber the Kenite; for there was friendship between King Jabin of Hazor and the family of Heber the Kenite. 18Jael came out to greet Sisera and said to him, "Come in, my lord, come in here, do not be afraid." So he entered her tent, and she covered him with a blanket. 19He said to her, "Please let me have some water; I am thirsty." She opened a skin of milk and gave him some to drink; and she covered him again. 20He said to her, "Stand at the entrance of the tent. If anybody comes and asks you if there is anybody here, say 'No.'" 21Then Jael wife of Heber took a tent pin and grasped the mallet. When he was fast asleep from exhaustion, she approached him stealthily and drove the pin through his temple till it went down to the ground. Thus he died.

22Now Barak appeared in pursuit of Sisera. Jael went out to greet him and said, "Come, I will show you the man you are looking for." He went inside with her, and there Sisera was lying dead, with the pin in his temple.

23On that day God subdued King Jabin of Hazor before the Israelites. 24The hand of the Israelites bore harder and harder on King Jabin of Canaan, until they destroyed King Jabin of Canaan.

a-a *Lit. "at his feet."*
b-b *Lit. "from Cain"; cf. 1.16.*
c-c *Lit. "at the edge of the sword before Barak."*

5
On that day Deborah and Barak son of Abinoam sang:

2a When b-locks go untrimmed-b in Israel,
When people dedicate themselves—
Bless the LORD!

3 Hear, O kings! Give ear, O potentates!
I will sing, will sing to the LORD,
Will hymn the LORD, the God of Israel.

4 O LORD, when You came forth from Seir,
Advanced from the country of Edom,
The earth trembled;
The heavens dripped,
Yea, the clouds dripped water,
5 The mountains quaked c—
Before the LORD, Him of Sinai,
Before the LORD, God of Israel.

6 In the days of Shamgar d-son of Anath,-d
In the days of Jael, caravans e ceased,
And wayfarers went
By roundabout paths.
7 Deliverance ceased,
Ceased in Israel,
Till you f arose, O Deborah,
Arose, O mother, in Israel!
8 When they chose new gods,
g-Was there a fighter then in the gates?-g
No shield or spear was seen
Among forty thousand in Israel!

9 My heart is with Israel's leaders,
With the dedicated of the people—
Bless the LORD!
10 You riders on tawny she-asses,
You who sit on saddle rugs,

---

a *In many parts of this poem the meaning is uncertain.*
b-b *Apparently an expression of dedication; cf. Num. 6.5.*
c *Taking* nazelu *as a by-form of* nazollu; *cf. Targum.*
d-d *Or "the Beth-anathite."*
e *Or "roads."*
f *Heb.* qamti, *archaic second-person singular feminine.*
g-g *Meaning of Heb. uncertain; others "then was war in the gates."*

And you wayfarers, declare it!
¹¹Louder than the ʰ⁻sound of archers,⁻ʰ
There among the watering places
Let them chant the gracious acts of the LORD,
His gracious deliverance of Israel.
Then did the people of the LORD
March down to the gates!
¹²Awake, awake, O Deborah!
Awake, awake, strike up the chant!
Arise, O Barak;
Take your captives, O son of Abinoam!

¹³Then was the remnant made victor over the mighty,
The LORD's peopleⁱ won my victory over the warriors.

¹⁴From Ephraim came they whose roots are in Amalek;
After you, your kin Benjamin;
From Machir came down leaders,
From Zebulun such as hold the marshal's staff.
¹⁵And Issachar's chiefs were with Deborah;
As Barak, so was Issachar—
Rushing after him into the valley.

Among the clans of Reuben
Were great decisions of heart.
¹⁶Why then did you stay among the sheepfolds
And listen as they pipe for the flocks?
Among the clans of Reuben
Were great searchings of heart!
¹⁷Gilead tarried beyond the Jordan;
And Dan—why did he linger ʲ⁻by the ships?⁻ʲ
Asher remained at the seacoast
And tarried at his landings.
¹⁸Zebulun is a people ᵏ⁻that mocked at death,⁻ᵏ
Naphtali—on the open heights.

¹⁹Then the kings came, they fought:
The kings of Canaan fought

ʰ⁻ʰ Or "thunder peals"; meaning of Heb. uncertain.
ⁱ Reading 'am (with pathaḥ) Adonai; so many Heb. mss.
ʲ⁻ʲ Or "at Onioth," a presumed designation of Dan's region.
ᵏ⁻ᵏ Lit. "belittled its life to die."

At Taanach, by Megiddo's waters—
They got no spoil of silver.
[20]The stars fought from heaven,
From their courses they fought against Sisera.
[21]The torrent Kishon swept them[l] away,
The raging torrent, the torrent Kishon.

March on, my soul, with courage!

[22]Then the horses' hoofs pounded
m-As headlong galloped the steeds.-m
[23]"Curse Meroz!" said the angel of the LORD.
"Bitterly curse its inhabitants,
Because they came not to the aid of the LORD,
To the aid of the LORD among[n] the warriors."

[24]Most blessed of women be Jael,
Wife of Heber the Kenite,
Most blessed of women in tents.
[25]He asked for water, she offered milk;
In a princely bowl she brought him curds.
[26]Her [left] hand reached for the tent pin,
Her right for the workmen's hammer.
She struck Sisera, crushed his head,
Smashed and pierced his temple.
[27]At her feet he sank, lay outstretched,
At her feet he sank, lay still;
Where he sank, there he lay—destroyed.

[28]Through the window peered Sisera's mother,
Behind the lattice she whined:[o]
"Why is his chariot so long in coming?
Why so late the clatter of his wheels?"
[29]The wisest of her ladies give answer;
She, too, replies to herself:
[30]"They must be dividing the spoil they have found:
A damsel or two for each man,

---

l *I.e., the kings of Canaan (v. 19).*
m-m *Lit. "From the gallopings, the gallopings of his steeds."*
n *Or "against."*
o *Or "gazed"; meaning of Heb. uncertain.*

Spoil of dyed cloths for Sisera,
Spoil of embroidered cloths,
A couple of embroidered cloths
Round every neck as spoil."

31So may all Your enemies perish, O LORD!
But may His friends be as the sun rising in might!

And the land was tranquil forty years.

6 Then the Israelites did what was offensive to the LORD, and the LORD delivered them into the hands of the Midianites for seven years. 2The hand of the Midianites prevailed over Israel; and because of Midian, the Israelites a-provided themselves with refuges in the caves and strongholds of the mountains.-a 3After the Israelites had done their sowing, Midian, Amalek, and the Kedemites would come up and raid them; 4they would attack them, destroyb the produce of the land all the way to Gaza, and leave no means of sustenance in Israel, not a sheep or an ox or an ass. 5For they would come up with their livestock and their tents, swarming as thick as locusts; they and their camels were innumerable. Thus they would invade the land and ravage it. 6Israel was reduced to utter misery by the Midianites, and the Israelites cried out to the LORD.

7When the Israelites cried to the LORD on account of Midian, 8the LORD sent a prophet to the Israelites who said to them, "Thus said the LORD, the God of Israel: I brought you up out of Egypt and freed you from the house of bondage. 9I rescued you from the Egyptians and from all your oppressors; I drove them out before you, and gave you their land. 10And I said to you, 'I the LORD am your God. You must not worship the gods of the Amorites in whose land you dwell.' But you did not obey Me."

11An angel of the LORD came and sat under the terebinth at Ophrah, which belonged to Joash the Abiezrite. His son Gideon was then beating out wheat inside a winepress in order to keep it safe from the Midianites. 12The angel of the LORD appeared to him and said to him, "The LORD is with you, valiant warrior!" 13Gideon said to him, "Please, my lord, if

---

a-a Meaning of Heb. uncertain.
b I.e., by grazing their livestock.

the LORD is with us, why has all this befallen us? Where are all His wondrous deeds about which our fathers told us, saying, 'Truly the LORD brought us up from Egypt'? Now the LORD has abandoned us and delivered us into the hands of Midian!" 14The LORD turned to him and said, "Go in this strength of yours and deliver Israel from the Midianites. I herewith make you My messenger." 15He said to Him, "Please, my lord, how can I deliver Israel? Why, my clan is the humblest in Manasseh, and I am the youngest in my father's household." 16The LORD replied, "I will be with you, and you shall defeat Midian to a man." 17And he said to Him, "If I have gained Your favor, give me a sign that it is You who are speaking to me: 18do not leave this place until I come back to You and bring out my offering and place it before You." And He answered, "I will stay until you return."

19So Gideon went in and prepared a kid, and [baked] unleavened bread from an ephah of flour. He put the meat in a basket and poured the broth into a pot, and he brought them out to Him under the terebinth. As he presented them, 20the angel of God said to him, "Take the meat and the unleavened bread, put them on yonder rock, and spill out the broth." He did so. 21The angel of the LORD held out the staff that he carried, and touched the meat and the unleavened bread with its tip. A fire sprang up from the rock and consumed the meat and the unleavened bread. And the angel of the LORD vanished from his sight. 22Then Gideon realized that it was an angel of the LORD; and Gideon said, "Alas, O Lord GOD! For I have seen an angel of the LORD face to face."

23But the LORD said to him, "All is well; have no fear, you shall not die." 24So Gideon built there an altar to the LORD and called it c-Adonai-shalom.-c To this day it stands in Ophrah of the Abiezrites.

25That night the LORD said to him: "Take the a-young bull-a belonging to your father and another bull seven years old; pull down the altar of Baal which belongs to your father, and cut down the sacred post which is beside it. 26Then build an altar to the LORD your God, on a-the level ground-a on top of this stronghold. Take the other bull and offer it as a burnt offering, using the wood of the sacred post that you have cut down." 27So Gideon took ten of his servants and did as the LORD had told him; but as he was afraid to do it by day, on account of his father's household and the townspeople, he did it by night. 28Early the next morning, the townspeople found that the altar of Baal had been torn down and the sacred post beside it had been cut down, and that the second bull

c-c *I.e., "My lord, 'All-is-well.' "*

had been offered on the newly built altar. [29]They said to one another, "Who did this thing?" Upon inquiry and investigation, they were told, "Gideon son of Joash did this thing!" [30]The townspeople said to Joash, "Bring out your son, for he must die: he has torn down the altar of Baal and cut down the sacred post beside it!" [31]But Joash said to all who had risen against him, "Do you have to contend for Baal? Do you have to vindicate him? Whoever fights his battles shall be dead by morning! If he is a god, let him fight his own battles, since it is his altar that has been torn down!" [32]That day they named him[d] Jerubbaal, meaning "Let Baal contend with him, since he tore down his altar."

[33]All Midian, Amalek, and the Kedemites joined forces; they crossed over and encamped in the Valley of Jezreel. [34]The spirit of the LORD enveloped Gideon; he sounded the horn, and the Abiezrites rallied behind him. [35]And he sent messengers throughout Manasseh, and they too rallied behind him. He then sent messengers through Asher, Zebulun, and Naphtali, and they came up to meet the Manassites.[e]

[36]And Gideon said to God, "If You really intend to deliver Israel through me as You have said—[37]here I place a fleece of wool on the threshing floor. If dew falls only on the fleece and all the ground remains dry, I shall know that You will deliver Israel through me, as You have said." [38]And that is what happened. Early the next day, he squeezed the fleece and wrung out the dew from the fleece, a bowlful of water. [39]Then Gideon said to God, "Do not be angry with me if I speak just once more. Let me make just one more test with the fleece: let the fleece alone be dry, while there is dew all over the ground." [40]God did so that night: only the fleece was dry, while there was dew all over the ground.

7 Early next day, Jerubbaal—that is, Gideon—and all the troops with him encamped above En-harod,[a] while the camp of Midian was in the plain to the north of him, at Gibeath-moreh.[b] [2]The LORD said to Gideon, "You have too many troops with you for Me to deliver Midian into their hands; Israel might claim for themselves the glory due to Me, thinking, 'Our own hand has brought us victory.' [3]Therefore, announce to the men, 'Let anybody who is timid and fearful turn back, [c-]as a bird flies from Mount Gilead.' "[-c] Thereupon, 22,000 of the troops turned back and 10,000 remained.

[4]"There are still too many troops," the LORD said to Gideon. "Take

---

[d] I.e., Gideon.
[e] Heb. "them."

[a] Or "the Spring of Harod."
[b] Or "the Hill of Moreh."
[c-c] Meaning of Heb. uncertain.

them down to the water and I will sift[d] them for you there. Anyone of whom I tell you, 'This one is to go with you,' that one shall go with you; and anyone of whom I tell you, 'This one is not to go with you,' that one shall not go." 5So he took the troops down to the water. Then the LORD said to Gideon, "Set apart all those who [c-]lap up the water with their tongues like dogs[-c] from all those who get down on their knees to drink." 6Now those who "lapped" the water into their mouths by hand numbered three hundred; all the rest of the troops got down on their knees to drink. 7Then the LORD said to Gideon, "I will deliver you and I will put Midian into your hands through the three hundred 'lappers'; let the rest of the troops go home." 8c-So [the lappers] took the provisions and horns that the other men had with them,-c and he sent the rest of the men of Israel back to their homes, retaining only the three hundred men.

The Midianite camp was below him, in the plain. 9That night the LORD said to him, "Come, attack[f] the camp, for I have delivered it into your hands. 10And if you are afraid to attack, first go down to the camp with your attendant Purah 11and listen to what they say; after that you will have the courage to attack the camp." So he went down with his attendant Purah to the outposts of the warriors who were in the camp.—12Now Midian, Amalek, and all the Kedemites were spread over the plain, as thick as locusts; and their camels were countless, as numerous as the sands on the seashore.—13Gideon came there just as one man was narrating a dream to another. "Listen," he was saying, "I had this dream: There was a commotion[c]—a loaf of barley bread was whirling through the Midianite camp. It came to a tent and struck it, and it fell; it turned it upside down, and the tent collapsed." 14To this the other responded, "That can only mean the sword of the Israelite Gideon son of Joash. God is delivering Midian and the entire camp into his hands."[g]

15When Gideon heard the dream told and interpreted, he bowed low. Returning to the camp of Israel, he shouted, "Come on! The LORD has delivered the Midianite camp into your hands!" 16He divided the three hundred men into three columns and equipped every man with a ram's horn and an empty jar, with a torch in each jar. 17"Watch me," he said, "and do the same. When I get to the outposts of the camp, do exactly as I do. 18When I and all those with me blow our horns, you too, all around the camp, will blow your horns and shout, 'For the LORD and for Gideon!' "

19Gideon and the hundred men with him arrived at the outposts of the

---

d Lit. "smelt."

c-c Actually, using their hands as a dog uses its tongue; see v. 6.

f Lit. "descend upon"; so in vv. 10 and 11.

g The loaf of bread symbolizes the agricultural Israelites; the tent, the nomadic Midianites.

camp, at the beginning of the middle watch, just after the sentries were posted. ^h-They sounded the horns and smashed the jars that they had with them,^-h 20and the three columns blew their horns and broke their jars. Holding the torches in their left hands and the horns for blowing in their right hands, they shouted, "A sword for the LORD and for Gideon!" 21They remained standing where they were, surrounding the camp; but the entire camp ran about yelling, and took to flight. 22For when the three hundred horns were sounded, the LORD turned every man's sword against his fellow, throughout the camp, and the entire host fled as far as Beth-shittah and on to Zererah—as far as the outskirts of Abel-meholah near Tabbath.

23And now the men of Israel from Naphtali and Asher and from all of Manasseh rallied for the pursuit of the Midianites. 24Gideon also sent messengers all through the hill country of Ephraim with this order: ^i"Go down ahead of the Midianites and seize their access to the water all along the Jordan down to Beth-barah." So all the men of Ephraim rallied and seized the waterside down to Beth-barah by the Jordan. 25They pursued the Midianites and captured Midian's two generals, Oreb and Zeeb. They killed Oreb at the Rock of Oreb and they killed Zeeb at the Winepress of Zeeb; and they brought the heads of Oreb and Zeeb from the other side of the Jordan to Gideon.

8 And the men of Ephraim said to him, "Why did you do that to us—not calling us when you went to fight the Midianites?" And they rebuked him severely. 2But he answered them, "After all, what have I accomplished compared to you? Why, Ephraim's gleanings are better than Abiezer's vintage! 3God has delivered the Midianite generals Oreb and Zeeb into your hands, and what was I able to do compared to you?" And when he spoke in this fashion, their anger against him abated.

4Gideon came to the Jordan and crossed it. The three hundred men with him were famished, but still in pursuit. 5He said to the people of Succoth, "Please give some loaves of bread to the men who are following me, for they are famished, and I am pursuing Zebah and Zalmunna, the kings of Midian." 6But the officials of Succoth replied, ^a-"Are Zebah and Zalmunna already in your hands,^-a that we should give bread to your troops?" 7"I swear," declared Gideon, "when the LORD delivers Zebah and Zalmunna into my hands, I'll thresh^b your bodies upon desert thorns

---

h-h *Emendation yields "He sounded the horn and smashed the jar that he had with him."*
i *Meaning of rest of verse uncertain.*

a-a *Lit. "Is the palm of Zebah and Zalmunna in your hand."*
b *I.e., throw them naked in a bed of thorns and trample them; but exact meaning uncertain.*

and briers!" [8]From there he went up to Penuel and made the same request of them; but the people of Penuel gave him the same reply as the people of Succoth. [9]So he also threatened the people of Penuel: "When I come back safe, I'll tear down this tower!"

[10]Now Zebah and Zalmunna were at Karkor with their army of about 15,000; these were all that remained of the entire host of the Kedemites, for the slain numbered 120,000 fighting men.[c] [11]Gideon marched up the road of the tent dwellers, up to east of Nobah and Jogbehah, and routed the camp, which was off guard. [12]Zebah and Zalmunna took to flight, with Gideon[d] in pursuit. He captured Zebah and Zalmunna, the two kings of Midian, and threw the whole army into panic.

[13]On his way back from the battle at the Ascent of Heres, Gideon son of Joash [14]captured a boy from among the people of Succoth and interrogated him. The latter drew up for him a list of the officials and elders of Succoth, seventy-seven in number. [15]Then he came to the people of Succoth and said, "Here are Zebah and Zalmunna, about whom you mocked me, saying, [a-]'Are Zebah and Zalmunna already in your hands,[-a] that we should give your famished men bread?' " [16]And he took the elders of the city and, [bringing] desert thorns and briers, he punished[e] the people of Succoth with them. [17]As for Penuel, he tore down its tower and killed the townspeople.

[18]Then he asked Zebah and Zalmunna, "Those men you killed at Tabor, [f-]what were they like?"[-f] "They looked just like you," they replied, "like sons of a king." [19]"They were my brothers," he declared, "the sons of my mother. As the LORD lives, if you had spared them, I would not kill you." [20]And he commanded his oldest son Jether, "Go kill them!" But the boy did not draw his sword, for he was timid, being still a boy. [21]Then Zebah and Zalmunna said, "Come, you slay us; for strength comes with manhood." So Gideon went over and killed Zebah and Zalmunna, and he took the crescents that were on the necks of their camels.

[22]Then the men of Israel said to Gideon, "Rule over us—you, your son, and your grandson as well; for you have saved us from the Midianites." [23]But Gideon replied, "I will not rule over you myself, nor shall my son rule over you; the LORD alone shall rule over you." [24]And Gideon said to them, "I have a request to make of you: Each of you give me the earring he received as booty." (They[g] had golden earrings, for they were Ishmaelites.) [25]"Certainly!" they replied. And they spread out a cloth, and

---

[c] Lit. "men who drew the sword."

[d] Heb. "him."

[e] Meaning of Heb. uncertain; emendation yields "threshed"; cf. v. 7.

[f-f] Others "Where are they?"

[g] I.e., the Midianites. The author explains that the Midianites wore earrings like the Ishmaelites, who were better known to his contemporaries.

everyone threw onto it the earring he had received as booty. 26The weight of the golden earrings that he had requested came to 1,700 shekels of gold; this was in addition to the crescents and the pendants and the purple robes worn by the kings of Midian and in addition to the collars on the necks of their camels. 27Gideon made an ephod of h-this gold-h and set it up in his own town of Ophrah. There all Israel went astray after it, and it became a snare to Gideon and his household.

28Thus Midian submitted to the Israelites and did not raise its head again; and the land was tranquil for forty years in Gideon's time.

29So Jerubbaal son of Joash retired to his own house. 30Gideon had seventy sons of his own issue, for he had many wives. 31A son was also born to him by his concubine in Shechem, and he named him Abimelech. 32Gideon son of Joash died at a ripe old age, and was buried in the tomb of his father Joash at Ophrah of the Abiezrites.

33After Gideon died, the Israelites again went astray after the Baalim, and they adopted Baal-berith as a god. 34The Israelites gave no thought to the LORD their God, who saved them from all the enemies around them. 35Nor did they show loyalty to the house of Jerubbaal-Gideon in return for all the good that he had done for Israel.

9 Abimelech son of Jerubbaal went to his mother's brothers in Shechem and spoke to them and to the whole clan of his mother's family. He said, 2"Put this question to all the citizens of Shechem: Which is better for you, to be ruled by seventy men—by all the sons of Jerubbaal—or to be ruled by one man? And remember, I am your own a-flesh and blood."-a 3His mother's brothers said all this in his behalf to all the citizens of Shechem, and they were won over to Abimelech; for they thought, "He is our kinsman." 4They gave him seventy shekels from the temple of Baal-berith; and with this Abimelech hired some worthless and reckless fellows, and they followed him. 5Then he went to his father's house in Ophrah and killed his brothers, the sons of Jerubbaal, seventy men on one stone. Only Jotham, the youngest son of Jerubbaal, survived, because he went into hiding.

6All the citizens of Shechem and all Beth-millo convened, and they proclaimed Abimelech king at the terebinth of the pillarb at Shechem.

h-h Heb. "it."

a-a Lit. "bone and flesh."
b Meaning of Heb. uncertain.

7When Jotham was informed, he went and stood on top of Mount Gerizim and called out to them in a loud voice. "Citizens of Shechem!" he cried, "listen to me, that God may listen to you.

8"Once the trees went to anoint a king over themselves. They said to the olive tree, 'Reign over us.' 9But the olive tree replied, 'Have I, through whom God and men are honored, stopped yielding my rich oil, that I should go and wave above the trees?' 10So the trees said to the fig tree, 'You come and reign over us.' 11But the fig tree replied, 'Have I stopped yielding my sweetness, my delicious fruit, that I should go and wave above the trees?' 12So the trees said to the vine, 'You come and reign over us.' 13But the vine replied, 'Have I stopped yielding my new wine, which gladdens God and men, that I should go and wave above the trees?' 14Then all the trees said to the thornbush, 'You come and reign over us.' 15And the thornbush said to the trees, 'If you are acting honorably in anointing me king over you, come and take shelter in my shade; but if not, may fire issue from the thornbush and consume the cedars of Lebanon!'

16"Now then, if you acted honorably and loyally in making Abimelech king, if you have done right by Jerubbaal and his house and have requited him according to his deserts—17considering that my father fought for you and saved you from the Midianites at the risk of his life, 18and now you have turned on my father's household, killed his sons, seventy men on one stone, and set up Abimelech, the son of his handmaid, as king over the citizens of Shechem just because he is your kinsman—19if, I say, you have this day acted honorably and loyally toward Jerubbaal and his house, have joy in Abimelech and may he likewise have joy in you. 20But if not, may fire issue from Abimelech and consume the citizens of Shechem and Beth-millo, and may fire issue from the citizens of Shechem and Beth-millo and consume Abimelech!"

21With that, Jotham fled. He ran to Beer and stayed there, because of his brother Abimelech.

22Abimelech held sway over Israel for three years. 23Then God sent a spirit of discord between Abimelech and the citizens of Shechem, and the citizens of Shechem broke faith with Abimelech—24to the end that the crime committed against the seventy sons of Jerubbaal might be avenged, and their blood recoil upon their brother Abimelech, who had slain them, and upon the citizens of Shechem, who had abetted him in the slaying of his brothers. 25The citizens of Shechem planted ambuscades against him on the hilltops; and they robbed whoever passed by them on the road. Word of this reached Abimelech.

26Then Gaal son of Ebed and his companions came passing through Shechem, and the citizens of Shechem gave him their confidence. 27They went out into the fields, gathered and trod out the vintage of their vineyards, and made a festival. They entered the temple of their god, and as they ate and drank they reviled Abimelech. 28Gaal son of Ebed said, "Who is Abimelech and who are [we] Shechemites, that we should serve him? b-This same son of Jerubbaal and his lieutenant Zebul once served the men of Hamor, the father of Shechem;-b so why should we serve him? 29Oh, if only this people were under my command, I would get rid of Abimelech! Onec would challenge Abimelech, 'Fill up your ranks and come out here!' "

30When Zebul, the governor of the city, heard the words of Gaal son of Ebed, he was furious. 31He sent messages to Abimelech at Tormahd to say, "Gaal son of Ebed and his companions have come to Shechem and they are incitingb the city against you. 32Therefore, set out at night with the forces you have with you and conceal yourself in the fields. 33Early next morning, as the sun rises, advance on the city. He and his men will thereupon come out against you, and you will do to him whatever you find possible."

34Abimelech and all the men with him set out at night and disposed themselves against Shechem in four hiding places. 35When Gaal son of Ebed came out and stood at the entrance to the city gate, Abimelech and the army with him emerged from concealment. 36Gaal saw the army and said to Zebul, "That's an army marching down from the hilltops!" But Zebul said to him, "The shadows of the hills look to you like men." 37Gaal spoke up again, "Look, an army is marching down from Tabbur-erez, and another column is coming from the direction of Elon-meonenim." 38"Well," replied Zebul, "where is your boast, 'Who is Abimelech that we should serve him'? There is the army you sneered at; now go out and fight it!"

39So Gaal went out at the head of the citizens of Shechem and gave battle to Abimelech. 40But he had to flee before him, and Abimelech pursued him, and many fell slain, all the way to the entrance of the gate. 41Then Abimelech stayed in Arumah,e while Zebul expelled Gaal and his companions and kept them out of Shechem.

42The next day, when people went out into the fields, Abimelech was

c Septuagint reads "I."
d Called "Arumah" in v. 41.
e Cf. "Tormah" in v. 31.

informed. 43Taking the army, he divided it into three columns and lay in ambush in the fields; and when he saw the people coming out of the city, he pounced upon them and struck them down. 44While Abimelech and the column^f that followed him dashed ahead and took up a position at the entrance of the city gate, the other two columns rushed upon all that were in the open and struck them down. 45Abimelech fought against the city all that day. He captured the city and massacred the people in it; he razed the town and sowed it with salt.

46When all the citizens of the Tower of Shechem^g learned of this, they went into the tunnel^h of the temple of El-berith.^i 47When Abimelech was informed that all the citizens of the Tower of Shechem had gathered [there], 48Abimelech and all the troops he had with him went up on Mount Zalmon. Taking an ax^j in his hand, Abimelech lopped off a tree limb and lifted it onto his shoulder. Then he said to the troops that accompanied him, "What you saw me do—quick, do the same!" 49So each of the troops also lopped off a bough; then they marched behind Abimelech and laid them against the tunnel, and set fire to the tunnel over their heads. Thus all the people of the Tower of Shechem also perished, about a thousand men and women.

50Abimelech proceeded to Thebez; he encamped at Thebez and occupied it. 51Within the town was a fortified tower; and all the citizens of the town, men and women, took refuge there. They shut themselves in, and went up on the roof of the tower. 52Abimelech pressed forward to the tower and attacked it. He approached the door of the tower to set it on fire. 53But a woman dropped an upper millstone on Abimelech's head and cracked his skull. 54He immediately cried out to his attendant, his arms-bearer, "Draw your dagger and finish me off, that they may not say of me, 'A woman killed him!' " So his attendant stabbed him, and he died. 55When the men of Israel saw that Abimelech was dead, everyone went home.

56Thus God repaid Abimelech for the evil he had done to his father by slaying his seventy brothers; 57and God likewise repaid the men of Shechem for all their wickedness. And so the curse of Jotham son of Jerubbaal was fulfilled upon them.

10 After Abimelech, Tola son of Puah son of Dodo, a man of Issachar, arose to deliver Israel. He lived at Shamir in the hill country of Ephraim.

---

f Heb. "columns."
g Perhaps identical with Beth-millo of vv. 6 and 20.
h Cf. 1 Sam. 13.6; others "citadel."
i Called "Baal-berith" in v. 4.
j Heb. plural.

²He led Israel for twenty-three years; then he died and was buried at Shamir.

³After him arose Jair the Gileadite, and he led Israel for twenty-two years. (⁴He had thirty sons, who rode on thirty burros and owned thirty boroughsᵃ in the region of Gilead; these are called Havvoth-jairᵇ to this day.) ⁵Then Jair died and was buried at Kamon.

⁶The Israelites again did what was offensive to the LORD. They served the Baalim and the Ashtaroth, and the gods of Aram, the gods of Sidon, the gods of Moab, the gods of the Ammonites, and the gods of the Philistines; they forsook the LORD and did not serve Him. ⁷And the LORD, incensed with Israel, surrendered them to the Philistines and to the Ammonites. ⁸That year they battered and shattered the Israelites— forᶜ eighteen years—all the Israelites beyond the Jordan, in [what had been] the land of the Amorites in Gilead. ⁹The Ammonites also crossed the Jordan to make war on Judah, Benjamin, and the House of Ephraim. Israel was in great distress.

¹⁰Then the Israelites cried out to the LORD, "We stand guilty before You, for we have forsaken our God and served the Baalim." ¹¹But the LORD said to the Israelites, "[I have rescued you] from the Egyptians, from the Amorites, from the Ammonites, and from the Philistines. ¹²The Sidonians, Amalek, and Maonᵈ also oppressed you; and when you cried out to Me, I saved you from them. ¹³Yet you have forsaken Me and have served other gods. No, I will not deliver you again. ¹⁴Go cry to the gods you have chosen; let them deliver you in your time of distress!" ¹⁵But the Israelites implored the LORD: "We stand guilty. Do to us as You see fit; only save us this day!" ¹⁶They removed the alien gods from among them and served the LORD; and He could not bear the miseries of Israel.

¹⁷The Ammonites mustered and they encamped in Gilead; and the Israelites massed and they encamped at Mizpah. ¹⁸The troops—the officers of Gilead—said to one another, "Let the man who is the first to fight the Ammonites be chieftain over all the inhabitants of Gilead."

11 Jephthah the Gileadite was an able warrior, who was the son of a prostitute. Jephthah's father was Gilead; ²but Gilead also had sons by his wife, and when the wife's sons grew up, they drove Jephthah out. They said to him, "You shall have no share in our father's property, for you are the son of an outsider."ᵃ ³So Jephthah fled from his brothers and settled

---

ᵃ Imitating the pun in the Heb., which employs ᶜayarim first in the sense of "donkeys" and then in the sense of "towns."
ᵇ I.e., "the villages of Jair"; cf. Num. 32.41.
ᶜ Meaning of Heb. uncertain; perhaps "enough for" or "continuing for."
ᵈ Septuagint reads "Midian."

ᵃ Lit. "another woman."

in the Tob country. Men of low character gathered about Jephthah and went out raiding with him.

4Some time later, the Ammonites went to war against Israel. 5And when the Ammonites attacked Israel, the elders of Gilead went to bring Jephthah back from the Tob country. 6They said to Jephthah, "Come be our chief, so that we can fight the Ammonites." 7Jephthah replied to the elders of Gilead, "You are the very people who rejected me and drove me out of my father's house. How can you come to me now when you are in trouble?" 8The elders of Gilead said to Jephthah, "Honestly, we have now turned back to you. If you come with us and fight the Ammonites, you shall be our commander over all the inhabitants of Gilead." 9Jephthah said to the elders of Gilead, "[Very well,] if you bring me back to fight the Ammonites and the LORD delivers them to me, I am to be your commander." 10And the elders of Gilead answered Jepthah, "The LORD Himself shall be witness between us: we will do just as you have said."

11Jephthah went with the elders of Gilead, and the people made him their commander and chief. And Jephthah repeated all these terms before the LORD at Mizpah.

12Jephthah then sent messengers to the king of the Ammonites, saying, "What have you against me that you have come to make war on my country?" 13The king of the Ammonites replied to Jephthah's messengers, "When Israel came from Egypt, they seized the land which is mine, from the Arnon to the Jabbok as far as the Jordan. Now, then, restore it peaceably."

14Jephthah again sent messengers to the king of the Ammonites. 15He said to him, "Thus said Jephthah: Israel did not seize the land of Moab or the land of the Ammonites. 16When they left Egypt, Israel traveled through the wilderness to the Sea of Reeds and went on to Kadesh. 17Israel then sent messengers to the king of Edom, saying, 'Allow us to cross your country.' But the king of Edom would not consent. They also sent a mission to the king of Moab, and he refused. So Israel, after staying at Kadesh, 18traveled on through the wilderness, skirting the land of Edom and the land of Moab. They kept to the east of the land of Moab until they encamped on the other side of the Arnon; and, since Moab ends at the Arnon, they never entered Moabite territory.

19"Then Israel sent messengers to Sihon king of the Amorites, the king of Heshbon. Israel said to him, 'Allow us to cross through your country to our homeland.' ²⁰But Sihon would not trust Israel to pass through his territory. Sihon mustered all his troops, and they encamped at Jahaz; he engaged Israel in battle. ²¹But the LORD, the God of Israel, delivered Sihon and all his troops into Israel's hands, and they defeated them; and Israel took possession of all the land of the Amorites, the inhabitants of that land. ²²Thus they possessed all the territory of the Amorites from the Arnon to the Jabbok and from the wilderness to the Jordan.

²³"Now, then, the LORD, the God of Israel, dispossessed the Amorites before His people Israel; and should you possess their land? ²⁴Do you not hold what Chemosh your god gives you to possess? So we will hold on to everything that the LORD our God has given us to possess.

²⁵"Besides, are you any better than Balak son of Zippor, king of Moab? Did he start a quarrel with Israel or go to war with them?

²⁶"While Israel has been inhabiting Heshbon and its dependencies, and Aroer and its dependencies, and all the towns along the Arnon for three hundred years, why have you not tried to recover them all this time? ²⁷I have done you no wrong; yet you are doing me harm and making war on me. May the LORD, who judges, decide today between the Israelites and the Ammonites!"

²⁸But the king of the Ammonites paid no heed to the message that Jephthah sent him.

²⁹Then the spirit of the LORD came upon Jephthah. He marched through Gilead and Manasseh, passing Mizpeh of Gilead; and from Mizpeh of Gilead he crossed over [to] the Ammonites. ³⁰And Jephthah made the following vow to the LORD: "If you deliver the Ammonites into my hands, ³¹then whatever comes out of the door of my house to meet me on my safe return from the Ammonites shall be the LORD's and shall be offered by me as a burnt offering."

³²Jephthah crossed over to the Ammonites and attacked them, and the LORD delivered them into his hands. ³³He utterly routed them—from Aroer as far as Minnith, twenty towns—all the way to Abel-cheramim. So the Ammonites submitted to the Israelites.

³⁴When Jephthah arrived at his home in Mizpah, there was his daughter coming out to meet him, with timbrel and dance! She was an only child; he had no other son or daughter. ³⁵On seeing her, he rent his clothes and said, "Alas, daughter! You have brought me low; you have become my troubler! For I have ᵇ-uttered a vow-ᵇ to the LORD and I cannot retract."

---

b-b *Lit. "opened my mouth."*

³⁶"Father," she said, "you have uttered a vow to the LORD; do to me as you have vowed, seeing that the LORD has vindicated you against your enemies, the Ammonites." ³⁷She further said to her father, "Let this be done for me: let me be for two months, and I will go with my companions and lament^c upon the hills and there bewail my maidenhood." ³⁸"Go," he replied. He let her go for two months, and she and her companions went and bewailed her maidenhood upon the hills. ³⁹After two months' time, she returned to her father, and he did to her as he had vowed. She had never known a man. So it became a custom in Israel ⁴⁰for the maidens of Israel to go every year, for four days in the year, and chant dirges for the daughter of Jephthah the Gileadite.

12 The men of Ephraim mustered and crossed [the Jordan] to Zaphon. They said to Jephthah, "Why did you march to fight the Ammonites without calling us to go with you? We'll burn your house down over you!" ²Jephthah answered them, "I and my people were in a bitter conflict with the Ammonites; and I summoned you, but you did not save me from them. ³When I saw that you were no saviors, I risked my life and advanced against the Ammonites; and the LORD delivered them into my hands. Why have you come here now to fight against me?" ⁴And Jephthah gathered all the men of Gilead and fought the Ephraimites. The men of Gilead defeated the Ephraimites; for ^athey had said, "You Gileadites are nothing but fugitives from Ephraim—being in Manasseh is like being in Ephraim."^{-a} ⁵The Gileadites held the fords of the Jordan against the Ephraimites. And when any fugitive from Ephraim said, "Let me cross," the men of Gilead would ask him, "Are you an Ephraimite?"; if he said "No," ⁶they would say to him, "Then say *shibboleth*"; but he would say "*sibboleth*," not being able to pronounce it correctly. Thereupon they would seize him and slay him by the fords of the Jordan. Forty-two thousand Ephraimites fell at that time.

⁷Jephthah led Israel six years. Then Jephthah the Gileadite died and he was buried in one of the towns of Gilead.

⁸After him, Ibzan of Bethlehem^b led Israel. ⁹He had thirty sons, and he married off thirty daughters outside the clan and brought in thirty girls from outside the clan for his sons. He led Israel seven years. ¹⁰Then Ibzan died and was buried in Bethlehem.

---

^c Lit. "descend," i.e., with weeping; cf. Isa. 15.3.

^{a-a} Meaning of Heb. uncertain.
^b I.e., Bethlehem in Zebulun; cf. Josh. 19.15.

¹¹After him, Elon the Zebulunite led Israel; he led Israel for ten years. ¹²Then Elon the Zebulunite died and was buried in Aijalon, in the territory of Zebulun.

¹³After him, Abdon son of Hillel the Pirathonite led Israel. ¹⁴He had forty sons and thirty grandsons, who rode on seventy jackasses. He led Israel for eight years. ¹⁵Then Abdon son of Hillel the Pirathonite died. He was buried in Pirathon, in the territory of Ephraim, on the hill of the Amalekites.

13 The Israelites again did what was offensive to the LORD, and the LORD delivered them into the hands of the Philistines for forty years.

²There was a certain man from Zorah, of the stock of Dan, whose name was Manoah. His wife was barren and had borne no children. ³An angel of the LORD appeared to the woman and said to her, "You are barren and have borne no children; but you shall conceive and bear a son. ⁴Now be careful not to drink wine or other intoxicant, or to eat anything unclean. ⁵For you are going to conceive and bear a son; let no razor touch his head, for the boy is to be a nazirite to God from the womb on. He shall be the first to deliver Israel from the Philistines."

⁶The woman went and told her husband, "A man of God came to me; he looked like an angel of God, very frightening. I did not ask him where he was from, nor did he tell me his name. ⁷He said to me, 'You are going to conceive and bear a son. Drink no wine or other intoxicant, and eat nothing unclean, for the boy is to be a nazirite to God from the womb to the day of his death!' "

⁸Manoah pleaded with the LORD. "Oh, my Lord!" he said, "please let the man of God that You sent come to us again, and let him instruct us how to act with the child that is to be born." ⁹God heeded Manoah's plea, and the angel of God came to the woman again. She was sitting in the field and her husband Manoah was not with her. ¹⁰The woman ran in haste to tell her husband. She said to him, "The man who came to me before^a has just appeared to me." ¹¹Manoah promptly followed his wife. He came to the man and asked him: "Are you the man who spoke to my wife?" "Yes," he answered. ¹²Then Manoah said, "May your words soon come true! What rules shall be observed for the boy?" ¹³The angel of the LORD said to Manoah, "The woman must abstain from all the things against which I warned her. ¹⁴She must not eat anything that comes from

---

^a Lit. "in the day."

the grapevine, or drink wine or other intoxicant, or eat anything unclean. She must observe all that I commanded her.'"

15Manoah said to the angel of the LORD, "Let us detain you and prepare a kid for you." 16But the angel of the LORD said to Manoah, "If you detain me, I shall not eat your food; and if you present a burnt offering, offer it to the LORD."—For Manoah did not know that he was an angel of the LORD. 17So Manoah said to the angel of the LORD, "What is your name? We should like to honor you when your words come true." 18The angel said to him, "You must not ask for my name; it is unknowable!"

19Manoah took the kid and the meal offering and offered them up on the rock to the LORD; b-and a marvelous thing happened-b while Manoah and his wife looked on. 20As the flames leaped up from the altar toward the sky, the angel of the LORD ascended in the flames of the altar, while Manoah and his wife looked on; and they flung themselves on their faces to the ground.—21The angel of the LORD never appeared again to Manoah and his wife.—Manoah then realized that it had been an angel of the LORD. 22And Manoah said to his wife, "We shall surely die, for we have seen a divine being." 23But his wife said to him, "Had the LORD meant to take our lives, He would not have accepted a burnt offering and meal offering from us, nor let us see all these things; and He would not have made such an announcement to us."

24The woman bore a son, and she named him Samson. The boy grew up, and the LORD blessed him. 25The spirit of the LORD first moved him in the encampment of Dan, between Zorah and Eshtaol.

14 Once Samson went down to Timnah; and while in Timnah, he noticed a girl among the Philistine women. 2On his return, he told his father and mother, "I noticed one of the Philistine women in Timnah; please get her for me as a wife." 3His father and mother said to him, "Is there no one among the daughters of your own kinsmen and among all oura people, that you must go and take a wife from the uncircumcised Philistines?" But Samson answered his father, "Get me that one, for she is the one that pleases me." 4His father and mother did not realize that this was the LORD's doing: He was seeking a pretext against the Philistines, for the Philistines were ruling over Israel at that time. 5So Samson and his father and mother went down to Timnah.

When heb came to the vineyards of Timnah [for the first time], a full-

b-b Meaning of Heb. uncertain.

a Heb. "my."
b Heb. "they."

grown lion came roaring at him. 6The spirit of the LORD gripped him, and he tore him asunder with his bare hands as one might tear a kid asunder; but he did not tell his father and mother what he had done. 7Then he went down and spoke to the woman, and she pleased Samson.

8Returning the following year to marry her, he turned aside to look at the remains of the lion; and in the lion's skeleton he found a swarm of bees, and honey. 9He scooped it into his palms and ate it as he went along. When he rejoined his father and mother, he gave them some and they ate it; but he did not tell them that he had scooped the honey out of a lion's skeleton.

10So his father came down to the woman, and Samson made a feast there, as young men used to do. 11When theyc saw him, they designated thirty companions to be with him. 12Then Samson said to them, "Let me propound a riddle to you. If you can give me the right answer during the seven days of the feast, I shall give you thirty linen tunics and thirty sets of clothing; 13but if you are not able to tell it to me, you must give me thirty linen tunics and thirty sets of clothing." And they said to him, "Ask your riddle and we will listen." 14So he said to them:

"Out of the eater came something to eat,
Out of the strong came something sweet."

For three days they could not answer the riddle.

15On the seventhd day, they said to Samson's wife, "Coax your husband to provide us with the answer to the riddle; else we shall put you and your father's household to the fire; have you invited us heree in order to impoverish us?" 16Then Samson's wife harassed him with tears, and she said, "You really hate me, you don't love me. You asked my countrymen a riddle, and you didn't tell me the answer." He replied, "I haven't even told my father and mother; shall I tell you?" 17During the rest of the seven days of the feast she continued to harass him with her tears, and on the seventh day he told her, because she nagged him so. And she explained the riddle to her countrymen. 18On the seventh day, before the sunset, the townsmen said to him:

"What is sweeter than honey,
And what is stronger than a lion?"

He responded:

"Had you not plowed with my heifer,
You would not have guessed my riddle!"

19The spirit of the LORD gripped him. He went down to Ashkelon and

---

c *I.e., the people of Timnah.*
d *Septuagint and Syriac read "fourth."*
e *Reading* halom, *with some Heb. mss. and Targum.*

killed thirty of its men. He stripped them and gave the sets of clothing to those who had answered the riddle. And he left in a rage for his father's house.

²⁰Samson's wife then married one of those who had been his wedding companions.

15 Some time later, in the season of the wheat harvest, Samson came to visit his wife, bringing a kid as a gift. He said, "Let me go into the chamber to my wife." But her father would not let him go in. ²"I was sure," said her father, "that you had taken a dislike to her, so I gave her to your wedding companion. But her younger sister is more beautiful than she; let her become your wife instead." ³Thereupon Samson declared, "Now the Philistines can have no claim against me for the harm I shall do them."

⁴Samson went and caught three hundred foxes. He took torches and, turning [the foxes] tail to tail, he placed a torch between each pair of tails. ⁵He lit the torches and turned [the foxes] loose among the standing grain of the Philistines, setting fire to stacked grain, standing grain, vineyards, [and]ᵃ olive trees.

⁶The Philistines asked, "Who did this?" And they were told, "It was Samson, the son-in-law of the Timnite, who took Samson'sᵇ wife and gave her to his wedding companion." Thereupon the Philistines came up and put her and her fatherᶜ to the fire. ⁷Samson said to them, "If that is how you act, I will not rest until I have taken revenge on you." ⁸ᵈ⁻He gave them a sound and thorough thrashing.⁻ᵈ Then he went down and stayed in the cave of the rock of Etam.

⁹The Philistines came up, pitched camp in Judah and spread out over Lehi. ¹⁰The men of Judah asked, "Why have you come up against us?" They answered, "We have come to take Samson prisoner, and to do to him as he did to us." ¹¹Thereupon three thousand men of Judah went down to the cave of the rock of Etam, and they said to Samson, "You knew that the Philistines rule over us; why have you done this to us?" He replied, "As they did to me, so I did to them." ¹²"We have come down," they told him, "to take you prisoner and to hand you over to the Philistines." "But swear to me," said Samson to them, "that you yourselves will not attack me." ¹³"We won't," they replied. "We will only take you

ᵃ So Targum.
ᵇ Heb. "his."
ᶜ Many mss. read "her father's household"; cf. 14.15.
ᵈ⁻ᵈ Lit. "He smote them leg as well as thigh, a great smiting."

prisoner and hand you over to them; we will not slay you." So they bound him with two new ropes and brought him up from the rock.

[14]When he reached Lehi, the Philistines came shouting to meet him. Thereupon the spirit of the LORD gripped him, and the ropes on his arms became like flax that catches fire; the bonds melted off his hands. [15]He came upon a fresh jawbone of an ass and he picked it up; and with it he killed a thousand men. [16]Then Samson said:

"With the jaw of an ass,
Mass upon mass!
With the jaw of an ass
I have slain a thousand men."

[17]As he finished speaking, he threw the jawbone away; hence that place was called Ramath-lehi.[e]

[18]He was very thirsty and he called to the LORD, "You Yourself have granted this great victory through Your servant; and must I now die of thirst and fall into the hands of the uncircumcised?" [19]So God split open the hollow which is at Lehi, and the water gushed out of it; he drank, regained his strength, and revived. That is why it is called to this day "En-hakkore[f] of Lehi."

[20]He led Israel in the days of the Philistines for twenty years.

16

Once Samson went to Gaza; there he met a whore and slept with her. [2][a]The Gazites [learned][b] that Samson had come there, so they gathered and lay in ambush for him in the town gate the whole night; and all night long they kept whispering to each other, "When daylight comes, we'll kill him." [3]But Samson lay in bed only till midnight. At midnight he got up, grasped the doors of the town gate together with the two gateposts, and pulled them out along with the bar. He placed them on his shoulders and carried them off to the top of the hill that is near Hebron.

[4]After that, he fell in love with a woman in the Wadi Sorek, named Delilah. [5]The lords of the Philistines went up to her and said, "Coax him and find out what makes him so strong, and how we can overpower him, tie him up, and make him helpless; and we'll each give you eleven hundred shekels of silver."

---

[e] I.e., "Jawbone Heights."
[f] Understood as "The Spring of the Caller."

[a] Meaning of parts of verse uncertain.
[b] Septuagint reads "were told."

⁶So Delilah said to Samson, "Tell me, what makes you so strong? And how could you be tied up and made helpless?" ⁷Samson replied, "If I were to be tied with seven fresh tendons that had not been dried,ᶜ I should become as weak as an ordinary man." ⁸So the lords of the Philistines brought up to her seven fresh tendons that had not been dried. She bound him with them, ⁹while an ambush was waiting in her room. Then she called out to him, "Samson, the Philistines are upon you!" Whereat he pulled the tendons apart, as a strand of tow comes apart at the touch of fire. So the secret of his strength remained unknown.

¹⁰Then Delilah said to Samson, "Oh, you deceived me; you lied to me! Do tell me now how you could be tied up." ¹¹He said, "If I were to be bound with new ropes that had never been used, I would become as weak as an ordinary man." ¹²So Delilah took new ropes and bound him with them, while an ambush was waiting in a room. And she cried, "Samson, the Philistines are upon you!" But he tore them off his arms like a thread. ¹³Then Delilah said to Samson, "You have been deceiving me all along; you have been lying to me! Tell me, how could you be tied up?" He answered her, "If you weave seven locks of my head into the web."ᵈ ¹⁴And she pinned it with a pegᵉ and cried to him, "Samson, the Philistines are upon you!" Awaking from his sleep, he pulled out the peg, the loom,ᶠ and the web.

¹⁵Then she said to him, "How can you say you love me, when you don't confide in me? This makes three times that you've deceived me and haven't told me what makes you so strong." ¹⁶Finally, after she had nagged him and pressed him constantly, he was wearied to death ¹⁷and he confided everything to her. He said to her, "No razor has ever touched my head, for I have been a nazirite to God since I was in my mother's womb. If my hair were cut, my strength would leave me and I should become as weak as an ordinary man."

¹⁸Sensing that he had confided everything to her, Delilah sent for the lords of the Philistines, with this message: "Come up once more, for he has confided everything to me." And the lords of the Philistines came up and brought the money with them. ¹⁹She lulled him to sleep on her lap. Then she called in a man, and she had him cut off the seven locks of his head; thus she weakened himᵍ and made him helpless: his strength slipped away from him. ²⁰She cried, "Samson, the Philistines are upon you!" And he awoke from his sleep, thinking he would break looseᶠ and shake himself

---

ᶜ For use as bowstrings.

ᵈ Septuagint adds "and pin it with a peg to the wall, I shall become as weak as an ordinary man. So Delilah put him to sleep and wove the seven locks of his head into the web."

ᵉ Septuagint adds "to the wall."

ᶠ Meaning of Heb. uncertain.

ᵍ Taking wattaḥel as equivalent to wattaḥal; cf. vv. 7, 11, and 17.

free as he had the other times. For he did not know that the LORD had departed from him. ²¹The Philistines seized him and gouged out his eyes. They brought him down to Gaza and shackled him in bronze fetters, and he became a mill slave in the prison. ²²After his hair was cut off, it began to grow back.

²³Now the lords of the Philistines gathered to offer a great sacrifice to their god Dagon and to make merry. They chanted,

"Our god has delivered into our hands
Our enemy Samson."

²⁴ʰWhen the people saw him, they sang praises to their god, chanting,

"Our god has delivered into our hands
The enemy who devastated our land,
And who slew so many of us."

²⁵As their spirits rose, they said, "Call Samson here and let him dance for us." Samson was fetched from the prison, and he danced for them. Then they put him between the pillars. ²⁶And Samson said to the boy who was leading him by the hand, "Let go of me and let me feel the pillars that the temple rests upon, that I may lean on them." ²⁷Now the temple was full of men and women; all the lords of the Philistines were there, and there were some three thousand men and women on the roof watching Samson dance. ²⁸Then Samson called to the LORD, "O Lord GOD! Please remember me, and give me strength just this once, O God, to take revenge of the Philistines, if only for one of my two eyes." ²⁹He embraced the two middle pillars that the temple rested upon, one with his right arm and one with his left, and leaned against them; ³⁰Samson cried, "Let me die with the Philistines!" and he pulled with all his might. The temple came crashing down on the lords and on all the people in it. Those who were slain by him as he died outnumbered those who had been slain by him when he lived.

³¹His brothers and all his father's household came down and carried him up and buried him in the tomb of his father Manoah, between Zorah and Eshtaol. He had led Israel for twenty years.

17

There was a man in the hill country of Ephraim whose name was Micah.ᵃ ²He said to his mother, "The eleven hundred shekels of silver that were taken from you, so that you uttered an imprecationᵇ which you

---

ʰ This verse would read well after v. 25.

ᵃ "Micaihu" here and in v. 4.

ᵇ Cursing anyone who knew the whereabouts of the silver and did not disclose it; cf. Lev. 5.1; 1 Kings 8.31.

repeated in my hearing—I have that silver; I took it." "Blessed of the LORD be my son," said his mother.^c ³He returned the eleven hundred shekels of silver to his mother; but his mother said, "I herewith consecrate the silver to the LORD, transferring it to my son to make a sculptured image and a molten image. I now return it to you." ⁴So when he gave the silver back to his mother, his mother took two hundred shekels of silver and gave it to a smith. He made of it a sculptured image and a molten image, which were kept in the house of Micah.

⁵Now the man Micah had a house of God; he had made an ephod and teraphim and he had inducted one of his sons to be his priest. ⁶In those days there was no king in Israel; every man did as he pleased.

⁷There was a young man from Bethlehem of Judah, from the clan seat of Judah; he was a Levite and had resided there as a sojourner. ⁸This man had left the town of Bethlehem of Judah to take up residence wherever he could find a place. On his way, he came to the house of Micah in the hill country of Ephraim. ⁹"Where do you come from?" Micah asked him. He replied, "I am a Levite from Bethlehem of Judah, and I am traveling to take up residence wherever I can find a place." ¹⁰"Stay with me," Micah said to him, "and be a father and a priest to me, and I will pay you ten shekels of silver a year, an allowance of clothing, and your food." ^{d-}The Levite went.^{-d} ¹¹The Levite agreed to stay with the man, and the youth became like one of his own sons. ¹²Micah inducted the Levite, and the young man became his priest and remained in Micah's shrine. ¹³"Now I know," Micah told himself, "that the LORD will prosper me, since the Levite has become my priest."

18 In those days there was no king in Israel, and in those days the tribe of Dan was seeking a territory in which to settle; for to that day no territory had fallen to their lot among the tribes of Israel. ²The Danites sent out five of their number, from their clan seat at Zorah and Eshtaol— valiant men—to spy out the land and explore it. "Go," they told them, "and explore the land." When they had advanced into the hill country of Ephraim as far as the house of Micah, they stopped there for the night. ³While in the vicinity of Micah's house, they recognized the speech^a of the young Levite, so they went over and asked him, "Who brought you to these parts? What are you doing in this place? What is your business here?" ⁴He replied, "Thus and thus Micah did for me—he hired me and

^c *In order to nullify the imprecation.*
^{d-d} *Force of Heb. uncertain.*

^a *Lit. "voice." The men could tell by his dialect that he came from Judah and was therefore a former neighbor of the Danites; cf. vv. 11–12.*

I became his priest." ⁵They said to him, "Please, inquire of God; we would like to know if the mission on which we are going will be successful." ⁶"Go in peace," the priest said to them, "the LORD views with favor the mission you are going on." ⁷The five men went on and came to Laish. They observed the people in it dwelling carefree, after the manner of the Sidonians, a tranquil and unsuspecting people, with no one in the land to molest them and ᵇ⁻with no hereditary ruler.⁻ᵇ Moreover, they were distant from the Sidonians and had no dealings with anybody.

⁸When [the men] came back to their kinsmen at Zorah and Eshtaol, their kinsmen asked them, "How did you fare?" ⁹They replied, "Let us go at once and attack them! For we found that the land was very good, and you are sitting idle! Don't delay; go and invade the land and take possession of it, ¹⁰for God has delivered it into your hand. When you come, you will come to an unsuspecting people; and the land is spacious and nothing on earth is lacking there."

¹¹They departed from there, from the clan seat of the Danites, from Zorah and Eshtaol, six hundred strong, girt with weapons of war. ¹²They went up and encamped at Kiriath-jearim in Judah. That is why that place is called "the Camp of Dan" to this day; it lies west of Kiriath-jearim. ¹³From there they passed on to the hill country of Ephraim and arrived at the house of Micah. ¹⁴Here the five men who had gone to spy out the Laish region remarked to their kinsmen, "Do you know, there is an ephod in these houses, and teraphim, and a sculptured image and a molten image? Now you know what you have to do." ¹⁵So they turned off there and entered the home of the young Levite at Micah's house and greeted him. ¹⁶The six hundred Danite men, girt with their weapons of war, stood at the entrance of the gate, ¹⁷while the five men who had gone to spy out the land went inside and took the sculptured image, the ephod, the teraphim, and the molten image. The priest was standing at the entrance of the gate, and the six hundred men girt with their weapons of war, ¹⁸while those men entered Micah's house and took ᶜ⁻the sculptured image, the molten image, the ephod, and the household gods.⁻ᶜ The priest said to them, "What are you doing?" ¹⁹But they said to him, "Be quiet; put your hand on your mouth! Come with us and be our father and priest. Would you rather be priest to one man's household or be priest to a tribe and clan in Israel?" ²⁰The priest was delighted. He took the ephod, the household gods, and the sculptured image, and he joined the people.

²¹They set out again, placing the children, the cattle, and their house-

ᵇ⁻ᵇ *Meaning of Heb. uncertain.*
ᶜ⁻ᶜ *Lit. "the sculptured image of the ephod, and the household gods, and the molten image."*

hold goods in front. ²²They had already gone some distance from Micah's house, when the men in the houses near Micah's mustered and caught up with the Danites. ²³They called out to the Danites, who turned around and said to Micah, "What's the matter? Why have you mustered?" ²⁴He said, "You have taken my priest and the gods that I made, and walked off! What do I have left? How can you ask, 'What's the matter'?" ²⁵But the Danites replied, "Don't do any shouting at us, or some desperate men might attack you, and you and your family would lose your lives." ²⁶So Micah, realizing that they were stronger than he, turned back and went home; and the Danites went on their way, ²⁷taking the things Micah had made and the priest he had acquired. They proceeded to Laish, a people tranquil and unsuspecting, and they put them to the sword and burned down the town. ²⁸There was none to come to the rescue, for it was distant from Sidon and they had no dealings with anyone; it lay in the valley of Beth-rehob.

They rebuilt the town and settled there, ²⁹and they named the town Dan, after their ancestor Dan who was Israel's son. Originally, however, the name of the town was Laish. ³⁰The Danites set up the sculptured image for themselves; and Jonathan son of Gershom son of Manasseh,ᵈ and his descendants, served as priests to the Danite tribe until the land went into exile. ³¹They maintainedᵇ the sculptured image that Micah had made throughout the time that the House of God stood at Shiloh.

19

In those days, when there was no king in Israel, a Levite residing at the other end of the hill country of Ephraim took to himself a concubine from Bethlehem in Judah. ²Once his concubine desertedᵃ him, leaving him for her father's house in Bethlehem in Judah; and she stayed there a full four months. ³Then her husband set out, with an attendant and a pair of donkeys, and went after her to woo her and to win her back. She admitted him into her father's house; and when the girl's father saw him, he received him warmly. ⁴His father-in-law, the girl's father, pressed him, and he stayed with him three days; they ate and drank and lodged there. ⁵Early in the morning of the fourth day, he started to leave; but the girl's father said to his son-in-law, "Eat something to give you strength, then you can leave." ⁶So the two of them sat down and they feasted together. Then the girl's father said to the man, "Won't you stay overnight and

---

ᵈ *Heb.* מנשׁה *with* נ *suspended, indicating an earlier reading* "Moses"; *cf. Exod. 2.22.*

ᵃ *Lit.* "played the harlot."

enjoy yourself?" ⁷The man started to leave, but his father-in-law kept urging him until he turned back and spent the night there. ⁸Early in the morning of the fifth day, he was about to leave, when the girl's father said, "Come, have a bite." The two of them ate, dawdling until past noon. ⁹Then the man, his concubine, and his attendant started to leave. His father-in-law, the girl's father, said to him, "Look, the day is waning toward evening; do stop for the night. See, the day is declining; spend the night here and enjoy yourself. You can start early tomorrow on your journey and head for home."

¹⁰But the man refused to stay for the night. He set out and traveled as far as the vicinity of Jebus—that is, Jerusalem; he had with him a pair of laden donkeys, and his concubine ᵇ-was with him.-ᵇ ¹¹Since they were close to Jebus, and the day was very far spent, the attendant said to his master, "Let us turn aside to this town of the Jebusites and spend the night in it." ¹²But his master said to him, "We will not turn aside to a town of aliens who are not of Israel, but will continue to Gibeah. ¹³Come," he said to his attendant, "let us approach one of those places and spend the night either in Gibeah or in Ramah." ¹⁴So they traveled on, and the sun set when they were near Gibeah of Benjamin.

¹⁵They turned off there and went in to spend the night in Gibeah. He went and sat down in the town square, but nobody took them indoors to spend the night. ¹⁶In the evening, an old man came along from his property ᶜ-outside the town.-ᶜ (This man hailed from the hill country of Ephraim and resided at Gibeah, where the townspeople were Benjaminites.) ¹⁷He happened to see the wayfarer in the town square. "Where," the old man inquired, "are you going to, and where do you come from?" ¹⁸He replied, "We are traveling from Bethlehem in Judah to the other end of the hill country of Ephraim. That is where I live. I made a journey to Bethlehem of Judah, and now I am on my way ᵈ-to the House of the LORD,-ᵈ and nobody has taken me indoors. ¹⁹We have both bruised straw and feed for our donkeys, and bread and wine for me and your handmaid,ᵉ and for the attendant ᶠ-with your servants.-ᶠ We lack nothing." ²⁰"Rest easy," said the old man. "Let me take care of all your needs. Do not on any account spend the night in the square." ²¹And he took him into his house. He mixed fodder for the donkeys; then they bathed their feet and ate and drank.

²²While they were enjoying themselves, the men of the town, a de-

---

ᵇ⁻ᵇ *Emendation yields "and his attendant."*
ᶜ⁻ᶜ *Lit. "in the field."*
ᵈ⁻ᵈ *Meaning of Heb. uncertain; emendation yields "to my home"; cf. v. 29.*
ᵉ *I.e., the concubine.*
ᶠ⁻ᶠ *I.e., "with us."*

praved lot, had gathered about the house and were pounding on the door. They called to the aged owner of the house, "Bring out the man who has come into your house, so that we can be intimate with him." 23The owner of the house went out and said to them, "Please, my friends, do not commit such a wrong. Since this man has entered my house, do not perpetrate this outrage. 24Look, here is my virgin daughter, and his concubine. Let me bring them out to you. Have your pleasure of them, do what you like with them; but don't do that outrageous thing to this man." 25But the men would not listen to him, so the man seized his concubine and pushed her out to them. They raped her and abused her all night long until morning; and they let her go when dawn broke.

26Toward morning the woman came back; and as it was growing light, she collapsed at the entrance of the man's house where her husband was. 27When her husband arose in the morning, he opened the doors of the house and went out to continue his journey; and there was the woman, his concubine, lying at the entrance of the house, with her hands on the threshold. 28"Get up," he said to her, "let us go." But there was no reply. So the man placed her on the donkey and set out for home. 29When he came home, he picked up a knife, and took hold of his concubine and cut her up limb by limb into twelve parts. He sent them throughout the territory of Israel. 30And everyone who saw it cried out, "Never has such a thing happened or been seen from the day the Israelites came out of the land of Egypt to this day! Put your mind to this; take counsel and decide."

20 Thereupon all the Israelites—from Dan to Beer-sheba and [from] the land of Gilead—marched forth, and the community assembled to a man before the LORD at Mizpah. 2All the leaders of the people [and] all the tribes of Israel presented themselves in the assembly of God's people, 400,000 fighting men on foot.—3The Benjaminites heard that the Israelites had come up to Mizpah.ᵃ—The Israelites said, "Tell us, how did this evil thing happen?" 4And the Levite, the husband of the murdered woman, replied, "My concubine and I came to Gibeah of Benjamin to spend the night. 5The citizens of Gibeah set out to harm me. They gathered against me around the house in the night; they meant to kill me, and they ravished my concubine until she died. 6So I took hold of my concubine and I cut her in pieces and sent them through every part of

---

ᵃ *This sentence is continued at v. 14 below.*

Israel's territory. For an outrageous act of depravity had been committed in Israel. [7]Now you are all Israelites; produce a plan of action here and now!"

[8]Then all the people rose, as one man, and declared, "We will not go back to our homes, we will not enter our houses! [9]But this is what we will do to Gibeah: [we will wage war] against it according to lot. [10]We will take from all the tribes of Israel ten men to the hundred, a hundred to the thousand, and a thousand to the ten thousand to supply provisions for the troops—[b-]to prepare for their going to Geba in Benjamin[-b] for all the outrage it has committed in Israel." [11]So all the men of Israel, united as one man, massed against the town. [12]And the tribes of Israel sent men through the whole tribe[c] of Benjamin, saying, "What is this evil thing that has happened among you? [13]Come, hand over those scoundrels in Gibeah so that we may put them to death and stamp out the evil from Israel." But the Benjaminites would not yield to the demand of their fellow Israelites.

[14]So the Benjaminites gathered from their towns to Gibeah in order to take the field against the Israelites. [15d]On that day the Benjaminites mustered from the towns 26,000 fighting men, mustered apart from the inhabitants of Gibeah; 700 picked men [16]of all this force—700 picked men— were left-handed. Every one of them could sling a stone at a hair and not miss. [17]The men of Israel other than Benjamin mustered 400,000 fighting men, warriors to a man. [18]They proceeded to Bethel and inquired of God; the Israelites asked, "Who of us shall advance first to fight the Benjaminites?" And the LORD replied, "Judah first." [19]So the Israelites arose in the morning and encamped against Gibeah.

[20]The men of Israel took the field against the Benjaminites; the men of Israel drew up in battle order against them at Gibeah. [21]But the Benjaminites issued from Gibeah, and that day they struck down 22,000 men of Israel.

[22]Now the army—the men of Israel—rallied and again drew up in battle order at the same place as they had on the first day. [23]For the Israelites had gone up and wept before the LORD until evening. They had inquired of the LORD, "Shall we again join battle with our kinsmen the Benjaminites?" And the LORD had replied, "March against them." [24]The Israelites advanced against the Benjaminites on the second day. [25]But the Benjaminites came out from Gibeah against them on the second day and struck down 18,000 more of the Israelites, all of them fighting men.

[b-b] *Emendation yields "for those who go to requite Gibeah."*
[c] *Heb. plural.*
[d] *Meaning of parts of vv. 15 and 16 uncertain.*

²⁶Then all the Israelites, all the army, went up and came to Bethel and they sat there, weeping before the LORD. They fasted that day until evening, and presented burnt offerings and offerings of well-being to the LORD. ²⁷The Israelites inquired of the LORD (for the Ark of God's Covenant was there in those days, ²⁸and Phinehas son of Eleazar son of Aaron the priest ministered before Him in those days), "Shall we again take the field against our kinsmen the Benjaminites, or shall we not?" The LORD answered, "Go up, for tomorrow I will deliver them into your hands."

²⁹Israel put men in ambush against Gibeah on all sides. ³⁰And on the third day, the Israelites went up against the Benjaminites, as before, and engaged them in battle at Gibeah. ³¹The Benjaminites dashed out to meet the army and were drawn away from the town onto the roads, of which one runs to Bethel and the other to Gibeah. As before, they started out by striking some of the men dead in the open field, about 30 men of Israel.

³²The Benjaminites thought, "They are being routed before us as previously." But the Israelites had planned: "We will take to flight and draw them away from the town to the roads." ³³And while the main body of the Israelites had moved away from their positions and had drawn up in battle order at Baal-tamar, the Israelite ambush was rushing out from its position at Maareh-geba.ᶜ ³⁴Thus 10,000 picked men of all Israel came to a point south ofᶠ Gibeah, and the battle was furious. Before they realized that disaster was approaching, ³⁵the LORD routed the Benjaminites before Israel. That day the Israelites slew 25,100 men of Benjamin, all of them fighting men. ³⁶Then the Benjaminites realized that they were routed.ᵍ Now the Israelites had yielded ground to the Benjaminites, for they relied on the ambush which they had laid against Gibeah. ³⁷One ambush quickly deployed against Gibeah, and the other ambush advanced and put the whole town to the sword.

³⁸A time had been agreed upon by the Israelite men with those in ambush: When a huge column of smoke was sent up from the town, ³⁹the Israelite men were to turn about in battle. Benjamin had begun by striking dead about 30 Israelite men, and they thought, "They are being routed before us as in the previous fighting." ⁴⁰But when the column, the pillar of smoke, began to rise from the city, the Benjaminites looked behind them, and there was the whole town going up in smoke to the sky! ⁴¹And now the Israelites turned about, and the men of Benjamin were thrown

---

ᶜ Emendation yields "west of Gibeah."
ᶠ So many Heb. mss. and Targum; most mss. and the editions read "opposite."
ᵍ This sentence is continued by v. 45.

into panic, for they realized that disaster had overtaken them. ⁴²They retreated before the men of Israel along the road to the wilderness, where the fighting caught up with them; meanwhile those ʰ⁻from the towns⁻ʰ were massacring them in it. ⁴³ⁱThey encircled the Benjaminites, pursued them, and trod them down [from] Menuhah to a point opposite Gibeah on the east. ⁴⁴That day 18,000 men of Benjamin fell, all of them brave men. ⁴⁵They turned and fled to the wilderness, to the Rock of Rimmon; but [the Israelites] picked off another 5,000 on the roads and, continuing in hot pursuit of them up to Gidom, they slew 2,000 more. ⁴⁶Thus the total number of Benjaminites who fell that day came to 25,000 fighting men, all of them brave. ⁴⁷But 600 men turned and fled to the wilderness, to the Rock of Rimmon; they remained at the Rock of Rimmon four months. ⁴⁸The men of Israel, meanwhile, turned back to the rest of the Benjaminites and put them to the sword—towns, people, cattle—everything that remained. Finally, they set fire to all the towns that were left.

21

Now the men of Israel had taken an oath at Mizpah: "None of us will give his daughter in marriage to a Benjaminite."

²The people came to Bethel and sat there before God until evening. They wailed and wept bitterly, ³and they said, "O LORD God of Israel, why has this happened in Israel, that one tribe must now be missing from Israel?" ⁴Early the next day, the people built an altar there, and they brought burnt offerings and offerings of well-being.

⁵The Israelites asked, "Is there anyone from all the tribes of Israel who failed to come up to the assembly before the LORD?" For a solemn oath had been taken concerning anyone who did not go up to the LORD at Mizpah: "He shall be put to death." ⁶The Israelites now relented toward their kinsmen the Benjaminites, and they said, "This day one tribe has been cut off from Israel! ⁷What can we do to provide wives for those who are left, seeing that we have sworn by the LORD not to give any of our daughters to them in marriage?"

⁸They inquired, "Is there anyone from the tribes of Israel who did not go up to the LORD at Mizpah?" Now no one from Jabesh-gilead had come to the camp, to the assembly. ⁹For, when the roll of the troops was taken, not one of the inhabitants of Jabesh-gilead was present. ¹⁰So the assemblage dispatched 12,000 of the warriors, instructing them as follows: "Go and put the inhabitants of Jabesh-gilead to the sword, women

---

ʰ⁻ʰ *Meaning of Heb. uncertain; emendation yields "in the town" (i.e., Gibeah).*
ⁱ *Meaning of verse uncertain.*

and children included. [11]This is what you are to do: Proscribe every man, and every woman who has known a man carnally." [12]They found among the inhabitants of Jabesh-gilead 400 maidens who had not known a man carnally; and they brought them to the camp at Shiloh, which is in the land of Canaan.[a]

[13]Then the whole community sent word to the Benjaminites who were at the Rock of Rimmon, and offered them terms of peace. [14]Thereupon the Benjaminites returned, and they gave them the girls who had been spared from the women of Jabesh-gilead. [b-]But there were not enough of them.[-b]

[15]Now the people had relented toward Benjamin, for the LORD had made a breach in the tribes of Israel. [16]So the elders of the community asked, "What can we do about wives for those who are left, since the women of Benjamin have been killed off?" [17]For they said, "There must be a saving remnant for Benjamin, that a tribe may not be blotted out of Israel; [18]yet we cannot give them any of our daughters as wives," since the Israelites had taken an oath: "Cursed be anyone who gives a wife to Benjamin!"

[19]They said, "The annual feast of the LORD is now being held at Shiloh." (It lies north of Bethel, east of the highway that runs from Bethel to Shechem, and south of Lebonah.)

[20]So they instructed the Benjaminites as follows: "Go and lie in wait in the vineyards. [21]As soon as you see the girls of Shiloh coming out to join in the dances, come out from the vineyards; let each of you seize a wife from among the girls of Shiloh, and be off for the land of Benjamin. [22]And if their fathers or brothers come to us to complain, we shall say to them, [b-]'Be generous to them for our sake! We could not provide any of them with a wife on account of the war, and you would have incurred guilt if you yourselves had given them [wives].' "[-b]

[23]The Benjaminites did so. They took to wife, from the dancers whom they carried off, as many as they themselves numbered. Then they went back to their own territory, and rebuilt their towns and settled in them. [24]Thereupon the Israelites dispersed, each to his own tribe and clan; everyone departed for his own territory.

[25]In those days there was no king in Israel; everyone did as he pleased.

---

[a] *I.e., west of the Jordan, while Jabesh-gilead is east of the Jordan.*
[b-b] *Meaning of Heb. uncertain.*

I SAMUEL

1 There was a man from a-Ramathaim of the Zuphites,-a in the hill country of Ephraim, whose name was Elkanah son of Jeroham son of Elihu son of Tohu son of Zuph, an Ephraimite. 2He had two wives, one named Hannah and the other Peninnah; Peninnah had children, but Hannah was childless. 3This man used to go up from his town every year to worship and to offer sacrifice to the LORD of Hosts at Shiloh.—Hophni and Phinehas, the two sons of Eli, were priests of the LORD there.

4One such day, Elkanah offered a sacrifice. He used to give portions to his wife Peninnah and to all her sons and daughters; 5but to Hannah he would give one portion b-only—though-b Hannah was his favorite—for the LORD had closed her womb. 6Moreover, her rival, to make her miserable, would taunt her that the LORD had closed her womb. 7c-This happened-c year after year: Every time she went up to the House of the LORD, the other would taunt her, so that she wept and would not eat. 8Her husband Elkanah said to her, "Hannah, why are you crying and why aren't you eating? Why are you so sad? Am I not more devoted to you than ten sons?"

9After they had eaten and drunk at Shiloh, Hannah rose.d—The priest Eli was sitting on the seat near the doorpost of the temple of the LORD.— 10In her wretchedness, she prayed to the LORD, weeping all the while. 11And she made this vow: "O LORD of Hosts, if You will look upon the suffering of Your maidservant and will remember me and not forget Your maidservant, and if You will grant Your maidservant a male child, I will dedicate him to the LORD for all the days of his life; and no razor shall ever touch his head."

12As she kept on praying before the LORD, Eli watched her mouth. 13Now Hannah was praying in her heart; only her lips moved, but her voice could not be heard. So Eli thought she was drunk. 14Eli said to her,

a-a *Heb. "Ramathaim-zophim." In 1.19, 2.11, 7.17, 15.34, 19.18, etc., the town is called Ramah; and 9.5 ff. shows that it was in the district of Zuph.*
b-b *Meaning of Heb. uncertain.*
c-c *Lit. "Thus he did."*
d *Septuagint adds "and stood before the LORD."*

"How long will you make a drunken spectacle of yourself? e-Sober up!"-e 15And Hannah replied, "Oh no, my lord! I am a very unhappy woman. I have drunk no wine or other strong drink, but I have been pouring out my heart to the LORD. 16Do not take your maidservant for a worthless woman; I have only been speaking all this time out of my great anguish and distress." 17"Then go in peace," said Eli, "and may the God of Israel grant you what you have asked of Him." 18She answered, "You are most kind to your handmaid." So the woman left, and she ate, and was no longer downcast. 19Early next morning they bowed low before the LORD, and they went back home to Ramah.

Elkanah knewf his wife Hannah and the LORD remembered her. 20Hannah conceived, and at the turn of the year bore a son. She named him Samuel,g meaning, "I asked the LORD for him." 21And when the man Elkanah and all his household were going up to offer to the LORD the annual sacrifice and his votive sacrifice, 22Hannah did not go up. She said to her husband, "When the child is weaned, I will bring him. For when he has appeared before the LORD, he must remain there for good." 23Her husband Elkanah said to her, "Do as you think best. Stay home until you have weaned him. May the LORD fulfill h-His word."-h So the woman stayed home and nursed her son until she weaned him.

24When she had weaned him, she took him up with her, along with i-three bulls,-i one ephah of flour, and a jar of wine. And b-though the boy was still very young,-b she brought him to the House of the LORD at Shiloh. 25After slaughtering the bull, they brought the boy to Eli. 26She said, "Please, my lord! As you live, my lord, I am the woman who stood here beside you and prayed to the LORD. 27It was this boy I prayed for; and the LORD has granted me what I asked of Him. 28I, in turn, hereby lendj him to the LORD. For as long as he lives he is lent to the LORD." And theyk bowed low there before the LORD.

2

And Hannah prayed:

My heart exults in the LORD;
a-I have triumphed-a through the LORD.

---

e-e *Lit. "Remove your wine from you."*
f *Cf. note at Gen. 4.1.*
g *Connected with sha'ul me'el "asked of God"; cf. vv. 17, 27–28.*
h-h *Septuagint and 4QSama (a Samuel fragment from Qumran) read "the utterance of your mouth." The translators express their thanks to Professor Frank M. Cross, Jr., for graciously making available to them copies of his unpublished Samuel fragments.*
i-i *Septuagint and 4QSama read "a three-year-old [cf. Gen. 15.9] bull and bread"; cf. v. 25.*
j *From the same root as that of the verb rendered "asked for" in v. 20.*
k *Heb. "he"; cf. 2.11. A reading in the Talmud (Berakot 61a) implies that Elkanah was there.*

a-a *Lit. "My horn is high."*

b-I gloat-b over my enemies;
I rejoice in Your deliverance.

²There is no holy one like the LORD,
Truly, there is none beside You;
There is no rock like our God.

³Talk no more with lofty pride,
Let no arrogance cross your lips!
For the LORD is an all-knowing God;
By Him actions are measured.

⁴The bows of the mighty are broken,
And the faltering are girded with strength.
⁵Men once sated must hire out for bread;
Men once hungry hunger no more.
While the barren woman bears seven,
The mother of many is forlorn.
⁶The LORD deals death and gives life,
Casts down into Sheol and raises up.
⁷The LORD makes poor and makes rich;
He casts down, He also lifts high.
⁸He raises the poor from the dust,
Lifts up the needy from the dunghill,
Setting them with nobles,
Granting them seats of honor.
For the pillars of the earth are the LORD's;
He has set the world upon them.
⁹He guards the steps of His faithful,
But the wicked perish in darkness—
For not by strength shall man prevail.

¹⁰The foes of the LORD shall be shattered;
He will thunder against them in the heavens.
The LORD will judge the ends of the earth.

b-b *Lit. "My mouth is wide."*

He will give power to His king,
c-And triumph to-c His anointed one.

11Then Elkanahd [and Hannah] went home to Ramah; and the boy entered the service of the LORD under the priest Eli.

12Now Eli's sons were scoundrels; they paid no heed to the LORD.
13This is how the priests used to deal with the people: When anyone brought a sacrifice, the priest's boy would come along with a three-pronged fork while the meat was boiling, 14and he would thrust it into e-the cauldron, or the kettle, or the great pot, or the small cooking-pot;-e and whatever the fork brought up, the priest would take away f-on it.-f This was the practice at Shiloh with all the Israelites who came there. 15[But now] even before the suet was turned into smoke, the priest's boy would come and say to the man who was sacrificing, "Hand over some meat to roast for the priest; for he won't accept boiled meat from you, only raw."
16And if the man said to him, "Let them first turn the suet into smoke, and then take as much as you want," he would reply, "No, hand it over at once or I'll take it by force." 17The sin of the young men against the LORD was very great, for the men treated the LORD's offerings impiously.

18Samuel was engaged in the service of the LORD as an attendant, girded with a linen ephod. 19His mother would also make a little robe for him and bring it up to him every year, when she made the pilgrimage with her husband to offer the annual sacrifice. 20Eli would bless Elkanah and his wife, and say, "May the LORD grantg you offspring by this woman in place of the loan she made to the LORD." Then they would return home. 21Forh the LORD took note of Hannah; she conceived and bore three sons and two daughters. Young Samuel meanwhile grew up in the service of the LORD.

22Now Eli was very old. When he heard all that his sons were doing to all Israel, and how they lay with the women who i-performed tasks-i at the entrance of the Tent of Meeting, 23he said to them, "Why do you do such things? I get evil reports about you from the people on all hands. 24Don't, my sons! It is no favorable report I hear the people of the LORD spreading about. 25If a man sins against a man, the LORD may pardoni him; but if a man offends against God, who can i-obtain pardon-i for him?" But they ignored their father's plea; for the LORD was resolved

c-c Lit. "And will raise the horn of."
d See note k at 1.28.
e-e These vessels have not been distinguished precisely.
f-f Targum and Septuagint add "for himself."
g 4QSamᵃ and Septuagint read "repay."
h 4QSamᵃ reads "And."
i-i Meaning of Heb. uncertain.

that they should die. 26Young Samuel, meanwhile, grew in esteem and favor both with God and with men.

27A man of God came to Eli and said to him, "Thus said the LORD: Lo, I revealed Myself to your father's house in Egypt when they were subject to the House of Pharaoh, 28and I chose them from among all the tribes of Israel to be My priests—to ascend My altar, to burn incense, [and] to carry an ephod^j before Me—and I assigned to your father's house all offerings by fire of the Israelites. 29Why, then, do you k-maliciously trample upon the sacrifices and offerings that I have commanded?-k You have honored your sons more than Me, feeding on the first portions of every offering of My people Israel.^l 30Assuredly—declares the LORD, the God of Israel—I intended for you and your father's house to remain in My service forever. But now—declares the LORD—far be it from Me! For I honor those who honor Me, but those who spurn Me shall be dishonored. 31A time is coming when I will break your power and that of your father's house, and there shall be no elder in your house. 32You will gaze grudgingly^m at all the bounty that will be bestowed on Israel, but there shall never be an elder in your house. 33i-I shall not cut off all your offspring from My altar; [but,] to make your eyes pine and your spirit languish, all the increase in your house shall die as [ordinary] men.-i 34And this shall be a sign for you: The fate of your two sons Hophni and Phinehas—they shall both die on the same day. 35And I will raise up for Myself a faithful priest, who will act in accordance with My wishes and My purposes. I will build for him an enduring house, and he shall walk before My anointed evermore. 36And all the survivors of your house shall come and bow low to him for the sake of a money fee and a loaf of bread, and shall say, 'Please, assign me to one of the priestly duties, that I may have a morsel of bread to eat.' "

3 Young Samuel was in the service of the LORD under Eli. In those days the word of the LORD was rare; prophecy was not widespread. 2One day, Eli was asleep in his usual place; his eyes had begun to fail and he could barely see. 3The lamp of God had not yet gone out, and Samuel was sleeping in the temple of the LORD where the Ark of God was. 4The LORD called out to Samuel, and he answered, "I'm coming." 5He ran to Eli and said, "Here I am; you called me." But he replied, "I didn't call

---

ⁱ Here a device for obtaining oracles (cf. 14.3; 23.6, 9–12), not a garment as in v. 18 above.
^{k-k} Meaning of Heb. uncertain. Emendation yields "gaze [cf. Septuagint] grudgingly upon the sacrifices and offerings which I have commanded" (connecting ma'on with 'oyen, "keeping a jealous eye"; see 1 Sam. 18.9); cf. v. 32 and note m below.
^l See vv. 15–16.
^m Cf. note k-k above.

you; go back to sleep." So he went back and lay down. ⁶Again the LORD called, "Samuel!" Samuel rose and went to Eli and said, "Here I am; you called me." But he replied, "I didn't call, my son; go back to sleep."—⁷Now Samuel had not yet experienced the LORD; the word of the LORD had not yet been revealed to him.—⁸The LORD called Samuel again, a third time, and he rose and went to Eli and said, "Here I am; you called me." Then Eli understood that the LORD was calling the boy. ⁹And Eli said to Samuel, "Go lie down. If you are called again, say, 'Speak, LORD, for Your servant is listening.'" And Samuel went to his place and lay down.

¹⁰The LORD came, and stood there, and He called as before: "Samuel! Samuel!" And Samuel answered, "Speak, for Your servant is listening." ¹¹The LORD said to Samuel: "I am going to do in Israel such a thing that both ears of anyone who hears about it will tingle. ¹²In that day I will fulfill against Eli all that I spoke concerning his house, from beginning to end. ¹³And I declare to him that I sentence his house to endless punishment for the iniquity he knew about—how his sons committed sacrilege ᵃ⁻at will⁻ᵃ—and he did not rebuke them. ¹⁴Assuredly, I swear concerning the house of Eli that the iniquity of the house of Eli will never be expiated by sacrifice or offering."

¹⁵Samuel lay there until morning; and then he opened the doors of the House of the LORD. Samuel was afraid to report the vision to Eli, ¹⁶but Eli summoned Samuel and said, "Samuel, my son"; and he answered, "Here." ¹⁷And [Eli] asked, "What did He say to you? Keep nothing from me. ᵇ⁻Thus and more may God do to you⁻ᵇ if you keep from me a single word of all that He said to you!" ¹⁸Samuel then told him everything, withholding nothing from him. And [Eli] said, "He is the LORD; He will do what He deems right."

¹⁹Samuel grew up and the LORD was with him: He did not leave any of Samuel'sᶜ predictions unfulfilled. ²⁰All Israel, from Dan to Beersheba, knew that Samuel was trustworthy as a prophet of the LORD. ²¹And the LORD continued to appear at Shiloh: the LORD revealed Himself to Samuel at Shiloh with the word of the LORD; ¹and Samuel's word went forth to all Israel.

ᵃIsrael marched out to engage the Philistines in battle; they encamped near Eben-ezer, while the Philistines encamped at Aphek. ²The Philistines

---

ᵃ⁻ᵃ *Meaning of Heb. uncertain. Septuagint reads "against God."*
ᵇ⁻ᵇ *A formula of adjuration.*
ᶜ *Heb. "his."*

ᵃ *Preceding this, Septuagint has "In those days, the Philistines gathered for war against Israel."*

arrayed themselves against Israel; and when the battle was fought,[b] Israel was routed by the Philistines, who slew about four thousand men on the field of battle. [3]When the [Israelite] troops returned to the camp, the elders of Israel asked, "Why did the LORD put us to rout today before the Philistines? Let us fetch the Ark of the Covenant of the LORD from Shiloh; thus He will be present among us and will deliver us from the hands of our enemies." [4]So the troops sent men to Shiloh; there Eli's two sons, Hophni and Phinehas, were in charge of the Ark of the Covenant of God, and they brought down from there the Ark of the Covenant of the LORD of Hosts Enthroned on the Cherubim.

[5]When the Ark of the Covenant of the LORD entered the camp, all Israel burst into a great shout, so that the earth resounded. [6]The Philistines heard the noise of the shouting and they wondered, "Why is there such a loud shouting in the camp of the Hebrews?" And when they learned that the Ark of the LORD had come to the camp, [7]the Philistines were frightened; for they said, "God has come to the camp." And they cried, "Woe to us! Nothing like this has ever happened before. [8]Woe to us! Who will save us from the power of this mighty God? He is the same God who struck the Egyptians with every kind of plague in the wilderness! [9]Brace yourselves and be men, O Philistines! Or you will become slaves to the Hebrews as they were slaves to you. Be men and fight!" [10]The Philistines fought; Israel was routed, and they all fled to their homes. The defeat was very great, thirty thousand foot soldiers of Israel fell there. [11]The Ark of God was captured, and Eli's two sons, Hophni and Phinehas, were slain.

[12]A Benjaminite ran from the battlefield and reached Shiloh the same day; his clothes were rent and there was earth on his head.[c] [13]When he arrived, he found Eli sitting on a seat, waiting beside the road—his heart trembling for the Ark of God. The man entered the city to spread the news, and the whole city broke out in a cry. [14]And when Eli heard the sound of the outcry and asked, "What is the meaning of this uproar?" the man rushed over to tell Eli. [15]Now Eli was ninety-eight years old; his eyes were fixed in a blind stare. [16]The man said to Eli, "I am the one who came from the battlefield; I have just fled from the battlefield." [Eli] asked, "What happened, my son?" [17]The bearer of the news replied, "Israel fled before the Philistines and the troops also suffered a great slaughter. Your two sons, Hophni and Phinehas, are dead, and the Ark of God has been

---

b *Meaning of Heb. uncertain.*
c *I.e., as a sign of mourning.*

captured." ¹⁸When he mentioned the Ark of God, [Eli] fell backward off the seat beside[b] the gate, broke his neck and died; for he was an old man and heavy. He had been a chieftain of Israel for forty years.

¹⁹His daughter-in-law, the wife of Phinehas, was with child, about to give birth. When she heard the report that the Ark of God was captured and that her father-in-law and her husband were dead, she was seized with labor pains, and she crouched down and gave birth. ²⁰As she lay dying, the women attending her said, "Do not be afraid, for you have borne a son." But she did not respond or pay heed. ²¹She named the boy Ichabod, meaning, "The glory has departed from Israel"—referring to the capture of the Ark of God and to [the death of] her father-in-law and her husband. ²²"The glory is gone from Israel," she said, "for the Ark of God has been captured."

5 When the Philistines captured the Ark of God, they brought it from Eben-ezer to Ashdod. ²The Philistines took the Ark of God and brought it into the temple of Dagon and they set it up beside Dagon. ³Early the next day, the Ashdodites found Dagon lying face down on the ground in front of the Ark of the LORD. They picked Dagon up and put him back in his place; ⁴but early the next morning, Dagon was again lying prone on the ground in front of the Ark of the LORD. The head and both hands of Dagon were cut off, lying on the threshold; only [a-]Dagon's trunk was left intact.[-a] ⁵That is why, to this day, the priests of Dagon and all who enter the temple of Dagon do not tread on the threshold of Dagon in Ashdod.

⁶The hand of the LORD lay heavy upon the Ashdodites, and He wrought havoc among them: He struck [b-]Ashdod and its territory[-b] with hemorrhoids. ⁷When the men of Ashdod saw how matters stood, they said, "The Ark of the God of Israel must not remain with us, for His hand has dealt harshly with us and with our god Dagon." ⁸They sent messengers and assembled all the lords of the Philistines and asked, "What shall we do with the Ark of the God of Israel?" They answered, "Let the Ark of the God of Israel be removed to Gath." So they moved the Ark of the God of Israel [to Gath]. ⁹And after they had moved it, the hand of the LORD came against the city, causing great panic; He struck the people of the city, young and old, so that hemorrhoids [a-]broke out[-a] among them. ¹⁰Then they sent the Ark of God to Ekron. But when the Ark of God

a-a *Meaning of Heb. uncertain.*
b-b *Meaning of Heb. uncertain. Septuagint reads differently from our Heb. text; it also mentions mice swarming in the Philistine ships and invading their fields. Cf. the mention of "mice" in 6.4, 18; and the note at 6.1.*

came to Ekron, the Ekronites cried out, "They have moved the Ark of the God of Israel to us to slay us and our kindred." [11]They too sent messengers and assembled all the lords of the Philistines and said, "Send the Ark of the God of Israel away, and let it return to its own place, that it may not slay us and our kindred." For the panic of death pervaded the whole city, so heavily had the hand of God fallen there; [12]and the men who did not die were stricken with hemorrhoids. The outcry of the city went up to heaven.

6 The Ark of the LORD remained in the territory of the Philistines seven months.[a] [2]Then the Philistines summoned the priests and the diviners and asked, "What shall we do about the Ark of the Lord? Tell us with what we shall send it off to its own place." [3]They answered, "If you are going to send the Ark of the God of Israel away, do not send it away without anything; you must also pay an indemnity to Him. Then you will be healed, and [b-]He will make Himself known to you; otherwise His hand will not turn away from you."[-b] [4]They asked, "What is the indemnity that we should pay to Him?" They answered, "Five golden hemorrhoids and five golden mice, corresponding to the number of lords of the Philistines; for the same plague struck all of you[c] and your lords. [5]You shall make figures of your hemorrhoids and of the mice that are ravaging your land; thus you shall honor the God of Israel, and perhaps He will lighten the weight of His hand upon you and your gods and your land. [6]Don't harden your hearts as the Egyptians and Pharaoh hardened their hearts. As you know, when He made a mockery of them, they had to let Israel[c] go, and they departed. [7]Therefore, get a new cart ready and two milch cows that have not borne a yoke; harness the cows to the cart, but take back indoors the calves that follow them. [8]Take the Ark of the LORD and place it on the cart; and put next to it in a chest the gold objects you are paying Him as indemnity. Send it off, and let it go its own way. [9]Then watch: If it goes up the road to Beth-shemesh, to His own territory, it was He who has inflicted this great harm on us. But if not, we shall know that it was not His hand that struck us; it just happened to us by chance."

[10]The men did so. They took two milch cows and harnessed them to the cart, and shut up their calves indoors. [11]They placed the Ark of the LORD on the cart together with the chest, the golden mice, and the figures of their hemorrhoids. [12]The cows went straight ahead along the road to

---

[a] *Septuagint continues "and mice invaded their fields"; cf. vv. 4, 5, 18, and note at 5.6.*
[b-b] *Or "and you will know why His hand would not turn away from you." Meaning of Heb. uncertain.*
[c] *Heb. "them."*

Beth-shemesh. They went along a single highroad, lowing as they went, and turning off neither to the right nor to the left; and the lords of the Philistines walked behind them as far as the border of Beth-shemesh.

13The people of Beth-shemesh were reaping their wheat harvest in the valley. They looked up and saw the Ark, and they rejoiced d-when they saw [it].-d 14The cart came into the field of Joshua of Beth-shemesh and it stopped there. They split up the wood of the cart and presented the cows as a burnt offering to the LORD. A large stone was there; 15and the Levites took down the Ark of the LORD and the chest beside it containing the gold objects and placed them on the large stone. Then the men of Beth-shemesh presented burnt offerings and other sacrifices to the LORD that day. 16The five lords of the Philistines saw this and returned the same day to Ekron.

17The following were the golden hemorrhoids that the Philistines paid as an indemnity to the LORD: For Ashdod, one; for Gaza, one; for Ashkelon, one; for Gath, one; for Ekron, one. 18eAs for the golden mice, their number accorded with all the Philistine towns that belonged to the five lords—both fortified towns and unwalled f-villages, as far as-f the great stoneg on which the Ark of the LORD was set down, to this day, in the field of Joshua of Beth-shemesh.

19[The LORD] struck at the men of Beth-shemesh because h-they looked into the Ark of the LORD; He struck down seventy men among the people [and] fifty thousand men.-h The people mourned, for He had inflicted a great slaughter upon the population. 20And the men of Beth-shemesh asked, "Who can stand in attendance on the LORD, this holy God? And to whom shall He go up from us?" 21They sent messengers to the inhabitants of Kiriath-jearim to say, "The Philistines have sent back the Ark of the LORD. Come down and take it into your keeping." 1The men of 7 Kiriath-jearim came and took up the Ark of the LORD and brought it into the house of Abinadab on the hill; and they consecrated his son Eleazar to have charge of the Ark of the LORD.

2A long time elapsed from the day that the Ark was housed in Kiriath-jearim, twenty years in all; and all the House of Israel a-yearned after-a the LORD. 3And Samuel said to all the House of Israel, "If you mean to return to the LORD with all your heart, you must remove the alien gods and the Ashtaroth from your midst and direct your heart to the LORD and serve Him alone. Then He will deliver you from the hands of the

---

d-d Septuagint reads "As they met it."

e Meaning of vv. 18 and 19 uncertain in part.

f-f Emendation yields "villages, as witness there is."

g Reading 'eben with some Heb. mss., Septuagint, and Targum; most mss. and editions 'abel, "meadow [?]."

h-h Force of Heb. uncertain.

a-a Meaning of Heb. uncertain.

Philistines." ⁴And the Israelites removed the Baalim and Ashtaroth and they served the LORD alone.

⁵Samuel said, "Assemble all Israel at Mizpah, and I will pray to the LORD for you." ⁶They assembled at Mizpah, and they drew water and poured it out before the LORD; they fasted that day, and there they confessed that they had sinned against the LORD. And Samuel acted as chieftain of the Israelites at Mizpah.

⁷When the Philistines heard that the Israelites had assembled at Mizpah, the lords of the Philistines marched out against Israel. Hearing of this, the Israelites were terrified of the Philistines ⁸and they implored Samuel, "Do not neglect us and do not refrain from crying out to the LORD our God to save us from the hands of the Philistines." ⁹Thereupon Samuel took a suckling lamb and sacrificed it as a whole burnt offering to the LORD; and Samuel cried out to the LORD in behalf of Israel, and the LORD responded to him. ¹⁰For as Samuel was presenting the burnt offering and the Philistines advanced to attack Israel, the LORD thundered mightily against the Philistines that day. He threw them into confusion, and they were routed by Israel. ¹¹The men of Israel sallied out of Mizpah and pursued the Philistines, striking them down to a point below Beth-car.

¹²Samuel took a stone and set it up between Mizpah and Shen,ᵇ and named it Eben-ezer:ᶜ "For up to now," he said, "the LORD has helped us." ¹³The Philistines were humbled and did not invade the territory of Israel again; and the hand of the LORD was set against the Philistines as long as Samuel lived. ¹⁴The towns which the Philistines had taken from Israel, from Ekron to Gath, were restored to Israel; Israel recovered all her territory from the Philistines. There was also peace between Israel and the Amorites.

¹⁵Samuel judged Israel as long as he lived. ¹⁶Each year he made the rounds of Bethel, Gilgal, and Mizpah, and acted as judge over Israel at all those places. ¹⁷Then he would return to Ramah, for his home was there, and there too he would judge Israel. He built an altar there to the LORD.

8

When Samuel grew old, he appointed his sons judges over Israel. ²The name of his first-born son was Joel, and his second son's name was

ᵇ Otherwise unknown; perhaps identical with "Jeshanah"; cf. Septuagint; also 2 Chron. 13.19.
ᶜ I.e., "Stone of Help."

Abijah; they sat as judges in Beer-sheba. ³But his sons did not follow in his ways; they were bent on gain, they accepted bribes, and they subverted justice.

⁴All the elders of Israel assembled and came to Samuel at Ramah, ⁵and they said to him, "You have grown old, and your sons have not followed your ways. Therefore appoint a king for us, to govern us like all other nations." ⁶Samuel was displeased that they said "Give us a king to govern us." Samuel prayed to the LORD, ⁷and the LORD replied to Samuel, "Heed the demand of the people in everything they say to you. For it is not you that they have rejected; it is Me they have rejected as their king. ⁸Like everything else they have done ever since I brought them out of Egypt to this day—forsaking Me and worshiping other gods—so they are doing to you. ⁹Heed their demand; but warn them solemnly, and tell them about the practices of any king who will rule over them."

¹⁰Samuel reported all the words of the LORD to the people, who were asking him for a king. ¹¹He said, "This will be the practice of the king who will rule over you: He will take your sons and appoint them as his charioteers and horsemen, and they will serve as outrunners for his chariots. ¹²He will appoint them as his chiefs of thousands and of fifties; or they will have to plow his fields, reap his harvest, and make his weapons and the equipment for his chariots. ¹³He will take your daughters as perfumers, cooks, and bakers. ¹⁴He will seize your choice fields, vineyards, and olive groves, and give them to his courtiers. ¹⁵He will take a tenth part of your grain and vintage and give it to his eunuchs and courtiers. ¹⁶He will take your male and female slaves, your choice ᵃ-young men,-ᵃ and your asses, and put them to work for him. ¹⁷He will take a tenth part of your flocks, and you shall become his slaves. ¹⁸The day will come when you cry out because of the king whom you yourselves have chosen; and the LORD will not answer you on that day."

¹⁹But the people would not listen to Samuel's warning. "No," they said. "We must have a king over us, ²⁰that we may be like all the other nations: Let our king rule over us and go out at our head and fight our battles." ²¹When Samuel heard all that the people said, he reported it to the LORD. ²²And the LORD said to Samuel, "Heed their demands and appoint a king for them." Samuel then said to the men of Israel, "All of you go home."

ᵃ⁻ᵃ *Septuagint reads "cattle."*

9 There was a man of Benjamin whose name was Kish son of Abiel son of Zeror son of Becorath son of Aphiah, a Benjaminite, a man of substance. ²He had a son whose name was Saul, an excellent young man; no one among the Israelites was handsomer than he; ᵃ⁻he was a head taller⁻ᵃ than any of the people.

³Once the asses of Saul's father Kish went astray, and Kish said to his son Saul, "Take along one of the servants and go out and look for the asses." ⁴He passed into the hill country of Ephraim. He crossed the district of Shalishah, but they did not find them. They passed through the district of Shaalim, but they were not there. They traversed the [entire] territory of Benjamin, and still they did not find them. ⁵When they reached the district of Zuph, Saul said to the servant who was with him, "Let us turn back, or my father will stop worrying about the asses and begin to worry about us." ⁶But he replied, "There is a man of God in that town, and the man is highly esteemed; everything that he says comes true. Let us go there; perhaps he will tell us about the errand on which we set out." ⁷"But if we go," Saul said to his servant, "what can we bring the man? For the food in our bags is all gone, and there is nothing we can bring to the man of God as a present. What have we got?" ⁸The servant answered Saul again, "I happen to have a quarter-shekel of silver. I can give that to the man of God and he will tell us about our errand."—⁹ᵇFormerly in Israel, when a man went to inquire of God, he would say, "Come, let us go to the seer," for the prophet of today was formerly called a seer.—¹⁰Saul said to his servant, "A good idea; let us go." And they went to the town where the man of God lived.

¹¹As they were climbing the ascent to the town, they met some girls coming out to draw water, and they asked them, "Is the seer in town?" ¹²"Yes," they replied. "He is up there ahead of you. ᶜ⁻Hurry, for he has just come to the town⁻ᶜ because the people have a sacrifice at the shrine today. ¹³As soon as you enter the town, you will find him before he goes up to the shrine to eat; the people will not eat until he comes; for he must first bless the sacrifice and only then will the guests eat. Go up at once, for you will find him right away." ¹⁴So they went up to the town; and as they were entering the town,ᵈ Samuel came out toward them, on his way up to the shrine.

¹⁵Now the day before Saul came, the LORD had revealed the following to Samuel: ¹⁶"At this time tomorrow, I will send a man to you from the

---

ᵃ⁻ᵃ Lit. "taller from his shoulders up."
ᵇ This verse explains the term "seer" in v. 11.
ᶜ⁻ᶜ Emendation yields "Hurry, for he has just reached ('attah kayyom ba, so Septuagint) the gate"; cf. v. 18.
ᵈ Emendation yields "gate"; cf. v. 18.

territory of Benjamin, and you shall anoint him ruler of My people Israel. He will deliver My people from the hands of the Philistines; for I have taken note of c-My people,-c their outcry has come to Me."

17As soon as Samuel saw Saul, the LORD declared to him, "This is the man that I told you would govern My people." 18Saul approached Samuel inside the gate and said to him, "Tell me, please, where is the house of the seer?" 19And Samuel answered Saul, "I am the seer. Go up ahead of me to the shrine, for you shall eat with me today; and in the morning I will let you go, after telling you whatever may be on your mind. 20As for your asses that strayed three days ago, do not concern yourself about them, for they have been found. And for whom is all Israel yearning, if not for you and all your ancestral house?" 21Saul replied, "But I am only a Benjaminite, from the smallest of the tribes of Israel, and my clan is the least of all the clans of the tribef of Benjamin! Why do you say such things to me?"

22Samuel took Saul and his servant and brought them into the hall, and gave them a place at the head of the guests, who numbered about thirty. 23And Samuel said to the cook, "Bring the portion which I gave you and told you to set aside." 24The cook lifted up the thigh and g-what was on it,-g and set it before Saul. And [Samuel] said, h-"What has been reserved is set before you. Eat; it has been kept for you for this occasion, when I said I was inviting the people."-h So Saul ate with Samuel that day. 25They then descended from the shrine to the town, and i-[Samuel] talked with Saul on the roof.

26Early, at-i the break of day, Samuel called to Saul on the roof. He said, "Get up, and I will send you off." Saul arose, and the two of them, Samuel and he, went outside. 27As they were walking toward the end of the town, Samuel said to Saul, "Tell the servant to walk ahead of us"— and he walked ahead—"but you stop here a moment and I will make known to you the word of God."

10 Samuel took a flask of oil and poured some on Saul'sa head and kissed him, and said, "The LORD herewith b-anoints you ruler-b over His

---

c-c *Septuagint and Targum read "the plight of My people"; cf. Exod. 3.7.*
f *Heb. plural.*
g-g *Meaning of Heb. uncertain. Emendation yields "the broad tail."*
h-h *Meaning of Heb. uncertain.*
i-i *Meaning of Heb. uncertain. Septuagint reads "They spread a bed for Saul on the roof, and he lay down. At. . . ."*

a *Heb. "his."*
b-b *Septuagint and Vulgate read "anoints you ruler over His people Israel, and you will govern the people of the LORD and deliver them from the hands of their foes roundabout. And this is the sign for you that the LORD anoints you."*

own people. ²When you leave me today, you will meet two men near the tomb of Rachel in the territory of Benjamin, ᶜ⁻at Zelzah,⁻ᶜ and they will tell you that the asses you set out to look for have been found, and that your father has stopped being concerned about the asses and is worrying about you, saying: 'What shall I do about my son?' ³You shall pass on from there until you come to the terebinth of Tabor. There you will be met by three men making a pilgrimage to God at Bethel. One will be carrying three kids, another will be carrying three loaves of bread, and the third will be carrying a jar of wine. ⁴They will greet you and offer you two loaves of bread, which you shall accept. ⁵After that, you are to go on to ᵈ⁻the Hill⁻ᵈ of God, where the Philistine prefects reside. There, as you enter the town, you will encounter a band of prophets coming down from the shrine, preceded by lyres, timbrels, flutes, and harps, and they will be ᵉ⁻speaking in ecstasy.⁻ᵉ ⁶The spirit of the LORD will grip you, and you will speak in ecstasy along with them; you will become another man. ⁷And once these signs have happened to you, ᶠ⁻act when the occasion arises,⁻ᶠ for God is with you. ⁸After that, you are to go down to Gilgal ahead of me, and I will come down to you to present burnt offerings and offer sacrifices of well-being.ᶠ Wait seven days until I come to you and instruct you what you are to do next."

⁹As [Saul] turned around to leave Samuel, God gave him another heart; and all those signs were fulfilled that same day. ¹⁰And when they came there, to ᵈ⁻the Hill,⁻ᵈ he saw a band of prophets coming toward him. Thereupon the spirit of God gripped him, and he spoke in ecstasy among them. ¹¹When all who knew him previously saw him speaking in ecstasy together with the prophets, the people said to one another, "What's happened to ᵍ⁻the son of Kish?⁻ᵍ Is Saul too among the prophets?" ¹²But another person there spoke up and said, "And who are their fathers?" Thus the proverb arose: "Is Saul too among the prophets?" ¹³And when he stopped speaking in ecstasy, he entered the shrine.

¹⁴Saul's uncle asked him and his servant, "Where did you go?" "To look for the asses," he replied. "And when we saw that they were not to be found, we went to Samuel." ¹⁵"Tell me," said Saul's uncle, "what did Samuel say to you?" ¹⁶Saul answered his uncle, "He just told us that the

ᶜ⁻ᶜ *Meaning of Heb. uncertain.*
ᵈ⁻ᵈ *Or "Gibeah."*
ᵉ⁻ᵉ *Others "prophesying"; cf. Num. 11.25 and note.*
ᶠ⁻ᶠ *See 11.5–15.*
ᵍ⁻ᵍ *To refer to a person merely as "the son (ben) of. . ." is slighting; cf. 20, 27, 30, 31; Isa. 7.4.*

asses had been found." But he did not tell him anything of what Samuel had said about the kingship.

17Samuel summoned the people to the LORD at Mizpah 18and said to them, "Thus said the LORD, the God of Israel: 'I brought Israel out of Egypt, and I delivered you from the hands of the Egyptians and of all the kingdoms that oppressed you.' 19But today you have rejected your God who delivered you from all your troubles and calamities. For you said, 'No,h set up a king over us!' Now station yourselves before the LORD, by your tribes and clans."

20Samuel brought forward each of the tribes of Israel, and the lot indicated the tribe of Benjamin. 21Then Samuel brought forward the tribe of Benjamin by its clans, and the clan of the Matrites was indicated; and theni Saul son of Kish was indicated. But when they looked for him, he was not to be found. 22They inquired of the LORD again, j-"Has anyone else come here?"-j And the LORD replied, "Yes; he is hiding among the baggage." 23So they ran over and brought him from there; and when he took his place among the people, he stood a head taller than all the people. 24And Samuel said to the people, "Do you see the one whom the LORD has chosen? There is none like him among all the people." And all the people acclaimed him, shouting, "Long live the king!"

25Samuel expounded to the people the rules of the monarchy, and recorded them in a document which he deposited before the LORD. Samuel then sent the people back to their homes. 26Saul also went home to Gibeah, accompanied by k-upstanding men-k whose hearts God had touched. 27But some scoundrels said, "How can this fellow save us?" So they scorned him and brought him no gift. l-But he pretended not to mind.-l

11 Nahash the Ammonite marched up and besieged Jabesh-gilead. All the men of Jabesh-gilead said to Nahash, "Make a pact with us, and we will serve you." 2But Nahash the Ammonite answered them, "I will make a pact with you on this condition, that everyone's right eye be gouged out; I will make this a humiliation for all Israel." 3The elders of Jabesh said to him, "Give us seven days' respite, so that we may send messengers throughout the territory of Israel; if no one comes to our aid,

---

h *So many Heb. mss. and ancient versions. Other mss. and editions read "to Him."*
i *Septuagint reads "then he brought up the family of the Matrites by their men and...."*
j-j *Septuagint reads "Has the man come here?"*
k-k *In contrast to "scoundrels" (v. 27); understanding Heb. ḥayil as the equivalent of bene hayil, as read by Septuagint and 4QSamª.*
l-l *Lit. "But he was as one who holds his peace." Septuagint and 4QSamª read "About a month later," connecting with what follows.*

we will surrender to you." ⁴When the messengers came to Gibeah of Saul and gave this report in the hearing of the people, all the people broke into weeping.

⁵Saul was just coming from the field driving the cattle; and Saul asked, "Why are the people crying?" And they told him about the situation of the men of Jabesh. ⁶When he heard these things, the spirit of God gripped Saul and his anger blazed up. ⁷He took a yoke of oxen and cut them into pieces, which he sent by messengers throughout the territory of Israel, with the warning, "Thus shall be done to the cattle of anyone who does not follow Saul and Samuel into battle!" Terror from the LORD fell upon the people, and they came out as one man. ⁸[Saul] mustered them in Bezek, and the Israelites numbered 300,000, the men of Judah 30,000. ⁹The messengers who had come were told, "Thus shall you speak to the men of Jabesh-gilead: Tomorrow, when the sun grows hot, you shall be saved." When the messengers came and told this to the men of Jabesh-gilead, they rejoiced. ¹⁰The men of Jabesh then told [the Ammonites], "Tomorrow we will surrender to you, and you can do to us whatever you please."

¹¹The next day, Saul divided the troops into three columns; at the morning watch they entered the camp and struck down the Ammonites until the day grew hot. The survivors scattered; no two were left together.

¹²The people then said to Samuel, "Who was it said, 'Shall Saul be king over us?' Hand the men over and we will put them to death!" ¹³But Saul replied, "No man shall be put to death this day! For this day the LORD has brought victory to Israel."

¹⁴Samuel said to the people, "Come, let us go to Gilgal and there inaugurate the monarchy." ¹⁵So all the people went to Gilgal, and there at Gilgal they declared Saul king before the LORD. They offered sacrifices of well-being there before the LORD; and Saul and all the men of Israel held a great celebration there.

12 Then Samuel said to all Israel, "I have yielded to you in all you have asked of me and have set a king over you. ²Henceforth the king will be your leader.

"As for me, I have grown old and gray—but my sons are still with you—and I have been your leader from my youth to this day. ³Here I am! Testify against me, in the presence of the LORD and in the presence of His anointed one: Whose ox have I taken, or whose ass have I taken? Whom have I defrauded or whom have I robbed? From whom have I taken a bribe ᵃ⁻to look the other way?⁻ᵃ I will return it to you." ⁴They responded, "You have not defrauded us, and you have not robbed us, and you have taken nothing from anyone." ⁵He said to them, "The LORD then is witness, and His anointed is witness, ᵇ⁻to your admission⁻ᵇ this day that you have found nothing in my possession." Theyᶜ responded, "He is!"

⁶Samuel said to the people, ᵈ⁻"The LORD [is witness], He who appointed⁻ᵈ Moses and Aaron and who brought your fathers out of the land of Egypt. ⁷Come, stand before the LORD while I cite against you all the kindnesses that the LORD has done to you and your fathers.

⁸"When Jacob came to Egypt,ᵉ . . . your fathers cried out to the LORD, and the LORD sent Moses and Aaron, who brought your fathers out of Egypt and settled them in this place. ⁹But they forgot the LORD their God; so He delivered them into the hands of Sisera the military commander of Hazor, into the hands of the Philistines, and into the hands of the king of Moab; and these made war upon them. ¹⁰They cried to the LORD, 'We are guilty, for we have forsaken the LORD and worshiped the Baalim and the Ashtaroth. Oh, deliver us from our enemies and we will serve You.' ¹¹And the Lord sent Jerubbaal and Bedanᶠ and Jephthah and Samuel, and delivered you from the enemies around you; and you dwelt in security. ¹²But when you saw that Nahash king of the Ammonites was advancing against you, you said to me, 'No, we must have a king reigning over us'—though the LORD your God is your King.

¹³"Well, the LORD has set a king over you! Here is the king that you have chosen, that you have asked for.

¹⁴"If you will revere the LORD, worship Him, and obey Him, and will not flout the LORD's command, if both you and the king who reigns over you will follow the LORD your God, [well and good]. ¹⁵But if you do not obey the LORD and you flout the LORD's command, the hand of the LORD will strike you ᵈ⁻as it did your fathers.⁻ᵈ

¹⁶"Now stand by and see the marvelous thing that the LORD will do before your eyes. ¹⁷It is the season of the wheat harvest.ᵍ I will pray to

---

ᵃ⁻ᵃ *Septuagint reads "or a pair of sandals? [cf. Amos 2.6] Testify against me."*
ᵇ⁻ᵇ *Lit. "against you."*
ᶜ *Heb. "he."*
ᵈ⁻ᵈ *Meaning of Heb. uncertain.*
ᵉ *Septuagint adds "the Egyptians oppressed them."*
ᶠ *Septuagint "Barak."*
ᵍ *When thunderstorms do not occur in the land of Israel.*

the LORD and He will send thunder and rain; then you will take thought and realize what a wicked thing you did in the sight of the LORD when you asked for a king."

18Samuel prayed to the LORD, and the LORD sent thunder and rain that day, and the people stood in awe of the LORD and of Samuel. 19The people all said to Samuel, "Intercede for your servants with the LORD your God that we may not die, for we have added to all our sins the wickedness of asking for a king." 20But Samuel said to the people, "Have no fear. You have, indeed, done all those wicked things. Do not, however, turn away from the LORD, but serve the LORD with all your heart. 21Do not turn away to follow worthless things, which can neither profit nor save but are worthless. 22For the sake of His great name, the LORD will never abandon His people, seeing that the LORD undertook to make you His people.

23"As for me, far be it from me to sin against the LORD and refrain from praying for you; and I will continue to instruct you in the practice of what is good and right. 24Above all, you must revere the LORD and serve Him faithfully with all your heart; and consider how grandly He has dealt with you. 25For if you persist in your wrongdoing, both you and your king shall be swept away."

13 Saul was . . .a years old when he became king, and he reigned over Israel two years. 2Saul picked 3,000 Israelites, of whom 2,000 were with Saul in Michmasb and in the hill country of Bethel, and 1,000 with Jonathan in Gibeah of Benjamin; the rest of the troops he sent back to their homes. 3Jonathan struck down the Philistine prefect in Geba;c and the Philistines heard about it. d-Saul had the ram's horn sounded throughout the land, saying, "Let the Hebrews hear."-d

4When all Israel heard that Saul had struck down the Philistine prefect, and that Israel had e-incurred the wrath of-e the Philistines, all the people rallied to Saul at Gilgal. 5The Philistines, in turn, gathered to attack Israel: 30,000f chariots and 6,000 horsemen, and troops as numerous as the sands of the seashore. They marched up and encamped at Michmas, east of Beth-aven.

6d-When the men of Israel saw that they were in trouble—for the troops were hard pressed—the people hid in caves, among thorns, among rocks,

---

a The number is lacking in the Heb. text; also, the precise context of the "two years" is uncertain. The verse is lacking in the Septuagint.
b So in oldest mss.; other mss. and editions read "Michmash" throughout the chapter.
c Apparently identical with Gibeah in v. 2.
d-d Meaning of Heb. uncertain.
e-e Lit. "became malodorous to."
f Septuagint and other versions read "three thousand."

in tunnels, and in cisterns. 7Some Hebrews crossed the Jordan, [to] the territory of Gad and Gilead. Saul was still at Gilgal, and the rest of the people rallied to him in alarm.-d

8He waited seven days, the time that Samuel [had set].g But when Samuel failed to come to Gilgal, and the people began to scatter, 9Saul said, "Bring me the burnt offering and the sacrifice of well-being"; and he presented the burnt offering. 10He had just finished presenting the burnt offering when Samuel arrived; and Saul went out to meet him and welcome him. 11But Samuel said, "What have you done?" Saul replied, "I saw the people leaving me and scattering; you had not come at the appointed time, and the Philistines had gathered at Michmas. 12I thought the Philistines would march down against me at Gilgal before I had entreated the LORD, so I d-forced myself-d to present the burnt offering." 13Samuel answered Saul, h-"You acted foolishly in not keeping the commandments that the LORD your God laid upon you! Otherwise-h the LORD would have established your dynasty over Israel forever. 14But now your dynasty will not endure. The LORD will seek out a man after His own heart, and the LORD will appoint him ruler over His people, because you did not abide by what the LORD had commanded you."

15i-Samuel arose and went up from Gilgal-i to Gibeahj of Benjamin. Saul numbered the troops who remained with him—about 600 strong. 16Saul and his son Jonathan, and the troops who remained with them, stayed in Geba of Benjamin, while the Philistines were encamped at Michmas. 17The raiders came out of the Philistine camp in three columns: One column headed for the Ophrah road that leads to the district of Shual, 18another column headed for the Beth-horon road, and the third column headed for the borderk road that overlooks the valley of Zeboim toward the desert.

19No smith was to be found in all the land of Israel, for the Philistines were afraid that the Hebrews would make swords or spears. 20So all the Israelites had to go down to the Philistines to have their plowshares, their mattocks, axes, and coltersl sharpened. 21m The charge for sharpening was a pimn for plowshares, mattocks, three-pronged forks, and axes, and for setting the goads. 22Thus on the day of the battle, no sword or spear was

---

g So some Heb. mss.; other mss., Septuagint, and Targum read "said." Cf. 10.8.
h-h Change of vocalization yields, "You acted foolishly. If you had kept the commandment the LORD your God laid upon you. . . ."
i-i Septuagint reads here, "Samuel rose and left Gilgal and went his way. The rest of the people followed Saul to meet the soldiers, and they went from Gilgal."
j Sometimes called Geba; cf. vv. 3, 16; 14.5.
k Septuagint reads "Geba."
l Meaning of Heb. uncertain. Septuagint reads "sickle."
mMeaning of several terms in this verse uncertain.
n I.e., two-thirds of a shekel.

to be found in the possession of any of the troops with Saul and Jonathan; only Saul and Jonathan had them.

²³Now the Philistine garrison had marched out to the pass of Michmas.

14 One day, Jonathan son of Saul said to the attendant who carried his arms, "Come, let us cross over to the Philistine garrison on the other side"; but he did not tell his father. ²Now Saul was staying on the outskirts of Gibeah,ᵃ under the pomegranate tree at Migron, and the troops with him numbered about 600. ³Ahijah son of Ahitub brother of Ichabod son of Phinehas son of Eli, the priest of the LORD at Shiloh, was there bearing an ephod.—The troops did not know that Jonathan had gone. ⁴ᵇ⁻At the crossing⁻ᵇ by which Jonathan sought to reach the Philistine garrison, there was a rocky crag on one side, and another rocky crag on the other, the one called Bozez and the other Seneh. ⁵One crag was located on the north, near Michmas, and the other on the south, near Geba.

⁶Jonathan said to the attendant who carried his arms, "Come, let us cross over to the outpost of those uncircumcised fellows. Perhaps the LORD will act in our behalf, for nothing prevents the LORD from winning a victory by many or by few." ⁷His arms-bearer answered him, "Do whatever ᶜ⁻you like. You go first,⁻ᶜ I am ᵈ⁻with you, whatever you decide."⁻ᵈ ⁸Jonathan said, "We'll cross over to those men and let them see us. ⁹If they say to us, 'Wait until we get to you,' then we'll stay where we are, and not go up to them. ¹⁰But if they say, 'Come up to us,' then we will go up, for the LORD is delivering them into our hands. That shall be our sign." ¹¹They both showed themselves to the Philistine outpost and the Philistines said, "Look, some Hebrews are coming out of the holes where they have been hiding." ¹²The men of the outpost shouted to Jonathan and his arms-bearer, "Come up to us, and we'll teach you a lesson." Then Jonathan said to his arms-bearer, "Follow me, for the LORD will deliver them into the hands of Israel." ¹³And Jonathan clambered up on his hands and feet, his arms-bearer behind him; [the Philistines] fell before Jonathan, and his arms-bearer finished them off behind him. ¹⁴The initial attack that Jonathan and his arms-bearer made accounted for some twenty

---

ᵃ *See note j at 13.15.*
ᵇ⁻ᵇ *Meaning of Heb. uncertain.*
ᶜ⁻ᶜ *Lit. "is in your heart. Incline yourself." Septuagint reads "your heart inclines to."*
ᵈ⁻ᵈ *Lit. "with you, according to your heart." Septuagint reads "with you; my heart is like your heart."*

men, b-within a space about half a furrow long [in] an acre of land.-b
15Terror broke out among all the troops both in the camp [and] in the field; the outposts and the raiders were also terrified. The very earth quaked, and a terror from God ensued.

16Saul's scouts in Gibeah of Benjamin saw that the multitude was e-scattering in all directions.-e 17And Saul said to the troops with him, "Take a count and see who has left us." They took a count and found that Jonathan and his arms-bearer were missing. 18Thereupon Saul said to Ahijah, "Bring the Arkf of God here"; for the Arkf of God was at the time amongg the Israelites. 19But while Saul was speaking to the priest, the confusion in the Philistine camp kept increasing; and Saul said to the priest, "Withdraw your hand." 20Saul and the troops with him assembled and rushed into battle; they found [the Philistines] in very great confusion, every man's sword turned against his fellow. 21b-And the Hebrews who had previously sided with the Philistines, who had come up with them in the army [from] round about—they too joined the Israelites-b who were with Saul and Jonathan. 22When all the men of Israel who were hiding in the hill country of Ephraim heard that the Philistines were fleeing, they too pursued them in battle. 23Thus the LORD brought victory to Israel that day.

The fighting passed beyond Beth-aven. 24h-The men of Israel were distressed-h that day. For Saul had laid an oath upon the troops: "Cursed be the man who eats any food before night falls and I take revenge on my enemies." So none of the troops ate anything. 25Everybody came to a i-stack of beehives-i where some honey had spilled on the ground. 26When the troops came to the beehivesi and found the flow of honey there, no one putb his hand to his mouth, for the troops feared the oath. 27Jonathan, however, had not heard his father adjure the troops. So he put out the stick he had with him, dipped it into the beehive of honey, and brought his hand back to his mouth; and his eyes lit up. 28At this one of the soldiers spoke up, "Your father adjured the troops: 'Cursed be the man who eats anything this day.' And so the troops are faint." 29Jonathan answered, "My father has brought trouble on the people. See for yourselves how my eyes lit up when I tasted that bit of honey. 30If only the troops had eaten today of spoil captured from the enemy, the defeat of the Philistines would have been greater still!"

e-e *Lit. "shaken and going thither." Meaning of Heb. uncertain.*
f *Septuagint reads "ephod," and cf. vv. 3, 23.9, 30.7.*
g *Heb. "and."*
h-h *Meaning of Heb. uncertain. Septuagint reads "And all the troops, about 10,000 men, were with Saul; and the battle spread into the hill country of Ephraim. Now Saul committed a rash act."*
i-i *Meaning of Heb. uncertain; cf. Song of Songs 5.1.*

³¹They struck down the Philistines that day from Michmas to Aijalon, and the troops were famished. ³²The troops pounced on the spoil; they took the sheep and cows and calves and slaughtered them on the ground, and the troops ate with the blood.ʲ ³³When it was reported to Saul that the troops were sinning against the LORD, eating with the blood, he said, "You have acted faithlessly. Roll a large stone over to me today."ᵏ ³⁴And Saul ordered, "Spread out among the troops and tell them that everyone must bring me his ox or his sheep and slaughter it here, and then eat. You must not sin against the LORD and eat with the blood." Every one of the troops brought ˡ-his own ox with him-ˡ that night and slaughtered it there. ³⁵Thus Saul set up an altar to the LORD; it was the first altar he erected to the LORD.

³⁶Saul said, "Let us go down after the Philistines by night and plunder among them until the light of morning; and let us not leave a single survivor among them." "Do whatever you please," they replied. But the priest said, "Let us approach God here." ³⁷So Saul inquired of God, "Shall I go down after the Philistines? Will You deliver them into the hands of Israel?" But this time He did not respond to him. ³⁸Then Saul said, "Come forward, all chief officers of the troops, and find out how this guilt was incurred today. ³⁹For as the LORD lives who brings victory to Israel, even if it was through my son Jonathan, he shall be put to death!" Not one soldier answered him. ⁴⁰And he said to all the Israelites, "You stand on one side, and my son Jonathan and I shall stand on the other." The troops said to Saul, "Do as you please." ⁴¹Saul then said to the LORD, the God of Israel, ᵐ-"Show Thammim."-ᵐ Jonathan and Saul were indicated by lot, and the troops were cleared. ⁴²And Saul said, "Cast the lots between my son and me"; and Jonathan was indicated.

⁴³Saul said to Jonathan, "Tell me, what have you done?" And Jonathan told him, "I only tasted a bit of honey with the tip of the stick in my hand. I am ready to die." ⁴⁴Saul said, "Thus and more may God do:ⁿ You shall be put to death, Jonathan!" ⁴⁵But the troops said to Saul, "Shall Jonathan die, after bringing this great victory to Israel? Never! As the LORD lives, not a hair of his head shall fall to the ground! For he brought this day to pass with the help of God." Thus the troops saved Jonathan and he did not die. ⁴⁶Saul broke off his pursuit of the Philistines, and the Philistines returned to their homes.

ʲ *I.e., without the proper rites.*
ᵏ *Septuagint reads "here."*
ˡ⁻ˡ *Septuagint reads "whatever he had in his possession."*
ᵐ⁻ᵐ*Meaning of Heb. uncertain. Septuagint reads "Why have You not responded to Your servant today? If this iniquity was due to my son Jonathan or to me, O LORD, God of Israel, show Urim; and if You say it was due to Your people Israel, show Thummim."*
ⁿ *Many mss. and Septuagint add "to me."*

47After Saul had secured his kingship over Israel, he waged war on every side against all his enemies: against the Moabites, Ammonites, Edomites, the Philistines, and the kings° of Zobah; and wherever he turned he worsted [them]. 48He was triumphant, defeating the Amalekites and saving Israel from those who plundered it.

49Saul's sons were: Jonathan, Ishvi,P and Malchishua; and the names of his two daughters were Merab, the older, and Michal, the younger. 50The name of Saul's wife was Ahinoam daughter of Ahimaaz; and the name of his army commander was Abiner9 son of Saul's uncle Ner. 51Kish, Saul's father, and Ner, Abner's father, were sons of Abiel.

52There was bitter war against the Philistines all the days of Saul; and whenever Saul noticed any stalwart man or warrior, he would take him into his service.

15 Samuel said to Saul, "I am the one the LORD sent to anoint you king over His people Israel. Therefore, listen to the LORD's command!

2"Thus said the LORD of Hosts: I am exacting the penalty for what Amalek did to Israel, for the assault he made upon them on the road, on their way up from Egypt. 3Now go, attack Amalek, and proscribea all that belongs to him. Spare no one, but kill alike men and women, infants and sucklings, oxen and sheep, camels and asses!"

4Saul mustered the troops and enrolled them at Telaim: 200,000 men on foot, and 10,000 men of Judah. 5Then Saul advanced as far as the city of Amalek and b-lay in wait-b in the wadi. 6Saul said to the Kenites, "Come, withdraw at once from among the Amalekites, that I may not destroy you along with them; for you showed kindness to all the Israelites when they left Egypt." So the Kenites withdrew from among the Amalekites.

7Saul destroyed Amalek from Havilah all the way to Shur, which is close to Egypt, 8and he captured King Agag of Amalek alive. He proscribed all the people, putting them to the sword; 9but Saul and the troops spared Agag and the best of the sheep, the oxen, the second-born,c the lambs, and all else that was of value. They would not proscribe them; they proscribed only b-what was cheap and worthless.-b

10The word of the LORD then came to Samuel: 11"I regret that I made Saul king, for he has turned away from Me and has not carried out My

o *Septuagint and 4QSama read "king."*
p *The same as Ishbosheth (2 Sam. 2.8) and Eshbaal (1 Chron. 8.33).*
q *Usually "Abner."*

a *See note at Josh. 6.18.*
b-b *Meaning of Heb. uncertain.*
c *Targum and Syriac read "fatlings."*

commands." Samuel was distressed and he entreated the LORD all night long. [12]Early in the morning Samuel went to meet Saul. Samuel was told, "Saul went to Carmel, where he erected a monument for himself; then he left and went on down to Gilgal."

[13]When Samuel came to Saul, Saul said to him, "Blessed are you of the LORD! I have fulfilled the LORD's command." [14]"Then what," demanded Samuel, "is this bleating of sheep in my ears, and the lowing of oxen that I hear?" [15]Saul answered, "They were brought from the Amalekites, for the troops spared the choicest of the sheep and oxen for sacrificing to the LORD your God. And we proscribed the rest." [16]Samuel said to Saul, "Stop! Let me tell you what the LORD said to me last night!" "Speak," he replied. [17]And Samuel said, "You may look small to yourself, but you are the head of the tribes of Israel. The LORD anointed you king over Israel, [18]and the LORD sent you on a mission, saying, 'Go and proscribe the sinful Amalekites; make war on them until you have exterminated them.' [19]Why did you disobey the LORD and swoop down on the spoil d-in defiance of the LORD's will?"-d [20]Saul said to Samuel, "But I did obey the LORD! I performed the mission on which the LORD sent me: I captured King Agag of Amalek, and I proscribed Amalek, [21]and the troops took from the spoil some sheep and oxen—the best of what had been proscribed—to sacrifice to the LORD your God at Gilgal." [22]But Samuel said:

> "Does the LORD delight in burnt offerings and sacrifices
> As much as in obedience to the LORD's command?
> Surely, obedience is better than sacrifice,
> Compliance than the fat of rams.
> [23]For rebellion is like the sin of divination,
> Defiance, like the iniquity of teraphim.e
> Because you rejected the LORD's command,
> He has rejected you as king."

[24]Saul said to Samuel, "I did wrong to transgress the LORD's command and your instructions; but I was afraid of the troops and I yielded to them. [25]Please, forgive my offense and come back with me, and I will bow low to the LORD." [26]But Samuel said to Saul, "I will not go back with you; for you have rejected the LORD's command, and the LORD has rejected you as king over Israel."

[27]As Samuel turned to leave, Saul seized the corner of his robe, and it

---

d-d Lit. "and do what was evil in the sight of the LORD."
e Idols consulted for oracles; see Ezek. 21.26; Zech. 10.2

NEVI'IM I SAMUEL 15.28

tore. ²⁸And Samuel said to him, "The LORD has this day torn the kingship over Israel away from you and has given it to another who is worthier than you. ²⁹Moreover, the Glory^b of Israel does not deceive or change His mind, for He is not human that He should change His mind." ³⁰But [Saul] pleaded, "I did wrong. Please, honor me in the presence of the elders of my people and in the presence of Israel, and come back with me until I have bowed low to the LORD your God." ³¹So Samuel followed Saul back, and Saul bowed low to the LORD.

³²Samuel said, "Bring forward to me King Agag of Amalek." Agag approached him ^{f-}with faltering steps;^{-f} and Agag said, "Ah, bitter death is at hand!"^b

³³Samuel said:

> "As your sword has bereaved women,
> So shall your mother be bereaved among women."

And Samuel ^{b-}cut Agag down^{-b} before the LORD at Gilgal.

³⁴Samuel then departed for Ramah, and Saul went up to his home at Gibeah of Saul.

³⁵Samuel never saw Saul again to the day of his death. But Samuel grieved over Saul, because the LORD regretted that He had made Saul **16** king over Israel. ¹And the LORD said to Samuel, "How long will you grieve over Saul, since I have rejected him as king over Israel? Fill your horn with oil and set out; I am sending you to Jesse the Bethlehemite, for I have decided on one of his sons to be king." ²Samuel replied, "How can I go? If Saul hears of it, he will kill me." The LORD answered, "Take a heifer with you, and say, 'I have come to sacrifice to the LORD.' ³Invite Jesse to the sacrificial feast, and then I will make known to you what you shall do; you shall anoint for Me the one I point out to you." ⁴Samuel did what the LORD commanded. When he came to Bethlehem, the elders of the city went out in alarm to meet him and said, "Do you come on a peaceful errand?" ⁵"Yes," he replied, "I have come to sacrifice to the LORD. Purify yourselves and join me in the sacrificial feast." He also instructed Jesse and his sons to purify themselves and invited them to the sacrificial feast.

⁶When they arrived and he saw Eliab, he thought: "Surely the LORD's anointed stands before Him." ⁷But the LORD said to Samuel, "Pay no attention to his appearance or his stature, for I have rejected him. For not as man sees [does the LORD see];^a man sees only what is visible, but the LORD sees into the heart." ⁸Then Jesse called Abinadab and had him pass

---

^{f-f} *From root* ma'ad, *"to falter"; cf. Septuagint.*

^a *These words are preserved in the Septuagint.*

before Samuel; but he said, "The LORD has not chosen this one either." [9]Next Jesse presented Shammah; and again he said, "The LORD has not chosen this one either." [10]Thus Jesse presented seven of his sons before Samuel, and Samuel said to Jesse, "The LORD has not chosen any of these."

[11]Then Samuel asked Jesse, "Are these all the boys you have?" He replied, "There is still the youngest; he is tending the flock." And Samuel said to Jesse, "Send someone to bring him, for we will not [b-]sit down to eat[-b] until he gets here." [12]So they sent and brought him. He was [b-]ruddy-cheeked, bright-eyed,[-b] and handsome. And the LORD said, "Rise and anoint him, for this is the one." [13]Samuel took the horn of oil and anointed him in the presence of his brothers; and the spirit of the LORD gripped David from that day on. Samuel then set out for Ramah.

[14]Now the spirit of the LORD had departed from Saul, and an evil spirit from the LORD began to terrify him. [15]Saul's courtiers said to him, "An evil spirit of God is terrifying you. [16]Let our lord give the order [and] the courtiers in attendance on you will look for someone who is skilled at playing the lyre; whenever the evil spirit of God comes over you, he will play it[b] and you will feel better." [17]So Saul said to his courtiers, "Find me someone who can play well and bring him to me." [18]One of the attendants spoke up, "I have observed a son of Jesse the Bethlehemite who is skilled in music; he is a stalwart fellow and a warrior, sensible in speech, and handsome in appearance, and the LORD is with him." [19]Whereupon Saul sent messengers to Jesse to say, "Send me your son David, who is with the flock." [20]Jesse took [b-]an ass [laden with][-b] bread, a skin of wine, and a kid, and sent them to Saul by his son David. [21]So David came to Saul and entered his service; [Saul] took a strong liking to him and made him one of his arms-bearers. [22]Saul sent word to Jesse, "Let David remain in my service, for I am pleased with him." [23]Whenever the [evil] spirit of God came upon Saul, David would take the lyre and play it;[b] Saul would find relief and feel better, and the evil spirit would leave him.

17

The Philistines assembled their forces for battle; they massed at Socoh of Judah, and encamped at Ephes-dammim, between Socoh and Azekah. [2]Saul and the men of Israel massed and encamped in the valley of Elah. They drew up their line of battle against the Philistines, [3]with

---

[b-b] *Meaning of Heb. uncertain.*

the Philistines stationed on one hill and Israel stationed on the opposite hill; the ravine was between them. 4A champion[a] of the Philistine forces stepped forward; his name was Goliath of Gath, and he was six cubits and a span tall. 5He had a bronze helmet on his head, and wore a breastplate of scale armor, a bronze breastplate weighing five thousand shekels. 6He had bronze greaves on his legs, and a bronze javelin [slung] from his shoulders. 7The shaft of his spear was like a weaver's bar, and the iron head of his spear weighed six hundred shekels; and the shield-bearer marched in front of him.

8He stopped and called out to the ranks of Israel and he said to them, "Why should you come out to engage in battle? I am the Philistine [champion], and you are Saul's servants. Choose[b] one of your men and let him come down against me. 9If he bests me in combat and kills me, we will become your slaves; but if I best him and kill him, you shall be our slaves and serve us." 10And the Philistine ended, "I herewith defy the ranks of Israel. Get me a man and let's fight it out!" 11When Saul and all Israel heard these words of the Philistine, they were dismayed and terror-stricken.

12David was the son of a certain Ephrathite of Bethlehem in Judah whose name was Jesse. He had eight sons, and in the days of Saul the man was already old, advanced in years.[b] 13The three oldest sons of Jesse had left and gone with Saul to the war. The names of his three sons who had gone to the war were Eliab the first-born, the next Abinadab, and the third Shammah; 14and David was the youngest. The three oldest had followed Saul, 15and David would go back and forth from attending on Saul to shepherd his father's flock at Bethlehem.

16The Philistine stepped forward morning and evening and took his stand for forty days.

17Jesse said to his son David, "Take an ephah of this parched corn and these ten loaves of bread for your brothers, and carry them quickly to your brothers in camp. 18Take these ten cheeses[b] to the captain of their thousand. Find out how your brothers are and bring some token[b] from them." 19Saul and [c]the brothers[c] and all the men of Israel were in the valley of Elah, in the war against the Philistines.

20Early next morning, David left someone in charge of the flock, took [the provisions], and set out, as his father Jesse had instructed him. He reached the barricade[b] as the army was going out to the battle lines shouting the war cry. 21Israel and the Philistines drew up their battle lines

---

a Lit. "the man of the space between," i.e., between the armies.
b Meaning of Heb. uncertain.
c-c Heb. "they."

opposite each other. ²²David left his baggage with the man in charge of the baggage and ran toward the battle line and went to greet his brothers. ²³While he was talking to them, the champion, whose name was Goliath, the Philistine of Gath, stepped forward from the Philistine ranks and spoke the same words as before; and David heard him.

²⁴When the men of Israel saw the man, they fled in terror. ²⁵And the men of Israel were saying [among themselves], "Do you see that man coming out? He comes out to defy Israel! The man who kills him will be rewarded by the king with great riches; he will also give him his daughter in marriage and grant exemption^d to his father's house in Israel." ²⁶David asked the men standing near him, "What will be done for the man who kills that Philistine and removes the disgrace from Israel? Who is that uncircumcised Philistine that he dares defy the ranks of the living God?" ²⁷The troops told him in the same words what would be done for the man who killed him.

²⁸When Eliab, his oldest brother, heard him speaking to the men, Eliab became angry with David and said, "Why did you come down here, and with whom did you leave those few sheep in the wilderness? I know your impudence and your impertinence:^e you came down to watch the fighting!" ²⁹But David replied, "What have I done now? I was only asking!" ³⁰And he turned away from him toward someone else; he asked the same question, and the troops gave him the same answer as before.

³¹The things David said were overheard and were reported to Saul, who had him brought over. ³²David said to Saul, "Let ^f no man's^-f courage fail him. Your servant will go and fight that Philistine!" ³³But Saul said to David, "You cannot go to that Philistine and fight him; you are only a boy, and he has been a warrior from his youth!" ³⁴David replied to Saul, "Your servant has been tending his father's sheep, and if a lion or^b a bear came and carried off an animal from the flock, ³⁵I would go after it and fight it and rescue it from its mouth. And if it attacked me, I would seize it by the beard and strike it down and kill it. ³⁶Your servant has killed both lion and bear; and that uncircumcised Philistine shall end up like one of them, for he has defied the ranks of the living God. ³⁷The LORD," David went on, "who saved me from lion and bear will also save me from that Philistine." "Then go," Saul said to David, "and may the LORD be with you!"

³⁸Saul clothed David in his own garment; he placed a bronze helmet

---

^d I.e., freedom from royal levies.

^e Lit. "badness of heart."

^f-f Septuagint reads "not my lord's."

on his head and fastened ᵍ⁻a breastplate on him.⁻ᵍ ³⁹David girded his
sword over his garment. Then he ʰ⁻tried to walk; but⁻ʰ he was not used
to it. And David said to Saul, "I cannot walk in these, for I am not used
to them." So David took them off. ⁴⁰He took his stick, picked a fewⁱ
smooth stones from the wadi, put them in the pocketᵇ of his shepherd's
bag and, sling in hand, he went toward the Philistine.

⁴¹The Philistine, meanwhile, was coming closer to David, preceded by
his shield-bearer. ⁴²When the Philistine caught sight of David, he scorned
him, for he was but a boy, ruddy and handsome. ⁴³And the Philistine
called out to David, "Am I a dog that you come against me with sticks?"
The Philistine cursed David by his gods; ⁴⁴and the Philistine said to
David, "Come here, and I will give your flesh to the birds of the sky and
the beasts of the field."

⁴⁵David replied to the Philistine, "You come against me with sword
and spear and javelin; but I come against you in the name of the LORD
of Hosts, the God of the ranks of Israel, whom you have defied. ⁴⁶This
very day the LORD will deliver you into my hands. I will kill you and cut
off your head; and I will give ʲ⁻the carcasses⁻ʲ of the Philistine camp to
the birds of the sky and the beasts of the earth. All the earth shall know
that there is a God inᵏ Israel. ⁴⁷And this whole assembly shall know that
the LORD can give victory without sword or spear. For the battle is the
LORD's, and He will deliver you into our hands."

⁴⁸When the Philistine began to advance toward him again, David quickly
ran up to the battle line to face the Philistine. ⁴⁹David put his hand into
the bag; he took out a stone and slung it. It struck the Philistine in the
forehead; the stone sank into his forehead, and he fell face down on the
ground. ⁵⁰Thus David bested the Philistine with sling and stone; he struck
him down and killed him. David had no sword; ⁵¹so David ran up and
stood over the Philistine, grasped his sword and pulled it from its sheath;
and with it he dispatched him and cut off his head.

When the Philistines saw that their warrior was dead, they ran. ⁵²The
men of Israel and Judah rose up with a war cry and they pursued the
Philistines all the way to Gaiˡ and up to the gates of Ekron; the Philistines
fell mortally wounded along the road to Shaarim up to Gath and Ekron.
⁵³Then the Israelites returned from chasing the Philistines and looted their
camp.

ᵍ⁻ᵍ *Heb. "clothed him in a breastplate" (cf. v. 5), because a breastplate was combined with a leather*
jerkin.
ʰ⁻ʰ *Septuagint reads "was unable to walk, for. . . ."*
ⁱ *Lit. "five."*
ʲ⁻ʲ *Septuagint reads "your carcass and the carcasses."*
ᵏ *So many Heb. mss. and ancient versions; other mss. and the editions read "to."*
ˡ *Septuagint reads "Gath"; cf. end of verse.*

54David took the head of the Philistine and brought it to Jerusalem;m and he put his weapons in his own tent.

55When Saul saw David going out to assault the Philistine, he asked his army commander Abner, "Whose son is that boy, Abner?" And Abner replied, "By your life, Your Majesty, I do not know." 56"Then find out whose son that young fellow is," the king ordered. 57So when David returned after killing the Philistine, Abner took him and brought him to Saul, with the head of the Philistine still in his hand. 58Saul said to him, "Whose son are you, my boy?" And David answered, "The son of your servant Jesse the Bethlehemite."

18

When [David] finished speaking with Saul, Jonathan's soul became bound up with the soul of David; Jonathan loved David as himself. 2Saul took him [into his service] that day and would not let him return to his father's house.—3Jonathan and David made a pact, because [Jonathan] loved him as himself. 4Jonathan took off the cloak and tunic he was wearing and gave them to David, together with his sword, bow, and belt. 5David went out [with the troops], and he was successful in every mission on which Saul sent him, and Saul put him in command of all the soldiers; this pleased all the troops and Saul's courtiers as well. 6When the [troops] came home [and] David returned from killing the Philistine, a-the women of all the towns of Israel came out singing and dancing to greet King Saul-a with timbrels, shouting, and sistrums.b 7The women sang as they danced, and they chanted:

Saul has slain his thousands;
David, his tens of thousands!

8Saul was much distressed and greatly vexed about the matter. For he said, "To David they have given tens of thousands, and to me they have given thousands. All that he lacks is the kingship!" 9From that day on Saul kept a jealous eye on David. 10The next day an evil spirit of God gripped Saul and he began to rave in the house, while David was playing [the lyre], as he did daily. Saul had a spear in his hand, 11and Saul threwc the spear, thinking to pin David to the wall. But David eluded him twice. 12Saul was afraid of David, for the LORD was with him and had turned away from Saul. 13So Saul removed him from his presence and appointed

m I.e., after David's capture of Jerusalem (2 Sam. 5).

a-a Meaning of Heb. uncertain; Septuagint reads "the dancing women came out to meet David from all the towns of Israel."

b Meaning of Heb. uncertain.

c Change of vocalization yields "raised."

him chief of a thousand, ^{d-}to march at the head of the troops.^{-d} ¹⁴ David was successful in all his undertakings, for the LORD was with him; ¹⁵and when Saul saw that he was successful, he dreaded him. ¹⁶All Israel and Judah loved David, for he marched at their head.

¹⁷Saul said to David, "Here is my older daughter, Merab; I will give her to you in marriage; in return, you be my warrior and fight the battles of the LORD." Saul thought: "Let not my hand strike him; let the hand of the Philistines strike him." ¹⁸David replied to Saul, "Who am I and ^{e-}what is my life^{-e}—my father's family in Israel—that I should become Your Majesty's son-in-law?" ¹⁹But at the time that Merab, daughter of Saul, should have been given to David, she was given in marriage to Adriel the Meholathite. ²⁰Now Michal daughter of Saul had fallen in love with David; and when this was reported to Saul, he was pleased. ²¹Saul thought: "I will give her to him, and she can serve as a snare for him, so that the Philistines may kill him." So Saul said to David, ^{b-}"You can become my son-in-law even now through the second one."^{-b} ²²And Saul instructed his courtiers to say to David privately, "The king is fond of you and all his courtiers like you. So why not become the king's son-in-law?" ²³When the king's courtiers repeated these words to David, David replied, "Do you think that becoming the son-in-law of a king is a small matter, when I am but a poor man of no consequence?" ²⁴Saul's courtiers reported to him, "This is what David answered." ²⁵And Saul said, "Say this to David: 'The king desires no other bride-price than the foreskins of a hundred Philistines, as vengeance on the king's enemies.' "—Saul intended to bring about David's death at the hands of the Philistines.— ²⁶When his courtiers told this to David, David was pleased with the idea of becoming the king's son-in-law. ^{b-}Before the time had expired,^{-b} ²⁷David went out with his men and killed two hundred^f Philistines; David brought their foreskins and ^{b-}they were counted out^{-b} for the king, that he might become the king's son-in-law. Saul then gave him his daughter Michal in marriage. ²⁸When Saul realized that the LORD was with David ^{g-}and that Michal daughter of Saul loved him,^{-g} ²⁹Saul grew still more afraid of David; and Saul was David's enemy ever after.

³⁰The Philistine chiefs marched out [to battle]; and every time they marched out, David was more successful than all the other officers of Saul. His reputation soared.

d-d *Lit. "and he went out and came in before the troops."*
e-e *Meaning of Heb. uncertain. Change of vocalization yields "who are my kin."*
f *Septuagint reads "one hundred" and cf. 2 Sam. 3.14.*
g-g *Septuagint reads "and that all Israel loved him."*

19

Saul urged his son Jonathan and all his courtiers to kill David. But Saul's son Jonathan was very fond of David, ²and Jonathan told David, "My father Saul is bent on killing you. Be on your guard tomorrow morning; get to a secret place and remain in hiding. ³I will go out and stand next to my father in the field where you will be, and I will speak to my father about you. If I learn anything, I will tell you." ⁴So Jonathan spoke well of David to his father Saul. He said to him, "Let not Your Majesty wrong his servant David, for he has not wronged you; indeed, all his actions have been very much to your advantage. ⁵He took his life in his hands and killed the Philistine, and the LORD wrought a great victory for all Israel. You saw it and rejoiced. Why then should you incur the guilt of shedding the blood of an innocent man, killing David without cause?" ⁶Saul heeded Jonathan's plea, and Saul swore, "As the LORD lives, he shall not be put to death!" ⁷Jonathan called David, and Jonathan told him all this. Then Jonathan brought David to Saul, and he served him as before.

⁸Fighting broke out again. David went out and fought the Philistines. He inflicted a great defeat upon them and they fled before him. ⁹Then an evil spirit of the LORD came upon Saul while he was sitting in his house with his spear in his hand, and David was playing [the lyre]. ¹⁰Saul tried to pin David to the wall with the spear, but he eluded Saul, so that he drove the spear into the wall. David fled and got away.

That night ¹¹Saul sent messengers to David's home to keep watch on him and to kill him in the morning. But David's wife Michal told him, "Unless you run for your life tonight, you will be killed tomorrow." ¹²Michal let David down from the window and he escaped and fled. ¹³Michal then took the household idol, laid it on the bed, and covered it with a cloth; and at its head she put a net of goat's hair. ¹⁴Saul sent messengers to seize David; but she said, "He is sick." ¹⁵Saul, however, sent back the messengers to see David for themselves. "Bring him up to me in the bed," he ordered, "that he may be put to death." ¹⁶When the messengers came, they found the household idol in the bed, with the net of goat's hair at its head. ¹⁷Saul said to Michal, "Why did you play that trick on me and let my enemy get away safely?" "Because," Michal answered Saul, "he said to me: 'Help me get away or I'll kill you.'"

¹⁸David made good his escape, and he came to Samuel at Ramah and told him all that Saul had done to him. He and Samuel went and stayed at Naioth. ¹⁹Saul was told that David was at Naioth in Ramah, ²⁰and Saul sent messengers to seize David. They^a saw a band of prophets ^b-speaking in ecstasy,-^b with Samuel standing by ^c-as their leader;-^c and the spirit of God came upon Saul's messengers and they too began to speak in ecstasy. ²¹When Saul was told about this, he sent other messengers; but they too spoke in ecstasy. Saul sent a third group of messengers; and they also spoke in ecstasy. ²²So he himself went to Ramah. When he came to ^d-the great cistern at Secu,-^d he asked, "Where are Samuel and David?" and was told that they were at Naioth in Ramah. ²³He was on his way there, to Naioth in Ramah, when the spirit of God came upon him too; and he walked on, speaking in ecstasy, until he reached Naioth in Ramah. ²⁴Then he too stripped off his clothes and he too spoke in ecstasy before Samuel; and he lay naked all that day and all night. That is why people say, "Is Saul too among the prophets?"

20 David fled from Naioth in Ramah; he came to Jonathan and said, "What have I done, what is my crime and my guilt against your father, that he seeks my life?" ²He replied, "Heaven forbid! You shall not die. My father does not do anything, great or small, without disclosing it to me; why should my father conceal this matter from me? It cannot be!" ³David ^a-swore further,-^a "Your father knows well that you are fond of me and has decided: Jonathan must not learn of this or he will be grieved. But, as the LORD lives and as you live, there is only a step between me and death." ⁴Jonathan said to David, "Whatever you want, I will do it for you."

⁵David said to Jonathan, "Tomorrow is the new moon, and I ^b-am to sit with the king at the meal. Instead, let-^b me go and I will hide in the countryside until the third^c evening. ⁶If your father notes my absence, you say, 'David asked my permission to run down to his home town, Bethlehem, for the whole family has its annual sacrifice there.' ⁷If he says 'Good,' your servant is safe; but if his anger flares up, know that he is resolved to do [me] harm. ⁸Deal faithfully with your servant, since you

---

ᵃ Heb. "He."
ᵇ⁻ᵇ Cf. note at 10.5.
ᶜ⁻ᶜ Meaning of Heb. uncertain.
ᵈ⁻ᵈ Septuagint reads "the cistern of the threshing floor on the bare height."

ᵃ⁻ᵃ Septuagint reads "replied to him."
ᵇ⁻ᵇ Septuagint reads "will not sit . . . meal. Let. . . ."
ᶜ Septuagint lacks "third."

have taken your servant into a covenant of the LORD with you. And if I am guilty, kill me yourself, but don't make me go back to your father." 9Jonathan replied, "Don't talk like that! If I learn that my father has resolved to kill you, I will surely tell you about it." 10David said to Jonathan, "Who will tell me if[d] your father answers you harshly?" 11Jonathan said to David, "Let us go into the open"; and they both went out into the open.

12eThen Jonathan said to David, "By the LORD, the God of Israel! I will sound out my father at this time tomorrow, [or] on the third day; and if [his response] is favorable for David, I will send a message to you at once and disclose it to you. 13But if my father intends to do you harm, may the LORD do thus to Jonathan and more if I do [not] disclose it to you and send you off to escape unharmed. May the LORD be with you, as He used to be with my father. 14Nor shall you fail to show me the f-LORD's faithfulness,-f while I am alive; nor, when I am dead, 15shall you ever discontinue your faithfulness to my house—not even after the LORD has wiped out every one of David's enemies from the face of the earth. 16Thus has Jonathan covenanted with the house of David; and may the LORD requite the enemies of David!"

17Jonathan, out of his love for David, adjured[g] him again, for he loved him as himself. 18Jonathan said to him, "Tomorrow will be the new moon; and you will be missed when your seat remains vacant.[h] 19So the day after tomorrow, go down i-all the way-i to the place where you hid j-the other time,-j and stay close to the Ezel stone. 20Now I will shoot three arrows to one side of it, as though I were shooting at a mark, 21and I will order the boy to go and find the arrows. If I call to the boy, 'Hey! the arrows are on this side of you,' be reassured[k] and come, for you are safe and there is no danger—as the LORD lives! 22But if, instead, I call to the lad, 'Hey! the arrows are beyond you,' then leave, for the LORD has sent you away. 23As for the promise we made to each other,[l] may the LORD be [witness] between you and me forever."

24David hid in the field. The new moon came, and the king sat down to partake of the meal. 25When the king took his usual place on the seat by the wall, Jonathan rose[m] and Abner sat down at Saul's side; but David's place remained vacant. 26That day, however, Saul said nothing. "It's ac-

---

d *Meaning of Heb. uncertain.*
e *The meaning of several parts of vv. 12–16 is uncertain.*
f-f *I.e., the faithfulness pledged in the covenant before the LORD.*
g *Septuagint reads "swore to."*
h *At the festal meal.*
i-i *Lit. "very much."*
j-j *Lit. "on the day of the incident"; see 19.2 ff.*
k *Lit. "accept it."*
l *See above, vv. 12–17.*
m *Force of Heb. uncertain; Septuagint "faced him."*

cidental," he thought. n-"He must be unclean and not yet cleansed."-n
27But on the day after the new moon, the second day, David's place was
vacant again. So Saul said to his son Jonathan, "Why didn't the son of
Jesseo come to the meal yesterday or today?" 28Jonathan answered Saul,
"David begged leave of me to go to Bethlehem. 29He said, 'Please let me
go, for we are going to have a family feast in our town and my brother
has summoned me to it. Do me a favor, let me slip away to see my
kinsmen.' That is why he has not come to the king's table."

30Saul flew into a rage against Jonathan. "You son of a perverse, rebellious woman!" he shouted. "I know that you side with the son of
Jesse—to your shame, and to the shame of your mother's nakedness! 31For
as long as the son of Jesse lives on earth, neither you nor your kingship
will be secure. Now then, have him brought to me, for he is marked for
death." 32But Jonathan spoke up and said to his father, "Why should he
be put to death? What has he done?" 33At that, Saul threwp his spear at
him to strike him down; and Jonathan realized that his father was determined to do away with David. 34Jonathan rose from the table in a rage.
He ate no food on the second day of the new moon, because he was
grieved about David, and because his father had humiliated him.

35In the morning, Jonathan went out into the open for the meeting
with David, accompanied by a young boy. 36He said to the boy, "Run
ahead and find the arrows that I shoot." And as the boy ran, he shot the
arrows past him. 37When the boy came to the place where the arrows
shot by Jonathan had fallen, Jonathan called out to the boy, "Hey, the
arrows are beyond you!" 38And Jonathan called after the boy, "Quick,
hurry up. Don't stop!" So Jonathan's boy gathered the arrows and came
back to his master.—39The boy suspected nothing; only Jonathan and
David knew the arrangement.—40Jonathan handed the gear to his boy
and told him, "Take these back to the town." 41When the boy got there,
David q-emerged from his concealment at-q the Negeb.r He flung himself
face down on the ground and bowed low three times. They kissed each
other and wept together; David wept the longer.

42Jonathan said to David, "Go in peace! For we two have sworn to
each other in the name of the LORD: 'May the LORD be [witness] between

21 you and me, and between your offspring and mine, forever!'"
1David then went his way, and Jonathan returned to the town.

---

n-n Heb. construction unclear.
o See note at 10.11.
p See 18.11 and note.
q-q Lit. "rose up from beside."
r Identical with the "Ezel Stone," v. 19.

²David went to the priest Ahimelech at Nob. Ahimelech came out in alarm to meet David, and he said to him, "Why are you alone, and no one with you?" ³David answered the priest Ahimelech, "The king has ordered me on a mission, and he said to me, 'No one must know anything about the mission on which I am sending you and for which I have given you orders.' So I have ᵃ-directed [my] young men to-ᵃ such and such a place. ⁴Now then, what have you got on hand? Anyᵇ loaves of bread? Let me have them—or whatever is available." ⁵The priest answered David, "I have no ordinary bread on hand; there is only consecrated bread—provided the young men have kept away from women." ⁶In reply to the priest, David said, "I assure you that women have been kept from us, as always. Whenever I went on a mission, even if the journey was a common one, the vessels of the young men were consecrated; all the more then ᶜ-may consecrated food be put into their vessels today."-ᶜ ⁷So the priest gave him consecrated bread, because there was none there except the bread of display, which had been removed from the presence of the LORD, to be replaced by warm bread as soon as it was taken away.—⁸Now one of Saul's officials was there that day, ᵈ-detained before the LORD;-ᵈ his name was Doeg the Edomite, Saul's ᵉ-chief herdsman.-ᵉ

⁹David said to Ahimelech, "Haven't you got a spear or sword on hand? I didn't take my sword or any of my weapons with me, because the king's mission was urgent." ¹⁰The priest said, "There is the sword of Goliath the Philistine whom you slew in the valley of Elah; it is over there, wrapped in a cloth, behind the ephod. If you want to take that one, take it, for there is none here but that one." David replied, "There is none like it; give it to me."

¹¹That day David continued on his flight from Saul and he came to King Achish of Gath. ¹²The courtiers of Achish said to him, "Why, that's David, king of the land! That's the one of whom they sing as they dance:

Saul has slain his thousands;

David, his tens of thousands."

¹³These words worried David and he became very much afraid of King Achish of Gath. ¹⁴So he concealed his good sense from them; he feigned madness ᶠ-for their benefit.-ᶠ He scratched marks on the doors of the gate and let his saliva run down his beard. ¹⁵And Achish said to his courtiers, "You see the man is raving; why bring him to me? ¹⁶Do I lack madmen

---

ᵃ⁻ᵃ *Meaning of Heb. uncertain. 4QSamᵇ (cf. Septuagint) reads "made an appointment with [my] young men at. . . ."*

ᵇ *Lit. "five."*

ᶜ⁻ᶜ *Meaning of Heb. uncertain in part.*

ᵈ⁻ᵈ *I.e., excluded from the shrine, perhaps because of ritual impurity.*

ᵉ⁻ᵉ *Meaning of Heb. uncertain.*

ᶠ⁻ᶠ *Lit. "in their hand"; meaning of Heb. uncertain.*

that you have brought this fellow to rave for me? Should this fellow enter my house?"

22 David departed from there and escaped to the cave[a] of Adullam; and when his brothers and all his father's house heard, they joined him down there. [2]Everyone who was in straits and everyone who was in debt and everyone who was desperate joined him, and he became their leader; there were about four hundred men with him. [3]David went from there to Mizpeh of Moab, and he said to the king of Moab, "Let my father and mother come [and stay] with you, until I know what God will do for me." [4]So he [b-]led them to[-b] the king of Moab, and they stayed with him as long as David remained in the stronghold.[a] [5]But the prophet Gad said to David, "Do not stay in the stronghold; go at once to the territory of Judah." So David left and went to the forest of Hereth.

[6]When Saul heard that David and the men with him had been located— Saul was then in Gibeah, sitting under the tamarisk tree on the height, spear in hand, with all his courtiers in attendance upon him—[7]Saul said to the courtiers standing about him, "Listen, men of Benjamin! Will the son of Jesse[c] give fields and vineyards to every one of you? And will he make all of you captains of thousands or captains of hundreds? [8]Is that why all of you have conspired against me? For no one informs me when my own son makes a pact with the son of Jesse; no one is concerned[d] for me and no one informs me when my own son has set my servant [e-]in ambush[-e] against me, as is now the case."

[9]Doeg the Edomite, who was standing among the courtiers of Saul, spoke up: "I saw the son of Jesse come to Ahimelech son of Ahitub at Nob. [10]He inquired of the LORD on his behalf and gave him provisions; he also gave him the sword of Goliath the Philistine." [11]Thereupon the king sent for the priest Ahimelech son of Ahitub and for all the priests belonging to his father's house at Nob. They all came to the king, [12]and Saul said, "Listen to me, son[c] of Ahitub." "Yes, my lord," he replied. [13]And Saul said to him, "Why have you and the son of Jesse conspired against me? You gave him food and a sword, and inquired of God for him—that he may rise [e-]in ambush[-e] against me, as is now the case."

[14]Ahimelech replied to the king, "But who is there among all your courtiers as trusted as David, son-in-law of Your Majesty and [f-]obedient

---

[a] *The "cave" in v. 1 is referred to as "stronghold" in vv. 4–5; cf. the same variation in 2 Sam. 23.13–14; 1 Chron. 11.15–16.*
[b-b] *Targum and Syriac read "left them with."*
[c] *See note at 10.11.*
[d] *For this meaning of* holeh, *cf. Amos 6.6.*
[e-e] *Septuagint reads "as an enemy."*
[f-f] *Cf. Isa. 11.14; but meaning of Heb. uncertain.*

to your bidding,⁻ᶠ and esteemed in your household? ¹⁵This is the first time that I inquired of God for him; ᵍ⁻I have done no wrong.⁻ᵍ Let not Your Majesty find fault with his servant [or] with any of my father's house; for your servant knew nothing whatever about all this." ¹⁶But the king said, "You shall die, Ahimelech, you and all your father's house." ¹⁷And the king commanded the guards standing by, "Turn about and kill the priests of the LORD, for they are in league with David; they knew he was running away and they did not inform me." But the king's servants would not raise a hand to strike down the priests of the LORD. ¹⁸Thereupon the king said to Doeg, "You, Doeg, go and strike down the priests." And Doeg the Edomite went and struck down the priests himself; that day, he killed eighty-five men ʰ⁻who wore the linen ephod.⁻ʰ ¹⁹He put Nob, the town of the priests, to the sword: men and women, children and infants, oxen, asses, and sheep—[all] to the sword.

²⁰But one son of Ahimelech son of Ahitub escaped—his name was Abiathar—and he fled to David. ²¹When Abiathar told David that Saul had killed the priests of the LORD, ²²David said to Abiathar, "I knew that day, when Doeg the Edomite was there, that he would tell Saul. I ⁱ⁻am to blame for all the deaths⁻ⁱ in your father's house. ²³Stay with me; do not be afraid; for ⁱ⁻whoever seeks your life must seek my life also.⁻ⁱ It will be my care to guard you."

23 David was told: "The Philistines are raiding Keilah and plundering the threshing floors." ²David consulted the LORD, "Shall I go and attack those Philistines?" And the LORD said to David, "Go; attack the Philistines and you will save Keilah." ³But David's men said to him, "Look, we are afraid here in Judah, how much more if we go to Keilah against the forces of the Philistines!" ⁴So David consulted the LORD again, and the LORD answered him, "March down at once to Keilah, for I am going to deliver the Philistines into your hands." ⁵David and his men went to Keilah and fought against the Philistines; he drove off their cattle and inflicted a severe defeat on them. Thus David saved the inhabitants of Keilah.

⁶When Abiathar son of Ahimelech fled to David at Keilah, ᵃ⁻he brought down an ephod with him.⁻ᵃ

⁷Saul was told that David had come to Keilah, and Saul thought, "God

ᵍ⁻ᵍ Lit. "Far be it from me!"
ʰ⁻ʰ Septuagint reads "bearers of the ephod"; cf. note at 2.28.
ⁱ⁻ⁱ Meaning of Heb. uncertain.

ᵃ⁻ᵃ Meaning of Heb. uncertain.

has delivered[a] him into my hands, for he has shut himself in by entering a town with gates and bars." [8]Saul summoned all the troops for war, to go down to Keilah and besiege David and his men. [9]When David learned that Saul was planning[a] to harm him, he told the priest Abiathar to bring the ephod forward. [10]And David said, "O LORD, God of Israel, Your servant has heard that Saul intends to come to Keilah and destroy the town because of me. [11]Will the citizens of Keilah deliver me into his hands? Will Saul come down, as Your servant has heard? O LORD, God of Israel, tell Your servant!" And the LORD said, "He will." [12]David continued, "Will the citizens of Keilah deliver me and my men into Saul's hands?" And the LORD answered, "They will." [13]So David and his men, about six hundred in number, left Keilah at once and moved about wherever they could. And when Saul was told that David had got away from Keilah, he did not set out.

[14]David was staying [a]in the strongholds of the wilderness [of Judah];[-a] he stayed in the hill country, in the wilderness of Ziph. Saul searched for him constantly, but God did not deliver him into his hands. [15]David was once at Horesh in the wilderness of Ziph, when David learned that Saul had come out to seek his life. [16]And Saul's son Jonathan came to David at Horesh and encouraged him in [the name of] God. [17]He said to him, "Do not be afraid: the hand of my father Saul will never touch you. You are going to be king over Israel and I shall be second to you; and even my father Saul knows this is so." [18]And the two of them entered into a pact before the LORD. David remained in Horesh, and Jonathan went home.

[19][b]Some Ziphites went up to Saul in Gibeah and said, "David is hiding among us in the strongholds of Horesh, at the hill of Hachilah south of Jeshimon. [20]So if Your Majesty has the desire to come down, come down, and it will be our task to deliver him into Your Majesty's hands." [21]And Saul replied, "May you be blessed of the LORD for the compassion you have shown me! [22]Go now and prepare further. Look around and learn what places he sets foot on [and] who has seen him there, for I have been told he is a very cunning fellow. [23]Look around and learn in which of all his hiding places he has been hiding, and return to me when you are certain. I will then go with you, and if he is in the region, I will search him out among all the clans of Judah."

[24]They left at once for Ziph, ahead of Saul; David and his men were

---

[b] *The meaning of many parts of 23.19 ff. is uncertain. The events described in 23.19—24.22 are partly paralleled in chapter 26, with variations.*

then in the wilderness of Maon, in the Arabah, to the south of Jeshimon. ²⁵When Saul and his men came to search, David was told about it; and he went down to ᵃ⁻the rocky region⁻ᵃ and stayed in the wilderness of Maon. On hearing this, Saul pursued David in the wilderness of Maon. ²⁶Saul was making his way along one side of a hill, and David and his men were on the other side of the hill. ᵃ⁻David was trying hard to elude Saul, and Saul and his men were trying to encircle David and his men and capture them,⁻ᵃ ²⁷when a messenger came and told Saul, "Come quickly, for the Philistines have invaded the land." ²⁸Saul gave up his pursuit of David and went to meet the Philistines. That is why that place came to be called the Rock of Separation.ᵃ

24 David went from there and stayed in the wildernesses of En-gedi. ²When Saul returned from pursuing the Philistines, he was told that David was in the wilderness of En-gedi. ³So Saul took three thousand picked men from all Israel and went in search of David and his men ᵃ⁻in the direction of the rocks of the wild goats;⁻ᵃ ⁴and he came to the sheepfolds along the way. There was a cave there, and Saul went in ᵇ⁻to relieve himself.⁻ᵇ Now David and his men were sitting in the back of the cave.

⁵David's men said to him, "This is the day of which the LORD said to you, 'I will deliver your enemy into your hands; you can do with him as you please.' " ᶜDavid went and stealthily cut off the corner of Saul's cloak. ⁶But afterward ᵈ⁻David reproached himself⁻ᵈ for cutting off ᵉ⁻the corner of Saul's cloak.⁻ᵉ ⁷He said to his men, "The LORD forbid that I should do such a thing to my lord—the LORD's anointed—that I should raise my hand against him; for he is the LORD's anointed." ⁸David rebukedᵃ his men and did not permit them to attack Saul.

Saul left the cave and started on his way. ⁹Then David also went out of the cave and called after Saul, "My lord king!" Saul looked around and David bowed low in homage, with his face to the ground. ¹⁰And David said to Saul, "Why do you listen to the people who say, 'David is out to do you harm?' ¹¹You can see for yourself now that the LORD delivered you into my hands in the cave today. And though ᵃ⁻I was urged⁻ᵃ to kill you, I showed you pity;ᶠ for I said, 'I will not raise a hand against my lord, since he is the LORD's anointed.' ¹²Please, sir,ᵍ take a close look at the corner of your cloak in my hand; for when I cut off the corner of

ᵃ⁻ᵃ *Meaning of Heb. uncertain.*
ᵇ⁻ᵇ *Lit. "to cover his feet."*
ᶜ *Vv. 5b-6 read well after 8a.*
ᵈ⁻ᵈ *Lit. "David's heart struck him."*
ᵉ⁻ᵉ *So several mss. and ancient versions; cf. v. 5. Most mss. and editions read "Saul's corner."*
ᶠ *Understanding the Heb. as an ellipsis of* wattahos 'eni *(cf., e.g., Deut. 7.16).*
ᵍ *Lit. "[my] father," cf. 2 Kings 5.13.*

your cloak, I did not kill you. You must see plainly that I have done nothing evil or rebellious, and I have never wronged you. Yet you are bent on taking my life. [13]May the LORD judge between you and me! And may He take vengeance upon you for me, but my hand will never touch you. [14]As the ancient proverb has it: 'Wicked deeds come from wicked men!' My hand will never touch you. [15]Against whom has the king of Israel come out? Whom are you pursuing? A dead dog? A single flea? [16]May the LORD be arbiter and may He judge between you and me! May He take note and uphold my cause, and vindicate me against you."

[17]When David finished saying these things to Saul, Saul said, "Is that your voice, my son David?" And Saul broke down and wept. [18]He said to David, "You are right, not I; for you have treated me generously, but I have treated you badly. [19]Yes, you have just revealed how generously you treated me, for the LORD delivered me into your hands and you did not kill me. [20]If a man meets his enemy, does he let him go his way unharmed? Surely, the LORD will reward you generously for [h-]what you have done for me this day.[-h] [21]I know now that you will become king, and that the kingship over Israel will remain in your hands. [22]So swear to me by the LORD that you will not destroy my descendants or wipe out my name from my father's house." [23]David swore to Saul, Saul went home, and David and his men went up to the strongholds.

25
Samuel died, and all Israel gathered and made lament for him; and they buried him in Ramah, his home.

David went down to the wilderness of Paran.[a]

[2]There was a man in Maon whose possessions were in Carmel. The man was very wealthy; he owned three thousand sheep and a thousand goats. At the time, he was shearing his sheep in Carmel. [3]The man's name was Nabal, and his wife's name was Abigail. The woman was intelligent and beautiful, but the man, a Calebite, was a hard man and an evildoer. [4]David was in the wilderness when he heard that Nabal was shearing his sheep. [5]David dispatched ten young men, and David instructed the young men, "Go up to Carmel. When you come to Nabal, greet him in my name. [6]Say [b-]as follows: 'To life![-b] Greetings to you and to your household and to all that is yours! [7]I hear that you are now doing your shearing. As you know, your shepherds have been with us; we did not harm them, and nothing of theirs was missing all the time they were in Carmel. [8]Ask

---

h-h *Meaning of Heb. uncertain. Emendation yields "the generosity you have shown me."*

a *Septuagint reads "Maon," cf. v. 2 and 23.24, 25.*

b-b *Meaning of Heb. uncertain.*

your young men and they will tell you. So receive these young men graciously, for we have come on a festive occasion. Please give your servants and your son David whatever you can.' "

⁹David's young men went and delivered this message to Nabal in the name of David. When they stopped speaking, ¹⁰Nabal answered David's servants, "Who is David? Who is the son of Jesse? There are many slaves nowadays who run away from their masters. ¹¹Should I then take my bread and my water,ᶜ and the meat that I slaughtered for my own shearers, and give them to men who come from I don't know where?" ¹²Thereupon David's young men retraced their steps; and when they got back, they told him all this. ¹³And David said to his men, "Gird on your swords." Each girded on his sword; David too girded on his sword. About four hundred men went up after David, while two hundred remained with the baggage.

¹⁴One of [Nabal's] young men told Abigail, Nabal's wife, that David had sent messengers from the wilderness to greet their master, and that he had spurnedᵇ them. ¹⁵"But the men had been very friendly to us; we were not harmed, nor did we miss anything all the time that we went about with them while we were in the open. ¹⁶They were a wall about us both by night and by day all the time that we were with them tending the flocks. ¹⁷So consider carefully what you should do, for harm threatens our master and all his household; he is such a nasty fellow that no one can speak to him."

¹⁸Abigail quickly got together two hundred loaves of bread, two jars of wine, five dressed sheep, five *seah*s of parched corn, one hundred cakes of raisin, and two hundred cakes of pressed figs. She loaded them on asses, ¹⁹and she told her young men, "Go on ahead of me, and I'll follow you"; but she did not tell her husband Nabal. ²⁰She was riding on the ass and going down a trailᵇ on the hill, when David and his men appeared, coming down toward her; and she met them.—²¹Now David had been saying, "It was all for nothing that I protected that fellow's possessions in the wilderness, and that nothing he owned is missing. He has paid me back evil for good. ²²May God do thus and more to ᵈ-the enemies of-ᵈ David if, by the light of morning, I leave ᵉ-a single male-ᵉ of his."—²³When Abigail saw David, she quickly dismounted from the ass and threw herself face down beforeᵇ David, bowing to the ground. ²⁴Prostrate at his feet, she pleaded, "Let the blame be mine, my lord, but let your handmaid speak to you; hear your maid's plea. ²⁵Please, my lord, pay no

ᶜ *Septuagint reads "wine," and cf. v. 18.*
ᵈ⁻ᵈ *The phrase is intended to avoid the imprecation of David against himself; it is lacking in the Septuagint.*
ᵉ⁻ᵉ *Lit. "one who pees against a wall."*

attention to that wretched fellow Nabal. For he is just what his name says: His name means 'boor' and he is a boor.

"Your handmaid did not see the young men whom my lord sent. 26I swear, my lord, as the LORD lives and as you live—the LORD who has kept you from seeking redress by blood with your own hands—let your enemies and all who would harm my lord fare like Nabal! 27Here is the present which your maidservant has brought to my lord; let it be given to the young men who are the followers of my lord. 28Please pardon your maid's boldness. For the LORD will grant my lord an enduring house, because my lord is fighting the battles of the LORD, and no wrong is ever to be found in you. 29And if anyone sets out to pursue you and seek your life, the life of my lord will be bound up in the bundle of life in the care of the LORD; but He will fling away the lives of your enemies as from the hollow of a sling. 30And when the LORD has accomplished for my lord all the good He has promised you, and has appointed you ruler of Israel, 31do not let this be a cause of stumbling and of faltering courage to my lord that you have shed blood needlessly and that my lord sought redress with his own hands. And when the LORD has prospered my lord, remember your maid."

32David said to Abigail, "Praised be the LORD, the God of Israel, who sent you this day to meet me! 33And blessed be your prudence, and blessed be you yourself for restraining me from seeking redress in blood by my own hands. 34For as sure as the LORD, the God of Israel, lives—who has kept me from harming you—had you not come quickly to meet me, not ᶜ-a single maleᶜ of Nabal's line would have been left by daybreak." 35David then accepted from her what she had brought him, and he said to her, "Go up to your home safely. See, I have heeded your plea and respected your wish."

36When Abigail came home to Nabal, he was having a feast in his house, a feast fit for a king; Nabal was in a merry mood and very drunk, so she did not tell him anything at all until daybreak. 37The next morning, when Nabal had slept off the wine, his wife told him everything that had happened; and his courage died within him, and he became like a stone. 38About ten days later the LORD struck Nabal and he died. 39When David heard that Nabal was dead, he said, "Praised be the LORD who championed my cause against the insults of Nabal and held back His servant from wrongdoing; the LORD has brought Nabal's wrongdoing down on his own head."

David sent messengers f-to propose marriage to-f Abigail, to take her as his wife. 40When David's servants came to Abigail at Carmel and told her that David had sent them to her to make her his wife, 41she immediately bowed low with her face to the ground and said, "Your handmaid is ready to be your maidservant, to wash the feet of my lord's servants." 42Then Abigail rose quickly and mounted an ass, and with five of her maids in attendance she followed David's messengers; and she became his wife.

43Now David had taken Ahinoam of Jezreel; so both of them became his wives. 44Saul had given his daughter Michal, David's wife, to Palti son of Laish from Gallim.

26 aThe Ziphites came to Saul at Gibeah and said, "David is hiding in the hill of Hachilah facing Jeshimon." 2Saul went down at once to the wilderness of Ziph, together with three thousand picked men of Israel, to search for David in the wilderness of Ziph, 3and Saul encamped on the hill of Hachilah which faces Jeshimon, by the road. When David, who was then living in the wilderness, learned that Saul had come after him into the wilderness, 4David sent out scouts and made sure that Saul had come. 5David went at once to the place where Saul had encamped, and David saw the spot where Saul and his army commander, Abner son of Ner, lay asleep. Saul lay asleep inside the barricadeb and the troops were posted around him.

6David spoke up and asked Ahimelech the Hittite and Abishai son of Zeruiah, Joab's brother, "Who will go down with me into the camp to Saul?" And Abishai answered, "I will go down with you." 7So David and Abishai approached the troops by night, and found Saul fast asleep inside the barricade,b his spear stuck in the ground at his head, and Abner and the troops sleeping around him. 8And Abishai said to David, "God has delivered your enemy into your hands today. Let me pin him to the ground with a single thrust of the spear. I will not have to strike him twice." 9But David said to Abishai, "Don't do him violence! No one can lay hands on the LORD's anointed with impunity." 10And David went on, "As the LORD lives, the LORD Himself will strike him down, or his time will come and he will die, or he will go down to battle and perish. 11But the LORD forbid that I should lay a hand on the LORD's anointed! Just take the spear and the water jar at his head and let's be off." 12So David

---

f-f Lit. "and spoke for"; cf. Song of Songs 8.8.

a Cf. 23.19 and note.

b Meaning of Heb. uncertain; cf. 17.20.

took away the spear and the water jar at Saul's head, and they left. No one saw or knew or woke up; all remained asleep; a deep sleep from the LORD had fallen upon them.

¹³David crossed over to the other side and stood afar on top of a hill; there was considerable distance between them. ¹⁴And David shouted to the troops and to Abner son of Ner, "Abner, aren't you going to answer?" And Abner shouted back, "Who are you to shout at the king?" ¹⁵And David answered Abner, "You are a man, aren't you? And there is no one like you in Israel! So why didn't you keep watch over your lord the king? For one of [our] troops came to do violence to your lord the king. ¹⁶You have not given a good account of yourself! As the LORD lives, [all of] you deserve to die, because you did not keep watch over your lord, the LORD's anointed. Look around, where are the king's spear and the water jar that were at his head?"

¹⁷Saul recognized David's voice, and he asked, "Is that your voice, my son David?" And David replied, "It is, my lord king." ¹⁸And he went on, "But why does my lord continue to pursue his servant? What have I done, and what wrong am I guilty of? ¹⁹Now let my lord the king hear his servant out. If the LORD has incited you against me, let Him be appeased[c] by an offering; but if it is men, may they be accursed of the LORD! For they have driven me out today, so that I cannot have a share in the LORD's possession, but am told, 'Go and worship other gods.' ²⁰Oh, let my blood not fall to the ground, away from the presence of the LORD! For the king of Israel has come out to seek a single flea—as if he were hunting a partridge in the hills."

²¹And Saul answered, "I am in the wrong. Come back, my son David, for I will never harm you again, seeing how you have held my life precious this day. Yes, I have been a fool, and I have erred so very much." ²²David replied, "Here is Your Majesty's spear. Let one of the young men come over and get it. ²³And the LORD will requite every man for his right conduct and loyalty—for this day the LORD delivered you into my[d] hands and I would not raise a hand against the LORD's anointed. ²⁴And just as I valued your life highly this day, so may the LORD value my life and may He rescue me from all trouble." ²⁵Saul answered David, "May you be blessed, my son David. You shall achieve, and you shall prevail."

David then went his way, and Saul returned home.

---

c Cf. Amos 5.21.
d So many mss.; other mss. and editions omit.

27 David said to himself, "Some day I shall certainly perish at the hands of Saul. The best thing for me is to flee to the land of the Philistines; Saul will then give up hunting me throughout the territory of Israel, and I will escape him." ²So David and the six hundred men with him went and crossed over to King Achish son of Maoch of Gath. ³David and his men stayed with Achish in Gath, each man with his family, and David with his two wives, Ahinoam the Jezreelite and Abigail wife of Nabal the Carmelite. ⁴And when Saul was told that David had fled to Gath, he did not pursue him any more.

⁵David said to Achish, "If you please, let a place be granted me in one of the country towns where I can live; why should your servant remain with you in the royal city?" ⁶At that time Achish granted him Ziklag; that is how Ziklag came to belong to the kings of Judah, as is still the case. ⁷The length of time that David lived in Philistine territory was a year and four months.

⁸David and his men went up and raided the Geshurites, the Gizrites, and the Amalekites—who were the inhabitants of the region of Olam,ᵃ all the way to Shur and to the land of Egypt.—⁹When David attacked a region, he would leave no man or woman alive; he would take flocks, herds, asses, camels, and clothing. When he returned and cameᵇ to Achish, ¹⁰Achish would ask, "Whereᶜ did you raid today?" and David would reply, "The Negebᵈ of Judah," or "the Negeb of the Jerahmeelites," or "the Negeb of the Kenites." ¹¹David would leave no man or woman alive to be brought to Gath; for he thought, "They might tell about us: David did this." Such was his practice as long as he stayed in the territory of the Philistines. ¹²Achish trusted David. He thought: ᵉ‑"He has aroused the wrath ofᵉ his own people Israel, and so he will be my vassal forever."

28 At that time the Philistines mustered their forces for war, to take the field against Israel. Achish said to David, "You know, of course, that you and your men must march out with my forces." ²David answered Achish, "You surely know what your servant will do." "In that case," Achish replied to David, "I will appoint you my bodyguard for life."

³ᵃNow Samuel had died and all Israel made lament for him; and he was

---

ᵃ *Septuagint reads "Telam" (cf. "Telaim" in 15.4; and "Telem" in Josh. 15.24).*
ᵇ *Change of vocalization yields "brought it"; cf. v. 11.*
ᶜ *So some mss. and Targum; Septuagint and 4QSamᵃ read "Whom."*
ᵈ *I.e., the part of the Negeb occupied by these clans.*
ᵉ‑ᵉ *Cf. note at 13.4.*

ᵃ *The rest of this chapter would read well after chapters 29 and 30.*

buried in his own town of Ramah. And Saul had forbidden [recourse to] ghosts and familiar spirits in the land.

⁴The Philistines mustered and they marched to Shunem and encamped; and Saul gathered all Israel, and they encamped at Gilboa. ⁵When Saul saw the Philistine force, his heart trembled with fear. ⁶And Saul inquired of the LORD, but the LORD did not answer him, either by dreams or by Urimᵇ or by prophets. ⁷Then Saul said to his courtiers, "Find me a woman who consults ghosts, so that I can go to her and inquire through her." And his courtiers told him that there was a woman in En-dor who consulted ghosts.

⁸Saul disguised himself; he put on different clothes and set out with two men. They came to the woman by night, and he said, "Please divine for me by a ghost. Bring up for me the one I shall name to you." ⁹But the woman answered him, "You know what Saul has done, how he has banned [the use of] ghosts and familiar spirits in the land. So why are you laying a trap for me, to get me killed?" ¹⁰Saul swore to her by the LORD: "As the LORD lives, you won't get into trouble over this." ¹¹At that, the woman asked, "Whom shall I bring up for you?" He answered, "Bring up Samuel for me." ¹²Then the woman recognized Samuel,ᶜ and she shrieked loudly, and said to Saul, "Why have you deceived me? You are Saul!" ¹³The king answered her, "Don't be afraid. What do you see?" And the woman said to Saul, "I see a divine being coming up from the earth." ¹⁴"What does he look like?" he asked her. "It is an old man coming up," she said, "and he is wrapped in a robe." Then Saul knew that it was Samuel; and he bowed low in homage with his face to the ground.

¹⁵Samuel said to Saul, "Why have you disturbed me and brought me up?" And Saul answered, "I am in great trouble. The Philistines are attacking me and God has turned away from me; He no longer answers me, either by prophets or in dreams. So I have called you to tell me what I am to do." ¹⁶Samuel said, "Why do you ask me, seeing that the LORD has turned away from you and has become your adversary?ᵈ ¹⁷The LORD has done ᵉ-for Himself-ᵉ as He foretold through me: The LORD has torn the kingship out of your hands and has given it to your fellow, to David, ¹⁸because you did not obey the LORD and did not execute His wrath upon the Amalekites. That is why the LORD has done this to you today. ¹⁹Further, the LORD will deliver the Israelites who are with you into the hands of the Philistines. Tomorrow your sons and you will be with me; and the LORD will also deliver the Israelite forces into the hands of the Philistines."

ᵇ *A kind of oracle; see note at Exod. 28.30 and 1 Sam. 14.41.*
ᶜ *Some Septuagint mss. read "Saul."*
ᵈ *Meaning of Heb. uncertain.*
ᵉ⁻ᵉ *Some mss. and Septuagint read "to you."*

²⁰At once Saul flung himself prone on the ground, terrified by Samuel's words. Besides, there was no strength in him, for he had not eaten anything all day and all night. ²¹The woman went up to Saul and, seeing how greatly disturbed he was, she said to him, "Your handmaid listened to you; I took my life in my hands and heeded the request you made of me. ²²So now you listen to me: Let me set before you a bit of food. Eat, and then you will have the strength to go on your way." ²³He refused, saying, "I will not eat." But when his courtiers as well as the woman urged him, he listened to them; he got up from the ground and sat on the bed. ²⁴The woman had a stall-fed calf in the house; she hastily slaughtered it, and took flour and kneaded it, and baked some unleavened cakes. ²⁵She set this before Saul and his courtiers, and they ate. Then they rose and left the same night.

29 The Philistines mustered all their forces at Aphek, while Israel was encamping at the spring in Jezreel. ²The Philistine lords came marching, each with his units of hundreds and of thousands; and David and his men came marching last, with Achish. ³The Philistine officers asked, "Who are those Hebrews?" "Why, that's David, the servant of King Saul of Israel," Achish answered the Philistine officers. "He has been with me ᵃ‑for a year or more,‑ᵃ and I have found no fault in him from the day he defected until now." ⁴But the Philistine officers were angry with him; and the Philistine officers said to him, "Send the man back; let him go back to the place you assigned him. He shall not march down with us to the battle, or else he may become our adversary in battle. For with what could that fellow appease his master if not with ᵇ‑the heads of these men?‑ᵇ ⁵Remember, he is the David of whom they sang as they danced:

Saul has slain his thousands;

David, his tens of thousands."

⁶Achish summoned David and said to him, "As the LORD lives, you are an honest man, and I would like to have you serveᶜ in my forces; for I have found no fault with you from the day you joined me until now. But you are not acceptable to the other lords. ⁷So go back in peace, and do nothing to displease the Philistine lords."

⁸David, however, said to Achish, "But what have I done, what fault have you found in your servant from the day I appeared before you to this day, that I should not go and fight against the enemies of my lord the king?" ⁹Achish replied to David, "I know; you are as acceptable to

---

ᵃ⁻ᵃ *Meaning of phrase uncertain.*
ᵇ⁻ᵇ *A euphemism for "our heads."*
ᶜ *Lit. "go out and come in."*

me as an angel of God. But the Philistine officers have decided that you must not march out with us to the battle. ¹⁰So rise early in the morning, you and your lord's servants who came with you—ᵈ⁻rise early in the morning,⁻ᵈ and leave as soon as it is light." ¹¹Accordingly, David and his men rose early in the morning to leave, to return to the land of the Philistines, while the Philistines marched up to Jezreel.

30 By the time David and his men arrived in Ziklag, on the third day, the Amalekites had made a raid into the Negeb and against Ziklag; they had stormed Ziklag and burned it down. ²They had taken the women in it captive, low-born and high-born alike; they did not kill any, but carried them off and went their way. ³When David and his men came to the town and found it burned down, and their wives and sons and daughters taken captive, ⁴David and the troops with him broke into tears, until they had no strength left for weeping. ⁵David's two wives had been taken captive, Ahinoam of Jezreel and Abigail wife of Nabal from Carmel. ⁶David was in great danger, for the troops threatened to stone him; for all the troops were embittered on account of their sons and daughters.

But David sought strength in the LORD his God. ⁷David said to the priest Abiathar son of Ahimelech, "Bring the ephod up to me." When Abiathar brought up the ephodᵃ to David, ⁸David inquired of the LORD, "Shall I pursue those raiders? Will I overtake them?" And He answered him, "Pursue, for you shall overtake and you shall rescue."

⁹So David and the six hundred men with him set out, and they came to the Wadi Besor, where a halt was made by those who were to be left behind. ¹⁰David continued the pursuit with four hundred men; two hundred men had halted, too faint to cross the Wadi Besor. ¹¹They came upon an Egyptian in the open country and brought him to David. They gave him food to eat and water to drink; ¹²he was also given a piece of pressed fig cake and two cakes of raisins. He ate and regained his strength, for he had eaten no food and drunk no water for three days and three nights. ¹³Then David asked him, "To whom do you belong and where are you from?" "I am an Egyptian boy," he answered, "the slave of an Amalekite. My master abandoned me when I fell ill three days ago. ¹⁴We had raided the Negeb of the Cherethites, and [the Negeb] of Judah, and the Negeb of Caleb; we also burned down Ziklag." ¹⁵And David said to him, "Can you lead me down to that band?" He replied, "Swear to me by God that

---

ᵈ⁻ᵈ *Meaning of parts of verse uncertain. Septuagint reads "and go to the place that I have assigned you; and harbor no evil thought in your heart, for you are acceptable to me."*

ᵃ *See note at 2.28.*

you will not kill me or deliver me into my master's hands, and I will lead you down to that band." ¹⁶So he led him down, and there they were, scattered all over the ground, eating and drinking and making merry because of all the vast spoil they had taken from the land of the Philistines and from the land of Judah. ¹⁷David attacked them from ᵇ⁻before dawn until the evening of the next day;⁻ᵇ none of them escaped, except four hundred young men who mounted camels and got away. ¹⁸David rescued everything the Amalekites had taken; David also rescued his two wives. ¹⁹Nothing of theirs was missing—young or old, sons or daughters, spoil or anything else that had been carried off—David recovered everything. ²⁰David took all the flocks and herds, ᵇ⁻which [the troops] drove ahead of the other livestock;⁻ᵇ and they declared, "This is David's spoil."

²¹When David reached the two hundred men who were too faint to follow David and who had been left at the Wadi Besor, they came out to welcome David and the troops with him; David came forward with the troops and greeted them. ²²But all the mean and churlish fellows among the men who had accompanied David spoke up, "Since they did not accompany us,ᶜ we will not give them any of the spoil that we seized— except that each may take his wife and children and go." ²³David, how-ever, spoke up, "You must not do that, ᵈ⁻my brothers, in view of⁻ᵈ what the LORD has granted us, guarding us and delivering into our hands the band that attacked us. ²⁴How could anyone agree with you in this matter? The share of those who remain with the baggage shall be the same as the share of those who go down to battle; they shall share alike." ²⁵So from that day on it was made a fixed rule for Israel, continuing to the present day.

²⁶When David reached Ziklag, he sent some of the spoil to the elders of Judah ᵇ⁻[and] to his friends,⁻ᵇ saying, "This is a present for you from our spoil of the enemies of the LORD." ²⁷[He sent the spoil to the elders] in Bethel,ᵉ Ramoth-negeb, and Jattir; ²⁸in Aroer, Siphmoth, and Eshte-moa; ²⁹in Racal, in the towns of the Jerahmeelites, and in the towns of the Kenites; ³⁰in Hormah, Bor-ashan, and Athach; ³¹and to those in Hebron—all the places where David and his men had roamed.

31

ᵃThe Philistines attacked Israel, and the men of Israel fled before the Philistines and [many] fell on Mount Gilboa. ²The Philistines pursued Saul and his sons, and the Philistines struck down Jonathan, Abinadab,

---

ᵇ⁻ᵇ *Meaning of Heb. uncertain.*
ᶜ *So some mss. and versions; most mss. and editions read "me."*
ᵈ⁻ᵈ *Meaning of Heb. uncertain. Septuagint reads "after."*
ᵉ *Called Bethul in Josh. 19.4.*

ᵃ *1 Chron. 10 reproduces this chapter, with minor variations.*

and Malchi-shua, sons of Saul. [3]The battle raged around Saul, and [b]some of the archers[-b] hit him, and he [c]was severely wounded[-c] by the archers. [4]Saul said to his arms-bearer, "Draw your sword and run me through, so that the uncircumcised may not run me through and make sport of me." But his arms-bearer, in his great awe, refused; whereupon Saul grasped the sword and fell upon it. [5]When his arms-bearer saw that Saul was dead, he too fell on his sword and died with him. [6]Thus Saul and his three sons and his arms-bearer, [d]as well as all his men,[-d] died together on that day. [7]And when the men of Israel [e]on the other side of the valley and on the other side of the Jordan[-e] saw that the men of Israel had fled and that Saul and his sons were dead, they abandoned the towns and fled; the Philistines then came and occupied them.

[8]The next day the Philistines came to strip the slain, and they found Saul and his three sons lying on Mount Gilboa. [9]They cut off his head and stripped him of his armor, and they sent them throughout the land of the Philistines, to spread the news [f]in the temples of their idols[-f] and among the people. [10]They placed his armor in the temple of Ashtaroth, and they impaled his body on the wall of Beth-shan. [11]When [g]the inhabitants of Jabesh-gilead heard about it—what[-g] the Philistines had done to Saul—[12]all their stalwart men set out and marched all night; they removed the bodies of Saul and his sons from the wall of Beth-shan and came[h] to Jabesh and burned them there. [13]Then they took the bones and buried them under the tamarisk tree in Jabesh, and they fasted for seven days.

---

b-b *Meaning of Heb. uncertain. Lit. "the archers, men with the bow."*
c-c *Construed as hophal form; cf. 1 Kings 2.34.*
d-d *Lacking in the Septuagint; 1 Chron. 10.6 reads "all his house."*
e-e *Meaning of Heb. uncertain. 1 Chron. 10.7 reads "in the valley."*
f-f *Septuagint and 1 Chron. 10.9 read "among their idols."*
g-g *1 Chron. 10.11 reads "all [the inhabitants of] Jabesh-gilead heard all that."*
h *1 Chron. 10.12 reads "brought them."*

שמואל ב

II SAMUEL

1 After the death of Saul—David had already returned from defeating the Amalekites—David stayed two days in Ziklag. ²On the third day, a man came from Saul's camp, with his clothes rent and earth on his head; and as he approached David, he flung himself to the ground and bowed low. ³David said to him, "Where are you coming from?" He answered, "I have just escaped from the camp of Israel." ⁴"What happened?" asked David. "Tell me!" And he told him how the troops had fled the battlefield, and that, moreover, many of the troops had fallen and died; also that Saul and his son Jonathan were dead. ⁵"How do you know," David asked the young man who brought him the news, "that Saul and his son Jonathan are dead?" ⁶The young man who brought him the news answered, "I happened to be at Mount Gilboa, and I saw Saul leaning on his spear, and the chariots and horsemen closing in on him. ⁷He looked around and saw me, and he called to me. When I responded, 'At your service,' ⁸he asked me, 'Who are you?' And I told him that I was an Amalekite. ⁹Then he said to me, 'Stand over me, and finish me off, ᵃ-for I am in agony and am barely alive.'-ᵃ ¹⁰So I stood over him and finished him off, for I knew that ᵃ-he would never rise from where he was lying.-ᵃ Then I took the crown from his head and the armlet from his arm, and I have brought them here to my lord."

¹¹David took hold of his clothes and rent them, and so did all the men with him. ¹²They lamented and wept, and they fasted until evening for Saul and his son Jonathan, and for the soldiers of the Lordᵇ and the House of Israel who had fallen by the sword. ¹³David said to the young man who had brought him the news, "Where are you from?" He replied, "I am the son of a resident alien, an Amalekite." ¹⁴"How did you dare," David said to him, "to lift your hand and kill the Lord's anointed?" ¹⁵Thereupon David called one of the attendants and said to him, "Come

ᵃ⁻ᵃ *Meaning of Heb. uncertain.*
ᵇ *Septuagint reads "Judah."*

over and strike him!" He struck him down and he died. [16]And David said to him, "Your blood be on your own head! Your own mouth testified against you when you said, 'I put the LORD's anointed to death.' "

[17]And David intoned this dirge over Saul and his son Jonathan— [18a-]He ordered the Judites to be taught [The Song of the] Bow. [-a] It is recorded in the Book of Jashar.[c]

> [19]Your glory, O Israel,
> Lies slain on your heights;
> How have the mighty fallen!
> [20]Tell it not in Gath,
> Do not proclaim it in the streets of Ashkelon,
> Lest the daughters of the Philistine rejoice,
> Lest the daughters of the uncircumcised exult.

> [21]O hills of Gilboa—
> Let there be no dew or rain on you,
> [d-]Or bountiful fields,[-d]
> For there the shield of warriors lay rejected,
> The shield of Saul,
> Polished with oil no more.

> [22]From the blood of slain,
> From the fat of warriors—
> The bow of Jonathan
> Never turned back;
> The sword of Saul
> Never withdrew empty.

> [23]Saul and Jonathan,
> Beloved and cherished,
> Never parted
> In life or in death!
> They were swifter than eagles,
> They were stronger than lions!

> [24]Daughters of Israel,
> Weep over Saul,

---

[c] *See note at Josh. 10.13.*
[d-d] *Meaning of Heb. uncertain. Emendation yields "springs from the deep" (cf. Ugaritic* shr'thmtm, *and Gen. 7.11; 8.2).*

Who clothed you in crimson and finery,
Who decked your robes with jewels of gold.

25How have the mighty fallen
In the thick of battle—
Jonathan, slain on your heights!
26I grieve for you,
My brother Jonathan,
You were most dear to me.
Your love was wonderful to me
More than the love of women.

27How have the mighty fallen,
The e-weapons of war-e perished!

2 Sometime afterward, David inquired of the LORD, "Shall I go up to one of the towns of Judah?" The LORD answered, "Yes." David further asked, "Which one shall I go up to?" And the LORD replied, "To Hebron." 2So David went up there, along with his two wives, Ahinoam of Jezreel and Abigail wife of Nabal the Carmelite. 3David also took the men who were with him, each with his family, and they settled in the towns about Hebron. 4The men of Judah came and there they anointed David king over the House of Judah.

David was told about the men of Jabesh-gilead who buried Saul. 5So David sent messengers to the men of Jabesh-gilead and said to them, "May you be blessed of the LORD because you performed this act of faithfulness to your lord Saul and buried him. 6May the LORD in turn show you true faithfulness; and I too will reward you generously because you performed this act. 7Now take courage and be brave men; for your lord Saul is dead and the House of Judah have already anointed me king over them."

8But Abner son of Ner, Saul's army commander, had taken Ish-bosheth[a] son of Saul and brought him across to Mahanaim 9and made him king over Gilead, the Ashurites,[b] Jezreel, Ephraim, and Benjamin—over all Israel. 10Ish-bosheth[a] son of Saul was forty years old when he became king of Israel, and he reigned two years. But the House of Judah sup-

e-e *I.e., Saul and Jonathan.*

a *Meaning "Man of Shame," deliberately altered from* Ish-baal, *"man of Baal"; cf. 1 Chron. 8.33; 9.39, and note at 2 Sam. 4.4.*
b *Meaning of Heb. uncertain.*

ported David. 11The length of time that David reigned in Hebron over the House of Judah was seven years and six months.

12Once Abner son of Ner and the soldiers of Ish-bosheth son of Saul marched out from Mahanaim to Gibeon, 13and Joab son of Zeruiah and the soldiers of David [also] came out.c They confronted one another at the pool of Gibeon: one group sat on one side of the pool, and the other group on the other side of the pool. 14Abner said to Joab, "Let the young men come forward and sportd before us." "Yes, let them," Joab answered. 15They came forward and were counted off, twelve for Benjamin and Ish-bosheth son of Saul, and twelve of David's soldiers. 16Each one grasped his opponent's heade [and thrust] his dagger into his opponent's side; thus they fell together. That place, which is in Gibeon, was called Helkath-hazzurim.f

17A fierce battle ensued that day, and Abner and the men of Israel were routed by David's soldiers. 18The three sons of Zeruiahg were there—Joab, Abishai, and Asahel. Asahel was swift of foot, like a gazelle in the open field. 19And Asahel ran after Abner, swerving neither right nor left in his pursuit of Abner. 20Abner looked back and shouted, "Is that you, Asahel?" "Yes, it is," he called back. 21Abner said to him, "Turn to the right or to the left, and seize one of our boys and strip off his tunic." But Asahel would not leave off. 22Abner again begged Asahel, "Stop pursuing me, or I'll have to strike you down. How will I look your brother Joab in the face?" 23When he refused to desist, Abner struck him in the belly with b-a backward thrust-b of his spear and the spear protruded from his back. He fell there and died on the spot. And all who came to the place where Asahel fell and died halted; 24but Joab and Abishai continued to pursue Abner. And the sun was setting as they reached the hill of Ammah, b-which faces Giah on the road to the wilderness of Gibeon.-b

25The Benjaminites rallied behind Abner, forming a single company; and they took up a position on the top of a hill. 26Abner then called out to Joab, "Must the sword devour forever? You know how bitterly it's going to end! How long will you delay ordering your troops to stop the pursuit of their kinsmen?" 27And Joab replied, "As God lives, h-if you hadn't spoken up, the troops would have given up the pursuit of their kinsmen only the next morning."-h 28Joab then sounded the horn, and all

---

c Septuagint adds "from Hebron."
d I.e., engage in single combat.
e Septuagint adds "with his hand."
f Meaning perhaps "the Field of the Flints (or Blades)."
g A sister of David, 1 Chron. 2.16.
h-h Emendation yields "If you had only spoken up, the troops would already have given up the pursuit of their kinsmen this morning."

the troops halted; they ceased their pursuit of Israel and stopped the fighting. ²⁹Abner and his men marched through the Arabah all that night and, after crossing the Jordan, they marched ᵇ-through all of Bithron-ᵇ until they came to Mahanaim. ³⁰After Joab gave up the pursuit of Abner, he assembled all the troops and found nineteen of David's soldiers missing, besides Asahel. ³¹David's soldiers, on the other hand, ᵇ-defeated the Benjaminites and the men under Abner and killed three hundred and sixty men.⁻ᵇ ³²They bore Asahel away and buried him in his father's tomb in Bethlehem. Then Joab and his men marched all night; day broke upon them in Hebron.

3 The war between the House of Saul and the House of David was long-drawn-out; but David kept growing stronger, while the House of Saul grew weaker.

²ᵃSons were born to David in Hebron: His first-born was Amnon, by Ahinoam of Jezreel; ³his second was Chileab, by Abigail wife of Nabal the Carmelite; the third was Absalom son of Maacah, daughter of King Talmai of Geshur; ⁴the fourth was Adonijah son of Haggith; the fifth was Shephatiah son of Abital; ⁵and the sixth was Ithream, by David's wife Eglah. These were born to David in Hebron.

⁶During the war between the House of Saul and the House of David, Abner supported the House of Saul. ⁷Now Saul had a concubine named Rizpah, daughter of Aiah; and [Ish-bosheth] said to Abner, "Why have you lain with my father's concubine?" ⁸Abner was very upset by what Ish-bosheth said, and he replied, "Am I a dog's head ᵇ-from Judah?-ᵇ Here I have been loyally serving the House of your father Saul and his kinsfolk and friends, and I have not betrayed you into the hands of David; yet this day you reproach me over a woman! ⁹May God do thus and more to Abner if I do not do for David as the LORD swore to him—¹⁰to transfer the kingship from the House of Saul, and to establish the throne of David over Israel and Judah from Dan to Beer-sheba." ¹¹[Ish-bosheth] could say nothing more in reply to Abner, because he was afraid of him.

¹²Abner immediatelyᵇ sent messengers to David, saying, ᵇ-"To whom shall the land belong?" and to say [further],-ᵇ "Make a pact with me, and

---

ᵃ *The list of David's wives and sons in vv. 2–5 differs somewhat from the parallel list in 1 Chron. 3.1–3. The narrative in v. 1 is resumed in v. 6.*
ᵇ⁻ᵇ *Meaning of Heb. uncertain.*

I will help you and bring all Israel over to your side." ¹³He replied, "Good; I will make a pact with you. But I make one demand upon you: Do not appear before me unless you bring Michal daughter of Saul when you come before me." ¹⁴David also sent messengers to Ish-bosheth son of Saul, to say, "Give me my wife Michal, for whom I paid the bride-price^c of one hundred Philistine foreskins."^d ¹⁵So Ish-bosheth sent and had her taken away from [her] husband, Paltiel son of Laish. ¹⁶Her husband walked with her as far as Bahurim, weeping as he followed her; then Abner ordered him to turn back, and he went back.

¹⁷Abner had conferred with the elders of Israel, saying, "You have wanted David to be king over you all along. ¹⁸Now act! For the LORD has said concerning David: ^{e-}I will deliver^{-e} My people Israel from the hands of the Philistines and all its other enemies through My servant David." ¹⁹Abner also talked with the Benjaminites; then Abner went and informed David in Hebron of all the wishes of Israel and of the whole House of Benjamin.

²⁰When Abner came to David in Hebron, accompanied by twenty men, David made a feast for Abner and the men with him. ²¹Abner said to David, "Now I will go and rally all Israel to Your Majesty. They will make a pact with you, and you can reign over all that your heart desires." And David dismissed Abner, who went away unharmed.

²²Just then David's soldiers and Joab returned from a raid, bringing much plunder with them; Abner was no longer with David in Hebron, for he had been dismissed and had gone away unharmed. ²³When Joab and the whole force with him arrived, Joab was told that Abner son of Ner had come to the king, had been dismissed by him, and had gone away unharmed. ²⁴Joab went to the king and said, "What have you done? Here Abner came to you; why did you let him go? Now he has gotten away! ²⁵Don't you know that Abner son of Ner came only to deceive you, to learn your comings and goings and to find out all that you are planning?" ²⁶Joab left David and sent messengers after Abner, and they brought him back from the cistern of Sirah; but David knew nothing about it. ²⁷When Abner returned to Hebron, Joab took him aside within the gate to talk to him privately;^b there he struck him in the belly. Thus [Abner] died for shedding the blood of Asahel, Joab's^f brother.

²⁸Afterward, when David heard of it, he said, "Both I and my kingdom are forever innocent before the LORD of shedding the blood of Abner

---

^c Cf. Exod. 22.15; Deut. 20.7; 22.23–29.
^d Cf. 1 Sam. 18.27 (where the number is given as "two hundred").
^{e-e} So many mss. and versions; most mss. and editions have "He has delivered."
^f Heb. "his."

son of Ner. ²⁹May [the guilt] fall upon the head of Joab and all his father's house. May the house of Joab never be without someone suffering from a discharge or an eruption, or ᵍ⁻a male who handles the spindle,⁻ᵍ or one slain by the sword, or one lacking bread."—³⁰Now Joab and his brother Abishai had killed Abner because he had killed their brother Asahel during the battle at Gibeon.—³¹David then ordered Joab and all the troops with him to rend their clothes, gird on sackcloth, and make lament beforeʰ Abner; and King David himself walked behind the bier. ³²And so they buried Abner at Hebron; the king wept aloud by Abner's grave, and all the troops wept. ³³And the king intoned this dirge over Abner,

"Should Abner have died the death of a churl?
³⁴Your hands were not bound,
Your feet were not put in fetters;
But you fell as one falls
Before treacherous men!"

And all the troops continued to weep over him.

³⁵All the troops came to urge David to eat something while it was still day; but David swore, "May God do thus to me and more if I eat bread or anything else before sundown." ³⁶All the troops ᵇ⁻took note of it⁻ᵇ and approved, ᵇ⁻just as all the troops approved everything else the king did.⁻ᵇ ³⁷That day all the troops and all Israel knew that it was not by the king's will that Abner son of Ner was killed. ³⁸And the king said to his soldiers, "You well know that a prince, a great man in Israel, has fallen this day. ³⁹And today I am weak, even though anointed king; those men, the sons of Zeruiah, are too savage for me. May the LORD requite the wicked for their wickedness!"

4 When [Ish-bosheth] son of Saul heard that Abner had died in Hebron, ᵃ⁻he lost heart⁻ᵃ and all Israel was alarmed. ²The son of Saul [had] two company commanders, one named Baanah and the other Rechab, sons of Rimmon the Beerothite—Benjaminites, since Beeroth too was considered part of Benjamin. ³The Beerothites had fled to Gittaim,ᵇ where they have sojourned to this day. (⁴Jonathan son of Saul had a son whose feet were crippled. He was five years old when the news about Saul and Jonathan came from Jezreel, and his nurse picked him up and fled; but as she was fleeing in haste, he fell and was lamed. His name was Mephibosheth.ᶜ)

g-g *I.e., a man fit only for woman's work.*
h *I.e., in the procession.*

a-a *Lit. "his hands weakened"; and so frequently.*
b *Gittaim was likewise in Benjamin; cf. Neh. 11.31 ff.*
c *The original form of the name, Merib-baal, is preserved in 1 Chron. 8.34; 9.40. Cf. Ish-bosheth (Eshbaal) in 2 Sam. 2.8, note a. This subject is resumed in chapter 9.*

⁵Rechab and Baanah, sons of Rimmon the Beerothite, started out, and they reached the home of Ish-bosheth at the heat of the day, when he was taking his midday rest. ⁶ᵈ⁻So they went inside the house, as though fetching wheat, and struck him in the belly.⁻ᵈ Rechab and his brother Baanah slipped by, ⁷and entered the house while he was asleep on his bed in his bedchamber; and they stabbed him to death. They cut off his head and took his head and made their way all night through the Arabah. ⁸They brought the head of Ish-bosheth to David in Hebron. "Here," they said to the king, "is the head of your enemy, Ish-bosheth son of Saul, who sought your life. This day the LORD has avenged my lord the king upon Saul and his offspring."

⁹But David answered Rechab and his brother Baanah, the sons of Rimmon the Beerothite, and said to them, "As the LORD lives, who has rescued me from every trouble: ¹⁰The man who told me in Ziklag that Saul was dead thought he was bringing good news. But instead of rewarding him for the news, I seized and killed him. ¹¹How much more, then, when wicked men have killed a blameless man in bed in his own house! I will certainly avenge his blood on you, and I will rid the earth of you." ¹²David gave orders to the young men, who killed them; they cut off their hands and feet and hung them up by the pool in Hebron. And they took the head of Ish-bosheth and buried it in the grave of Abner at Hebron.

5 ᵃAll the tribes of Israel came to David at Hebron and said, "We are your own flesh and blood. ²Long before now, when Saul was king over us, it was you who ᵇ⁻led Israel in war;⁻ᵇ and the LORD said to you: You shall shepherd My people Israel; you shall be ruler of Israel." ³All the elders of Israel came to the king at Hebron, and King David made a pact with them in Hebron before the LORD. And they anointed David king over Israel.

⁴David was thirty years old when he became king, and he reigned forty years. ⁵In Hebron he reigned over Judah seven years and six months, and in Jerusalem he reigned over all Israel and Judah thirty-three years.

⁶The king and his men set out for Jerusalem against the Jebusites who inhabited the region. David was told, "You will never get in here! ᶜ⁻Even

ᵈ⁻ᵈ *Meaning of Heb. uncertain. Septuagint reads, "And behold, the woman who kept the door of the house was cleaning wheat. She became drowsy and fell asleep."*

ᵃ *The account in vv. 1–3 and 6–10 is to be found also, with variations, in 1 Chron. 11.1–9.*
ᵇ⁻ᵇ *Lit. "led Israel out and in."*
ᶜ⁻ᶜ *Meaning of Heb. uncertain.*

the blind and the lame will turn you back." (They meant: David will never enter here.)-c 7But David captured the stronghold of Zion; it is now the City of David. 8On that occasion David said, "Those who attack the Jebusites c-shall reach the water channel and [strike down] the lame and the blind, who are hateful to David." That is why they say: "No one who is blind or lame may enter the House."-c

9David occupied the stronghold and renamed it the City of David; David also fortified the surrounding area, from the Millod inward. 10David kept growing stronger, for the LORD, the God of Hosts, was with him.

11eKing Hiram of Tyre sent envoys to David with cedar logs, carpenters, and stonemasons; and they built a palace for David. 12Thus David knew that the LORD had established him as king over Israel and had exalted his kingship for the sake of His people Israel.

13After he left Hebron, David took more concubines and wives in Jerusalem, and more sons and daughters were born to David. 14These are the names of the children born to him in Jerusalem: fShammua, Shobab, Nathan, and Solomon; 15Ibhar, Elishua, Nepheg, and Japhia; 16Elishama, Eliada, and Eliphelet.

17gWhen the Philistines heard that David had been anointed king over Israel, the Philistines marched up in search of David; but David heard of it, and he went down to the fastness.h 18The Philistines came and spread out over the Valley of Rephaim. 19David inquired of the LORD, "Shall I go up against the Philistines? Will You deliver them into my hands?" And the LORD answered David, "Go up, and I will deliver the Philistines into your hands." 20Thereupon David marched to Baal-perazim, and David defeated them there. And he said, "The LORD has broken through my enemies before me as waters break through [a dam]." That is why that place was named Baal-perazim.i 21The Philistines abandoned their idols there, and David and his men carried them off.

22Once again the Philistines marched up and spread out over the Valley of Rephaim. 23David inquired of the LORD, and He answered, "Do not go up, but circle around behind them and confront them at the bacac trees. 24And when you hear the sound of marching in the tops of the baca trees, then go into action, for the LORD will be going in front of you to attack the Philistine forces." 25David did as the LORD had commanded him; and he routed the Philistines from Geba all the way to Gezer.

d A citadel.
e The account in vv. 11–25 is to be found also, with variations, in 1 Chron. 14.1–16.
f The list in vv. 14–16 is found, in addition to 1 Chron. 14.4–7, in 1 Chron. 3.5–8, with variations.
g Vv. 17–25 continue the narrative of v. 3.
h Probably the stronghold of Adullam (cf. 1 Sam. 22.4–5).
i Interpreted as "Baal of Breaches." Cf. 6.8 below, and the name Perez in Gen. 38.29 and note.

6 David again assembled all the picked men of Israel, thirty thousand strong. [2a]Then David and all the troops that were with him set out from Baalim[b] of Judah to bring up from there the Ark of God to which the Name was attached, the name LORD of Hosts Enthroned on the Cherubim.

[3]They loaded the Ark of God onto a new cart and conveyed it from the house of Abinadab, which was on the hill; and Abinadab's sons, Uzza and Ahio, guided the [c]new cart. [4]They conveyed it from Abinadab's house on the hill, [Uzzah walking][d] alongside[-c] the Ark of God and Ahio walking in front of the Ark. [5]Meanwhile, David and all the House of Israel danced before the LORD to [c-][the sound of] all kinds of cypress wood [instruments],[-c] with lyres, harps, timbrels, sistrums, and cymbals.

[6]But when they came to the threshing floor of Nacon, Uzzah reached out for the Ark of God and grasped it, for the oxen had stumbled.[f] [7]The LORD was incensed at Uzzah. And God struck him down on the spot [g-]for his indiscretion,[-g] and he died there beside the Ark of God. [8]David was distressed because the LORD had inflicted a breach upon Uzzah; and that place was named Perez-uzzah,[h] as it is still called.

[9]David was afraid of the LORD that day; he said, "How can I let the Ark of the LORD come to me?" [10]So David would not bring the Ark of the LORD to his place in the City of David; instead, David diverted it to the house of Obed-edom the Gittite. [11]The Ark of the LORD remained in the house of Obed-edom the Gittite three months, and the LORD blessed Obed-edom and his whole household.

[12]It was reported to King David: "The LORD has blessed Obed-edom's house and all that belongs to him because of the Ark of God." [i]Thereupon David went and brought up the Ark of God from the house of Obededom to the City of David, amid rejoicing. [13]When the bearers of the Ark of the LORD had moved forward six paces, he sacrificed [j-]an ox and a fatling.[-j] [14]David whirled with all his might before the LORD; David was girt with a linen ephod. [15]Thus David and all the House of Israel

---

a *Vv. 2–12 are found also in 1 Chron. 13.5–14, with variations.*

b *Identical with Baalah, another name for Kiriath-jearim, where the Ark had been kept (cf. 1 Sam. 6.21; 1 Chron. 13.6; Josh. 15.9).*

c-c *Septuagint and 4QSam[a] read "cart alongside."*

d *Cf. vv. 6–7.*

e-e *Cf. Kimhi; the parallel passage 1 Chron. 13.8 reads "with all their might and with songs."*

f *Meaning of Heb. uncertain.*

g-g *So Targum; 1 Chron. 13.10 reads "because he had laid a hand on the Ark."*

h *I.e., "the Breach of Uzzah"; cf. 5.20 and note.*

   Vv. 12b–14 are found, with variations, in 1 Chron. 15.25–27; vv. 15–19a, with variations, in 1 Chron. 15.28—16.3; vv. 19b–20a, with variations, in 1 Chron. 16.43.

i-i *4QSam[a] reads "seven oxen and seven [rams]"; cf. 1 Chron. 15.26.*

brought up the Ark of the LORD with shouts and with blasts of the horn.

¹⁶As the Ark of the LORD entered the City of David, Michal daughter of Saul looked out of the window and saw King David leaping and whirling before the LORD; and she despised him for it.

¹⁷They brought in the Ark of the LORD and set it up in its place inside the tent which David had pitched for it, and David sacrificed burnt offerings and offerings of well-being before the LORD. ¹⁸When David finished sacrificing the burnt offerings and the offerings of well-being, he blessed the people in the name of the LORD of Hosts. ¹⁹And he distributed among all the people—the entire multitude of Israel, man and woman alike—to each a loaf of bread, [f]-a cake made in a pan, and a raisin cake.-[f] Then all the people left for their homes.

²⁰David went home to greet his household. And Michal daughter of Saul came out to meet David and said, "Didn't the king of Israel do himself honor today—exposing himself today in the sight of the slavegirls of his subjects, as one of the riffraff might expose himself!" ²¹David answered Michal, "It was before the LORD who chose me instead of your father and all his family and appointed me ruler over the LORD's people Israel! I will dance before the LORD ²²and dishonor myself even more, and be low in [k]-my own-[k] esteem; but among the slavegirls that you speak of I will be honored." ²³So to her dying day Michal daughter of Saul had no children.

7 [a]When the king was settled in his palace and the LORD had granted him safety from all the enemies around him, ²the king said to the prophet Nathan: "Here I am dwelling in a house of cedar, while the Ark of the LORD abides in a tent!" ³Nathan said to the king, "Go and do whatever you have in mind, for the LORD is with you."

⁴But that same night the word of the LORD came to Nathan: ⁵"Go and say to My servant David: Thus said the LORD: Are you the one to build a house for Me to dwell in? ⁶From the day that I brought the people of Israel out of Egypt to this day I have not dwelt in a house, but have moved about in Tent and Tabernacle. ⁷As I moved about wherever the Israelites went, did I ever reproach any of the tribal leaders[b] whom I

[k-k] *Septuagint reads "your."*

[a] *This chapter is found, with variations, also in 1 Chron. 17.*

[b] *Understanding* shibṭe *as "scepters"; so Kimḥi. 1 Chron. 17.6 reads "chieftains"; cf. below, v. 11.*

appointed to care for My people Israel: Why have you not built Me a house of cedar?

8"Further, say thus to My servant David: Thus said the LORD of Hosts: I took you from the pasture, from following the flock, to be ruler of My people Israel, 9and I have been with you wherever you went, and have cut down all your enemies before you. Moreover, I will give you great renown like that of the greatest men on earth. 10I will establish a home for My people Israel and will plant them firm, so that they shall dwell secure and shall tremble no more. Evil men shall not oppress them any more as in the past, 11ever since I appointed chieftains over My people Israel. I will give you safety from all your enemies.

"The LORD declares to you that He, the LORD, will establish a house^c for you. 12When your days are done and you lie with your fathers, I will raise up your offspring after you, one of your own issue, and I will establish his kingship. 13He shall build a house for My name, and I will establish his royal throne forever. 14I will be a father to him, and he shall be a son to Me. When he does wrong, I will chastise him d-with the rod of men and the affliction of mortals;-d 15but I will never withdraw My favor from him as I withdrew it from Saul, whom I removed e-to make room for you.-e 16Your house and your kingship shall ever be secure before you;f your throne shall be established forever."

17Nathan spoke to David in accordance with all these words and all this prophecy. 18Then King David came and sat before the LORD, and he said, "What am I, O Lord GOD, and what is my family, that You have brought me thus far? 19Yet even this, O Lord GOD, has seemed too little to You; for You have spoken of Your servant's house also for the future. g-May that be the law for the people,-g O Lord GOD. 20What more can David say to You? You know Your servant, O Lord GOD. 21g-For Your word's sake and of Your own accord-g You have wrought this great thing, and made it known to Your servant. 22You are great indeed, O LORD God! There is none like You and there is no other God but You, as we have always heard. 23And who is like Your people Israel, a unique nation on earth, whom God went and redeemed as His people, winning renown for Himself and doing great and marvelous deeds for them^h [and] for Your land—[driving out]ⁱ nations and their gods before Your people, whom You redeemed for Yourself from Egypt. 24You have established

---

^c *I.e., a dynasty; play on "house" (i.e., Temple) in v. 5.*
^{d-d} *I.e., only as a human father would.*
^{e-e} *Lit. "from before you."*
^f *Septuagint reads "before Me," i.e., "by My favor."*
^{g-g} *Meaning of Heb. uncertain.*
^h *Heb. "you," apparently denoting Israel.*
ⁱ *So 1 Chron. 17.21.*

Your people Israel as Your very own people forever; and You, O LORD, have become their God.

²⁵"And now, O LORD God, fulfill Your promise to Your servant and his house forever; and do as You have promised. ²⁶And may Your name be glorified forever, in that men will say, 'The LORD of Hosts is God over Israel'; and may the house of Your servant David be established before You. ²⁷Because You, O LORD of Hosts, the God of Israel, have revealed to Your servant that You will build a house for him, Your servant has ventured to offer this prayer to You. ²⁸And now, O Lord GOD, You are God and Your words will surely come true, and You have made this gracious promise to Your servant. ²⁹Be pleased, therefore, to bless Your servant's house, that it abide before You forever; for You, O Lord GOD, have spoken. May Your servant's house be blessed forever by Your blessing."

8 ᵃSome time afterward, David attacked the Philistines and subdued them; and David took Metheg-ammahᵇ from the Philistines. ²He also defeated the Moabites. He made them lie down on the ground and he measured them off with a cord; he measured out two lengths of cord for those who were to be put to death, and one length for those to be spared.ᶜ And the Moabites became tributary vassals of David.

³David defeated Hadadezer son of Rehob, king of Zobah, who was then on his way to restore his monumentᵈ at the Euphrates River. ⁴David captured 1,700 horsemen and 20,000 foot soldiers of his force; and David hamstrung all the chariot horses, except for 100 which he retained. ⁵And when the Arameans of Damascus came to the aid of King Hadadezer of Zobah, David struck down 22,000 of the Arameans. ⁶David stationed garrisons in Aram of Damascus, and the Arameans became tributary vassals of David. The LORD gave David victory wherever he went. ⁷David took the gold shieldsᵉ carried by Hadadezer's retinue and brought them to Jerusalem; ⁸and from Betah and Berothai, towns of Hadadezer, King David took a vast amount of copper.

⁹When King Toi of Hamath heard that David had defeated the entire army of Hadadezer, ¹⁰Toi sent his son Joram to King David to greet him and to congratulate him on his military victory over Hadadezer—for Ha-

---

ᵃ *This chapter is reproduced, with some variations, in 1 Chron. 18.*
ᵇ *If not a place name, meaning of Heb. uncertain.*
ᶜ *I.e., he repeatedly doomed twice the number he spared.*
ᵈ *On* yad *in this sense, cf. 18.18; 1 Chron. 18.3; 1 Sam. 15.12. Others "dominion."*
ᵉ *Or "quivers."*

dadezer had been at war with Toi. [Joram] brought with him objects of silver, gold, and copper. [11]King David dedicated these to the LORD, along with the other silver and gold that he dedicated, [taken] from all the nations he had conquered: [12]from Edom,[f] Moab, and Ammon; from the Philistines and the Amalekites, and from the plunder of Hadadezer son of Rehob, king of Zobah.

[13]David gained fame [g-]when he returned from defeating[-g] Edom[f] in the Valley of Salt, 18,000 in all. [14]He stationed garrisons in Edom—[h-]he stationed garrisons in all of Edom[-h]—and all the Edomites became vassals of David. The LORD gave David victory wherever he went.

[15]David reigned over all Israel, and David executed true justice among all his people. [16]Joab son of Zeruiah was commander of the army; Jehoshaphat son of Ahilud was recorder; [17]Zadok son of Ahitub and [i-]Ahimelech son of Abiathar[-i] were priests; Seraiah[j] was scribe; [18]Benaiah son of Jehoiada was [k-]commander of[-k] the Cherethites and the Pelethites; and David's sons were priests.

9

David inquired, "Is there anyone still left of the House of Saul with whom I can keep faith for the sake of Jonathan?" [2]There was a servant of the House of Saul named Ziba, and they summoned him to David. "Are you Ziba?" the king asked him. [a-]"Yes, sir,"[-a] he replied. [3]The king continued, "Is there anyone at all left of the House of Saul with whom I can keep faith as pledged before God?"[b] Ziba answered the king, "Yes, there is still a son of Jonathan whose feet are crippled." [4]"Where is he?" the king asked, and Ziba said to the king, "He is in the house of Machir son of Ammiel, in Lo-debar." [5]King David had him brought from the house of Machir son of Ammiel, at Lo-debar; [6]and when Mephibosheth son of Jonathan son of Saul came to David, he flung himself on his face and prostrated himself. David said, "Mephibosheth!" and he replied, "At your service, sir." [7]David said to him, "Don't be afraid, for I will keep faith with you for the sake of your father Jonathan. I will give you back all the land of your grandfather Saul; moreover, you shall always eat at my table." [8][Mephibosheth] prostrated himself again, and said, "What is your servant, that you should show regard for a dead dog like me?"

[f] *So several mss., Septuagint, and 1 Chron. 18.11–13; and cf. v. 14 below. Printed editions and most mss. read "Aram."*

[g-g] *1 Chron. 18.12 and Ps. 60.1 read differently.*

[h-h] *This phrase is lacking in 1 Chron. 18.13.*

[i-i] *Emendation yields "Abiathar son of Ahimelech," cf., e.g., 20.25; 1 Sam. 22.20.*

[i] *"Sheva" in 20.25; "Shavsha" in 1 Chron. 18.16.*

[k-k] *So Targum (cf. 20.23; 1 Chron. 18.17); Heb. "and."*

[a-a] *Lit. "Your servant is."*

[b] *See 1 Sam. 20.14 and note.*

⁹The king summoned Ziba, Saul's steward, and said to him, "I give to your master's grandson everything that belonged to Saul and to his entire family. ¹⁰You and your sons and your slaves shall farm the land for him and shall bring in [its yield] to provide food for your master's grandsonᶜ to live on; but Mephibosheth, your master's grandson, shall always eat at my table."—Ziba had fifteen sons and twenty slaves.—¹¹Ziba said to the king, "Your servant will do just as my lord the king has commanded him." ᵈ-"Mephibosheth shall eat at my tableᵈ like one of the king's sons."

¹²Mephibosheth had a young son named Mica; and all the members of Ziba's household worked for Mephibosheth. ¹³Mephibosheth lived in Jerusalem, for he ate regularly at the king's table. He was lame in both feet.

10

ᵃSome time afterward, the king of Ammon died, and his son Hanun succeeded him as king. ²David said, "I will keep faith with Hanun son of Nahash, just as his father kept faith with me." He sent his courtiers with a message of condolence to him over his father. But when David's courtiers came to the land of Ammon, ³the Ammonite officials said to their lord Hanun, "Do you think David is really honoring your father just because he sent you men with condolences? Why, David has sent his courtiers to you to explore and spy out the city, and to overthrowᵇ it." ⁴So Hanun seized David's courtiers, clipped off one side of their beards and cut away half of their garments at the buttocks, and sent them off. ⁵When David was told of it, he dispatched men to meet them, for the men were greatly embarrassed. And the king gave orders: "Stop in Jericho until your beards grow back; then you can return."

⁶The Ammonites realized that they had ᶜ-incurred the wrath ofᶜ David; so the Ammonites sent agents and hired Arameans of Beth-rehob and Arameans of Zobah—20,000 foot soldiers—the king of Maacah [with] 1,000 men, and 12,000 men from Tob. ⁷On learning this, David sent out Joab and the whole army—[including] the professional fighters. ⁸The Ammonites marched out and took up their battle position at the entrance of the gate, while the Arameans of Zobah and Rehob and the men of Tob and Maacah took their stand separately in the open. ⁹Joab saw that there was a battle line against him both front and rear. So he made a

---

ᶜ *Septuagint reads "household."*
ᵈ⁻ᵈ *Septuagint reads "And Mephibosheth ate at David's table."*

ᵃ *This chapter is found also in 1 Chron. 19.*
ᵇ *Emendation yields "reconnoiter"; cf. Deut. 1.22; Josh. 2.2–3.*
ᶜ⁻ᶜ *See note at 1 Sam. 13.4.*

selection from all the picked men of Israel and arrayed them against the Arameans, ¹⁰and the rest of the troops he put under the command of his brother Abishai[d] and arrayed them against the Ammonites. ¹¹[Joab] said, "If the Arameans prove too strong for me, you come to my aid; and if the Ammonites prove too strong for you, I will come to your aid. ¹²Let us be strong and resolute for the sake of our people and the land[e] of our God; and the LORD will do what He deems right."

¹³Joab and the troops with him marched into battle against the Arameans, who fled before him. ¹⁴And when the Ammonites saw that the Arameans had fled, they fled before Abishai and withdrew into the city. So Joab broke off the attack against the Ammonites, and went to Jerusalem.

¹⁵When the Arameans saw that they had been routed by Israel, they regrouped their forces. ¹⁶Hadadezer[f] sent for and brought out the Arameans from across the Euphrates; they came to Helam, led by Shobach, Hadadezer's[f] army commander. ¹⁷David was informed of it; he assembled all Israel, crossed the Jordan, and came to Helam. The Arameans drew up their forces against David and attacked him; ¹⁸but the Arameans were put to flight by Israel. David killed 700 Aramean charioteers and 40,000 horsemen;[g] he also struck down Shobach, Hadadezer's[h] army commander, who died there. ¹⁹And when all the vassal kings of Hadadezer[f] saw that they had been routed by Israel, they submitted to Israel and became their vassals. And the Arameans were afraid to help the Ammonites any more.

11 At the turn of the year, the season when kings go out [to battle], David sent Joab with his officers and all Israel with him, and they devastated Ammon and besieged Rabbah; David remained in Jerusalem. ²Late one afternoon, David rose from his couch and strolled on the roof of the royal palace; and from the roof he saw a woman bathing. The woman was very beautiful, ³and the king sent someone to make inquiries about the woman. He reported, "She is Bathsheba daughter of Eliam [and] wife of Uriah the Hittite." ⁴David sent messengers to fetch her; she came to him and he lay with her—she had just purified herself after her period—and she went back home. ⁵The woman conceived, and she sent word to David, "I am pregnant." ⁶Thereupon David sent a message to Joab, "Send Uriah the Hittite to me"; and Joab sent Uriah to David.

d *Heb. "Abshai."*
e *Lit. "towns."*
f *Many editions read "Hadarezer . . . Hadarezer's."*
g *1 Chron. 19.18 reads "foot soldiers."*
h *Heb. "his."*

7When Uriah came to him, David asked him how Joab and the troops were faring and how the war was going. 8Then David said to Uriah, "Go down to your house and bathe your feet." When Uriah left the royal palace, a present from the king followed him. 9But Uriah slept at the entrance of the royal palace, along with the other officers of his lord, and did not go down to his house. 10When David was told that Uriah had not gone down to his house, he said to Uriah, "You just came from a journey; why didn't you go down to your house?" 11Uriah answered David, "The Ark and Israel and Judah are located at Succoth, and my master Joab and Your Majesty's men are camped in the open; how can I go home and eat and drink and sleep with my wife? a-As you live, by your very life,-a I will not do this!" 12David said to Uriah, "Stay here today also, and tomorrow I will send you off." So Uriah remained in Jerusalem that day. The next day, 13David summoned him, and he ate and drank with him until he got him drunk; but in the evening, [Uriah] went out to sleep in the same place, with his lord's officers; he did not go down to his home.

14In the morning, David wrote a letter to Joab, which he sent with Uriah. 15He wrote in the letter as follows: "Place Uriah in the front line where the fighting is fiercest; then fall back so that he may be killed." 16So when Joab was besieging the city, he stationed Uriah at the point where he knew that there were able warriors. 17The men of the city sallied out and attacked Joab, and some of David's officers among the troops fell; Uriah the Hittite was among those who died.

18Joab sent a full report of the battle to David. 19He instructed the messenger as follows: "When you finish reporting to the king all about the battle, 20the king may get angry and say to you, 'Why did you come so close to the city to attack it? Didn't you know that they would shoot from the wall? 21Who struck down Abimelech son of Jerubbesheth?b Was it not a woman who dropped an upper millstone on him from the wall at Thebez, from which he died? Why did you come so close to the wall?' Then say: 'Your servant Uriah the Hittite was among those killed.' "

22The messenger set out; he came and told David all that Joab had sent him to say.c 23The messenger said to David, "First the men prevailed against us and sallied out against us into the open; then we drove them back up to the entrance to the gate. 24But the archers shot at your men from the wall and some of Your Majesty's men fell; your servant Uriah the Hittite also fell." 25Whereupon David said to the messenger, "Give

---

a-a *Meaning of Heb. uncertain. Emendation yields "As the* LORD *lives and as you live" (cf. 1 Sam. 20.3; 25.26; etc.). Lit. "as you live and as your being lives."*

b *The earlier form is Jerubbaal (another name for Gideon), Judg. 7.1; on -bosheth/besheth for -baal, see note at 2 Sam. 4.4. For the event at Thebez described here, see Judg. 9.35 ff.*

c *Septuagint continues with a recapitulation of vv. 19–21.*

Joab this message: 'Do not be distressed about the matter. The sword d-always takes its toll.-d Press your attack on the city and destroy it!' Encourage him!"

26When Uriah's wife heard that her husband Uriah was dead, she lamented over her husband. 27After the period of mourning was over, David sent and had her brought into his palace; she became his wife and she bore him a son.

12 But the LORD was displeased with what David had done, 1and the LORD sent Nathan to David. He came to him and said, "There were two men in the same city, one rich and one poor. 2The rich man had very large flocks and herds, 3but the poor man had only one little ewe lamb that he had bought. He tended it and it grew up together with him and his children: it used to share his morsel of bread, drink from his cup, and nestle in his bosom; it was like a daughter to him. 4One day, a traveler came to the rich man, but he was loath to take anything from his own flocks or herds to prepare a meal for the guest who had come to him; so he took the poor man's lamb and prepared it for the man who had come to him."

5David flew into a rage against the man, and said to Nathan, "As the LORD lives, the man who did this deserves to die! 6He shall pay for the lamb four times over, because he did such a thing and showed no pity." 7And Nathan said to David, "That man is you! Thus said the LORD, the God of Israel: 'It was I who anointed you king over Israel and it was I who rescued you from the hand of Saul. 8I gave you your master's house and possession of your master's wives; and I gave you the House of Israel and Judah; and if that were not enough, I would give you twice as much more. 9Why then have you flouted the command of the LORD and done what displeases Him? You have put Uriah the Hittite to the sword; you took his wife and made her your wife and had him killed by the sword of the Ammonites. 10Therefore the sword shall never depart from your House—because you spurned Me by taking the wife of Uriah the Hittite and making her your wife.' 11Thus said the LORD: 'I will make a calamity rise against you from within your own house; I will take your wives and give them to another man before your very eyes and he shall sleep with your wives under this very sun. 12You acted in secret, but I will make this happen in the sight of all Israel and in broad daylight.'"

d-d Lit. "consumes the like and the like."

¹³David said to Nathan, "I stand guilty before the LORD!" And Nathan replied to David, "The LORD has remitted your sin; you shall not die. ¹⁴However, since you have spurned ^{a-}the enemies of-^a the LORD by this deed, even the child about to be born to you shall die."

¹⁵Nathan went home, and the LORD afflicted the child that Uriah's wife had borne to David, and it became critically ill. ¹⁶David entreated God for the boy; David fasted, and he went in and spent the night lying^b on the ground. ¹⁷The senior servants of his household tried to induce him to get up from the ground; but he refused, nor would he partake of food with them. ¹⁸On the seventh day the child died. David's servants were afraid to tell David that the child was dead; for they said, "We spoke to him when the child was alive and he wouldn't listen to us; how can we tell him that the child is dead? He might do something terrible." ¹⁹When David saw his servants talking in whispers, David understood that the child was dead; David asked his servants, "Is the child dead?" "Yes," they replied.

²⁰Thereupon David rose from the ground; he bathed and anointed himself, and he changed his clothes. He went into the House of the LORD and prostrated himself. Then he went home and asked for food, which they set before him, and he ate. ²¹His courtiers asked him, "Why have you acted in this manner? While the child was alive, you fasted and wept; but now that the child is dead, you rise and take food!" ²²He replied, "While the child was still alive, I fasted and wept because I thought: 'Who knows? The LORD may have pity on me, and the child may live.' ²³But now that he is dead, why should I fast? Can I bring him back again? I shall go to him, but he will never come back to me."

²⁴David consoled his wife Bathsheba; he went to her and lay with her. She bore a son and she named him Solomon. The LORD favored him, ²⁵and He sent a message through the prophet Nathan; and he was named Jedidiah^c at the instance of the LORD.

^{26d}Joab attacked Rabbah of Ammon and captured the royal city. ²⁷Joab sent messengers to David and said, "I have attacked Rabbah and I have already captured ^{e-}the water city.-^e ²⁸Now muster the rest of the troops and besiege the city and capture it; otherwise I will capture the city myself, and my name will be connected with it." ²⁹David mustered all the troops and marched on Rabbah, and he attacked it and captured it. ^{30f}The crown

---

^{a-a} *The phrase is intended to avoid saying "spurned the LORD"; cf. note d-d at 1 Sam. 25.22.*
^b *Some Septuagint mss. and 4QSam^a add "in sackcloth"; cf. 1 Kings 21.27.*
^c *I.e., "Beloved of the LORD."*
^d *Vv. 26–29 are abridged in 1 Chron. 20.1b.*
^{e-e} *Meaning of Heb. uncertain; perhaps the source of the water supply.*
^f *Vv. 30–31 are found also in 1 Chron. 20.2–3.*

was taken from the head of their king[g] and it was placed on David's head—it weighed a talent of gold, and [on it][h] were precious stones. He also carried off a vast amount of booty from the city. [31]He led out the people who lived there and set them to work with saws, iron threshing boards, and iron axes, or assigned them to brickmaking; David did this to all the towns of Ammon. Then David and all the troops returned to Jerusalem.

13 This happened sometime afterward: Absalom son of David had a beautiful sister named Tamar, and Amnon son of David became infatuated with her. [2]Amnon was so distraught because of his [half-]sister Tamar that he became sick; for she was a virgin, and it seemed impossible to Amnon to do anything to her. [3]Amnon had a friend named Jonadab, the son of David's brother Shimah; Jonadab was a very clever man. [4]He asked him, "Why are you so dejected, O prince, morning after morning? Tell me!" Amnon replied, "I am in love with Tamar, the sister of my brother Absalom!" [5]Jonadab said to him, "Lie down in your bed and pretend you are sick. When your father comes to see you, say to him, 'Let my sister Tamar come and give me something to eat. Let her prepare the food in front of me, so that I may look on, and let her serve it to me.' "

[6]Amnon lay down and pretended to be sick. The king came to see him, and Amnon said to the king, "Let my sister Tamar come and prepare a couple of cakes in front of me, and let her bring them to me." [7]David sent a message to Tamar in the palace, "Please go to the house of your brother Amnon and prepare some food for him." [8]Tamar went to the house of her brother Amnon, who was in bed. She took dough and kneaded it into cakes in front of him, and cooked the cakes. [9]She took the [a-]pan and set out [the cakes],[-a] but Amnon refused to eat and ordered everyone to withdraw. After everyone had withdrawn, [10]Amnon said to Tamar, "Bring the food inside and feed me." Tamar took the cakes she had made and brought them to her brother inside. [11]But when she served them to him, he caught hold of her and said to her, "Come lie with me, sister." [12]But she said to him, "Don't, brother. Don't force me. Such things are not done in Israel! Don't do such a vile thing! [13]Where will I carry my shame? And you, you will be like any of the scoundrels in Israel!

[g] *Heb.* "malkam," *perhaps equivalent to "Milcom," the Ammonite deity; cf. 1 Kings 11.5.*
[h] *So Targum and 1 Chron. 20.2.*

[a-a] *Meaning of Heb. uncertain.*

Please, speak to the king; he will not refuse me to you." [14]But he would not listen to her; he overpowered her and lay with her by force.

[15]Then Amnon felt a very great loathing for her; indeed, his loathing for her was greater than the passion he had felt for her. And Amnon said to her, "Get out!" [16]She pleaded with him, "Please don't ᵃ-commit this wrong; to send me away would be even worse-ᵃ than the first wrong you committed against me." But he would not listen to her. [17]He summoned his young attendant and said, "Get that woman out of my presence, and bar the door behind her."—[18]She was wearing an ornamented tunic,ᵇ for maiden princesses were customarily dressed ᶜ-in such garments.-ᶜ—His attendant took her outside and barred the door after her. [19]Tamar put dust on her head and rent the ornamented tunic she was wearing; she put her hands on her head,ᵈ and walked away, screaming loudly as she went. [20]Her brother Absalom said to her, "Was it your brother Amnonᵉ who did this to you? For the present, sister, keep quiet about it; he is your brother. Don't brood over the matter." And Tamar remained in her brother Absalom's house, forlorn. [21]When King David heard about all this, he was greatly upset.ᶠ [22]Absalom didn't utter a word to Amnon, good or bad; but Absalom hated Amnon because he had violated his sister Tamar.

[23]Two years later, when Absalom was having his flocks sheared at Baal-hazor near Ephraim, Absalom invited all the king's sons. [24]And Absalom came to the king and said, "Your servant is having his flocks sheared. Would Your Majesty and your retinue accompany your servant?" [25]But the king answered Absalom, "No, my son. We must not all come, or we'll be a burden to you." He urged him, but he would not go, and he said good-bye to him. [26]Thereupon Absalom said, "In that case, let my brother Amnon come with us," to which the king replied, "He shall not go with you." [27]But Absalom urged him, and he sent with him Amnon and all the other princes.ᵍ

[28]Now Absalom gave his attendants these orders: "Watch, and when Amnon is merry with wine and I tell you to strike down Amnon, kill him! Don't be afraid, for it is I who give you the order. Act with determination, like brave men!" [29]Absalom's attendants did to Amnon as Absalom had ordered; whereupon all the other princes mounted their mules and fled. [30]They were still on the road when a rumor reached David that Absalom had killed all the princes, and that not one of them had survived.

ᵇ *See Gen. 37.3 and note.*

ᶜ⁻ᶜ *Meaning of Heb. uncertain. Emendation yields "(thus) in olden times,"* meʿolam.

ᵈ *A gesture of wild grief; cf. Jer. 2.37.*

ᵉ *Heb. "Aminon."*

ᶠ *Septuagint adds "but he did not rebuke his son Amnon, for he favored him, since he was his first-born"; cf. 1 Kings 1.6.*

ᵍ *Septuagint adds "and Absalom made a feast fit for a king."*

³¹At this, David rent his garment and lay down on the ground, ʰ⁻and all his courtiers stood by with their clothes rent.⁻ʰ ³²But Jonadab, the son of David's brother Shimah, said, "My lord must not think that all the young princes have been killed. Only Amnon is dead; for this has been ⁱ⁻decided by⁻ⁱ Absalom ever since his sister Tamar was violated. ³³So my lord the king must not think for a moment that all the princes are dead; Amnon alone is dead."

³⁴Meanwhile Absalom had fled.

The watchman on duty looked up and saw a large crowd coming ʲ⁻from the road to his rear,⁻ʲ from the side of the hill. ³⁵Jonadab said to the king, "See, the princes have come! It is just as your servant said." ³⁶As he finished speaking, the princes came in and broke into weeping; and David and all his courtiers wept bitterly, too.

³⁷Absalom had fled, and he came to Talmai son of Ammihud, king of Geshur. And [King David] mourned over his son a long time. ³⁸Absalom, who had fled to Geshur, remained there three years. ³⁹And ᵏ⁻King David⁻ᵏ was pining away for Absalom, for [the king] had gotten over Amnon's death.

14

Joab son of Zeruiah could see that the king's mind was on Absalom; ²so Joab sent to Tekoa and brought a clever woman from there. He said to her, "Pretend you are in mourning; put on mourning clothes and don't anoint yourself with oil; and act like a woman who has grieved a long time over a departed one. ³Go to the king and say to him thus and thus." And Joab told her what to say.ᵃ

⁴The woman of Tekoa cameᵇ to the king, flung herself face down to the ground, and prostrated herself. She cried out, "Help, O king!" ⁵The king asked her, "What troubles you?" And she answered, "Alas, I am a widow, my husband is dead. ⁶Your maidservant had two sons. The two of them came to blows out in the fields where there was no one to stop them, and one of them struck the other and killed him. ⁷Then the whole clan confronted your maidservant and said, 'Hand over the one who killed his brother, that we may put him to death for the slaying of his brother, ᶜ⁻even though we wipe out the heir.'⁻ᶜ Thus they would quench the last ember remaining to me, and leave my husband without name or remnant

---

ʰ⁻ʰ *Septuagint reads "and all his courtiers who were standing by him rent their clothes."*
ⁱ⁻ⁱ *Lit. "determined by the command of."*
ʲ⁻ʲ *Emendation yields "down the slope of the Horonaim road. The watchman came and told the king 'I see men coming from the Horonaim road.'" Cf. Septuagint.*
ᵏ⁻ᵏ *Some Septuagint mss. and 4QSamᵃ read "the spirit [ruaḥ] of the king."*

ᵃ *Lit. "and he put words into her mouth."*
ᵇ *So many mss. and printed editions. Most mss. and printed editions read "said."*
ᶜ⁻ᶜ *Emendation yields "Thus they would destroy the [last] heir and. . . ."*

upon the earth." [8]The king said to the woman, "Go home. I will issue an order in your behalf." [9]And the woman of Tekoa said to the king, "My lord king, may the guilt be on me and on my ancestral house; Your Majesty and his throne are guiltless." [10]The king said, "If anyone says anything more to you, have him brought to me, and he will never trouble you again." [11]She replied, "Let Your Majesty be mindful of the LORD your God and restrain the blood avenger bent on destruction, so that my son may not be killed." And he said, "As the LORD lives, not a hair of your son shall fall to the ground."

[12]Then the woman said, "Please let your maidservant say another word to my lord the king." "Speak on," said the king. [13]And the woman said, "Why then have you planned the like against God's people? In making this pronouncement, Your Majesty condemns himself in that Your Majesty does not bring back his own banished one. [14]We must all die; we are like water that is poured out on the ground and cannot be gathered up. [d-]God will not take away the life of one who makes plans so that no one may be kept banished.[-d] [15]And the reason I have come to say these things to the king, my lord, is that the people have frightened me. Your maidservant thought I would speak to Your Majesty; perhaps Your Majesty would act on his handmaid's plea. [16]For Your Majesty would surely agree to deliver his handmaid from the hands of anyone [who would seek to] cut off both me and my son from the heritage[e] of God. [17]Your maidservant thought, 'Let the word of my lord the king provide comfort; for my lord the king is like an angel of God, understanding everything, good and bad.' May the LORD your God be with you."

[18]In reply, the king said to the woman, "Do not withhold from me anything I ask you!" The woman answered, "Let my lord the king speak." [19]The king asked, "Is Joab in league with you in all this?" The woman replied, "As you live, my lord the king, [f-]it is just as my lord the king says.[-f] Yes, your servant Joab was the one who instructed me, and it was he who [g-]told your maidservant everything she was to say.[-g] [20]It was to conceal the real purpose of the matter that your servant Joab did this thing. My lord is as wise as an angel of God, and he knows all that goes on in the land."

[21]Then the king said to Joab, "I will do this thing. Go and bring back my boy Absalom." [22]Joab flung himself face down on the ground and

---

[d-d] *Meaning of Heb. uncertain. The apparent sense is: God will not punish you for bringing back the banished Absalom.*

[e] *I.e., people.*

[f-f] *Lit. "there is no turning to the right or to the left of what my lord the king says."*

[g-g] *See note a above.*

prostrated himself. Joab blessed the king and said, "Today your servant knows that he has found favor with you, my lord king, for Your Majesty has granted his servant's request." 23And Joab went at once to Geshur and brought Absalom to Jerusalem. 24But the king said, "Let him go directly to his house and not present himself to me." So Absalom went directly to his house and did not present himself to the king.

25No one in all Israel was so admired for his beauty as Absalom; from the sole of his foot to the crown of his head he was without blemish. 26When he cut his hair—he had to have it cut every year, for it grew too heavy for him—the hair of his head weighed two hundred shekels by the royal weight. 27Absalom had three sons and a daughter whose name was Tamar; she was a beautiful woman.

28Absalom lived in Jerusalem two years without appearing before the king. 29Then Absalom sent for Joab, in order to send him to the king; but Joab would not come to him. He sent for him a second time, but he would not come. 30So [Absalom] said to his servants, "Look, Joab's field is next to mine, and he has barley there. Go and set it on fire." And Absalom's servants set the field on fire. 31Joab came at once to Absalom's house and said to him, "Why did your servants set fire to my field?" 32Absalom replied to Joab, "I sent for you to come here; I wanted to send you to the king to say [on my behalf]: 'Why did I leave Geshur? I would be better off if I were still there. Now let me appear before the king; and if I am guilty of anything, let him put me to death!' " 33Joab went to the king and reported to him; whereupon he summoned Absalom. He came to the king and flung himself face down to the ground before the king. And the king kissed Absalom.

15 Sometime afterward, Absalom provided himself with a chariot, horses, and fifty outrunners. 2Absalom used to rise early and stand by the road to the city gates; and whenever a man had a case that was to come before the king for judgment, Absalom would call out to him, "What town are you from?" And when he answered, "Your servant is from a-such and such a tribe-a in Israel," 3Absalom would say to him, "It is clear that your claim is right and just, but there is no one assigned to you

a-a Lit. "one of the tribes."

by the king to hear it." [4]And Absalom went on, "If only I were appointed judge in the land and everyone with a legal dispute came before me, I would see that he got his rights." [5]And if a man approached to bow to him, [Absalom] would extend his hand and take hold of him and kiss him. [6]Absalom did this to every Israelite who came to the king for judgment. Thus Absalom won away the hearts of the men of Israel.

[7]After a period of forty[b] years had gone by, Absalom said to the king, "Let me go to Hebron and fulfill a vow that I made to the LORD. [8]For your servant made a vow when I lived in Geshur of Aram: If the LORD ever brings me back to Jerusalem, I will worship the LORD."[c] [9]The king said to him, "Go in peace"; and so he set out for Hebron.

[10]But Absalom sent agents to all the tribes of Israel to say, "When you hear the blast of the horn, announce that Absalom has become king in Hebron." [11]Two hundred men of Jerusalem accompanied Absalom; they were invited and went in good faith, suspecting nothing. [12]Absalom also [d-]sent [to fetch][-d] Ahithophel the Gilonite, David's counselor, from his town, Giloh, when the sacrifices were to be offered. The conspiracy gained strength, and the people supported Absalom in increasing numbers.

[13]Someone came and told David, "The loyalty of the men of Israel has veered toward Absalom." [14]Whereupon David said to all the courtiers who were with him in Jerusalem, "Let us flee at once, or none of us will escape from Absalom. We must get away quickly, or he will soon overtake us and bring down disaster upon us and put the city to the sword." [15]The king's courtiers said to the king, "Whatever our lord the king decides, your servants are ready." [16]So the king left, followed by his entire household, except for ten concubines whom the king left to mind the palace.

[17]The king left, followed by [e-]all the people,[-e] and they stopped at [f-]the last house.[-f] [18]All [g-]his followers[-g] marched past him, including all the Cherethites and all the Pelethites; and[h] all the Gittites, six hundred men who had accompanied him from Gath, also marched by the king. [19]And the king said to Ittai the Gittite, "Why should you too go with us? Go back and stay with the [new] king, for you are a foreigner and you are also an exile from[i] your country. [20]You came only yesterday; should I make you wander about with us today, when I myself must go wherever I can? Go back, and take your kinsmen with you, [in][j] true faithfulness." [21]Ittai replied to the king, "As the LORD lives and as my lord the king

b *Some Septuagint mss. and Syriac read "four."*
c *Some Septuagint mss. add "in Hebron."*
d-d *Some Septuagint mss. and 4QSam[a] read "sent and summoned."*
e-e *Septuagint reads "his courtiers."*
f-f *Meaning of Heb. uncertain.*
g-g *Septuagint reads "the people."*
h *Emendation yields "and Ittai and."*
i *So one Heb. ms. and several ancient versions; most mss. and editions read "to."*
j *Meaning of Heb. uncertain. Septuagint reads "and may the LORD show you" (cf., e.g., 2.6).*

lives, wherever my lord the king may be, there your servant will be, whether for death or for life!" 22And David said to Ittai, "Then march by." And Ittai the Gittite and all his men and all the children who were with him marched by.

23The whole countryside wept aloud as the troops marched by. The king k-crossed the Kidron Valley, and all the troops crossed by the road to-k the wilderness. 24Then Zadok appeared, with all the Levites carrying the Ark of the Covenant of God; and they set down the Ark of God until all the people had finished marching out of the city. f-Abiathar also came up.-f 25But the king said to Zadok, "Take the Ark of God back to the city. If I find favor with the LORD, He will bring me back and let me see it and its abode. 26And if He should say, 'I do not want you,' I am ready; let Him do with me as He pleases." 27And the king said to the priest Zadok, l-"Do you understand? You return-l to the safety of the city with your two sons, your own son Ahimaaz and Abiathar's son Jonathan. 28Look, I shall linger in the steppes of the wilderness until word comes from you to inform me." 29Zadok and Abiathar brought the Ark of God back to Jerusalem, and they stayed there.

30David meanwhile went up the slope of the [Mount of] Olives, weeping as he went; his head was covered and he walked barefoot. And all the people who were with him covered their heads and wept as they went up. 31David [was] told that Ahithophel was among the conspirators with Absalom, and he prayed, "Please, O LORD, frustrate Ahithophel's counsel!"

32When David reached the top, where people would prostrate themselves to God, Hushai the Archite was there to meet him, with his robe torn and with earth on his head. 33David said to him, "If you march on with me, you will be a burden to me. 34But if you go back to the city and say to Absalom, 'I will be your servant, O king; I was your father's servant formerly, and now I will be yours,' then you can nullify Ahithophel's counsel for me. 35You will have the priests Zadok and Abiathar there, and you can report everything that you hear in the king's palace to the priests Zadok and Abiathar. 36Also, their two sons are there with them, Zadok's son Ahimaaz and Abiathar's son Jonathan; and through them you can report to me everything you hear." 37And so Hushai, the friend of David, reached the city as Absalom was entering Jerusalem.

---

k-k *Meaning of Heb. uncertain. Emendation yields "stopped in the Kidron Valley, while all the people marched on before him by way of the Mount of Olives to. . . ."*
l-l *Meaning of Heb. uncertain. Emendation yields "Look, you and Abiathar return."*

16

David had passed a little beyond the summit when Ziba the servant of Mephibosheth came toward him with a pair of saddled asses carrying two hundred loaves of bread, one hundred cakes of raisin, one hundred cakes of figs,ᵃ and a jar of wine. ²The king asked Ziba, "What are you doing with these?" Ziba answered, "The asses are for Your Majesty's family to ride on, the bread and figs are for the attendants to eat, and the wine is to be drunk by any who are exhausted in the wilderness." ³"And where is your master's son?" the king asked. "He is staying in Jerusalem," Ziba replied to the king, "for he thinks that the House of Israel will now give him back the throne of his grandfather." ⁴The king said to Ziba, "Then all that belongs to Mephibosheth is now yours!" And Ziba replied, "I bow low. Your Majesty is most gracious to me."

⁵As King David was approaching Bahurim, a member of Saul's clan— a man named Shimei son of Gera—came out from there, hurling insults as he came. ⁶He threw stones at David and all King David's courtiers, while all the troops and all the warriors were at his right and his left. ⁷And these are the insults that Shimei hurled: "Get out, get out, you criminal, you villain! ⁸The LORD is paying you back for all your crimes against the family of Saul, whose throne you seized. The LORD is handing over the throne to your son Absalom; you are in trouble because you are a criminal!"

⁹Abishai son of Zeruiah said to the king, "Why let that dead dog abuse my lord the king? Let me go over and cut off his head!" ¹⁰But the king said, ᵇ"What has this to do with you,ᵇ you sons of Zeruiah? He is abusing [me] only because the LORD told him to abuse David; and who is to say, 'Why did You do that?'" ¹¹David said further to Abishai and all the courtiers, "If my son, my own issue, seeks to kill me, how much more the Benjaminite! Let him go on hurling abuse, for the LORD has told him to. ¹²Perhaps the LORD will look upon my punishmentᶜ and recompense me for the abuse [Shimei] has uttered today." ¹³David and his men continued on their way, while Shimei walked alongside on the slope of the hill, insulting him as he walked, and throwing stones at him and flinging dirt. ¹⁴The king and all who accompanied him arrivedᵈ exhausted, and he rested there.

¹⁵Meanwhile Absalom and all the people, the men of Israel, arrived in Jerusalem, together with Ahithophel. ¹⁶When Hushai the Archite, David's

---

ᵃ Lit. "summer fruit."
ᵇ⁻ᵇ Lit. "What have I and you."
ᶜ So kethib; qere "eye." Ancient versions read "suffering."
ᵈ Some Septuagint mss. add "at the Jordan."

friend, came before Absalom, Hushai said to Absalom, "Long live the king! Long live the king!" [17]But Absalom said to Hushai, "Is this your loyalty to your friend? Why didn't you go with your friend?" [18]"Not at all!" Hushai replied. "I am for the one whom the LORD and this people and all the men of Israel have chosen, and I will stay with him. [19]Furthermore, whom should I serve, if not David's[e] son? As I was in your father's service, so I will be in yours."

[20]Absalom then said to Ahithophel, "What do you advise us to do?" [21]And Ahithophel said to Absalom, "Have intercourse with your father's concubines, whom he left to mind the palace; and when all Israel hears that you have dared the wrath of your father, all who support you will be encouraged." [22]So they pitched a tent for Absalom on the roof, and Absalom lay with his father's concubines [f]with the full knowledge[f] of all Israel.—[23]In those days, the advice which Ahithophel gave was accepted like an oracle sought from God; that is how all the advice of Ahithophel was esteemed both by David and by Absalom.

17

And Ahithophel said to Absalom, "Let me pick twelve thousand men and set out tonight in pursuit of David. [2]I will come upon him when he is weary and disheartened, and I will throw him into a panic; and when all the troops with him flee, I will kill the king alone. [3]And I will bring back all the people [a]to you; when all have come back [except] the man you are after,[a] all the people will be at peace." [4]The advice pleased Absalom and all the elders of Israel. [5]But Absalom said, "Summon Hushai the Archite as well, so we can hear what he too has to say." [6]Hushai came to Absalom, and Absalom said to him, "This is what Ahithophel has advised. Shall we follow his advice? If not, what do you say?"

[7]Hushai said to Absalom, "This time the advice that Ahithophel has given is not good. [8]You know," Hushai continued, "that your father and his men are courageous fighters, and they are as desperate as a bear in the wild robbed of her whelps. Your father is an experienced soldier, and he will not spend the night with the troops; [9]even now he must be hiding in one of the pits or in some other place. And if any of them[b] fall at the first attack, whoever hears of it will say, 'A disaster has struck the troops that follow Absalom'; [10]and even if he is a brave man with the heart of a lion, he will be shaken—for all Israel knows that your father and the soldiers with him are courageous fighters. [11]So I advise that all Israel from

---

[e] Heb. "his."

[f-f] Lit. "before the eyes."

[a-a] Meaning of Heb. uncertain. Septuagint reads "to you as a bride comes back to her husband; you seek the life of but one man, and. . . ."

[b] Some Septuagint mss. read "the troops" (i.e., Absalom's).

Dan to Beersheba—as numerous as the sands of the sea—be called up to join you, and that you yourself march c-into battle.-c 12When we come upon him in whatever place he may be, we'll descend on him [as thick] as dew falling on the ground; and no one will survive, neither he nor any of the men with him. 13And if he withdraws into a city, all Israel will bring ropes to that city and drag d-its stones-d as far as the riverbed, until not even a pebble of it is left." 14Absalom and all Israel agreed that the advice of Hushai the Archite was better than that of Ahithophel.—The LORD had decreed that Ahithophel's sound advice be nullified, in order that the LORD might bring ruin upon Absalom.

15Then Hushai told the priests Zadok and Abiathar, "This is what Ahithophel advised Absalom and the elders of Israel; this is what I advised. 16Now send at once and tell David, 'Do not spend the night at the fords of the wilderness, but cross over at once; otherwise the king and all the troops with him will be annihilated.' " 17Jonathan and Ahimaaz were staying at En-rogel, and a slave girl would go and bring them word and they in turn would go and inform King David. For they themselves dared not be seen entering the city. 18But a boy saw them and informed Absalom. They left at once and came to the house of a man in Bahurim who had a well in his courtyard. They got down into it, 19and the wife took a cloth, spread it over the mouth of the well, and scattered groats on top of it, so that nothing would be noticed. 20When Absalom's servants came to the woman at the house and asked where Ahimaaz and Jonathan were, the woman told them that they had crossed e-a bit beyond the water.-e They searched, but found nothing; and they returned to Jerusalem.

21After they were gone, [Ahimaaz and Jonathan] came up from the well and went and informed King David. They said to David, "Go and cross the water quickly, for Ahithophel has advised thus and thus concerning you." 22David and all the troops with him promptly crossed the Jordan, and by daybreak not one was left who had not crossed the Jordan.

23When Ahithophel saw that his advice had not been followed, he saddled his ass and went home to his native town. He set his affairs in order, and then he hanged himself. He was buried in his ancestral tomb.

24David had reached Mahanaim when Absalom and all the men of Israel with him crossed the Jordan. 25Absalom had appointed Amasa army commander in place of Joab; Amasa was the son of a man named Ithra the f-Israelite, who had married Abigal, daughter of Nahash and sister of Joab's mother Zeruiah.-f 26The Israelites and Absalom encamped in the

---

c-c Ancient versions read "among them."
d-d Heb. "it."
e-e Meaning of Heb. uncertain. Targum reads "the Jordan."
f-f Some Septuagint mss. and 1 Chron. 2.12–17 read "Ishmaelite" and give a somewhat different genealogy.

district of Gilead. ²⁷When David reached Mahanaim, Shobi son of Nahash from Rabbath-ammon, Machir son of Ammiel from Lo-debar, and Barzillai the Gileadite from Rogelim ²⁸presentedᵍ couches, basins, and earthenware; also wheat, barley, flour, parched grain, beans, lentils, ʰ⁻parched grain,⁻ʰ ²⁹honey, ⁱ⁻curds, a flock,⁻ⁱ and cheeseʲ from the herd for David and the troops with him to eat. For they knew that the troops must have grown hungry, faint, and thirsty in the wilderness.

18 David mustered the troops who were with him and set over them captains of thousands and captains of hundreds. ²David ᵃ⁻sent out the troops,⁻ᵃ one-third under the command of Joab, one-third under the command of Joab's brother Abishai son of Zeruiah, and one-third under the command of Ittai the Gittite. And David said to the troops, "I myself will march out with you." ³But the troops replied, "No! For if some of us flee, the rest will not be concerned about us; even if half of us should die, the others will not be concerned about us. But ᵇ⁻you are worth ten thousand of us.⁻ᵇ Therefore, it is better for you to support us from the town." ⁴And the king said to them, "I will do whatever you think best."

So the king stood beside the gate as all the troops marched out by their hundreds and thousands. ⁵The king gave orders to Joab, Abishai, and Ittai: "Deal gently with my boy Absalom, for my sake." All the troops heard the king give the order about Absalom to all the officers.

⁶The troops marched out into the open to confront the Israelites,ᶜ and the battle was fought in the forest of Ephraim.ᵈ ⁷The Israelite troops were routed by David's followers, and a great slaughter took place there that day—twenty thousand men. ⁸The battle spread out over that whole region, and the forest devoured more troops that day than the sword.

⁹Absalom encountered some of David's followers. Absalom was riding on a mule, and as the mule passed under the tangled branches of a great terebinth, his hair got caught in the terebinth; he ᵉ⁻was held⁻ᵉ between heaven and earth as the mule under him kept going. ¹⁰One of the men saw it and told Joab, "I have just seen Absalom hanging from a terebinth."

g *Brought up from v. 29 for clarity.*
h-h *Lacking in the Septuagint and Syriac.*
i-i *Emendation yields "curds from the flock."*
j *Meaning of Heb. uncertain.*
a-a *Some Septuagint mss. read "divided the troops into three."*
b-b *So two Heb. mss., Septuagint, and Vulgate; cf. 1 Kings 1.18 and note. Most mss. and the editions read "Now there are ten thousand like us."*
c *The usual term in this narrative for the supporters of Absalom.*
d *Some Septuagint mss. read "Mahanaim"; cf. 17.24.*
e-e *Meaning of Heb. uncertain. Ancient versions and 4QSamᵃ read "was left hanging"; cf. v. 10.*

11Joab said to the man who told him, "You saw it! Why didn't you kill him f-then and there?-f I would have owed you teng shekels of silver and a belt." 12But the man answered Joab, "Even if I had a thousand shekels of silver in my hands, I would not raise a hand against the king's son. For the king charged you and Abishai and Ittai in our hearing, 'Watch over my boy Absalom, h-for my sake.'-h 13If I betrayed myselfi—and nothing is hidden from the king—you would have stood aloof." 14Joab replied, j-"Then I will not wait for you."-j He took three darts in his hand and drove them into Absalom's chest. [Absalom] was still alive in the thick growth of the terebinth, 15when ten of Joab's young arms-bearers closed in and struck at Absalom until he died. 16Then Joab sounded the horn, and the troops gave up their pursuit of the Israelites; for Joab held the troops in check. 17They took Absalom and flung him into a large pit in the forest, and they piled up a very great heap of stones over it. Then all the Israelites fled to their homes.—18Now Absalom, in his lifetime, had taken the pillar which is in the Valley of the King and set it up for himself; for he said, "I have no son to keep my name alive." He had named the pillar after himself, and it has been called Absalom's Monument to this day.

19Ahimaaz son of Zadok said, "Let me run and report to the king that the LORD has vindicated him against his enemies." 20But Joab said to him, "You shall not be the one to bring tidings today. You may bring tidings some other day, but you'll not bring any today; for the king's son is dead!" 21And Joab said to a Cushite, "Go tell the king what you have seen." The Cushite bowed to Joab and ran off. 22But Ahimaaz son of Zadok again said to Joab, "No matter what, let me run, too, behind the Cushite." Joab asked, "Why should you run, my boy, when you have no news k-worth telling?"-k 23"I am going to run anyway." "Then run," he said. So Ahimaaz ran by way of the Plain, and he passed the Cushite.

24David was sitting between the two gates.l The watchman on the roof of the gate walked over to the city wall. He looked up and saw a man running alone. 25The watchman called down and told the king; and the king said, "If he is alone, he has news to report." As he was coming nearer, 26the watchman saw another man running; and he called out to

f-f Lit. "to the ground."
g Some Septuagint mss. and 4QSama read "fifty."
h-h So some Heb. mss. and ancient versions. Most mss. and editions read "who"—perhaps meaning "whoever you are."
i I.e., by killing Absalom.
j-j Some Septuagint mss. and Targum read "Therefore, I will begin before you."
k-k Meaning of Heb. uncertain.
l I.e., the inner and outer gateways.

the gatekeeper, "There is another man running alone." And the king said, "That one, too, brings news." 27The watchman said, "I can see that the first one runs like Ahimaaz son of Zadok"; to which the king replied, "He is a good man, and he comes with good news." 28Ahimaaz called out and said to the king, "All is well!" He bowed low with his face to the ground and said, "Praised be the LORD your God, who has delivered up the men who raised their hand against my lord the king." 29The king asked, "Is my boy Absalom safe?" And Ahimaaz answered, "I saw k-a large crowd when Your Majesty's servant Joab was sending your servant off,-k but I don't know what it was about." 30The king said, "Step aside and stand over there"; he stepped aside and waited.

31Just then the Cushite came up; and the Cushite said, "Let my lord the king be informed that the LORD has vindicated you today against all who rebelled against you!" 32The king asked the Cushite, "Is my boy Absalom safe?" And the Cushite replied, "May the enemies of my lord the king and all who rose against you to do you harm fare like that young man!" 1aThe king was shaken. He went up to the upper chamber of the gateway and wept, moaning these words as he went,b "My son Absalom! O my son, my son Absalom! If only I had died instead of you! O Absalom, my son, my son!"

2Joab was told that the king was weeping and mourning over Absalom. 3And the victory that day was turned into mourning for all the troops, for that day the troops heard that the king was grieving over his son. 4The troops stole into town that day like troops ashamed after running away in battle. 5The king covered his face and the king kept crying aloud, "O my son Absalom! O Absalom, my son, my son!"

6Joab came to the king in his quarters and said, "Today you have humiliated all your followers, who this day saved your life, and the lives of your sons and daughters, and the lives of your wives and concubines, 7by showing love for those who hate you and hate for those who love you. For you have made clear today that the officers and men mean nothing to you. I am sure that if Absalom were alive today and the rest of us dead, you would have preferred it. 8Now arise, come out and placate your followers! For I swear by the LORD that ifc you do not come out, not a single man will remain with you overnight; and that would be a greater disaster for you than any disaster that has befallen you from your youth until now." 9So the king arose and sat down in the gateway; and

---

a *Counted as 18.33 in some versions.*

b *Some Septuagint mss. read "wept."*

c *So Septuagint, 4QSam*a*, and some other Heb. mss., and an ancient masoretic tradition; ordinary texts omit "if."*

when all the troops were told that the king was sitting in the gateway, all the troops presented themselves to the king.

Now the Israelites had fled to their homes. ¹⁰All the people throughout the tribes of Israel were arguing: Some said, "The king saved us from the hands of our enemies, and he delivered us from the hands of the Philistines; and just now he had to flee the country because of Absalom. ¹¹But Absalom, whom we anointed over us, has died in battle; why then do you sit idle instead of escorting the king back?" ¹²The talk of all Israel reached the king in his quarters. So King David sent this message to the priests Zadok and Abiathar: "Speak to the elders of Judah and say, 'Why should you be the last to bring the king back to his palace? ¹³You are my kinsmen, my own flesh and blood! Why should you be the last to escort the king back?' ¹⁴And to Amasa say this, 'You are my own flesh and blood. May God do thus and more to me if you do not become my army commander permanently in place of Joab!' " ¹⁵So [Amasa] swayed the hearts of all the Judites as one man; and they sent a message to the king: "Come back with all your followers."

¹⁶The king started back and arrived at the Jordan; and the Judites went to Gilgal to meet the king and to conduct the king across the Jordan. ¹⁷Shimei son of Gera, the Benjaminite from Bahurim, hurried down with the Judites to meet King David, ¹⁸accompanied by a thousand Benjaminites. ᵈAnd Ziba, the servant of the House of Saul, together with his fifteen sons and twenty slaves, rushed down to the Jordan ahead of the king ¹⁹while the crossing was being made, to escort the king's family over, and to do whatever he wished. Shimei son of Gera flung himself before the king as he was about to cross the Jordan. ²⁰He said to the king, "Let not my lord hold me guilty, and do not remember the wrong your servant committed on the day my lord the king left Jerusalem; let Your Majesty give it no thought. ²¹For your servant knows that he has sinned; so here I have come down today, the first of all the House of Joseph, to meet my lord the king." ²²Thereupon Abishai son of Zeruiah spoke up, "Shouldn't Shimei be put to death for that—insulting the LORD's anointed?" ²³But David said, ᵉ"What has this to do with you,ᵉ you sons of Zeruiah, that you should cross me today? Should a single Israelite be put to death today? Don't Iᶠ know that today I am again king over Israel?" ²⁴Then the king said to Shimei, "You shall not die"; and the king gave him his oath.

²⁵Mephibosheth, the grandson of Saul, also came down to meet the king. He had not pared his toenails, or trimmed his mustache, or washed

---

ᵈ Meaning of parts of the rest of vv. 18 and 19 uncertain.
ᵉ⁻ᵉ See note at 16.10.
ᶠ Some Septuagint mss. read "you."

his clothes from the day that the king left until the day he returned safe. [26]When he g-came [from]-g Jerusalem to meet the king, the king asked him, "Why didn't you come with me, Mephibosheth?" [27]He replied, "My lord the king, my own servant[h] deceived me. i-Your servant planned to saddle his ass and ride-i on it and go with Your Majesty—for your servant is lame. [28][Ziba] has slandered your servant to my lord the king. But my lord the king is like an angel of the LORD; do as you see fit. [29]For all the members of my father's family deserved only death from my lord the king; yet you set your servant among those who ate at your table. What right have I to appeal further to Your Majesty?" [30]The king said to him, "You need not speak further. I decree that you and Ziba shall divide the property." [31]And Mephibosheth said to the king, "Let him take it all, as long as my lord the king has come home safe."

[32]Barzillai the Gileadite had come down from Rogelin and j-passed on to the Jordan with the king, to see him off at-j the Jordan. [33]Barzillai was very old, eighty years of age; and he had provided the king with food during his stay at Mahanaim, for he was a very wealthy man. [34]The king said to Barzillai, "Cross over with me, and I will provide for you in Jerusalem at my side." [35]But Barzillai said to the king, "How many years are left to me that I should go up with Your Majesty to Jerusalem? [36]I am now eighty years old. Can I tell the difference between good and bad? Can your servant taste what he eats and drinks? Can I still listen to the singing of men and women? Why then should your servant continue to be a burden to my lord the king? [37] j-Your servant could barely cross the Jordan-j with your Majesty! Why should Your Majesty reward me so generously? [38]Let your servant go back, and let me die in my own town, near the graves of my father and mother. But here is your servant Chimham; let him cross with my lord the king, and do for him as you see fit." [39]And the king said, "Chimham[k] shall cross with me, and I will do for him as you see fit; and anything you want me to do, I will do for you."

[40]All the troops crossed the Jordan; and when the king was ready to cross, the king kissed Barzillai and bade him farewell; and [Barzillai] returned to his home. [41]The king passed on to Gilgal, with Chimham[k] accompanying him; and all the Judite soldiers and part of the Israelite army escorted the king across.

[42]Then all the men of Israel came to the king and said to the king, "Why did our kinsmen, the men of Judah, steal you away and escort the king and his family across the Jordan, along with all David's men?" [43]All

g-g *So Septuagint. Heb. "entered."*

h *I.e., Ziba (cf. v. 30 and 9.2 ff.).*

i-i *Ancient versions read "Your servant said to him, 'Saddle my ass, that I may ride....'"*

j-j *Meaning of Heb. uncertain.*

k *Heb. Chimhan.*

l *Meaning of parts of vv. 40–44 uncertain.*

the men of Judah replied to the men of Israel, "Because the king is our relative! Why should this upset you? Have we consumed anything that belongs to the king? Has he given us any gifts?" ⁴⁴But the men of Israel answered the men of Judah, "We have ten shares in the king, and ^{m-}in David, too, we have more than you.^{-m} Why then have you slighted us? Were we not the first to propose that our king be brought back?" However, the men of Judah prevailed over the men of Israel.

20

A scoundrel named Sheba son of Bichri, a Benjaminite, happened to be there. He sounded the horn and proclaimed:

"We have no portion in David,
No share in Jesse's son!
Every man to his tent, O Israel!"

²All the men of Israel left David and followed Sheba son of Bichri; but the men of Judah accompanied their king from the Jordan to Jerusalem. ³David went to his palace in Jerusalem, and the king took the ten concubines he had left to mind the palace and put them in a guarded place; he provided for them, but he did not cohabit with them. They remained in seclusion until the day they died, in living widowhood.

⁴The king said to Amasa, "Call up the men of Judah to my standard, and report here three days from now." ⁵Amasa went to call up Judah, but he took longer than the time set for him. ⁶And David said to Abishai, "Now Sheba son of Bichri will cause us more trouble than Absalom. So take your lord's servants and pursue him, before he finds fortified towns and ^{a-}eludes us."^{-a} ^{7b-}Joab's men, the Cherethites and Pelethites, and all the warriors, marched out behind him.^{-b} They left Jerusalem in pursuit of Sheba son of Bichri. ⁸They were near the great stone in Gibeon when Amasa appeared before them. ^{a-}Joab was wearing his military dress, with his sword girded over it and fastened around his waist in its sheath; and, as he stepped forward, it fell out.^{-a} ⁹Joab said to Amasa, "How are you, brother?" and with his right hand Joab took hold of Amasa's beard as if to kiss him. ¹⁰Amasa was not on his guard against the sword in Joab's [left] hand, and [Joab] drove it into his belly so that his entrails poured out on the ground and he died; he did not need to strike him a second time.

Joab and his brother Abishai then set off in pursuit of Sheba son of Bichri, ¹¹while one of Joab's henchmen stood by ^{c-}the corpse^{-c} and called

---

^{m-m} *Septuagint reads "we are the first-born, rather than you."*

^{a-a} *Meaning of Heb. uncertain.*
^{b-b} *Emendation yields "Joab, the Cherethites and Pelethites, and all the warriors marched out behind Abishai."*
^{c-c} *Heb. "him."*

out, "Whoever favors Joab, and whoever is on David's side, follow Joab!"
12Amasa lay in the middle of the road, drenched in his blood; and the
man saw that everyone stopped. And when he saw that all the people
were stopping, he dragged Amasa from the road into the field and covered
him with a garment. 13Once he was removed from the road, everybody
continued to follow Joab in pursuit of Sheba son of Bichri. 14[Sheba] had
passed through all the tribes of Israel up to Abel of·d Beth-maacah; and
all the Beerites·e assembled and followed him inside. 15[Joab's men] came
and besieged him in Abel of Beth-maacah; they threw up a siegemound
against the city ·f-and it stood against the rampart.·f

All the troops with Joab were ·g-engaged in battering the wall,·g 16when
a clever woman shouted from the city, "Listen! Listen! Tell Joab to come
over here so I can talk to him." 17He approached her, and the woman
asked, "Are you Joab?" "Yes," he answered; and she said to him, "Listen
to what your handmaid has to say." "I'm listening," he replied. 18And she
continued, "In olden times people used to say, ·a-'Let them inquire of
Abel,'·a and that was the end of the matter. 19I am one of those who seek
the welfare of the faithful in Israel. But you seek to bring death upon a
mother city in Israel! Why should you destroy the LORD's possession?"
20Joab replied, "Far be it, far be it from me to destroy or to ruin! 21Not
at all! But a certain man from the hill country of Ephraim, named Sheba
son of Bichri, has rebelled against King David. Just hand him alone over
to us, and I will withdraw from the city." The woman assured Joab, "His
head shall be thrown over the wall to you." 22The woman came to all the
people with her clever plan; and they cut off the head of Sheba son of
Bichri and threw it down to Joab. He then sounded the horn; all the men
dispersed to their homes, and Joab returned to the king in Jerusalem.

23Joab was commander of the whole army [of] Israel; Benaiah son of
Jehoiada was commander of the Cherethites and the Pelethites; 24Adoramh
was in charge of forced labor; Jehoshaphat son of Ahilud was recorder;
25Shevai was scribe; and Zadok and Abiathar were priests. 26Ira the Jairite
also served David as priest.

21 There was a famine during the reign of David, year after year for
three years. David inquired of the LORD, and the LORD replied, "It is

---

d *Heb. "and." Cf. v. 15 (and "Abel-beth-maacah" in 1 Kings 15.20 and 2 Kings 15.29).*

e *Emendation yields "Bichrites"; cf. Septuagint.*

f-f *Meaning of Heb. uncertain. The phrase would read well in the next verse (". . . a clever woman
stood on the rampart and shouted. . . .").*

g-g *Lit. "destroying, to topple the wall." Septuagint and Targum read "were planning to topple
the wall."*

h *So in 1 Kings 12.18 and 2 Chron. 10.18 ("Hadoram"); elsewhere "Adoniram."*

i *See note j at 8.17.*

because of the bloodguilt of Saul and [his] house, for he put some Gibeonites to death." ²The king summoned the Gibeonites and spoke to them.—Now the Gibeonites were not of Israelite stock, but a remnant of the Amorites, to whom the Israelites had given an oath; and Saul had tried to wipe them out in his zeal for the people of Israel and Judah.— ³David asked the Gibeonites, "What shall I do for you? How shall I make expiation, so that you may bless the LORD's own people?" ⁴The Gibeonites answered him, "We have no claim for silver or gold against Saul and his household; and we have no claim on the life of any other man in Israel." And [David] responded, "Whatever you say I will do for you." ⁵Thereupon they said to the king, "The man who massacred us and planned to ᵃ-exterminate us, so that we-ᵃ should not survive in all the territory of Israel—⁶let seven of his male issue be handed over to us, and we will impale them before the LORD in ᵇ-Gibeah of Saul, the chosen of the LORD."-ᵇ And the king replied, "I will do so."

⁷The king spared Mephibosheth son of Jonathan son of Saul, because of the oath before the LORD between the two, between David and Jonathan son of Saul. ⁸Instead, the king took Armoni and Mephibosheth, the two sons that Rizpah daughter of Aiah bore to Saul, and the five sons that Merabᶜ daughter of Saul bore to Adriel son of Barzillai the Meholathite, ⁹and he handed them over to the Gibeonites. They impaled them on the mountain before the LORD; all seven of them perished at the same time. They were put to death in the first days of the harvest, the beginning of the barley harvest.

¹⁰Then Rizpah daughter of Aiah took sackcloth and spread it on a rock for herself, and she stayed there from the beginning of the harvest until rain from the sky fell on ᵈ-the bodies;-ᵈ she did not let the birds of the sky settle on them by day or the wild beasts [approach] by night. ¹¹David was told what Saul's concubine Rizpah daughter of Aiah had done. ¹²And David went and took the bones of Saul and of his son Jonathan from the citizens of Jabesh-gilead, who had made off with them from the public square of Beth-shan, where the Philistines had hung them up on the day the Philistines killed Saul at Gilboa. ¹³He brought up the bones of Saul and of his son Jonathan from there; and he gathered the bones of those who had been impaled. ¹⁴And they buried the bones of Saul and of his son Jonathanᵉ in Zela, in the territory of Benjamin, in the tomb of his

---

ᵃ⁻ᵃ *Meaning of Heb. uncertain.*
ᵇ⁻ᵇ *Emendation yields "at Gibeon, on the mountain of the LORD" (cf. Septuagint and v. 9).*
ᶜ *So two Heb. mss., many Septuagint mss., and Peshitta; and cf. Targum, Sanhedrin 19b, and*
  1 Sam. 18.19. Most mss. and the printed editions read "Michal."
ᵈ⁻ᵈ *Heb. "them."*
ᵉ *Septuagint adds "and the bones of those impaled."*

father Kish. And when all that the king had commanded was done, God responded to the plea of the land thereafter.

¹⁵Again war broke out between the Philistines and Israel, and David and the men with him went down and fought the Philistines; David grew weary, ¹⁶and ᵃ⁻Ishbi-benob⁻ᵃ tried to kill David.—He was a descendant of the Raphah;ᶠ his bronze spear weighed three hundred shekels and he wore new armor.—¹⁷But Abishai son of Zeruiah came to his aid; he attacked the Philistine and killed him. It was then that David's men declared to him on oath, "You shall not go with us into battle any more, lest you extinguish the lamp of Israel!"

¹⁸ᵍAfter this, fighting broke out again with the Philistines, at Gob; that was when Sibbecai the Hushathite killed Saph, a descendant of the Raphah.ᶠ ¹⁹Again there was fighting with the Philistines at Gob; and Elhanan son of Jaare-oregimʰ the Bethlehemite killed Goliath the Gittite, whose spear had a shaft like a weaver's bar. ²⁰Once again there was fighting, at Gath. There was a ᵃ⁻giant of a man,⁻ᵃ who had six fingers on each hand and six toes on each foot, twenty-four in all; he too was descended from the Raphah. ²¹When he taunted Israel, Jonathan, the son of David's brother Shimei, killed him. ²²Those four were descended from the Raphah in Gath, and they fell by the hands of David and his men.

22

ᵃDavid addressed the words of this song to the LORD, after the LORD had saved him from the hands of all his enemies and from the hands of Saul. ²He said:

> O LORD, my crag, my fastness, my deliverer!
> ³O ᵇ⁻God, the rock⁻ᵇ wherein I take shelter:
> My shield, my ᶜ⁻mighty champion,⁻ᶜ my fortress and refuge!
> My savior, You who rescue me from violence!

> ⁴ᵈ⁻All praise! I called on the LORD,⁻ᵈ
> And I was delivered from my enemies.

> ⁵For the breakers of Death encompassed me,

ᶠ *Apparently a race of giants.*

ᵍ *This paragraph is found also in 1 Chron. 20.4–8; in part, also in 1QSamᵃ, with some variations.*

ʰ *Perhaps a duplicate of* 'oregim *("weavers") at the end of the verse; meaning of Heb. uncertain.*
1 Chron. 20.5 reads "And Elhanan son of Jair killed Lahmi, the brother of Goliath the Gittite."

ᵃ *This poem occurs again as Ps. 18, with a number of variations, some of which are cited in the following notes.*

ᵇ⁻ᵇ *Lit. "the God of my rock"; Ps. 18.3 "my God, my rock."*

ᶜ⁻ᶜ *Lit. "horn of rescue."*

ᵈ⁻ᵈ *Construction of Heb. uncertain.*

The torrents of Belial[c] terrified me;
⁶The snares of Sheol encircled me,
The toils of Death engulfed me.

⁷In my anguish I called on the LORD,
Cried out to my God;
In His Abode[f] He heard my voice,
My cry entered His ears.

⁸Then the earth rocked and quaked,
The foundations of heaven[g] shook—
Rocked by His indignation.
⁹Smoke went up from His nostrils,
From His mouth came devouring fire;
Live coals blazed forth from Him.
¹⁰He bent the sky and came down,
Thick cloud beneath His feet.
¹¹He mounted a cherub and flew;
[h-]He was seen[-h] on the wings of the wind.
¹²He made pavilions of darkness about Him,
Dripping clouds, huge thunderheads;
¹³In the brilliance before Him
Blazed fiery coals.
¹⁴The LORD thundered forth from heaven,
The Most High sent forth His voice;
¹⁵He let loose bolts, and scattered them;[i]
Lightning, and put them to rout.
¹⁶The bed of the sea was exposed,
The foundations of the world were laid bare
By the mighty roaring of the LORD,
At the blast of the breath of His nostrils.
¹⁷He reached down from on high, He took me,
Drew me out of the mighty waters;[j]
¹⁸He rescued me from my enemy so strong,
From foes too mighty for me.
¹⁹They attacked me on my day of calamity,

c *I.e., the netherworld, like "Death" and "Sheol."*
f *Lit. "Temple."*
g *Ps. 18.8 "mountains."*
h-h *Ps. 18.11 "Gliding."*
i *I.e., the enemies in v. 4.*
j *Cf. v. 5.*

But the LORD was my stay.
20He brought me out to freedom,
He rescued me because He was pleased with me.
21The LORD rewarded me according to my merit,
He requited the cleanness of my hands.

22For I have kept the ways of the LORD
And have not been guilty before my God;
23I am mindful of all His rules
And have not departed from His laws.
24I have been blameless before Him,
And have guarded myself against sinning—
25And the LORD has requited my merit,
According to my purity in His sight.
26With the loyal You deal loyally;
With the blameless hero,k blamelessly.
27With the pure You act in purity,
And with the perverse You are wily.
28To humble folk You give victory,
l-And You look with scorn on the haughty.-l

29You, O LORD, are my lamp;
The LORD lights up my darkness.
30With You, I can rush a barrier,m
With my God, I can scale a wall.
31The way of God is perfect,
The word of the LORD is pure.
He is a shield to all who take refuge in Him.
32Yea, who is a god except the LORD,
Who is a rock except God—
33The God, n-my mighty stronghold,-n
Who kepto my path secure;
34Who made my legs like a deer's,
And set me firm on thep heights;
35Who trained my hands for battle,
So that my arms can bend a bow of bronze!
36You have granted me the shield of Your protection

k Ps. 18.26 "man."
l-l Lit. "And lower Your eyes on the haughty"; Ps. 18.28 "But haughty eyes You humble."
m Cf. postbiblical gedudiyyoth "walls," Aramaic gudda, "wall."
n-n Ps. 18.33 "who girded me with might."
o Meaning of Heb. uncertain; Ps. 18.33 "made."
p Taking bamothai as a poetic form of bamoth; cf. Hab. 3.19; others "my."

^{q-}And Your providence has made me great.^{-q}
³⁷You have let me stride on freely,
And my feet have not slipped.
³⁸I pursued my enemies and wiped them out,
I did not turn back till I destroyed them.
³⁹I destroyed them, I struck them down;
They rose no more, they lay at my feet.
⁴⁰You have girt me with strength for battle,
Brought low my foes before me,
⁴¹Made my enemies turn tail before me,
My foes—and I wiped them out.
⁴²They looked,^r but there was none to deliver;
To the LORD, but He answered them not.
⁴³I pounded them like dust of the earth,
Stamped, crushed them like dirt of the streets.
⁴⁴You have rescued me from the strife of peoples,^s
^{t-}Kept me to be^{-t} a ruler of nations;
Peoples I knew not must serve me.
⁴⁵Aliens have cringed before me,
Paid me homage at the mere report of me.
⁴⁶Aliens have lost courage
^{q-}And come trembling out of their fastnesses.^{-q}

⁴⁷The LORD lives! Blessed is my rock!
Exalted be God, the rock
Who gives me victory;
⁴⁸The God who has vindicated me
And made peoples subject to me,
⁴⁹Rescued me from my enemies,
Raised me clear of my foes,
Saved me from lawless men!
⁵⁰For this I sing Your praise among the nations
And hymn Your name:
^{51u-}Tower of victory^{-u} to His king,
Who deals graciously with His anointed,
With David and his offspring evermore.

---

^{q-q} *Meaning of Heb. uncertain.*
^r *Ps. 18.42 "cried."*
^s *So some mss. and the Septuagint; most mss. and the printed editions "my people."*
^{t-t} *Ps. 18.44 "made me."*
^{u-u} Kethib *and Ps. 18.51 read "He accords wondrous victories."*

23 These are the last words of David:

aThe utterance of David son of Jesse,
The utterance of the man b-set on high,-b
The anointed of the God of Jacob,
c-The favorite of the songs of Israel:-c
2The spirit of the LORD has spoken through me,
His message is on my tongue;
3The God of Israel has spoken,
The Rock of Israel said concerning me:
"He who rules men justly,
He who rules ind awe of God
4Is like the light of morning at sunrise,
A morning without clouds—
e-Through sunshine and rain
[Bringing]-e vegetation out of the earth."
5Is not my House established before God?
For He has granted me an eternal pact,
Drawn up in full and secured.
Will He not cause all my success
And [my] every desire to blossom?
6But the wicked shall all
Be raked aside like thorns;
For no one will take them in his hand.
7Whoever touches them
Must arm himself with iron
And the shaft of a spear;
And they must be burned up on the spot.

8These are the namesf of David's warriors: Josheb-basshebeth, a Tah-chemonite, the chief officer—he is Adino the Eznite; g-[he wielded his spear]-g against eight hundred h-and slew them-h on one occasion.

9Next to him was Eleazar son of Dodo son of Ahohi. He was one of

a Meaning of much of this poem (vv. 1–7) uncertain.
b-b 4QSamª reads "God raised up."
c-c Or "The favorite of the Mighty One of Israel"; cf. Exod. 15.2. Others "The sweet singer of Israel."
d So many Heb. mss. Most mss. and the printed editions lack "in."
e-e Meaning of Heb. uncertain.
f A number of these names, with variations, are found in 1 Chron. 11 and 27.
g-g Preserved in 1 Chron. 11.11; similarly some Septuagint mss. of 2 Sam.
h-h Lit. "slain."

the three warriors with David when they defied the Philistines gathered there for battle. The Israelite soldiers retreated, [10]but he held his ground. He struck down Philistines until his arm grew tired and his hand stuck to his sword; and the LORD wrought a great victory that day. Then the troops came back to him—but only to strip [the slain].

[11]Next to him was Shammah son of Age the Ararite. The Philistines had gathered e-in force-e where there was a plot of ground full of lentils; and the troops fled from the Philistines. [12]But [Shammah] took his stand in the middle of the plot and defended it, and he routed the Philistines. Thus the LORD wrought a great victory.

[13]e-Once, during the harvest,-e three of the thirty chiefs went down to David at the cave[i] of Adullam, while a force of Philistines was encamped in the Valley of Rephaim. [14]David was then in the stronghold,[i] and a Philistine garrison was then at Bethlehem. [15]David felt a craving and said, "If only I could get a drink of water from the cistern which is by the gate of Bethlehem!" [16]So the three warriors got through the Philistine camp and drew water from the cistern which is by the gate of Bethlehem, and they carried it back. But when they brought it to David he would not drink it, and he poured it out as a libation to the LORD. [17]For he said, "The LORD forbid that I should do this! Can [I drink][j] the blood of the men who went at the risk of their lives?" So he would not drink it. Such were the exploits of the three warriors.

[18]Abishai, the brother of Joab son of Zeruiah, was head of k-another three.-k He once wielded his spear against three hundred h-and slew them.-h [19]He won a name among the three;[l] since he was the most highly regarded among the three,[l] he became their leader. However, he did not attain to the three.

[20]Benaiah son of Jehoiada, from Kabzeel, was m-a brave soldier-m who performed great deeds. He killed the two e-[sons] of Ariel of Moab.-e Once, on a snowy day, he went down into a pit and killed a lion. [21]He also killed an Egyptian, a huge[n] man. The Egyptian had a spear in his hand, yet [Benaiah] went down against him with a club, wrenched the spear out of the Egyptian's hand, and killed him with his own spear. [22]Such were the exploits of Benaiah son of Jehoiada; and he won a name among the three[l] warriors. [23]He was highly regarded among the thirty,

---

i *See note at 1 Sam. 22.1.*
j *So Septuagint and 1 Chron. 11.19.*
k-k *Two Heb. mss. and Syriac read "the thirty"; cf. vv. 23–24.*
l *Emendation yields "thirty."*
m-m *Heb. "the son of a brave soldier."*
n *Meaning of Heb. uncertain. 1 Chron. 11.23 reads "a giant of a man."*

but he did not attain to the three. David put him in charge of his body-guard.[e]

24Among the thirty were Asahel, the brother of Joab; Elhanan son of Dodo [from] Bethlehem, 25Shammah the Harodite, Elika the Harodite, 26Helez the Paltite, Ira son of Ikkesh from Tekoa, 27Abiezer of Anathoth, Mebunnai the Hushathite, 28Zalmon the Ahohite, Maharai the Neto-phathite, 29Heleb son of Baanah the Netophathite, Ittai son of Ribai from Gibeah of the Benjaminites, 30Benaiah of Pirathon, Hiddai of Nahale-gaash, 31Abi-albon the Arbathite, Azmaveth the Barhumite, 32Eliahba of Shaalbon, sons of [e-]Jashen, Jonathan,[-e] 33Shammah the Ararite, Ahiam son of Sharar the Ararite, 34Eliphelet son of Ahasbai son of the Maacath-ite, Eliam son of Ahithophel the Gilonite, 35Hezrai the Carmelite, Paarai the Arbite, 36Igal son of Nathan from Zobah, Bani the Gadite, 37Zelek the Ammonite, Naharai the Beerothite—the arms-bearer of Joab son of Zeruiah—38Ira the Ithrite, Gareb the Ithrite, 39Uriah the Hittite: thirty-seven in all.[o]

24

[a]The anger of the LORD again[b] flared up against Israel; and He incited David against them, saying, "Go and number Israel and Judah." 2The king said to Joab, [c-]his army commander,[-c] "Make the rounds of all the tribes of Israel, from Dan to Beer-sheba, and take a census of the people, so that I may know the size of the population." 3Joab answered the king, "May the LORD your God increase the number of the people a hundredfold, while your own eyes see it! But why should my lord king want this?" 4However, the king's command to Joab and to the officers of the army remained firm; and Joab and the officers of the army set out, at the instance of the king, to take a census of the people of Israel.

5They crossed the Jordan and [d-]encamped at Aroer, on the right side of the town, which is in the middle of the wadi of Gad, and[-d] [went on] to Jazer. 6They continued to Gilead and to the region of [e-]Tahtim-hodshi, and they came to Dan-jaan and around to[-e] Sidon. 7They went onto the fortress of Tyre and all the towns of the Hivites and Canaanites, and finished at Beer-sheba in southern Judah. 8They traversed the whole coun-try, and then they came back to Jerusalem at the end of nine months and

---

o *Septuagint and 1 Chron. 11 differ from the foregoing lists in vv. 8–38, and from each other in the number and forms of the names.*

a *This chapter is also found, with some variations, in 1 Chron. 21.1–7.*

b *Cf. above 21.1–14.*

c-c *1 Chron. 21.2 reads "and to the officers of the army"; cf. below v. 4.*

d-d *Some Septuagint mss. read "began at Aroer, and from the town, which is . . . Gad, they."*

e-e *Meaning of Heb. uncertain.*

twenty days. 9Joab reported to the king the number of the people that had been recorded: in Israel there were 800,000 soldiers ready to draw the sword, and the men of Judah numbered 500,000.

10But afterward David f-reproached himself-f for having numbered the people. And David said to the LORD, "I have sinned grievously in what I have done. Please, O LORD, remit the guilt of Your servant, for I have acted foolishly." 11When David rose in the morning, the word of the LORD had come to the prophet Gad, David's seer: 12"Go and tell David, 'Thus said the LORD: I hold three things over you; choose one of them, and I will bring it upon you.'" 13Gad came to David and told him; he asked, "Shall a seven-year famine come upon you in the land, or shall you be in flight from your adversaries for three months while they pursue you, or shall there be three days of pestilence in your land? Now consider carefully what reply I shall take back to Him who sent me." 14David said to Gad, "I am in great distress. Let us fall into the hands of the LORD, for His compassion is great; and let me not fall into the hands of men."g

15The LORD sent a pestilence upon Israel from morning e-until the set time;-e and 70,000 of the people died, from Dan to Beer-sheba. 16But when the angel extended his hand against Jerusalem to destroy it, the LORD renounced further punishment and said to the angel who was destroying the people, "Enough! Stay your hand!" The angel of the LORD was then by the threshing floor of Araunah the Jebusite. 17When David saw the angel who was striking down the people, he said to the LORD, "I alone am guilty, I alone have done wrong; but these poor sheep, what have they done? Let Your hand fall upon me and my father's house!"

18Gad came to David the same day and said to him, "Go and set up an altar to the LORD on the threshing floor of Araunah the Jebusite." 19David went up, following Gad's instructions, as the LORD had commanded. 20Araunah looked out and saw the king and his courtiers approaching him.h So Araunah went out and bowed low to the king, with his face to the ground. 21And Araunah asked, "Why has my lord the king come to his servant?" David replied, "To buy the threshing floor from you, that I may build an altar to the LORD and that the plague against the people may be checked." 22And Araunah said to David, "Let my lord the king take it and offer up whatever he sees fit. Here are oxen for a burnt offering, and the threshing boards and the gear of the oxen for wood. 23All this, e-O king,-e Araunah gives to Your Majesty. And may the LORD your God," Araunah added, "respond to you with favor!"

f-f *See note at 1 Sam. 24.6.*
g *Septuagint adds "So David chose the pestilence. It was the time of the wheat harvest."*
h *4QSamᵃ and 1 Chron. 21.20 add "Araunah (Ornan) was threshing wheat."*

24But the king replied to Araunah, "No, I will buy them from you at a price. I cannot sacrifice to the LORD my God burnt offerings that have cost me nothing." So David bought the threshing floor and the oxen for fifty shekels of silver. 25And David built there an altar to the LORD and sacrificed burnt offerings and offerings of well-being. The LORD responded to the plea for the land, and the plague against Israel was checked.

I KINGS

מְלָכִים א

1 King David was now old, advanced in years; and though they covered him with bedclothes, he never felt warm. [2]His courtiers said to him, "Let a young virgin be sought for my lord the king, to wait upon Your Majesty and be his attendant;[a] and let her lie in your bosom, and my lord the king will be warm." [3]So they looked for a beautiful girl throughout the territory of Israel. They found Abishag the Shunammite and brought her to the king. [4]The girl was exceedingly beautiful. She became the king's attendant[a] and waited upon him; but the king was not intimate with her.

[5]Now Adonijah son of Haggith [b-]went about boasting,[-b] "I will be king!" He provided himself with chariots and horses,[c] and an escort of fifty outrunners. [6]His father had never scolded him: "Why did you do that?" He was the one born after Absalom[d] and, like him, was very handsome.

[7]He conferred with Joab son of Zeruiah and with the priest Abiathar, and they supported Adonijah; [8]but the priest Zadok, Benaiah son of Jehoiada, the prophet Nathan, Shimei and Rei, and David's own fighting men did not side with Adonijah. [9]Adonijah made a sacrificial feast of sheep, oxen, and fatlings at the Zoheleth stone which is near En-rogel; he invited all his brother princes[e] and all the king's courtiers of the tribe of Judah; [10]but he did not invite the prophet Nathan, or Benaiah, or the fighting men, or his brother Solomon.

[11]Then Nathan said to Bathsheba, Solomon's mother, "You must have heard that Adonijah son of Haggith has assumed the kingship without the knowledge of our lord David. [12]Now take my advice, so that you may save your life and the life of your son Solomon. [13]Go immediately to King David and say to him, 'Did not you, O lord king, swear to your maidservant: "Your son Solomon shall succeed me as king, and he shall sit upon my throne"? Then why has Adonijah become king?' [14]While you

---

[a] *Meaning of Heb. uncertain.*
[b-b] *Or "presumed to think."*
[c] *Others "horsemen"; meaning of Heb.* parash(im) *not always certain.*
[d] *Thus, Absalom having died, Adonijah was David's oldest living son.*
[e] *Lit. "all his brothers, sons of the king."*

are still there talking with the king, I will come in after you and confirm your words."

¹⁵So Bathsheba went to the king in his chamber.—The king was very old, and Abishag the Shunammite was waiting on the king.—¹⁶Bathsheba bowed low in homage to the king; and the king asked, "What troubles you?" ¹⁷She answered him, "My lord, you yourself swore to your maid-servant by the LORD your God: 'Your son Solomon shall succeed me as king, and he shall sit upon my throne.' ¹⁸Yet now Adonijah has become king, and you,ᶠ my lord the king, know nothing about it. ¹⁹He has pre-pared a sacrificial feast of a great many oxen, fatlings, and sheep, and he has invited all the king's sons and Abiathar the priest and Joab commander of the army; but he has not invited your servant Solomon. ²⁰And so the eyes of all Israel are upon you, O lord king, to tell them who shall succeed my lord the king on the throne. ²¹Otherwise, when my lord the king lies down with his fathers, my son Solomon and I will be regarded as traitors."

²²She was still talking to the king when the prophet Nathan arrived. ²³They announced to the king, "The prophet Nathan is here," and he entered the king's presence. Bowing low to the king with his face to the ground, ²⁴Nathan said, "O lord king, ᵍyou must have said,ᵍ 'Adonijah shall succeed me as king and he shall sit upon my throne.' ²⁵For he has gone down today and prepared a sacrificial feast of a great many oxen, fatlings, and sheep. He invited all the king's sons and the army officers and Abiathar the priest. At this very moment they are eating and drinking with him, and they are shouting, 'Long live King Adonijah!' ²⁶But he did not invite me your servant, or the priest Zadok, or Benaiah son of Je-hoiada, or your servant Solomon. ²⁷Can this decision have come from my lord the king, without your telling your servant who is to succeed to the throne of my lord the king?"

²⁸King David's response was: "Summon Bathsheba!" She entered the king's presence and stood before the king. ²⁹And the king took an oath, saying, "As the LORD lives, who has rescued me from every trouble: ³⁰The oath I swore to you by the LORD, the God of Israel, that your son Solomon should succeed me as king and that he should sit upon my throne in my stead, I will fulfill this very day!" ³¹Bathsheba bowed low in homage to the king with her face to the ground, and she said, "May my lord King David live forever!"

³²Then King David said, "Summon to me the priest Zadok, the prophet Nathan, and Benaiah son of Jehoiada." When they came before the king,

ᶠ So many mss. and ancient versions; usual editions "now."
ᵍ⁻ᵍ Or (cf. Rashi, Ralbag, Radak) "have you said. . . ?"

³³the king said to them, "Take ^{h-}my loyal soldiers,^{-h} and have my son Solomon ride on my mule and bring him down to Gihon. ³⁴Let the priest Zadok and the prophet Nathan anoint him there king over Israel, whereupon you shall sound the horn and shout, 'Long live King Solomon!' ³⁵Then march up after him, and let him come in and sit on my throne. For he shall succeed me as king; him I designate to be ruler of Israel and Judah." ³⁶Benaiah son of Jehoiada spoke up and said to the king, "Amen! And may the LORD, the God of my lord the king, so ordain. ³⁷As the LORD was with my lord the king, so may He be with Solomon; and may He exalt his throne even higher than the throne of my lord King David."

³⁸Then the priest Zadok, and the prophet Nathan, and Benaiah son of Jehoiada went down with the Cherethites and the Pelethites. They had Solomon ride on King David's mule and they led him to Gihon. ³⁹The priest Zadok took the horn of oil from the Tent and anointed Solomon. They sounded the horn and all the people shouted, "Long live King Solomon!" ⁴⁰All the people then marched up behind him, playing on flutes and making merry till the earth was split open by the uproar.

⁴¹Adonijah and all the guests who were with him, who had just finished eating, heard it. When Joab heard the sound of the horn, he said, "Why is the city in such an uproar?" ⁴²He was still speaking when the priest Jonathan son of Abiathar arrived. "Come in," said Adonijah. "You are a worthy man, and you surely bring good news." ⁴³But Jonathan replied to Adonijah, "Alas, our lord King David has made Solomon king! ⁴⁴The king sent with him the priest Zadok and the prophet Nathan and Benaiah son of Jehoiada, and the Cherethites and Pelethites. They had him ride on the king's mule, ⁴⁵and the priest Zadok and the prophet Nathan anointed him king at Gihon. Then they came up from there making merry, and the city went into an uproar. That's the noise you heard. ⁴⁶Further, Solomon seated himself on the royal throne; ⁴⁷further, the king's courtiers came to congratulate our lord King David, saying, 'May God make the renown of Solomon even greater than yours, and may He exalt his throne even higher than yours!' And the king bowed low on his couch. ⁴⁸And further, this is what the king said, 'Praised be the LORD, the God of Israel who has this day provided a successor to my throne, while my own eyes can see it.' " ⁴⁹Thereupon, all of Adonijah's guests rose in alarm and each went his own way.

⁵⁰Adonijah, in fear of Solomon, went at once [to the Tent] and grasped

h-h *Lit. "your lord's men."*

the horns of the altar. [51]It was reported to Solomon: "Adonijah is in fear of King Solomon and has grasped the horns of the altar, saying, 'Let King Solomon first swear to me that he will not put his servant to the sword.'" [52]Solomon said, "If he behaves worthily, not a hair of his head shall fall to the ground; but if he is caught in any offense, he shall die." [53]So King Solomon sent and had him taken down from the altar. He came and bowed before King Solomon, and Solomon said to him, "Go home."

2 When David's life was drawing to a close, he instructed his son Solomon as follows: [2]"I am going the way of all the earth; be strong and show yourself a man. [3]Keep the charge of the LORD your God, walking in His ways and following His laws, His commandments, His rules, and His admonitions as recorded in the Teaching of Moses, in order that you may succeed in whatever you undertake and wherever you turn. [4]Then the LORD will fulfill the promise that He made concerning me: 'If your descendants are scrupulous in their conduct, and walk before Me faithfully, with all their heart and soul, [a-]your line on the throne of Israel shall never end!'[-a]

[5]"Further, you know what Joab son of Zeruiah did to me, what he did to the two commanders of Israel's forces, Abner son of Ner and Amasa son of Jether: he killed them, shedding[b] blood of war in peacetime, staining the girdle of his loins and the sandals on his feet with blood of war.[c] [6]So act in accordance with your wisdom, and see that his white hair does not go down to Sheol in peace.

[7]"But deal graciously with the sons of Barzillai the Gileadite, for they befriended me when I fled from your brother Absalom; let them be among those that eat at your table.[d]

[8]"You must also deal with Shimei son of Gera, the Benjaminite from Bahurim. He insulted me outrageously when I was on my way to Mahanaim; but he came down to meet me at the Jordan,[e] and I swore to him by the LORD: 'I will not put you to the sword.' [9]So do not let him go unpunished; for you are a wise man and you will know how to deal with him and send his gray hair down to Sheol in blood."

[10]So David slept with his fathers, and he was buried in the City of David. [11]The length of David's reign over Israel was forty years: he reigned seven years in Hebron, and he reigned thirty-three years in Jerusalem.

[a-a] *Lit. "there shall never cease to be a man of yours on the throne of Israel." Cf. 2 Sam. 7.12–16.*

[b] *Meaning of Heb. uncertain.*

[c] *I.e., Joab had thus brought bloodguilt on David's house; see 2 Sam. 3.27 and 20.10.*

[d] *I.e., for whose maintenance you provide; see 2 Sam. 19.32 ff.*

[e] *See 2 Sam. 16.5 ff; 19.17 ff.*

¹²And Solomon sat upon the throne of his father David, and his rule was firmly established.

¹³Adonijah son of Haggith came to see Bathsheba, Solomon's mother. She said, "Do you come with friendly intent?" "Yes," he replied; ¹⁴and he continued, "I would like to have a word with you." "Speak up," she said. ¹⁵Then he said, "You know that the kingship was rightly mine and that all Israel wanted me to reign. But the kingship passed on to my brother; it came to him by the will of the LORD. ¹⁶And now I have one request to make of you; do not refuse me." She said, "Speak up." ¹⁷He replied, "Please ask King Solomon—for he won't refuse you—to give me Abishag the Shunammite as wife." ¹⁸"Very well," said Bathsheba, "I will speak to the king in your behalf."

¹⁹So Bathsheba went to King Solomon to speak to him about Adonijah. The king rose to greet her and bowed down to her. He sat on his throne; and he had a throne placed for the queen mother, and she sat on his right. ²⁰She said, "I have one small request to make of you, do not refuse me." He responded, "Ask, Mother; I shall not refuse you." ²¹Then she said, "Let Abishag the Shunammite be given to your brother Adonijah as wife." ²²The king replied to his mother, "Why request Abishag the Shunammite for Adonijah? Request the kingship for him! For he is my older brother, ᶠ⁻and the priest Abiathar and Joab son of Zeruiah are on his side."⁻ᶠ

²³Thereupon, King Solomon swore by the LORD, saying, "So may God do to me and even more, if broaching this matter does not cost Adonijah his life! ²⁴Now, as the LORD lives, who has established me and set me on the throne of my father David and who has provided himᵍ with a house, as he promised, Adonijah shall be put to death this very day!" ²⁵And Solomon instructed Benaiah son of Jehoiada, who struck Adonijahʰ down; and so he died.

²⁶To the priest Abiathar, the king said, "Go to your estate at Anathoth! You deserve to die, but I shall not put you to death at this time, because you carried the Ark of my Lord GOD before my father David and because you shared all the hardships that my father endured." ²⁷So Solomon dismissed Abiathar from his office of priest of the LORD—thus fulfilling what the LORD had spoken at Shilohⁱ regarding the house of Eli.

²⁸When the news reached Joab, he fled to the Tent of the LORD and grasped the horns of the altar—for Joab had sided with Adonijah, though

---

ᶠ⁻ᶠ Lit. "And for him and for Abiathar and for Joab son of Zeruiah." Meaning of Heb. uncertain.
ᵍ Heb. "me."
ʰ Heb. "him."
ⁱ Cf. 1 Sam. 3.14.

he had not sided with Absalom. ²⁹King Solomon was told that Joab had fled to the Tent of the LORD and that he was there by the altar; so Solomon sent Benaiah son of Jehoiada, saying, "Go and strike him down." ³⁰Benaiah went to the Tent of the LORD and said to him, "Thus said the king: Come out!" "No!" he replied; "I will die here." Benaiah reported back to the king that Joab had answered thus and thus, ³¹and the king said, "Do just as he said; strike him down and bury him, and remove guilt from me and my father's house for the blood of the innocent that Joab has shed. ³²Thus the LORD will bring his blood guilt down upon his own head, because, unbeknown to my father, he struck down with the sword two men more righteous and honorable than he—Abner son of Ner, the army commander of Israel, and Amasa son of Jether, the army commander of Judah. ³³May the guilt for their blood come down upon the head of Joab and his descendants forever, and may good fortune from the LORD be granted forever to David and his descendants, his house and his throne." ³⁴So Benaiah son of Jehoiada went up and struck him down. And he was buried at his home in the wilderness. ³⁵In his place, the king appointed Benaiah son of Jehoiada over the army, and in place of Abiathar, the king appointed the priest Zadok.

³⁶Then the king summoned Shimei and said to him, "Build yourself a house in Jerusalem and stay there—do not ever go out from there anywhere else. ³⁷On the very day that you go out and cross the Wadi Kidron, you can be sure that you will die; your blood shall be on your own head." ³⁸"That is fair," said Shimei to the king, "your servant will do just as my lord the king has spoken." And for a long time, Shimei remained in Jerusalem.

³⁹Three years later, two slaves of Shimei ran away to King Achish son of Maacah of Gath. Shimei was told, "Your slaves are in Gath." ⁴⁰Shimei thereupon saddled his ass and went to Achish in Gath to claim his slaves; and Shimei returned from Gath with his slaves. ⁴¹Solomon was told that Shimei had gone from Jerusalem to Gath and back, ⁴²and the king summoned Shimei and said to him, "Did I not adjure you by the LORD and warn you, 'On the very day that you leave and go anywhere else, you can be sure that you will die,' and did you not say to me, 'It is fair; I accept'? ⁴³Why did you not abide by the oath before the LORD and by the orders which I gave you?" ⁴⁴The king said further to Shimei, "You know all the wrong, which you remember very well, that you did to my father David.

Now the LORD brings down your wrongdoing upon your own head. [45]But King Solomon shall be blessed, and the throne of David shall be established before the LORD forever."

[46]The king gave orders to Benaiah son of Jehoiada and he went out and struck Shimei[h] down; and so he died.

Thus the kingdom was secured in Solomon's hands.

3 Solomon allied himself by marriage with Pharaoh king of Egypt. He married Pharaoh's daughter and brought her to the City of David [to live there] until he had finished building his palace, and the House of the LORD, and the walls around Jerusalem.

[2]The people, however, continued to offer sacrifices at the open shrines, because up to that time no house had been built for the name of the LORD. [3]And Solomon, though he loved the LORD and followed the practices of his father David, also sacrificed and offered at the shrines.

[4]The king went to Gibeon to sacrifice there, for that was the largest shrine; on that altar Solomon presented a thousand burnt offerings. [5]At Gibeon the LORD appeared to Solomon in a dream by night; and God said, "Ask, what shall I grant you?" [6]Solomon said, "You dealt most graciously with Your servant my father David, because he walked before You in faithfulness and righteousness and in integrity of heart. You have continued this great kindness to him by giving him a son to occupy his throne, as is now the case. [7]And now, O LORD my God, You have made Your servant king in place of my father David; but I am a young lad, [a-]with no experience in leadership.[-a] [8]Your servant finds himself in the midst of the people You have chosen, a people too numerous to be numbered or counted. [9]Grant, then, Your servant an understanding mind to judge Your people, to distinguish between good and bad; for who can judge this vast people of Yours?"

[10]The LORD was pleased that Solomon had asked for this. [11]And God said to him, "Because you asked for this—you did not ask for long life, you did not ask for riches, you did not ask for the life of your enemies, but you asked for discernment in dispensing justice—[12]I now do as you have spoken. I grant you a wise and discerning mind; there has never been anyone like you before, nor will anyone like you arise again. [13]And I also grant you what you did not ask for—both riches and glory all your

a-a Lit. *"do not know to go out and come in"*; cf. *Num. 27.17.*

life—the like of which no king has ever had. ¹⁴And I will further grant you long life, if you will walk in My ways and observe My laws and commandments, as did your father David."

¹⁵Then Solomon awoke: it was a dream! He went to Jerusalem, stood before the Ark of the Covenant of the LORD, and sacrificed burnt offerings and presented offerings of well-being; and he made a banquet for all his courtiers.

¹⁶Later two prostitutes came to the king and stood before him. ¹⁷The first woman said, "Please, my lord! This woman and I live in the same house; and I gave birth to a child while she was in the house. ¹⁸On the third day after I was delivered, this woman also gave birth to a child. We were alone; there was no one else with us in the house, just the two of us in the house. ¹⁹During the night this woman's child died, because she lay on it. ²⁰She arose in the night and took my son from my side while your maidservant was asleep, and laid him in her bosom; and she laid her dead son in my bosom. ²¹When I arose in the morning to nurse my son, there he was, dead; but when I looked at him closely in the morning, it was not the son I had borne."

²²The other woman spoke up, "No, the live one is my son, and the dead one is yours!" But the first insisted, "No, the dead boy is yours; mine is the live one!" And they went on arguing before the king.

²³The king said, "One says, 'This is my son, the live one, and the dead one is yours'; and the other says, 'No, the dead boy is yours, mine is the live one.' ²⁴So the king gave the order, "Fetch me a sword." A sword was brought before the king, ²⁵and the king said, "Cut the live child in two, and give half to one and half to the other."

²⁶But the woman whose son was the live one pleaded with the king, for she was overcome with compassion for her son. "Please, my lord," she cried, "give her the live child; only don't kill it!" The other insisted, "It shall be neither yours nor mine; cut it in two!" ²⁷Then the king spoke up. "Give the live child to her," he said, "and do not put it to death; she is its mother."

²⁸When all Israel heard the decision that the king had rendered, they stood in awe of the king; for they saw that he possessed divine wisdom to execute justice.

4 King Solomon was now king over all Israel. ²These were his officials:
Azariah son of Zadok—the priest;
³Elihoreph and Ahijah sons of Shisha—scribes;
Jehoshaphat son of Ahilud—recorder;
⁴Benaiah son of Jehoiada—over the army;
Zadok and Abiathar—priests;
⁵Azariah son of Nathan—in charge of the prefects;
Zabud son of Nathan the priest—companion of the king;
⁶Ahishar—in charge of the palace; and
Adoniram son of Abda—in charge of the forced labor.

⁷Solomon had twelve prefects governing all Israel, who provided food for the king and his household; each had to provide food for one month in the year. ⁸And these were their names: Ben-hur, in the hill country of Ephraim; ⁹Ben-deker, in Makaz, Shaalbim, Beth-shemesh, and Elon-beth-hanan; ¹⁰Ben-hesed in Arubboth—he governed Socho and all the Hepher area; ¹¹Ben-abinadab, [in] all of Naphath-dor (Solomon's daughter Taphath was his wife); ¹²Baana son of Ahilud [in] Taanach and Megiddo and all Beth-shean, which is beside Zarethan, below Jezreel—from Beth-shean to Abel-meholah as far as the other side of Jokmeam; ¹³Ben-geber, in Ramoth-gilead—he governed the villages of Jair son of Manasseh which are in Gilead, and he also governed the district of Argob which is in Bashan, sixty large towns with walls and bronze bars; ¹⁴Ahinadab son of Iddo, in Mahanaim; ¹⁵Ahimaaz, in Naphtali (he too took a daughter of Solomon—Basemath—to wife); ¹⁶Baanah son of Hushi, in Asher and Bealoth;ᵃ ¹⁷Jehoshaphat son of Paruah, in Issachar; ¹⁸Shimei son of Ela, in Benjamin; ¹⁹Geber son of Uri, in the region of Gilead, the country of Sihon, king of the Amorites, and Og, king of Bashan; ᵇ⁻and one prefect who was in the land.⁻ᵇ

²⁰Judah and Israel were as numerous as the sands of the sea; they ate and drank and were content.

5 Solomon's rule extended over all the kingdoms from the Euphrates to the land of the Philistines and the boundary of Egypt. They brought Solomon tribute and were subject to him all his life. ²Solomon's daily provisions consisted of 30 *kor*s of semolina, and 60 *kor*s of [ordinary] flour, ³10 fattened oxen, 20 pasture-fed oxen, and 100 sheep and goats,

ᵃ Or "*in Aloth.*"
ᵇ⁻ᵇ *Meaning of Heb. uncertain.*

besides deer and gazelles, roebucks and a-fatted geese.-a 4For he controlled the whole region west of the Euphrates—all the kings west of the Euphrates, from Tiphsah to Gaza—and he had peace on all his borders roundabout. 5All the days of Solomon, Judah and Israel from Dan to Beer-sheba dwelt in safety, everyone under his own vine and under his own fig tree. 6Solomon had 40,000 stalls of horses for his chariotry and 12,000 horsemen.

7bAll those prefects, each during his month, would furnish provisions for King Solomon and for all who were admitted to King Solomon's table; they did not fall short in anything. 8They would also, each in his turn, deliver barley and straw for the horses and the swift steeds to the places where they were stationed.

9The LORD endowed Solomon with wisdom and discernment in great measure, with understanding as vast as the sands on the seashore. 10Solomon's wisdom was greater than the wisdom of all the Kedemites and than all the wisdom of the Egyptians. 11He was the wisest of all men: [wiser] than Ethan the Ezrahite, and Heman, Chalkol, and Darda the sons of Mahol. His fame spread among all the surrounding nations. 12He composed three thousand proverbs, and his songs numbered one thousand and five. 13He discoursed about trees, from the cedar in Lebanon to the hyssop that grows out of the wall; and he discoursed about beasts, birds, creeping things, and fishes. 14Men of all peoples came to hear Solomon's wisdom, [sent] by all the kings of the earth who had heard of his wisdom.

15King Hiram of Tyre sent his officials to Solomon when he heard that he had been anointed king in place of his father; for Hiram had always been a friend of David. 16Solomon sent this message to Hiram: 17"You know that my father David could not build a house for the name of the LORD his God because of the enemiesc that encompassed him, until the LORD had placed them under the soles of his feet. 18But now the LORD my God has given me respite all around; there is no adversary and no mischance. 19And so I propose to build a house for the name of the LORD my God, as the LORD promised my father David, saying, 'Your son, whom I will set on your throne in your place, shall build the house for My name.' 20Please, then, give orders for cedars to be cut for me in the Lebanon. My servants will work with yours, and I will pay you any wages

---

a-a *Exact meaning of Heb. uncertain.*
b *Resuming the account begun in 4.2.*
c *Heb. "war"; cf. Targum.*

you may ask for your servants; for as you know, there is none among us who knows how to cut timber like the Sidonians."

21When Hiram heard Solomon's message, he was overjoyed. "Praised be the LORD this day," he said, "for granting David a wise son to govern this great people." 22So Hiram sent word to Solomon: "I have your message; I will supply all the cedar and cypress logs you require. 23My servants will bring them down to the sea from the Lebanon; and at the sea I will make them into floats and [deliver them] to any place that you designate to me. There I shall break them up for you to carry away. You, in turn, will supply the food I require for my household." 24So Hiram kept Solomon provided with all the cedar and cypress wood he required, 25and Solomon delivered to Hiram 20,000 *kors* of wheat as provisions for his household and d-20 *kors*-d of beaten oil. Such was Solomon's annual payment to Hiram.

26The LORD had given Solomon wisdom, as He had promised him. There was friendship between Hiram and Solomon, and the two of them made a treaty.

27King Solomon imposed forced labor on all Israel; the levy came to 30,000 men. 28He sent them to the Lebanon in shifts of 10,000 a month: they would spend one month in the Lebanon and two months at home. Adoniram was in charge of the forced labor. 29Solomon also had 70,000 porters and 80,000 quarriers in the hills, 30apart from Solomon's 3,300 officials who were in charge of the work and supervised the gangs doing the work. 31The king ordered huge blocks of choice stone to be quarried, so that the foundations of the house might be laid with hewn stones. 32Solomon's masons, Hiram's masons, and the men of Gebal shaped them. Thus the timber and the stones for building the house were made ready.

6 In the four hundred and eightieth year after the Israelites left the land of Egypt, in the month of Ziv—that is, the second month—in the fourth year of his reign over Israel, Solomon began to build the House of the LORD. 2The House which King Solomon built for the LORD was 60 cubits long, 20 cubits wide, and 30 cubits high. 3The portico in front of

d-d *Septuagint reads, "20,000 baths."*

the Great Hall of the House was 20 cubits long—along the width of the House—and 10 cubits deep to the front of the House. ⁴ᵃHe made windows for the House, recessed and latticed. ⁵Against the outside wall of the House—the outside walls of the House enclosing the Great Hall and the Shrineᵇ—he built a storied structure; and he made side chambers all around. ⁶The lowest story was 5 cubits wide, the middle one 6 cubits wide, and the third 7 cubits wide; for he had provided recesses around the outside of the House so as not to penetrate the walls of the House.

⁷When the House was built, only finished stones cut at the quarry were used, so that no hammer or ax or any iron tool was heard in the House while it was being built.

⁸The entrance to the middleᶜ [story of] the side chambers was on the right side of the House; and winding stairs led up to the middle chambers, and from the middle chambers to the third story. ⁹When he finished building the House, ᵈ⁻he paneled the House with beams and planks of cedar.⁻ᵈ ¹⁰He built the storied structure against the entire House—each story 5 cubits high, so that it encased the House with timbers of cedar.

¹¹Then the word of the LORD came to Solomon, ¹²"With regard to this House you are building—if you follow My laws and observe My rules and faithfully keep My commandments, I will fulfill for you the promise that I gave to your father David: ¹³I will abide among the children of Israel, and I will never forsake My people Israel."

¹⁴When Solomon had completed the construction of the House, ¹⁵he paneled the walls of the House on the inside with planks of cedar. He also overlaid the walls on the inside with wood, from the floor of the House to the ceiling. And he overlaid the floor of the House with planks of cypress. ¹⁶Twenty cubits from the rear of the House, he built [a partition] of cedar planks from the floor to the walls;ᵉ he furnished its interior to serve as a shrine, as the Holy of Holies. ¹⁷ᶠThe front part of the House, that is, the Great Hall, measured 40 cubits. ¹⁸The cedar of the interior of the House had carvings of gourds and calyxes; it was all cedar, no stone was exposed. ¹⁹In the innermost part of the House, he fixed a Shrine in which to place the Ark of the LORD's Covenant. ²⁰ᵇ⁻The interior of the⁻ᵇ Shrine was 20 cubits long, 20 cubits wide, and 20 cubits high. He overlaid it with solid gold; he similarly overlaid [its] cedar altar. ²¹Solomon overlaid the interior of the House with solid gold; and he inserted golden chains ᵍ⁻into the door of⁻ᵍ the Shrine. He overlaid [the Shrine] with gold,

---

ᵃ *Meaning of parts of vv. 4–6 uncertain.*
ᵇ *I.e., the inner sanctuary, designated in v. 16 and elsewhere as the "Holy of Holies."*
ᶜ *Septuagint and Targum read "lowest."*
ᵈ⁻ᵈ *Meaning of Heb. uncertain.*
ᵉ *Septuagint reads "rafters."*
ᶠ *Meaning of vv. 17–22 is unclear in part.*
ᵍ⁻ᵍ *Heb. "in front of."*

²²so that the entire House was overlaid with gold; he even overlaid with gold the entire altar of the Shrine. And so the entire House was completed.

²³In the Shrine he made two cherubim of olive wood, each 10 cubits high. ²⁴[One] had a wing measuring 5 cubits and another wing measuring 5 cubits, so that the spread from wingtip to wingtip was 10 cubits; ²⁵and the wingspread of the other cherub was also 10 cubits. The two cherubim had the same measurements and proportions: ²⁶the height of the one cherub was 10 cubits, and so was that of the other cherub.

²⁷He placed the cherubim inside the ^{h-}inner chamber.^{-h} Since the wings of the cherubim were extended, a wing of the one touched one wall and a wing of the other touched the other wall, while their wings in the center of the chamber touched each other. ²⁸He overlaid the cherubim with gold. ²⁹All over the walls of the House, of both the inner area and the outer area, he carved reliefs of cherubim, palms, and calyxes, ³⁰and he overlaid the floor of the House with gold, both the inner and the outer areas.

³¹For the entrance of the Shrine he made doors of olive wood, ^{d-}the pilasters and the doorposts having five sides.^{-d} ³²The double doors were of olive wood, and on them he carved reliefs of cherubim, palms, and calyxes. He overlaid them with gold, hammering the gold onto the cherubim and the palms. ³³For the entrance of the Great Hall, too, he made doorposts of oleaster wood, ^{d-}having four sides,^{-d} ³⁴and the double doors of cypress wood, each door consisting of two rounded planks. ³⁵On them he carved cherubim, palms, and calyxes, overlaying them with gold applied evenly over the carvings. ³⁶He built the inner enclosure of three courses of hewn stones and one course of cedar beams.

³⁷In the fourth year, in the month of Ziv, the foundations of the House were laid; ³⁸and in the eleventh year, in the month of Bul—that is, the eighth month—the House was completed according to all its details and all its specifications. It took him seven years to build it. ¹And it took Solomon thirteen years to build his palace, until his whole palace was completed.

²He built the ^{a-}Lebanon Forest House with four rows^{-a} of cedar columns, and with hewn cedar beams above the columns. Its length was 100 cubits, its breadth 50 cubits, and its height 30 cubits. ³It was paneled above with cedar, with the planks^b that were above on the 45 columns—

---

^{h-h} *I.e., the Shrine.*

^{a-a} *So called because of the rows of cedar columns. Septuagint reads "three rows" instead of "four rows"; cf. v. 3.*

^b *Apparently the "planks" connected the columns longitudinally, and the "beams" (v. 2) connected the planks transversely.*

15 in each row. [4]And there were three rows of window frames, with three tiers of windows facing each other. [5]All the doorways and doorposts[c] had square frames—with three tiers of windows facing each other.

[6]He made the portico of columns 50 cubits long and 30 cubits wide; [d-]the portico was in front of [the columns], and there were columns with a canopy in front of them.[-d] [7]He made the throne portico, where he was to pronounce judgment—the Hall of Judgment. It was paneled with cedar from floor to floor.[e]

[8]The house that he used as a residence, in the rear courtyard, back of the portico, was of the same construction. Solomon also constructed a palace like that portico for the daughter of Pharaoh, whom he had married.

[9]All these buildings, from foundation to coping and all the way out to the great courtyard, were of choice stones, hewn according to measure, smooth on all sides.[f] [10]The foundations were huge blocks of choice stone, stones of 10 cubits and stones of 8 cubits; [11]and above were choice stones, hewn according to measure, and cedar wood. [12]The large surrounding courtyard had three tiers of hewn stone and a row of cedar beams, the same as for the inner court of the House of the LORD, and for the portico of the House.

[13]King Solomon sent for Hiram and brought him down from Tyre. [14]He was the son of a widow of the tribe of Naphtali, and his father had been a Tyrian, a coppersmith. He was endowed with skill, ability, and talent for executing all work in bronze.[g] He came to King Solomon and executed all his work. [15]He cast two columns of bronze; one column was 18 cubits high and measured 12 cubits in circumference, [and similarly] the other column. [16]He made two capitals, cast in bronze, to be set upon the two columns, the height of each of the two capitals being 5 cubits; [17]also nets of meshwork with festoons of chainwork for the capitals that were on the top of the columns, seven for each of the two capitals. [18]He made the columns[h] so that there were two rows [of pomegranates] encircling the top of the one network, to cover the capitals that were on the top of the pomegranates;[i] and he did the same for [the network on] the second capital. [19]The capitals upon the columns of the portico were of lily design, 4 cubits high; [20]so also the capitals upon the two columns

---

c *Septuagint reads "windows."*
d-d *Meaning of Heb. uncertain.*
e *Syriac reads "rafters."*
f *Lit. "sawed with a saw in the inside and outside."*
g *Heb.* nehosheth *means both copper and bronze. In the translation "copper" is ordinarily used to denote the natural product and "bronze" for the artifacts.*
h *Two Heb. mss. read "pomegranates."*
i *About fifty Heb. mss. read "columns."*

extended above and next to the bulge[j] that was beside the network. There were 200 pomegranates in rows around the top of the second capital.[k]

²¹He set up the columns at the portico of the Great Hall; he set up one column on the right and named it Jachin, and he set up the other column on the left and named it Boaz. ²²Upon the top of the columns there was a lily design. Thus the work of the columns was completed.

²³Then he made the tank[l] of cast metal, 10 cubits across from brim to brim, completely round; it was 5 cubits high, and it measured 30 cubits in circumference. ²⁴There were gourds below the brim completely encircling it—ten to a cubit, encircling the tank; the gourds were in two rows, cast in one piece with it. ²⁵It stood upon twelve oxen: three facing north, three facing west, three facing south, and three facing east, with the tank resting upon them; their haunches were all turned inward. ²⁶It was a handbreadth thick, and its brim was made like that of a cup, like the petals of a lily. Its capacity was 2,000 *baths*.

²⁷He made the ten laver stands of bronze. The length of each laver stand was 4 cubits and the width 4 cubits, and the height was 3 cubits. ²⁸The structure of the laver stands was as follows: They had insets,[m] and there were insets within the frames; ²⁹and on the insets within the frames were lions, oxen, and cherubim. Above the frames was a stand; and both above and below the lions and the oxen were spirals of hammered metal. ³⁰Each laver stand had four bronze wheels and [two] bronze axletrees. Its four legs had brackets; the brackets were under the laver, cast ᵈ⁻with spirals beyond each.⁻ᵈ ³¹Its funnel, within the crown, rose a cubit above it; this funnel was round, in the fashion of a stand, a cubit and a half in diameter. On the funnel too there were carvings.

But the insets were square, not round. ³²And below the insets were the four wheels. The axletrees of the wheels were [fixed] in the laver stand, and the height of each wheel was a cubit and a half. ³³The structure of the wheels was like the structure of chariot wheels; and their axletrees, their rims, their spokes, and their hubs were all of cast metal. ³⁴Four brackets ran to the four corners of each laver stand; the brackets were of a piece with the laver stand. ³⁵At the top of the laver stand was a round band half a cubit high, and together with the top of the laver stand; its sides and its insets were of one piece with it. ³⁶ᵈ⁻On its surface—on its sides—and on its insets [Hiram] engraved cherubim, lions, and palms, as

---

j Lit. *"belly"*; *exact force of Heb. uncertain.*

k *I.e., each of the two capitals.*

l Lit. *"sea."*

m *Emendation yields "frames."*

the clear space on each allowed,⁻ᵈ with spirals roundabout. ³⁷It was after this manner that he made the ten laver stands, all of them cast alike, of the same measure and the same form. ³⁸Then he made ten bronze lavers, one laver on each of the ten laver stands, each laver measuring 4 cubits and each laver containing forty *bath*s.

³⁹He disposed the laver stands, five at the right side of the House and five at its left side; and the tank he placed on the right side of the House, at the southeast [corner].

⁴⁰Hiram also made the lavers, the scrapers, and the sprinkling bowls.

So Hiram finished all the work that he had been doing for King Solomon on the House of the LORD: ⁴¹the two columns, the two globes of the capitals upon the columns; and the two pieces of network to cover the two globes of the capitals upon the columns; ⁴²the four hundred pomegranates for the two pieces of network, two rows of pomegranates for each network, to cover the two globes of the capitals upon the columns; ⁴³the ten stands and the ten lavers upon the stands; ⁴⁴the one tank with the twelve oxen underneath the tank; ⁴⁵the pails, the scrapers, and the sprinkling bowls. All those vessels in the House of the LORD that Hiram made for King Solomon were of burnished bronze. ⁴⁶The king had them cast ⁿ⁻in earthen molds,⁻ⁿ in the plain of the Jordan between Succoth and Zarethan. ⁴⁷Solomon left all the vessels [unweighed] because of their very great quantity; the weight of the bronze was not reckoned.

⁴⁸And Solomon made all the furnishings that were in the House of the LORD: the altar, of gold; the table for the bread of display, of gold; ⁴⁹the lampstands—five on the right side and five on the left—in front of the Shrine, of solid gold; and the petals, lamps, and tongs, of gold; ⁵⁰the basins, snuffers, sprinkling bowls, ladles, and fire pans, of solid gold; and the hinge sockets for the doors of the innermost part of the House, the Holy of Holies, and for the doors of the Great Hall of the House, of gold.

⁵¹When all the work that King Solomon had done in the House of the LORD was completed, Solomon brought in the sacred donations of his father David—the silver, the gold, and the vessels—and deposited them in the treasury of the House of the LORD.

ⁿ⁻ⁿ *Lit. "in the thick of the earth."*

8 Then Solomon convoked the elders of Israel—all the heads of the tribes and the ancestral chieftains of the Israelites—before King Solomon in Jerusalem, to bring up the Ark of the Covenant of the LORD from the City of David, that is, Zion. ²All the men of Israel gathered before King Solomon at the Feast,ᵃ in the month of Ethanim—that is, the seventh month. ³When all the elders of Israel had come, the priests lifted the Ark ⁴and carried up the Ark of the LORD. Then the priests and the Levites brought the Tent of Meeting and all the holy vessels that were in the Tent. ⁵Meanwhile, King Solomon and the whole community of Israel, who were assembled with him before the Ark, were sacrificing sheep and oxen in such abundance that they could not be numbered or counted.

⁶The priests brought the Ark of the LORD's Covenant to its place underneath the wings of the cherubim, in the Shrine of the House, in the Holy of Holies; ⁷for the cherubim had their wings spread out over the place of the Ark, so that the cherubim shielded the Ark and its poles from above. ⁸The poles projected so that the ends of the poles were visible in the sanctuary in front of the Shrine, but they could not be seen outside; and there they remain to this day. ⁹There was nothing inside the Ark but the two tablets of stone which Moses placed there at Horeb, when the LORD made [a covenant] with the Israelites after their departure from the land of Egypt.

¹⁰When the priests came out of the sanctuary—for the cloud had filled the House of the LORD ¹¹and the priests were not able to remain and perform the service because of the cloud, for the Presence of the LORD filled the House of the LORD—¹²then Solomon declared:

> "The LORD has chosen
> To abide in a thick cloud:
> ¹³I have now built for You
> A stately House,
> A place where You
> May dwell forever."

¹⁴Then, with the whole congregation of Israel standing, the king faced about and blessed the whole congregation of Israel. ¹⁵He said:

"Praised be the LORD, the God of Israel, ᵇwho has fulfilled with deeds the promise He made-ᵇ to my father David. For He said, ¹⁶'Ever since I brought My people Israel out of Egypt, I have not chosen a city among

---

ᵃ *I.e., of Booths. Cf. Lev. 23.34.*
ᵇ⁻ᵇ *Lit. "who spoke with His own mouth . . . and has fulfilled with His own hand."*

all the tribes of Israel for building a House where My name might abide; but I have chosen David to rule My people Israel.'

17"Now my father David had intended to build a House for the name of the LORD, the God of Israel. 18But the LORD said to my father David, 'As regards your intention to build a House for My name, you did right to have that intention. 19However, you shall not build the House yourself; instead, your son, the issue of your loins, shall build the House for My name.'

20"And the LORD has fulfilled the promise that He made: I have suc-ceeded^c my father David and have ascended the throne of Israel, as the LORD promised. I have built the House for the name of the LORD, the God of Israel; 21and I have set a place there for the Ark, containing the covenant which the LORD made with our fathers when He brought them out from the land of Egypt."

22Then Solomon stood before the altar of the LORD in the presence of the whole community of Israel; he spread the palms of his hands toward heaven 23and said, "O LORD God of Israel, in the heavens above and on the earth below there is no god like You, who keep Your gracious cov-enant with Your servants when they walk before You in wholehearted devotion; 24You who have kept the promises You made to Your servant, my father David, fulfilling with deeds the promise You made—as is now the case. 25And now, O LORD God of Israel, keep the further promise that You made to Your servant, my father David: 'Your line on the throne of Israel shall never end, if only your descendants will look to their way and walk before Me as you have walked before Me.' 26Now, therefore, O God of Israel, let the promise that You made to Your servant my father David be fulfilled.

27"But will God really dwell^d on earth? Even the heavens to their ut-termost reaches cannot contain You, how much less this House that I have built! 28Yet turn, O LORD my God, to the prayer and supplication of Your servant,and hear the cry and prayer which Your servant offers before You this day. 29May Your eyes be open day and night toward this House, toward the place of which You have said, 'My name shall abide there'; may You heed the prayers which Your servant will offer toward this place. 30And when You hear the supplications which Your servant and Your people Israel offer toward this place, give heed in Your heavenly abode—give heed and pardon.

31"Whenever one man commits an offense against another, and the

---

c Lit. "risen in place of."
d 2 Chron. 6.18 adds "with man."

latter utters an imprecation to bring a curse upon him, and comes with his imprecation before Your altar in this House, 32oh, hear in heaven and take action to judge Your servants, condemning him who is in the wrong and bringing down the punishment of his conduct on his head, vindicating him who is in the right by rewarding him according to his righteousness.

33"Should Your people Israel be routed by an enemy because they have sinned against You, and then turn back to You and acknowledge Your name, and they offer prayer and supplication to You in this House, 34oh, hear in heaven and pardon the sin of Your people Israel, and restore them to the land that You gave to their fathers.

35"Should the heavens be shut up and there be no rain, because they have sinned against You, and then they pray toward this place and acknowledge Your name and repent of their sins, when You answer[c] them, 36oh, hear in heaven and pardon the sin of Your servants, Your people Israel, after You have shown them the proper way in which they are to walk; and send down rain upon the land which You gave to Your people as their heritage. 37So, too, if there is a famine in the land, if there is pestilence, blight, mildew, locusts or caterpillars, or if an enemy oppresses them in any of the settlements of the land.

"In any plague and in any disease, 38in any prayer or supplication offered by any person among all Your people Israel—each of whom knows his own affliction—when he spreads his palms toward this House, 39oh, hear in Your heavenly abode, and pardon and take action! Render to each man according to his ways as You know his heart to be—for You alone know the hearts of all men—40so that they may revere You all the days that they live on the land that You gave to our fathers.

41"Or if a foreigner who is not of Your people Israel comes from a distant land for the sake of Your name—42for they shall hear about Your great name and Your mighty hand and Your outstretched arm—when he comes to pray toward this House, 43oh, hear in Your heavenly abode and grant all that the foreigner asks You for. Thus all the peoples of the earth will know Your name and revere You, as does Your people Israel; and they will recognize that Your name is attached to this House that I have built.

44"When Your people take the field against their enemy by whatever way You send them, and they pray to the LORD in the direction of the city which You have chosen, and of the House which I have built to Your

---

c *The Septuagint, with a different vocalization, reads "chastise."*

name, ⁴⁵oh, hear in heaven their prayer and supplication and uphold their cause.

⁴⁶"When they sin against You—for there is no man who does not sin—and You are angry with them and deliver them to the enemy, and their captors carry them off to an enemy land, near or far; ⁴⁷and then they take it to heart in the land to which they have been carried off, and they repent and make supplication to You in the land of their captors, saying: 'We have sinned, we have acted perversely, we have acted wickedly,' ⁴⁸and they turn back to You with all their heart and soul, in the land of the enemies who have carried them off, and they pray to You in the direction of their land which You gave to their fathers, of the city which You have chosen, and of the House which I have built to Your name—⁴⁹oh, give heed in Your heavenly abode to their prayer and supplication, uphold their cause, ⁵⁰and pardon Your people who have sinned against You for all the transgressions that they have committed against You. Grant them mercy in the sight of their captors that they may be merciful to them. ⁵¹For they are Your very own people that You freed from Egypt, from the midst of the iron furnace. ⁵²May Your eyes be open to the supplication of Your servant and the supplication of Your people Israel, and may You heed them whenever they call upon You. ⁵³For You, O Lord GOD, have set them apart for Yourself from all the peoples of the earth as Your very own, as You promised through Moses Your servant when You freed our fathers from Egypt."

⁵⁴When Solomon finished offering to the LORD all this prayer and supplication, he rose from where he had been kneeling, in front of the altar of the LORD, his hands spread out toward heaven. ⁵⁵He stood, and in a loud voice blessed the whole congregation of Israel:

⁵⁶"Praised be the LORD who has granted a haven to His people Israel, just as He promised; not a single word has failed of all the gracious promises that He made through His servant Moses. ⁵⁷May the LORD our God be with us, as He was with our fathers. May He never abandon or forsake us. ⁵⁸May He incline our hearts to Him, that we may walk in all His ways and keep the commandments, the laws, and the rules, which He enjoined upon our fathers. ⁵⁹And may these words of mine, which I have offered in supplication before the LORD, be close to the LORD our God day and night, that He may provide for His servant and for His people Israel, according to each day's needs—⁶⁰to the end that all the

peoples of the earth may know that the LORD alone is God, there is no other. 61And may you be wholehearted with the LORD our God, to walk in His ways and keep His commandments, even as now."

62The king and all Israel with him offered sacrifices before the LORD. 63Solomon offered 22,000 oxen and 120,000 sheep as sacrifices of well-being to the LORD. Thus the king and all the Israelites dedicated the House of the LORD. 64That day the king consecrated the center of the court that was in front of the House of the LORD. For it was there that he presented the burnt offerings, the meal offerings, and the fat parts of the offerings of well-being, because the bronze altar that was before the LORD was too small to hold the burnt offerings, the meal offerings, and the fat parts of the offerings of well-being.

65So Solomon and all Israel with him—a great assemblage, [coming] from Lebo-hamath to the Wadi of Egypt[f]—observed the Feast[a] at that time before the LORD our God, seven days and again seven days, fourteen days in all. 66On the eighth day[g] he let the people go. They bade the king good-bye and went to their homes, joyful and glad of heart over all the goodness that the LORD had shown to His servant David and His people Israel.

9 When Solomon had finished building the House of the LORD and the royal palace and everything that Solomon had set his heart on constructing, 2the LORD appeared to Solomon a second time, as He had appeared to him at Gibeon. 3The LORD said to him, "I have heard the prayer and the supplication which you have offered to Me. I consecrate this House which you have built and I set My name there forever. My eyes and My heart shall ever be there. 4As for you, if you walk before Me as your father David walked before Me, wholeheartedly and with uprightness, doing all that I have commanded you [and] keeping My laws and My rules, 5then I will establish your throne of kingship over Israel forever, as I promised your father David, saying, 'Your line on the throne of Israel shall never end.' 6[But] if you and your descendants turn away from Me and do not keep the commandments [and] the laws which I have set before you, and go and serve other gods and worship them, 7then I will sweep[a] Israel off the land which I gave them; I will reject[b] the House which I have consecrated to My name; and Israel shall become a proverb

---

f *I.e., coming from one end of the country to the other.*
g *I.e., of the second seven-day feast; cf. 2 Chron. 7.8–10.*

a *Lit. "cut."*
b *Lit. "dismiss from My presence."*

and a byword among all peoples. [8]And [c-]as for this House, once so exalted,[-c] everyone passing by it shall be appalled and shall hiss.[d] And when they ask, 'Why did the LORD do thus to the land and to this House?' [9]they shall be told, 'It is because they forsook the LORD their God who freed them from the land of Egypt, and they embraced other gods and worshiped them and served them; therefore the LORD has brought all this calamity upon them.' "

[10]At the end of the twenty years[e] during which Solomon constructed the two buildings, the LORD's House and the royal palace—[11]since King Hiram of Tyre had supplied Solomon with all the cedar and cypress timber and gold that he required—King Solomon in turn gave Hiram twenty towns in the region of Galilee. [12]But when Hiram came from Tyre to inspect the towns that Solomon had given him, he was not pleased with them. [13]"My brother," he said, "what sort of towns are these you have given me?" So they were named the land of Cabul,[f] as is still the case. [14]However, Hiram sent the king one hundred and twenty talents of gold.

[15]This was the purpose of the forced labor which Solomon imposed: It was to build the House of the LORD, his own palace, the Millo,[g] and the wall of Jerusalem, and [to fortify] Hazor, Megiddo, and Gezer. ([16]Pharaoh king of Egypt had come up and captured Gezer; he destroyed it by fire, killed the Canaanites who dwelt in the town, and gave it as dowry to his daughter, Solomon's wife.) [17]So Solomon fortified Gezer, lower Beth-horon, [18]Baalith, and Tamar[h] in the wilderness, in the land [of Judah], [19]and all of Solomon's garrison towns, chariot towns, and cavalry towns—everything that Solomon set his heart on building in Jerusalem and in the Lebanon, and throughout the territory that he ruled. [20]All the people that were left of the Amorites, Hittites, Perizzites, Hivites, and Jebusites who were not of the Israelite stock—[21]those of their descendants who remained in the land and whom the Israelites were not able to annihilate—of these Solomon made a slave force, as is still the case. [22]But he did not reduce any Israelites to slavery; they served, rather, as warriors and as his attendants, officials, and officers, and as commanders of his chariotry and cavalry.

[23]These were the prefects that were in charge of Solomon's works and were foremen over the people engaged in the work, who numbered 550.[i]

c-c *Targum and some other ancient versions read "and this House shall become a ruin."*
d *An action performed at the sight of ruin to ward off a like fate from the observer; cf. note at Jer. 18.16.*
e *See 6.38—7.1.*
f *Perhaps taken to mean "as nothing."*
g *A citadel.*
h *So kethib, cf. Ezek. 47.19, 48.28; qere Tadmor.*
i *Their names are not listed in the text.*

24As soon as Pharaoh's daughter went up from the City of David to the palace that he had built for her, he built the Millo.g

25Solomon used to offer burnt offerings and sacrifices of well-being three times a year on the altar that he had built for the LORD, and j-he used to offer incense on the one that was before the LORD. And he kept the House in repair.-j

26King Solomon also built a fleet of ships at Ezion-geber, which is near Elothk on the shore of the Sea of Reeds in the land of Edom. 27Hiram sent servants of his with the fleet, mariners who were experienced on the sea, to serve with Solomon's men. 28They came to Ophir; there they obtained gold in the amount of four hundred and twenty talents, which they delivered to King Solomon.

10 The queen of Sheba heard of Solomon's fame, a-through the name of the LORD,-a and she came to test him with hard questions. 2She arrived in Jerusalem with a very large retinue, with camels bearing spices, a great quantity of gold, and precious stones. When she came to Solomon, she asked him all that she had in mind. 3Solomon had answers for all her questions; there was nothing that the king did not know, [nothing] to which he could not give her an answer. 4When the queen of Sheba observed all of Solomon's wisdom, and the palace he had built, 5the fare of his table, the seating of his courtiers, the service and attire of his attendants, and his wine service, b-and the burnt offerings that he offered at-b the House of the LORD, she was left breathless.

6She said to the king, "The report I heard in my own land about you and your wisdom was true. 7But I did not believe the reports until I came and saw with my own eyes that not even the half had been told me; your wisdom and wealth surpass the reports that I heard. 8How fortunate are your men and how fortunate are these your courtiers, who are always in attendance on you and can hear your wisdom! 9Praised be the LORD your God, who delighted in you and set you on the throne of Israel. It is because of the LORD's everlasting love for Israel that He made you king to administer justice and righteousness."

10She presented the king with one hundred and twenty talents of gold, and a large quantity of spices, and precious stones. Never again did such

j-j *Meaning of Heb. uncertain.*
k *Elsewhere called Elath.*

a-a *The force of the phrase is uncertain.*
b-b *2 Chron. 9.4 reads ". . . and the procession with which he went up to. . . ."*

a vast quantity of spices arrive as that which the queen of Sheba gave to King Solomon.—[11]Moreover, Hiram's fleet, which carried gold from Ophir, brought in from Ophir a huge quantity of *almug* wood[c] and precious stones. [12]The king used the *almug* wood for decorations in the House of the LORD and in the royal palace, and for harps and lyres for the musicians. Such a quantity of *almug* wood has never arrived or been seen to this day.—[13]King Solomon, in turn, gave the queen of Sheba everything she wanted and asked for, in addition to what King Solomon gave her out of his royal bounty. Then she and her attendants left and returned to her own land.

[14]The weight of the gold which Solomon received every year was 666 talents of gold, [15]besides what came from tradesmen, from the traffic of the merchants, and from all the kings of Arabia and the governors of the regions. [16]King Solomon made 200 shields of beaten gold—600 shekels of gold to each shield—[17]and 300 bucklers of beaten gold—three *minas* of gold to each buckler. The king placed them in the Lebanon Forest House.

[18]The king also made a large throne of ivory, and he overlaid it with refined gold. [19]Six steps led up to the throne, and the throne had a back with a rounded top, and arms on either side of the seat. Two lions stood beside the arms, [20]and twelve lions stood on the six steps, six on either side. No such throne was ever made for any other kingdom.[d]

[21]All King Solomon's drinking cups were of gold, and all the utensils of the Lebanon Forest House were of pure gold: silver did not count for anything in Solomon's days. [22]For the king had a Tarshish[e] fleet on the sea, along with Hiram's fleet. Once every three years, the Tarshish fleet came in, bearing gold and silver, ivory, apes, and peacocks.

[23]King Solomon excelled all the kings on earth in wealth and in wisdom. [24]All the world came to pay homage to Solomon and to listen to the wisdom with which God had endowed him; [25]and each one would bring his tribute—silver and gold objects, robes, weapons and spices, horses and mules—in the amount due each year.

[26]Solomon assembled chariots and horses. He had 1,400 chariots and 12,000 horses, which he stationed[f] in the chariot towns and with the king in Jerusalem. [27]The king made silver as plentiful in Jerusalem as stones, and cedars as plentiful as sycamores in the Shephelah. [28]Solomon's horses were procured from Mizraim[g] and Kue. The king's dealers would buy them from Kue at a fixed price. [29]A chariot imported from Mizraim[g] cost

---

[c] *Others "sandalwood."*
[d] *Or "prince"; like Phoenician* mamlakt.
[e] *Probably a fleet of large ships.*
[f] *So 2 Chron. 1.14; 9.25; Heb. here "led."*
[g] *Usually Egypt, here perhaps Muṣru, a neighbor of Kue (Cilicia).*

600 shekels of silver, and a horse 150; these in turn were exported by them[h] to all the kings of the Hittites and the kings of the Arameans.

11 King Solomon loved many foreign women in addition to Pharaoh's daughter—Moabite, Ammonite, Edomite, Phoenician, and Hittite women, [2]from the nations of which the LORD had said to the Israelites, "None of you shall join them and none of them shall join you,[a] lest they turn your heart away to follow their gods." Such Solomon clung to and loved. [3]He had seven hundred royal wives and three hundred concubines; and his wives turned his heart away. [4]In his old age, his wives turned away Solomon's heart after other gods, and he was not as wholeheartedly devoted to the LORD his God as his father David had been. [5]Solomon followed Ashtoreth the goddess of the Phoenicians, and Milcom the abomination of the Ammonites.

[6]Solomon did what was displeasing to the LORD and did not remain loyal to the LORD like his father David. [7]At that time, Solomon built a shrine for Chemosh the abomination of Moab on the hill near Jerusalem, and one for Molech the abomination of the Ammonites. [8]And he did the same for all his foreign wives who offered and sacrificed to their gods.

[9]The LORD was angry with Solomon, because his heart turned away from the LORD, the God of Israel, who had appeared to him twice [10]and had commanded him about this matter, not to follow other gods; he did not obey what the LORD had commanded. [11]And the LORD said to Solomon, [b]"Because you are guilty of this[b]—you have not kept My covenant and the laws which I enjoined upon you—I will tear the kingdom away from you and give it to one of your servants. [12]But, for the sake of your father David, I will not do it in your lifetime; I will tear it away from your son. [13]However, I will not tear away the whole kingdom; I will give your son one tribe, for the sake of My servant David and for the sake of Jerusalem which I have chosen."

[14]So the LORD raised up an adversary against Solomon, the Edomite Hadad, who was of the royal family of Edom. [15]When David [c]was in[c] Edom, Joab the army commander went up to bury the slain, and he killed every male in Edom; [16]for Joab and all Israel stayed there for six months until he had killed off every male in Edom. [17]But Hadad,[d] together with some Edomite men, servants of his father, escaped and headed for Egypt; Hadad was then a young boy. [18]Setting out from Midian, they came to

---

h *I.e., Solomon's dealers.*

a *I.e., in marriage; cf. Deut. 7.3–4; 23.4, 8–9.*
b-b *Lit. "This is with you."*
c-c *Emendation yields "defeated"; cf. 2 Sam. 8.13.*
d *Heb. Adad.*

Paran and took along with them men from Paran. Thus they came to Egypt, to Pharaoh king of Egypt, who gave him a house, assigned a food allowance to him, and granted him an estate. ¹⁹Pharaoh took a great liking to Hadad and gave him his sister-in-law, the sister of Queen Tahpenes, as wife. ²⁰The sister of Tahpenes bore him a son, Genubath. Tahpenes weaned^e him in Pharaoh's palace, and Genubath remained in Pharaoh's palace among the sons of Pharaoh. ²¹When Hadad heard in Egypt that David had been laid to rest with his fathers and that Joab the army commander was dead, Hadad said to Pharaoh, "Give me leave to go to my own country." ²²Pharaoh replied, "What do you lack with me, that you want to go to your own country?" But he said, "Nevertheless, give me leave to go."

²³Another adversary that God raised up against Solomon^f was Rezon son of Eliada, who had fled from his lord, King Hadadezer of Zobah, ²⁴when David was slaughtering them. He gathered men about him and became captain over a troop; they went to Damascus and settled there, and they established a kingdom in Damascus. ²⁵He was an adversary of Israel all the days of Solomon, adding to the trouble [caused by] Hadad; he repudiated [the authority of] Israel and reigned over Aram.

²⁶Jeroboam son of Nebat, an Ephraimite of Zeredah, the son of a widow whose name was Zeruah, was in Solomon's service; he raised his hand against the king. ²⁷The circumstances under which he raised his hand against the king were as follows: Solomon built the Millo and repaired the breach of the city of his father, David. ²⁸This Jeroboam was an able man, and when Solomon saw that the young man was a capable worker, he appointed him over all the forced labor of the House of Joseph.

²⁹During that time Jeroboam went out of Jerusalem and the prophet Ahijah of Shiloh met him on the way. He had put on a new robe; and when the two were alone in the open country, ³⁰Ahijah took hold of the new robe he was wearing and tore it into twelve pieces. ³¹"Take ten pieces," he said to Jeroboam. "For thus said the LORD, the God of Israel: I am about to tear the kingdom out of Solomon's hands, and I will give you ten tribes. ³²But one tribe shall remain his—for the sake of My servant David and for the sake of Jerusalem, the city that I have chosen out of all the tribes of Israel. ³³For they have forsaken Me; they have worshiped Ashtoreth the goddess of the Phoenicians, Chemosh the god of Moab, and Milcom the god of the Ammonites; they have not walked in My ways, or done what is pleasing to Me, or [kept] My laws and rules, as his

---

^e *Septuagint reads "reared."*
^f *Heb. "him."*

father David did. ³⁴However, I will not take the entire kingdom away from him, but will keep him as ruler as long as he lives for the sake of My servant David whom I chose, and who kept My commandments and My laws. ³⁵But I will take the kingship out of the hands of his son and give it to you—the ten tribes. ³⁶To his son I will give one tribe, so that there may be a lamp for My servant David forever before Me in Jerusalem—the city where I have chosen to establish My name. ³⁷But you have been chosen by Me; reign[g] wherever you wish, and you shall be king over Israel. ³⁸If you heed all that I command you, and walk in My ways, and do what is right in My sight, keeping My laws and commandments as My servant David did, then I will be with you and I will build for you a lasting dynasty as I did for David. I hereby give Israel to you; ³⁹and I will chastise David's descendants for that [sin], though not forever."

⁴⁰Solomon sought to put Jeroboam to death, but Jeroboam promptly fled to King Shishak of Egypt; and he remained in Egypt till the death of Solomon.

⁴¹The other events of Solomon's reign, and all his actions and his wisdom, are recorded in the book of the Annals of Solomon. ⁴²The length of Solomon's reign in Jerusalem, over all Israel, was forty years. ⁴³Solomon slept with his fathers and was buried in the city of his father David; and his son Rehoboam succeeded him as king.

12 Rehoboam went to Shechem, for all Israel had come to Shechem to acclaim him as king. ²Jeroboam son of Nebat learned of it while he was still in Egypt; for Jeroboam had fled from King Solomon, [a-]and had settled in Egypt.[-a] ³They sent for him; and Jeroboam and all the assembly of Israel came and spoke to Rehoboam as follows: ⁴"Your father made our yoke heavy. Now lighten the harsh labor and the heavy yoke which your father laid on us, and we will serve you." ⁵He answered them, "Go away for three days and then come back to me." So the people went away.

⁶King Rehoboam took counsel with the elders who had served his father Solomon during his lifetime. He said, "What answer do you advise [me] to give to this people?" ⁷They answered him, "If you will be a servant to those people today and serve them, and if you respond to them with kind words, they will be your servants always." ⁸But he ignored the advice that the elders gave him, and took counsel with the young men who had grown up with him and were serving him. ⁹"What," he asked, "do you

---

g *I.e., establish your residence.*

a-a *2 Chron. 10.2 reads "So Jeroboam returned from Egypt."*

advise that we reply to the people who said to me, 'Lighten the yoke that your father placed upon us'?" [10]And the young men who had grown up with him answered, "Speak thus to the people who said to you, 'Your father made our yoke heavy, now you make it lighter for us.' Say to them, 'My little finger is thicker than my father's loins. [11]My father imposed a heavy yoke on you, and I will add to your yoke; my father flogged you with whips, but I will flog you with scorpions.' "

[12]Jeroboam and all the people came to Rehoboam on the third day, since the king had told them: "Come back on the third day." [13]The king answered the people harshly, ignoring the advice that the elders had given him. [14]He spoke to them in accordance with the advice of the young men, and said, "My father made your yoke heavy, but I will add to your yoke; my father flogged you with whips, but I will flog you with scorpions." [15](The king did not listen to the people; for the LORD had brought it about in order to fulfill the promise that the LORD had made through Ahijah the Shilonite to Jeroboam son of Nebat.) [16]When all Israel saw that the king had not listened to them, the people answered the king:

"We have no portion in David,
No share in Jesse's son!
To your tents, O Israel!
Now look to your own House, O David."

So the Israelites returned to their homes.[b] [17]But Rehoboam continued to reign over the Israelites who lived in the towns of Judah.

[18]King Rehoboam sent Adoram,[c] who was in charge of the forced labor, but all Israel pelted him to death with stones. Thereupon King Rehoboam hurriedly mounted his chariot and fled to Jerusalem. [19]Thus Israel revolted against the House of David, as is still the case.

[20]When all Israel heard that Jeroboam had returned, they sent messengers and summoned him to the assembly and made him king over all Israel. Only the tribe of Judah remained loyal to the House of David.

[21]On his return to Jerusalem, Rehoboam mustered all the House of Judah and the tribe of Benjamin, 180,000 picked warriors, to fight against the House of Israel, in order to restore the kingship to Rehoboam son of Solomon. [22]But the word of God came to Shemaiah, the man of God: [23]"Say to King Rehoboam son of Solomon of Judah, and to all the House of Judah and Benjamin and the rest of the people: [24]Thus said the LORD: You shall not set out to make war on your kinsmen the Israelites. Let every man return to his home, for this thing has been brought about by

---

b *Lit. "tents."*
c *Elsewhere called Adoniram; cf. 2 Sam. 20.24 and note.*

Me." They heeded the word of the LORD and turned back, in accordance with the word of the LORD.

²⁵Jeroboam fortified Shechem in the hill country of Ephraim and resided there; he moved out from there and fortified Penuel. ²⁶Jeroboam said to himself, "Now the kingdom may well return to the House of David. ²⁷If these people still go up to offer sacrifices at the House of the LORD in Jerusalem, the heart of these people will turn back to their master, King Rehoboam of Judah; they will kill me and go back to King Rehoboam of Judah." ²⁸So the king took counsel and made two golden calves. He said to ᵈ⁻the people,⁻ᵈ "You have been going up to Jerusalem long enough. This is your god, O Israel, who brought you up from the land of Egypt!" ²⁹He set up one in Bethel and placed the other in Dan. ³⁰That proved to be a cause of guilt, for the people went to worship [the calf at Bethel and] the one at Dan. ³¹He also made cult places and appointed priests from the ranks of the people who were not of Levite descent.

³²He stationed at Bethel the priests of the shrines that he had appointed to sacrifice to the calves that he had made. And Jeroboam established a festival on the fifteenth day of the eighth month; in imitation of the festival in Judah, he established one at Bethel, and he ascended the altar [there]. ³³On the fifteenth day of the eighth month—the month in which he had contrived of his own mind to establish a festival for the Israelites—Jeroboam ascended the altar that he had made in Bethel.

13 As he ascended the altar to present an offering, ¹a man of God arrived at Bethel from Judah at the command of the LORD. While Jeroboam was standing on the altarᵃ to present the offering, the man of God, at the command of the LORD, cried out against the altar: ²"O altar, altar! Thus said the LORD: A son shall be born to the House of David, Josiah by name; and he shall slaughter upon you the priests of the shrines who bring offerings upon you. And human bones shall be burned upon you." ³He gave a portent on that day, saying, "Here is the portent that the LORD has decreed: This altar shall break apart, and the ashes on it shall be spilled." ⁴When the king heard what the man of God had proclaimed against the altar in Bethel, Jeroboam stretched out his arm above the altar and cried, "Seize him!" But the arm that he stretched out against him became rigid, and he could not draw it back. ⁵The altar broke apart and its ashes were spilled—the very portent that the man of God had

ᵈ⁻ᵈ *Heb. "them."*

ᵃ *I.e., at the top of the steps or ramp.*

announced at the LORD's command. ⁶Then the king spoke up and said to the man of God, "Please entreat the LORD your God and pray for me that I may be able to draw back my arm." The man of God entreated the LORD and the king was able to draw his arm back; it became as it was before.

⁷The king said to the man of God, "Come with me to my house and have some refreshment; and I shall give you a gift." ⁸But the man of God replied to the king, "Even if you give me half your wealth, I will not go in with you, nor will I eat bread or drink water in this place; ⁹for so I was commanded by the word of the LORD: You shall eat no bread and drink no water, nor shall you go back by the road by which you came." ¹⁰So he left by another road and did not go back by the road on which he had come to Bethel.

¹¹There was an old prophet living in Bethel; and his sons^b came and told him all the things that the man of God had done that day in Bethel [and] the words that he had spoken to the king. When they told it to their father, ¹²their father said to them, "Which road did he leave by?" ^{c-}His sons had seen^{-c} the road taken by the man of God who had come from Judah. ¹³"Saddle the ass for me," he said to his sons. They saddled the ass for him, and he mounted it ¹⁴and rode after the man of God. He came upon him sitting under a terebinth and said to him, "Are you the man of God who came from Judah?" "Yes, I am," he answered. ¹⁵"Come home with me," he said, "and have something to eat." ¹⁶He replied, "I may not go back with you and enter your home; and I may not eat bread or drink water in this place; ¹⁷the order I received by the word of the LORD was: You shall not eat bread or drink water there; nor shall you return by the road on which you came." ¹⁸"I am a prophet, too," said the other, "and an angel said to me by command of the LORD: Bring him back with you to your house, that he may eat bread and drink water." He was lying to him. ¹⁹So he went back with him, and he ate bread and drank water in his house.

²⁰While they were sitting at the table, the word of the LORD came to the prophet who had brought him back. ²¹He cried out to the man of God who had come from Judah: "Thus said the LORD: Because you have flouted the word of the LORD and have not observed what the LORD your God commanded you, ²²but have gone back and eaten bread and drunk water in the place of which He said to you, 'Do not eat bread or

---

b *Heb. "son."*
c-c *Septuagint reads "And his sons showed."*

drink water [there],' your corpse shall not come to the grave of your fathers." 23After he had eaten bread and had drunk, he saddled the ass for him—for the prophet whom he had brought back. 24He set out, and a lion came upon him on the road and killed him. His corpse lay on the road, with the ass standing beside it, and the lion also standing beside the corpse. 25Some men who passed by saw the corpse lying on the road and the lion standing beside the corpse; they went and told it in the town where the old prophet lived. 26And when the prophet who had brought him back from the road heard it, he said, "That is the man of God who flouted the LORD's command; the LORD gave him over to the lion, which mauled him and killed him in accordance with the word that the LORD had spoken to him." 27He said to his sons, "Saddle the ass for me," and they did so. 28He set out and found the corpse lying on the road, with the ass and the lion standing beside the corpse; the lion had not eaten the corpse nor had it mauled the ass. 29The prophet lifted up the corpse of the man of God, laid it on the ass, and brought it back; d-it was brought-d to the town of the old prophet for lamentation and burial. 30He laid the corpse in his own burial place; and they lamented over it, "Alas, my brother!" 31After burying him, he said to his sons, "When I die, bury me in the grave where the man of God lies buried; lay my bones beside his. 32For what he announced by the word of the LORD against the altar in Bethel, and against all the cult places in the towns of Samaria, shall surely come true."

33Even after this incident, Jeroboam did not turn back from his evil way, but kept on appointing priests for the shrines from the ranks of the people. He ordained as priests of the shrines any who so desired. 34Thereby the House of Jeroboam incurred guilt—to their utter annihilation from the face of the earth.

14 At that time, Abijah, a son of Jeroboam, fell sick. 2Jeroboam said to his wife, "Go and disguise yourself, so that you will not be recognized as Jeroboam's wife, and go to Shiloh. The prophet Ahijah lives there, the one who predicted that I would be king over this people. 3Take with you ten loaves, some wafers, and a jug of honey, and go to him; he will tell you what will happen to the boy." 4Jeroboam's wife did so; she left and went to Shiloh and came to the house of Ahijah. Now Ahijah could not

---

d-d Lit. "it came."

see, for his eyes had become sightless with age; ⁵but the LORD had said to Ahijah, "Jeroboam's wife is coming to inquire of you concerning her son, who is sick. Speak to her thus and thus. When she arrives, she will be in disguise."

⁶Ahijah heard the sound of her feet as she came through the door, and he said, "Come in, wife of Jeroboam. Why are you disguised? I have a harsh message for you. ⁷Go tell Jeroboam: Thus said the LORD, the God of Israel: I raised you up from among the people and made you a ruler over My people Israel; ⁸I tore away the kingdom from the House of David and gave it to you. But you have not been like My servant David, who kept My commandments and followed Me with all his heart, doing only what was right in My sight. ⁹You have acted worse than all those who preceded you; you have gone and made for yourself other gods and molten images to vex Me; and Me you have cast behind your back. ¹⁰Therefore I will bring disaster upon the House of Jeroboam and will cut off from Jeroboam every male, ᵃ⁻bond and free,⁻ᵃ in Israel. I will sweep away the House of Jeroboam utterly, as dung is swept away. ¹¹Anyone belonging to Jeroboam who dies in the town shall be devoured by dogs; and anyone who dies in the open country shall be eaten by the birds of the air; for the LORD has spoken. ¹²As for you, go back home; as soon as you set foot in the town, the child will die. ¹³And all Israel shall lament over him and bury him; he alone of Jeroboam's family shall be brought to burial, for in him alone of the House of Jeroboam has some devotion been found to the LORD, the God of Israel. ¹⁴Moreover, the LORD will raise up a king over Israel who will destroy the House of Jeroboam, ᵇ⁻this day and even now.⁻ᵇ

¹⁵"The LORD will strike Israel until it sways like a reed in water. He will uproot Israel from this good land that He gave to their fathers, and will scatter them beyond the Euphrates, because they have provoked the LORD by the sacred posts that they have made for themselves. ¹⁶He will forsake Israel because of the sins that Jeroboam committed and led Israel to commit."

¹⁷Jeroboam's wife got up and left, and she went to Tirzah. As soon as she stepped over the threshold of her house, the child died. ¹⁸They buried him and all Israel lamented over him, in accordance with the word that the LORD had spoken through His servant the prophet Ahijah.

¹⁹The other events of Jeroboam's reign, how he fought and how he ruled, are recorded in the Annals of the Kings of Israel. ²⁰Jeroboam reigned

ᵃ⁻ᵃ *Meaning of Heb. uncertain; possibly "kinsman and friend," cf. 16.11.*
ᵇ⁻ᵇ *Meaning of Heb. uncertain.*

twenty-two years; then he slept with his fathers, and his son Nadab succeeded him as king.

²¹Meanwhile, Rehoboam son of Solomon had become king in Judah. Rehoboam was forty-one years old when he became king, and he reigned seventeen years in Jerusalem—the city the LORD had chosen out of all the tribes of Israel to establish His name there. His mother's name was Naamah the Ammonitess. ²²Judah did what was displeasing to the LORD, and angered Him more than their fathers had done by the sins that they committed. ²³They too built for themselves shrines, pillars, and sacred posts on every high hill and under every leafy tree; ²⁴there were also male prostitutes in the land. [Judah] imitated all the abhorrent practices of the nations that the LORD had dispossessed before the Israelites.

²⁵In the fifth year of King Rehoboam, King Shishak of Egypt marched against Jerusalem ²⁶and carried off the treasures of the House of the LORD and the treasures of the royal palace. He carried off everything; he even carried off all the golden shields that Solomon had made. ²⁷King Rehoboam had bronze shields made instead, and he entrusted them to the officers of the guardᶜ who guarded the entrance to the royal palace. ²⁸Whenever the king went into the House of the LORD, the guards would carry them and then bring them back to the armory of the guards.

²⁹The other events of Rehoboam's reign, and all his actions, are recorded in the Annals of the Kings of Judah. ³⁰There was continual war between Rehoboam and Jeroboam. ³¹Rehoboam slept with his fathers and was buried with his fathers in the City of David; his mother's name was Naamah the Ammonitess. His son Abijam succeeded him as king.

15

In the eighteenth year of King Jeroboam son of Nebat, Abijam became king over Judah. ²He reigned three years in Jerusalem; his mother's name was ᵃ⁻Maacah daughter of Abishalom.⁻ᵃ ³He continued in all the sins that his father before him had committed; he was not wholehearted with the LORD his God, like his father David. ⁴Yet, for the sake of David, the LORD his God gave him a lamp in Jerusalem, by raising up his descendant after him and by preserving Jerusalem. ⁵For David had done what was pleasing to the LORD and never turned throughout his life from all that He had commanded him, except in the matter of Uriah the Hittite. ⁶There was war between Abijamᵇ and Jeroboam all the days

---

ᶜ *Lit. "runners."*

ᵃ⁻ᵃ *2 Chron. 13.2 reads "Micaiah daughter of Uriel of Gibeah"; cf. v. 10 below, where Maacah, daughter of Abishalom, appears as mother of Asa.*
ᵇ *So several mss.; most mss. and the editions read "Rehoboam."*

of his life. 7The other events of Abijam's reign and all his actions are recorded in the Annals of the Kings of Judah. 8Abijam slept with his fathers; he was buried in the City of David, and his son Asa succeeded him as king.

9In the twentieth year of King Jeroboam of Israel, Asa became king over Judah. 10He reigned forty-one years in Jerusalem; his mother's name was Maacah daughter of Abishalom. 11Asa did what was pleasing to the LORD, as his father David had done. 12He expelled the male prostitutes from the land, and he removed all the idols that his ancestors had made. 13He also deposed his mother Maacah from the rank of queen mother, because she had made c-an abominable thing-c for [the goddess] Asherah. Asa cut down her abominable thing and burnt it in the Wadi Kidron. 14The shrines, indeed, were not abolished; however, Asa was whole-hearted with the LORD his God all his life. 15He brought d-into the House of the LORD all the consecrated things of his father and his own consecrated things-d—silver, gold, and utensils.

16There was war between Asa and King Baasha of Israel all their days. 17King Baasha of Israel advanced against Judah, and he fortified Ramah to prevent anyone belonging to King Asa from going out or coming in. 18So Asa took all the silver and gold that remained in the treasuries of the House of the LORD as well as the treasuries of the royal palace, and he entrusted them to his officials. King Asa sent them to King Ben-hadad son of Tabrimmon son of Hezion of Aram, who resided in Damascus, with this message: 19"There is a pact between you and me, and between your father and my father. I herewith send you a gift of silver and gold: Go and break your pact with King Baasha of Israel, so that he may withdraw from me." 20Ben-hadad responded to King Asa's request; he sent his army commanders against the towns of Israel and captured Ijon, Dan, Abel-beth-maacah, and all Chinneroth, as well as all the land of Naphtali. 21When Baasha heard about it, he stopped fortifying Ramah and remained in Tirzah.

22Then King Asa mustered all Judah, with no exemptions; and they carried away the stones and timber with which Baasha had fortified Ramah. With these King Asa fortified Geba of Benjamin, and Mizpah.

23All the other events of Asa's reign, and all his exploits, and all his actions, and the towns that he fortified, are recorded in the Annals of the Kings of Judah. However, in his old age he suffered from a foot ailment. 24Asa slept with his fathers and was buried with his fathers in the city of his father David. His son Jehoshaphat succeeded him as king.

c-c *Exact meaning of Heb. uncertain.*
d-d *So* kethib *and 2 Chron. 15.18.*

²⁵Nadab son of Jeroboam had become king over Israel in the second year of King Asa of Judah, and he reigned over Israel for two years. ²⁶He did what was displeasing to the LORD; he continued in the ways of his father, in the sins which he caused Israel to commit. ²⁷Then Baasha son of Ahijah, of the House of Issachar, conspired against him; and Baasha struck him down at Gibbethon of the Philistines, while Nadab and all Israel were laying siege to Gibbethon. ²⁸Baasha killed him in the third year of King Asa of Judah and became king in his stead. ²⁹As soon as he became king, he struck down all the House of Jeroboam; he did not spare a single soul belonging to Jeroboam until he destroyed it—in accordance with the word that the LORD has spoken through His servant, Ahijah the Shilonite—³⁰because of the sins which Jeroboam committed and which he caused Israel to commit thereby vexing the LORD, the God of Israel.

³¹The other events of Nadab's reign and all his actions are recorded in the Annals of the Kings of Israel.

³²There was war between Asa and King Baasha of Israel all their days. ³³In the third year of King Asa of Judah, Baasha son of Ahijah became king in Tirzah over all Israel—for twenty-four years. ³⁴He did what was displeasing to the LORD; he followed the ways of Jeroboam and the sins which he caused Israel to commit.

16 The word of the LORD came to Jehu son of Hanani against Baasha: ²"Because I lifted you up from the dust and made you a ruler over My people Israel, but you followed the way of Jeroboam and caused My people Israel to sin, vexing Me with their sins—³I am going to sweep away Baasha and his house. I will make your house like the House of Jeroboam son of Nebat. ⁴Anyone belonging to Baasha who dies in the town shall be devoured by dogs, and anyone belonging to him who dies in the open country shall be devoured by the birds of the sky."

⁵The other events of Baasha's reign and his actions and his exploits are recorded in the Annals of the Kings of Israel. ⁶Baasha slept with his fathers and was buried in Tirzah. His son Elah succeeded him as king.

⁷But the word of the LORD had come through the prophet Jehu son of Hanani against Baasha and against his house, that it would fare like the House of Jeroboam, ^awhich he himself had struck down,^{-a} because of all the evil he did which was displeasing to the LORD, vexing him with his deeds.

⁸In the twenty-sixth year of King Asa of Judah, Elah son of Baasha

---

a-a *Syntax of Heb. unclear.*

became king over Israel, at Tirzah—for two years. ⁹His officer Zimri, commander of half the chariotry, committed treason against him while he was at Tirzah drinking himself drunk in the house of Arza, who was in charge of the palace at Tirzah. ¹⁰Zimri entered, struck him down, and killed him; he succeeded him as king in the twenty-seventh year of King Asa of Judah. ¹¹No sooner had he become king and ascended the throne than he struck down all the House of Baasha; he did not leave a single male of his, nor any kinsman or friend. ¹²Thus Zimri destroyed all the House of Baasha, in accordance with the word that the LORD had spoken through the prophet Jehu—¹³because of the sinful acts which Baasha and his son Elah committed, and which they caused Israel to commit, vexing the LORD, the God of Israel, with their false gods. ¹⁴The other events of Elah's reign and all his actions are recorded in the Annals of the Kings of Israel.

¹⁵During the twenty-seventh year of King Asa of Judah, Zimri reigned in Tirzah for seven days. At the time, the troops were encamped at Gibbethon of the Philistines. ¹⁶When the troops who were encamped there learned that Zimri had committed treason and had struck down the king, that very day, in the camp, all Israel acclaimed the army commander Omri king over Israel. ¹⁷Omri and all Israel then withdrew from Gibbethon and laid siege to Tirzah. ¹⁸When Zimri saw that the town was taken, he went into the citadel of the royal palace and burned down the royal palace over himself. And so he died—¹⁹because of the sins which he committed and caused Israel to commit, doing what was displeasing to the LORD and following the ways of Jeroboam. ²⁰The other events of Zimri's reign, and the treason which he committed, are recorded in the Annals of the Kings of Israel.

²¹Then the people of Israel split into two factions: a part of the people followed Tibni son of Ginath to make him king, and the other part followed Omri. ²²Those who followed Omri proved stronger than those who followed Tibni son of Ginath; Tibni died and Omri became king.

²³In the thirty-first year of King Asa of Judah, Omri became king over Israel—for twelve years. He reigned in Tirzah six years. ²⁴Then he bought the hill of Samaria from Shemer for two talents of silver; he built [a town] on the hill and named the town which he built Samaria, after Shemer, the owner of the hill.

²⁵Omri did what was displeasing to the LORD; he was worse than all

who preceded him. ²⁶He followed all the ways of Jeroboam son of Nebat and the sins which he committed and caused Israel to commit, vexing the LORD, the God of Israel, with their futilities. ²⁷The other events of Omri's reign, [and] his actions, and the exploits he performed, are recorded in the Annals of the Kings of Israel. ²⁸Omri slept with his fathers and was buried in Samaria; and his son Ahab succeeded him as king.

²⁹Ahab son of Omri became king over Israel in the thirty-eighth year of King Asa of Judah, and Ahab son of Omri reigned over Israel in Samaria for twenty-two years. ³⁰Ahab son of Omri did what was displeasing to the LORD, more than all who preceded him. ³¹Not content to follow the sins of Jeroboam son of Nebat, he took as wife Jezebel daughter of King Ethbaal of the Phoenicians, and he went and served Baal and worshiped him. ³²He erected an altar to Baal in the temple of Baal which he built in Samaria. ³³Ahab also made a sacred post. Ahab did more to vex the LORD, the God of Israel, than all the kings of Israel who preceded him.

³⁴During his reign, Hiel the Bethelite fortified Jericho. He laid its foundations at the cost of Abiram his first-born, and set its gates in place at the cost of Segub his youngest, in accordance with the words that the LORD had spoken through Joshua son of Nun.ᵇ

17 Elijah the Tishbite, an inhabitant of Gilead, said to Ahab, "As the LORD lives, the God of Israel whom I serve, there will be no dew or rain except at my bidding."

2 The word of the LORD came to him: ³"Leave this place; turn eastward and go into hiding by the Wadi Cherith, which is east of the Jordan. ⁴You will drink from the wadi, and I have commanded the ravens to feed you there." ⁵He proceeded to do as the LORD had bidden: he went, and he stayed by the Wadi Cherith, which is east of the Jordan. ⁶The ravens brought him bread and meat every morning and every evening, and he drank from the wadi.

7 After some time the wadi dried up, because there was no rain in the land. ⁸And the word of the LORD came to him: ⁹"Go at once to Zarephath of Sidon, and stay there; I have designated a widow there to feed you." ¹⁰So he went at once to Zarephath. When he came to the entrance of the town, a widow was there gathering wood. He called out to her, "Please

ᵇ Cf. Josh. 6.26.

bring me a little water in your pitcher, and let me drink." ¹¹As she went to fetch it, he called out to her, "Please bring along a piece of bread for me." ¹²"As the LORD your God lives," she replied, "I have nothing baked, nothing but a handful of flour in a jar and a little oil in a jug. I am just gathering a couple of sticks, so that I can go home and prepare it for me and my son; we shall eat it and then we shall die." ¹³"Don't be afraid," said Elijah to her. "Go and do as you have said; but first make me a small cake from what you have there, and bring it out to me; then make some for yourself and your son. ¹⁴For thus said the LORD, the God of Israel: The jar of flour shall not give out and the jug of oil shall not fail until the day that the LORD sends rain upon the ground." ¹⁵She went and did as Elijah had spoken, and she and he and her household had food for a long time. ¹⁶The jar of flour did not give out, nor did the jug of oil fail, just as the LORD had spoken through Elijah.

¹⁷After a while, the son of the mistress of the house fell sick, and his illness grew worse, until he had no breath left in him. ¹⁸She said to Elijah, "What harm have I done you, O man of God, that you should come here to recall my sin and cause the death of my son?" ¹⁹"Give me the boy," he said to her; and taking him from her arms, he carried him to the upper chamber where he was staying, and laid him down on his own bed. ²⁰He cried out to the LORD and said, "O LORD my God, will You bring calamity upon this widow whose guest I am, and let her son die?" ²¹Then he stretched out over the child three times, and cried out to the LORD, saying, "O LORD my God, let this child's life return to his body!" ²²The LORD heard Elijah's plea; the child's life returned to his body, and he revived. ²³Elijah picked up the child and brought him down from the upper room into the main room, and gave him to his mother. "See," said Elijah, "your son is alive." ²⁴And the woman answered Elijah, "Now I know that you are a man of God and that the word of the LORD is truly in your mouth."

18

Much later, in the third year,ᵃ the word of the LORD came to Elijah: "Go, appear before Ahab; then I will send rain upon the earth." ²Thereupon Elijah set out to appear before Ahab.

The famine was severe in Samaria. ³Ahab had summoned Obadiah, the steward of the palace. (Obadiah revered the LORD greatly. ⁴When Jezebel was killing off the prophets of the LORD, Obadiah had taken a hundred

---

ᵃ *I.e., of the drought; see 17.1.*

prophets and hidden them, fifty to a cave, and provided them with food and drink.) ⁵And Ahab had said to Obadiah, "Go through the land, to all the springs of water and to all the wadis. Perhaps we shall find some grass to keep horses and mules alive, so that we are not left without beasts."

⁶They divided the country between them to explore it, Ahab going alone in one direction and Obadiah going alone in another direction. ⁷Obadiah was on the road, when Elijah suddenly confronted him. [Obadiah] recognized him and flung himself on his face, saying, "Is that you, my lord Elijah?" ⁸"Yes, it is I," he answered. "Go tell your lord: Elijah is here!" ⁹But he said, "What wrong have I done, that you should hand your servant over to Ahab to be killed? ¹⁰As the LORD your God lives, there is no nation or kingdom to which my lord has not sent to look for you; and when they said, 'He is not here,' he made that kingdom or nation swear that you could not be found. ¹¹And now you say, 'Go tell your lord: Elijah is here!' ¹²When I leave you, the spirit of the LORD will carry you off I don't know where; and when I come and tell Ahab and he does not find you, he will kill me. Yet your servant has revered the LORD from my youth. ¹³My lord has surely been told what I did when Jezebel was killing the prophets of the LORD, how I hid a hundred of the prophets of the LORD, fifty men to a cave, and provided them with food and drink. ¹⁴And now you say, 'Go tell your lord: Elijah is here.' Why, he will kill me!"

¹⁵Elijah replied, "As the LORD of Hosts lives, whom I serve, I will appear before him this very day."

¹⁶Obadiah went to find Ahab, and informed him; and Ahab went to meet Elijah. ¹⁷When Ahab caught sight of Elijah, Ahab said to him, "Is that you, you troubler of Israel?" ¹⁸He retorted, "It is not I who have brought trouble on Israel, but you and your father's House, by forsaking the commandments of the LORD and going after the Baalim. ¹⁹Now summon all Israel to join me at Mount Carmel, together with the four hundred and fifty prophets of Baal and the four hundred prophets of Asherah, ᵇ-who eat at Jezebel's table."-ᵇ

²⁰Ahab sent orders to all the Israelites and gathered the prophets at Mount Carmel. ²¹Elijah approached all the people and said, "How long will you keep hopping ᶜ-between two opinions?-ᶜ If the LORD is God, follow Him; and if Baal, follow him!" But the people answered him not

---

ᵇ-ᵇ *I.e., who are maintained by Jezebel.*
ᶜ-ᶜ *Lit. "on the two boughs."*

a word. ²²Then Elijah said to the people, "I am the only prophet of the LORD left, while the prophets of Baal are four hundred and fifty men. ²³Let two young bulls be given to us. Let them choose one bull, cut it up, and lay it on the wood, but let them not apply fire; I will prepare the other bull, and lay it on the wood, and will not apply fire. ²⁴You will then invoke your god by name, and I will invoke the LORD by name; ^{d-}and let us agree:^{-d} the god who responds with fire, that one is God." And all the people answered, "Very good!"

²⁵Elijah said to the prophets of Baal, "Choose one bull and prepare it first, for you are the majority; invoke your god by name, but apply no fire." ²⁶They took the bull that was given them; they prepared it, and invoked Baal by name from morning until noon, shouting, "O Baal, answer us!" But there was no sound, and none who responded; so they performed a hopping dance about the altar that had been set up. ²⁷When noon came, Elijah mocked them, saying, "Shout louder! After all, he is a god. ^{e-}But he may be in conversation, he may be detained, or he may be on a journey,^{-e} or perhaps he is asleep and will wake up." ²⁸So they shouted louder, and gashed themselves with knives and spears, according to their practice, until the blood streamed over them. ²⁹When noon passed, they ^{f-}kept raving^{-f} until the hour of presenting the meal offering. Still there was no sound, and none who responded or heeded.

³⁰Then Elijah said to all the people, "Come closer to me"; and all the people came closer to him. He repaired the damaged altar of the LORD. ³¹Then Elijah took twelve stones, corresponding to the number of the tribes of the sons of Jacob—to whom the word of the LORD had come: "Israel shall be your name"^g—³²and with the stones he built an altar in the name of the LORD. Around the altar he made a trench large enough for two *seah*s of seed.^h ³³He laid out the wood, and he cut up the bull and laid it on the wood. ³⁴And he said, "Fill four jars with water and pour it over the burnt offering and the wood." Then he said, "Do it a second time"; and they did it a second time. "Do it a third time," he said; and they did it a third time. ³⁵The water ran down around the altar, and even the trench was filled with water.

³⁶When it was time to present the meal offering, the prophet Elijah came forward and said, "O LORD, God of Abraham, Isaac, and Israel! Let it be known today that You are God in Israel and that I am Your servant, and that I have done all these things at Your bidding. ³⁷Answer

---

^{d-d} *Lit. "and it shall be."*
^{e-e} *Meaning of Heb. uncertain.*
^{f-f} *Others "prophesied"; see Num. 11.25–26.*
^g *See Gen. 35.10.*
^h *I.e., of an area which would require two* seah*s of seed if sown. Cf. Lev. 27.16; Isa. 5.10.*

me, O LORD, answer me, that this people may know that You, O LORD, are God; c-for You have turned their hearts backward."-c

38Then fire from the LORD descended and consumed the burnt offering, the wood, the stones, and the earth; and it licked up the water that was in the trench. 39When they saw this, all the people flung themselves on their faces and cried out: "The LORD alone is God, The LORD alone is God!"

40Then Elijah said to them, "Seize the prophets of Baal, let not a single one of them get away." They seized them, and Elijah took them down to the Wadi Kishon and slaughtered them there.

41Elijah said to Ahab, "Go up, eat and drink, for there is a rumbling of [approaching] rain," 42and Ahab went up to eat and drink. Elijah meanwhile climbed to the top of Mount Carmel, crouched on the ground, and put his face between his knees. 43And he said to his servant, "Go up and look toward the Sea." He went up and looked and reported, "There is nothing." Seven times [Elijah] said, "Go back," 44and the seventh time, [the servant] reported, "A cloud as small as a man's hand is rising in the west." Then [Elijah] said, "Go say to Ahab, 'Hitch up [your chariot] and go down before the rain stops you.' " 45Meanwhile the sky grew black with clouds; there was wind, and a heavy downpour fell; Ahab mounted his chariot and drove off to Jezreel. 46The hand of the LORD had come upon Elijah. i-He tied up his skirts-i and ran in front of Ahab all the way to Jezreel.

19 When Ahab told Jezebel all that Elijah had done and how he had put all the prophetsa to the sword, 2Jezebel sent a messenger to Elijah, saying, b-"Thus and more may the gods do-b if by this time tomorrow I have not made you like one of them."

3Frightened,c he fled at once for his life. He came to Beer-sheba, which is in Judah, and left his servant there; 4he himself went a day's journey into the wilderness. He came to a broom bush and sat down under it, and prayed that he might die. "Enough!" he cried. "Now, O LORD, take my life, for I am no better than my fathers."

5He lay down and fell asleep under a broom bush. Suddenly an angel touched him and said to him, "Arise and eat." 6He looked about; and there, beside his head, was a cake baked on hot stones and a jar of water!

i-i Lit. "He bound up his loins."

a Of Baal; see 18.40.
b-b A formula of imprecation. Many Heb. mss. and Septuagint add "to me."
c So many Heb. mss. and Septuagint; most mss., and the editions, read "And he saw, and."

He ate and drank, and lay down again. ⁷The angel of the LORD came a second time and touched him and said, "Arise and eat, or the journey will be too much for you." ⁸He arose and ate and drank; and with the strength from that meal he walked forty days and forty nights as far as the mountain of God at Horeb. ⁹There he went into a cave, and there he spent the night.

Then the word of the LORD came to him. He said to him, "Why are you here, Elijah?" ¹⁰He replied, "I am moved by zeal for the LORD, the God of Hosts, for the Israelites have forsaken Your covenant, torn down Your altars, and put Your prophets to the sword. I alone am left, and they are out to take my life." ¹¹"Come out," He called, "and stand on the mountain before the LORD."

And lo, the LORD passed by. There was a great and mighty wind, splitting mountains and shattering rocks by the power of the LORD; but the LORD was not in the wind. After the wind—an earthquake; but the LORD was not in the earthquake. ¹²After the earthquake—fire; but the LORD was not in the fire. And after the fire—a soft murmuring sound.ᵈ ¹³When Elijah heard it, he wrapped his mantle about his face and went out and stood at the entrance of the cave. Then a voice addressed him: "Why are you here, Elijah?" ¹⁴He answered, "I am moved by zeal for the LORD, the God of Hosts; for the Israelites have forsaken Your covenant, torn down Your altars, and have put Your prophets to the sword. I alone am left, and they are out to take my life."

¹⁵The LORD said to him, "Go back by the way you came, [and] on to the wilderness of Damascus. When you get there, anoint Hazael as king of Aram. ¹⁶Also anoint Jehu son of Nimshi as king of Israel, and anoint Elisha son of Shaphat of Abel-meholah to succeed you as prophet. ¹⁷Whoever escapes the sword of Hazael shall be slain by Jehu, and whoever escapes the sword of Jehu shall be slain by Elisha. ¹⁸I will leave in Israel only seven thousand—every knee that has not knelt to Baal and every mouth that has not kissed him."

¹⁹He set out from there and came upon Elisha son of Shaphat as he was plowing. There were twelve yoke of oxen ahead of him, and he was with the twelfth. Elijah came over to him and threw his mantle over him. ²⁰He left the oxen and ran after Elijah, saying: "Let me kiss my father and mother good-by, and I will follow you." And he answered him, "Go back. What have I done to you?"ᵉ ²¹He turned back from him and took the yoke of oxen and slaughtered them; he boiled ᶠtheir meatᶠ with the

---

ᵈ Others "a still, small voice."
ᵉ I.e., I am not stopping you.
ᶠ⁻ᶠ Lit. "them, the flesh."

gear^g of the oxen and gave it to the people, and they ate. Then he arose and followed Elijah and became his attendant.

20 King Ben-hadad of Aram gathered his whole army; thirty-two kings accompanied him with horses and chariots. He advanced against Samaria, laid siege to it, and attacked it. ²And he sent messengers to Ahab inside the city ³to say to him, "Thus said Ben-hadad: Your silver and gold are mine, and your beautiful wives and children are mine." ⁴The king of Israel replied, "As you say, my lord king: I and all I have are yours." ⁵Then the messengers came again and said, "Thus said Ben-hadad: When I sent you the order to give me your silver and gold, and your wives and children, ⁶I meant that tomorrow at this time I will send my servants to you and they will search your house and the houses of your courtiers and seize everything you^a prize and take it away."

⁷Then the king of Israel summoned all the elders of the land, and he said, "See for yourselves how that man is bent on evil! For when he demanded my wives and my children, my silver and my gold, I did not refuse him." ⁸All the elders and all the people said, "Do not obey and do not submit!" ⁹So he said to Ben-hadad's messengers, "Tell my lord the king: All that you first demanded of your servant I shall do, but this thing I cannot do." The messengers went and reported this to him. ¹⁰Thereupon Ben-hadad sent him this message: $^{b\text{-}}$"May the gods do thus to me and even more,$^{\text{-}b}$ if the dust of Samaria will provide even a handful for each of the men who follow me!"

¹¹The king of Israel replied, "Tell him: Let not him who girds on his sword boast like him who ungirds it!"

¹²On hearing this reply—while he and the other kings were drinking together at Succoth—he^c commanded his followers, "Advance!" And they advanced against the city. ¹³Then a certain prophet went up to King Ahab of Israel and said, "Thus said the LORD: Do you see that great host? I will deliver it into your hands today, and you shall know that I am the LORD." ¹⁴"Through whom?" asked Ahab. He answered, "Thus said the LORD: Through the aides of the provincial governors." He asked, "Who shall begin the battle?" And he answered, "You."

¹⁵So he mustered the aides of the provincial governors, 232 strong, and then he mustered all the troops—all the Israelites—7,000 strong. ¹⁶They marched out at noon, while Ben-hadad was drinking himself drunk

---

^{g} *I.e., using it as firewood; cf. 2 Sam. 24.22.*

^{a} *Several ancient versions read "they."*

$^{b\text{-}b}$ *See note at 19.2.*

^{c} *I.e., Ben-hadad.*

at Succoth together with the thirty-two kings allied with him. ¹⁷The aides of the provincial governors rushed out first. Ben-hadad sent [scouts], who told him, "Some men have come out from Samaria." ¹⁸He said, "If they have come out to surrender, take them alive; and if they have come out for battle, take them alive anyhow." ¹⁹But the others—the aides of the provincial governors, with the army behind them—had already rushed out of the city, ²⁰and each of them struck down his opponent. The Arameans fled, and Israel pursued them; but King Ben-hadad of Aram escaped on a horse with other horsemen. ²¹The king of Israel came out and attacked the horses and chariots, and inflicted a great defeat on the Arameans. ²²Then the prophet approached the king of Israel and said to him, "Go, keep up your efforts, and consider well what you must do; for the king of Aram will attack you at the turn of the year."

²³Now the ministers of the king of Aram said to him, "Their God is a God of mountains; that is why they got the better of us. But if we fight them in the plain, we will surely get the better of them. ²⁴Do this: Remove all the kings from their posts and appoint governors in their place. ²⁵Then muster for yourself an army equal to the army you lost, horse for horse and chariot for chariot. And let us fight them in the plain, and we will surely get the better of them." He took their advice and acted accordingly.

²⁶At the turn of the year, Ben-hadad mustered the Arameans and advanced on Aphek to fight Israel. ²⁷Now the Israelites had been mustered and provisioned, and they went out against them; but when the Israelites encamped against them, they looked like two flocksᵈ of goats, while the Arameans covered the land. ²⁸Then the man of God approached and spoke to the king of Israel, "Thus said the LORD: Because the Arameans have said, 'The LORD is a God of mountains, but He is not a God of lowlands,' I will deliver that great host into your hands; and you shall know that I am the LORD."

²⁹For seven days they were encamped opposite each other. On the seventh day, the battle was joined and the Israelites struck down 100,000 Aramean foot soldiers in one day. ³⁰The survivors fled to Aphek, inside the town, and the wall fell on the 27,000 survivors.

Ben-hadad also fled and took refuge inside the town, in an inner chamber. ³¹His ministers said to him, "We have heard that the kings of the House of Israel are magnanimous kings. Let us put sackcloth on our loins and ropes on our heads, and surrender to the king of Israel; perhaps he will spare your life." ³²So they girded sackcloth on their loins and wound

---

ᵈ Meaning of Heb. uncertain.

ropes around their heads, and came to the king of Israel and said, "Your servant Ben-hadad says, 'I beg you, spare my life.'" He replied, "Is he still alive? He is my brother." ³³The men divined his meaning and quickly d-caught the word from him,-d saying, "Yes, Ben-hadad is your brother." "Go, bring him," he said. Ben-hadad came out to him, and he invited him into his chariot. ³⁴Ben-hadad said to him, "I will give back the towns that my father took from your father, and you may set up bazaars for yourself in Damascus as my father did in Samaria." "And I, for my part," [said Ahab,] "will let you go home under these terms." So he made a treaty with him and dismissed him.

³⁵A certain man, a disciple of the prophets, said to another, at the word of the LORD, "Strike me"; but the man refused to strike him. ³⁶He said to him, "Because you have not obeyed the LORD, a lion will strike you dead as soon as you leave me." And when he left, a lion came upon him and killed him. ³⁷Then he met another man and said, "Come, strike me." So the man struck him and wounded him. ³⁸Then the prophet, disguised by a cloth over his eyes, went and waited for the king by the road. ³⁹As the king passed by, he cried out to the king and said, "Your servant went out into the thick of the battle. Suddenly a man came over and brought a man to me, saying, 'Guard this man! If he is missing, it will be your life for his, or you will have to pay a talent of silver.' ⁴⁰While your servant was busy here and there, [the man] got away." The king of Israel responded, "You have your verdict; you pronounced it yourself." ⁴¹Quickly he removed the cloth from his eyes, and the king recognized him as one of the prophets. ⁴²He said to him, "Thus said the LORD: Because you have set free the man whom I doomed, your life shall be forfeit for his life and your people for his people." ⁴³Dispirited and sullen, the king of Israel left for home and came to Samaria.

21 [The following events] occurred sometime afterward: Naboth the Jezreelite owned a vineyard in Jezreel, adjoining the palace of King Ahab of Samaria. ²Ahab said to Naboth, "Give me your vineyard, so that I may have it as a vegetable garden, since it is right next to my palace. I will give you a better vineyard in exchange; or, if you prefer, I will pay you the price in money." ³But Naboth replied, "The LORD forbid that I should give up to you what I have inherited from my fathers!" ⁴Ahab went home dispirited and sullen because of the answer that Naboth the Jezreelite had given him: "I will not give up to you what I have inherited from my fathers!" He lay down on his bed and turned away his face, and he would not eat. ⁵His wife Jezebel came to him and asked him, "Why are you so dispirited that you won't eat?" ⁶So he told her, "I spoke to Naboth the Jezreelite and proposed to him, 'Sell me your vineyard for money, or if you prefer, I'll give you another vineyard in exchange'; but he answered, 'I will not give my vineyard to you.' " ⁷His wife Jezebel said to him, "Now is the time to show yourself king over Israel. Rise and eat something, and be cheerful; I will get the vineyard of Naboth the Jezreelite for you."

⁸So she wrote letters in Ahab's name and sealed them with his seal, and sent the letters to the elders and the nobles who lived in the same town with Naboth. ⁹In the letters she wrote as follows: "Proclaim a fast and seat Naboth at the front of the assembly. ¹⁰And seat two scoundrels opposite him, and let them testify against him: 'You have reviled God and king!' Then take him out and stone him to death."

¹¹His townsmen—the elders and nobles who lived in his town—did as Jezebel had instructed them, just as was written in the letters she had sent them: ¹²They proclaimed a fast and seated Naboth at the front of the assembly. ¹³Then the two scoundrels came and sat down opposite him; and the scoundrels testified against Naboth publicly as follows: "Naboth has reviled God and king." Then they took him outside the town and stoned him to death. ¹⁴Word was sent to Jezebel: "Naboth has been stoned to death." ¹⁵As soon as Jezebel heard that Naboth had been stoned to death, she said to Ahab, "Go and take possession of the vineyard which Naboth the Jezreelite refused to sell you for money; for Naboth is no longer alive, he is dead." ¹⁶When Ahab heard that Naboth was dead, Ahab set out for the vineyard of Naboth the Jezreelite to take possession of it.

¹⁷Then the word of the LORD came to Elijah the Tishbite: ¹⁸"Go down and confront King Ahab of Israel who [resides] in Samaria. He is now in Naboth's vineyard; he has gone down there to take possession of it. ¹⁹Say to him, 'Thus said the LORD: Would you murder and take possession? Thus said the LORD: In the very place where the dogs lapped up Naboth's blood, the dogs will lap up your blood too.' "

²⁰Ahab said to Elijah, "So you have found me, my enemy?" "Yes, I have found you," he replied. "Because you have committed yourself to doing what is evil in the sight of the LORD, ²¹I will bring disaster upon you. I will make a clean sweep of you, I will cut off from Israel every male belonging to Ahab,ᵃ⁻bond and free.⁻ᵃ ²²And I will make your house

---

ᵃ⁻ᵃ *See note at 14.10.*

like the House of Jeroboam son of Nebat and like the House of Baasha son of Ahijah, because of the provocation you have caused by leading Israel to sin. 23And the LORD has also spoken concerning Jezebel: 'The dogs shall devour Jezebel in the field[b] of Jezreel. 24All of Ahab's line who die in the town shall be devoured by dogs, and all who die in the open country shall be devoured by the birds of the sky.' "

(25Indeed, there never was anyone like Ahab, who committed himself to doing what was displeasing to the LORD, at the instigation of his wife Jezebel. 26He acted most abominably, straying after the fetishes just like the Amorites, whom the LORD had dispossessed before the Israelites.)

27When Ahab heard these words, he rent his clothes and put sackcloth on his body. He fasted and lay in sackcloth and walked about subdued. 28Then the word of the LORD came to Elijah the Tishbite: 29"Have you seen how Ahab has humbled himself before Me? Because he has humbled himself before Me, I will not bring the disaster in his lifetime; I will bring the disaster upon his house in his son's time."

22 a-There was a lull of-a three years, with no war between Aram and Israel. 2In the third year, King Jehoshaphat of Judah came to visit the king of Israel. 3The king of Israel said to his courtiers, "You know that Ramoth-gilead belongs to us, and yet we do nothing to recover it from the hands of the king of Aram." 4And he said to Jehoshaphat, "Will you come with me to battle at Ramoth-gilead?" Jehoshaphat answered the king of Israel, "I will do what you do; my troops shall be your troops, my horses shall be your horses." 5But Jehoshaphat said further to the king of Israel, "Please, first inquire of the LORD."

6So the king of Israel gathered the prophets, about four hundred men, and asked them, "Shall I march upon Ramoth-gilead for battle, or shall I not?" "March," they said, "and the LORD will deliver [it] into Your Majesty's hands." 7Then Jehoshaphat asked, "Isn't there another prophet of the LORD here through whom we can inquire?" 8And the king of Israel answered Jehoshaphat, "There is one more man through whom we can inquire of the LORD; but I hate him, because he never prophesies anything good for me, but only misfortune—Micaiah son of Imlah." But King Jehoshaphat said, "Don't say that, Your Majesty." 9So the king of Israel summoned an officer and said, "Bring Micaiah son of Imlah at once."

10The king of Israel and King Jehoshaphat of Judah were seated on

b *So nine Heb. mss. and the parallel 2 Kings 9.36, as well as Targum and other ancient versions. Most texts read here "rampart."*

a-a *Lit. "They remained."*

their thrones, arrayed in their robes, on the threshing floor at the entrance of the gate of Samaria; and all the prophets were prophesying before them. 11Zedekiah son of Chenaanah had provided himself with iron horns; and he said, "Thus said the LORD: With these you shall gore the Arameans till you make an end of them." 12And all the other prophets were prophesying similarly, "March upon Ramoth-gilead and triumph! The LORD will deliver it into Your Majesty's hands."

13The messenger who had gone to summon Micaiah said to him: "Look, the words of the prophets are with one accord favorable to the king. Let your word be like that of the rest of them; speak a favorable word." 14"As the LORD lives," Micaiah answered, "I will speak only what the LORD tells me." 15When he came before the king, the king said to him, "Micaiah, shall we march upon Ramoth-gilead for battle, or shall we not?" He answered him, "March and triumph! The LORD will deliver [it] into Your Majesty's hands." 16The king said to him, "How many times must I adjure you to tell me nothing but the truth in the name of the LORD?" 17Then he said, "I saw all Israel scattered over the hills like sheep without a shepherd; and the LORD said, 'These have no master; let everyone return to his home in safety.'" 18"Didn't I tell you," said the king of Israel to Jehoshaphat, "that he would not prophesy good fortune for me, but only misfortune?" 19But [Micaiah] said, "I call upon you to hear the word of the LORD! I saw the LORD seated upon His throne, with all the host of heaven standing in attendance to the right and to the left of Him. 20The LORD asked, 'Who will entice Ahab so that he will march and fall at Ramoth-gilead?' Then one said thus and another said thus, 21until a certain spirit came forward and stood before the LORD and said, 'I will entice him.' 'How?' the LORD asked him. 22And he replied, 'I will go out and be a lying spirit in the mouth of all his prophets.' Then He said, 'You will entice and you will prevail. Go out and do it.' 23So the LORD has put a lying spirit in the mouth of all these prophets of yours; for the LORD has decreed disaster upon you."

24Thereupon Zedekiah son of Chenaanah stepped up and struck Micaiah on the cheek, and demanded, "Which way did the spirit of the LORD pass from me to speak with you?" 25And Micaiah replied, "You'll find out on the day when you try to hide in the innermost room." 26Then the king of Israel said, "Take Micaiah and turn him over to Amon, the city's governor, and to Prince Joash, 27and say, 'The king's orders are: Put this fellow in prison, and let his fare be scant bread and scant water until I come home safe.' " 28To which Micaiah retorted, "If you ever come home safe, the LORD has not spoken through me." b-He said further, "Listen, all you peoples!"-b

29So the king of Israel and King Jehoshaphat of Judah marched upon Ramoth-gilead. 30The king of Israel said to Jehoshaphat, c-"Disguise yourself and go-c into the battle; but you, wear your robes." So the king of Israel went into the battle disguised. 31Now the king of Aram had instructed his thirty-two chariot officers: "Don't attack anyone, small or great, except the king of Israel." 32So when the chariot officers saw Jehoshaphat, whom they took for the king of Israel, they turned upon him to attack him, and Jehoshaphat cried out. 33And when the chariot officers became aware that he was not the king of Israel, they turned back from pursuing him. 34Then a man drew his bow at random and he hit the king of Israel between d-the plates of-d the armor; and he said to his charioteer, "Turn e-the horses-e around and get me f-behind the lines;-f I'm wounded." 35The battle d-raged all day long,-d and the king remained propped up in the chariot facing Aram; the blood from the wound ran down into the hollow of the chariot, and at dusk he died. 36As the sun was going down, a shout went through the army: "Every man to his own town! Every man to his own district."

37So the king died g-and was brought-g to Samaria. They buried the king in Samaria, 38and they flushed out the chariot at the pool of Samaria. Thus the dogs lapped up his blood and the whores bathed [in it], in accordance with the word that the LORD had spoken.h

39The other events of Ahab's reign, and all his actions—the ivory palace that he built and all the towns that he fortified—are all recorded in the Annals of the Kings of Israel. 40Ahab slept with his fathers, and his son Ahaziah succeeded him as king.

41Jehoshaphat son of Asa had become king of Judah in the fourth year of King Ahab of Israel. 42Jehoshaphat was thirty-five years old when he became king, and he reigned in Jerusalem for twenty-five years. His mother's name was Azubah daughter of Shilhi. 43He followed closely the course of his father Asa and did not deviate from it, doing what was pleasing to

b-b *Perhaps a notation suggesting that Micaiah was identical with Micah, whose prophecies begin,* "Listen, all you peoples," *Mic. 1.2.*
c-c *Targum and Septuagint read,* "I will disguise myself and go."
d-d *Meaning of Heb. uncertain.*
e-e *Lit.* "your hand," *because horses are guided by a pull on the appropriate rein; cf. 2 Kings 9.23.*
f-f *Lit.* "outside the camp."
g-g *Lit.* "he came."
h *Cf. 21.19.*

the LORD. [44]However, the shrines did not cease to function; the people still sacrificed and offered at the shrines. [45]And further, Jehoshaphat submitted to the king of Israel. [46]As for the other events of Jehoshaphat's reign and the valor he displayed in battle, they are recorded in the Annals of the Kings of Judah. ([47]He also stamped out the remaining male prostitutes who had survived in the land from the time of his father Asa.)

[48]There was no king in Edom; i-a viceroy acted as king. [49]Jehoshaphat-i constructed Tarshishj ships to sail to Ophir for gold. But he did not sail because the ships were wrecked at Ezion-geber. [50]Then Ahaziah son of Ahab proposed to Jehoshaphat, "Let my servants sail on the ships with your servants"; but Jehoshaphat would not agree. [51]Jehoshaphat slept with his fathers and was buried with his fathers in the city of his father David, and his son Jehoram succeeded him as king.

[52][Meanwhile,] Ahaziah son of Ahab had become king of Israel, in Samaria, in the seventeenth year of King Jehoshaphat of Judah; he reigned over Israel two years. [53]He did what was displeasing to the LORD, following in the footsteps of his father and his mother, and in those of Jeroboam son of Nebat who had caused Israel to sin. [54]He worshiped Baal and bowed down to him; he vexed the LORD, the God of Israel, just as his father had done.

i-i *Emendation yields "the viceroy of King Jehoshaphat."*
i *See note at 10.22.*

II KINGS

1 After Ahab's death, Moab rebelled against Israel.
²Ahaziah fell through the lattice in his upper chamber at Samaria and was injured. So he sent messengers, whom he instructed: "Go inquire of Baal-zebub, the god of Ekron, whether I shall recover from this injury."
³But an angel of the LORD said to Elijah the Tishbite, "Go and confront the messengers of the king of Samaria and say to them, 'Is there no God in Israel that you go to inquire of Baal-zebub, the god of Ekron? ⁴Assuredly, thus said the LORD: You shall not ᵃ⁻rise from the bed you are lying on,⁻ᵃ but you shall die.' " And Elijah went.

⁵The messengers returned to Ahaziah;ᵇ and he asked, "Why have you come back?" ⁶They answered him, "A man came toward us and said to us, 'Go back to the king who sent you, and say to him: Thus said the LORD: Is there no God in Israel that you must send to inquire of Baal-zebub, the god of Ekron? Assuredly, you shall not rise from the bed you are lying on, but shall die.' " ⁷"What sort of man was it," he asked them, "who came toward you and said these things to you?" ⁸"A hairy man," they replied, "with a leather belt tied around his waist." "That's Elijah the Tishbite!" he said.

⁹Then he sent to him a captain of fifty with his fifty men. He climbed up to him, and found him sitting at the top of a hill. "Man of God," he said to him, "by order of the king, come down!" ¹⁰Elijah replied to the captain of the fifty, "If I am a man of God, let fire come down from heaven and consume you with your fifty men!" And fire came down from heaven and consumed him and his fifty men. ¹¹The king then sent to him another captain with his fifty men; and he ᶜ⁻addressed him⁻ᶜ as follows: "Man of God, by order of the king, come down at once!" ¹²But Elijah answered him, "If I am a man of God, let fire come down from heaven and consume you with your fifty men!" And fire of God came down from heaven and consumed him and his fifty men. ¹³Then he sent a third captain

of fifty with his fifty men. The third captain of fifty climbed to the top, knelt before Elijah, and implored him, saying, "Oh, man of God, please have regard for my life and the lives of these fifty servants of yours! [14]Already fire has come from heaven and consumed the first two captains of fifty and their men;[d] I beg you, have regard for my life!"

[15]Then the angel of the LORD said to Elijah, "Go down with him, do not be afraid of him." So he rose and went down with him to the king. [16]He said to him, "Because you sent messengers to inquire of Baal-zebub the god of Ekron—as if there were no God in Israel whose word you could seek—assuredly, you shall not rise from the bed which you are lying on; but you shall die."

[17]And [Ahaziah] died, according to the word of the LORD that Elijah had spoken. Jehoram[e] succeeded him as king, in the second year of King Jehoram son of Jehoshaphat of Judah, for he had no son. [18]The other events of Ahaziah's reign [and] his actions are recorded in the Annals of the Kings of Israel.

2 When the LORD was about to take Elijah up to heaven in a whirlwind, Elijah and Elisha had set out from Gilgal. [2]Elijah said to Elisha, "Stay here, for the LORD has sent me on to Bethel." "As the LORD lives and as you live," said Elisha, "I will not leave you." So they went down to Bethel. [3]Disciples of the prophets at Bethel came out to Elisha and said to him, "Do you know that the LORD will take your master [a-]away from you[-a] today?" He replied, "I know it, too; be silent."

[4]Then Elijah said to him, "Elisha, stay here, for the LORD has sent me on to Jericho." "As the LORD lives and as you live," said Elisha, "I will not leave you." So they went on to Jericho. [5]The disciples of the prophets who were at Jericho came over to Elisha and said to him, "Do you know that the LORD will take your master [a-]away from you[-a] today?" He replied, "I know it, too; be silent."

[6]Elijah said to him, "Stay here, for the LORD has sent me on to the Jordan." "As the LORD lives and as you live, I will not leave you," he said, and the two of them went on. [7]Fifty men of the disciples of the prophets followed and stood by at a distance from them as the two of them stopped at the Jordan. [8]Thereupon Elijah took his mantle and, rolling it up, he struck the water; it divided to the right and left, so that the two of them crossed over on dry land. [9]As they were crossing, Elijah

---

[d] Lit. "fifties."

[e] Brother of Ahaziah.

[a-a] Lit. "from your head."

said to Elisha, "Tell me, what can I do for you before I am taken from you?" Elisha answered, "Let a ᵇ⁻double portion⁻ᵇ of your spirit pass on to me." ¹⁰"You have asked a difficult thing," he said. "If you see me as I am being taken from you, this will be granted to you; if not, it will not." ¹¹As they kept on walking and talking, a fiery chariot with fiery horses suddenly appeared and separated one from the other; and Elijah went up to heaven in a whirlwind. ¹²Elisha saw it, and he cried out, "Oh, father, father! Israel's chariots and horsemen!" When he could no longer see him, he grasped his garments and rent them in two.

¹³He picked up Elijah's mantle, which had dropped from him; and he went back and stood on the bank of the Jordan. ¹⁴Taking the mantle which had dropped from Elijah, he struck the water and said, "Where is the LORD, the God of Elijah?" As he too struck the water, it parted to the right and to the left, and Elisha crossed over. ¹⁵When the disciples of the prophets at Jericho saw him from a distance, they exclaimed, "The spirit of Elijah has settled on Elisha!" And they went to meet him and bowed low before him to the ground.

¹⁶They said to him, "Your servants have fifty able men with them. Let them go and look for your master; perhaps the spirit of the LORD has carried him off and cast him upon some mountain or into some valley." "Do not send them," he replied. ¹⁷But they kept pressing him for a long time, until he said, "Send them." So they sent out fifty men, who searched for three days but did not find him. ¹⁸They came back to him while he was still in Jericho; and he said to them, "I told you not to go."

¹⁹The men of the town said to Elisha, "Look, the town is a pleasant place to live in, as my lord can see; but the water is bad and the land causes bereavement." ²⁰He responded, "Bring me a new dish and put salt in it." They brought it to him; ²¹he went to the spring and threw salt into it. And he said, "Thus said the LORD: I heal this water; no longer shall death and bereavement come from it!" ²²The water has remained wholesome to this day, in accordance with the word spoken by Elisha.

²³From there he went up to Bethel. As he was going up the road, some little boys came out of the town and jeered at him, saying, "Go away, baldhead! Go away, baldhead!" ²⁴He turned around and looked at them and cursed them in the name of the LORD. Thereupon, two she-bears came out of the woods and mangled forty-two of the children. ²⁵He went on from there to Mount Carmel, and from there he returned to Samaria.

ᵇ⁻ᵇ Lit. "two-thirds"; cf. Zech. 13.8.

3 Jehoram son of Ahab became king of Israel in Samaria in the eighteenth year of King Jehoshaphat of Judah; and he reigned twelve years. ²He did what was displeasing to the LORD, yet not like his father and mother, for he removed the pillars of Baal that his father had made. ³However, he clung to the sins which Jeroboam son of Nebat caused Israel to commit; he did not depart from them.

⁴Now King Mesha of Moab was a sheep breeder; and he used to pay as tribute to the king of Israel ᵃ⁻ᵃ hundred thousand lambs and the wool of a hundred thousand rams.⁻ᵃ ⁵But when Ahab died, the king of Moab rebelled against the king of Israel. ⁶So King Jehoram promptly set out from Samaria and mustered all Israel. ⁷At the same time, he sent this message to King Jehoshaphat of Judah: "The king of Moab has rebelled against me; will you come with me to make war on Moab?" He replied, "I will go. I will do what you do: my troops shall be your troops, my horses shall be your horses." ⁸And he asked, "Which route shall we take?" [Jehoram] replied, "The road through the wilderness of Edom."

⁹So the king of Israel, the king of Judah, and the king of Edom set out, and they marched for seven days until they rounded [the tip of the Dead Sea]; and there was no water left for the army or for the animals that were with them. ¹⁰"Alas!" cried the king of Israel. "The LORD has brought these three kings together only to deliver them into the hands of Moab." ¹¹But Jehoshaphat said, "Isn't there a prophet of the LORD here, through whom we may inquire of the LORD?" One of the courtiers of the king of Israel spoke up and said, "Elisha son of Shaphat, who ᵇ⁻poured water on the hands of⁻ᵇ Elijah, is here." ¹²"The word of the LORD is with him," said Jehoshaphat. So the king of Israel and Jehoshaphat and the king of Edom went down to him. ¹³Elisha said to the king of Israel, "What have you to do with me? Go to your father's prophets or your mother's prophets." But the king of Israel said, "Don't [say that], for the LORD has brought these three kings together only to deliver them into the hands of Moab." ¹⁴"As the LORD of Hosts lives, whom I serve," Elisha answered, "were it not that I respect King Jehoshaphat of Judah, I wouldn't look at you or notice you. ¹⁵Now then, get me a musician."

As the musician played, the hand of the LORD came upon him, ¹⁶and he said, "Thus said the LORD: This wadi shall be full of pools. ¹⁷For thus

---

ᵃ⁻ᵃ *Or "the wool of 100,000 lambs and of 100,000 rams."*
ᵇ⁻ᵇ *I.e., personally attended.*

said the LORD: You shall see no wind, you shall see no rain, and yet the wadi shall be filled with water; and you and your cattle and your pack animals shall drink. ¹⁸And this is but a slight thing in the sight of the LORD, for He will also deliver Moab into your hands. ¹⁹You shall conquer every fortified town and every splendid city; you shall fell every good tree and stop up all wells of water; and every fertile field you shall ruin with stones." ²⁰And in the morning, when it was time to present the meal offering, water suddenly came from the direction of Edom and the land was covered by the water.

²¹Meanwhile, all the Moabites had heard that the kings were advancing to make war on them; ᶜ⁻every man old enough to bear arms⁻ᶜ rallied, and they stationed themselves at the border. ²²Next morning, when they rose, the sun was shining over the water, and from the distance the water appeared to the Moabites as red as blood. ²³"That's blood!" they said. "The kings must have fought among themselves and killed each other. Now to the spoil, Moab!"

²⁴They entered the Israelite camp, and the Israelites arose and attacked the Moabites, who fled before them. ᵈ⁻They advanced, constantly attacking⁻ᵈ the Moabites, ²⁵and they destroyed the towns. Every man threw a stone into each fertile field, so that it was covered over; and they stopped up every spring and felled every fruit tree. ᵉ⁻Only the walls of⁻ᵉ Kir-hareseth were left, and then the slingers surrounded it and attacked it. ²⁶Seeing that the battle was going against him, the king of Moab led an attempt of seven hundred swordsmen to break a way through to the king of Edom;ᶠ but they failed. ²⁷So he took his first-born son, who was to succeed him as king, and offered him up on the wall as a burnt offering. A great wrath came upon Israel, so they withdrew from him and went back to [their own] land.

4 A certain woman, the wife of one of the disciples of the prophets, cried out to Elisha: "Your servant my husband is dead, and you know how your servant revered the LORD. And now a creditor is coming to seize my two children as slaves." ²Elisha said to her, "What can I do for you? Tell me, what have you in the house?" She replied, "Your maidservant has nothing at all in the house, except a jug of oil." ³"Go," he said, "and borrow vessels outside, from all your neighbors, empty vessels,

---

ᶜ⁻ᶜ *Lit. "from all those old enough to gird on a sword."*
ᵈ⁻ᵈ *Meaning of Heb. uncertain.*
ᵉ⁻ᵉ *Lit. "Until the stones in"; meaning of Heb. uncertain.*
ᶠ *Emendation yields "Aram."*

as many as you can. ⁴Then go in and shut the door behind you and your children, and pour [oil] into all those vessels, removing each one as it is filled."

⁵She went away and shut the door behind her and her children. They kept bringing [vessels] to her and she kept pouring. ⁶When the vessels were full, she said to her son, "Bring me another vessel." He answered her, "There are no more vessels"; and the oil stopped. ⁷She came and told the man of God, and he said, "Go sell the oil and pay your debt, and you and your children can live on the rest."

⁸One day Elisha visited Shunem. A wealthy woman lived there, and she urged him to have a meal; and whenever he passed by, he would stop there for a meal. ⁹Once she said to her husband, "I am sure it is a holy man of God who comes this way regularly. ¹⁰Let us make a small ᵃ⁻enclosed upper chamber⁻ᵃ and place a bed, a table, a chair, and a lampstand there for him, so that he can stop there whenever he comes to us." ¹¹One day he came there; he retired to the upper chamber and lay down there. ¹²He said to his servant Gehazi, "Call that Shunammite woman." He called her, and she stood before him. ¹³He said to him, "Tell her, 'You have gone to all this trouble for us. What can we do for you? Can we speak in your behalf to the king or to the army commander?'" She replied, "I live among my own people." ¹⁴"What then can be done for her?" he asked. "The fact is," said Gehazi, "she has no son, and her husband is old." ¹⁵"Call her," he said. He called her, and she stood in the doorway. ¹⁶And Elisha said, "At this season next year, you will be embracing a son." She replied, "Please, my lord, man of God, do not delude your maidservant."

¹⁷The woman conceived and bore a son at the same season the following year, as Elisha had assured her. ¹⁸The child grew up. One day, he went out to his father among the reapers. ¹⁹[Suddenly] he cried to his father, "Oh, my head, my head!" He said to a servant, "Carry him to his mother." ²⁰He picked him up and brought him to his mother. And the child sat on her lap until noon; and he died. ²¹She took him up and laid him on the bed of the man of God, and left him and closed the door. ²²Then she called to her husband: "Please, send me one of the servants and one of the she-asses, so I can hurry to the man of God and back." ²³But he said, "Why are you going to him today? It is neither new moon nor sabbath." She answered, ᵇ⁻"It's all right."⁻ᵇ

ᵃ⁻ᵃ Or "upper wall-chamber"; lit. "an upper chamber of wall(s)."
ᵇ⁻ᵇ Heb. Shalom.

24She had the ass saddled, and said to her servant, "Urge [the beast] on;c see that I don't slow down unless I tell you." 25She went on until she came to the man of God on Mount Carmel. When the man of God saw her from afar, he said to his servant Gehazi, "There is that Shunammite woman. 26Go, hurry toward her and ask her, 'How are you? How is your husband? How is the child?' " "We are well," she replied. 27But when she came up to the man of God on the mountain, she clasped his feet. Gehazi stepped forward to push her away; but the man of God said, "Let her alone, for she is in bitter distress; and the LORD has hidden it from me and has not told me." 28Then she said, "Did I ask my lord for a son? Didn't I say: 'Don't mislead me'?"

29He said to Gehazi, d-"Tie up your skirts,-d take my staff in your hand, and go. If you meet anyone, do not greet him; and if anyone greets you, do not answer him. And place my staff on the face of the boy." 30But the boy's mother said, "As the LORD lives and as you live, I will not leave you!" So he arose and followed her.

31Gehazi had gone on before them and had placed the staff on the boy's face; but there was no sound or response. He turned back to meet him and told him, "The boy has not awakened." 32Elisha came into the house, and there was the boy, laid out dead on his couch. 33He went in, shut the door behind the two of them, and prayed to the LORD. 34Then he mounted [the bed] and placed himself over the child. He put his mouth on its mouth, his eyes on its eyes, and his hands on its hands, as he bent over it. And the body of the child became warm. 35He stepped down, walked once up and down the room, then mounted and bent over him. Thereupon, the boy sneezed seven times, and the boy opened his eyes. 36[Elisha] called Gehazi and said, "Call the Shunammite woman," and he called her. When she came to him, he said, "Pick up your son." 37She came and fell at his feet and bowed low to the ground; then she picked up her son and left.

38Elisha returned to Gilgal. There was a famine in the land, and the disciples of the prophets were sitting before him. He said to his servant, "Set the large pot [on the fire] and cook a stew for the disciples of the prophets." 39So one of them went out into the fields to gather sprouts. He came across a wild vine and picked from it wild gourds, as many as his garment would hold. Then he came back and sliced them into the pot of stew, for they did not know [what they were]; 40and they served it for

---

c *The servant runs behind the donkey and urges it on with a stick.*
d-d *Lit. "Gird your loins"; cf. 1 Kings 18.46.*

the men to eat. While they were still eating of the stew, they began to cry out: "O man of God, there is death in the pot!"ᶜ And they could not eat it. ⁴¹"Fetch some flour," [Elisha] said. He threw it into the pot and said, "Serve it to the people and let them eat." And there was no longer anything harmful in the pot.

⁴²A man came from Baal-shalishah and he brought the man of God some bread of the first reaping—twenty loaves of barley bread, and some fresh grain ᶠin his sack.ᶠ And [Elisha] said, "Give it to the people and let them eat." ⁴³His attendant replied, "How can I set this before a hundred men?" But he said, "Give it to the people and let them eat. For thus said the LORD: They shall eat and have some left over." ⁴⁴So he set it before them; and when they had eaten, they had some left over, as the LORD had said.

5 Naaman, commander of the army of the king of Aram, was important to his lord and high in his favor, for through him the LORD had granted victory to Aram. But the man, though a great warrior, was a leper.ᵃ ²Once, when the Arameans were out raiding, they carried off a young girl from the land of Israel, and she became an attendant to Naaman's wife. ³She said to her mistress, "I wish Master could come before the prophet in Samaria; he would cure him of his leprosy." ⁴[Naaman] went and told his lord just what the girl from the land of Israel had said. ⁵And the king of Aram said, "Go to the king of Israel, and I will send along a letter."

He set out, taking with him ten talents of silver, six thousand shekels of gold, and ten changes of clothing. ⁶He brought the letter to the king of Israel. It read: "Now, when this letter reaches you, know that I have sent my courtier Naaman to you, that you may cure him of his leprosy." ⁷When the king of Israel read the letter, he rent his clothes and cried, "Am I God, to deal death or give life, that this fellow writes to me to cure a man of leprosy? Just see for yourselves that he is seeking a pretext against me!"

⁸When Elisha, the man of God, heard that the king of Israel had rent his clothes, he sent a message to the king: "Why have you rent your clothes? Let him come to me, and he will learn that there is a prophet in Israel."

ᶜ *The wild gourds cause severe cramps.*
ᶠ⁻ᶠ *Or "on the stalk"; perhaps connected with Ugaritic* bṣql.
ᵃ *Cf. note on Lev. 13.3.*

⁹So Naaman came with his horses and chariots and halted at the door of Elisha's house. ¹⁰Elisha sent a messenger to say to him, "Go and bathe seven times in the Jordan, and your flesh shall be restored and you shall be clean." ¹¹But Naaman was angered and walked away. "I thought," he said, "he would surely come out to me, and would stand and invoke the LORD his God by name, and would wave his hand toward the spot, and cure the affected part. ¹²Are not the Amanah and the Pharpar, the rivers of Damascus, better than all the waters of Israel? I could bathe in them and be clean!" And he stalked off in a rage.

¹³But his servants came forward and spoke to him. "Sir,"ᵇ they said, "if the prophet told you to do something difficult, would you not do it? How much more when he has only said to you, 'Bathe and be clean.' " ¹⁴So he went down and immersed himself in the Jordan seven times, as the man of God had bidden; and his flesh became like a little boy's, and he was clean. ¹⁵Returning with his entire retinue to the man of God, he stood before him and exclaimed, "Now I know that there is no God in the whole world except in Israel! So please accept a gift from your servant." ¹⁶But he replied, "As the LORD lives, whom I serve, I will not accept anything." He pressed him to accept, but he refused. ¹⁷And Naaman said, "Then at least let your servant be given two mule-loads of earth; for your servant will never again offer up burnt offering or sacrifice to any god, except the LORD. ¹⁸But may the LORD pardon your servant for this: When my master enters the temple of Rimmon to bow low in worship there, and he is leaning on my arm so that I must bow low in the temple of Rimmon—when I bow low in the temple of Rimmon, may the LORD pardon your servant in this." ¹⁹And he said to him, "Go in peace."

When he had gone some distance from him, ²⁰Gehazi, the attendant of Elisha the man of God, thought: "My master ᶜ⁻has let that Aramean Naaman off without accepting what he brought!⁻ᶜ As the LORD lives, I will run after him and get something from him." ²¹So Gehazi hurried after Naaman. When Naaman saw someone running after him, he alighted from his chariot to meet him and said, "Is all well?" ²²"All is well," he replied. "My master has sent me to say: Two youths, disciples of the prophets, have just come to me from the hill country of Ephraim. Please give them a talent of silver and two changes of clothing." ²³Naaman said, "Please take two talents." He urged him, and he wrapped the two talents of silver in two bags and gave them, along with two changes of clothes,

---

ᵇ Lit. "[My] father."
ᶜ⁻ᶜ Lit. "has prevented that Aramean Naaman from having what he brought accepted."

to two of his servants, who carried them ahead of him. [24]When [Gehazi] arrived at the citadel, he took [the things] from them and deposited them in the house. Then he dismissed the men and they went their way.

[25]He entered and stood before his master; and Elisha said to him, "Where have you been, Gehazi?" He replied, "Your servant has not gone anywhere." [26]Then [Elisha] said to him, "Did not my spirit[d] go along when a man got down from his chariot to meet you? Is this a time to take money in order to buy clothing and olive groves and vineyards, sheep and oxen, and male and female slaves? [27]Surely, the leprosy of Naaman shall cling to you and to your descendants forever." And as [Gehazi] left his presence, he was snow-white with leprosy.

6 The disciples of the prophets said to Elisha, "See, the place where we live under your direction is too cramped for us. [2]Let us go to the Jordan, and let us each get a log there and build quarters there for ourselves to live in." "Do so," he replied. [3]Then one of them said, "Will you please come along with your servants?" "Yes, I will come," he said; [4]and he accompanied them. So they went to the Jordan and cut timber. [5]As one of them was felling a trunk, the iron ax head fell into the water. And he cried aloud, "Alas, master, it was a borrowed one!" [6]"Where did it fall?" asked the man of God. He showed him the spot; and he cut off a stick and threw it in, and he made the ax head float. [7]"Pick it up," he said; so he reached out and took it.

[8]While the king of Aram was waging war against Israel, he took counsel with his officers and said, [a-]"I will encamp[-a] in such and such a place." [9]But the man of God sent word to the king of Israel, "Take care not to pass through that place, for the Arameans are encamped there." [10]So the king of Israel sent word to the place of which the man of God had told him. [b-]Time and again[-b] he alerted [c-]such a place[-c] and took precautions there. [11]Greatly agitated about this matter, the king of Aram summoned his officers and said to them, "Tell me! Who of us is on the side of the king of Israel?" [12]"No one, my lord king," said one of the officers. "Elisha, that prophet in Israel, tells the king of Israel the very words you speak in your bedroom." [13]"Go find out where he is," he said, "so that I can have him seized." It was reported to him that [Elisha] was in Dothan; [14]so he sent horses and chariots there and a strong force. They arrived at night and encircled the town.

---

d Lit. "heart."

a-a Meaning of Heb. uncertain.
b-b Lit. "not once or twice."
c-c Heb. "it."

¹⁵When the attendant of the man of God rose early and went outside, he saw a force, with horses and chariots, surrounding the town. "Alas, master, what shall we do?" his servant asked him. ¹⁶"Have no fear," he replied. "There are more on our side than on theirs." ¹⁷Then Elisha prayed: "LORD, open his eyes and let him see." And the LORD opened the servant's eyes and he saw the hills all around Elisha covered with horses and chariots of fire. ¹⁸[The Arameans] came down against him, and Elisha prayed to the LORD: "Please strike this people with a blinding light." And He struck them with a blinding light, as Elisha had asked.

¹⁹Elisha said to them, "This is not the road, and that is not the town; follow me, and I will lead you to the man you want." And he led them to Samaria. ²⁰When they entered Samaria, Elisha said, "O LORD, open the eyes of these men so that they may see." The LORD opened their eyes and they saw that they were inside Samaria. ²¹When the king of Israel saw them, he said to Elisha, "Father, shall I strike them down?" ²²"No, do not," he replied. "Did you take them captive with your sword and bow that you would strike them down? Rather, set food and drink before them, and let them eat and drink and return to their master." ²³So he prepared a lavish feast for them and, after they had eaten and drunk, he let them go, and they returned to their master. And the Aramean bands stopped invading the land of Israel.

²⁴Sometime later, King Ben-hadad of Aram mustered his entire army and marched upon Samaria and besieged it. ²⁵There was a great famine in Samaria, and the siege continued until a donkey's head sold for eighty [shekels] of silver and a quarter of a *kab* of ᵈ⁻doves' dung⁻ᵈ for five shekels. ²⁶Once, when the king of Israel was walking on the city wall, a woman cried out to him: "Help me, Your Majesty!" ²⁷"Don't [ask me]," he replied. "Let the LORD help you! Where could I get help for you, from the threshing floor or from the winepress? ²⁸But what troubles you?" the king asked her. The woman answered, "That woman said to me, 'Give up your son and we will eat him today; and tomorrow we'll eat my son.' ²⁹So we cooked my son and we ate him. The next day I said to her, 'Give up your son and let's eat him'; but she hid her son." ³⁰When the king heard what the woman said, he rent his clothes; and as he walked along the wall, the people could see that he was wearing sackcloth underneath. ³¹He said, "Thus and more may God do to me if the head of Elisha son of Shaphat remains on ᵉ⁻his shoulders⁻ᵉ today." ³²Now Elisha was sitting at home and the elders were sitting with him. The king had sent

ᵈ⁻ᵈ *Apparently a popular term for "carob pods," as in Akkadian.*
ᵉ⁻ᵉ *Lit. "him."*

ahead one of his men; but before the messenger arrived, [Elisha] said to the elders, "Do you see—that murderer has sent someone to cut off my head! Watch when the messenger comes, and shut the door and hold the door fast against him. No doubt the sound of his master's footsteps will follow."

33While he was still talking to them, the messenger[f] came to him and said, "This calamity is from the LORD. What more can I hope for 7 from the LORD?" 1And Elisha replied, "Hear the word of the LORD. Thus said the LORD: This time tomorrow, a *seah* of choice flour shall sell for a shekel at the gate of Samaria, and two *seah*s of barley for a shekel." 2The aide on whose arm the king was leaning spoke up and said to the man of God, "Even if the LORD were to make windows in the sky, could this come to pass?" And he retorted, "You shall see it with your own eyes, but you shall not eat of it."

3There were four men, lepers, outside the gate. They said to one another, "Why should we sit here waiting for death? 4If we decide to go into the town, what with the famine in the town, we shall die there; and if we just sit here, still we die. Come, let us desert to the Aramean camp. If they let us live, we shall live; and if they put us to death, we shall but die."

5They set out at twilight for the Aramean camp; but when they came to the edge of the Aramean camp, there was no one there. 6For the LORD had caused the Aramean camp to hear a sound of chariots, a sound of horses—the din of a huge army. They said to one another, "The king of Israel must have hired the kings of the Hittites and the kings of Mizraim[a] to attack us!" 7And they fled headlong in the twilight, abandoning their tents and horses and asses—the [entire] camp just as it was—as they fled for their lives.

8When those lepers came to the edge of the camp, they went into one of the tents and ate and drank; then they carried off silver and gold and clothing from there and buried it. They came back and went into another tent, and they carried off what was there and buried it. 9Then they said to one another, "We are not doing right. This is a day of good news, and we are keeping silent! If we wait until the light of morning, we shall incur guilt. Come, let us go and inform the king's palace." 10They went and called out to the gatekeepers of the city and told them, "We have been to the Aramean camp. There is not a soul there, nor any human sound;

f Emendation yields "king."

a Cf. 1 Kings 10.28 and note g there.

but the horses are tethered and the asses are tethered and the tents are undisturbed."

11The gatekeepers called out, and the news was passed on into the king's palace. 12The king rose in the night and said to his courtiers, "I will tell you what the Arameans have done to us. They know that we are starving, so they have gone out of camp and hidden in the fields, thinking: When they come out of the town, we will take them alive and get into the town." 13But one of the courtiers spoke up, "Let a few*b* of the remaining horses that are still here be taken—*c*they are like those that are left here of the whole multitude of Israel, out of the whole multitude of Israel that have perished*c*—and let us send and find out."

14They took two teams*c* of horses and the king sent them after the Aramean army, saying, "Go and find out." 15They followed them as far as the Jordan, and found the entire road full of clothing and gear which the Arameans had thrown away in their haste; and the messengers returned and told the king. 16The people then went out and plundered the Aramean camp. So a *seah* of choice flour sold for a shekel, and two *seah*s of barley for a shekel—as the LORD had spoken.

17Now the king had put the aide on whose arm he leaned in charge of the gate; and he was trampled to death in the gate by the people—just as the man of God had spoken, as he had spoken when the king came down to him. 18For when the man of God said to the king, "This time tomorrow two *seah*s of barley shall sell at the gate of Samaria for a shekel, and a *seah* of choice flour for a shekel," 19the aide answered the man of God and said, "Even if the LORD made windows in the sky, could this come to pass?" And he retorted, "You shall see it with your own eyes, but you shall not eat of it." 20That is exactly what happened to him: The people trampled him to death in the gate.

8 Elisha had said to the woman whose son he revived, "Leave immediately with your family and go sojourn *a*somewhere else;*a* for the LORD has decreed a seven-year famine upon the land, and it has already begun." 2The woman had done as the man of God had spoken; she left with her family and sojourned in the land of the Philistines for seven years. 3At the end of the seven years, the woman returned from the land of the Philistines and went to the king to complain about her house and farm. 4Now the king was talking to Gehazi, the servant of the man of God, and

b *Lit. "five."*
c-c *Meaning of Heb. uncertain.*
a-a *Lit. "wherever you may sojourn."*

he said, "Tell me all the wonderful things that Elisha has done." [5]While he was telling the king how [Elisha] had revived a dead person, in came the woman whose son he had revived, complaining to the king about her house and farm. "My lord king," said Gehazi, "this is the woman and this is her son whom Elisha revived." [6]The king questioned the woman, and she told him [the story]; so the king assigned a eunuch to her and instructed him: "Restore all her property, and all the revenue from her farm from the time she left the country until now."

[7]Elisha arrived in Damascus at a time when King Ben-hadad of Aram was ill. [b-]The king[-b] was told, "The man of God is on his way here," [8]and he said to Hazael, "Take a gift with you and go meet the man of God, and through him inquire of the LORD: Will I recover from this illness?" [9]Hazael went to meet him, taking with him as a gift forty camel-loads of all the bounty of Damascus. He came and stood before him and said, "Your son, King Ben-hadad of Aram, has sent me to you to ask: Will I recover from this illness?" [10]Elisha said to him, "Go and say to him, 'You will recover.' However, the LORD has revealed to me that he will die." [11]The man of God [c-]kept his face expressionless[-c] for a long time; and then he wept. [12]"Why does my lord weep?" asked Hazael. "Because I know," he replied, "what harm you will do to the Israelite people: you will set their fortresses on fire, put their young men to the sword, dash their little ones in pieces, and rip open their pregnant women." [13]"But how," asked Hazael, "can your servant, who is a mere dog, perform such a mighty deed?" Elisha replied, "The LORD has shown me a vision of you as king of Aram." [14]He left Elisha and returned to his master, who asked him, "What did Elisha say to you?" He replied, "He told me that you would recover." [15]The next day, [Hazael] took [c-]a piece of netting,[-c] dipped it in water, and spread it over his face. So [Ben-hadad] died, and Hazael succeeded him as king.

[16]In the fifth year of King Joram[d] son of Ahab of Israel—Jehoshaphat had been king of Judah—Joram son of King Jehoshaphat of Judah became king. [17]He was thirty-two years old when he became king, and he reigned in Jerusalem eight years. [18]He followed the practices of the kings of Israel—whatever the House of Ahab did, for he had married a daughter[e] of Ahab—and he did what was displeasing to the LORD. [19]However, the LORD refrained from destroying Judah, for the sake of His servant David,

b-b Brought up from v. 8 for clarity.
c-c Meaning of Heb. uncertain.
d Throughout this chapter, the name Joram is sometimes written Jehoram.
e Emendation yields "sister"; cf. v. 26.

in accordance with His promise to maintain a lamp for his descendants for all time. [20]During his reign, the Edomites rebelled against Judah's rule and set up a king of their own. [21]Joram crossed over to Zair with all his chariotry. [c-]He arose by night and attacked the Edomites, who were surrounding him and the chariot commanders; but[-c] his troops fled to their homes. [22]Thus Edom fell away from Judah, as is still the case. Libnah likewise fell away at that time.

[23]The other events of Joram's reign, and all his actions, are recorded in the Annals of the Kings of Judah. [24]Joram slept with his fathers and was buried with his fathers in the City of David; his son Ahaziah succeeded him as king.

[25]In the twelfth year of King Joram son of Ahab of Israel, Ahaziah son of Joram became king of Judah. [26]Ahaziah was twenty-two years old when he became king, and he reigned in Jerusalem one year; his mother's name was Athaliah daughter of King Omri of Israel. [27]He walked in the ways of the House of Ahab and did what was displeasing to the LORD, like the House of Ahab, for he was related by marriage to the House of Ahab. [28]He marched with Joram son of Ahab to battle against King Hazael of Aram at Ramoth-gilead, but the Arameans wounded Joram. [29]King Joram retired to Jezreel to recover from the wounds which the Arameans had inflicted upon him at Ramah, when he fought against King Hazael of Aram. And King Ahaziah son of Joram of Judah went down to Jezreel to visit Joram son of Ahab while he was ill.

9 Then the prophet Elisha summoned one of the disciples of the prophets and said to him, "Tie up your skirts,[a] and take along this flask of oil, and go to Ramoth-gilead. [2]When you arrive there, go and see Jehu son of Jehoshaphat son of Nimshi; get him to leave his comrades, and take him into an inner room. [3]Then take the flask of oil and pour some on his head, and say, 'Thus said the LORD: I anoint you king over Israel.' Then open the door and flee without delay."

[4]The young man, the servant of the prophet, went to Ramoth-gilead. [5]When he arrived, the army commanders were sitting together. He said, "Commander, I have a message for you." "For which one of us?" Jehu asked. He answered, "For you, commander." [6]So [Jehu] arose and went inside; and [the disciple] poured the oil on his head, and said to him,

---

[a] See note at 4.29.

"Thus said the LORD, the God of Israel: I anoint you king over the people of the LORD, over Israel. 7You shall strike down the House of Ahab your master; thus will I avenge on Jezebel the blood of My servants the prophets, and the blood of the other servants of the LORD. 8The whole House of Ahab shall perish, and I will cut off every male belonging to Ahab, b-bond and free-b in Israel. 9I will make the House of Ahab like the House of Jeroboam son of Nebat, and like the House of Baasha son of Ahijah. 10The dogs shall devour Jezebel in the field of Jezreel, with none to bury her." Then he opened the door and fled.

11Jehu went out to the other officers of his master, and they asked him, "Is all well? What did that madman come to you for?" He said to them, "You know the man and his ranting!" 12"You're lying," they said. "Tell us [the truth]." Then he replied, "Thus and thus he said: Thus said the LORD: I anoint you king over Israel!" 13Quickly each man took his cloak and placed it under him,c on d-the top step.-d They sounded the horn and proclaimed, "Jehu is king!" 14Thus Jehu son of Jehoshaphat son of Nimshi conspired against Joram.

Joram and all Israel had been defending Ramoth-gilead against King Hazael of Aram, 15but King Joram had gone back to Jezreel to recover from the wounds which the Arameans had inflicted on him in his battle with King Hazael of Aram.

Jehu said, "If such is your wish, allow no one to slip out of the town to go and report this in Jezreel." 16Then Jehu mounted his chariot and drove to Jezreel; for Joram was lying ill there, and King Ahaziah of Judah had gone down to visit Joram. 17The lookout was stationed on the tower in Jezreel, and he saw the troop of Jehu as he approached. He called out, "I see a troop!" Joram said, "Dispatch a horseman to meet them and let him ask: Is all well?" 18The horseman went to meet him, and he said, "The king inquires: Is all well?" Jehu replied, "What concern of yours is it whether all is well? Fall in behind me." The lookout reported: "The messenger has reached them, but has not turned back." 19So he sent out a second horseman. He came to them and said, "Thus says the king: Is all well?" Jehu answered, "What concern of yours is it whether all is well? Fall in behind me." 20And the lookout reported, "The messenger has

b-b *See note at 1 Kings 14.10.*
c *I.e., Jehu.*
d-d *Meaning of Heb. uncertain.*

reached them, but has not turned back. And it looks like the driving of Jehu son of Nimshi, who drives wildly."

21Joram ordered, "Hitch up [the chariot]!" They hitched up his chariot; and King Joram of Israel and King Ahaziah of Judah went out, each in his own chariot, to meet Jehu. They met him at the field of Naboth the Jezreelite. 22When Joram saw Jehu, he asked, "Is all well, Jehu?" But Jehu replied, "How can all be well as long as your mother Jezebel carries on her countless harlotries and sorceries?" 23Thereupon Joram turned his horses^c around and fled, crying out to Ahaziah, "Treason, Ahaziah!" 24But Jehu drew his bow and hit Joram between the shoulders,^f so that the arrow pierced his heart; and he collapsed in his chariot.

25Jehu thereupon ordered his officer Bidkar, "Pick him up and throw him into the field of Naboth the Jezreelite. Remember how you and I were riding side by side behind his father Ahab, when the LORD made this pronouncement about him: 26'I swear, I have taken note of the blood of Naboth and the blood of his sons yesterday—declares the LORD. And I will requite you in this plot—declares the LORD.' So pick him up and throw him unto the plot in accordance with the word of the LORD."

27On seeing this, King Ahaziah of Judah fled along the road to Beth-haggan. Jehu pursued him and said, "Shoot him down too!" [And they shot him] in his chariot at the ascent of Gur, which is near Ibleam. He fled to Megiddo and died there. 28His servants conveyed him in a chariot to Jerusalem, and they buried him in his grave with his fathers, in the City of David. (29Ahaziah had become king over Judah in the eleventh year of Joram son of Ahab.)

30Jehu went on to Jezreel. When Jezebel heard of it, she painted her eyes with kohl and dressed her hair, and she looked out of the window. 31As Jehu entered the gate, she called out, "Is all well, Zimri, murderer of your master?"^g 32He looked up toward the window and said, "Who is on my side, who?" And two or three eunuchs leaned out toward him. 33"Throw her down," he said. They threw her down; and her blood spattered on the wall and on the horses, and they trampled her. 34Then he went inside and ate and drank. And he said, "Attend to that cursed woman and bury her, for she was a king's daughter." 35So they went to bury her; but all they found of her were the skull, the feet, and

---

^c Lit. "hands"; see note at 1 Kings 22.34.
^f Lit. "arms."
^g See 1 Kings 16.8–10.

the hands. ³⁶They came back and reported to him; and he said, "It is just as the LORD spoke through His servant Elijah the Tishbite: The dogs shall devour the flesh of Jezebel in the field of Jezreel; ³⁷and the carcass of Jezebel shall be like dung on the ground, in the field of Jezreel, so that none will be able to say: 'This was Jezebel.' "

10

Ahab had seventy descendants in Samaria. Jehu wrote letters and sent them to Samaria, to the elders and officials of Jezreelᵃ and to the guardians of [the children] of Ahab, as follows: ²"Now, when this letter reaches you—since your master's sons are with you and you also have chariots and horses, and a fortified city and weapons—³select the best and the most suitable of your master's sons and set him on his father's throne, and fight for your master's house." ⁴But they were overcome by fear, for they thought, "If the two kings could not stand up to him, how can we?" ⁵The steward of the palace and the governor of the city and the elders and the guardians sent this message to Jehu: "We are your subjects, and we shall do whatever you tell us to. We shall not proclaim anyone king; do whatever you like."

⁶He wrote them a second time: "If you are on my side and are ready to obey me, take the heads of the attendants of your master's sons and comeᵇ to me in Jezreel tomorrow at this time." Now the princes, seventy in number, were with the notables of the town, who were rearing them. ⁷But when the letter reached them, they took the princes and slaughtered all seventy of them; they put their heads in baskets and sent them to him in Jezreel. ⁸A messenger came and reported to him: "They have brought the heads of the princes." He said, "Pile them up in two heaps at the entrance of the gate before morning." ⁹In the morning he went out and stood there; and he said to all the people, "Are you blameless?ᶜ True, I conspired against my master and killed him; but who struck down all of these? ¹⁰Know, then, that nothing that the LORD has spoken concerning the House of Ahab shall remain unfulfilled, for the LORD has done what he announced through His servant Elijah." ¹¹And Jehu struck down all that were left of the House of Ahab in Jezreel—and all his notables, intimates, and priests—till he left him no survivor.

¹²He then set out for Samaria. On the way, when he was at Beth-eked of the shepherds, ¹³Jehu came upon the kinsmen of King Ahaziah of Judah. "Who are you?" he asked. They replied, "We are the kinsmen of

---

ᵃ Emendation yields "of the city."
ᵇ Targum and Septuagint read "and bring them."
ᶜ Or "You are blameless."

Ahaziah, and we have come to pay our respects to the sons of the king and the sons of the queen mother." 14"Take them alive!" he said. They took them alive and then slaughtered them at the pit of Beth-eked, forty-two of them; he did not spare a single one.

15He went on from there, and he met Jehonadab son of Rechab coming toward him. He greeted him and said to him, "Are you as wholehearted with me as I am with you?" "I am," Jehonadab replied. "If so," [said Jehu,] "give me your hand." He gave him his hand and [Jehu] helped him into the chariot. 16"Come with me," he said, "and see my zeal for the LORD." And he was taken along in the chariot. 17Arriving in Samaria, [Jehu] struck down all the survivors of [the House of] Ahab in Samaria, until he wiped it out, fulfilling the word that the LORD had spoken to Elijah.

18Jehu assembled all the people and said to them, "Ahab served Baal little; Jehu shall serve him much! 19Therefore, summon to me all the prophets of Baal, all his worshipers, and all his priests: let no one fail to come, for I am going to hold a great sacrifice for Baal. Whoever fails to come shall forfeit his life." Jehu was acting with guile in order to exterminate the worshipers of Baal. 20Jehu gave orders to convoke a solemn assembly for Baal, and one was proclaimed. 21Jehu sent word throughout Israel, and all the worshipers of Baal came, not a single one remained behind. They came into the temple of Baal, and the temple of Baal was filled from end to end. 22He said to the man in charge of the wardrobe,d "Bring out the vestments for all the worshipers of Baal"; and he brought vestments out for them. 23Then Jehu and Jehonadab son of Rechab came into the temple of Baal, and they said to the worshipers of Baal, "Search and make sure that there are no worshipers of the LORD among you, but only worshipers of Baal." 24So they went in to offer sacrifices and burnt offerings. But Jehu had stationed eighty of his men outside and had said, "Whoever permits the escape of a single one of the men I commit to your charge shall forfeit life for life."

25When Jehu had finished presenting the burnt offering, he said to the guards and to the officers, "Come in and strike them down; let no man get away!" The guards and the officers struck them down with the sword and left them lying where they were; then they proceeded to the interiore of the temple of Baal. 26They brought out the pillarsf of the temple of Baal and burned them. 27They destroyed the pillarg of Baal, and they tore down the temple of Baal and turned it into latrines, as is still the case.

---

d *Meaning of Heb. uncertain.*
e *Lit. "city."*
f *Emendation yields "sacred posts"; cf. Deut. 12.3.*
g *Emendation yields "altar."*

28Thus Jehu eradicated the Baal from Israel. 29However, Jehu did not turn away from the sinful objects by which Jeroboam son of Nebat had caused Israel to sin, namely, the golden calves at Bethel and at Dan.

30The LORD said to Jehu, "Because you have acted well and done what was pleasing to Me, having carried out all that I desired upon the House of Ahab, four generations of your descendants shall occupy the throne of Israel." 31But Jehu was not careful to follow the Teaching of the LORD, the God of Israel, with all his heart; he did not turn away from the sins that Jeroboam had caused Israel to commit.

32In those days the LORD began to reduce Israel; and Hazael harassed them throughout the territory of Israel 33east of the Jordan, all the land of Gilead—the Gadites, the Reubenites, and the Manassites—from Aroer, by the Wadi Arnon, up to Gilead and Bashan.

34The other events of Jehu's reign, and all his actions, and all his exploits, are recorded in the Annals of the Kings of Israel. 35Jehu slept with his fathers and he was buried in Samaria; he was succeeded as king by his son Jehoahaz. 36Jehu reigned over Israel for twenty-eight years in Samaria.

11 When Athaliah, the mother of Ahaziah, learned that her son was dead, she promptly killed off all who were of royal stock. 2But Jehosheba, daughter of King Joram and sister of Ahaziah, secretly took Ahaziah's son Joash away from among the princes who were being slain, and [put]a him and his nurse in a bedroom. And theyb kept him hidden from Athaliah so that he was not put to death. 3He stayed with her for six years, hidden in the House of the LORD,c while Athaliah reigned over the land.

4In the seventh year, Jehoiada sent for the chiefs of the hundreds of the Caritesd and of the guards, and had them come to him in the House of the LORD. He made a pact with them, exacting an oath from them in the House of the LORD, and he showed them the king's son. 5He instructed them: "This is what you must do: One-third of those who are on duty for the week e-shall maintain guard-e over the royal palace; 6another third shall be [stationed] at the f-Sur Gate;-f and the other third shall be at the gate behind g-the guards; you shall keep guard over the House on every side.-g 7The two divisions of yours who are off duty this week shall keep

a Cf. 2 Chron. 22.11.
b 2 Chron. 22.11 reads "she."
c Jehosheba was the wife of the high priest Jehoiada; cf. 2 Chron. 22.11.
d Perhaps the Cherethites (cf. 2 Sam. 20.23) or the Carians. They were members of the king's bodyguard.
e-e Heb. "and who keep guard."
f-f 2 Chron. 23.5 reads "Foundation Gate."
g-g Meaning of Heb. uncertain.

guard over the House of the LORD for the protection of the king. 8You shall surround the king on every side, every man with his weapons at the ready; and whoever breaks through the ranks shall be killed. Stay close to the king in his comings and goings."

9The chiefs of hundreds did just as Jehoiada ordered: Each took his men—those who were on duty that week and those who were off duty that week—and they presented themselves to Jehoiada the priest. 10The priest gave the chiefs of hundreds King David's spears[h] and quivers that were kept in the House of the LORD. 11The guards, each with his weapons at the ready, stationed themselves—from the south end of the House to the north end of the House, at the altar and the House—to guard the king on every side. 12[Jehoiada] then brought out the king's son, and placed upon him the crown and the insignia.[g] They anointed him and proclaimed him king; they clapped their hands and shouted, "Long live the king!"

13When Athaliah heard the shouting of the guards [and] the people, she came out to the people in the House of the LORD. 14She looked about and saw the king standing by the pillar, as was the custom, the chiefs with their trumpets beside the king, and all the people of the land rejoicing and blowing trumpets. Athaliah rent her garments and cried out, "Treason, treason!" 15Then the priest Jehoiada gave the command to the army officers, the chiefs of hundreds, and said to them, "Take her out [g]-between the ranks-[g] and, if anyone follows her, put him to the sword." For the priest thought: "Let her not be put to death in the House of the LORD." 16They cleared a passageway for her and she entered the royal palace through the horses' entrance: there she was put to death.

17And Jehoiada solemnized the covenant between the LORD, on the one hand, and the king and the people, on the other—as well as between the king and the people—that they should be the people of the LORD. 18Thereupon all the people of the land went to the temple of Baal. They tore it down and smashed its altars and images to bits, and they slew Mattan, the priest of Baal, in front of the altars. [Jehoiada] the priest then placed guards over the House of the LORD. 19He took the chiefs of hundreds, the Carites,[d] the guards, and all the people of the land, and they escorted the king from the House of the LORD into the royal palace

h 2 Chron. 23.9 adds "and shields."

by the gate of the guards. And he ascended the royal throne. 20All the people of the land rejoiced, and the city was quiet. As for Athaliah, she had been put to the sword in the royal palace.

12 Jehoash was seven years old when he became king. 2Jehoash began his reign in the seventh year of Jehu, and he reigned in Jerusalem forty years. His mother's name was Zibiah of Beer-sheba. 3All his days Jehoash did what was pleasing to the LORD, as the priest Jehoiada instructed him. 4The shrines, however, were not removed; the people continued to sacrifice and offer at the shrines.

5Jehoash said to the priests, "All the money, current money, brought into the House of the LORD as sacred donations—a-any money a man may pay as the money equivalent of persons,-a or any other money that a man may be minded to bring to the House of the LORD—6let the priests receive it, each from his benefactor; they, in turn, shall make repairs on the House, wherever damage may be found."

7But in the twenty-third year of King Jehoash, [it was found that] the priests had not made the repairs on the House. 8So King Jehoash summoned the priest Jehoiada and the other priests and said to them, "Why have you not kept the House in repair? Now do not accept money from your benefactors any more, but have it donated for the repair of the House." 9The priests agreed that they would neither accept money from the people nor make repairs on the House.

10And the priest Jehoiada took a chest and bored a hole in its lid. He placed it at the right side of the altar as one entered the House of the LORD, and the priestly guards of the threshold deposited there all the money that was brought into the House of the LORD. 11Whenever they saw that there was much money in the chest, the royal scribe and the high priest would come up and put the money accumulated in the House of the LORD into bags, and they would count it. 12Then they would deliver the money b-that was weighed out-b to the overseers of the work, who were in charge of the House of the LORD. These, in turn, used to pay the carpenters and the laborers who worked on the House of the LORD, 13and the masons and the stonecutters. They also paid for wood and for quarried stone with which to make the repairs on the House of the LORD, and for every other expenditure that had to be made in repairing the

---

a-a *See Lev. 27.2–8.*
b-b *Meaning of Heb. uncertain.*

House. ¹⁴However, no silver bowls and no snuffers, basins, or trumpets—no vessels of gold or silver—were made at the House of the LORD from the money brought into the House of the LORD; ¹⁵this was given only to the overseers of the work for the repair of the House of the LORD. ¹⁶No check was kept on the men to whom the money was delivered to pay the workers; for they dealt honestly.

¹⁷Money brought ᶜ⁻as a guilt offering or as a sin offering⁻ᶜ was not deposited in the House of the LORD; it went to the priests.

¹⁸At that time, King Hazael of Aram came up and attacked Gath and captured it; and Hazael proceeded to march on Jerusalem. ¹⁹Thereupon King Joash of Judah took all the objects that had been consecrated by his fathers, Kings Jehoshaphat, Jehoram, and Ahaziah of Judah, and by himself, and all the gold that there was in the treasuries of the Temple of the LORD and in the royal palace, and he sent them to King Hazael of Aram, who then turned back from his march on Jerusalem.

²⁰The other events of Joash's reign, and all his actions, are recorded in the Annals of the Kings of Judah. ²¹His courtiers formed a conspiracy against Joash and assassinated him at Beth-millo ᵇ⁻that leads down to Silla.⁻ᵇ ²²The courtiers who assassinated him were Jozacar son of Shimeath and Jehozabad son of Shomer. He died and was buried with his fathers in the City of David; and his son Amaziah succeeded him as king.

13

In the twenty-third year of King Joash son of Ahaziah of Judah, Jehoahaz son of Jehu became king over Israel in Samaria—for seventeen years. ²He did what was displeasing to the LORD. He persisted in the sins which Jeroboam son of Nebat had caused Israel to commit; he did not depart from them. ³The LORD was angry with Israel and He repeatedly delivered them into the hands of King Hazael of Aram and into the hands of Ben-hadad son of Hazael. ⁴But Jehoahaz pleaded with the LORD; and the LORD listened to him, for He saw the suffering that the king of Aram inflicted upon Israel. ⁵So the LORD granted Israel a deliverer, and they gained their freedom from Aram; and Israel dwelt in its homes as before. ⁶However, they did not depart from the sins which the House of Jeroboam had caused Israel to commit; they persisted in them. Even the sacred post stood in Samaria. ⁷ᵃIn fact, Jehoahaz was left with a force of only fifty horsemen, ten chariots, and ten thousand foot soldiers; for the

---

ᶜ⁻ᶜ *See Lev. 5.15.*

ᵃ *This verse would read well after v. 3.*

king of Aram had decimated them and trampled them like the dust under his feet.

⁸The other events of Jehoahaz's reign, and all his actions and his exploits, are recorded in the Annals of the Kings of Israel. ⁹Jehoahaz slept with his fathers and he was buried in Samaria; his son Joash succeeded him as king.

¹⁰In the thirty-seventh year of King Joash of Judah, Jehoash son of Jehoahaz became king of Israel in Samaria—for sixteen years. ¹¹He did what was displeasing to the LORD; he did not depart from any of the sins which Jeroboam son of Nebat had caused Israel to commit; he persisted in them.

¹²The other events of Joash's reign, and all his actions, and his exploits in his war with King Amaziah of Judah, are recorded in the Annals of the Kings of Israel. ¹³Joash slept with his fathers and Jeroboam occupied his throne; Joash was buried in Samaria with the kings of Israel.

¹⁴Elisha had been stricken with the illness of which he was to die, and King Joash of Israel went down to see him. He wept over him and cried, "Father, father! ᵇ⁻Israel's chariots and horsemen!"⁻ᵇ ¹⁵Elisha said to him, "Get a bow and arrows"; and he brought him a bow and arrows. ¹⁶Then he said to the king of Israel, "Grasp the bow!" And when he had grasped it, Elisha put his hands over the king's hands. ¹⁷"Open the window toward the east," he said; and he opened it. Elisha said, "Shoot!" and he shot. Then he said, "An arrow of victory for the LORD! An arrow of victory over Aram! You shall rout Aram completely at Aphek." ¹⁸He said, "Now pick up the arrows." And he picked them up. "Strike the ground!" he said to the king of Israel; and he struck three times and stopped. ¹⁹The man of God was angry with him and said to him, ᶜ⁻"If only you had struck⁻ᶜ five or six times! Then you would have annihilated Aram; as it is, you shall defeat Aram only three times."

²⁰Elisha died and he was buried. Now bands of Moabites used to invade the land ᵈ⁻at the coming of every year.⁻ᵈ ²¹Once a man was being buried, when the people caught sight of such a band; so they threw the corpseᵉ into Elisha's grave and ᶠmade off.⁻ᶠ When the [dead] man came in contact with Elisha's bones, he came to life and stood up.

²²King Hazael of Aram had oppressed the Israelites throughout the reign of Jehoahaz. ²³But the LORD was gracious and merciful to them,

ᵇ⁻ᵇ *On Elisha as defender of Israel, see chapters 6—8.*
ᶜ⁻ᶜ *Lit. "to strike."*
ᵈ⁻ᵈ *Meaning of Heb. uncertain; emendation yields "year by year."*
ᵉ *Heb. "the man."*
ᶠ⁻ᶠ *Heb. "he made off."*

and He turned back to them for the sake of His covenant with Abraham, Isaac, and Jacob. He refrained from destroying them, and He still did not cast them out from His presence. ²⁴When King Hazael of Aram died, his son Ben-hadad succeeded him as king; ²⁵and then Jehoash son of Jehoahaz recovered from Ben-hadad son of Hazael the towns which had been taken from his father Jehoahaz in war. Three times Joash defeated him, and he recovered the towns of Israel.

14 In the second year of King Joash son of Joahaz of Israel, Amaziah son of King Joash of Judah became king. ²He was twenty-five years old when he became king, and he reigned twenty-nine years in Jerusalem; his mother's name was Jehoaddan of Jerusalem. ³He did what was pleasing to the LORD, but not like his ancestor David; he did just as his father Joash had done. ⁴However, the shrines were not removed; the people continued to sacrifice and make offerings at the shrines. ⁵Once he had the kingdom firmly in his grasp, he put to death the courtiers who had assassinated his father the king. ⁶But he did not put to death the children of the assassins, in accordance with what is written in the Book of the Teaching of Moses, where the LORD commanded, "Parents shall not be put to death for children, nor children be put to death for parents; a person shall be put to death only for his own crime."ª

⁷He defeated ten thousand Edomites in the Valley of Salt, and he captured Sela in battle and renamed it Joktheel, as is still the case. ⁸Then Amaziah sent envoys to King Jehoash son of Jehoahaz son of Jehu of Israel, with this message: "Come, let us confrontᵇ each other." ⁹King Jehoash of Israel sent back this message to King Amaziah of Judah: "The thistle in Lebanon sent this message to the cedar in Lebanon, 'Give your daughter to my son in marriage.' But a wild beast in Lebanon went by and trampled down the thistle. ¹⁰Because you have defeated Edom, you have become arrogant. Stay home and enjoy your glory, rather than provoke disaster and fall, dragging Judah down with you."

¹¹But Amaziah paid no heed; so King Jehoash of Israel advanced, and he and King Amaziah of Judah confronted each other at Beth-shemesh in Judah. ¹²The Judites were routed by Israel, and they all fled to their homes. ¹³King Jehoash of Israel captured King Amaziah son of Jehoash son of Ahaziah of Judah at Beth-shemesh. He marched on Jerusalem, and he made a breach of four hundred cubits in the wall of Jerusalem, fromᶜ

ª *Deut. 24.16.*
ᵇ *I.e., in battle.*
ᶜ *Heb. "at."*

the Ephraim Gate to the Corner Gate. ¹⁴He carried off all the gold and silver and all the vessels that there were in the House of the LORD and in the treasuries of the royal palace, as well as hostages; and he returned to Samaria.

¹⁵The other events of Jehoash's reign, and all his actions and exploits, and his war with King Amaziah of Judah, are recorded in the Annals of the Kings of Israel. ¹⁶Jehoash slept with his fathers, and was buried in Samaria with the kings of Israel; his son Jeroboam succeeded him as king.

¹⁷King Amaziah son of Joash of Judah lived fifteen years after the death of King Jehoash son of Jehoahaz of Israel. ¹⁸The other events of Amaziah's reign are recorded in the Annals of the Kings of Judah. ¹⁹A conspiracy was formed against him in Jerusalem and he fled to Lachish; but they sent men after him to Lachish, and they killed him there. ²⁰They brought back his body on horses, and he was buried with his fathers in Jerusalem, in the City of David.

²¹Then all the people of Judah took Azariah, who was sixteen years old, and proclaimed him king to succeed his father Amaziah. ²²It was he who rebuilt Elath and restored it to Judah, after King [Amaziah] slept with his fathers.

²³In the fifteenth year of King Amaziah son of Joash of Judah, King Jeroboam son of Joash of Israel became king in Samaria—for forty-one years. ²⁴He did what was displeasing to the LORD; he did not depart from all the sins that Jeroboam son of Nebat had caused Israel to commit. ²⁵It was he who restored the territory of Israel from Lebo-hamath to the sea of the Arabah, in accordance with the promise that the LORD, the God of Israel, had made through His servant, the prophet Jonah son of Amittai from Gath-hepher. ²⁶For the LORD saw the very bitter plight of Israel, with neither ^{d-}bond nor free^{-d} left, and with none to help Israel. ²⁷And the LORD resolved not to blot out the name of Israel from under heaven; and he delivered them through Jeroboam son of Joash.

²⁸The other events of Jeroboam's reign, and all his actions and exploits, how he fought and recovered Damascus and Hamath ^{e-}for Judah in Israel,^{-e} are recorded in the Annals of the Kings of Israel. ²⁹Jeroboam slept with his fathers, the kings of Israel, and his son Zechariah succeeded him as king.

^{d-d} *See note at 1 Kings 14.10.*
^{e-e} *Emendation yields "for Israel."*

15

In the twenty-seventh year of King Jeroboam of Israel, Azariah son of King Amaziah of Judah became king. ²He was sixteen years old when he became king, and he reigned fifty-two years in Jerusalem; his mother's name was Jecoliah of Jerusalem. ³He did what was pleasing to the LORD, just as his father Amaziah had done. ⁴However, the shrines were not removed; the people continued to sacrifice and make offerings at the shrines. ⁵The LORD struck the king with a plague, and he was a leper until the day of his death; he lived ᵃ⁻in isolated quarters,⁻ᵃ while Jotham, the king's son, was in charge of the palace and governed the people of the land.

⁶The other events of Azariah's reign, and all his actions, are recorded in the Annals of the Kings of Judah. ⁷Azariah slept with his fathers, and he was buried with his fathers in the City of David; his son Jotham succeeded him as king.

⁸In the thirty-eighth year of King Azariah of Judah, Zechariah son of Jeroboam became king over Israel in Samaria—for six months. ⁹He did what was displeasing to the LORD, as his fathers had done; he did not depart from the sins which Jeroboam son of Nebat had caused Israel to commit. ¹⁰Shallum son of Jabesh conspired against him and struck him down ᵇ⁻before the people⁻ᵇ and killed him, and succeeded him as king. ¹¹The other events of Zechariah's reign are recorded in the Annals of the Kings of Israel. ¹²This was in accord with the word that the LORD had spoken to Jehu: "Four generations of your descendants shall occupy the throne of Israel." And so it came about.ᶜ

¹³Shallum son of Jabesh became king in the thirty-ninth year of King Uzziah of Judah, and he reigned in Samaria one month. ¹⁴Then Menahem son of Gadi set out from Tirzah and came to Samaria; he attacked Shallum son of Jabesh in Samaria and killed him, and he succeeded him as king. ¹⁵The other events of Shallum's reign, and the conspiracy that he formed, are recorded in the Annals of the Kings of Israel.

¹⁶At that time, ᵃ⁻[marching] from Tirzah,⁻ᵃ Menahem subdued Tiphsah and all who were in it, and its territory; and because it did not surrender, he massacred [its people] and ripped open all its pregnant women.

ᵃ⁻ᵃ *Meaning of Heb. uncertain.*
ᵇ⁻ᵇ *Some Septuagint mss. read "at Ibleam."*
ᶜ *Cf. 10.30.*

¹⁷In the thirty-ninth year of King Azariah of Judah, Menahem son of Gadi became king over Israel in Samaria—for ten years. ¹⁸He did what was displeasing to the LORD; throughout his days he did not depart from the sins which Jeroboam son of Nebat had caused Israel to commit. ¹⁹King Pul of Assyria invaded the land, and Menahem gave Pul a thousand talents of silver that he might support him and strengthen his hold on the kingdom. ²⁰Menahem exacted the money from Israel: every man of means had to pay fifty shekels of silver for the king of Assyria. The king of Assyria withdrew and did not remain in the land. ²¹The other events of Menahem's reign, and all his actions, are recorded in the Annals of the Kings of Israel. ²²Menahem slept with his fathers, and his son Pekahiah succeeded him as king.

²³In the fiftieth year of King Azariah of Judah, Pekahiah son of Menahem became king over Israel in Samaria—for two years. ²⁴He did what was displeasing to the LORD; he did not depart from the sins which Jeroboam son of Nebat had caused Israel to commit. ²⁵His aide, Pekah son of Remaliah, conspired against him and struck him down in the royal palace in Samaria; with him were fifty Gileadites, ᵃ⁻with men from Argob and Arieh;⁻ᵃ and he killed him and succeeded him as king.

²⁶The other events of Pekahiah's reign, and all his actions, are recorded in the Annals of the Kings of Israel.

²⁷In the fifty-second year of King Azariah of Judah, Pekah son of Remaliah became king over Israel and Samaria—for twenty years. ²⁸He did what was displeasing to the LORD; he did not depart from the sins which Jeroboam son of Nebat had caused Israel to commit. ²⁹In the days of King Pekah of Israel, King Tiglath-pileser of Assyria came and captured Ijon, Abel-beth-maacah, Janoah, Kedesh, Hazor—Gilead, Galilee, the entire region of Naphtali; and he deported ᵈ⁻the inhabitants⁻ᵈ to Assyria.

³⁰Hoshea son of Elah conspired against Pekah son of Remaliah, attacked him, and killed him. He succeeded him as king in the twentieth year of Jotham son of Uzziah. ³¹The other events of Pekah's reign, and all his actions, are recorded in the Annals of the Kings of Israel.

³²In the second year of King Pekah son of Remaliah of Israel, Jotham son of King Uzziah of Judah became king. ³³He was twenty-five years old when he became king, and he reigned sixteen years in Jerusalem; his

ᵈ⁻ᵈ *Heb. "them."*

mother's name was Jerusha daughter of Zadok. ³⁴He did what was pleasing to the LORD, just as his father Uzziah had done. ³⁵However, the shrines were not removed; the people continued to sacrifice and make offerings at the shrines. It was he who built the Upper Gate of the House of the LORD. ³⁶The other events of Jotham's reign, and all his actions, are recorded in the Annals of the Kings of Judah. ³⁷In those days, the LORD began to incite King Rezin of Aram and Pekah son of Remaliah against Judah. ³⁸Jotham slept with his fathers, and he was buried with his fathers in the city of his ancestor David; his son Ahaz succeeded him as king.

16 In the seventeenth year of Pekah son of Remaliah, Ahaz son of King Jotham of Judah became king. ²Ahaz was twenty years old when he became king, and he reigned sixteen years in Jerusalem. He did not do what was pleasing to the LORD his God, as his ancestor David had done, ³but followed the ways of the kings of Israel. He even consigned his son to the fire, in the abhorrent fashion of the nations which the LORD had dispossessed before the Israelites. ⁴He sacrificed and made offerings at the shrines, on the hills, and under every leafy tree.

⁵Then King Rezin of Aram and King Pekah son of Remaliah of Israel advanced on Jerusalem for battle. They besieged Ahaz, but could not overcome [him]. ⁶At that time King Rezin of Aram recovered Elath for Aram;ᵃ he drove out the Judites from Elath, and Edomites came to Elath and settled there, as is still the case.

⁷Ahaz sent messengers to King Tiglath-pileser of Assyria to say, "I am your servant and your son; come and deliver me from the hands of the king of Aram and from the hands of the king of Israel, who are attacking me." ⁸Ahaz took the gold and silver that were on hand in the House of the LORD and in the treasuries of the royal palace and sent them as a gift to the king of Assyria. ⁹The king of Assyria responded to his request; the king of Assyria marched against Damascus and captured it. He deported ᵇ-its inhabitants-ᵇ to Kir and put Rezin to death.

¹⁰When King Ahaz went to Damascus to greet King Tiglath-pileser of Assyria, he saw the altar in Damascus. King Ahaz sent the priest Uriah a sketch of the altar and a detailed plan of its construction. ¹¹The priest Uriah did just as King Ahaz had instructed him from Damascus; the priest Uriah built the altar before King Ahaz returned from Damascus. ¹²When

---

ᵃ Emendation yields "Edom."
ᵇ⁻ᵇ Heb. "it."

the king returned from Damascus, and when the king saw the altar, the king drew near the altar, ascended it, 13and offered his burnt offering and meal offering; he poured his libation, and he dashed the blood of his offering of well-being against the altar. 14As for the bronze altar which had been before the LORD, he moved it from its place in front of the Temple, c-between the [new] altar and the House of the LORD,-c and placed it on the north side of the [new] altar. 15And King Ahaz commanded the priest Uriah: "On the greatd altar you shall offer the morning burnt offering and the evening meal offering and the king's burnt offering and his meal offering, with the burnt offerings of all the people of the land, their meal offerings and their libations. And against it you shall dash the blood of all the burnt offerings and all the blood of the sacrifices. And I will decidec about the bronze altar."e 16Uriah did just as King Ahaz commanded.

17King Ahaz cut off the insets—the laver stands—and removed the lavers from them. He also removed the tank from the bronze oxen that supported it and set it on a stone pavement—18on account of the king of Assyria.f He also extended to the House of the LORD c-the sabbath passage that had been built in the palace and the king's outer entrance.-c

19The other events of Ahaz's reign, and his actions, are recorded in the Annals of the Kings of Judah. 20Ahaz slept with his fathers and was buried with his fathers in the City of David; his son Hezekiah succeeded him as king.

17

In the twelfth year of King Ahaz of Judah, Hoshea son of Elah became king over Israel in Samaria—for nine years. 2He did what was displeasing to the LORD, though not as much as the kings of Israel who preceded him. 3King Shalmaneser marched against him, and Hoshea became his vassal and paid him tribute. 4But the king of Assyria caught Hoshea in an act of treachery: he had sent envoys to King So of Egypt, and he had not paid the tribute to the king of Assyria, as in previous years. And the king of Assyria arrested him and put him in prison. 5Then the king of Assyria marched against the whole land; he came to Samaria and besieged it for three years. 6In the ninth year of Hoshea, the king of Assyria captured Samaria. He deported the Israelites to Assyria and settled them in Halah, at the [River] Habor, at the River Gozan, and in the towns of Media.

---

c-c *Meaning of Heb. uncertain.*
d *I.e., the new one.*
e *I.e., the old one, cf. v. 14.*
f *I.e., because of the metal given him in tribute.*

⁷This happened because the Israelites sinned against the LORD their God, who had freed them from the land of Egypt, from the hand of Pharaoh king of Egypt. They worshiped other gods ⁸and followed the customs of the nations which the LORD had dispossessed before the Israelites and the customs which the kings of Israel had practiced. ⁹The Israelites committedᵃ against the LORD their God acts which were not right: They built for themselves shrines in all their settlements, from watchtowers to fortified cities; ¹⁰they set up pillars and sacred posts for themselves on every lofty hill and under every leafy tree; ¹¹and they offered sacrifices there, at all the shrines, like the nations whom the LORD had driven into exile before them. They committed wicked acts to vex the LORD, ¹²and they worshiped fetishes concerning which the LORD had said to them, "You must not do this thing."

¹³The LORD warned Israel and Judah by every prophet [and] every seer, saying: "Turn back from your wicked ways, and observe My commandments and My laws, according to all the Teaching that I commanded your fathers and that I transmitted to you through My servants the prophets." ¹⁴But they did not obey; they stiffened their necks, like their fathers who did not have faith in the LORD their God; ¹⁵they spurned His laws and the covenant that He had made with their fathers, and the warnings He had given them. They went after delusion and were deluded; [they imitated] the nations that were about them, which the LORD had forbidden them to emulate. ¹⁶They rejected all the commandments of the LORD their God; they made molten idols for themselves—two calves—and they made a sacred post and they bowed down to all the host of heaven, and they worshiped Baal. ¹⁷They consigned their sons and daughters to the fire; they practiced augury and divination, and gave themselves over to what was displeasing to the LORD and vexed Him. ¹⁸The LORD was incensed at Israel and He banished them from His presence; none was left but the tribe of Judah alone.

¹⁹Nor did Judah keep the commandments of the LORD their God; they followed the customs that Israel had practiced. ²⁰So the LORD spurned all the offspring of Israel, and He afflicted them and delivered them into the hands of plunderers, and finally He cast them out from His presence.

²¹For Israel broke away from the House of David, and they made Jeroboam son of Nebat king. Jeroboam caused Israel to stray from the LORD and to commit great sin, ²²and the Israelites persisted in all the sins which Jeroboam had committed; they did not depart from them. ²³In

---

ᵃ *Meaning of Heb. uncertain.*

the end, the LORD removed Israel from His presence, as He had warned them through all His servants the prophets. So the Israelites were deported from their land to Assyria, as is still the case.

24The king of Assyria brought [people] from Babylon, Cuthah, Avva, Hamath, and Sepharvaim, and he settled them in the towns of Samaria in place of the Israelites; they took possession of Samaria and dwelt in its towns. 25When they first settled there, they did not worship the LORD; so the LORD sent lions against them which killed some of them. 26They said to the king of Assyria: "The nations which you deported and resettled in the towns of Samaria do not know the rules of the God of the land; therefore He has let lions loose against them which are killing them—for they do not know the rules of the God of the land."

27The king of Assyria gave an order: "Send there one of the priests whom you have deported; let himb go and dwell there, and let him teach them the practices of the God of the land." 28So one of the priests whom they had exiled from Samaria came and settled in Bethel; he taught them how to worship the LORD. 29However, each nation continued to make its own gods and to set them up in the cult places which had been made by the people of Samaria; each nation [set them up] in the towns in which it lived. 30The Babylonians made Succoth-benoth, and the men of Cuth made Nergal, and the men of Hamath made Ashima, 31and the Avvites made Nibhaz and Tartak; and the Sepharvites burned their children [as offerings] to Adrammelech and Anamelech, the gods of Sepharvaim. 32They worshiped the LORD, but they also appointed from their own ranks priests of the shrines, who officiated for them in the cult places. 33They worshiped the LORD, while serving their own gods according to the practices of the nations from which they had been deported. 34To this day, they follow their former practices. They do not worship the LORD [properly]. They do not follow the laws and practices, the Teaching and Instruction that the LORD enjoined upon the descendants of Jacob—who was given the name Israel—35with whom He made a covenant and whom He commanded: "You shall worship no other gods; you shall not bow down to them nor serve them nor sacrifice to them. 36You must worship only the LORD your God, who brought you out of the land of Egypt with great might and with an outstretched arm: to Him alone shall you bow down and to Him alone shall you sacrifice. 37You shall observe faithfully, all your days, the laws and the practices; the Teaching and Instruction that

b Heb. "them."

I[c] wrote down for you; do not worship other gods. [38]Do not forget the covenant that I made with you; do not worship other gods. [39]Worship only the LORD your God, and He will save you from the hands of all your enemies." [40]But they did not obey; they continued their former practices. [41]Those nations worshiped the LORD, but they also served their idols. To this day their children and their children's children do as their ancestors did.

18 In the third year of King Hoshea son of Elah of Israel, Hezekiah son of King Ahaz of Judah became king. [2]He was twenty-five years old when he became king, and he reigned in Jerusalem twenty-nine years; his mother's name was Abi[a] daughter of Zechariah. [3]He did what was pleasing to the LORD, just as his father David had done. [4]He abolished the shrines and smashed the pillars and cut down the sacred post. He also broke into pieces the bronze serpent that Moses had made, for until that time the Israelites had been offering sacrifices to it; it was called Nehushtan. [5]He trusted only in the LORD the God of Israel; there was none like him among all the kings of Judah after him, nor among those before him. [6]He clung to the LORD; he did not turn away from following Him, but kept the commandments that the LORD had given to Moses. [7]And the LORD was always with him; he was successful wherever he turned. He rebelled against the king of Assyria and would not serve him. [8]He overran Philistia as far as Gaza and its border areas, from watchtower to fortified town.

[9]In the fourth year of King Hezekiah, which was the seventh year of King Hoshea son of Elah of Israel, King Shalmaneser of Assyria marched against Samaria and besieged it, [10]and he[b] captured it at the end of three years. In the sixth year of Hezekiah, which was the ninth year of King Hoshea of Israel, Samaria was captured; [11]and the king of Assyria deported the Israelites to Assyria. He [c-]settled them in-[c] Halah, along the Habor [and] the River Gozan, and in the towns of Media. [12][This happened] because they did not obey the LORD their God; they transgressed His covenant—all that Moses the servant of the LORD had commanded. They did not obey and they did not fulfill it.

[13]In the fourteenth year of King Hezekiah, King Sennacherib of Assyria marched against all the fortified towns of Judah and seized them. [14]King

---

[c] *Heb. "He."*

[a] *2 Chron. 29.1 reads "Abijah."*

[b] *So some mss. and ancient versions; most mss. and editions read "they."*

[c-c] *Lit. "led them to."*

Hezekiah sent this message to the king of Assyria at Lachish: "I have done wrong; withdraw from me; and I shall bear whatever you impose on me." So the king of Assyria imposed upon King Hezekiah of Judah a payment of three hundred talents of silver and thirty talents of gold. 15Hezekiah gave him all the silver that was on hand in the House of the LORD and in the treasuries of the palace. 16At that time Hezekiah cut down the doors and the doorposts^d of the Temple of the LORD, which King Hezekiah had overlaid [with gold], and gave them to the king of Assyria.

17But the king of Assyria sent ^{e-}the Tartan, the Rabsaris, and the Rabshakeh^{-e} from Lachish with a large force to King Hezekiah in Jerusalem. They marched up to Jerusalem; and when they arrived, they took up a position near the conduit of the Upper Pool, by the road of the Fuller's Field. 18They summoned the king; and Eliakim son of Hilkiah, who was in charge of the palace, Shebna the scribe, and Joah son of Asaph the recorder went out to them.

19The Rabshakeh said to them, "You tell Hezekiah: Thus said the Great King, the King of Assyria: What makes you so confident? 20You must think that mere talk is counsel and valor for war! Look, on whom are you relying, that you have rebelled against me? 21You rely, of all things, on Egypt, that splintered reed of a staff, which enters and punctures the palm of anyone who leans on it! That's what Pharaoh king of Egypt is like to all who rely on him. 22And if you tell me that you are relying on the LORD your God, He is the very one whose shrines and altars Hezekiah did away with, telling Judah and Jerusalem, 'You must worship only at this altar in Jerusalem.' 23Come now, make this wager with my master, the king of Assyria: I'll give you two thousand horses if you can produce riders to mount them. 24So how could you refuse anything even to the deputy of one of my master's lesser servants, relying on Egypt for chariots and horsemen? 25And do you think I have marched against this land to destroy it without the LORD? The LORD Himself told me: Go up against that land and destroy it."

26Eliakim son of Hilkiah, Shebna, and Joah replied to the Rabshakeh, "Please, speak to your servants in Aramaic, for we understand it; do not speak to us in Judean in the hearing of the people on the wall." 27But the Rabshakeh answered them, "Was it to your master and to you that my master sent me to speak those words? It was precisely to the men who are sitting on the wall—who will have to eat their dung and drink their

---

^d *Meaning of Heb. uncertain.*
^{e-e} *Assyrian titles.*

urine with you." 28And the Rabshakeh stood and called out in a loud voice in Judean: "Hear the words of the Great King, the King of Assyria. 29Thus said the king: Don't let Hezekiah deceive you, for he will not be able to deliver you from my[f] hands. 30Don't let Hezekiah make you rely on the LORD, saying: The LORD will surely save us: this city will not fall into the hands of the king of Assyria. 31Don't listen to Hezekiah. For thus said the king of Assyria: Make your peace with me and come out to me,[g] so that you may all eat from your vines and your fig trees and drink water from your cisterns, 32until I come and take you away to a land like your own, a land of grain [fields] and vineyards, of bread and wine, of olive oil and honey, so that you may live and not die. Don't listen to Hezekiah, who misleads you by saying, 'The LORD will save us.' 33Did any of the gods of other nations save his land from the king of Assyria? 34Where were the gods of Hamath and Arpad? Where were the gods of Sepharvaim, Hena, and Ivvah? [And] did they[h] save Samaria from me? 35Which among all the gods of [those] countries saved their countries from me, that the LORD should save Jerusalem from me?" 36But the people were silent and did not say a word in reply; for the king's order was: "Do not answer him." 37And so Eliakim son of Hilkiah, who was in charge of the palace, Shebna the scribe, and Joah son of Asaph the recorder came to Hezekiah with their clothes rent, and they reported to him what the Rabshakeh had said.

19

When King Hezekiah heard this, he rent his clothes, and covered himself with sackcloth, and went into the House of the LORD. 2He also sent Eliakim, who was in charge of the palace, Shebna the scribe, and the senior priests, covered with sackcloth, to the prophet Isaiah son of Amoz. 3They said to him, "Thus said Hezekiah: This day is a day of distress, of chastisement, and of disgrace. a-The babes have reached the birthstool, but the strength to give birth is lacking.-a 4Perhaps the LORD your God will take note of all the words of the Rabshakeh, whom his master the king of Assyria has sent to blaspheme the living God, and will mete out judgment for the words that the LORD your God has heard—if you will offer up prayer for the surviving remnant."

5When King Hezekiah's ministers came to Isaiah, 6Isaiah said to them, "Tell your master as follows: Thus said the LORD: Do not be frightened

---

f So several mss. and ancient versions; most mss. and editions read "his."
g I.e., to my representative the Rabshakeh.
h I.e., the gods of Samaria.
a-a I.e., the situation is desperate and we are at a loss.

by the words of blasphemy against Me that you have heard from the minions of the king of Assyria. [7]I will delude[b] him; he will hear a rumor and return to his land, and I will make him fall by the sword in his land."

[8]The Rabshakeh, meanwhile, heard that [the king] had left Lachish; he turned back and found the king of Assyria attacking Libnah. [9]But [the king of Assyria] learned that King Tirhakah of Nubia had come out to fight him; so he again sent messengers to Hezekiah, saying, [10]"Tell this to King Hezekiah of Judah: Do not let your God, on whom you are relying, mislead you into thinking that Jerusalem will not be delivered into the hands of the king of Assyria. [11]You yourself have heard what the kings of Assyria have done to all the lands, how they have annihilated them; and can you escape? [12]Were the nations that my predecessors[c] destroyed—Gozan, Haran, Rezeph, and the Beth-edenites in Telassar—saved by their gods? [13]Where is the king of Hamath? And the king of Arpad? And the kings of Lair, Sepharvaim, Hena, and Ivvah?"

[14]Hezekiah took the letter from the messengers and read it. Hezekiah then went up to the House of the LORD and spread it out before the LORD. [15]And Hezekiah prayed to the LORD and said, "O LORD of Hosts, Enthroned on the Cherubim! You alone are God of all the kingdoms of the earth. You made the heavens and the earth. [16]O LORD, incline Your ear and hear; open Your eyes and see. Hear the words that Sennacherib has sent to blaspheme the living God! [17]True, O LORD, the kings of Assyria have annihilated the nations and their lands, [18]and have committed their gods to the flames and have destroyed them; for they are not gods, but man's handiwork of wood and stone. [19]But now, O LORD our God, deliver us from his hands, and let all the kingdoms of the earth know that You alone, O LORD, are God."

[20]Then Isaiah son of Amoz sent this message to Hezekiah: "Thus said the LORD, the God of Israel: I have heard the prayer you have offered to Me concerning King Sennacherib of Assyria. [21]This is the word that the LORD has spoken concerning him:

> "Fair Maiden Zion despises you,
> She mocks at you;
> Fair Jerusalem shakes
> Her head at you.
> [22]Whom have you blasphemed and reviled?
> Against whom made loud your voice

b Lit. "put a spirit in."
c Lit. "fathers."

And haughtily raised your eyes?
Against the Holy One of Israel!
²³Through your envoys you have blasphemed my Lord.
Because you thought,
'Thanks to my vast chariotry,
It is I who have climbed the highest mountains,
To the remotest parts of the Lebanon,
And have cut down its loftiest cedars,
Its choicest cypresses,
And have reached its ᵈ-remotest lodge,-ᵈ
ᵉ-Its densest forest.-ᵉ
²⁴It is I who have drawnᶠ and drunk the waters of strangers;
I have dried up with the soles of my feet
All the streams of Egypt.'
²⁵Have you not heard? Of old
I planned that very thing,
I designed it long ago,
And now have fulfilled it.
And it has come to pass,
Laying waste fortified towns
In desolate heaps.
²⁶Their inhabitants are helpless,
Dismayed and shamed.
They were but grass of the field
And green herbage,
Grass of the roofs that is blasted
Before the ᵍ-standing grain.-ᵍ
²⁷I know your stayings
And your goings and comings,
And how you have raged against Me.
²⁸Because you have raged against Me,
And your tumult has reached My ears,
I will place My hook in your nose
And My bit between your jaws;
And I will make you go back by the road
By which you came.

²⁹"And this is the sign for you:ʰ This year you eat what grows of itself,

ᵈ⁻ᵈ *Isa. 37.24 reads "highest peak."*
ᵉ⁻ᵉ *Lit. "Its farmland forest"; exact meaning of Heb. uncertain.*
ᶠ *Or "dug"; meaning of Heb. uncertain.*
ᵍ⁻ᵍ *Emendation yields "east wind"; see note at Isa. 37.27.*
ʰ *I.e., Hezekiah.*

and the next year what springs from that; and in the third year, sow and reap, and plant vineyards and eat their fruit. ³⁰And the survivors of the House of Judah that have escaped shall regenerate its stock below and produce boughs above.

³¹For a remnant shall come forth from Jerusalem,
Survivors from Mount Zion.
The zeal of the LORD of Hosts
Shall bring this to pass.

³²Assuredly, thus said the LORD concerning the king of Assyria:

He shall not enter this city:
He shall not shoot an arrow at it,
Or advance upon it with a shield,
Or pile up a siege mound against it.
³³He shall go back
By the way he came;
He shall not enter this city

—declares the LORD.
³⁴I will protect and save this city for My sake,
And for the sake of My servant David."

³⁵That night an angel of the LORD went out and struck down one hundred and eighty-five thousand in the Assyrian camp, and the following morning they were all dead corpses.

³⁶So King Sennacherib of Assyria broke camp and retreated, and stayed in Nineveh. ³⁷While he was worshiping in the temple of his god Nisroch, his sons Adrammelech and Sarezer struck him down with the sword. They fled to the land of Ararat, and his son Esarhaddon succeeded him as king.

20 In those days Hezekiah fell dangerously ill. The prophet Isaiah son of Amoz came and said to him, "Thus said the LORD: Set your affairs in order, for you are going to die; you will not get well." ²Thereupon Hezekiah turned his face to the wall and prayed to the LORD. He said, ³"Please, O LORD, remember how I have walked before You sincerely and whole-heartedly, and have done what is pleasing to You." And Hezekiah wept profusely.

⁴Before Isaiah had gone out of the middle court, the word of the LORD came to him: ⁵"Go back and say to Hezekiah, the ruler of My people:

Thus said the LORD, the God of your father David: I have heard your prayer, I have seen your tears. I am going to heal you; on the third day you shall go up to the House of the LORD. ⁶And I will add fifteen years to your life. I will also rescue you and this city from the hands of the king of Assyria. I will protect this city for My sake and for the sake of My servant David."—⁷Then Isaiah said, "Get a cake of figs." And they got one, and they applied it to the rash, and he recovered.—⁸Hezekiah asked Isaiah, "What is the sign that the LORD will heal me and that I shall go up to the House of the LORD on the third day?" ⁹Isaiah replied, "This is the sign for you from the LORD that the LORD will do the thing that He has promised: Shallᵃ the shadow advance ten steps or recede ten steps?" ¹⁰Hezekiah said, "It is easy for the shadow to lengthen ten steps, but not for the shadow to recede ten steps." ¹¹So the prophet Isaiah called to the LORD, and He made the shadow which had descended on the dialᵇ of Ahaz recede ten steps.

¹²At that time, King Berodach-ᶜbaladan son of Baladan of Babylon sent [envoys with] a letter and a gift to Hezekiah, for he had heard about Hezekiah's illness. ¹³ᵈ⁻Hezekiah heard about them⁻ᵈ and he showed them all his treasurehouse—the silver, the gold, the spices, and the fragrant oil—and his armory, and everything that was to be found in his storehouses. There was nothing in his palace or in all his realm that Hezekiah did not show them. ¹⁴Then the prophet Isaiah came to King Hezekiah. "What," he demanded of him, "did those men say to you? Where have they come to you from?" "They have come," Hezekiah replied, "from a far country, from Babylon." ¹⁵Next he asked, "What have they seen in your palace?" And Hezekiah replied, "They have seen everything that is in my palace. There was nothing in my storehouses that I did not show them."

¹⁶Then Isaiah said to Hezekiah, "Hear the word of the LORD: ¹⁷A time is coming when everything in your palace which your ancestors have stored up to this day will be carried off to Babylon; nothing will remain behind, said the LORD. ¹⁸And some of your sons, your own issue, whom you will have fathered, will be taken to serve as eunuchs in the palace of the king of Babylon." ¹⁹Hezekiah declared to Isaiah, "The word of the LORD that you have spoken is good." For he thought, "It means that ᵉ⁻safety is assured for⁻ᵉ my time."

²⁰The other events of Hezekiah's reign, and all his exploits, and how he made the pool and the conduit and brought the water into the city,

---

ᵃ Cf. Targum.
ᵇ Heb. "steps." A model of a dial with steps has been discovered in Egypt.
ᶜ Several mss. and the parallel Isa. 39.1 read "Merodach."
ᵈ⁻ᵈ Isa. 39.2 reads "Hezekiah was pleased by their coming."
ᵉ⁻ᵉ Lit. "there shall be safety and faithfulness in."

are recorded in the Annals of the Kings of Judah. ²¹Hezekiah slept with his fathers, and his son Manasseh succeeded him as king.

21

Manasseh was twelve years old when he became king, and he reigned fifty-five years in Jerusalem; his mother's name was Hephzibah. ²He did what was displeasing to the LORD, following the abhorrent practices of the nations that the LORD had dispossessed before the Israelites. ³He rebuilt the shrines that his father Hezekiah had destroyed; he erected altars for Baal and made a sacred post, as King Ahab of Israel had done. He bowed down to all the host of heaven and worshiped them, ⁴and he built altars for them in the House of the LORD, of which the LORD had said, "I will establish My name in Jerusalem." ⁵He built altars for all the hosts of heaven in the two courts of the House of the LORD. ⁶He consigned his son to the fire; he practiced soothsaying and divination, and consulted ghosts and familiar spirits; he did much that was displeasing to the LORD, to vex Him. ⁷The sculptured image of Asherah that he made he placed in the House concerning which the LORD had said to David and to his son Solomon, "In this House and in Jerusalem, which I chose out of all the tribes of Israel, I will establish My name forever. ⁸And I will not again cause the feet of Israel to wander from the land that I gave to their fathers, if they will but faithfully observe all that I have commanded them—all the Teachings with which My servant Moses charged them." ⁹But they did not obey, and Manasseh led them astray to do greater evil than the nations that the LORD had destroyed before the Israelites. ¹⁰Therefore the LORD spoke through His servants the prophets: ¹¹"Because King Manasseh of Judah has done these abhorrent things— he has outdone in wickedness all that the Amorites did before his time— and because he led Judah to sin with his fetishes, ¹²assuredly, thus said the LORD, the God of Israel: I am going to bring such a disaster on Jerusalem and Judah that both ears of everyone who hears about it will tingle. ¹³I will ^aapply to Jerusalem the measuring line of Samaria and the weights of the House of Ahab;^{-a} I will wipe Jerusalem clean as one wipes a dish and turns it upside down. ¹⁴And I will cast off the remnant of My own people and deliver them into the hands of their enemies. They shall be plunder and prey to all their enemies ¹⁵because they have done what

---

^{a-a} *I.e., I will bring the same fate upon it.*

is displeasing to Me and have been vexing Me from the day that their fathers came out of Egypt to this day."

16Moreover, Manasseh put so many innocent persons to death that he filled Jerusalem [with blood] from end to end—besides the sin he committed in causing Judah to do what was displeasing to the LORD.

17The other events of Manasseh's reign, and all his actions, and the sins he committed, are recorded in the Annals of the Kings of Judah. 18Manasseh slept with his fathers and was buried in the garden of his palace, in the garden of Uzza; and his son Amon succeeded him as king.

19Amon was twenty-two years old when he became king, and he reigned two years in Jerusalem; his mother's name was Meshullemeth daughter of Haruz of Jotbah. 20He did what was displeasing to the LORD, as his father Manasseh had done. 21He walked in all the ways of his father, worshiping the fetishes which his father had worshiped and bowing down to them. 22He forsook the LORD, the God of his fathers, and did not follow the way of the LORD.

23Amon's courtiers conspired against him; and they killed the king in his palace. 24But the people of the land put to death all who had conspired against King Amon, and the people of the land made his son Josiah king in his stead. 25The other events of Amon's reign [and] his actions are recorded in the Annals of the Kings of Judah. 26He was buried in his tomb in the garden of Uzza; and his son Josiah succeeded him as king.

22 Josiah was eight years old when he became king, and he reigned thirty-one years in Jerusalem. His mother's name was Jedidah daughter of Adaiah of Bozkath. 2He did what was pleasing to the LORD and he followed all the ways of his ancestor David; he did not deviate to the right or to the left.

3In the eighteenth year of King Josiah, the king sent the scribe Shaphan son of Azaliah son of Meshullam to the House of the LORD, saying, 4"Go to the high priest Hilkiah and let him weigha the silver that has been deposited in the House of the LORD, which the guards of the threshold have collected from the people. 5And let it be delivered to the overseers of the work who are in charge at the House of the LORD, that they in

---

a *Meaning of Heb. uncertain. Emendation yields "melt down," cf. v. 9.*

turn may pay it out to the workmen that are in the House of the LORD, for the repair of the House: ⁶to the carpenters, the laborers, and the masons, and for the purchase of wood and quarried stones for repairing the House. ⁷However, no check is to be kept on them for the silver that is delivered to them, for they deal honestly."

⁸Then the high priest Hilkiah said to the scribe Shaphan, "I have found a scroll of the Teaching in the House of the LORD." And Hilkiah gave the scroll to Shaphan, who read it. ⁹The scribe Shaphan then went to the king and reported to the king: "Your servants have melted down the silver that was deposited in the House, and they have delivered it to the overseers of the work who are in charge at the House of the LORD." ¹⁰The scribe Shaphan also told the king, "The high priest Hilkiah has given me a scroll"; and Shaphan read it to the king.

¹¹When the king heard the words of the scroll of the Teaching, he rent his clothes. ¹²And the king gave orders to the priest Hilkiah, and to Ahikam son of Shaphan, Achbor son of Michaiah, the scribe Shaphan, and Asaiah the king's minister: ¹³"Go, inquire of the LORD on my behalf, and on behalf of the people, and on behalf of all Judah, concerning the words of this scroll that has been found. For great indeed must be the wrath of the LORD that has been kindled against us, because our fathers did not obey the words of this scroll to do all that has been prescribed for us."

¹⁴So the priest Hilkiah, and Ahikam, Achbor, Shaphan, and Asaiah went to the prophetess Huldah—the wife of Shallum son of Tikvah son of Harhas, the keeper of the wardrobe—who was living in Jerusalem in the Mishneh,ᵇ and they spoke to her. ¹⁵She responded: "Thus said the LORD, the God of Israel: Say to the man who sent you to me: ¹⁶Thus said the LORD: I am going to bring disaster upon this place and its inhabitants, in accordance with all the words of the scroll which the king of Judah has read. ¹⁷Because they have forsaken Me and have made offerings to other gods and vexed Me with all their deeds, My wrath is kindled against this place and it shall not be quenched. ¹⁸But say this to the king of Judah, who sent you to inquire of the LORD: Thus said the LORD, the God of Israel: As for the words which you have heard— ¹⁹because your heart was softened and you humbled yourself before the LORD when you heard what I decreed against this place and its inhabitants—that it will become a desolation and a curse—and because you rent

ᵇ A quarter in Jerusalem; cf. Zeph. 1.10.

your clothes and wept before Me, I for My part have listened—declares the LORD. ²⁰Assuredly, I will gather you to your fathers and you will be laid in your tomb in peace. Your eyes shall not see all the disaster which, I will bring upon this place." So they brought back the reply to the king.

23 At the king's summons, all the elders of Judah and Jerusalem assembled before him. ²The king went up to the House of the LORD, together with all the men of Judah and all the inhabitants of Jerusalem, and the priests and prophets—all the people, young and old. And he read to them the entire text of the covenant scroll which had been found in the House of the LORD. ³The king stood ᵃ⁻by the pillar⁻ᵃ and solemnized the covenant before the LORD: that they would follow the LORD and observe His commandments, His injunctions, and His laws with all their heart and soul; that they would fulfill all the terms of this covenant as inscribed upon the scroll. And all the people ᵇ⁻entered into⁻ᵇ the covenant.

⁴Then the king ordered the high priest Hilkiah, the priests of the second rank, and the guards of the threshold to bring out of the Temple of the LORD all the objects made for Baal and Asherahᶜ and all the host of heaven. He burned them outside Jerusalem in the fieldsᵈ of Kidron, and he removed the ashes to Bethel. ⁵He suppressed the idolatrous priests whom the kings of Judah had appointed ᵉ⁻to make offerings⁻ᵉ at the shrines in the towns of Judah and in the environs of Jerusalem, and those who made offerings to Baal, to the sun and moon and constellations—all the host of heaven. ⁶He brought out the [image of] Asherah from the House of the LORD to the Kidron Valley outside Jerusalem, and burned it in the Kidron Valley; he beat it to dust and scattered its dust over the burial ground of the common people. ⁷He tore down the cubicles of the male prostitutes in the House of the LORD, at the place where the women wove coveringsᵈ for Asherah.

⁸He brought all the priests from the towns of Judah [to Jerusalem] and defiled the shrines where the priests had been making offerings—from Geba to Beer-sheba. He also demolished the shrines of the gates, which were at the entrance of the gate of Joshua, the city prefect—ᵈ⁻which were on a person's left [as he entered] the city gate.⁻ᵈ ⁹ᶠ⁻The priests of the shrines, however, did not ascend the altar of the LORD in Jerusalem, but they ate unleavened bread along with their kinsmen.⁻ᶠ ¹⁰He also defiled

---

ᵃ⁻ᵃ *Or "on a platform," cf. Targum.*
ᵇ⁻ᵇ *Cf. Targum.*
ᶜ *For this goddess, cf. 1 Kings 18.19; ordinarily* asherah *is rendered "sacred post," e.g., 2 Kings 17.16.*
ᵈ *Meaning of Heb. uncertain.*
ᵉ⁻ᵉ *Lit. "and he offered."*
ᶠ⁻ᶠ *This verse may be understood in connection with vv. 21–23.*

Topheth, which is in the Valley of Ben-hinnom, so that no one might consign his son or daughter to the fire of Molech. ¹¹He did away with the horses that the kings of Judah had dedicated to the sun, ᵍ⁻at the entrance⁻ᵍ of the House of the LORD, near the chamber of the eunuch Nathan-melech, which was in the precincts.ᵈ He burned the chariots of the sun. ¹²And the king tore down the altars made by the kings of Judah on the roof by the upper chamber of Ahaz, and the altars made by Manasseh in the two courts of the House of the LORD. He ʰ⁻removed them quickly from there⁻ʰ and scattered their rubble in the Kidron Valley. ¹³The king also defiled the shrines facing Jerusalem, to the south of the ⁱ⁻Mount of the Destroyer,⁻ⁱ which King Solomon of Israel had built for Ashtoreth, the abomination of the Sidonians, for Chemosh, the abomination of Moab, and for Milcom, the detestable thing of the Ammonites.ʲ ¹⁴He shattered their pillars and cut down their sacred posts and covered their sites with human bones.

¹⁵As for the altar in Bethel [and] the shrine made by Jeroboam son of Nebat who caused Israel to sin—that altar, too, and the shrine as well, he tore down. He burned down the shrine and beat it to dust, and he burned the sacred post.

¹⁶Josiah turned and saw the graves that were there on the hill; and he had the bones taken out of the graves and burned on the altar. Thus he defiled it, in fulfillment of the word of the LORD foretold by the man of God who foretold these happenings. ¹⁷He asked, "What is the marker I see there?" And the men of the town replied, "That is the grave of the man of God who came from Judah and foretold these things that you have done to the altar of Bethel."ᵏ ¹⁸"Let him be," he said, "let no one disturb his bones." So they left his bones undisturbed together with the bones of the prophetˡ who came from Samaria.ᵐ

¹⁹Josiah also abolished all the cult places in the towns of Samaria, which the kings of Israel had built, vexing [the LORD]. He dealt with them just as he had done to Bethel: ²⁰He slew on the altars all the priests of the shrines who were there, and he burned human bones on them. Then he returned to Jerusalem.

²¹The king commanded all the people, "Offer the passover sacrifice to the LORD your God as prescribed in this scroll of the covenant." ²²Now

---

ᵍ⁻ᵍ *Heb. "from entering."*
ʰ⁻ʰ *Heb. "ran from there." Emendation yields "smashed them there."*
ⁱ⁻ⁱ *Heb.* har ha-mashḥith: *a derogatory play on* har ha-mishḥah *("Mount of Ointment"); Mishnah Middoth 2.4.*
ʲ *Cf. 1 Kings 11.5, 7.*
ᵏ *Cf. 1 Kings 13.2–3.*
ˡ *See 1 Kings 13.31–32 and note m below.*
ᵐ *The prophet lived in Bethel, which, in Josiah's time, was part of the Assyrian province of Samaria.*

the passover sacrifice had not been offered in that manner in the days of the chieftains who ruled Israel, or during the days of the kings of Israel and the kings of Judah. [23]Only in the eighteenth year of King Josiah was such a passover sacrifice offered in that manner to the LORD in Jerusalem. [24]Josiah also did away with [n]the necromancers and the mediums,[n] the idols and the fetishes—all the detestable things that were to be seen in the land of Judah and Jerusalem. Thus he fulfilled the terms of the Teaching recorded in the scroll that the priest Hilkiah had found in the House of the LORD. [25]There was no king like him before who turned back to the LORD with all his heart and soul and might, in full accord with the Teaching of Moses; nor did any like him arise after him.

[26]However, the LORD did not turn away from His awesome wrath which had blazed up against Judah because of all the things Manasseh did to vex Him. [27]The LORD said, "I will also banish Judah from My presence as I banished Israel; and I will reject the city of Jerusalem which I chose and the House where I said My name would abide."

[28]The other events of Josiah's reign, and all his actions, are recorded in the Annals of the Kings of Judah. [29]In his days, Pharaoh Neco, king of Egypt, marched against the king of Assyria[o] to the River Euphrates; King Josiah marched toward him, but when he confronted him at Megiddo, [Pharaoh Neco] slew him. [30]His servants conveyed his body in a chariot from Megiddo to Jerusalem, and they buried him in his tomb. Then the people of the land took Jehoahaz; they anointed him and made him king in place of his father.

[31]Jehoahaz was twenty-three years old when he became king, and he reigned three months in Jerusalem; his mother's name was Hamutal daughter of Jeremiah of Libnah. [32]He did what was displeasing to the LORD, just as his fathers had done. [33]Pharaoh Neco imprisoned him in Riblah in the region of Hamath, to keep him from reigning in Jerusalem. And he imposed on the land an indemnity of one hundred talents of silver and a talent of gold. [34]Then Pharaoh Neco appointed Eliakim son of Josiah king in place of his father Josiah, changing his name to Jehoiakim. He took Jehoahaz and [p]brought him[p] to Egypt, where he died. [35]Jehoiakim gave Pharaoh the silver and the gold, and he made an assessment on the land to pay the money demanded by Pharaoh. He exacted from the people

[n-n] Lit. "the ghosts and the familiar spirits."
[o] I.e., the Chaldean Empire; cf. Isa. 52.4 and note.
[p-p] So 2 Chron. 36.4; Heb. here "he came."

of the land the silver and gold to be paid Pharaoh Neco, according to each man's assessment.

³⁶Jehoiakim was twenty-five years old when he became king, and he reigned eleven years in Jerusalem; his mother's name was Zebudah daughter of Pedaiah of Rumah. ³⁷He did what was displeasing to the LORD, just as his ancestors had done.

24 In his days, King Nebuchadnezzar of Babylon came up, and Jehoiakim became his vassal for three years. Then he turned and rebelled against him. ²The LORD let loose against him the raiding bands of the Chaldeans, Arameans, Moabites, and Ammonites; He let them loose against Judah to destroy it, in accordance with the word that the LORD had spoken through His servants the prophets. ³All this befell Judah at the command of the LORD, who banished [them] from His presence because of all the sins that Manasseh had committed, ⁴and also because of the blood of the innocent that he shed. For he filled Jerusalem with the blood of the innocent, and the LORD would not forgive.

⁵The other events of Jehoiakim's reign, and all of his actions, are recorded in the Annals of the Kings of Judah. ⁶Jehoiakim slept with his fathers, and his son Jehoiachin succeeded him as king. ⁷The king of Egypt did not venture out of his country again, for the king of Babylon had seized all the land that had belonged to the king of Egypt, from the Wadi of Egypt to the River Euphrates.

⁸Jehoiachin was eighteen years old when he became king, and he reigned three months in Jerusalem; his mother's name was Nehushta daughter of Elnathan of Jerusalem. ⁹He did what was displeasing to the LORD, just as his father had done. ¹⁰At that time, the troopsᵃ of King Nebuchadnezzar of Babylon marched against Jerusalem, and the city came under siege. ¹¹King Nebuchadnezzar of Babylon advanced against the city while his troops were besieging it. ¹²Thereupon King Jehoiachin of Judah, along with his mother, and his courtiers, commanders, and officers, surrendered to the king of Babylon. The king of Babylon took him captive in the eighth year of his reign. ¹³He carried off ᵇ⁻from Jerusalem⁻ᵇ all the treasures of the House of the LORD and the treasures of the royal palace; he stripped off all the golden decorations in the Temple of the LORD—which

---

ᵃ *Heb. "servants."*
ᵇ⁻ᵇ *Heb. "from there."*

King Solomon of Israel had made—as the LORD had warned. ¹⁴He exiled all of Jerusalem: all the commanders and all the warriors—ten thousand exiles—as well as all the craftsmen and smiths; only the poorest people in the land were left. ¹⁵He deported Jehoiachin to Babylon; and the king's mother and wives and officers and the notables of the land were brought as exiles from Jerusalem to Babylon. ¹⁶All the able men, to the number of seven thousand—all of them warriors, trained for battle—and a thousand craftsmen and smiths were brought to Babylon as exiles by the king of Babylon. ¹⁷And the king of Babylon appointed Mattaniah, Jehoiachin's^c uncle, king in his place, changing his name to Zedekiah.

^{18d}Zedekiah was twenty-one years old when he became king, and he reigned eleven years in Jerusalem; his mother's name was Hamutal daughter of Jeremiah of Libnah. ¹⁹He did what was displeasing to the LORD, just as Jehoiakim had done. ²⁰Indeed, Jerusalem and Judah ^{e-}were a cause of anger for the LORD, so that^{-e} He cast them out of His presence.

25 Zedekiah rebelled against the king of Babylon. ¹And in the ninth year of his^a reign, on the tenth day of the tenth month, Nebuchadnezzar moved against Jerusalem with his whole army. He besieged it; and they built towers against it all around. ²The city continued in a state of siege until the eleventh year of King Zedekiah. ³By the ninth day [of the fourth month]^b the famine had become acute in the city; there was no food left for the common people.

⁴Then [the wall of] the city was breached. All the soldiers [left the city] by night through the gate between the double walls, which is near the king's garden—the Chaldeans were all around the city; and [the king] set out for the Arabah.^c ⁵But the Chaldean troops pursued the king, and they overtook him in the steppes of Jericho as his entire force left him and scattered. ⁶They captured the king and brought him before the king of Babylon at Riblah; and they put him on trial. ⁷They slaughtered Zedekiah's sons before his eyes; then Zedekiah's eyes were put out. He was chained in bronze fetters and he was brought to Babylon.

⁸On the seventh day of the fifth month—that was the nineteenth year of King Nebuchadnezzar of Babylon—Nebuzaradan, the chief of the guards, an officer of the king of Babylon, came to Jerusalem. ⁹He burned the House of the LORD, the king's palace, and all the houses of Jerusalem; he burned down ^{d-}the house of every notable person.^{-d} ¹⁰The entire Chal-

---

^c Heb. "his."
^d For the rest of this book cf. Jer. 39 and 52.
^{e-e} Meaning of Heb. uncertain.

^a I.e., Zedekiah's.
^b Cf. Jer. 52.6.
^c Hoping to escape across the Jordan.
^{d-d} Meaning of Heb. uncertain.

dean force that was with the chief of the guard tore down the walls of Jerusalem on every side. 11The remnant of the people that was left in the city, the defectors who had gone over to the king of Babylon—and the remnant of the population—were taken into exile by Nebuzaradan, the chief of the guards. 12But some of the poorest in the land were left by the chief of the guards, to be vinedressers and field hands.

13The Chaldeans broke up the bronze columns of the House of the LORD, the stands, and the bronze tank that was in the House of the LORD; and they carried the bronze away to Babylon. 14They also took all the pails, scrapers, snuffers, ladles, and all the other bronze vessels used in the service. 15The chief of the guards took whatever was of gold and whatever was of silver: firepans and sprinkling bowls. 16The two columns, the one tank, and the stands that Solomon provided for the House of the LORD—all these objects contained bronze beyond weighing. 17The one column was eighteen cubits high. It had a bronze capital above it; the height of the capital was three cubits, and there was a meshwork [decorated] with pomegranates about the capital, all made of bronze. And the like was true of the other column with its meshwork.

18The chief of the guards also took Seraiah, the chief priest, Zephaniah, the deputy priest, and the three guardians of the threshold. 19And from the city he took a eunuch who was in command of the soldiers; five royal privy councillors who were present in the city; the scribe of the army commander, who was in charge of mustering the people of the land; and sixty of the common people who were inside the city. 20Nebuzaradan, the chief of the guards, took them and brought them to the king of Babylon at Riblah. 21The king of Babylon had them struck down and put to death at Riblah, in the region of Hamath.

Thus Judah was exiled from its land. 22King Nebuchadnezzar of Babylon put Gedaliah son of Ahikam son of Shaphan in charge of the people whom he left in the land of Judah. 23When the officers of the troops and their men heard that the king of Babylon had put Gedaliah in charge, they came to Gedaliah at Mizpah with Ishmael son of Nethaniah, Johanan son of Kareah, Seraiah son of Tanhumeth the Netophathite, and Jaazaniah son of the Maachite, together with their men. 24Gedaliah reassured[e] them and their men, saying, "Do not be afraid [f]of the servants of the Chaldeans.[f] Stay in the land and serve the king of Babylon, and it will go well with you."

e Lit. "took an oath to them."
f-f Jer. 40.9 reads "to serve the Chaldeans."

²⁵In the seventh month, Ishmael son of Nethaniah son of Elishama, who was of royal descent, came with ten men, and they struck down Gedaliah and he died; [they also killed] the Judeans and the Chaldeans who were present with him at Mizpah. ²⁶And all the people, young and old, and the officers of the troops set out and went to Egypt because they were afraid of the Chaldeans.

²⁷In the thirty-seventh year of the exile of King Jehoiachin of Judah, on the twenty-seventh day of the twelfth month, King Evil-merodach of Babylon, in the year he became king, ᵍ‑took note of‑ᵍ King Jehoiachin of Judah and released him from prison. ²⁸He spoke kindly to him, and gave him a throne above those of other kings who were with him in Babylon. ²⁹His prison garments were removed, and [Jehoiachin] received regular rations by his favor for the rest of his life. ³⁰A regular allotment of food was given him at the instance of the king—an allotment for each day— all the days of his life.

ᵍ‑ᵍ Lit. "raised the head of."

ISAIAH

1 The prophecies of Isaiah son of Amoz, who prophesied concerning Judah and Jerusalem in the reigns of Uzziah, Jotham, Ahaz, and Hezekiah, kings of Judah.

2Hear, O heavens, and give ear, O earth,
For the LORD has spoken:
"I reared children and brought them up—
And they have rebelled against Me!
3An ox knows its owner,
An ass its master's crib:
Israel does not know,
My people takes no thought."

4Ah, sinful nation!
People laden with iniquity!
Brood of evildoers!
Depraved children!
They have forsaken the LORD,
Spurned the Holy One of Israel,
Turned their backs [on Him].

5Why do you seek further beatings,
That you continue to offend?
Every head is ailing,
And every heart is sick.
6From head to foot
No spot is sound:
All bruises, and welts,
And festering sores—

Not pressed out, not bound up,
Not softened with oil.
⁷Your land is a waste,
Your cities burnt down;
Before your eyes, the yield of your soil
Is consumed by strangers—
A wasteland ᵃ⁻as overthrown by strangers!⁻ᵃ
⁸Fairᵇ Zion is left
Like a booth in a vineyard,
Like a hut in a cucumber field,
Like a city beleaguered.
⁹Had not the LORD of Hosts
Left us some survivors,
We should be like Sodom,
Another Gomorrah.

¹⁰Hear the word of the LORD,
You chieftains of Sodom;
Give ear to our God's instruction,
You folk of Gomorrah!
¹¹"What need have I of all your sacrifices?"
Says the LORD.
"I am sated with burnt offerings of rams,
And suet of fatlings,
And blood of bulls;
And I have no delight
In lambs and he-goats.
¹²That you come to appear before Me—
Who asked that ᶜ⁻of you?
Trample My courts
¹³   no more;
Bringing oblations is futile,⁻ᶜ
Incense is offensive to Me.
New moon and sabbath,
Proclaiming of solemnities,
ᵈ⁻Assemblies with iniquity,⁻ᵈ
I cannot abide.

ᵃ⁻ᵃ *Emendation yields "like Sodom overthrown."*
ᵇ *Lit. "Daughter."*
ᶜ⁻ᶜ *Others "To trample My courts? /¹³Bring no more vain oblations."*
ᵈ⁻ᵈ *Septuagint "Fast and assembly"; cf. Joel 1.14.*

14Your new moons and fixed seasons
Fill Me with loathing;
They are become a burden to Me,
I cannot endure them.
15And when you lift up your hands,
I will turn My eyes away from you;
Though you pray at length,
I will not listen.
Your hands are stained with crime—
16Wash yourselves clean;
Put your evil doings
Away from My sight.
Cease to do evil;
17Learn to do good.
Devote yourselves to justice;
e-Aid the wronged.-e
Uphold the rights of the orphan;
Defend the cause of the widow.

18"Come, e-let us reach an understanding,-e

                         —says the LORD.

Be your sins like crimson,
They can turn snow-white;
Be they red as dyed wool,
They can become like fleece."
19If, then, you agree and give heed,
You will eat the good things of the earth;
20But if you refuse and disobey,
f-You will be devoured [by] the sword.-f—
For it was the LORD who spoke.

21Alas, she has become a harlot,
The faithful city
That was filled with justice,
Where righteousness dwelt—
But now murderers.
22Yourg silver has turned to dross;

e-e Meaning of Heb. uncertain.
f-f Or "you will be fed the sword."
g I.e., Jerusalem's.

c-Your wine is cut with water.-c
²³Your rulers are rogues
And cronies of thieves,
Every one avid for presents
And greedy for gifts;
They do not judge the case of the orphan,
And the widow's cause never reaches them.

²⁴Assuredly, this is the declaration
Of the Sovereign, the LORD of Hosts,
The Mighty One of Israel:
"Ah, I will get satisfaction from My foes;
I will wreak vengeance on My enemies!
²⁵I will turn My hand against you,
And smelt out your dross h-as with lye,-h
And remove all your slag:
²⁶I will restore your magistrates as of old,
And your counselors as of yore.
After that you shall be called
City of Righteousness, Faithful City."

²⁷iZion shall be saved in the judgment;
Her repentant ones, in the retribution.j
²⁸But rebels and sinners shall all be crushed,
And those who forsake the LORD shall perish.

²⁹Truly, youk shall be shamed
Because of the terebinths you desired,
And you shall be confounded
Because of the gardens you coveted.
³⁰For you shall be like a terebinth
Wilted of leaf,
And like a garden
That has no water,
³¹l-Stored wealth-l shall become as tow,
And he who amassed it a spark;
And the two shall burn together,
With none to quench.

h-h *Emendation yields "in a crucible"; cf. 48.10.*
i *Others "Zion shall be saved by justice, /Her repentant ones by righteousness."*
j *For this meaning cf. 5.16; 10.22.*
k *Heb. "they."*
l-l *Connecting* hason *with* hasan, *"to store" (23.18), and* hosen, *"treasure" (33.6).*

2 The word that Isaiah son of Amoz prophesied concerning Judah and Jerusalem.

²In the days to come,
The Mount of the LORD's House
Shall stand firm above the mountains
And tower above the hills;
And all the nations
Shall gaze on it with joy.
³And the many peoples shall go and say:
"Come,
Let us go up to the Mount of the LORD,
To the House of the God of Jacob;
That He may instruct us in His ways,
And that we may walk in His paths."
For instruction shall come forthᵃ from Zion,
The word of the LORD from Jerusalem.
⁴Thus He will judge among the nations
And arbitrate for the many peoples,
And they shall beat their swords into plowsharesᵇ
And their spears into pruning hooks:
Nation shall not take up
Sword against nation;
They shall never again knowᶜ war.

⁵O House of Jacob!
Come, let us walk
By the light of the LORD.
⁶For you have forsaken [the ways of] your people,
O House of Jacob!
ᵈ⁻For they are full [of practices] from the East,
And of soothsaying like the Philistines;
They abound in customsᵉ of the aliens.⁻ᵈ
⁷Their land is full of silver and gold,
There is no limit to their treasures;
Their land is full of horses,
There is no limit to their chariots.

ᵃ I.e., oracles will be obtainable.
ᵇ More exactly, the iron points with which wooden plows were tipped.
ᶜ Cf. Judg. 3.2.
ᵈ⁻ᵈ Emendation yields "For they are full of divination/and have abundance of soothsaying,/Like Philistines/And like alien folk."
ᵉ Cf. Targum; lit. "children."

⁸And their land is full of idols;
They bow down to the work of their hands,
To what their own fingers have wrought.
⁹But man shall be humbled,
And mortal brought low—
^{f-}Oh, do not forgive them!^{-f}

¹⁰Go deep into the rock,
Bury yourselves in the ground,
Before the terror of the LORD
And His dread majesty!
¹¹Man's haughty look shall be brought low,
And the pride of mortals shall be humbled.
None but the LORD shall be
Exalted in that day.

¹²For the LORD of Hosts has ready a day
Against all that is proud and arrogant,
Against all that is lofty—so that it is brought low:
¹³Against all the cedars of Lebanon,
Tall and stately,
And all the oaks of Bashan;
¹⁴Against all the high mountains
And all the lofty hills;
¹⁵Against every soaring tower
And every mighty wall;
¹⁶Against all the ^{g-}ships of Tarshish^{-g}
And all the gallant barks.
¹⁷Then man's haughtiness shall be humbled
And the pride of man brought low.
None but the LORD shall be
Exalted in that day.

¹⁸As for idols, they shall vanish completely.
¹⁹And men shall enter caverns in the rock
And hollows in the ground—
Before the terror of the LORD
And His dread majesty,
When He comes forth to overawe the earth.

---

^{f-f} *Meaning of Heb. uncertain. Emendation yields "And their idols with them"; cf. vv. 17–21.*
^{g-g} *Probably a type of large ship.*

²⁰On that day, men shall fling away,
To the ʰ-flying foxes-ʰ and the bats,
The idols of silver
And the idols of gold
Which they made for worshiping.
²¹And they shall enter the clefts in the rocks
And the crevices in the cliffs,
Before the terror of the LORD
And His dread majesty,
When He comes forth to overawe the earth.

²²Oh, cease to glorify man,
Who has only a breath in his nostrils!
For by what does he merit esteem?

3 For lo!
The Sovereign LORD of Hosts
Will remove from Jerusalem and from Judah
Prop and stay,
Every prop of food
And every prop of water:ᵃ
²Soldier and warrior,
Magistrate and prophet,
Augur and elder;
³Captain of fifty,
Magnate and counselor,
Skilled artisan and expert enchanter;ᵇ
⁴And Heᶜ will make boys their rulers,
And babes shall govern them.
⁵So the people shall oppress one another—
Each oppressing his fellow:
The young shall bully the old;
And the despised [shall bully] the honored.

⁶For should a man seize his brother,
ᵈ-In whose father's house there is clothing:-ᵈ
"Come, be a chief over us,

h-h *Exact meaning of Heb. uncertain.*

a *Emendation yields "clothing"; cf. v. 7; 4.1.*
b *Emendation yields "craftsman."*
c *Heb. "I."*
d-d *Emendation yields "His father's son, saying. . . ."*

And let this ruin[c] be under your care,"
[7]The other will thereupon protest,
"I will not be a dresser of wounds,
With no food or clothing in my own house.
You shall not make me chief of a people!"

[8]Ah, Jerusalem has stumbled,
And Judah has fallen,
Because by word and deed
They insult the LORD,
Defying His majestic glance.
[9]Their partiality in judgment[f] accuses them;
They avow their sins like Sodom,
They do not conceal them.
Woe to them! For ill
Have they served themselves.
[10](Hail[g] the just man, for he shall fare well;
He shall eat the fruit of his works.
[11]Woe to the wicked man, for he shall fare ill;
As his hands have dealt, so shall it be done to him.)
[12]My people's rulers are babes,
It is governed by women.[h]
O my people!
Your leaders are misleaders;
They have confused the course of your paths.

[13]The LORD stands up to plead a cause,
He rises to champion peoples.[i]
[14]The LORD will bring this charge
Against the elders and officers of His people:
"It is you who have ravaged the vineyard;
That which was robbed from the poor is in your houses.
[15]How dare you crush My people
And grind the faces of the poor?"
           —says my Lord GOD of Hosts.

[16]The LORD said:
"Because the daughters of Zion

---

[c] *Meaning of Heb. uncertain. Emendation yields "wound."*
[f] *So Targum; cf. Deut. 1.17; 16.19.*
[g] *Emendation yields "Happy is."*
[h] *Emendation yields "boys"; cf. v. 4 (and v. 5).*
[i] *Septuagint "His people"; cf. vv. 14, 15.*

Are so vain
And walk with [j-]heads thrown back,[-j]
With roving eyes,
And with mincing gait,
Making a tinkling with their feet"—
[17]My Lord will bare[k] the pates
Of the daughters of Zion,
The LORD will uncover their heads.

[18]In that day, my LORD will strip off the finery[l] of the anklets, the fillets, and the crescents; [19]of the eardrops, the bracelets, and the veils; [20]the turbans, the armlets, and the sashes; of the talismans and the amulets; [21]the signet rings and the nose rings; [22]of the festive robes, the mantles, and the shawls; the purses, [23]the lace gowns, and the linen vests; and the kerchiefs and the capes.

[24]And then—
Instead of perfume, there shall be rot;
And instead of an apron, a rope;
Instead of a diadem of beaten-work,
A shorn head;
Instead of a rich robe,
A girding of sackcloth;
[m-]A burn instead of beauty.[-m]

[25]Her[n] men shall fall by the sword,
Her fighting manhood in battle;
[26]And her gates shall lament and mourn,
And [o-]she shall be emptied,[-o]
Shall sit on the ground.

4 In that day, seven women shall take hold of one man, saying,
"We will eat our own food
And wear our own clothes;
Only let us be called by your name—
Take away our disgrace!"

[j-j] *Lit. "throats bent back."*
[k] *So Saadia. To bare a woman's head in public was an intolerable humiliation; cf. Mishnah Baba Kamma 8.6.*
[l] *Many of the articles named in vv. 18–24 cannot be identified with certainty.*
[m-m] *The complete Isaiah scroll from Qumran, hereafter 1QIs[a], reads "For shame shall take the place of beauty"; cf. note k.*
[n] *I.e., Zion's; cf. vv. 16, 17; Heb. "your."*
[o-o] *Meaning of Heb. uncertain. Emendation yields "her wall"; cf. Lam. 2.8.*

2ªIn that day,
The radiance of the LORD
Will lend beauty and glory,
And the splendor of ᵇ⁻the land⁻ᵇ
[Will give] dignity and majesty,
To the survivors of Israel.
³And those who remain in Zion
And are left in Jerusalem—
All who are inscribed for life in Jerusalem—
Shall be called holy.

⁴When my Lord has washed away
The filth of ᶜ⁻the daughters of Zion,⁻ᶜ
And from Jerusalem's midst
Has rinsed out her infamy—
In a spirit of judgment
And in a spirit of purging—

⁵the LORD will createᵈ over the whole shrine and meeting place of Mount Zion cloud by day and smoke with a glow of flaming fire by night. Indeed, over ᵉ⁻all the glory⁻ᵉ shall hang a canopy, ⁶which shall serve as a pavilion for shade from heat by day and as a shelter for protection against drenching rain.

5   Let me sing for my beloved
A song of my lover about his vineyard.

My beloved had a vineyard
ª⁻On a fruitful hill.⁻ª
²He broke the ground, cleared it of stones,
And planted it with choice vines.
He built a watchtower inside it,
He even hewed a wine press in it;
For he hoped it would yield grapes.
Instead, it yielded wild grapes.

ª *For the interpretation of this verse, cf. 28.5. For "radiance," cf. Septuagint and the Syriac ṣemḥa, and for "splendor," cf. the meaning of peri in 10.12.*
ᵇ⁻ᵇ *Emendation yields "my Lord"; cf. the parallelism (in reverse order) in 3.17.*
ᶜ⁻ᶜ *Emendation yields "Daughter Zion," i.e., Zion personified; cf. 1.8 and note.*
ᵈ *Emendation yields "spread"; cf. Ps. 105.39.*
ᵉ⁻ᵉ *Emendation yields "His whole shrine."*

ª⁻ª *Meaning of Heb. uncertain.*

3"Now, then,
Dwellers of Jerusalem
And men of Judah,
You be the judges
Between Me and My vineyard:
4What more could have been done for My vineyard
That I failed to do in it?
Why, when I hoped it would yield grapes,
Did it yield wild grapes?

5"Now I am going to tell you
What I will do to My vineyard:
I will remove its hedge,
That it may be ravaged;
I will break down its wall,
That it may be trampled.
6And I will ª-make it a desolation;-ª
It shall not be pruned or hoed,
And it shall be overgrown with briers and thistles.
And I will command the clouds
To drop no rain on it."

7For the vineyard of the LORD of Hosts
Is the House of Israel,
And the seedlings he lovingly tended
Are the men of Judah.
bAnd He hoped for justice,
But behold, injustice;
For equity,
But behold, iniquity!

8Ah,
Those who add house to house
And join field to field,
Till there is room for none but you
To dwell in the land!
9In my hearing [said] the LORD of Hosts:

---

b *This sentence contains two word-plays: "And He hoped for* mishpaṭ, *And there is* mispaḥ [*exact meaning uncertain*];/*For* ṣedaqah, *But there is* śeʿaqah [*lit.* ʿoutcryʾ]."

Surely, great houses
Shall lie forlorn,
Spacious and splendid ones
Without occupants.
[10]For ten acres of vineyard
Shall yield just one *bath*,[c]
And a field sown with a *homer* of seed
Shall yield a mere *ephah*.

[11]Ah,
Those who chase liquor
From early in the morning,
And till late in the evening
Are inflamed by wine!
[12][d-]Who, at their banquets,
Have[-d] lyre and lute,
Timbrel, flute, and wine;
But who never give a thought
To the plan of the LORD,
And take no note
Of what He is designing.
[13]Assuredly,
My people will suffer exile
For not giving heed,
Its multitude victims of hunger
And its masses parched with thirst.
[14]Assuredly,
Sheol has opened wide its gullet
And parted its jaws in a measureless gape;
And down into it shall go,
That splendor and tumult,
That din and revelry.
[15]Yea, man is bowed,
And mortal brought low;
Brought low is the pride of the haughty.
[16]And the LORD of Hosts is exalted by judgment,
The Holy God proved holy by retribution.

---

[c] *I.e., of wine. The* bath *was the liquid equivalent of the* ephah; *and the* homer *was ten* baths *or* ephahs (*Ezek 45.11*).

[d-d] *Emendation yields "whose interests are"* (mish'ehem, *from* sha'ah *"to turn to," 17.7, 8; 31.1*).

17cThen lambs shall graze
As in their meadows,
And strangers shall feed
On the ruins of the stout.

18Ah,

Those who haul sin with cords of falsehood
And iniquity as with cart ropes!
19Who say,f
"Let Him speed, let Him hasten His purpose,
If we are to give thought;
Let the plans of the Holy One of Israel
Be quickly fulfilled,
If we are to give heed."

20Ah,

Those who call evil good
And good evil;
Who present darkness as light
And light as darkness;
Who present bitter as sweet
And sweet as bitter!
21Ah,

Those who are so wise—
In their own opinion;
So clever—
In their own judgment!

22Ah,

Those who are so doughty—
As drinkers of wine,
And so valiant—
As mixers of drink!
23Who vindicate him who is in the wrong
In return for a bribe,
And withhold vindication
From him who is in the right.

---

c *Meaning of verse uncertain. Emendation yields "The lambs shall graze/In the pasture of the fat [rams],/And the kids shall feed/On the ranges of the stout [bucks]." The lambs and the kids are the poor and the rams and bucks are the rich oppressors (cf. Ezek. 34.17–22).*
f *By way of retort to v. 12.*

²⁴Assuredly,
As straw is consumed by a tongue of fire
And hay ^{g-}shrivels as it burns,^{-g}
Their stock shall become like rot,
And their buds shall blow away like dust.
For they have rejected the instruction of the LORD of Hosts,
Spurned the word of the Holy One of Israel.

²⁵That is why
The LORD's anger was roused
Against His people,
Why He stretched out His arm against it
And struck it,
So that the mountains quaked,^h
And its corpses lay
Like refuse in the streets.
Yet his anger has not turned back,
And His arm is outstretched still.
²⁶He will raise an ensign to a nationⁱ afar,
Whistle to one at the end of the earth.
There it comes with lightning speed!
²⁷In its ranks, none is weary or stumbles,
They never sleep or slumber;
The belts on their waists do not come loose,
Nor do the thongs of their sandals break.
²⁸Their arrows are sharpened,
And all their bows are drawn.
Their horses' hoofs are like flint,
Their chariot wheels like the whirlwind.
²⁹Their roaring is like a lion's,
They roar like the great beasts;
When they growl and seize a prey,
They carry it off and none can recover it.

³⁰But in that day, a roaring shall resound over him like that of the sea;^j
and then he shall look below and, behold,
Distressing darkness, with light;
Darkness, ^{a-}in its lowering clouds.^{-a}

---

^{g-g} *Emendation yields "is burned by flame"; cf. 33.11–12; 47.14.*
^h *An allusion to the destructive earthquake in the reign of King Uzziah: Amos 1.1; Zech. 14.5; cf. Isa. 9.18a.*
ⁱ *Heb. "nations."*
^j *I.e., the LORD will intervene and come to his aid. Cf. 29.6–7; 30.27. This verse may constitute a transition between chaps. 8 and 9.*

6 In the year that King Uzziah died, I beheld my Lord seated on a high and lofty throne; and the skirts of His robe filled the Temple. ²Seraphs stood in attendance on Him. Each of them had six wings: with two he covered his face, with two he covered his legs, and with two he would fly.

³And one would call to the other,
"Holy, holy, holy!
The LORD of Hosts!
His presence fills all the earth!"

⁴The doorposts[a] would shake at the sound of the one who called, and the House kept filling with smoke. ⁵I cried,
"Woe is me; I am lost!
For I am a man [b-]of unclean lips[-b]
And I live among a people
Of unclean lips;
Yet my own eyes have beheld
The King LORD of Hosts."

⁶Then one of the seraphs flew over to me with a live coal, which he had taken from the altar with a pair of tongs. ⁷He touched it to my lips and declared,

"Now that this has touched your lips,
Your guilt shall depart
And your sin be purged away."

⁸Then I heard the voice of my Lord saying, "Whom shall I send? Who will go for us?" And I said, "Here am I; send me." ⁹And He said, "Go, say to that people:
'Hear, indeed, but do not understand;
See, indeed, but do not grasp.'
¹⁰Dull that people's mind,
Stop its ears,
And seal its eyes—

---

[a] *Meaning of Heb. uncertain.*
[b-b] *I.e., speaking impiety; cf. 9.16, and contrast "pure of speech [lit. 'lip']" in Zeph. 3.9.*

> Lest, seeing with its eyes
> And hearing with its ears,
> It also grasp with its mind,
> And repent and save^c itself."

11I asked, "How long, my Lord?" And He replied:
> "Till towns lie waste without inhabitants
> And houses without people,
> And the ground lies waste and desolate—
> 12For the LORD will banish the population—
> And deserted sites are many
> In the midst of the land.

13"But while a tenth part yet remains in it, it shall repent. It shall be ravaged like the terebinth and the oak, of which stumps are left even when they are felled: its stump shall be a holy seed."

7 In the reign of Ahaz son of Jotham son of Uzziah, king of Judah, King Rezin of Aram and King Pekah son of Remaliah of Israel marched upon Jerusalem to attack it; but they were not able to attack it.

2Now, when it was reported to the House of David that Aram had allied itself with Ephraim, their hearts and the hearts of their people trembled as trees of the forest sway before a wind. 3But the LORD said to Isaiah, "Go out with your son Shear-jashub^a to meet Ahaz at the end of the conduit of the Upper Pool, by the road of the Fuller's Field. 4And say to him: Be firm and be calm. Do not be afraid and do not lose heart on account of those two smoking stubs of firebrands, on account of the raging of Rezin and his Arameans and the son of Remaliah.^b 5Because the Arameans—with Ephraim and the son of Remaliah—have plotted against you, saying, 6'We will march against Judah and invade and conquer it, and we will set up as king in it the son of Tabeel,'^b 7thus said my Lord GOD:
> It shall not succeed,
> It shall not come to pass.
> 8For the chief city of Aram is Damascus,
> And the chief of Damascus is Rezin;
> 9The chief city of Ephraim is Samaria,
> And the chief of Samaria is the son of Remaliah.^c

c Lit. "heal."
a Meaning "[only] a remnant will turn back," i.e., repent; cf. 6.13; 10.21.
b To refer to a person only as "the son of—" is slighting; cf. note at 1 Sam. 10.11.
c The thought is continued by 8.8b–10; cf. 2 Chron. 13.8–12.

d-And in another sixty-five years,
Ephraim shall be shattered as a people.-d
If you will not believe, for you e-cannot be trusted-e. . ."

10The LORD spoke further to Ahaz: 11"Ask for a sign from the LORD your God, anywhere down to Sheol or up to the sky." 12But Ahaz replied, "I will not ask, and I will not test the LORD." 13"Listen, House of David," [Isaiah] retorted, "is it not enough for you to treat men as helpless that you also treat my God as helpless?f 14Assuredly, my Lord will give you a sign of His own accord! Look, the young woman is with child and about to give birth to a son. Let her name him Immanuel.g 15(By the time he learns to reject the bad and choose the good, people will be feeding on curds and honey.) 16For before the lad knows to reject the bad and choose the good, the ground whose two kings you dread shall be abandoned. 17The LORD will cause to come upon you and your people and your ancestral house such days as never have come since Ephraim turned away from Judah—that selfsame king of Assyria!h

18"In that day, the LORD will whistle to the flies at the ends of the water channels of Egypt and to the bees in the land of Assyria; 19and they shall all come and alight in the rugged wadis, and in the clefts of the rocks, and in all the thornbrakes, and in all the watering places.

20"In that day, my Lord will cut away with the razor that is hired beyond the Euphrates—with the king of Assyriai—the hair of the head and j-the hair of the legs,-j and it shall clip off the beard as well. 21And in that day, each man shall save alive a heifer of the herd and two animals of the flock. 22(And he shall obtain so much milk that he shall eat curds.) Thus everyone who is left in the land shall feed on curds and honey.

23"For in that day, every spot where there could stand a thousand vines worth a thousand shekels of silverk shall become a wilderness of thornbush and thistle. 24One will have to go there with bow and arrows,l for the country shall be all thornbushes and thistles. 25But the perils of thornbush and thistle shall not spread to any of the hills that could only be tilled with a hoe;m and here cattle shall be let loose, and n-sheep and goats-n shall tramp about."

---

d-d Brought down from v. 8 for clarity.
e-e Others "surely, you shall not be established."
f By insisting on soliciting the aid of Assyria (see 2 Kings 16.7 ff.; cf. below, v. 20). "Treat as helpless" follows the translation of Saadia; cf. Gen. 19.11.
g Meaning "with us is God."
h Cf. note on v. 13.
i Who was hired by Ahaz; cf. notes on vv. 13 and 17.
j-j I.e., the pubic hair.
k I.e., all the best farm land, corresponding to the hairiest parts of the body; v. 20.
l Because of dangerous beasts.
m Marginal farm land, too rocky for the plow, corresponding to areas of the body with scant hair.
n-n See note at Exod. 12.3.

8 The LORD said to me, "Get yourself a large sheet and write on it ᵃ⁻in common script⁻ᵃ 'For Maher-shalal-hash-baz';ᵇ ²and call reliable witnesses, the priest Uriah and Zechariah son of Jeberechiah, to witness for Me." ³I was intimate with the prophetess,ᶜ and she conceived and bore a son; and the LORD said to me, "Name him Maher-shalal-hash-baz.ᵇ ⁴For before the boy learns to call 'Father' and 'Mother,' the wealth of Damascus and the spoils of Samaria, ᵈ⁻and the delights of Rezin and of the son of Remaliah,⁻ᵈ shall be carried off before the king of Assyria."

⁵Again the LORD spoke to me, thus:
⁶"Because that people has spurned
The gently flowing waters of Siloam"ᵉ—
⁷Assuredly,
My Lord will bring up against them
The mighty, massive waters of the Euphrates,
The king of Assyria and all his multitude.
It shall rise above all its channels,
And flow over all its beds,
⁸And swirl through Judah like a flash flood
Reaching up to the neck.ᶠ

ᵍBut with us is God,
Whose wings are spread
As wide as your land is broad!
⁹Band together, O peoples—you shall be broken!
Listen to this, you remotest parts of the earth:
Gird yourselves—you shall be broken;
Gird yourselves—you shall be broken!
¹⁰Hatch a plot—it shall be foiled;
Agree on action—it shall not succeed.
For with us is God!

¹¹For this is what the LORD said to me, when He took me by the handʰ and charged me not to walk in the path of that people:

ᵃ⁻ᵃ *Meaning of Heb. uncertain.*
ᵇ *I.e., "Pillage hastens, looting speeds," indicating that two cities are to be pillaged at an early date; see v. 4.*
ᶜ *I.e., Isaiah's wife.*
ᵈ⁻ᵈ *Brought up from v. 6 for clarity.*
ᵉ *The conduit—and later the tunnel—of Siloam conveyed into Jerusalem the waters of Gihon, which symbolize "the LORD of Hosts who dwells on Mount Zion" (v. 18). For the nature of the rejection see note at 7.13.*
ᶠ *I.e., Judah shall be imperiled, but, in contrast to Aram and Ephraim (v. 4), not destroyed.*
ᵍ *See note c at 7.9.*
ʰ *I.e., singled me out; cf. 41.9, 13; 42.6; 45.1; Jer. 31.32 [31].*

12i"You must not call conspiracyj
All that that people calls conspiracy,j
Nor revere what it reveres,
Nor hold it in awe.
13None but the LORD of Hosts
Shall you account holy;
Give reverence to Him alone,
Hold Him alone in awe.
14He shall be k-for a sanctuary,
A stone-k men strike against:
A rock men stumble over
For the two Houses of Israel,
And a trap and a snare for those
Who dwell in Jerusalem.
15The masses shall trip over these
And shall fall and be injured,
Shall be snared and be caught.
16Bind up the message,
Seal the instruction with My disciples."

17So I will wait for the LORD, who is hiding His face from the House of Jacob, and I will trust in Him. 18Here stand I and the children the LORD has given me as signs and portents in Israel from the LORD of Hosts, who dwells on Mount Zion.

19Now, should people say to you, "Inquire of the ghosts and familiar spirits that chirp and moan; for a people may inquire of its divine beingsl— of the dead on behalf of the living—20for instruction and message," surely, for one who speaks thus there shall be no dawn. 21m-And he shall go about in it wretched and hungry; and when he is hungry, he shall rage and revolt against his king and his divine beings.-m He may turn his face upward 22or he may look below, but behold,

Distress and darkness, n-with no daybreak;-n
Straitness and gloom, n-with no dawn.-n

23For o-if there were to be-o any break of day for that [land] which is in straits, only the former [king] would have brought abasement to the land of Zebulun and the land of Naphtali—while the later one would

---

i The Heb. forms here and in vv. 13 and 19 are plural to include the disciples (v. 16) and the children (v. 18).
j Meaning of Heb. uncertain. Emendation yields "holy"; cf. v. 13.
k-k Emendation yields ". . . for His holy domain [cf. Ps. 114.2]/A stone. . . ."
l I.e., the shades of the dead; cf. 1 Sam. 28.13.
m-m This sentence would read well after v. 22.
n-n Meaning of Heb. uncertain.
o-o So 1QIsᵃ; the others have "there is not."

have brought honor to the Way of the Sea, the other side of the Jordan, and Galilee of the Nations.ᴾ

9

ᵃThe people that walked in darkness
Have seen a brilliant light;
On those who dwelt in a land of gloom
Light has dawned.
²You have magnified that nation,
Have given it great joy;
They have rejoiced before You
As they rejoice at reaping time,
As they exult
When dividing spoil.

³For the yoke that they bore
And the stick on their back—
The rod of their taskmaster—
You have broken as on the day of Midian.ᵇ
⁴Truly, all the boots put on ᶜto stamp withᶜ
And all the garments donned in infamy
Have been fed to the flames,
Devoured by fire.
⁵For a child has been born to us,
A son has been given us.
And authority has settled on his shoulders.
He has been named
"The Mighty God is planning grace;ᵈ
The Eternal Father, a peaceable ruler"—
⁶In token of abundant authority
And of peace without limit
Upon David's throne and kingdom,
That it may be firmly established
In justice and in equity
Now and evermore.
The zeal of the LORD of Hosts
Shall bring this to pass.

ᴾ *Meaning of verse uncertain. The rendering here assumes that "the former [king]" refers to Pekah (cf. 2 Kings 15.29) and "the later" to Hoshea (ibid. 30). For the construction* lu ... ka'eth, *see Judg. 13—23.*

ᵃ *See note j at 5.30.*
ᵇ *See Judg. 7—8.*
ᶜ⁻ᶜ *Meaning of Heb. uncertain; emendation yields "in wickedness"; cf. Targum.*
ᵈ *As in 25.1.*

⁷My Lord
ᵉ⁻Let loose a word⁻ᵉ against Jacob
And it fell upon Israel.
⁸But all the people notedᶠ—
Ephraim and the inhabitants of Samaria—
In arrogance and haughtiness:
⁹"Bricks have fallen—
We'll rebuild with dressed stone;
Sycamores have been felled—
We'll grow cedars instead!"
¹⁰So the LORD let ᵍ⁻the enemies of Rezin⁻ᵍ
Triumph over it
And stirred up its foes—
¹¹Aram from the east
And Philistia from the west—
Who devoured Israel
With greedy mouths.

Yet His anger has not turned back,
And His arm is outstretched still.

¹²For the people has not turned back
To Him who struck it
And has not sought
The LORD of Hosts.
¹³So the LORD will cut off from Israel
Head and tail,
Palm branch and reed,
In a single day.
¹⁴Elders ʰ⁻and magnates⁻ʰ—
Such are the heads;
Prophets who give false instruction,
Such are the tailsⁱ
¹⁵That people's leaders have been misleaders,
So they that are led have been confused.
¹⁶That is why my Lord

ᵉ⁻ᵉ *Septuagint reads "Let loose pestilence"; cf. Amos 4.10. In vv. 7–20 Isaiah alludes to and builds
    upon Amos 4.10–12.*
ᶠ *1QIsᵃ reads "shouted."*
ᵍ⁻ᵍ *Emendation yields "its enemies."*
ʰ⁻ʰ *Emendation yields "who practice partiality."*
ⁱ *Emendation yields "palm branches"; the elders and the prophets are the leaders, the people are
    the led; cf. 3.1–2, 12.*

Will not spare[j] their youths,
Nor show compassion
To their orphans and widows;
For all are ungodly and wicked,
And every mouth speaks impiety.

[17]Already wickedness has blazed forth like a fire
Devouring thorn and thistle.
It has kindled the thickets of the wood,
[k]Which have turned into billowing smoke.[-k]

[l]Yet His anger has not turned back,
And His arm is outstretched still.[-l]

[18]By the fury of the LORD of Hosts,
The earth was shaken.[m]
Next, the people became like devouring fire:
No man spared his countryman.
[19]They snatched on the right, but remained hungry,
And consumed on the left without being sated.
Each devoured the flesh of his [n]own kindred[-n]—
[20]Manasseh Ephraim's, and Ephraim Manasseh's,[o]
And both of them against Judah![p]

Yet His anger has not turned back,
And His arm is outstretched still.

10 Ha!

Those who write out evil writs
And compose iniquitous documents,
[2]To subvert the cause of the poor,
To rob of their rights the needy of My people;
That widows may be their spoil,
And fatherless children their booty!
[3]What will you do on the day of punishment,
When the calamity comes from afar?

j Cf. Arabic samuha. 1QIs[a] reads yhmw.
k-k Meaning of Heb. uncertain.
l-l Moved down from v. 16 for clarity.
m Cf. note at 5.25.
n-n Meaning of Heb. uncertain. Emendation yields "fellow"; cf. Targum.
o Alludes to the civil wars of 2 Kings 15.10, 14–16, 25.
p Cf. 7.1–9.

To whom will you flee for help,
And how will you save your carcasses[a]
[4]From collapsing under [fellow] prisoners,
From falling beneath the slain?

Yet His anger has not turned back,
And his arm is outstretched still.

[5]Ha!
Assyria, rod of My anger,
[b-]In whose hand, as a staff, is My fury![-b]
[6]I send him against an ungodly nation,
I charge him against a people that provokes Me,
To take its spoil and to seize its booty
And to make it a thing trampled
Like the mire of the streets.
[7]But he has evil plans,
His mind harbors evil designs;
For he means to destroy,
To wipe out nations, not a few.
[8]For he thinks,
"After all, [c-]I have kings as my captains![-c]
[9]Was Calno any different from Carchemish?
Or Hamath from Arpad?
Or Samaria from Damascus?
[10][d-]Since I was able to seize
The insignificant kingdoms,
Whose images exceeded
Jersualem's and Samaria's,[-d]
[11]Shall I not do to Jerusalem and her images
What I did to Samaria and her idols?"

[12]But when my Lord has carried out all his purpose on Mount Zion and in Jerusalem, He[e] will punish the majestic pride and overbearing arrogance of the king of Assyria. [13]For he thought,
"By the might of my hand have I wrought it,
By my skill, for I am clever:

[a] Meaning of Heb. uncertain; for "carcasses," compare the rendering of kabod in v. 16; 22.18.
[b-b] Emendation yields "Who is a staff in the hand of my fury."
[c-c] Emendation yields "all the kingdoms fared alike!"
[d-d] Emendation yields "Since I was able to seize/those kingdoms and their images,/Why is Jerusalem better than Samaria?"
[e] Heb. "I."

I have erased the borders of peoples;
I have plundered their treasures,
And exiled their vast populations.[f]
14I was able to seize, like a nest,
The wealth of peoples;
As one gathers abandoned eggs,
So *I* gathered all the earth:
Nothing so much as flapped a wing
Or opened a mouth to peep."

15Does an ax boast over him who hews with it,
Or a saw magnify itself above him who wields it?
As though the rod raised him who lifts it,
As though the staff lifted the man![g]

16Assuredly,
The Sovereign LORD of Hosts will send
A wasting away in its[h] fatness;
And under its body[i] shall burn
A burning like that of fire,
[j-]Destroying frame and flesh.
It shall be like a sick man who pines away.[-j]
17The Light of Israel will be fire
And its Holy One flame.
It will burn and consume its thorns
And its thistles in a single day,
18And the mass of its scrub and its farm land.
19What trees remain of its scrub
Shall be so few that a boy may record them.

20And in that day,
The remnant of Israel
And the escaped of the House of Jacob
Shall lean no more upon him that beats it,[k]
But shall lean sincerely

---

f *According to vv. 6–7, Assyria was to plunder, but not to exile.*
g *Lit. "not-wood."*
h *Presumably Israel's. These verses would read well after 9.16.*
i *Cf. note at v. 3.*
j-j *Brought up from v. 18 for clarity.*
k *I.e., upon Assyria (see v. 24). Ahaz's reliance on Assyria was interpreted by Isaiah as lack of faith in the Lord; see 7.13 with note.*

On the LORD, the Holy One of Israel.
21Only a remnant shall return,
Only a remnant of Jacob,
To Mighty God.
22Even if your people, O Israel,
Should be as the sands of the sea,
Only a remnant of it shall return.
Destruction is decreed;
Retribution comes like a flood!
23For my Lord GOD of Hosts is carrying out
A decree of destruction upon all the land.

24Assuredly, thus said my Lord GOD of Hosts: "O My people that dwells in Zion, have no fear of Assyria, who beats you with a rod and wields his staff over you as did the Egyptians. 25For very soon My wrath will have spent itself, and l-My anger that was bent on wasting them."-l 26The LORD of Hosts will brandish a scourge over him as when He beat Midian at the Rock of Oreb,m and will wield His staff as He did over the Egyptians by the sea.

27And in that day,
His burden shall drop from your back,
n-And his yoke from your neck;
The yoke shall be destroyed because of fatness.

28He advanced upon Aiath,
He proceeded to Migron,
At Michmas he deposited his baggage.
29They made the crossing;
"Geba is to be our night quarters!"-n
Ramah was alarmed;
Gibeah of Saul took to flight.
30"Give a shrill cry, O Bath-gallim!
Hearken, Laishah!
Take up the cry, Anathoth!"
31Madmenah ran away;

---

l-l *Presumably Assyria; meaning of Heb. uncertain. Emendation yields "My anger against the world shall cease."*
m *See Judg. 7.25.*
n-n *Emendation yields "And his yoke shall leave your neck./He came up from Jeshimon/ 28By the ascent of Aiath,/He proceeded to Migron;/At Michmas he commanded his forces:/29Make the crossing;/Geba is to be our night quarters!" Jeshimon is the southeast corner of the Jordan Valley, Num. 21.20; 23.28; Aiath is elsewhere called Ai.*

The dwellers of Gebim sought refuge.
³²This same day at Nob
He shall stand and wave his hand.^o

O mount of Fair Zion!
O hill of Jerusalem!
³³Lo! The Sovereign LORD of Hosts
Will hew off the tree-crowns with an ax:
The tall ones shall be felled,
The lofty ones cut down:
³⁴The thickets of the forest shall be hacked away
   with iron,
And the Lebanon trees shall fall ^{p-}in their majesty.^{-p}

11
But a shoot shall grow out of the stump of Jesse,
A twig shall sprout from his stock.
²The spirit of the LORD shall alight upon him:
A spirit of wisdom and insight,
A spirit of counsel and valor,
A spirit of devotion and reverence for the LORD.
^{3a-}He shall sense the truth^{-a} by his reverence for the LORD:
He shall not judge by what his eyes behold,
Nor decide by what his ears perceive.
⁴Thus he shall judge the poor with equity
And decide with justice for the lowly of the land.
He shall strike down a land^b with the rod of his mouth
And slay the wicked with the breath of his lips.
⁵Justice shall be the girdle of his loins,
And faithfulness the girdle of his waist.
⁶The wolf shall dwell with the lamb,
The leopard lie down with the kid;
^{c-}The calf, the beast of prey, and the fatling^{-c} together,
With a little boy to herd them.
⁷The cow and the bear shall graze,

---

^o *I.e., the Assyrian king, arriving at Nob (close to Jerusalem), shall beckon his army onward; cf. 13.2.*

^{p-p} *Or "by the bronze," connecting Heb.* 'addir *with Akkadian* urudu, *"bronze."*

^{a-a} *Lit. "His sensing [shall be]"; meaning of Heb. uncertain.*

^b *Emendation yields "the ruthless."*

^{c-c} *1QIs^a reads: "The calf and the beast of prey shall feed"; so too the Septuagint.*

Their young shall lie down together;
And the lion, like the ox, shall eat straw.
8A babe shall play
Over a viper's hole,
And an infant pass[d] his hand
Over an adder's den.
9In all of [e-]My sacred mount[-e]
Nothing evil or vile shall be done;
For the land shall be filled with devotion to the LORD
As water covers the sea.

10In that day,
The stock of Jesse that has remained standing
Shall become a standard to peoples—
Nations shall seek his counsel
And his abode shall be honored.

11In that day, My Lord will apply His hand again to redeeming the other part[f] of His people from Assyria—as also from Egypt, Pathros, Nubia, Elam, Shinar, Hamath, and the coastlands.

12He will hold up a signal to the nations
And assemble the banished of Israel,
And gather the dispersed of Judah
From the four corners of the earth.

13Then Ephraim's envy shall cease
And Judah's harassment shall end;
Ephraim shall not envy Judah,
And Judah shall not harass Ephraim.
14They shall pounce on the back of Philistia to the west,
And together plunder the peoples of the east;
Edom and Moab shall be subject to them
And the children of Ammon shall obey them.

15The LORD will dry up the tongue of the Egyptian sea.—He will raise His hand over the Euphrates with the might[d] of His wind and break it

d Meaning of Heb. uncertain.
e-e I.e., the Holy Land; cf. Exod. 15.17; Ps. 78.54.
f I.e., the part outside the Holy Land; lit. "the rest that will remain."

641

into seven wadis, so that it can be trodden dry-shod. [16]Thus there shall be a highway for the other part[f] of His people out of Assyria, such as there was for Israel when it left the land of Egypt.

12

In that day, you shall say:
"I give thanks to You, O LORD!
Although You were wroth with me,
Your wrath has turned back and You comfort me,
[2]Behold the God who gives me triumph!
I am confident, unafraid;
For Yah the LORD is my strength and might,[a]
And He has been my deliverance."

[3]Joyfully shall you draw water
From the fountains of triumph,
[4]And you shall say on that day:
"Praise the LORD, proclaim His name.
Make His deeds known among the peoples;
Declare that His name is exalted.
[5]Hymn the LORD,
For He has done gloriously;
Let this be made known
In all the world!
[6]Oh, shout for joy,
You who dwell in Zion!
For great in your midst
Is the Holy One of Israel."

13

The "Babylon" Pronouncement, a prophecy of Isaiah son of Amoz.

[2]"Raise a standard upon a bare hill,
Cry aloud to them;
Wave a hand, and let them enter
The gates of the nobles!
[3]I have summoned My purified guests
To execute My wrath;

a Others "song."

Behold, I have called My stalwarts,
My proudly exultant ones."a

⁴Hark! a tumult on the mountains—
As ofᵇ a mighty force;
Hark! an uproar of kingdoms,
Nations assembling!
The LORD of Hosts is mustering
A host for war.
⁵They come from a distant land,
From the end of the sky—
The LORD with the weapons of His wrath—
To ravage all the earth!

⁶Howl!
For the day of the LORD is near;
It shall come like havoc from Shaddai.ᶜ
⁷Therefore all hands shall grow limp,
And all men's hearts shall sink;
⁸And, overcome by terror,
They shall be seized by pangs and throes,
Writhe like a woman in travail.
They shall gaze at each other in horror,
Their faces ᵈ⁻livid with fright.⁻ᵈ

⁹Lo! The day of the LORD is coming
With pitiless fury and wrath,
To make the earth a desolation,
To wipe out the sinners upon it.
¹⁰The stars and constellations of heaven
Shall not give off their light;
The sun shall be dark when it rises,
And the moon shall diffuse no glow.

¹¹"And I will requite to the world its evil,
And to the wicked their iniquity;
I will put an end to the pride of the arrogant
And humble the haughtiness of tyrants.

ᵃ *The impending slaughter is spoken of as a sacrificial meal, for which the guests were notified to purify themselves ritually; cf. Zeph. 1.7.*
ᵇ *Meaning of Heb. uncertain.*
ᶜ *Traditionally rendered "the Almighty."*
ᵈ⁻ᵈ *Taking the root lhb as a variant of bhl: others "shall be faces of flame."*

¹²I will make people scarcer than fine gold,
And men than gold of Ophir."

¹³Therefore ᵉ⁻shall heaven be shaken,⁻ᵉ
And earth leap out of its place,
At the fury of the LORD of Hosts
On the day of His burning wrath.
¹⁴Then like gazelles that are chased,
And like sheep that no man gathers,
Each man shall turn back to his people,
They shall flee every one to his land.
¹⁵All who remain shall be pierced through,
All who ᶠ⁻are caught⁻ᶠ
Shall fall by the sword.
¹⁶And their babes shall be dashed to pieces in their sight,
Their homes shall be plundered,
And their wives shall be raped.

¹⁷"Behold,
I stir up the Medes against them,
Who do not value silver
Or delight in gold.
¹⁸Their bows shall shatter the young;
They shall show no pity to infants,
They shall not spare the children."

¹⁹And Babylon, glory of kingdoms,
Proud splendor of the Chaldeans,
Shall become like Sodom and Gomorrah
Overturned by God.
²⁰Nevermore shall it be settled
Nor dwelt in through all the ages.
No Arab shall pitch his tent there,
No shepherds make flocks lie down there.
²¹But beastsᵇ shall lie down there,
And the houses be filled with owls;ᵇ
There shall ostriches make their home,
And there shall satyrs dance.

ᵉ⁻ᵉ *Lit. "I will shake heaven."*
ᶠ⁻ᶠ *Meaning of Heb. uncertain; emendation yields "flee."*

22And jackals[b] shall abide in its castles
And dragons[b] in the palaces of pleasure.
Her hour is close at hand;
Her days will not be long.

14
But the LORD will pardon Jacob, and will again choose Israel, and will settle them on their own soil. And strangers shall join them and shall cleave to the House of Jacob. 2For peoples shall take them[a] and bring them to their homeland; and the House of Israel shall possess them[b] as slaves and handmaids on the soil of the LORD. They shall be captors of their captors and masters to their taskmasters.

3And when the LORD has given you rest from your sorrow and trouble, and from the hard service that you were made to serve, 4you shall recite this song of scorn over the king of Babylon:

How is the taskmaster vanished,
How is oppression[c] ended!
5The LORD has broken the staff of the wicked,
The rod of tyrants,
6That smote peoples in wrath
With stroke unceasing,
That belabored nations in fury
In relentless pursuit.

7All the earth is calm, untroubled;
Loudly it cheers.
8Even pines rejoice at your fate,
And cedars of Lebanon:
"Now that you have lain down,
None shall come up to fell us."

9Sheol below was astir
To greet your coming—
Rousing for you the shades
Of all earth's chieftains,
Raising from their thrones
All the kings of nations.

---

[a] I.e., the House of Jacob.
[b] I.e., the peoples.
[c] Reading marhebah with 1QIs[a] (cf. Septuagint). The traditional reading madhebah is of unknown meaning.

10All speak up and say to you,
"So you have been stricken as we were,
You have become like us!
11Your pomp is brought down to Sheol,
And the strains of your lutes!
Worms are to be your bed,
Maggots your blanket!"

12How are you fallen from heaven,
O Shining One, son of Dawn!d
How are you felled to earth,
O vanquisher of nations!

13Once you thought in your heart,
"I will climb to the sky;
Higher than the stars of God
I will set my throne.
I will sit in the mount of assembly,e
On the summit of Zaphon:f
14I will mount the back of a cloud—
I will match the Most High."
15Instead, you are brought down to Sheol,
To g-the bottom of the Pit.-g
16They who behold you stare;
They peer at you closely:
"Is this the man
Who shook the earth,
Who made realms tremble,
17Who made the world like a waste
And wrecked its towns,
h-Who never released his prisoners to their homes?"
18All the kings of nations
Were laid, every one, in honor-h
Each in his tomb;
19While you were left lying unburied,
Like loathsome carrion,i

d A character in some lost myth.
e I.e., the assembly of the gods in council.
f The abode of the gods; cf. Ps. 48.3.
g-g A region of the netherworld reserved for those who have not received decent burial; cf. Ezek. 32.21 ff.
h-h Emendation yields "Who chained to his palace gate/All the kings of nations?/Yet they were all laid in honor. . . ." The practice of chaining captive chieftains to gates is attested in Mesopotamia.
i So several ancient versions; cf. postbiblical nesel, "putrefying flesh or blood."

Like a trampled corpse
[In] the clothing of slain gashed by the sword
Who sink to the very stones of the Pit.
20You shall not have a burial like them;
Because you destroyed ʲyour country,
Murdered your people.ʲ

Let the breed of evildoers
Nevermore be named!
21Prepare a slaughtering block for his sons
Because of the guilt of their father.ᵏ
Let them not arise to possess the earth!
Then the world's face shall be covered with towns.

22I will rise up against them—declares the LORD of Hosts—and will wipe out from Babylon name and remnant, kith and kin—declares the LORD—23and I will make it a home of bitterns,ˡ pools of water. I will sweep it with a broom of extermination—declares the LORD of Hosts.

24The LORD of Hosts has sworn this oath:
"As I have designed, so shall it happen;
What I have planned, that shall come to pass:
25To break Assyria in My land,
To crush him on My mountain."ᵐ
And his yoke shall drop off them,
And his burden shall drop from theirⁿ backs.
26That is the plan that is planned
For all the earth;
That is why an arm is poised
Over all the nations.
27For the LORD of Hosts has planned,
Who then can foil it?
It is His arm that is poised,
And who can stay it?

28This pronouncement was made in the year that King Ahaz died:

ʲ⁻ʲ *Emendation yields ". . . countries,/Murdered peoples."*
ᵏ *Heb. "fathers."*
ˡ *Meaning of Heb. uncertain.*
ᵐ*Heb. "mountains"; for the designation of the entire land of Israel as the Lord's mountain, cf. 11.9.*
ⁿ *Heb. "his." The last two lines of this verse would read well after v. 26.*

[29]Rejoice not, all Philistia,
Because the staff of him that beat you is broken.
For from the stock of a snake there sprouts an asp,
A flying seraph[o] branches out from it.
[30][p-]The first-born of the poor shall graze[-p]
And the destitute lie down secure.
[q-]I will kill your stock by famine,[-q]
And it shall slay the very last of you.
[31]Howl, O gate; cry out, O city;
Quake, all Philistia!
[r-]For a stout one is coming from the north
And there is no straggler in his ranks.[-r]

[32]And what will he answer the messengers of any nation?
That Zion has been established by the LORD:
In it, the needy of His people shall find shelter.

15

The "Moab" Pronouncement.

Ah, in the night Ar was sacked,
Moab was ruined;
Ah, in the night Kir was sacked,
Moab was ruined.

[2]He went up to the temple to weep,
Dibon[a] [went] to the outdoor shrines.
Over Nebo and Medeba
Moab is wailing;
On every head is baldness,
Every beard is shorn.
[3]In its streets, they are girt with sackcloth;
On its roofs, in its squares,
Everyone is wailing,
Streaming with tears.
[4]Heshbon and Elealeh cry out,
Their voice carries to Jahaz.

[o] *Others "fiery serpent"; cf. Num. 21.6, 8.*
[p-p] *Emendation yields "The poor shall graze in his pasture." This line and the next would read well after v. 32.*
[q-q] *Emendation yields "It shall kill your offspring with its venom (*zar'ekh berosho*)."*
[r-r] *Meaning of Heb. uncertain; the rendering "stout one" is suggested by the Syriac* 'ashshīn.

[a] *Regarded as the principal city of Moab.*

Therefore,
^{b-}The shock troops of Moab shout,^{-b}
His body is convulsed.
⁵My heart cries out for Moab—
His fugitives flee down to Zoar,
To Eglath-shelishiyah.
For the ascent of Luhith
They ascend with weeping;
On the road to Horonaim
They raise a cry of anguish.

⁶Ah, the waters of Nimrim
Are become a desolation;
The grass is sear,
The herbage is gone,
Vegetation is vanished.

⁷Therefore,
The gains they have made, and their stores,
They carry to the Wadi of Willows.

⁸Ah, the cry has compassed
The country of Moab:
All the way to Eglaim her wailing,
Even at Beer-elim her wailing!

⁹Ah, the waters of Dimon are full of blood[c]
For I pour added [water] on Dimon;
I drench[d] it—for Moab's refugees—
With soil[e] for its remnant.

16 ^aDispatch as messenger
The ruler of the land,
From Sela in the wilderness
To the mount of Fair Zion:

b-b *Change of vocalization yields "The loins of Moab are trembling."*
c *Emendation yields "tears."*
d *Cf. 16.9.*
e *Emendation yields "tears"; cf. Ugaritic 'dm't.*

a *Meaning of vv. 1 and 2 uncertain.*

2"Like fugitive birds,
Like nestlings driven away,
Moab's villagers linger
By the fords of the Arnon.
3 Give advice,
b-Offer counsel.-b
At high noon make
Your shadow like night:
Conceal the outcasts,
Betray not the fugitives.
4 Let c-Moab's outcasts-c
Find asylum in you;
Be a shelter for them
Against the despoiler."

For violence has vanished,
Rapine is ended,
And marauders have perished from this land.
5 And a throne shall be established in goodness
In the tent of David,
And on it shall sit in faithfulness
A ruler devoted to justice
And zealous for equity.d

6 "We have heard of Moab's pride—
Most haughty is he—
Of his pride and haughtiness and arrogance,
And of the iniquity in him."e

7 Ah, let Moab howl;
Let all in Moab howl!
For the raisin-cakesf of Kir-hareseth
You shall moan most pitifully.
8 The vineyards of Heshbon are withered,
And the vines of Sibmah;
b-Their tendrils spread
To Baale-goiim,-b

b-b *Meaning of Heb. uncertain.*
c-c *Heb. "my outcasts, Moab."*
d *14.32, above, would read well here.*
e *Baddaw is a suffixed form of the preposition* bede: *Nah. 2.13; Hab. 2.13; Job 39.25; with suffixes, Job 11.3, 41.4.*
f *Jer. 48.36 has "men."*

And reached to Jazer,
And strayed to the desert;
Their shoots spread out
And crossed the sea.

⁹Therefore,
As I weep for Jazer,
So I weep for Sibmah's vines;
O Heshbon and Elealeh,
I drench you with my tears.
ᵍ⁻Ended are the shouts
Over your fig and grain harvests.⁻ᵍ
¹⁰Rejoicing and gladness
Are gone from the farm land;
In the vineyards no shouting
Or cheering is heard.
No more does the treader
Tread wine in the presses—
The shouts ʰ⁻have been silenced.⁻ʰ

¹¹Therefore,
Like a lyre my heart moans for Moab,
And my very soul for Kir-heres.

¹²And when it has become apparent that Moab has gained nothing in the outdoor shrine, he shall come to pray in his temple—but to no avail.
¹³That is the word that the LORD spoke concerning Moab long ago. ¹⁴And now the LORD has spoken: In three years, fixed like the years of a hired laborer, Moab's population, with all its huge multitude, shall shrink. Only a remnant shall be left, of no consequence.

17 The "Damascus" Pronouncement.

Behold,
Damascus shall cease to be a city;
It shall become a heap of ruins.

ᵍ⁻ᵍ *Jer. 48.32 reads "A ravager has come down/Upon your fig and grape harvests."*
ʰ⁻ʰ *Lit. "I have silenced."*

2a-The towns of Aroer shall be deserted;-a
They shall be a place for flocks
To lie down, with none disturbing.

3Fortresses shall cease from Ephraim,b
And sovereignty from Damascus;
The remnant of Aram shall become
Like the mass of Israelites

—declares the LORD of Hosts.

4In that day,
The mass of Jacob shall dwindle,
And the fatness of his body become lean:
5After being like the standing grain
Harvested by the reaper—
Who reaps ears by the armful—
He shall be like the ears that are gleaned
In the Valley of Rephaim.
6Only gleanings shall be left of him,
As when one beats an olive tree:
Two berries or three on the topmost branch,
Four or five c-on the boughs of the crown-c

—declares the LORD, the God of Israel.

7In that day, men shall turn to their Maker, their eyes look to the Holy One of Israel; 8they shall not turn to the altars that their own hands made, or look to the sacred posts and incense stands that their own fingers wrought.

9In that day, their fortress cities shall be like the deserted sites which d-the Horesh and the Amir-d abandoned because of the Israelites; and there shall be desolation.

10Truly, you have forgotten the God who saves you
And have not remembered the Rock who shelters you;
That is why, though you plant a delightfule sapling,
What you sow proves a disappointing slip.
11On the day that you plant, you see it grow;

a-a *Emendation yields (cf. Septuagint) "Its towns shall be deserted forevermore."*
b *Emendation yields "Aram."*
c-c *Lit. "on her boughs, the many-branched one."*
d-d *Septuagint reads "the Amorites and the Hivites."*
e *Emendation yields "true." So Vulgate (cf. Septuagint); cf. Jer. 2.21.*

On the morning you sow, you see it bud—
But the branches wither away
On a day of sickness and mortal agony.

12Ah, the roar of many peoples
That roar as roars the sea,
The rage of nations that rage
As rage the mighty waters—
13Nations raging like massive waters!
But He shouts at them, and they flee far away,
Driven like chaff before winds in the hills,
And like tumbleweed before a gale.
14At eventide, lo, terror!
By morning, it is no more.
Such is the lot of our despoilers,
The portion of them that plunder us.

18 Ah,
a-land in the deep shadow of wings,-a
Beyond the rivers of Nubia!

2Go, swift messengers,
To a nation b-far and remote,
To a people thrust forth and away-b—
A nation of gibber and chatterc—
Whose land is cut off by streams;
d-Which sends out envoys by sea,
In papyrus vessels upon the water!-d

3[Say this:]
"All you who live in the world
And inhabit the earth,
When a flag is raised in the hills, take note!
When a ram's horn is blown, give heed!"
4For thus the LORD said to me:
"I rest calm and confidente in My habitation—

---

a-a *Or "Most sheltered land"; cf., e.g., 30.2, 3; Ps. 36.8; 57.2; 61.5.*
b-b *Meaning of Heb. uncertain.*
c *Meaning of Heb. uncertain; cf. 28.10. Biblical writers often characterize distant nations by their unintelligible speech; cf. 33.19; Deut. 28.49; Jer. 5.15.*
d-d *Brought down from beginning of verse for clarity. The Hebrew verb for "sends" agrees in gender with "nation," not with "land."*
e *Cf. hibbit "to rely" (Job 6.19). The related noun* mabbaṭ *occurs with similar meaning in Isa. 20.5, 6.*

Like a scorching heat upon sprouts,
ᶠ-Like a rain-cloud in the heat of reaping time."-ᶠ
⁵For before the harvest,ᵍ yet after the budding,
When the blossom has hardened into berries,
He will trim away the twigs with pruning hooks,
And lop off the trailing branches.ʰ
⁶They shall all be left
To the kites of the hills
And to the beasts of the earth;
The kites shall summer on them
And all the beasts of the earth shall winter on them.

⁷In that time,
Tribute shall be brought to the LORD of Hosts
[From] a people far and remote,
From a people thrust forth and away—
A nation of gibber and chatter,
Whose land is cut off by streams—
At the place where the name of the LORD of Hosts abides,
At Mount Zion.

19 The "Egypt" Pronouncement.

Mounted on a swift cloud,
The LORD will come to Egypt;
Egypt's idols shall tremble before Him,
And the heart of the Egyptians shall sink within them.

²"I will incite Egyptian against Egyptian:
They shall war with each other,
Every man with his fellow,
City with city
And kingdom with kingdom.ᵃ
³Egypt shall be drained of spirit,
And I will confound its plans;
So they will consult the idols and the shades
And the ghosts and the familiar spirits.
⁴And I will place the Egyptians

ᶠ⁻ᶠ *I.e., like a threat of disaster; cf. Eccl. 11.4.*
ᵍ *Emendation yields "vintage."*
ʰ *A figure of speech for the defeated enemy.*

ᵃ *I.e., the various districts of Egypt, which is Isaiah's time were governed by hereditary princes.*

At the mercy of a harsh master,
And a ruthless king shall rule them"
                    —declares the Sovereign, the LORD of Hosts.

⁵Water shall fail from the seas,
Rivers dry up and be parched,
⁶Channels turn foul as they ebb,
And Egypt's canals run dry.
Reed and rush shall decay,
⁷ᵇ⁻And the Nile papyrus by the Nile-side⁻ᵇ
And everything sown by the Nile
Shall wither, blow away, and vanish.
⁸The fishermen shall lament;
All who cast lines in the Nile shall mourn,
And those who spread nets on the water shall languish.
⁹The flax workers, too, shall be dismayed,
Both carders and weavers chagrined.ᵇ
¹⁰ᶜHer foundations shall be crushed,
And all who make dams shall be despondent.

¹¹Utter fools are the nobles of Tanis;
The sagest of Pharaoh's advisers
[Have made] absurd predictions.
How can you say to Pharaoh,
"I am a scion of sages,
A scion of Kedemite kings"?ᵈ
¹²Where, indeed, are your sages?
Let them tell you, let them discover
What the LORD of Hosts has planned against Egypt.
¹³The nobles of Tanis have been fools,
The nobles of Memphis deluded;
Egypt has been led astray
By the chiefs of her tribes.
¹⁴The LORD has mixed within her
A spirit of distortion,
Which shall lead Egypt astray in all her undertakings
As a vomiting drunkard goes astray;
¹⁵Nothing shall be achieved in Egypt
By either head or tail,
Palm branch or reed.ᶜ

ᵇ⁻ᵇ *Meaning of Heb. uncertain.*
ᶜ *Meaning of verse uncertain; emendation yields "Her drinkers shall be dejected,/And all her brewers despondent."*
ᵈ *Or "advisers." The wisdom of the Kedemites was proverbial; cf. 1 Kings 5.10.*
ᵉ *I.e., a man of either high or low station; cf. 9.13, 14.*

¹⁶In that day, the Egyptians shall be like women, trembling and terrified because the LORD of Hosts will raise His hand against them. ¹⁷And the land of Judah shall also be the dread of the Egyptians; they shall quake whenever anybody mentions it to them, because of what the LORD of Hosts is planning against them. ¹⁸In that day, there shall be several[f] towns in the land of Egypt speaking the language of Canaan and swearing loyalty to the LORD of Hosts; one[g] shall be called Town of Heres.[h]

¹⁹In that day, there shall be an altar to the LORD inside the land of Egypt and a pillar to the LORD at its border.[i] ²⁰They shall serve as a symbol and reminder of the LORD of Hosts in the land of Egypt, so that when [the Egyptians] cry out to the LORD against oppressors, He will send them a savior and champion to deliver them. ²¹For the LORD will make Himself known to the Egyptians, and the Egyptians shall acknowledge the LORD in that day, and they shall serve [Him] with sacrifice and oblation and shall make vows to the LORD and fulfill them. ²²The LORD will first afflict and then heal the Egyptians; when they turn back to the LORD, He will respond to their entreaties and heal them.

²³In that day, there shall be a highway from Egypt to Assyria. The Assyrians shall join with the Egyptians and Egyptians with the Assyrians, and then the Egyptians together with the Assyrians shall serve [the LORD].

²⁴In that day, Israel shall be a third partner with Egypt and Assyria as a blessing[j] on earth; ²⁵for the LORD of Hosts will bless them, saying, "Blessed be My people Egypt, My handiwork Assyria, and My very own Israel."

20 It was the year that the Tartan[a] came to Ashdod—being sent by King Sargon of Assyria—and attacked Ashdod and took it. ²Previously,[b] the LORD had spoken to Isaiah son of Amoz, saying, "Go, untie the sackcloth from your loins and take your sandals off your feet," which he had done, going naked and barefoot. ³And now the LORD said, "It is a sign and a portent for Egypt and Nubia. Just as My servant Isaiah has gone naked and barefoot for three years, ⁴so shall the king of Assyria

---

f Lit. "five."
g Or "each one."
h Meaning uncertain. Many Heb. mss. read heres, "sun," which may refer to Heliopolis, i.e., Sun City, in Egypt. Targum's "Beth Shemesh" (cf. Jer. 43.13) has the same meaning.
i As a symbol of the Lord's sovereignty over Egypt.
j I.e., a standard by which blessing is invoked; cf. Gen. 12.2 with note.

a An Assyrian title meaning "General"; cf. 2 Kings 18.17 and note.
b Lit. "At that time."

drive off the captives of Egypt and the exiles of Nubia, young and old, naked and barefoot and with bared buttocks—to the shame of Egypt! ⁵And they shall be dismayed and chagrined because of Nubia their hope and Egypt their boast. ⁶In that day, the dwellers of this coastland shall say, 'If this could happen to those we looked to, to whom we fled for help and rescue from the king of Assyria, how can we ourselves escape?' "

21 ᵃ⁻The "Desert of the Sea" Pronouncement.⁻ᵃ

> Like the gales
> That race through the Negeb,
> It comes from the desert,
> The terrible land.
> ²A harsh prophecy
> Has been announced to me:
> "The betrayer is ᵇ⁻betraying,
> The ravager ravaging.⁻ᵇ
> Advance, Elam!
> Lay siege, Media!
> ᶜ⁻I have put an end
> To all her sighing."⁻ᶜ
>
> ³Therefore my loins
> Are seized with trembling;
> I am gripped by pangs
> Like a woman in travail,
> Too anguished to hear,
> Too frightened to see.
> ⁴My mind is confused,
> I shudder in panic.
> My night of pleasure
> He has turned to terror:
> ⁵"Set the table!"
> To "Let the watchman watch!"

ᵃ⁻ᵃ *Emendation yields "The 'From the Desert' Pronouncement," agreeing with the phrase farther on in the verse.*
ᵇ⁻ᵇ *Emendation yields "betrayed . . . ravaged"; cf. 33.1.*
ᶜ⁻ᶜ *Emendation yields "Put an end to all her merrymaking!"*

"Eat and drink!"
To "Up, officers! grease[d] the shields!"

6For thus my LORD said to me:
"Go, set up a sentry;
Let him announce what he sees.
7He will see mounted men,
Horsemen in pairs—
Riders on asses,
Riders on camels—
And he will listen closely,
Most attentively."
8And [e-[like] a lion he]-e called out:
[f-"On my Lord's lookout]-f I stand
Ever by day,
And at my post I watch
Every night.
9And there they come, mounted men—
Horsemen in pairs!"
Then he spoke up and said,
"Fallen, fallen is Babylon,
And all the images of her gods
Have crashed to the ground!"
10[g-My threshing, the product of my threshing floor:]-g
What I have heard from the LORD of Hosts,
The God of Israel—
That I have told to you.

11The "Dumah"[h] Pronouncement.

A call comes to me from Seir:
"Watchman, what of the night?
Watchman, what of the night?"
12The watchman replied,
"Morning came, and so did night.
If you would inquire, inquire.
Come back again."

d *Emendation yields "grasp."*
e-e *1QIs[a] reads "The watcher."*
f-f *Or "On a lookout, my lord."*
g-g *Connection of Heb. uncertain.*
h *Name of a people; cf. Gen. 25.14.*

¹³The "In the Steppe" Pronouncement.

In the scrub, in the steppe, you will lodge,
O caravans of the Dedanites!
¹⁴Meet the thirsty with water,
You who dwell in the land of Tema;
Greet the fugitive with bread.
¹⁵For they have fled before swords:
Before the whetted sword,
Before the bow that was drawn,
Before the stress of war.

¹⁶For thus my Lord has said to me: "In another year, fixed like the years of a hired laborer, all the multitude of Kedar shall vanish; ¹⁷the remaining bows of Kedar's warriors shall be few in number; for the LORD, the God of Israel, has spoken.

22 The ᵃ⁻"Valley of Vision"⁻ᵃ Pronouncement.

ᵇWhat can have happened to you
That you have gone, all of you, up on the roofs,
²O you who were full of tumult,
You clamorous town,
You city so gay?
Your slain are not the slain of the sword
Nor the dead of battle.ᶜ
³Your officers have all departed,
They fled far away;
Your survivors were all taken captive,
ᵃ⁻Taken captive without their bows.⁻ᵃ
⁴That is why I say, "Let me be,
I will weep bitterly.
Press not to comfort me
For the ruin of ᵈ⁻my poor people."⁻ᵈ

⁵For my Lord GOD of Hosts had a day
Of tumult and din and confusion—

ᵃ⁻ᵃ *Meaning of Heb. uncertain.*
ᵇ *Vv. 1–3 describe a scene of mourning to take place in Jerusalem in the near future. In the ancient Near East, public weeping took place on the low flat roofs as well as in the streets and squares; cf. above, 15.3; Jer. 48.38.*
ᶜ *I.e., executed, instead of dying in battle.*
ᵈ⁻ᵈ *Lit. "the young woman, my people."*

^{c-}Kir raged in the Valley of Vision,
And Shoa on the hill;^{-c}
⁶While Elam bore the quiver
In troops of mounted men,
And Kir bared the shield—
⁷And your choicest lowlands
Were filled with chariots and horsemen:
They stormed at Judah's^f gateway
⁸And pressed beyond its screen.^g
You gave thought on that day
To the arms in the Forest House,^h
⁹And you took note of the many breaches
In the City of David.

¹⁰ⁱ⁻And you collected the water of the Lower Pool;⁻ⁱ and you counted the houses of Jerusalem and pulled houses down to fortify the wall; ¹¹and you constructed a basin between the two walls for the water of the old pool.

But you gave no thought to Him who planned it,
You took no note of Him who designed it long before.
¹²My Lord GOD of Hosts summoned on that day
To weeping and lamenting,
To tonsuring and girding with sackcloth.
¹³Instead, there was rejoicing and merriment,
Killing of cattle and slaughtering of sheep,
Eating of meat and drinking of wine:
"Eat and drink, for tomorrow we die!"
¹⁴Then the LORD of Hosts revealed Himself to my ears:
"This iniquity shall never be forgiven you
Until you die," said my Lord GOD of Hosts.

¹⁵Thus said my Lord GOD of Hosts: Go in to see that steward, that Shebna, in charge of the palace:
¹⁶What have you here, and whom have you here,
That you have hewn out a tomb for yourself here?—
O you who have hewn your^j tomb on high;
O you who have hollowed out for yourself^j an abode in the
cliff!

---

^{c-c} *Meaning of Heb. uncertain. On Kir see 2 Kings 16.9; Amos 1.5; 9.7; on Shoa see Ezek. 23.23.*
^f *Brought up from 8a for clarity.*
^g *Judah's gateway is the upper course of the Valley of Elah. The screen is the fortress Azekah, at the mouth of the gateway, which was captured by the Assyrians.*
^h *See 1 Kings 7.2–5; 10.16–17.*
ⁱ⁻ⁱ *This clause would read well after the prose part of v. 11a.*
^j *Heb. "his," "himself."*

[17]The LORD is about to shake you
k-Severely, fellow,-k and then wrap you around Himself.[1]
[18]Indeed, He will wind you about Him m-as a headdress, a
   turban.-m
Off to a broad land!
There shall you die, and there shall be the n-chariots bearing
   your body,-n
O shame of your master's house!
[19]For I will hurl you from your station
And you shall be torn down from your stand.

[20]And in that day, I will summon My servant Eliakim son of Hilkiah,
[21]and I will invest him with your tunic, gird him with your sash, and
deliver your authority into his hand; and he shall be a father to the inhabitants of Jerusalem and the men of Judah. [22]I will place the keys of
David's palace on his shoulders; and what he unlocks none may shut, and
what he locks none may open. [23]He shall be a seat of honor to his father's[o]
household. I will fix him as a peg in a firm place, [24]on which all the
substance of his father's[o] household shall be hung: a-the sprouts and the
leaves-a—all the small vessels, from bowls to all sorts of jars.

[25p]In that day—declares the LORD of Hosts—the peg fixed in a firm
place shall give way: it shall be cut down and shall fall, and the weight it
supports shall be destroyed. For it is the LORD who has spoken.

23 The "Tyre" Pronouncement.

Howl, you a-ships of Tarshish!-a
For havoc has been wrought, not a house is left;
As they came from the land of Kittim,
This was revealed to them.

[2]Moan, you coastland dwellers,
You traders of Sidon,
Once thronged by seafarers,
[3]Over many waters
Your[b] revenue came:

k-k Emendation yields "as a garment is shaken out."
[1] I.e., and walk off with you; cf. Jer. 43.12.
m-mEmendation yields "as a turban is wound about."
n-n Emendation yields "abode [cf. v. 16] of your body" [cf. 10.3, 16].
o Emendation yields "master's"; cf. v. 18 end.
p Apparently continues v. 19.

a-a See note at 2.16.
b Heb. "her."

From the trade of nations,
From the grain of Shihor,
The harvest of the Nile.
⁴Be ashamed, O Sidon!
For the sea—this stronghold of the sea—declares,
ᶜ-"I am as one who has-ᶜ never labored,
Never given birth,
Never raised youths
Or reared maidens!"
⁵When the Egyptians heard it, they quailed
As when they heard about Tyre.

⁶Pass on to Tarshish—
Howl, you coastland dwellers!
⁷Was such your merry city
In former times, of yore?
Did her feet carry her off
To sojourn far away?
⁸Who was it that planned this
For crown-wearing Tyre,
Whose merchants were nobles,
Whose traders the world honored?
⁹The LORD of Hosts planned it—
To defile all glorious beauty,
To shame all the honored of the world.

¹⁰ᵈ-Traverse your land like the Nile,
Fair Tarshish;-ᵈ
This is a harborᵉ no more.

¹¹The LORD poised His arm o'er the sea
And made kingdoms quake;
It was He decreed destruction
For Phoenicia'sᶠ strongholds,
¹²And said,
"You shall be gay no more,
O plundered one, Fair Maiden Sidon.

ᶜ⁻ᶜ *Lit. "I have."*
ᵈ⁻ᵈ *Meaning of Heb. uncertain. Emendation yields "Pass on to the land of Kittim,/You ships of Tarshish."*
ᵉ *Meaning of Heb. uncertain; taking* mezah *as a by-form of* mahoz: *cf. Ps. 107.30.*
ᶠ *Heb. "Canaan's."*

Up, cross over to Kittim—
Even there you shall have no rest."

13gBehold the land of Chaldea—
This is the people that has ceased to be.
Assyria, which founded it for ships,
Which raised its watchtowers,
Erected its ramparts,
Has turned it into a ruin.

14Howl, O ships of Tarshish,
For your stronghold is destroyed!

15In that day, Tyre shall remain forgotten for seventy years, equaling
the lifetime of one king. After a lapse of seventy years, it shall go with
Tyre as with the harlot in the ditty:

16Take a lyre, go about the town,
Harlot long forgotten;
Sweetly play, make much music,
To bring you back to mind.

17For after a lapse of seventy years, the LORD will take note of Tyre,
and she shall resume her h-"fee-taking" and "play the harlot"-h with all
the kingdoms of the world, on the face of the earth. 18But her profits and
"hire" shall be consecrated to the LORD. They shall not be treasured or
stored; rather shall her profits go to those who abide before the LORD,
that they may eat their fill and clothe themselves elegantly.

24 Behold,

The LORD will strip the earth bare,
And lay it waste,
And twist its surface,
And scatter its inhabitants.
2Layman and priest shall fare alike,
Slave and master,

---

g Meaning of verse uncertain. Emendation yields "The land of Kittim itself—/Which the Sidonian
people founded,/Whose watchtowers they raised,/Whose citadels they erected—/Exists no more;/
Assyria has turned it into a ruin."
h-h I.e., "trading . . . trade."

Handmaid and mistress,
Buyer and seller,
Lender and borrower,
Creditor and debtor.
³The earth shall be bare, bare;
It shall be plundered, plundered;
For it is the LORD who spoke this word.

⁴The earth is withered, sear;
The world languishes, it is sear;
ᵃ⁻The most exalted people of the earth⁻ᵃ languish.
⁵For the earth was defiled
Under its inhabitants;
Because they transgressed teachings,
Violated laws,
Broke the ancient covenant.ᵇ
⁶That is why a curse consumes the earth,
And its inhabitants pay the penalty;
That is why earth's dwellers have dwindled,
And but few men are left.
⁷The new wine fails,
The vine languishes;
And all the merry-hearted sigh.
⁸Stilled is the merriment of timbrels,
Ended the clamor of revelers,
Stilled the merriment of lyres.
⁹They drink their wine without song;
Liquor tastes bitter to the drinker.
¹⁰Towns are broken,ᶜ empty;
Every house is shut, none enters;
¹¹Even over wine, a cry goes up in the streets:
The sun has set on all joy,
The gladness of the earth is banished.
¹²Desolation is left in the town
And the gate is battered to ruins.
¹³For thus shall it be among the peoples
In the midst of the earth:

ᵃ⁻ᵃ *Change of vocalization yields "both sky and earth."*
ᵇ *I.e., the moral law, which is binding on all men (cf. Gen. 9.4–6).*
ᶜ *Emendation yields "left."*

As when the olive tree is beaten out,
Like gleanings when the vintage is over.

¹⁴These shall lift up their voices,
Exult in the majesty of the LORD.
They shall shout from the sea:
¹⁵Therefore, honor the LORD with lights
In the coastlands of the sea—
The name of the LORD, the God of Israel.
¹⁶From the end of the earth
We hear singing:
Glory to the righteous!
d-And I said:-d
e-I waste away! I waste away! Woe is me!
The faithless have acted faithlessly;
The faithless have broken faith!-e

¹⁷f-Terror, and pit, and trap-f
Upon you who dwell on earth!
¹⁸He who flees at the report of the terror
Shall fall into the pit;
And he who climbs out of the pit
Shall be caught in the trap.
For sluices are opened on high,
And earth's foundations tremble.

¹⁹The earth is breaking, breaking;
The earth is crumbling, crumbling.
The earth is tottering, tottering;
²⁰The earth is swaying like a drunkard;
It is rocking to and fro like a hut.
Its iniquity shall weigh it down,
And it shall fall, to rise no more.

²¹In that day, the LORD will punish
The host of heaven in heaven
And the kings of the earth on earth.

---

d-d *Change of vocalization yields "They shall say."*
e-e *Meaning of Heb. uncertain. Emendation yields "Villain [Arabic* razīl], *foolish villain!/The
faithless who acted faithlessly/Have been betrayed in turn."*
f-f *Heb.* paḥad wa-paḥath, wa-paḥ.

²²They shall be gathered in a dungeon
As captives are gathered;
And shall be locked up in a prison.
But after many days they shall be remembered.

²³Then the moon shall be ashamed,
And the sun shall be abashed.
For the LORD of Hosts will reign
On Mount Zion and in Jerusalem,
And the Presence will be revealed to His elders.

25 O LORD, You are my God;
I will extol You, I will praise Your name.
For You planned graciousnessᵃ of old,
Counsels of steadfast faithfulness.

²For You have turned a city into a stone heap,
A walled town into a ruin,
The citadel of strangersᵇ into rubble,ᶜ
Never to be rebuilt.
³Therefore a fierce people must honor You,
A city of cruel nations must fear You.
⁴For You have been a refuge for the poor man,
A shelter for the needy man in his distress—
Shelter from rainstorm, shade from heat.
When the fury of tyrants was like a winterᶜ rainstorm,
⁵The rage of strangersᵇ like heat in the desert,
You subdued the heat with the shade of clouds,
The singingᵈ of the tyrants was vanquished.

⁶The LORD of Hosts will make on this mountᵉ
For all the peoples
A banquet of ᶜrich viands,
A banquet of choice wines—
Of rich viands seasoned with marrow,
Of choice wines⁻ᶜ well refined.

ᵃ See 9.5.
ᵇ Emendation yields "arrogant men."
ᶜ Meaning of Heb. uncertain.
ᵈ Meaning of Heb. uncertain. Emendation yields "rainstorm"; cf. 4d.

7And He will destroy on this mount[c] the shroud
That is drawn over the faces of all the peoples
And the covering that is spread
Over all the nations:
8He will destroy death[f] forever.
My Lord GOD will wipe the tears away
From all faces
And will put an end to the reproach of [g-]His people[-g]
Over all the earth—
For it is the LORD who has spoken.

9In that day they shall say:
This is our God;
We trusted in Him, and He delivered us.
This is the LORD, in whom we trusted;
Let us rejoice and exult in His deliverance!

10For the hand of the LORD shall descend
Upon this mount,[c]
And Moab[h] shall be trampled under Him
As straw is threshed to bits at Madmenah.[i]
11Then He will spread out His hands in their homeland,[j]
As a swimmer spreads his hands out to swim,
And He will humble their pride
Along with [k-]the emblems of their power.[-k]
12Yea, the secure fortification of their[l] walls
He will lay low and humble,
Will raze to the ground, to the very dust.

26 In that day, this song shall be sung
In the land of Judah:
Ours is a mighty city;
He makes victory our inner and outer wall.
2Open the gates, and let
A righteous nation enter,
[A nation] that keeps faith.

---

c *I.e., the Holy Land, as in 11.9; 14.25; 57.13.*
f *Perhaps an allusion to the mass killings committed by the Assyrians; cf. 10.7; 14.20.*
g-g *Emendation yields "peoples."*
h *Emendation yields "Assyria"; cf. 14.25.*
i *A village near Jerusalem; see 10.31. Emendation yields "As straw gets shredded in the threshing."*
j *Lit. "midst."*
k-k *Meaning of Heb. uncertain. Emendation yields "their citadels"; cf. the next verse.*
l *Heb. "your."*

³The confident mind You guard in safety,
In safety because it trusts in You.

⁴Trust in the LORD for ever and ever,
For in Yah the LORD you have an everlasting Rock.
⁵For He has brought low those who dwelt high up,
Has humbled the secure city,
Humbled it to the ground,
Leveled it with the dust—
⁶To be trampled underfoot,
By the feet of the needy,
By the soles of the poor.
⁷The path is level for the righteous man;
O Just One, You make smooth the course of the righteous.

⁸For Your just ways, O LORD, we look to You;
We long for the name by which You are called.
⁹At night I yearn for You with all my being,
I seek You with all ᵃ-the spirit within me.-ᵃ
For when Your judgments are wrought on earth,
The inhabitants of the world learn righteousness.
¹⁰But when the scoundrel is spared, he learns not righteousness;
In a place of integrity, he does wrong—
He ignores the majesty of the LORD.

¹¹O LORD!
They see not Your hand exalted.
Let them be shamed as they behold
Your zeal for Your people
And fire consuming Your adversaries.
¹²ᵇO LORD!
May You appoint well-being for us,
Since You have also requited all our misdeeds.

¹³O LORD our God!
Lords other than You possessed us,
But only Your name shall we utter.

ᵃ⁻ᵃ *Emendation yields "my spirit in the morning."*
ᵇ *Meaning of verse uncertain.*

¹⁴They are dead, they can never live;
Shades, they can never rise;
Of a truth, You have dealt with them and wiped them out,
Have put an end to all mention of them.
¹⁵ᶜWhen You added to the nation, O LORD,
When You added to the nation,
Extending all the boundaries of the land,
You were honored.
¹⁶O LORD! In their distress, they sought You;
Your chastisement reduced them
To anguishedᵈ whispered prayer.
¹⁷Like a woman with child
Approaching childbirth,
Writhing and screaming in her pangs,
So are we become because of You, O LORD.
¹⁸We were with child, we writhed—
It is as though we had given birth to wind;
We have won no victory on earth;
The inhabitants of the world have not ᶜ⁻come to life!⁻ᶜ
¹⁹Oh, let Your dead revive!
Let corpsesᶠ arise!
Awake and shout for joy,
You who dwell in the dust!—
For Your dew is like the dew on fresh growth;
You make the land of the shades ᶜ⁻come to life.⁻ᶜ

²⁰Go, my people, enter your chambers,
And lock your doors behind you.
Hide but a little moment,
Until the indignation passes.
²¹For lo!
The LORD shall come forth from His place
To punish the dwellers of the earth
For their iniquity;
And the earth shall disclose its bloodshed
And shall no longer conceal its slain.

ᶜ *Meaning of vv. 15–16 uncertain.*
ᵈ *Lit. "anguish"; taking ṣaqun as a noun formed like zadon and sason.*
ᶜ⁻ᶜ *Meaning of Heb. uncertain.*
ᶠ *Grammar of Heb. unclear.*

27
In that day the LORD will punish,
With His great, cruel, mighty sword
Leviathan the Elusive[a] Serpent—
Leviathan the Twisting[a] Serpent;
He will slay the Dragon of the sea.[b]

[2]In that day,
They shall sing of it:[c]
"Vineyard of Delight."[d]
[3]I the LORD keep watch over it,
I water it every moment;
[e-]That no harm may befall it,[-e]
I watch it night and day.
[4]There is no anger in Me:
[a-]If one offers Me thorns and thistles,
I will march to battle against him,
And set all of them on fire.[-a]
[5]But if he holds fast to My refuge,
[a-]He makes Me his friend;
He makes Me his friend.[-a]

[6][In days] to come Jacob shall strike root,
Israel shall sprout and blossom,
And the face of the world
Shall be covered with fruit.

[7]Was he beaten as his beater has been?
Did he suffer such slaughter as his slayers?
[8f-]Assailing them[-f] with fury unchained,
His pitiless blast bore them off
On a day of gale.

[9g]Assuredly, by this alone
Shall Jacob's sin be purged away;
This is the only price

---

[a] *Meaning of Heb. uncertain.*
[b] *The monster which the Lord vanquished of old (cf. 51.9; Ps. 74.13–14) was the embodiment of chaos; here it stands for the forces of evil in the present world.*
[c] *Apparently the earth; cf. 26.21.*
[d] *So some mss. (cf. Amos 5.11); other mss. and the editions have "Wine."*
[e-e] *Meaning of Heb. uncertain; emendation yields "My eye is open upon it."*
[f-f] *Lit. "Striving with her"; meaning of verse uncertain.*
[g] *This verse would read well before v. 6; the thought of vv. 7–8, dealing with the punishment of Israel's enemies, is continued in vv. 10–11.*

For removing his guilt:
That he make all the altar-stones
Like shattered blocks of chalk—
With no sacred post left standing,
Nor any incense altar.
¹⁰Thus fortified cities lie desolate,
Homesteads deserted, forsaken like a wilderness;
There calves graze, there they lie down
ʰ⁻And consume its boughs.
¹¹When its crown is withered, they break;⁻ʰ
Women come and make fires with them.
For they are a people without understanding;
That is why
Their Maker will show them no mercy,
Their Creator will deny them grace.

¹²And in that day, the LORD will beat out [the peoples like grain] from the channel of the Euphrates to the Wadi of Egypt; and you shall be picked up one by one, O children of Israel!

¹³And in that day, a great ram's horn shall be sounded; and the strayed who are in the land of Assyria and the expelled who are in the land of Egypt shall come and worship the LORD on the holy mount, in Jerusalem.

28

Ah, the proud crowns of the drunkards of Ephraim,
Whose glorious beauty is but wilted flowers
On the heads of men bloatedᵃ with rich food,
Who are overcome by wine!

²Lo, my Lord has something strong and mighty,
Like a storm of hail,
A shower of pestilence.
Something like a storm of massive, torrential rainᵇ
Shall be hurled with force to the ground.
³Trampled underfoot shall be
The proud crowns of the drunkards of Ephraim,

ʰ⁻ʰ *Meaning of Heb. uncertain. Emendation yields "Or like a terebinth whose boughs/Break when its crown is withered."*

ᵃ *Ge is contracted from ge'e; cf. Ibn Ezra.*
ᵇ *Lit. "water."*

⁴The wilted flowers—
On the heads of men bloatedᵃ with rich food—
That are his glorious beauty.
They shall be like an early fig
Before the fruit harvest;
Whoever sees it devours it
While it is still ᶜ⁻in his hand.⁻ᶜ

⁵In that day, the LORD of Hosts shall become a crown of beauty and a diadem of glory for the remnant of His people, ⁶and a spirit of judgment for him who sits in judgment and of valor for those who repel attacks at the gate.

⁷But these are also muddled by wine
And dazed by liquor:
Priest and prophet
Are muddled by liquor;
They are confused by wine,
They are dazed by liquor;
They are muddled in their visions,
They stumble in judgment.
⁸Yea, all tables are covered
With vomit and filth,
So that no space is left.

⁹ᵈ"To whom would he give instruction?
To whom expound a message?
To those newly weaned from milk,
Just taken away from the breast?
¹⁰That same mutter upon mutter,
Murmur upon murmur,
Now here, now there!"

¹¹Truly, as one who speaks to that people in a stammering jargon and an alien tongue ¹²is he who declares to them, "This is the resting place, let the weary rest;ᵉ this is the place of repose." They refuse to listen. ¹³To them the word of the LORD is:

ᶜ⁻ᶜ *Emendation yields "on the bough."*
ᵈ *This is the drunkards' reaction to Isaiah's reproof.*
ᵉ *I.e., do not embark on any political adventure at this time.*

"Mutter upon mutter,
Murmur upon murmur,
Now here, now there."
And so they will march,[f]
But they shall fall backward,
And be injured and snared and captured.

[14]Hear now the word of the LORD,
You men of mockery,
[g]Who govern that people[g]
In Jerusalem!
[15]For you have said,
"We have made a covenant with Death,
Concluded a pact with Sheol.
When the sweeping flood passes through,
It shall not reach us;
For we have made falsehood our refuge,
Taken shelter in treachery."
[16]Assuredly,
Thus said the Lord GOD:
"Behold, I will found in Zion,
Stone by stone,
[h]A tower of precious cornerstones,[h]
Exceedingly firm;
He who trusts need not fear.
[17]But I will apply judgment as a measuring line
And retribution[i] as weights;[j]
Hail shall sweep away the refuge of falsehood,
And flood-waters engulf your shelter.
[18]Your covenant with Death shall be annulled,
Your pact with Sheol shall not endure;
When the sweeping flood passes through,
You shall be its victims.
[19]It shall catch you
Every time it passes through;
It shall pass through every morning,
Every day and every night.

f *I.e., embark on the political adventure.*
g-g *Or "composers of taunt-verses for that people."*
h-h *Meaning of Heb. uncertain.*
i *As in 1.27; 5.16; 10.22.*
j *I.e., I will make judgment and retribution My plan of action; cf. 34.11; 2 Kings 21.13.*

And it shall be sheer horror
To grasp the message."

²⁰The couch is too short for stretching out,
And the cover too narrow for curling up!

²¹For the LORD will arise
As on the hill of Perazim,
He will rouse Himself
As in the vale of Gibeon,
To do His work—
Strange is His work!
And to perform His task—
Astounding is His task!^k
²²Therefore, refrain from mockery,
Lest your bonds be tightened.
For I have heard a decree of destruction
From my Lord GOD of Hosts
Against all the land.

²³Give diligent ear to my words,
Attend carefully to what I say.
²⁴Does he who plows to sow
Plow all the time,
Breaking up and furrowing his land?
²⁵When he has smoothed its surface,
Does he not rather broadcast black cumin
And scatter cumin,
Or set wheat in a row,^l
Barley in a strip,
And emmer in a patch?
²⁶For He teaches him the right manner,
His God instructs him.
²⁷So, too, black cumin is not threshed with a threshing board,
Nor is the wheel of a threshing sledge rolled over cumin;
But black cumin is beaten out with a stick
And cumin with a rod.
²⁸It is cereal that is crushed.^m

k *Instead of giving victory, as at Baal-perazim and Gibeon (cf. 2 Sam. 5.19–25; 1 Chron. 14.9–16), He will inflict punishment.*
l *In some Near Eastern countries, wheat is actually planted rather than scattered.*
m *Emendation yields "threshed."*

For ⁿ-even if-ⁿ he threshes it thoroughly,
And the wheel of his sledge ʰ-and his horses overwhelm it,-ʰ
He does not crush it.
²⁹That, too, is ordered by the LORD of Hosts;
His counsel is unfathomable,
His wisdom marvelous.

29 "Ah, Ariel,ᵃ Ariel,
City where David camped!
Add year to year,
Let festivals come in their cycles!
²And I will harass Ariel,
And there shall be sorrow and sighing.
ᵇ-She shall be to Me like Ariel.-ᵇ
³And I will camp against you ᶜ-round about;-ᶜ
I will lay siege to you ᵇ-with a mound,-ᵇ
And I will set up siegeworks against you.
⁴And you shall speak from lower than the ground,
Your speech shall be humbler than the sod;
Your speech shall sound like a ghost's from the ground,
Your voice shall chirp from the sod.
⁵And like fine dust shall be
The multitude of ᵈ-your strangers;-ᵈ
And like flying chaff,
The multitude of tyrants."

And suddenly, in an instant,
⁶She shall be remembered of the LORD of Hosts
With roaring, and shaking, and deafening noise,
Storm, and tempest, and blaze of consuming fire.
⁷Then, like a dream, a vision of the night,
Shall be the multitude of nations
That war upon Ariel,
And all her besiegers, and the siegeworks against her,
And those who harass her.
⁸Like one who is hungry
And dreams he is eating,

n-n *Taking* lo *as equivalent to* lu.

ᵃ *A poetic name of Jerusalem; cf. 33.7.*
ᵇ⁻ᵇ *Meaning of Heb. uncertain.*
ᶜ⁻ᶜ *Meaning of Heb. uncertain; Septuagint reads "like David"; cf. v. 1.*
ᵈ⁻ᵈ *Manuscript 1QIsᵃ reads "haughty men."*

But wakes to find himself empty;
And like one who is thirsty
And dreams he is drinking,
But wakes to find himself faint
And utterly parched—
So shall be all the multitude of nations
That war upon Mount Zion.

9Act stupid and be stupefied!
Act blind and be blinded!
(They are drunk, but not from wine,
They stagger, but not from liquor.)
10For the LORD has spread over you
A spirit of deep sleep,
And has shut your eyes, the prophets,
And covered your heads, the seers;
11So that all prophecy has been to you
Like the words of a sealed document.

If it is handed to one who can read and he is asked to read it, he will
say, "I can't, because it is sealed"; 12and if the document is handed to one
who cannot read and he is asked to read it, he will say, "I can't read."

13My Lord said:
Because that people has approached [Me] with its mouth
And honored Me with its lips,
But has kept its heart far from Me,
And its worship of Me has been
A commandment of men, learned by rote—
14Truly, I shall further baffle that people
With bafflement upon bafflement;
And the wisdom of its wise shall fail,
And the prudence of its prudent shall vanish.

15Ha! Those who would hide their plans
Deep from the LORD!
Who do their work in dark places

And say, "Who sees us, who takes note of us?"
16e-How perverse of you!
Should the potter be accounted as the clay?-e
Should what is made say of its Maker,
"He did not make me,"
And what is formed say of Him who formed it,
f-"He did not understand?"-f
17Surely, in a little while,
Lebanon will be transformed into farm land,
And farm land accounted as mere brush.
18In that day, the deaf shall hear even written words,
And the eyes of the blind shall see
Even in darkness and obscurity.
19Then the humble shall have increasing joy through the LORD,
And the neediest of men shall exult
In the Holy One of Israel.
20For the tyrant shall be no more,
The scoffer shall cease to be;
And those diligent for evil shall be wiped out,
21Who cause men to lose their lawsuits,
Laying a snare for the arbiter at the gate,
And wronging by falsehood
Him who was in the right.

22Assuredly, thus said the LORD to the House of Jacob, g-Who redeemed Abraham:-g

No more shall Jacob be shamed,
No longer his face grow pale.

23For when he—that is, his children—behold what My hands have wrought in his midst, they will hallow My name.

Men will hallow the Holy One of Jacob
And stand in awe of the God of Israel.
24And the confused shall acquire insight
And grumblers accept instruction.

e-e *Meaning of first line uncertain; emendation yields "Should the potter be accounted/Like the jugs or like the clay?"*
f-f *Emendation yields "He did not fashion me."*
g-g *Emendation yields "Whose fathers He redeemed."*

30 Oh, disloyal sons!

—declares the LORD—

Making plans
Against My wishes,
Weaving schemes
Against My will,
Thereby piling
Guilt on guilt—
²Who set out to go down to Egypt
Without asking Me,
To seek refuge with Pharaoh,
To seek shelter under the protection of Egypt.

³The refuge with Pharaoh shall result in your shame;
The shelter under Egypt's protection, in your chagrin.
⁴Though his officers are present in Zoan,ᵃ
And his messengersᵇ reach as far as Hanes,
⁵They all shall come to shame
Because of a people that does not avail them,
That is of no help or avail,
But [brings] only chagrin and disgrace.

⁶ᶜ⁻The "Beasts of the Negeb" Pronouncement.

Through aᶜ land of distress and hardship,
Of lion and roaringᵈ king-beast,
Of viper and flying seraph,ᵉ
They convey their wealth on the backs of asses,
Their treasures on camels' humps,
To a people of no avail.
⁷For the help of Egypt
Shall be vain and empty.
Truly, I call this,
ᶠ⁻"They are a threat that has ceased."⁻ᶠ

⁸Now,
Go, write it down on a tablet

ᵃ Or "Tanis."
ᵇ Emendation yields "kings"; cf. 19.2 with note.
ᶜ⁻ᶜ Meaning of Heb. uncertain; emendation yields "Through the wasteland of the Negeb/Through a. . . ."
ᵈ Meaning of Heb. uncertain.
ᵉ See note on 14.29.
ᶠ⁻ᶠ Meaning of Heb. uncertain. Emendation yields "Disgrace and chagrin"; cf. v. 5.

And inscribe it in a record,
That it may be with them for future days,
A witness[g] forever.
⁹For it is a rebellious people,
Faithless children,
Children who refused to heed
The instruction of the LORD;
¹⁰Who said to the seers,
"Do not see,"
To the prophets, "Do not prophesy truth to us;
Speak to us falsehoods,
Prophesy delusions.
¹¹Leave the way!
Get off the path!
Let us hear no more
About the Holy One of Israel!"

¹²Assuredly,
Thus said the Holy One of Israel:
Because you have rejected this word,
And have put your trust and reliance
In that which is fraudulent and tortuous—
¹³Of a surety,
This iniquity shall work on you
Like a spreading breach that occurs in a lofty wall,
Whose crash comes sudden and swift.
¹⁴It is smashed as one smashes an earthen jug,
Ruthlessly shattered
So that no shard is left in its breakage
To scoop coals from a brazier,
Or ladle water from a puddle.

¹⁵For thus said my Lord GOD,
The Holy One of Israel,
"You shall triumph by stillness and quiet;
Your victory shall come about
Through calm and confidence."
But you refused.

g Understanding 'ad, with Targum, as a variant of 'ed.

¹⁶"No," you declared.
"We shall flee on steeds"—
Therefore you shall flee!
"We shall ride on swift mounts"—
Therefore your pursuers shall prove swift!
¹⁷One thousand before the shout of one—
You shall flee at the shout of five;
Till what is left of you
Is like a mast on a hilltop,
Like a pole upon a mountain.

¹⁸Truly, the LORD is waiting to show you grace,
Truly, He will arise to pardon you.
For the LORD is a God of justice;
Happy are all who wait for Him.

¹⁹Indeed, O people in Zion, dwellers of Jerusalem, you shall not have cause to weep. He will grant you His favor at the sound of your cry; He will respond as soon as He hears it. ²⁰My Lord will provide for you meager bread and scant water. Then your Guide will no more ᵈ⁻be ignored,⁻ᵈ but your eyes will watch your Guide; ²¹and, whenever you deviate to the right or to the left, your ears will heed the command from behind you: "This is the road; follow it!" ²²And you will treat as unclean the silver overlay of your images and the golden plating of your idols. You will castʰ them away like a menstruous woman. "Out!" you will call to them.

²³So rain shall be provided for the seed with which you sow the ground, and the bread that the ground brings forth shall be rich and fat. Your livestock, in that day, shall graze in broad pastures; ²⁴as for the cattle and the asses that till the soil, they shall partake of salted fodder that has been winnowed with shovel and fan.

²⁵And on every high mountain and on every lofty hill, there shall appear brooks and watercourses—on a day of heavy slaughter, when towers topple. ²⁶And the light of the moon shall become like the light of the sun, and the light of the sun shall become sevenfold, like the light of the seven days, when the LORD binds up His people's wounds and heals the injuries it has suffered.

ʰ *Change of vocalization yields "keep."*

[27]Behold the [i]-LORD Himself[i]
Comes from afar
In blazing wrath,
[j]With a heavy burden[j]—
His lips full of fury,
His tongue like devouring fire,
[28]And his breath like a raging torrent
Reaching halfway up the neck—
To set a misguiding yoke[k] upon nations
And a misleading bridle upon the jaws of peoples,

[29]For you, there shall be singing
As on a night when a festival is hallowed;
There shall be rejoicing as when they march
With flute, [l]with timbrels, and with lyres[l]
To the Rock of Israel on the Mount of the LORD.

[30]For the LORD will make His majestic voice heard
And display the sweep of His arm
In raging wrath,
In a devouring blaze of fire,
In tempest, and rainstorm, and hailstones.
[31]Truly, Assyria, who beats with the rod,
Shall be cowed by the voice of the LORD;
[32][d]-And each time the appointed staff passes by,
The LORD will bring down [His arm] upon him
And will do battle with him as he waves it.[-d]
[33]The Topheth[m] has long been ready for him;
He too is destined for Melech[n]—
His firepit has been made both wide and deep,
With plenty of fire and firewood,
And with the breath of the LORD
Burning in it like a stream of sulfur.

31 Ha!

Those who go down to Egypt for help

[i-i] Lit. "The name of the LORD."
[j-j] Presumably with a heavy load of punishment. Meaning of Heb. uncertain.
[k] Interpreting naphath like Arabic nāf; meaning of line uncertain.
[l-l] Brought from v. 32 for clarity.
[m] A site near Jerusalem at which human beings were sacrificed by fire in periods of paganizing; see 2 Kings 23.10.
[n] Cf. Molech, Lev. 18.21; 20.2–5.

And rely upon horses!
They have put their trust in abundance of chariots,
In vast numbers of riders,
And they have not turned to the Holy One of Israel,
They have not sought the LORD.

²But He too is wise!
He has brought on misfortune,
And has not canceled His word.
So He shall rise against the house of evildoers,
And the alliesᵃ of the workers of iniquity.
³For the Egyptians are man, not God,
And their horses are flesh, not spirit;
And when the LORD stretches out His arm,
The helper shall trip
And the helped one shall fall,
And both shall perish together.

⁴For thus the LORD has said to me:
As a lion—a great beast—
Growls over its prey
And, when the shepherds gather
In force against him,
Is not dismayed by their cries
Nor cowed by their noise—
So the LORD of Hosts will descend to make war
Against the mount and the hill of Zion.

⁵Like the birds that fly, even so will the LORD of Hosts shield Jerusalem, shielding and saving, protecting and rescuing.

⁶ᵇ⁻Return, O children of Israel,⁻ᵇ to Him to whom they have been so shamefully false; ⁷for in that day everyone will reject his idols of silver and idols of gold, which your hands have made for your guilt.

⁸Then Assyria shall fall,
Not by the sword of man;
A sword not of humans shall devour him.
He shall shrivelᶜ before the sword,
And his young men ᵈ⁻pine away.⁻ᵈ

ᵃ Lit. "help."
ᵇ⁻ᵇ Emendation yields "Then the children of Israel shall return."
ᶜ From root nss; cf. 10.18; others "flee."
ᵈ⁻ᵈ From root mss; cf. 10.18; others "become tributary."

⁹His rock shall melt with terror,
And his officers shall ᶜ⁻collapse from weakness⁻ᶜ—
Declares the LORD, who has a fire in Zion,
Who has an oven in Jerusalem.ᶠ

32

Behold, a king shall reign in righteousness,
And ministers shall govern with justice;
²Every one of them shall be
Like a refuge from gales,
A shelter from rainstorms;
Like brooks of water in a desert,
Like the shade of a massive rock
In a languishing land.

³Then the eyes of those who have sight shall not be sealed,
And the ears of those who have hearing shall listen;
⁴And the minds of the thoughtless shall attend and note,
And the tongues of mumblers shall speak with fluent eloquence.
⁵No more shall a villain be called noble,
Nor shall "gentleman" be said of a knave.
⁶For the villain speaks villainy
And plots treachery;
To act impiously
And to preach disloyalty against the LORD;
To leave the hungry unsatisfied
And deprive the thirsty of drink.
⁷As for the knave, his tools are knavish.
He forges plots
To destroy the poor with falsehoods
And the needy when they plead their cause.
⁸But the noble has noble intentions
And is constant in noble acts.

⁹You carefree women,
Attend, hear my words!
You confident ladies,
Give ear to my speech!
¹⁰ᵃ⁻In little more than a year,⁻ᵃ

ᶜ⁻ᶜ *Cf. note c; meaning of Heb. uncertain.*
ᶠ *Cf. 30.33.*

ᵃ⁻ᵃ *Meaning of Heb. uncertain.*

You shall be troubled, O confident ones,
When the vintage is over
And no ingathering takes place.
¹¹Tremble, you carefree ones!
Quake, O confident ones!
Strip yourselves naked,
Put the cloth about your loins!
¹²Lament ᵇ⁻upon the breasts,⁻ᵇ
For the pleasant fields,
For the spreading grapevines,
¹³For my people's soil—
It shall be overgrown with briers and thistles—
Aye, and for all the houses of delight,
For the city of mirth.
¹⁴For the castle shall be abandoned,
The noisy city forsaken;
Citadel and tower shall become
ᶜ⁻Bare places⁻ᶜ forever,
A stamping ground for wild asses,
A pasture for flocksᵈ—
¹⁵Till a spirit from on high is poured out on us,
And wilderness is transformed into farm land,
While farm land rates as mere brush.ᵉ
¹⁶Then justice shall abide in the wilderness
And righteousness shall dwell on the farm land.
¹⁷For the work of righteousness shall be peace,
And the effect of righteousness, calm and confidence forever.
¹⁸Then my people shall dwell in peaceful homes,
In secure dwellings,
In untroubled places of rest.
¹⁹ᶠAnd the brush shall sink and vanish,
Even as the city is laid low.

²⁰Happy shall you be who sow by all waters,
Who ᵍ⁻send out cattle and asses to pasture.⁻ᵍ

b-b *Emendation yields "for the fields."*
c-c *Meaning of Heb. uncertain; emendation yields "Brushland, desert."*
d *Emendation yields "onagers"; cf. Job 39.5.*
e *I.e., the transformed wilderness will surpass in fertility what is now used as farm land.*
f *Meaning of verse uncertain.*
g-g *Lit. "let loose the feet of cattle and asses"; cf. 7.25 end.*

33

Ha, you ravager who are not ravaged,
You betrayer who have not been betrayed!
When you have done ravaging, you shall be ravaged;
When you have finished betraying, you shall be betrayed.

²O LORD, be gracious to us!
It is to You we have looked;
ᵃ⁻Be their armᵃ every morning,
Also our deliverance in time of stress.
³At [Your] roaring, peoples have fled,
Before Your majesty nations have scattered;
⁴And spoilᵇ was gathered as locusts are gathered,
Itᶜ was amasseddᵈ as grasshoppers are amassed.ᵉ

⁵The LORD is exalted,
He dwells on high!
[Of old] He filled Zion
With justice and righteousness.
⁶Faithfulness to ᶠ⁻Your chargeᶠ was [her] wealth,
Wisdom and devotion [her] triumph,
Reverence for the LORD—that was herᵍ treasure.

⁷Hark! The Arielitesʰ cry aloud;
Shalom'sⁱ messengers weep bitterly.
⁸Highways are desolate,
Wayfarers have ceased.
A covenant has been renounced,
Citiesʲ rejected
ᵏ⁻Mortal manᵏ despised.
⁹The land is wilted and withered;
Lebanon disgraced and moldering,
Sharon is become like a desert,
And Bashan and Carmel are stripped bare.

ᵃ⁻ᵃ *Emendation yields "You have been our help."*
ᵇ *Heb. "your spoil."*
ᶜ *Meaning of Heb. uncertain. Emendation yields "booty"; cf. v. 23.*
ᵈ *Taking šqq as a cognate of qšš.*
ᵉ *Apparently for food; cf. Lev. 11.22.*
ᶠ⁻ᶠ *Meaning of Heb. uncertain.*
ᵍ *Heb. "his."*
ʰ *So a few manuscripts; cf. 29.1.*
ⁱ *I.e., Jerusalem's; cf. Salem (Heb. Shalem), Ps. 76.3.*
ʲ *1QIsᵃ reads "A pact."*
ᵏ⁻ᵏ *Emendation yields "an obligation."*

¹⁰"Now I will arise," says the LORD,
"Now I will exalt Myself, now raise Myself high.
¹¹You shall conceive hay,
Give birth to straw;
My[l] breath will devour you like fire.
¹²Peoples shall be burnings of lime,[m]
Thorns cut down that are set on fire.
¹³Hear, you who are far, what I have done;
You who are near, note My might."

¹⁴Sinners in Zion are frightened,
The godless are seized with trembling:
"Who of us can dwell with the devouring fire:
Who of us can dwell with the never-dying blaze?"
¹⁵He who walks in righteousness,
Speaks uprightly,
Spurns profit from fraudulent dealings,
Waves away a bribe instead of grasping it,
Stops his ears against listening to infamy,
Shuts his eyes against looking at evil—
¹⁶Such a one shall dwell in lofty security,
With inaccessible cliffs for his stronghold,
With his food supplied
And his drink assured.

¹⁷When your eyes behold [n-]a king in his beauty,[-n]
When they contemplate the land round about,
¹⁸Your throat[o] shall murmur in awe,
"Where is one who could count? Where is one who could
    weigh?
Where is one who could count [all these] towers?"
¹⁹No more shall you see the barbarian folk,
The people of speech too obscure to comprehend,
So stammering of tongue that they are not understood.

l *Heb. "your."*
m *Emendation yields "brambles"; cf. 32.13.*
n-n *Emendation yields "perfection of beauty"; cf. Ps. 50.2.*
o *As in 59.13 and elsewhere; others "heart."*

20When you gaze upon Zion, our city of assembly,
Your eyes shall behold Jerusalem
As a secure homestead,
A tent not to be transported,
Whose pegs shall never be pulled up,
And none of whose ropes shall break.
21For there the LORD in His greatness shall be for us
Like a region of rivers, of broad streams,
Where no floating vessels can sail
And no mighty craft can travel—
p-Their^q ropes are slack,
They cannot steady the sockets of their masts,
They cannot spread a sail.-p
22For the LORD shall be our ruler,
The LORD shall be our prince,
The LORD shall be our king:
He shall deliver us.
23Then r-shall indeed much spoil be divided,-r
Even the lame shall seize booty.
24And none who lives there shall say, "I am sick";
It shall be inhabited by folk whose sin has been forgiven.

34
Approach, O nations, and listen,
Give heed, O peoples!
Let the earth and those in it hear;
The world, and what it brings forth.
2For the LORD is angry at all the nations,
Furious at all their host;
He has doomed them, consigned them to slaughter.
3Their slain shall be left lying,
And the stench of their corpses shall mount;
And the hills shall be drenched with their blood,
4a-All the host of heaven shall molder.-a

p-p *Brought up from v. 23 for clarity. The passage means that the Lord will render Jerusalem as inaccessible to enemies as if it were surrounded by an impassable sea.*
q *Heb. "your."*
r-r *Meaning of Heb. uncertain; emendation yields "even a blind man shall divide much spoil."*
a-a *1QIs^a reads "And the valleys shall be cleft,/And all the host of heaven shall wither."*

The heavens shall be rolled up like a scroll,
And all their host shall wither
Like a leaf withering on the vine,
Or shriveled fruit on a fig tree.

⁵For My sword shall ᵇ⁻be drunk⁻ᵇ in the sky;
Lo, it shall come down upon Edom,
Upon the people I have doomed,
To wreak judgment.
⁶The LORD has a sword; it is sated with blood,
It is gorged with fat—
The blood of lambs and he-goats,
The kidney fat of rams.
For the LORD holds a sacrifice in Bozrah,
A great slaughter in the land of Edom.
⁷Wild oxen shall fall ᶜ⁻with them,⁻ᶜ
Young bulls with mighty steers;
And their land shall be drunk with blood,
Their soil shall be saturated with fat.
⁸For it is the LORD's day of retribution,
The year of vindication for Zion's cause.
⁹Itsᵈ streams shall be turned to pitch
And its soil to sulfur.
Its land shall become burning pitch,
¹⁰Night and day it shall never go out;
Its smoke shall rise for all time.
Through the ages it shall lie in ruins;
Through the aeons none shall traverse it.
¹¹ᵉ⁻Jackdaws and owls⁻ᵉ shall possess it;
Great owls and ravens shall dwell there.
He shall measure it with a line of chaos
And with weights of emptiness.ᶠ
¹²ᵉ⁻It shall be called, "No kingdom is there,"⁻ᵉ
Its nobles and all its lords shall be nothing.
¹³Thorns shall grow up in its palaces,
Nettles and briers in its strongholds.

ᵇ⁻ᵇ *1QIsᵃ reads "be seen"; cf. Targum.*
ᶜ⁻ᶜ *Emendation yields "with fatted calves."*
ᵈ *I.e., Edom's.*
ᵉ⁻ᵉ*Meaning of Heb. uncertain.*
ᶠ *I.e., He shall plan chaos and emptiness for it; cf. 28.17; Lam. 2.8.*

It shall be a home of jackals,
An abode of ostriches.
14gWildcats shall meet hyenas,
Goat-demons shall greet each other;
There too the lilithh shall repose
And find herself a resting place.
15There the arrow-snake shall nest and lay eggs,
And shall brood and hatch in its shade.
There too the buzzards shall gather
With one another.
16Search and read it in the scroll of the LORD:
Not one of these shall be absent,
Not one shall miss its fellow.
For Hisi mouth has spoken,
It is His spirit that has assembled them,
17And it is He who apportioned it to them by lot,
Whose hand divided it for them with the line.
They shall possess it for all time,
They shall dwell there through the ages.

35

The arid desert shall be glad,
The wilderness shall rejoice
And shall blossom like a rose.a
2It shall blossom abundantly,
It shall also exult and shout.
It shall receive the glory of Lebanon,
The splendor of Carmel and Sharon.
They shall behold the glory of the LORD,
The splendor of our God.

3Strengthen the hands that are slack;
Make firm the tottering knees!
4Say to the anxious of heart,
"Be strong, fear not;
Behold your God!

g *Most of the creatures in vv. 14–15 cannot be identified with certainty.*
h *A kind of demon.*
i *Heb. "My."*

a *Lit. "crocus."*

Requital is coming,
The recompense of God—
He Himself is coming to give you triumph."

5Then the eyes of the blind shall be opened,
And the ears of the deaf shall be unstopped.
6Then the lame shall leap like a deer,
And the tongue of the dumb shall shout aloud;
For waters shall burst forth in the desert,
Streams in the wilderness.
7Torrid earth shall become a pool;
Parched land, fountains of water;
The home of jackals, a pasture;b
The abode [of ostriches],c reeds and rushes.

8And a highway shall appear there,
Which shall be called the Sacred Way.
No one unclean shall pass along it,
But it shall be for them.d
e-No traveler, not even fools, shall go astray.-e
9No lion shall be there,
No ferocious beast shall set foot on it—
These shall not be found there.
But the redeemed shall walk it;
10And the ransomed of the LORD shall return,
And come with shouting to Zion,
Crowned with joy everlasting.
They shall attain joy and gladness,
While sorrow and sighing flee.

36 aIn the fourteenth year of King Hezekiah, King Sennacherib of Assyria marched against all the fortified towns of Judah and seized them. 2From Lachish, the king of Assyria sent the Rabshakeh,b with a large force, to King Hezekiah in Jerusalem. [The Rabshakeh] took up a position near the conduit of the Upper Pool, by the road of the Fuller's Field;

---

b *Meaning of Heb. uncertain; emendation yields "a marsh."*
c *Cf. 34.13.*
d *Emendation yields "for His people."*
e-e *Meaning of Heb. uncertain.*

a *Chaps. 36–39 occur also as 2 Kings 18.13–20.19, with a number of variants, some of which will be cited here in the footnotes.*
b *An Assyrian title; cf. "Tartan," 20.1.*

³and Eliakim son of Hilkiah who was in charge of the palace, Shebna the scribe, and Joah son of Asaph the recorder went out to him.

⁴The Rabshakeh said to them, "You tell Hezekiah: Thus said the Great King, the king of Assyria: What makes you so confident? ⁵I suppose ͨ mere talk makes counsel and valor for war! Look, on whom are you relying, that you have rebelled against me? ⁶You are relying on Egypt, that splintered reed of a staff, which enters and punctures the palm of anyone who leans on it. That's what Pharaoh king of Egypt is like to all who rely on him. ⁷And if you tell me that you are relying on the LORD your God, He is the very one whose shrines and altars Hezekiah did away with, telling Judah and Jerusalem, 'You must worship only at this altar!' ⁸Come now, make this wager with my master, the king of Assyria: I'll give you two thousand horses, if you can produce riders to mount them. ⁹So how could you refuse anything, even to the deputy of one of my master's lesser servants, relying on Egypt for chariots and horsemen? ¹⁰And do you think I have marched against this land to destroy it without the LORD? The LORD Himself told me: Go up against that land and destroy it."

¹¹Eliakim, Shebna, and Joah replied to the Rabshakeh, "Please, speak to your servants in Aramaic, since we understand it; do not speak to us in Judean in the hearing of the people on the wall." ¹²But the Rabshakeh replied, "Was it to your master and to you that my master sent me to speak those words? It was precisely to the men who are sitting on the wall—who will have to eat their dung and drink their urine with you." ¹³And the Rabshakeh stood and called out in a loud voice in Judean: ¹⁴"Hear the words of the Great King, the king of Assyria! Thus said the king: Don't let Hezekiah deceive you, for he will not be able to save you. ¹⁵Don't let Hezekiah make you rely on the LORD, saying, 'The LORD will surely save us; this city will not fall into the hands of Assyria!' ¹⁶Don't listen to Hezekiah. For thus said the king of Assyria: Make your peace with me and come out to me,ᵈ so that you may all eat from your vines and your fig trees and drink water from your cisterns, ¹⁷until I come and take you away to a land like your own, a land of bread and wine, of grain [fields] and vineyards. ¹⁸Beware of letting Hezekiah mislead you by saying, 'The LORD will save us.' Did any of the gods of the other nations save his land from the king of Assyria? ¹⁹Where were the gods of Hamath

ͨ 2 Kings 18.20 "You must think."
ᵈ I.e., to my representative the Rabshakeh.

and Arpad? Where were the gods of Sepharvaim? And did they^c save Samaria from me? 20Which among all the gods of those countries saved their countries from me, that the LORD should save Jerusalem from me?" 21But they were silent and did not answer him with a single word; for the king's order was: "Do not answer him."

22And so Eliakim son of Hilkiah who was in charge of the palace, Shebna the scribe, and Joah son of Asaph the recorder came to Hezekiah with their clothes rent, and they reported to him what the Rabshakeh had said.

37 When King Hezekiah heard this, he rent his clothes and covered himself with sackcloth and went into the House of the LORD. 2He also sent Eliakim, who was in charge of the palace, Shebna, the scribe, and the senior priests, covered with sackcloth, to the prophet Isaiah son of Amoz. 3They said to him, "Thus said Hezekiah: This day is a day of distress, of chastisement, and of disgrace. a-The babes have reached the birthstool, but the strength to give birth is lacking.-a 4Perhaps the LORD your God will take note of the words of the Rabshakeh, whom his master the king of Assyria has sent to blaspheme the living God, and will mete out judgment for the words that the LORD your God has heard—if you will offer up prayer for the surviving remnant."

5When King Hezekiah's ministers came to Isaiah, 6Isaiah said to them, "Tell your master as follows: Thus said the LORD: Do not be frightened by the words of blasphemy against Me that you have heard from the minions of the king of Assyria. 7I will delude^b him: He will hear a rumor and return to his land, and I will make him fall by the sword in his land."

8The Rabshakeh, meanwhile, heard that [the King] had left Lachish; he turned back and found the king of Assyria attacking Libnah. 9But [the king of Assyria] learned that King Tirhakah of Nubia had come out to fight him; and when he heard it, he sent messengers to Hezekiah, saying, 10"Tell this to King Hezekiah of Judah: Do not let your God, on whom you are relying, mislead you into thinking that Jerusalem will not be delivered into the hands of the king of Assyria. 11You yourself have heard what the kings of Assyria have done to all the lands, how they have annihilated them; and can you escape? 12Were the nations that my predecessors^c destroyed—Gozan, Haran, Rezeph, and the Bethedenites in

c _I.e., the gods of Samaria._

a-a _I.e., the situation is desperate, and we are at a loss._
b _Lit. "put a spirit in."_
c _Lit. "fathers."_

Telassar—saved by their gods? [13]Where is the king of Hamath? and the king of Arpad? and the kings of Lair, Sepharvaim, Hena, and Ivvah?"

[14]Hezekiah received the letter from the messengers and read it. Hezekiah then went up to the House of the LORD and spread it out before the LORD. [15]And Hezekiah prayed to the LORD: [16]"O LORD of Hosts, enthroned on the Cherubim! You alone are God of all the kingdoms of the earth. You made the heavens and the earth. [17]O LORD, incline Your ear and hear, open Your eye and see. Hear all the words that Sennacherib has sent to blaspheme the living God! [18]True, O LORD, the kings of Assyria have annihilated all the nations[d] and their lands [19]and have committed their gods to the flames and have destroyed them; for they are not gods, but man's handwork of wood and stone. [20]But now, O LORD our God, deliver us from his hands, and let all the kingdoms of the earth know that You, O LORD, alone [are God]."[e]

[21]Then Isaiah son of Amoz sent this message to Hezekiah: "Thus said the LORD, the God of Israel, to whom you have prayed, concerning King Sennacherib of Assyria—[22]this is the word that the LORD has spoken concerning him:

Fair Maiden Zion despises you,
She mocks at you;
Fair Jerusalem shakes
Her head at you.
[23]Whom have you blasphemed and reviled?
Against whom made loud your voice
And haughtily raised your eyes?
Against the Holy One of Israel!
[24]Through your servants you have blasphemed my Lord.
Because you thought,
'Thanks to my vast chariotry,
It is I who have climbed the highest mountains,
To the remotest parts of the Lebanon,
And have cut down its loftiest cedars,
Its choicest cypresses,
And have reached its highest peak,
[f-]Its densest forest.[-f]
[25]It is I who have drawn[g]

---

[d] So 2 Kings 19.17, and 13 mss. here; most mss. and editions read "lands."
[e] Supplied from 2 Kings 19.19.
[f-f] Lit. "Its farmland forest"; exact meaning of Heb. uncertain.
[g] Or "dug"; meaning of Heb. uncertain.

And drunk water.
I have dried up with the soles of my feet
All the streams of Egypt.'
26Have you not heard? Of old
I planned that very thing,
I designed it long ago,
And now have fulfilled it.
And it has come to pass,
Laying fortified towns waste in desolate heaps.
27Their inhabitants are helpless,
Dismayed and shamed.
They were but grass of the field
And green herbage,
Grass of the roofs h-that is blasted
Before the east wind.-h
28I know your stayings
And your goings and comings,
And how you have raged against Me,
29Because you have raged against Me,
And your tumult has reached My ears,
I will place My hook in your nose
And My bit between your jaws;
And I will make you go back by the road
By which you came.

30"And this is the sign for you:i This year you eat what grows of itself, and the next year what springs from that, and in the third year sow and reap and plant vineyards and eat their fruit. 31And the survivors of the House of Judah that have escaped shall renew its trunk below and produce boughs above.

32For a remnant shall come forth from Jerusalem,
Survivors from Mount Zion.
The zeal of the LORD of Hosts
Shall bring this to pass.

33"Assuredly, thus said the LORD concerning the king of Assyria:

h-h So ms. 1QIs^a; cf. 2 Kings 19.26. The usual reading in our passage means, literally, "and a field [?] before standing grain."
i I.e., Hezekiah.

He shall not enter this city;
He shall not shoot an arrow at it,
Or advance upon it with a shield,
Or pile up a siegemound against it.
³⁴He shall go back
By the way he came,
He shall not enter this city
                    —declares the LORD;
³⁵I will protect and save this city for My sake
And for the sake of My servant David."

³⁶[That night]ʲ an angel of the LORD went out and struck down one hundred and eighty-five thousand in the Assyrian camp, and the following morning they were all dead corpses.

³⁷So King Sennacherib of Assyria broke camp and retreated, and stayed in Nineveh. ³⁸While he was worshiping in the temple of his god Nisroch, he was struck down with the sword by his sons Adrammelech and Sarezer. They fled to the land of Ararat, and his son Esarhaddon succeeded him as king.

38 In those days Hezekiah fell dangerously ill. The prophet Isaiah son of Amoz came and said to him, "Thus said the LORD: Set your affairs in order, for you are going to die; you will not get well." ²Thereupon Hezekiah turned his face to the wall and prayed to the LORD. ³"Please, O LORD," he said, "remember how I have walked before You sincerely and wholeheartedly, and have done what is pleasing to You." And Hezekiah wept profusely.

⁴Then the word of the LORD came to Isaiah: ⁵"Go and tell Hezekiah: Thus said the LORD, the God of your father David: I have heard your prayer, I have seen your tears. I hereby add fifteen years to your life. ⁶I will also rescue you and this city from the hands of the king of Assyria. I will protect this city. ⁷And this is the sign for you from the LORD that the LORD will do the thing that He has promised: ⁸I am going to make the shadow on the steps, which has descended on the dialᵃ of Ahaz because of the sun, recede ten steps." And the sun['s shadow] receded ten steps, the same steps as it had descended.

ʲ *Supplied from 2 Kings 19.35.*

ᵃ *Heb. "steps." A model of a dial with steps has been discovered in Egypt.*

⁹A poem by King Hezekiah of Judah when he recovered from the illness he had suffered:

¹⁰ᵇI had thought:
I must depart in the middle of my days;
I have been consigned to the gates of Sheol
For the rest of my years.
¹¹I thought, I shall never see Yah,ᶜ
Yah in the land of the living,
Or ever behold men again
Among those who inhabit the earth.
¹²My dwelling is pulled up and removed from me
Like a tent of shepherds;
My life is rolled up like a web
And cut from the thrum.

ᵈ⁻Only from daybreak to nightfall
Was I kept whole,
¹³Then it was as though a lion
Were breaking all my bones;
I cried out until morning.
(Only from daybreak to nightfall
Was I kept whole.)⁻ᵈ
¹⁴I piped like a swift or a swallow,
I moaned like a dove,
As my eyes, all worn, looked to heaven:
"My Lord, I am in straits;
Be my surety!"

¹⁵What can I say? ᵈ⁻He promised me,⁻ᵈ
And He it is who has wrought it.
ᵈ⁻All my sleep had fled
Because of the bitterness of my soul.
¹⁶My Lord, for all that and despite it
My life-breath is revived;⁻ᵈ
You have restored me to health and revived me.
¹⁷Truly, it was for my own good
That I had such great bitterness:

ᵇ *Meaning of verse uncertain in part.*
ᶜ *I.e., visit His Temple. For "Yah" see 12.2; 26.4.*
ᵈ⁻ᵈ *Meaning of Heb. uncertain.*

You saved my life
From the pit of destruction,
For You have cast behind Your back
All my offenses.
18For it is not Sheol that praises You,
Not [the Land of] Death that extols You;
Nor do they who descend into the Pit
Hope for Your grace.
19The living, only the living
Can give thanks to You
As I do this day;
Fathersᵉ relate to children
Your acts of grace:
20"[It has pleased] the LORD to deliver us,ᵉ
That is why we offer up musicᶠ
All the days of our lives
At the House of the LORD."

21When Isaiah said, "Let them take a cake of figs and apply it to the rash, and he will recover," 22Hezekiah asked, "What will be the sign that I shall go up to the House of the LORD?"

39 At that time, Merodach-baladan son of Baladan, the king of Babylon, sent [envoys with] a letter and a gift to Hezekiah, for he had heard about his illness and recovery. 2Hezekiah was pleased by their coming, and he showed them his treasure house—the silver, the gold, the spices, and the fragrant oil—and all his armory, and everything that was to be found in his storehouses. There was nothing in his palace or in all his realm that Hezekiah did not show them. 3Then the prophet Isaiah came to King Hezekiah. "What," he demanded of him, "did those men say to you? Where have they come to you from?" "They have come to me," replied Hezekiah, "from a far country, from Babylon." 4Next he asked, "What have they seen in your palace?" And Hezekiah replied, "They have seen everything there is in my palace. There was nothing in my storehouses that I did not show them."

5Then Isaiah said to Hezekiah, "Hear the word of the LORD of Hosts: 6A time is coming when everything in your palace, which your ancestors

---

ᵉ Heb. singular.
ᶠ Neginothai is a poetic form of neginoth.

have stored up to this day, will be carried off to Babylon; nothing will be left behind, said the LORD. ⁷And some of your sons, your own issue, whom you will have fathered, will be taken to serve as eunuchs in the palace of the king of Babylon." ⁸Hezekiah declared to Isaiah, "The word of the LORD that you have spoken is good." For he thought, "It means that ᵃ⁻safety is assured for⁻ᵃ my time."

40 Comfort, oh comfort My people,
Says your God.
²Speak tenderly to Jerusalem,
And declare to her
That her term of service is over,
That her iniquity is expiated;
For she has received at the hand of the LORD
Double for all her sins.

³A voice rings out:
"Clear in the desert
A road for the LORD!
Level in the wilderness
A highway for our God!
⁴Let every valley be raised,
Every hill and mount made low.
Let the rugged ground become level
And the ridges become a plain.
⁵The Presence of the LORD shall appear,
And all flesh, as one, shall behold—
For the LORD Himself has spoken."

⁶A voice rings out: "Proclaim!"
ᵃ⁻Another asks,⁻ᵃ "What shall I proclaim?"
"All flesh is grass,
All its goodness like flowers of the field:
⁷Grass withers, flowers fade
When the breath of the LORD blows on them.

ᵃ⁻ᵃ *Lit. "there shall be safety and faithfulness in."*
ᵃ⁻ᵃ *1QIsᵃ and Septuagint read "And I asked."*

Indeed, man is but grass:
[8]Grass withers, flowers fade—
But the word of our God is always fulfilled!"

[9]Ascend a lofty mountain,
O herald of joy to Zion;
Raise your voice with power,
O herald of joy to Jerusalem—
Raise it, have no fear;
Announce to the cities of Judah:
Behold your God!
[10]Behold, the Lord GOD comes in might,
And His arm wins triumph for Him;
See, His reward[b] is with Him,
His recompense before Him.
[11]Like a shepherd He pastures His flock:
He gathers the lambs in His arms
And carries them in His bosom;
Gently He drives the mother sheep.

[12]Who measured the waters with the hollow of His hand,
And gauged the skies with a span,
And meted earth's dust with a measure,[c]
And weighed the mountains with a scale
And the hills with a balance?
[13]Who has plumbed the mind of the LORD,
What man could tell Him His plan?
[14]Whom did He consult, and who taught Him,
Guided Him in the way of right?
Who guided Him in knowledge
And showed Him the path of wisdom?

[15]The nations are but a drop in a bucket,
Reckoned as dust on a balance;
The very coastlands He lifts like motes.
[16]Lebanon is not fuel enough,

b *The reward and recompense to the cities of Judah; cf. Jer. 31.14, 16.*
c *Heb. shalish "third," probably a third of an ephah.*

Nor its beasts enough for sacrifice.
17All nations are as naught in His sight;
He accounts them as less than nothing.

18To whom, then, can you liken God,
What form compare to Him?
19The idol? A woodworker shaped it,
And a smith overlaid it with gold,
d-Forging links of silver.-d
20As a gift, he chooses the mulberry^e—
A wood that does not rot—
Then seeks a skillful woodworker
To make a firm idol,
That will not topple.

21Do you not know?
Have you not heard?
Have you not been told
From the very first?
Have you not discerned
d-How the earth was founded?-d
22It is He who is enthroned above the vault of the earth,
So that its inhabitants seem as grasshoppers;
Who spread out the skies like gauze,
Stretched them out like a tent to dwell in.
23He brings potentates to naught,
Makes rulers of the earth as nothing.
24Hardly are they planted,
Hardly are they sown,
Hardly has their stem
Taken root in earth,
When He blows upon them and they dry up,
And the storm bears them off like straw.

25To whom, then, can you liken Me,
To whom can I be compared?
—says the Holy One.

---

d-d *Meaning of Heb. uncertain.*
e *Heb.* mesukkan; *according to a Jewish tradition, preserved by Jerome, a kind of wood; a similar word denotes a kind of wood in Akkadian.*

²⁶Lift high your eyes and see:
Who created these?
He who sends out their host by count,
Who calls them each by name:
Because of His great might and vast power,
Not one fails to appear.

²⁷Why do you say, O Jacob,
Why declare, O Israel,
"My way is hid from the LORD,
My cause is ignored by my God"?
²⁸Do you not know?
Have you not heard?
The LORD is God from of old,
Creator of the earth from end to end,
He never grows faint or weary,
His wisdom cannot be fathomed.
²⁹He gives strength to the weary,
Fresh vigor to the spent.
³⁰Youths may grow faint and weary,
And young men stumble and fall;
³¹But they who trust in the LORD shall renew their strength
As eagles grow new plumes:[f]
They shall run and not grow weary,
They shall march and not grow faint.

41

Stand silent before Me, coastlands,
And let nations [a]renew their strength.[a]
Let them approach to state their case;
Let us come forward together for argument.
²Who has roused a victor[b] from the East,
Summoned him to His service?
Has delivered up nations to him,
And trodden sovereigns down?
Has rendered their[c] swords like dust,
Their[c] bows like wind-blown straw?

---

[f] *Alluding to a popular belief that eagles regain their youth when they molt; cf. Ps. 103.5.*

[a-a] *Connection of Heb. uncertain.*
[b] *Lit. "victory."*
[c] *Heb. "his."*

³He pursues them, he goes on unscathed;
No shackle^d is placed on his feet.
⁴Who has wrought and achieved this?
He who announced the generations from the start—
I, the LORD, who was first
And will be with the last as well.

⁵The coastlands look on in fear,
The ends of earth tremble.

They draw near and come;
⁶Each one helps the other,
Saying to his fellow, "Take courage!"
⁷The woodworker encourages the smith;
He who flattens with the hammer
[Encourages] him who pounds the anvil.
He says of the riveting, "It is good!"
And he fixes it with nails,
That it may not topple.

⁸But you, Israel, My servant,
Jacob, whom I have chosen,
Seed of Abraham My friend—
⁹You whom I drew from the ends of the earth
And called from its far corners,
To whom I said: You are My servant;
I chose you, I have not rejected you—
¹⁰Fear not, for I am with you,
Be not frightened, for I am your God;
I strengthen you and I help you,
I uphold you with My victorious right hand.
¹¹Shamed and chagrined shall be
All who contend with you;
They who strive with you
Shall become as naught and shall perish.
¹²You may seek, but shall not find
Those who struggle with you;
Less than nothing shall be
The men who battle against you.

d 'rh *has this meaning in Old Aramaic.*

¹³For I the LORD am your God,
Who grasped your right hand,
Who say to you: Have no fear;
I will be your help.
¹⁴Fear not, O worm Jacob,
O ᶜ⁻men ofᶜ Israel:
I will help you

—declares the LORD—

I your Redeemer, the Holy One of Israel.
¹⁵I will make of you a threshing board,
A new thresher, with many spikes;
You shall thresh mountains to dust,
And make hills like chaff.
¹⁶You shall winnow them
And the wind shall carry them off;
The whirlwind shall scatter them.
But you shall rejoice in the LORD,
And glory in the Holy One of Israel.

¹⁷The poor and the needy
Seek water,ᶠ and there is none;
Their tongue is parched with thirst.
I the LORD will respond to them.
I, the God of Israel, will not forsake them.
¹⁸I will open up streams on the bare hills
And fountains amid the valleys;
I will turn the desert into ponds,
The arid land into springs of water.
¹⁹I will plant cedars in the wilderness,
Acacias and myrtles and oleasters;
I will set cypresses in the desert,
Box trees and elms as well—
²⁰That men may see and know,
Consider and comprehend
That the LORD's hand has done this,
That the Holy One of Israel has wrought it.

²¹Submit your case, says the LORD;
Offer your pleas, says the King of Jacob.

ᶜ⁻ᶜ *Emendation yields "maggot."*
ᶠ *I.e., on the homeward march through the desert.*

²²Let them approach[g] and tell us what will happen.
Tell us what has occurred,[h]
And we will take note of it;
Or announce to us what will occur,
That we may know the outcome.
²³Foretell what is yet to happen,
That we may know that you are gods!
Do anything, good or bad,
That we may be awed and see.[i]
²⁴Why, you are less than nothing,
Your effect is less than nullity;
One who chooses you is an abomination.

²⁵I have roused him from the north, and he has come,
From the sunrise, one who invokes My name;
And he has trampled rulers like mud,
Like a potter treading clay.
²⁶Who foretold this from the start, that we may note it;
From aforetime, that we might say, "He is right"?
Not one foretold, not one announced;
No one has heard your utterance!
²⁷[j-The things once predicted to Zion—
Behold, here they are!-j]
And again I send a herald to Jerusalem.
²⁸But I look and there is not a man;
Not one of them can predict
Or can respond when I question him.
²⁹See, they are all nothingness,
Their works are nullity,
Their statues are naught and nil.

42 This is My servant, whom I uphold,
My chosen one, in whom I delight.
I have put My spirit upon him,
He shall teach the true way to the nations.
²He shall not cry out or shout aloud,
Or make his voice heard in the streets.

g *Taking* yaggishu *intransitively; cf.* hiqriv. Exod. 14.10.
h *I.e., former prophecies by your gods which have been fulfilled.*
i *Change of vocalization yields "fear"; cf. v. 10.*
j-j *Meaning of Heb. uncertain.*

3a-He shall not break even a bruised reed,
Or snuff out even a dim wick.-a
He shall bring forth the true way.
4He shall not grow dim or be bruised
Till he has established the true way on earth;
And the coastlands shall await his teaching.

5Thus said God the LORD,
Who created the heavens and stretched them out,
Who spread out the earth and what it brings forth,
Who gave breath to the people upon it
And life to those who walk thereon:
6I the LORD, in My grace, have summoned you,
And I have grasped you by the hand.
I created you, and appointed you
A b-covenant people,-b c-a light of nations-c—
7d-Opening eyes deprived of light,-d
Rescuing prisoners from confinement,
From the dungeon those who sit in darkness.
8I am the LORD, that is My name;
I will not yield My glory to another,
Nor My renown to idols.
9See, the things once predicted have come,
And now I foretell new things,
Announce to you ere they sprout up.
10Sing to the LORD a new song,
His praise from the ends of the earth—
e-You who sail the sea and you creatures in it,
You coastlands-e and their inhabitants!
11Let the desert and its towns cry aloud,
The villages where Kedar dwells;
Let Sela's inhabitants shout,
Call out from the peaks of the mountains.
12Let them do honor to the LORD,
And tell His glory in the coastlands.

13The LORD goes forth like a warrior,
Like a fighter He whips up His rage.

a-a *Or "A bruised reed, he shall not be broken;/A dim wick, he shall not be snuffed out."*
b-b *Lit. "covenants of a people"; meaning of Heb. uncertain.*
c-c *See 49.6 and note.*
d-d *An idiom meaning "freeing the imprisoned"; cf. 61.1.*
e-e *Emendation yields "Let the sea roar and its creatures,/The coastlands. . . ." Cf. Ps. 98.7.*

He yells, He roars aloud,
He charges upon His enemies.
14"I have kept silent ^{f-}far too long,^{-f}
Kept still and restrained Myself;
Now I will scream like a woman in labor,
I will pant and I will gasp.
15Hills and heights will I scorch,
Cause all their green to wither;
I will turn rivers into isles,^g
And dry the marshes up.
16I will lead the blind
By a road they did not know,
And I will make them walk
By paths they never knew.
I will turn darkness before them to light,
Rough places into level ground.
These are the promises—
I will keep them without fail.
17Driven back and utterly shamed
Shall be those who trust in an image,
Those who say to idols,
'You are our gods!' "

18Listen, you who are deaf;
You blind ones, look up and see!
19Who is so blind as My servant,
So deaf as the messenger I send?
Who is so blind as the chosen^h one,
So blind as the servant of the LORD?
20Seeing many things, ⁱ⁻he gives⁻ⁱ no heed;
With ears open, he hears nothing.
21^jThe LORD desires His [servant's] vindication,
That he may magnify and glorify [His] Teaching.

22Yet it is a people plundered and despoiled:
All of them are trapped in holes,
Imprisoned in dungeons.

---

f-f Lit. "from of old."
g Emendation yields "desert."
h Meaning of Heb. uncertain.
i-i Heb "you give."
j Meaning of verse uncertain; cf. 43.9–12.

They are given over to plunder, with none to rescue them;
To despoilment, with none to say "Give back!"
23If only you would listen to this,
Attend and give heed from now on!
24Who was it gave Jacob over to despoilment
And Israel to plunderers?
Surely, the LORD against whom they[k] sinned
In whose ways they would not walk
And whose Teaching they would not obey.
25So He poured out wrath upon them,
His anger and the fury of war.
It blazed upon them all about, but they heeded not;
It burned among them, but they gave it no thought.

43 But now thus said the LORD—
Who created you, O Jacob,
Who formed you, O Israel:
Fear not, for I will redeem you;
I have singled you out by name,
You are Mine.
2When you pass through water,
I will be with you;
Through streams,
They shall not overwhelm you.
When you walk through fire,
You shall not be scorched;
Through flame,
It shall not burn you.
3For I the LORD am your God,
The Holy One of Israel, your Savior.
I give Egypt as a ransom for you,
Nubia and Saba in exchange for you.
4Because you are precious to Me,
And honored, and I love you,
I give men in exchange for you
And peoples in your stead.

k *Heb. "we."*

⁵Fear not, for I am with you:
I will bring your folk from the East,
Will gather you out of the West;
⁶I will say to the North, "Give back!"
And to the South, "Do not withhold!
Bring My sons from afar,
And My daughters from the end of the earth—
⁷All who are linked to My name,
Whom I have created,
Formed, and made for My glory—
⁸Setting free that people,
Blind though it has eyes
And deaf though it has ears."

⁹All the nations assemble as one,
The peoples gather.
Who among them declared this,
Foretold to us the things that have happened?
Let them produce their witnesses and be vindicated,
That men, hearing them, may say, "It is true!"ᵃ
¹⁰My witnesses are *you*

—declares the LORD—

My servant, whom I have chosen.
To the end that youᵇ may take thought,
And believe in Me,
And understand that I am He:
Before Me no god was formed,
And after Me none shall exist—
¹¹None but me, the LORD;
Beside Me, none can grant triumph.
¹²I alone foretold the triumph
And I brought it to pass;
I announced it,
And no strange god was among you.
So you are My witnesses

—declares the LORD—

And I am God.
¹³Ever since day was, I am He;

ᵃ *I.e., that the other nations' gods are real.*
ᵇ *Emendation yields "they."*

None can deliver from My hand.
When I act, who can reverse it?

¹⁴Thus said the LORD,
Your Redeemer, the Holy One of Israel:
For your sake ᶜˉI send to Babylon;
I will bring down all [her] bars,
And the Chaldeans shall raise their voice in lamentation.ˉᶜ
¹⁵I am your Holy One, the LORD,
Your King, the Creator of Israel.

¹⁶Thus said the LORD,
Who made a road through the sea
And a path through mighty waters,
¹⁷Who destroyedᵈ chariots and horses,
And all the mighty host—
They lay down to rise no more,
They were extinguished, quenched like a wick:
¹⁸Do not recall what happened of old,
Or ponder what happened of yore!
¹⁹I am about to do something new;
Even now it shall come to pass,
Suddenly you shall perceive it:
I will make a road through the wilderness
And riversᵉ in the desert.
²⁰The wild beasts shall honor Me,
Jackals and ostriches,
For I provide water in the wilderness,
Rivers in the desert,
To give drink to My chosen people,
²¹The people I formed for Myself
That they might declare my praise.

²²But you have not worshiped Me, O Jacob,
That you should be weary of Me, O Israel.
²³You have not brought Me your sheep for burnt offerings,
Nor honored Me with your sacrifices.
I have not burdened you with meal offerings,

ᶜˉᶜ *Meaning of Heb. uncertain.*
ᵈ *Understanding* hoṣi, *here, as equivalent to Aramaic* shesi.
ᵉ *1QIsᵃ reads "paths"; cf. v. 16.*

Nor wearied you about frankincense.
24You have not bought Me fragrant reed with money,
Nor sated Me with the fat of your sacrifices.
Instead, you have burdened Me with your sins,
You have wearied Me with your iniquities.
25It is I, I who—for My own sake[f]—
Wipe your transgressions away
And remember your sins no more.
26Help me remember!
Let us join in argument,
Tell your version,
That you may be vindicated.
27Your earliest ancestor sinned,
And your spokesmen transgressed against Me.
28So I profaned [g-]the holy princes;[-g]
I abandoned Jacob to proscription[h]
And Israel to mockery.

44 But hear, now, O Jacob My servant,
Israel whom I have chosen!
2Thus said the LORD, your Maker,
Your Creator who has helped you since birth:
Fear not, My servant Jacob,
Jeshurun[a] whom I have chosen,
3Even as I pour water on thirsty soil,
And rain upon dry ground,
So will I pour My spirit on your offspring,
My blessing upon your posterity.
4And they shall sprout like[b] grass,
Like willows by watercourses.
5One shall say, "I am the LORD's,"
Another shall use the name of "Jacob,"
Another shall mark his arm "of the LORD"[c]
And adopt the name of "Israel."

6Thus said the LORD, the King of Israel,
Their Redeemer, the LORD of Hosts:

---

f *I.e., in order to put an end to the profanation of My holy name; cf. 48.9–11.*
g-g *Emendation yields "My holy name"; see preceding note.*
h *Emendation yields "insult."*

a *A name for Israel; see note on Num. 23.10; cf. Deut. 32.15; 33.5, 26.*
b *Lit. "in among."*
c *It was customary to mark a slave with the owner's name.*

I am the first and I am the last,
And there is no god but Me.
7dWho like Me can announce,
Can foretell it—and match Me thereby?
Even as I told the future to an ancient people,
So let him foretell coming events to them.
8Do not be frightened, do not be shaken!
Have I not from of old predicted to you?
I foretold, and you are My witnesses.
Is there any god, then, but Me?
"There is no other rock; I know none!"

9The makers of idols
All work to no purpose;
And the things they treasure
Can do no good,
As they themselves can testify.
They neither look nor think,
And so they shall be shamed.
10Who would fashion a god
Or cast a statue
That can do no good?
11Lo, all its adherents shall be shamed;
They are craftsmen, are merely human.
Let them all assemble and stand up!
They shall be cowed, and they shall be shamed.

12eThe craftsman in iron, with his tools,
Works itf over charcoal
And fashions it by hammering,
Working with the strength of his arm.
Should he go hungry, his strength would ebb;
Should he drink no water, he would grow faint.

13The craftsman in wood measures with a line
And marks out a shape with a stylus;
He forms it with scraping tools,
Marking it out with a compass.

---

d *Meaning of verse uncertain.*
e *The meaning of parts of vv. 12–13 is uncertain.*
f *I.e., the image he is making.*

He gives it a human form,
The beauty of a man, to dwell in a shrine.
¹⁴For his use he cuts down cedars;
He chooses plane trees and oaks.
He sets aside trees of the forest;
Or plants firs, and the rain makes them grow.
¹⁵All this serves man for fuel:
He takes some to warm himself,
And he builds a fire and bakes bread.
He also makes a god of it and worships it,
Fashions an idol and bows down to it!
¹⁶Part of it he burns in a fire:
On that part he roasts^g meat,
He eats^g the roast and is sated;
He also warms himself and cries, "Ah,
I am warm! I can feel^h the heat!"
¹⁷Of the rest he makes a god—his own carving!
He bows down to it, worships it;
He prays to it and cries,
"Save me, for you are my god!"

¹⁸They have no wit or judgment:
Their eyes are besmeared, and they see not;
Their minds, and they cannot think.
¹⁹They do not give thought,
They lack the wit and judgment to say:
"Part of it I burned in a fire;
I also baked bread on the coals,
I roasted meat and ate it—
Should I make the rest an abhorrence?
Should I bow to a block of wood?"
²⁰He pursues ashes!ⁱ
A deluded mind has led him astray,
And he cannot save himself;
He never says to himself,
"The thing in my hand is a fraud!"

g *Transposing the Heb. verbs for clarity.*
h *Lit. "see."*
i *Lit. "He shepherds ashes."*

21Remember these things, O Jacob
For you, O Israel, are My servant:
I fashioned you, you are My servant—
O Israel, never forget Me.ʲ
22I wipe away your sins like a cloud,
Your transgressions like mist—
Come back to Me, for I redeem you.

23Shout, O heavens, for the LORD has acted;
Shout aloud, O depths of the earth!
Shout for joy, O mountains,
O forests with all your trees!
For the LORD has redeemed Jacob,
Has glorified Himself through Israel.

24Thus said the LORD, your Redeemer,
Who formed you in the womb:
It is I, the LORD, who made everything,
Who alone stretched out the heavens
And unaidedᵏ spread out the earth;
25Who annul the omens of diviners,
And make fools of the augurs;
Who turn sages back
And make nonsense of their knowledge;
26But confirm the word of Myˡ servant
And fulfill the prediction of Myˡ messengers.
It is I who say of Jerusalem, "It shall be inhabited,"
And of the towns of Judah, "They shall be rebuilt;
And I will restore their ruined places."
27[I,] who said to the deep, "Be dry;
I will dry up your floods,"
28Am the same who says of Cyrus, "He is My shepherd;ᵐ
He shall fulfill all My purposes!
He shall say of Jerusalem, 'She shall be rebuilt,'
And to the Temple: 'You shall be founded again.' "

ʲ Emendation yields "them," these things.
ᵏ Lit. "with none beside me," or (following many Heb. mss., kethib, and ancient versions) "who was with me?"
ˡ Heb. "His."
ᵐ I.e., the king whom I have designated.

45 Thus said the LORD to Cyrus, His anointed one—
Whose right hand a-He has-a grasped,
Treading down nations before him,
b-Ungirding the loins of kings,-b
Opening doors before him
And letting no gate stay shut:
2I will march before you
And level c-the hills that loom up;-c
I will shatter doors of bronze
And cut down iron bars.
3I will give you treasures concealed in the dark
And secret hoards—
So that you may know that it is I the LORD,
The God of Israel, who call you by name.
4For the sake of My servant Jacob,
Israel My chosen one,
I call you by name,
I hail you by title, though you have not known Me.
5I am the LORD and there is none else;
Beside Me, there is no god.
I engird you, though you have not known Me,
6So that they may know, from east to west,
That there is none but Me.
I am the LORD and there is none else,
7I form light and create darkness,
I make weal and create woe—
I the LORD do all these things.
8Pour down, O skies, from above!
Let the heavens rain down victory!
Let the earth open up and triumph sprout,
Yes, let vindication spring up:
I the LORD have created it.

9Shame on him who argues with his Maker,
Though naught but a potsherd of earth!

a-a *Heb. "I have." Cf. note at 8.11.*
b-b *I.e., I made them helpless; one who wished to move freely belted his garment around the waist; cf. "engird," v. 5.*
c-c *Meaning of Heb. uncertain.*

Shall the clay say to the potter, "What are you doing?
d-Your work has no handles"?-d
10Shame on him who asks his father, "What are
   you begetting?"
Or a woman, "What are you bearing?"

11Thus said the LORD,
Israel's Holy One and Maker:
e-Will you question Me-e on the destiny of My children,
Will you instruct Me about the work of My hands?
12It was I who made the earth
And created man upon it;
My own hands stretched out the heavens,
And I marshaled all their host.
13It was I who roused himf for victory
And who level all roads for him.
He shall rebuild My city
And let My exiled people go
Without price and without payment
                          —said the LORD of Hosts.

14Thus said the LORD:
Egypt's wealth and Nubia's gains
And Sabaites, g-long of limb,-g
Shall pass over to you and be yours,
Pass over and follow you in fetters,
Bow low to you
And reverently address you:
"Only among you is God,
There is no other god at all!
15You are indeed a God who concealed Himself,
O God of Israel, who bring victory!
16Those who fabricate idols,
All are shamed and disgraced;
To a man, they slink away in disgrace.
17But Israel has won through the LORD

d-d Emendation yields "To its maker, 'You have no hands'?"
e-e Heb. imperative.
f I.e., Cyrus.
g-g Emendation yields "bearing tribute." For "tribute" cf. Ezra 4.20; 6.8; Neh. 5.4.

Triumph everlasting.
You shall not be shamed or disgraced
In all the ages to come!"

¹⁸For thus said the LORD,
The Creator of heaven who alone is God,
Who formed the earth and made it,
Who alone established it—
He did not create it a waste,
But formed it for habitation:
I am the LORD, and there is none else.
¹⁹I did not speak in secret,
At a site in a land of darkness;
I did not say to the stock of Jacob,
"Seek Me out in a wasteland"—
I the LORD, who foretell reliably,
Who announce what is true.

²⁰Come, gather together,
Draw nigh, you remnants of the nations!
No foreknowledge had they who carry their wooden images
And pray to a god who cannot give success.
²¹Speak up, compare testimony—
Let them even take counsel together!
Who announced this aforetime,
Foretold it of old?
Was it not I the LORD?
Then there is no god beside Me,
No God exists beside Me
Who foretells truly and grants success.
²²Turn to Me and gain success,
All the ends of earth!
For I am God, and there is none else.
²³By Myself have I sworn,
From My mouth has issued truth,
A word that shall not turn back:
To Me every knee shall bend,
Every tongue swear loyalty.

24h-They shall say: "Only through the LORD
Can I find victory and might.-h
When people i-trust in-i Him,
All their adversaries are put to shame.
25It is through the LORD that all the offspring of Israel
Have vindication and glory."

46

Bela is bowed, Neboa is cowering,
Their images are a burden for beasts and cattle;
The things youb would carry [in procession]
Are now piled as a burden
On tired [beasts].
2They cowered, they bowed as well,
They could not rescue the burden,c
And they themselves went into captivity.

3Listen to Me, O House of Jacob,
All that are left of the House of Israel,
Who have been carried since birth,
Supported since leaving the womb:
4Till you grow old, I will still be the same;
When you turn gray, it is I who will carry;
I was the Maker, and I will be the Bearer;
And I will carry and rescue [you].

5To whom can you compare Me
Or declare Me similar?
To whom can you liken Me,
So that we seem comparable?
6Those who squander gold from the purse
And weigh out silver on the balance,d
They hire a metal worker to make it into a god,
To which they bow down and prostrate themselves.
7They must carry it on their backs and transport it;
When they put it down, it stands,
It does not budge from its place.
If they cry out to it, it does not answer;

---

h-h *Emendation yields "Only in the* LORD/*Are there victory and might for man."*
i-i *Lit. "come to"; for this idiom cf. Ps. 65.3; Job 6.20.*

a *Babylonian deities.*
b *Emendation yields "they."*
c *Emendation yields "him who carried [them]"; cf. Targum.*
d *Lit. "beam [of the balance]."*

It cannot save them from their distress.
⁸Keep this in mind, and ᶜ‑stand firm!‑ᶜ
Take this to heart, you sinners!
⁹Bear in mind what happened of old;
For I am God, and there is none else,
I am divine, and there is none like Me.
¹⁰I foretell the end from the beginning,
And from the start, things that had not occurred.
I say: My plan shall be fulfilled;
I will do all I have purposed.
¹¹I summoned that swooping bird from the East;ᶠ
From a distant land, the man for My purpose.
I have spoken, so I will bring it to pass;
I have designed it, so I will complete it.
¹²Listen to Me, you ᵍ‑stubborn of heart,‑ᵍ
Who are far from victory:
¹³I am bringing My victory close;
It shall not be far,
And My triumph shall not be delayed.
I will grant triumph in Zion
To Israel, in whom I glory.

47 Get down, sit in the dust,
Fair Maiden Babylon;
Sit, dethroned, on the ground,
O Fair Chaldea;
Nevermore shall they call you
The tender and dainty one.
²Grasp the handmill and grind meal.
Remove your veil,
Strip off your train, bare your leg,
Wade through the rivers.
³Your nakedness shall be uncovered,
And your shame shall be exposed.
I will take vengeance,
ᵃ‑And let no man intercede.
⁴Our Redeemer—LORD of Hosts is His name—

ᶜ‑ᶜ *Meaning of Heb. uncertain.*
ᶠ *I.e., Cyrus; cf. 41.2–3; 44.28—45.1.*
ᵍ‑ᵍ *Septuagint reads, "who have lost heart."*

ᵃ‑ᵃ *Meaning of Heb. uncertain; emendation yields "And not be appeased,/Says our Redeemer, whose name is* LORD *of Hosts,/The Holy One of Israel."*

Is the Holy One of Israel.⁻ᵃ
⁵Sit silent; retire into darkness,
O Fair Chaldea;
Nevermore shall they call you
Mistress of Kingdoms.

⁶I was angry at My people,
I defiled My heritage;
I put them into your hands,
But you showed them no mercy.
Even upon the aged you made
Your yoke exceedingly heavy.
⁷You thought, "I shall always be
The mistress still."
You did not take these things to heart,
You gave no thought to the end of it.

⁸And now hear this, O pampered one—
Who dwell in security,
Who think to yourself,
"I am, and there is none but me;
I shall not become a widow
Or know loss of children"—
⁹These two things shall come upon you,
Suddenly, in one day:
Loss of children and widowhood
Shall come upon you in full measure,
Despite your many enchantments
And all your countless spells.
¹⁰You were secure in your wickedness;
You thought, "No one can see me."
It was your skill and your science
That led you astray.
And you thought to yourself,
"I am, and there is none but me."
¹¹Evil is coming upon you
Which you will not know how to ᵇ⁻charm away;⁻ᵇ
Disaster is falling upon you

b-b *Meaning of Heb. uncertain; emendation yields "bribe."*

Which you will not be able to appease;
Coming upon you suddenly
Is ruin of which you know nothing.
¹²Stand up, with your spells and your many enchantments
On which you labored since youth!
Perhaps you'll be able to profit,
Perhaps you ᶜ⁻will find strength.⁻ᶜ
¹³You are helpless, despite all your art.
Let them stand up and help you now,
The scannersᵈ of heaven, the star-gazers,
Who announce, month by month,
Whatever will come upon you.
¹⁴See, they are become like straw,
Fire consumes them;
They cannot save themselves
From the power of the flame;
This is no coal for warming oneself,
No fire to sit by!
¹⁵This is what they have profited you—
The traders you dealt with since youth—
Each has wandered off his own way,
There is none to save you.

48 Listen to this, O House of Jacob,
Who bear the name Israel
And have issued from the watersᵃ of Judah,
Who swear by the name of the LORD
And invoke the God of Israel—
Though not in truth and sincerity—
²For youᵇ are called after ᶜ⁻the Holy City⁻ᶜ
And youᵇ do lean on the God of Israel,
Whose name is LORD of Hosts:

³Long ago, I foretold things that happened,
From My mouth they issued, and I announced them;
Suddenly I acted, and they came to pass.
⁴Because I know how stubborn you are

ᶜ⁻ᶜ *Taking ʿaras as a variant of* ʿasar; *cf. 2 Chron. 20.37.*
ᵈ *Meaning of Heb. uncertain.*

ᵃ *Emendation yields "loins."*
ᵇ *Heb. "they."*
ᶜ⁻ᶜ *Emendation yields "the holy people."*

(Your neck is like an iron sinew
And your forehead bronze),
⁵Therefore I told you long beforehand,
Announced things to you ere they happened—
That you might not say, "My idol caused them,
My carved and molten images ordained them."
⁶You have ᵈ-heard all this; look, must you not acknowledge it?-ᵈ
As of now, I announce to you new things,
Well-guarded secrets you did not know.
⁷Only now are they created, and not of old;
ᵈ-Before today-ᵈ you had not heard them;
You cannot say, "I knew them already."
⁸You had never heard, you had never known,
Your ears were not opened of old.

Though I know that you are treacherous,
That you were called a rebel from birth,
⁹For the sake of My name I control My wrath;
To My own glory, ᵈ-I am patient-ᵈ with you,
And I will not destroy you.
¹⁰See, I refine you, but not as silver;
I test you in the furnace of affliction.
¹¹For My sake, My own sake, do I act—
Lest [My name]ᵉ be dishonored!
I will not give My glory to another.

¹²Listen to Me, O Jacob,
Israel, whom I have called:
I am He—I am the first,
And I am the last as well.
¹³My own hand founded the earth,
My right hand spread out the skies.

I call unto them, let them stand up.
¹⁴Assemble, all of you, and listen!
Who among youᶠ foretold these things:
ᵈ-"He whom the LORD loves
Shall work His will against Babylon,

ᵈ⁻ᵈ *Meaning of Heb. uncertain.*
ᵉ *These words are supplied in some ancient versions; cf. v. 9.*
ᶠ *Heb. "them."*

And, with His might, against Chaldea"?-d
¹⁵I, I predicted, and I called him;
I have brought him and he shall succeed in his mission.
¹⁶Draw near to Me and hear this:
From the beginning, I did not speak in secret;
From the time anything existed, I was there.ᵍ

"And now the Lord God has sent me, ʰ-endowed
   with His spirit."-ʰ

¹⁷Thus said the LORD your Redeemer,
The Holy One of Israel:
I the LORD am your God,
Instructing you for your own benefit.
Guiding you in the way you should go.
¹⁸If only you would heed My commands!
Then your prosperity would be like a river,
Your triumph like the waves of the sea.
¹⁹Your offspring would be as many as the sand,
Their issue as many as its grains.ᵈ
Their name would never be cut off
Or obliterated from before Me.

²⁰Go forth from Babylon,
Flee from Chaldea!
Declare this with loud shouting,
Announce this,
Bring out the word to the ends of the earth!
²¹Say: "The LORD has redeemed
His servant Jacob!"
They have known no thirst,
Though He led them through parched places;
He made water flow for them from the rock;
He cleaved the rock and water gushed forth.

²²There is no safety—said the LORD—for the wicked.

ᵍ I.e., I foretold it through prophets.
ʰ⁻ʰ Lit. "and His spirit."

49

Listen, O coastlands, to me,
And give heed, O nations afar:
The Lord appointed me before I was born,
He named me while I was in my mother's womb.
²He made my mouth like a sharpened blade,
He hid me in the shadow of His hand,
And He made me like a polished arrow;
He concealed me in His quiver.
³And He said to me, "You are My servant,
Israel in whom I glory."
⁴I thought, "I have labored in vain,
I have spent my strength for empty breath."
But my case rested with the Lord,
My recompense was in the hands of my God.
⁵And now the Lord has resolved—
He who formed me in the womb to be His servant—
To bring back Jacob to Himself,
That Israel may be restored to Him.
And I have been honored in the sight of the Lord,
My God has been my strength.
⁶For He has said:
"It is too little that you should be My servant
In that I raise up the tribes of Jacob
And restore the survivors of Israel:
I will also make you a light[a] of nations,
That My salvation may reach the ends of the earth."

⁷Thus said the Lord,
The Redeemer of Israel, his Holy One,
[b-]To the despised one,
To the abhorred nations,[-b]
To the slave of rulers:
Kings shall see and stand up;
Nobles, and they shall prostrate themselves—
To the honor of the Lord, who is faithful,
To the Holy One of Israel who chose you.

---

[a] *I.e., the agent of good fortune; cf. 42.1–4; 51.4–5.*
[b-b] *Meaning of Heb. uncertain. Emendation yields "Whose being is despised,/Whose body is detested"; cf. 51.23.*

⁸Thus said the LORD:
In an hour of favor I answer you,
And on a day of salvation I help you—
I created you and appointed you ᶜ⁻a covenant people⁻ᶜ—
Restoring the land,
Allotting anew the desolate holdings,
⁹Saying to the prisoners, "Go free,"
To those who are in darkness, "Show yourselves."
They shall pasture along the roads,
On every bare height shall be their pasture.
¹⁰They shall not hunger or thirst,
Hot wind and sun shall not strike them;
For He who loves them will lead them,
He will guide them to springs of water.
¹¹I will make all My mountains a road,
And My highways shall be built up.
¹²Look! These are coming from afar,
These from the north and the west,
And these from the land of Sinim.ᵈ
¹³Shout, O heavens, and rejoice, O earth!
Break into shouting, O hills!
For the LORD has comforted His people,
And has taken back His afflicted ones in love.

¹⁴Zion says,
"The LORD has forsaken me,
My Lord has forgotten me."
¹⁵Can a woman forget her baby,
Or disown the child of her womb?
Though she might forget,
I never could forget you.
¹⁶See, I have engraved you
On the palms of My hands,
Your walls are ever before Me.
¹⁷Swiftly your children are coming;
Those who ravaged and ruined you shall leave you.
¹⁸Look up all around you and see:

ᶜ⁻ᶜ *See note b-b at 42.6.*
ᵈ *1QIsᵃ reads "the Syenians"; cf. Ezek. 30.6.*

They are all assembled, are come to you!
As I live

—declares the LORD—

You shall don them all like jewels,
Deck yourself with them like a bride.
¹⁹As for your ruins and desolate places
And your land laid waste—
You shall soon be crowded with settlers,
While destroyers stay far from you.
²⁰The children ᶜ⁻you thought you had lostᶜ
Shall yet say in your hearing,
"The place is too crowded for me;
Make room for me to settle."
²¹And you will say to yourself,
"Who bore these for me
When I was bereaved and barren,
Exiled and disdainedᶠ—
By whom, then, were these reared?
I was left all alone—
And where have these been?"

²²Thus said the Lord GOD:
I will raise My hand to nations
And lift up My ensign to peoples;
And they shall bring your sons in their bosoms,
And carry your daughters on their backs.
²³Kings shall tend your children,
Their queens shall serve you as nurses.
They shall bow to you, face to the ground,
And lick the dust of your feet.
And you shall know that I am the LORD—
Those who trust in Me shall not be shamed.

²⁴Can spoil be taken from a warrior,
Or captives retrieved from a victor?
²⁵Yet thus said the LORD:
Captives shall be taken from a warrior

ᶜ⁻ᶜ Lit. "of your bereavement."
ᶠ Meaning of Heb. uncertain.

And spoil shall be retrieved from a tyrant;
For *I* will contend with your adversaries,
And *I* will deliver your children.
²⁶I will make your oppressors eat their own flesh,
They shall be drunk with their own blood as with wine.
And all mankind shall know
That I the LORD am your Savior,
The Mighty One of Jacob, your Redeemer.

50 Thus said the LORD:
ªWhere is the bill of divorce
Of your mother whom I dismissed?
And which of My creditors was it
To whom I sold you off?
You were only sold off for your sins,
And your mother dismissed for your crimes.
²Why, when I came, was no one there,
Why, when I called, would none respond?
Is my arm, then, too short to rescue,
Have I not the power to save?
With a mere rebuke I dry up the sea,
And turn rivers into desert.
Their fish stink from lack of water;
They lie dead ᵇ⁻of thirst.⁻ᵇ
³I clothe the skies in blackness
And make their raiment sackcloth.

⁴ᶜ⁻The Lord GOD gave me a skilled tongue,
To know how to speak timely words to the weary.⁻ᶜ
Morning by morning, He rouses,
He rouses my ear
To give heed like disciples.
⁵The Lord GOD opened my ears,
And I did not disobey,
I did not run away.
⁶I offered my back to the floggers,
And my cheeks to those who tore out my hair.

ª *The mother (the country) has not been formally divorced, nor the children (the people) sold because of poverty. Therefore there is no obstacle to their restoration.*
ᵇ⁻ᵇ *Change of vocalization yields "on the parched ground"; cf. 44.3.*
ᶜ⁻ᶜ *Meaning of Heb. uncertain.*

I did not hide my face
From insult and spittle.
[7] But the Lord GOD will help me—
Therefore I feel no disgrace;
Therefore I have set my face like flint,
And I know I shall not be shamed.
[8] My Vindicator is at hand—
Who dares contend with me?
Let us stand up together![d]
Who would be my opponent?
Let him approach me!
[9] Lo, the Lord GOD will help me—
Who can get a verdict against me?
They shall all wear out like a garment,
The moth shall consume them.

[10] Who among you reveres the LORD
And heeds the voice of His servant?—
Though he walk in darkness
And have no light,
Let him trust in the name of the LORD
And rely upon his God.
[11] But you are all kindlers of fire,
[e-]Girding on[-e] firebrands.
Walk by the blaze of your fire,
By the brands that you have lit!
This has come to you from My hand:
[c-]You shall lie down in pain.[-c]

51

Listen to Me, you who pursue justice,
You who seek the LORD:
Look to the rock you were hewn from,
To the quarry you were dug from.
[2] Look back to Abraham your father
And to Sarah who brought you forth.
For he was only one when I called him,
But I blessed him and made him many.

---

[d] *I.e., as opponents in court; cf. Num. 35.12.*
[e-e] *Emendation yields "Lighters of."*

³Truly the LORD has comforted Zion,
Comforted all her ruins;
He has made her wilderness like Eden,
Her desert like the Garden of the LORD.
Gladness and joy shall abide there,
Thanksgiving and the sound of music.

⁴Hearken to Me, ᵃ-My people,-ᵃ
And give ear to Me, O ᵃ-My nation,-ᵃ
For teaching shall go forthᵇ from Me,
My way for the light of peoples.
In a moment I will bring it:
⁵The triumph I grant is near,
The success I give has gone forth.
My arms shall ᶜ-provide for-ᶜ the peoples;
The coastlands shall trust in Me,
They shall look to My arm.

⁶Raise your eyes to the heavens,
And look upon the earth beneath:
Though the heavens should melt away like smoke,
And the earth wear out like a garment,
And its inhabitants die out ᵈ-as well,-ᵈ
My victory shall stand forever,
My triumph shall remain unbroken.

⁷Listen to Me, you who care for the right,
O people who lay My instruction to heart!
Fear not the insults of men,
And be not dismayed at their jeers;
⁸For the moth shall eat them up like a garment,
The wormᵉ shall eat them up like wool.
But My triumph shall endure forever,
My salvation through all the ages.

⁹Awake, awake, clothe yourself with splendor.
O arm of the LORD!
Awake as in days of old,

ᵃ⁻ᵃ *Several mss. read "O peoples . . . O nations"; cf. end of this verse and v. 5.*
ᵇ *I.e., through My servant Israel; cf. 42.1–4; 49.6.*
ᶜ⁻ᶜ *Lit. "judge."*
ᵈ⁻ᵈ *Emendation yields "like gnats."*
ᵉ *Heb. sas, another word for "moth."*

As in former ages!
It was you that hacked Rahab[f] in pieces,
That pierced the Dragon.[f]
10It was you that dried up the Sea,
The waters of the great deep;
That made the abysses of the Sea
A road the redeemed might walk.
11So let the ransomed of the LORD return,
And come with shouting to Zion,
Crowned with joy everlasting.
Let them attain joy and gladness,
While sorrow and sighing flee.

12I, I am He who comforts you!
What ails you that you fear
Man who must die,
Mortals who fare like grass?
13You have forgotten the LORD your Maker,
Who stretched out the skies and made firm the earth!
And you live all day in constant dread
Because of the rage of an oppressor
Who is aiming to cut [you] down.
Yet of what account is the rage of an oppressor?
14gQuickly the crouching one is freed;
He is not cut down and slain,
And he shall not want for food.
15For I the LORD your God—
Who stir up the sea into roaring waves,
Whose name is LORD of Hosts—
16h-Have put My words in your mouth
And sheltered you with My hand;-h
I, who planted[i] the skies and made firm the earth,
Have said to Zion: You are My people!
17Rouse, rouse yourself!
Arise, O Jerusalem,
You who from the LORD's hand
Have drunk the cup of His wrath,
You who have drained to the dregs

f *Names of primeval monsters.*
g *Meaning of verse uncertain. Emendation yields (cf. Jer. 11.19; Job 14.7–9) "Quickly the tree buds anew;/It does not die though cut down,/And its sap does not fail."*
h-h *I.e., I have chosen you to be a prophet-nation; cf. 49.2; 59.21.*
i *Emendation yields "stretched out"; cf. Syriac version and v. 13.*

The bowl, the cup of reeling!
¹⁸She has none to guide her
Of all the sons she bore;
None takes her by the hand,
Of all the sons she reared.^j
¹⁹These two things have befallen you:
Wrack and ruin—who can console you?
Famine and sword—^{k-}how shall I^{-k} comfort you?
²⁰Your sons lie in a swoon
At the corner of every street—
Like an antelope caught in a net—
Drunk with the wrath of the LORD,
With the rebuke of your God.
²¹Therefore,
Listen to this, unhappy one,
Who are drunk, but not with wine!
²²Thus said the LORD, your Lord,
Your God who champions His people:
Herewith I take from your hand
The cup of reeling,^l
The bowl, the cup of My wrath;
You shall never drink it again.
²³I will put it in the hands of your tormentors,
Who have commanded you,
"Get down, that we may walk over you"—
So that you made your back like the ground,
Like a street for passersby.

52
Awake, awake, O Zion!
Clothe yourself in splendor;
Put on your robes of majesty,
Jerusalem, holy city!
For the uncircumcised and the unclean
Shall never enter you again.
²Arise, shake off the dust,
Sit [on your throne], Jerusalem!

---

^j To guide a drunken parent home was a recognized filial duty in ancient Canaan and Egypt.
^{k-k} Several ancient versions render "who can."
^l A figure of speech for a dire fate; cf. Jer. 25.15 ff.

Loose the bonds from your neck,
O captive one, Fair Zion!

³For thus said the LORD:
You were sold for no price,
And shall be redeemed without money.
⁴For thus said the Lord GOD:
Of old, My people went down
To Egypt to sojourn there;
But Assyria has robbed them,
Giving nothing in return.ᵃ
⁵What therefore do I gain here?

—declares the LORD—

For My people has been carried off for nothing,
Their mockers howl

—declares the LORD—

And constantly, unceasingly,
My name is reviled.
⁶Assuredly, My people shall learn My name,
Assuredly [they shall learn] on that day
That I, the One who promised,
Am now at hand.

⁷How welcome on the mountain
Are the footsteps of the herald
Announcing happiness,
Heralding good fortune,
Announcing victory,
Telling Zion, "Your God is King!"
⁸Hark!
Your watchmen raise their voices,
As one they shout for joy;
For every eye shall behold
The LORD's return to Zion.
⁹Raise a shout together,
O ruins of Jerusalem!
For the LORD will comfort His people,

ᵃ *Whereas the Israelites themselves sought hospitality in Egypt, Assyria (i.e., the Chaldean Empire)
has exiled them by force.*

Will redeem Jerusalem.
¹⁰The LORD will bare His holy arm
In the sight of all the nations,
And the very ends of earth shall see
The victory of our God.

¹¹Turn, turn away, touch naught unclean
As you depart from there;
Keep pure, as you go forth from there,
You who bear the vessels of the LORD!ᵇ
¹²For you will not depart in haste,
Nor will you leave in flight;
For the LORD is marching before you,
The God of Israel is your rear guard.

¹³"Indeed, My servant shall prosper,
Be exalted and raised to great heights.
¹⁴Just as the many were appalled at himᶜ—
So marred was his appearance, unlike that of man,
His form, beyond human semblance—
¹⁵Just so he shall startleᵈ many nations.
Kings shall be silenced because of him,
For they shall see what has not been told them,
Shall behold what they never have heard."

53 "Who can believe what we have heard?
Upon whom has ᵃ⁻the arm of the LORD⁻ᵃ been revealed?
²For he has grown, by His favor, like a tree crown,
Like a tree trunk out of arid ground.
He had no form or beauty, that we should look at him:
No charm, that we should find him pleasing.
³He was despised, ᵇ⁻shunned by men,⁻ᵇ
A man of suffering, familiar with disease.
ᶜ⁻As one who hid his face from us,⁻ᶜ
He was despised, we held him of no account.
⁴Yet it was our sickness that he was bearing,

ᵇ Cf. Ezra 1.7–8; 5.14–15.
ᶜ Heb. "you."
ᵈ Meaning of Heb. uncertain.

ᵃ⁻ᵃ I.e., the vindication which the arm of the LORD effects.
ᵇ⁻ᵇ Meaning of Heb. uncertain.
ᶜ⁻ᶜ I.e., as a leper; cf. Lev. 13.45 ff.

Our suffering that he endured.
We accounted him plagued,
Smitten and afflicted by God;
5But he was wounded because of our sins,
Crushed because of our iniquities.
He bore the chastisement that made us whole,
And by his bruises we were healed.
6We all went astray like sheep,
Each going his own way;
And the LORD visited upon him
The guilt of all of us."

7He was maltreated, yet he was submissive,
He did not open his mouth;
Like a sheep being led to slaughter,
Like a ewe, dumb before those who shear her,
He did not open his mouth.
8By oppressive judgment he was taken away,
b-Who could describe his abode?-b
For he was cut off from the land of the living
Through the sin of my people, who deserved the punishment.
9And his grave was set among the wicked,
d-And with the rich, in his death-d—
Though he had done no injustice
And had spoken no falsehood.
10But the LORD chose to crush him b-by disease,
That, if he made himself an offering for guilt,-b
He might see offspringᵉ and have long life,
And that through him the LORD's purpose might prosper.
11Out of his anguish he shall see it;ᶠ
He shall enjoy it to the full through his devotion.ᵍ

"My righteous servant makes the many righteous,
It is their punishment that he bears;
12Assuredly, I will give him the many as his portion,
He shall receive the multitude as his spoil.
For he exposed himself to death

---

d-d *Emendation yields "And his tomb with evildoers."*
ᵉ *Emendation yields "His arm," i.e., His vindication; cf. v. 1 with note.*
ᶠ *I.e., the arm of the Lord; see preceding note.*
ᵍ *For this sense of* da'ath *see 11.2, 9.*

And was numbered among the sinners,
Whereas he bore the guilt of the many
And made intercession for sinners."

54 Shout, O barren one,
You who bore no child!
Shout aloud for joy,
You who did not travail!
For the children of the wife forlorn
Shall outnumber those of the espoused

        —said the LORD.

²Enlarge the site of your tent,
ᵃ⁻Extend the size of your dwelling,⁻ᵃ
Do not stint!
Lengthen the ropes, and drive the pegs firm.
³For you shall spread out to the right and the left;
Your offspring shall dispossess nationsᵇ
And shall people the desolate towns.

⁴Fear not, you shall not be shamed;
Do not cringe, you shall not be disgraced.
For you shall forget
The reproach of your youth,
And remember no more
The shame of your widowhood.
⁵For He who made you will espouse you—
His name is "LORD of Hosts."
The Holy One of Israel will redeem you—
He is called "God of all the Earth."

⁶The LORD has called you back
As a wife forlorn and forsaken.
Can one cast off the wife of his youth?

        —said your God.

⁷For a little while I forsook you,
But with vast love I will bring you back.
⁸In slight anger, for a moment,

ᵃ⁻ᵃ Lit. "Let the cloths of your dwelling extend."
ᵇ I.e., the foreigners who had occupied regions from which Israelites had been exiled; cf. 2 Kings
17.24.

I hid My face from you;
But with kindness everlasting
I will take you back in love

          —said the LORD your Redeemer.

⁹For this to Me is like the waters^c of Noah:
As I swore that the waters of Noah
Nevermore would flood the earth,
So I swear that I will not
Be angry with you or rebuke you.
¹⁰For the mountains may move
And the hills be shaken,
But my loyalty shall never move from you,
Nor My covenant of friendship be shaken

          —said the LORD, who takes you back in love.

¹¹Unhappy, storm-tossed one, uncomforted!
I will lay carbuncles^d as your building stones
And make your foundations of sapphires.
¹²I will make your battlements of rubies,
Your gates of precious stones,
The whole encircling wall of gems.
¹³And all your children shall be disciples of the LORD,
And great shall be the happiness of your children;
¹⁴You shall be established through righteousness.
You shall be safe from oppression,
And shall have no fear;
From ruin, and it shall not come near you.
¹⁵ᵉSurely no harm can be done
Without My consent:
Whoever would harm you
Shall fall because of you.
¹⁶It is I who created the smith
To fan the charcoal fire
And produce the tools for his work;
So it is I who create
The instruments of havoc.
¹⁷No weapon formed against you
Shall succeed,

---

^c *Other Heb. mss. and the ancient versions read "days."*
^d *Taking* pukh *as a byform of* nophekh; *so already Rashi.*
^e *Meaning of verse uncertain.*

And every tongue that contends with you at law
You shall defeat.
Such is the lot of the servants of the LORD,
Such their triumph through Me

—declares the LORD.

55

Ho, all who are thirsty,
Come for water,
Even if you have no money;
Come, buy food and eat:
Buy food without money,
Wine and milk without cost.
2Why do you spend money for what is not bread,
Your earnings for what does not satisfy?
Give heed to Me,
And you shall eat choice food
And enjoy the richest viands.
3Incline your ear and come to Me;
Hearken, and you shall be revived.
And I will make with you an everlasting covenant,
The enduring loyalty promised to David.
4a-As I made him a leaderb of peoples,
A prince and commander of peoples,
5So you shall summon a nation you did not know,
And a nation that did not know you
Shall come running to you-a—
For the sake of the LORD your God,
The Holy One of Israel who has glorified you.

6Seek the LORD while He can be found,
Call to Him while He is near.
7Let the wicked give up his ways,
The sinful man his plans;
Let him turn back to the LORD,
And He will pardon him;
To our God,
For he freely forgives.

a-a Cf. 2 Sam. 22.44–45//Ps. 18.44–45.
b Cf. Targum; others "witness."

⁸For My plans are not your plans,
Nor are My ways^c your ways^c

—declares the LORD.

⁹But as the heavens are high above the earth,
So are My ways^c high above your ways^c
And My plans above your plans.
¹⁰For as the rain or snow drops from heaven
And returns not there,
But soaks the earth
And makes it bring forth vegetation,
Yielding ^{d-}seed for sowing and bread for eating,^{-d}
¹¹So is the word that issues from My mouth:
It does not come back to Me unfulfilled,
But performs what I purpose,
Achieves what I sent it to do.
¹²Yea, you shall leave^e in joy and be led home secure.
Before you, mount and hill shall shout aloud,
And all the trees of the field shall clap their hands.
¹³Instead of the brier, a cypress shall rise;
Instead of the nettle, a myrtle shall rise.
These shall stand as a testimony to the LORD,
As an everlasting sign that shall not perish.

56

Thus said the LORD:
Observe what is right and do what is just;
For soon My salvation shall come,
And my deliverance be revealed.

²Happy is the man who does this,
The man who holds fast to it:
Who keeps the sabbath and does not profane it,
And stays his hand from doing any evil.

³Let not the foreigner say,
Who has attached himself to the LORD,
"The LORD will keep me apart from His people";
And let not the eunuch say,

---

^c *Emendation yields "words"; cf. v. 11 and 40.8.*
^{d-d} *Lit. "seed for the sower and bread for the eater."*
^e *I.e., leave the Babylonian exile.*

"I am a withered tree."
⁴For thus said the LORD:
"As for the eunuchs who keep My sabbaths,
Who have chosen what I desire
And hold fast to My covenant—
⁵I will give them, in My House
And within My walls,
A monument and a name
Better than sons or daughters.
I will give them an everlasting name
Which shall not perish.
⁶As for the foreigners
Who attach themselves to the LORD,
To minister to Him,
And to love the name of the LORD,
To be His servants—
All who keep the sabbath and do not profane it,
And who hold fast to My covenant—
⁷I will bring them to My sacred mount
And let them rejoice in My house of prayer.
Their burnt offerings and sacrifices
Shall be welcome on My altar;
For My House shall be called
A house of prayer for all peoples."
⁸Thus declares the Lord GOD,
Who gathers the dispersed of Israel:
"I will gather still more to those already gathered."

⁹All you wild beasts, come and devour,
All you beasts of the forest!
¹⁰Theᵃ watchmen are blind, all of them,
They perceive nothing.
They are all dumb dogs
That cannot bark;
They lie sprawling,ᵇ
They love to drowse.

ᵃ Heb. "his."
ᵇ Meaning of Heb. uncertain.

¹¹Moreover, the dogs are greedy;
They never know satiety.
ᶜ⁻As for the shepherds, they know not
What it is to give heed.⁻ᶜ
Everyone has turned his own way,
Every last one seeks his own advantage.
¹²"Come, I'll get some wine;
Let us swill liquor.
And tomorrow will be just the same,
Or even much grander!"

57

The righteous man perishes,
And no one considers;
Pious men are taken away,
And no one gives thought
That because of evil
The righteous was taken away.
²Yet he shall come to peace,
ᵃ⁻He shall have rest on his couch⁻ᵃ
Who walked straightforward.

³But as for you, come closer,
You sons of a sorceress,
You offspring of an adulterer and a harlot!ᵇ
⁴With whom do you act so familiarly?
At whom do you open your mouth
And stick out your tongue?
Why, you are children of iniquity,
Offspring of treachery—
⁵You who inflameᶜ yourselves
Among the terebinths,
Under every verdant tree;
Who slaughter children in the wadis,
Amongᵈ the clefts of the rocks.
⁶ᵉ⁻With suchᶠ are your share and portion,⁻ᵉ

ᶜ⁻ᶜ *Meaning of Heb. uncertain. Emendation yields "Neither do the shepherds ever know sufficiency (hon)." Cf. hon in Prov. 30.15, 16.*

ᵃ⁻ᵃ *Heb. "They shall have rest on their couches."*
ᵇ *Lit. "she acts the harlot."*
ᶜ *I.e., in some frenzied idolatrous rite.*
ᵈ *Heb. "under."*
ᵉ⁻ᵉ *Meaning of Heb. uncertain.*
ᶠ *The cult-trees referred to above in v. 5.*

They, they are your allotment;
To them you have poured out libations,
Presented offerings.
Should I relent in the face of this?

7On a high and lofty hill
You have set your couch;
There, too, you have gone up
To perform sacrifices.
8Behind the door and doorpost
You have directed your thoughts;
e-Abandoning Me, you have gone up
On the couch you made so wide.
You have made a covenant with them,f
You have loved bedding with them;g
You have chosen lust.h
9You have approached-e the kingi with oil,
You have provided many perfumes.
And you have sent your envoys afar,
Even down to the netherworld.j
10Though wearied by much travel,
You never said, "I give up!"
You found gratification for your lust,
And so you never cared.
11k-Whom do you dread and fear,
That you tell lies?-k
But you gave no thought to Me,
You paid no heed.
It is because I have stood idly by l-so long-l
That you have no fear of Me.
12I hereby pronounce m-judgment upon your deeds:-m
n-Your assorted [idols]-n shall not avail you,
13Shall not save you when you cry out.
They shall all be borne off by the wind,
Snatched away by a breeze.
But those who trust in Me shall inherit the land

g I.e., with the objects behind door and doorpost.
h Like Ugaritic yd, from root ydd, "to love."
i Or "Molech."
j I.e., you have brought tribute to alien cults as to a king.
k-k Emendation yields "Them you dreaded and feared,/And so you gave them thought."
l-l Emendation yields "and shut My eyes."
m-mLit. "your retribution and your deeds."
n-n Brought up from v. 13 for clarity.

And possess My sacred mount.
14[The Lord] says:
Build up, build up a highway!
Clear a road!
Remove all obstacles
From the road of My people!
15For thus said He who high aloft
Forever dwells, whose name is holy:
I dwell on high, in holiness;
Yet with the contrite and the lowly in spirit—
Reviving the spirits of the lowly,
Reviving the hearts of the contrite.
16For I will not always contend,
I will not be angry forever:
Nay, I [e]who make spirits flag,[e]
Also create the breath of life.
17For their[o] sinful greed I was angry;
I struck them and turned away in My wrath.
[p]Though stubborn, they follow the way of their hearts,[p]
18I note how they fare and will heal them:
I will guide them and mete out solace to them,
And to the mourners among them
19 heartening,[q] comforting[r] words:
It shall be well,
Well with the far and the near
—said the LORD—
And I will heal them.
20But the wicked are like the troubled sea
Which cannot rest,
Whose waters toss up mire and mud.
21There is no safety
—said my God—
For the wicked.

58 Cry with full throat, without restraint;
Raise your voice like a ram's horn!

[o] *I.e., Israel's. Cf. "My people," v. 14.*

[p-p] *Meaning of Heb. uncertain. Emendation yields "When they have walked broken in the contrition of their hearts."*

[q] *Lit. "the vigor of"; cf. Eccl. 12.1 and postbiblical* bori.

[r] *The Heb.* nib *is otherwise unknown; its meaning is inferred from that of* nid *(cf. the verb* nad *"to condole") in the parallel expression in Job 16.5.*

Declare to My people their transgression,
To the House of Jacob their sin.

²To be sure, they seek Me daily,
Eager to learn My ways.
Like a nation that does what is right,
That has not abandoned the laws of its God,
They ask Me for the right way,
They are eager for the nearness of God:
³"Why, when we fasted, did You not see?
When we starved our bodies, did You pay no heed?"
Because on your fast day
You see to your business
And oppress all your laborers!
⁴Because you fast in strife and contention,
And you strike with a wicked fist!
Your fasting today is not such
As to make your voice heard on high.
⁵Is such the fast I desire,
A day for men to starve their bodies?
Is it bowing the head like a bulrush
And lying in sackcloth and ashes?
Do you call that a fast,
A day when the LORD is favorable?
⁶No, this is the fast I desire:
To unlock fetters of wickedness,
And untie the cords of ᵃ‑the yoke‑ᵃ
To let the oppressed go free;
To break off every yoke.
⁷It is to share your bread with the hungry,
And to take the wretched poor into your home;
When you see the naked, to clothe him,
And not to ignore your own kin.

⁸Then shall your light burst through like the dawn
And your healing spring up quickly;
Your Vindicator shall march before you,

ᵃ‑ᵃ *Change of vocalization yields "lawlessness"; cf.* muṭṭeh, *Ezek. 9.9.*

The Presence of the LORD shall be your rear guard.
⁹Then, when you call, the LORD will answer;
When you cry, He will say: Here I am.
If you banish the yokeª from your midst,
ᵇ⁻The menacing hand,⁻ᵇ and evil speech,
¹⁰And you offer your compassionᶜ to the hungry
And satisfy the famished creature—
Then shall your light shine in darkness,
And your gloom shall be like noonday.
¹¹The LORD will guide you always;
He will slake your thirst in ᵈ⁻parched places⁻ᵈ
And give strength to your bones.
You shall be like a watered garden,
Like a spring whose waters do not fail.
¹²Men from your midst shall rebuild ancient ruins,
You shall restore foundations laid long ago.
And you shall be called
"Repairer of fallen walls,
Restorer of lanes for habitation."
¹³If you ᵉ⁻refrain from trampling⁻ᵉ the sabbath,
From pursuing your affairs on My holy day;
If you call the sabbath "delight,"
The LORD's holy day "honored";
And if you honor it and go not your ways
Nor look to your affairs, nor strike bargains—
¹⁴Then you ᶠ⁻can seek the favor of the LORD.⁻ᶠ
I will set you astride the heights of the earth,
And let you enjoy the heritage of your father Jacob—
For the mouth of the LORD has spoken.

59 No, the LORD's arm is not too short to save,
Or His ear too dull to hear;
²But your iniquities have been a barrier
Between you and your God,
Your sins have made Him turn His face away
And refuse to hear you.

ᵇ⁻ᵇ *Lit. "Extending the finger."*
ᶜ *Some Heb. mss. and ancient versions read "bread."*
ᵈ⁻ᵈ *Meaning of Heb. uncertain.*
ᵉ⁻ᵉ *Lit. "turn back your foot from."*
ᶠ⁻ᶠ *Cf. Ps. 37.4; Job 22.26–27; 27.10.*

³For your hands are defiled with crime^a
And your fingers with iniquity.
Your lips speak falsehood,
Your tongue utters treachery.
⁴No one sues justly
Or pleads honestly;
They rely on emptiness and speak falsehood,
Conceiving wrong and begetting evil.

⁵They hatch adder's eggs
And weave spider webs;
He who eats of those eggs will die,
And if one is crushed, it hatches out a viper.
⁶Their webs will not serve as a garment,
What they make cannot serve as clothing;
Their deeds are deeds of mischief,
Their hands commit lawless acts,
⁷Their feet run after evil,
They hasten to shed the blood of the innocent.
Their plans are plans of mischief,
Destructiveness and injury are on their roads.
⁸They do not care for the way of integrity,
There is no justice on their paths.
They make their courses crooked,
No one who walks in them cares for integrity.

⁹"That is why redress is far from us,
And vindication does not reach us.
We hope for light, and lo! there is darkness;
For a gleam, and we must walk in gloom.
¹⁰We grope, like blind men along a wall;
Like those without eyes we grope.
We stumble at noon, as if in darkness;
^{b-}Among the sturdy, we are-^b like the dead.
¹¹We all growl like bears
And moan like doves.
We hope for redress, and there is none;

---

^a *Or "blood."*
^{b-b} *Meaning of Heb. uncertain. Emendation yields "In the daytime. . . ."*

For victory, and it is far from us.
¹²For our many sins are before You,
Our guilt testifies against us.
We are aware of our sins,
And we know well our iniquities:
¹³Rebellion, faithlessness to the LORD,
And turning away from our God,
Planning fraud and treachery,
Conceiving lies and uttering them with the throat.ᶜ
¹⁴And so redress is turned back
And vindication stays afar,
Because honesty stumbles in the public square
And uprightness cannot enter.
¹⁵Honesty has been lacking,
He who turns away from evil is despoiled."

The LORD saw and was displeased
That there was no redress.
¹⁶He saw that there was no man,
He gazed long, but no one intervened.
Then His own arm won Him triumph,
His victorious right handᵈ supported Him.
¹⁷He donned victory like a coat of mail,
With a helmet of triumph on His head;
He clothed Himself with garments of retribution,
Wrapped himself in zeal as in a robe.
¹⁸ᵉ⁻According to their deserts,
So shall He repayᵉ fury to His foes;
He shall make requital to His enemies,
Requital to the distant lands.
¹⁹From the west, they shall revereᶠ the name of the LORD,ᶠ
And from the east, His Presence.
For He shall come like a hemmed-in stream
Which the wind of the LORD drives on;
²⁰He shall come as redeemer to Zion,
To those in Jacob who turn back from sin
                                    —declares the LORD.

ᶜ Lit. "heart"; see note at 33.18 and frequently elsewhere.
ᵈ Cf. Ps. 98.1–2.
ᵉ⁻ᵉ Meaning of Heb. uncertain.
ᶠ Or (with a number of mss. and editions) "see."

²¹And this shall be My covenant with them, said the LORD: My spirit^g which is upon you, and the words which I have placed in your mouth, shall not be absent from your mouth, nor from the mouth of your children, nor from the mouth of your children's children—said the LORD— from now on, for all time.^h

60

Arise, shine, for your light has dawned;
The Presence of the LORD has shone upon you!
²Behold! Darkness shall cover the earth,
And thick clouds the peoples;
But upon you the LORD will shine,
And His Presence be seen over you.
³And nations shall walk by your light,
Kings, by your shining radiance.

⁴Raise your eyes and look about:
They have all gathered and come to you.
Your sons shall be brought from afar,
Your daughters like babes on shoulders.
⁵As you behold, you will glow;
Your heart will throb and thrill—
For the wealth of the sea^a shall pass on to you,
The riches of nations shall flow to you.
⁶Dust clouds of camels shall cover you,
Dromedaries of Midian and Ephah.
They all shall come from Sheba;
They shall bear gold and frankincense,
And shall herald the glories of the LORD.
⁷All the flocks of Kedar shall be assembled for you,
The rams of Nebaioth shall serve your needs;
They shall be welcome offerings on My altar,
And I will add glory to My glorious House.

⁸Who are these that float like a cloud,
Like doves to their cotes?
⁹^{b-}Behold, the coastlands await me,^{-b}
With ^{c-}ships of Tarshish^{-c} in the lead,

---

^g *I.e., the gift of prophecy; cf., e.g., 61.1.*
^h *Israel is to be a prophet-nation; cf. 51.16.*

^a *Emendation yields "coastlands."*
^{b-b} *Emendation yields "The vessels of the coastlands are gathering."*
^{c-c} *See note at 2.16.*

To bring your sons from afar,
And their[d] silver and gold as well—
For the name of the LORD your God,
For the Holy One of Israel, who has glorified you.
10Aliens shall rebuild your walls,
Their kings shall wait upon you—
For in anger I struck you down,
But in favor I take you back.
11Your gates shall always stay open—
Day and night they shall never be shut—
To let in the wealth of the nations,
With their kings in procession.

12For the nation or the kingdom
That does not serve you shall perish;
Such nations shall be destroyed.

13The majesty of Lebanon shall come to you—
Cypress and pine and box—
To adorn the site of My Sanctuary,
To glorify the place where My feet rest.

14Bowing before you, shall come
The children of those who tormented you;
Prostrate at the soles of your feet
Shall be all those who reviled you;
And you shall be called
"City of the LORD,
Zion of the Holy One of Israel."
15Whereas you have been forsaken,
Rejected, with none passing through,
I will make you a pride everlasting,
A joy for age after age.
16You shall suck the milk of the nations,
Suckle at royal breasts.[e]
And you shall know
That I the LORD am your Savior,
I, The Mighty One of Jacob, am your Redeemer.

d *I.e., of the people of the coastlands.*
e *Lit. "breasts of kings" or "breasts of kingdoms."*

¹⁷Instead of copper I will bring gold,
Instead of iron I will bring silver;
Instead of wood, copper;
And instead of stone, iron.
And I will appoint Well-being as your government,
Prosperity as your officials.
¹⁸The cry "Violence!"
Shall no more be heard in your land,
Nor "Wrack and ruin!"
Within your borders.
And you shall name your walls "Victory"
And your gates "Renown."

¹⁹No longer shall you need the sun
For light by day,
Nor the shining of the moon
For radiance [by night[f]];
For the LORD shall be your light everlasting,
Your God shall be your glory.
²⁰Your sun shall set no more,
Your moon no more withdraw;
For the LORD shall be a light to you forever,
And your days of mourning shall be ended.
²¹And your people, all of them righteous,
Shall possess the land for all time;
They are the shoot that I planted,
My handiwork in which I glory.
²²The smallest shall become a clan;
The least, a mighty nation.
I the LORD will speed it in due time.

61

The spirit of the Lord GOD is upon me,
Because the LORD has anointed me;
He has sent me as a herald of joy to the humble,
To bind up the wounded of heart,
To proclaim release to the captives,

---

f *So 1QIs^a, Septuagint, and Targum.*

Liberation to the imprisoned;
²To proclaim a year of the LORD's favor
And a day of vindication by our God;
To comfort all who mourn—
³ᵃ⁻To provide for⁻ᵃ the mourners in Zion—
To give them a turban instead of ashes,
The festive ointment instead of mourning,
A garment of splendor instead of a drooping spirit.
They shall be called terebinths of victory,
Planted by the LORD for His glory.
⁴And they shall build the ancient ruins,
Raise up the desolations of old,
And renew the ruined cities,
The desolations of many ages.
⁵Strangers shall stand and pasture your flocks,
Aliens shall be your plowmen and vine-trimmers;
⁶While you shall be called "Priests of the LORD,"
And termed "Servants of our God."
You shall enjoy the wealth of nations
And revel ᵃ in their riches.
⁷Because your shame was double—
ᵇ⁻Men cried, "Disgrace is their portion"⁻ᵇ—
Assuredly,
They shall have a double share in their land,
Joy shall be theirs for all time.
⁸For I the LORD love justice,
I hate ᶜ⁻robbery with a burnt offering.⁻ᶜ
I will pay them their wages faithfully,
And make a covenant with them for all time.
⁹Their offspring shall be known among the nations,
Their descendants in the midst of the peoples.
All who see them shall recognize
That they are a stock the LORD has blessed.

¹⁰I greatly rejoice in the LORD,
My whole being exults in my God.
For He has clothed me with garments of triumph,

ᵃ⁻ᵃ *Meaning of Heb. uncertain.*
ᵇ⁻ᵇ *Emendation yields "They inherited disgrace as their portion."*
ᶜ⁻ᶜ *Emendation yields "the robbing of wages."*

749

Wrapped me in a robe of victory,
Like a bridegroom adorned with a turban,
Like a bride bedecked with her finery.
¹¹For as the earth brings forth her growth
And a garden makes the seed shoot up,
So the Lord GOD will make
Victory and renown shoot up
In the presence of all the nations.

62For the sake of Zion I will not be silent,
For the sake of Jerusalem I will not be still,
Till her victory emerge resplendent
And her triumph like a flaming torch.
²Nations shall see your victory,
And every king your majesty;
And you shall be called by a new name
Which the LORD Himself shall bestow.
³You shall be a glorious crown
In the hand of the LORD,
And a royal diadem
In the palm of your God.

⁴Nevermore shall you be called "Forsaken,"
Nor shall your land be called "Desolate";
But you shall be called "I delight in her,"
And your land "Espoused."
For the LORD takes delight in you,
And your land shall be espoused.
⁵As a youth espouses a maiden,
ᵃ⁻Your sonsᵃ shall espouse you;
And as a bridegroom rejoices over his bride,
So will your God rejoice over you.

⁶Upon your walls, O Jerusalem,
I have set watchmen,
Who shall never be silent

ᵃ⁻ᵃ *Change of vocalization yields "He who rebuilds you."*

By day or by night.
O you, the LORD's remembrancers,[b]
Take no rest
[7]And give no rest to Him,
Until He establish Jerusalem
And make her renowned on earth.

[8]The LORD has sworn by His right hand,
By His mighty arm:
Nevermore will I give your new grain
To your enemies for food,
Nor shall foreigners drink the new wine
For which you have labored.
[9]But those who harvest it shall eat it
And give praise to the LORD;
And those who gather it shall drink it
In My sacred courts.
[10]Pass through, pass through the gates!
Clear the road for the people;
Build up, build up the highway,
Remove the rocks!
Raise an ensign over the peoples!
[11]See, the LORD has proclaimed
To the end of the earth:
Announce to Fair Zion,
Your Deliverer is coming!
See, his reward is with Him,
His recompense before Him.[c]
[12]And they shall be called, "The Holy People,
The Redeemed of the LORD,"
And you shall be called, "Sought Out,
A City Not Forsaken."

63

Who is this coming from Edom,
In crimsoned garments from Bozrah—
Who is this, majestic in attire,

[b] *I.e., the watchmen just mentioned.*
[c] *See note at 40.10.*

a-Pressing forward-a in His great might?
"It is I, who contend victoriously,
Powerful to b-give triumph."-b

²Why is your clothing so red,
Your garments like his who treads grapes?c
³"I trod out a vintage alone;
d-Of the peoples-d no man was with Me.
I trod them down in My anger,
Trampled them in My rage;
Their life-bloode bespattered My garments,
And all My clothing was stained.
⁴For I had planned a day of vengeance,
And My year of redemption arrived.
⁵Then I looked, but there was none to help;
I stared, but there was none to aid—
So My own arm wrought the triumph,
And f-My own rage-f was My aid.
⁶I trampled peoples in My anger,
g-I made them drunk with-g My rage,
And I hurled their glory to the ground."

⁷I will recount the kind acts of the LORD,
The praises of the LORD—
For all that the LORD has wrought for us,
The vast bounty to the House of Israel
That He bestowed upon them
According to His mercy and His great kindness.
⁸He thought: Surely they are My people,
Children who will not play false.
h-So He was their Deliverer.
⁹In all their troubles He was troubled,
And the angel of His Presence delivered them.-h
In His love and pity
He Himself redeemed them,
Raised them, and exalted them

---

a-a *Meaning of Heb. uncertain; emendation yields "striding."*
b-b *Change of vocalization yields "Who contest triumphantly"; cf. 19.20.*
c *Lit. "in a press."*
d-d *Emendation yields "Peoples, and. . . ."*
e *Meaning of Heb. uncertain.*
f-f *Many mss. read* weṣidqathi *"My victorious [right hand]"; cf. 59.16.*
g-g *Many mss. and Targum read "I shattered them in"; cf. 14.25.*
h-h *Ancient versions read "So He was their Deliverer/⁹In all their troubles./No [so* kethib] *angel or messenger,/His own Presence delivered them." Cf. Deut. 4.37 and note.*

All the days of old.
10But they rebelled, and grieved
His holy spirit;
Then He became their enemy,
And Himself made war against them.
11Then theyⁱ remembered the ancient days,
ʲ᠆Him, who pulled His people᠆ʲ out [of the water]:
"Where is He who brought them up from the Sea
Along with the shepherdᵏ of His flock?
Where is He who put
In their midst His holy spirit,
12Who made His glorious arm
March at the right hand of Moses,
Who divided the waters before them
To make Himself a name for all time,
13Who led them through the deeps
So that they did not stumble—
As a horse in a desert,
14Like a beast descending to the plain?"
'Twas the spirit of the LORD ˡ᠆gave them rest;᠆ˡ
Thus did You shepherd Your people
To win for Yourself a glorious name.

15Look down from heaven and see,
From Your holy and glorious height!
Where is Your zeal, Your power?
Your yearning and Your love
Are being withheld from us!ᵐ
16Surely You are our Father:
Though Abraham regard us not,
And Israel recognize us not,
You, O LORD, are our Father;
From of old, Your name is "Our Redeemer."
17Why, LORD, do You make us stray from Your ways,
And turn our hearts away from revering You?
Relent for the sake of Your servants,

ⁱ Heb. "he."
ʲ᠆ʲ Heb. moshe 'ammo, a play on the name Moshe (Moses).
ᵏ So many mss. and ancient versions; other texts "shepherds."
ˡ᠆ˡ Emendation yields "guided them."
ᵐ Heb. "me." Emendation yields "[Where are] Your yearning and Your love?/Let them not be restrained!"

The tribes that are Your very own!
18 Our foes have trampled Your Sanctuary,
Which Your holy people n-possessed but a little while.-n
19 We have become as a people You never ruled,
To which Your name was never attached.

64 If You would but tear open the heavens and come down,
So that mountains would quake before You—
aAs when fire kindles brushwood,
And fire makes water boil—
To make Your name known to Your adversaries
So that nations will tremble at Your Presence,
2 When You did wonders we dared not hope for,
You came down
And mountains quaked before You.
3 Such things had never been heard or noted.
No eye has seen [them], O God, but You,
Who act for those who trust in You.b
4 Yet you have struck him who would gladly do justice,
And remember You in Your ways.
It is because You are angry that we have sinned;
c-We have been steeped in them from of old,
And can we be saved?-c
5 We have all become like an unclean thing,
And all our virtues like a filthy rag.
We are all withering like leaves,
And our iniquities, like a wind, carry us off.
6 Yet no one invokes Your name,
Rouses himself to cling to You.
For You have hidden Your face from us,
And d-made us melt because of-d our iniquities.
7 But now, O LORD, You are our Father;
We are the clay, and You are the Potter,
We are all the work of Your hands.
8 Be not implacably angry, O LORD,
Do not remember iniquity forever.
Oh, look down to Your people, to us all!
9 Your holy cities have become a desert:

n-n Meaning of Heb. uncertain.

a Meaning of vv. 1–4 uncertain.
b Heb. "Him."
c-c Emendation yields "Because You have hidden Yourself we have offended." For the thought cf.
63.17.
d-d Emendation yields "delivered us into the hands of. . . ."

Zion has become a desert,
Jerusalem a desolation.
¹⁰Our holy Temple, our pride,
Where our fathers praised You,
Has been consumed by fire:
And all that was dear to us is ruined.
¹¹At such things will You restrain Yourself, O LORD,
Will You stand idly by and let us suffer so heavily?

65

ᵃ⁻I responded to⁻ᵃ those who did not ask,
I was at hand to those who did not seek Me;
I said, "Here I am, here I am,"
To a nation that did not invoke My name.
²I constantly spread out My hands
To a disloyal people,
Who walk the way that is not good,
Following their own designs;
³The people who provoke My anger,
Who continually, to My very face,
Sacrifice in gardens and burn incense on tiles;
⁴Who sit inside tombs
And pass the night in secret places;
Who eat the flesh of swine,
With broth of unclean things in their bowls;
⁵Who say, "Keep your distance! Don't come closer!
ᵇ⁻For I would render you consecrated."⁻ᵇ
Such things make My anger rage,
Like fire blazing all day long.
⁶See, this is recorded before Me;
I will not stand idly by, but will repay,
Deliver ᶜ⁻theirᵈ sins⁻ᶜ into their bosom,
⁷And the sins of their fathers as well

—said the LORD—

For they made offerings upon the mountains
And affronted Me upon the hills.
I will count out their recompense in full,ᵉ
Into their bosoms.

ᵃ⁻ᵃ *Lit.* "I let Myself be inquired of. . . ."
ᵇ⁻ᵇ *Taking* qedashtikha *as equivalent to* qiddashtikha,/ *cf. Ezek. 49.19; others* "For I am holier than thou."
ᶜ⁻ᶜ *Brought up from v. 7 for clarity.*
ᵈ *Heb.* "your."
ᵉ *Taking* rishonah *as equivalent to* beroshah; *cf. Lev. 5.24; Jer. 16.18. Meaning of Heb. uncertain.*

⁸Thus said the LORD:
As, when new wine is present in the cluster,
One says, "Don't destroy it; there's good in it,"
So will I do for the sake of My servants,
And not destroy everything.
⁹I will bring forth offspring from Jacob,
From Judah heirs to My mountains;
My chosen ones shall take possession,
My servants shall dwell thereon.
¹⁰Sharonᶠ shall become a pasture for flocks,
And the Valley of Achor a place for cattle to lie down,
For My people who seek Me.

¹¹But as for you who forsake the LORD,
Who ignore My holy mountain,
Who set a table for Luckᵍ
And fill a mixing bowl for Destiny:ᵍ
¹²I will destine you for the sword,
You will all kneel down, to be slaughtered—
Because, when I called, you did not answer,
When I spoke, you would not listen.
You did what I hold evil,
And chose what I do not want.

¹³Assuredly, thus said the Lord GOD:
My servants shall eat, and you shall hunger;
My servants shall drink, and you shall thirst;
My servants shall rejoice, and you shall be shamed;
¹⁴My servants shall shout in gladness,
And you shall cry out in anguish,
Howling in heartbreak.
¹⁵You shall leave behind a name
By which My chosen ones shall curse:
"So may the Lord GOD slay you!"
But His servants shall be given a ʰ⁻different name.⁻ʰ
¹⁶For whoever blesses himself in the land
Shall bless himself by the true God;
And whoever swears in the land

ᶠ *Emendation yields "Jeshimon," the bleak southeast corner of the Jordan Valley; cf. Num. 21.20; 23.8.*
ᵍ *Names of heathen deities.*
ʰ⁻ʰ *I.e., a name to be used in blessing.*

Shall swear by the true God.
The former troubles shall be forgotten,
Shall be hidden from My eyes.

17For behold! I am creating
A new heaven and a new earth;
The former things shall not be remembered,
They shall never come to mind.
18Be glad, then, and rejoice forever
In what I am creating.
For I shall create Jerusalem as a joy,
And her people as a delight;
19And I will rejoice in Jerusalem
And delight in her people.
Never again shall be heard there
The sounds of weeping and wailing.
20No more shall there be an infant or graybeard
Who does not live out his days.
He who dies at a hundred years
Shall be reckoned a youth,
And he who fails to reach a hundred
Shall be reckoned accursed.
21They shall build houses and dwell in them,
They shall plant vineyards and enjoy their fruit.
22They shall not build for others to dwell in,
Or plant for others to enjoy.
For the days of My people shall be
As long as the days of a tree,
My chosen ones shall outlive^i
The work of their hands.
23They shall not toil to no purpose;
They shall not bear children ^j-for terror,-^j
But they shall be a people blessed by the LORD,
And their offspring shall remain with them.
24Before they pray, I will answer;
While they are still speaking, I will respond.
25The wolf and the lamb shall graze together,
And the lion shall eat straw like the ox,

i *Lit. "wear out."*
j-j *Emendation yields "in vain."*

And the serpent's food shall be earth.
In all My sacred mount[k]
Nothing evil or vile shall be done

—said the LORD.

66 Thus said the LORD:
The heaven is My throne
And the earth is My footstool:
Where could you build a house for Me,
What place could serve as My abode?
[2]All this was made by My hand,
And thus it all came into being

—declares the LORD.

Yet to such a one I look:
To the poor and brokenhearted,
Who is concerned about My word.

[3a]As for those who slaughter oxen and slay humans,
Who sacrifice sheep and immolate[b] dogs,
Who present as oblation the blood of swine,
Who offer[c] incense and worship false gods—
Just as they have chosen their ways
And take pleasure in their abominations,
[4]So will I choose to mock them,
To bring on them the very thing they dread.
For I called and none responded,
I spoke and none paid heed.
They did what I deem evil
And chose what I do not want.

[5]Hear the word of the LORD,
You who are concerned about His word!
Your kinsmen who hate you,
Who spurn you because of Me,[d] are saying,
"Let the LORD manifest His Presence,
So that we may look upon your joy."
But theirs shall be the shame.

[k] *See note at 11.9.*

[a] *Vv. 3–4 refer to practitioners of idolatrous rites; cf. v. 17 and 57.5–8; 65.1–12.*
[b] *Lit. "break the necks of."*
[c] *Heb. mazkir refers to giving the "token portion" ('azkarah); cf. Lev. 2.2, etc.*
[d] *Lit. "My name."*

⁶Hark, tumult from the city,
Thunder from the Temple!
It is the thunder of the LORD
As He deals retribution to His foes.

⁷Before she labored, she was delivered;
Before her pangs came, she bore a son.
⁸Who ever heard the like?
Who ever witnessed such events?
Can a land pass through travail
In a single day?
Or is a nation born
All at once?
Yet Zion travailed
And at once bore her children!
⁹Shall I who bring on labor not bring about birth?
                              —says the LORD.

Shall I who cause birth shut the womb?
                              —said your God.

¹⁰Rejoice with Jerusalem and be glad for her,
All you who love her!
Join in her jubilation,
All you who mourned over her—
¹¹That you may suck from her breast
Consolation to the full,
That you may draw from her bosomᵉ
Glory to your delight.

¹²For thus said the LORD:
I will extend to her
Prosperity like a stream,
The wealth of nations
Like a wadi in flood;
And you shall drink of it.
You shall be carried on shoulders
And dandled upon knees.
¹³As a mother comforts her son
So I will comfort you;

ᵉ Cf. Akkadiam zīzu, Arabic zīzat, "udder."

759

You shall find comfort in Jerusalem.
[14]You shall see and your heart shall rejoice,
Your limbs shall flourish like grass.
The power of the LORD shall be revealed
In behalf of His servants;
But He shall rage against His foes.

[15]See, the LORD is coming with fire—
His chariots are like a whirlwind—
To vent His anger in fury,
His rebuke in flaming fire.
[16]For with fire will the LORD contend,
With His sword, against all flesh;
And many shall be the slain of the LORD.

[17]Those who sanctify and purify themselves to enter the groves, f-imitating one in the center,-f eating the flesh of the swine, the reptile, and the mouse, shall one and all come to an end—declares the LORD. [18]gFor I [know] their deeds and purposes.

[The time] has come to gather all the nations and tongues; they shall come and behold My glory. [19]I will set a sign among them, and send from them survivors to the nations: to Tarshish, Pul, and Lud—that draw the bow—to Tubal, Javan, and the distant coasts, that have never heard My fame nor beheld My glory. They shall declare My glory among these nations. [20]And out of all the nations, said the LORD, they shall bring all your brothers on horses, in chariots and drays, on mules and dromedaries, to Jerusalem My holy mountain as an offering to the LORD—just as the Israelites bring an offering in a pure vessel to the House of the LORD. [21]And from them likewise I will take some to be h-levitical priests,-h said the LORD.

[22]For as the new heaven and the new earth
Which I will make
Shall endure by My will

—declares the LORD—

---

f-f *Meaning of Heb. uncertain.*
g *Exact construction of this verse uncertain; for the insertions in brackets, cf. Kimhi.*
h-h *Some Heb. mss. read "priests and Levites."*

So shall your seed and your name endure.
23And new moon after new moon,
And sabbath after sabbath,
All flesh shall come to worship Me

—said the LORD.

24They shall go out and gaze
On the corpses of the men who rebelled against Me:
Their worms shall not die,
Nor their fire be quenched;
They shall be a horror
To all flesh.

  And new moon after new moon,
  And sabbath after sabbath,
  All flesh shall come to worship Me

—said the LORD.

JEREMIAH

1 The words of Jeremiah son of Hilkiah, one of the priests at Anathoth in the territory of Benjamin. ²The word of the LORD came to him in the days of King Josiah son of Amon of Judah, in the thirteenth year of his reign, ³and throughout the days of King Jehoiakim son of Josiah of Judah, and until the end of the eleventh year of King Zedekiah son of Josiah of Judah, when Jerusalem went into exile in the fifth month.

⁴The word of the LORD came to me:

⁵Before I created you in the womb, I selected you;
Before you were born, I consecrated you;
I appointed you a prophet concerning the nations.

⁶I replied:
Ah, Lord GOD!
I don't know how to speak,
For I am still a boy.
⁷And the LORD said to me:
Do not say, "I am still a boy,"
But go wherever I send you
And speak whatever I command you.
⁸Have no fear of them,
For I am with you to deliver you

—declares the LORD.

⁹The LORD put out His hand and touched my mouth, and the LORD said to me: Herewith I put My words into your mouth.
¹⁰See, I appoint you this day
Over nations and kingdoms:

To uproot and to pull down,
To destroy and to overthrow,
To build and to plant.

¹¹The word of the LORD came to me: What do you see, Jeremiah? I replied: I see a branch of an almond tree.ª
¹²The LORD said to me:
You have seen right,
For I am watchfulᵇ to bring My word to pass.

¹³And the word of the LORD came to me a second time: What do you see? I replied:
I see a steaming pot,
ᶜTipped away from the north.⁻ᶜ
¹⁴And the LORD said to me:
From the north shall disaster break loose
Upon all the inhabitants of the land!
¹⁵For I am summoning all the peoples
  of the kingdoms of the north
                                    —declares the LORD.
They shall come, and shall each set up a throne
Before the gates of Jerusalem,
Against its walls roundabout,
And against all the towns of Judah.
¹⁶And I will argue My case against themᵈ
For all their wickedness:
They have forsaken Me
And sacrificed to other gods
And worshiped the works of their hands.

¹⁷So you, gird up your loins,
Arise and speak to them
All that I command you.
Do not break down before them,
Lest I break you before them.
¹⁸I make you this day
A fortified city,
And an iron pillar,

ª *Heb.* shaqed.
ᵇ *Heb.* shoqed.
ᶜ⁻ᶜ *Meaning of Heb. uncertain.*
ᵈ *I.e., against Jerusalem and Judah.*

And bronze walls
Against the whole land—
Against Judah's kings and officers,
And against its priests and citizens.[c]
19They will attack you,
But they shall not overcome you;
For I am with you—declares the LORD—to save you.

2 The word of the LORD came to me, saying, 2Go proclaim to Jerusalem: Thus said the LORD:
I accounted to your favor
The devotion of your youth,
Your love as a bride—
How you followed Me in the wilderness,
In a land not sown.
3Israel was holy to the LORD,
The first fruits of His harvest.
All who ate of it were held guilty;
Disaster befell them

—declares the LORD.

4Hear the word of the LORD, O House of Jacob,
Every clan of the House of Israel!
5Thus said the LORD:
What wrong did your fathers find in Me
That they abandoned Me
And went after delusion and were deluded?
6They never asked themselves, "Where is the LORD,
Who brought us up from the land of Egypt,
Who led us through the wilderness,
A land of deserts and pits,
A land of drought and darkness,
A land no man had traversed,
Where no human being had dwelt?"
7I brought you to this country of farm land
To enjoy its fruit and its bounty;

c Lit. "the people of the land."

But you came and defiled My land,
You made My possession abhorrent.
⁸The priests never asked themselves, "Where is the LORD?"
The guardians of the Teaching ignored Me;
The rulersᵃ rebelled against Me,
And the prophets prophesied by Baal
And followed what can do no good.

⁹Oh, I will go on accusing you

—declares the LORD—

And I will accuse your children's children!
¹⁰Just cross over to the isles of the Kittim and look,
Send to Kedar and observe carefully;
See if aught like this has ever happened:
¹¹Has any nation changed its gods
Even though they are no-gods?
But My people has exchanged its glory
For what can do no good.
¹²Be appalled, O heavens, at this;
Be horrified, utterly dazed!

—says the LORD.

¹³For My people have done a twofold wrong:
They have forsaken Me, the Fount of living waters,
And hewed them out cisterns, broken cisterns,
Which cannot even hold water.

¹⁴Is Israel a bondman?
Is he a home-born slave?
Then why is he given over to plunder?
¹⁵Lions have roared over him,
Have raised their cries.
They have made his land a waste,
His cities desolate, without inhabitants.
¹⁶Those, too, in Noph and Tahpanhesᵇ
ᶜ⁻Will lay bare⁻ᶜ your head.
¹⁷See, ᵈ⁻that is the price you have paid
For forsaking the LORD your God⁻ᵈ
ᶜ⁻While He led you in the way.⁻ᶜ

ᵃ Lit. "shepherds"; cf. 3.15; 23.1 ff.
ᵇ Cities in Egypt. The Egyptians, like the Assyrians, will prove a disappointment; cf. v. 36.
ᶜ⁻ᶜ Meaning of Heb. uncertain.
ᵈ⁻ᵈ Lit. "that is what your forsaking the LORD your God is doing to you."

¹⁸What, then, is the good of your going to Egypt
To drink the waters of the Nile?
And what is the good of your going to Assyria
To drink the waters of the Euphrates?
¹⁹Let your misfortune reprove you,
Let your afflictions rebuke you;
Mark well how bad and bitter it is
That you forsake the LORD your God,
That awe for Me is not in you

—declares the Lord GOD of Hosts.

²⁰For long ago you^e broke your yoke,
Tore off your yoke-bands,
And said, "I will not work!"^f
On every high hill and under every verdant tree,
You recline as a whore.
²¹I planted you with noble vines,
All with choicest seed;
Alas, I find you changed
Into a base, an alien vine!
²²Though you wash with natron
And use much lye,
Your guilt is ingrained before Me

—declares the Lord GOD.

²³How can you say, "I am not defiled,
I have not gone after the Baalim"?
Look at your deeds in the Valley,^g
Consider what you have done!
Like a lustful she-camel,
^{c-}Restlessly running about,^{-c}
²⁴Or like a wild ass used to the desert,
Snuffing the wind in her eagerness,
Whose passion none can restrain,
None that seek her need grow weary—
In her season, they'll find her!

²⁵Save your foot from going bare,
And your throat from thirst.
But you say, "It is no use.

---

^e *For the form, cf.* shaqqamti, *Judg. 5.7; others "I."*
^f *Following the* kethib; *qere "transgress."*
^g *I.e., of Hinnom; cf. 7.31–32; 32.35.*

No, I love the strangers,[h]
And after them I must go."
26Like a thief chagrined when he is caught,
So is the House of Israel chagrined—
They, their kings, their officers,
And their priests and prophets.
27They said to wood, "You are my father,"
To stone, "You gave birth to me,"
While to Me they turned their backs
And not their faces.
But in their hour of calamity they cry,
"Arise and save us!"
28And where are those gods
You made for yourself?
Let them arise and save you, if they can,
In your hour of calamity.
For your gods have become, O Judah,
As many as your towns!
29Why do you call Me to account?
You have all rebelled against Me

　　　　　　　　　　　　　　—declares the LORD.

30To no purpose did I smite your children;
They would not accept correction.
Your sword has devoured your prophets
Like a ravening lion.
31 c-O generation, behold-c the word of the LORD!
Have I been like a desert to Israel,
Or like a land of deep gloom?
Then why do My people say, "We have broken loose,
We will not come to You any more?"
32Can a maiden forget her jewels,
A bride her adornments?
Yet My people have forgotten Me—
Days without number.

33How skillfully you plan your way
To seek out love!
Why, you have even taught

h *I.e., other gods.*

The worst of women your ways.
34Moreover, on your garments is found
The lifeblood of the innocent poor—
You did not catch them breaking in.i
c-Yet, despite all these things,-c
35You say, "I have been acquitted;
Surely, His anger has turned away from me."
Lo, I will bring you to judgment
For saying, "I have not sinned."

36How you cheapen yourself,
By changing your course!
You shall be put to shame through Egypt,
Just as you were put to shame through Assyria.
37From this way, too, you will come out
j-With your hands on your head;-j
For the LORD has rejected those you trust,
You will not prosper with them.

3 [The word of the LORD came to me] as follows: If a man divorces his wife, and she leaves him and marries another man, can he ever go back to her? Would not such a land be defiled?a Now you have whored with many lovers: can you return to Me?—says the LORD.

2Look up to the bare heights, and see:
Where have they not lain with you?
You waited for them on the roadside
Like a banditb in the wilderness.
And you defiled the land
With your whoring and your debauchery.
3And when showers were withheld
And the late rains did not come,
You had the brazennessc of a street woman,
You refused to be ashamed.
4Just now you called to Me, "Father!
You are the Companion of my youth.
5Does one hated for all time?

---

i *In which case there might have been an excuse for killing them; cf. Exod. 22.1.*
j-j *A gesture of wild grief; cf. 2 Sam. 13.19.*

a *Cf. Deut. 24.1–4.*
b *Lit. "Arab."*
c *Lit. "forehead."*
d *Cf. Akkadian parallels nadāru and shamāru.*

Does one rage[d] forever?"
That is how you spoke;
You did wrong, and [e-]had your way.[-e]

[6]The LORD said to me in the days of King Josiah: Have you seen what Rebel Israel did, going to every high mountain and under every leafy tree, and whoring there? [7]I thought: After she has done all these things, she will come back to Me. But she did not come back; and her sister, Faithless Judah, saw it. [8]I noted: Because Rebel Israel had committed adultery, I cast her off and handed her a bill of divorce; yet her sister, Faithless Judah, was not afraid—she too went and whored. [9]Indeed, the land was defiled by her casual immorality, as she committed adultery with stone and with wood.[f] [10]And after all that, her sister, Faithless Judah, did not return to Me wholeheartedly, but insincerely—declares the LORD.

[11]And the LORD said to me: Rebel Israel has shown herself more in the right than Faithless Judah. [12]Go, make this proclamation toward the north, and say: Turn back, O Rebel Israel—declares the LORD. I will not look on you in anger, for I am compassionate—declares the LORD; I do not bear a grudge for all time. [13]Only recognize your sin; for you have transgressed against the LORD your God, and scattered your favors[g] among strangers under every leafy tree, and you have not heeded Me—declares the LORD.

[14]Turn back, rebellious children—declares the LORD. Since I have espoused[h] you, I will take you, one from a town and two from a clan, and bring you to Zion. [15]And I will give you shepherds[c] after My own heart, who will pasture you with knowledge and skill.

[16]And when you increase and are fertile in the land, in those days—declares the LORD—men shall no longer speak of the Ark of the Covenant of the LORD, nor shall it come to mind. They shall not mention it, or miss it, or make another. [17]At that time, they shall call Jerusalem "Throne of the LORD," and all nations shall assemble there, in the name of the LORD, at Jerusalem. They[i] shall no longer follow the willfulness of their evil hearts. [18]In those days, the House of Judah shall go with the House of Israel; they shall come together from the land of the north to the land I gave your fathers as a possession.

[19]I had resolved to adopt you as My child, and I gave you a desirable land—the fairest heritage of all the nations; and I thought you would surely call Me "Father," and never cease to be loyal to Me. [20]Instead, you

---

[e-e] *Meaning of Heb. uncertain.*
[f] *She deserted her God for idols of stone and wood.*
[g] *Lit. "ways."*
[h] *Meaning of Heb.* ba'alti *uncertain; compare 31.32.*
[i] *I.e., Israel and Judah.*

have broken faith with Me, as a woman breaks faith with a paramour, O House of Israel—declares the LORD.

²¹Hark! On the bare heights is heard
The supliant weeping of the people of Israel,
For they have gone a crooked way,
Ignoring the LORD their God.

²²Turn back, O rebellious children,
I will heal your afflictions!

"Here we are, we come to You,
For You, O LORD, are our God!
²³ ʲ⁻Surely, futility comes from the hills,
Confusion from the mountains.⁻ʲ
Only through the LORD our God
Is there deliverance for Israel.
²⁴But the Shameful Thingᵏ has consumed
The possessions of our fathers ever since our youth—
Their flocks and herds,
Their sons and daughters.
²⁵Let us lie down in our shame,
Let our disgrace cover us;
For we have sinned against the LORD our God,
We and our fathers from our youth to this day,
And we have not heeded the LORD our God."

4 If you return, O Israel

—declares the LORD—

If you return to Me,
If you remove your abominations from My presence
And do not waver,
²And ᵃ⁻swear, "As the LORD lives,"⁻ᵃ
In sincerity, justice, and righteousness—
Nations shall bless themselves by youᵇ
And praise themselves by you.ᵇ

ʲ⁻ʲ *I.e., the pagan rites celebrated on the hills are futile; exact force of Heb. uncertain.*
ᵏ *Heb.* Bosheth, *a contemptuous substitute for Baal.*

ᵃ⁻ᵃ *I.e., profess the worship of the LORD.*
ᵇ *Heb.* "him."

³For thus said the LORD to the men of Judah and to Jerusalem:

Break up the untilled ground,
And do not sow among thorns.
⁴Openᶜ your hearts to the LORD,
Remove the thickening about your hearts—
O men of Judah and inhabitants of Jerusalem—
Lest My wrath break forth like fire,
And burn, with none to quench it,
Because of your wicked acts.

⁵Proclaim in Judah,
Announce in Jerusalem,
And say:
"Blow the horn in the land!"
Shout aloud and say:
"Assemble, and let us go
Into the fortified cities!"
⁶Set up a signpost: To Zion.
Take refuge, do not delay!
For I bring evil from the north,
And great disaster.
⁷The lion has come up from his thicket:
The destroyer of nations has set out,
Has departed from his place,
To make your land a desolation;
Your cities shall be ruined,
Without inhabitants.
⁸For this, put on sackcloth,
Mourn and wail;
For the blazing anger of the LORD
Has not turned away from us.
⁹And in that day

—declares the LORD—

The mind of the king
And the mind of the nobles shall fail,
The priests shall be appalled,
And the prophets shall stand aghast.

ᶜ *Lit. "circumcise"; cf. Deut. 10.16 and 30.6.*

10d-And I said:-d Ah, Lord GOD! Surely You have deceived this people
and Jerusalem, saying:
>It shall be well with you—
>Yet the sword threatens the very life!

11At that time, it shall be said concerning this people and Jerusalem:
>The conduct of e-My poor people-e is like searing wind
>From the bare heights of the desert—
>It will not serve to winnow or to fan.
>12A full blast from them comes against Me:
>Now I in turn will bring charges against them.

13Lo, hef ascends like clouds,
>His chariots are like a whirlwind,
>His horses are swifter than eagles.
>Woe to us, we are ruined!
>14Wash your heart clean of wickedness,
>O Jerusalem, that you may be rescued.
>How long will you harbor within you
>Your evil designs?

15Hark, one proclaims from Dan
>And announces calamity from Mount Ephraim!
>16Tell the nations: Here they are!
>Announce concerning Jerusalem:
>Watchersf are coming from a distant land,
>They raise their voices against the towns of Judah.
>17Like guards of fields, they surround her on every side.
>For she has rebelled against Me

>>—declares the LORD.

18Your conduct and your acts
>Have brought this upon you;
>This is your bitter punishment;
>It pierces your very heart.

19Oh, my suffering,g my suffering!
>How I writhe!
>Oh, the walls of my heart!

---

d-d *Septuagint reads "And they shall say."*
e-e *Lit. "the daughter that is My people"; so, frequently, in poetry.*
f *I.e., the invader of v. 7.*
g *Lit. "entrails."*

My heart moans within me,
I cannot be silent;
For h-I hear-h the blare of horns,
Alarms of war.
²⁰Disaster overtakes disaster,
For all the land has been ravaged.
Suddenly my tents have been ravaged,
In a moment, my tent cloths.
²¹How long must I see standards
And hear the blare of horns?

²²For My people are stupid,
They give Me no heed;
They are foolish children,
They are not intelligent.
They are clever at doing wrong,
But unable to do right.

²³I look at the earth,
It is unformed and void;
At the skies,
And their light is gone.
²⁴I look at the mountains,
They are quaking;
And all the hills are rocking.
²⁵I look: no man is left,
And all the birds of the sky have fled.
²⁶I look: the farm land is desert,
And all its towns are in ruin—
Because of the LORD,
Because of His blazing anger.
(²⁷For thus said the LORD:
The whole land shall be desolate,
But I will not make an end of it.)
²⁸For this the earth mourns,

---

h-h *Lit. "you, O my being, hear." Change of vocalization yields "I hear the blare of horns,/My inner being, alarms of war."*

And skies are dark above—
Because I have spoken, I have planned,
And I will not relent or turn back from it.

29At the shout of horseman and bowman
The whole city flees.
They enter the thickets,
They clamber up the rocks.
The whole city is deserted,
Not a man remains there.
30And you, who are doomed to ruin,
What do you accomplish by wearing crimson,
By decking yourself in jewels of gold,
By enlarging your eyes with kohl?
You beautify yourself in vain:
Lovers despise you,
They seek your life!
31I hear a voice as of one in travail,
Anguish as of a woman bearing her first child,
The voice of Fair Zion
Panting, stretching out her hands:
"Alas for me! I faint
Before the killers!"

5 Roam the streets of Jerusalem,
Search its squares,
Look about and take note:
You will not find a man,
There is none who acts justly,
Who seeks integrity—
That I should pardon her.
2Even when they say, "As the LORD lives,"
They are sure to be swearing falsely.
3O LORD, Your eyes look for integrity.

You have struck them, but they sensed no pain;
You have consumed them, but they would accept
  no discipline.
They made their faces harder than rock,
They refused to turn back.

⁴Then I thought: These are just poor folk;
They act foolishly;
For they do not know the way of the LORD,
The rules of their God.
⁵So I will go to the wealthy
And speak with them:
Surely they know the way of the LORD,
The rules of their God.
But they as well had broken the yoke,
Had snapped the bonds.
⁶Therefore,
The lion of the forest strikes them down,
The wolf of the desert ravages them.
A leopard lies in wait by their towns;
Whoever leaves them will be torn in pieces.
For their transgressions are many,
Their rebellious acts unnumbered.

⁷Why should I forgive you?
Your children have forsaken Me
And sworn by no-gods.
When I fed them their fill,
They committed adultery
And went trooping to the harlot's house.
⁸They were ᵃ⁻well-fed, lusty⁻ᵃ stallions,
Each neighing at another's wife.
⁹Shall I not punish such deeds?

—says the LORD—

Shall I not bring retribution
On a nation such as this?
¹⁰Go up among her vinesᵇ and destroy;
Lop off her trailing branches,

ᵃ⁻ᵃ *Meaning of Heb. uncertain.*
ᵇ *Lit. "rows."*

For they are not of the LORD.
(But do not make an end.)
¹¹For the House of Israel and the House of Judah
Have betrayed Me

—declares the LORD.

¹²They have been false to the LORD
And said: "ᶜ⁻It is not so!⁻ᶜ
No trouble shall come upon us,
We shall not see sword or famine.
¹³The prophets shall prove mere wind
For the Word is not in them;
Thus-and-thus shall be done to them!"

¹⁴Assuredly, thus said the LORD,
The God of Hosts:
Because theyᵈ said that,
I am putting My words into your mouth as fire,
And this people shall be firewood,
Which it will consume.
¹⁵Lo, I am bringing against you, O House of Israel,
A nation from afar

—declares the LORD;

It is an enduring nation,
It is an ancient nation;
A nation whose language you do not know—
You will not understand what they say.
¹⁶ᵉ⁻Their quivers⁻ᵉ are like a yawning grave—
They are all mighty men.
¹⁷They will devour your harvest and food,
They will devour your sons and daughters,
They will devour your flocks and herds,
They will devour your vines and fig trees.
They will batter down with the sword
The fortified towns on which you rely.

¹⁸But even in those days—declares the LORD—I will not make an end
of you. ¹⁹And when theyᵈ ask, "Because of what did the LORD our God
do all these things?" you shall answer them, "Because you forsook Me

---

ᶜ⁻ᶜ *Or "Not He"; cf. Deut. 32.39; Isa. 43.13.*
ᵈ *Heb. "you."*
ᵉ⁻ᵉ *Emendation yields "Whose mouths."*

and served alien gods on your own land, you will have to serve foreigners in a land not your own."

20Proclaim this to the House of Jacob
And announce it in Judah:
21Hear this, O foolish people,
Devoid of intelligence,
That have eyes but can't see,
That have ears but can't hear!
22Should you not revere Me

—says the LORD—

Should you not tremble before Me,
Who set the sand as a boundary to the sea,
As a limit for all time, not to be transgressed?
Though its waves toss, they cannot prevail;
Though they roar, they cannot pass it.
23Yet this people has a wayward and defiant heart;
They have turned aside and gone their way.
24They have not said to themselves,
"Let us revere the LORD our God,
Who gives the rain,
The early and late rain in season,
Who keeps for our benefit
The weeks appointed for harvest."
25It is your iniquities that have diverted these things,
Your sins that have withheld the bounty from you.
26For among My people are found wicked men,
a-Who lurk, like fowlers lying in wait;-a
They set up a trap to catch men.
27As a cage is full of birds,
So their houses are full of guile;
That is why they have grown so wealthy.
28They have become fat and sleek;
They f-pass beyond the bounds of wickedness,-f
And they prosper.
They will not judge the case of the orphan,
Nor give a hearing to the plea of the needy.

f-f Some ancient versions read "have transgressed My words for evil."

²⁹Shall I not punish such deeds

—says the LORD—

Shall I not bring retribution
On a nation such as this?
³⁰An appalling, horrible thing
Has happened in the land:
³¹The prophets prophesy falsely,
And the priests ᵃ⁻rule accordingly;⁻ᵃ
And My people like it so.
But what will you do at the end of it?

6 Flee for refuge, O people of Benjamin,
Out of the midst of Jerusalem!
Blow the horn in Tekoa,
Set up a signal at Beth-haccherem!
For evil is appearing from the north,
And great disaster.
²ᵃ⁻Fair Zion, the lovely and delicate,
I will destroy.⁻ᵃ
³Against her come shepherds with their flocks,
They pitch tents all around her;
Each grazes ᵇ⁻the sheep under his care.⁻ᵇ
⁴ᶜ⁻Prepare for⁻ᶜ battle against her:
"Up! we will attack at noon."
"Alas for us! for day is declining,
The shadows of evening grow long."
⁵"Up! let us attack by night,
And wreck her fortresses."

⁶For thus said the LORD of Hosts:
Hew down her trees,
And raise a siegemound against Jerusalem.
ᵈ⁻She is the city destined for punishment;⁻ᵈ
Only fraud is found in her midst.
⁷As a well flows with water,
So she flows with wickedness.

ᵃ⁻ᵃ *Meaning of Heb. uncertain.*
ᵇ⁻ᵇ *Understanding* yado *as in Ps. 95.7.*
ᶜ⁻ᶜ *Lit. "Consecrate."*
ᵈ⁻ᵈ *Emendation yields "She is the city of falseness."*

Lawlessness and rapine are heard in her;
Before Me constantly are sickness and wounds.
⁸Accept rebuke, O Jerusalem,
Lest I come to loathe you,
Lest I make you a desolation,
An uninhabited land.

⁹Thus said the LORD of Hosts:
ᵉ⁻Let them glean⁻ᵉ over and over, as a vine,
The remnant of Israel.
Pass your hand again,
Like a vintager,
Over its branches.

¹⁰ᶠTo whom shall I speak,
Give warning that they may hear?
Their ears are blocked
And they cannot listen.
See, the word of the LORD has become for them
An object of scorn; they will have none of it.
¹¹But I am filled with the wrath of the LORD,
I cannot hold it in.

Pour it on the infant in the street,
And on the company of youths gathered together!
Yes, men and women alike shall be captured,
Elders and those of advanced years.
¹²Their houses shall pass to others,
Fields and wives as well,
For I will stretch out My arm
Against the inhabitants of the country

　　　　　　　　　　　　　　—declares the LORD.

¹³For from the smallest to the greatest,
They are all greedy for gain;
Priest and prophet alike,
They all act falsely.
¹⁴They offer healing offhand

ᵉ⁻ᵉ *Emendation yields "Glean" (singular).*
ᶠ *The prophet speaks.*

For the wounds of My people,
Saying, "All is well, all is well,"
When nothing is well.
15They have acted shamefully;
They have done abhorrent things—
Yet they do not feel shame,
And they cannot be made to blush.
Assuredly, they shall fall among the falling,
They shall stumble at the time when I punish them
—said the LORD.

16Thus said the LORD:
Stand by the roads and consider,
Inquire about ancient paths:
Which is the road to happiness?
Travel it, and find tranquillity for yourselves.
But they said, "We will not."
17And I raised up watchmeng for you:
"Hearken to the sound of the horn!"
But they said, "We will not."
18Hear well, O nations,
And know, a-O community, what is in store for them.-a
19Hear, O earth!
I am going to bring disaster upon this people,
The outcome of their own schemes;
For they would not hearken to My words,
And they rejected My Instruction.
20What need have I of frankincense
That comes from Sheba,
Or fragrant cane from a distant land?
Your burnt offerings are not acceptable
And your sacrifices are not pleasing to Me.
21Assuredly, thus said the LORD:
I shall put before this people stumbling blocks
Over which they shall stumble—
Fathers and children alike,
Neighbor and friend shall perish.

g *I.e., prophets.*

²²Thus said the LORD:
See, a people comes from the northland,
A great nation is roused
From the remotest parts of the earth.
²³They grasp the bow and javelin;
They are cruel, they show no mercy;
The sound of them is like the roaring sea.
They ride upon horses,
Accoutered like a man for battle,
Against you, O Fair Zion!

²⁴"We have heard the report of them,
Our hands fail;
Pain seizes us,
Agony like a woman in childbirth.
²⁵Do not go out into the country,
Do not walk the roads!
For the sword of the enemy is there,
Terror on every side."

²⁶^{h-}My poor people,^{-h}
Put on sackcloth
And strew dust on yourselves!
Mourn, as for an only child;
Wail bitterly,
For suddenly the destroyer
Is coming upon us.

²⁷I have made you an assayer of My people
—A refiner^a—
You are to note and assay their ways.
²⁸They are copper and iron:
They are all stubbornly defiant;
They ⁱ⁻deal basely⁻ⁱ
All of them act corruptly.
²⁹^{a-}The bellows puff;
The lead is consumed by fire.^{-a}
Yet the smelter smelts to no purpose—

---

^{h-h} Lit. *"Daughter that is My people"*; *so, frequently, in poetry. See 4.11 and note.*
ⁱ⁻ⁱ *See note at Lev. 19.16.*

The dross[a] is not separated out.
30 They are called "rejected silver,"
For the LORD has rejected them.

7 The word which came to Jeremiah from the LORD: 2 Stand at the gate of the House of the LORD, and there proclaim this word: Hear the word of the LORD, all you of Judah who enter these gates to worship the LORD! 3 Thus said the LORD of Hosts, the God of Israel: Mend your ways and your actions, and I will [a-]let you dwell[-a] in this place. 4 Don't put your trust in illusions and say, "The Temple of the LORD, the Temple of the LORD, the Temple of the LORD are these [buildings]." 5 No, if you really mend your ways and your actions; if you execute justice between one man and another; 6 if you do not oppress the stranger, the orphan, and the widow; if you do not shed the blood of the innocent in this place; if you do not follow other gods, to your own hurt— 7 then only will I [a-]let you dwell[-a] in this place, in the land that I gave to your fathers for all time. 8 See, you are relying on illusions that are of no avail. 9 Will you steal and murder and commit adultery and swear falsely, and sacrifice to Baal, and follow other gods whom you have not experienced,[b] 10 and then come and stand before Me in this House which bears My name and say, "We are safe"?—[Safe] to do all these abhorrent things! 11 Do you consider this House, which bears My name, to be a den of thieves? As for Me, I have been watching—declares the LORD.

12 Just go to My place at Shiloh, where I had established My name formerly, and see what I did to it because of the wickedness of My people Israel. 13 And now, because you do all these things—declares the LORD— and though I spoke to you persistently, you would not listen; and though I called to you, you would not respond— 14 therefore I will do to the House which bears My name, on which you rely, and to the place which I gave you and your fathers, just what I did to Shiloh. 15 And I will cast you out of My presence as I cast out your brothers, the whole brood of Ephraim.

16 As for you, do not pray for this people, do not raise a cry of prayer on their behalf, do not plead with Me; for I will not listen to you. 17 Don't you see what they are doing in the towns of Judah and in the streets of Jerusalem? 18 The children gather sticks, the fathers build the fire, and the mothers knead dough, to make cakes for the Queen of Heaven,[c] and they

---

a-a *Meaning of Heb. uncertain. Change of vocalization yields "dwell with you"; so Aquila and Vulgate.*
b *See note at Deut. 11.28.*
c *I.e., the mother goddess (Ishtar, Astarte) in whose honor these cakes were baked.*

pour libations to other gods, to vex Me. ¹⁹Is it Me they are vexing?—says the LORD. It is rather themselves, to their own disgrace. ²⁰Assuredly, thus said the Lord GOD: My wrath and My fury will be poured out upon this place, on man and on beast, on the trees of the field and the fruit of the soil. It shall burn, with none to quench it.

²¹Thus said the LORD of Hosts, the God of Israel: Add your burnt offerings to your other sacrifices and eat the meat! ²²For when I freed your fathers from the land of Egypt, I did not speak with them or command them concerning burnt offerings or sacrifice. ²³But this is what I commanded them: Do My bidding, that I may be your God and you may be My people; walk only in the way that I enjoin upon you, that it may go well with you. ²⁴Yet they did not listen or give ear; they followed their own counsels, the willfulness of their evil hearts. They have gone backward, not forward, ²⁵from the day your fathers left the land of Egypt until today. And though I kept sending all My servants, the prophets, to them[d] daily and persistently, ²⁶they would not listen to Me or give ear. They stiffened their necks, they acted worse than their fathers.

²⁷You shall say all these things to them, but they will not listen to you; you shall call to them, but they will not respond to you. ²⁸Then say to them: This is the nation that would not obey the LORD their God, that would not accept rebuke. Faithfulness has perished, vanished from their mouths.

²⁹Shear your locks and cast them away,
Take up a lament on the heights,
For the LORD has spurned and cast off
The brood that provoked His wrath.

³⁰For the people of Judah have done what displeases Me—declares the LORD. They have set up their abominations in the House which is called by My name, and they have defiled it. ³¹And they have built the shrines of Topheth in the Valley of Ben-hinnom to burn their sons and daughters in fire—which I never commanded, which never came to My mind.

³²Assuredly, a time is coming—declares the LORD—when men shall no longer speak of Topheth or the Valley of Ben-hinnom, but of the Valley of Slaughter; and they shall bury in Topheth until no room is left. ³³The

d *Heb. "you."*

784

carcasses of this people shall be food for the birds of the sky and the beasts of the earth, with none to frighten them off. ³⁴And I will silence in the towns of Judah and the streets of Jerusalem the sound of mirth and gladness, the voice of bridegroom and bride. For the whole land shall fall to ruin.

8 At that time—declares the LORD—the bones of the kings of Judah, of its officers, of the priests, of the prophets, and of the inhabitants of Jerusalem shall be taken out of their graves ²and exposed to the sun, the moon, and all the host of heaven which they loved and served and followed, to which they turned and bowed down. They shall not be gathered for reburial; they shall become dung upon the face of the earth. ³And death shall be preferable to life for all that are left of this wicked folk, in all the other places to which I shall banish them—declares the LORD of Hosts.

⁴Say to them: Thus said the LORD:
When men fall, do they not get up again?
If they turn aside, do they not turn back?
⁵Why is this people—Jerusalem—rebellious
With a persistent rebellion?
They cling to deceit,
They refuse to return.
⁶I have listened and heard:
They do not speak honestly.
No one regrets his wickedness
And says, "What have I done!"
They all persist in their wayward course
Like a steed dashing forward in the fray.
⁷Even the stork in the sky knows her seasons,
And the turtledove, swift, and crane
Keep the time of their coming;
But My people pay no heed
To the law of the LORD.
⁸How can you say, "We are wise,
And we possess the Instruction of the LORD"?
Assuredly, for naught has the pen labored,
For naught the scribes!

⁹The wise shall be put to shame,
Shall be dismayed and caught;
See, they reject the word of the LORD,
So their wisdom amounts to nothing.

¹⁰Assuredly, I will give their wives to others,
And their fields to dispossessors;
For from the smallest to the greatest,
They are all greedy for gain;
Priest and prophet alike,
They all act falsely.
¹¹They offer healing offhand
For the wounds of My poor people,
Saying, "All is well, all is well,"
When nothing is well.
¹²They have acted shamefully;
They have done abhorrent things—
Yet they do not feel shame,
They cannot be made to blush.
Assuredly, they shall fall among the falling,
They shall stumble at the time of their doom

—said the LORD.

¹³ᵃ-I will make an end of them⁻ᵃ

—declares the LORD:

No grapes left on the vine,
No figs on the fig tree,
The leaves all withered;
ᵇ-Whatever I have given them is gone.⁻ᵇ
¹⁴Why are we sitting by?
Let us gather into the fortified cities
And meet our doom there.
For the LORD our God has doomed us,
He has made us drink a bitter draft,
Because we sinned against the LORD.
¹⁵We hoped for good fortune, but no happiness came;
For a time of relief—instead there is terror!
¹⁶The snorting of their horses was heard from Dan;

ᵃ⁻ᵃ *Meaning of Heb. uncertain; change of vocalization yields "Their fruit harvest has been gathered in."*
ᵇ⁻ᵇ *Meaning of Heb. uncertain.*

At the loud neighing of their steeds
The whole land quaked.
They came and devoured the land and what was in it,
The towns and those who dwelt in them.

¹⁷Lo, I will send serpents against you,
Adders that cannot be charmed,
And they shall bite you

                            —declares the LORD.

^{18b-}When in grief I would seek comfort,^{-b}
My heart is sick within me.

^{19c}"Is not the LORD in Zion?
Is not her King within her?
Why then did they anger Me with their images,
With alien futilities?"

Hark! The outcry of my poor people
From the land far and wide:
²⁰"Harvest is past,
Summer is gone,
But we have not been saved."
²¹Because my people is shattered I am shattered;
I am dejected, seized by desolation.
²²Is there no balm in Gilead?
Can no physician be found?
Why has healing not yet
Come to my poor people?
²³Oh, that my head were water,
My eyes a fount of tears!
Then would I weep day and night
For the slain of my poor people.

9

Oh, to be in the desert,
At an encampment for wayfarers!
Oh, to leave my people,
To go away from them—

^c *Here God is speaking.*

For they are all adulterers,
A band of rogues.

²They bend their tongues like bows;
They are valorous in the land
For treachery, not for honesty;
They advance from evil to evil.
And they do not heed Me

—declares the LORD.

³Beware, every man of his friend!
Trust not even a brother!
For every brother takes advantage,
Every friend ᵃ⁻is base in his dealings.⁻ᵃ
⁴One man cheats the other,
They will not speak truth;
They have trained their tongues to speak falsely;
ᵇ⁻They wear themselves out working iniquity.
⁵You dwell in the midst of deceit.
In their deceit,⁻ᵇ they refuse to heed Me

—declares the LORD.

⁶Assuredly, thus said the LORD of Hosts:
Lo, I shall smelt and assay them—
ᵇ⁻For what else can I do because of My poor people?⁻ᵇ
⁷Their tongue is a sharpened arrow,
They use their mouths to deceive.
One speaks to his fellow in friendship,
But lays an ambush for him in his heart.
⁸Shall I not punish them for such deeds?

—says the LORD—

Shall I not bring retribution
On such a nation as this?

⁹For the mountains I take up weeping and wailing,
For the pastures in the wilderness, a dirge.
They are laid waste; no man passes through,
And no sound of cattle is heard.

ᵃ⁻ᵃ *See note at Lev. 19.16.*
ᵇ⁻ᵇ *Meaning of Heb. uncertain.*

Birds of the sky and beasts as well
Have fled and are gone.

10I will turn Jerusalem into rubble,
Into dens for jackals;
And I will make the towns of Judah
A desolation without inhabitants.

11What man is so wise
That he understands this?
To whom has the LORD's mouth spoken,
So that he can explain it:
Why is the land in ruins,
Laid waste like a wilderness,
With none passing through?

12The LORD replied: Because they forsook the Teaching I had set before them. They did not obey Me and they did not follow it, 13but followed their own willful heart and followed the Baalim, as their fathers had taught them. 14Assuredly, thus said the LORD of Hosts, the God of Israel: I am going to feed that people wormwood and make them drink a bitter draft. 15I will scatter them among nations which they and their fathers never knew; and I will dispatch the sword after them until I have consumed them.

16Thus said the LORD of Hosts:
Listen!
Summon the dirge-singers, let them come;
17Send for the skilled women, let them come.
Let them quickly start a wailing for us,
That our eyes may run with tears,
Our pupils flow with water.

18For the sound of wailing
Is heard from Zion:
How we are despoiled!
How greatly we are shamed!

Ah, we must leave our land,
Abandon^c our dwellings!

¹⁹Hear, O women, the word of the LORD,
Let your ears receive the word of His mouth,
And teach your daughters wailing,
And one another lamentation.
²⁰For death has climbed through our windows,
Has entered our fortresses,
To cut off babes from the streets,
Young men from the squares.

²¹Speak thus—says the LORD:
The carcasses of men shall lie
Like dung upon the fields,
Like sheaves behind the reaper,
With none to pick them up.

²²Thus said the LORD:
Let not the wise man glory in his wisdom;
Let not the strong man glory in his strength;
Let not the rich man glory in his riches.
²³But only in this should one glory:
In his earnest devotion to Me.
For I the LORD act with kindness,
Justice, and equity in the world;
For in these I delight

—declares the LORD.

²⁴Lo, days are coming—declares the LORD—when I will take note of everyone ^{d-}circumcised in the foreskin:^{-d} ²⁵of Egypt, Judah, Edom, the Ammonites, Moab, and all the desert dwellers who have the hair of their temples clipped. For all these nations are uncircumcised, but all the House of Israel are ^{e-}uncircumcised of heart.^{-e}

---

^c *Lit. "They abandoned."*
^{d-d} *Force of Heb. uncertain.*
^{e-e} *I.e., their minds are blocked to God's commandments.*

10

Hear the word which the LORD has spoken to you, O House of Israel!

²Thus said the LORD:
Do not learn to go the way of the nations,
And do not be dismayed by portents in the sky;
Let the nations be dismayed by them!
³For ª-the laws of the nations-ª are delusions:
For it is the work of a craftsman's hands.
He cuts down a tree in the forest with an ax,
⁴He adorns it with silver and gold,
He fastens itᵇ with nails and hammer,
So that it does not totter.
⁵They are like a scarecrow in a cucumber patch,
They cannot speak.
They have to be carried,
For they cannot walk.
Be not afraid of them, for they can do no harm;
Nor is it in them to do any good.

⁶O LORD, there is none like You!
You are great and Your name is great in power.
⁷Who would not revere You, O King of the nations?
For that is Your due,
Since among all the wise of the nations
And among all their royalty
There is none like You.
⁸But they are both dull and foolish;
ᶜ-[Their] doctrine is but delusion;-ᶜ
It is a piece of wood,
⁹Silver beaten flat, that is brought from Tarshish,
And gold from Uphaz,
The work of a craftsman and the goldsmith's hands;
Their clothing is blue and purple,
All of them are the work of skilled men.

ª-ª *Emendation yields "the objects that the nations fear."*
ᵇ *Heb. "them."*
ᶜ-ᶜ *Meaning of Heb. uncertain.*

¹⁰But the L𝚘ʀᴅ is truly God:
He is a living God,
The everlasting King.
At His wrath, the earth quakes,
And nations cannot endure His rage.

¹¹ᵈThus shall you say to them: Let the gods, who did not make heaven and earth, perish from the earth and from under these heavens.

¹²He made the earth by His might,
Established the world by His wisdom,
And by His understanding stretched out the skies.
¹³ᵉ⁻When He makes His voice heard,⁻ᵉ
There is a rumbling of water in the skies;
He makes vapors rise from the end of the earth,
He makes lightning for the rain,
And brings forth wind from His treasuries.
¹⁴Every man is proved dull, without knowledge;
Every goldsmith is put to shame because of the idol,
For his molten image is a deceit—
There is no breath in them.
¹⁵They are delusion, a work of mockery;
In their hour of doom, they shall perish.
¹⁶Not like these is the Portion of Jacob;
For it is He who formed all things,
And Israel is His very own tribe:
L𝚘ʀᴅ of Hosts is His name.

¹⁷Gather up your bundleᶜ from the ground,
You who dwell under siege!
¹⁸For thus said the L𝚘ʀᴅ: I will fling away the inhabitants of the land this time: I will harass them so that they shall ᶠ⁻feel it.⁻ᶠ

¹⁹Woe unto me for my hurt,
My wound is severe!
I thought, "This is but a sickness
And I must bear it."

ᵈ This verse is in Aramaic.
ᵉ⁻ᵉ Lit. "At the sound of His making."
ᶠ⁻ᶠ Emendation yields "have to leave."

20My tents are ravaged,
All my tent cords are broken.
My children have gone forth from me
And are no more;
No one is left to stretch out my tents
And hang my tent cloths.
21For the shepherdsᵍ are dull
And did not seek the LORD;
Therefore they have not prospered
And all their flock is scattered.
22Hark, a noise! It is coming,
A great commotion out of the north,
That the towns of Judah may be made a desolation,
A haunt of jackals.

23I know, O LORD, that man's road is not his [to choose],
That man, as he walks, cannot direct his own steps.
24Chastise me, O LORD, but in measure;
Not in Your wrath, lest You reduce me to naught.
25Pour out Your wrath on the nations who have not heeded You,
Upon the clans that have not invoked Your name.
For they have devoured Jacob,
Have devoured and consumed him,
And have laid desolate his homesteads.

11 The word which came to Jeremiah from the LORD:

2"Hear the terms of this covenant, and recite them to the men of Judah and the inhabitants of Jerusalem! 3And say to them, Thus said the LORD, the God of Israel: Cursed be the man who will not obey the terms of this covenant, 4which I enjoined upon your fathers when I freed them from the land of Egypt, the iron crucible, saying, 'Obey Me and observe them,ᵃ just as I command you, that you may be My people and I may be your God'—5in order to fulfill the oath which I swore to your fathers, to give them a land flowing with milk and honey, as is now the case." And I responded, "Amen, LORD."

ᵍ *I.e., rulers; cf. note at 2.8.*
ᵃ *I.e., the terms of the covenant.*

⁶And the LORD said to me, "Proclaim all these things through the towns of Judah and the streets of Jerusalem: Hear the terms of this covenant, and perform them. ⁷For I have repeatedly and persistently warned your fathers from[b] the time I brought them out of Egypt to this day, saying: Obey My commands. ⁸But they would not listen or give ear; they all followed the willfulness of their evil hearts. So I have brought upon them all the terms[c] of this covenant, because they did not do what I commanded them to do."

⁹The LORD said to me, "A conspiracy exists among the men of Judah and the inhabitants of Jerusalem. ¹⁰They have returned to the iniquities of their fathers of old, who refused to heed My words. They, too, have followed other gods and served them. The House of Israel and the House of Judah have broken the covenant that I made with their fathers."

¹¹Assuredly, thus said the LORD: I am going to bring upon them disaster from which they will not be able to escape. Then they will cry out to me, but I will not listen to them. ¹²And the townsmen[d] of Judah and the inhabitants of Jerusalem will go and cry out to the gods to which they sacrifice; but they will not be able to rescue them in their time of disaster. ¹³For your gods have become as many as your towns, O Judah, and you have set up as many altars to Shame[e] as there are streets in Jerusalem—altars for sacrifice to Baal.

¹⁴As for you, do not pray for this people, do not raise a cry of prayer on their behalf; for I will not listen when they call to Me on account of their disaster.

¹⁵Why should My beloved be in My House,
[f-]Who executes so many vile designs?
The sacral flesh will pass away from you,
For you exult while performing your evil deeds.[-f]
¹⁶The LORD named you
"Verdant olive tree,
Fair, with choice fruit."
But with a great roaring sound
He has set it on fire,
And its boughs are broken.[g]

---

b *Lit. "at."*
c *I.e., the punishments prescribed for violation.*
d *Lit. "towns."*
e *See note at 3.24.*
f-f *Meaning of Heb. uncertain. Emendation yields "Who does such vile deeds? / Can your treacheries be canceled by sacral flesh / That you exult while performing your evil deeds?"*
g *Emendation yields "burned."*

¹⁷The LORD of Hosts, who planted you, has decreed disaster for you, because of the evil wrought by the House of Israel and the House of Judah, who angered Me by sacrificing to Baal.

> ¹⁸The LORD informed me, and I knew—
> Then You let me see their deeds.
> ¹⁹For I was like a docile lamb
> Led to the slaughter;
> I did not realize
> That it was against me
> They fashioned their plots:
> "Let us destroy the tree with its fruit,^h
> Let us cut him off from the land of the living.
> That his name be remembered no more!"
> ²⁰O LORD of Hosts, O just Judge,
> Who test the thoughts and the mind,
> Let me see Your retribution upon them,
> For I lay my case before You.

²¹Assuredly, thus said the LORD of Hosts concerning the men of Anathoth who seek your life and say, "You must not prophesy any more in the name of the LORD, or you will die by our hand"—²²Assuredly, thus said the LORD of Hosts: "I am going to deal with them: the young men shall die by the sword, their boys and girls shall die by famine. ²³No remnant shall be left of them, for I will bring disaster on the men of Anathoth, the year of their doom."

12 You will win,^a O LORD, if I make claim against You,
Yet I shall present charges against You:
Why does the way of the wicked prosper?
Why are the workers of treachery at ease?
²You have planted them, and they have taken root,
They spread, they even bear fruit.
You are present in their mouths,

h *Or "sap."*
a *Lit. "be in the right."*

But far from their thoughts.
³Yet You, LORD, have noted and observed me;
You have tested my heart, and found it with You.
Drive them out like sheep to the slaughter,
Prepare them for the day of slaying!

⁴How long must the land languish,
And the grass of all the countryside dry up?
Must beasts and birds perish,
Because of the evil of its inhabitants,
Who say, "He will not look upon our future"?^b

^{5c}If you race with the foot-runners and they exhaust you,
How then can you compete with horses?
If you are ^{d-}secure only^{-d} in a tranquil land,
How will you fare in the jungle of the Jordan?
⁶For even your kinsmen and your father's house,
Even they are treacherous toward you,
They cry after you as a mob.
Do not believe them
When they speak cordially to you.

⁷I have abandoned My House,
I have deserted My possession,
I have given over My dearly beloved
Into the hands of her enemies.
⁸My own people^e acted toward Me
Like a lion in the forest;
She raised her voice against Me—
Therefore I have rejected her.
^{9f-}My own people acts toward Me
Like a bird of prey [or] a hyena;
Let the birds of prey surround her!^{-f}
Go, gather all the wild beasts,
Bring them to devour!

---

^b *Septuagint reads "ways."*
^c *God here replies to Jeremiah's plea in vv. 1–3.*
^{d-d} *Some Septuagint mss. read "not secure."*
^e *Lit. "possession"; the land as well as the people, as is clear in v. 14.*
^{f-f} *Meaning of Heb. uncertain.*

¹⁰Many shepherds have destroyed My vineyard,
Have trampled My field,
Have made My delightful field
A desolate wilderness.
¹¹ᵍ⁻They have⁻ᵍ made her a desolation;
Desolate, she pours out grief to Me.
The whole land is laid desolate,
But no man gives it thought.
¹²Spoilers have come
Upon all the bare heights of the wilderness.
For a sword of the LORD devours
From one end of the land to the other;
No flesh is safe.
¹³They have sown wheat and reaped thorns,
They have endured pain to no avail.
Be shamed, then, by your harvest—
By the blazing wrath of the LORD!

¹⁴Thus said the LORD: As for My wicked neighbors who encroach on the heritage that I gave to My people Israel—I am going to uproot them from their soil, and I will uproot the House of Judah out of the midst of them. ¹⁵Then, after I have uprooted them, I will take them back into favor, and restore them each to his own inheritance and his own land. ¹⁶And if they learn the ways of My people, to swear by My name—"As the LORD lives"—just as they once taught My people to swear by Baal, then they shall be ʰ⁻built up in the midst ofʰ My people. ¹⁷But if they do not give heed, I will tear out that nation, tear it out and destroy it— declares the LORD.

13

Thus the LORD said to me: "Go buy yourself a loincloth of linen, and put it around your loins, but do not dip it into water." ²So I bought the loincloth in accordance with the LORD's command, and put it about my loins. ³And the word of the LORD came to me a second time: ⁴"Take the loincloth which you bought, which is about your loins, and go at

ᵍ⁻ᵍ *Heb. "He has."*
ʰ⁻ʰ *Or "incorporated into."*

once to Perath[a] and cover it up there in a cleft of the rock." 5I went and buried it at Perath, as the LORD had commanded me. 6Then, after a long time, the LORD said to me, "Go at once to Perath and take there the loincloth which I commanded you to bury there." 7So I went to Perath and dug up the loincloth from the place where I had buried it; and found the loincloth ruined; it was not good for anything.

8The word of the LORD came to me: 9Thus said the LORD: Even so will I ruin the overweening pride of Judah and Jerusalem. 10This wicked people who refuse to heed My bidding, who follow the willfulness of their own hearts, who follow other gods and serve them and worship them, shall become like that loincloth, which is not good for anything. 11For as the loincloth clings close to the loins of a man, so I brought close to Me the whole House of Israel and the whole House of Judah—declares the LORD—that they might be My people, for fame, and praise, and splendor. But they would not obey.

12And speak this word to them: Thus said the LORD, the God of Israel: "Every jar should be filled with wine." And when they say to you, "Don't we know that every jar should be filled with wine?" 13say to them, "Thus said the LORD: I am going to fill with drunkenness all the inhabitants of this land, and the kings who sit on the throne of David, and the priests and the prophets, and all the inhabitants of Jerusalem. 14And I will smash them one against the other, parents and children alike—declares the LORD; no pity, compassion, or mercy will stop Me from destroying them."

15Attend and give ear; be not haughty,
For the LORD has spoken.
16Give honor to the LORD your God
Before He brings darkness,
Before your feet stumble
On the mountains in shadow—
When you hope for light,
And it is turned to darkness
And becomes deep gloom.
17For if you will not give heed,
My inmost self must weep,
Because of your arrogance;
My eye must stream and flow
With copious tears,

---

a Or "the Euphrates"; cf. "Parah," Josh. 18.23.

Because the flock of the LORD
Is taken captive.

¹⁸Say to the king and the queen mother,
"Sit in a lowly spot;
For your diadems are abased,
Your glorious crowns."
¹⁹The cities of the Negeb are shut,
There is no one to open them;
ᵇ⁻Judah is exiled completely,
All of it exiled.⁻ᵇ
²⁰Raise your eyes and behold
Those who come from the north:
Where are the sheep entrusted to you,
The flock you took pride in?
²¹ᶜ⁻What will you say when they appoint as your heads
Those among you whom you trained to be tame?⁻ᶜ
Shall not pangs seize you
Like a woman in childbirth?
²²And when you ask yourself,
"Why have these things befallen me?"
It is because of your great iniquity
That your skirts are lifted up,
Your limbs exposed.

²³Can the Cushite change his skin,
Or the leopard his spots?
Just as much can you do good,
Who are practiced in doing evil!
²⁴So I will scatter youᵈ like straw that flies
Before the desert wind.
²⁵This shall be your lot,
Your measured portion from Me

                        —declares the LORD.

Because you forgot Me
And trusted in falsehood,
²⁶I in turn will lift your skirts over your face
And your shame shall be seen.

ᵇ⁻ᵇ *I.e., most of Judah has been annexed by an alien people.*
ᶜ⁻ᶜ *Meaning of Heb. uncertain.*
ᵈ *Heb. "them."*

²⁷I behold your adulteries,
Your lustful neighing,
Your unbridled depravity, your vile acts
On the hills of the countryside.
Woe to you, O Jerusalem,
Who will not be clean!
How much longer shall it be?

14 The word of the LORD which came to Jeremiah concerning the droughts.

²Judah is in mourning,
Her settlements languish.
Men are bowed to the ground,
And the outcry of Jerusalem rises.
³Their nobles sent their servants for water;
They came to the cisterns, they found no water.
They returned, their vessels empty.
They are shamed and humiliated,
They cover their heads.
⁴ᵃ⁻Because of the ground there is dismay,⁻ᵃ
For there has been no rain on the earth.
The plowmen are shamed,
They cover their heads.
⁵Even the hind in the field
Forsakes her new-born fawn,
Because there is no grass.
⁶And the wild asses stand on the bare heights,
Snuffing the air like jackals;
Their eyes pine,
Because there is no herbage.

⁷Though our iniquities testify against us,
Act, O LORD, for the sake of Your name;
Though our rebellions are many
And we have sinned against You.
⁸O Hope of Israel,

ᵃ⁻ᵃ *Meaning of Heb. uncertain.*

Its deliverer in time of trouble,
Why are You like a stranger in the land,
Like a traveler who stops only for the night?
9Why are You like a man who is stunned,
Like a warrior who cannot give victory?
Yet You are in our midst, O LORD,
And Your name is attached to us—
Do not forsake us!

10Thus said the LORD concerning this people: "Truly, they love to stray, they have not restrained their feet; so the LORD has no pleasure in them. Now He will recall their iniquity and punish their sin."

11And the LORD said to me, "Do not pray for the benefit of this people. 12When they fast, I will not listen to their outcry; and when they present burnt offering and meal offering, I will not accept them. I will exterminate them by war, famine, and disease."

13I said, "Ah, Lord GOD! The prophets are saying to them, 'You shall not see the sword, famine shall not come upon you, but I will give you unfailing security in this place.' "

14The LORD replied: It is a lie that the prophets utter in My name. I have not sent them or commanded them. I have not spoken to them. A lying vision, an empty divination, the deceit of their own contriving—that is what they prophesy to you! 15Assuredly, thus said the LORD concerning the prophets who prophesy in My name though I have not sent them, and who say, "Sword and famine shall not befall this land"; those very prophets shall perish by sword and famine. 16And the people to whom they prophesy shall be left lying in the streets of Jerusalem because of the famine and the sword, with none to bury them—they, their wives, their sons, and their daughters. I will pour out upon them [the requital of] their wickedness.

17And do you speak to them thus:
Let my eyes run with tears,
Day and night let them not cease,
For b-my hapless people-b has suffered
A grievous injury, a very painful wound.
18If I go out to the country—
Lo, the slain of the sword.

b-b Lit. "the maiden daughter, My people."

If I enter the city—
Lo, ᶜ⁻those who are sick with⁻ᶜ famine.
Both priest and prophet roamᵃ the land,
They know not where.

¹⁹Have You, then, rejected Judah?
Have You spurned Zion?
Why have You smitten us
So that there is no cure?
Why do we hope for happiness,
But find no good;
For a time of healing,
And meet terror instead?
²⁰We acknowledge our wickedness, O LORD—
The iniquity of our fathers—
For we have sinned against You.
²¹For Your name's sake, do not disown us;
Do not dishonor Your glorious throne.
Remember, do not annul Your covenant with us.
²²Can any of the false gods of the nations give rain?
Can the skies of themselves give showers?
Only You can, O LORD our God!
So we hope in You,
For only You made all these things.

15 The LORD said to me, "Even if Moses and Samuel were to ᵃ⁻intercede with Me,⁻ᵃ I would not be won over to that people. Dismiss them from My presence, and let them go forth! ²And if they ask you, 'To what shall we go forth?' answer them, 'Thus said the LORD:

Those destined for the plague, to the plague;
Those destined for the sword, to the sword;
Those destined for famine, to famine;
Those destined for captivity, to captivity.

³And I will appoint over them four kindsᵇ [of punishment]—declares the LORD—the sword to slay, the dogs to drag, the birds of the sky, and the beasts of the earth to devour and destroy. ⁴I will make them a horror to all the kingdoms of the earth, on account of King Manasseh son of Hezekiah of Judah, and of what he did in Jerusalem.'"

ᶜ⁻ᶜ *Lit. "the sicknesses of."*

ᵃ⁻ᵃ *Lit. "stand before Me," as Jeremiah is doing now; cf. 18.20.*
ᵇ *Meaning of Heb. uncertain.*

⁵But who will pity you, O Jerusalem,
Who will console you?
Who will turn aside to inquire
About your welfare?
⁶You cast Me off

—declares the LORD—

You go ever backward.
So I have stretched out My hand to destroy you;
I cannot relent.
⁷I will scatter them as with a winnowing fork
Through the settlements of the earth.
I will bereave, I will destroy My people,
For they would not turn back from their ways.
⁸Their widows shall be more numerous
Than the sands of the seas.
I will bring against them—
ᵇ⁻Young men and mothers together⁻ᵇ—
A destroyer at noonday.
I will bring down suddenly upon them
Alarmᵇ and terror.
⁹She who bore seven is forlorn,
Utterly disconsolate;
Her sun has set while it is still day,
She is shamed and humiliated.
The remnant of them I will deliver to the sword,
To the power of their enemies

—declares the LORD.

¹⁰Woe is me, my mother, that you ever bore me—
A man of conflict and strife with all the land!
I have not lent,
And I have not borrowed;
Yet everyone curses me.

¹¹The LORD said:
ᵇ⁻Surely, a mere remnant of you
Will I spare for a better fate!⁻ᵇ
By the enemy ᶜ⁻from the north⁻ᶜ
In a time of distress and a time of disaster,

c-c *Moved up from v. 12 for clarity.*

803

Surely, I will have you struck down!
12d-Can iron break iron and bronze?-d
13b-I will hand over your wealth and your treasures
As a spoil, free of charge,
Because of all your sins throughout your territory.
14And I will bring your enemies
By way of a land you have not known.-b
For a fire has flared in My wrath,
It blazes against you.

15O LORD, you know—
Remember me and take thought of me,
Avenge me on those who persecute me;
Do not yield to Your patience,
e-Do not let me perish!-e
Consider how I have borne insult
On Your account.
16When Your words were offered, I devoured them;
Your word brought me the delight and joy
Of knowing that Your name is attached to me,
O LORD, God of Hosts.
17I have not sat in the company of revelers
And made merry!
I have sat lonely because of Your hand upon me,
For You have filled me with gloom.
18Why must my pain be endless,
My wound incurable,
Resistant to healing?
You have been to me like a spring that fails,
Like waters that cannot be relied on.

19Assuredly, thus said the LORD:
If you turn back, I shall take you back
And you shall stand before Me;
If you produce what is noble
Out of the worthless,
You shall be My spokesman.

d-d *Emendation yields "He shall shatter iron—iron and bronze!"*
e-e *Lit. "Do not take me away."*

They shall come back to you,
Not you to them.
20Against this people I will make you
As a fortified wall of bronze:
They will attack you,
But they shall not overcome you,
For I am with you to deliver and save you

—declares the LORD.
21I will save you from the hands of the wicked
And rescue you from the clutches of the violent.

16 The word of the LORD came to me:

2You are not to marry and not to have sons and daughters in this place. 3For thus said the LORD concerning any sons and daughters that may be born in this place, and concerning the mothers who bear them, and concerning the fathers who beget them in this land: 4They shall die gruesome deaths. They shall not be lamented or buried; they shall be like dung on the surface of the ground. They shall be consumed by the sword and by famine, and their corpses shall be food for the birds of the sky and the beasts of the earth.

5For thus said the LORD:
Do not enter a house of mourning,a
Do not go to lament and to condole with them;
For I have withdrawn My favor from that people

—declares the LORD—
My kindness and compassion.
6Great and small alike shall die in this land,
They shall not be buried; men shall not lament them,
Nor gash and tonsure themselves for them.
7They shall not break breadb for a mournerc
To comfort him for a bereavement,
Nor offer one a cup of consolation
For the loss of his father or mother.
8Nor shall you enter a house of feasting,
To sit down with them to eat and drink.

a Lit. "religious gathering."
b So a few mss. Most mss. and editions read "to them."
c Lit. "mourning."

⁹For thus said the LORD of Hosts, the God of Israel: I am going to banish from this place, in your days and before your eyes, the sound of mirth and gladness, the voice of bridegroom and bride.

¹⁰And when you announce all these things to that people, and they ask you, "Why has the LORD decreed upon us all this fearful evil? What is the iniquity and what the sin that we have committed against the LORD our God?" ¹¹say to them, "Because your fathers deserted Me—declares the LORD—and followed other gods and served them and worshiped them; they deserted Me and did not keep My Instruction. ¹²And you have acted worse than your fathers, every one of you following the willfulness of his evil heart and paying no heed to Me. ¹³Therefore I will hurl you out of this land to a land that neither you nor your fathers have known, and there you will serve other gods, day and night; for I will show you no mercy."

¹⁴Assuredly, a time is coming—declares the LORD—when it shall no more be said, "As the LORD lives who brought the Israelites out of the land of Egypt," ¹⁵but rather, "As the LORD lives who brought the Israelites out of the northland, and out of all the lands to which He had banished them." For I will bring them back to their land, which I gave to their fathers.

¹⁶Lo, I am sending for many fishermen

—declares the LORD—

And they shall haul them out;
And after that I will send for many hunters,
And they shall hunt them
Out of every mountain and out of every hill
And out of the clefts of the rocks.
¹⁷For My eyes are on all their ways,
They are not hidden from My presence,
Their iniquity is not concealed from My sight.
¹⁸I will pay them in full[d]—
Nay, doubly for their iniquity and their sins—
Because they have defiled My land
With the corpses of their abominations,[e]
And have filled My own possession
With their abhorrent things.

d *See note to Isa. 65.7.*
e *I.e., their lifeless idols.*

¹⁹O LORD, my strength and my stronghold,
My refuge in a day of trouble,
To You nations shall come
From the ends of the earth and say:
Our fathers inherited utter delusions,
Things that are futile and worthless.
²⁰Can a man make gods for himself?
No-gods are they!
²¹Assuredly, I will teach them,
Once and for all I will teach them
My power and My might.
And they shall learn that My name is LORD.

17

The guilt of Judah is inscribed
With a stylus of iron,
Engraved with an adamant point
On the tablet of their hearts,
^{a-}And on the horns of their altars,
²While their children remember^{-a}
Their altars and sacred posts,
By verdant trees,
Upon lofty hills.
^{3b-}Because of the sin of your shrines
Throughout your borders,
I will make your rampart a heap in the field,
And all your treasures a spoil.^{-b}
^{4c-}You will forfeit,^{-c} by your own act,
The inheritance I have given you;
I will make you a slave to your enemies
In a land you have never known.
For you have kindled the flame of My wrath
Which shall burn for all time.

⁵Thus said the LORD:
Cursed is he who trusts in man,
Who makes mere flesh his strength,
And turns his thoughts from the LORD.

---

^{a-a} *Meaning of Heb. uncertain. Emendation yields "Surely the horns of their altars / Are as a memorial against them."*
^{b-b} *Meaning of Heb. uncertain.*
^{c-c} *Meaning of Heb. uncertain. Emendation yields "Your hand must let go."*

6He shall be like a bushd in the desert,
Which does not sense the coming of good:
It is set in the scorched places of the wilderness,
In a barren land without inhabitant.
7Blessed is he who trusts in the LORD,
Whose trust is the LORD alone.
8He shall be like a tree planted by waters,
Sending forth its roots by a stream:
It does not sense the coming of heat,
Its leaves are ever fresh;
It has no care in a year of drought,
It does not cease to yield fruit.

9Most devious is the heart;
It is perverse—who can fathom it?
10I the LORD probe the heart,
Search the mind—
To repay every man according to his ways,
With the proper fruit of his deeds.

11b-Like a partridge hatching what she did not lay,-b
So is one who amasses wealth by unjust means;
In the middle of his life it will leave him,
And in the end he will be proved a fool.

12O Throne of Glory exalted from of old,
Our Sacred Shrine!
13O Hope of Israel! O LORD!
All who forsake You shall be put to shame,
Those in the land who turn from Youe
Shall be doomedf men,
For they have forsaken the LORD,
The Fount of living waters.

14Heal me, O LORD, and let me be healed;
Save me, and let me be saved;
For You are my glory.

d Or "tamarisk"; exact meaning of Heb. uncertain.
e Lit. "Me."
f Lit. "inscribed"; meaning of line uncertain.

¹⁵See, they say to me:
"Where is the prediction of the LORD?
Let it come to pass!"
¹⁶But I have not ^gevaded
Being a shepherd in your service,^{-g}
Nor have I longed for the fatal day.
You know the utterances of my lips,
They were ever before You.
¹⁷Do not be a cause of dismay to me;
You are my refuge in a day of calamity.
¹⁸Let my persecutors be shamed,
And let not me be shamed;
Let them be dismayed,
And let not me be dismayed.
Bring on them the day of disaster,
And shatter them with double destruction.

¹⁹Thus said the LORD to me: Go and stand in the People's Gate, by which the kings of Judah enter and by which they go forth, and in all the gates of Jerusalem, ²⁰and say to them: Hear the word of the LORD, O kings of Judah, and all Judah, and all the inhabitants of Jerusalem who enter by these gates! ²¹Thus said the LORD: Guard yourselves for your own sake against carrying burdens^h on the sabbath day, and bringing them through the gates of Jerusalem. ²²Nor shall you carry out burdens from your houses on the sabbath day, or do any work, but you shall hallow the sabbath day, as I commanded your fathers. (²³But they would not listen or turn their ear; they stiffened their necks and would not pay heed or accept discipline.) ²⁴If you obey Me—declares the LORD—and do not bring in burdens through the gates of this city on the sabbath day, but hallow the sabbath day and do no work on it, ²⁵then through the gates of this city shall enter kings who sit upon the throne of David, with their officers—riding on chariots and horses, they and their officers—and the men of Judah and the inhabitants of Jerusalem. And this city shall be inhabited for all time. ²⁶And people shall come from the towns of Judah and from the environs of Jerusalem, and from the land of Benjamin, and from the Shephelah, and from the hill country, and from the Negeb, bringing burnt

g-g *Exact force of Heb. uncertain. Emendation yields "urged you to [bring] misfortune."*
h *Or "merchandise."*

offerings and sacrifices, meal offerings and frankincense, and bringing offerings of thanksgiving to the House of the LORD. 27But if you do not obey My command to hallow the sabbath day and to carry in no burdens through the gates of Jerusalem on the sabbath day, then I will set fire to its gates; it shall consume the fortresses of Jerusalem and it shall not be extinguished.

18

The word which came to Jeremiah from the LORD: 2"Go down to the house of a potter, and there I will impart My words to you." 3So I went down to the house of a potter, and found him working at the wheel. 4a-And if the vessel he was making was spoiled, as happens to clay in the potter's hands,-a he would make it into another vessel, such as the potter saw fit to make.

5Then the word of the LORD came to me: 6O House of Israel, can I not deal with you like this potter?—says the LORD. Just like clay in the hands of the potter, so are you in My hands, O House of Israel! 7At one moment I may decree that a nation or a kingdom shall be uprooted and pulled down and destroyed; 8but if that nation against which I made the decree turns back from its wickedness, I change My mind concerning the punishment I planned to bring on it. 9At another moment I may decree that a nation or a kingdom shall be built and planted; 10but if it does what is displeasing to Me and does not obey Me, then I change My mind concerning the good I planned to bestow upon it.

11And now, say to the men of Judah and the inhabitants of Jerusalem: Thus said the LORD: I am devisingb disaster for you and laying plans against you. Turn back, each of you, from your wicked ways, and mend your ways and your actions! 12But they will say, "It is no use. We will keep on following our own plans; each of us will act in the willfulness of his evil heart."

13Assuredly, thus said the LORD:
Inquire among the nations:
Who has heard anything like this?
Maiden Israel has done
A most horrible thing.
14cDoes one forsake Lebanon snow
From the mountainous rocks?

---

a-a *So some mss. and one early edition. Most mss. and editions read "And if the vessel that he was making with clay in the potter's hands was spoiled."*
b *The same Hebrew word as is used above for "potter."*
c *Meaning of verse uncertain; cf. 2.13, 17.13.*

Does one abandon cool water
Flowing from afar?
15Yet My people have forgotten Me:
They sacrifice to a delusion;
They are made to stumble in their ways—
The ancient paths—
And to walk instead on byways,
On a road not built up.
16So their land will become a desolation,
An object of hissingd for all time.
Every passerby will be appalled
And will shake his head.d
17Like the east wind, I will scatter them
Before the enemy.
e-I will look upon their back, not their face,-e
In their day of disaster.

18They said,f "Come let us devise a plot against Jeremiah—for instruction shall not fail from the priest, nor counsel from the wise, nor oracle from the prophet. Come, let us strike him with the tongue, and we shall no longer have to listen to all those words of his."

19Listen to me, O LORD—
And take note of g-what my enemies say!-g
20Should good be repaid with evil?
Yet they have dug a pit for me.
Remember how I stood before You
To plead in their behalf,
To turn Your anger away from them!
21Oh, give their children over to famine,
Mow them down by the sword.
Let their wives be bereaved
Of children and husbands,
Let their men be struck down by the plague,
And their young men be slain in battle by the sword.
22Let an outcry be heard from their houses
When You bring sudden marauders against them;
For they have dug a pit to trap me,

---

d These actions were performed at the sight of ruin to ward off a like fate from the observer; cf. Lam. 2.15.
e-e Change of vocalization yields "I will show them [My] back and not [My] face."
f Cf. 20.10.
g-g Emendation yields "my case."

And laid snares for my feet.
²³O LORD, You know
All their plots to kill me.
Do not pardon their iniquity,
Do not blot out their guilt from Your presence.
Let them be made to stumble before You—
Act against them in Your hour of wrath!

19 Thus said the LORD: Go buy a jug of potter's ware. And [take] some of the elders of the people and the priests, ²and go out to the Valley of Ben-hinnom—ᵃ⁻at the entrance of the Harsith Gate⁻ᵃ—and proclaim there the words which I will speak to you.

³Say: "Hear the word of the LORD, O kings of Judah and inhabitants of Jerusalem! Thus said the LORD of Hosts, the God of Israel: I am going to bring such disaster upon this place that the ears of all who hear about it will tingle. ⁴For they and their fathers and the kings of Judah have forsaken Me, and have made this place alien [to Me]; they have sacrificed in it to other gods whom they have not experienced,ᵇ and they have filled this place with the blood of the innocent. ⁵They have built shrines to Baal, to put their children to the fire as burnt offerings to Baal—which I never commanded, never decreed, and which never came to My mind. ⁶Assuredly, a time is coming—declares the LORD—when this place shall no longer be called Topheth or Valley of Ben-hinnom, but Valley of Slaughter.

⁷"And I will frustrateᶜ the plans of Judah and Jerusalem in this place. I will cause them to fall by the sword before their enemies, by the hand of those who seek their lives; and I will give their carcasses as food to the birds of the sky and the beasts of the earth. ⁸And I will make this city an object of horror and hissing;ᵈ everyone who passes by it will be appalled and will hiss over all its wounds. ⁹And I will cause them to eat the flesh of their sons and the flesh of their daughters, and they shall devour one another's flesh—because of the desperate straits to which they will be reduced by their enemies, who seek their life."

¹⁰Then you shall smash the jug in the sight of the men who go with you, ¹¹and say to them: "Thus said the LORD of Hosts: So will I smash this people and this city, as one smashes a potter's vessel, which can never be mended. And they shall bury in Topheth until no room is left for

ᵃ⁻ᵃ *Others "by way of the Potsherd Gate"; meaning of Heb. uncertain.*
ᵇ *See note at Deut. 11.28.*
ᶜ *Lit. "empty," Heb. u-baqqothi, a play on baqbuq, "jug" in v. 1.*
ᵈ *See note at 18.16.*

burying. ¹²That is what I will do to this place and its inhabitants—declares the LORD. I will make this city like Topheth: ¹³the houses of Jerusalem and the houses of the kings of Judah shall be unclean, like that place Topheth—all the houses on the roofs of which offerings were made to the whole host of heaven and libations were poured out to other gods."

¹⁴When Jeremiah returned from Topheth, where the LORD had sent him to prophesy, he stood in the court of the House of the LORD and said to all the people: ¹⁵"Thus said the LORD of Hosts, the God of Israel: I am going to bring upon this city and upon all its villages all the disaster which I have decreed against it, for they have stiffened their necks and refused to heed My words."

20 Pashhur son of Immer, the priest who was chief officer of the House of the LORD, heard Jeremiah prophesy these things. ²Pashhur thereupon had Jeremiah flogged and put in the cell[a] at the Upper Benjamin Gate in the House of the LORD. ³The next day, Pashhur released Jeremiah from the cell.

But Jeremiah said to him, "The LORD has named you not Pashhur, but Magor-missabib.[b] ⁴For thus said the LORD: I am going to deliver you and all your friends over to terror: they will fall by the sword of their enemies while you look on. I will deliver all Judah into the hands of the king of Babylon; he will exile them to Babylon or put them to the sword. ⁵And I will deliver all the wealth, all the riches, and all the prized possessions of this city, and I will also deliver all the treasures of the kings of Judah into the hands of their enemies: they shall seize them as plunder and carry them off to Babylon. ⁶As for you, Pashhur, and all who live in your house, you shall go into captivity. You shall come to Babylon; there you shall die and there you shall be buried, and so shall all your friends to whom you prophesied falsely."

⁷You enticed me, O LORD, and I was enticed;
You overpowered me and You prevailed.
I have become a constant laughingstock,
Everyone jeers at me.
⁸For every time I speak, I must cry out,
Must shout, "Lawlessness and rapine!"

---

a *Meaning of Heb. uncertain.*
b *I.e., "Terror all around"; cf. v. 10.*

For the word of the LORD causes me
Constant disgrace and contempt.
⁹I thought, "I will not mention Him,
No more will I speak in His name"—
But [His word] was like a raging fire in my heart,
Shut up in my bones;
I could not hold it in, I was helpless.
¹⁰I heard the whispers of the crowd—
Terror all around:
"Inform! Let us inform against him!"
All my [supposed] friends
Are waiting for me to stumble:
"Perhaps he can be entrapped,
And we can prevail against him
And take our vengeance on him."
¹¹But the LORD is with me like a mighty warrior;
Therefore my persecutors shall stumble;
They shall not prevail and shall not succeed.
They shall be utterly shamed
With a humiliation for all time,
Which shall not be forgotten.
¹²O LORD of Hosts, You who test the righteous,
Who examine the heart and the mind,
Let me see Your retribution upon them,
For I lay my case before You.
¹³Sing unto the LORD,
Praise the LORD,
For He has rescued the needy
From the hands of evildoers!

¹⁴Accursed be the day
That I was born!
Let not the day be blessed
When my mother bore me!
¹⁵Accursed be the man
Who brought my father the news
And said, "A boy

Is born to you,"
And gave him such joy!
¹⁶Let that man^c become like the cities
Which the LORD overthrew without relenting!
Let him hear shrieks in the morning
And battle shouts at noontide—
¹⁷Because he did not kill me before birth
So that my mother might be my grave,
And her womb big [with me] for all time.
¹⁸Why did I ever issue from the womb,
To see misery and woe,
To spend all my days in shame!

21 The word which came to Jeremiah from the LORD, when King Zedekiah sent to him Pashhur son of Malchiah and the priest Zephaniah, son of Maaseiah, to say, ²"Please inquire of the LORD on our behalf, for King Nebuchadrezzar of Babylon is attacking us. Perhaps the LORD will act for our sake in accordance with all His wonders, so that [Nebuchadrezzar] will withdraw from us."

³Jeremiah answered them, "Thus shall you say to Zedekiah: ⁴Thus said the LORD, the God of Israel: I am going to turn around the weapons in your hands with which you are battling outside the wall against those who are besieging you—the king of Babylon and the Chaldeans—and I will take them into the midst of this city; ⁵and I Myself will battle against you with an outstretched mighty arm, with anger and rage and great wrath. ⁶I will strike the inhabitants of this city, man and beast: they shall die by a terrible pestilence. ⁷And then—declares the LORD—I will deliver King Zedekiah of Judah and his courtiers and the people—those in this city who survive the pestilence, the sword, and the famine—into the hands of King Nebuchadrezzar of Babylon, into the hands of their enemies, into the hands of those who seek their lives. He will put them to the sword without pity, without compassion, without mercy.

⁸"And to this people you shall say: Thus said the LORD: I set before you the way of life and the way of death. ⁹Whoever remains in this city shall die by the sword, by famine, and by pestilence; but whoever leaves and goes over to the Chaldeans who are besieging you shall live; ^{a-}he shall

---

^c *Emendation yields "day."*
^{a-a} *Lit. "he shall have his life as booty."*

at least gain his life.⁻ᵃ ¹⁰For I have set My face against this city for evil and not for good—declares the LORD. It shall be delivered into the hands of the king of Babylon, who will destroy it by fire."

¹¹To the House of the king of Judah: Hear the word of the LORD! ¹²O House of David, thus said the LORD:

> Render just verdicts
> Morning by morning;
> Rescue him who is robbed
> From him who defrauded him.
> Else My wrath will break forth like fire
> And burn, with none to quench it,
> Because of your wicked acts.
> ¹³I will deal with you, ᵇ⁻O inhabitants of the valley,
> O rock of the plain⁻ᵇ—declares the LORD—
> You who say, "Who can come down against us?
> Who can get into our lairs?"
> ¹⁴I will punish you according to your deeds
> —declares the LORD.
> I will set fire to its forest;ᶜ
> It shall consume all that is around it.

22 Thus said the LORD: Go down to the palace of the king of Judah, where you shall utter this word. ²Say: "Hear the word of the LORD: O king of Judah, you who sit on the throne of David, and your courtiers and your subjects who enter these gates! ³Thus said the LORD: Do what is just and right; rescue from the defrauder him who is robbed; do not wrong the stranger, the fatherless, and the widow; commit no lawless act, and do not shed the blood of the innocent in this place. ⁴For if you fulfill this command, then through the gates of this palace shall enter kings of David's line who sit upon his throne, riding horse-drawn chariots, with their courtiers and their subjects. ⁵But if you do not heed these commands, I swear by Myself—declares the LORD—that this palace shall become a ruin."

⁶For thus said the LORD concerning the royal palace of Judah:

> You are as Gilead to Me,
> As the summit of Lebanon;

ᵇ⁻ᵇ *Force of Heb. uncertain.*
ᶜ *Perhaps a reference to the royal palace; cf. 1 Kings 7.2.*

But I will make you a desert,
Uninhabited towns.
7I will appoint destroyers against you,
Each with his tools;
They shall cut down your choicest cedars
And make them fall into the fire.

8And when many nations pass by this city and one man asks another,
"Why did the LORD do thus to that great city?" 9the reply will be, "Because they forsook the covenant with the LORD their God and bowed
down to other gods and served them."

10Do not weep for the dead^a
And do not lament for him;
Weep rather for ^b-him who is leaving,-^b
For he shall never come back
To see the land of his birth!

11For thus said the LORD concerning Shallum^b son of King Josiah of
Judah, who succeeded his father Josiah as king, but who has gone forth
from this place: He shall never come back. 12He shall die in the place to
which he was exiled, and he shall not see this land again.

13Ha! he who builds his house with unfairness
And his upper chambers with injustice,
Who makes his fellow man work without pay
And does not give him his wages,
14Who thinks: I will build me a vast palace
With spacious upper chambers,
Provided with windows,
Paneled in cedar,
Painted with vermilion!
15Do you think you are more a king
Because you compete in cedar?
Your father ^c-ate and drank-^c
And dispensed justice and equity—
Then all went well with him.
16He upheld the rights of the poor and needy—
Then all was well.

---

a I.e., Josiah; see 2 Kings 23.29–30.
b-b I.e., the king called by his throne name Jehoahaz in 2 Kings 23.31 ff., and by his private name
   Shallum here in v. 11 and in 1 Chron. 3.15.
c-c I.e., he was content with the simple necessities of life.

d-That is truly heeding Me-d

—declares the LORD.

17But your eyes and your mind are only
On ill-gotten gains,
On shedding the blood of the innocent,
On committing fraud and violence.
18Assuredly, thus said the LORD concerning Jehoiakim son of Josiah,
king of Judah:
e-They shall not mourn for him,
"Ah, brother! Ah, sister!"
They shall not mourn for him,
"Ah, lord! Ah, his majesty!"-e
19He shall have the burial of an ass,
Dragged out and left lying
Outside the gates of Jerusalem.

20fClimb Lebanon and cry out,
Raise your voice in Bashan,
Cry out from Abarim,
For all your lovers are crushed.
21I spoke to you when you were prosperous;
You said, "I will not listen."
That was your way ever since your youth,
You would not heed Me.
22All your shepherdsg shall be devoured by the wind,
And your lovers shall go into captivity.
Then you shall be shamed and humiliated
Because of all your depravity.
23You who dwell in Lebanon,
Nestled among the cedars,
h-How much grace will you have-h
When pains come upon you,
Travail as in childbirth!

24As I live—declares the LORD—i-if you, O King Coniah, son of Jehoiakim, of Judah, were-i a signet on my right hand, I would tear you off

---

d-d Or "That is the reward for heeding Me."
e-e They shall express neither sorrow at the loss of a relative nor grief at the death of a ruler.
f Israel is addressed.
g Change of vocalization yields "paramours."
h-h Septuagint reads "How you will groan."
i-i Heb. "If Coniah . . . were . . ."; Coniah (Jeconiah in 24.1) is identical with Jehoiachin, 2
   Kings 24.8 ff.

even from there. ²⁵I will deliver you into the hands of those who seek your life, into the hands of those you dread, into the hands of King Nebuchadrezzar of Babylon and into the hands of the Chaldeans. ²⁶I will hurl you and the mother who bore you into another land, where you were not born; there you shall both die. ²⁷They shall not return to the land that they yearn to come back to.

²⁸Is this man Coniah
A wretched broken pot,
A vessel no one wants?
Why are he and his offspring hurled out,
And cast away in a land they knew not?
²⁹O land, land, land,
Hear the word of the LORD!
³⁰Thus said the LORD:
Record this man as without succession,
One who shall never be found acceptable;
For no man of his offspring shall be accepted
To sit on the throne of David
And to rule again in Judah.

23 Ah, shepherds who let the flock of My pasture stray and scatter!—declares the LORD. ²Assuredly, thus said the LORD, the God of Israel, concerning the shepherds who should tend My people: It is you who let My flock scatter and go astray. You gave no thought to them, but I am going to give thought to you, for your wicked acts—declares the LORD. ³And I Myself will gather the remnant of My flock from all the lands to which I have banished them, and I will bring them back to their pasture, where they shall be fertile and increase. ⁴And I will appoint over them shepherds who will tend them; they shall no longer fear or be dismayed, and none of them shall be missing—declares the LORD.

⁵See, a time is coming—declares the LORD—when I will raise up a true branch of David's line. He shall reign as king and shall prosper, and he shall do what is just and right in the land. ⁶In his days Judah shall be delivered and Israel shall dwell secure. And this is the name by which he shall be called: "The LORD is our Vindicator."

⁷Assuredly, a time is coming—declares the LORD—when it shall no

more be said, "As the LORD lives, who brought the Israelites out of the land of Egypt," 8but rather, "As the LORD lives, who brought out and led the offspring of the House of Israel from the northland and from all the lands to which I have banished them." And they shall dwell upon their own soil.

9Concerning the prophets.

My heart is crushed within me,
All my bones are trembling;ª
I have become like a drunken man,
Like one overcome by wine—
Because of the LORD and His holy word.
10For the land is full of adulterers,
The land mourns because of b-a curse;-b
The pastures of the wilderness are dried up.
c-For they run to do evil,
They strain to do wrong.-c
11For both prophet and priest are godless;
Even in My House I find their wickedness

—declares the LORD.

12Assuredly,
Their path shall become
Like slippery ground;
They shall be thrust into darkness
And there they shall fall;
For I will bring disaster upon them,
The year of their doom

—declares the LORD.

13In the prophets of Samaria
I saw a repulsive thing:
They prophesied by Baal
And led My people Israel astray.
14But what I see in the prophets of Jerusalem
Is something horrifying:
Adultery and false dealing.
They encourage evildoers,
So that no one turns back from his wickedness.

ª Meaning of Heb. uncertain.
b-b A few Heb. mss. and Septuagint read "these."
c-c Lit. "Their running is wickedness, / Their straining is iniquity."

To Me they are all like Sodom,
And [all] its inhabitants like Gomorrah.

¹⁵Assuredly, thus said the LORD of Hosts concerning the prophets:

I am going to make them eat wormwood
And drink a bitter draft;
For from the prophets of Jerusalem
Godlessness has gone forth to the whole land.

¹⁶Thus said the LORD of Hosts:
Do not listen to the words of the prophets
Who prophesy to you.
They are deluding you,
The prophecies they speak are from their own minds,
Not from the mouth of the LORD.
¹⁷They declare to men who despise Me:
The LORD has said:
"All shall be well with you";
And to all who follow their willful hearts they say:
"No evil shall befall you."
¹⁸But he who has stood in the council of the LORD,
And seen, and heard His word—
He who has listened to His word must obey.ᵈ
¹⁹ᵉ⁻Lo, the storm of the LORD goes forth in fury,
A whirling storm,
It shall whirl down upon the heads of the wicked.
²⁰The anger of the LORD shall not turn back
Till it has fulfilled and completed His purposes.⁻ᵉ
In the days to come
You shall clearly perceive it.

²¹I did not send those prophets,
But they rushed in;
I did not speak to them,
Yet they prophesied.
²²If they have stood in My council,
Let them announce My words to My people

ᵈ Change of vocalization yields "announce it"; cf. vv. 22, 28.
ᵉ⁻ᵉ This section constitutes the word of God to which Jeremiah refers.

And make them turn back
From their evil ways and wicked acts.

23Am I only a God near at hand

           —says the LORD—

And not a God far away?
24If a man enters a hiding place,
Do I not see him?

           —says the LORD.

For I fill both heaven and earth

           —declares the LORD.

25I have heard what the prophets say, who prophesy falsely in My name: "I had a dream, I had a dream." 26 a-How long will there be-a in the minds of the prophets who prophesy falsehood—the prophets of their own deceitful minds— 27the plan to make My people forget My name, by means of the dreams which they tell each other, just as their fathers forgot My name because of Baal? 28Let the prophet who has a dream tell the dream; and let him who has received My word report My word faithfully! How can straw be compared to grain?—says the LORD. 29Behold, My word is like fire—declares the LORD—and like a hammer that shatters rock!

30Assuredly, I am going to deal with the prophets—declares the LORD—who steal My words from one another. 31I am going to deal with the prophets—declares the LORD—who waga their tongues and make oracular utterances. 32I am going to deal with those who prophesy lying dreams—declares the LORD—who relate them to lead My people astray with their reckless lies, when I did not send them or command them. They do this people no good—declares the LORD.

33And when this people—or a prophet or a priest—asks you, "What is the burdenf of the LORD?" you shall answer them, g-"What is the burden?-g I will cast you off" —declares the LORD.

34As for the prophet or priest or layman who shall say "the burden of the LORD," I will punish that person and his house. 35Thus you shall speak to each other, every one to his fellow, "What has the LORD answered?" or "What has the LORD spoken?" 36But do not mention "the burden of the LORD" any more. a-Does a man regard his own word as a "burden,"-a that you pervert the words of the living God, the LORD of

f I.e., pronouncement; cf. Isa. 13.1, 15.1, etc., where the word rendered "pronouncement" can also mean "burden."
g-g Septuagint and other versions read "You are the burden!"

Hosts, our God? ³⁷Thus you shall speak to the prophet: "What did the LORD answer you?" or "What did the LORD speak?" ³⁸But if you say "the burden of the LORD"—assuredly, thus said the LORD: Because you said this thing, "the burden of the LORD," whereas I sent word to you not to say "the burden of the LORD," ³⁹I will utterly ʰ-forget you-ʰ and I will cast you away from My presence, together with the city that I gave to you and your fathers. ⁴⁰And I will lay upon you a disgrace for all time, shame for all time, which shall never be forgotten.

24 The LORD showed me two baskets of figs, placed in front of the Temple of the LORD. This was after King Nebuchadrezzar of Babylon had exiled King Jeconiah son of Jehoiakim of Judah, and the officials of Judah, and the craftsmen and smiths, from Jerusalem, and had brought them to Babylon. ²One basket contained very good figs, like first-ripened figs, and the other basket contained very bad figs, so bad that they could not be eaten.

³And the LORD said to me, "What do you see, Jeremiah?" I answered, "Figs—the good ones are very good, and the bad ones very bad, so bad that they cannot be eaten."

⁴Then the word of the LORD came to me:

⁵Thus said the LORD, the God of Israel: As with these good figs, so will I single out for good the Judean exiles whom I have driven out from this place to the land of the Chaldeans. ⁶I will look upon them favorably, and I will bring them back to this land; I will build them and not overthrow them; I will plant them and not uproot them. ⁷And I will give them the understanding to acknowledge Me, for I am the LORD. And they shall be My people and I will be their God, when they turn back to Me with all their heart.

⁸And like the bad figs, which are so bad that they cannot be eaten— thus said the Lord—so will I treat King Zedekiah of Judah and his officials and the remnant of Jerusalem that is left in this land, and those who are living in the land of Egypt: ⁹I will make them a horror—an evil—to all the kingdoms of the earth, a disgrace and a proverb, a byword and a curseᵃ in all the places to which I banish them. ¹⁰I will send the sword, famine, and pestilence against them until they are exterminated from the land that I gave to them and their fathers.

ʰ-ʰ *Some Heb. mss., Septuagint, and other versions read "lift you up," a word from the same root as "burden."*

ᵃ *I.e., a standard by which men curse; cf. Gen. 12.2 and note; Zech. 8.13.*

25 The word which came to Jeremiah concerning all the people of Judah, in the fourth year of King Jehoiakim son of Josiah of Judah, which was the first year of King Nebuchadrezzar of Babylon. ²This is what the prophet Jeremiah said to all the people of Judah and to all the inhabitants of Jerusalem:

³From the thirteenth year of King Josiah son of Amon of Judah, to this day—these twenty-three years—the word of the LORD has come to me. I have spoken to you persistently, but you would not listen. ⁴Moreover, the LORD constantly sent all his servants the prophets to you, but you would not listen or incline your ears to hear ⁵when they said, "Turn back, every one, from your evil ways and your wicked acts, that you may remain throughout the ages on the soil which the LORD gave to you and your fathers. ⁶Do not follow other gods, to serve them and worship them. Do not vex Me with what your own hands have made,ª and I will not bring disaster upon you." ⁷But you would not listen to Me—declares the LORD— but vexed Me with what your hands made, to your own hurt.

⁸Assuredly, thus said the LORD of Hosts: Because you would not listen to My words, ⁹I am going to send for all the peoples of the north— declares the LORD—and for My servant, King Nebuchadrezzar of Babylon, and bring them against this land and its inhabitants, and against all those nations roundabout. I will exterminate them and make them a desolation, an object of hissingᵇ—ruins for all time. ¹⁰And I will banish from them the sound of mirth and gladness, the voice of bridegroom and bride, and the sound of the mill and the light of the lamp. ¹¹This whole land shall be a desolate ruin.

And those nations shall serve the king of Babylon seventy years. ¹²When the seventy years are over, I will punish the king of Babylon and that nation and the land of the Chaldeans for their sins—declares the LORD— and I will make it a desolation for all time. ¹³And I will bring upon that land all that I have decreed against it, all that is recorded in this book— that which Jeremiah prophesied against all the nations. ¹⁴For they too shall be enslaved by many nations and great kings; and I will requite them according to their acts and according to their conduct.

¹⁵For thus said the LORD, the God of Israel, to me: "Take from My hand this cup of wine—of wrath—and make all the nations to whom I

ª *I.e., idols.*
ᵇ *Cf. note at 18.16.*

send you drink of it. ¹⁶Let them drink and retch and act crazy, because of the sword that I am sending among them."

¹⁷So I took the cup from the hand of the LORD and gave drink to all the nations to whom the LORD had sent me: ¹⁸Jerusalem and the towns of Judah, and its kings and officials, to make them a desolate ruin, an object of hissing and a curse^c—as is now the case; ¹⁹Pharaoh king of Egypt, his courtiers, his officials, and all his people; ²⁰all ^{d-}the mixed peoples;^{-d} all the kings of the land of Uz; all the kings of the land of the Philistines—Ashkelon, Gaza, Ekron, and what is left of Ashdod; ²¹Edom, Moab, and Ammon; ²²all the kings of Tyre and all the kings of Sidon, and all the kings of the coastland across the sea; ²³Dedan, Tema, and Buz, and all those who have their hair clipped; ²⁴all the kings of Arabia, and all the kings of ^{d-}the mixed peoples^{-d} who live in the desert; ²⁵all the kings of Zimri^d and all the kings of Elam and all the kings of Media; ²⁶all the kings of the north, whether far from or close to each other—all the ^{d-}royal lands which are on the earth.^{-d} And last of all, the king of She-shach^e shall drink.

²⁷Say to them: "Thus said the LORD of Hosts, the God of Israel: Drink and get drunk and vomit; fall and never rise again, because of the sword that I send among you." ²⁸And if they refuse to take the cup from your hand and drink, say to them, "Thus said the LORD of Hosts: You must drink! ²⁹If I am bringing the punishment first on the city that bears My name, do you expect to go unpunished? You will not go unpunished, for I am summoning the sword against all the inhabitants of the earth—declares the LORD of Hosts."

³⁰You are to prophesy all those things to them, and then say to them:

> The LORD roars from on high,
> He makes His voice heard from His holy dwelling;
> He roars aloud over His [earthly] abode;
> He utters shouts like the grape-treaders,
> Against all the dwellers on earth.
> ³¹Tumult has reached the ends of the earth,
> For the LORD has a case against the nations,
> He contends with all flesh.
> He delivers the wicked to the sword
>
>   —declares the LORD.

³²Thus said the LORD of Hosts:

---

^c *Cf. note at 24.9.*
^{d-d} *Meaning of Heb. uncertain.*
^e *A cipher for* Babel, Babylon.

Disaster goes forth
From nation to nation;
A great storm is unleashed
From the remotest parts of earth.

³³In that day, the earth shall be strewn with the slain of the LORD from one end to the other. They shall not be mourned, or gathered and buried; they shall become dung upon the face of the earth.

³⁴Howl, you shepherds, and yell,
Strew [dust] on yourselves, you lords of the flock!
For the day of your slaughter draws near.
^{d-}I will break you in pieces,^{-d}
And you shall fall like a precious vessel.
³⁵Flight shall fail the shepherds,
And escape, the lords of the flock.
³⁶Hark, the outcry of the shepherds,
And the howls of the lords of the flock!
For the LORD is ravaging their pasture.
³⁷The peaceful meadows shall be wiped out
By the fierce wrath of the LORD.
³⁸Like a lion, He has gone forth from His lair;
The land has become a desolation,
Because of the oppressive^d wrath,
Because of His fierce anger.

26 At the beginning of the reign of King Jehoiakim son of Josiah of Judah, this word came from the LORD:
²"Thus said the LORD: Stand in the court of the House of the LORD, and speak to [the men of] all the towns of Judah, who are coming to worship in the House of the LORD, all the words which I command you to speak to them. Do not omit anything. ³Perhaps they will listen and turn back, each from his evil way, that I may renounce the punishment I am planning to bring upon them for their wicked acts.

⁴"Say to them: Thus said the LORD: If you do not obey Me, abiding by the Teaching that I have set before you, ⁵heeding the words of My

servants the prophets whom I have been sending to you persistently—
but you have not heeded—⁶then I will make this House like Shiloh, and
I will make this city a curse^a for all the nations of earth."

⁷The priests and prophets and all the people heard Jeremiah speaking
these words in the House of the LORD. ⁸And when Jeremiah finished
speaking all that the LORD had commanded him to speak to all the people,
the priests and the prophets and all the people seized him, shouting, "You
shall die! ⁹How dare you prophesy in the name of the LORD that this
House shall become like Shiloh and this city be made desolate, without
inhabitants?" And all the people crowded about Jeremiah in the House
of the LORD.

¹⁰When the officials of Judah heard about this, they went up from the
king's palace to the House of the LORD and held a session at the entrance
of the New Gate of $^{b\text{-}}$the House of$^{\text{-}b}$ the LORD. ¹¹The priests and prophets
said to the officials and to all the people, "This man deserves the death
penalty, for he has prophesied against this city, as you yourselves have
heard."

¹²Jeremiah said to the officials and to all the people, "It was the LORD
who sent me to prophesy against this House and this city all the words
you heard. ¹³Therefore mend your ways and your acts, and heed the LORD
your God, that the LORD may renounce the punishment He has decreed
for you. ¹⁴As for me, I am in your hands: do to me what seems good and
right to you. ¹⁵But know that if you put me to death, you and this city
and its inhabitants will be guilty of shedding the blood of an innocent
man. For in truth the LORD has sent me to you, to speak all these words
to you."

¹⁶Then the officials and all the people said to the priests and prophets,
"This man does not deserve the death penalty, for he spoke to us in the
name of the LORD our God."

¹⁷And some of the elders of the land arose and said to the entire assemblage of the people, ¹⁸"Micah the Morashtite, who prophesied in the days
of King Hezekiah of Judah, said to all the people of Judah: 'Thus said
the LORD of Hosts:

Zion shall be plowed as a field,
Jerusalem shall become heaps of ruins
And the Temple Mount a shrine in the woods.'^{c}

¹⁹"Did King Hezekiah of Judah, and all Judah, put him to death? Did

---

^{a} *Cf. note at 24.9.*
$^{b\text{-}b}$ *So many mss. and ancient versions; other mss. and the editions omit these words.*
^{c} *Cf. Mic. 3.12.*

he not rather fear the LORD and implore the LORD, so that the LORD renounced the punishment He had decreed against them? We are about to do great injury to ourselves!"

20There was also a man prophesying in the name of the LORD, Uriah son of Shemaiah from Kiriath-jearim, who prophesied against this city and this land the same things as Jeremiah. 21King Jehoiakim and all his warriors and all the officials heard about his address, and the king wanted to put him to death. Uriah heard of this and fled in fear, and came to Egypt. 22But King Jehoiakim sent men to Egypt, Elnathan son of Achbor and men with him to Egypt. 23They took Uriah out of Egypt and brought him to King Jehoiakim, who had him put to the sword and his body thrown into the burial place of the common people. 24However, Ahikam son of Shaphan protected Jeremiah, so that he was not handed over to the people for execution.

27 At the beginning of the reign of King Jehoiakima son of Josiah of Judah, this word came to Jeremiah from the LORD:

2Thus said the LORD to me: Make for yourself thongs and bars of a yoke, and put them on your neck. 3b-And send them-b to the king of Edom, the king of Moab, the king of the Ammonites, the king of Tyre, and the king of Sidon, by envoys who have come to King Zedekiah of Judah in Jerusalem; 4and give them this charge to their masters: Thus said the LORD of Hosts, the God of Israel: Say this to your masters:

5"It is I who made the earth, and the men and beasts who are on the earth, by My great might and My outstretched arm; and I give it to whomever I deem proper. 6I herewith deliver all these lands to My servant, King Nebuchadnezzar of Babylon; I even give him the wild beasts to serve him. 7All nations shall serve him, his son and his grandson—until the turn of his own land comes, when many nations and great kings shall subjugate him. 8The nation or kingdom that does not serve him—King Nebuchadnezzar of Babylon—and does not put its neck under the yoke of the king of Babylon, that nation I will visit—declares the LORD—with sword, famine, and pestilence, until I have destroyed it by his hands. 9As for you, give no heed to your prophets, augurs, dreamers,c diviners, and sorcerers, who say to you, 'Do not serve the king of Babylon.' 10For they

---

a Emendation yields "Zedekiah"; so a few mss. and Syriac; cf. vv. 3 and 12.
b-b Emendation yields "And send," i.e., a message.
c Lit. "dreams."

prophesy falsely to you—with the result that you shall be banished from your land; I will drive you out and you shall perish. [11]But the nation that puts its neck under the yoke of the king of Babylon, and serves him, will be left by Me on its own soil—declares the LORD—to till it and dwell on it."

[12]I also spoke to King Zedekiah of Judah in just the same way: "Put your necks under the yoke of the king of Babylon; serve him and his people, and live! [13]Otherwise you will die together with your people, by sword, famine, and pestilence, as the LORD has decreed against any nation that does not serve the king of Babylon. [14]Give no heed to the words of the prophets who say to you, 'Do not serve the king of Babylon,' for they prophesy falsely to you. [15]I have not sent them—declares the LORD—and they prophesy falsely in My name, with the result that I will drive you out and you shall perish, together with the prophets who prophesy to you."

[16]And to the priests and to all that people I said: "Thus said the LORD: Give no heed to the words of the prophets who prophesy to you, 'The vessels of the House of the LORD shall shortly be brought back from Babylon,' for they prophesy falsely to you. [17]Give them no heed. Serve the king of Babylon, and live! Otherwise this city shall become a ruin. [18]If they are really prophets and the word of the LORD is with them, let them intercede with the LORD of Hosts not to let the vessels remaining in the House of the LORD, in the royal palace of Judah, and in Jerusalem, go to Babylon!

[19]"For thus said the LORD of Hosts concerning the columns, the tank,[d] the stands, and the rest of the vessels remaining in this city, [20]which King Nebuchadnezzar of Babylon did not take when he exiled King Jeconiah son of Jehoiakim of Judah, from Jerusalem to Babylon, with all the nobles of Judah and Jerusalem; [21]for thus said the LORD of Hosts, the God of Israel, concerning the vessels remaining in the House of the LORD, in the royal palace of Judah, and in Jerusalem: [22]They shall be brought to Babylon, and there they shall remain, until I take note of them—declares the LORD of Hosts—and bring them up and restore them to this place."

28

That year, early in the reign of King Zedekiah of Judah, in the fifth month of the fourth year, the prophet Hananiah son of Azzur, who

---

[d] Lit. "sea"; cf. 1 Kings 7.23 ff.

was from Gibeon, spoke to me in the House of the LORD, in the presence of the priests and all the people. He said: ²"Thus said the LORD of Hosts, the God of Israel: I hereby break the yoke of the king of Babylon. ³In two years, I will restore to this place all the vessels of the House of the LORD which King Nebuchadnezzar of Babylon took from this place and brought to Babylon. ⁴And I will bring back to this place King Jeconiah son of Jehoiakim of Judah, and all the Judean exiles who went to Babylon—declares the LORD. Yes, I will break the yoke of the king of Babylon."

⁵Then the prophet Jeremiah answered the prophet Hananiah in the presence of the priests and of all the people who were standing in the House of the LORD. ⁶The prophet Jeremiah said: "Amen! May the LORD do so! May the LORD fulfill what you have prophesied and bring back from Babylon to this place the vessels of the House of the LORD and all the exiles! ⁷But just listen to this word which I address to you and to all the people: ⁸The prophets who lived before you and me from ancient times prophesied war, disaster, and pestilence against many lands and great kingdoms. ⁹So if a prophet prophesies good fortune, then only when the word of the prophet comes true can it be known that the LORD really sent him."

¹⁰But the prophet Hananiah removed the bar from the neck of the prophet Jeremiah, and broke it; ¹¹and Hananiah said in the presence of all the people, "Thus said the LORD: So will I break the yoke of King Nebuchadnezzar of Babylon from off the necks of all the nations, in two years." And the prophet Jeremiah went on his way.

¹²After the prophet Hananiah had broken the bar from off the neck of the prophet Jeremiah, the word of the LORD came to Jeremiah: ¹³"Go say to Hananiah: Thus said the LORD: You broke bars of wood, but ᵃ⁻you shall⁻ᵃ make bars of iron instead. ¹⁴For thus said the LORD of Hosts, the God of Israel: I have put an iron yoke upon the necks of all those nations, that they may serve King Nebuchadnezzar of Babylon—and serve him they shall! I have even given the wild beasts to him."

¹⁵And the prophet Jeremiah said to the prophet Hananiah, "Listen, Hananiah! The LORD did not send you, and you have given this people lying assurances. ¹⁶Assuredly, thus said the LORD: I am going to banish you from off the earth. This year you shall die, for you have urged disloyalty to the LORD."

¹⁷And the prophet Hananiah died that year, in the seventh month.

ᵃ⁻ᵃ *Septuagint reads "I will."*

29

This is the text of the letter which the prophet Jeremiah sent from Jerusalem to the priests, the prophets, the rest of the elders of the exile community, and to all the people whom Nebuchadnezzar had exiled from Jerusalem to Babylon—²after King Jeconiah, the queen mother, the eunuchs, the officials of Judah and Jerusalem, and the craftsmen and smiths had left Jerusalem. ³[The letter was sent] through Elasah son of Shaphan and Gemariah son of Hilkiah, whom King Zedekiah of Judah had dispatched to Babylon, to King Nebuchadnezzar of Babylon.

⁴Thus said the LORD of Hosts, the God of Israel, to the whole community which I exiled from Jerusalem to Babylon: ⁵Build houses and live in them, plant gardens and eat their fruit. ⁶Take wives and beget sons and daughters; and take wives for your sons, and give your daughters to husbands, that they may bear sons and daughters. Multiply there, do not decrease. ⁷And seek the welfare of the city to which I have exiled you and pray to the LORD in its behalf; for in its prosperity you shall prosper.

⁸For thus said the LORD of Hosts, the God of Israel: Let not the prophets and diviners in your midst deceive you, and pay no heed to the dreams theyᵃ dream. ⁹For they prophesy to you in My name falsely; I did not send them—declares the LORD.

¹⁰For thus said the LORD: When Babylon's seventy years are over, I will take note of you, and I will fulfill to you My promise of favor—to bring you back to this place. ¹¹For I am mindful of the plans I have made concerning you—declares the LORD—plans for your welfare, not for disaster, to give you a hopeful future. ¹²When you call Me, and come and pray to Me, I will give heed to you. ¹³You will search for Me and find Me, if only you seek Me wholeheartedly. ¹⁴I will be at hand for you— declares the LORD—and I will restore your fortunes. And I will gather you from all the nations and from all the places to which I have banished you—declares the LORD—and I will bring you back to the place from which I have exiled you.

¹⁵But you say, "The LORD has raised up prophets for us in Babylon."ᵇ

¹⁶Thus said the LORD concerning the king who sits on the throne of David, and concerning all the people who dwell in this city, your brothers who did not go out with you into exile—¹⁷thus said the LORD of Hosts: I am going to let loose sword, famine, and pestilence against them and I will treat them as loathsome figs, so bad that they cannot be eaten.ᶜ ¹⁸I

ᵃ *Heb. "you."*
ᵇ *This verse is continued in vv. 20 ff.*
ᶜ *Cf. 24.1 ff.*

will pursue them with the sword, with famine, and with pestilence; and I will make them a horror to all the kingdoms of the earth, a curse and an object of horror and hissing[d] and scorn among all the nations to which I shall banish them, [19] because they did not heed My words—declares the LORD—when I persistently sent to them My servants, the prophets, and they[a] did not heed—declares the LORD.

[20]But you, the whole exile community which I banished from Jerusalem to Babylon, hear the word of the LORD! [21]Thus said the LORD of Hosts, the God of Israel, concerning Ahab son of Kolaiah and Zedekiah son of Maaseiah, who prophesy falsely to you in My name: I am going to deliver them into the hands of King Nebuchadrezzar of Babylon, and he shall put them to death before your eyes. [22]And the whole community of Judah in Babylonia shall use a curse derived from their fate: "May God make you like Zedekiah and Ahab, whom the king of Babylon consigned to the flames!"—[23]because they did vile things in Israel, committing adultery with the wives of their fellows and speaking in My name false words which I had not commanded them. I am He who knows and bears witness—declares the LORD.

[24]Concerning Shemaiah the Nehelamite you[e] shall say: [25]Thus said the LORD of Hosts, the God of Israel: Because you sent letters in your own name to all the people in Jerusalem, to Zephaniah son of Maaseiah and to the rest of the priests, as follows, [26]"The LORD appointed you priest in place of the priest Jehoiada, [f]to exercise authority[f] in the House of the LORD over every madman who wants to play the prophet, to put him into the stocks[g] and into the pillory.[g] [27]Now why have you not rebuked Jeremiah the Anathothite, who plays the prophet among you? [28]For he has actually sent a message to us in Babylon to this effect: It will be a long time. Build houses and live in them, plant gardens and enjoy their fruit."—

[29]When the priest Zephaniah read this letter in the hearing of the prophet Jeremiah, [30]the word of the LORD came to Jeremiah: [31]Send a message to the entire exile community: "Thus said the LORD concerning Shemaiah the Nehelamite: Because Shemaiah prophesied to you, though I did not send him, and made you false promises, [32]assuredly, thus said the LORD: I am going to punish Shemaiah the Nehelamite and his offspring. There shall be no man of his line dwelling among this people or seeing the good

---

d *Cf. note at 18.16.*
e *I.e., Jeremiah.*
f-f *Lit. "that there might be officials."*
g *Meaning of Heb. uncertain.*

things I am going to do for My people—declares the LORD—for he has urged disloyalty toward the LORD."

30 The word which came to Jeremiah from the LORD: ²Thus said the LORD, the God of Israel: Write down in a scroll all the words that I have spoken to you. ³For days are coming—declares the LORD—when I will restore the fortunes of My people Israel and Judah, said the LORD; and I will bring them back to the land that I gave their fathers, and they shall possess it. ⁴And these are the words that the LORD spoke concerning Israel and Judah:

⁵Thus said the LORD:
We have heard cries of panic,
Terror without relief.
⁶Ask and see:
Surely males do not bear young!
Why then do I see every man
With his hands on his loins
Like a woman in labor?
Why have all faces turned pale?
⁷Ah, that day is awesome;
There is none like it!
It is a time of trouble for Jacob,
But he shall be delivered from it.

⁸In that day—declares the LORD of Hosts—I will break the yoke from off your neck and I will rip off your bonds. Strangers shall no longer make slaves of them; ⁹instead, they shall serve the LORD their God and David, the king whom I will raise up for them.

¹⁰But you,
Have no fear, My servant Jacob

—declares the LORD—

Be not dismayed, O Israel!
I will deliver you from far away,
Your folk from their land of captivity.
And Jacob shall again have calm

And quiet with none to trouble him;
¹¹For I am with you to deliver you

—declares the LORD.

I will make an end of all the nations
Among which I have dispersed you;
But I will not make an end of you!
I will not leave you unpunished,
But will chastise you in measure.

¹²For thus said the LORD:
Your injury is incurable,
Your wound severe;
¹³ª-No one pleads for the healing of your sickness,-ª
There is no remedy, no recovery for you.
¹⁴All your lovers have forgotten you,
They do not seek you out;
For I have struck you as an enemy strikes,
With cruel chastisement,
Because your iniquity was so great
And your sins so many.
¹⁵Why cry out over your injury,
That your wound is incurable?
I did these things to you
Because your iniquity was so great
And your sins so many.

¹⁶Assuredly,
All who wanted to devour you shall be devoured,
And every one of your foes shall go into captivity;
Those who despoiled you shall be despoiled,
And all who pillaged you I will give up to pillage.
¹⁷But I will bring healing to you
And cure you of your wounds

—declares the LORD.

Though they called you "Outcast,
That Zion whom no one seeks out,"
¹⁸Thus said the LORD:

ª-ª *Meaning of Heb. uncertain.*

I will restore the fortunes of Jacob's tents
And have compassion upon his dwellings.
The city shall be rebuilt on its mound,[b]
And the fortress in its proper place.
19From them shall issue thanksgiving
And the sound of dancers.
I will multiply them,
And they shall not be few;
I will make them honored,
And they shall not be humbled.
20His children shall be as of old,
And his community shall be established by My grace;
And I will deal with all his oppressors.
21His chieftain shall be one of his own,
His ruler shall come from his midst;
I will bring him near, that he may approach Me

       —declares the LORD—

For who would otherwise dare approach Me?
22You shall be My people,
And I will be your God.

23Lo, the storm of the LORD goes forth in fury,
A raging tempest;
It shall whirl down upon the head of the wicked.
24The anger of the LORD shall not turn back
Till it has fulfilled and completed His purposes.
In the days to come
You shall perceive it.
[31]1cAt that time—declares the LORD—I will be God to all the clans
of Israel, and they shall be My people.

31
2Thus said the LORD:
The people escaped from the sword,
Found favor in the wilderness;
When Israel was marching homeward
3The LORD revealed Himself to me[a] of old.
Eternal love I conceived for you then;

---

b *I.e., on the mound of ruins left after its previous destruction.*
c *In some editions this verse is 30.25.*

a *Emendation yields "him."*

Therefore I continue My grace to you.
⁴I will build you firmly again,
O Maiden Israel!
Again you shall take up your timbrels
And go forth to the rhythm of the dancers.
⁵Again you shall plant vineyards
On the hills of Samaria;
Men shall plant and live to enjoy them.
⁶For the day is coming when watchmen
Shall proclaim on the heights of Ephraim:
Come, let us go up to Zion,
To the LORD our God!

⁷For thus said the LORD:
Cry out in joy for Jacob,
Shout at the crossroads^b of the nations!
Sing aloud in praise, and say:
^c-Save, O LORD, Your people,-^c
The remnant of Israel.
⁸I will bring them in from the northland,
Gather them from the ends of the earth—
The blind and the lame among them,
Those with child and those in labor—
In a vast throng they shall return here.
⁹They shall come with weeping,
And with compassion^d will I guide them.
I will lead them to streams of water,
By a level road where they will not stumble.
For I am ever a Father to Israel,
Ephraim is My first-born.

¹⁰Hear the word of the LORD, O nations,
And tell it in the isles afar.
Say:
He who scattered Israel will gather them,
And will guard them as a shepherd his flock.
¹¹For the LORD will ransom Jacob,
Redeem him from one too strong for him.

---

b *Lit. "head."*
c-c *Emendation yields "The LORD has saved His people."*
d *For this meaning, cf. Zech. 12.10.*

¹²They shall come and shout on the heights of Zion,
Radiant over the bounty of the LORD—
Over new grain and wine and oil,
And over sheep and cattle.
They shall fare like a watered garden,
They shall never languish again.
¹³Then shall maidens dance gaily,
Young men and old alike.
I will turn their mourning to joy,
I will comfort them and cheer them in their grief.
¹⁴I will give the priests their fill of fatness,
And My people shall enjoy My full bounty

—declares the LORD.

¹⁵Thus said the LORD:
A cry is heard ^{e-}in Ramah^{-e}—
Wailing, bitter weeping—
Rachel weeping for her children.
She refuses to be comforted
For her children, who are gone.
¹⁶Thus said the LORD:
Restrain your voice from weeping,
Your eyes from shedding tears;
For there is a reward for your labor

—declares the LORD:

They shall return from the enemy's land.
¹⁷And there is hope for your future

—declares the LORD:

Your children shall return to their country.

¹⁸I can hear Ephraim lamenting:
You have chastised me, and I am chastised
Like a calf that has not been broken.
Receive me back, let me return,
For You, O LORD, are my God.
¹⁹Now that I have turned back, I am filled with remorse;
Now that I am made aware, I strike my thigh.^f
I am ashamed and humiliated,
For I bear the disgrace of my youth.
²⁰Truly, Ephraim is a dear son to Me,

---

^{e-e} Or *"on a height."*
^f *I.e., as a gesture of self-reproach.*

A child that is dandled!
Whenever I have turned[g] against him,
My thoughts would dwell on him still.
That is why My heart yearns for him;
I will receive him back in love

—declares the LORD.

21Erect markers,
Set up signposts;[h]
Keep in mind the highway,
The road that you traveled.
Return, Maiden Israel!
Return to these towns of yours!
22How long will you waver,
O rebellious daughter?
(For the LORD has created something new on earth:
A woman courts[h] a man.)

23Thus said the LORD of Hosts, the God of Israel: They shall again say this in the land of Judah and in its towns, when I restore their fortunes:

"The LORD bless you,
Abode of righteousness,
O holy mountain!"

24Judah and all its towns alike shall be inhabited by the farmers and [i]such as move about[i] with the flocks. 25For I will give the thirsty abundant drink, and satisfy all who languish.

26At this I awoke and looked about, and my sleep[j] had been pleasant to me.

27See, a time is coming—declares the LORD—when I will sow the House of Israel and the House of Judah with seed of men and seed of cattle; 28and just as I was watchful over them to uproot and to pull down, to overthrow and to destroy and to bring disaster, so I will be watchful over them to build and to plant—declares the LORD. 29In those days, they shall no longer say, "Parents have eaten sour grapes and children's teeth are blunted."[k] 30But every one shall die for his own sins: whosoever eats sour grapes, his teeth shall be blunted.

g Lit. "spoken."
h Meaning of Heb. uncertain.
i-i Lit. "they shall travel."
j I.e., the vision in the preceding verses.
k Others "set on edge."

³¹See, a time is coming—declares the LORD—when I will make a new covenant with the House of Israel and the House of Judah. ³²It will not be like the covenant I made with their fathers, when I took them by the hand to lead them out of the land of Egypt, a covenant which they broke, though I espoused¹ them—declares the LORD. ³³But such is the covenant I will make with the House of Israel after these days—declares the LORD: I will put My Teaching into their inmost being and inscribe it upon their hearts. Then I will be their God, and they shall be My people. ³⁴No longer will they need to teach one another and say to one another, "Heed the LORD"; for all of them, from the least of them to the greatest, shall heed Me—declares the LORD.

> For I will forgive their iniquities,
> And remember their sins no more.

³⁵Thus said the LORD,
Who established the sun for light by day,
The laws of moon and stars for light by night,
Who stirs up the sea into roaring waves,
Whose name is LORD of Hosts:
³⁶If these laws should ever be annulled by Me
—declares the LORD—
Only then would the offspring of Israel cease
To be a nation before Me for all time.

³⁷Thus said the LORD: If the heavens above could be measured, and the foundations of the earth below could be fathomed, only then would I reject all the offspring of Israel for all that they have done—declares the LORD.

³⁸See, a time is coming—declares the LORD—when the city shall be rebuilt for the LORD from the Tower of Hananel to the Corner Gate; ³⁹and the measuring line shall go straight out to the Gareb Hill, and then turn toward Goah. ⁴⁰And the entire Valley of the Corpses and Ashes, and all the fields as far as the Wadi Kidron, and the corner of the Horse Gate on the east, shall be holy to the LORD. They shall never again be uprooted or overthrown.

¹ *Meaning of Heb. uncertain; compare 3.14.*

32 The word which came to Jeremiah from the LORD in the tenth year of King Zedekiah of Judah, which was the eighteenth year of Nebuchadrezzar. ²At that time the army of the king of Babylon was besieging Jerusalem, and the prophet Jeremiah was confined in the prison compound attached to the palace of the king of Judah. ³For King Zedekiah of Judah had confined him, saying, "How dare you prophesy: 'Thus said the LORD: I am delivering this city into the hands of the king of Babylon, and he shall capture it. ⁴And King Zedekiah of Judah shall not escape from the Chaldeans; he shall be delivered into the hands of the king of Babylon, ᵃ⁻and he shall speak to him face to face and see him in person.⁻ᵃ ⁵And Zedekiah shall be brought to Babylon, there to remain until I take note of him—declares the LORD. When you wage war against the Chaldeans, you shall not be successful.' "

⁶Jeremiah said: The word of the LORD came to me: ⁷Hanamel, the son of your uncle Shallum, will come to you and say, "Buy my land in Anathoth, ᵇ⁻for you are next in succession to redeem it by purchase."⁻ᵇ ⁸And just as the LORD had said, my cousin Hanamel came to me in the prison compound and said to me, "Please buy my land in Anathoth, in the territory of Benjamin; for the right of succession is yours, and you have the duty of redemption. Buy it." Then I knew that it was indeed the word of the LORD.

⁹So I bought the land in Anathoth from my cousin Hanamel. I weighed out the money to him, seventeen shekels of silver. ¹⁰I wrote a deed, sealed it, and had it witnessed; and I weighed out the silver on a balance. ¹¹I took the deed of purchase, the sealed text and the open one ᶜ⁻according to rule and law,⁻ᶜ ¹²and gave the deed to Baruch son of Neriah son of Mahseiah in the presence of my kinsman Hanamel, of the witnesses ᵈ⁻who were named⁻ᵈ in the deed, and all the Judeans who were sitting in the prison compound. ¹³In their presence I charged Baruch as follows: ¹⁴Thus said the LORD of Hosts, the God of Israel: "Take these documents, this deed of purchase, the sealed text and the open one, and put them into an earthen jar, so that they may last a long time." ¹⁵For thus said the LORD of Hosts, the God of Israel: "Houses, fields, and vineyards shall again be purchased in this land."

¹⁶But after I had given the deed to Baruch son of Neriah, I prayed to

---

ᵃ⁻ᵃ Lit. "and his mouth shall speak with his mouth, and his eyes shall see his eyes."
ᵇ⁻ᵇ Lit. "for yours is the procedure of redemption by purchase."
ᶜ⁻ᶜ Force of Heb. uncertain.
ᵈ⁻ᵈ With many mss. and ancient versions; so ancient Near Eastern practice. Other mss. and the editions read "who wrote" (i.e., signed their names).

the LORD: 17"Ah, Lord GOD! You made heaven and earth with Your great might and outstretched arm. Nothing is too wondrous for You! 18You show kindness to the thousandth generation, but visit the guilt of the fathers upon their children after them. O great and mighty God whose name is LORD of Hosts, 19wondrous in purpose and mighty in deed, whose eyes observe all the ways of men, so as to repay every man according to his ways, and with the proper fruit of his deeds! 20You displayed signs and marvels in the land of Egypt e-with lasting effect,-e and won renown in Israel and among mankind to this very day. 21You freed Your people Israel from the land of Egypt with signs and marvels, with a strong hand and an outstretched arm, and with great terror. 22You gave them this land that You had sworn to their fathers to give them, a land flowing with milk and honey, 23and they came and took possession of it. But they did not listen to You or follow Your Teaching; they did nothing of what You commanded them to do. Therefore you have caused all this misfortune to befall them. 24Here are the siegemounds, raised against the city to storm it; and the city, because of sword and famine and pestilence, is at the mercy of the Chaldeans who are attacking it. What You threatened has come to pass—as You see. 25Yet You, Lord GOD, said to me: Buy the land for money and call in witnesses—when the city is at the mercy of the Chaldeans!"

26Then the word of the LORD came to Jeremiah: 27"Behold I am the LORD, the God of all flesh. Is anything too wondrous for Me? 28Assuredly, thus said the LORD: I am delivering this city into the hands of the Chaldeans and of King Nebuchadrezzar of Babylon, and he shall capture it. 29And the Chaldeans who have been attacking this city shall come and set this city on fire and burn it down—with the houses on whose roofs they made offerings to Baal and poured out libations to other gods, so as to vex Me. 30For the people of Israel and Judah have done nothing but evil in My sight since their youth; the people of Israel have done nothing but vex Me by their conduct—declares the LORD. 31This city has aroused My anger and My wrath from the day it was built until this day; so that it must be removed from My sight 32because of all the wickedness of the people of Israel and Judah who have so acted as to vex Me—they, their kings, their officials, their priests and prophets, and the men of Judah and the inhabitants of Jerusalem. 33They turned their backs to Me, not their faces; though I have taught them persistently, they

e-e Lit. "to this day."

do not give heed or accept rebuke. ³⁴They placed their abominations in the House which bears My name and defiled it; ³⁵and they built the shrines of Baal which are in the Valley of Ben-hinnom, where they offered up their sons and daughters to Molech—when I had never commanded, or even thought [of commanding], that they should do such an abominable thing, and so bring guilt on Judah.

³⁶But now, assuredly, thus said the LORD, the God of Israel, concerning this city of which you say, "It is being delivered into the hands of the king of Babylon through the sword, through famine, and through pestilence": ³⁷See, I will gather them from all the lands to which I have banished them in My anger and wrath, and in great rage; and I will bring them back to this place and let them dwell secure. ³⁸They shall be My people, and I will be their God. ³⁹I will give them a single heart and a single nature to revere Me for all time, and it shall be well with them and their children after them. ⁴⁰And I will make an everlasting covenant with them that I will not turn away from them and that I will treat them graciously; and I will put into their hearts reverence for Me, so that they do not turn away from Me. ⁴¹I will delight in treating them graciously, and I will plant them in this land faithfully, with all My heart and soul.

⁴²For thus said the LORD: As I have brought this terrible disaster upon this people, so I am going to bring upon them the vast good fortune which I have promised for them. ⁴³And fields shall again be purchased in this land of which you say, "It is a desolation, without man or beast; it is delivered into the hands of the Chaldeans."

⁴⁴Fields shall be purchased, and deeds written and sealed, and witnesses called in the land of Benjamin and in the environs of Jerusalem, and in the towns of Judah; the towns of the hill country, the towns of the Shephelah, and the towns of the Negeb. For I will restore their fortunes— declares the LORD.

33

The word of the LORD came to Jeremiah a second time, while he was still confined in the prison compound, as follows:

²Thus said the LORD who is planning it,
The LORD who is shaping it to bring it about,

Whose name is LORD:
³Call to Me, and I will answer you,
And I will tell you wondrous things,
Secrets you have not known.

⁴For thus said the LORD, the God of Israel, concerning the houses of this city and the palaces of the kings of Judah that were torn down ᵃ⁻for [defense] against the siegemounds and against the sword, ⁵and were filled by those who went to fight the Chaldeans,⁻ᵃ—with the corpses of the men whom I struck down in My anger and rage, hiding My face from this city because of all their wickedness: ⁶I am going to bring her relief and healing. I will heal them and reveal to them abundanceᵃ of true favor. ⁷And I will restore the fortunes of Judah and Israel, and I will rebuild them as of old. ⁸And I will purge them of all the sins which they committed against Me, and I will pardon all the sins which they committed against Me, by which they rebelled against Me. ⁹And she shall gain through Me renown, joy, fame, and glory above all the nations on earth, when they hear of all the good fortune I provide for them.ᵇ They will thrill and quiver because of all the good fortune and all the prosperity that I provide for her.

¹⁰Thus said the LORD: Again there shall be heard in this place, which you say is ruined, without man or beast—in the towns of Judah and the streets of Jerusalem that are desolate, without man, without inhabitants, without beast—¹¹the sound of mirth and gladness, the voice of bridegroom and bride, the voice of those who cry, "Give thanks to the LORD of Hosts, for the LORD is good, for His kindness is everlasting!" as they bring thanksgiving offerings to the House of the LORD. For I will restore the fortunes of the land as of old—said the LORD.

¹²Thus said the LORD of Hosts: In this ruined place, without man and beast, and in all its towns, there shall again be a pasture for shepherds, where they can rest their flocks. ¹³In the towns of the hill country, in the towns of the Shephelah, and in the towns of the Negeb, in the land of Benjamin and in the environs of Jerusalem and in the towns of Judah, sheep shall pass again under the hands of one who counts them—said the LORD. ¹⁴See, days are coming—declares the LORD—when I will fulfill the promise that I made concerning the House of Israel and the House of Judah. ¹⁵In those days and at that time, I will raise up a true branch of David's line, and he shall do what is just and right in the land. ¹⁶In those days Judah shall be delivered and Israel shall dwell secure. And this is what she shall be called: "The LORD is our Vindicator." ¹⁷For thus said

---

ᵃ⁻ᵃ *Meaning of Heb. uncertain.*
ᵇ *I.e., for Judah and Israel.*

the LORD: There shall never be an end to men of David's line who sit upon the throne of the House of Israel. ¹⁸Nor shall there ever be an end to the line of the levitical priests before Me, of those who present burnt offerings and turn the meal offering to smoke and perform sacrifices.

¹⁹The word of the LORD came to Jeremiah: ²⁰Thus said the LORD: If you could break My covenant with the day and My covenant with the night, so that day and night should not come at their proper time, ²¹only then could My covenant with My servant David be broken—so that he would not have a descendant reigning upon his throne—or with My ministrants, the levitical priests. ²²Like the host of heaven which cannot be counted, and the sand of the sea which cannot be measured, so will I multiply the offspring of My servant David, and of the Levites who minister to Me.

²³The word of the LORD came to Jeremiah: ²⁴You see what this people said: "The two families which the LORD chose have now been rejected by Him." Thus they despise My people, ᵃ⁻and regard them as no longer a nation.⁻ᵃ ²⁵Thus said the LORD: As surely as I have established My covenant with day and night—the laws of heaven and earth—²⁶so I will never reject the offspring of Jacob and My servant David; I will never fail to take from his offspring rulers for the descendants of Abraham, Isaac, and Jacob. Indeed, I will restore their fortunes and take them back in love.

34 The word which came to Jeremiah from the LORD, when King Nebuchadrezzar of Babylon and all his army, and all the kingdoms of the earth and all the peoples under his sway, were waging war against Jerusalem and all its towns:

²Thus said the LORD, the God of Israel: Go speak to King Zedekiah of Judah, and say to him: "Thus said the LORD: I am going to deliver this city into the hands of the king of Babylon, and he will destroy it by fire. ³And you will not escape from him; you will be captured and handed over to him. ᵃ⁻And you will see the king of Babylon face to face and speak to him in person;⁻ᵃ and you will be brought to Babylon. ⁴But hear the word of the LORD, O King Zedekiah of Judah! Thus said the LORD concerning you: You will not die by the sword. ⁵You will die a peaceful

---

ᵃ⁻ᵃ *For the idiom see note at 32.4.*

death; and as incense[b] was burned for your ancestors, the earlier kings who preceded you, so they will burn incense[b] for you, and they will lament for you 'Ah, lord!' For I Myself have made the promise—declares the LORD."

[6] The prophet Jeremiah spoke all these words to King Zedekiah of Judah in Jerusalem, [7] when the army of the king of Babylon was waging war against Jerusalem and against the remaining towns of Judah—against Lachish and Azekah, for they were the only fortified towns of Judah that were left.

[8] The word which came to Jeremiah from the LORD after King Zedekiah had made a covenant with all the people in Jerusalem to proclaim a release[c] among them—[9] that everyone should set free his Hebrew slaves, both male and female, and that no one should keep his fellow Judean enslaved.

[10] Everyone, officials and people, who had entered into the covenant agreed to set their male and female slaves free and not keep them enslaved any longer; they complied and let them go. [11] But afterward they turned about and brought back the men and women they had set free, and forced them into slavery again. [12] Then it was that the word of the LORD came to Jeremiah from the LORD:

[13] Thus said the LORD, the God of Israel: I made a covenant with your fathers when I brought them out of the land of Egypt, the house of bondage, saying: [14] "In the seventh year[d] each of you must let go any fellow Hebrew [e-]who may be sold[-e] to you; when he has served you six years, you must set him free." But your fathers would not obey Me or give ear. [15] Lately you turned about and did what is proper in My sight, and each of you proclaimed a release to his countrymen; and you made a covenant accordingly before Me in the House which bears My name. [16] But now you have turned back and have profaned My name; each of you has brought back the men and women whom you had given their freedom, and forced them to be your slaves again.

[17] Assuredly, thus said the LORD: You would not obey Me and proclaim a release, each to his kinsman and countryman. Lo! I proclaim your release—declares the LORD—to the sword, to pestilence, and to famine; and I will make you a horror to all the kingdoms of the earth. [18] I will make the men who violated My covenant, who did not fulfill the terms of the covenant which they made before Me, [like] the calf which they

b *Lit. "burnings."*
c *Others "liberty."*
d *I.e., of servitude. Lit. "After a period of seven years"; cf. Deut. 14.28 and 15.1.*
e-e *Or "who sells himself."*

cut in two so as to pass between the halves:[f] 19The officers of Judah and Jerusalem, the officials, the priests, and all the people of the land who passed between the halves of the calf 20shall be handed over to their enemies, to those who seek to kill them. Their carcasses shall become food for the birds of the sky and the beasts of the earth. 21I will hand over King Zedekiah of Judah and his officers to their enemies, who seek to kill them—to the army of the king of Babylon which has withdrawn from you. 22I hereby give the command—declares the LORD—by which I will bring them back against this city. They shall attack it and capture it, and burn it down. I will make the towns of Judah a desolation, without inhabitant.

35

The word which came to Jeremiah from the LORD in the days of King Jehoiakim son of Josiah of Judah:

2Go to the house of the Rechabites and speak to them, and bring them to the House of the LORD, to one of the chambers, and give them wine to drink.

3So I took Jaazaniah son of Jeremiah son of Habazziniah, and his brothers, all his sons, and the whole household of the Rechabites; 4and I brought them to the House of the LORD, to the chamber of the sons of Hanan son of Igdaliah, the man of God, which is next to the chamber of the officials and above the chamber of Maaseiah son of Shallum, the guardian of the threshold. 5I set bowls full of wine and cups before the men of the house of the Rechabites, and said to them, "Have some wine."

6They replied, "We will not drink wine, for our ancestor, Jonadab son of Rechab, commanded us: 'You shall never drink wine, either you or your children. 7Nor shall you build houses or sow fields[a] or plant vineyards, nor shall you own such things; but you shall live in tents all your days, so that you may live long upon the land where you sojourn.' 8And we have obeyed our ancestor Jonadab son of Rechab in all that he commanded us: we never drink wine, neither we nor our wives nor our sons and daughters. 9Nor do we build houses to live in, and we do not own vineyards or fields for sowing; 10but we live in tents. We have obeyed and done all that our ancestor Jonadab commanded us. 11But when King Nebuchadrezzar of Babylon invaded the country, we said, 'Come, let us go into Jerusalem because of the army of the Chaldeans and the army of Aram.' And so we are living in Jerusalem."

f Cf. Gen. 15.9–10, 17–21.
a Lit. "seed."

12Then the word of the Lord came to Jeremiah:

13Thus said the LORD of Hosts, the God of Israel: Go say to the men of Judah and the inhabitants of Jerusalem: "You can learn a lesson [here] about obeying My commands—declares the LORD. 14The commands of Jonadab son of Rechab have been fulfilled: he charged his children not to drink wine, and to this day they have not drunk, in obedience to the charge of their ancestor. But I spoke to you persistently, and you did not listen to Me. 15I persistently sent you all My servants, the prophets, to say: 'Turn back, every one of you, from your wicked ways and mend your deeds; do not follow other gods or serve them. Then you may remain on the land that I gave to you and your fathers.' But you did not give ear or listen to Me. 16The family of Jonadab son of Rechab have indeed fulfilled the charge which their ancestor gave them; but this people has not listened to Me. 17Assuredly, thus said the LORD, the God of Hosts, the God of Israel: I am going to bring upon Judah and upon all the inhabitants of Jerusalem all the disaster with which I have threatened them; for I spoke to them, but they would not listen; I called to them, but they would not respond."

18And to the family of the Rechabites Jeremiah said: "Thus said the LORD of Hosts, the God of Israel: Because you have obeyed the charge of your ancestor Jonadab and kept all his commandments, and done all that he enjoined upon you, 19assuredly, thus said the LORD of Hosts, the God of Israel: There shall never cease to be a man of the line of Jonadab son of Rechab standing before Me."

36 In the fourth year of King Jehoiakim son of Josiah of Judah, this word came to Jeremiah from the LORD:

2Get a scroll and write upon it all the words that I have spoken to you—concerning Israel and Judah and all the nations—from the time I first spoke to you in the days of Josiah to this day. 3Perhaps when the House of Judah hear of all the disasters I intend to bring upon them, they will turn back from their wicked ways, and I will pardon their iniquity and their sin. 4So Jeremiah called Baruch son of Neriah; and Baruch wrote down in the scroll, at Jeremiah's dictation, all the words which the LORD had spoken to him.

5Jeremiah instructed Baruch, "I am in hiding; I cannot go to the House of the LORD. 6But you go and read aloud the words of the LORD from the scroll which you wrote at my dictation, to all the people in the House of the LORD on a fast day; thus you will also be reading them to all the Judeans who come in from the towns. 7Perhaps their entreaty will be accepted by the LORD, if they turn back from their wicked ways. For great is the anger and wrath with which the LORD has threatened this people."

8Baruch son of Neriah did just as the prophet Jeremiah had instructed him, about reading the words of the LORD from the scroll in the House of the LORD. 9In the ninth month of the fifth year of King Jehoiakim son of Josiah of Judah, all the people in Jerusalem and all the people coming from Judah proclaimed a fast before the LORD in Jerusalem. 10It was then that Baruch—in the chamber of Gemariah son of Shaphan the scribe, in the upper court, near the new gateway of the House of the LORD—read the words of Jeremiah from the scroll to all the people in the House of the LORD.

11Micaiah son of Gemariah son of Shaphan heard all the words of the LORD [read] from the scroll, 12and he went down to the king's palace, to the chamber of the scribe. There he found all the officials in session: Elishama the scribe, Delaiah son of Shemaiah, Elnathan son of Achbor, Gemariah son of Shaphan, Zedekiah son of Hananiah, and all the other officials. 13And Micaiah told them all that he had heard as Baruch read from the scroll in the hearing of the people.

14Then all the officials sent Jehudi son of Nethaniah son of Shelemiah son of Cushi to say to Baruch, "Take that scroll from which you read to the people, and come along!" And Baruch took the scroll and came to them.

15They said, a-"Sit down and read it-a to us." And Baruch read it to them. 16When they heard all these words, they turned to each other in fear; and they said to Baruch, "We must report all this to the king."

17And they questioned Baruch further, "Tell us how you wrote down all these words b-that he spoke."-b 18He answered them, "He himself recited all those words to me, and I would write them down in the scroll in ink."

19The officials said to Baruch, "Go into hiding, you and Jeremiah. Let no man know where you are!" 20And they went to the king in the court, after leaving the scroll in the chamber of the scribe Elishama. And they reported all these matters to the king.

a-a *Change of vocalization yields "Read it again"; cf. Targum and Septuagint.*
b-b *Force of Heb. uncertain.*

21The king sent Jehudi to get the scroll and he fetched it from the chamber of the scribe Elishama. Jehudi read it to the king and to all the officials who were in attendance on the king. 22Since it was the ninth month, the king was sitting in the winter house, with a fire burning in the brazier before him. 23And every time Jehudi read three or four columns, [the king] would cut it up with a scribe's knife and throw it into the fire in the brazier, until the entire scroll was consumed by the fire in the brazier. 24Yet the king and all his courtiers who heard all these words showed no fear and did not tear their garments; 25moreover, Elnathan, Delaiah, and Gemariah begged the king not to burn the scroll, but he would not listen to them.

26The king ordered Jerahmeel, the king's son, and Seraiah son of Azriel, and Shelemiah son of Abdeel to arrest the scribe Baruch and the prophet Jeremiah. But the LORD hid them.

27The word of the LORD came to Jeremiah after the king had burned the scroll containing the words that Baruch had written at Jeremiah's dictation: 28Get yourself another scroll, and write upon it the same words that were in the first scroll that was burned by King Jehoiakim of Judah. 29And concerning King Jehoiakim of Judah you shall say: Thus said the LORD: You burned that scroll, saying, "How dare you write in it that the king of Babylon will come and destroy this land and cause man and beast to cease from it?" 30Assuredly, thus said the LORD concerning King Jehoiakim of Judah: He shall not have any of his line sitting on the throne of David; and his own corpse shall be left exposed to the heat by day and the cold by night. 31And I will punish him and his offspring and his courtiers for their iniquity; I will bring on them and on the inhabitants of Jerusalem and on all the men of Judah all the disasters of which I have warned them—but they would not listen.

32So Jeremiah got another scroll and gave it to the scribe Baruch son of Neriah. And at Jeremiah's dictation, he wrote in it the whole text of the scroll that King Jehoiakim of Judah had burned; and more of the like was added.

37 Zedekiah son of Josiah became king instead of Coniah son of Jehoiakim, for King Nebuchadrezzar of Babylon set him up as king over the land of Judah. 2Neither he nor his courtiers nor the people of the land gave heed to the words which the LORD spoke through the prophet Jeremiah.

³Yet King Zedekiah sent Jehucal son of Shelemiah and Zephaniah son of the priest Maaseiah to the prophet Jeremiah, to say, "Please pray on our behalf to the LORD our God." (⁴Jeremiah could still go in and out among the people, for they had not yet put him in prison. ⁵The army of Pharaoh had set out from Egypt; and when the Chaldeans who were besieging Jerusalem heard the report, they raised the siege of Jerusalem.)

⁶Then the word of the LORD came to the prophet Jeremiah: ⁷Thus said the LORD, the God of Israel: Thus shall you say to the king of Judah who sent you to Me to inquire of Me: "The army of Pharaoh, which set out to help you, will return to its own land, to Egypt. ⁸And the Chaldeans will come back and attack this city and they will capture it and destroy it by fire."

⁹Thus said the LORD: Do not delude yourselves into thinking, "The Chaldeans will go away from us." They will not. ¹⁰Even if you defeated the whole army of the Chaldeans that are fighting against you, and only wounded men were left lying in their tents, they would get up and burn this city down!

¹¹When the army of the Chaldeans raised the siege of Jerusalem on account of the army of Pharaoh, ¹²Jeremiah was going to leave Jerusalem and go to the territory of Benjamin ᵃ⁻to share in some property there⁻ᵃ among the people. ¹³When he got to the Benjamin Gate, there was a guard officer there named Irijah son of Shelemiah son of Hananiah; and he arrested the prophet Jeremiah, saying, "You are defecting to the Chaldeans!" ¹⁴Jeremiah answered, "That's a lie! I'm not defecting to the Chaldeans!" But Irijah would not listen to him; he arrested Jeremiah and brought him to the officials. ¹⁵The officials were furious with Jeremiah; they beat him and put him into prison, in the house of the scribe Jonathan—for it had been made into a jail. ¹⁶Thus Jeremiah came to the ᵃ⁻pit and the cells,⁻ᵃ and Jeremiah remained there a long time.

¹⁷Then King Zedekiah sent for him, and the king questioned him secretly in his palace. He asked, "Is there any word from the LORD?" "There is!" Jeremiah answered, and he continued, "You will be delivered into the hands of the king of Babylon." ¹⁸And Jeremiah said to King Zedekiah, "What wrong have I done to you, to your courtiers, and to this people,

---

ᵃ⁻ᵃ *Meaning of Heb. uncertain.*

that you have put me in jail? ¹⁹And where are those prophets of yours who prophesied to you that the king of Babylon would never move against you and against this land? ²⁰Now, please hear me, O lord king, and grant my plea: Don't send me back to the house of the scribe Jonathan ᵇ⁻to die there."⁻ᵇ

²¹So King Zedekiah gave instructions to lodge Jeremiah in the prison compound and to supply him daily with a loaf of bread from the Bakers' Street—until all the bread in the city was gone. Jeremiah remained in the prison compound.

38

Shephatiah son of Mattan, Gedaliah son of Pashhur, Jucal son of Shelemiah, and Pashhur son of Malchiah heard what Jeremiah was saying to all the people: ²"Thus said the LORD: Whoever remains in this city shall die by the sword, by famine, and by pestilence; but whoever surrenders to the Chaldeans shall live; ᵃ⁻he shall at least gain his life⁻ᵃ and shall live. ³Thus said the LORD: This city shall be delivered into the hands of the king of Babylon's army, and he shall capture it."

⁴Then the officials said to the king, "Let that man be put to death, for he disheartensᵇ the soldiers, and all the people who are left in this city, by speaking such things to them. That man is not seeking the welfare of this people, but their harm!" ⁵King Zedekiah replied, "He is in your hands; the king cannot oppose you in anything!"

⁶So they took Jeremiah and put him down in the pit of Malchiah, the king's son, which was in the prison compound; they let Jeremiah down by ropes. There was no water in the pit, only mud, and Jeremiah sank into the mud.

⁷Ebed-melech the Cushite, a eunuch who was in the king's palace, heard that they had put Jeremiah in the pit. The king was then sitting at the Benjamin Gate; ⁸so Ebed-melech left the king's palace, and spoke to the king: ⁹"O lord king, those men have acted wickedly in all they did to the prophet Jeremiah; they have put him down in the pit, to die there of hunger." For there was no more bread in the city.

¹⁰Then the king instructed Ebed-melech the Cushite, "Take with you thirtyᶜ men from here, and pull the prophet Jeremiah up from the pit before he dies." ¹¹So Ebed-melech took the men with him, and went to the king's palace, to ᵈ⁻a place below⁻ᵈ the treasury. There they got worn cloths and rags, which they let down to Jeremiah in the pit by ropes.

ᵇ⁻ᵇ Lit. "and let me not die there."

ᵃ⁻ᵃ Lit. "he shall have his life as booty"; cf. 21.9.
ᵇ Lit. "weakens the hands of."
ᶜ One ms. reads "three."
ᵈ⁻ᵈ Emendation yields "the wardrobe of."

¹²And Ebed-melech the Cushite called to Jeremiah, "Put the worn cloths and rags under your armpits, inside the ropes." Jeremiah did so, ¹³and they pulled Jeremiah up by the ropes and got him out of the pit. And Jeremiah remained in the prison compound.

¹⁴King Zedekiah sent for the prophet Jeremiah, and had him brought to him at the third entrance of the House of the LORD. And the king said to Jeremiah, "I want to ask you something; don't conceal anything from me."

¹⁵Jeremiah answered the king, "If I tell you, you'll surely kill me; and if I give you advice, you won't listen to me."

¹⁶Thereupon King Zedekiah secretly promised Jeremiah on oath: "As the LORD lives who has ᶜ⁻given us this life,⁻ᶜ I will not put you to death or leave you in the hands of those men who seek your life."

¹⁷Then Jeremiah said to Zedekiah, "Thus said the LORD, the God of Hosts, the God of Israel: If you surrender to the officers of the king of Babylon, your life will be spared and this city will not be burned down. You and your household will live. ¹⁸But if you do not surrender to the officers of the king of Babylon, this city will be delivered into the hands of the Chaldeans, who will burn it down; and you will not escape from them."

¹⁹King Zedekiah said to Jeremiah, "I am worried about the Judeans who have defected to the Chaldeans; that they [the Chaldeans] might hand me over to them to abuse me."

²⁰"They will not hand you over," Jeremiah replied. "Listen to the voice of the LORD, to what I tell you, that it may go well with you and your life be spared. ²¹For this is what the LORD has shown me if you refuse to surrender: ²²All the women who are left in the palace of the king of Judah shall be brought out to the officers of the king of Babylon; and they shall say:

> The men who were your friends
> Have seduced you and vanquished you.
> Now that your feet are sunk in the mire,
> They have turned their backs [on you].

²³They will bring out all your wives and children to the Chaldeans, and

ᶜ⁻ᶜ *Meaning of Heb. uncertain.*

you yourself will not escape from them. You will be captured by the king of Babylon, and f-this city shall be burned down."-f

24Zedekiah said to Jeremiah, "Don't let anyone know about this conversation, g-or you will die.-g 25If the officials should hear that I have spoken with you, and they should come and say to you, 'Tell us what you said to the king; hide nothing from us, h-or we'll kill you.-h And what did the king say to you?' 26say to them, 'I was presenting my petition to the king not to send me back to the house of Jonathan to die there.' "

27All the officials did come to Jeremiah to question him; and he replied to them just as the king had instructed him. So they stopped questioning him, for the conversation had not been overheard. 28Jeremiah remained in the prison compound until the day Jerusalem was captured.

When Jerusalem was captured . . .i

39 In the ninth year of King Zedekiah of Judah, in the tenth month, King Nebuchadrezzar of Babylon moved against Jerusalem with his whole army, and they laid siege to it. 2And in the eleventh year of Zedekiah, on the ninth day of the fourth month, the [walls of] the city were breached. 3All the officers of the king of Babylon entered, and took up quarters at the middle gate—Nergal-sarezer, Samgar-nebo, Sarsechim the Rab-saris,a Nergal-sarezer the Rab-mag,a and all the rest of the officers of the king of Babylon.

4When King Zedekiah of Judah saw them, he and all the soldiers fled. They left the city at night, by way of the king's garden, through the gate between the double walls; and he set out toward the Arabah.b 5But the Chaldean troops pursued them, and they overtook Zedekiah in the steppes of Jericho. They captured him and brought him before King Nebuchadrezzar of Babylon at Riblah in the region of Hamath; and he put him on trial. 6The king of Babylon had Zedekiah's children slaughtered at Riblah before his eyes; the king of Babylon had all the nobles of Judah slaughtered. 7Then the eyes of Zedekiah were put out and he was chained in bronze fetters, that he might be brought to Babylon.

8The Chaldeans burned down the king's palace and the housesc of the people by fire, and they tore down the walls of Jerusalem. 9The remnant

---

f-f *So Targum and Septuagint and some mss. Most mss. and the editions read "you will burn down this city by fire."*
g-g *Lit. "that you may not die."*
h-h *Lit. "that we may not kill you."*
i *This clause would read well before 39.3.*

a *Titles of officers.*
b *Hoping to escape across the Jordan.*
c *Taking Heb. singular as collective, with Kimhi.*

of the people that was left in the city, and the defectors who had gone over to him—the remnant of the people that was left—were exiled by Nebuzaradan, the chief of the guards, to Babylon. [10]But some of the poorest people who owned nothing were left in the land of Judah by Nebuzaradan, the chief of the guards, and he gave them vineyards and fields at that time.

[11]King Nebuchadrezzar of Babylon had given orders to Nebuzaradan, the chief of the guards, concerning Jeremiah: [12]"Take him and look after him; do him no harm, but grant whatever he asks of you." [13]So Nebuzaradan, the chief of the guards, and Nebushazban the Rab-saris, and Nergal-sarezer the Rab-mag, and all the commanders of the king of Babylon sent [14]and had Jeremiah brought from the prison compound. They committed him to the care of Gedaliah son of Ahikam son of Shaphan, [d-]that he might be left at liberty in a house.[-d] So he dwelt among the people.

[15]The word of the LORD had come to Jeremiah while he was still confined in the prison compound: [16]Go and say to Ebed-melech the Ethiopian: "Thus said the LORD of Hosts, the God of Israel: I am going to fulfill My words concerning this city—for disaster, not for good—and they shall come true on that day in your presence. [17]But I will save you on that day—declares the LORD; you shall not be delivered into the hands of the men you dread. [18]I will rescue you, and you shall not fall by the sword. [e-]You shall escape with your life,[-e] because you trusted Me—declares the LORD."

40 The word that came to Jeremiah from the LORD, after Nebuzaradan, the chief of the guards, set him free at Ramah, to which he had taken him, chained in fetters, among those from Jerusalem and Judah who were being exiled to Babylon.

[2]The chief of the guards took charge of Jeremiah, and he said to him, "The LORD your God threatened this place with this disaster; [3]and now the LORD has brought it about. He has acted as He threatened, because you sinned against the LORD and did not obey Him. That is why this has happened to you. [4]Now, I release you this day from the fetters which

---

[d-d] *Meaning of Heb. uncertain.*
[e-e] *See note at 38.2.*

were on your hands. If you would like to go with me to Babylon, come, and I will look after you. And if you don't want to come with me to Babylon, you need not. See, the whole land is before you: go wherever seems good and right to you."—⁵ᵃ⁻But [Jeremiah] still did not turn back.⁻ᵃ—"Or go to Gedaliah son of Ahikam son of Shaphan, whom the king of Babylon has put in charge of the towns of Judah, and stay with him among the people, or go wherever you want to go."

The chief of the guards gave him an allowance of food, and dismissed him. ⁶So Jeremiah came to Gedaliah son of Ahikam at Mizpah, and stayed with him among the people who were left in the land.

⁷The officers of the troops in the open country, and their men with them, heard that the king of Babylon had put Gedaliah son of Ahikam in charge of the region, and that he had put in his charge the men, women, and children—of the poorest in the land—those who had not been exiled to Babylon. ⁸So they with their men came to Gedaliah at Mizpah—Ishmael son of Nethaniah; Johanan and Jonathan the sons of Kareah; Seraiah son of Tanhumeth; the sons of Ephai the Netophathite; and Jezaniah son of the Maacathite. ⁹Gedaliah son of Ahikam son of Shaphan reassuredᵇ them and their men, saying, "Do not be afraid to serve the Chaldeans. Stay in the land and serve the king of Babylon, and it will go well with you. ¹⁰I am going to stay in Mizpah to attend upon the Chaldeans who will come to us. But you may gather wine and figsᶜ and oil and put them in your own vessels, and settle in the towns you have occupied."

¹¹Likewise, all the Judeans who were in Moab, Ammon, and Edom, or who were in other lands, heard that the king of Babylon had let a remnant stay in Judah, and that he had put Gedaliah son of Ahikam son of Shaphan in charge of them. ¹²All these Judeans returned from all the places to which they had scattered. They came to the land of Judah, to Gedaliah at Mizpah, and they gathered large quantities of wine and figs.ᶜ

¹³Johanan son of Kareah, and all the officers of the troops in the open country, came to Gedaliah at Mizpah ¹⁴and said to him, "Do you know that King Baalis of Ammon has sent Ishmael son of Nethaniah to kill you?" But Gedaliah son of Ahikam would not believe them. ¹⁵Johanan son of Kareah also said secretly to Gedaliah at Mizpah, "Let me go and

---

ᵃ⁻ᵃ *Meaning of Heb. uncertain.*
ᵇ *Lit. "swore to."*
ᶜ *Lit. "summer fruit."*

strike down Ishmael son of Nethaniah before anyone knows about it; otherwise he will kill you, and all the Judeans who have gathered about you will be dispersed, and the remnant of Judah will perish!"

¹⁶But Gedaliah son of Ahikam answered Johanan son of Kareah, "Do not do such a thing: what you are saying about Ishmael is not true!"

41 In the seventh month, Ishmael son of Nethaniah son of Elishama, who was of royal descent and one of the king's commanders, came with ten men to Gedaliah son of Ahikam at Mizpah; and they ate together there at Mizpah. ²Then Ishmael son of Nethaniah and the ten men who were with him arose and struck down Gedaliah son of Ahikam son of Shaphan with the sword and killed him, because the king of Babylon had put him in charge of the land. ³Ishmael also killed all the Judeans who were with him—with Gedaliah in Mizpah—and the Chaldean soldiers who were stationed there.

⁴The second day after Gedaliah was killed, when no one yet knew about it, ⁵eighty men came from Shechem, Shiloh, and Samaria, their beards shaved, their garments torn, and their bodies gashed, carrying meal offerings and frankincense to present at the House of the LORD. ⁶Ishmael son of Nethaniah went out from Mizpah to meet them, weeping as he walked. As he met them, he said to them, "Come to Gedaliah son of Ahikam." ⁷When they came inside the town, Ishmael son of Nethaniah and the men who were with him slaughtered them [and threw their bodies] into a cistern.

⁸But there were ten men among them who said to Ishmael, "Don't kill us! We have stores hidden in a field—wheat, barley, oil, and honey." So he stopped, and did not kill them along with their fellows.— ⁹The cistern into which Ishmael threw all the corpses of the men he had killed ᵃ-in the affair of Gedaliah was the one thatᵃ King Asa had constructed on account of King Baasha of Israel. That was the one which Ishmael son of Nethaniah filled with corpses.— ¹⁰Ishmael carried off all the rest of the people who were in Mizpah, including the daughters of the king—all the people left in Mizpah, over whom Nebuzaradan, the chief of the guards, had appointed Gedaliah son of Ahikam. Ishmael son of Nethaniah carried them off, and set out to cross over to the Ammonites.

¹¹Johanan son of Kareah, and all the army officers with him, heard of all the crimes committed by Ishmael son of Nethaniah. ¹²They took all

---

ᵃ⁻ᵃ *Septuagint reads "was a large cistern, which. . . ."*

their men and went to fight against Ishmael son of Nethaniah; and they encountered him by the great pool in Gibeon. 13When all the people held by Ishmael saw Johanan son of Kareah and all the army officers with him, they were glad; 14all the people whom Ishmael had carried off from Mizpah turned back and went over to Johanan son of Kareah. 15But Ishmael son of Nethaniah escaped from Johanan with eight men, and went to the Ammonites.

16Johanan son of Kareah and all the army officers with him took all the rest of the people whom b-he had rescued from Ishmael son of Nethaniah-b from Mizpah after he had murdered Gedaliah son of Ahikam—the men, soldiers, women, children, and eunuchs whom [Johanan] had brought back from Gibeon. 17They set out, and they stopped at Geruthc Chimham, near Bethlehem, on their way to go to Egypt 18because of the Chaldeans. For they were afraid of them, because Ishmael son of Nethaniah had killed Gedaliah son of Ahikam, whom the king of Babylon had put in charge of the land.

42 Then all the army officers, with Johanan son of Kareah, Jezaniah son of Hoshaiah, and all the rest of the people, great and small, approached 2the prophet Jeremiah and said, "Grant our plea, and pray for us to the LORD your God, for all this remnant! For we remain but a few out of many, as you can see. 3Let the LORD your God tell us where we should go and what we should do."

4The prophet Jeremiah answered them, "Agreed: I will pray to the LORD your God as you request, and I will tell you whatever response the LORD gives for you. I will withhold nothing from you."

5Thereupon they said to Jeremiah, "Let the LORD be a true and faithful witness against us! We swear that we will do exactly as the LORD your God instructs us through you—6Whether it is pleasant or unpleasant, we will obey the LORD our God to whom we send you, in order that it may go well with us when we obey the LORD our God."

7After ten days, the word of the LORD came to Jeremiah. 8He called Johanan son of Kareah and all the army officers, and the rest of the people, great and small, 9and said to them, "Thus said the LORD, the God of Israel, to whom you sent me to present your supplication before Him: 10If you remain in this land, I will build you and not overthrow, I will

b-b *Emendation yields "Ishmael son of Nethaniah had carried off."*
c *Aquila reads "the sheepfolds of."*

plant you and not uproot; for I regret the punishment I have brought upon you. ¹¹Do not be afraid of the king of Babylon, whom you fear; do not be afraid of him—declares the LORD—for I am with you to save you and to rescue you from his hands. ¹²I will dispose him to be merciful to you: he shall show you mercy and ᵃ⁻bring you back to⁻ᵃ your own land.

¹³"But if you say, 'We will not stay in this land'—thus disobeying the LORD your God— ¹⁴if you say, 'No! We will go to the land of Egypt, so that we may not see war or hear the sound of the horn, and so that we may not hunger for bread; there we will stay,' ¹⁵then hear the word of the LORD, O remnant of Judah! Thus said the LORD of Hosts, the God of Israel: If you turn your faces toward Egypt, and you go and sojourn there, ¹⁶the sword that you fear shall overtake you there, in the land of Egypt, and the famine you worry over shall follow at your heels in Egypt too; and there you shall die. ¹⁷All the men who turn their faces toward Egypt, in order to sojourn there, shall die by the sword, by famine, and by pestilence. They shall have no surviving remnant of the disaster that I will bring upon them. ¹⁸For thus said the LORD of Hosts, the God of Israel: As My anger and wrath were poured out upon the inhabitants of Jerusalem, so will My wrath be poured out on you if you go to Egypt. You shall become ᵇ⁻an execration of woe, a curse⁻ᵇ and a mockery; and you shall never again see this place. ¹⁹The LORD has spoken against you, O remnant of Judah! Do not go to Egypt! Know well, then—for I warn you this day ²⁰that you were deceitful at heart when you sent me to the LORD your God, saying, 'Pray for us to the LORD our God; and whatever the LORD our God may say, just tell us and we will do it.' ²¹I told you today, and you have not obeyed the LORD your God in respect to all that He sent me to tell you—²²know well, then, that you shall die by the sword, by famine, and by pestilence in the place where you want to go and sojourn."

43 When Jeremiah had finished speaking all these words to all the people—all the words of the LORD their God, with which the LORD their God had sent him to them—²Azariah son of Hoshaiah and Johanan son of Kareah and all the arrogant men said to Jeremiah, "You are lying! The LORD our God did not send you to say, 'Don't go to Egypt and sojourn there'! ³It is Baruch son of Neriah who is inciting you against us, so that

ᵃ⁻ᵃ *Change of vocalization yields "let you dwell in."*
ᵇ⁻ᵇ *I.e., a standard by which men execrate and curse; cf. note at 24.9.*

we will be delivered into the hands of the Chaldeans to be killed or to be exiled to Babylon!"

⁴So Johanan son of Kareah and all the army officers and the rest of the people did not obey the LORD's command to remain in the land of Judah. ⁵Instead, Johanan son of Kareah and all the army officers took the entire remnant of Judah—those who had returned from all the countries to which they had been scattered and had sojourned in the land of Judah, ⁶men, women, and children; and the daughters of the king and all the people whom Nebuzaradan the chief of the guards had left with Gedaliah son of Ahikam son of Shaphan, as well as the prophet Jeremiah and Baruch son of Neriah—⁷and they went to Egypt. They did not obey the LORD.

They arrived at Tahpanhes, ⁸and the word of the LORD came to Jeremiah in Tahpanhes: ⁹Get yourself large stones, and embed them in mortar in the brick structure at the entrance to Pharaoh's palace in Tahpanhes, with some Judeans looking on. ¹⁰And say to them: "Thus said the LORD of Hosts, the God of Israel: I am sending for My servant King Nebuchadrezzar of Babylon, and Iᵃ will set his throne over these stones which I have embedded. He will spread out his pavilionᵇ over them. ¹¹He will come and attack the land of Egypt, delivering

Those destined for the plague, to the plague,
Those destined for captivity, to captivity,
And those destined for the sword, to the sword.

¹²And Iᵃ will set fire to the temples of the gods of Egypt; he will burn them down and carry themᶜ off. He shall wrap himself up in the land of Egypt, as a shepherd wraps himself up in his garment. And he shall depart from there in safety. ¹³He shall smash the obelisks of the Temple of the Sun which is in the land of Egypt, and he shall burn down the temples of the gods of Egypt.

44

The word which came to Jeremiah for all the Judeans living in the land of Egypt, living in Migdol, Tahpanhes, and Noph, and in the land of Pathros:

²Thus said the LORD of Hosts, the God of Israel: You have seen all

---

ᵃ Septuagint reads "he."
ᵇ Meaning of Heb. uncertain.
ᶜ I.e., the gods.

the disaster that I brought on Jerusalem and on all the towns of Judah. They are a ruin today, and no one inhabits them, ³on account of the wicked things they did to vex Me, going to make offerings in worship of other gods which they had not known—neither they nor you nor your fathers. ⁴Yet I persistently sent to you all My servants the prophets, to say, "I beg you not to do this abominable thing which I hate." ⁵But they would not listen or give ear, to turn back from their wickedness and not make offerings to other gods; ⁶so My fierce anger was poured out, and it blazed against the towns of Judah and the streets of Jerusalem. And they became a desolate ruin, as they still are today.

⁷And now, thus said the LORD, the God of Hosts, the God of Israel: Why are you doing such great harm to yourselves, so that every man and woman, child and infant of yours shall be cut off from the midst of Judah, and no remnant shall be left of you? ⁸For you vex me by your deeds, making offering to other gods in the land of Egypt where you have come to sojourn, so that you shall be cut off and become a curse*a* and a mockery among all the nations of earth. ⁹Have you forgotten the wicked acts of your forefathers, of the kings of Judah and their*b* wives, and your own wicked acts and those of your wives, which were committed in the land of Judah and in the streets of Jerusalem? ¹⁰No one has shown contrition to this day, and no one has shown reverence. You*c* have not followed the Teaching and the laws that I set before you and before your fathers.

¹¹Assuredly, thus said the LORD of Hosts, the God of Israel: I am going to set My face against you for punishment, to cut off all of Judah. ¹²I will take the remnant of Judah who turned their faces toward the land of Egypt, to go and sojourn there, and they shall be utterly consumed in the land of Egypt. They shall fall by the sword, they shall be consumed by famine; great and small alike shall die by the sword and by famine, and they shall become an execration*a* and a desolation, a curse*a* and a mockery. ¹³I will punish those who live in the land of Egypt as I punished Jerusalem, with the sword, with famine, and with pestilence. ¹⁴Of the remnant of Judah who came to sojourn here in the land of Egypt, no survivor or fugitive shall be left to return to the land of Judah. Though they all long to return and dwell there, none shall return except [a few] survivors.

¹⁵Thereupon they answered Jeremiah—all the men who knew that their

---

ᵃ *See note at 24.9; 42.18.*
ᵇ *Heb. "his."*
ᶜ *Heb. "They."*

wives made offerings to other gods; all the women present, a large gathering; and all the people who lived in Pathros in the land of Egypt: 16"We will not listen to you in the matter about which you spoke to us in the name of the LORD. 17On the contrary, we will do d-everything that we have vowed-d—to make offerings to the Queen of Heaven and to pour libations to her, as we used to do,e we and our fathers, our kings and our officials, in the towns of Judah and the streets of Jerusalem. For then we had plenty to eat, we were well-off, and suffered no misfortune. 18But ever since we stopped making offerings to the Queen of Heaven and pouring libations to her, we have lacked everything, and we have been consumed by the sword and by famine. 19And when we make offerings to the Queen of Heaven and pour libations to her, is it without our husbands' approval that we have made cakes f-in her likeness-f and poured libations to her?"

20Jeremiah replied to all the people, men and women—all the people who argued with him. He said, 21"Indeed, the offerings you presented in the towns of Judah and the streets of Jerusalem—you, your fathers, your kings, your officials, and the people of the land—were remembered by the LORD and brought to mind! 22When the LORD could no longer bear your evil practices and the abominations you committed, your land became a desolate ruin and a curse,a without inhabitant, as is still the case. 23Because you burned incense and sinned against the LORD and did not obey the LORD, and because you did not follow His Teaching, His laws, and His exhortations, therefore this disaster has befallen you, as is still the case."

24Jeremiah further said to all the people and to all the women: "Hear the word of the LORD, all Judeans in the land of Egypt! 25Thus said the LORD of Hosts, the God of Israel: You and your wives have g-confirmed by deed what you spoke in words:-g 'We will fulfill the vows which we made, to burn incense to the Queen of Heaven and to pour libations to her.' So fulfill your vows; perform your vows!

26"Yet hear the word of the LORD, all Judeans who dwell in the land of Egypt! Lo, I swear by My great name—said the LORD—that none of the men of Judah in all the land of Egypt shall ever again invoke My name, saying, 'As the Lord GOD lives!' 27I will be watchful over them to their hurt, not to their benefit; all the men of Judah in the land of Egypt shall be consumed by sword and by famine, until they cease to be. 28Only

---

d-d Lit. "everything that has gone forth from our mouth."
e Cf. 7.18.
f-f Meaning of Heb. uncertain.
g-g Lit. "spoken with your mouth and fulfilled by your hands."

the few who survive the sword shall return from the land of Egypt to the land of Judah. All the remnant of Judah who came to the land of Egypt to sojourn there shall learn whose word will be fulfilled—Mine or theirs!

²⁹"And this shall be the sign to you—declares the LORD—that I am going to deal with you in this place, so that you may know that My threats of punishment against you will be fulfilled: ³⁰Thus said the LORD: I will deliver Pharaoh Hophra, king of Egypt, into the hands of his enemies, those who seek his life, just as I delivered King Zedekiah of Judah into the hands of King Nebuchadrezzar of Babylon, his enemy who sought his life."

45 The word which the prophet Jeremiah spoke to Baruch son of Neriah, when he was writing these words in a scroll at Jeremiah's dictation, in the fourth year of King Jehoiakim son of Josiah of Judah:

²Thus said the LORD, the God of Israel, concerning you, Baruch: ³You say, "Woe is me! The LORD has added grief to my pain. I am worn out with groaning, and I have found no rest." ⁴Thus shall you speak to him: "Thus said the LORD: I am going to overthrow what I have built, and uproot what I have planted—ᵃ·this applies to the whole land.·ᵃ ⁵And do you expect great things for yourself? Don't expect them. For I am going to bring disaster upon all flesh—declares the LORD—but I will ᵇ·at least grant you your life·ᵇ in all the places where you may go."

46 The word of the LORD to the prophet Jeremiah concerning the nations.

²Concerning Egypt, about the army of Pharaoh Neco, king of Egypt, which was at the river Euphrates near Carchemish, and which was defeated by King Nebuchadrezzar of Babylon, in the fourth year of King Jehoiakim son of Josiah of Judah.

> ³Get ready buckler and shield,
> And move forward to battle!
> ⁴Harness the horses;
> Mount, you horsemen!
> Fall in line, helmets on!

ᵃ⁻ᵃ *Meaning of Heb. uncertain.*
ᵇ⁻ᵇ *Cf. note at 21.9.*

Burnish the lances,
Don your armor!
⁵Why do I see them dismayed,
Yielding ground?
Their fighters are crushed,
They flee in haste
And do not turn back—
Terror all around!

—declares the LORD.

⁶ᵃ⁻The swift cannot get away,
The warrior cannot escape.⁻ᵃ
In the north, by the river Euphrates,
They stagger and fall.

⁷Who is this that rises like the Nile,
Like streams whose waters surge?
⁸It is Egypt that rises like the Nile,
Like streams whose waters surge,
That said, "I will rise,
I will cover the earth,
I will wipe out towns
And those who dwell in them.
⁹Advance, O horses,
Dash madly, O chariots!
Let the warriors go forth,
Cush and Put, that grasp the shield,
And the Ludim who grasp and draw the bow!"

¹⁰But that day shall be for the Lord GOD of Hosts a day when He exacts retribution from His foes. The sword shall devour; it shall be sated and drunk with their blood. For the Lord GOD of Hosts is preparing a sacrifice in the northland, by the river Euphrates.

¹¹Go up to Gilead and get balm,
Fair Maiden Egypt.
In vain do you seek many remedies,
There is no healing for you.
¹²Nations have heard your shame;

ᵃ⁻ᵃ *Lit. "Let not the swift get away, / Let not the warrior escape."*

863

The earth resounds with your screams.
For warrior stumbles against warrior;
The two fall down together.

13 The word which the LORD spoke to the prophet Jeremiah about the coming of King Nebuchadrezzar of Babylon to attack the land of Egypt:

14 Declare in Egypt, proclaim in Migdol,
Proclaim in Noph and Tahpanhes!
Say: Take your posts and stand ready,
For the sword has devoured all around you!
15 Why are your stalwarts swept away?
They did not stand firm,
For the LORD thrust them down;
16 He made many stumble,
They fell over one another.

They said:
"Up! let us return to our people,
To the land of our birth,
Because of the deadly[b] sword."
17 There they called Pharaoh king of Egypt:
[b]-"Braggart who let the hour go by."-[b]

18 As I live—declares the King,
Whose name is LORD of Hosts—
[b]-As surely as Tabor is among the mountains
And Carmel is by the sea,
So shall this come to pass.-[b]
19 Equip yourself for exile,
Fair Egypt, you who dwell secure!
For Noph shall become a waste,
Desolate, without inhabitants.
20 Egypt is a handsome heifer—
A gadfly[c] from the north [d]-is coming, coming!-[d]
21 The mercenaries, too, in her midst
Are like stall-fed calves;
They too shall turn tail,

b Meaning of Heb. uncertain.
c Or "butcher"; meaning of Heb. uncertain.
d-d Many mss. read "will come upon her."

Flee as one, and make no stand.
Their day of disaster is upon them,
The hour of their doom.
22b-She shall rustle away like a snake-b
As they come marching in force;
They shall come against her with axes,
Like hewers of wood.
23They shall cut down her forest

—declares the LORD—

Though it cannot be measured;
For they are more numerous than locusts,
And cannot be counted.
24Fair Egypt shall be shamed,
Handed over to the people of the north.

25The LORD of Hosts, the God of Israel, has said: I will inflict punishment on Amonᵉ of No and on Pharaoh—on Egypt, her gods, and her kings—on Pharaoh and all who rely on him. 26I will deliver them into the hands of those who seek to kill them, into the hands of King Nebuchadrezzar of Babylon and into the hands of his subjects. But afterward she shall be inhabited again as in former days, declares the LORD.

27But you,
Have no fear, My servant Jacob,
Be not dismayed, O Israel!
I will deliver you from far away,
Your folk from their land of captivity;
And Jacob again shall have calm
And quiet, with none to trouble him.
28But you, have no fear,
My servant Jacob

—declares the LORD—

For I am with you.
I will make an end of all the nations
Among which I have banished you,
But I will not make an end of you!
I will not leave you unpunished,
But I will chastise you in measure.

ᵉ Tutelary deity of the city No (Thebes); cf. Nah. 3.8.

47

The word of the LORD that came to the prophet Jeremiah concerning the Philistines, before Pharaoh conquered Gaza.

²Thus said the LORD:
See, waters are rising from the north,
They shall become a raging torrent,
They shall flood the land and its creatures,
The towns and their inhabitants.
Men shall cry out,
All the inhabitants of the land shall howl,
³At the clatter of the stamping hoofs of his stallions,
At the noise of his chariots,
The rumbling of their wheels,
Fathers shall not look to their children
Out of ᵃ⁻sheer helplessness⁻ᵃ
⁴Because of the day that is coming
For ravaging all the Philistines,
For cutting off every last ally
Of Tyre and Sidon.
For the LORD will ravage the Philistines,
The remnant from the island of Caphtor.
⁵Baldnessᵇ has come upon Gaza,
Ashkelon is destroyed.
O remnant of ᶜ⁻their valley,⁻ᶜ
How long will you ᵇ⁻gash yourself?⁻ᵇ

⁶"O sword of the LORD,
When will you be quiet at last?
Withdraw into your sheath,
Rest and be still!"

⁷How can itᵈ be quiet
When the LORD has given it orders
Against Ashkelon and the seacoast,
Given it assignment there?

ᵃ⁻ᵃ *Lit. "weakness of hands."*
ᵇ *Shaving the head and gashing the body were expressions of mourning; cf. Deut. 14.1.*
ᶜ⁻ᶜ *Septuagint reads "the Anakites"; cf. Josh. 11.22.*
ᵈ *Heb. "you."*

48 Concerning Moab.[a]

Thus said the LORD of Hosts, the God of Israel:
Alas, that Nebo should be ravaged,
Kiriathaim captured and shamed,
[b-]The stronghold[-b] shamed and dismayed!
[2]Moab's glory is no more;
In Heshbon they have planned[c] evil against her:
"Come, let us make an end of her as a nation!"
You too, O Madmen, shall be silenced;[d]
The sword is following you.
[3]Hark! an outcry from Horonaim,
Destruction and utter ruin!

[4]Moab is broken;
[e-]Her young ones cry aloud;[-e]
[5]They climb to Luhith
Weeping continually;
On the descent to Horonaim
A distressing cry of anguish is heard:
[6]Flee, save your lives!
[f-]And be like Aroer in the desert.[-f]

[7]Surely, because of your trust
In your wealth and in your treasures,
You too shall be captured.
And Chemosh shall go forth to exile,
Together with his priests and attendants.
[8]The ravager shall come to every town;
No town shall escape.
The valley shall be devastated
And the tableland laid waste

—because the LORD has spoken.

[9]Give [f-]wings to Moab,
For she must go hence.[-f]

---

[a] A number of parallels to this chapter occur in Isa. 15–16.
[b-b] Or "Misgab."
[c] Heb. hashebu, play on Heshbon.
[d] Heb. tiddommi, play on Madmen, the name of a town.
[e-e] Emendation yields "They cry aloud as far as Zoar"; cf. Isa. 15.5.
[f-f] Meaning of Heb. uncertain.

Her towns shall become desolate,
With no one living in them.

10Cursed be he who is slack in doing the LORD's work! Cursed be he who withholds his sword from blood!

11Moab has been secure from his youth on—
He is settled on his lees
And has not been poured from vessel to vessel—
He has never gone into exile.
Therefore his fine flavor has remained
And his bouquet is unspoiled.

12But days are coming—declares the LORD—when I will send men against him to tip him over; they shall empty his vessels and smash his jars. 13And Moab shall be shamed because of Chemosh, as the House of Israel were shamed because of Bethel, on whom they relied.

14How can you say: We are warriors,
Valiant men for war?
15Moab is ravaged,
His towns have been entered,
His choice young men
Have gone down to the slaughter
          —declares the King whose name is LORD of Hosts.
16The doom of Moab is coming close,
His downfall is approaching swiftly.
17Condole with him, all who live near him,
All you who know him by name!
Say: "Alas, the strong rod is broken,
The lordly staff!"

18Descend from glory
And sit in thirst,f
O inhabitant of Fair Dibon;
For the ravager of Moab has entered your town,
He has destroyed your fortresses.
19Stand by the road and look out,

O inhabitant of Aroer.
Ask of him who is fleeing
And of her who is escaping:
Say, "What has happened?"
20Moab is shamed and dismayed;
Howl and cry aloud!
Tell at the Arnon
That Moab is ravaged!

21Judgment has come upon the tableland—upon Holon, Jahzah, and
Mephaath; 22upon Dibon, Nebo, and Beth-diblathaim; 23upon Kiriathaim, Beth-gamul, and Beth-meon; 24upon Kerioth and Bozrah—upon
all the towns of the land of Moab, far and near.

25The might of Moab has been cut down,
His strength is broken
                                        —declares the LORD.
26Get him drunk
For he vaunted himself against the LORD.
Moab shall vomit till he is drained,
And he too shall be a laughingstock.
27Wasn't Israel a laughingstock to you?
Was he ever caught among thieves,
That you should g-shake your head-g
Whenever you speak of him?
28Desert the cities
And dwell in the crags,
O inhabitants of Moab!
Be like a dove that nests
In the sides of a pit.

29We have heard of Moab's pride—
Most haughty is he—
Of his arrogance and pride,
His haughtiness and self-exaltation.
30I know his insolence—declares the LORD—the wickedness that is in
him,h the wickedness i-he has-i committed.
31Therefore I will howl for Moab,

g-g *I.e., in mockery.*
h *Cf. note at Isa. 16.6.*
i-i *Heb. "they have."*

I will cry out for all Moab,
I⟩ will moan for the men of Kir-heres.
³²With greater weeping than for Jazer
I weep for you, O vine of Sibmah,
Whose tendrils crossed the sea,
Reached to the sea,^f to Jazer.
A ravager has come down
Upon your fig and grape harvests.
³³Rejoicing and gladness
Are gone from the farm land,
From the country of Moab;
I have put an end to wine in the presses,
No one treads [the grapes] with shouting—
^{f-}The shout is a shout no more.^{-f}
³⁴There is an outcry from Heshbon to Elealeh,
They raise their voices as far as Jahaz,
From Zoar to Horonaim and Eglath-shelishiah.
The waters of Nimrim
Shall also become desolation.
³⁵And I will make an end in Moab

—declares the LORD—

Of those who offer at a shrine
And burn incense to their god.
³⁶Therefore,
My heart moans for Moab like a flute;
Like a flute my heart moans
For the men of Kir-heres—
^{f-}Therefore,
The gains they have made shall vanish^{-f}—
³⁷For every head is bald
And every beard is shorn;
On all hands there are gashes,
And on the loins sackcloth.
³⁸On all the roofs of Moab,
And in its squares
There is naught but lamentation;
For I have broken Moab
Like a vessel no one wants

—declares the LORD.

ⁱ *Heb. "He."*

³⁹How he is dismayed! Wail!
How Moab has turned his back in shame!
Moab shall be a laughingstock
And a shock to all those near him.

⁴⁰For thus said the LORD:
See, he soars like an eagle
And spreads out his wings against Moab!
⁴¹Kerioth shall be captured
And the strongholds shall be seized.
In that day, the heart of Moab's warriors
Shall be like the heart of a woman in travail.
⁴²And Moab shall be destroyed as a people,
For he vaunted himself against the LORD.
⁴³ ^{k-}Terror, and pit, and trap^{-k}
Upon you who dwell in Moab!

—declares the LORD.

⁴⁴He who flees from the terror
Shall fall into the pit;
And he who climbs out of the pit
Shall be caught in the trap.
For I will bring upon Moab
The year of their doom

—declares the LORD.

⁴⁵In the shelter of Heshbon
Fugitives halt exhausted;
For fire went forth from Heshbon,
Flame from the midst^l of Sihon,
Consuming the brow of Moab,
The pate of the people of Shaon.^m
⁴⁶Woe to you, O Moab!
The people of Chemosh are undone,
For your sons are carried off into captivity,
Your daughters into exile.
⁴⁷But I will restore the fortunes of Moab in the days to come—
declares the LORD.

Thus far is the judgment on Moab.

---

k-k *See note at Isa. 24.17.*
l *Emendation yields "house."*
m *Or "tumult."*

49 Concerning the Ammonites.

Thus said the LORD:
Has Israel no sons,
Has he no heir?
Then why has Milcom[a] dispossessed Gad,
And why have his people settled in Gad's[b] towns?
²Assuredly, days are coming

—declares the LORD—

When I will sound the alarm of war
Against Rabbah of the Ammonites;
It shall become a desolate mound,
And its villages shall be set on fire.
And Israel shall dispossess
Those who dispossessed him

—said the LORD.

³Howl, O Heshbon, for Ai is ravaged!
Cry out, O daughters of Rabbah!
Gird on sackcloth, lament,
[c-]And run to and fro in the sheepfolds.[-c]
For Milcom shall go into exile,
Together with his priests and attendants.

⁴[d-]Why do you glory in strength,
Your strength is drained,[-d]
O rebellious daughter,
You who relied on your treasures,
[Who said:] Who dares attack me?
⁵I am bringing terror upon you

—declares the Lord GOD of Hosts—

From all those around you.
Every one of you shall be driven [e-]in every direction,[-e]
And none shall gather in the fugitives.

⁶But afterward I will restore the fortunes of the Ammonites—declares the LORD.

⁷Concerning Edom.

ᵃ *The name of the Ammonite deity; vocalized Malcam here and in v. 3.*
ᵇ *Heb. "his."*
ᶜ⁻ᶜ *Meaning of Heb. uncertain.*
ᵈ⁻ᵈ *Meaning of Heb. uncertain; for "strength" cf. Akkadian emuqu.*
ᵉ⁻ᵉ *Lit. "each man straight ahead."*

Thus said the LORD of Hosts:
Is there no more wisdom in Teman?
Has counsel vanished from the prudent?
Has their wisdom gone stale?
⁸Flee, turn away, sit down low,
O inhabitants of Dedan,
For I am bringing Esau's doom upon him,
The time when I deal with him.
⁹ᶠ⁻If vintagers were to come upon you,
Would they leave no gleanings?
Even thieves in the night
Would destroy only for their needs!⁻ᶠ
¹⁰But it is I who have bared Esau,
Have exposed his place of concealment;
He cannot hide.
His offspring is ravaged,
His kin and his neighbors—
ᵍ⁻He is no more.⁻ᵍ
¹¹"Leave your orphans with me,
I will rear them;
Let your widows rely on me!"

¹²For thus said the LORD: If they who rightly should not drink of the
cup must drink it, are you the one to go unpunished? You shall not go
unpunished: you will have to drink! ¹³For by Myself I swear—declares
the LORD—Bozrah shall become a desolation, a mockery, a ruin, and a
curse;ʰ and all its towns shall be ruins for all time.

¹⁴I have received tidings from the LORD,
And an envoy is sent out among the nations:
Assemble, and move against her,
And rise up for war!
¹⁵For I will make you least among nations,
Most despised among men.
¹⁶ᶜ⁻Your horrible nature,⁻ᶜ
Your arrogant heart has seduced you,
You who dwell in clefts of the rock,
Who occupy the height of the hill!
Should you nest as high as the eagle,

ᶠ⁻ᶠ *Obad. 1.5 reads: "If thieves were to come to you, / Marauders by night, / They would steal no*
  more than they needed. / If vintagers came to you, / They would surely leave some gleanings."
ᵍ⁻ᵍ *Some Septuagint mss. read "And there is none to say."*
ʰ *Cf. note at 24.9 and 42.18.*

From there I will pull you down

—declares the LORD.

[17]And Edom shall be a cause of appallment; whoever passes by will be appalled and will hiss[i] at all its wounds. [18]It shall be like the overthrow of Sodom and Gomorrah and their neighbors—said the LORD: no man shall live there, no human shall sojourn there. [19]It shall be as when a lion comes up out of the jungle of the Jordan against a secure pasture: in a moment [j-]I can harry him out of it and appoint over it anyone I choose.[-j] Then who is like Me? Who can summon Me? Who is the shepherd that can stand up against Me? [20]Hear, then, the plan which the LORD has devised against Edom, and what He has purposed against the inhabitants of Teman:

Surely the shepherd boys
Shall drag them away;
Surely the pasture shall be
Aghast because of them.
[21]At the sound of their downfall
The earth shall shake;
The sound of screaming
Shall be heard at the Sea of Reeds.
[22]See, like an eagle he flies up,
He soars and spreads his wings against Bozrah;
And the heart of Edom's warriors in that day
Shall be like the heart of a woman in travail.

[23]Concerning Damascus.

Hamath and Arpad are shamed,
For they have heard bad news.
They shake with anxiety,
Like[k] the sea which cannot rest.
[24]Damascus has grown weak,
She has turned around to flee;
Trembling has seized her,
Pain and anguish have taken hold of her,
Like a woman in childbirth.

---

i *Cf. note at 18.16.*
j-j *Emendation yields "he can harry them [i.e., the sheep] out of it; and what champion could one place in charge of them?"*
k *So a few mss. Most mss. and editions read "In."*

²⁵·How has the glorious city not been deserted,·[1]
The citadel of my joy!
²⁶Assuredly, her young men shall lie fallen in her squares.
And all her warriors shall be stilled in that day
     —declares the LORD of Hosts.
²⁷I will set fire to the wall of Damascus,
And it shall consume the fortresses of Ben-hadad.

²⁸Concerning Kedar and the kingdoms of Hazor, which King
Nebuchadrezzar of Babylon conquered.

Thus said the LORD:
Arise, march against Kedar,
And ravage the Kedemites!
²⁹They will take away their tents and their flocks,
Their tent cloths and all their gear;
They shall carry off their camels,
And shall proclaim against them:
Terror all around!
³⁰Flee, wander far,
Sit down low, O inhabitants of Hazor
     —says the LORD.

For King Nebuchadrezzar of Babylon
Has devised a plan against you
And formed a purpose against you:
³¹Rise up, attack a tranquil nation
That dwells secure
     —says the LORD—

That has no barred gates,
That dwells alone.
³²Their camels shall become booty,
And their abundant flocks a spoil;
And I will scatter to every quarter
Those who have their hair clipped;
And from every direction I will bring
Disaster upon them
     —says the LORD.
³³Hazor shall become a lair of jackals,
A desolation for all time.

---

[1] Emendation yields "How has the glorious city been deserted"; so Vulgate.

No man shall live there,
No human shall sojourn there.

[34]The word of the LORD that came to the prophet Jeremiah concerning Elam, at the beginning of the reign of King Zedekiah of Judah:

[35]Thus said the LORD of Hosts: I am going to break the bow of Elam, the mainstay of their strength. [36]And I shall bring four winds against Elam from the four quarters of heaven, and scatter them to all those winds. There shall not be a nation to which the fugitives from Elam do not come. [37]And I will break Elam before their enemies, before those who seek their lives; and I will bring disaster upon them, My flaming wrath—declares the LORD. And I will dispatch the sword after them until I have consumed them.

[38]And I will set My throne in Elam,
And wipe out from there king and officials
—says the LORD.

[39]But in the days to come I will restore the fortunes of Elam—declares the LORD.

50

The word which the LORD spoke concerning Babylon, the land of the Chaldeans, through the prophet Jeremiah:

[2]Declare among the nations, and proclaim;
Raise a standard, proclaim;
Hide nothing! Say:
Babylon is captured,
Bel[a] is shamed,
Merodach[a] is dismayed.
Her idols are shamed,
Her fetishes dismayed.
[3]For a nation from the north has attacked her,
It will make her land a desolation.
No one shall dwell in it,
Both man and beast shall wander away.

[4]In those days and at that time—declares the LORD—the people of

---

[a] Names of the city god of Babylon.

Israel together with the people of Judah shall come, and they shall weep as they go to seek the LORD their God. ⁵They shall inquire for Zion; in that direction their faces shall turn; ᵇ⁻they shall come⁻ᵇ and attach themselves to the LORD by a covenant for all time, which shall never be forgotten. ⁶My people were lost sheep: their shepherds led them astray, they drove them out to the mountains, they roamed from mount to hill, they forgot their own resting place. ⁷All who encountered them devoured them; and their foes said, "We shall not be held guilty, because they have sinned against the LORD, the true Pasture, the Hope of their fathers—the LORD."

⁸Flee from Babylon,
Leave the land of the Chaldeans,
And be like he-goats that lead the flock!
⁹For see, I am rousing and leading
An assemblage of great nations against Babylon
From the lands of the north.
They shall draw up their lines against her,
There she shall be captured.
Their arrows are like those of ᶜ⁻a skilled warrior⁻ᶜ
Who does not turn back without hitting the mark.
¹⁰Chaldea shall be despoiled,
All her spoilers shall be sated

—declares the LORD.

¹¹For you rejoiced, you exulted,
You who plundered My possession;
You stamped like a heifer treading grain,
You neighed like steeds.
¹²So your mother will be utterly shamed,
She who bore you will be disgraced.
Behold the end of the nations—
Wilderness, desert, and steppe!
¹³Because of the LORD's wrath she shall not be inhabited;
She shall be utterly desolate.
Whoever passes by Babylon will be appalled
And will hiss at all her wounds.

¹⁴Range yourselves roundabout Babylon,
All you who draw the bow;

ᵇ⁻ᵇ *Heb. "come ye."*
ᶜ⁻ᶜ *So many mss., editions, and versions; other mss. and editions read "a warrior who bereaves."*

Shoot at her, don't spare arrows,
For she has sinned against the LORD.
¹⁵Raise a shout against her all about!
^{d-}She has surrendered;^{-d}
Her bastions have fallen,
Her walls are thrown down—
This is the LORD's vengeance.
Take vengeance on her,
Do to her as she has done!
¹⁶Make an end in Babylon of sowers,
And of wielders of the sickle at harvest time.
Because of the deadly^e sword,
Each man shall turn back to his people,
They shall flee every one to his land.

¹⁷Israel are scattered sheep, harried by lions. First the king of Assyria devoured them, and in the end King Nebuchadrezzar of Babylon crunched their bones. ¹⁸Assuredly, thus said the LORD of Hosts, the God of Israel: I will deal with the king of Babylon and his land as I dealt with the king of Assyria. ¹⁹And I will lead Israel back to his pasture, and he shall graze in Carmel and Bashan, and eat his fill in the hill country of Ephraim and in Gilead.

²⁰In those days and at that time

—declares the LORD—

The iniquity of Israel shall be sought,
And there shall be none;
The sins of Judah,
And none shall be found;
For I will pardon those I allow to survive.

²¹Advance against her—^{e-} the land of Merathaim^{-e}—
And against the inhabitants of Pekod;
Ruin and destroy after them to the last

—says the LORD—

Do just as I have commanded you.

---

^{d-d} Lit. "She has given her hand"; meaning of Heb. uncertain.
^e Meaning of Heb. uncertain.

²²Hark! War in the land
And vast destruction!
²³How the hammer of the whole earth
Has been hacked and shattered!
How Babylon has become
An appallment among the nations!
²⁴I set a snare for you, O Babylon,
And you were trapped unawares;
You were found and caught,
Because you challenged the LORD.
²⁵The LORD has opened His armory
And brought out the weapons of His wrath;
For that is the task
Of my Lord GOD of Hosts
In the land of the Chaldeans.
²⁶Come against her ^{e-}from every quarter;^{-e}
Break open her granaries,
^{e-}Pile her up like heaps of grain,^{-e}
And destroy her, let her have no remnant!
^{27f-}Destroy all^{-f} her bulls,
Let them go down to slaughter.
Alas for them, their day is come,
The hour of their doom!
²⁸Hark! fugitives are escaping
From the land of Babylon,
To tell in Zion of the vengeance of the LORD our God,
Vengeance for His Temple.

²⁹Summon archers against Babylon,
All who draw the bow!
Encamp against her roundabout,
Let none of her people escape.
Pay her back for her actions,
Do to her just what she has done;
For she has acted insolently against the LORD,
The Holy One of Israel.

f-f *Emendation yields "A sword against"; cf. vv. 35 ff.*

³⁰Assuredly, her young men shall fall in her squares,
And all her warriors shall perish in that day
                              —declares the LORD.
³¹I am going to deal with you, O Insolence
                    —declares the Lord GOD of Hosts—
For your day is come, the time when I doom you:
³²Insolence shall stumble and fall,
With none to raise her up.
I will set her cities on fire,
And it shall consume everything around her.

³³Thus said the LORD of Hosts:
The people of Israel are oppressed,
And so too the people of Judah;
All their captors held them,
They refused to let them go.
³⁴Their Redeemer is mighty,
His name is LORD of Hosts.
He will champion their cause—
So as to give rest to the earth,
And unrest to the inhabitants of Babylon.

³⁵A sword against the Chaldeans
                              —declares the LORD—
And against the inhabitants of Babylon,
Against its officials and its wise men!
³⁶A sword against the diviners, that they be made fools of!
A sword against the warriors, that they be dismayed!
³⁷A sword against its horses and chariots,
And against all the motley crowd in its midst,
That they become like women!
A sword against its treasuries, that they be pillaged!
³⁸A drought ͨ against its waters, that they be dried up!
For it is a land of idols;
They are besotted by their ͨ⁻dread images.⁻ͨ
³⁹Assuredly,

ᵍ Horeb, *play on* ḥereb, *"sword" in preceding verses.*

e-Wildcats and hyenas-e shall dwell [there],
And ostriches shall dwell there;
It shall never be settled again,
Nor inhabited throughout the ages.

⁴⁰It shall be as when God overthrew Sodom and Gomorrah and their neighbors—declares the LORD; no man shall live there, no human shall sojourn there.

⁴¹Lo, a people comes from the northland;
A great nation and many kings are roused
From the remotest parts of the earth.
⁴²They grasp the bow and javelin,
They are cruel, they show no mercy;
The sound of them is like the roaring sea.
They ride upon horses,
Accoutered like a man for battle,
Against you, O Fair Babylon!
⁴³The king of Babylon has heard the report of them,
And his hands are weakened;
Anguish seizes him,
Pangs like a woman in childbirth.

⁴⁴It shall be as when a lion comes out of the jungle of the Jordan against a secure pasture: in a moment h-I can harry them out of it and appoint over it anyone I choose.-h Then who is like Me? Who can summon Me? Who is the shepherd that can stand up against Me? ⁴⁵Hear, then, the plan that the LORD has devised against Babylon, and has purposed against the land of Chaldea:
Surely the shepherd boys
Shall drag them away;
Surely the pasture shall be
Aghast because of them.
⁴⁶At the sound of Babylon's capture
The earth quakes,
And an outcry is heard among the nations.

h-h *See note at 49.19.*

51
Thus said the LORD:
See, I am rousing a destructive wind
Against Babylon and the inhabitants of Leb-kamai.ᵃ
²I will send strangersᵇ against Babylon, and they
   shall winnow her.
And they shall strip her land bare;
They shall beset her on all sides
On the day of disaster.
³Letᶜ the archer draw his bow,
And let him stand ready in his coat of mail!
Show no pity to her young men,
Wipe out all her host!
⁴Let them fall slain in the land of Chaldea,
Pierced through in her streets.

⁵For Israel and Judah were not bereftᵈ
Of their God the LORD of Hosts,
But their land was filled with guilt
Before the Holy One of Israel.

⁶Flee from the midst of Babylon
And save your lives, each of you!
Do not perish for her iniquity;
For this is a time of vengeance for the LORD,
He will deal retribution to her.

⁷Babylon was a golden cup in the LORD's hand,
It made the whole earth drunk;
The nations drank of her wine—
That is why the nations are mad.
⁸Suddenly Babylon has fallen and is shattered;
Howl over her!
Get balm for her wounds:
Perhaps she can be healed.
⁹We tried to cure Babylon
But she was incurable.
Let us leave her and go,

ᵃ A cipher for Kasdim, "Chaldea."
ᵇ Change of vocalization yields "winnowers."
ᶜ Some Heb. mss. and ancient versions read "Let not" here and in next line.
ᵈ Lit. "widowed."

882

Each to his own land;
For her punishment reaches to heaven,
It is as high as the sky.
¹⁰The LORD has proclaimed our vindication;
Come, let us recount in Zion
The deeds of the LORD our God.

¹¹Polish the arrows,
Fill the quivers!
The LORD has roused the spirit of the kings of Media,
For His plan against Babylon is to destroy her.
This is the vengeance of the LORD,
Vengeance for His Temple.

¹²Raise a standard against the walls of Babylon!
Set up a blockade; station watchmen;
Prepare those in ambush.
For the LORD has both planned and performed
What He decreed against the inhabitants of Babylon.

¹³O you who dwell by great waters,
With vast storehouses,
Your time is come, ᵉ⁻the hour of your end.⁻ᵉ
¹⁴The LORD of Hosts has sworn by Himself:
I will fill you with men like a locust swarm,
They will raise a shout against you.

¹⁵He made the earth by His might,
Established the world by His wisdom,
And by His understanding stretched out the skies.
¹⁶ᶠ⁻When He makes His voice heard,⁻ᶠ
There is a rumbling of waters in the skies;
He makes vapors rise from the end of the earth,
He makes lightning for the rain,
And brings forth wind from His treasuries.
¹⁷Every man is proved dull, without knowledge;
Every goldsmith is put to shame because of the idol,
For his molten image is a deceit—

ᵉ⁻ᵉ *Meaning of Heb. uncertain.*
ᶠ⁻ᶠ *Lit. "At the sound of His making."*

There is no breath in them.
¹⁸They are delusion, a work of mockery;
In their hour of doom, they shall perish.
¹⁹Not like these in the Portion of Jacob,
For it is He who formed all things;
And [Israel is] His very own tribe.
LORD of Hosts is His name.

²⁰You are My war club, [My] weapons of battle;
With you I clubbed nations,
With you I destroyed kingdoms;
²¹With you I clubbed horse and rider,
With you I clubbed chariot and driver,
²²With you I clubbed man and woman,
With you I clubbed graybeard and boy,
With you I clubbed youth and maiden;
²³With you I clubbed shepherd and flock,
With you I clubbed plowman and team,
With you I clubbed governors and prefects.
²⁴But I will requite Babylon and all the inhabitants of Chaldea
For all the wicked things they did to Zion before your eyes
　　　　　　　　　　　　　　　　—declares the LORD.
²⁵See, I will deal with you, O mountain of the destroyer
　　　　　　　　　　　　　　　　—declares the LORD—
Destroyer of the whole earth!
I will stretch out My hand against you
And roll you down from the crags,
And make you a burnt-out mountain.
²⁶They shall never take from you
A cornerstone or foundation stone;
You shall be a desolation for all time
　　　　　　　　　　　　　　　　—declares the LORD.
²⁷Raise a standard on earth,
Sound a horn among the nations,
Appoint nations against her,
Assemble kingdoms against her—
Ararat, Minni, and Ashkenaz—
Designate a marshal against her,

Bring up horses like swarming[e] locusts!
28Appoint nations for war against her—
The kings of Media,
Her governors and all her prefects,
And all the lands they rule!

29Then the earth quakes and writhes,
For the LORD's purpose is fulfilled against Babylon,
To make the land of Babylon
A waste without inhabitant.
30The warriors of Babylon stop fighting,
They sit in the strongholds,
Their might is dried up,
They become women.
Her dwellings are set afire,
Her bars are broken.
31Runner dashes to meet runner,
Messenger to meet messenger,
To report to the king of Babylon
That his city is captured, from end to end.
32The fords are captured,
And the swamp thickets[e] are consumed in fire;
And the fighting men are in panic.

33For thus said the LORD of Hosts, the God of Israel:
Fair Babylon is like a threshing floor
Ready to be trodden;
In a little while her harvesttime will come.

34"Nebuchadrezzar king of Babylon
Devoured me and discomfited me;
He swallowed me like a dragon,
He filled his belly with my dainties,
And set me down like an empty dish;
Then he [e-rinsed me out.-e]
35Let the violence done me and my kindred
Be upon Babylon,"
Says the inhabitant of Zion;

"And let my blood be upon the inhabitants of Chaldea,"
Says Jerusalem.

36Assuredly, thus said the LORD:
I am going to uphold your cause
And take vengeance for you;
I will dry up her sea
And make her fountain run dry.
37Babylon shall become rubble,
A den for jackals,
An object of horror and hissing,g
Without inhabitant.
38Like lions, they roar together,
They growl like lion cubs.
39h-When they are heated, I will set out their drink
And get them drunk, that they may become hilarious-h
And then sleep an endless sleep,
Never to awake

—declares the LORD.

40I will bring them down like lambs for slaughter,
Like rams and he-goats.
41How has Sheshachi been captured,
The praise of the whole earth been taken!
How has Babylon become
A horror to the nations!
42The sea has risen over Babylon,
She is covered by its roaring waves.
43Her towns are a desolation,
A land of desert and steppe,
A land no man lives in
And no human passes through.
44And I will deal with Bel in Babylon,
And make him disgorge what he has swallowed,
And nations shall no more gaze on him with joy.
Even the wall of Babylon shall fall.

45Depart from there, O My people,

g See note at 18.16.
h-h Emendation yields "With poison [so Syriac] will I set out their drink / And get them drunk till
they fall unconscious" (so ancient versions).
i See note at 25.26.

Save your lives, each of you,
From the furious anger of the LORD.
⁴⁶Do not be downhearted or afraid
At the rumors heard in the land:
A rumor will come one year,
And another rumor the next year
Of violence in the land,
And of ruler against ruler.
⁴⁷Assuredly, days are coming,
When I will deal with Babylon's images;
Her whole land shall be shamed,
And all her slain shall fall in her midst.
⁴⁸Heavens and earth and all that is in them
Shall shout over Babylon;
For the ravagers shall come upon her from the north
                                    —declares the LORD.

⁴⁹Yes, Babylon is to fall
[For] the slain of Israel,
As the slain of all the earth
Have fallen through Babylon.

⁵⁰You fugitives from the sword,
Go, don't delay!
Remember the LORD from afar,
And call Jerusalem to mind.
⁵¹"We were shamed, we heard taunts;
Humiliation covered our faces,
When aliens entered
The sacred areas of the LORD's House."
⁵²Assuredly, days are coming
                                    —declares the LORD—
When I will deal with her images,
And throughout her land the dying shall groan.
⁵³Though Babylon should climb to the skies,
Though she fortify her strongholds up to heaven,
The ravagers would come against her from Me
                                    —declares the LORD.

⁵⁴Hark! an outcry from Babylon,
Great destruction from the land of the Chaldeans.
⁵⁵For the LORD is ravaging Babylon;
He will put an end to her great din,
Whose roar is like waves of mighty waters,
Whose tumultuous noise resounds.
⁵⁶For a ravager is coming upon Babylon,
Her warriors shall be captured, their bows shall be snapped.
For the LORD is a God of requital,
He deals retribution.
⁵⁷I will make her officials and wise men drunk,
Her governors and prefects and warriors;
And they shall sleep an endless sleep,
Never to awaken
　　　　　　—declares the King whose name is LORD of Hosts.
⁵⁸Thus said the LORD of Hosts:
Babylon's broad wall shall be knocked down,
And her high gates set afire.
Peoples shall labor for naught,
And nations have wearied themselves for fire.

⁵⁹The instructions that the prophet Jeremiah gave to Seraiah son of Neriah son of Mahseiah, when the latter went withʲ King Zedekiah of Judah to Babylonia, in the fourth year of [Zedekiah's] reign. Seraiah was quartermaster.ᵉ ⁶⁰Jeremiah wrote down in one scroll all the disaster that would come upon Babylon, all these things that are written concerning Babylon. ⁶¹And Jeremiah said to Seraiah, "When you get to Babylon, see that you read out all these words. ⁶²And say, 'O LORD, You Yourself have declared concerning this place that it shall be cut off, without inhabitant, man or beast; that it shall be a desolation for all time.' ⁶³And when you finish reading this scroll, tie a stone to it and hurl it into the Euphrates. ⁶⁴And say, 'Thus shall Babylon sink and never rise again, because of the disaster that I will bring upon it. And [nations] shall have wearied themselves [for fire].' "ᵏ

Thus far the words of Jeremiah.

ʲ *Emendation yields "at the instance of."*
ᵏ *Cf. v. 58, last line.*

52

ᵃZedekiah was twenty-one years old when he became king, and he reigned in Jerusalem for eleven years. His mother's name was Hamutal, daughter of Jeremiah of Libnah. ²He did what was displeasing to the LORD, just as Jehoiakim had done. ³Indeed, Jerusalem and Judah ᵇ⁻were a cause of anger for the LORD, so that⁻ᵇ He cast them out of His presence.

Zedekiah rebelled against the king of Babylon. ⁴And in the ninth year of hisᶜ reign, on the tenth day of the tenth month, King Nebuchadrezzar moved against Jerusalem with his whole army. They besieged it and built towers against it all around. ⁵The city continued in a state of siege until the eleventh year of King Zedekiah. ⁶By the ninth day of the fourth month, the famine had become acute in the city; there was no food left for the common people.

⁷Then [the wall of] the city was breached. All the soldiers fled; they left the city by night through the gate between the double walls, which is near the king's garden—the Chaldeans were all around the city—and they set out for the Arabah.ᵈ ⁸But the Chaldean troops pursued the king, and they overtook Zedekiah in the steppes of Jericho, as his entire force left him and scattered. ⁹They captured the king and brought him before the king of Babylon at Riblah, in the region of Hamath; and he put him on trial. ¹⁰The king of Babylon had Zedekiah's sons slaughtered before his eyes; he also had all the officials of Judah slaughtered at Riblah. ¹¹Then the eyes of Zedekiah were put out, and he was chained in bronze fetters. The king of Babylon brought him to Babylon and put him in prison, [where he remained] to the day of his death.

¹²On the tenth day of the fifth month—that was the nineteenth year of King Nebuchadrezzar, the king of Babylon—Nebuzaradan, the chief of the guards, came ᵉ⁻to represent⁻ᵉ the king of Babylon in Jerusalem. ¹³He burned the House of the LORD, the king's palace, and all the houses of Jerusalem; he burned down the house of ᵇ⁻every notable person.⁻ᵇ ¹⁴The entire Chaldean force that was with the chief of the guards tore down all the walls of Jerusalem on every side. ¹⁵The remnant of the people left in the city, the defectors who had gone over to the king of Babylon, and what remained of the craftsmenᶠ were taken into exile by Nebuzaradan, the chief of the guards. But some of the poorest elements of the

---

ᵃ For this chapter cf. chap. 39 above and 2 Kings 24–25.
ᵇ⁻ᵇ Meaning of Heb. uncertain.
ᶜ I.e., Zedekiah's.
ᵈ See note at 39.4.
ᵉ⁻ᵉ Lit. "he stood before."
ᶠ Apparently after the deportation of 2 Kings 24.14; meaning of Heb. uncertain.

population—¹⁶some of the poorest in the land—were left by Nebuzara-dan, the chief of the guards, to be vine-dressers and field hands.

¹⁷The Chaldeans broke up the bronze columns of the House of the LORD, the stands, and the bronze tank that was in the House of the LORD; and they carried all the bronze away to Babylon. ¹⁸They also took the pails, scrapers, snuffers, sprinkling bowls, ladles, and all the other bronze vessels used in the service. ¹⁹The chief of the guards took whatever was of gold and whatever was of silver: basins, fire pans, sprinkling bowls, pails, lampstands, ladles, and jars. ²⁰The two columns, the one tank and the twelve bronze oxen which supported it, and the stands, which King Solomon had provided for the House of the LORD—all these objects contained bronze beyond weighing. ²¹As for the columns, each was eight-een cubits high and twelve cubits in circumference; it was hollow, and [the metal] was four fingers thick. ²²It had a bronze capital above it; the height of each capital was five cubits, and there was a meshwork [deco-rated] with pomegranates about the capital, all made of bronze; and so for the second column, also with pomegranates. ²³There were ninety-six pomegranates ᵇ⁻facing outward;⁻ᵇ all the pomegranates around the mesh-work amounted to one hundred.

²⁴The chief of the guards also took Seraiah the chief priest and Zeph-aniah, the deputy priest, and the three guardians of the threshold. ²⁵And from the city he took a eunuch who was in command of the soldiers; seven royal privy councilors, who were present in the city; the scribe of the army commander, who was in charge of mustering the people of the land; and sixty of the common people who were inside the city. ²⁶Nebuzaradan, the chief of the guards, took them and brought them to the king of Babylon at Riblah. ²⁷The king of Babylon had them struck down and put to death at Riblah, in the region of Hamath.

Thus Judah was exiled from its land. ²⁸This is the number of those whom Nebuchadrezzar exiled in the seventh year: 3,023 Judeans. ²⁹In the eighteenth year of Nebuchadrezzar, 832 persons [were exiled] from Jerusalem. ³⁰And in the twenty-third year of Nebuchadrezzar, Nebuza-radan, the chief of the guards, exiled 745 Judeans. The total amounted to 4,600 persons.

³¹In the thirty-seventh year of the exile of King Jehoiachin of Judah, on the twenty-fifth day of the twelfth month, King Evil-merodach of

Babylon, in the year he became king, ᵍ‑took note of‑ᵍ King Jehoiachin of Judah and released him from prison. ³²He spoke kindly to him, and gave him a throne above those of other kings who were with him in Babylon. ³³He removed his prison garments and [Jehoiachin] ate regularly in his presence the rest of his life. ³⁴A regular allotment of food was given him by order of the king of Babylon, an allotment for each day, to the day of his death—all the days of his life.

ᵍ‑ᵍ *Lit. "raised the head of."*

יחזקאל

EZEKIEL

1 In the thirtieth year,[a] on the fifth day of the fourth month, when I was in the community of exiles by the Chebar Canal, the heavens opened and I saw visions of God. [2]On the fifth day of the month—it was the fifth year of the exile of King Jehoiachin—[3]the word of the LORD came to the priest Ezekiel son of Buzi, by the Chebar Canal, in the land of the Chaldeans. And the hand of the LORD came upon him there.

[4]I looked, and lo, a stormy wind came sweeping out of the north—a huge cloud and flashing fire, surrounded by a radiance; and in the center of it, in the center of the fire, a gleam as of amber. [5]In the center of it were also the figures of four creatures. And this was their appearance:

They had the figures of human beings. [6]However, each had four faces, and each of them had four wings; [7]the legs of each were [fused into] a single rigid leg, and the feet of each were like a single calf's hoof;[b] and their sparkle[c] was like the luster of burnished bronze. [8]They had human hands below their wings. The four of them had their faces and their wings on their four sides. [9]Each one's wings touched those of the other. They did not turn when they moved; each could move in the direction of any of its faces.

[10]Each of them had a human face [at the front]; each of the four had the face of a lion on the right; each of the four had the face of an ox on the left; and each of the four had the face of an eagle [at the back]. [11]Such were their faces. As for their wings, they were separated: above, each had two touching those of the others, while the other two covered its body. [12]And each could move in the direction of any of its faces; they went wherever the spirit impelled them to go, without turning when they moved.

[13]Such then was the appearance of the creatures. With them was something that looked like burning coals of fire. This fire, suggestive of torches, kept moving about among the creatures; the fire had a radiance, and

---

a *We do not know the 30th of what.*
b *I.e., cleft in front.*
c *Or "plumage."*

lightning issued from the fire. [14d-]Dashing to and fro [among] the creatures was something that looked like flares.[-d]

[15]As I gazed on the creatures, I saw one wheel on the ground next to each of the four-faced creatures. [16]As for the appearance and structure of the wheels, they gleamed like beryl. All four had the same form; the appearance and structure of each was as of two wheels cutting through each other. [17]And when they moved, each could move in the direction of any of its four quarters; they did not veer when they moved. [18]Their rims were tall and frightening, for the rims of all four were covered all over with eyes. [19]And when the creatures moved forward, the wheels moved at their sides; and when the creatures were borne above the earth, the wheels were borne too. [20]Wherever the spirit impelled them to go, they went—wherever the spirit impelled them—and the wheels were borne alongside them; for the spirit of the creatures was in the wheels. [21]When those moved, these moved; and when those stood still, these stood still; and when those were borne above the earth, the wheels were borne alongside them—for the spirit of the creatures was in the wheels.

[22]Above the heads of the creatures was a form: an expanse, with an awe-inspiring gleam as of crystal, was spread out above their heads. [23]Under the expanse, each had one pair of wings extended toward those of the others; and each had another pair covering its body. [24]When they moved, I could hear the sound of their wings like the sound of mighty waters, like the sound of Shaddai,[c] a tumult like the din of an army. When they stood still, they would let their wings droop. [25d-]From above the expanse over their heads came a sound.[-d] When they stood still, they would let their wings droop.

[26]Above the expanse over their heads was the semblance of a throne, in appearance like sapphire; and on top, upon this semblance of a throne, there was the semblance of a human form. [27]From what appeared as his loins up, I saw a gleam as of amber—[d-]what looked like a fire encased in a frame;[-d] and from what appeared as his loins down, I saw what looked like fire. There was a radiance all about him. [28]Like the appearance of the bow which shines in the clouds on a day of rain, such was the appearance of the surrounding radiance. That was the appearance of the semblance of the Presence of the LORD. When I beheld it, I flung myself down on my face. And I heard the voice of someone speaking.

[d-d] *Meaning of Heb. uncertain.*
[c] *Traditionally "the Almighty"; see Gen. 17.1.*

2 And He said to me, "O mortal, stand up on your feet that I may speak to you." ²As He spoke to me, a spirit entered into me and set me upon my feet; and I heard what was being spoken to me. ³He said to me, "O mortal, I am sending you to the people of Israel, that nation of rebels, who have rebelled against Me.—They as well as their fathers have defied Me to this very day; ⁴for the sons are brazen of face and stubborn of heart. I send you to them, and you shall say to them: 'Thus said the Lord GOD'—⁵whether they listen or not, for they are a rebellious breed—that they may know that there was a prophet among them.

⁶"And you, mortal, do not fear them and do not fear their words, though thistles and thorns ᵃ⁻press against⁻ᵃ you, and you sit upon scorpions. Do not be afraid of their words and do not be dismayed by them, though they are a rebellious breed; ⁷but speak My words to them, whether they listen or not, for they are rebellious.

⁸"And you, mortal, heed what I say to you: Do not be rebellious like that rebellious breed. Open your mouth and eat what I am giving you." ⁹As I looked, there was a hand stretched out to me, holding a written scroll. ¹⁰He unrolled it before me, and it was inscribed on both the front and the back; on it were written lamentations, dirges, and woes.

3 He said to me, "Mortal, eat what is offered you; eat this scroll, and go speak to the House of Israel." ²So I opened my mouth, and He gave me this scroll to eat, ³as He said to me, "Mortal, feed your stomach and fill your belly with this scroll that I give you." I ate it, and it tasted as sweet as honey to me.

⁴Then He said to me, "Mortal, go to the House of Israel and repeat My very words to them. ⁵For you are sent, not to a people of unintelligible speech and difficult language, but to the House of Israel—⁶not to the many peoples of unintelligible speech and difficult language, whose talk you cannot understand. If I sent you to them, they would listen to you. ⁷But the House of Israel will refuse to listen to you, for they refuse to listen to Me; for the whole House of Israel are brazen of forehead and stubborn of heart. ⁸But I will make your face as hard as theirs, and your forehead as brazen as theirs. ⁹I will make your forehead like adamant,

---

ᵃ⁻ᵃ Lit. "are with."

harder than flint. Do not fear them, and do not be dismayed by them, though they are a rebellious breed."

¹⁰Then He said to me: "Mortal, listen with your ears and receive into your mind all the words that I speak to you. ¹¹Go to your people, the exile community, and speak to them. Say to them: Thus says the Lord GOD—whether they listen or not." ¹²Then a spirit carried me away, and behind me I heard a great roaring sound: ᵃ-"Blessed is the Presence of the LORD, in His place,"-ᵃ ¹³with the sound of the wings of the creatures beating against one another, and the sound of the wheels beside them— a great roaring sound. ¹⁴A spirit seized me and carried me away. I went in bitterness, in the fury of my spirit, while the hand of the LORD was strong upon me. ¹⁵And I came to the exile community that dwelt in Tel Abib by the Chebar Canal, and I remained where they dwelt. And for seven days I sat there stunned among them.

¹⁶After those seven days, the word of the LORD came to me: ¹⁷"O mortal, I appoint you watchman for the House of Israel; and when you hear a word from My mouth, you must warn them for Me. ¹⁸If I say to a wicked man, 'You shall die,' and you do not warn him—you do not speak to warn the wicked man of his wicked course in order to save his life—he, the wicked man, shall die for his iniquity, but I will require a reckoning for his blood from you. ¹⁹But if you do warn the wicked man, and he does not turn back from his wickedness and his wicked course, he shall die for his iniquity, but you will have saved your own life. ²⁰Again, if a righteous man abandons his righteousness and does wrong, when I put a stumbling block before him, he shall die. He shall die for his sins; the righteous deeds that he did shall not be remembered; but because you did not warn him, I will require a reckoning for his blood from you. ²¹If, however, you warn the righteous man not to sin, and he, the righteous, does not sin, he shall live because he took warning, and you will have saved your own life."

²²Then the hand of the LORD came upon me there, and He said to me, "Arise, go out to the valley, and there I will speak with you." ²³I arose and went out to the valley, and there stood the Presence of the LORD, like the Presence that I had seen at the Chebar Canal; and I flung myself down on my face. ²⁴And a spirit entered into me and set me upon my feet. And He spoke to me, and said to me: "Go, shut yourself up in your house. ²⁵As for you, O mortal, cords have been placed upon you, and you have been bound with them, and you shall not go out among

---

ᵃ⁻ᵃ *Emendation yields "as the Presence of the LORD rose from where it stood."*

them.b 26And I will make your tongue cleave to your palate, and you shall be dumb; you shall not be a reprover to them, for they are a rebellious breed. 27But when I speak with you, I will open your mouth, and you shall say to them, 'Thus says the Lord GOD!' He who listens will listen, and he who does not will not—for they are a rebellious breed."

4 "And you, O mortal, take a brick and put it in front of you, and incise on it a city, Jerusalem. 2Set up a siege against it, and build towers against it, and cast a mound against it; pitch camps against it, and bring up battering rams roundabout it. 3Then take an iron plate and place it as an iron wall between yourself and the city, and set your face against it. aThus it shall be under siege, you shall besiege it. This shall be an omen for the House of Israel.

4"Then lie on your left side, and let it bear the punishment of the House of Israel;b for as many days as you lie on it you shall bear their punishment. 5For I impose upon you three hundred and ninety days, corresponding to the number of the years of their punishment; and so you shall bear the punishment for the House of Israel. 6When you have completed these, you shall lie another forty days on your right side, and bear the punishment of the House of Judah.b I impose on you one day for each year.

7"Then, with bared arm, set your face toward besieged Jerusalem and prophesy against it. 8Now I put cords upon you, so that you cannot turn from side to side until you complete your days of siege.

9"Further, take wheat, barley, beans, lentils, millet, and emmer. Put them into one vessel and bake them into bread. Eat it as many days as you lie on your side: three hundred and ninety. 10The food that you eat shall be by weight, twenty shekels a day; this you shall eat in the space of a day. 11And you shall drink water by measure; drink a sixth of a *hin* in the space of a day.

12"Eat it as a barleyc cake; you shall bake it on human excrement before their eyes. 13So," said the LORD, "shall the people of Israel eat their bread, unclean, among the nations to which I will banish them." 14Then I said, "Ah, Lord GOD, my person was never defiled; nor have I eaten anything that died of itself or was torn by beasts from my youth until now, nor has foul flesh entered my mouth." 15He answered me, "See, I allow you cow's dung instead of human excrement; prepare your bread on that."

16dAnd He said to me, "O mortal, I am going to break the staff of

---

b *I.e., the people.*

a *I.e., in hostility.*

b *Since left and right also denote north and south (e.g., 16.46), the left side represents Israel, the northern kingdom, and the right side Judah, the southern kingdom.*

c *Meaning of Heb. uncertain.*

d *Resuming the thought of v. 11.*

bread in Jerusalem, and they shall eat bread by weight, in anxiety, and drink water by measure, in horror, [17]so that, lacking bread and water, they shall stare at each other, heartsick over their iniquity. [1]"And you, O mortal, take a sharp knife; use it as a barber's razor and pass it over your head and beard. Then take scales and divide the hair.[a] [2]When the days of siege are completed, destroy a third part in fire in the city, take a third and strike it with the sword all around [b-]the city,[-b] and scatter a third to the wind and unsheathe[c] a sword after them.

[3]"Take also a few [hairs] from there and tie them up in your skirts. [4]And take some more of them and cast them into the fire, and burn them in the fire. From this a fire shall go out upon the whole House of Israel."

[5]Thus said the Lord GOD: I set this Jerusalem in the midst of nations, with countries round about her. [6]But she rebelled against My rules and My laws, acting more wickedly than the nations and the countries round about her; she[d] rejected My rules and disobeyed My laws. [7]Assuredly, thus said the Lord GOD: Because you have outdone the nations that are round about you—you have not obeyed My laws or followed My rules, nor have you observed the rules of the nations round about you—[8]assuredly, thus said the Lord GOD: I, in turn, am going to deal with you, and I will execute judgments in your midst in the sight of the nations. [9]On account of all your abominations, I will do among you what I have never done, and the like of which I will never do again.

[10]Assuredly, parents shall eat their children in your midst, and children shall eat their parents. I will execute judgments against you, and I will scatter all your survivors in every direction.

[11]Assuredly, as I live—said the Lord GOD—because you defiled My Sanctuary with all your detestable things and all your abominations, I in turn will shear [you] away[e] and show no pity. I in turn will show no compassion: [12]One-third of you shall die of pestilence or perish in your midst by famine, one-third shall fall by the sword around you, and I will scatter one-third in every direction and will unsheathe the sword after them. [13]I will vent all My anger and satisfy My fury upon them; and when I vent all My fury upon them, they shall know that I the LORD have spoken in My passion. [14]I will make you a ruin and a mockery among the nations roundabout you, in the sight of every passerby. [15]And when I execute judgment upon you in anger and rage and furious chastisement,

---

[a] Lit. "them."
[b-b] Heb. "it."
[c] Cf. v. 12; lit. "I will unsheathe."
[d] Heb. "they."
[e] Cf. Isa. 15.2 and Jer. 48.37; here an allusion to the symbolism in v. 1.

you[f] shall be a mockery and a derision, a warning and a horror, to the nations roundabout you: I the LORD have spoken. [16]When I loose the deadly arrows of famine against those doomed to destruction, when I loose them against you to destroy you, I will heap more famine upon you and break your staff of bread. [17]I will let loose against you famine and wild beasts and they shall bereave you; pestilence and bloodshed shall sweep through you, and I will bring the sword upon you. I the LORD have spoken.

6 The word of the LORD came to me: [2]O mortal, turn your face toward the mountains of Israel and prophesy to them [3]and say: O mountains of Israel, hear the word of the Lord GOD. Thus said the Lord GOD to the mountains and the hills, to the streams and the valleys: See, I will bring a sword against you and destroy your shrines. [4]Your altars shall be wrecked and your incense stands smashed, and I will hurl down your slain in front of your fetishes. [5]I will cast the corpses of the people of Israel in front of their fetishes, and scatter your bones around your altars [6]in all your settlements. The towns shall be laid waste and the shrines shall be devastated. Thus your altars shall be laid waste and [a-]bear their punishment;[-a] your fetishes shall be smashed and annihilated, your incense stands cut down, and your handiwork wiped out; [7]and the slain shall fall in your midst. Then you shall know that I am the LORD. [8]Yet I will leave a remnant, in that some of you shall escape the sword among the nations and be scattered through the lands. [9]And those of you that escape will remember Me among the nations where they have been taken captive, [b-]how I was brokenhearted through[-b] their faithless hearts which turned away from Me, and through their eyes which lusted after their fetishes. And they shall loathe themselves for all the evil they committed and for all their abominable deeds. [10]Then they shall realize it was not without cause that I the LORD resolved to bring this evil upon them.

[11]Thus said the Lord GOD: Strike your hands together and stamp your feet and cry: Aha! over all the vile abominations of the House of Israel who shall fall by the sword, by famine, and by pestilence. [12]He who is far away shall die of pestilence, and he who is near shall fall by the sword, and he who survives and is protected shall die of famine. Thus I will spend My fury upon them. [13]And you shall know that I am the LORD, when

---

[f] *Heb. "she."*

[a-a] *Targum and other ancient versions read "shall be devastated."*
[b-b] *Emendation yields "how I broke."*

your slain lie among the fetishes round about their altars, on every high hill, on all the mountaintops, under every green tree, and under every leafy oak—wherever they presented pleasing odors to all their fetishes.

¹⁴I will stretch out My hand against them, and lay the land waste and desolate in all their settlements, from the wilderness as far as Diblah;ᶜ then they shall know that I am the LORD.

7 The word of the LORD came to me: ²You, O mortal, [say:] Thus said the Lord GOD to the land of Israel: Doom! Doom is coming upon the four corners of the land. ³Now doom is upon you! I will let loose My anger against you and judge you according to your ways; I will requite you for all your abominations. ⁴I will show you no pity and no compassion; but I will requite you for your ways and for the abominations in your midst. And you shall know that I am the LORD.

⁵Thus said the Lord GOD: ᵃ⁻A singular disaster; a disasterᵃ is coming. ⁶Doom is coming! The hour of doom is coming! It stirs against you; there it comes! ⁷ᵇ⁻The cycle has come around for you, O inhabitants of the land; the time has come; the day is near. There is panic on the mountains, not joy.⁻ᵇ ⁸Very soon I will pour out My wrath upon you and spend My anger on you; I will judge you according to your ways, and I will requite you for all your abominations. ⁹I will show you no pity and no compassion; but I will requite you for your ways, and for the abominations in your midst. And you shall know it was I the LORD who punished.

¹⁰Here is the day! See, the ᵇ⁻cycle has come round; it has appeared. The rod has blossomed; arrogance has budded, ¹¹lawlessness has grown into a rod of wickedness. Nothing comes of them, nor of their abundance, nor of their wealth; nor is there preeminence among them.⁻ᵇ ¹²The time has come, the day has arrived. Let not the buyer rejoice nor the seller mourn—for divine wrath shall overtake all her multitude. ¹³For the seller shall not return to what he sold so long as they remain among the living. For the vision concerns all her multitude, it shall not be revoked. And because of his guilt, no man shall hold fast to his life.

¹⁴They have sounded the horn, and all is prepared; but no one goes to battle, for My wrath is directed against all her multitude. ¹⁵The sword is outside and pestilence and famine are inside; he who is in the open shall die by the sword, he who is in the town shall be devoured by famine and

---

ᶜ A few Heb. mss. read "Riblah"; cf. 2 Kings 23.33; 25.6 ff.

ᵃ⁻ᵃ A number of mss. and editions, as well as Targum, read "Disaster after disaster."
ᵇ⁻ᵇ Meaning of Heb. uncertain.

pestilence. [16]And if any survive, they shall take to the mountains; they shall be [c]like doves of the valley, moaning together[c]—every one for his iniquity. [17]All hands shall grow weak, and all knees shall turn to water. [18]They shall gird on sackcloth, and horror shall cover them; every face shall betray shame, and every head shall be made bald.

[19]They shall throw their silver into the streets, and their gold shall be treated as something unclean. Their silver and gold shall not avail to save them in the day of the LORD's wrath—to satisfy their hunger or to fill their stomachs. Because they made them stumble into guilt—[20]for out of their beautiful adornments, in which they took pride, they made their images and their detestable abominations—therefore I will make them[d] an unclean thing to them. [21]I will give them as spoil to strangers, and as plunder to the wicked of the earth; and they shall defile them. [22]I will turn My face from them, and My treasures shall be defiled; ruffians shall invade it and defile it.

[23][b]Forge the chain,[b] for the land is full of bloody crimes, and the city is full of lawlessness. [24]I will bring in the worst of the nations to take possession of their houses; so shall I turn to naught the pride of the powerful, and their sanctuaries shall be defiled.

[25]Horror[b] comes, and they shall seek safety, but there shall be none. [26]Calamity shall follow calamity, and rumor follow rumor. Then they shall seek vision from the prophet in vain; instruction shall perish from the priest, and counsel from the elders. [27]The king shall mourn, the prince shall clothe himself with desolation, and the hands of the people of the land shall tremble. I will treat them in accordance with their own ways and judge them according to their deserts. And they shall know that I am the LORD.

8 In the sixth year, on the fifth day of the sixth month, I was sitting at home, and the elders of Judah were sitting before me, and there the hand of the Lord GOD fell upon me. [2]As I looked, there was a figure that had the appearance of fire:[a] from what appeared as his loins down, [he was] fire; and from his loins up, his appearance was resplendent and had the color of amber. [3]He stretched out the form of a hand, and took me by the hair of my head. A spirit lifted me up between heaven and earth and brought me in visions of God to Jerusalem, to the entrance of the Penimith[b]

[c-c] *Emendation yields "like moaning doves. All of them shall perish."*
[d] *I.e., their adornments.*

[a] *Septuagint "a man."*
[b] *Meaning of Heb. uncertain.*

Gate that faces north; that was the site of the infuriating image that provokes fury. 4And the Presence of the God of Israel appeared there, like the vision that I had seen in the valley.c

5And He said to me, "O mortal, turn your eyes northward." I turned my eyes northward, and there, d-north of the gate of the altar, was-d that infuriating image on the approach.b 6And He said to me, "Mortal, do you see what they are doing, the terrible abominations that the House of Israel is practicing here, e-to drive Me far-e from My Sanctuary? You shall yet see even greater abominations!"

7Then He brought me to the entrance of the court;f and I looked, and there was a hole in the wall. 8He said to me, "Mortal, break through the wall"; so I broke through the wall and found an entrance. 9And He said to me, "Enter and see the vile abominations that they are practicing here." 10I entered and looked, and there all detestable forms of creeping things and beasts and all the fetishes of the House of Israel were depicted over the entire wall. 11Before them stood seventy men, elders of the House of Israel, with Jaazaniah son of Shaphan standing in their midst. Everyone had a censer in his hand, and a thick cloud of incense smoke ascended. 12Again He spoke to me, "O mortal, have you seen what the elders of the House of Israel are doing in the darkness, everyone in his image-covered chamber? For they say, 'The LORD does not see us; the LORD has abandoned the country.' " 13And He said to me, "You shall see even more terrible abominations which they practice."

14Next He brought me to the entrance of the north g-gate of the House of the LORD;-g and there sat the women bewailing Tammuz.h 15He said to me, "Have you seen, O mortal? You shall see even more terrible abominations than these."

16Then He brought me into the inner court of the House of the LORD, and there, at the entrance to the Temple of the LORD, between the portico and the altar, were about twenty-five men, their backs to the Temple of the LORD and their faces to the east; they were bowing low to the sun in the east. 17And He said to me, "Do you see, O mortal? Is it not enough for the House of Judah to practice the abominations that they have committed here, that they must fill the country with lawlessness and provoke Me still further and i-thrust the branch to their nostrils?-i 18I in turn will act with fury, I will show no pity or compassion; though they cry aloud to Me, I will not listen to them."

---

c See chap. 1 and 3.22–23.
d-d Meaning of Heb. uncertain; emendation yields "north of the gate was the altar of."
e-e Or "at a distance."
f I.e., the outer court of the Temple.
g-g I.e., the gate of the inner court.
h A Babylonian god.
i-i Apparently meaning "goad Me to fury"; "their" is a euphemism for "My."

9 Then He called loudly in my hearing, saying, "Approach, you men in charge of the city, each bearing his weapons of destruction!" ²And six men entered by way of the upper gate that faces north, each with his club in his hand; and among them was another, clothed in linen, with a writing case at his waist. They came forward and stopped at the bronze altar. ³Now the Presence of the God of Israel had moved from the cherub on which it had rested to the platform^a of the House. He called to the man clothed in linen with the writing case at his waist; ⁴and the LORD said to him, "Pass through the city, through Jerusalem, and put a mark on the foreheads of the men who moan and groan because of all the abominations that are committed in it." ⁵To the others He said in my hearing, "Follow him through the city and strike; show no pity or compassion. ⁶Kill off graybeard, youth and maiden, women and children; but do not touch any person who bears the mark. Begin here at My Sanctuary." So they began with the elders who were in front of the House. ⁷And He said to them, "Defile the House and fill the courts with the slain. Then go forth." So they went forth and began to kill in the city. ⁸When they were out killing, and I remained alone, I flung myself on my face and cried out, "Ah, Lord GOD! Are you going to annihilate all that is left of Israel, pouring out Your fury upon Jerusalem?" ⁹He answered me, "The iniquity of the Houses of Judah and Israel is very very great, the land is full of crime and the city is full of corruption. For they say, 'The LORD has forsaken the land, and the LORD does not see.' ¹⁰I, in turn, will show no pity or compassion; I will give them their deserts." ¹¹And then the man clothed in linen with the writing case at his waist brought back word, saying, "I have done as You commanded me."

10 I looked, and on the expanse over the heads of the cherubs, there was something like a sapphire stone; an appearance resembling a throne could be seen over them. ²He spoke to the man clothed in linen and said, "Step inside the wheelwork, under the cherubs, and fill your hands with glowing coals from among the cherubs, and scatter them over the city." And he went in as I looked on. ³Now the cherubs were standing on the south side of the House when the man entered, and the cloud filled the inner court. ⁴But when the Presence of the LORD moved from the cherubs

---

^a *The raised platform on which the Temple stood; cf. 47.1.*

to the platform[a] of the House, the House was filled with the cloud, and the court was filled with the radiance of the Presence of the LORD. [5]The sound of the cherubs' wings could be heard as far as the outer court, like the voice of El Shaddai[b] when He speaks.

[6]When He commanded the man dressed in linen: "Take fire from among the cherubs within the wheelwork," he went in and stood beside a wheel. [7]And a cherub stretched out his hand among the cherubs to the fire that was among the cherubs; he took some and put it into the hands of him who was clothed in linen, who took it and went out. [8]The cherubs appeared to have the form of a man's hand under their wings.

[9]I could see that there were four wheels beside the cherubs, one wheel beside each of the cherubs; as for the appearance of the wheels, they gleamed like the beryl stone. [10]In appearance, the four had the same form, as if there were two wheels cutting through each other. [11]And when they moved, each could move in the direction of any of its four quarters; they did not veer as they moved. The [cherubs] moved in the direction in which one of the heads faced, without turning as they moved. [12]Their entire bodies—backs, hands, and wings—and the wheels, the wheels of the four of them, were covered all over with eyes. [13]It was these wheels that I had heard called "the wheelwork."[c] [14]Each one had four faces: One was a cherub's face, the second a human face, the third a lion's face, and the fourth an eagle's face.

[15]The cherubs ascended; those were the creatures that I had seen by the Chebar Canal. [16]Whenever the cherubs went, the wheels went beside them; and when the cherubs lifted their wings to ascend from the earth, the wheels did not roll away from their side. [17]When those stood still, these stood still; and when those ascended, these ascended with them, for the spirit of the creature was in them.

[18]Then the Presence of the LORD left the platform[a] of the House and stopped above the cherubs. [19]And I saw the cherubs lift their wings and rise from the earth, with the wheels beside them as they departed; and they[d] stopped at the entrance of the eastern gate of the House of the LORD, with the Presence of the God of Israel above them. [20]They were the same creatures that I had seen below the God of Israel at the Chebar Canal; so now I knew that they were cherubs.[e] [21]Each one had four faces and each had four wings, with the form of human hands under the wings. [22]As for the form of their faces, they were the very faces that I had seen

---

[a] *See note at 47.1.*
[b] *See note at Gen. 17.1.*
[c] *See v. 2.*
[d] *Lit. "it."*
[e] *Because they had been called "cherubs." (cf. v. 2.).*

by the Chebar Canal—their appearance and ᶠ·their features·ᶠ—and each could move in the direction of any of its faces.

11 Then a spirit lifted me up and brought me to the east gate of the House of the LORD, which faces eastward; and there, at the entrance of the gate, were twenty-five men, among whom I saw Jaazaniah son of Azzur and Pelatiah son of Benaiah, leaders of the people. ²[The LORD] said to me, "O mortal, these are the men who plan iniquity and plot wickedness in this city, ³who say: 'There is no need now to build houses; this [city] is the pot, and we are the meat.'ᵃ ⁴I adjure you, prophesy against them; prophesy, O mortal!"

⁵Thereupon the spirit of the LORD fell upon me, and He said to me, "Speak: Thus said the LORD: Such are your thoughts, O House of Israel; I know what comes into your mind. ⁶Many have you slain in this city; you have filled its streets with corpses. ⁷Assuredly, thus says the Lord GOD: The corpses that you have piled up in it are the meat for which it is the pot; but you shall be taken out of it. ⁸You feared the sword, and the sword I will bring upon you—declares the Lord GOD. ⁹I will take you out of it and deliver you into the hands of strangers, and I will execute judgments upon you. ¹⁰You shall fall by the sword; I will punish you at the border of Israel. And you shall know that I am the LORD. ¹¹This [city] shall not be a pot for you, nor you the meat in it; I will punish you at the border of Israel. ¹²Then you shall know that I am the LORD, whose laws you did not follow and whose rules you did not obey, acting instead according to the rules of the nations around you."

¹³Now, as I prophesied, Pelatiah son of Benaiah dropped dead. I threw myself upon my face and cried out aloud, "Ah, Lord GOD! You are wiping out the remnant of Israel!"

¹⁴Then the word of the LORD came to me: ¹⁵"O mortal, [I will save] your brothers, your brothers, the men of your kindred,ᵇ all of that very House of Israel to whom the inhabitants of Jerusalem say, 'Keep far from the LORD; the land has been given as a heritage to us.' ¹⁶Say then: Thus said the Lord GOD: I have indeed removed them far among the nations and have scattered them among the countries, and I have become to them a diminished sanctity in the countries whither they have gone. ¹⁷Yet say: Thus said the Lord GOD: I will gather youᵇ from the peoples and assemble

ᶠ·ᶠ *Lit. "themselves."*
ᵃ *I.e., the exiles will not return.*
ᵇ *I.e., the exiles.*

you out of the countries where you have been scattered, and I will give you the Land of Israel. [18]And they shall return there, and do away with all its detestable things and all its abominations. [19]I will give them one heart and put a new spirit in them;[c] I will remove the heart of stone from their bodies and give them a heart of flesh, [20]that they may follow My laws and faithfully observe My rules. Then they shall be My people and I will be their God. [21]But as for them whose heart is set upon their detestable things and their abominations, I will repay them for their conduct—declares the Lord GOD."

[22]Then the cherubs, with the wheels beside them, lifted their wings, while the Presence of the God of Israel rested above them. [23]The Presence of the LORD ascended from the midst of the city and stood on the hill east of the city. [24]A spirit carried me away and brought me in a vision by the spirit of God to the exile community in Chaldea. Then the vision that I had seen left me, [25]and I told the exiles all the things that the LORD had shown me.

12 The word of the LORD came to me: [2]O mortal, you dwell among the rebellious breed. They have eyes to see but see not, ears to hear but hear not; for they are a rebellious breed. [3]Therefore, mortal, get yourself gear for exile, and go into exile by day before their eyes. Go into exile from your home to another place before their very eyes; perhaps they will take note, even though they are a rebellious breed. [4]Carry out your gear as gear for exile by day before their very eyes; and go out again in the evening before their eyes, as one who goes out into exile. [5]Before their eyes, break through the wall and carry [the gear] out through it; [6]before their eyes, carry it on your shoulder. Take it out in the dark, and cover your face that you may not see the land; for I make you a portent to the House of Israel.

[7]I did just as I was ordered: I took out my gear by day as gear for exile, and in the evening I broke through the wall [a-]with my own hands.[-a] In the darkness I carried [the gear] out on my shoulder, carrying it before their eyes.

[8]In the morning, the word of the LORD came to me: [9]O mortal, did not the House of Israel, that rebellious breed, ask you, "What are you doing?" [10]Say to them: "Thus said the Lord GOD: This pronouncement concerns the prince in Jerusalem and all the House of Israel who are in

---

[c] Heb. "you."

[a-a] Lit. "by hand."

it." [11]Say: "I am a portent for you: As I have done, so shall it be done to them; they shall go into exile, into captivity. [12]And the prince among them shall carry his gear on his shoulder as he goes out in the dark. He[b] shall break through the wall in order to carry [his gear] out through it; he shall cover his face, because he himself shall not see the land with his eyes." [13]I will spread My net over him, and he shall be caught in My snare. I will bring him to Babylon, the land of the Chaldeans, but he shall not see it;[c] and there he shall die. [14]And all those around him, his helpers and all his troops, I will scatter in every direction; and I will unsheathe the sword after them. [15]Then, when I have scattered them among the nations and dispersed them through the countries, they shall know that I am the LORD. [16]But I will spare a few of them from the sword, from famine, and from pestilence, that they may recount all their abominable deeds among the nations to which they come; and they shall know that I am the LORD!

[17]The word of the LORD came to me: [18]O mortal, eat your bread in trembling and drink your water in fear and anxiety. [19]And say to the people of the land: Thus said the Lord GOD concerning the inhabitants of Jerusalem in the land of Israel: They shall eat their bread in anxiety and drink their water in desolation, because their land will be desolate of its multitudes on account of the lawlessness of all its inhabitants. [20]The inhabited towns shall be laid waste and the land shall become a desolation; then you shall know that I am the LORD.

[21]The word of the LORD came to me: [22]O mortal, what is this proverb that you have in the land of Israel, that you say, "The days grow many and every vision comes to naught?" [23]Assuredly, say to them, Thus said the Lord GOD: I will put an end to this proverb; it shall not be used in Israel any more. Speak rather to them: The days draw near, and the fulfillment of every vision. [24]For there shall no longer be any false vision or soothing divination in the House of Israel. [25]But whenever I the LORD speak what I speak, that word shall be fulfilled without any delay; in your days, O rebellious breed, I will fulfill every word I speak—declares the Lord GOD.

[26]The word of the LORD came to me: [27]See, O mortal, the House of Israel says, "The vision that he sees is far ahead, and he prophesies for the distant future." [28]Assuredly, say to them: Thus said the Lord GOD: There shall be no more delay; whenever I speak a word, that word shall be fulfilled—declares the Lord GOD.

[b] *Heb. "They."*
[c] *Cf. 2 Kings 25.7.*

13
The word of the LORD came to me: ²O mortal, prophesy against the prophets of Israel who prophesy; say to those who prophesy out of their own imagination: Hear the word of the LORD! ³Thus said the Lord GOD: Woe to the degenerate prophets, who follow their own fancy, without having had a vision! ⁴Your prophets, O Israel, have been like jackals among ruins. ⁵You did not enter the breaches and repair the walls for the House of Israel, that they might stand up in battle in the day of the LORD. ⁶They prophesied falsehood and lying divination; they said, "Declares the LORD," when the LORD did not send them, and then they waited for their word to be fulfilled. ⁷It was false visions you prophesied and lying divination you uttered, saying, "Declares the LORD," when I had not spoken.

⁸Assuredly, thus said the Lord GOD: Because you speak falsehood and prophesy lies, assuredly, I will deal with you—declares the Lord GOD. ⁹My hand will be against the prophets who prophesy falsehood and utter lying divination. They shall not remain in the assembly of My people, they shall not be inscribed in the lists of the House of Israel, and they shall not come back to the land of Israel. Thus shall you know that I am the Lord GOD.

¹⁰Inasmuch as they have misled My people, saying, "It is well," when nothing is well, daubing with plaster the flimsy wall which ªthe people-ª were building, ¹¹say to those daubers of plaster: It shall collapse; a driving rain shall descend—and you, O great hailstones, shall fall—and a hurricane wind shall rend it. ¹²Then, when the wall collapses, you will be asked, "What became of the plaster you daubed on?"

¹³Assuredly, thus said the Lord GOD: In My fury I will let loose hurricane winds; in My anger a driving rain shall descend, and great hailstones in destructive fury. ¹⁴I will throw down the wall that you daubed with plaster, and I will raze it to the ground so that its foundation is exposed; and when it falls, you shall perish in its midst; then you shall know that I am the LORD. ¹⁵And when I have spent My fury upon the wall and upon those who daubed it with plaster, I will say to you: Gone is the wall and gone are its daubers, ¹⁶the prophets of Israel who prophesy about Jerusalem and see a vision of well-being for her when there is no well-being—declares the Lord GOD.

ª-ª *Heb.* "*it.*"

¹⁷And you, O mortal, set your face against the women of your people, who prophesy out of their own imagination. Prophesy against them ¹⁸and say: Thus said the Lord GOD: Woe to those who sew pads^b on all arm-joints and make bonnets^b for the head of every person, in order to entrap! Can you hunt down lives among My people, while you preserve your own lives? ¹⁹You have profaned ^{c-}My name^{-c} among My people in return for handfuls of barley and morsels of bread; you have announced the death of persons who will not die and the survival of persons who will not live—lying to My people, who listen to your lies.

²⁰Assuredly, thus said the Lord GOD: I am going to deal with your pads,^b ^{d-}by which^{-d} you hunt down lives like birds, and I will tear them from your arms and free the persons whose lives you hunt down like birds. ²¹I will tear off your bonnets^b and rescue My people from your hands, and they shall no longer be prey in your hands; then you shall know that I am the LORD. ²²Because you saddened the heart of the innocent with lies, when I would not inflict suffering on him, and encouraged the wicked not to repent of his evil ways and so gain life—²³assuredly, you shall no longer prophesy lies or practice divination! I will save My people from your hands, and you shall know that I am the LORD.

14 Certain elders of Israel came to me and sat down before me. ²And the word of the LORD came to me: ³O mortal, these men have turned their thoughts upon their fetishes and set their minds upon the sin through which they stumbled: Shall I respond to their inquiry? ⁴Now speak to them and tell them: Thus said the Lord GOD: If anyone of the House of Israel turns his thoughts upon his fetishes and sets his mind upon the sin through which he stumbled, and yet comes to the prophet, I the LORD will respond to him ^{a-}as he comes with^{-a} his multitude of fetishes. ⁵Thus I will hold the House of Israel to account for their thoughts, because they have all been estranged from Me through their fetishes.

⁶Now say to the House of Israel: Thus said the Lord GOD: Repent, and turn back from your fetishes and turn your minds away from all your abominations. ⁷For if any man of the House of Israel, or of the strangers who dwell in Israel, breaks away from Me and turns his thoughts upon his fetishes and sets his mind upon the sins through which he stumbled,

^b *Meaning of Heb. uncertain.*
^{c-c} *Heb. "Me."*
^{d-d} *Heb. "where."*

^{a-a} *Emendation yields "directly, because of"; cf. v. 7.*

and then goes to the prophet to inquire of Me through him, I the LORD will respond to him directly. [8]I will set My face against that man and make him a sign and a byword, and I will cut him off from the midst of My people. Then you shall know that I am the LORD.

[9]And if a prophet is seduced and does speak a word [to such a man], it was I the LORD who seduced that prophet; I will stretch out My hand against him and destroy him from among My people Israel. [10]Thus they shall bear their punishment: The punishment of the inquirer and the punishment of the prophet shall be the same, [11]so that the House of Israel may never again stray from Me and defile itself with all its transgressions. Then they shall be My people and I will be their God—declares the Lord GOD.

[12]The word of the LORD came to me: [13]O mortal, if a land were to sin against Me and commit a trespass, and I stretched out My hand against it and broke its staff of bread, and sent famine against it and cut off man and beast from it, [14]even if these three men—Noah, Daniel, and Job—should be in it, they would by their righteousness save only themselves—declares the Lord GOD. [15]Or, if I were to send wild beasts to roam the land and they depopulated it, and it became a desolation with none passing through it because of the beasts, [16]as I live—declares the Lord GOD—those three men in it would save neither sons nor daughters; they alone would be saved, but the land would become a desolation. [17]Or, if I were to bring the sword upon that land and say, "Let a sword sweep through the land so that I may cut off from it man and beast," [18]if those three men should be in it, as I live—declares the Lord GOD—they would save neither sons nor daughters, but they alone would be saved. [19]Or, if I let loose a pestilence against that land, and poured out My fury upon it in blood, cutting off from it man and beast, [20]should Noah, Daniel, and Job be in it, as I live—declares the Lord GOD—they would save neither son nor daughter; they would save themselves alone by their righteousness.

[21]Assuredly, thus said the Lord GOD: How much less [should any escape] now that I have let loose against Jerusalem all four of My terrible punishments—the sword, famine, wild beasts, and pestilence—to cut off man and beast from it! [22]Yet there are survivors left of it, b-sons and daughters who are being brought out.-b They are coming out to you; and when you see their ways and their deeds, you will be consoled for the disaster that I brought on Jerusalem, for all that I brought on it. [23]You will be consoled through them, when you see their ways and their deeds

b-b *Several ancient versions read "who are bringing out sons and daughters."*

and realize that not without cause did I do all that I did in it—declares the Lord GOD.

15 The word of the LORD came to me: ²O mortal, how is the wood of the grapevine better than the wood of any branch to be found among the trees of the forest? ³Can wood be taken from it for use in any work? Can one take a peg from it to hang any vessel on? ⁴Now suppose it was thrown into the fire as fuel and the fire consumed its two ends and its middle was charred—is it good for any use? ⁵Even when it was whole it could not be used for anything; how much less when fire has consumed it and it is charred! Can it still be used for anything?

⁶Assuredly, thus said the Lord GOD: Like the wood of the grapevine among the trees of the forest, which I have designated to be fuel for fire, so will I treat the inhabitants of Jerusalem. ⁷I will set My face against them; they escaped from fire, but fire shall consume them. When I set my face against them, you shall know that I am the LORD. ⁸I will make the land a desolation, because they committed trespass—declares the Lord GOD.

16 The word of the LORD came to me: ²O mortal, proclaim Jerusalem's abominations to her, ³and say: Thus said the Lord GOD to Jerusalem: By origin and birth you are from the land of the Canaanites—your father was an Amorite and your mother a Hittite. ⁴As for your birth, when you were born your navel cord was not cut, and you were not bathed in water to ᵃ-smooth you;-ᵃ you were not rubbed with salt, nor were you swaddled. ⁵No one pitied you enough to do any one of these things for you out of compassion for you; on the day you were born, you were left lying, rejected, in the open field. ⁶When I passed by you and saw you wallowing in your blood, I said to you: "Live in spite of your blood." ᵇ-Yea, I said to you: "Live in spite of your blood."-ᵇ ⁷I let you grow like the plants of the field; and you continued to grow up until you attained ᵃ-to womanhood,-ᵃ until your breasts became firm and your hair sprouted.

You were still naked and bare ⁸when I passed by you [again] and saw that your time for love had arrived. ᶜ-So I spread My robe over you-ᶜ and covered your nakedness, and I entered into a covenant with you by oath—

ᵃ⁻ᵃ *Meaning of Heb. uncertain.*
ᵇ⁻ᵇ *This sentence is missing from some ancient versions and a few Heb. mss.*
ᶜ⁻ᶜ *An act symbolizing espousal; cf. note at Deut. 23.1, Ruth 3.9.*

declares the Lord GOD; thus you became Mine. [9]I bathed you in water, and washed the blood off you, and anointed you with oil. [10]I clothed you with embroidered garments, and gave you sandals of [d-]dolphin leather[-d] to wear, and wound fine linen about your head, and dressed you in silks. [11]I decked you out in finery and put bracelets on your arms and a chain around your neck. [12]I put a ring in your nose, and earrings in your ears, and a splendid crown on your head. [13]You adorned yourself with gold and silver, and your apparel was of fine linen, silk, and embroidery. Your food was choice flour, honey, and oil. You grew more and more beautiful, and became fit for royalty. [14]Your beauty won you fame among the nations, for it was perfected through the splendor which I set upon you—declares the Lord GOD.

[15]But confident in your beauty and fame, you played the harlot: you lavished your favors on every passerby; [a-]they were his.[-a] [16]You even took some of your cloths and made yourself [a-]tapestried platforms[-a] and fornicated on them—[d-]not in the future; not in time to come.[-d] [17]You took your beautiful things, made of the gold and silver that I had given you, and you made yourself phallic images and fornicated with them. [18]You took your embroidered cloths to cover them; and you set My oil and My incense before them. [19]The food that I had given you—the choice flour, the oil, and the honey, which I had provided for you to eat—you set it before them for a pleasing odor.[e] And so it went—declares the Lord GOD. [20]You even took the sons and daughters that you bore to Me and sacrificed them to those [images] as food—as if your harlotries were not enough, [21]you slaughtered My children and presented them as offerings to them! [22]In all your abominations and harlotries, you did not remember the days of your youth, when you were naked and bare, and lay wallowing in your blood.

[23]After all your wickedness (woe, woe to you!)—declares the Lord GOD—[24]you built yourself an eminence and made yourself a mound in every square. [25]You built your mound at every crossroad; and you sullied your beauty and spread your legs to every passerby, and you multiplied your harlotries. [26]You played the whore with your neighbors, the lustful[f] Egyptians—you multiplied your harlotries to anger Me. [27]Now, I will stretch out My arm against you and withhold your maintenance; and I will surrender you to the will of your enemies, the Philistine women, who are shocked by your lewd behavior.

[28]In your insatiable lust you also played the whore with the Assyrians;

[d-d] *See note at Ex. 25:4.*
[e] *I.e., as a sacrifice; cf. Lev. 2.2.*
[f] *Lit. "big of phallus"; cf. 23.20.*

you played the whore with them, but were still unsated. ²⁹You multiplied your harlotries with Chaldea, that land of traders; yet even with this you were not satisfied.

³⁰ᵍ⁻How sick was your heart ᵍ—declares the Lord GOD—when you did all those things, the acts of a self-willed whore, ³¹building your eminence at every crossroad and setting your mound in every square! Yet you were not like a prostitute, for you spurned fees; ³²[you were like] the adulterous wife who welcomes strangers instead of her husband. ³³Gifts are made to all prostitutes, but you made gifts to all your lovers, and bribed them to come to you from every quarter for your harlotries. ³⁴You were the opposite of other women: you solicited instead of being solicited; you paid fees instead of being paid fees. Thus you were just the opposite!

³⁵Now, O harlot, hear the word of the LORD. ³⁶Thus said the Lord GOD: Because of your brazen effrontery, offering your nakedness to your lovers for harlotry—ʰ⁻just like the blood of your children, which you gave to all your abominable fetishes:⁻ʰ—³⁷I will assuredly assemble all the lovers to whom you gave your favors, along with everybody you accepted and everybody you rejected. I will assemble them against you from every quarter, and I will expose your nakedness to them, and they shall see all your nakedness. ³⁸I will inflict upon you the punishment of women who commit adultery and murder, and I will direct bloody and impassioned fury against you. ³⁹I will deliver you into their hands, and they shall tear down your eminence and level your mounds; and they shall strip you of your clothing and take away your dazzling jewels, leaving you naked and bare. ⁴⁰Then they shall assemble a mob against you to pelt you with stones and pierce you with their swords. ⁴¹They shall put your houses to the flames and execute punishment upon you in the sight of many women; thus I will put a stop to your harlotry, and you shall pay no more fees. ⁴²When I have satisfied My fury upon you and My rage has departed from you, then I will be tranquil; I will be angry no more.

⁴³Because you did not remember the days of your youth, but infuriated Me with all those things, I ʰ⁻will pay you back for your conduct⁻ʰ— declares the Lord GOD.

Have you not committed depravity on top of all your other abominations? ⁴⁴Why, everyone who uses proverbs applies to you the proverb "Like mother, like daughter." ⁴⁵You are the daughter of your mother, who rejected her husband and children. And you are the sister of your sisters, who rejected their husbands and children; for you are daughters

---

ᵍ⁻ᵍ *Change of vocalization yields "How furious I was with you"; lit. "How I was filled with your fury"* (libbat, *as in Akkadian and Old Aramaic*).
ʰ⁻ʰ *Construction of Heb. uncertain.*

of a Hittite mother and an Amorite father. ⁴⁶Your elder sister was Samaria, who lived with her daughters to the north of you; your younger sister was Sodom, who lived with her daughters to the south of you. ⁴⁷Did you not walk in their ways and practice their abominations? Why, you were almostᵃ more corrupt than they in all your ways. ⁴⁸As I live—declares the Lord GOD—your sister Sodom and her daughters did not do what you and your daughters did. ⁴⁹Only this was the sin of your sister Sodom: arrogance! She and her daughters had plenty of bread and untroubled tranquillity; yet she did not support the poor and the needy. ⁵⁰In their haughtiness, they committed abomination before Me; and so I removed them, as you saw.ⁱ ⁵¹Nor did Samaria commit even half your sins. You committed more abominations than they, and by all the abominations that you committed you made your sisters look righteous. ⁵²Truly, you must bear the disgrace of serving as your sisters' advocate: Since you have sinned more abominably than they, they appear righteous in comparison. So be ashamed and bear your disgrace, because you have made your sisters look righteous.

⁵³I will restore their fortunes—the fortunes of Sodom and her daughters and the fortunes of Samaria and her daughters—and your fortunes along with theirs. ⁵⁴Thus you shall bear your disgrace and feel your disgrace for behaving in such a way that they could take comfort. ⁵⁵Then your sister Sodom and her daughters shall return to their former state, and Samaria and her daughters shall return to their former state, and you and your daughters shall return to your former state. ⁵⁶Was not your sister Sodom a byword in your mouth in the days of your pride, ⁵⁷before your own wickedness was exposed? So must you now bear the mockery of the daughters of Aramʲ and all her neighbors, the daughters of Philistia who jeer at you on every side. ⁵⁸You yourself must bear your depravity and your abominations—declares the LORD.

⁵⁹Truly, thus said the Lord GOD: I will deal with you as you have dealt, for you have spurned the pact and violated the covenant. ⁶⁰Nevertheless, I will remember the covenant I made with you in the days of your youth, and I will establish it with you as an everlasting covenant. ⁶¹You shall remember your ways and feel ashamed, when you receive your older sisters and your younger sisters, and I give them to you as daughters, though they are not of your covenant. ⁶²I will establish My covenant with you, and you shall know that I am the LORD. ⁶³Thus you shall remember and

---

ⁱ *Construed as second-person feminine; cf.* qere, *vv. 47 and 51; and see above vv. 13, 18, 22, 31, 43.*

ʲ *Many Heb. mss. and editions read "Edom."*

feel shame, and you shall be too abashed to open your mouth again, when I have forgiven you for all that you did—declares the Lord GOD.

17 The word of the LORD came to me: [2]O mortal, propound a riddle and relate an allegory to the House of Israel. [3]Say: Thus said the Lord GOD: The great eagle with the great wings and the long pinions, a-with the full plumage and the brilliant colors,-a came to the Lebanon range and seized the top of the cedar. [4]He plucked off its topmost bough and carried it off to the land of traders[b] and set it in a city of merchants. [5]He then took some of the seed of the land[c] and planted it in a fertile field; d-he planted and set it like a willow-d beside abundant waters. [6]It grew and became a spreading vine of low stature; it became a vine, produced branches, and sent out boughs. [He had intended] that its twigs should turn to him, and that its roots should stay under him.

[7]But there was another great eagle with great wings and full plumage; and this vine now bent its roots in his direction and sent out its twigs toward him, that he might water it more than the bed where it was planted—[8]though it was planted in rich soil beside abundant water—so that it might grow branches and produce boughs and be a noble vine.

[9]Say: Thus said the Lord GOD: Will it thrive? Will he[e] not tear out its roots and rip off its crown, so that its entire foliage withers? It shall wither, despite any strong arm or mighty army [that may come] to remove it from its roots. [10]And suppose it is transplanted, will it thrive? When the east wind strikes it, it shall wither—wither upon the bed where it is growing.

[11]Then the word of the LORD came to me: [12]Say to the rebellious breed: Do you not know what these things mean? Say: The king of Babylon came to Jerusalem, and carried away its king and its officers and brought them back with him to Babylon. [13]He took one of the seed royal and made a covenant with him and imposed an oath on him, and he carried away the nobles of the land—[14]so that it might be a humble kingdom and not exalt itself, but keep his covenant and so endure.

[15]But [that prince] rebelled against him and sent his envoys to Egypt to get horses and a large army. Will he succeed? Will he who does such things escape? Shall he break a covenant and escape? [16]As I live—declares the Lord GOD—in the very homeland of the king who made him king,

---

a-a *This description suggests the golden eagle; the vulture, called by the same word in Heb.* (nesher) *has a bald head (Mic. 1.16) and dark feathers.*
b *Cf. 16.29.*
c *Emendation yields "cedar."*
d-d *Meaning of Heb. uncertain.*
e *I.e., the first eagle.*

whose oath he flouted and whose covenant he broke—right there, in Babylon, he shall die. [17]Pharaoh will not fight at his side with a great army and with numerous troops in the war, when mounds are thrown up and siege towers erected to destroy many lives. [18]He flouted a pact and broke a covenant; he gave his promise and did all these things—he shall not escape. [19]Assuredly, thus said the Lord GOD: As I live, I will pay him back for flouting My pact and breaking My covenant. [20]I will spread My net over him and he shall be caught in My snare; I will carry him to Babylon and enter with him into judgment there for the trespass which he committed against Me. [21]And all the fugitives[f] of all his battalions shall fall by the sword, and those who remain shall scatter in every direction; then you will know that I the LORD have spoken.

[22]Thus said the Lord GOD: Then I in turn will take and set [in the ground a slip] from the lofty top of the cedar; I will pluck a tender twig from the tip of its crown, and I will plant it on a tall, towering mountain. [23]I will plant it in Israel's lofty highlands, and it shall bring forth boughs and produce branches[g] and grow into a noble cedar. Every bird of every feather shall take shelter under it, shelter in the shade of its boughs. [24]Then shall all the trees of the field know that it is I the LORD who have abased the lofty tree and exalted the lowly tree, who have dried up the green tree and made the withered tree bud. I the LORD have spoken, and I will act.

18

The word of the LORD came to me: [2]What do you mean by quoting this proverb upon the soil of Israel, "Parents eat sour grapes and their children's teeth are blunted"?[a] [3]As I live—declares the Lord GOD— this proverb shall no longer be current among you in Israel. [4]Consider, all lives are Mine; the life of the parent and the life of the child are both Mine. The person who sins, only he shall die.

[5]Thus, if a man is righteous and does what is just and right: [6]If he has not eaten on the mountains[b] or raised his eyes to the fetishes of the House of Israel; if he has not defiled another man's wife or approached a menstruous woman; [7]if he has not wronged anyone; if he has returned the debtor's pledge to him and has taken nothing by robbery; if he has given bread to the hungry and clothed the naked; [8]if he has not lent at advance interest or exacted accrued interest;[c] if he has abstained from wrongdoing

---

[f] *Many mss. read "picked men."*
[g] *Others "fruit."*

[a] *Others "set on edge."*
[b] *I.e., in idolatry. Emendation yields "with the blood"; cf. 33.25; Lev. 17.10–11, 19.26.*
[c] *I.e., interest deducted in advance or interest added at the time of repayment; cf. Lev. 25.36.*

and executed true justice between man and man; 9if he has followed My laws and kept My rules and acted honestly—he is righteous. Such a man shall live—declares the Lord GOD.

10Suppose, now, that he has begotten a son who is a ruffian, a shedder of blood, who d-does any of these things,-d 11whereas he himself did none of these things. That is, [the son] has eaten on the mountains,b has defiled another man's wife, 12has wronged the poor and the needy, has taken by robbery, has not returned a pledge, has raised his eyes to the fetishes, has committed abomination, 13has lent at advance interest, or exacted accrued interest—shall he live? He shall not live! If he has committed any of these abominations, he shall die; he has forfeited his life.

14Now suppose that he, in turn, has begotten a son who has seen all the sins that his father committed, but has taken heed and has not imitated them: 15He has not eaten on the mountainsb or raised his eyes to the fetishes of the House of Israel; he has not defiled another man's wife; 16he has not wronged anyone; he has not seized a pledge or taken anything by robbery; he has given his bread to the hungry and clothed the naked; 17he has e-refrained from oppressing the poor;-e he has not exacted advance or accrued interest; he has obeyed My rules and followed My laws— he shall not die for the iniquity of his father, but shall live. 18To be sure, his father, because he practiced fraud, robbed his brother, and acted wickedly among his kin, did die for his iniquity; 19and now you ask, "Why has not the son shared the burden of his father's guilt?" But the son has done what is right and just, and has carefully kept all My laws: he shall live!

20The person who sins, he alone shall die. A child shall not share the burden of a parent's guilt, nor shall a parent share the burden of a child's guilt; the righteousness of the righteous shall be accounted to him alone, and the wickedness of the wicked shall be accounted to him alone.

21Moreover, if the wicked one repents of all the sins that he committed and keeps all My laws and does what is just and right, he shall live; he shall not die. 22None of the transgressions he committed shall be remembered against him; because of the righteousness he has practiced, he shall live. 23Is it my desire that a wicked person shall die?—says the Lord GOD. It is rather that he shall turn back from his ways and live.

24So, too, if a righteous person turns away from his righteousness and does wrong, practicing the very abominations that the wicked person

---

d-d Meaning of Heb. uncertain.
e-e Lit. "turned his hand back from the poor." Emendation yields "abstained from wrongdoing"; cf. v. 8.

practiced, shall he live? None of the righteous deeds that he did shall be remembered; because of the treachery he has practiced and the sins he has committed—because of these, he shall die.

25Yet you say, "The way of the Lord is unfair." Listen, O House of Israel: Is My way unfair? It is your ways that are unfair! 26When a righteous person turns away from his righteousness and does wrong, he shall die for it; he shall die for the wrong he has done. 27And if a wicked person turns back from the wickedness that he practiced and does what is just and right, such a person shall save his life. 28Because he took heed and turned back from all the transgressions that he committed, he shall live; he shall not die.

29Yet the House of Israel say, "The way of the LORD is unfair." Are My ways unfair, O House of Israel? It is your ways that are unfair! 30Be assured, O House of Israel, I will judge each one of you according to his ways—declares the Lord GOD. Repent and turn back from all your transgressions; let them not be a stumbling block of guilt for you. 31Cast away all the transgressions by which you have offended, and get yourselves a new heart and a new spirit, that you may not die, O House of Israel. 32For it is not My desire that anyone shall die—declares the Lord GOD. Repent, therefore, and live!

19

And you are to intone a dirge over the princes of Israel, 2and say:

What a lioness was your mother
Among the lions!
Crouching among the great beasts,
She reared her cubs.
3She raised up one of her cubs,
He became a great beast;
He learned to hunt prey—
He devoured men.
4Nations heeded [the call] against him;
He was caught in their snare.
They dragged him off with hooks
To the land of Egypt.
5When she saw herself frustrated,
Her hope defeated,

She took another of her cubs
And set him up as a great beast.
⁶He stalked among the lions,
He was a great beast;
He learned to hunt prey—
He devoured men.
⁷He ᵃ‑ravished their widows,‑ᵃ
Laid waste their cities;
The land and all in it were appalled
At the sound of his roaring.
⁸Nations from the countries roundabout
Arrayed themselves against him.
They spread their net over him,
He was caught in their snare.
⁹With hooks he was put in a cage,
They carried him off to the king of Babylon
And confined him in a fortress,
So that never again should his roar be heard
On the hills of Israel.

¹⁰Your mother was like a vine ᵇ‑in your blood,‑ᵇ
Planted beside streams,
With luxuriant boughs and branches
Thanks to abundant waters.
¹¹And she had a mighty rodᶜ
Fit for a ruler's scepter.ᶜ
It towered highest ᵈ‑among the leafy trees,‑ᵈ
It was conspicuous by its height,
By the abundance of its boughs.
¹²But plucked up in a fury,
She was hurled to the ground.
The east wind withered her branches,
They broke apart and dried up;
And her mighty rod was consumed by fire.
¹³Now she is planted in the desert,
In ground that is arid and parched.
¹⁴Fire has issued from her twig-laden branch
And has consumed her boughs,

ᵃ⁻ᵃ *Emendation yields "ravaged their castles."*
ᵇ⁻ᵇ *Meaning of Heb. uncertain; emendation yields "in a vineyard."*
ᶜ *Heb. plural.*
ᵈ⁻ᵈ *Meaning of Heb. uncertain.*

She is left without a mighty rod,
A scepter to rule with.

This is a dirge, and it has become a [familiar] dirge.

20

In the seventh year, on the tenth day of the fifth month, certain elders of Israel came to inquire of the LORD, and sat down before me. ²And the word of the LORD came to me:

³O mortal, speak to the elders of Israel and say to them: Thus said the Lord GOD: Have you come to inquire of Me? As I live, I will not respond to your inquiry—declares the Lord GOD.

⁴ᵃ-Arraign, arraign them, O mortal!-ᵃ Declare to them the abhorrent deeds of their fathers. ⁵Say to them: Thus said the Lord GOD:

On the day that I chose Israel, I ᵇ-gave My oath-ᵇ to the stock of the House of Jacob; when I made Myself known to them in the land of Egypt, I gave my oath to them. When I said, "I the LORD am your God," ⁶that same day I swore to them to take them out of the land of Egypt into a land flowing with milk and honey, a land which I had sought out for them, the fairest of all lands.

⁷I also said to them: Cast away, every one of you, the detestable things ᶜ-that you are drawn to,-ᶜ and do not defile yourselves with the fetishes of Egypt—I the LORD am your God. ⁸But they defied Me and refused to listen to Me. They did not cast away the detestable things they were drawn to, nor did they give up the fetishes of Egypt. Then I resolved to pour out My fury upon them, to vent all My anger upon them there, in the land of Egypt. ⁹But I acted for the sake of My name, that it might not be profaned in the sight of the nations among whom they were. For it was before their eyes that I had made Myself known to Israelᵈ to bring them out of the land of Egypt.

¹⁰I brought them out of the land of Egypt and I led them into the wilderness. ¹¹I gave them My laws and taught them My rules, by the pursuit of which a man shall live. ¹²Moreover, I gave them My sabbaths to serve as a sign between Me and them, that they might know that it is I the LORD who sanctify them. ¹³But the House of Israel rebelled against Me in the wilderness; they did not follow My laws and they rejected My rules—by the pursuit of which a man shall live—and they grossly desecrated My sabbaths. Then I thought to pour out My fury upon them in

---

ᵃ⁻ᵃ Lit. "Will you arraign them, will you arraign, O mortal?"
ᵇ⁻ᵇ Lit. "raised My hand."
ᶜ⁻ᶜ Lit. "of his eyes."
ᵈ Lit. "them."

the wilderness and to make an end of them; ¹⁴but I acted for the sake of My name, that it might not be profaned in the sight of the nations before whose eyes I had led them out. ¹⁵However, I swore[b] to them in the wilderness that I would not bring them into the land flowing with milk and honey, the fairest of all lands, which I had assigned [to them], ¹⁶for they had rejected My rules, disobeyed My laws, and desecrated My sabbaths; their hearts followed after their fetishes. ¹⁷But I had pity on them and did not destroy them; I did not make an end of them in the wilderness.

¹⁸I warned their children in the wilderness: Do not follow the practices of your fathers, do not keep their ways, and do not defile yourselves with their fetishes. ¹⁹I the LORD am your God: Follow My laws and be careful to observe My rules. ²⁰And hallow My sabbaths, that they may be a sign between Me and you, that you may know that I the LORD am your God.

²¹But the children rebelled against Me: they did not follow My laws and did not faithfully observe My rules, by the pursuit of which man shall live; they profaned My sabbaths. Then I resolved to pour out My fury upon them, to vent all My anger upon them, in the wilderness. ²²But I held back My hand and acted for the sake of My name, that it might not be profaned in the sight of the nations before whose eyes I had led them out. ²³However, I swore[b] to them in the wilderness that I would scatter them among the nations and disperse them through the lands, ²⁴because they did not obey My rules, but rejected My laws, profaned My sabbaths, and looked with longing to the fetishes of their fathers. ²⁵Moreover, I gave them laws that were not good and rules by which they could not live: ²⁶When they set aside every first issue of the womb, I defiled them by their very gifts[e]—that I might render them desolate,[f] that they might know that I am the LORD.

²⁷Now, O mortal, speak to the House of Israel and say to them: Thus said the Lord GOD: By this too your fathers affronted Me and committed trespass against Me: ²⁸When I brought them to the land that I had sworn[b] to give them, and they saw any high hill or any leafy tree, they slaughtered their sacrifices there and presented their offensive offerings there; there they produced their pleasing odors and poured out their libations. ²⁹Then I said to them, "What is this shrine which you visit?" (Therefore such [a shrine] is called *bamah*[g] to this day.)

³⁰Now say to the House of Israel: Thus said the Lord GOD: If you defile yourselves as your fathers did and go astray after their detestable

---

[e] *See v. 31.*
[f] *Emendation yields "guilty."*
[g] *As if from* ba *"visit" and* mah *"what."*

things, [31]and if to this very day you defile yourselves in the presentation of your gifts by making your children pass through the fire to all your fetishes, shall I respond to your inquiry, O House of Israel? As I live— declares the Lord GOD—I will not respond to you. [32]And what you have in mind shall never come to pass—when you say, "We will be like the nations, like the families of the lands, worshiping wood and stone." [33]As I live—declares the Lord GOD—I will reign over you with a strong hand, and with an outstretched arm, and with overflowing fury. [34]With a strong hand and an outstretched arm and overflowing fury I will bring you out from the peoples and gather you from the lands where you are scattered, [35]and I will bring you into the wilderness of the peoples; and there I will enter into judgment with you face to face. [36]As I entered into judgment with your fathers in the wilderness of the land of Egypt, so will I enter into judgment with you—declares the Lord GOD. [37]I will make you pass under the shepherd's staff,[h] and I will bring you into the bond[i] of the covenant. [38]I will remove from you those who rebel and transgress against Me; I will take them out of the countries where they sojourn, but they shall not enter the land of Israel. Then you shall know that I am the LORD.

[39]As for you, O House of Israel, thus said the Lord GOD: Go, every one of you, and worship his fetishes and continue,[i] if you will not obey Me; but do not profane My holy name any more with your idolatrous gifts. [40]For only on My holy mountain, on the lofty mount of Israel— declares the Lord GOD—there, in the land, the entire House of Israel, all of it, must worship Me. There I will accept them, and there I will take note of your contributions and the choicest offerings of all your sacred things. [41]When I bring you out from the peoples and gather you from the lands in which you are scattered, I will accept you as a pleasing odor; and I will be sanctified through you in the sight of the nations. [42]Then, when I have brought you to the land of Israel, to the country that I swore[b] to give to your fathers, you shall know that I am the LORD. [43]There you will recall your ways and all the acts by which you defiled yourselves; and you will loathe yourselves for all the evils that you committed. [44]Then, O House of Israel, you shall know that I am the LORD, when I deal with you for My name's sake—not in accordance with your evil ways and corrupt acts—declares the Lord GOD.

h *I.e., to be counted; see Lev. 27.32.*
i *Meaning of Heb. uncertain.*

21 The word of the LORD came to me: ²O mortal, set your face toward Teman,ª and proclaim to Darom,ª and prophesy against the brushland of the Negeb.ª ³Say to the brushland of the Negeb: Hear the word of the LORD. Thus said the Lord GOD: I am going to kindle a fire in you, which shall devour every tree of yours, both green and withered. Its leaping flame shall not go out, and every face from south to north shall be scorched by it. ⁴Then all flesh shall recognize that I the LORD have kindled it; it shall not go out. ⁵And I said, "Ah, Lord GOD! They say of me: He is just a riddlemonger."

⁶Then the word of the LORD came to me: ⁷O mortal, set your face toward Jerusalem and proclaim against her sanctuaries and prophesy against the land of Israel. ⁸Say to the land of Israel: Thus said the LORD: I am going to deal with you! I will draw My sword from its sheath, and I will wipe out from you both the righteous and the wicked. ⁹In order to wipe out from you both the righteous and the wicked, My sword shall assuredly be unsheathed against all flesh from south to north; ¹⁰and all flesh shall know that I the LORD have drawn My sword from its sheath, not to be sheathed again.

¹¹And you, O mortal, sigh; with tottering limbs and bitter grief, sigh before their eyes. ¹²And when they ask you, "Why do you sigh?" answer, "Because of the tidings that have come." Every heart shall sink and all hands hang nerveless; every spirit shall grow faint and all knees turn to water because of the tidings that have come. It is approaching, it shall come to pass—declares the Lord GOD.

¹³The word of the LORD came to me: ¹⁴O mortal, prophesy and say: Thus said the Lord GOD: A sword! A sword has been whetted and polished. ¹⁵It has been whetted to wreak slaughter; ᵇ⁻[therefore] it has been ground to a brilliant polish.⁻ᵇ ᶜ⁻How can we rejoice? My son, it scorns⁻ᶜ the rod and every stick. ¹⁶It has been given to be polished and then grasped in the hand; for this has the sword been whetted, for this polished—to be put into the hand of a slayer. ¹⁷Cry and wail, O mortal, for this shall befall My people, this shall befall all the chieftains of Israel: they shall be cast before the sword together with My people; oh, strike the thigh [in grief]. ¹⁸ᶜ⁻Consider: How shall it fail to happen, seeing that it even scorns the rod?⁻ᶜ—says the Lord GOD.

ª *Teman, Darom, Negeb are three terms for "the south." The allusion is to Jerusalem (v. 7), which was always approached from Babylon by way of the north.*
ᵇ⁻ᵇ *Lit. "it has been polished in order that it may have lightning."*
ᶜ⁻ᶜ *Meaning of Heb. uncertain.*

¹⁹Further, O mortal, prophesy, striking hand against hand. Let the sword strike a second time and yet a third time; it is a sword for massacre, a sword for great carnage, that presses^c upon them. ²⁰Thus hearts shall lose courage and many shall fall. At all their gates I have appointed slaughter^c by the sword. Ah! it is made to flash brilliantly, it is honed^c for slaughter. ²¹Be united,^d go to the right, turn left; whither are you bound? ²²I, too, will strike hand against hand and will satisfy My fury upon you; I the LORD have spoken.

²³The word of the LORD came to me: ²⁴And you, O mortal, choose two roads on which the sword of the king of Babylon may advance, both issuing from the same country; and select a spot, select it where roads branch off to [two] cities. ²⁵Choose a way for the sword to advance on Rabbah of the Ammonites or on fortified Jerusalem in Judah. ²⁶For the king of Babylon has stood at the fork of the road, where two roads branch off, to perform divination: He has shaken arrows, consulted teraphim, and inspected the liver.^e ²⁷In his right hand came up the omen against Jerusalem—to set battering rams, to proclaim murder, to raise battle shouts, to set battering rams against the gates, to cast up mounds, to erect towers.

²⁸ᶠIn their eyes, the oaths they had sworn to them were like empty divination; but this shall serve to recall their guilt, for which they shall be taken to task. ²⁹Assuredly, thus said the Lord GOD: For causing your guilt to be recalled, your transgressions to be uncovered, and your sins to be revealed—all your misdeeds—because you have brought yourselves to [My] mind, you shall be taken to task.

³⁰And to you, O dishonored wicked prince of Israel, whose day has come—the time set for your punishment—³¹thus said the Lord GOD: Remove the turban and lift off the crown! This shall not remain as it is; exalt the low and abase the high. ³²Ruin, an utter ruin I will make it. ^{c-}It shall be no more^{-c} until he comes to whom it rightfully belongs; and I will give it to him.

³³Further, O mortal, prophesy and say: Thus said the Lord GOD concerning the Ammonites and their blasphemies: Proclaim: O sword! O sword unsheathed for slaughter, polished to the utmost, to a flashing brilliance! ³⁴Because they have prophesied falsely about you and have divined deceitfully concerning you, you shall be wielded over the necks

---

^d *Meaning of Heb. uncertain; Targum reads "Be whetted." Cf. vv. 14–16.*
^e *I.e., of a sacrificed animal.*
^f *The inhabitants of Jerusalem disregarded their oaths to the Babylonians; cf. 17.13 ff.*

of the dishonored wicked ones, for their day has come, the time ᶜ⁻set for their punishment.⁻ᶜ

³⁵ᵍ⁻Return it to its sheath!⁻ᵍ In the place where you were created, in the land of your origin, I will judge you. ³⁶I will pour out My indignation upon you, I will blow upon you with the fire of My wrath; and I will deliver you into the hands of barbarians, craftsmen of destruction. ³⁷You shall be fuel for the fire, your blood shall sink into the earth, you shall not be remembered, for I the LORD have spoken.

22 The word of the LORD came to me: ²Further, O mortal, ᵃ⁻arraign, arraign⁻ᵃ the city of bloodshed; declare to her all her abhorrent deeds! ³Say: Thus said the Lord GOD: O city in whose midst blood is shed, so that your hour is approaching; within which fetishes are made, so that you have become unclean! ⁴You stand guilty of the blood you have shed, defiled by the fetishes you have made. You have brought on your day; ᵇ⁻you have reached your year.⁻ᵇ Therefore I will make you the mockery of the nations and the scorn of all the lands. ⁵Both the near and the far shall scorn you, O besmirched of name, O laden with iniquity!

⁶Every one of the princes of Israel in your midst used his strength for the shedding of blood. ⁷Fathers and mothers have been humiliated within you; strangers have been cheated in your midst; orphans and widows have been wronged within you. ⁸You have despised My holy things and profaned My sabbaths.

⁹Baseᶜ men in your midst were intent on shedding blood; in you they have eaten ᵈ⁻upon the mountains;⁻ᵈ and they have practiced depravity in your midst. ¹⁰In you they have uncovered their fathers' nakedness;ᵉ in you they have ravished women during their impurity. ¹¹They have committed abhorrent acts with other men's wives; in their depravity they have defiled their own daughters-in-law; in you they have ravished their own sisters, daughters of their fathers. ¹²They have taken bribes within you to shed blood. You have taken advance and accrued interest;ᶠ you have defrauded your countrymen to your profit. You have forgotten Me—declares the Lord GOD.

¹³Lo, I will strike My hands over the ill-gotten gains that you have amassed, and over the bloodshed that has been committed in your midst. ¹⁴Will your courage endure, will your hands remain firm in the days when

ᵍ⁻ᵍ *Emendation yields "Return to your scabbard!" In this and the following verses, the prophet describes the future punishment of Babylon, still symbolized by the sword.*

ᵃ⁻ᵃ *Lit. "will you arraign, arraign."*

ᵇ⁻ᵇ *Some Babylonian mss. and ancient versions read "the time of your years has come."*

ᶜ *Meaning of Heb. uncertain.*

ᵈ⁻ᵈ *I.e., in idolatry. Emendation yields "with the blood"; cf. Lev. 19.26.*

ᵉ *I.e., have cohabited with a former wife of the father; cf. Lev. 18.7–8.*

ᶠ *Cf. note at 18.8.*

I deal with you? I the LORD have spoken and I will act. [15]I will scatter you among the nations and disperse you through the lands; I will consume the uncleanness out of you. [16]You shall be dishonored in the sight of nations, and you shall know that I am the LORD.

[17]The word of the LORD came to me: [18]O mortal, the House of Israel has become dross to Me; they are all copper, tin, iron, and lead. c-But in a crucible, the dross shall turn into silver.-c [19]Assuredly, thus said the Lord GOD: Because you have all become dross, I will gather you into Jerusalem. [20]As silver, copper, iron, lead, and tin are gathered into a crucible to blow the fire upon them, so as to melt them, so will I gather you in My fierce anger and cast you [into the fire] and melt you. [21]I will gather you and I will blow upon you the fire of My fury, and you shall be melted in it. [22]As silver is melted in a crucible, so shall you be melted in it. And you shall know that I the LORD have poured out My fury upon you.

[23]The word of the LORD came to me: [24]O mortal, say to her: You are an uncleansed land, c-not to be washed with rain-c on the day of indignation. [25]g-Her gang of prophets-g are like roaring lions in her midst, rending prey. They devour human beings; they seize treasure and wealth; they have widowed many women in her midst. [26]Her priests have violated My Teaching: they have profaned what is sacred to Me, they have not distinguished between the sacred and the profane, they have not taught the difference between the unclean and the clean, and they have closed their eyes to My sabbaths. I am profaned in their midst. [27]Her officials are like wolves rending prey in her midst; they shed blood and destroy lives to win ill-gotten gain. [28]Her prophets, too, daub the wall for them with plaster:h They prophesy falsely and divine deceitfully for them; they say, "Thus said the Lord GOD," when the LORD has not spoken. [29]And the people of the land have practiced fraud and committed robbery; they have wronged the poor and needy, have defrauded the stranger without redress. [30]And I sought a man among them to repair the wall or to stand in the breach before Me in behalf of this land, that I might not destroy it; but I found none. [31]I have therefore poured out My indignation upon them; I will consume them with the fire of My fury. I will repay them for their conduct—declares the Lord GOD.

g-g *Septuagint reads "Whose chieftains."*
h *Cf. 13.10 ff.*

23

The word of the LORD came to me: [2]O mortal, once there were two women, daughters of one mother. [3]They played the whore in Egypt; they played the whore while still young. There their breasts were squeezed, and there their virgin nipples were handled. [4]Their names were: the elder one, Oholah;[a] and her sister, Oholibah.[b] They became Mine, and they bore sons and daughters. As for their names, Oholah is Samaria, and Oholibah is Jerusalem.

[5]Oholah whored while she was Mine, and she lusted after her lovers, after the Assyrians, warriors[c] [6]clothed in blue, governors and prefects, horsemen mounted on steeds—all of them handsome young fellows. [7]She bestowed her favors upon them—upon all the pick of the Assyrians—and defiled herself with all their fetishes after which she lusted. [8]She did not give up the whoring she had begun with the Egyptians; for they had lain with her in her youth, and they had handled her virgin nipples and had poured out their lust upon her. [9]Therefore I delivered her into the hands of her lovers, into the hands of the Assyrians after whom she lusted. [10]They exposed her nakedness; they seized her sons and daughters, and she herself was put to the sword. And because of the punishment inflicted upon her, she became a byword among women.

[11]Her sister Oholibah saw this; yet her lusting was more depraved than her sister's, and her whoring more debased. [12]She lusted after the Assyrians, governors and prefects, warriors[c] gorgeously clad, horsemen mounted on steeds—all of them handsome young fellows. [13]And I saw how she had defiled herself. Both of them followed the same course, [14]but she carried her harlotries further. For she saw men sculptured upon the walls, figures of Chaldeans drawn in vermilion, [15]girded with belts round their waists, and with flowing turbans on their heads, all of them looking like officers—a picture of Babylonians whose native land was Chaldea. [16]At the very sight of them she lusted after them, and she sent messengers for them to Chaldea. [17]So the Babylonians came to her for lovemaking and defiled her with their whoring; and she defiled herself with them until she turned from them in disgust. [18]She flaunted her harlotries and exposed her nakedness, and I turned from her in disgust, as I had turned disgusted from her sister. [19]But she whored still more, remembering how in her youth she had played the whore in the land of Egypt; [20]she lusted for

---

a *I.e., "Tent."*
b *I.e., "My Tent Is in Her."*
c *Meaning of Heb. uncertain.*

concubinage with them, whose members were like those of asses and whose organs^c were like those of stallions. 21Thus you reverted to the wantonness of your youth, remembering^d your youthful breasts, when the men of Egypt handled your nipples.

22Assuredly, Oholibah, thus said the Lord GOD: I am going to rouse against you the lovers from whom you turned in disgust, and I will bring them upon you from all around—23the Babylonians and all the Chaldeans, [the people of] Pekod, Shoa, and Koa, and all the Assyrians with them, all of them handsome young fellows, governors and prefects, officers and warriors,^c all of them riding on horseback. 24They shall attack you with fleets^c of wheeled chariots and a host of troops; they shall set themselves against you on all sides with bucklers, shields, and helmets. And I will entrust your punishment to them, and they shall inflict their punishments on you. 25I will direct My passion against you, and they shall deal with you in fury: they shall cut off your nose and ears. The last of you shall fall by the sword; they^e shall take away your sons and daughters, and your remnant shall be devoured by fire. 26They shall strip you of your clothing and take away your dazzling jewels. 27I will put an end to your wantonness and to your whoring in the land of Egypt, and you shall not long for them or remember Egypt any more.

28For thus said the Lord GOD: I am going to deliver you into the hands of those you hate, into the hands of those from whom you turned in disgust. 29They shall treat you with hate, and they shall take away all you have toiled for, and leave you naked and bare; your naked whoredom, wantonness, and harlotry will be exposed. 30These things shall be done to you for your harlotries with the nations, for defiling yourself with their fetishes. 31You walked in your sister's path; therefore I will put her cup into your hand.

32Thus said the Lord GOD:

You shall drink of your sister's cup,
So deep and wide;
It shall cause derision and scorn,
It holds so much.
33You shall be filled with drunkenness and woe.
The cup of desolation and horror,
The cup of your sister Samaria—

---

^d Lit. "for the sake of."
^e I.e., the former lovers, vv. 22 ff.

³⁴You shall drink it and drain it,

ᶜ⁻And gnaw its shards;⁻ᶜ

And you shall tear your breasts.

For I have spoken—declares the Lord GOD.

³⁵Assuredly, thus said the Lord GOD: Because you have forgotten Me and cast Me behind your back, you in turn must suffer for your wanton whoring.

³⁶Then the LORD said to me: O mortal, arraignᶠ Oholah and Oholibah, and charge them with their abominations. ³⁷For they have committed adultery, and blood is on their hands; truly they have committed adultery with their fetishes, and have even offered to them as food the children they bore to Me. ³⁸At the same time they also did this to Me: they defiled My Sanctuary and profaned My sabbaths. ³⁹On the very day that they slaughtered their children to their fetishes, they entered My Sanctuary to desecrate it. That is what they did in My House.

⁴⁰Moreover, they sent for men to come from afar, [men] to whom a messenger was sent; and they came. For them, [Oholibah,] you bathed, painted your eyes, and donned your finery; ⁴¹and you sat on a grand couch with a set table in front of it—and it was My incense and My oil you laid upon it. ⁴²And the noise of a carefree multitude was there, ᶜ⁻of numerous men brought drunk from the desert;⁻ᶜ and they put bracelets on their arms and splendid crowns upon their heads. ⁴³Then I said, ᶜ⁻"To destruction with adultery! Look, they are still going on with those same fornications of hers."⁻ᶜ ⁴⁴And they would go to her as one goes to a prostitute; that is how they went to Oholah and Oholibah, wanton women. ⁴⁵But righteous men shall punish them with the punishments for adultery and for bloodshed, for they are adulteresses and have blood on their hands.

⁴⁶For thus said the Lord GOD: Summon an assembly against them, and make them an object of horror and plunder. ⁴⁷Let the assembly pelt them with stones and cut them down with their swords; let them kill their sons and daughters, and burn down their homes. ⁴⁸I will put an end to wantonness in the land; and all the women shall take warning not to imitate your wantonness. ⁴⁹They shall punish you for your wantonness, and you shall suffer the penalty for your sinful idolatry. And you shall know that I am the Lord GOD.

ᶠ Lit. "will you arraign"; cf. 22.2.

24 In the ninth year, on the tenth day of the tenth month, the word of the LORD came to me: ²O mortal, record this date, this exact day; for this very day the king of Babylon has laid siege to Jerusalem. ³Further, speak in an allegory to the rebellious breed and say to them: Thus said the Lord GOD:

Put the caldron [on the fire], put it on,
And then pour water into it.
⁴Collect in it the pieces [of meat].
Every choice piece, thigh and shoulder;
Fill it with the best cuts^a—
⁵Take the best of the flock.
Also pile the cuts^b under it;
Get it boiling briskly,
And cook the cuts in it.
⁶Assuredly, thus said the Lord GOD:
Woe to the city of blood—
A caldron whose scum^c is in it,
Whose scum has not been cleaned out!
Empty it piece by piece;
^{d-}No lot has fallen upon it.^{-d}
⁷For the blood she shed is still in her;
She set it upon a bare rock;
She did not pour it out on the ground
To cover it with earth.
⁸She^e set her blood upon the bare rock,
So that it was not covered,
So that it may stir up [My] fury
To take vengeance.
⁹Assuredly, thus said the Lord GOD:
Woe to the city of blood!
I in turn will make a great blaze.
¹⁰Pile on the logs,
Kindle the fire,
Cook the meat through
And ^{f-}stew it completely,^{-f}
And let the bones be charred.
¹¹Let it stand empty on the coals,

---

^a *Lit. "limbs."*
^b *Emendation yields "wood"; cf. v. 10.*
^c *Or "rust."*
^{d-d} *Meaning of Heb. uncertain.*
^e *Heb. "I."*
^{f-f} *Emendation yields "Pour out the broth."*

Until it becomes so hot
That the copper glows.
Then its uncleanness shall melt away in it,
And its rust be consumed.
12d-It has frustrated all effort,
Its thick scum will not leave it—
Into the fire with its scum!-d

13For your vile impurity—because I sought to cleanse you of your impurity, but you would not be cleansed—you shall never be clean again until I have satisfied My fury upon you. 14I the LORD have spoken: It shall come to pass and I will do it. I will not refrain or spare or relent. You shall be punished according to your ways and your deeds—declares the Lord GOD.

15The word of the LORD came to me: 16O mortal, I am about to take away the delight of your eyes from you through pestilence; but you shall not lament or weep or let your tears flow. 17Moan softly; observe no mourning for the dead: Put on your turban and put your sandals on your feet; do not cover over your upper lip, and do not eat the bread of comforters."g

18In the evening my wife died, and in the morning I did as I had been commanded. And when I spoke to the people that morning, 19the people asked me, "Will you not tell us what these things portend for us, that you are acting so?" 20I answered them, "The word of the LORD has come to me: 21Tell the House of Israel: Thus said the Lord GOD: 'I am going to desecrate My Sanctuary, your pride and glory, the delight of your eyes and the desire of your heart; and the sons and daughters you have left behind shall fall by the sword. 24hAnd Ezekiel shall become a portent for you: you shall do just as he has done, when it happens; and you shall know that I am the Lord GOD.' 22Accordingly, you shall do as I have done: you shall not cover over your upper lips or eat the bread of comforters;g 23and your turbans shall remain on your heads, and your sandals upon your feet. You shall not lament or weep, but you shall be heartsick because of your iniquities and shall moan to one another."h

25You, O mortal, take note: On the day that I take their stronghold from them, their pride and joy, the delight of their eyes and the longing

g Lit. "men."
h V. 24 moved up for clarity.

of their hearts—their sons and daughters—²⁶on that day a fugitive will come to you, to let you hear it with your own ears. ²⁷On that day your mouth shall be opened to the fugitive, and you shall speak and no longer be dumb. So you shall be a portent for them, and they shall know that I am the LORD.

25 The word of the LORD came to me: ²O mortal, set your face toward the Ammonites and prophesy against them. ³Say to the Ammonites: Hear the word of the Lord GOD! Thus said the Lord GOD: Because you cried "Aha!" over My Sanctuary when it was desecrated, and over the land of Israel when it was laid waste, and over the House of Judah when it went into exile—⁴assuredly, I will deliver you to the Kedemites as a possession. They shall set up their encampments among you and pitch their dwellings in your midst; they shall eat your produce and they shall drink your milk. ⁵I will make Rabbah a pasture for camels and Ammon a place for sheep to lie down. And you shall know that I am the LORD.

⁶For thus said the Lord GOD: Because you clapped your hands and stamped your feet and rejoiced over the land of Israel with such utter scorn—⁷assuredly, I will stretch out My hand against you and give you as booty to the nations; I will cut you off from among the peoples and wipe you out from among the countries and destroy you. And you shall know that I am the LORD.

⁸Thus said the Lord GOD: Because Moab ᵃ-and Seir-ᵃ said, "See, the House of Judah is like all other nations"—⁹assuredly, I will lay bare the flank of Moab, all its towns to the last one—Beth-jeshimoth, Baal-meon, and Kiriathaim, the glory of the country. ¹⁰I will deliver it, together with Ammon, to the Kedemites as their possession. Thus Ammon shall not be remembered among the nations, ¹¹and I will mete out punishments to Moab. And they shall know that I am the LORD.

¹²Thus said the Lord GOD: Because Edom acted vengefully against the House of Judah and incurred guilt by wreaking revenge upon it—¹³assuredly, thus said the Lord GOD: I will stretch out My hand against Edom and cut off from it man and beast, and I will lay it in ruins; from Tema to Dedan they shall fall by the sword. ¹⁴I will wreak My vengeance on Edom through My people Israel, and they shall take action against

---

ᵃ⁻ᵃ *Lacking in some Septuagint mss.*

932

Edom in accordance with My blazing anger; and they shall know My vengeance—declares the Lord GOD.

[15]Thus said the Lord GOD: Because the Philistines, in their ancient hatred, acted vengefully, and with utter scorn sought revenge and destruction—[16]assuredly, thus said the Lord GOD: I will stretch out My hand against the Philistines and cut off the Cherethites and wipe out the last survivors of the seacoast. [17]I will wreak frightful vengeance upon them by furious punishment; and when I inflict My vengeance upon them, they shall know that I am the LORD.

26 In the eleventh year, on the first of the month,[a] the word of the LORD came to me: [2]O mortal, because Tyre gloated over Jerusalem, "Aha! The gateway[b] of the peoples is broken, it has become mine; I shall be filled, now that it is laid in ruins"—[3]assuredly, thus said the Lord GOD:

I am going to deal with you, O Tyre!
I will hurl many nations against you,
As the sea hurls its waves.
[4]They shall destroy the walls of Tyre
And demolish her towers;
And I will scrape her soil off her
And leave her a naked rock.
[5]She shall be in the heart of the sea
A place for drying[c] nets;
For I have spoken it
                                    —declares the Lord GOD.
She shall become spoil for the nations,
[6]And her daughter-towns in the country
Shall be put to the sword.
And they shall know that I am the LORD.

[7]For thus said the Lord GOD: I will bring from the north, against Tyre, King Nebuchadrezzar of Babylon, a king of kings, with horses, chariots, and horsemen—a great mass of troops.

[8]Your daughter-towns in the country
He shall put to the sword;
He shall erect towers against you,

---

[a] *The month is not indicated.*
[b] *Targum reads "trafficker"; cf. 27.3.*
[c] *Lit. "spreading out."*

And cast up mounds against you,
And raise [a wall of] bucklers against you.
⁹He shall turn the force of his battering rams
Against your walls
And smash your towers with his axes.ᵈ
¹⁰From the cloud raised by his horses
Dust shall cover you;
From the clatter of horsemen
And wheels and chariots,
Your walls shall shake—
When he enters your gates
As men enter a breached city.
¹¹With the hoofs of his steeds
He shall trample all your streets.
He shall put your people to the sword,
And your mighty pillars shall crash to the ground.
¹²They shall plunder your wealth
And loot your merchandise.
They shall raze your walls
And tear down your splendid houses,
And they shall cast into the water
Your stones and timber and soil.
¹³I will put an end to the murmur of your songs,
And the sound of your lyres shall be heard no more.
¹⁴I will make you a naked rock,
You shall be a place for dryingᶜ nets;
You shall never be rebuilt.
For I have spoken

——declares the Lord GOD.

¹⁵Thus said the Lord GOD to Tyre: The coastlands shall quake at the sound of your downfall, when the wounded groan, when slaughter is rife within you. ¹⁶All the rulers of the sea shall descend from their thrones; they shall remove their robes and strip off their embroidered garments. They shall clothe themselves with trembling, and shall sit on the ground; they shall tremble every moment, and they shall be aghast at you. ¹⁷And they shall intone a dirge over you, and they shall say to you:

How you have perished, ᶜ-you who were peopledᶜ from the
seas,

ᵈ *Lit. "swords."*
ᶜ⁻ᶜ *Septuagint reads "vanished."*

O renowned city!
Mighty on the sea were she and her inhabitants,
Who cast their terror on all [f]its inhabitants.[f]
[18]Now shall the coastlands tremble
On the day of your downfall,
And the coastlands by the sea
Be terrified at your end.

[19]For thus said the Lord GOD: When I make you a ruined city, like cities empty of inhabitants; when I bring the deep over you, and its mighty waters cover you, [20]then I will bring you down, with those who go down to the Pit, to the people of old. I will install you in the netherworld, with those that go down to the Pit, like the ruins of old, so that you shall not be inhabited and shall not radiate[g] splendor in the land of the living. [21]I will make you a horror, and you shall cease to be; you shall be sought, but shall never be found again—declares the Lord GOD.

27

The word of the LORD came to me: [2]Now you, O mortal, intone a dirge over Tyre. [3]Say to Tyre:

O you who dwell at the gateway of the sea,
Who trade with the peoples on many coastlands:
Thus said the Lord GOD:
[a]O Tyre, you boasted,
I am perfect in beauty.[a]
[4]Your frontiers were on the high seas,
Your builders perfected your beauty.
[5]From cypress trees of Senir
They fashioned your planks;
They took a cedar from Lebanon
To make a mast for you.
[6]From oak trees of Bashan
They made your oars;
Of boxwood from the isles of Kittim,
Inlaid with ivory,
They made your decks.
[7]Embroidered linen from Egypt
Was the cloth

[f-f] *I.e., of the sea. Emendation yields "the dry land."*
[g] *Understanding* nathatti *as second-person singular feminine; cf. 16.50 and note. But meaning of Heb. uncertain.*

[a-a] *Emendation yields: "O Tyre, you are a ship / Perfect in beauty."*

That served you for sails;
Of blue and purple from the coasts of Elishah
Were your awnings.
⁸The inhabitants of Sidon and Arvad
Were your rowers;
ᵇ⁻Your skilled men, O Tyre,⁻ᵇ were within you,
They were your pilots.
⁹Gebal's elders and craftsmen were within you,
Making your repairs.

All the ships of the sea, with their crews,
Were ᶜ⁻in your harborᶜ
To traffic in your wares.
¹⁰Men of Paras, Lud, and Put
Were in your army,
Your fighting men;
They hung shields and helmets in your midst,
They lent splendor to you.
¹¹Men of Arvad and Helech
Manned your walls all around,
And men of Gammad were stationed in your towers;
They hung their quivers all about your walls;
They perfected your beauty.

¹²Tarshish traded with you because of your wealth of all kinds of goods; they bartered silver, iron, tin, and lead for your wares. ¹³Javan, Tubal, and Meshech—they were your merchants; they trafficked with you in human beings and copper utensils. ¹⁴From Beth-togarmah they bartered horses, horsemen, and mules for your wares. ¹⁵The people of Dedan were your merchants; many coastlands traded under your rule and rendered you tribute in ivory tusks and ebony. ¹⁶Aram traded with you because of your wealth of merchandise, dealing with you in turquoise, purple stuff, embroidery, fine linen, coral, and agate.ᵈ ¹⁷Judah and the land of Israel were your merchants; they trafficked with you in wheat of ᵉ⁻Minnith and Pannag,⁻ᵉ honey, oil, and balm. ¹⁸Because of your wealth of merchandise, because of your great wealth, Damascus traded with you in Helbon wine and white wool. ¹⁹ᶠ⁻Vedan and Javan from Uzal traded for your wares; they trafficked with you in polished iron, cassia, and calamus. ²⁰Dedan

ᵇ⁻ᵇ *Emendation yields "The skilled men of Zemar"; cf. Gen. 10.18.*
ᶜ⁻ᶜ *Lit. "in you."*
ᵈ *The exact identity of these stones is uncertain.*
ᵉ⁻ᵉ *Meaning of Heb. uncertain; cf. "Minnith," Judg. 11.33.*
ᶠ⁻ᶠ *Meaning of Heb. uncertain.*

was your merchant in saddlecloths for riding.-f ²¹Arabia and all Kedar's chiefs were traders under your rule; they traded with you in lambs, rams, and goats. ²²The merchants of Sheba and Raamah were your merchants; they bartered for your wares all the finest spices, all kinds of precious stones, and gold. ²³Haran, Canneh, and Eden, the merchants of Sheba, Assyria, and Chilmad traded with you. ²⁴f These were your merchants in choice fabrics, embroidered cloaks of blue, and many-colored carpets tied up with cords and preserved with cedar—among your wares.-f ²⁵The ships of Tarshish were in the service of your trade.

gSo you were full and richly laden
On the high seas.
²⁶Your oarsmen brought you out
Into the mighty waters;
The tempest wrecked you
On the high seas.
²⁷Your wealth, your wares, your merchandise,
Your sailors and your pilots,
The men who made your repairs,
Those who carried on your traffic,
And all the fighting men within you—
All the multitude within you—
Shall go down into the depths of the sea
On the day of your downfall.
²⁸At the outcry of your pilots
The billows shall heave;
²⁹And all the oarsmen and mariners,
All the pilots of the sea,
Shall come down from their ships
And stand on the ground.
³⁰They shall raise their voices over you
And cry out bitterly;
They shall cast dust on their heads
And strew ashes on themselves.
³¹On your account, they shall make
Bald patches on their heads,
And shall gird themselves with sackcloth.
They shall weep over you, brokenhearted,

ᵍ *Resuming the description of Tyre as a ship, as in vv. 3b–9a.*

With bitter lamenting;
32They shall intone a dirge over you as they wail,
And lament for you thus:

Who was like Tyre when she was silenced
In the midst of the sea?
33When your wares were unloaded from the seas,
You satisfied many peoples;
With your great wealth and merchandise
You enriched the kings of the earth.
34But when you were wrecked on the seas,
In the deep waters sank your merchandise
And all the crew aboard you.
35All the inhabitants of the coastlands
Are appalled over you;
Their kings are aghast,
Their faces contorted.f
36The merchants among the peoples hissedh at you;
You have become a horror,
And have ceased to be forever.

28

The word of the LORD came to me: 2O mortal, say to the prince of Tyre: Thus said the Lord GOD:

Because you have been so haughty and have said, "I am a god; I sit enthroned like a god in the heart of the seas," whereas you are not a god but a man, though you deemed your mind equal to a god'sa—

3Yes, you are wiser than Daniel;
In no hidden matter can anyone
Compare to you.
4By your shrewd understanding
You have gained riches,
And have amassed gold and silver
In your treasuries.
5By your great shrewdness in trade
You have increased your wealth,
And you have grown haughty
Because of your wealth.

h *I.e., to ward off the calamity from the viewer; cf. Jer. 18.16, 49.17; Job 27.23; Lam. 2.15.*

a *This sentence is continued in v. 6; vv. 3–5 are parenthetical.*

⁶Assuredly, thus said the Lord GOD: Because you have deemed your mind equal to a god's,

⁷I swear I will bring against you
Strangers, the most ruthless of nations.
They shall unsheathe their swords
Against your prized shrewdness,
And they shall strike down[b] your splendor.
⁸They shall bring you down to the Pit;
In the heart of the sea you shall die
The death of the slain.
⁹Will you still say, "I am a god"
Before your slayers,
When you are proved a man, not a god,
At the hands of those who strike you down?
¹⁰By the hands of strangers you shall die
The death of the uncircumcised;[c]
For I have spoken

—declares the Lord GOD.

¹¹The word of the LORD came to me: ¹²O mortal, intone a dirge over the king of Tyre and say to him: Thus said the Lord GOD:

You were the seal of perfection,
Full of wisdom and flawless in beauty.
¹³You were in Eden, the garden of God;
Every precious stone was your adornment:
Carnelian, chrysolite, and amethyst;
Beryl, lapis lazuli, and jasper;
Sapphire, turquoise, and emerald;
And gold [d-]beautifully wrought for you,
Mined for you, prepared the day you were created.[-d]
¹⁴[b-]I created you as a cherub
With outstretched shielding wings;[-b]
And you resided on God's holy mountain;
You walked among stones of fire.
¹⁵You were blameless in your ways,
From the day you were created
Until wrongdoing was found in you.
¹⁶By your far-flung commerce

---

[b] *Meaning of Heb. uncertain.*
[c] *According to popular belief, those who die uncircumcised and those left unburied are relegated to the lower level of the netherworld; cf. 31.18; 32.19 ff.*
[d-d] *Meaning of Heb. uncertain. On the stones, see note at Exod. 28.17.*

You were filled with lawlessness
And you sinned.
So I have struck you down
From the mountain of God,
And I have destroyed you, O shielding cherub,
From among the stones of fire.
17You grew haughty because of your beauty,
You debased your wisdom for the sake of your splendor;
I have cast you to the ground,
I have made you an object for kings to stare at.
18By the greatness of your guilt,
Through the dishonesty of your trading,
You desecrated your sanctuaries.
So I made a fire issue from you,
And it has devoured you;
I have reduced you to ashes on the ground,
In the sight of all who behold you.
19All who knew you among the peoples
Are appalled at your doom.
You have become a horror
And have ceased to be forever.

20The word of the LORD came to me: 21O mortal, set your face toward Sidon and prophesy against her. 22Say: Thus said the Lord GOD:

I am going to deal with you, O Sidon.
I will gain glory in your midst;
And they shall know that I am the LORD,
When I wreak punishment upon her
And show Myself holy through her.
23I will let pestilence loose against her
And bloodshed into her streets.
And the slain shall fall in her midst
When the sword comes upon her from all sides.
And they shall know that I am the LORD.

24Then shall the House of Israel no longer be afflicted with prickling briers and lacerating thorns from all the neighbors who despise them; and they shall know that I am the Lord GOD.

²⁵Thus said the Lord GOD: When I have gathered the House of Israel from the peoples among which they have been dispersed, and have shown Myself holy through them in the sight of the nations, they shall settle on their own soil, which I gave to My servant Jacob, ²⁶and they shall dwell on it in security. They shall build houses and plant vineyards, and shall dwell on it in security, when I have meted out punishment to all those about them who despise them. And they shall know that I the LORD am their God.

29 In the tenth year, on the twelfth day of the tenth month, the word of the LORD came to me: ²O mortal, turn your face against Pharaoh king of Egypt, and prophesy against him and against all Egypt. ³Speak these words:

Thus said the Lord GOD:
I am going to deal with you, O Pharaoh king of Egypt,
Mighty monster, sprawling in your^a channels,
Who said,
My Nile is my own;
I made it for myself.
⁴I will put hooks in your jaws,
And make the fish of your channels
Cling to your scales;
I will haul you up from your channels,
With all the fish of your channels
Clinging to your scales.
⁵And I will fling you into the desert,
With all the fish of your channels.
You shall be left lying in the open,
Ungathered and unburied:
I have given you as food
To the beasts of the earth
And the birds of the sky.
⁶Then all the inhabitants of Egypt shall know
That I am the LORD.
Because you^b were a staff of reed

---

^a Lit. "its."
^b Lit. "they."

To the House of Israel:

⁷When they grasped you with the hand, you would splinter,
And wound all their shoulders,^c
And when they leaned on you, you would break,
And make all their loins unsteady.^d

⁸Assuredly, thus said the Lord GOD: Lo, I will bring a sword against you, and will cut off man and beast from you, ⁹so that the land of Egypt shall fall into desolation and ruin. And they shall know that I am the LORD—because he boasted, "The Nile is mine, and I made it." ¹⁰Assuredly, I am going to deal with you and your channels, and I will reduce the land of Egypt to utter ruin and desolation, ^{e-}from Migdol to Syene, all the way to the border of Nubia.^{-e} ¹¹No foot of man shall traverse it, and no foot of beast shall traverse it; and it shall remain uninhabited for forty years. ¹²For forty years I will make the land of Egypt the most desolate of desolate lands, and its cities shall be the most desolate of ruined cities. And I will scatter the Egyptians among the nations and disperse them throughout the countries.

¹³Further, thus said the Lord GOD: After a period of forty years I will gather the Egyptians from the peoples among whom they were dispersed. ¹⁴I will restore the fortunes of the Egyptians and bring them back to the land of their origin, the land of Pathros,^f and there they shall be a lowly kingdom. ¹⁵It shall be the lowliest of all the kingdoms, and shall not lord it over the nations again. I will reduce the Egyptians,^g so that they shall have no dominion over the nations. ¹⁶Never again shall they be the trust of the House of Israel, recalling its guilt in having turned to them. And they shall know that I am the Lord GOD.

¹⁷In the twenty-seventh year, on the first day of the first month, the word of the LORD came to me: ¹⁸O mortal, King Nebuchadrezzar of Babylon has made his army expend vast labor on Tyre; every head is rubbed bald and every shoulder scraped. But he and his army have had no return for the labor he expended on Tyre. ¹⁹Assuredly, thus said the Lord GOD: I will give the land of Egypt to Nebuchadrezzar, king of Babylon. He shall carry off her wealth and take her spoil and seize her booty; and she shall be the recompense of his army. ²⁰As the wage for which he labored, for what they did for Me, I give him the land of Egypt—declares the Lord GOD.

^c *Septuagint and Syriac read "palms"; cf. 2 Kings 18.21; Isa. 36.6.*
^d *Taking* 'amad *as a byform of* ma'ad; *cf. Syriac translation.*
^{e-e} *I.e., the length of Egypt, from north to south. Syene is modern Aswan.*
^f *I.e., southern Egypt.*
^g *Heb. "them."*

21On that day I will h-endow the House of Israel with strength, and you shall be vindicated-h among them. And they shall know that I am the LORD.

30

The word of the LORD came to me: 2O mortal, prophesy and say: Thus said the Lord GOD:

Wail, alas for the day!
3For a day is near;
A day of the LORD is near.
It will be a day of cloud,
An hour of [invading] nations.
4A sword shall pierce Egypt,
And Nubia shall be seized with trembling,
When men fall slain in Egypt
And her wealth is seized
And her foundations are overthrown.

5Nubia, Put, and Lud, and all a-the mixed populations,-a and Cub, and the inhabitants of the allied countries shall fall by the sword with them. 6Thus said the LORD:

Those who support Egypt shall fall,
And her proud strength shall sink;
There they shall fall by the sword,
From Migdol to Syene

—declares the Lord GOD.

7They shall be the most desolate of desolate lands, and her cities shall be the most ruined of cities, 8when I set fire to Egypt and all who help her are broken. Thus they shall know that I am the LORD.

9On that day, messengers shall set out at My bidding to strike terror into confident Nubia. And they shall be seized with trembling on Egypt's day [of doom]—for it is at hand.

10Thus said the Lord GOD: I will put an end to the wealth of Egypt through King Nebuchadrezzar of Babylon. 11He, together with his troops, the most ruthless of the nations, shall be brought to ravage the land. And they shall unsheathe the sword against Egypt and fill the land with the slain.

h-h *Lit. "cause a horn to sprout for the House of Israel, and I will grant you opening of the mouth."*
a-a *Meaning of Heb. uncertain.*

¹²I will turn the channels into dry ground, and I will deliver the land into the hands of evil men. I will lay waste the land and everything in it by the hands of strangers. I the LORD have spoken.

¹³Thus said the Lord GOD: I will destroy the fetishes and make an end of the idols in Noph; and no longer shall there be a prince in the land of Egypt; and I will strike the land of Egypt with fear. ¹⁴I will lay Pathros waste, I will set fire to Zoan, and I will execute judgment on No. ¹⁵I will pour out my anger upon Sin, the stronghold of Egypt, and I will destroy the wealth of No. ¹⁶I will set fire to Egypt; Sin shall writhe in anguish and No shall be torn apart; ᵃ⁻and Noph [shall face] adversaries in broad daylight.⁻ᵃ ¹⁷The young men of Avenᵇ and Pi-beseth shall fall by the sword, and those [towns] shall go into captivity. ¹⁸In Tehaphnehesᶜ daylight shall be withheld,ᵈ when I break there the power of Egypt, and there her proud strength comes to an end. [The city] itself shall be covered with cloud, and its daughter towns shall go into captivity.
¹⁹Thus I will execute judgment on Egypt;
And they shall know that I am the LORD.

²⁰In the eleventh year, on the seventh day of the first month, the word of the LORD came to me: ²¹O mortal, I have broken the arm of Pharaoh king of Egypt; it has not been bound up to be healed nor firmly bandaged to make it strong enough to grasp the sword. ²²Assuredly, thus said the Lord GOD: I am going to deal with Pharaoh king of Egypt. I will break his arms, both the sound one and the injured, and make the sword drop from his hand. ²³I will scatter the Egyptians among the nations and disperse them throughout the countries. ²⁴I will strengthen the arms of the king of Babylon and put My sword in his hand; and I will break the arms of Pharaoh, and he shall groan before him with the groans of one struck down. ²⁵I will make firm the arms of the king of Babylon, but the arms of Pharaoh shall fail. And they shall know that I am the LORD, when I put My sword into the hand of the king of Babylon, and he lifts it against the land of Egypt. ²⁶I will scatter the Egyptians among the nations and disperse them throughout the countries. Thus they shall know that I am the LORD.

ᵇ Elsewhere called "On"; cf. Gen. 41.45, 50; 46.20.
ᶜ Elsewhere vocalized "Tahpanhes"; e.g., Jer. 2.16; 44.1.
ᵈ Some Heb. mss. and editions read "darkened."

31 In the eleventh year, on the first day of the third month, the word of the LORD came to me: ²O mortal, say to Pharaoh king of Egypt and his hordes:

> Who was comparable to you in greatness?
> ³Assyria was a cedar in Lebanon
> With beautiful branches and ᵃ-shady thickets,⁻ᵃ
> Of lofty stature,
> With its top among ᵇ-leafy trees.⁻ᵇ
> ⁴Waters nourished it,
> The deep made it grow tall,
> Washing with its streams
> The place where it was planted,
> Making its channels well up
> ᶜ-To all⁻ᶜ the trees of the field.
> ⁵Therefore it exceeded in stature
> All the trees of the field;
> Its branches multiplied and its boughs grew long
> Because of the abundant water
> That welled up for it.
> ⁶In its branches nested
> All the birds of the sky;
> All the beasts of the field
> Bore their young under its boughs,
> And in its shadow lived
> All the great nations.
> ⁷It was beautiful in its height,
> In the length of its branches,
> Because its stock stood
> By abundant waters.
> ⁸Cedars in the garden of God
> Could not compare with it;
> Cypresses could not match its boughs,
> And plane trees could not vie with its branches;

ᵃ⁻ᵃ *Meaning of Heb. uncertain.*
ᵇ⁻ᵇ *Septuagint reads "clouds."*
ᶜ⁻ᶜ *Meaning of Heb. uncertain; emendation yields "more than for all."*

No tree in the garden of God
Was its peer in beauty.
⁹I made it beautiful
In the profusion of its branches;
And all the trees of Eden envied it
In the garden of God.

¹⁰Assuredly, thus said the Lord GOD: Because it^d towered high in stature, and thrust its top up among the ^b-leafy trees,-^b and it was arrogant in its height, ¹¹I delivered it into the hands of the mightiest of nations. They treated it as befitted its wickedness. I banished it. ¹²Strangers, the most ruthless of nations, cut it down and abandoned it; its branches fell on the mountains and in every valley; its boughs were splintered in every watercourse of the earth; and all the peoples of the earth departed from its shade and abandoned it. ¹³Upon its fallen trunk all the birds of the sky nest, and all the beasts of the field lodge among its boughs—¹⁴so that no trees by water should exalt themselves in stature or set their tops among the ^b-leafy trees,-^b and that no well-watered tree may reach up to them in height. For they are all consigned to death, to the lowest part of the netherworld,^e together with human beings who descend into the Pit.

¹⁵Thus said the Lord GOD: On the day it went down to Sheol, I closed^f the deep over it and covered it; I held back its streams, and the great waters were checked. I made Lebanon mourn deeply for it, and all the trees of the field languished on its account. ¹⁶I made nations quake at the crash of its fall, when I cast it down to Sheol with those who descend into the Pit; and all the trees of Eden, the choicest and best of Lebanon, all that were well watered, were consoled in the lowest part of the netherworld. ¹⁷They also descended with it into Sheol, to those slain by the sword, together with its supporters,^g they who had lived under its shadow among the nations.

¹⁸[Now you know] who is comparable to you in glory and greatness among the trees of Eden. And you too shall be brought down with the trees of Eden to the lowest part of the netherworld; you shall lie among the uncircumcised and those slain by the sword. Such shall be [the fate of] Pharaoh and all his hordes—declares the Lord GOD.

---

^d *Heb. "you."*
^e *To which popular belief relegated those who died uncircumcised or by the sword; cf. v. 18.*
^f *Cf. Aramaic 'abulla, "gate."*
^g *Heb. "arm."*

32 In the twelfth year, on the first day of the twelfth month, the word of the LORD came to me: ²O mortal, intone a dirge over Pharaoh king of Egypt. Say to him:

ᵃ⁻O great beast among the nations,⁻ᵃ you are doomed!
You are like the dragon in the seas,
Thrusting through theirᵇ streams,
Stirring up the water with your feet
And muddying their streams!
³Thus said the Lord GOD:
I will cast My net over you
In an assembly of many peoples,
And you shall be hauled up in My toils.
⁴And I will fling you to the ground,
Hurl you upon the open field.
I will cause all the birds of the sky
To settle upon you.
I will cause the beasts of all the earth
To batten on you.
⁵I will cast your carcass upon the hills
And fill the valleys with your ᵃ⁻rotting flesh.⁻ᵃ
⁶I will drench the earth
With your oozing blood upon the hills,
And the watercourses shall be filled with your [gore].
⁷When you are snuffed out,
I will cover the sky
And darken its stars;
I will cover the sun with clouds
And the moon shall not give its light.
⁸All the lights that shine in the sky
I will darken above you;
And I will bring darkness upon your land
　　　　　　　　　　　　　　　—declares the Lord GOD.
⁹I will vex the hearts of many peoples
When I bring your ᶜ⁻shattered remnants⁻ᶜ among the nations,

ᵃ⁻ᵃ *Meaning of Heb. uncertain.*
ᵇ *Heb. "your."*
ᶜ⁻ᶜ *Septuagint reads "captives."*

To countries which you never knew.
¹⁰I will strike many peoples with horror over your fate;
And their kings shall be aghast over you,
When I brandish My sword before them.
They shall tremble continually,
Each man for his own life,
On the day of your downfall.
¹¹For thus said the Lord GOD:
The sword of the king of Babylon shall come upon you.
¹²I will cause your multitude to fall
By the swords of warriors,
All the most ruthless among the nations.
They shall ravage the splendor of Egypt,
And all her masses shall be wiped out.
¹³I will make all her cattle vanish from beside abundant waters;
The feet of man shall not muddy them any more,
Nor shall the hoofs of cattle muddy them.
¹⁴Then I will let their waters settle,
And make their rivers flow like oil

—declares the Lord GOD:
¹⁵When I lay the land of Egypt waste,
When the land is emptied of [the life] that filled it,
When I strike down all its inhabitants.
And they shall know that I am the LORD.
¹⁶This is a dirge, and it shall be intoned;
The women of the nations shall intone it,
They shall intone it over Egypt and all her multitude

—declares the Lord GOD.

¹⁷In the twelfth year, on the fifteenth day of the month,^d the word of the LORD came to me: ^{18e}O mortal, wail [the dirge]—along with the women of the mighty nations—over the masses of Egypt, accompanying their descent to the lowest part of the netherworld, among those who have gone down into the Pit. ^{19f-}Whom do you surpass in beauty? Down with you, and be laid to rest with the uncircumcised! ²⁰They shall lie amid those slain by the sword,^{-f e}[amid those slain by] the sword [Egypt] has been dragged and left with all her masses.

²¹From the depths of Sheol the mightiest of warriors speak to him and

---

^d *Presumably the twelfth month; cf. v. 1.*
^e *Construction of these verses uncertain.*
^{f-f} *Cf. 31.18 ff. and note e on 31.14.*

his allies; the uncircumcised, the slain by the sword, have gone down and lie [there]. ²²Assyria is there with all her company, their graves round about, all of them slain, fallen by the sword. ²³Their graves set in the farthest recesses of the Pit, all her company are round about her tomb, all of them slain, fallen by the sword—they who struck terror in the land of the living. ²⁴There too is Elam and all her masses round about her tomb, all of them slain, fallen by the sword—they who descended uncircumcised to the lowest part of the netherworld, who struck terror in the land of the living—now they bear their shame with those who have gone down to the Pit. ²⁵They made a bed for her among the slain, with all her masses; their graves are round about her. They are all uncircumcised, slain by the sword. Though their terror was once spread over the land of the living, they bear their shame with those who have gone into the Pit; they are placed among the slain. ²⁶Meshech and Tubal and all their masses are there; their graves are round about. They are all uncircumcised, pierced through by the sword—they who once struck terror in the land of the living. ²⁷And they do not lie with the fallen uncircumcised warriors, who went down to Sheol with their battle gear, who put their swords beneath their heads and their iniquitiesᵍ upon their bones—for the terror of the warriors was upon the land of the living. ²⁸And you too shall be shattered amid the uncircumcised, and lie among those slain by the sword. ²⁹Edom is there, her kings and all her chieftains, who, for all their might, are laid among those who are slain by the sword; they too lie with the uncircumcised and with those who have gone down to the Pit. ³⁰All the princes of the north and all the Sidonians are there, who went down in disgrace with the slain, in spite of the terror that their might inspired; and they lie, uncircumcised, with those who are slain by the sword, and bear their shame with those who have gone down to the Pit.

³¹These Pharaoh shall see, and he shall be consoled for all his masses, those of Pharaoh's men slain by the sword and all his army—declares the Lord GOD. ³²ʰ⁻I strike terror into the land of the living; Pharaoh⁻ʰ and all his masses are laid among the uncircumcised, along with those who were slain by the sword—said the Lord GOD.

33 The word of the LORD came to me: ²O mortal, speak to your fellow countrymen and say to them: When I bring the sword against a country, the citizens of that country take one of their number and appoint

ᵍ Emendation yields "shields."
ʰ⁻ʰ Emendation yields "because he struck terror in the land of the living, Pharaoh."

him their watchman. ³Suppose he sees the sword advancing against the country, and he blows the horn and warns the people. ⁴If anybody hears the sound of the horn but ignores the warning, and the sword comes and dispatches him, his blood shall be on his own head. ⁵Since he heard the sound of the horn but ignored the warning, his bloodguilt shall be upon himself; had he taken the warning, he would have saved his life. ⁶But if the watchman sees the sword advancing and does not blow the horn, so that the people are not warned, and the sword comes and destroys one of them, that person was destroyed for his own sins; however, I will demand a reckoning for his blood from the watchman.

⁷Now, O mortal, I have appointed you a watchman for the House of Israel; and whenever you hear a message from My mouth, you must transmit My warning to them. ⁸When I say to the wicked, "Wicked man, you shall die," but you have not spoken to warn the wicked man against his way, he, that wicked man, shall die for his sins, but I will demand a reckoning for his blood from you. ⁹But if you have warned the wicked man to turn back from his way, and he has not turned from his way, he shall die for his own sins, but you will have saved your life.

¹⁰Now, O mortal, say to the House of Israel: This is what you have been saying: "Our transgressions and our sins weigh heavily upon us; we are sick at heart about them. How can we survive?" ¹¹Say to them: As I live—declares the Lord GOD—it is not My desire that the wicked shall die, but that the wicked turn from his [evil] ways and live. Turn back, turn back from your evil ways, that you may not die, O House of Israel!

¹²Now, O mortal, say to your fellow countrymen: The righteousness of the righteous shall not save him when he transgresses, nor shall the wickedness of the wicked cause him to stumble when he turns back from his wickedness. The righteous shall not survive through ᵃhis righteous-ness-ᵃ when he sins. ¹³When I say of the righteous "He shall surely live," and, relying on his righteousness, he commits iniquity, none of his right-eous deeds shall be remembered; but for the iniquity that he has com-mitted he shall die. ¹⁴So, too, when I say to the wicked, "You shall die," and he turns back from his sinfulness and does what is just and right—¹⁵if the wicked man restores a pledge, makes good what he has taken by robbery, follows the laws of life,ᵇ and does not commit iniquity—he shall live, he shall not die. ¹⁶None of the sins that he committed shall be remembered against him; since he does what is just and right, he shall live.

¹⁷Your fellow countrymen say, "The way of the Lord is unfair." But it

---

ᵃ⁻ᵃ *Heb. "it."*
ᵇ *Cf. Lev. 18.5.*

is their way that is unfair! ¹⁸When a righteous man turns away from his righteous deeds and commits iniquity, he shall die ᶜ⁻for it.⁻ᶜ ¹⁹And when a wicked man turns back from his wickedness and does what is just and right, it is he who shall live by virtue of these things. ²⁰And will you say, "The way of the Lord is unfair"? I will judge each one of you according to his ways, O House of Israel!

²¹In the twelfth year of our exile, on the fifth day of the tenth month, a fugitive came to me from Jerusalem and reported, "The city has fallen." ²²Now the hand of the LORD had come upon me the evening before the fugitive arrived, and He opened my mouth before he came to me in the morning; thus my mouth was opened and I was no longer speechless.

²³The word of the LORD came to me: ²⁴O mortal, those who live in these ruins in the land of Israel argue, "Abraham was but one man, yet he was granted possession of the land. We are many; surely, the land has been given as a possession to us." ²⁵Therefore say to them: Thus said the Lord GOD: You eat with the blood, you raise your eyes to your fetishes, and you shed blood—yet you expect to possess the land! ²⁶You have relied on your sword, you have committed abominations, you have all defiled other men's wives—yet you expect to possess the land!

²⁷Thus shall you speak to them: Thus said the Lord GOD: As I live, those who are in the ruins shall fall by the sword, and those who are in the open I have allotted as food to the beasts, and those who are in the strongholds and caves shall die by pestilence. ²⁸I will make the land a desolate waste, and her proud glory shall cease; and the mountains of Israel shall be desolate, with none passing through. ²⁹And they shall know that I am the LORD, when I make the land a desolate waste on account of all the abominations which they have committed.

³⁰Note well, O mortal: your fellow countrymen who converse about you by the walls and in the doorways of their houses and say to each other and propose to one another, "Come and hear what word has issued from the LORD." ³¹They will come to you ᵈ⁻in crowds and sit before you in throngs⁻ᵈ and will hear your words, but they will not obey them. For ᵉ⁻they produce nothing but lust with their mouths;⁻ᵉ and their hearts pursue nothing but gain. ³²To them you are just a singer of bawdy songs, who has a sweet voice and plays skillfully; they hear your words, but will not obey them. ³³But when itᶠ comes—and come it will—they shall know that a prophet has been among them.

ᶜ⁻ᶜ *Or "in spite of them," i.e., his righteous deeds.*
ᵈ⁻ᵈ *Meaning of Heb. uncertain. Lit. "as a people come, and sit before you as My people."*
ᵉ⁻ᵉ *Meaning of Heb. uncertain.*
ᶠ *I.e., the punishment predicted.*

34

The word of the LORD came to me: ²O mortal, prophesy against the shepherdsᵃ of Israel. Prophesy, and say to them:

To the shepherds: Thus said the Lord GOD: Ah, you shepherds of Israel, who have been tending yourselves! Is it not the flock that the shepherds ought to tend? ³You partake of the fat,ᵇ you clothe yourselves with the wool, and you slaughter the fatlings; but you do not tend the flock. ⁴You have not sustained the weak, healed the sick, or bandaged the injured; you have not brought back the strayed, or looked for the lost; but you have driven them with harsh rigor, ⁵and they have been scattered for want of anyone to tend them; scattered, they have become prey for every wild beast. ⁶My sheep stray through all the mountains and over every lofty hill; My flock is scattered all over the face of the earth, with none to take thought of them and none to seek them. ⁷Hear then, O shepherds, the word of the LORD! ⁸As I live—declares the Lord GOD: Because My flock has been a spoil—My flock has been a prey for all the wild beasts, for want of anyone to tend them since My shepherds have not taken thought of My flock, for the shepherds tended themselves instead of tending the flock—⁹hear indeed, O shepherds, the word of the LORD: ¹⁰Thus said the Lord GOD: I am going to deal with the shepherds! I will demand a reckoning of them for My flock, and I will dismiss them from tending the flock. The shepherds shall not tend themselves any more; for I will rescue My flock from their mouths, and it shall not be their prey. ¹¹For thus said the Lord GOD: Here am I! I am going to take thought for My flock and I will seek them out. ¹²As a shepherd seeks out his flock when some [animals] in his flock have gotten separated, so I will seek out My flock, I will rescue them from all the places to which they were scattered on a day of cloud and gloom. ¹³I will take them out from the peoples and gather them from the countries, and I will bring them to their own land, and will pasture them on the mountains of Israel, by the watercourses and in all the settled portions of the land. ¹⁴I will feed them in good grazing land, and the lofty hills of Israel shall be their pasture. There, in the hills of Israel, they shall lie down in a good pasture and shall feed on rich grazing land. ¹⁵I Myself will graze My flock, and I Myself will let them lie down—declares the Lord GOD. ¹⁶I will look for the lost, and I will bring back the strayed; I will bandage the injured, and I will sustain the weak; and the fat and healthy ones I will destroy.ᶜ I will tend them rightly.

ᵃ *I.e., rulers.*
ᵇ *Septuagint and Vulgate, reading the Hebrew consonants with different vowels, translate "milk."*
ᶜ *Several ancient versions read "guard."*

¹⁷And as for you, My flock, thus said the Lord GOD: I am going to judge between one animal and another.

To the rams and the bucks: ¹⁸Is it not enough for you to graze on choice grazing ground, but you must also trample with your feet what is left from your grazing? And is it not enough for you to drink ᵈ⁻clear water,⁻ᵈ but you must also muddy with your feet what is left? ¹⁹And must My flock graze on what your feet have trampled and drink what your feet have muddied? ²⁰Assuredly, thus said the Lord GOD to them: Here am I, I am going to decide between the stout animals and the lean. ²¹Because you pushed with flank and shoulder against the feeble ones and butted them with your horns until you scattered them abroad, ²²I will rescue My flock and they shall no longer be a spoil. I will decide between one animal and another.

²³Then I will appoint a single shepherd over them to tend them—My servant David. He shall tend them, he shall be a shepherd to them. ²⁴I the LORD will be their God, and My servant David shall be a ruler among them—I the LORD have spoken. ²⁵And I will grant them a covenant of friendship. I will banish vicious beasts from their land, and they shall live secure in the wasteland, they shall even sleep in the woodland. ²⁶I will make ᵉ⁻these and the environs of My hill⁻ᵉ a blessing: I will send down the rain in its season, rains that bring blessing. ²⁷The trees of the field shall yield their fruit and the land shall yield its produce. [My people] shall continue secure on its own soil. They shall know that I am the LORD when I break the bars of their yoke and rescue them from those who enslave them. ²⁸They shall no longer be a spoil for the nations, and the beasts of the earth shall not devour them; they shall dwell secure and untroubled. ²⁹I shall establish for them ᵉ⁻a planting of renown;⁻ᵉ they shall no more be carried off by famine, and they shall not have to bear again the taunts of the nations.ᶠ ³⁰They shall know that I the LORD their God am with them and they, the House of Israel, are My people—declares the Lord GOD.

³¹For you, My flock, flock that I tend, are men; and I am your God—declares the Lord GOD.

35 The word of the LORD came to me: ²O mortal, set your face against Mount Seir and prophesy against it. ³Say to it: Thus said the Lord GOD: I am going to deal with you, Mount Seir: I will stretch out My

---

ᵈ⁻ᵈ *Lit. "water that has settled."*
ᵉ⁻ᵉ *Meaning of Heb. uncertain.*
ᶠ *Cf. 36.30.*

hand against you and make you an utter waste. 4I will turn your towns into ruins, and you shall be a desolation; then you shall know that I am the LORD. 5Because you harbored an ancient hatred and handed the people of Israel over to the sword in their time of calamity, the time set for their punishment—6assuredly, as I live, declares the Lord GOD, a-I will doom you with blood; blood shall pursue you; I swear that, for your bloodthirsty hatred, blood shall pursue you.-a 7I will make Mount Seir an utter waste, and I will keep all passersby away from it. 8I will cover its mountains with the slain; men slain by the sword shall lie on your hills, in your valleys, and in all your watercourses. 9I will make you a desolation for all time; your towns shall never be inhabited. And you shall know that I am the LORD.

10Because you thought "The two nations and the two lands shall be mine and we shall possess them"—b-although the LORD was there-b— 11assuredly, as I live, declares the Lord GOD, I will act with the same anger and passion that you acted with in your hatred of them. And I will make Myself known through them when I judge you. 12You shall know that I the LORD have heard all the taunts you uttered against the hills of Israel: "They have been laid waste; they have been given to us as prey." 13And you spoke arrogantly against Me and c-multiplied your words-c against Me: I have heard it.

14Thus said the LORD God: When the whole earth rejoices, I will make you a desolation. 15As you rejoiced when the heritage of the House of Israel was laid waste, so will I treat you: the hill country of Seir and the whole of Edom, all of it, shall be laid waste. And they shall know that I am the LORD.

36 And you, O mortal, prophesy to the mountains of Israel and say: O mountains of Israel, hear the word of the LORD:

2Thus said the Lord GOD: Because the enemy gloated over you, "Aha! Those ancient heights have become our possession!" 3therefore prophesy, and say: Thus said the Lord GOD: Just because a-they eagerly lusted to see you become a possession of the other nations round about, so that you have become the butt of gossip in every language and of the jibes from every people-a—4truly, you mountains of Israel, hear the word of the Lord GOD: Thus said the Lord GOD to the mountains and the hills, to the watercourses and the valleys, and to the desolate wastes and deserted

---

a-a Meaning of Heb. uncertain.
b-b Meaning of Heb. uncertain; emendation yields "and the LORD heard it."
c-c Emendation yields "and spoke arrogantly."

a-a Meaning of Heb. uncertain.

cities which have become a prey and a laughingstock to the other nations round about:

⁵Assuredly, thus said the Lord GOD: I have indeed spoken in My blazing wrath against the other nations and against all of Edom which, ᵃ⁻with wholehearted glee and with contempt, have made My land a possession for themselves for pasture and for prey.⁻ᵃ ⁶Yes, prophesy about the land of Israel, and say to the mountains and the hills, to the watercourses and to the valleys, Thus said the Lord GOD: Behold, I declare in My blazing wrath: Because you have suffered the taunting of the nations, ⁷thus said the Lord GOD: I hereby swear that the nations which surround you shall, in their turn, suffer disgrace. ⁸But you, O mountains of Israel, shall yield your produce and bear your fruit for My people Israel, for their return is near. ⁹For I will care for you: I will turn to you, and you shall be tilled and sown. ¹⁰I will settle a large population on you, the whole House of Israel; the towns shall be resettled, and the ruined sites rebuilt. ¹¹I will multiply men and beasts upon you, and they shall increase and be fertile, and I will resettle you as you were formerly, and will make you more prosperous than you were at first. And you shall know that I am the LORD. ¹²I will lead men—My people Israel—to you, and they shall possess you. You shall be their heritage, and you shall not again cause them to be bereaved.

¹³Thus said the Lord GOD: Because they say to you, "You are [a land] that devours men, you have been a bereaver of your nations,"ᵇ ¹⁴assuredly, you shall devour men no more, you shall never again bereave your nations—declares the Lord GOD. ¹⁵No more will I allow the jibes of the nations to be heard against you, no longer shall you suffer the taunting of the peoples; and never again shall you cause your nations to stumbleᶜ— declares the Lord GOD.

¹⁶The word of the LORD came to me: ¹⁷O mortal, when the House of Israel dwelt on their own soil, they defiled it with their ways and their deeds; their ways were in My sight like the uncleanness of a menstruous woman. ¹⁸So I poured out My wrath on them for the blood which they shed upon their land, and for the fetishes with which they defiled it. ¹⁹I scattered them among the nations, and they were dispersed through the countries: I punished them in accordance with their ways and their deeds. ²⁰But when they came ᵈ⁻to those nations,⁻ᵈ they caused My holy name to be profaned,ᵉ in that it was said of them, "These are the people of the

ᵇ *I.e., Israel and Judah; cf. 37.15–22.*
ᶜ *Many mss. read "be bereaved"; cf. vv. 13–14.*
ᵈ⁻ᵈ *Lit. "the nations they came to."*
ᵉ *I.e., the exile of Israel was taken by the nations to be evidence of the LORD's weakness.*

LORD, yet they had to leave His land." ²¹Therefore I am concerned for My holy name, which the House of Israel have caused to be profaned among the nations to which they have come.

²²Say to the House of Israel: Thus said the Lord GOD: Not for your sake will I act, O House of Israel, but for My holy name, which you have caused to be profaned among the nations to which you have come. ²³I will sanctify My great name which has been profaned among the nations— among whom you have caused it to be profaned. And the nations shall know that I am the LORD—declares the Lord GOD—when I manifest My holiness before their eyes through you. ²⁴I will take you from among the nations and gather you from all the countries, and I will bring you back to your own land. ²⁵I will sprinkle clean water upon you, and you shall be clean: I will cleanse you from all your uncleanness and from all your fetishes. ²⁶And I will give you a new heart and put a new spirit into you: I will remove the heart of stone from your body and give you a heart of flesh; ²⁷and I will put My spirit into you. Thus I will cause you to follow My laws and faithfully to observe My rules. ²⁸Then you shall dwell in the land which I gave to your fathers, and you shall be My people and I will be your God.

²⁹And when I have delivered you from all your uncleanness, I will summon the grain and make it abundant, and I will not bring famine upon you. ³⁰I will make the fruit of your trees and the crops of your fields abundant, so that you shall never again be humiliated before the nations because of famine. ³¹Then you shall recall your evil ways and your base conduct, and you shall loathe yourselves for your iniquities and your abhorrent practices. ³²Not for your sake will I act—declares the Lord GOD—take good note! Be ashamed and humiliated because of your ways, O House of Israel!

³³Thus said the Lord GOD: When I have cleansed you of all your iniquities, I will people your settlements, and the ruined places shall be rebuilt; ³⁴and the desolate land, after lying waste in the sight of every passerby, shall again be tilled. ³⁵And men shall say, "That land, once desolate, has become like the garden of Eden; and the cities, once ruined, desolate, and ravaged, are now populated and fortified." ³⁶And the nations that are left around you shall know that I the LORD have rebuilt the ravaged places and replanted the desolate land. I the LORD have spoken and will act.

³⁷Thus said the Lord GOD: Moreover, in this I will respond to the

House of Israel and act for their sake: I will multiply their people like sheep. 38As Jerusalem is filled with sacrificial sheep during her festivals, so shall the ruined cities be filled with flocks of people. And they shall know that I am the LORD.

37 The hand of the LORD came upon me. He took me out by the spirit of the LORD and set me down in the valley. It was full of bones. 2He led me all around them; there were very many of them spread over the valley, and they were very dry. 3He said to me, "O mortal, can these bones live again?" I replied, "O Lord GOD, only You know." 4And He said to me, "Prophesy over these bones and say to them: O dry bones, hear the word of the LORD! 5Thus said the Lord GOD to these bones: I will cause breath to enter you and you shall live again. 6I will lay sinews upon you, and cover you with flesh, and form skin over you. And I will put breath into you, and you shall live again. And you shall know that I am the LORD!"

7I prophesied as I had been commanded. And while I was prophesying, suddenly there was a sound of rattling, and the bones came together, bone to matching bone. 8I looked, and there were sinews on them, and flesh had grown, and skin had formed over them; but there was no breath in them. 9Then He said to me, "Prophesy to the breath, prophesy, O mortal! Say to the breath: Thus said the Lord GOD: Come, O breath, from the four winds, and breathe into these slain, that they may live again." 10I prophesied as He commanded me. The breath entered them, and they came to life and stood up on their feet, a vast multitude.

11And He said to me, "O mortal, these bones are the whole House of Israel. They say, 'Our bones are dried up, our hope is gone; we are doomed.' 12Prophesy, therefore, and say to them: Thus said the Lord GOD: I am going to open your graves and lift you out of the graves, O My people, and bring you to the land of Israel. 13You shall know, O My people, that I am the LORD, when I have opened your graves and lifted you out of your graves. 14I will put My breath into you and you shall live again, and I will set you upon your own soil. Then you shall know that I the LORD have spoken and have acted"—declares the LORD.

15The word of the LORD came to me: 16And you, O mortal, take a stick and write on it, "Of Judah and the Israelites associated with him";

and take another stick and write on it, "Of Joseph—the stick of Ephraim—and all the House of Israel associated with him." 17Bring them close to each other, so that they become one stick, joined together in your hand. 18And when any of your people ask you, "Won't you tell us what these actions of yours mean?" 19answer them, "Thus said the Lord GOD: I am going to take the stick of Joseph—which is in the hand of Ephraim—and of the tribes of Israel associated with him, and I will place the stick of Judah a-upon it-a and make them into one stick; they shall be joined in My hand." 20You shall hold up before their eyes the sticks which you have inscribed, 21and you shall declare to them: Thus said the Lord GOD: I am going to take the Israelite people from among the nations they have gone to, and gather them from every quarter, and bring them to their own land. 22I will make them a single nation in the land, on the hills of Israel, and one king shall be king of them all. Never again shall they be two nations, and never again shall they be divided into two kingdoms. 23Nor shall they ever again defile themselves by their fetishes and their abhorrent things, and by their other transgressions. I will save them in all their settlements where they sinned, and I will cleanse them. Then they shall be My people, and I will be their God.

24My servant David shall be king over them; there shall be one shepherd for all of them. They shall follow My rules and faithfully obey My laws. 25Thus they shall remain in the land which I gave to My servant Jacob and in which your fathers dwelt; they and their children and their children's children shall dwell there forever, with My servant David as their prince for all time. 26I will make a covenant of friendship with them—it shall be an everlasting covenant with them—I will establisha them and multiply them, and I will place My Sanctuary among them forever. 27My Presenceb shall rest over them; I will be their God and they shall be My people. 28And when My Sanctuary abides among them forever, the nations shall know that I the LORD do sanctify Israel.

38 The word of the LORD came to me: 2O mortal, turn your face toward Gog of the land of Magog, the chief prince of Meshech and Tubal. Prophesy against him 3and say: Thus said the Lord GOD: Lo, I am coming to deal with you, O Gog, chief prince of Meshech and Tubal! 4I will turn you around and put hooks in your jaws, and lead you out with all your army, horses, and horsemen, all of them clothed in splendor, a vast as-

a-a *Meaning of Heb. uncertain.*
b *Lit. "dwelling place."*

sembly, all of them with bucklers and shields, wielding swords. ⁵Among them shall be Persia, Nubia, and Put, everyone with shield and helmet; ⁶Gomer and all its cohorts, Beth-togarmah [in] the remotest parts of the north and all its cohorts—the many peoples with you.ᵃ ⁷Be ready, prepare yourselves, you and all the battalions mustered about you, and hold yourself in reserve for them.ᵇ ⁸After a long time you shall be summoned; in the distant future you shall march against the land [of a people] restored from the sword, gathered from the midst of many peoples—against the mountains of Israel, which have long lain desolate—[a people] liberated from the nations, and now all dwelling secure. ⁹You shall advance, coming like a storm; you shall be like a cloud covering the earth, you and all your cohorts, and the many peoples with you.

¹⁰Thus said the Lord GOD: On that day, a thought will occur to you, and you will conceive a wicked design. ¹¹You will say, "I will invade a land of open towns, I will fall upon a tranquil people living secure, all of them living in unwalled towns and lacking bars and gates, ¹²in order to take spoil and seize plunder"—to turn your hand against repopulated wastes, and against a people gathered from among nations, acquiring livestock and possessions, living at the center of the earth. ¹³Sheba and Dedan, and the merchants and all the magnates of Tarshish will say to you, "Have you come to take spoil? Is it to seize plunder that you assembled your hordes—to carry off silver and gold, to make off with livestock and goods, to gather an immense booty?"

¹⁴Therefore prophesy, O mortal, and say to Gog: Thus said the Lord GOD: Surely, on that day, when My people Israel are living secure, you will ᶜ⁻take note,⁻ᶜ ¹⁵and you will come from your home in the farthest north, you and many peoples with you—all of them mounted on horses, a vast horde, a mighty army—¹⁶and you will advance upon My people Israel, like a cloud covering the earth. This shall happen on that distant day: I will bring you to My land, that the nations may know Me when, before their eyes, I manifest My holiness through you, O Gog!

¹⁷Thus said the Lord GOD: Why, you are the one I spoke of in ancient days through My servants, the prophets of Israel, who prophesied for years in those days that I would bring you against them!

¹⁸On that day, when Gog sets foot on the soil of Israel—declares the Lord GOD—My raging anger shall flare up. ¹⁹For I have decreed in My indignation and in My blazing wrath: On that day, a terrible earthquake shall befall the land of Israel. ²⁰The fish of the sea, the birds of the sky,

---

ᵃ I.e., with Gog.
ᵇ Septuagint reads "Me."
ᶜ⁻ᶜ Septuagint reads "rouse yourself."

the beasts of the field, all creeping things that move on the ground, and every human being on earth shall quake before Me. Mountains shall be overthrown, cliffs shall topple, and every wall shall crumble to the ground. 21d-I will then summon the sword against him throughout My mountains-d—declares the Lord GOD—and every man's sword shall be turned against his brother. 22I will punish him with pestilence and with bloodshed; and I will pour torrential rain, hailstones, and sulfurous fire upon him and his hordes and the many peoples with him. 23Thus will I manifest My greatness and My holiness, and make Myself known in the sight of many nations. And they shall know that I am the LORD.

39 And you, O mortal, prophesy against Gog and say: Thus said the Lord GOD: I am going to deal with you, O Gog, chief prince of Meshech and Tubal! 2I will turn you around and a-drive you on,-a and I will take you from the far north and lead you toward the mountains of Israel. 3I will strike your bow from your left hand and I will loosen the arrows from your right hand. 4You shall fall on the mountains of Israel, you and all your battalions and the peoples who are with you; and I will give you as food to carrion birds of every sort and to the beasts of the field, 5as you lie in the open field. For I have spoken—declares the Lord GOD. 6And I will send a fire against Magog and against those who dwell secure in the coastlands. And they shall know that I am the LORD. 7I will make My holy name known among My people Israel, and never again will I let My holy name be profaned. And the nations shall know that I the LORD am holy in Israel. 8Ah! it has come, it has happened—declares the Lord GOD: this is that day that I decreed.

9Then the inhabitants of the cities of Israel will go out and make fires and feed them with the weapons—shields and bucklers, bows and arrows, clubs and spears; they shall use them as fuel for seven years. 10They will not gather firewood in the fields or cut any in the forests, but will use the weapons as fuel for their fires. They will despoil those who despoiled them and plunder those who plundered them—declares the Lord GOD.

11On that day I will assign to Gog a burial site there in Israel—the Valley of the Travelers, east of the Sea. It shall block the path of travelers, for there Gog and all his multitude will be buried. It shall be called the Valley of Gog's Multitude. 12The House of Israel shall spend seven months burying them, in order to cleanse the land; 13all the people of the land

d-d *Meaning of Heb. uncertain.*

a-a *Meaning of Heb. uncertain.*

shall bury them. a-The day I manifest My glory shall bring renown to them-a—declares the Lord GOD. 14And they shall appoint men to serve permanently, to traverse the land and bury any invaders who remain above ground, in order to cleanse it. The search shall go on for a period of seven months. 15As those who traverse the country make their rounds, any one of them who sees a human bone shall erect a marker beside it, until the buriers have interred them in the Valley of Gog's Multitude. 16a-There shall also be a city named Multitude.-a And thus the land shall be cleansed.

17And you, O mortal, say to every winged bird and to all the wild beasts: Thus said the Lord GOD: Assemble, come and gather from all around for the sacrificial feast that I am preparing for you—a great sacrificial feast—upon the mountains of Israel, and eat flesh and drink blood. 18You shall eat the flesh of warriors and drink the blood of the princes of the earth: rams, lambs, he-goats, and bulls—fatlings of Bashan all of them. 19You shall eat fat to satiety and drink your fill of blood from the sacrificial feast that I have prepared for you. 20And you shall sate yourselves at My table with horses, charioteers,b warriors, and all fighting men—declares the Lord GOD. 21Thus will I manifest My glory among the nations, and all the nations shall see the judgment that I executed and the power that I wielded against them.

22From that time on, the House of Israel shall know that I the LORD am their God. 23And the nations shall know that the House of Israel were exiled only for their iniquity, because they trespassed against Me, so that I hid My face from them and delivered them into the hands of their adversaries, and they all fell by the sword. 24When I hid My face from them, I dealt with them according to their uncleanness and their transgressions.

25Assuredly, thus said the Lord GOD: I will now restore the fortunes of Jacob and take the whole House of Israel back in love; and I will be zealous for My holy name. 26They will bearc their shame and all their trespasses that they committed against Me, when they dwell in their land secure and untroubled, 27when I have brought them back from among the peoples and gathered them out of the lands of their enemies and have manifested My holiness through them in the sight of many nations. 28They shall know that I the Lord am their GOD when, having exiled them among the nations, I gather them back into their land and leave none of them

b *Lit. "chariots"; Septuagint reads "riders."*
c *Change of diacritical point yields "forget."*

behind. ²⁹I will never again hide My face from them, for I will pour out My spirit upon the House of Israel—declares the Lord GOD.

40

In the twenty-fifth year of our exile,^a the fourteenth year after the city had fallen, at the beginning of the year, the tenth day of the month—on that very day—the hand of the LORD came upon me, and He brought me there. ²He brought me, in visions of God, to the Land of Israel, and He set me down on a very high mountain^b on which there seemed to be the outline of a city ^{c-}on the south.^{-c} ³He brought me over to it, and there, standing at the gate, was a man who shone like copper. In his hand were a cord of linen and a measuring rod. ⁴The man spoke to me: "Mortal, look closely and listen attentively and note well everything I am going to show you—for you have been brought here in order to be shown—and report everything you see to the House of Israel."

⁵Along the outside of the Temple [area] ran a wall on every side. The rod that the man held was six cubits long, plus one handbreadth for each cubit; and when he applied it to that structure, it measured one rod deep^d and one rod high.

⁶He went up to the gate that faced eastward and mounted its steps. He measured the threshold of the gate; it was one rod deep^d—^{e-}the one threshold was one rod deep.^{-e} ⁷Each recess was one rod wide and one rod deep, with [a partition of] 5 cubits between recesses; and the threshold of the gate, at the inner vestibule of the gate, was one rod deep. ^{8e-}For when he measured it at the inner vestibule of the gate, it was one rod [deep].^{-e} ⁹Next he measured the vestibule of the gate, and it measured 8 cubits and its supports 2 cubits; the vestibule of the gate was at its inner end. ^{10f}On either side of this eastern gate there were three recesses, all three of the same size; of identical sizes were also the supports^g on either side. ¹¹He measured the opening of the gate and found it 10 cubits wide, while the gate itself measured 13 cubits across.^h ¹²At the fronts of the recesses on either side were ^{e-}barriers of one cubit;^{-e} the recesses on either side were 6 cubits [deep]. ¹³Their openings faced each other directly across the gate passage, so that when he measured from rear^e of recess to rear^e

---

^a *I.e., the exile of King Jehoiachin; see 1.2.*
^b *Cf. Isa. 2.1; Mic. 4.1.*
^{c-c} *Septuagint reads "in the distance."*
^d *In this description, the Hebrew word which ordinarily corresponds to English "width" sometimes designates a measurement from an opening or outer surface inward, and so corresponds to the English "depth"; and the word which ordinarily corresponds to English "length" designates the distance from side to side of a vestibule or a passage, and so corresponds to the English "width."*
^{e-e} *Meaning of Heb. uncertain.*
^f *This verse would read well before v. 7.*
^g *In connection with recesses, the "supports" are partitions.*
^h *The opening was perhaps narrowed by a stone on each side for receiving the hinge of a door-leaf.*

of recess he obtained a width of 25 cubits.[i] [14e-]He made the vestibule[j]—60 cubits—and the gate next to the support on every side of the court.[-e] [15]And [the distance] from the front of the outer[e] gate to the front of the inner vestibule of the gate was 50 cubits. [16]The recesses—and their supports—had windows [e-]with frames[-e] on the interior of the gate complex on both sides, and the interiors of the vestibules also had windows on both sides; and the supports were adorned with palms.

[17]He took me into the outer court. There were chambers there, and there was a pavement laid out all around the court. There were 30 chambers on the pavement. [18]The pavements flanked the gates; the depth of the lower[k] pavements paralleled that of the gates. [19]Then he measured the width of [l-]the lower[k] court, from in front of the inner gate to in front of the outer gate[-l]—100 cubits.

[e-]After the east [gate], the north [gate].[-e] [20]Next he measured the gate of the outer court that faced north: its length and its width, [21]its three recesses on either side and its supports, as also its vestibule. It measured, like the first gate, 50 cubits in length and 25 cubits in width. [22]Its windows and [those of] its vestibule, as also its palm trees, corresponded to those of the gate that faced east. [From the outside] one had to climb 7 steps to reach it, and its vestibule was [m-]ahead of them.[-m] [23]Like the east gate, the north gate faced a gate leading into the inner forecourt; and when he measured the distance from gate to gate, it was 100 cubits.

[24]Then he took me to the south side. There was also a gate on the south side, and he got the same measurements as before for its supports and its vestibule. [25]Both it and its vestibule had windows like the aforementioned ones. It was 50 cubits long and 25 cubits wide. [26]Its staircase consisted of 7 steps; its vestibule was [m-]ahead of them,[-m] and its supports were decorated on both sides with palm trees. [27]The inner court likewise had a gate facing south; and on the south side, too, he measured a distance of 100 cubits from the [outer] gate to the [inner] gate.

[28]He now took me into the inner forecourt through its south gate. When he measured this south gate, it had the same measurements as the foregoing. [29]Its recesses, its supports, and its vestibule had the same measurements. Both it and its vestibule had windows on both sides; it

---

i *Since each of the recesses was 6 cubits deep (v. 7a) and the passage in the middle was 13 cubits wide (v. 11).*

j *Elim here is the same as elam in vv. 16, 21, 22, etc.*

k *The outer court and its gates were 8 steps lower than the inner ones: v. 34.*

l-l *In this rendering, the adjectives "lower" and "inner" are construed, not with the nouns they stand next to in the Hebrew, but with those with which they agree in gender.*

m-m *Septuagint reads "at its inner end."*

was 50 cubits long and 25 cubits wide—[30n-]vestibules on both sides, 25 cubits long, 5 cubits wide.[-n] [31]Its vestibule, however, gave on the outer court.[o] Its supports were adorned on either side with palms, and its staircase consisted of 8 steps.

[32]Then he took me to the eastern side of the inner forecourt; and when he measured the gate there, he got the same measurements: [33]its recesses, supports, and vestibule had the above measurements. Both it and its vestibule had windows on both sides; it was 50 cubits long and 25 cubits wide, [34]and its vestibule gave on the outer court. Its supports were decorated on both sides with palm trees, and its staircase consisted of 8 steps.

[35]Then he took me to the north gate, and found its measurements to be identical, [36]with the same recesses, supports, vestibule, windows on both sides, and a length of 50 cubits and a width of 25 cubits. [37]Its supports[p] gave on the outer court; its supports were decorated on both sides with palm trees; and its staircase consisted of eight steps.

[38]A chamber opened into the gate;[q] there the burnt offering would be washed. [39]And inside the vestibule of the gate, there were two tables on each side, at which the burnt offering, the sin offering, and the guilt offering were to be slaughtered; [40]while outside—[r-]as one goes up toward[-r] the opening of the north gate—there were two tables on one side, and there were two tables on the other side of the gate's vestibule. [41]Thus there were four tables on either flank of the gate—eight tables in all—at which [the sacrifices] were to be slaughtered. [42]As for the four tables for the burnt offering[s]—they were of hewn stone, one and a half cubits long, one and a half cubits wide, and one cubit high—[t-]on them were laid out the instruments with which burnt offerings and sacrifices were slaughtered.[-t] [43]Shelves,[e] one handbreadth wide, were attached all around the inside; and the sacrificial flesh was [laid] on the tables.

[44]There were [u-]chambers for singers[-u] in the inner forecourt: [one] beside the north gate facing south, and one beside the east[v] gate facing north. [45][The man] explained to me: "The chamber that faces south is for the priests who perform the duties of the Temple; [46]and the chamber that faces north is for the priests who perform the duties of the altar—

---

n-n *Connection unclear; wanting in some Heb. mss. and versions.*
o *I.e., in the inner gates the vestibules were situated at their entrances, and so they were true vestibules, in contrast to the "inner vestibules" of the outer gates.*
p *Septuagint reads "vestibules"; cf. vv. 31, 34.*
q *Heb. "gates"; the reference is apparently to the north gate; cf. v. 40 and Lev. 1.11; 4.24; 7.2.*
r-r *Emendation yields "the vestibule at."*
s *See v. 39.*
t-t *This clause would read well after v. 43.*
u-u *Septuagint reads "two chambers."*
v *Septuagint reads "south."*

they are the descendants of Zadok, who alone of the descendants of Levi may approach the LORD to minister to Him."

⁴⁷He then measured the forecourt: 100 cubits long and 100 cubits broad—foursquare. In front of the Temple stood the altar. ⁴⁸He took me into the portico of the Temple and measured it. The jambsʷ of the portico were 5 cubits deep on either side. The width of the gate-opening was ˣ⁻[14 cubits, and the flanking wall of the gate was]⁻ˣ 3 cubits on either side. ⁴⁹The portico was 20 cubits wideʸ and 11ᶻ cubits deep, and ᵃᵃ⁻it was by steps that it was reached.⁻ᵃᵃ There were columns by the jambs on either side.

41
He then led me into the great hall. He measured the jambs, 6 cubits on either side; such was the depthᵃ of each jamb.ᵇ ²The entrance was 10 cubits wide, and the flanking walls of the entrance were each 5 cubits wide. Next he measured the depth [of the hall], 40 cubits, and the width, 20 cubits. ³And then he entered the inner room. He measured each jamb of the entrance, 2 cubits [deep]; the entrance itself, 6 cubits across; and the width of ᶜ⁻[the flanking wall on either side of]⁻ᶜ the entrance, 7 cubits. ⁴Then he measured the depth, 20 cubits; and the width at the inner end of the great hall was also 20 cubits. And he said to me, "This is the Holy of Holies."

⁵Then he measured the wall of the Temple. [It was] 6 cubits [thick] on every side of the Temple, and the side-chamber measured 4 cubits [across].ᵈ ⁶The side chambers were arranged one above the other, in 33 sections.ᵉ All around, there were projections in the Temple wall to serve the side chambers as supports, so that [their] supports should not be the Temple wall itself. ⁷The ᶠ⁻winding passage⁻ᶠ of the side chambers widened from story to story; ᵍ⁻and since the structure was furnished all over with winding passages from story to story, the structure itself became wider from story to story.⁻ᵍ It was by this means that one ascended from the bottom story to the top one by way of the middle one.

ʷ *I.e., the edges of the flanking walls.*
ˣ⁻ˣ *Preserved in the Septuagint.*
ʸ *See note on v. 5.*
ᶻ *Septuagint reads "12"; see note j on 41.13.*
ᵃᵃ⁻ᵃᵃ*Septuagint reads "it was reached by ten steps."*

ᵃ *See note on 40.5.*
ᵇ *This sense is demanded by the context; usually,* ohel *means "tent."*
ᶜ⁻ᶜ *Preserved in the Septuagint.*
ᵈ *I.e., on the ground level; cf. v. 7.*
ᵉ *Lit. "times." Emendation yields "in three sections of three tiers each," i.e., one section next to each of the two side walls of the Temple and one next to its rear wall; cf. v. 7.*
ᶠ⁻ᶠ *So Targum; cf. Mishnah Tamid 1.1.*
ᵍ⁻ᵍ *Exact meaning of Heb. uncertain, but for the general sense cf. 1 Kings 6.6a, 8b.*

[8]I observed that the Temple was surrounded by a raised pavement—the foundations of the side chambers; its elevation was a rod's length, or 6 cubits. [9]The outer wall of the side chamber was 5 cubits thick, and that which served as a walk between the Temple's side chambers [10]and the chamber complexes[h] was 20 cubits wide all around the Temple. [11]Of entrances to the side chambers giving on the walk, there was one entrance on the north side and one entrance on the south side; and the space[i] of the walk was 5 cubits thick all around. [12]And the structure that fronted on the vacant space at the [Temple's] western end was 70 cubits deep;[a] the walls of the structure were 5 cubits thick on every side; and it was 90 cubits wide.[a]

[13]He measured the [total] depth of the Temple, 100 cubits;[j] and the depth of the vacant space and of the structure, with its walls, also came to 100 cubits.[k] [14]The front side of the Temple, like the vacant space on the east, was 100 cubits wide.[l] [15]He also measured the width[a] of the structure facing the vacant space in the rear, inclusive of its ledges,[m] 100 cubits.

Both the great hall inside and the portico next to the court [16]—[n]the thresholds-[n]—and the windows [o]with frames-[o] and the ledges[p] at the threshold, all over the three parts of each, were completely overlaid[o] with wood. There was wainscoting from the floor to the windows, including the window [frame]s [17]and extending above the openings, [q]both in the inner Temple and outside.[q] And all over the wall, [q]both in the inner one and in the outer,[q] ran a pattern.[o] [18]It consisted of cherubs and palm trees, with a palm tree between every two cherubs. Each cherub had two faces: [19]a human face turned toward the palm tree on one side and a lion's face turned toward the palm tree on the other side. This was repeated all over the Temple; [20]the cherubs and the palm trees were carved on[r] the wall from the floor to above the openings.

As regards the great hall, [21]the great hall had four doorposts; and before

---

[h] See 42.1 ff.

[i] Emendation yields "parapet."

[j] Comprising the 5 cubits of 40.48, the 12 of 40.49 (see note there), the 6 of 41.1, the 40 of 41.2, the 2 of 41.3, the 20 of 41.4, the 6 of 41.5a, the 4 of 41.5b, and the 5 of 41.9.

[k] The structure was 70 cubits deep and its front and rear walls each 5 cubits thick (v. 12). The remaining 20 cubits are accounted for by the vacant space; cf. 42.1-2.

[l] To the inside width of 20 cubits (40.49; 41.2–4) must be added on each side: one Temple wall of 6 cubits equals 12; one side-chamber wall of 5 cubits equals 10; one side chamber's inner depth of 4 cubits equals 8; a walk's width of 20 cubits (40.9–10) equals 40; and a parapet's thickness of 5 cubits (v. 11) equals 10; totaling 100 cubits.

[m] Emendation yields "walls"; cf. v. 12.

[n-n] Septuagint reads "were paneled."

[o-o] Meaning of Heb. uncertain.

[p] Here perhaps designating the door frames, since it is these that (as required by the continuation of the verse) are situated at the threshold and consist of three parts (a lintel and two doorposts).

[q-q] Meaning perhaps the great hall and the vestibule; cf. v. 5.

[r] Heb. "and."

the Shrine was something resembling ²²a wooden altar 3 cubits high and
2 cubits long and having inner corners;ˢ and its lengthᵗ and its walls were
of wood. And he said to me, "This is the tableᵘ that stands before the
LORD." ²³The great hall had a double door, and the Shrine likewise had
²⁴a double door, and each door had two ᵒ⁻swinging leaves:⁻ᵒ two for the
one door and two ᵒ⁻such leaves⁻ᵒ for the other. ²⁵Cherubs and palm trees
were carved on these—on the doors of the hall—just as they were carved
on the walls; and there was a latticeᵒ of wood outside in front of the
portico. ²⁶And there were windows ᵒ⁻with frames⁻ᵒ and palm trees on the
flanking walls of the portico on either side [of the entrance] ᵒ⁻and [on]⁻
the Temple's side chambers and [on] the lattices.⁻ᵒ

42

He took me out, by way of the northern gate, into the outer court,
and he led me [westward] up to a ᵃ⁻complex of chambers⁻ᵃ that ran parallel
to the northern ends of the vacant space and the structure. ²The widthᵇ
of its façade—ᶜ⁻its north side, the one from which it was entered⁻ᶜ—was
100 cubits, and its depthᵇ was 50 cubits. ³At right angles to the 20 cubitsᵈ
of the inner court and to the pavement of the outer court,ᵉ the complex
rose ledge by ledgeᶠ in three tiers. ⁴There was an areaway, 10 cubits wide
and ᵍ⁻a road of one cubit,⁻ᵍ running along the inner-court side of the
chamber complex, but its entrances were on its north side. ⁵Here its upper
chambers were cut back, because ledges took away from them as construction proceeded backward from the bottom ones and then from the middle
ones. ⁶For they were arranged in three tiers, and they had no columns
like those of the chambers in the courts.ʰ That is why the rise proceeded
by stages: from the ground, from the bottom ones, and from the middle
ones. ⁷In the outer court, a wall 50 cubits long ran parallel to the chamber
complex up to the chambers in the outer court;ʰ ⁸for the chambers in the
outer court were themselves 50 cubits deep, thus completing 100 cubits

---

ˢ *Apparently meaning that it had a rim around the top, like the table of Exod. 25.25; see the*
  final note on the present verse.
ᵗ *Septuagint reads "base."*
ᵘ *Serving to hold the bread of display; cf. Exod. 25.30; 40.22–23; 1 Kings 7.48.*

ᵃ⁻ᵃ *Heb. simply "chambers," and so elsewhere.*
ᵇ *See note a at 40.6.*
ᶜ⁻ᶜ *Lit. "the north entrance"; but cf. v. 4.*
ᵈ *I.e., the vacant space; cf. 41.13 with note k.*
ᵉ *Cf. 40.17.*
ᶠ *Because this part of the inner court was considerably higher than the outer; 40.28–31 and 41.8,*
  9b–10.
ᵍ⁻ᵍ *Septuagint and Syriac read "and 100 cubits long"; cf. vv. 2–3.*
ʰ *See vv. 8–9 referring to chambers along the west wall.*

alongside the edifice.[i] [9]Thus, at the foot of that complex of chambers ran a passage[j]—[k]of a width set by the wall in the outer court[k]—which one entered from the east in order to gain access to them from the outer court.

[10]There was another chamber complex to the east[l] of the vacant space and the structure, [11]likewise with a passage in front—just like the complex on the north side, with which this one agreed in width[b] and depth[b] and in the exact layout of its exits and entrances. [12]Accordingly, the entrances to the chamber complex on the south side were approached from the east by the entrance at the head of [m]the corresponding passage along the matching wall.[m]

[13]And he said to me, "The northern chambers and the southern chambers by the vacant space are the consecrated chambers in which the priests who have access to the LORD shall eat the most holy offerings. There they shall deposit the most holy offerings—the meal offerings, the sin offerings, and the guilt offerings, for the place is consecrated. [14]When the priests enter, they shall not proceed from the consecrated place to the outer court without first leaving here the vestments in which they minister; for the [vestments] are consecrated. Before proceeding to the area open to the people,[n] they shall put on other garments."

[15]When he had finished the measurements of the inner Temple [area], he led me out by way of the gate which faces east, and he measured off the entire area. [16]He measured the east side with the measuring rod, 500 [cubits]—in rods, by the measuring rod. He turned [17][and] measured the north side: 500 [cubits]—in rods, by the measuring rod. He turned [18][and] measured the south side: 500 [cubits]—in rods, by the measuring rod. [19]Then he turned to the west side [and] measured it: 500 cubits—in rods, by the measuring rod. [20]Thus he measured it on the four sides; it had a wall completely surrounding it, 500 [cubits] long [o]on each side,[o] to separate the consecrated from the unconsecrated.

43

Then he led me to a gate, the gate that faced east. [2]And there, coming from the east with a roar like the roar of mighty waters, was the

[i] *Apparently meaning the chamber complex of v. 1.*
[j] *So kethib; qere "thing giving access."*
[k-k] *Brought up from v. 10 for clarity.*
[l] *Septuagint reads "south"; cf. v. 13.*
[m-m] *Exact meaning of Heb. uncertain; the phrase apparently refers to vv. 7–8.*
[n] *Cf. 44.19 and note d.*
[o-o] *Lit. "and 500 wide."*

Presence of the God of Israel, and the earth was lit up by His Presence. [3]The vision was like the vision I had seen when I[a] came to destroy the city, the very same vision that I had seen by the Chebar Canal. Forthwith, I fell on my face.

[4]The Presence of the LORD entered the Temple by the gate that faced eastward. [5]A spirit carried me into the inner court, and lo, the Presence of the LORD filled the Temple; [6]and I heard speech addressed to me from the Temple, though [the] man[b] was standing beside me. [7]It said to me:

O mortal, this is the place of My throne and the place for the soles of My feet, where I will dwell in the midst of the people Israel forever. The House of Israel and their kings must not again defile My holy name by their apostasy and by the corpses of their kings [c-]at their death.[-c] [8]When they placed their threshold next to My threshold and their doorposts next to My doorposts with only a wall between Me and them,[d] they would defile My holy name by the abominations that they committed, and I consumed them in My anger. [9]Therefore, let them put their apostasy and the corpses of their kings far from Me, and I will dwell among them forever.

[10][Now] you, O mortal, describe the Temple to the House of Israel,[e] and let them measure its design. But let them be ashamed of their iniquities: [11]When they are ashamed of all they have done, make known to them the plan of the Temple and its layout, its exits and entrances—its entire plan, and all the laws and instructions pertaining to its entire plan. Write it down before their eyes, that they may faithfully follow its entire plan and all its laws. [12]Such are the instructions for the Temple on top of the mountain: the entire area of its enclosure shall be most holy. Thus far the instructions for the Temple.

[13][f]And these are the dimensions of the altar, in cubits where each is a cubit and a handbreadth. The trench[g] shall be a cubit deep and a cubit wide, with a rim one span high around its edge. And the height[h] shall be as follows: [14]From the trench in the ground to the lower ledge, which shall be a cubit wide: 2 cubits; from the [i-]lower ledge to the upper[-i] ledge, which shall likewise be a cubit wide: 4 cubits; [15]and the height of the

---

a *Six mss. and two ancient versions read "He."*

b *I.e., the guide of 40.3 ff.*

c-c *So with a number of Heb. mss. The usual vocalization yields "their shrines."*

d *The south wall of the First Temple enclosure was also the north wall of the royal enclosure; the two communicated by the Gate of the Guard (2 Kings 11.19). Thus Temple and palace could be regarded as a single dwelling ("tent") in the sense of Num. 19.14, and the death of a king in the palace would defile the Temple. Hence the zoning provisions of 45.2 ff.*

e *In accordance with the three preceding chapters; cf. 40.4.*

f *Some of the terms and details in vv. 13–17 are obscure.*

g *Lit. "bosom."*

h *Lit. "bulge."*

i-i *Lit. "lesser ledge to the greater."*

altar hearth shall be 4 cubits, with 4 horns projecting upward from the hearth: 4 cubits. [16]Now the hearth shall be 12 cubits long and 12 broad, square, with 4 equal sides. [17]Hence, the [upper] base[j] shall be 14 cubits broad, with 4 equal sides. The surrounding rim shall be half a cubit [high],[k] and the surrounding trench shall measure one cubit. And the ramp[l] shall face east.

[18]Then he[b] said to me: O mortal, thus said the Lord GOD: These are the directions for the altar on the day it is erected, so that burnt offerings may be offered up on it and blood dashed against it. [19]You shall give to the levitical priests who are of the stock of Zadok, and so eligible to minister to Me—declares the Lord GOD—a young bull of the herd for a sin offering. [20]You shall take some of its blood and apply it to [m-]the four horns [of the altar],[-m] to the four corners of the base, and to the surrounding rim; thus you shall purge it and perform purification upon it. [21]Then you shall take the bull of sin offering and burn it in the [n-]designated area[-n] of the Temple, outside the Sanctuary.

[22]On the following day, you shall offer a goat without blemish as a sin offering; and the altar shall be purged [with it] just as it was purged with the bull. [23]When you have completed the ritual of purging, you shall offer a bull of the herd without blemish and a ram of the flock without blemish. [24]Offer them to the LORD; let the priests throw salt on them and offer them up as a burnt offering to the LORD. [25]Every day, for seven days, you shall present a goat of sin offering, as well as a bull of the herd and a ram of the flock; you[o] shall present unblemished ones. [26]Seven days they shall purge the altar and cleanse it; [p-]thus shall it be consecrated.[-p]

[27]And when these days are over, then from the eighth day onward the priests shall offer your burnt offerings and your offerings of well-being on the altar; and I will extend My favor to you—declares the Lord GOD.

44

Then he led me back to the outer gate of the Sanctuary that faced eastward; it was shut. [2]And the LORD said to me: This gate is to be kept shut and is not to be opened! No one shall enter by it because the LORD, the God of Israel, has entered by it; therefore it shall remain shut. [3]Only the prince may sit in it and eat bread before the LORD, since he is a

---

[j] Heb. 'azarah, which in v. 14 means "ledge." The altar consists of 3 blocks, each smaller than the one below it.

[k] Half a cubit is identical with the one span of v. 13.

[l] Leading up to the altar; cf. Exod. 20.23.

[m-m] Heb. "its four horns."

[n-n] Meaning of Heb. uncertain. Emendation yields "burning place"; cf. Lev. 6.2; Isa. 33.14; Ps. 102.4 (for the word), and Lev. 4.12; 6.4 (for the place).

[o] Heb. "they."

[p-p] Lit. "they shall fill its hands"; cf. note at Exod. 28.41.

prince; he shall enter by way of ᵃ⁻the vestibule of the gate,⁻ᵃ and shall depart by the same way.

⁴Then he led me, by way of the north gate, to the front of the Temple. I looked, and lo! the Presence of the LORD filled the Temple of the LORD; and I fell upon my face. ⁵Then the LORD said to me: O mortal, mark well, look closely and listen carefully to everything that I tell you regarding all the laws of the Temple of the LORD and all the instructions regarding it. Note well who may enter the Temple and all who must be excluded from the Sanctuary. ⁶And say to the rebellious House of Israel: Thus said the Lord GOD: Too long, O House of Israel, have you committed all your abominations, ⁷admitting aliens, uncircumcised of spirit and uncircumcised of flesh, to be in My Sanctuary and profane My very Temple, when you offer up My food—the fat and the blood. Youᵇ have broken My covenant with all your abominations. ⁸You have not discharged the duties concerning My sacred offerings, but have appointed them to discharge the duties of My Sanctuary for you.

⁹Thus said the Lord GOD: Let no alien, uncircumcised in spirit and flesh, enter My Sanctuary—no alien whatsoever among the people of Israel. ¹⁰But the Levites who forsook Me when Israel went astray—straying from Me to follow their fetishes—shall suffer their punishment: ¹¹They shall be servitors in My Sanctuary, appointed over the Temple gates, and performing the chores of My Temple; they shall slaughter the burnt offerings and the sacrifices for the people. They shall attend on them and serve them. ¹²Because they served the House of Israel in the presence of their fetishes and made them stumble into guilt, therefore—declares the Lord GOD—I have sworn concerning them that they shall suffer their punishment: ¹³They shall not approach Me to serve Me as priests, to come near any of My sacred offerings, the most holy things. They shall bear their shame for the abominations that they committed. ¹⁴I will make them watchmen of the Temple, to perform all its chores, everything that needs to be done in it.

¹⁵ᶜ⁻But the levitical priests descended from Zadok,⁻ᶜ who maintained the service of My Sanctuary when the people of Israel went astray from Me—they shall approach Me to minister to Me; they shall stand before Me to offer Me fat and blood—declares the Lord GOD. ¹⁶They alone may

---

ᵃ⁻ᵃ *This does not contradict v. 2 because the vestibule is at the inner end of the gate; cf. 40.9.*
ᵇ *Heb. "They."*
ᶜ⁻ᶜ *By contrast with the Levite-priests whose demotion has just been announced.*

enter My Sanctuary and they alone shall approach My table to minister to Me; and they shall keep My charge. 17And when they enter the gates of the inner court, they shall wear linen vestments: they shall have nothing woolen upon them when they minister inside the gates of the inner court. 18They shall have linen turbans on their heads and linen breeches on their loins; they shall not gird themselves with anything that causes sweat. 19When they go out to the outer court—the outer court where the people are—they shall remove the vestments in which they minister and shall deposit them in the sacred chambers;d they shall put on other garments, lest they make the people consecratede by [contact with] their vestments. 20They shall neither shave their heads nor let their hair go untrimmed; they shall keep their hair trimmed. 21No priest shall drink wine when he enters into the inner court. 22They shall not marry widowsf or divorced women; they may marry only virgins of the stock of the House of Israel, or widows who are widows of priests.

23They shall declare to My people what is sacred and what is profane, and inform them what is clean and what is unclean. 24In lawsuits, too, it is they who shall act as judges; they shall decide them in accordance with My rules. They shall preserve My teachings and My laws regarding all My fixed occasions; and they shall maintain the sanctity of My sabbaths.

25[A priest] shall not defile himself by entering [a house] where there is a dead person. He shall defile himself only for father or mother, son or daughter, brother or unmarried sister. 26After he has become clean, seven days shall be counted off for him; 27and on the day that he reenters the inner court of the Sanctuary to minister in the Sanctuary, he shall present his sin offering—declares the Lord GOD.

28This shall be their portion, for I am their portion; and no holding shall be given them in Israel, for I am their holding. 29The meal offerings, sin offerings, and guilt offerings shall be consumed by them. Everything proscribedg in Israel shall be theirs. 30All the choice first fruits of every kind, and all the gifts of every kind—of all your contributions—shall go to the priests. You shall further give the first of the yield of your bakingh to the priest, that a blessing may rest upon your home.

31Priests shall not eat anything, whether bird or animal, that died or was torn by beasts.

d Cf. 42.13–14.
e Thereby rendering the people unfit for ordinary activity.
f I.e., of laymen.
g See Lev. 27.28.
h See Num. 15.20–21.

45

When you allot the land as an inheritance, you shall set aside from the land, as a gift sacred to the LORD, an area[a] 25,000 [cubits] long and 10,000[b] wide: this shall be holy through its entire extent. [2]Of this, a square measuring a full 500 by 500 shall be reserved for the Sanctuary,[c] and 50 cubits for an open space all around it. [3]Of the aforesaid area, you shall measure off, as most holy and destined to include the Sanctuary, [a space] 25,000 long by 10,000 wide; [4]it is a sacred portion of the land; it shall provide space for houses for the priests, the ministrants of the Sanctuary who are qualified to minister to the LORD, as well as holy ground for the Sanctuary. [5]Another [space], 25,000 long by 10,000 wide, shall be the property of the Levites, the servants of the Temple—[d]twenty chambers.[-d] [6]Alongside the sacred reserve, you shall set aside [a space] 25,000 long by 5,000 wide, as the property of the city; it shall belong to the whole House of Israel. [7]And to the prince shall belong, on both sides of the sacred reserve and the property of the city and alongside the sacred reserve and the property of the city, on the west extending westward and on the east extending eastward, a portion[a] corresponding to one of the [tribal] portions that extend from the western border to the eastern border [8]of the land.[e] That shall be his property in Israel; and My princes shall no more defraud My people, but shall leave the rest of the land to the several tribes of the House of Israel.

[9]Thus said the Lord GOD: Enough, princes of Israel! Make an end of lawlessness and rapine, and do what is right and just! Put a stop to your evictions of My people—declares the Lord GOD. [10]Have honest balances, an honest *ephah*, and an honest *bath*.[f] [11]The *ephah* and the *bath* shall comprise the same volume, the *bath* a tenth of a *homer* and the *ephah* a tenth of a *homer*; their capacity shall be gauged by the *homer*. [12]And the shekel shall weigh 20 *gerah*s. [g]20 shekels, 25 shekels [and] 10 plus 5 shekels shall count with you as a *mina*.[-g]

[13]This is the contribution you shall make: One-sixth of an *ephah* from every *homer* of wheat and one-sixth of an *ephah* from every *homer* of barley, [14]while the due from the oil—[h]the oil being measured by the *bath*[-h]— shall be one-tenth of a *bath* from every *kor*.—As 10 *bath*s make a *homer*, so 10 *bath*s make a *homer*.[i]—[15]And [the due] from the flock shall be one

---

a Lit. *"length."*
b *Septuagint reads 20,000; cf. vv. 3–5.*
c *Cf. 42.15 ff.*
d-d *Septuagint reads "for towns to dwell in."*
e *Cf. for all the foregoing 48.1 ff.*
f *The ephah is used for dry measure and the bath for liquid measure.*
g-g *The Mesopotamian mina of 60 shekels; but meaning of Heb. uncertain.*
h-h *Meaning of Heb. uncertain.*
i *The Vulgate reads "kor"; homer and kor are synonyms.*

animal from every 200. [All these shall be contributed] from Israel's products[h] for meal offerings, burnt offerings, and offerings of well-being, to make expiation for them—declares the Lord GOD. [16]In this contribution, the entire population must join with the prince in Israel.

[17]But the burnt offerings, the meal offerings, and the libations on festivals, new moons, sabbaths—all fixed occasions—of the House of Israel shall be the obligation of the prince; he shall provide the sin offerings, the meal offerings, the burnt offerings, and the offerings of well-being, to make expiation for the House of Israel.

[18]Thus said the Lord GOD: On the first day of the first month, you shall take a bull of the herd without blemish, and you shall cleanse the Sanctuary. [19]The priest shall take some of the blood of the sin offering and apply it to the doorposts of the Temple, to the four corners of the ledge[h] of the altar, and to the doorposts of the gate of the inner court. [20]You shall do the same [j-]on the seventh day of the month[-j] to purge the Temple from uncleanness caused by unwitting or ignorant persons.

[21]On the fourteenth day of the first month you shall have the passover sacrifice; and during a festival of seven days unleavened bread shall be eaten. [22]On that day, the prince shall provide a bull of sin offering on behalf of himself and of the entire population; [23]and during the seven days of the festival, he shall provide daily—for seven days—seven bulls and seven rams, without blemish, for a burnt offering to the LORD, and one goat daily for a sin offering. [24]He shall provide a meal offering of an *ephah*[k] for each bull and an *ephah* for each ram, with a *hin* of oil to every *ephah*. [25]So, too, during the festival of the seventh month, for seven days from the fifteenth day on, he shall provide the same sin offerings, burnt offerings, meal offerings, and oil.

46

Thus said the Lord GOD: The gate of the inner court which faces east shall be closed on the six working days; it shall be opened on the sabbath day and it shall be opened on the day of the new moon. [2]The prince shall enter by way of the vestibule outside the gate, and shall attend at the gatepost while the priests sacrifice his burnt offering and his offering of well-being; he shall then bow low at the threshold of the gate and depart. The gate, however, shall not be closed until evening. [3]The common people[a] shall worship before the LORD on sabbaths and new moons at the entrance of the same gate.

[4]The burnt offering which the prince presents to the LORD on the

---

[j-j] *Septuagint reads "in the seventh month."*
[k] *Of choice flour.*

[a] *I.e., those other than the priests, the Levites, and the prince; lit. "the people of the land."*

sabbath day shall consist of six lambs without blemish and one ram without blemish—[5]with a meal offering of an *ephah* for the ram, a meal offering of as much as he wishes for the lambs, and a *hin* of oil with every *ephah*. [6]And on the day of the new moon, it shall consist of a bull of the herd without blemish, and six lambs and a ram—they shall be without blemish. [7]And he shall provide a meal offering of an *ephah* for the bull, an *ephah* for the ram, and as much as he can afford for the lambs, with a *hin* of oil to every *ephah*.

[8]When the prince enters, he shall come in by way of the vestibule of the gate, and he shall go out the same way.

[9]But on the fixed occasions, when the common people come before the LORD, whoever enters by the north gate to bow low shall leave by the south gate; and whoever enters by the south gate shall leave by the north gate. They shall not go back through the gate by which they came in, but shall go out b-by the opposite one.-b [10]And as for the prince, he shall enter with them when they enter and leave when they leave.

[11]On festivals and fixed occasions, the meal offering shall be an *ephah* for each bull, an *ephah* for each ram, and as much as he wishes for the lambs, with a *hin* of oil for every *ephah*.

[12]The gate that faces east shall also be opened for the prince whenever he offers a freewill offering—be it burnt offering or offering of well-being—freely offered to the LORD, so that he may offer his burnt offering or his offering of well-being just as he does on the sabbath day. Then he shall leave, and the gate shall be closed after he leaves.

[13]Each day you shall offer a lamb of the first year without blemish, as a daily burnt offering to the LORD; you shall offer one every morning. [14]And every morning regularly you shall offer a meal offering with it: a sixth of an *ephah*, with a third of a *hin* of oil to moisten the choice flour, as a meal offering to the LORD—a law for all time. [15]The lamb, the meal offering, and oil shall be presented every morning as a regular burnt offering.

[16]Thus said the Lord GOD: If the prince makes a gift to any of his sons, it shall become the latter's inheritance; it shall pass on to his sons; it is their holding by inheritance. [17]But if he makes a gift from his inheritance to any of his subjects, it shall only belong to the latter until the year of release.c Then it shall revert to the prince; his inheritance must by all means pass on to his sons.

[18]But the prince shall not take property away from any of the people

---

b-b *Lit. "straight before him."*
c *Cf. Lev. 25.10.*

and rob them of their holdings. Only out of his own holdings shall he endow his sons, in order that My people may not be dispossessed of their holdings.

19Then he led me into the passage at the side of the gate to the sacred chambers of the priests, which face north, and there, at the rear of it, in the west, I saw a space. 20He said to me, "This is the place where the priests shall boil the guilt offerings and the sin offerings, and where they shall bake the meal offerings, so as not to take them into the outer court and d-make the people consecrated."-d 21Then he led me into the outer court and led me past the four corners of the court; and in each corner of the court there was an enclosure. 22These unroofede enclosures, [each] 40 [cubits] long and 30 wide, were in the four corners of the court; the four corner enclosures had the same measurements. 23[On the inside,] running round the four of them, there was a row of masonry, equipped with hearths under the rows all around. 24He said to me, "These are the kitchens where the Temple servitors shall boil the sacrifices of the people."

47 He led me back to the entrance of the Temple, and I found that water was issuing from below the platforma of the Temple—eastward, since the Temple faced east—but the water was running out at the b-south of the altar,-b under the south wall of the Temple. 2Then he led me out by way of the northern gate and led me around to the outside of the outer gate that faces in the direction of the east;c and I found that water was gushing from [under] the south wall. 3As the man went on eastward with a measuring line in his hand, he measured off a thousand cubits and led me across the water; the water was ankle deep. 4Then he measured off another thousand and led me across the water; the water was knee deep. He measured off a further thousand and led me across the water; the water was up to the waist. 5When he measured yet another thousand, it was a stream I could not cross; for the water had swollen into a stream that could not be crossed except by swimming. 6"Do you see, O mortal?" he said to me; and he led me back to the bank of the stream.

7As I came back, I saw trees in great profusion on both banks of the stream. 8"This water," he told me, "runs out to the eastern region, and

---

d-d See note e at 44.19.

e So Mishnah Middoth 2.5; emendation yields "small."

a See note at 9.3.

b-b Connection unclear. Emendation yields "southeast."

c The end of the verse explains why he could not have made the detour by way of the south gate. For the reasons why he could not have proceeded to his present position directly by way of the east gate, see 43.1–2; 44.1–2.

flows into the Arabah; and when it comes into the sea, into ᵈ-the sea of foul waters,-ᵈ the water will become wholesome. ⁹Every living creature that swarms will be able to live wherever this stream goes; the fish will be very abundant once these waters have reached there. It will be wholesome, and everything will live wherever this stream goes. ¹⁰Fishermen shall stand beside it all the way from En-gedi to En-eglaim; it shall be a place for drying nets; and the fish will be of various kinds [and] most plentiful, like the fish of the Great Sea. ¹¹But its swamps and marshes shall not become wholesome; they will serve to [supply] salt. ¹²All kinds of trees for food will grow up on both banks of the stream. Their leaves will not wither nor their fruit fail; they will yield new fruit every month, because the water for them flows from the Temple. Their fruit will serve for food and their leaves for healing."

¹³Thus said the Lord GOD: These shall be the boundaries of the land that you shall allot to the twelve tribes of Israel. Joseph shall receive two portions, ¹⁴and you shall share the rest equally. As I swore to give it to your fathers, so shall this land fall to you as your heritage. ¹⁵These are the boundaries of the land:

As the northern limit: From the Great Sea by way of Hethlon, Lebo-ᵉ-hamath,-ᵉ Zedad, ¹⁶Berathah, Sibraim—which lies between the border of Damascus and the border of Hamath—[down to] Hazer-hatticon, which is on the border of Hauran. ¹⁷Thus the boundary shall run from the Sea to ᶠ-Hazar-enon,-ᶠ to the north of the territory of Damascus, with the territory of Hamath to the north of it. That shall be the northern limit.

¹⁸As the eastern limit: A line between Hauran and Damascus, and between Gilead and the land of Israel: with the Jordan as a boundary, you shall measure down to the ᵈ-Eastern Sea.-ᵈ That shall be the eastern limit.

¹⁹The southern limit shall run: A line from Tamar to the waters of Meriboth-kadesh, along the Wadi [of Egypt and] the Great Sea. That is the southern limit.

²⁰And as the western limit: The Great Sea shall be the boundary up to a point opposite Lebo-hamath. That shall be the western limit.

²¹This land you shall divide for yourselves among the tribes of Israel.

ᵈ⁻ᵈ *I.e., the Dead Sea.*
ᵉ⁻ᵉ *Brought up from v. 16 for clarity.*
ᶠ⁻ᶠ *Apparently identical with Hazer-hatticon in v. 16.*

²²You shall allot it as a heritage for yourselves and for the strangers who reside among you, who have begotten children among you. You shall treat them as Israelite citizens; they shall receive allotments along with you among the tribes of Israel. ²³You shall give the stranger an allotment within the tribe where he resides—declares the Lord GOD.

48 These are the names of the tribes:

At the northern end, along the Hethlon road, [from] Lebo-hamath to Hazar-enan—which is the border of Damascus, with Hamath to the north—from the eastern border to the Sea: Dan—one [tribe].

²Adjoining the territory of Dan, from the eastern border to the western border: Asher—one.

³Adjoining the territory of Asher, from the eastern border to the western border: Naphtali—one.

⁴Adjoining the territory of Naphtali, from the eastern border to the western border: Manasseh—one.

⁵Adjoining the territory of Manasseh, from the eastern border to the western border: Ephraim—one.

⁶Adjoining the territory of Ephraim, from the eastern border to the western border: Reuben—one.

⁷Adjoining the territory of Reuben, from the eastern border to the western border: Judah—one.

⁸Adjoining the territory of Judah, from the eastern border to the western border, shall be the reserve that you set aside: 25,000 [cubits] in breadth and in length equal to one of the portions from the eastern border to the western border; the Sanctuary shall be in the middle of it. ⁹The reserve that you set aside for the LORD shall be 25,000 long and 10,000^a wide. ¹⁰It shall be apportioned to the following: The sacred reserve for the priests shall measure 25,000 [cubits] on the north, ^{b-}10,000 on the west, 10,000 on the east, and 25,000 on the south,^{-b} with the LORD's Sanctuary in the middle of it. ¹¹This consecrated area shall be for the priests of the line of Zadok, who kept My charge and did not go astray, as the Levites did when the people of Israel went astray. ¹²It shall be a special reserve for them out of the [total] reserve from the land, most holy, adjoining the territory of the Levites. ¹³Alongside the territory of the priests, the Levites shall have [an area] 25,000 long by 10,000 wide; the total length shall be 25,000 and the breadth 10,000.^c ¹⁴None of it—

---

^a *Emendation yields "25,000"; cf. 45.3–6.*
^{b-b} *Lit. "10,000 in breadth on the west; 10,000 in breadth on the east; and 25,000 in length on the south."*
^c *Septuagint reads "20,000"; cf. note a.*

the choicest of the land—may be sold, exchanged, or transferred; it is sacred to the LORD.

15The remaining 5,000 in breadth by 25,000 shall be for common use—serving the city for dwellings and pasture. The city itself shall be in the middle of it; 16and these shall be its measurements: On the north side 4,500 cubits, on the south side 4,500, on the east side 4,500, and on the west side 4,500. 17The pasture shall extend 250 cubits to the north of the city, 250 to the south, 250 to the east, and 250 to the west. 18As for the remaining 10,000 to the east and 10,000 to the west, adjoining the long sided of the sacred reserve, the produce of these areas adjoining the sacred reserve shall serve as food for the workers in the city; 19the workers in the city from all the tribes of Israel shall cultivate it. 20The entire reserve, 25,000 square, you shall set aside as the sacred reserve plus the city property. 21What remains on either side of the sacred reserve and the city property shall belong to the prince. The prince shall own [the land] from the border of the 25,000 e-of the reserve-e up to the eastern boundary, and from the border of the 25,000 on the west up to the western boundary, corresponding to the [tribal] portions. The sacred reserve, with the Temple Sanctuary in the middle of it 22and the property of the Levites and the city property as well, shall be in the middle of the [area belonging] to the prince; [the rest of the land] between the territory of Judah and the territory of Benjamin shall belong to the prince.

23As for the remaining tribes:f From the eastern border to the western border: Benjamin—one.

24Adjoining the territory of Benjamin, from the eastern border to the western border: Simeon—one.

25Adjoining the territory of Simeon, from the eastern border to the western border: Issachar—one.

26Adjoining the territory of Issachar, from the eastern border to the western border: Zebulun—one.

27Adjoining the territory of Zebulun, from the eastern border to the western border: Gad—one.

28The other border of Gad shall be the southern boundary. This boundary shall run from Tamar to the waters of Meribath-kadesh, to the Wadi [of Egypt], and to the Great Sea.

29That is the land which you shall allot as a heritage to the tribes of Israel, and those are their portions—declares the Lord GOD.

d I.e., the south side.
e-e Emendation yields "on the east."
f The tribes not provided for in vv. 1–7, and lying south of the sacred gift.

30And these are the exits from the city: On its northern side, measuring 4,500 cubits, 31the gates of the city shall be—three gates on the north—named for the tribes of Israel: the Reuben Gate: one; the Judah Gate: one; the Levi Gate: one. 32On the eastern side, [measuring] 4,500 cubits—there shall be three gates: the Joseph Gate: one; the Benjamin Gate: one; and the Dan Gate: one. 33On the southern side, measuring 4,500 cubits, there shall be three gates: the Simeon Gate: one; the Issachar Gate: one; and the Zebulun Gate: one. 34And on the western side, [measuring] 4,500 cubits—there shall be three gates: the Gad Gate: one; the Asher Gate: one; the Naphtali Gate: one.

35Its circumference [shall be] 18,000 [cubits]; and the name of the city from that day on shall be "The LORD Is There."

HOSEA

1 The word of the LORD that came to Hosea son of Beeri, in the reigns of Kings Uzziah, Jotham, Ahaz, and Hezekiah of Judah, and in the reign of King Jeroboam son of Joash of Israel.

²When the LORD first spoke to Hosea, the LORD said to Hosea, "Go, get yourself ᵃ⁻ᵃ wife of whoredom and children of whoredom; for the land will strayᵇ from following the LORD."⁻ᵃ ³So he went and married Gomer daughter of Diblaim. She conceived and bore him a son, ⁴and the LORD instructed him, "Name him Jezreel; for, I will soon punish the House of Jehuᶜ for the ᵈ⁻bloody deeds at Jezreel⁻ᵈ and put an end to the monarchy of the House of Israel. ⁵In that day, I will break the bow of Israel in the Valley of Jezreel."

⁶She conceived again and bore a daughter; and He said to him, "Name her Lo-ruhamah;ᵉ for I will no longer accept the House of Israel ᶠ⁻or pardon them.⁻ᶠ (⁷But I will accept the House of Judah. And I will give them victory through the LORD their God; I will not give them victory with bow and sword and battle, by horses and riders.)"

⁸After weaning Lo-ruhamah, she conceived and bore a son. ⁹Then He said, "Name him Lo-ammi;ᵍ for youʰ are not My people, and ⁱ⁻I will not be your [God]."⁻ⁱ

2 ᵃThe number of the people of Israel shall be like that of the sands of the sea, which cannot be measured or counted; and instead of being told, "You are Not-My-People,"ᵇ they shall be called Children-of-the-Living-God. ²The people of Judah and the people of Israel shall assemble together

---

ᵃ⁻ᵃ *Force of Heb. uncertain.*
ᵇ *Lit. "whore away."*
ᶜ *Emendation yields "Israel"; cf. next note.*
ᵈ⁻ᵈ *See 1 Kings 21.1–24; 2 Kings 9.21–35. Emendation yields "the Baal days"; cf. 2.15.*
ᵉ *I.e., "Not-accepted"; cf. 2.3, 6, and 25.*
ᶠ⁻ᶠ *Meaning of Heb. uncertain; emendation yields "but will disown them"; cf. 9.15 and elsewhere.*
ᵍ *I.e., "Not-My-People."*
ʰ *I.e., you and your fellow countrymen.*
ⁱ⁻ⁱ *Cf. 2.25.*

ᵃ *Vv. 1–3 anticipate the conclusion of the chapter.*
ᵇ *See 1.9.*

and appoint one head over them; and they shall rise from the ground^c—
for marvelous shall be ^{d-}the day of Jezreel!^{-d}

³Oh, call^e your brothers "My People,"
And your sisters "Lovingly Accepted!"

⁴Rebuke^e your mother, rebuke her—
For she is not My wife
And I am not her husband—
And let her put away her harlotry from her face
And her adultery from between her breasts.
⁵Else will I strip her naked
And leave her as on the day she was born:
And I will make her like a wilderness,
Render her like desert land,
And let her die of thirst.
⁶I will also disown her children;
For they are now a harlot's brood,
⁷In that their mother has played the harlot,
She that conceived them has acted shamelessly—
Because she thought,
"I will go after my lovers,
Who supply my bread and my water,
My wool and my linen,
My oil and my drink."

⁸Assuredly,
I will hedge up her^f roads with thorns
And raise walls against her,
And she shall not find her paths.
⁹Pursue her lovers as she will,
She shall not overtake them;
And seek them as she may,
She shall never find them.
Then she will say,
"I will go and return
To my first husband,
For then I fared better than now."

---

^c *Meaning, perhaps, "from their wretched condition," or "to ascendancy over the land."*
^{d-d} *I.e., the day when the name Jezreel will convey a promise (2.23–25) instead of a threat (1.4-5).*
^e *The Lord addresses Hosea and his fellow North Israelites; see 1.9. The mother is the nation; her children the individual North Israelites.*
^f *Heb. "your." Vv. 8–9 would read well after v. 15.*

¹⁰And she did not consider this:
It was I who bestowed on her
The new grain and wine and oil;
I who lavished silver on her
And gold—which they used for Baal.
¹¹Assuredly,
I will take back My new grain in its time
And My new wine in its season,
And I will snatch away My wool and My linen
That serve to cover her nakedness.
¹²Now will I uncover her shame
In the very sight of her lovers,
And none shall save her from Me.
¹³And I will end all her rejoicing:
Her festivals, new moons, and sabbaths—
All her festive seasons.
¹⁴I will lay waste her vines and her fig trees,
Which she thinks are a fee
She received from her lovers;
I will turn them into brushwood,
And beasts of the field shall devour them.
¹⁵Thus will I punish her
For the days of the Baalim,
On which she brought them offerings;
When, decked with earrings and jewels,
She would go after her lovers,
Forgetting Me

         —declares the LORD.

¹⁶Assuredly,
I will speak coaxingly to her
And lead her through the wilderness^g
And speak to her tenderly.
¹⁷I will give her her vineyards from there,
And the Valley of Achor^h as a ^i-plowland of hope.^-i
There she shall respond as in the days of her youth,
When she came up from the land of Egypt.

g *I.e., her ravaged land (see vv. 5, 10–11, 14); so Ibn Ezra.*
h *A desolate region; cf. Isa. 65.10; see further Josh. 7.25–26.*
i-i *Connecting* pethah *with* pittah *"to plow" (see Isa. 28.24). Meaning of Heb. uncertain; others*
"door of hope."

¹⁸And in that day

—declares the LORD—

You will call [Me] Ishi,ʲ
And no more will you call Me Baali.ʲ
¹⁹For I will remove the names of the Baalim from her mouth,
And they shall nevermore be mentioned by name.

²⁰In that day, I will make a covenant for them with the beasts of the field, the birds of the air, and the creeping things of the ground; I will also banishᵏ bow, sword, and war from the land. Thus I will let them lie down in safety.

²¹And I will espouse you forever:
I will espouse you ˡ⁻with righteousness and justice,
And with goodness and mercy,
²²And I will espouse you with faithfulness;⁻ˡ
Then you shall be devoted to the LORD.
²³In that day,
I will respond

—declares the LORD—

I will respond to the sky,
And it shall respond to the earth;
²⁴And the earth shall respond
With new grain and wine and oil,
And they shall respond to Jezreel.ᵐ
²⁵I will sow her in the land as My own;
And take Lo-ruhamah back in favor;
And I will say to Lo-ammi, "You are My people,"
And he will respond, "[You are] my God."

3 The LORD said to me further, "Go, ᵃ⁻befriend a woman who, while befriended by a companion, consorts with others, just as the LORD befriends the Israelites,⁻ᵃ but they turn ᵇ⁻to other gods and love the cups of the grape."⁻ᵇ

ʲ *Both* Ishi *and* Baali *mean "my husband," but the latter also means "my Baal."*
ᵏ *Lit. "break."*
ˡ⁻ˡ *As the bride-price which the bridegroom will pay, He will confer these qualities on her, so that she will never offend again.*
ᵐ *I.e., "God sows." The names of Hosea's children (1.3–8) are applied here to Israel.*

ᵃ⁻ᵃ *For "befriend," see Deut. 10.19. For God's befriending Israel, see Hos. 2.10.*
ᵇ⁻ᵇ *Meaning of Heb. uncertain; emendation yields " 'to other gods.' And so I befriended a woman of lust."*

²Then I hired her for fifteen [shekels of] silver, a *homer* of barley, and ᶜ⁻a *lethech* of barley;⁻ᶜ ³and I stipulated with her, ᵈ⁻"In return,⁻ᵈ you are to go a long time without either fornicating or marrying; even I [shall not cohabit] with you."

⁴For the Israelites shall go a long time without king and without officials, without sacrificeᵉ and without cult pillars, and without ephod and teraphim. ⁵Afterward, the Israelites will turn back and will seek the LORD their God and David their king—and they will thrill over the LORD and over His bounty in the days to come.

4
Hear the word of the LORD,
O people of Israel!
For the LORD has a case
Against the inhabitants of this land,
Because there is no honesty and no goodness
And no obedience to God in the land.
²[False] swearing, dishonesty, and murder,
And theft and adultery are rife;
Crime follows upon crime!
³For that, the earth is withered:
Everything that dwells on it languishes—
Beasts of the field and birds of the sky—
Even the fish of the sea perish.

⁴"Let no man rebuke, let no man protest!"
ᵃ⁻For this your people has a grievance against [you],
    O priest!⁻ᵃ
⁵So you shall stumble by day,
And by night ᵇ⁻a prophet⁻ᵇ shall stumble as well,
And I will destroy your kindred.ᶜ
⁶My people is destroyed because of [your] disobedience!
Because you have rejected obedience,
I reject you as My priest;
Because you have spurned the teaching of your God,

ᶜ⁻ᶜ *Septuagint reads "a jar of wine."*
ᵈ⁻ᵈ *Lit. "for me."*
ᵉ *Emendation yields "altar."*

ᵃ⁻ᵃ *For failing to reprove; but meaning of Heb. uncertain.*
ᵇ⁻ᵇ *Emendation yields "your children"; cf. v. 6 end.*
ᶜ *Lit. "mother."*

I, in turn, will spurn your children.

⁷The more they increased, the more they sinned against Me:
I will change their dignity to dishonor.

⁸They feed on My people's sin offerings,
And so they desire its iniquity.

⁹Therefore, the people shall fare like the priests:
I will punish it for its conduct,
I will requite it for its deeds.

¹⁰Truly, they shall eat, but not be sated;
They shall swill,ᵈ but not be satisfied,
Because they have forsaken the LORD
To practiceᵉ

¹¹   lechery.
Wineᶠ and new wine destroy
The mind of

¹²   My people:
It consults its stick,ᵍ
Its rodᵍ directs it!
A lecherous impulse has made them go wrong,
And they have strayedʰ from submission to their God.

¹³They sacrifice on the mountaintops
And offer on the hills,
Under oaks, poplars, and terebinths
Whose shade is so pleasant.
That is why theirⁱ daughters fornicate
And their daughters-in-law commit adultery!

¹⁴I will not punish their daughters for fornicating
Nor their daughters-in-law for committing adultery;
For they themselves ʲ-turn aside-ʲ with whores
And sacrifice with prostitutes,
And a people that is without senseᵏ must stumble.

¹⁵If you are a lecher, Israel—
Let not Judah incur guilt—
Do not come to Gilgal,ˡ

ᵈ *For this meaning of* hiznah *cf. v. 18.*
ᵉ *Cf. 12.7.*
ᶠ *Emendation yields "New grain"; cf. 7.14; 9.1–2.*
ᵍ *I.e., its phallus, meaning "its lust."*
ʰ *See note b at 1.2.*
ⁱ *Heb. "your," here and through v. 14.*
ʲ⁻ʲ *Meaning of Heb. uncertain.*
ᵏ *Cf. vv. 11–12.*
ˡ *One who participates in the debaucheries of the open-air shrines is not fit to visit a temple building.*

Do not make pilgrimages to Beth-aven,[m]
And do not swear by the LORD![n]

[16]Ah, Israel has balked
Like a stubborn cow;
Therefore,
The LORD will graze him
On the range, like a sheep.[o]
[17][p]Ephraim is addicted to images—
Let him be.
[18]They drink to excess—
Their liquor turns against them.
They "love" beyond measure—
Disgrace is the "gift"
[19]Which the wind [q-]is bringing;[-q]
They shall garner shame from their sacrifices.

5 Hear this, O priests,
Attend, O House[a] of Israel,
And give ear, O royal house;
For right conduct is your responsibility!
But you have been a snare to Mizpah
And a net spread out over Tabor;
[2][b-]For when trappers dug deep pitfalls,
I was the only reprover of them all.[-b]
[3]Yes, I have watched Ephraim,
Israel has not escaped my notice:
Behold, you have fornicated, O Ephraim;
Israel has defiled himself!
[4]Their habits do not let them
Turn back to their God;
Because of the lecherous impulse within them,
They pay no heed to the LORD.

---

[m] Lit. "House of Delusion," substituted for Bethel (cf. Amos 4.4).
[n] I.e., you are not fit to profess His religion; see Jer. 12.16.
[o] Instead of giving them fodder in return for their work; cf. Isa. 30.23–24.
[p] Meaning of vv. 17–19 uncertain in part.
[q-q] Lit. "has bound up in the corners of its garment"; see note at Mal. 3.20.

[a] Emendation yields "prophets."
[b-b] Meaning of Heb. uncertain.

5c-Israel's pride shall be humbled before his very eyes,
As Israel and Ephraim fall because of their sin
(And Judah falls with them).
6Then they will go with their sheep and cattle
To seek the LORD, but they will not find Him.-c

b-He has cast them off:-b
7[Because] they have broken faith with the LORD,
Because d-they have-d begotten
Alien children.
Therefore, b-the new moon
Shall devour their portion.-b

8Sound a ram's horn in Gibeah,
A trumpet in Ramah;
Give the alarm in Beth-aven;e
f-After you,-f Benjamin!
9Ephraim is stricken with horror
On a day of chastisement.

Against the tribesg of Israel
I proclaim certainties:
10The officers of Judah have acted
Like shifters of field boundaries;
On them I will pour out
My wrath like water.
11Ephraim is defrauded,
Robbed of redress,
Because he has witlessly
Gone after futility.h
12For it is I who am like rot to Ephraim,
Like decay to the House of Judah;i
13Yet when Ephraim became aware of his sickness,
Judahi of his sores,
Ephraim repaired to Assyria—
He sent envoys to a patronj king!

c-c *This passage would read well after 5.15; cf. 5.6 with 6.6.*
d-d *Emendation yields "He has."*
e *The three towns named, in the territory of Benjamin, are now being wrested from Israel by Judah; see v. 10.*
f-f *Emendation yields "Stir up."*
g *I.e., the kingdoms of Judah and Israel (Ephraim).*
h *Cf. Targum and Septuagint; but meaning of Heb. uncertain.*
i *Emendation yields "Israel."*
j *Compare the verb* ryb *in the sense of "to champion, uphold the cause of," in Isa. 1.17; 3.13; 19.20 end; 51.22.*

He will never be able to cure you,
Will not heal you of your sores.
¹⁴No, I will be like a lion to Ephraim,
Like a great beast to the House of Judah;ⁱ
I, I will attack and stride away,
Carrying the prey that no one can rescue;
¹⁵And I will return to My abode—
Till they realize their guilt.
In their distress, they will seek Me
And beg for My favor.

6 ᵃ"Come, let us turn back to the LORD:
He attacked, and He can heal us;
He wounded, and He can bind us up.
²In two days He will make us whole again;
On the third day He will raise us up,
And we shall be whole by His favor.
³Let us pursue obedience to the LORD,
And we shall become obedient.
His appearance is as sure as daybreak,
And He will come to us like rain,
Like latter rain that refreshesᵇ the earth."

⁴What can I do for you, Ephraim,
What can I do for you, Judah,ᶜ
When your goodness is like morning clouds,
Like dew so early gone?
⁵That is why I have hewn down ᵈ⁻the prophets,⁻ᵈ
Have slain them with the words of My mouth:
ᵉ⁻And the day that dawned [brought on] your punishment.⁻ᵉ
⁶For I desire goodness, not sacrifice;
Obedience to God, rather than burnt offerings.
⁷ᶠBut they, to a man, have transgressed the Covenant.
This is where they have been false to Me:
⁸Gilead is a city of evildoers,

ᵃ *As anticipated at the end of chapter 5, Israel seeks the Lord's favor; His answer begins with v. 4.*
ᵇ *Taking* yoreh *as equivalent of* yarweh.
ᶜ *Emendation yields "Israel"; cf. "Ephraim . . . Israel" in v. 10.*
ᵈ⁻ᵈ *Emendation yields "your children"; cf. 9.13.*
ᵉ⁻ᵉ *Cf. v. 3; but meaning of Heb. uncertain.*
ᶠ *Meaning of vv. 7–11 unclear in part.*

Tracked up with blood.
⁹The gang of priests is
Like the ambuscade of bandits
Who murder on the road to Shechem,
For they have encouraged^g depravity.
¹⁰In ^{h-}the House of Israel^{-h} I have seen
A horrible thing;
Ephraim has fornicated there,
Israel has defiled himself.
¹¹ⁱ⁻(Even Judah has reaped a harvest of you!)⁻ⁱ

7 When I would restore My people's fortunes,
¹When I would heal Israel,
The guilt of Ephraim reveals itself
And the wickedness of Samaria.
For they have acted treacherously,
With thieves breaking in
And bands raiding outside.
²And they do not consider
That I remembered all their wickedness.
Why, their misdeeds have been all around them,^a
They have been ever before Me.

³^bIn malice they make a king merry,
And officials in treachery.
⁴They ^{c-}commit adultery,^{-c} all of them,
Like an oven fired by a baker,
Who desists from stoking only
From the kneading of the dough to its leavening.
⁵The day they made our king sick
[And] officials with the poison of wine,
^{d-}He gave his hand to traitors.^{-d}
⁶^{e-}For they approach their ambush
With their hearts like an oven:^{-e}
Through the night

g *Heb. "done"; cf. 5.1–3.*
h-h *Emendation yields "Beth-shean."*
i-i *Cf. 5.9–10; but meaning of clause uncertain.*

a *Emendation yields "Me."*
b *Vv. 3–6 would read well in the order 4, 6, 3, 5.*
c-c *Emendation yields "rage."*
d-d *I.e., he trusted traitors; but meaning of verse uncertain.*
e-e *Meaning of Heb. uncertain.*

Their baker^c has slept;
In the morning, it flares up
Like a blazing fire.
⁷They all get heated like an oven
And devour their rulers—
None of them calls to Me.
All their kings have fallen [by their hand].

^{8c-}Ephraim is among the peoples;
He is rotting away.
Ephraim is like a cake—
Incapable of turning.^{-c}
⁹Strangers have consumed his strength,
But he has taken no notice;
Also, mold^f is scattered over him,
But he has taken no notice.
¹⁰Though Israel's pride has been humbled
Before his very eyes,
They have not turned back
To their God the LORD;
They have not sought Him
In spite of everything.
¹¹Instead, Ephraim has acted
Like a silly dove with no mind:
They have appealed to Egypt!
They have gone to Assyria!
¹²When they go, I will spread
My net over them,
I will bring them down
Like birds of the sky;
^{e-}I will chastise them
When I hear their bargaining.^{-e}
¹³Woe to them
For straying from Me;
Destruction to them

^f *Like Akkadian* shību; *others "gray hairs."*

For rebelling against Me!
For I was their Redeemer;
Yet they have plotted treason against Me.

^{14g}But they did not cry out to Me sincerely
As they ^{h-}lay wailing.^{-h}
They debauchⁱ over new grain and new wine,
They are faithless^j to Me.

¹⁵*I* braced, *I* strengthened their arms,
And they plot evil against *Me!*
¹⁶They come back;
They have been of no use,^c
Like a slack bow.
Their officers shall fall by the sword,
Because of the stammering^k of their tongues.
Such shall be [the results of] their jabbering^l
In the land of Egypt.

8

[Put] a ram's horn to your mouth—
^{a-}Like an eagle^{-a} over the House of ^{b-}the LORD;^{-b}
Because they have transgressed My covenant
And been faithless to My teaching.
²Israel cries out to Me,
"O my God, we are devoted to You."^c

³Israel rejects what is good;
^{d-}An enemy shall pursue him.^{-d}
⁴They have made kings,
But not with My sanction;
They have made officers,
But not of My choice.
Of their silver and gold
They have made themselves images,

g *This verse would read well after 8.2.*
h-h *I.e., in penitence; cf. Isa. 58.5.*
i *Cf. Aramaic gar/yegur "to commit adultery"; for the thought, cf. 4.11.*
j *Taking yasuru as equivalent to yasoru, from sarar; cf. 9.15 end.*
k *Cf. Arabic zaghūm and zughmūm "a stammerer."*
l *I.e., the negotiations conducted in the Egyptian language.*

a-a *Meaning of Heb. uncertain.*
b-b *Emendation yields "Israel."*
c *See note g at 7.14.*
d-d *Emendation yields "They pursue delusion."*

To their own undoing.
5 e-He rejects-e your calf, Samaria!
I am furious with them!
Will they never be capable of f-purity?
6 For it was Israel's doing;-f
It was only made by a joiner,
It is not a god.
No, the calf of Samaria shall be
Reduced to splinters!

7 They sow wind,
And they shall reap whirlwind—
Standing stalks devoid of ears
And yielding no flour.
If they do yield any,
Strangers shall devour it.
8 Israel is bewildered;[g]
They have now become among the nations
Like an unwanted vessel,
9 [Like] a lonely wild ass.
For they have gone up to Assyria,
h-Ephraim has-h courted friendship.
10 And while they are courting among the nations,
i-There I will hold them fast;-i
a-And they shall begin to diminish in number
From the burden of king [and] officers.-a

11 For Ephraim has multiplied altars—for guilt;
His altars have redounded to his guilt:
12 The many teachings I wrote for him
Have been treated as something alien.
13 a-When they present sacrifices to Me,-a
It is but flesh for them to eat:
The LORD has not accepted them.
Behold, He remembers their iniquity,

e-e *Emendation yields "I reject."*
f-f *Emendation yields "understanding, / That House of Israel?"*
g *A play on words: The Heb. root* bala', *which means "bewildered" here (cf. Isa. 28.7), means "devour" in the preceding verse.*
h-h *Emendation yields "In Egypt they have."*
i-i *Cf. 9.6; but meaning of Heb. uncertain.*

He will punish their sins:
Back to Egypt with them!
14Israel has ignored his Maker
And built temples
(And Judah has fortified many cities).
So I will set fire to his cities,
And it shall consume their fortresses.

9 Rejoice not, O Israel,
As other peoples exult;
For you have strayed
Away from your God:
a-You have loved a harlot's fee
By every threshing floor of new grain.
2Threshing floor and winepress
Shall not join them,
And the new wine shall betray her.-a
3They shall not be able to remain
In the land of the LORD.
But Ephraim shall return to Egypt
And shall eat unclean food in Assyria.b
4It shall be for them like the food of mourners,
All who partake of which are defiled.
They will offer no libations of wine to the LORD,
And no sacrifices of theirs will be pleasing to Him;
But their food will be only for their hunger,
It shall not come into the House of the LORD.
5What will you do about feast days,
About the festivals of the LORD?
6Behold, they have gone c-from destruction-c
[With] the silver they treasure.
Egypt shall d-hold them fast,-d
Mophe shall receive them in burial.
Weeds are their heirs;
Prickly shrubs occupy their [old] homes.

a-a *Emendation and rearrangement yield: "You have loved fornication / By every threshing floor
and press; / The new grain shall not join them, / And the new wine shall fail them."*
b *The lands of the heathen and the food there are unclean; cf. Ezek. 4.13; Amos 7.17.*
c-c *Emendation yields "to Assyria."*
d-d *Cf. 8.10.*
e *Believed to be Memphis, elsewhere called Noph.*

⁷The days of punishment have come
For your heavy guilt;
The days of requital have come—
Let Israel know it!

The prophet was distraught,
The inspired man driven mad
By constant harassment.
⁸Ephraim watches for ᶠ⁻my God.
As for the prophet,⁻ᶠ
Fowlers' snares are on all his paths,
Harassment in the House of his God.
⁹They have been as grievously corrupt
As in the days of Gibeah;ᵍ
He will remember their iniquity,
He will punish their sins.

¹⁰I found Israel [as pleasing]
As grapes in the wilderness;
Your fathers seemed to Me
ʰ⁻Like the first fig to ripen on a fig tree.⁻ʰ
But when they came to Baal-peor,
They turned aside to shamefulness;ⁱ
ʲ⁻Then they became as detested
As they had been loved.⁻ʲ
¹¹From birth, from the womb, from conception
Ephraim's glory shall be
Like birds that fly away.ᵏ
¹²Even if they rear their infants,
I will bereave them of men.
ˡ⁻Woe to them indeed
When I turn away from them!⁻ˡ
¹³ʲ⁻It shall go with Ephraim
As I have seen it go with Tyre,
Which was planted in a meadow;⁻ʲ
Ephraim too must bring out

ᶠ⁻ᶠ *Emendation yields "the prophet of my God."*
ᵍ *See Judg. 19—20.*
ʰ⁻ʰ *Emendation yields "like a ripe fig in a waterless waste"; cf. 13.5.*
ⁱ *Cf. Num. 25.1–3.*
ʲ⁻ʲ *Meaning of Heb. uncertain.*
ᵏ *V. 16 would read well after v. 11.*
ˡ⁻ˡ *Emendation yields: "Even if they wean their babes, / They shall be dismayed because of them."*

His children to slayers.
14Give them, O LORD—give them what?
Give them a womb that miscarries,
And shriveled breasts!
15All their misfortune [began] at Gilgal,
For there I disowned them.m
For their evil deeds
I will drive them out of My House.
I will accept them no more;
n-All their officials are-n disloyal.

16kEphraimo is stricken,
Their stock is withered;
They can produce no fruit.
Even if they do bear children,
I will slay their cherished offspring.

17My God rejects them
Because they have not obeyed Him,
And they shall go wandering
Among the nations.

10 Israel is a ravaged vine
And its fruit is like it.
When his fruit was plentiful,
He made altars aplenty;
When his land was bountiful,
Cult pillars abounded.
2Now that his boughsa are broken up,
He feels his guilt;
He himself pulls apart his altars,
Smashes his pillars.

3Truly, now they say,
"We have no king;
For, since we do not fear the LORD,

m The specific allusion is uncertain.
n-n Emendation yields "They are all."
o Targum reads "Their crown," i.e., of a tree.

a Cf. 2 Sam. 18.14, where the word is rendered "thick growth."

What can a king do to us?"
⁴So they conclude agreements and make covenants
With false oaths,
And justice ᵇ⁻degenerates into poison weeds,
Breaking out⁻ᵇ on the furrows of the fields.

⁵The inhabitants of Samaria fear
For the calf of Beth-aven;ᶜ
Indeed, its people and priestlings,
ᵈ⁻Whose joy it once was,⁻ᵈ
Mourn over it for the glory
That is departed from it.
⁶It too shall be brought to Assyria
As tribute to a patronᵉ king;
Ephraim shall be chagrined,
Israel shall be dismayed
Because of his plans.ᶠ
⁷Samaria's monarchyᵍ is vanishing
Like foam upon water,
⁸Ruined shall be the shrines of [Beth-]aven,ᶜ
That sin of Israel.
Thorns and thistles
Shall grow on their altars.
They shall call to the mountains, "Bury us!"
To the hills, "Fall on us!"

⁹You have sinned more, O Israel,
Than in the days of Gibeah.ʰ
ᵈ⁻There they stand [as] at Gibeah!
Shall they not be overtaken
By a war upon scoundrels
¹⁰As peoples gather against them?⁻ᵈ

When I chose [them], I broke them in,
Harnessing them for two furrows.
¹¹Ephraim became a trained heifer,
But preferred to thresh;

ᵇ⁻ᵇ *Cf. Amos 6.12; lit. "breaks out like poison weeds."*
ᶜ *See note m at 4.15.*
ᵈ⁻ᵈ *Meaning of Heb. uncertain.*
ᵉ *See note j at 5.13.*
ᶠ *Emendation yields "image," referring to the calf.*
ᵍ *The Heb. verb agrees with this word, not with "Samaria."*
ʰ *See note at 9.9.*

I ⁱ⁻placed a yoke
Upon her sleek neck.⁻ⁱ
I will make Ephraim ^{j-}do advance plowing;^{-j}
Judah^k shall do [main] plowing!
Jacob shall do final plowing!
12"Sow righteousness for yourselves;
Reap ^{l-}the fruits of^{-l} goodness;
Break for yourselves betimes fresh ground
Of seeking the LORD,
So that you may obtain ^{m-}a teacher^{-m} of righteousness."
13You have plowed wickedness,
You have reaped iniquity—
[And] you shall eat the fruits of treachery—
Because you relied on your way,ⁿ
On your host of warriors.
14But the din of war shall arise in your own people,
And all your fortresses shall be ravaged
As Beth-arbel was ravaged by Shalman^o
On a day of battle,
When mothers and babes were dashed to death together.
15This ^{p-}is what Bethel has done to you^{-p}
For your horrible wickedness:
^{q-}At dawn^{-q} shall Israel's monarchy
Utterly perish.

11 I fell in love with Israel
When he was still a child;
And I have called [him] My son
Ever since Egypt.
2aThus were they called,
But they went their own way;
They sacrifice to Baalim^b
And offer to carved images.

ⁱ⁻ⁱ *Lit. "passed over the comeliness of its neck."*
^{j-j} *Taking rkb in the sense of the Arabic krb.*
^k *Emendation yields "Israel."*
^{l-l} *Lit. "according to."*
^{m-m}*Meaning of Heb. uncertain; Septuagint reads "the fruits."*
ⁿ *Septuagint reads "chariots."*
^o *Perhaps identical with the Shallum of 2 Kings 15.10 ff.; cf. the atrocities of Shallum's rival, ibid., v. 16.*
^{p-p} *Emendation yields "will I do to you, O House of Israel."*
^{q-q} *Meaning, perhaps, "swiftly as the dawn"; cf. v. 7 above, "like foam upon water."*

^a *Meaning of parts of vv. 2–7 uncertain.*
^b *Emendation yields "calves"; cf. 8.4–6; 13.2.*

³I have pampered Ephraim,
Taking them in My^c arms;
But they have ignored
My healing care.
⁴I drew them with human ties,
With cords of love;
But I seemed to them as one
Who imposed a yoke on their jaws,
Though I was offering them food.
⁵No!
They return to the land of Egypt,
And Assyria is their king.
Because they refuse to repent,
⁶A sword shall descend upon their towns^d
And consume their limbs
And devour ᶜ-[them] because of their designs.⁻ᶜ
⁷ᶠ-For My people persists
In its defection from Me;
When it is summoned upward,
It does not rise at all.⁻ᶠ

⁸How can I give you up, O Ephraim?
How surrender you, O Israel?
How can I make you like Admah,
Render you like Zeboiim?ᵍ
I have had a change of heart,
All My tenderness is stirred.
⁹I will not act on My wrath,
Will not turn to destroy Ephraim.
For I am God, not man,
ᶠ-The Holy One in your midst:
I will not come in fury.⁻ᶠ

¹⁰The LORD will roar like a lion,

---

^c Heb. "his."
^d Emendation yields "bodies," lit. "skins"; cf. Job. 18.13.
^{e-e} Emendation yields "their bones."
^{f-f} Meaning of Heb. uncertain.
^g Admah and Zeboiim were destroyed with neighboring Sodom and Gomorrah; cf. Gen. 10.19;
    14.2, 8; Deut. 29.22.

And they shall march behind Him;
When He roars, His children shall come
Fluttering out of the west.
¹¹They shall flutter from Egypt like sparrows,
From the land of Assyria like doves;
And I will settle them in their homes

—declares the LORD.

12Ephraim surrounds Me with deceit,
The House of Israel with guile.ᵃ
ᵇ⁻(But Judah stands firm with God
And is faithful to the Holy One.)⁻ᵇ
²Ephraim tends the wind
And pursues the gale;
He is forever adding
Illusion to calamity.ᶜ
Now they make a covenant with Assyria,
Now oil is carried to Egypt.ᵈ

³The LORD once indicted Judah,ᵉ
And punished Jacob for his conduct,
Requited him for his deeds.
⁴In the womb he tried to supplant his brother;
Grown to manhood, he strove with a divine being,ᶠ
⁵He strove with an angel and prevailed—
The other had to weep and implore him.
At Bethel [Jacob] would meet him,
There to commune with him.ᵍ
⁶Yet the LORD, the God of Hosts,
Must be invoked as "LORD."ʰ
⁷You must return to your God!
Practice goodness and justice,
And constantly trust in your God.

⁸A trader who uses false balances,

ᵃ *I.e., the deceit and guile they practice on each other (below vv. 8–9) is constantly noted by the* LORD.
ᵇ⁻ᵇ *Meaning of Heb. uncertain.*
ᶜ *Septuagint reads "futility."*
ᵈ *I.e., they foolishly depend on alliances instead of on the* LORD; *cf. 5.13; 7.10–11.*
ᵉ *Presumably the patriarch Judah. Emendation would yield "Israel"; cf. next note.*
ᶠ *Cf. Gen. 25.26 and 32.29.*
ᵍ *Heb. "us."*
ʰ *I.e., one should not invoke any of the angelic hosts.*

Who loves to overreach,
9Ephraim thinks,
"Ah, I have become rich;
I have gotten power!
b-All my gains do not amount
To an offense which is real guilt."-b
10I the LORD have been your God
Ever since the land of Egypt.
I will let you dwell in your tentsⁱ again
As in the days of old,ʲ
11When I spoke to the prophets;
For I granted many visions,
b-And spoke parables through the prophets.
12As for Gilead, it is worthless;
And to no purpose-b have they
Been sacrificing oxen in Gilgal:
The altars of these are also
Like stone heaps upon a plowed field.ᵏ

13Then Jacob had to fleeˡ to the land of Aram;
There Israel served for a wife,
For a wife he had to guard [sheep].
14But when the LORD
Brought Israel up from Egypt,
It was through a prophet;ᵐ
Through a prophetᵐ they were guarded.
15ⁿEphraim gave bitter offense,
And his Lord cast his crimes upon him
And requited him for his mockery.

13

When Ephraim spoke piety,
He was exalted in Israel;
But he incurred guilt through Baal,ᵃ
And so he died.
2And now they go on sinning;

ⁱ *I.e., securely; see 2 Kings 13.5.*
ʲ *Lit. "fixed season."*
ᵏ *I.e., the cults of Gilead and Gilgal are as worthless as that of Bethel.*
ˡ *This is the punishment mentioned in 12.3.*
ᵐ *I.e., not through an angel.*
ⁿ *Meaning of 12.15—13.1 uncertain.*

ᵃ *I.e., Baal-peor; cf. 9.10.*

They have made them molten images,
Idols, by their skill, from their silver,
Wholly the work of craftsmen.
b-Yet for these they appoint men to sacrifice;-b
They are wont to kiss calves!
³Assuredly,
They shall be like morning clouds,
Like dew so early gone;
Like chaff whirled away from the threshing floor.
And like smoke from a lattice.
⁴Only I the LORD have been your God
Ever since the land of Egypt;
You have never known a [true] God but Me,
You have never had a helper other than Me.
⁵I looked after you in the desert,
In a thirsty land.
⁶When they grazed, they were sated;
When they were sated, they grew haughty;
And so they forgot Me.
⁷So I am become like a lion to them,
Like a leopard I lurk on the way;
⁸Like a bear robbed of her young I attack them
And rip open the casing of their hearts;
c-I will devour them there like a lion,-c
The beasts of the field shall mangle them.

9b-You are undone, O Israel!
You had no help but Me.-b
¹⁰Where now is your king?
Let him save you!
Where are the chieftains in all your towns
Whom you demanded:
"Give me a king and officers"?
¹¹I give you kings in my ire,
And take them away in My wrath.

¹²Ephraim's guilt is bound up,
His sin is stored away.d

b-b *Meaning of Heb. uncertain.*
c-c *Emendation yields "There dogs shall devour them"; cf. Septuagint.*
d *I.e., for future retribution.*

1002

13Pangs of childbirth assail him,
b-And the babe is not wise—
For this is no time to survive
At the birthstool of babes.-b

14cFrom Sheol itself I will save them,
Redeem them from very Death.
Where, O Death, are your plagues?
Your pestilence where, O Sheol?
f-Revenge shall be far from My thoughts.-f
15For though he flourish among reeds,
A blast, a wind of the LORD,
Shall come blowing up from the wilderness;
His fountain shall be parched,
His spring dried up.
That [wind] shall plunder treasures,

14 Every lovely object.
Samaria must bear her guilt,
For she has defied her God.
They shall fall by the sword,
Their infants shall be dashed to death,
And their women with child ripped open.

2Return, O Israel, to the LORD your God,
For you have fallen because of your sin.
3Take words with you
And return to the LORD.
Say to Him:
a-"Forgive all guilt
And accept what is good;
Instead of bulls we will pay
[The offering of] our lips.-a
4Assyria shall not save us,
No more will we ride on steeds;b
Nor ever again will we call
Our handiwork our god,
Since in You alone orphans find pity!"

---

c *This verse would read well before 14.5.*
f-f *Lit. "Satisfaction (for this meaning of* nḥm *see Deut. 32.36; Isa. 1.24) shall be hidden from My eyes."*
a-a *Meaning of Heb. uncertain.*
b *I.e., we will no longer depend on an alliance with Egypt; cf. 2 Kings 18.24 // Isa. 36.9; Isa. 30.16.*

⁵I will heal their affliction,ᶜ
Generously will I take them back in love;
For My anger has turned away from them.ᵈ
⁶I will be to Israel like dew;
He shall blossom like the lily,
He shall strike root like a ᵉ⁻Lebanon tree.⁻ᵉ
⁷His boughs shall spread out far,
His beauty shall be like the olive tree's,
His fragrance like that of Lebanon.
⁸They who sit in his shade shall be revived:
They shall bring to life new grain,
They shall blossom like the vine;
His scent shall be like the wine of Lebanon.ᶠ
⁹Ephraim [shall say]:
"What more have I to do with idols?
When I respond and look to Him,
I become like a verdant cypress."
ᵃ⁻Your fruit is provided by Me.⁻ᵃ

¹⁰He who is wise will consider these words,
He who is prudent will take note of them.
For the paths of the LORD are smooth;
The righteous can walk on them,
While sinners stumble on them.

ᶜ For this meaning of meshubah see Jer. 2.19; 3.22.
ᵈ Heb. "him."
ᵉ⁻ᵉ Emendation yields "poplar."
ᶠ Emendation yields "Helbon"; cf. Ezek. 27.18.

JOEL

1 The word of the LORD that came to Joel son of Pethuel.

²Listen to this, O elders,
Give ear, all inhabitants of the land.
Has the like of this happened in your days
Or in the days of your fathers?
³Tell your children about it,
And let your children tell theirs,
And their children the next generation!
⁴What the cutterᵃ has left, the locust has devoured;
What the locust has left, the grub has devoured;
And what the grub has left, the hopper has devoured.
⁵Wake up, you drunkards, and weep,
Wail, all you swillers of wine—
For the new wine that is ᵇ⁻denied you!⁻ᵇ
⁶For a nation has invaded my land,
Vast beyond counting,
With teeth like the teeth of a lion,
With the fangs of a lion's breed.
⁷They have laid my vines waste
And splintered my fig trees:
They have stripped off their bark and thrown [it] away;
Their runners have turned white.

⁸Lament—like a maiden girt with sackcloth
For the husband of her youth!
⁹Offering and libation have ceased
From the House of the LORD;
The priests must mourn

ᵃ The Heb. terms translated "cutter, locust, grub, and hopper" are of uncertain meaning; they probably designate stages in the development of the locust.
ᵇ⁻ᵇ Lit. "cut off from your mouth."

Who minister to the LORD.
¹⁰The country is ravaged,
The ground must mourn;
For the new grain is ravaged,
The new wine is dried up,
The new oil has failed.
¹¹Farmers are dismayed
And vine dressers wail
Over wheat and barley;
For the crops of the field are lost.
¹²The vine has dried up,
The fig tree withers,
Pomegranate, palm, and apple—
All the trees of the field are sear.
And joy has dried up
Among men.

¹³Gird yourselves and lament, O priests,
Wail, O ministers of the altar;
Come, spend the night in sackcloth,
O ministers of my God.
For offering and libation are withheld
From the House of your God.
¹⁴Solemnize a fast,
Proclaim an assembly;
Gather the elders—all the inhabitants of the land—
In the House of the LORD your God,
And cry out to the LORD.

¹⁵Alas for the day!
For the day of the LORD is near;
It shall come like havoc from Shaddai.ᶜ
¹⁶For food is cut off
Before our very eyes,
And joy and gladness
From the House of our God.
¹⁷ᵈ⁻The seeds have shriveled
Under their clods.⁻ᵈ

ᶜ *Traditionally "the Almighty"; see Gen. 17.1.*
ᵈ⁻ᵈ *Meaning of Heb. uncertain.*

The granaries are desolate,
Barns are in ruins,
For the new grain has failed.
18How the beasts groan!
The herds of cattle are bewildered
Because they have no pasture,
And the flocks of sheep are dazed.ᵈ

19To You, O LORD, I call.
For fireᵉ has consumed
The pastures in the wilderness,
And flameᵉ has devoured
All the trees of the countryside.
20The very beasts of the field
Cry out to You;
For the watercourses are dried up,
And fire has consumed
The pastures in the wilderness.

2 Blow a horn in Zion,
Sound an alarm on My holy mount!
Let all dwellers on earth tremble,
For the day of the LORD has come!
It is close—
2A day of darkness and gloom,
A day of densest cloud
Spread like soot over the hills.
A vast, enormous horde—
Nothing like it has ever happened,
And it shall never happen again
Through the years and ages.

3Their vanguard is a consuming fire,
Their rear guard a devouring flame.
Before them the land was like the Garden of Eden,
Behind them, a desolate waste:
Nothing has escaped them.

ᵉ *I.e., scorching heat.*

⁴They have the appearance of horses,
They gallop just like steeds.
⁵With a clatter as of chariots
They bound on the hilltops,
With a noise like a blazing fire
Consuming straw;
Like an enormous horde
Arrayed for battle.
⁶Peoples tremble before them,
All faces ᵃ⁻turn ashen.⁻ᵃ
⁷They rush like warriors,
They scale a wall like fighters.
And each keeps to his own track.
Their paths never cross;ᵇ
⁸No one jostles another,
Each keeps to his own course.
ᵇ⁻And should they fall through a loophole,
They do not get hurt.⁻ᵇ
⁹They rush up the wall,
They dash about in the city;
They climb into the houses,
They enter like thieves
By way of the windows.
¹⁰Before them earth trembles,
Heaven shakes,
Sun and moon are darkened,
And stars withdraw their brightness.
¹¹And the LORD roars aloud
At the head of His army;
For vast indeed is His host,
Numberless are those that do His bidding.
For great is the day of the LORD,
Most terrible—who can endure it?
¹²"Yet even now"—says the LORD—
"Turn back to Me with all your hearts,
And with fasting, weeping, and lamenting."
¹³Rend your hearts
Rather than your garments,

ᵃ⁻ᵃ *Meaning of Heb. uncertain; cf. Nah. 2.11.*
ᵇ *Meaning of Heb. uncertain.*

And turn back to the LORD your God.
For He is gracious and compassionate,
Slow to anger, abounding in kindness,
And renouncing punishment.
14Who knows but He may turn and relent,
And leave a blessing behind
For meal offering and drink offering
To the LORD your God?c

15Blow a horn in Zion,
Solemnize a fast,
Proclaim an assembly!
16Gather the people,
Bid the congregation purify themselves.d
Bring together the old,
Gather the babes
And the sucklings at the breast;
Let the bridegroom come out of his chamber,
The bride from her canopied couch.
17Between the portico and the altar,
Let the priests, the LORD's ministers, weep
And say:
"Oh, spare Your people, LORD!
Let not Your possession become a mockery,
To be taunted by nations!
Let not the peoples say,
'Where is their God?' "

18Then the LORD was roused
On behalf of His land
And had compassion
Upon His people.
19In response to His people
The LORD declared:
"I will grant you the new grain,
The new wine, and the new oil,
And you shall have them in abundance.
Nevermore will I let you be

c *When the locusts depart, there will again be yield enough for offerings; see 1.9.*
d *Cf. Exod. 19.10; Zeph. 1.7.*

A mockery among the nations.
²⁰I will drive the northerner^c far from you,
I will thrust it into a parched and desolate land—
Its van to the Eastern Sea^f
And its rear to the Western Sea;^g
And the stench of it shall go up,
And the foul smell rise."
For [the LORD] shall work great deeds.

²¹Fear not, O soil, rejoice and be glad;
For the LORD has wrought great deeds.
²²Fear not, O beasts of the field,
For the pastures in the wilderness
Are clothed with grass.
The trees have borne their fruit;
Fig tree and vine
Have yielded their strength.
²³O children of Zion, be glad,
Rejoice in the LORD your God.
For He has given you the early rain in [His] kindness,
Now He makes the rain fall [as] formerly—
The early rain and the late—
²⁴And threshing floors shall be piled with grain,
And vats shall overflow with new wine and oil.

²⁵"I will repay you ^{h-}for the years^{-h}
Consumed by swarms and hoppers,
By grubs and locusts,
The great army I let loose against you.
²⁶And you shall eat your fill
And praise the name of the LORD your God
Who dealt so wondrously with you—
My people shall be shamed no more.
²⁷And you shall know
That I am in the midst of Israel:
That I the LORD am your God
And there is no other.
And My people shall be shamed no more."

^c *I.e., the locusts. Emendation yields "My multitude"; cf. "nation" (1.6), "horde," "army," and*
"host" (2.2, 5, 11, and 25).
^f *The Dead Sea.*
^g *The Mediterranean Sea.*
^{h-h} *Emendation yields "double what was."*

3 After that,
I will pour out My spirit on all flesh;
Your sons and daughters shall prophesy;
Your old men shall dream dreams,
And your young men shall see visions.
²I will even pour out My spirit
Upon male and female slaves in those days.

³ᵃ⁻Before the great and terrible day of the LORD comes,⁻ᵃ
I will set portents in the sky and on earth:
Blood and fire and pillars of smoke;
⁴The sun shall turn into darkness
And the moon into blood.

⁵But everyone who invokes the name of the LORD shall escape; for there shall be a remnant on Mount Zion and in Jerusalem, as the LORD promised. ᵇ⁻Anyone who invokes the LORD will be among the survivors.⁻ᵇ

4 For lo! in those days
And in that time,
When I restore the fortunes
Of Judah and Jerusalem,
²I will gather all the nations
And bring them down to the Valley of Jehoshaphat.ᵃ
There I will contend with them
Over My very own people, Israel,
Which they scattered among the nations.
For they divided My land among themselves
³And cast lots over My people;
And they bartered a boy for a whore,
And sold a girl for wine, which they drank.

⁴What is this you are doing to Me, O Tyre, Sidon, and all the districts of Philistia? Are you requiting Me for something I have done, or are you doing something for My benefit? Quick as a flash, I will pay you back; ⁵for you have taken My gold and My silver, and have carried off My

---

ᵃ⁻ᵃ *Brought up from v. 4 for clarity.*
ᵇ⁻ᵇ *Meaning of Heb. uncertain.*

ᵃ *Here understood as "The LORD contends"; contrast v. 12.*

precious treasures to your palaces; 6and you have sold the people of Judah
and the people of Jerusalem to the Ionians, so that you have removed
them far away from their homeland. 7Behold, I will rouse them to leave
the place you have sold them to, and I will pay you back: 8I will deliver
your sons and daughters into the hands of the people of Judah, and they
will sell them into captivity to a distant nation—for the LORD has spoken.

9Proclaim this among the nations:
Prepare for battle!
Arouse the warriors,
Let all the fighters come and draw near!
10Beat your plowsharesb into swords,
And your pruning hooks into spears.
Let even the weakling say, "I am strong."
11c-Rouse yourselves-c and come,
All you nations;
Come together
From roundabout.
There c-bring down-c
Your warriors, O LORD!
12Let the nations rouse themselves and march up
To the Valley of Jehoshaphat;d
For there I will sit in judgment
Over all the nations roundabout.
13Swing the sickle,
For the crop is ripe;
Come and tread,
For the winepress is full,
The vats are overflowing!
For great is their wickedness.

14Multitudes upon multitudes
In the Valley of Decision!
For the day of the LORD is at hand
In the Valley of Decision.
15Sun and moon are darkened,
And stars withdraw their brightness.
16And the LORD will roar from Zion,

b See note at Isa. 2.4.
c-c Meaning of Heb. uncertain.
d Here understood as "The LORD judges"; contrast v. 2.

And shout aloud from Jerusalem,
So that heaven and earth tremble.
But the LORD will be a shelter to His people,
A refuge to the children of Israel.
¹⁷And you shall know that I the LORD your God
Dwell in Zion, My holy mount.
And Jerusalem shall be holy;
Nevermore shall strangers pass through it.
¹⁸And in that day,
The mountains shall drip with wine,
The hills shall flow with milk,
And all the watercourses of Judah shall flow with water;
A spring shall issue from the House of the LORD
And shall water the Wadi of the Acacias.
¹⁹Egypt shall be a desolation,
And Edom a desolate waste,
Because of the outrage to the people of Judah,
In whose land they shed the blood of the innocent.
²⁰But Judah shall be inhabited forever,
And Jerusalem throughout the ages.
²¹Thus ^{c-}I will treat as innocent their blood
Which I have not treated as innocent;^{-c}
And the LORD shall dwell in Zion.

---

^{c-c} *Emendation yields "their unavenged blood shall be avenged."*

AMOS

1 The words of Amos, a sheepbreeder from Tekoa, who prophesied concerning Israel in the reigns of Kings Uzziah of Judah and Jeroboam son of Joash of Israel, two years before the earthquake.[a]

2He proclaimed:

The LORD roars from Zion,
Shouts aloud from Jerusalem;
And the pastures of the shepherds shall languish,
And the summit of Carmel shall wither.

3Thus said the LORD:
For three transgressions of Damascus,
For four, I will not revoke it:[b]
Because they threshed Gilead
With threshing boards of iron.
4I will send down[c] fire upon the palace of Hazael,
And it shall devour the fortresses of Ben-hadad.[d]
5I will break the gate bars of Damascus,
And wipe out the inhabitants from the Vale of Aven
And the sceptered ruler of Beth-eden;
And the people of Aram shall be exiled to Kir

—said the LORD.

6Thus said the LORD:
For three transgressions of Gaza,
For four, I will not revoke it:
Because they exiled[e] an entire population,
Which they delivered to Edom.[f]
7I will send down fire upon the wall of Gaza,

---

[a] See Zech. 14.5.
[b] I.e, the decree of punishment.
[c] Cf. Lam. 1.13.
[d] Cf. 2 Kings 13.22–25.
[e] I.e., they cooperated in the annexation of Israelite territory; cf. Jer. 13.19 with note.
[f] Emendation yields "Aram"; cf. Isa. 9.11.

And it shall devour its fortresses;
⁸And I will wipe out the inhabitants of Ashdod
And the sceptered ruler of Ashkelon;
And I will turn My hand against Ekron,
And the Philistines shall perish to the last man
—said the Lord GOD.

⁹Thus said the LORD:
For three transgressions of Tyre,
For four, I will not revoke it:
Because they handed over
An entire population to Edom,ᵍ
Ignoring the covenant of brotherhood.ʰ
¹⁰I will send down fire upon the wall of Tyre,
And it shall devour its fortresses.

¹¹Thus said the LORD:
For three transgressions of Edom,
For four, I will not revoke it:
Because he pursued his brother with the sword
And repressed all pity,
Because his anger raged unceasing
And his fury stormedⁱ unchecked.
¹²I will send down fire upon Teman,
And it shall devour the fortresses of Bozrah.

¹³Thus said the LORD:
For three transgressions of the Ammonites,
For four, I will not revoke it:
Because they ripped open the pregnant women of Gilead
In order to enlarge their own territory.
¹⁴I will set fire to the wall of Rabbah,
And it shall devour its fortresses,
Amid shouting on a day of battle,
On a day of violent tempest.
¹⁵Their king and his officers shall go
Into exile together
—said the LORD.

ᵍ *Emendation yields "Aram."*
ʰ *Cf. 1 Kings 5.26; 9.12–13.*
ⁱ *Cf. Akkadian* shamaru *and Jer. 3.5.*

2

Thus said the LORD:
For three transgressions of Moab,
For four, I will not revoke it:
Because he burned the bones
Of the king of Edom to lime.
²I will send down fire upon Moab,
And it shall devour the fortresses of Kerioth.
And Moab shall die in tumult,
Amid shouting and the blare of horns;
³I will wipe out the ruler from within her
And slay all her officials along with him

—said the LORD.

⁴Thus said the LORD:
For three transgressions of Judah,
For four, I will not revoke it:
Because they have spurned the Teaching of the LORD
And have not observed His laws;
They are beguiled by the delusions
After which their fathers walked.
⁵I will send down fire upon Judah,
And it shall devour the fortresses of Jerusalem.

⁶Thus said the LORD:
For three transgressions of Israel,
For four, I will not revoke it:
Because they have sold for silver
Those whose cause was just,
And the needy for a pair of sandals.
⁷[Ah,] you ᵃ⁻who trample the heads of the poor
Into the dust of the ground,
And make the humble walk a twisted course!⁻ᵃ
Father and son go to the same girl,
And thereby profane My holy name.
⁸They recline by every altar
On garments taken in pledge,
And drink in the House of their God

ᵃ⁻ᵃ *Understanding* sho'afim *as equivalent to* shafim. *Emendation yields:* "Who crush on the ground / The heads of the poor, / And push off the road / The humble of the land"; *cf. Job 24.4.*

Wine bought with fines they imposed.
⁹Yet I
Destroyed the Amorite before them,
Whose stature was like the cedar's
And who was stout as the oak,
Destroying his boughs above
And his trunk below!
¹⁰And I
Brought you up from the land of Egypt
And led you through the wilderness forty years,
To possess the land of the Amorite!
¹¹And I raised up prophets from among your sons
And nazirites from among your young men.
Is that not so, O people of Israel?

　　　　　　　　　　　　　　　—says the LORD.

¹²But you made the nazirites drink wine
And ordered the prophets not to prophesy.
¹³ᵇ⁻Ah, I will slow your movements
As a wagon is slowed
When it is full of cut grain.⁻ᵇ
¹⁴Flight shall fail the swift,
The strong shall find no strength,
And the warrior shall not save his life.
¹⁵The bowman shall not hold his ground,
And the fleet-footed shall not escape,
Nor the horseman save his life.
¹⁶Even the most stouthearted warrior
Shall run away unarmedᶜ that day

　　　　　　　　　　　　　　　—declares the LORD.

3 Hear this word, O people of Israel,
That the LORD has spoken concerning you,
Concerning the whole family that I brought up from the land of
　　Egypt:
²You alone have I singled out
Of all the families of the earth—

ᵇ⁻ᵇ *Meaning of verse uncertain; alternatively: "I will slow your movements / As a threshing sledge*
　(cf. Isa. 28.27–28) is slowed / When clogged by cut grain."
ᶜ *Lit. "naked."*

That is why I will call you to account
For all your iniquities.

³Can two walk together
Without having met?
⁴Does a lion roar in the forest
When he has no prey?
Does a great beast let out a cry from its den
Without having made a capture?
⁵Does a bird drop on the ground—in a trap—
With no snare there?
Does a trap spring up from the ground
Unless it has caught something?
⁶When a ram's horn is sounded in a town,
Do the people not take alarm?
Can misfortune come to a town
If the LORD has not caused it?
⁷Indeed, my Lord GOD does nothing
Without having revealed His purpose
To His servants the prophets.
⁸A lion has roared,
Who can but fear?
My Lord GOD has spoken,
Who can but prophesy?
⁹Proclaim in the fortresses of Ashdodᵃ
And in the fortresses of the land of Egypt!
Say:
Gather on the hillᵇ of Samaria
And witness the great outrages within her
And the oppression in her midst.
¹⁰They are incapable of doing right

                              —declares the LORD;

They store up lawlessness and rapine
In their fortresses.
¹¹Assuredly,
Thus said my Lord GOD:
An enemy, all about the land!
He shall strip you of your splendor,

ᵃ *Septuagint reads "Assyria."*
ᵇ *Heb. plural; but cf. 4.1; 6.1.*

And your fortresses shall be plundered.
¹²Thus said the LORD:
As a shepherd rescues from the lion's jaws
Two shank bones or the tip of an ear,
So shall the Israelites escape
Who dwell in Samaria—
With the leg^c of a bed or the head^c of a couch.

¹³Hear [this], and warn the House of Jacob
— says my Lord GOD, the God of Hosts—
¹⁴That when I punish Israel for its transgressions,
I will wreak judgment on the altar^d of Bethel,
And the horns of the altar shall be cut off
And shall fall to the ground.
¹⁵I will wreck the winter palace
Together with the summer palace;
The ivory palaces shall be demolished,
And the great houses shall be destroyed
—declares the LORD.

4 Hear this word, you cows of Bashan
On the hill of Samaria—
Who defraud the poor,
Who rob the needy;
Who say to your^a husbands,
"Bring, and let's carouse!"
²My Lord GOD swears by His holiness:
Behold, days are coming upon you
^{b-}When you will be carried off in baskets,
And, to the last one, in fish baskets,
³And taken out [of the city]—
Each one through a breach straight ahead—
And flung on the refuse heap^{-b}
—declares the LORD.

---

^c *Meaning of Heb. uncertain.*
^d *Heb. plural, but cf. "altar" in next line.*

^a *Heb. "their."*
^{b-b} *Meaning of Heb. uncertain.*

⁴Come to Bethel and transgress;
To Gilgal, and transgress even more:
Present your sacrifices the next morning
And your tithes on the third day;
⁵And burn a thank offering of leavened bread;ᶜ
And proclaim freewill offerings loudly.
For you love that sort of thing, O Israelites

—declares my Lord GOD.

⁶I, on My part, have given you
Cleanness of teeth in all your towns,
And lack of food in all your settlements.
Yet you did not turn back to Me

—declares the LORD.

⁷I therefore withheld the rain from you
Three months before harvesttime:
I would make it rain on one town
And not on another;
One field would be rained upon
While another on which it did not rain
Would wither.
⁸So two or three towns would wander
To a single town to drink water,
But their thirst would not be slaked.
Yet you did not turn back to Me

—declares the LORD.

⁹I scourged you with blight and mildew;
Repeatedlyᵇ your gardens and vineyards,
Your fig trees and olive trees
Were devoured by locusts.
Yet you did not turn back to Me

—declares the LORD.

¹⁰I sent against you pestilence
In the manner of Egypt;ᵈ
I slew your young men with the sword,
Together with your captured horses,

ᶜ Cf. Lev. 7.12–14; where, however, the bread is not to be burned.
ᵈ Alluding to the plagues at the time of the Exodus.

And I made the stench of your armies
Rise in your very nostrils.
Yet you did not turn back to Me

      —declares the LORD.

¹¹I have wrought destruction among you
As when God destroyed Sodom and Gomorrah;
You have become like a brand plucked from burning.
Yet you have not turned back to Me

      —declares the LORD.

¹²Assuredly,
ᵉ⁻Because I am doing that to you,⁻ᵉ
Even so will I act toward you, O Israel—
Prepare to meet your God, O Israel!

¹³Behold,
He who formed the mountains,
And created the wind,
And has told man what His wishᵇ is,
Who turns blacknessᶠ into daybreak,
And treads upon the high places of the earth—
His name is the LORD, the God of Hosts.

5 Hear this word which I intone
As a dirge over you, O House of Israel:
²Fallen, not to rise again,
Is Maiden Israel;
Abandoned on her soil
With none to lift her up.
³For thus said my Lord GOD
About the House of Israel:
The town that marches out a thousand strong
Shall have a hundred left,
And the one that marches out a hundred strong
Shall have but ten left.

ᵉ⁻ᵉ *Emendation yields "Because you are acting thus toward Me."*
ᶠ *Cf. Joel 2.2. Emendation yields "darkness"; cf. 5.8.*

⁴Thus said the LORD
To the House of Israel:
Seek Me, and you will live.
⁵Do not seek Bethel,
Nor go to Gilgal,
Nor cross overᵃ to Beer-sheba;
For Gilgal shall go into exile,
And Bethel shall become a delusion.
⁶Seek the LORD, and you will live,
ᵇ⁻Else He will rush like fire upon⁻ᵇ the House of Joseph
And consume Bethelᶜ with none to quench it.

⁷[Ah,] you who turn justice into wormwood
And hurl righteousness to the ground!
[Seek the LORD,]
⁸Who made the Pleiades and Orion,
Who turns deep darkness into dawn
And darkens day into night,
Who summons the waters of the sea
And pours them out upon the earth—
His name is the LORD!
⁹ᵇ⁻It is He who hurls destruction upon strongholds,
So that ruin comes upon fortresses!⁻ᵇ

¹⁰They hate the arbiter in the gate,
And detest him whose plea is just.
¹¹Assuredly,
Because you ᵇ⁻impose a tax⁻ᵇ on the poor
And exact from him a levy of grain,
You have built houses of hewn stone,
But you shall not live in them;
You have planted delightful vineyards,
But shall not drink their wine.
¹²For I have noted how many are your crimes,
And how countless your sins—
You enemies of the righteous,

ᵃ I.e., into Judah; cf. 1 Kings 19.3.
ᵇ⁻ᵇ Meaning of Heb. uncertain.
ᶜ Septuagint reads "the House of Israel."

You takers of bribes,
You who subvert in the gate
The cause of the needy!

¹³Assuredly,
At such a time the prudent man keeps silent,
For it is an evil time.

¹⁴Seek good and not evil,
That you may live,
And that the LORD, the God of Hosts,
May truly be with you,
As you think.
¹⁵Hate evil and love good,
And establish justice in the gate;
Perhaps the LORD, the God of Hosts,
Will be gracious to the remnant of Joseph.

¹⁶Assuredly,
Thus said the LORD,
My Lord, the God of Hosts:
In every square there shall be lamenting,
In every street cries of "Ah, woe!"
And the farm hand shall be
Called to mourn,
And those skilled in wailing
To lament;
¹⁷For there shall be lamenting
In every vineyard, too,
When I pass through your midst

                                    —said the LORD.

¹⁸Ah, you who wish
For the day of the LORD!
Why should you want
The day of the LORD?
It shall be darkness, not light!
¹⁹—As if a man should run from a lion

And be attacked by a bear;
Or if he got indoors,
Should lean his hand on the wall
And be bitten by a snake!
20Surely the day of the LORD shall be
Not light, but darkness,
Blackest night without a glimmer.

21I loathe, I spurn your festivals,
I am not appeased by your solemn assemblies.
22If you offer Me burnt offerings—or your meal offerings—
I will not accept them;
I will pay no heed
To your gifts of fatlings.
23Spare Me the sound of your hymns,
And let Me not hear the music of your lutes.
24But let justice well up like water,
Righteousness like an unfailing stream.
25Did you offer sacrifice and oblation to Me
Those forty years in the wilderness,
O House of Israel?

26dAnd you shall carry off your "king"—
Sikkuthe and Kiyyun,e
The images you have made for yourselves
Of your astral deity—
27As I drive you into exile beyond Damascus
—Said the LORD, whose name is God of Hosts.f

6

Ah, you who are at ease in Ziona
And confident on the hill of Samaria,
You notables of the leading nation
On whom the House of Israel b-pin their hopes:-b
2Cross over to Calneh and see,
Go from there to Great Hamath,
And go down to Gath of the Philistines:
Are [you] better than those kingdoms,

---

d Vv. 26–27 would read well after 6.14.
e Two Akkadian names applied to Saturn, here deliberately pointed with the vowels of Heb. shiqquṣ,
"detestable thing."
f I.e., who is Lord of all the astral bodies.

a Emendation yields "Joseph," cf. v. 6, and 5.6, 15, where "Joseph" denotes the northern kingdom.
b-b Taking ba l- as synonymous with ba 'ad; see Isa. 45.24 and note i-i.

ᶜ-Or is their territory larger than yours?-ᶜ
³ᵈ-Yet you ward off [the thought of] a day of woe
And convene a session of lawlessness. -ᵈ
⁴They lie on ivory beds,
Lolling on their couches,
Feasting on lambs from the flock
And on calves from the stalls.
⁵ᵈ-They hum snatches of song
To the tune of the lute—
They account themselves musicians-ᵈ like David.
⁶They drink [straight] from the wine bowls
And anoint themselves with the choicest oils—
But they are not concerned about the ruin of Joseph.
⁷Assuredly, right soon
They shall head the column of exiles;
They shall loll no more at festive meals.

⁸My Lord GOD swears by Himself:
I loathe ᶜ-the Pride of Jacob,-ᶜ
And I detest his fortresses.
I will declare forfeit city and inhabitants alike
                    —declares the LORD, the God of Hosts.
⁹If ten people are left in one house, they shall die. ¹⁰ᵈ-And if someone's kinsman—who is to burn incense for him—comes to carry the remains out of a house,-ᵈ and he calls to the one at the rear of the house, "Are there any alive besides you?" he will answer, "No, none." And he will say, "Hush!"—so that no one may utter the name of the LORD.
¹¹For the LORD will command,
And the great house shall be smashed to bits,
And the little house to splinters.

¹²Can horses gallop on a rock?
ᶠ-Can it be plowed with oxen?-ᶠ
Yet you have turned justice into poison weed
And the fruit of righteousness to wormwood.
¹³[Ah,] those who are so happy about Lo-dabar,ᵍ

ᶜ⁻ᶜ *Emendation yields "Or is your territory larger than theirs?"*
ᵈ⁻ᵈ *Meaning of Heb. uncertain.*
ᵉ⁻ᵉ *A poetic designation of the northern kingdom.*
ᶠ⁻ᶠ *Meaning of Heb. uncertain; emendation yields "Can one plow the sea with oxen?"*
ᵍ *Two towns east of the Jordan recovered for Israel by Jeroboam II (see 2 Kings 14.25). For Lo-dabar, cf. 2 Sam. 9.4, 5; 17.27; for Karnaim, cf. Gen. 14.5.*

Who exult, "By our might
We have captured Karnaim"!ᵍ
¹⁴But I, O House of Israel,
Will raise up a nation against you
       —declares the LORD, the God of Hosts—
Who will harass you from Lebo-Hamath
To the Wadi Arabah.

7 This is what my Lord GOD showed me: He was creating [a plague of] locusts at the time when the late-sown crops were beginning to sprout—ᵃ⁻the late-sown crops after the king's reaping.⁻ᵃ ²When it had finished devouring the herbage in the land, I said, "O Lord GOD, pray forgive. How will Jacob survive? He is so small." ³The LORD relented concerning this. "It shall not come to pass," said the LORD.

⁴This is what the Lord GOD showed me: Lo, my Lord GOD was summoning ᵇ⁻to contend by⁻ᵇ fire which consumed the Great Deep and was consuming the fields. ⁵I said, "Oh, Lord GOD, refrain! How will Jacob survive? He is so small." ⁶The LORD relented concerning this. "That shall not come to pass, either," said my Lord GOD.

⁷This is what He showed me: He was standing on a wall ᶜ⁻checked with a plumb line⁻ᶜ and He was holding a plumb line.ᵈ ⁸And the LORD asked me, "What do you see, Amos?" "A plumb line,"ᵈ I replied. And my Lord declared, "I am going to apply a plumb lineᵈ to My people Israel; I will pardon them no more. ⁹The shrines of Isaac shall be laid waste, and the sanctuaries of Israel reduced to ruins; and I will turn upon the House of Jeroboam with the sword."

¹⁰Amaziah, the priest of Bethel, sent this message to King Jeroboam of Israel: "Amos is conspiring against you within the House of Israel. The country cannot endure the things he is saying. ¹¹For Amos has said, 'Jeroboam shall die by the sword, and Israel shall be exiled from its soil.' "

¹²Amaziah also said to Amos, "Seer, off with you to the land of Judah! ᵉ⁻Earn your living⁻ᵉ there, and do your prophesying there. ¹³But don't ever prophesy again at Bethel; for it is a king's sanctuary and a royal palace." ¹⁴Amos answered Amaziah: "I am not a prophet,ᶠ and I am not

---

ᵃ⁻ᵃ *Meaning of Heb. uncertain. The king's reaping of fodder apparently occurred near the end of the rainy season, and whatever the locust destroyed after that could not be replaced for another year.*

ᵇ⁻ᵇ *Emendation yields "flaming."*

ᶜ⁻ᶜ *Or "destined for the pickax"; meaning of Heb. uncertain.*

ᵈ *Or "pickax"; meaning of Heb. uncertain.*

ᵉ⁻ᵉ *Lit. "eat bread."*

ᶠ *I.e., by profession.*

a prophet's disciple. I am a cattle breeder[g] and a tender of sycamore figs. [15]But the LORD took me away from following the flock, and the LORD said to me, 'Go, prophesy to My people Israel.' [16]And so, hear the word of the LORD. You say I must not prophesy about the House of Israel or preach about the House of Isaac; [17]but this, I swear, is what the LORD said: Your wife shall [h-]play the harlot[-h] in the town, your sons and daughters shall fall by the sword, and your land shall be divided up with a measuring line. And you yourself shall die on unclean soil;[i] for Israel shall be exiled from its soil."

8 This is what my Lord GOD showed me: There was a basket of figs.[a] [2]He said, "What do you see, Amos?" "A basket of figs," I replied. And the LORD said to me: "The [b-]hour of doom[-b] has come for My people Israel; I will not pardon them again. [3]And the singing women of the palace shall howl on that day—declares my Lord GOD:

> So many corpses
> Left lying everywhere!
> Hush!"

[4]Listen to this, you [c-]who devour the needy, annihilating the poor of the land,[-c] [5]saying, "If only the new moon were over, so that we could sell grain; the sabbath, so that we could offer wheat for sale, [d-]using an *ephah* that is too small, and a shekel that is too big,[-d] tilting a dishonest scale, [6]and selling grain refuse as grain! We will buy the poor for silver, the needy for a pair of sandals." [7]The LORD swears by[e] the Pride of Jacob: "I will never forget any of their doings."

> [8]Shall not the earth shake for this
> And all that dwell on it mourn?
> Shall it not all rise like the Nile
> And surge and subside like the Nile of Egypt?
> [9]And in that day

> > —declares my Lord GOD—

> I will make the sun set at noon,
> I will darken the earth on a sunny day.
> [10]I will turn your festivals into mourning

---

g *Meaning of Heb. uncertain; emendation yields "sheep breeder"; cf. the next verse and 1.1.*
h-h *Emendation yields "be ravished"; cf. Lam. 5.11.*
i *Cf. Hos. 9.3 and note.*

a *Heb. qayiṣ, lit. "summer fruit."*
b-b *Heb. qeṣ.*
c-c *Emendation yields "who on every new moon devour the needy, and on every sabbath the humble of the land"; cf. v. 5.*
d-d *Giving short measures of grain, but using oversize weights for the silver received in payment.*
e *Or "concerning"; cf. 6.8 with note.*

And all your songs into dirges;
I will put sackcloth on all loins
And tonsures on every head.
I will make it[f] mourn as for an only child,
All[g] of it as on a bitter day.

[11]A time is coming—declares my Lord GOD—when I will send a famine upon the land: not a hunger for bread or a thirst for water, but for hearing the words of the LORD. [12]Men shall wander from [h]sea to sea[h] and from north to east to seek the word of the LORD, but they shall not find it.

[13]In that day, the beautiful maidens and the young men shall faint with thirst—

[14]Those who swear by the guilt of Samaria,
Saying, "As your god lives, Dan,"[i]
And "As the way to Beer-sheba lives"[j]—
They shall fall to rise no more.

9 I saw my LORD standing by the altar, and He said: [a]Strike the capitals so that the thresholds quake, and make an end of the first of them all.[a] And I will slay the last of them with the sword; not one of them shall escape, and not one of them shall survive.

[2]If they burrow down to Sheol,
From there My hand shall take them;
And if they ascend to heaven,
From there I will bring them down.
[3]If they hide on the top of Carmel,
There I will search them out and seize them;
And if they conceal themselves from My sight
At the bottom of the sea,
There I will command
The serpent to bite them.
[4]And if they go into captivity
Before their enemies,
There I will command

---

[f] *I.e., the earth; cf. vv. 8 and 9d.*
[g] *Lit. "the end."*
[h-h] *Emendation yields "south to west."*
[i] *See 1 Kings 12.28–29.*
[j] *See 5.5 with note.*

[a-a] *Meaning of Heb. uncertain.*

The sword to slay them.
I will fix My eye on them for evil
And not for good.

⁵It is my Lord the GOD of Hosts
At whose touch the earth trembles
And all who dwell on it mourn,
And all of it swells like the Nile
And subsides like the Nile of Egypt;
⁶Who built His chambers in heaven
And founded His vault on the earth,
Who summons the waters of the sea
And pours them over the land—
His name is the LORD.

⁷To Me, O Israelites, you are
Just like the Ethiopians

          —declares the LORD.

True, I brought Israel up
From the land of Egypt,
But also the Philistines from Caphtor
And the Arameans from Kir.
⁸Behold, the Lord GOD has His eye
Upon the sinful kingdom:
I will wipe it off
The face of the earth!

But, I will not wholly wipe out
The House of Jacob

          —declares the LORD.

⁹For I will give the order
And shake the House of Israel—
Through all the nations—
As one shakes [sand] in a sieve,ᵇ
And not a pebble falls to the ground.
¹⁰All the sinners of My people
Shall perish by the sword,
Who boast,

ᵇ *A coarse sieve used for cleansing grain of straw and stones, or sand of pebbles and shells.*

"Never shall the evil
Overtake us or come near us."

[11]In that day,
I will set up again the fallen booth of David:
I will mend its breaches and set up its ruins anew.
I will build it firm as in the days of old,
[12c-]So that they shall possess the rest of Edom
And all the nations once attached to My name[-c]
—declares the LORD who will bring this to pass.
[13]A time is coming

—declares the LORD—

When the plowman shall meet the reaper,[d]
And the treader of grapes
Him who holds the [bag of] seed;
When the mountains shall drip wine
And all the hills shall wave [with grain].

[14]I will restore My people Israel.
They shall rebuild ruined cities and inhabit them;
They shall plant vineyards and drink their wine;
They shall till gardens and eat their fruits.
[15]And I will plant them upon their soil,
Nevermore to be uprooted
From the soil I have given them

—said the LORD your God.

c-c *I.e., the House of David shall reestablish its authority over the nations that were ruled by David.*
d *Cf. Lev. 26.5.*

OBADIAH

1 The prophecy of Obadiah.

We have received tidings from the LORD,
And an envoy has been sent out among the nations:
"Up! Let us rise up against her for battle."

Thus said my Lord GOD concerning Edom:
²I will make you least among nations,
You shall be most despised.
³Your arrogant heart has seduced you,
You who dwell in clefts of the rock,
In your lofty abode.
You think in your heart,
"Who can pull me down to earth?"
⁴Should you nest as high as the eagle,
Should your eyrie be lodged 'mong the stars,
Even from there I will pull you down

—declares the LORD.

⁵If thieves were to come to you,
Marauders by night,
They would steal no more than they needed.
If vintagers came to you,
They would surely leave some gleanings.
How utterly you are destroyed!
⁶How thoroughly rifled is Esau,
How ransacked his hoards!
⁷All your allies turned you back
At the frontier;
Your own confederates

Have duped and overcome you;
[Those who ate] your bread
Have planted snares under you.

He is bereft of understanding.
⁸In that day

—declares the LORD—

I will make the wise vanish from Edom,
Understanding from Esau's mount.
⁹Your warriors shall lose heart, O Teman,
And not a man on Esau's mount
Shall survive the slaughter.

¹⁰For the outrage to your brother Jacob,
Disgrace shall engulf you,
And you shall perish forever.
¹¹On that day when you stood aloof,
When aliens carried off his goods,
When foreigners entered his gates
And cast lots for Jerusalem,
You were as one of them.

¹²ᵃ⁻How could youᵃ gaze with glee
On your brother that day,
On his day of calamity!
How could you gloat
Over the people of Judah
On that day of ruin!
How could you loudly jeer
On a day of anguish!
¹³How could you enter the gate of My people
On its day of disaster,
Gaze in glee with the others
On its misfortune
On its day of disaster,
And lay hands on its wealth
On its day of disaster!
¹⁴How could you stand at the passesᵇ

ᵃ⁻ᵃ *Lit. "Do not," and so through v. 14.*
ᵇ *Meaning of Heb. uncertain.*

To cut down its fugitives!
How could you betray those who fled
On that day of anguish!
¹⁵As you did, so shall it be done to you;
Your conduct shall be requited.

Yea, against all nations
The day of the LORD is at hand.
¹⁶That same cup that you^c drank on My Holy Mount
Shall all nations drink evermore,^d
Drink till their speech grows thick,
And they become as though they had never been.
¹⁷But on Zion's mount a remnant shall survive,
And it shall be holy.^e
The House of Jacob shall dispossess
Those who dispossessed them.
¹⁸The House of Jacob shall be fire,
And the House of Joseph flame,
And the House of Esau shall be straw;
They shall burn it and devour it,
And no survivor shall be left of the House of Esau
——for the LORD has spoken.

¹⁹^fThus they shall possess the Negeb and Mount Esau as well, the Shephelah and Philistia. They shall possess the Ephraimite country and the district of Samaria,^g and Benjamin^h along with Gilead. ²⁰And that exiled force of Israelites [shall possess] what belongs to the Phoenicians as far as Zarephath,^i while the Jerusalemite exile community of Sepharad^j shall possess the towns of the Negeb. ²¹For ^k-liberators shall march up-^k on Mount Zion to wreak judgment on Mount Esau; and dominion shall be the LORD's.

---

c *I.e., the Israelites.*
d *Emendation yields "at My hand," cf. Isa. 51.17; Jer. 25.15; Ps. 75.9.*
e *I.e., inviolate; cf. Jer. 2.3.*
f *Meaning of parts of vv. 19–21 uncertain.*
g *After the exile of the northern tribes, the city and district of Samaria were occupied mainly by non-Israelites.*
h *Emendation yields "the land of the Ammonites."*
i *A town in southern Phoenicia; see 1 Kings 17.9.*
j *Probably Asia Minor, called Saparda in Persian cuneiform inscriptions.*
k-k *Several ancient versions read, "they [the exiles from Jerusalem named in the preceding verse] shall march up victorious."*

JONAH

1 The word of the LORD came to Jonah[a] son of Amittai: 2Go at once to Nineveh, that great city, and proclaim judgment upon it; for their wickedness has come before Me.

3Jonah, however, started out to flee to Tarshish from the LORD's service. He went down to Joppa and found a ship going to Tarshish. He paid the fare and went aboard to sail with the others to Tarshish, away from the service of the LORD.

4But the LORD cast a mighty wind upon the sea, and such a great tempest came upon the sea that the ship was in danger of breaking up. 5In their fright, the sailors cried out, each to his own god; and they flung the ship's cargo overboard to make it lighter for them. Jonah, meanwhile, had gone down into the hold of the vessel where he lay down and fell asleep. 6The captain went over to him and cried out, "How can you be sleeping so soundly! Up, call upon your god! Perhaps the god will be kind to us and we will not perish."

7The men said to one another, "Let us cast lots and find out on whose account this misfortune has come upon us." They cast lots and the lot fell on Jonah. 8They said to him, "Tell us, you who have brought this misfortune upon us, what is your business? Where have you come from? What is your country, and of what people are you?" 9"I am a Hebrew," he replied. "I worship the LORD, the God of Heaven, who made both sea and land." 10The men were greatly terrified, and they asked him, "What have you done?" And when the men learned that he was fleeing from the service of the LORD—for so he told them—11they said to him, "What must we do to you to make the sea calm around us?" For the sea was growing more and more stormy. 12He answered, "Heave me overboard, and the sea will calm down for you; for I know that this terrible storm came upon you on my account." 13Nevertheless, the men rowed hard to regain the shore, but they could not, for the sea was growing

---

[a] *Mentioned in 2 Kings 14.25.*

more and more stormy about them. ¹⁴Then they cried out to the LORD: "Oh, please, LORD, do not let us perish on account of this man's life. Do not hold us guilty of killing an innocent person! For You, O LORD, by Your will, have brought this about." ¹⁵And they heaved Jonah overboard, and the sea stopped raging.

¹⁶The men feared the LORD greatly; they offered a sacrifice to the LORD and they made vows.

2 The LORD provided a huge fish to swallow Jonah; and Jonah remained in the fish's belly three days and three nights. ²Jonah prayed to the LORD his God from the belly of the fish. ³He said:

> In my trouble I called to the LORD,
> And He answered me;
> From the belly of Sheol I cried out,
> And You heard my voice.
> ⁴You cast me into the depths,
> Into the heart of the sea,
> The floods engulfed me;
> All Your breakers and billows
> Swept over me.
> ⁵I thought I was driven away
> Out of Your sight:
> Would I ever gaze again
> Upon Your holy Temple?
> ⁶The waters closed in over me,
> The deep engulfed me.
> Weeds twined around my head.
> ⁷I sank to the base of the mountains;
> The bars of the earth closed upon me forever.
> Yet You brought my life up from the pit,
> O LORD my God!
> ⁸When my life was ebbing away,
> I called the LORD to mind;
> And my prayer came before You,
> Into Your holy Temple.

⁹They who cling to empty folly
Forsake their own welfare,ᵃ
¹⁰But I, with loud thanksgiving,
Will sacrifice to You;
What I have vowed I will perform.
Deliverance is the LORD's!

¹¹The LORD commanded the fish, and it spewed Jonah out upon dry land.

3 The word of the LORD came to Jonah a second time: ²"Go at once to Nineveh, that great city, and proclaim to it what I tell you." ³Jonah went at once to Nineveh in accordance with the LORD's command.

Nineveh was ᵃ⁻an enormously large cityᵃ a three days' walk across. ⁴Jonah started out and made his way into the city the distance of one day's walk, and proclaimed: "Forty days more, and Nineveh shall be overthrown!"

⁵The people of Nineveh believed God. They proclaimed a fast, and great and small alike put on sackcloth. ⁶When the news reached the king of Nineveh, he rose from his throne, took off his robe, put on sackcloth, and sat in ashes. ⁷And he had the word cried through Nineveh: "By decree of the king and his nobles: No man or beast—of flock or herd—shall taste anything! They shall not graze, and they shall not drink water! ⁸They shall be covered with sackcloth—man and beast—and shall cry mightily to God. Let everyone turn back from his evil ways and from the injustice of which he is guilty. ⁹Who knows but that God may turn and relent? He may turn back from His wrath, so that we do not perish."

¹⁰God saw what they did, how they were turning back from their evil ways. And God renounced the punishment He had planned to bring upon them, and did not carry it out.

4 This displeased Jonah greatly, and he was grieved. ²He prayed to the LORD, saying, "O LORD! Isn't this just what I said when I was still in my own country? That is why I fled beforehand to Tarshish. For I know that You are a compassionate and gracious God, slow to anger, abounding

---

ᵃ Meaning of Heb. uncertain.

ᵃ⁻ᵃ Lit. "a large city of God."

in kindness, renouncing punishment. ³Please, LORD, take my life, for I would rather die than live." ⁴The LORD replied, "Are you that deeply grieved?"

⁵Now Jonah had left the city and found a place east of the city. He made a booth there and sat under it in the shade, until he should see what happened to the city. ⁶The LORD God provided a ricinus plant,ᵃ which grew up over Jonah, to provide shade for his head and save him from discomfort. Jonah was very happy about the plant. ⁷But the next day at dawn God provided a worm, which attacked the plant so that it withered. ⁸And when the sun rose, God provided a sultryᵇ east wind; the sun beat down on Jonah's head, and he became faint. He begged for death, saying, "I would rather die than live." ⁹Then God said to Jonah, "Are you so deeply grieved about the plant?" "Yes," he replied, "so deeply that I want to die."

¹⁰Then the LORD said: "You cared about the plant, which you did not work for and which you did not grow, which appeared overnight and perished overnight. ¹¹And should not I care about Nineveh, that great city, in which there are more than a hundred and twenty thousand persons who do not yet know their right hand from their left, and many beasts as well!"ᶜ

ᵃ *Meaning of Heb. uncertain; others "gourd."*
ᵇ *Meaning of Heb. uncertain.*
ᶜ *Infants and beasts are not held responsible for their actions.*

MICAH

1 The word of the LORD that came to Micah the Morashtite, who prophesied concerning Samaria and Jerusalem in the reigns of Kings Jotham, Ahaz, and Hezekiah of Judah.

> ²Listen, all you peoples,
> Give heed, O earth, and all it holds;
> And let my Lord GOD be your accuser—
> My Lord from His holy abode.
> ³For lo! the LORD
> Is coming forth from His dwelling-place,
> He will come down and stride
> Upon the heights of the earth.
> ⁴The mountains shall melt under Him
> And the valleys burst open—
> Like wax before fire,
> Like water cascading down a slope.

> ⁵All this is for the transgression of Jacob,
> And for the sins of the House of Israel.
> What is the transgression of Jacob
> But Samaria,
> And what the shrinesᵃ of Judah
> But Jerusalem?
> ⁶So I will turn Samaria
> Into a ruin in open country,
> Into ground for planting vineyards;
> For I will tumble her stones into the valley
> And lay her foundations bare.
> ⁷All her sculptured images shall be smashed,

ᵃ Emendation yields "sins."

And all her harlot's wealth be burned,
And I will make a waste heap of all her idols,
For they were amassed from fees for harlotry,
And they shall become harlots' fees again.

⁸Because of this I will lament and wail;
I will go stripped and naked!
I will lament as sadly as the jackals,
As mournfully as the ostriches.
⁹For her[b] wound is incurable,
It has reached Judah,
It has spread to the gate of my people,
To Jerusalem.

¹⁰[c]Tell it not in Gath,
Refrain from weeping;[d]
In Beth-leaphrah,
Strew dust[e] over your [head].
¹¹Pass on, inhabitants of Shaphir!
Did not the inhabitants of Zaanan
Have to go forth naked in shame?
There is lamentation in Beth-ezel—
It will withdraw its support from you.
¹²Though the inhabitants of Maroth
Hoped for good,
Yet disaster from the LORD descended
Upon the gate of Jerusalem.
¹³Hitch the steeds to the chariot,
Inhabitant of Lachish!
It is the beginning
Of Fair Zion's guilt;
Israel's transgressions
Can be traced to you!
¹⁴Truly, you must give a farewell gift
To Moresheth-gath.
[f]The houses of Achzib are[f]
To the kings of Israel

---

b I.e., the nation's.
c Meaning of much of vv. 10–13 uncertain. They may refer to the transfer of part of western Judah to Philistine rule by Sennacherib of Assyria in the year 701 B.C.E.
d So that enemies may not gloat; cf. 2 Sam. 1.20.
e Heb. 'aphar, a play on Beth-leaphrah; vv. 10–15 contain several similar puns.
f-f Emendation yields "Fair Achzib is."

Like a spring that fails.
15A dispossessor will I bring to you
Who dwell in Mareshah;
At Adullam the glory
Of Israel shall set.
16gShear off your hair and make yourself bald
For the children you once delighted in;
Make yourself as bald as a vulture,
For they have been banished from you.

2

Ah, those who plan iniquity
And design evil on their beds;
When morning dawns, they do it,
For they have the power.
2They covet fields, and seize them;
Houses, and take them away.
They defraud men of their homes,
And people of their land.

3Assuredly, thus said the LORD: I am planning such a misfortune against this clan that you will not be able to free your necks from it. You will not be able to walk erect; it will be such a time of disaster.

4In that day,
One shall recite a poem about you,
And utter a bitter lament,
And shall say:
a-"My people's portion changes hands;
How it slips away from me!
Our field is allotted to a rebel.b
We are utterly ravaged."-a
5Truly, none of you
Shall cast a lot cordc
In the assembly of the LORD!

6"Stop preaching!" they preach.
"That's no way to preach;
a-Shame shall not overtake [us].

g *A common rite of mourning; cf. Jer. 7.29.*

a-a *Meaning of Heb. uncertain.*
b *Emendation yields "ravager."*
c *On a piece of land, thus acquiring title to it; cf. Josh. 18.6 and Ps. 16.6.*

⁷Is the House of Jacob condemned?⁻ᵃ
Is the LORD's patience short?
Is such His practice?"

To be sure, My words are friendly
To those who walk in rectitude;
⁸But ᵈ⁻an enemy arises against⁻ᵈ My people.
You strip the mantle ᵉ⁻with the cloak⁻ᵉ
Off such as pass unsuspecting,
ᵃ⁻Who are turned away from war.⁻ᵃ
⁹You drive the women of My people away
From their pleasant homes;
You deprive their infants
Of My glory forever.
¹⁰Up and depart!
This is no resting place
ᵃ⁻Because of [your] defilement.
Terrible destruction shall befall.⁻ᵃ

¹¹If a man were to go about uttering
Windy, baseless falsehoods:
"I'll preach to you in favor of wine and liquor"—
He would be a preacher [acceptable] to that people.

¹²ᶠI will assemble Jacob, all of you;
I will bring together the remnant of Israel;
I will make them all like sheep ᵍ⁻of Bozrah,⁻ᵍ
Like a flock inside its penᵃ—
They will be noisy with people.
¹³One who makes a breach
Goes before them;
They enlarge it to a gate
And leave by it.
Their king marches before them,
The LORD at their head.

ᵈ⁻ᵈ *Meaning of Heb. uncertain; emendation yields "you arise as enemies against."*
ᵉ⁻ᵉ *Meaning of Heb. uncertain; emendation yields "off peaceful folk."*
ᶠ *Vv. 12–13 may be an example of such "acceptable" preaching.*
ᵍ⁻ᵍ *Emendation yields "in a fold [Arabic sīrah]."*

3 I said:

Listen, you rulers of Jacob,
You chiefs of the House of Israel!
For you ought to know what is right,
²ᵃBut you hate good and love evil.
³You have devoured My people's flesh;
You have flayed the skin off them,
And their flesh off their bones.
ᵇ⁻And after tearing their skins off them,
And their flesh off their bones,⁻ᵇ
And breaking their bones to bits,
You have cut it up ᶜ⁻as into⁻ᶜ a pot,
Like meat in a caldron.
⁴Someday they shall cry out to the LORD,
But He will not answer them;
At that time He will hide His face from them,
In accordance with the wrongs they have done.

⁵Thus said the LORD to the prophets
Who lead My people astray,
Who cry "Peace!"
When they have something to chew,
But launch a war on him
Who fails to fill their mouths:
⁶Assuredly,
It shall be night for you
So that you cannot prophesy,
And it shall be dark for you
So that you cannot divine;
The sun shall set on the prophets,
And the day shall be darkened for them.
⁷The seers shall be shamed
And the diviners confounded;
They shall cover their upper lips,ᵈ

ᵃ *Syntax of vv. 2–3 uncertain.*
ᵇ⁻ᵇ *Brought down from v. 2 for clarity.*
ᶜ⁻ᶜ *Meaning of Heb. uncertain; Septuagint and Syriac read "like flesh in."*
ᵈ *As a sign of mourning; cf. Ezek. 24.17, 22; Lev. 13.45.*

Because no response comes from God.
⁸But I,
I am filled with strength by the spirit of the LORD,
And with judgment and courage,
To declare to Jacob his transgressions
And to Israel his sin.

⁹Hear this, you rulers of the House of Jacob,
You chiefs of the House of Israel,
Who detest justice
And make crooked all that is straight,
¹⁰Who build Zion with crime,
Jerusalem with iniquity!
¹¹Her rulers judge for gifts,
Her priests give rulings for a fee,
And her prophets divine for pay;
Yet they rely upon the LORD, saying,
"The LORD is in our midst;
No calamity shall overtake us."
¹²Assuredly, because of you
Zion shall be plowed as a field,
And Jerusalem shall become heaps of ruins,
And the Temple Mount
A shrine in the woods.

4 ᵃIn the days to come,
The Mount of the LORD's House shall stand
Firm above the mountains;
And it shall tower above the hills.
The peoples shall gaze on it with joy,
²And the many nations shall go and shall say:
"Come,
Let us go up to the Mount of the LORD,
To the House of the God of Jacob;
That He may instruct us in His ways,
And that we may walk in His paths."
For instruction shall come forthᵇ from Zion,

ᵃ For vv. 1–3 cf. Isa. 2.2–4.
ᵇ I.e., oracles will be obtainable.

The word of the LORD from Jerusalem.
³Thus He will judge among the many peoples,
And arbitrate for the multitude of nations,
However distant;
And they shall beat their swords into plowsharesᶜ
And their spears into pruning hooks.
Nation shall not take up
Sword against nation;
They shall never again knowᵈ war;
⁴But every man shall sit
Under his grapevine or fig tree
With no one to disturb him.
For it was the LORD of Hosts who spoke.
⁵Though all the peoples walk
Each in the names of its gods,
We will walk
In the name of the LORD our God
Forever and ever.

⁶In that day

—declares the LORD—

I will assemble the lame [sheep]
And will gather the outcast
And those I have treated harshly;
⁷And I will turn the lame into a remnant
And the expelledᵉ into a populous nation.
And the LORD will reign over them on Mount Zion
Now and for evermore.

⁸And you, O Migdal-eder,ᶠ
ᵍ⁻Outpost of Fair Zion,
It shall come to you:⁻ᵍ
The former monarchy shall return—
The kingship of ʰ⁻Fair Jerusalem.⁻ʰ

⁹Now why do you utter such cries?
Is there no king in you,
Have your advisors perished,

ᶜ More exactly, the iron points with which wooden plows were tipped.
ᵈ Cf. Judg. 3.2.
ᵉ Meaning of Heb. uncertain; emendation yields "weaklings"; cf. Ezek. 34.4.
ᶠ Apparently near Bethlehem; see Gen. 35.19–21.
ᵍ⁻ᵍ Meaning of Heb. uncertain.
ʰ⁻ʰ Emendation yields "the House of Israel"; cf. 5.1–2.

That you have been seized by writing
Like a woman in travail?
¹⁰Writhe and scream,ᵍ Fair Zion,
Like a woman in travail!
For now you must leave the city
And dwell in the country—
And you will reach Babylon.
There you shall be saved,
There the LORD will redeem you
From the hands of your foes.
¹¹Indeed, many nations
Have assembled against you
Who think, "Let our eye
ᵍ-Obscenely gaze-ᵍ on Zion."
¹²But they do not know
The design of the LORD,
They do not divine His intent:
He has gathered them
Like cut grain to the threshing floor.
¹³Up and thresh, Fair Zion!
For I will give you horns of iron
And provide you with hoofs of bronze,
And you will crush the many peoples.
Youⁱ will devote their riches to the LORD,
Their wealth to the Lord of all the earth.

¹⁴Now you gash yourself ᵍ-in grief.-ᵍ
They have laid siege to us;
They strike the ruler of Israel
On the cheek with a staff.

5 And you, O Bethlehem of Ephrath,ᵃ
Least among the clans of Judah,
From you one shall come forth
To rule Israel for Me—
One whose origin is from of old,
From ancient times.

ⁱ *Heb. -ti serves here as the ending of the second-person singular feminine; cf. Judg. 5.7 and note; Jer. 2.20; etc.*

ᵃ *The clan to which the Bethlehemites belonged; see 1 Sam. 17.12; Ruth 1.2; 4.11.*

2b-Truly, He will leave them [helpless]
Until she who is to bear has borne;c
Then the rest of his countrymen
Shall return to the children of Israel.-b
3He shall stand and shepherd
By the might of the LORD,
By the power of the name
Of the LORD his God,
And they shall dwell [secure].
For lo, he shall wax great
To the ends of the earth;
4And that shall afford safety.
Should Assyria invade our land
And tread upon our fortresses,d
We will set up over ite seven shepherds,
Eight princes of men,
5Who will shepherd Assyria's land with swords,
The land of Nimrod f-in its gates.-f
Thus he will deliver [us]
From Assyria, should it invade our land,
And should it trample our country.

6The remnant of Jacob shall be,
In the midst of the many peoples,
Like dew from the LORD,
Like droplets on grass—
Which do not look to any man
Nor place their hope in mortals.

7The remnant of Jacob
Shall be among the nations,
In the midst of the many peoples,
Like a lion among beasts of the wild,
Like a fierce lion among flocks of sheep,
Which tramples wherever it goes
And rends, with none to deliver.
8Your hand shall prevail over your foes,
And all your enemies shall be cut down!

---

b-b *Meaning of Heb. uncertain.*
c *I.e., a ruler, shepherd (v. 3), to deliver Israel from the Assyrians (vv. 4–5).*
d *Septuagint and Syriac read "soil"; cf. v. 5.*
e *I.e., Assyria.*
f-f *Emendation yields "with drawn blades"; cf. Ps. 37.14; 55.22.*

⁹In that day

—declares the LORD—

I will destroy the horses in your midst
And wreck your chariots.
¹⁰I will destroy the cities of your land
And demolish all your fortresses.
¹¹I will destroy the sorcery you practice,
And you shall have no more soothsayers.
¹²I will destroy your idols
And the sacred pillars in your midst;
And no more shall you bow down
To the work of your hands.
¹³I will tear down the sacred posts in your midst
And destroy your cities.ᵍ
¹⁴In anger and wrath
Will I wreak retribution
On the nationsʰ that have not obeyed.

6
Hear what the LORD is saying:
Come, present [My] case before the mountains,
And let the hills hear you pleading.

²Hear, you mountains, the case of the LORD—
ᵃ-You firm-ᵃ foundations of the earth!
For the LORD has a case against His people,
He has a suit against Israel.

³"My people!
What wrong have I done you?
What hardship have I caused you?
Testify against Me.
⁴In fact,
I brought you up from the land of Egypt,
I redeemed you from the house of bondage,
And I sent before you
Moses, Aaron, and Miriam.

ᵍ *Emendation yields "idols."*
ʰ *Emendation yields "arrogant."*

ᵃ-ᵃ *Emendation yields "Give ear, you."*

⁵"My people,
Remember what Balak king of Moab
Plotted against you,
And how Balaam son of Beor
Responded to him.
[Recall your passage]
From Shittim to Gilgalᵇ—
And you will recognize
The gracious acts of the LORD."

⁶With what shall I approach the LORD,
Do homage to God on high?
Shall I approach Him with burnt offerings,
With calves a year old?
⁷Would the LORD be pleased with thousands of rams,
With myriads of streams of oil?
Shall I give my first-born for my transgression,
The fruit of my body for my sins?

⁸"He has told you, O man, what is good,
And what the LORD requires of you:
Only to do justice
And to love goodness,
And ᶜ-to walk modestly with your God;-ᶜ
⁹ᵈ-Then will your name achieve wisdom."-ᵈ

Hark! The LORD
Summons the city:
ᵉ-Hear, O scepter;
For who can direct her
10   but you?-ᵉ
Will I overlook,ᶠ in the wicked man's house,
The granaries of wickedness
And the accursed short *ephah*?ᵍ
¹¹Shall heʰ be acquitted despite wicked balances
And a bag of fraudulent weights?—
¹²ⁱWhose rich men are full of lawlessness,

ᵇ *I.e., the crossing of the Jordan; see Josh. 3.1, 14—4.19.*
ᶜ⁻ᶜ *Or "It is prudent to serve your God."*
ᵈ⁻ᵈ *Emendation yields "And it is worthwhile to revere His name."*
ᵉ⁻ᵉ *Meaning of Heb. uncertain.*
ᶠ *Taking* ish *as from* nashah *"to forget"; cf. Deut. 32.18.*
ᵍ *Cf. Amos 8.4–5.*
ʰ *Heb. "I"; change of vocalization yields "Will I acquit him."*
ⁱ *This verse would read well after "city" in v. 9.*

And whose inhabitants speak treachery,
With tongues of deceit in their mouths.

¹³I, in turn, have beaten you sore,
Have stunned [you] for your sins:
¹⁴You have been eating without getting your fill,
ᶜ-And there is a gnawing at your vitals;
You have been conceiving without bearing young,-ᶜ
And what you bore I would deliver to the sword.
¹⁵You have been sowing, but have nothing to reap;
You have trod olives, but have no oil for rubbing,
And grapesʲ but have no wine to drink.
¹⁶Yet ᵏ-you have kept-ᵏ the laws of Omri,
And all the practices of the House of Ahab,
And have followed what they devised.
Therefore I will make you an object of horror
And ˡ-her inhabitants-ˡ an object of hissing;ᵐ
And you shall bear the mockery of peoples.ⁿ

7 Woe is me!ᵃ
I am become like leavings of a fig harvest,
Like gleanings when the vintage is over,
There is not a cluster to eat,
Not a ripe fig I could desire.
²The pious are vanished from the land,
None upright are left among men;
All lie in wait to commit crimes,
One traps the other in his net.
³ᵇ-They are eager to do evil:
The magistrate makes demands,
And the judge [judges] for a fee;
The rich man makes his crooked plea,
And they grant it.-ᵇ
⁴The best of them is like a prickly shrub;
The [most] upright, worse than a barrier of thorns.
ᵇ-On the day you waited for,-ᵇ your doom has come—

ʲ *Lit. "new wine."*
ᵏ⁻ᵏ *Heb. "is kept."*
ˡ⁻ˡ *I.e., those of the city of v. 9, apparently Samaria.*
ᵐ *See note at Jer. 18.16.*
ⁿ *Heb. "My people."*

ᵃ *The speaker is feminine (cf. 'elohayikh, v. 10), probably Samaria personified; cf. note l-l at 6.16.*
ᵇ⁻ᵇ *Meaning of Heb. uncertain.*

Now their confusion shall come to pass.
⁵Trust no friend,
Rely on no intimate;
Be guarded in speech
With her who lies in your bosom.
⁶For son spurns father,
Daughter rises up against mother,
Daughter-in-law against mother-in-law—
A man's own household
Are his enemies.
⁷Yet I will look to the LORD,
I will wait for the God who saves me,
My God will hear me.

⁸Do not rejoice over me,
O my enemy!ᶜ
Though I have fallen, I rise again;
Though I sit in darkness, the LORD is my light.
⁹I must bear the anger of the LORD,
Since I have sinned against Him,
Until He champions my cause
And upholds my claim.
He will let me out into the light;
I will enjoy vindication by Him.
¹⁰When my enemyᶜ sees it,
She shall be covered with shame,
She who taunts me with "Where is He,
The LORD your God?"
My eyes shall behold her [downfall];
Lo, she shall be for trampling
Like mud in the streets.
¹¹A day for mending your wallsᵈ—
That is a far-off day.
¹²This is rather a day when to you
[Tramplers] will come streaming
From Assyria and the towns of Egypt—
From [every land from] Egypt to the Euphrates,

ᶜ Heb. feminine, apparently referring to Damascus.
ᵈ To keep out tramplers (end of preceding verse); cf. Isa. 5.5; Ps. 80.13–14.

From sea to sea and from mountain to mountain—
¹³And your^e land shall become a desolation—
Because of those who dwell in it—
As the fruit of their misdeeds.

¹⁴Oh, shepherd Your people with Your staff,
Your very own flock.
May they who dwell isolated
ᶠ-In a woodland surrounded by farmland-ᶠ
Graze^g Bashan and Gilead
As in olden days.
¹⁵ʰ-I will show him-ʰ wondrous deeds
As in the days when You sallied forth from the land of Egypt.
¹⁶Let nations behold and be ashamed
Despite all their might;
Let them put hand to mouth;
Let their ears be deafened!
¹⁷Let them lick dust like snakes,
Like crawling things on the ground!
ᵇ-Let them come trembling out of their strongholds-ᵇ
To the LORD our God;
Let them fear and dread You!

¹⁸Who is a God like You,
Forgiving iniquity
And remitting transgression;
Who has not maintained His wrath forever
Against the remnant of His own people,
Because He loves graciousness!
¹⁹He will take us back in love;
He will cover up our iniquities,
You will hurl all ourⁱ sins
Into the depths of the sea.
²⁰You will keep faith with Jacob,
Loyalty to Abraham,
As You promised on oath to our fathers
In days gone by.

ᵉ *Heb. "the."*
ᶠ⁻ᶠ *I.e., the land west of the Jordan, which is represented as far less fertile than adjacent regions.*
ᵍ *Emendation yields "possess."*
ʰ⁻ʰ *Emendation yields "Show us."*
ⁱ *Heb. "their."*

NAHUM

1 A pronouncement on Nineveh: The Book of the Prophecy of Nahum the Elkoshite.

²The LORD is a passionate, avenging God;
The LORD is vengeful and fierce in wrath.
The LORD takes vengeance on His enemies,
He rages against His foes.
³The LORD is slow to anger and of great forbearance,
But the LORD does not remit all punishment.
He travels in whirlwind and storm,
And clouds are the dust on His feet.
⁴He rebukes the sea and dries it up,
And He makes all rivers fail;
Bashan and Carmel languish,
And the blossomsᵃ of Lebanon wither.
⁵The mountains quake because of Him,
And the hills melt.
The earth heavesᵇ before Him,
The world and all that dwell therein.
⁶Who can stand before His wrath?
Who can resist His fury?
His anger pours out like fire,
And rocks are shattered because of Him.
⁷The LORD is good to [those who hope in Him],
A haven on a day of distress;
He is mindful of those who seek refuge in Him.
⁸And with a sweeping flood

ᵃ Lit. "bud."
ᵇ Meaning of Heb. uncertain.

He makes an end of ᶜher place,ᶜ
And chases His enemies into darkness.
⁹Why will you plot against the LORD?
He wreaks utter destruction:
No adversaryᵈ opposes Him twice!
¹⁰ᵇFor like men besotted with drink,
They are burned up like tangled thorns,
Like straw that is thoroughly dried.ᵇ

¹¹ᵉThe base plotter
Who designed evil against the LORD
Has left you.
¹²Thus said the LORD:
ᵇ"Even as theyᶠ were full and many,
Even so are they over and gone;
As surely as I afflicted you,
I will afflict you no more."ᵇ
¹³And now
I will break off his yoke bar from you
And burst your cords apart.
¹⁴The LORD has commanded concerning him:ᵍ
ᵇNo posterity shall continue your name.ᵇ
I will do away with
The carved and graven images
In the temples of your gods;
I will make your grave
ᵇAccord with your worthlessness.ᵇ

2 Behold on the hills
The footsteps of a herald
Announcing good fortune!
"Celebrate your festivals, O Judah,
Fulfill your vows.

ᶜ⁻ᶜ *Meaning of Heb. uncertain; emendation yields "those who oppose Him."*
ᵈ *Cf. Ugaritic* srt.
ᵉ *Vv. 11–14 would read well after 2.1.*
ᶠ *I.e., the days of your affliction.*
ᵍ *Heb. "you."*

Never again shall scoundrels invade you,
They have totally vanished."

²ᵃA shatterer has come up against you.
Man the guard posts,
Watch the road;
Steady your loins,
Brace all your strength!

³For the LORD has restored ᵇ⁻the Prideᶜ of Jacob
As well as the Prideᶜ of Israel,⁻ᵇ
Though marauders have laid them waste
And ravaged their branches.

⁴His warriors' shields are painted red,
And the soldiers are clothed in crimson;
The chariots are like flaming torches,ᵈ
On the day they are made ready.
ᵉ⁻The [arrows of] cypress wood are poisoned,⁻ᵉ
⁵The chariots dash about frenzied in the fields,
They rush through the meadows.
They appear like torches,
They race like streaks of lightning.
⁶ᶠ⁻He commands his burly men;
They stumble as they advance,
They hasten up to her wall,
Where ᵍ⁻wheeled shelters⁻ᵍ are set up.⁻ᶠ
⁷ʰ⁻The floodgates are opened,
And the palace is deluged.⁻ʰ
⁸ⁱ⁻And Huzzab is exiled and carried away,⁻ⁱ
While her handmaidens ʲ⁻escort [her]⁻ʲ
As with the voices of doves,
Beating their breasts.
⁹Nineveh has been like a [placid] pool of water

ᵃ *This verse would read well after v. 3.*
ᵇ⁻ᵇ *"Jacob" refers to the northern kingdom (cf. Amos 6.8; 8.7); Israel refers to the southern kingdom,*
regarded as the remnant of Israel after the fall of the northern kingdom (cf. Mic. 1.13–15).
ᶜ *Emendation yields "vine."*
ᵈ *Understanding* peladoth *as equivalent to* lappidoth.
ᵉ⁻ᵉ *Meaning of Heb. uncertain. Emendation yields "The horsemen charge"; cf. 3.3.*
ᶠ⁻ᶠ *Meaning of Heb. uncertain.*
ᵍ⁻ᵍ *To protect the crews that swung the battering rams.*
ʰ⁻ʰ *I.e., the walls are breached and the palace is overrun.*
ⁱ⁻ⁱ *Meaning of Heb. uncertain. Emendation yields "And its mistress is led out and exiled."*
ʲ⁻ʲ *Emendation yields "moan."*

f-From earliest times;-f
Now they flee.
"Stop! Stop!"—
But none can turn them back.
10"Plunder silver! Plunder gold!"
There is no limit to the treasure;
It is a hoard of all precious objects.

11Desolation, devastation, and destruction!
Spirits sink,
Knees buckle,
All loins tremble,
All faces k-turn ashen.-k
12What has become of that lions' den,
That pasturel of great beasts,
Where lion and lion's breed walked,
And lion's cub—with none to disturb them?
13[Where is] the lion that tore victims for his cubs
And strangled for his lionesses,
And filled his lairs with prey
And his dens with mangled flesh?
14I am going to deal with you
                              —declares the LORD of Hosts:
I will burn down m-her chariots in smoke,-m
And the sword shall devour your great beasts;
I will stamp out your killings from the earth,
And the sound of your messengersn
Shall be heard no more.

3 Ah, city of crime,
Utterly treacherous,
Full of violence,
Where killing never stops!

2Crack of whip
And rattle of wheel,
Galloping steed

k-k *Meaning of Heb. uncertain; cf. note at Joel 2.6.*
l *Emendation yields "cave."*
m-m *Emendation yields "your thicket in fire."*
n *Emendation yields "devouring."*

And bounding chariot!
³Charging horsemen,
Flashing swords,
And glittering spears!
Hosts of slain
And heaps of corpses,
Dead bodies without number—
They stumble over bodies.
⁴Because of the countless harlotries of the harlot,
The winsome mistress of sorcery,
Who ensnared[a] nations with her harlotries
And peoples with her sorcery,
⁵I am going to deal with you

          —declares the LORD of Hosts.

I will lift up your skirts over your face
And display your nakedness to the nations
And your shame to kingdoms.
⁶I will throw loathsome things over you
And disfigure you
And make a spectacle of you.
⁷All who see you will recoil from you
And will say,
"Nineveh has been ravaged!"
Who will console her?
Where shall I look for
Anyone to comfort you?
⁸Were you any better than No-amon,[b]
Which sat by the Nile,
Surrounded by water—
Its rampart a river,[c]
Its wall [d-consisting of sea?-d]
⁹Populous Nubia
And teeming Egypt,
Put and the Libyans—
They were her[e] helpers.
¹⁰Yet even she was exiled,
She went into captivity.
Her babes, too, were dashed in pieces

---

a Meaning of Heb. uncertain.
b Amon was the tutelary deity of No (Thebes; cf. Jer. 46.25), which the Assyrians had sacked in
  663 B.C.E.
c Heb. "sea."
d-d Change of vocalization yields "water."
e Heb. "your."

At every street corner.
Lots were cast for her honored men,
And all her nobles were bound in chains.
11You too shall be drunk
And utterly overcome;ᵃ
You too shall seek
A refuge from the enemy.
12All your forts are fig trees
Withᶠ ripe fruit;
If shaken they will fall
Into the mouths of devourers.
13Truly, the troops within you are women;
The gates of your land have opened themselves
To your enemies;
Fire has consumed your gate bars.

14Draw water for the siege,
Strengthen your forts;
Tread the clay,
Trample the mud,
Grasp the brick mold!
15There fire will devour you,
The sword will put an end to you;
It will devour you like the grub.
ᵃ⁻Multiply like grubs,
Multiply like locusts!⁻ᵃ

16You had more traders
Than the sky has stars—
The grubs cast their skins and fly away.
17Your guards were like locusts,
Your marshals like piles of hoppers
Which settle on the stone fences
On a chilly day;
When the sun comes out, they fly away,
And where they are nobody knows.

ᶠ *Emendation yields "Your troops are"*; cf. next verse.

¹⁸Your shepherds are slumbering,
O king of Assyria;
Your sheepmasters are ᵍ⁻lying inert;⁻ᵍ
Your people are scatteredᵃ over the hills,
And there is none to gather them.
¹⁹There is no healingʰ for your injury;
Your wound is grievous.
All who hear the news about you
Clap their hands over you.
For who has not suffered
From your constant malice?

ᵍ⁻ᵍ *Lit. "dwelling"; emendation yields "asleep."*
ʰ *Heb.* kehah, *a varient of* gehah; *see Prov. 17.22.*

HABAKKUK

1 The pronouncement made by the prophet Habakkuk.

²How long, O LORD, shall I cry out
And You not listen,
Shall I shout to You, "Violence!"
And You not save?
³Why do You make me see iniquity
a-[Why] do You look-a upon wrong?—
Raiding and violence are before me,
Strife continues and contention b-goes on.-b
⁴That is why decision fails
And justice never emerges;
For the villain hedges in the just man—
Therefore judgment emerges deformed.

⁵"Look among the nations,
Observe well and be utterly astounded;
For a work is being wrought in your days
Which you would not believe if it were told.
⁶For lo, I am raising up the Chaldeans,
That fierce, impetuous nation,
Who cross the earth's wide spaces
To seize homes not their own.
⁷They are terrible, dreadful;
c-They make their own laws and rules.-c
⁸Their horses are swifter than leopards,
Fleeter than wolves of the steppe.d
Their steeds gallop—e-their steeds-e
Come flying from afar.

---

a-a *Targum and Syriac "So that I look."*
b-b *Meaning of Heb. uncertain.*
c-c *Lit. "Their law and majesty proceed from themselves."*
d *Understanding* 'ereb *as synonymous with* 'arabah; *cf. Jer. 5.6.*
e-e *The Qumran Habakkuk commentary (hereafter 1QpHab) reads "and spread [wings]."*

Like vultures rushing toward food,
⁹They all come, bent on rapine.
The thrust[b] of their van is forward,
And they amass captives like sand.
¹⁰Kings they hold in derision,
And princes are a joke to them;
They laugh at every fortress,
They pile up earth and capture it.
¹¹[b-]Then they pass on like the wind,
They transgress and incur guilt,
For they ascribe their might to their god."[-b]

¹²You, O LORD, are from everlasting;
My holy God, You[f] never die.
O LORD, You have made them a subject of contention;
O Rock, You have made them a cause for complaint.
¹³You whose eyes are too pure to look upon evil,
Who cannot countenance wrongdoing,
Why do You countenance treachery,
And stand by idle
While the one in the wrong devours
The one in the right?
¹⁴You have made mankind like the fish of the sea,
Like creeping things [g-]that have no ruler.[-g]
¹⁵He has fished them all up with a line,
Pulled them up in his trawl,
And gathered them in his net.
ᐧThat is why he rejoices and is glad.
¹⁶That is why he sacrifices to his trawl
And makes offerings to his net;
For through them his portion[h] is rich
And his nourishment fat.
¹⁷Shall he then keep [i-]emptying his trawl,[-i]
And slaying nations without pity?

ᶠ *Heb. "we," a change made by a pious scribe.*
ᵍ ᵍ *1QpHab "[for him] to rule over"; cf. Gen. 1.28; Ps. 8.7–9.*
ʰ *Emendation yields "bread"; cf. Gen. 49.20.*
ⁱ⁻ⁱ *1QpHab "drawing his sword."*

2

I will stand on my watch,
Take up my station at the^a post,
And wait to see what He will say to me,
What He^b will reply to my complaint.

²The LORD answered me and said:
Write the prophecy down,
Inscribe it clearly on tablets,
So that it can be read easily.
³For ^{c-}there is yet a prophecy^{-c} for a set term,
A truthful witness for a time that will come.
Even if it tarries, wait for it still;
For it will surely come, without delay:
^{4d-}Lo, his spirit within him is puffed up, not upright,
But^{-d} the righteous man is rewarded with life
For his fidelity.
⁵How much less then shall the defiant^e go unpunished,
The treacherous, arrogant man
Who has made his maw as wide as Sheol,
Who is as insatiable as Death,
Who has harvested all the nations
And gathered in all the peoples!
⁶Surely all these shall pronounce a satire against him,
A pointed epigram concerning him.
They shall say:
Ah, you who pile up what is not yours—
How much longer?—
And make ever heavier your load of indebtedness!
⁷Right suddenly will your creditors^f arise,
And those who remind^g you will awake,
And you will be despoiled by them.
⁸Because you plundered many nations,
All surviving peoples shall plunder you—

---

^a *1QpHab reads "my."*
^b *Taking 'ashib as equivalent to yashib.*
^{c-c} *Emendation yields "the prophecy is a witness."*
^{d-d} *Meaning of Heb. uncertain. Emendation yields "Lo there is a reward for the upright—/the life breath within him—/And. . . ."*
^e *Connecting hyyn (1QpHab hwn) with the root hwn, Deut. 1.41; for the thought cf. Prov. 11.31. Meaning of rest of line uncertain.*
^f *Lit. "usurers."*
^g *Lit. "shake"; the same verb means "to call to mind" in Samaritan Aramaic.*

For crimes against men and wrongs against lands,
Against cities and all their inhabitants.

9Ah, you who have acquired gains
To the detriment of your own house,
h-Who have destroyed many peoples-h
In order to set your nest on high
To escape disaster!
10You have plotted shame for your own house,
And guilt for yourself;
11For a stone shall cry out from the wall,
And a rafter shall answer it from the woodwork.

12Ah, you who have built a town with crime,
And established a city with infamy,
13So that peoples have had to toil for the fire,i
And nations to weary themselves for naught!
iBehold, it is from the LORD of Hosts:
14k-For the earth shall be filled
With awe for the glory of the LORD
As water covers the sea.-k

15Ah, you who make others drink to intoxication
l-As you pour out-l your wrath,
In order to gaze upon their nakedness!m
16You shall be sated with shame
Rather than glory:
Drink in your turn and stagger!n
The cup in the right hand of the LORD
Shall come around to you,
And o-disgrace to-o your glory.
17p-For the lawlessness against Lebanon shall cover you,
The destruction of beasts shall overwhelm you-p—
For crimes against men and wrongs against lands,
Against cities and all their inhabitants.

h-h *Brought up from v. 10 for clarity.*
i *I.e., without profit.*
j *Connection with the next four lines uncertain; they might read better after v. 20.*
k-k *Cf. Isa. 11.9.*
l-l *Meaning of Heb. uncertain. Emendation yields "from the bowl of."*
m *Cf. Gen. 9.21–22.*
n *Emendation yields "uncover yourself"; cf. Lam. 4.21.*
o-o *Or "vomit of disgrace upon."*
p-p *Meaning of Heb. uncertain.*

18qWhat has the carved image availed,
That he who fashioned it has carved it
For an image and a false oracle—
That he who fashioned his product has trusted in it,
Making dumb idols?
19Ah, you who say, "Wake up" to wood,
"Awaken," to inert stone!
Can that give an oracle?
Why, it is encased in gold and silver,
But there is no breath inside it.
20But the LORD in His holy Abode—
Be silent before Him all the earth!

3 A prayer of the prophet Habakkuk. In the mode of *Shigionoth*.a

2O LORD! I have learned of Your renown;
I am awed, O LORD, by Your deeds.
Renew them in these years,
Oh, make them known in these years!
Though angry, may You remember compassion.

3God is coming from Teman,
The Holy One from Mount Paran.   *Selah*.b
His majesty covers the skies,
His splendor fills the earth:
4c-It is a brilliant light
Which gives off rays on every side—
And therein His glory is enveloped.-c
5Pestilence marches before Him,
And plague comes forth at His heels.
6When He stands, He makes the earth shake;d
When He glances, He makes nations tremble.
The age-old mountains are shattered,
The primeval hills sink low.

q *This verse would read well after v. 19.*

a *Meaning uncertain; perhaps "psalms of supplication"; cf. Ps. 7.1.*
b *A musical direction of uncertain meaning.*
c-c *Meaning of Heb. uncertain.*
d *Cf. Targum and Septuagint.*

^{c-}His are the ancient routes:
⁷As a scene of havoc I behold^{-c}
The tents of Cushan;
Shaken are the pavilions
Of the land of Midian!

⁸Are You wroth, O LORD, with Neharim?
Is Your anger against Neharim,
Your rage against Yam^e—
That You are driving Your steeds,
Your victorious chariot?
⁹All bared and ready is Your bow.
^{c-}Sworn are the rods of the word.^{-c}   *Selah.*
You make the earth burst into streams,
¹⁰The mountains rock at the sight of You,
A torrent of rain comes down;
Loud roars the deep,
^{c-}The sky returns the echo.^{-c}
¹¹Sun [and] moon stand still on high
As Your arrows fly in brightness,
Your flashing spear in brilliance.
¹²You tread the earth in rage,
You trample nations in fury.
¹³You have come forth to deliver Your people,
To deliver Your anointed.^f
^{g-}You will smash the roof of the villain's house,
Raze it from foundation to top.   *Selah.*
¹⁴You will crack [his] skull with Your^h bludgeon;
Blown away shall be his warriors,
Whose delight is to crush me suddenly,
To devour a poor man in an ambush.^{-g}
¹⁵ⁱ⁻You will make Your steeds tread the sea,
Stirring the mighty waters.

---

^e *Neharim (lit. "Floods") and Yam (lit. "Sea") were marine monsters vanquished by the* LORD
*in hoary antiquity. On Yam see Ps. 74.13; Job 7.12. A being called both Yam and Nahar
figures in early Canaanite literature.*
^f *I.e., the king of Judah.*
^{g-g} *Emendation yields: You will strike the heads of men of evil,/Smash the pates of Your adversaries.*
*Selah./You will crack their skulls with Your bludgeon;/Dispersed, blown like chaff shall be they/
Who lie in wait to swallow the innocent,/To devour the poor in an ambush.*
^h *Heb. "His."*
ⁱ⁻ⁱ *Or:* ¹⁵*You will make Your steeds tread the sea,/Stirring the mighty waters,/*¹⁶*That I may have
rest on a day of distress,/When a people come up to attack us./But this report made my bowels
quake,/These tidings made my lips quiver;/Rot entered into my bone,/I trembled where I stood:/*
¹⁷*That the fig tree does not bud,/And no yield is on the vine;/The olive crop has failed,/And the
fields produce no grain;/The sheep have vanished from the fold,/And no cattle are in the pen.*

¹⁶I heard and my bowels quaked,
My lips quivered at the sound;
Rot entered into my bone,
I trembled where I stood.
Yet I wait calmly for the day of distress,
For a people to come to attack us.
¹⁷Though the fig tree does not bud
And no yield is on the vine,
Though the olive crop has failed
And the fields produce no grain,
Though sheep have vanished from the fold
And no cattle are in the pen,⁻ⁱ
¹⁸Yet will I rejoice in the LORD,
Exult in the God who delivers me.
¹⁹My Lord GOD is my strength:
He makes my feet like the deer's
And lets me stride upon the heights.

^{c-}For the leader; with instrumental music.^{-c}

צפניה

ZEPHANIAH

1 The word of the LORD that came to Zephaniah son of Cushi son of Gedaliah son of Amariah son of Hezekiah, during the reign of King Josiah son of Amon of Judah.

> ²I will sweep everything away
> From the face of the earth
>
> > —declares the LORD.
>
> ³I will sweep away man and beast;
> I will sweep away the birds of the sky
> And the fish of the sea.
> a-I will make the wicked stumble,-a
> And I will destroy mankind
> From the face of the earth
>
> > —declares the LORD.
>
> ⁴I will stretch out My arm against Judah
> And against all who dwell in Jerusalem;
> And I will wipe out from this place
> Every vestige of Baal,
> And the name of the priestlingsᵇ along with the priests;
> ⁵And those who bow down on the roofs
> To the host of heaven;
> And those who bow down and swear to the LORD
> But also swear by Malcam;ᶜ
> ⁶And those who have forsaken the LORD,
> And those who have not sought the LORD
> And have not turned to Him.

---

a-a *Meaning of Heb. uncertain.*
b *Heb.* kemarim, *a term used only of priests of heathen gods.*
c *Apparently identical with "Milcom the abomination of the Ammonites"; cf. 1 Kings 11.5.*

⁷Be silent before my Lord GOD,
For the day of the LORD is approaching;
For the LORD has prepared a ᵈ⁻sacrificial feast,⁻ᵈ
Has bidden His guests purify themselves.
⁸And on the day of the LORD's sacrifice
I will punish the officials
And the king's sons,ᵉ
ᶠ⁻And all who don a foreign vestment.
⁹I will also punish on that day
Everyone who steps over the threshold,⁻ᶠ
Who fill their master'sᵍ palace
With lawlessness and fraud.
¹⁰In that day there shall be

—declares the LORD—

A loud outcry from the Fish Gate,
And howling from the Mishneh,ʰ
And a sound of great anguish from the hills.
¹¹The dwellers of the Machteshⁱ howl;
For all the tradesmen have perished,
All who weigh silver are wiped out.

¹²At that time,
I will search Jerusalem with lamps;
And I will punish the men
Who rest untroubled on their lees,
Who say to themselves,
"The LORD will do nothing, good or bad."
¹³Their wealth shall be plundered
And their homes laid waste.
They shall build houses and not dwell in them,
Plant vineyards and not drink their wine.
¹⁴The great day of the LORD is approaching,
Approaching most swiftly.
ʲ⁻Hark, the day of the LORD!
It is bitter:

ᵈ⁻ᵈ *I.e., a slaughter of sinners.*
ᵉ *Apparently brothers of King Amon, who exercised influence during the minority of King Josiah (2 Kings 22.1).*
ᶠ⁻ᶠ *Apparently references to two customs of heathen worship; cf. 2 Kings 10.22 and 1 Sam. 5.5.*
ᵍ *I.e., King Josiah's.*
ʰ *A quarter of Jerusalem; cf. 2 Kings 22.14.*
ⁱ *Another quarter of Jerusalem.*
ʲ⁻ʲ *Emendation yields: "The day of the LORD is faster than a runner,/Fleeter than a warrior"; cf. Ps. 19.6.*

There a warrior shrieks!-ʲ
¹⁵That day shall be a day of wrath,
A day of trouble and distress,
A day of calamity and desolation,
A day of darkness and deep gloom,
A day of densest clouds,
¹⁶A day of horn blasts and alarms—
Against the fortified towns
And the lofty corner towers.
¹⁷I will bring distress on the people,
And they shall walk like blind men,
Because they sinned against the LORD;
Their blood shall be spilled like dust,
And their fatᵏ like dung.
¹⁸Moreover, their silver and gold
Shall not avail to save them.
On the day of the LORD's wrath,
In the fire of His passion,
The whole land shall be consumed;
For He will make a terrible end
Of all who dwell in the land.

2

Gather together, gather,
ᵃ-O nation without shame,
²Before the day the decree is born—
The day flies by like chaff-ᵃ—
Before the fierce anger
Of the LORD overtakes you,
Before the day of anger
Of the LORD overtakes you.
³Seek the LORD,
All you humble of the land
Who have fulfilled His law;
Seek righteousness,

ᵏ *Or "marrow"; meaning of Heb. uncertain.*

ᵃ⁻ᵃ *Meaning of Heb. uncertain. Emendation yields: "O straw [Aramaic gel] not gathered in,/
Before you are driven like flying chaff"; cf. Ps. 35.5.*

Seek humility.
Perhaps you will find shelter
On the day of the LORD's anger.

⁴Indeed, Gaza shall be deserted
And Ashkelon desolate;
Ashdod's people shall be expelled in broad daylight,
And Ekron shall be uprooted.
⁵Ah, nation of Cherethites
Who inhabit the seacoast!
There is a word of the LORD against you,
O Canaan,ᵇ land of the Philistines:
I will lay you waste
Without inhabitants.

⁶The seacoast Cherothᶜ shall become
An abode for shepherds and folds for flocks,
⁷And shall be a portion for the remnant of the House of Judah;
On these [pastures] they shall graze [their flocks],
They shall ᵈ-lie down-ᵈ at eventide
In the houses of Ashkelon.
For the LORD their God will take note of them
And restore their fortunes.

⁸I have heard the insults of Moab
And the jeers of the Ammonites,
Who have insulted My people
And gloated over their country.
⁹Assuredly, as I live
        —declares the LORD of Hosts, the God of Israel—
Moab shall become like Sodom
And the Ammonites like Gomorrah:
Clumpsᶜ of weeds and patchesᶜ of salt,
And desolation evermore.
The remnant of My people shall plunder them,
The remainder of My nation shall possess them.
¹⁰That is what they'll get for their haughtiness,
For insulting and jeering

ᵇ Or "Phoenicia," of which Philistia is regarded as an extension southward.
ᶜ Meaning of Heb. uncertain.
ᵈ⁻ᵈ Change of vocalization yields "rest [them]"; cf. Song of Songs 1.7.

At the people of the LORD of Hosts.
¹¹The LORD will show Himself terrible against them,
Causing all the gods on earth to shrivel;ᶜ
And all the coastlands of the nations
Shall bow down to Him—
Every man in his own home.

¹²You Cushites too—
ᶜ-They shall be slain by My sword.⁻ᶜ
¹³And He will stretch out His arm against the north
And destroy Assyria;
He will make Nineveh a desolation,
Arid as the desert.
¹⁴In it flocks shall lie down,
Every ᶜ-species of beast,
While jackdaws and owls roost on its capitals,
The great owl hoots in the window,
And the raven [croaks] on the threshold.
For he has stripped its cedarwork bare.⁻ᶜ

¹⁵Is this the gay city
That dwelt secure,
That thought in her heart,
"I am, and there is none but me"?
Alas, she is become a waste,
A lair of wild beasts!
Everyone who passes by her
Hisses and gestures with his hand.ᶠ

3 Ah, sullied, polluted,
Overbearingᵃ city!
²She has been disobedient,
Has learned no lesson;
She has not trusted in the LORD,
Has not drawn near to her God.
³The officials within her
Are roaring lions;

ᶜ⁻ᶜ *Emendation yields "shall be slain by the sword of the LORD."*
ᶠ *To ward off a like fate from himself; cf. Jer. 18.16 and note.*

ᵃ *Meaning of Heb. uncertain. Emendation yields "harlot"; cf. Isa. 1.21.*

Her judges are wolves ^{b-}of the steppe,
They leave no bone until morning.^{-b}
⁴Her prophets are reckless,
Faithless fellows;
Her priests profane what is holy,
They give perverse rulings.
⁵But the LORD in her midst is righteous,
He does no wrong;
He issues judgment every morning,
As unfailing as the light.

The wrongdoer knows no shame!
⁶I wiped out nations:
Their corner towers are desolate;
I turned their thoroughfares into ruins,
With none passing by;
Their towns lie waste without people,
Without inhabitants.
⁷And I thought that she^c would fear Me,
Would learn a lesson,
And that the punishment I brought on them^d
Would not be ^{e-}lost on her.^{-e}
Instead, all the more eagerly
They have practiced corruption in all their deeds.

⁸But wait for Me—says the LORD—
For the day when I arise as an accuser;^f
When I decide to gather nations,
To bring kingdoms together,
To pour out My indignation on them,
All My blazing anger.
Indeed, by the fire of My passion
All the earth shall be consumed.
⁹For then I will make the peoples pure of speech,
So that they all invoke the LORD by name
And serve Him with one accord.^g
¹⁰From beyond the rivers of Cush, My suppliants^b

---

^{b-b} *Meaning of Heb. uncertain.*
^c *Heb. "you."*
^d *Heb. "her."*
^{e-e} *Lit. "cut off [from] her vision."*
^f *Understanding 'ad as equivalent to 'ed, with Septuagint and Syriac.*
^g *Lit. "back," i.e., like beasts of burden.*

Shall bring offerings to Me in Fair Puzai.[h]
[11]In that day,
You will no longer be shamed for all the deeds
By which you have defied Me.
For then I will remove
The proud and exultant within you,
And you will be haughty no more
On My sacred mount.[i]
[12]But I will leave within you
A poor, humble folk,
And they shall find refuge
In the name of the LORD.
[13]The remnant of Israel
Shall do no wrong
And speak no falsehood;
A deceitful tongue
Shall not be in their mouths.
Only such as these shall graze and lie down,
With none to trouble them.

[14]Shout for joy, Fair Zion,
Cry aloud, O Israel!
Rejoice and be glad with all your heart,
Fair Jerusalem!
[15]The LORD has annulled the judgment against you,
He has swept away your foes.
Israel's Sovereign the LORD is within you;
You need fear misfortune no more.

[16]In that day,
This shall be said to Jerusalem:
Have no fear, O Zion;
Let not your hands droop!
[17]Your God the LORD is in your midst,
A warrior who brings triumph.
He will rejoice over you and be glad,
He will shout over you with jubilation.

---

[h] *Emendation yields "Zion." For the thought, cf. Isa. 18.1, 7.*
[i] *I.e., in My holy land; cf. Isa. 11.9; 57.13; 65.25.*

He will [j]soothe with His love
[18]Those long disconsolate.[-j]
I will take away from you [b]the woe
Over which you endured mockery.[-b]
[19]At that time I will make [an end]
Of all who afflicted you.
And I will rescue the lame [sheep]
And gather the strayed;
And I will exchange their disgrace
For fame and renown in all the earth.
[20]At that time I will gather you,
And at [that] time I will bring you [home];
For I will make you renowned and famous
Among all the peoples on earth,
When I restore your fortunes
Before their[k] very eyes

                        —said the LORD.

[j-j] *Meaning of Heb. uncertain. Emendation yields "renew His love/As in the days of old."*
[k] *Heb. "your."*

HAGGAI

1 In the second year of King Darius, on the first day of the sixth month, this word of the LORD came through the prophet Haggai to Zerubbabel son of Shealtiel, the governor of Judah, and to Joshua son of Jehozadak, the high priest:

2Thus said the LORD of Hosts: These people say, a-"The time has not yet come-a for rebuilding the House of the LORD."

3And the word of the LORD through the prophet Haggai continued:

4Is it a time for you to dwell in your paneled houses, while this House is lying in ruins? 5Now thus said the LORD of Hosts: Consider how you have been faring! 6You have sowed much and brought in little; you eat without being satisfied; you drink without getting your fill; you clothe yourselves, but no one gets warm; and he who earns anything earns it for a leaky purse.

7bThus said the LORD of Hosts: Consider how you have fared: 8Go up to the hills and get timber, and rebuild the House; then I will look on it with favor and I will c-be glorified-c—said the LORD.

9You have been expecting much and getting little; and when you brought it home, I would blow on it!d Because of what?—says the LORD of Hosts. Because of My House which lies in ruins, while you all hurry to your own houses! 10That is why the skies above you have withheld [their] moisture and the earth has withheld its yield, 11and I have summoned fierce heat upon the land—upon the hills, upon the new grain and wine and oil, upon all that the ground produces, upon man and beast, and upon all the fruits of labor.

12Zerubbabel son of Shealtiel and the high priest Joshua son of Jehozadak and all the rest of the people gave heed to the summons of the LORD their God and to the words of the prophet Haggai, when the LORD

---

a-a Lit. "It is not time for the coming of the time."
b Vv. 7–8 would read well after v. 11.
c-c Emendation yields "glorify it"; see 2.7–9.
d Meaning, perhaps, cast a curse on.

their God sent him; the people feared the LORD. ¹³And Haggai, the LORD's messenger, fulfilling the LORD's mission, spoke to the people, "I am with you—declares the LORD."

¹⁴Then the LORD roused the spirit of Zerubbabel son of Shealtiel, the governor of Judah, and the spirit of the high priest Joshua son of Jehozadak, and the spirit of all the rest of the people: They came and set to work on the House of the LORD of Hosts, their God, ¹⁵on the twenty-fourth day of the sixth month. In the second year of King Darius, ¹on the twenty-first day of the seventh month, the word of the LORD came through the prophet Haggai:

²Speak to Zerubbabel son of Shealtiel, the governor of Judah, and to the high priest Joshua son of Jehozadak, and to the rest of the people: ³Who is there left among you who saw this House in its former splendor? How does it look to you now? It must seem like nothing to you. ⁴But be strong, O Zerubbabel—says the LORD—be strong, O high priest Joshua son of Jehozadak; be strong, all you people of the land—says the LORD— and act! For I am with you—says the LORD of Hosts. ⁵So I promised you when you came out of Egypt, and My spirit is still in your midst. Fear not!

⁶For thus said the LORD of Hosts: In just a little while longer I will shake the heavens and the earth, the sea and the dry land; ⁷I will shake all the nations. And the precious things of all the nations shall come [here], and I will fill this House with glory, said the LORD of Hosts. ⁸Silver is Mine and gold is Mine—says the LORD of Hosts. ⁹The glory of this latter House shall be greater than that of the former one, said the LORD of Hosts; and in this place I will grant prosperity—declares the LORD of Hosts.

¹⁰On the twenty-fourth day of the ninth [month], in the second year of Darius, the word of the LORD came to the prophet Haggai: ¹¹Thus said the LORD of Hosts: Seek a ruling from the priests, as follows: ¹²If a man is carrying sacrificial flesh in a fold of his garment, and with that fold touches bread, stew, wine, oil, or any other food, will the latter become holy? In reply, the priests said, "No." ¹³Haggai went on, "If someone defiled by a corpse touches any of these, will it be defiled?" And the priests responded, "Yes."

¹⁴Thereupon Haggai said: That is how this people and that is how this nation looks to Me—declares the LORD—and so, too, the work of their hands: Whatever they offer there is defiled. ¹⁵And now take thought, from this day backward:ᵃ As long as no stone had been laid on another in the House of the LORD, ¹⁶if one came to a heap of twenty measures,ᵇ it would yield only ten; and if one came to a wine vat to skim off fifty measures, the press would yield only twenty. ¹⁷I struck you—all the works of your hands—with blight and mildew and hail, but ᶜyou did not re-turnᶜ to Me—declares the LORD. ¹⁸Take note, from this day forward— from the twenty-fourth day of the ninth month, from the day when the foundation was laid for the LORD's Temple—take note ¹⁹while the seed is still in the granary, and the vine, fig tree, pomegranate, and olive tree have not yet borne fruit. For from this day on I will send blessings.

²⁰And the word of the LORD came to Haggai a second time on the twenty-fourth day of the month: ²¹Speak to Zerubbabel the governor of Judah: I am going to shake the heavens and the earth. ²²And I will over-turn the thrones of kingdoms and destroy the might of the kingdoms of the nations. I will overturn chariots and their drivers. Horses and their riders shall fall, each by the sword of his fellow. ²³On that day—declares the LORD of Hosts—I will take you, O My servant Zerubbabel son of Shealtiel—declares the LORD—and make you as a signet;ᵈ for I have chosen you—declares the LORD of Hosts.

ᵃ Or "forward."
ᵇ I.e., of grain.
ᶜ⁻ᶜ Lit. "there was not with you to Me"; cf. Amos 4.9.
ᵈ I.e., bring you close to Me; contrast Jer. 22.24–30.

ZECHARIAH

1 In the eighth month of the second year of Darius, this word of the LORD came to the prophet Zechariah son of Berechiah son of Iddo:[a] 2The LORD was very angry with your fathers. 3Say to them further:

Thus said the LORD of Hosts: Turn back to me—says the LORD of Hosts—and I will turn back to you—said the LORD of Hosts. 4Do not be like your fathers! For when the earlier prophets called to them, "Thus said the LORD of Hosts: Come, turn back from your evil ways and your evil deeds, they did not obey or give heed to Me—declares the LORD. 5Where are your fathers now? And did the prophets live forever? 6But the warnings and the decrees with which I charged My servants the prophets overtook your fathers—did they not?—and in the end they had to admit, 'The LORD has dealt with us according to our ways and our deeds, just as He purposed.' "

7On the twenty-fourth day of the eleventh month of the second year of Darius—the month of Shebat—this word of the LORD came to the prophet Zechariah son of Berechiah son of Iddo:

8In the night, I had a vision. I saw a man, mounted on a bay horse, standing b-among the myrtles-b in the Deep, and behind him were bay,c sorrel,d and white horses. 9I asked, "What are those, my lord?" And the angel who talked with me answered, "I will let you know what they are." 10Then the man who was standing b-among the myrtles-b spoke up and said, "These were sent out by the LORD to roam the earth."

11And in fact, they reported to the angel of the LORD who was standing b-among the myrtles,-b "We have roamed the earth, and have found all the earth dwelling in tranquility."e 12Thereupon the angel of the LORD exclaimed, "O LORD of Hosts! How long will You withhold pardon from

---

a *A clause like "Say to the people" is here understood; cf. 7.5.*
b-b *Septuagint reads "between the mountains"; cf. 6.1. In 6.1 ff. four teams of horses leave the LORD's abode to roam the four quarters of the earth; in 1.8 ff. they are about to reenter His abode after such a reconnaisance.*
c *Septuagint adds "dappled"; cf. 6.3.*
d *Meaning of Heb. uncertain. Emendation yields "black"; cf. 6.2.*
e *Upheavals at the start of Darius' reign had encouraged hopes of an early restoration of the Davidic dynasty (cf. Hag. 2.21 ff.). Now these hopes were dashed.*

Jerusalem and the towns of Judah, which You placed under a curse seventy years ago?"

¹³The LORD replied with kind, comforting words to the angel who talked with me.

¹⁴Then the angel who talked with me said to me: "Proclaim! Thus said the LORD of Hosts: I am very jealous for Jerusalem—for Zion—¹⁵and I am very angry with those nations that are at ease; for I was only angry a little, but they overdid the punishment. ¹⁶Assuredly, thus said the LORD: I graciously return to Jerusalem. My House shall be built in her—declares the LORD of Hosts—the measuring line is being applied to Jerusalem. ¹⁷Proclaim further: Thus said the LORD of Hosts: My towns shall yet overflow with bounty. For the LORD will again comfort Zion; He will choose Jerusalem again."

2 I looked up, and I saw four horns.ᵃ ²I asked the angel who talked with me, "What are those?" "Those," he replied, "are the horns that tossed Judah, Israel, and Jerusalem."ᵃ ³Then the LORD showed me four smiths. ⁴"What are they coming to do?" I asked. He replied: "Those are the horns that tossed Judah, so that no man could raise his head; and these men have come ᵇ⁻to throw them into a panic,⁻ᵇ to ᶜ⁻hew down⁻ᶜ the horns of the nations that raise a horn against the land of Judah, to toss it."

⁵I looked up, and I saw a man holding a measuring line. ⁶"Where are you going?" I asked. "To measure Jerusalem," he replied, "to see how long and wide it is to be." ⁷But the angel who talked with me came forward, and another angel came forward to meet him. ⁸The former said to him, "Run to that young man and tell him:

"Jerusalem shall be peopled as a city without walls, so many shall be the men and cattle it contains. ⁹And I Myself—declares the LORD—will be a wall of fire all around it, and I will be a glory inside it.

¹⁰"Away, away! Flee from the land of the north—says the LORD—though I swept you [there] like the four winds of heaven—declares the LORD."

¹¹Away, escape, O Zion, you who dwell in Fair Babylon! ¹²For thus said the LORD of Hosts—He ᵈ⁻who sent me after glory⁻ᵈ—concerning the nations that have taken you as spoil: "Whoever touches you touches

---

ᵃ *The four horns correspond to the four winds of v. 10.*
ᵇ⁻ᵇ *Meaning of Heb. uncertain; emendation yields "to sharpen ax heads."*
ᶜ⁻ᶜ *Meaning of Heb. uncertain.*
ᵈ⁻ᵈ *Emendation yields "whose Presence sent me."*

the pupil of ^{e-}his own^{-e} eye. ¹³For I will lift My hand against them, and they shall be spoil for those they enslaved."—Then you shall know that I was sent by the LORD of Hosts.

¹⁴Shout for joy, Fair Zion! For lo, I come; and I will dwell in your midst—declares the LORD. ¹⁵In that day many nations will attach themselves to the LORD and become His^f people, and He^g will dwell in your midst. Then you will know that I was sent to you by the LORD of Hosts.

¹⁶The LORD will ^{h-}take Judah to Himself as His portion^{-h} in the Holy Land, and He will choose Jerusalem once more.

¹⁷Be silent, all flesh, before the LORD!
For He is roused from His holy habitation.

3 He further showed me Joshua, the high priest, standing before the angel of the LORD, and the Accuser^a standing at his right to accuse him. ²But [the angel of] the LORD said to the Accuser, "The LORD rebuke you, O Accuser; may the LORD who has chosen Jerusalem rebuke you! For this is a brand plucked from the fire."^b ³Now Joshua was clothed in filthy garments when he stood before the angel. ⁴The latter spoke up and said to his attendants, "Take the filthy garments off him!" And he said to him, "See, I have removed your guilt from you, and you shall be clothed in [priestly] robes." ⁵Then he^c gave the order, "Let a pure^d diadem be placed on his head." And they placed the pure diadem on his head and clothed him in [priestly] garments,^e as the angel of the LORD stood by.

⁶And the angel of the LORD charged Joshua as follows: ⁷"Thus said the LORD of Hosts: If you walk in My paths and keep My charge, you in turn will rule My House and guard My courts, and I will permit you to move about among these attendants. ⁸Hearken well, O High Priest Joshua, you and your fellow priests sitting before you! For those men are a sign that I am going to bring My servant the Branch.^f ⁹For mark well

---

^{e-e} *According to ancient Jewish tradition, a scribal change for "My."*
^f *Heb. "My."*
^g *Heb. "I."*
^{h-h} *Emendation yields "allot to Judah its portion"; cf. Num. 34.17.*

^a *Others "Satan."*
^b *Joshua's father (Hag. 1.1; 1 Chron. 5.40–41) was exiled and his grandfather executed (2 Kings 25.18–21) by the Babylonians, but Joshua returned.*
^c *Heb. "I."*
^d *I.e., ritually pure.*
^e *Joshua has now been rendered fit to associate with the heavenly beings (v. 7); cf. Isa. 6.6–8.*
^f *I.e., the future king of David's line. See 6.12; Jer. 23.5–6; 33.15–16; cf. Isa. 11.1.*

this stone which I place before Joshua, a single stone with seven eyes.ᵍ I will execute its engraving—declares the LORD of Hosts—and I will remove that country's guilt in a single day. ¹⁰In that day—declares the LORD of Hosts—you will be inviting each other to the shade of vines and fig trees."

4 The angel who talked with me came back and woke me as a man is wakened from sleep. ²He said to me, "What do you see?" And I answered, "I see a lampstand all of gold, with a bowl above it. The lamps on it are seven in number, and the ᵃ⁻lamps above it have⁻ᵃ seven pipes; ³and by it are two olive trees, one on the right of the bowl and one on its left." ⁴I, in turn, asked the angel who talked with me, "What do those things mean, my lord?" ⁵"Do you not know what those things mean?" asked the angel who talked with me; and I said, "No, my lord." ⁶Then he explained to me as follows:ᵇ

"This is the word of the LORD to Zerubbabel:ᶜ Not by might, nor by power, but by My spiritᵈ—said the LORD of Hosts. ⁷Whoever you are, O great mountain in the path of Zerubbabel, turn into level ground! For he shall produce that excellent stone; it shall be greeted with shouts of 'Beautiful! Beautiful!' "

⁸And the word of the LORD came to me: ⁹"Zerubbabel's hands have founded this House and Zerubbabel's hands shall complete it. Then you shall know that it was the LORD of Hosts who sent me to you. ¹⁰Does anyone scorn a day of small beginnings? When they see ᶜ⁻the stone of distinction⁻ᶜ in the hand of Zerubbabel, they shall rejoice.

"Those seven are the eyes of the LORD, ranging over the whole earth."

¹¹"And what," I asked him, "are those two olive trees, one on the right and one on the left of the lampstand?" ¹²And I further asked him, "What are the two topsᶠ of the olive trees that feed their goldᵍ through those

---

ᵍ Meaning of Heb. uncertain. The stone apparently symbolizes the God-given power of the future Davidic ruler; see below 4.6–7.

ᵃ⁻ᵃ Emendation yields "bowl above it has."

ᵇ The explanation is given in the last sentence of v. 10.

ᶜ A grandson of King Jehoiachin (1 Chron. 3.17–19) and the secular head of the repatriated community (Hag. 1.1; etc.).

ᵈ I.e., Zerubbabel will succeed by means of spiritual gifts conferred upon him by the LORD; cf. Isa. 11.2. ff.

ᶜ⁻ᶜ Meaning of Heb. uncertain; others "plummet."

ᶠ Meaning of Heb. uncertain; literally "ears" (as of grain).

ᵍ Emendation yields "oil"; cf. v. 14.

two golden tubes?"ʰ ¹³He asked me, "Don't you know what they are?" And I replied, "No, my lord." ¹⁴Then he explained, "They are the two ⁱ⁻anointed dignitaries⁻ⁱ who attend the Lord of all the earth."

5 I looked up again, and I saw a flying scroll. ²"What do you see?" he asked. And I replied, "A flying scroll, twenty cubits long and ten cubits wide." ³"That," he explained to me, "is the curse which goes out over the whole land. ᵃ⁻For everyone who has stolen, as is forbidden on one side [of the scroll], has gone unpunished; and everyone who has sworn [falsely], as is forbidden on the other side of it, has gone unpunished.⁻ᵃ ⁴[But] I have sent it forth—declares the LORD of Hosts—and [the curse] shall enter the house of the thief and the house of the one who swears falsely by My name, and it shall lodge inside their houses and shall consume them to the last timber and stone."

⁵Then the angel who talked with me came forward and said, "Now look up and note this other object that is approaching." ⁶I asked, "What is it?" And he said, "This tubᵇ that is approaching—this," said he, "is their eyeᶜ in all the land." ⁷And behold, a disk of lead was lifted, revealing a woman seated inside the tub. ⁸"That," he said, "is Wickedness"; and, thrusting her down into the tub, he pressed the leaden weight into its mouth.

⁹I looked up again and saw two women come soaring with the wind in their wings—they had wings like those of a stork—and carry off the tub between earth and sky. ¹⁰"Where are they taking the tub?" I asked the angel who talked with me. ¹¹And he answered, "To build a shrine for it in the land of Shinar;ᵈ [a stand] shall be erected for it, and it shall be set down there upon the stand."

6 I looked up again, and I saw: Four chariots were coming out from between the two mountains; the mountains were of copper. ²The horses of the first chariot were bay, the horses of the second chariot were black; ³the horses of the third chariot were white, and the horses of the fourth chariot were spotted—dappled. ⁴And I spoke up and asked the angel who talked with me: "What are those, my lord?" ⁵In reply, the angel said to me, "Those are the four winds of heaven coming out after presenting

ʰ Or "funnels"; through them the oil runs from the olive trees into the bowl of vv. 2 and 3.
ⁱ⁻ⁱ I.e., the high priest and the king (cf. 3.8–9 with note); lit. "sons of oil."

ᵃ⁻ᵃ Meaning of Heb. uncertain.
ᵇ Heb. ephah, a measure of capacity.
ᶜ Septuagint and Syriac read "guilt."
ᵈ I.e., Babylonia; cf. Gen. 10.10; 11.2, 9.

themselves to the Lord of all the earth. 6The one with the black horses is going out to the region of the north; the white ones a-have gone out-a to b-what is to the west of them;-b the spotted ones a-have gone out-a to the region of the south; 7and c-the dappled ones have gone out. . . ."-c They were ready to start out and range the earth, and he gave them the order, "Start out and range the earth!" And they ranged the earth. 8Then he alerted me, and said to me, "Take good note! Those that went out to the region of the north have d-done my pleasure-d in the region of the north."e

9The word of the LORD came to me: 10Receive fromf the exiled community—from Heldai, Tobijah, and Jedaiah, who have come from Babylon—and you, in turn, proceed the same day to the house of Josiah son of Zephaniah. 11Take silver and gold and make crowns. Place [one] on the head of High Priest Joshua son of Jehozadak, 12and say to him, "Thus said the LORD of Hosts: Behold, a man called the Branchg shall branch out from the place where he is, and he shall build the Temple of the LORD. 13He shall build the Temple of the LORD and shall assume majesty, and he shall sit on his throne and rule. And there shall also be a priest h-seated on his throne,-h and harmonious understanding shall prevail between them."

14The crowns shall remain in the Temple of the LORD as a memorial to Helem,i Tobijah, Jedaiah, and Henj son of Zephaniah. 15Men from far away shall come and take part in the building of the Temple of the LORD, and you shall know that I have been sent to you by the LORD of Hosts— if only you will obey the LORD your God!

7 In the fourth year of King Darius, on the fourth day of the ninth month, Kislev, the word of the LORD came to Zechariah—2when Bethelsharezer a-and Regem-melech and his men sent-a to entreat the favor of the LORD, 3[and] to address this inquiry to the priests of the House of

a-a *Change of vocalization yields "will go out."*
b-b *Cf. 'ahor, "west," Isa. 9.11. Emendation yields "the region of the west."*
c-c *Emendation yields "the bay ones will go out to the region of the east."*
d-d *Cf. postbiblical* nahath ruaḥ, *"gratification." Emendation yields, "done the LORD's pleasure."*
e *I.e., Babylonia, whose communication with Judah was via North Mesopotamia and Syria; cf. 2.10–11.*
f *Emendation yields "the gift of."*
g *See note at 3.8.*
h-h *Septuagint reads "on his right side."*
i *The Syriac version reads "Heldai"; cf. v. 10.*
j *In v. 10, "Josiah."*
a-a *Emendation yields "sent Regem-melech and his men."*

the LORD and to the prophets: "Shall I weep and practice abstinence in the fifth month,[b] as I have been doing all these years?"

⁴Thereupon the word of the LORD of Hosts came to me: ⁵Say to all the people of the land and to the priests: When you fasted and lamented in the fifth and seventh months all these seventy years, did you fast for my benefit? ⁶And when you eat and drink, who but you does the eating, and who but you does the drinking? ⁷Look, this is the message that the LORD proclaimed through the earlier prophets, when Jerusalem and the towns about her were peopled and tranquil, when the Negeb and the Shephelah were peopled.

⁸And the word of the LORD to Zechariah continued: ⁹Thus said the LORD of Hosts: Execute true justice; deal loyally and compassionately with one another. ¹⁰Do not defraud the widow, the orphan, the stranger, and the poor; and do not plot evil against one another.—¹¹But they refused to pay heed. They presented a balky back and turned a deaf ear. ¹²They hardened their hearts like adamant against heeding the instruction and admonition that the LORD of Hosts sent to them by His spirit through the earlier prophets; and a terrible wrath issued from the LORD of Hosts. ¹³Even as He called and they would not listen, "So," said the LORD of Hosts, "let them call and I will not listen." ¹⁴I dispersed them among all those nations which they had not known, and the land was left behind them desolate, without any who came and went. They caused a delightful land to be turned into a desolation.

8

The word of the LORD of Hosts came [to me]:

²Thus said the LORD of Hosts: I am very jealous for Zion, I am fiercely jealous for her. ³Thus said the LORD: I have returned to Zion, and I will dwell in Jerusalem. Jerusalem will be called the City of Faithfulness, and the mount of the LORD of Hosts the Holy Mount.

⁴Thus said the LORD of Hosts: There shall yet be old men and women in the squares of Jerusalem, each with staff in hand because of their great age. ⁵And the squares of the city shall be crowded with boys and girls playing in the squares. ⁶Thus said the LORD of Hosts: Though it will seem impossible to the remnant of this people in those days, shall it also be impossible to Me?—declares the LORD of Hosts. ⁷Thus said the LORD of Hosts: I will rescue My people from the lands of the east and from the lands of the west, ⁸and I will bring them home to dwell in Jerusalem. They shall be My people, and I will be their God—in truth and sincerity.

b *Because of the destruction of the Temple and Jerusalem; cf. 2 Kings 25.8 ff.*

⁹Thus said the LORD of Hosts: Take courage, you who now hear these words which the prophets spoke when the foundations were laid for the rebuilding of the Temple, the House of the LORD of Hosts.

¹⁰ªFor before that time, the earnings of men were nil, and profits from beasts were nothing. It was not safe to go about one's business on account of enemies; and I set all men against one another. ¹¹But now I will not treat the remnant of this people as before—declares the LORD of Hosts— ¹²but what it sows shall prosper: The vine shall produce its fruit, the ground shall produce its yield, and the skies shall provide their moisture. I will bestow all these things upon the remnant of this people. ¹³And just as you were a curseᵇ among the nations, O House of Judah and House of Israel, so, when I vindicate you, you shall become a blessing.ᵇ Have no fear; take courage!

¹⁴For thus said the LORD of Hosts: Just as I planned to afflict you and did not relent when your fathers provoked Me to anger—said the LORD of Hosts—¹⁵so, at this time, I have turned and planned to do good to Jerusalem and to the House of Judah. Have no fear! ¹⁶These are the things you are to do: Speak the truth to one another, render true and perfect justice in your gates. ¹⁷And do not contrive evil against one another, and do not love perjury, because all those are things that I hate—declares the LORD.

¹⁸And the word of the LORD of Hosts came to me, saying, ¹⁹Thus said the LORD of Hosts: The fast of the fourth month, the fast of the fifth month, the fast of the seventh month, and the fast of the tenth monthᶜ shall become occasions for joy and gladness, happy festivals for the House of Judah; but you must love honesty and integrity.

²⁰Thus said the LORD of Hosts: Peoples and the inhabitants of many cities shall yet come—²¹the inhabitants of one shall go to the other and say, "Let us go and entreat the favor of the LORD, let us seek the LORD of Hosts; I will go, too." ²²The many peoples and the multitude of nations shall come to seek the LORD of Hosts in Jerusalem and to entreat the favor of the LORD. ²³Thus said the LORD of Hosts: In those days, ten men from nations of every tongue will take hold—they will take hold of every Jew by a corner of his cloak and say, "Let us go with you, for we have heard that God is with you."

ª Cf. Hag. 1.6.
ᵇ I.e., a standard by which men curse or bless; cf. Gen. 12.2 and note.
ᶜ Commemorating, respectively, the events of 2 Kings 25.3 ff. (Jer. 52.6 ff.); 2 Kings 25.8 ff. (Jer. 52.12 ff.); 2 Kings 25.25 ff. (Jer. 41); 2 Kings 25.1 ff. (Jer. 52.4).

9

A pronouncement: The word of the LORD.

He will reside in the land of Hadrach and Damascus;
For all men's eyes will turn to the LORD—
Like all the tribes of Israel—
²Including Hamath, which borders on it,ᵃ
And Tyre and Sidon, though they are very wise.
³Tyre has built herself a fortress;
She has amassed silver like dust,
And gold like the mud in the streets.
⁴But my Lord will impoverish her;
He will defeat her forces at sea,
And she herself shall be consumed by fire.

⁵Ashkelon shall see it and be frightened,
Gaza shall tremble violently,
And Ekron, at the collapse of her hopes.
Kingship shall vanish from Gaza,
Ashkelon shall be without inhabitants,
⁶And ᵇ⁻a mongrel people⁻ᵇ shall settle in Ashdod.
I will uproot the grandeur of Philistia.

⁷But I will clean out the blood from its mouth,
And the detestable things from between its teeth.
Its survivors, too, shall belong to our God:
They shall become like a clan in Judah,
And Ekron shall be like the Jebusites.

⁸And I will encamp in My House ᶜ⁻against armies,⁻ᶜ
Against any that come and go,
And no oppressor shall ever overrun them again;
For I have now taken note ᵈ⁻with My own eyes.⁻ᵈ

⁹Rejoice greatly, Fair Zion;
Raise a shout, Fair Jerusalem!
Lo, your king is coming to you.
He is victorious, triumphant,
Yet humble, riding on an ass,

ᵃ *I.e., on the land of Hadrach and Damascus.*
ᵇ⁻ᵇ *Heb.* mamzer; *cf. note at Deut. 23.3.*
ᶜ⁻ᶜ *Change of vocalization yields "as a garrison."*
ᵈ⁻ᵈ *Emendation yields "of their suffering"; cf. 1 Sam. 1.11.*

On a donkey foaled by a she-ass.
[10]He[e] shall banish chariots from Ephraim
And horses from Jerusalem;
The warrior's bow shall be banished.
He shall call on the nations to surrender,[f]
And his rule shall extend from sea to sea
And from ocean to land's end.

[11][g]You, for your part, have released[h]
Your prisoners from the dry pit,[i]
For the sake of the blood of your covenant,
[12][Saying], "Return to Bizzaron,[j]
You prisoners of hope."
In return [I] announce this day:
I will repay you double.
[13]For I have drawn Judah taut,
And applied [My hand] to Ephraim as to a bow,
And I will arouse your sons, O Zion,
Against your sons, O Javan,
And make you like a warrior's sword.

[14]And the LORD will manifest Himself to them,[k]
And His arrows shall flash like lightning;
My Lord GOD shall sound the ram's horn
And advance in a stormy tempest.[l]
[15]The LORD of Hosts will protect them:
[m][His] slingstones shall devour and conquer;
They shall [n]-drink, shall rage as with-[n] wine,
And be filled [with it] like a dashing bowl,
Like the corners of an altar.
[16]The LORD their God shall prosper them
On that day;
[He shall pasture] His people like sheep.
[They shall be] like crown jewels glittering on His soil.
[17]How lovely, how beautiful they shall be,

---

e *Heb. "I."*
f *Cf. Deut. 20.10–12 and note.*
g *Exact meaning and connection of vv. 11–12 uncertain.*
h *Taking shillaḥti as a second-person singular feminine form, with Septuagint; cf. Judg. 5.7 with note.*
i *I.e., a pit that serves as a dungeon rather than a cistern (both are called bor in Heb.).*
j *Perhaps a nickname ("fortress") for Samaria (Heb. Shomeron).*
k *I.e., Judah.*
l *Lit. "tempests of wind"; for teman in the sense of wind, cf. Job 9.9; 39.26.*
m *The meaning of much of the rest of the chapter is uncertain.*
n-n *Some Septuagint mss. read "drink blood like."*

Producing young men like new grain,
Young women like new wine!

10

Ask the LORD for rain
In the ᵃ⁻season of late rain.⁻ᵃ
It is the LORD who causes storms;ᵇ
And He will provide rainstorms ᶜ⁻for them,
Grass in the fields for everyone.⁻ᶜ

²For the teraphimᵈ spoke delusion,
The augurs predicted falsely;
And dreamers speak lies
And console with illusions.
That is why My people have strayedᵇ like a flock,
They sufferᵇ for lack of a shepherd.
³My anger is roused against the shepherds,
And I will punish the he-goats.ᵉ

For the LORD of Hosts has taken thought
In behalf of His flock, the House of Judah;
He will make them like majestic chargers in battle.
⁴From them shall come ᶠ⁻cornerstones,
From them tent pegs,⁻ᶠ
From them bows of combat,
And every captain shall also arise from them.
⁵And together they shall be like warriors in battle,
Tramping in the dirt of the streets;
They shall fight, for the LORD shall be with them,
And they shall put horsemen to shame.
⁶I will give victory to the House of Judah,
And triumph to the House of Joseph.
I will restore them, for I have pardoned them,
And they shall be as though I had never disowned them;
For I the LORD am their God,

ᵃ⁻ᵃ *Septuagint reads "in its season/The early rain and the late." Cf. Deut. 11.14.*
ᵇ *Meaning of Heb. uncertain.*
ᶜ⁻ᶜ *Emendation yields "[producing] food for men,/Grass in the fields for cattle." Cf. Deut.*
11.14–15.
ᵈ *Idols consulted for oracles; cf. 1 Sam. 15.23; Ezek. 21.26.*
ᵉ *I.e., oppressive leaders; cf. Ezek. 34.17 ff.*
ᶠ⁻ᶠ *Emendation yields "shields and bucklers."*

And I will answer their prayers.
7g-Ephraim shall be like a warrior,
And they-g shall exult as with wine;
Their children shall see it and rejoice,
They shall exult in the LORD.
8I will whistle to them and gather them,
For I will redeem them;
They shall increase b-and continue increasing.-b
9For though I sowed them among the nations,
In the distant places they shall remember Me,
They shall escape with their children and shall return.
10I will bring them back from the land of Egypt
And gather them from Assyria;
And I will bring them to the lands of Gilead and Lebanon,
And even they shall not suffice for them.
11b-A hemmed-in force shall pass over the sea
And shall stir up waves in the sea;-b
And all the deeps of the Nile shall dry up.
Down shall come the pride of Assyria,
And the scepter of Egypt shall pass away.
12But I will make themh mighty through the LORD,
And they shall i-march proudly-i in His name

—declares the LORD.

11 Throw open your gates, O Lebanon,
And let fire consume your cedars!
2Howl, cypresses, for cedars have fallen!
How the mighty are ravaged!
Howl, you oaks of Bashan,
For the stately forest is laid low!
3Hark, the wailing of the shepherds,
For their a-rich pastures-a are ravaged;
Hark, the roaring of the great beasts,
For the jungle of the Jordan is ravaged.

4Thus said my God the LORD: Tend the sheep meant for slaughter,
5whose buyers will slaughter them with impunity, whose seller will say,

g-g *Emendation yields "And when Ephraim is victorious,/They. . . ."*
h *I.e., Judah and Ephraim.*
i-i *Meaning of Heb. uncertain. Emendation yields "have glory"; cf. Isa. 45.25.*

a-a *Meaning of Heb. uncertain.*

"Praised be the LORD! I'll get rich," and whose shepherd will not pity them. ⁶For I will pity the inhabitants of the land no more—declares the LORD—but I will place every man at the mercy of every other man and at the mercy of his king; they shall break the country to bits, and I will not rescue it from their hands.

⁷So I tended the sheep meant for slaughter, ᵇ⁻for those poor men of the sheep.⁻ᵇ I got two staffs, one of which I named Favor and the other Unity, and I proceeded to tend the sheep. ⁸But I lost ᶜ⁻the three shepherds⁻ᶜ in one month; then my patience with them was at an end, and they in turn were disgusted with me. ⁹So I declared, "I am not going to tend you; let the one that is to die die and the one that is to get lost get lost; and let the rest devour each other's flesh!"

¹⁰Taking my staff Favor, I cleft it in two, so as to annul the covenant I had made with all the peoples;ᵈ ¹¹and when it was annulled that day, ᵉ⁻the same poor men of the sheep⁻ᵉ who watchedᶠ me realized that it was a message from the LORD. ¹²Then I said to them, "If you are satisfied, pay me my wages; if not, don't." So they weighed out my wages, thirty shekels of silver—¹³ᵃ⁻the noble sum that I was worth in their estimation.⁻ᵃ The LORD said to me, "Deposit it in the treasury."ᵃ And I took the thirty shekels and deposited it in the treasury in the House of the LORD. ¹⁴Then I cleft in two my second staff, Unity, in order to annul the brotherhood between Judah and Israel.ᵍ

¹⁵The LORD said to me further: Get yourself the gear of a foolish shepherd. ¹⁶For I am going to raise up in the land a shepherd who will neither miss the lost [sheep], nor seek the strayed,ᵃ nor heal the injured, nor sustain the frail,ᵃ but will feast on the flesh of the fat ones and ᵃ⁻tear off their hoofs.⁻ᵃ

> ¹⁷Oh, the worthless shepherd
> Who abandons the flock!
> Let a sword descend upon his arm
> And upon his right eye!
> His arm shall shrivel up;
> His right eye shall go blind.

ᵇ⁻ᵇ *Emendation yields "for the sheep dealers"; cf. the word rendered "trader" in 14.21.*
ᶜ⁻ᶜ *Emendation yields "a third of the flock."*
ᵈ *Perhaps alluding to the prediction of 14.1–3.*
ᵉ⁻ᵉ *Emendation yields "the sheep dealers."*
ᶠ *Emendation yields "hired."*
ᵍ *Two mss. of the Septuagint have "Jerusalem"; cf. 12.2–3; 14.14.*

12

A pronouncement: The word of the LORD concerning Israel.

The utterance of the LORD,
Who stretched out the skies
And made firm the earth,
And created man's breath within him:

²Behold, I will make Jerusalem a bowl of reeling for the peoples all around. Judah shall be caught up in the siege upon Jerusalem, ³when all the nations of the earth gather against her. In that day, I will make Jerusalem a stone for all the peoples to lift; all who lift it shall injure themselves. ⁴In that day—declares the LORD—I will strike every horse with panic and its rider with madness. But I will ᵃ⁻watch over the House of Judah while I strike every horse of⁻ᵃ the peoples with blindness. ⁵And the clans of Judah will say to themselves, ᵇ⁻"The dwellers of Jerusalem are a task set for us by⁻ᵇ their God, the LORD of Hosts." ⁶In that day, I will make the clans of Judah like a flaming brazier among sticks and like a flaming torch among sheaves. They shall devour all the besieging peoples right and left; and Jerusalem shall continue on its site, in Jerusalem.ᶜ

⁷The LORD will give victory to the tents of Judah first, so that the glory of the House of David and the glory of the inhabitants of Jerusalem may not be too great for Judah. ⁸In that day, the LORD will shield the inhabitants of Jerusalem; and the feeblest of them shall be in that day like David, and the House of David like a divine being—like an angel of the LORD—at their head.

⁹In that day I will ᵈ⁻all but annihilate⁻ᵈ all the nations that came up against Jerusalem. ¹⁰But I will fill the House of David and the inhabitants of Jerusalem with a spirit of pity and compassion; and they shall lamentᵉ to Me about those who are slain, wailing over them as over a favorite son and showing bitter grief as over a first-born. ¹¹In that day, the wailing in Jerusalem shall be as great as the wailing at Hadad-rimmon in the plain of Megiddon.ᶠ ¹²The land shall wail, each family by itself: The family of

---

ᵃ⁻ᵃ *Emendation yields "open the eyes of Judah while I strike all."*
ᵇ⁻ᵇ *Emendation yields "We will save the dwellers of Jerusalem with the help of."*
ᶜ *Emendation yields "safety."*
ᵈ⁻ᵈ *For the idiom cf. Gen. 43.30; it is also attested in postbiblical Hebrew.*
ᵉ *Meaning of Heb. uncertain.*
ᶠ *Usually "Megiddo."*

the House of David by themselves, and their womenfolk by themselves; the family of the House of Nathan by themselves, and their womenfolk by themselves; 13the family of the House of Levi by themselves, and their womenfolk by themselves; the family of the Shimeites by themselves, and their womenfolk by themselves; 14and all the other families, every family by itself, with their womenfolk by themselves.g

13 In that day a fountain shall be open to the House of David and the inhabitants of Jerusalem for purging and cleansing.

2In that day, too—declares the LORD of Hosts—I will erase the very names of the idols from the land; they shall not be uttered any more. And I will also make the "prophets" and the a-unclean spirit-a vanish from the land. 3If anyone "prophesies" thereafter, his own father and mother, who brought him into the world, will say to him, "You shall die, for you have lied in the name of the LORD"; and his own father and mother, who brought him into the world, will put him to death when he "prophesies." 4In that day, every "prophet" will be ashamed of the "visions" [he had] when he "prophesied." In order to deceive, heb will not wear a hairy mantle,c 5and he will declare, "I am not a 'prophet'; d-I am a tiller of the soil;-d you see, e-I was plied with the red stuffe from my youth on." 6And if he is asked, "What are those f-sores on your back?"-f he will reply, "From being beaten in the homes of my friends."g

> 7hO sword!
> Rouse yourself against My shepherd,
> The man i-in charge of My flock-i
>
> —says the LORD of Hosts.
>
> Strike down the shepherd
> And let the flock scatter;
> And I will also turn My hand
> Against all the shepherd boys.
> 8Throughout the land
>
> —declares the LORD—

---

g *In this way, apparently, they will prevail upon the LORD to spare the remnant of the besieging nations; cf. v. 10.*

a-a *To which abnormal human behavior was attributed.*

b *Heb. "They."*

c *In imitation of Elijah; cf. 2 Kings 1.8.*

d-d *I.e., I was addicted to wine like Noah, the tiller of the soil (cf. Gen. 9.20–21), hence my hallucinations and ravings; cf. Prov. 23.33.*

e-e *Connecting 'adam with 'adom "red" (cf. Prov. 23.31); but meaning of Heb. uncertain.*

f-f *Lit. "sores between your arms"; cf. 2 Kings 9.24. Sores are sometimes symptoms of hysteria.*

g *Presumably for making drunken scenes; cf. Prov. 23.35.*

h *Vv. 7–9 would read well after 11.17.*

i-i *Meaning of Heb. uncertain.*

Two-thirds shall perish, shall die,
And one-third of it shall survive.
9That third I will put into the fire,
And I will smelt them as one smelts silver
And test them as one tests gold.
They will invoke Me by name,
And I will respond to them.
I will declare, "You are My people,"
And they will declare,
"The LORD is our God!"

14 Lo, a day of the LORD is coming when your[a] spoil shall be divided in your very midst! 2For I will gather all the nations to Jerusalem for war: The city shall be captured, the houses plundered, and the women violated; and a part of the city shall go into exile. But the rest of the population shall not be uprooted from the city.

3Then the LORD will come forth and make war on those nations as He is wont to make war on a day of battle. 4On that day, He will set His feet on the Mount of Olives, near Jerusalem on the east; and the Mount of Olives shall split across from east to west, and one part of the Mount shall shift to the north and the other to the south, a huge gorge. 5bAnd the Valley in the Hills shall be stopped up, for the Valley of the Hills shall reach only to Azal; it shall be stopped up as it was stopped up as a result of the earthquake in the days of King Uzziah of Judah.—And the LORD my God, with all the holy beings, will come to you.

6cIn that day, there shall be neither sunlight nor cold moonlight, 7but there shall be a continuous day—only the LORD knows when—of neither day nor night, and there shall be light at eventide.

8In that day, fresh water shall flow from Jerusalem, part of it to the Eastern Sea[d] and part to the Western Sea,[e] throughout the summer and winter.

9And the LORD shall be king over all the earth; in that day there shall be one LORD with one name.[f]

---

a *Jerusalem is addressed.*
b *Vocalizing* [we] nistam *with Targum, Septuagint, and an old Heb. ms. Other mss. and printed editions read, "You [pl.] shall flee [to] the Valley in the Hills, for the Valley of the Hills shall reach up to Azal. You shall flee as you fled because of the earthquake. . . ."*
c *Meaning of verse uncertain; cf. Job 21.26.*
d *I.e., the Dead Sea; cf. Joel 2.20.*
e *I.e., the Mediterranean Sea; cf. Joel 2.20.*
f *I.e., the LORD alone shall be worshiped and shall be invoked by His true name.*

¹⁰Then the whole country shall become like the Arabah,^g ^{h-}from Geba to Rimmon south of Jerusalem.^{-h} The latter, however, shall perch high up where it is, and ⁱ⁻shall be inhabited⁻ⁱ from the Gate of Benjamin to the site of the Old Gate, down to the Corner Gate, and from the Tower of Hananel to the king's winepresses. ¹¹Never again shall destruction be decreed, and Jerusalem shall dwell secure.

¹²As for those peoples that warred against Jerusalem, the LORD will smite them with this plague: Their flesh shall rot away while they stand on their feet; their eyes shall rot away in their sockets; and their tongues shall rot away in their mouths.

¹³In that day, a great panic from the LORD shall fall upon them, and everyone shall snatch at the hand of another, and everyone shall raise his hand against everyone else's hand. ¹⁴Judah shall join the fighting in Jerusalem, and the wealth of all the nations roundabout—vast quantities of gold, silver, and clothing—shall be gathered in.

¹⁵The same plague shall strike the horses, the mules, the camels, and the asses; the plague shall affect all the animals in those camps.

¹⁶All who survive of all those nations that came up against Jerusalem shall make a pilgrimage year by year to bow low to the King LORD of Hosts and to observe the Feast of Booths. ¹⁷Any of the earth's communities that does not make the pilgrimage to Jerusalem to bow low to the King LORD of Hosts shall receive no rain. ¹⁸However, if the community of Egypt does not make this pilgrimage, it shall not be visited by the same affliction with which the LORD will strike the other nations that do not come up to observe the Feast of Booths.^j ¹⁹Such shall be the punishment of Egypt and of all other nations that do not come up to observe the Feast of Booths.

²⁰In that day, even the bells on the horses shall be inscribed "Holy to the LORD." The metal pots in the House of the LORD shall be like the basins before the altar; ²¹indeed, every metal pot in Jerusalem and in Judah shall be holy to the LORD of Hosts. And all those who sacrifice shall come and take of these to boil [their sacrificial meat] in; in that day there shall be no more traders^k in the House of the LORD of Hosts.

---

g *I.e., shall be depressed like the Jordan Valley.*
h-h *I.e., from the northern border of the Kingdom of Judah (1 Kings 15.22; 2 Kings 23.8) to the southern border (Josh. 15.32; 19.7).*
i-i *Brought up from v. 11 for clarity.*
j *Because Egypt is not dependent on rain, it will suffer some other punishment, presumably that described in v. 12.*
k *To sell ritually pure vessels.*

MALACHI

1 A pronouncement: The word of the LORD to Israel through Malachi.

²I have shown you love, said the LORD. But you ask, "How have You shown us love?" After all—declares the LORD—Esau is Jacob's brother; yet I have accepted Jacob ³and have rejected Esau. I have made his hills a desolation, his territory ᵃ⁻ᵃ home for beasts⁻ᵃ of the desert. ⁴If Edom thinks, "Though crushed, we can build the ruins again," thus said the LORD of Hosts: They may build, but I will tear down. And so they shall be known as the region of wickedness, the people damned forever of the LORD. ⁵Your eyes shall behold it, and you shall declare, "Great is the LORD beyond the borders of Israel!"

⁶A son should honor his father, and a slaveᵇ his master. Now if I am a father, where is the honor due Me? And if I am a master, where is the reverence due Me?—said the LORD of Hosts to you, O priests who scorn My name. But you ask, "How have we scorned Your name?" ⁷You offer defiled food on My altar. But you ask, "How have we defiled You?"ᶜ By saying, "The table of the LORD can be treated with scorn." ⁸When you present a blind animal for sacrifice—it doesn't matter! When you present a lame or sick one—it doesn't matter! Just offer it to your governor: Will he accept you? Will he show you favor?—said the LORD of Hosts. ⁹And now implore the favor of God! Will He be gracious to us? This is what you have done—will He accept any of you?

The LORD of Hosts has said: ¹⁰If only you would lock My doors, and not kindle fire on My altar to no purpose! I take no pleasure in you—said the LORD of Hosts—and I will accept no offering from you. ¹¹For from where the sun rises to where it sets, My name is honored among the nations, and everywhere incense and pure oblation are offered to My name; for My name is honored among the nations—said the LORD of

ᵃ⁻ᵃ *Meaning of Heb. uncertain.*
ᵇ *Septuagint and Targum add "should reverence"; cf. next part of verse.*
ᶜ *Septuagint "it."*

Hosts. ¹²But you profane it when you say, "The table of the LORD is defiled and the meat,^a the food, can be treated with scorn." ¹³You say, "Oh, what a bother!" And so you degrade^a it—said the LORD of Hosts— and you bring the stolen, the lame, and the sick; and you offer such as an oblation. Will I accept it from you?—said the LORD.

¹⁴A curse on the cheat who has an [unblemished] male in his flock, but for his vow sacrifices a blemished animal to the LORD! For I am a great King—said the LORD of Hosts—and My name is revered among the nations.

2 And now, O priests, this charge is for you: ²Unless you obey and unless you lay it to heart, and do honor to My name—said the LORD of Hosts—I will send a curse and turn your blessings into curses. (Indeed, I have turned them into curses, because you do not lay it to heart.) ³I will ^{a-}put your seed under a ban,^{-a} and I will strew dung upon your faces, the dung of your festal sacrifices, and you shall be carried out to its [heap].

⁴Know, then, that I have sent this charge to you that My covenant with Levi may endure—said the LORD of Hosts. ⁵I had with him a covenant of life and well-being, which I gave to him, and of reverence, which he showed Me. For he stood in awe of My name.

^{6b}Proper rulings were in his mouth,
And nothing perverse was on his lips;
He served Me with complete loyalty
And held the many back from iniquity.
^{7c-}For the lips of a priest guard knowledge,
And men seek rulings from his mouth;^{-c}
For he is a messenger of the LORD of Hosts.

⁸But you have turned away from that course: You have made the many stumble through your rulings;^d you have corrupted the covenant of the Levites—said the LORD of Hosts. ⁹And I, in turn, have made you despicable and vile in the eyes of all the people, because you disregard My ways and show partiality in your rulings.

¹⁰Have we not all one Father? Did not one God create us? Why do we break faith with one another, profaning the covenant of our ancestors? ¹¹Judah has broken faith; abhorrent things have been done in Israel and in Jerusalem. For Judah has profaned what is holy to the LORD—what He de-

---

^{a-a} *Meaning of Heb. uncertain.*
^b *See Hag. 2.10–13; cf. Lev. 10.8–11, Deut. 33.8, 10.*
^{c-c} *Or: For the lips of a priest are observed;/Knowledge and ruling are sought from his mouth.*
^d *By ruling falsely that an act was licit or an object ritually pure.*

sires—and espoused daughters of alien gods. 12May the LORD leave to him who does this a-no descendants-a dwelling in the tents of Jacob and presenting offerings to the LORD of Hosts. 13And this you do e-as well:-e You cover the altar of the LORD with tears, weeping, and moaning, so that He refuses to regard the oblation any more and to accept f-what you offer.-f 14But you ask, "Because of what?" Because the LORD is a witness between you and the wife of your youth with whom you have broken faith, though she is your partner and covenanted spouse. 15Did not the One make [all,] a-so that all remaining life-breath is His? And what does that One seek but godly folk? So be careful of your life-breath,-a and let no one break faith with the wife of his youth. 16For I detest divorce— said the LORD, the God of Israel—a-and covering oneself with lawlessness as with a garment-a—said the LORD of Hosts. So be careful of your life-breath and do not act treacherously.

17You have wearied the LORD with your talk. But you ask, "By what have we wearied [Him]?" By saying, "All who do evil are good in the sight of the LORD, and in them He delights," or else, "Where is the God of justice?"

3 Behold, I am sending My messenger to clear the way before Me, and the Lord whom you seek shall come to His Temple suddenly. As for the angel of the covenanta that you desire, he is already coming. 2But who can endure the day of his coming, and who can hold out when he appears? For he is like a smelter's fire and like fuller's lye. 3He shall actb like a smelter and purger of silver; and he shall purify the descendants of Levi and refine them like gold and silver, so that they shall present offerings in righteousness. 4Then the offerings of Judah and Jerusalem shall be pleasing to the LORD as in the days of yore and in the years of old. 5But [first] I will step forward to contend against you, and I will act as a relentless accuser against those who have no fear of Me: Who practice sorcery, who commit adultery, who swear falsely, who cheat laborers of their hire, and who subvert [the cause of] the widow, orphan, and stranger, said the LORD of Hosts.

6cFor I am the LORD—I have not changed; and you are the children of Jacob—you have not ceased to be. 7From the very days of your fathers

---

e-e Lit. "a second time"; Septuagint reads "which I detest"; cf. v. 16.
f-f Lit. "from your hand."

a Apparently the messenger of the previous sentence is regarded as Israel's tutelary angel.
b Lit. "sit."
c Vv. 6–12 resume the thought of 1.2–5.

you have turned away from My laws and have not observed them. Turn back to Me, and I will turn back to you—said the LORD of Hosts. But you ask, "How shall we turn back?" 8Ought man to defraud[d] God? Yet you are defrauding Me. And you ask, "How have we been defrauding You?" In tithe and contribution.[e] 9You are suffering under a curse, yet you go on defrauding Me—the whole nation of you. 10Bring the full tithe into the storehouse,[f] and let there be food in My House, and thus put Me to the test—said the LORD of Hosts. I will surely open the floodgates of the sky for you and pour down blessings on you; 11and I will banish the locusts[g] from you, so that they will not destroy the yield of your soil; and your vines in the field shall no longer miscarry—said the LORD of Hosts. 12And all the nations shall account you happy, for you shall be the most desired of lands—said the LORD of Hosts.

13You have spoken hard words against Me—said the LORD. But you ask, "What have we been saying among ourselves against You?" 14You have said, "It is useless to serve God. What have we gained by keeping His charge and walking in abject awe of the LORD of Hosts? 15And so, we account the arrogant happy: they have indeed done evil and endured; they have indeed dared God and escaped." 16In this vein have those who revere the LORD been talking to one another. The LORD has heard and noted it, and a scroll of remembrance has been written at His behest concerning those who revere the LORD and esteem His name. 17And on the day that I am preparing, said the LORD of Hosts, they shall be My treasured possession; I will be tender toward them as a man is tender toward a son who ministers to him. 18And you shall come to see the difference between the righteous and the wicked, between him who has served the LORD and him who has not served Him.

19For lo! That day is at hand, burning like an oven. All the arrogant and all the doers of evil shall be straw, and the day that is coming—said the LORD of Hosts—shall burn them to ashes and leave of them neither stock nor boughs. 20But for you who revere My name a sun of victory shall rise [h]-to bring healing.-[h] You shall go forth and stamp like stall-fed calves, 21and you shall trample the wicked to a pulp, for they shall be dust beneath your feet on the day that I am preparing—said the LORD of Hosts.

d *Heb.* qaba', *a play on the name of Jacob (v. 6); cf. Gen. 27.36.*
e *I.e., the contributions to the priests from the new grain, oil, and wine; see Num. 18.12.*
f *I.e., the public storehouse; see Neh. 13.10–13.*
g *Lit. "devourer."*
h-h *Lit. "with healing in the folds of its garments"; others "with healing in its wings."*

²²Be mindful of the Teaching of My servant Moses, whom I charged at Horeb with laws and rules for all Israel.

²³Lo, I will send the prophet Elijah to you before the coming of the awesome, fearful day of the LORD. ²⁴He shall reconcile parents with children and children with their parents, so that, when I come, I do not strike the whole land with utter destruction.

> Lo, I will send the prophet Elijah to you before
> the coming of the awesome, fearful day of the LORD.

כתובים

KETHUVIM

THE WRITINGS

PSALMS

BOOK ONE

1

Happy is the man who has not followed the counsel of the
wicked,
or taken the path of sinners,
or joined the company of the insolent;
²rather, the teaching of the LORD is his delight,
and he studiesª that teaching day and night.
³He is like a tree planted beside streams of water,
which yields its fruit in season,
whose foliage never fades,
and whatever ᵇ⁻it produces thrives.⁻ᵇ

⁴Not so the wicked;
rather, they are like chaff that wind blows away.
⁵Therefore the wicked will not survive judgment,
nor will sinners, in the assembly of the righteous.
⁶For the LORD cherishes the way of the righteous,
but the way of the wicked is doomed.

2

Why do nations assemble,
and peoples plotª vain things;
²kings of the earth take their stand,
and regents intrigue together
against the LORD and against His anointed?
³"Let us break the cords of their yoke,
shake off their ropes from us!"

ª Or "recites"; lit. "utters."
ᵇ⁻ᵇ Or "he does prospers."

ª Lit. "utter."

⁴He who is enthroned in heaven laughs;
 the Lord mocks at them.
⁵Then He speaks to them in anger,
 terrifying them in His rage,
⁶"But I have installed My king
 on Zion, My holy mountain!"
⁷Let me tell of the decree:
 the LORD said to me,
 ᵇ-"You are My son,
 I have fathered you this day.-ᵇ
⁸Ask it of Me,
 and I will make the nations your domain;
 your estate, the limits of the earth.
⁹You can smash them with an iron mace,
 shatter them like potter's ware."

¹⁰So now, O kings, be prudent;
 accept discipline, you rulers of the earth!
¹¹Serve the LORD in awe;
 ᶜ-tremble with fright,-ᶜ
12 ᵈ-pay homage in good faith,-ᵈ
 lest He be angered, and your way be doomed
 in the mere flash of His anger.
Happy are all who take refuge in Him.

3 A psalm of David when he fled from his son Absalom.

²O LORD, my foes are so many!
Many are those who attack me;
 ³many say of me,
 "There is no deliverance for him through God."   *Selah.*ᵃ
⁴But You, O LORD, are a shield about me,
 my glory, He who holds my head high.
⁵I cry aloud to the LORD,
 and He answers me from His holy mountain.   *Selah.*
⁶I lie down and sleep and wake again,
 for the LORD sustains me.

ᵇ-ᵇ *Compare 2 Sam. 7.14, and Ps. 89.27 ff.*
ᶜ-ᶜ *Meaning of Heb. uncertain; others "rejoice with trembling."*
ᵈ-ᵈ *Meaning of Heb. uncertain.*

ᵃ *A liturgical direction of uncertain meaning.*

⁷I have no fear of the myriad forces
    arrayed against me on every side.

⁸Rise, O Lord!
Deliver me, O my God!
For You slap all my enemies in the face;ᵇ
    You break the teeth of the wicked.
⁹Deliverance is the Lord's;
    Your blessing be upon Your people!   *Selah.*

4 ᵃ⁻For the leader; with instrumental music.⁻ᵃ A psalm of David.

²Answer me when I call,
    O God, my vindicator!
You freed me from distress;
    have mercy on me and hear my prayer.
³You men, how long will my glory be mocked,
    will you love illusions,
    have recourse to frauds?   *Selah.*
⁴Know that the Lord singles out the faithful for Himself;
    the Lord hears when I call to Him.
⁵So tremble, and sin no more;
    ponder it on your bed, and sigh.ᵇ
⁶Offer sacrifices in righteousness
    and trust in the Lord.

⁷Many say, "O for good days!"
ᶜ⁻Bestow Your favor on us,⁻ᶜ O Lord.
⁸You put joy into my heart
    when their grain and wine show increase.
⁹Safe and sound, I lie down and sleep,
    ᵈ⁻for You alone, O Lord, keep me secure.⁻ᵈ

5 ᵃ⁻For the leader; on *nehiloth*.⁻ᵃ A psalm of David.

²Give ear to my speech, O Lord;
    consider my utterance.

ᵇ *Lit. "cheek."*

ᵃ⁻ᵃ *Meaning of Heb. uncertain.*
ᵇ *Others "be still."*
ᶜ⁻ᶜ *Lit. "Lift up the light of Your countenance upon us"; cf. Num. 6.25 f.*
ᵈ⁻ᵈ *Or "for You, O Lord, keep me alone and secure."*

ᵃ⁻ᵃ *Meaning of Heb. uncertain.*

³Heed the sound of my cry,
  my king and God,
  for I pray to You.
⁴Hear my voice, O LORD, at daybreak;
  at daybreak I plead before You, and wait.

⁵For You are not a God who desires wickedness;
  evil cannot abide with You;
⁶wanton men cannot endure in Your sight.
You detest all evildoers;
  ⁷You doom those who speak lies;
  murderous, deceitful men the LORD abhors.

⁸But I, through Your abundant love, enter Your house;
  I bow down in awe at Your holy temple.
⁹O LORD, ᵇ⁻lead me along Your righteous [path]⁻ᵇ
  because of my watchful foes;
  make Your way straight before me.
¹⁰For there is no sincerity on their lips;ᶜ
  their heart is [filled with] malice;
  their throat is an open grave;
  their tongue slippery.
¹¹Condemn them, O God;
  let them fall by their own devices;
  cast them out for their many crimes,
  for they defy You.
¹²But let all who take refuge in You rejoice,
  ever jubilant as You shelter them;
  and let those who love Your name exult in You.
¹³For You surely bless the righteous man, O LORD,
  encompassing him with favor like a shield.

6 ᵃ⁻For the leader; with instrumental music on the *sheminith*.⁻ᵃ A psalm of David.

²O LORD, do not punish me in anger,
  do not chastise me in fury.

ᵇ⁻ᵇ *Or "as You are righteous, lead me."*
ᶜ *Lit. "mouth."*

ᵃ⁻ᵃ *Meaning of Heb. uncertain.*

³Have mercy on me, O LORD, for I languish;
  heal me, O LORD, for my bones shake with terror.
⁴My whole being is stricken with terror,
  while You, LORD—O, how long!
⁵O LORD, turn! Rescue me!
Deliver me as befits Your faithfulness.
⁶For there is no praise of You among the dead;
  in Sheol, who can acclaim You?

⁷I am weary with groaning;
  every night I drench my bed,
  I melt my couch in tears.
⁸My eyes are wasted by vexation,
  worn out because of all my foes.
⁹Away from me, all you evildoers,
  for the LORD heeds the sound of my weeping.
¹⁰The LORD heeds my plea,
  the LORD accepts my prayer.
¹¹All my enemies will be frustrated and stricken with terror;
  they will turn back in an instant, frustrated.

7 ᵃ⁻*Shiggaion* of David,⁻ᵃ which he sang to the LORD, concerning Cush,
a Benjaminite.

²O LORD, my God, in You I seek refuge;
  deliver me from all my pursuers and save me,
³lest, like a lion, they tear me apart,
  rending in pieces, and no one save me.
⁴O LORD, my God, if I have done such things,
  if my hands bear the guilt of wrongdoing,
⁵if I have dealt evil to my ally,
  —ᵇ⁻I who rescued my foe without reward⁻ᵇ—
⁶then let the enemy pursue and overtake me;
  let him trample my life to the ground,
  and lay my body in the dust.   *Selah.*

ᵃ⁻ᵃ *Meaning of Heb. uncertain.*
ᵇ⁻ᵇ *Meaning of Heb. uncertain; others "or stripped my foe clean."*

⁷Rise, O LORD, in Your anger;
    assert Yourself ^{c-}against the fury of my foes;^{-c}
    bestir Yourself on my behalf;
    You have ordained judgment.
⁸ ^{a-}Let the assembly of peoples gather about You,
    with You enthroned above, on high.^{-a}
⁹The LORD judges the peoples;
    vindicate me, O LORD,
    for the righteousness and blamelessness that are mine.
¹⁰Let the evil of the wicked come to an end,
    but establish the righteous;
    he who probes the mind and conscience^d is God the
      righteous.
¹¹^{e-}I look to God to shield me;^{-e}
    the deliverer of the upright.
¹²God vindicates the righteous;
    God ^{f-}pronounces doom^{-f} each day.
¹³^{g-}If one does not turn back, but whets his sword,
    bends his bow and aims it,
¹⁴then against himself he readies deadly weapons,
    and makes his arrows sharp.^{-g}
¹⁵See, he hatches evil, conceives mischief,
    and gives birth to fraud.
¹⁶He has dug a pit and deepened it,
    and will fall into the trap he made.
¹⁷His mischief will recoil upon his own head;
    his lawlessness will come down upon his skull.
¹⁸I will praise the LORD for His righteousness,
    and sing a hymn to the name of the LORD Most High.

8

^{a-}For the leader; on the *gittith.*^{-a} A psalm of David.

²O LORD, our Lord,
    How majestic is Your name throughout the earth,

c-c *Or "in Your fury against my foes."*
d *Lit. "kidneys."*
e-e *Cf. Ibn Ezra and Kimhi; lit. "My Shield is upon God."*
f-f *Others "has indignation."*
g-g *Meaning of vv. 13–14 uncertain; an alternate rendering, with God as the main subject, is:*
  13*If one does not turn back, He whets His sword,/bends His bow and aims it;/*14*deadly weapons*
    He prepares for him,/and makes His arrows sharp.

a-a *Meaning of Heb. uncertain.*

ᵇ⁻You who have covered the heavens with Your splendor! ⁻ᵇ
³ᵃ⁻From the mouths of infants and sucklings
  You have founded strength on account of Your foes,
  to put an end to enemy and avenger.⁻ᵃ
⁴When I behold Your heavens, the work of Your fingers,
  the moon and stars that You set in place,
  ⁵what is man that You have been mindful of him,
  mortal man that You have taken note of him,
  ⁶that You have made him little less than divine,ᶜ
  and adorned him with glory and majesty;
  ⁷You have made him master over Your handiwork,
  laying the world at his feet,
  ⁸sheep and oxen, all of them,
  and wild beasts, too;
  ⁹the birds of the heavens, the fish of the sea,
  whatever travels the paths of the seas.
  ¹⁰O LORD, our Lord, how majestic is Your name throughout
    the earth!

9

ᵃ⁻For the leader; *'almuth labben.*⁻ᵃ A psalm of David.

²I will praise You, LORD, with all my heart;
  I will tell all Your wonders.
³I will rejoice and exult in You,
  singing a hymn to Your name, O Most High.

⁴When my enemies retreat,
  they stumble to their doom at Your presence.
⁵For You uphold my right and claim,
  enthroned as righteous judge.
⁶You blast the nations;
  You destroy the wicked;
  You blot out their name forever.
⁷ᵇ⁻The enemy is no more—
  ruins everlasting;
  You have torn down their cities;
  their very names are lost.⁻ᵇ

ᵇ⁻ᵇ *Meaning of Heb. uncertain; or "You whose splendor is celebrated all over the heavens!"*
ᶜ *Or "the angels."*

ᵃ⁻ᵃ *Meaning of Heb. uncertain; some mss. and ancient versions,* 'al muth labben, *as though "over the death of the son."*
ᵇ⁻ᵇ *Meaning of Heb. uncertain.*

⁸But the LORD abides forever;
    He has set up His throne for judgment;
    ⁹it is He who judges the world with righteousness,
    rules the peoples with equity.
¹⁰The LORD is a haven for the oppressed,
    a haven in times of trouble.
¹¹Those who know Your name trust You,
    for You do not abandon those who turn to You, O LORD.
¹²Sing a hymn to the LORD, ᶜ⁻who reigns in Zion;⁻ᶜ
    declare His deeds among the peoples.
¹³ ᵈ⁻For He does not ignore the cry of the afflicted;
    He who requites bloodshed is mindful of them.⁻ᵈ
¹⁴Have mercy on me, O LORD;
    see my affliction at the hands of my foes,
    You who lift me from the gates of death,
    ¹⁵so that in the gates of ᵉ⁻Fair Zion⁻ᵉ
    I might tell all Your praise,
    I might exult in Your deliverance.
¹⁶The nations sink in the pit they have made;
    their own foot is caught in the net they have hidden.
¹⁷The LORD has made Himself known:
    He works judgment;
    the wicked man is snared by his own devices. *Higgaion.*ᵇ *Selah.*
¹⁸Let the wicked beᶠ in Sheol,
    all the nations who ignore God!
¹⁹Not always shall the needy be ignored,
    nor the hope of the afflicted forever lost.
²⁰Rise, O LORD!
Let not men have power;
    let the nations be judged in Your presence.
²¹ᵇ⁻Strike fear into them,⁻ᵇ O LORD;
    let the nations know they are only men.   *Selah.*

10

Why, O LORD, do You stand aloof,
    heedless in times of trouble?
²The wicked in his arrogance hounds the lowly—

ᶜ⁻ᶜ *Or "O You who dwell in Zion."*
ᵈ⁻ᵈ *Order of Hebrew clauses inverted for clarity.*
ᵉ⁻ᵉ *Lit. "the Daughter of Zion."*
ᶠ *Others "return to."*

^{a-}may they be caught in the schemes they devise! ^{-a}

^{3b-}The wicked crows about his unbridled lusts;
the grasping man reviles and scorns the LORD.

⁴The wicked, arrogant as he is,
in all his scheming [thinks],^{-b}
"He does not call to account;
^{c-}God does not care."^{-c}

⁵His ways prosper at all times;
Your judgments are far beyond him;
he snorts at all his foes.

⁶He thinks, "I shall not be shaken,
through all time never be in trouble."

⁷His mouth is full of oaths, deceit, and fraud;
mischief and evil are under his tongue.

⁸He lurks in outlying places;
from a covert he slays the innocent;
his eyes spy out the hapless.

⁹He waits in a covert like a lion in his lair;
waits to seize the lowly;
he seizes the lowly as he pulls his net shut;

¹⁰he stoops, he crouches,
^{b-}and the hapless fall prey to his might.^{-b}

¹¹He thinks, "God is not mindful,
He hides His face, He never looks."

¹²Rise, O LORD!
^{d-}Strike at him,^{-d} O God!
Do not forget the lowly.

¹³Why should the wicked man scorn God,
thinking You do not call to account?

¹⁴You do look!
You take note of mischief and vexation!
^{b-}To requite is in Your power.^{-b}
To You the hapless can entrust himself;
You have ever been the orphan's help.

¹⁵O break the power of the wicked and evil man,
so that when You ^{e-}look for^{-e} his wickedness
You will find it no more.

^{a-a} *Or "they (i.e., the lowly) are caught by the schemes they devised."*
^{b-b} *Meaning of Heb. uncertain.*
^{c-c} *Lit. "There is no God."*
^{d-d} *Lit. "Lift Your hand."*
^{e-e} *A play on* darash, *which in vv. 4 and 13 means "to call to account."*

¹⁶The LORD is king for ever and ever;
    the nations will perish from His land.
¹⁷You will listen to the entreaty of the lowly, O LORD,
    You will make their hearts firm;
    You will incline Your ear
      ¹⁸to champion the orphan and the downtrodden,
    b-that men who are of the earth tyrannize no more.-b

11

For the leader. Of David.

In the LORD I take refuge;
    how can you say to me,
    "Take to a-the hills like a bird! -a
²For see, the wicked bend the bow,
    they set their arrow on the string
    to shoot from the shadows at the upright.
³b-When the foundations are destroyed,
    what can the righteous man do?"-b

⁴The LORD is in His holy palace;
    the LORD—His throne is in heaven;
    His eyes behold, His gaze searches mankind.
⁵The LORD seeks out the righteous man,
    but loathes the wicked one who loves injustice.
⁶He will rain down upon the wicked blazing coals and sulfur;
    a scorching wind shall be c-their lot.-c
⁷For the LORD is righteous;
    He loves righteous deeds;
    the upright shall behold His face.

12

For the leader; on the *sheminith*. A psalm of David.

²Help, O LORD!
For the faithful are no more;
    the loyal have vanished from among men.

---

a-a *Meaning of Heb. uncertain; lit. "your hill, bird!"*
b-b *Or "For the foundations are destroyed; what has the Righteous One done?"*
   Or "If the foundations are destroyed, what has the righteous man accomplished?"
c-c *Lit. "the portion of their cup."*

³Men speak lies to one another;
 their speech is smooth;
 they talk with duplicity.
⁴May the Lord cut off all flattering lips,
 every tongue that speaks arrogance.
⁵They say, "By our tongues we shall prevail;
 with lips such as ours, who can be our master?"

⁶"Because of the groans of the plundered poor and needy,
 I will now act," says the Lord.
ᵃ-"I will give help," He affirms to him.⁻ᵃ
⁷The words of the Lord are pure words,
 silver purged in an earthen crucible,
 refined sevenfold.
⁸You, O Lord, will keep them,
 guarding each ᵃ-from this age⁻ᵃ evermore.
⁹On every side the wicked roam
 ᵃ-when baseness is exalted among men.⁻ᵃ

13 For the leader. A psalm of David.

²How long, O Lord; will You ignore me forever?
How long will You hide Your face from me?
³How long will I have cares on my mind,
 grief in my heart all day?
How long will my enemy have the upper hand?
⁴Look at me, answer me, O Lord, my God!
Restore the luster to my eyes,
 lest I sleep the sleep of death;
 ⁵lest my enemy say, "I have overcome him,"
 my foes exult when I totter.
⁶But I trust in Your faithfulness,
 my heart will exult in Your deliverance.
I will sing to the Lord,
 for He has been good to me.

ᵃ⁻ᵃ *Meaning of Heb. uncertain.*

14

aFor the leader. Of David.

The benighted man thinks,
  b-"God does not care."-b
Man's deeds are corrupt and loathsome;
    no one does good.
2The LORD looks down from heaven on mankind
    to find a man of understanding,
    a man mindful of God.
3All have turned bad,
    altogether foul;
    there is none who does good,
    not even one.
4Are they so witless, all those evildoers,
    who devour my people as they devour food,
    and do not invoke the LORD?
5There they will be seized with fright,
    for God is present in the circle of the righteous.
6You may set at naught the counsel of the lowly,
    but the LORD is his refuge.

7O that the deliverance of Israel might come from Zion!
When the LORD restores the fortunes of His people,
    Jacob will exult, Israel will rejoice.

15

A psalm of David.

LORD, who may sojourn in Your tent,
    who may dwell on Your holy mountain?
2He who lives without blame,
    who does what is right,
    and in his heart acknowledges the truth;
    3 a-whose tongue is not given to evil;-a
    who has never done harm to his fellow,
    or borne reproach for [his acts toward] his neighbor;
    4for whom a contemptible man is abhorrent,

a Cf. Ps. 53.
b-b Lit. "There is no God"; cf. Ps. 10.4.

a-a Meaning of Heb. uncertain; or "who has no slander upon his tongue."

but who honors those who fear the LORD;
who stands by his oath even to his hurt;
⁵who has never lent money at interest,
or accepted a bribe against the innocent.
The man who acts thus shall never be shaken.

16 A *michtam*ᵃ of David.

Protect me, O God, for I seek refuge in You.
²I say to the LORD,
"You are my Lord, ᵇ⁻my benefactor;
there is none above You."⁻ᵇ
³ ᶜ⁻As to the holy and mighty ones that are in the land,
my whole desire concerning them is that
⁴those who espouse another [god]
may have many sorrows! ⁻ᶜ
I will have no part of their bloody libations;
their names will not pass my lips.
⁵The LORD is my allotted share and portion;ᵈ
You control my fate.
⁶Delightful country has fallen to my lot;
lovely indeed is my estate.
⁷I bless the LORD who has guided me;
my conscienceᵉ admonishes me at night.
⁸I am ever mindful of the LORD's presence;
He is at my right hand; I shall never be shaken.
⁹So my heart rejoices,
my whole being exults,
and my body rests secure.
¹⁰For You will not abandon me to Sheol,
or let Your faithful one see the Pit.
¹¹You will teach me the path of life.
In Your presence is perfect joy;
delights are ever in Your right hand.

ᵃ *Meaning of Heb. uncertain.*
ᵇ⁻ᵇ *Others "I have no good but in You."*
ᶜ⁻ᶜ *Meaning of Heb. uncertain; "holy and mighty ones" taken as epithets for divine beings; cf.*
  qedoshim *in Ps. 89.6, 8, and* 'addirim *in 1 Sam. 4.8.*
ᵈ *Lit. "cup."*
ᵉ *Lit. "kidneys."*

17 A prayer of David.

Hear, O Lord, what is just;
  heed my cry, give ear to my prayer,
  uttered without guile.
²My vindication will come from You;
  Your eyes will behold what is right.
³You have visited me at night, probed my mind,
  You have tested me and found nothing amiss;
  ªᵃI determined that my mouth should not transgress.
⁴As for man's dealings,
  in accord with the command of Your lips,⁻ᵃ
  I have kept in view the fate^b of the lawless.
⁵My feet have held to Your paths;
  my legs have not given way.

⁶I call on You;
  You will answer me, God;
  turn Your ear to me,
  hear what I say.
⁷Display Your faithfulness in wondrous deeds,
  You who deliver with Your right hand
  those who seek refuge from assailants.
⁸Guard me like the apple of Your eye;
  hide me in the shadow of Your wings
  ⁹from the wicked who despoil me,
  ᶜmy mortal enemies who⁻ᶜ encircle me.
10 ªᵃTheir hearts are closed to pity;⁻ᵃ
  they mouth arrogance;
  ¹¹now they hem in our feet on every side;
  they set their eyes roaming over the land.
¹²He is like a lion eager for prey,
  a king of beasts lying in wait.

¹³Rise, O Lord! Go forth to meet him.
Bring him down;
  rescue me from the wicked with Your sword,

ᵃᵃ *Meaning of Heb. uncertain.*
ᵇ *Cf. Prov. 1.19; lit. "paths."*
ᶜᶜ *Or "from my enemies who avidly."*

14 a-from men, O LORD, with Your hand,
from men whose share in life is fleeting.
But as to Your treasured ones,
    fill their bellies.-a
Their sons too shall be satisfied,
    and have something to leave over for their young.
15Then I, justified, will behold Your face;
    awake, I am filled with the vision of You.

18 aFor the leader. Of David, the servant of the LORD, who addressed
the words of this song to the LORD after the LORD had saved him from
the hands of all his enemies and from the clutches of Saul.
    2He said:
        b-I adore you, O LORD, my strength,-b
        3O LORD, my crag, my fortress, my rescuer,
        my God, my rock in whom I seek refuge,
        my shield, my c-mighty champion,-c my haven.
4 d-All praise! I called on the LORD-d
    and was delivered from my enemies.
5Ropese of Death encompassed me;
    torrents of Belialf terrified me;
        6ropes of Sheol encircled me;
        snares of Death confronted me.
7In my distress I called on the LORD,
    cried out to my God;
        in His temple He heard my voice;
        my cry to Him reached His ears.
8Then the earth rocked and quaked;
    the foundations of the mountains shook,
    rocked by His indignation;
        9smoke went up from His nostrils,
        from His mouth came devouring fire;
        live coals blazed forth from Him.
10He bent the sky and came down,
    thick cloud beneath His feet.
11He mounted a cherub and flew,
    gliding on the wings of the wind.

---

a *This poem occurs again at 2 Sam. 22, with a number of variations, some of which are cited in
the following notes.*
b-b *Not in 2 Sam. 22.2.*
c-c *Lit. "horn of rescue."*
d-d *Construction of Heb. uncertain.*
e *2 Sam. 22.5, "breakers."*
f *I.e., the netherworld, like "Death" and "Sheol."*

¹²He made darkness His screen;
  dark thunderheads, dense clouds of the sky
  were His pavilion round about Him.
¹³Out of the brilliance before Him,
  hail and fiery coals ᵍ⁻pierced His clouds.⁻ᵍ
¹⁴Then the LORD thundered from heaven,
  the Most High gave forth His voice—
  ʰ⁻hail and fiery coals.⁻ʰ
¹⁵He let fly His shafts and scattered them;
  He discharged lightning and routed them.
¹⁶The ocean bed was exposed;
  the foundations of the world were laid bare
  by Your mighty roaring, O LORD,
  at the blast of the breath of Your nostrils.
¹⁷He reached down from on high, He took me;
  He drew me out of the mighty waters;
  ¹⁸He saved me from my fierce enemy,
  from foes too strong for me.
¹⁹They confronted me on the day of my calamity,
  but the LORD was my support.
²⁰He brought me out to freedom;
  He rescued me because He was pleased with me.

²¹The LORD rewarded me according to my merit;
  He requited the cleanness of my hands;
  ²²for I have kept to the ways of the LORD,
  and have not been guilty before my God;
  ²³for I am mindful of all His rules;
  I have not disregarded His laws.
²⁴I have been blameless toward Him,
  and have guarded myself against sinning;
  ²⁵and the LORD has requited me according to my merit,
  the cleanness of my hands in His sight.

²⁶With the loyal, You deal loyally;
  with the blameless man, blamelessly.
²⁷With the pure, You act purely,
  and with the perverse, You are wily.
²⁸It is You who deliver lowly folk,

ᵍ⁻ᵍ 2 Sam. 22.13, "blazed."
ʰ⁻ʰ Not in 2 Sam. 22.14.

but haughty eyes You humble.
²⁹It is You who light my lamp;
   the LORD, my God, lights up my darkness.
³⁰With You, I can rush a barrier;ⁱ
   with my God I can scale a wall;
     ³¹the way of God is perfect;
   the word of the LORD is pure;
   He is a shield to all who seek refuge in Him.
³²Truly, who is a god except the LORD,
   who is a rock but our God?—
     ³³the God who girded me with might,
   who made my way perfect;
     ³⁴who made my legs like a deer's,
   and let me stand firm on the^j heights;
     ³⁵who trained my hands for battle;
   my arms can bend a bow of bronze.
³⁶You have given me the shield of Your protection;
   Your right hand has sustained me,
   Your care^k has made me great.
³⁷You have let me stride on freely;
   my feet have not slipped.
³⁸I pursued my enemies and overtook them;
   I did not turn back till I destroyed them.
³⁹I struck them down,
   and they could rise no more;
   they lay fallen at my feet.
⁴⁰You have girded me with strength for battle,
   brought my adversaries low before me,
     ⁴¹made my enemies turn tail before me;
   I wiped out my foes.
⁴²They cried out, but there was none to deliver;
   [cried] to the LORD, but He did not answer them.
⁴³I ground them fine as windswept dust;
   I trod them flat as dirt of the streets.
⁴⁴You have rescued me from the strife of people;
   You have set me at the head of nations;
   peoples I knew not must serve me.
⁴⁵At the mere report of me they are submissive;

ⁱ *Cf. note to 2 Sam. 22.30; or "troop."*
^j *Taking* bamothai *as a poetic form of* bamoth; *cf. Hab. 3.19; others "my."*
^k *Meaning of Heb. uncertain; others "condescension."*

foreign peoples cower before me;
⁴⁶foreign peoples lose courage,
ˡ⁻and come trembling out of their strongholds.⁻ˡ

⁴⁷The LORD lives! Blessed is my rock!
Exalted be God, my deliverer,
⁴⁸the God who has vindicated me
and made peoples subject to me,
⁴⁹who rescued me from my enemies,
who raised me clear of my adversaries,
saved me from lawless men.
⁵⁰For this I sing Your praise among the nations, LORD,
and hymn Your name:
⁵¹ᵐ⁻He accords great victories⁻ᵐ to His king,
keeps faith with His anointed,
with David and his offspring forever.

19

For the leader. A psalm of David.

²The heavens declare the glory of God,
the sky proclaims His handiwork.
³Day to day makes utterance,
night to night speaks out.
⁴There is no utterance,
there are no words,
ᵃ⁻whose sound goes unheard.⁻ᵃ
⁵Their voiceᵇ carries throughout the earth,
their words to the end of the world.
He placed in themᶜ a tent for the sun,
⁶who is like a groom coming forth from the chamber,
like a hero, eager to run his course.
⁷His rising-place is at one end of heaven,
and his circuit reaches the other;
nothing escapes his heat.

⁸The teaching of the LORD is perfect,
renewing life;

ˡ⁻ˡ *Meaning of Heb. uncertain.*
ᵐ⁻ᵐ *2 Sam. 22.51, "Tower of victory."*

ᵃ⁻ᵃ *With Septuagint, Symmachus, and Vulgate; or "their sound is not heard."*
ᵇ *Cf. Septuagint, Symmachus, and Vulgate; Arabic qawwah, "to shout."*
ᶜ *Viz., the heavens.*

the decrees of the LORD are enduring,
　　making the simple wise;
9The precepts of the LORD are just,
　　rejoicing the heart;
　　the instruction of the LORD is lucid,
　　making the eyes light up.
10The fear of the LORD is pure,
　　abiding forever;
　　the judgments of the LORD are true,
　　righteous altogether,
　　11more desirable than gold,
　　than much fine gold;
　　sweeter than honey,
　　than drippings of the comb.
12Your servant pays them heed;
　　in obeying them there is much reward.
13Who can be aware of errors?
Clear me of unperceived guilt,
　　14and from d-willful sins-d keep Your servant;
　　let them not dominate me;
　　then shall I be blameless
　　and clear of grave offense.
15May the words of my mouth
　　and the prayer of my hearte
　　be acceptable to You,
　　O LORD, my rock and my redeemer.

20 For the leader. A psalm of David.

2May the LORD answer you in time of trouble,
　　the name of Jacob's God keep you safe.
3May He send you help from the sanctuary,
　　and sustain you from Zion.
4May He receive the tokensa of all your meal offerings,
　　and approveb your burnt offerings.　　　　　　　　　*Selah.*
5May He grant you your desire,
　　and fulfill your every plan.

d-d *Or "arrogant men"; cf. Ps. 119.51.*
e *For* leb *as a source of speech, see note to Eccl. 5.1.*

a *Reference to* azkara, *"token portion" of meal offering; Lev. 2.2, 9, 16, etc.*
b *Meaning of Heb. uncertain.*

⁶May we shout for joy in your victory,
   arrayed by standards in the name of our God.
May the LORD fulfill your every wish.

⁷Now I know that the LORD will give victory to His anointed,
   will answer him from His heavenly sanctuary
   with the mighty victories of His right arm.
⁸They [call] on chariots, they [call] on horses,
   but we call on the name of the LORD our God.
⁹They collapse and lie fallen,
   but we rally and gather strength.
¹⁰ᶜ⁻O LORD, grant victory!
May the King answer us when we call.⁻ᶜ

21 For the leader. A psalm of David.

²O LORD, the king rejoices in Your strength;
   how greatly he exults in Your victory!
³You have granted him the desire of his heart,
   have not denied the request of his lips.   *Selah.*
⁴You have proffered him blessings of good things,
   have set upon his head a crown of fine gold.
⁵He asked You for life; You granted it;
   a long life, everlasting.
⁶Great is his glory through Your victory;
   You have endowed him with splendor and majesty.
⁷You have made him blessed forever,
   gladdened him with the joy of Your presence.
⁸For the king trusts in the LORD;
   Through the faithfulness of the Most High
   he will not be shaken.
⁹Your hand is equal to all Your enemies;
   Your right hand overpowers Your foes.
¹⁰You set them ablaze like a furnace
      ᵃ⁻when You show Your presence.⁻ᵃ
The LORD in anger destroys them;

ᶜ⁻ᶜ *Or, in the light of v. 7, "O LORD, grant victory to the king; may He answer us when we call."*
ᵃ⁻ᵃ *Or "at the time of Your anger."*

fire consumes them.
11You wipe their offspring from the earth,
their issue from among men.
12For they schemed against You;
they laid plans,
but could not succeed.
13b-For You make them turn back-b
by Your bows aimed at their face.
14Be exalted, O LORD, through Your strength;
we will sing and chant the praises of Your mighty deeds.

22For the leader; on a-*ayyeleth ha-shahar.*-a A psalm of David.

2My God, my God,
why have You abandoned me;
why so far from delivering me
and from my anguished roaring?
3My God,
I cry by day—You answer not;
by night, and have no respite.

4b-But You are the Holy One,
enthroned,
the Praise of Israel.-b
5In You our fathers trusted;
they trusted, and You rescued them.
6To You they cried out
and they escaped;
in You they trusted
and were not disappointed.

7But I am a worm, less than human;
scorned by men, despised by people.
8All who see me mock me;
c-they curl their lips,-c
they shake their heads.

b-b *Meaning of Heb. uncertain.*

a-a *Meaning of Heb. uncertain.*
b-b *Or "But You are holy, enthroned upon the praises of Israel."*
c-c *Lit. "they open wide with a lip."*

⁹"Let him commit himself to the LORD;
    let Him rescue him,
    let Him save him,
    for He is pleased with him."
¹⁰You ª⁻drew me⁻ª from the womb,
    made me secure at my mother's breast.
¹¹I became Your charge at birth;
    from my mother's womb You have been my God.
¹²Do not be far from me,
    for trouble is near,
    and there is none to help.
¹³Many bulls surround me,
    mighty ones of Bashan encircle me.
¹⁴They open their mouths at me
    like tearing, roaring lions.
¹⁵ᵈ⁻My life ebbs away:⁻ᵈ
    all my bones are disjointed;
    my heart is like wax,
    melting within me;
    ¹⁶my vigor dries up like a shard;
    my tongue cleaves to my palate;
    You commit me to the dust of death.
¹⁷Dogs surround me;
    a pack of evil ones closes in on me,
    ᵉ⁻like lions [they maul] my hands and feet.⁻ᵉ
¹⁸I take the count of all my bones
    while they look on and gloat.
¹⁹They divide my clothes among themselves,
    casting lots for my garments.

²⁰But You, O LORD, be not far off;
    my strength, hasten to my aid.
²¹Save my life from the sword,
    my precious lifeᶠ from the clutches of a dog.
²²Deliver me from a lion's mouth;
    from the horns of wild oxen rescueᵍ me.
²³Then will I proclaim Your fame to my brethren,
    praise You in the congregation.

ᵈ⁻ᵈ *Lit. "I am poured out like water."*
ᵉ⁻ᵉ *With Rashi; cf. Isa. 38.13.*
ᶠ *Lit. "only one."*
ᵍ *Lit. "answer."*

24You who fear the LORD, praise Him!
All you offspring of Jacob, honor Him!
Be in dread of Him, all you offspring of Israel!
25For He did not scorn, He did not spurn
the plea^h of the lowly;
He did not hide His face from him;
when he cried out to Him, He listened.
26 i-Because of You I offer praise-i in the great congregation;
I pay my vows in the presence of His worshipers.
27Let the lowly eat and be satisfied;
let all who seek the LORD praise Him.
Always be of good cheer!
28Let all the ends of the earth pay heed and turn to the LORD,
and the peoples of all nations prostrate themselves before
You;
29for kingship is the LORD's
and He rules the nations.
30j-All those in full vigor shall eat and prostrate themselves;
all those at death's door, whose spirits flag,
shall bend the knee before Him.-j
31Offspring shall serve Him;
the LORD's fame shall be proclaimed to the generation
32to come;
they shall tell of His beneficence
to people yet to be born,
for He has acted.

23 A psalm of David.

The LORD is my shepherd;
I lack nothing.
2He makes me lie down in green pastures;
He leads me to a-water in places of repose;-a
3He renews my life;
He guides me in right paths
as befits His name.

---

h Or "plight."
i-i Lit. "From You is my praise."
j-j Meaning of Heb. uncertain; others "All the fat ones of the earth shall eat and worship;/All
they that go down to the dust shall kneel before Him,/Even he that cannot keep his soul alive."

a-a Others "still waters."

⁴Though I walk through ᵇ⁻a valley of deepest darkness,⁻ᵇ
    I fear no harm, for You are with me;
    Your rod and Your staff—they comfort me.

⁵You spread a table for me in full view of my enemies;
    You anoint my head with oil;
    my drink is abundant.
⁶Only goodness and steadfast love shall pursue me
    all the days of my life,
    and I shall dwell in the house of the LORD
    for many long years.

24 Of David. A psalm.

The earth is the LORD's and all that it holds,
    the world and its inhabitants.
²For He founded it upon the ocean,
    set it on the nether-streams.

³Who may ascend the mountain of the LORD?
Who may stand in His holy place?—
⁴He who has clean hands and a pure heart,
    who has not taken a false oath by Myᵃ life
    or sworn deceitfully.
⁵He shall carry away a blessing from the LORD,
    a just reward from God, his deliverer.
⁶Such is the circleᵇ of those who turn to Him,
    Jacob, who seek Your presence.   *Selah.*

⁷O gates, lift up your heads!
Up high, you everlasting doors,
    so the King of glory may come in!
⁸Who is the King of glory?—
    the LORD, mighty and valiant,
    the LORD, valiant in battle.
⁹O gates, lift up your heads!
Lift them up, you everlasting doors,
    so the King of glory may come in!

ᵇ⁻ᵇ *Others "the valley of the shadow of death."*

ᵃ *Ancient versions and some mss. read "His."*
ᵇ *Lit. "generation."*

¹⁰Who is the King of glory?—
the LORD of hosts,
He is the King of glory!   *Selah.*

25 Of David.

א   O LORD, I set my hope on You;
ב   ²my God, in You I trust;
        may I not be disappointed,
        may my enemies not exult over me.
ג   ³O let none who look to You be disappointed;
        let the faithless be disappointed, empty-handed.
ד   ⁴Let me know Your paths, O LORD;
        teach me Your ways;
ה ו   ⁵guide me in Your true way and teach me,
        for You are God, my deliverer;
        it is You I look to at all times.
ז   ⁶O LORD, be mindful of Your compassion
        and Your faithfulness;
        they are old as time.
ח   ⁷Be not mindful of my youthful sins and transgressions;
        in keeping with Your faithfulness consider what is in my
            favor,
        as befits Your goodness, O LORD.
ט   ⁸Good and upright is the LORD;
        therefore He shows sinners the way.
י   ⁹He guides the lowly in the right path,
        and teaches the lowly His way.
כ   ¹⁰All the LORD's paths are steadfast love
        for those who keep the decrees of His covenant.
ל   ¹¹As befits Your name, O LORD,
        pardon my iniquity though it be great.
מ   ¹²Whoever fears the LORD,
        he shall be shown what path to choose.
נ   ¹³He shall live a happy life,
        and his children shall inherit the land.
ס   ¹⁴The counselª of the LORD is for those who fear Him;

ª *Or "secret."*

to them He makes known His covenant.
15My eyes are ever toward the LORD,
    for He will loose my feet from the net.
16Turn to me, have mercy on me,
    for I am alone and afflicted.
17b-My deep distress-b increases;
    deliver me from my straits.
18Look at my affliction and suffering,
    and forgive all my sins.
19See how numerous my enemies are,
    and how unjustly they hate me!
20Protect me and save me;
    let me not be disappointed,
    for I have sought refuge in You.
21May integrity and uprightness watch over me,
    for I look to You.
22O God, redeem Israel
    from all its distress.

26 Of David.

Vindicate me, O LORD,
    for I have walked without blame;
    I have trusted in the LORD;
    I have not faltered.
2Probe me, O LORD, and try me,
    test my a-heart and mind;-a
    3 b-for my eyes are on Your steadfast love;
    I have set my course by it.-b
4I do not consort with scoundrels,
    or mix with hypocrites;
    5I detest the company of evil men,
    and do not consort with the wicked;
    6I wash my hands in innocence,
    and walk around Your altar, O LORD,
    7raising my voice in thanksgiving,
    and telling all Your wonders.

b-b *Lit. "The distress of my heart."*

a-a *Lit. "kidneys and heart."*
b-b *Or "I am aware of Your faithfulness, and always walk in Your true [path]."*

8O LORD, I love Your temple abode,
  the dwelling-place of Your glory.
9Do not sweep me away with sinners,
  or [snuff out] my life with murderers,
  10who have schemes at their fingertips,
  and hands full of bribes.
11But I walk without blame;
  redeem me, have mercy on me!
12My feet are on level ground.
In assemblies I will bless the LORD.

27 Of David.

The LORD is my light and my help;
  whom should I fear?
The LORD is the stronghold of my life,
  whom should I dread?
2When evil men assail me
  a-to devour my flesh-a—
  it is they, my foes and my enemies,
  who stumble and fall.
3Should an army besiege me,
  my heart would have no fear;
  should war beset me,
  still would I be confident.

4One thing I ask of the LORD,
  only that do I seek:
  to live in the house of the LORD
  all the days of my life,
  to gaze upon the beauty of the LORD,
  b-to frequent-b His temple.
5He will shelter me in His pavilion
  on an evil day,
  grant me the protection of His tent,
  raise me high upon a rock.
6Now is my head high

a-a Or "to slander me"; cf. Dan. 3.8; 6.25.
b-b Meaning of Heb. uncertain.

over my enemies roundabout;
   I sacrifice in His tent with shouts of joy,
   singing and chanting a hymn to the LORD.

7Hear, O LORD, when I cry aloud;
   have mercy on me, answer me.
8 b-In Your behalf-b my heart says:
   "Seek My face!"
O LORD, I seek Your face.
9Do not hide Your face from me;
   do not thrust aside Your servant in anger;
   You have ever been my help.
Do not forsake me, do not abandon me,
   O God, my deliverer.
10Though my father and mother abandon me,
   the LORD will take me in.
11Show me Your way, O LORD,
   and lead me on a level path
   because of my watchful foes.
12Do not subject me to the will of my foes,
   for false witnesses and unjust accusers
   have appeared against me.
13Had I not the assurance
   that I would enjoy the goodness of the LORD
   in the land of the living . . .

14Look to the LORD;
   be strong and of good courage!
O look to the LORD!

28 Of David.

O LORD, I call to You;
   my rock, do not disregard me,
   for if You hold aloof from me,
   I shall be like those gone down into the Pit.
2Listen to my plea for mercy

when I cry out to You,
  when I lift my hands
  toward Your inner sanctuary.
³Do not ᵃ⁻count me⁻ᵃ with the wicked and evildoers
  who profess goodwill toward their fellows
  while malice is in their heart.
⁴Pay them according to their deeds,
  their malicious acts;
  according to their handiwork pay them,
  give them their deserts.
⁵For they do not consider the LORD's deeds,
  the work of His hands.
May He tear them down,
  never to rebuild them!
⁶Blessed is the LORD,
  for He listens to my plea for mercy.
⁷The LORD is my strength and my shield;
  my heart trusts in Him.
I was helped,ᵇ and my heart exulted,
  so I will glorify Him with my song.
⁸The LORD is ᶜ⁻their strength;⁻ᶜ
  He is a stronghold for the deliverance of His anointed.
⁹Deliver and bless Your very own people;
  tend them and sustain them forever.

29 A psalm of David.

Ascribe to the LORD, O divine beings,
  ascribe to the LORD glory and strength.
²Ascribe to the LORD the glory of His name;
  bow down to the LORD, majestic in holiness.
³The voice of the LORD is over the waters;
  the God of glory thunders,
  the LORD, over the mighty waters.
⁴The voice of the LORD is power;
  the voice of the LORD is majesty;
  ⁵the voice of the LORD breaks cedars;

ᵃ⁻ᵃ Or "drag me off"; meaning of Heb. uncertain.
ᵇ Or "strengthened."
ᶜ⁻ᶜ Septuagint, Saadia, and others render, and some mss. read, ʿoz leʿammo, "the strength of His people."

the LORD shatters the cedars of Lebanon.
6a-He makes Lebanon skip like a calf,-a
   Sirion, like a young wild ox.
7The voice of the LORD kindles flames of fire;
   8the voice of the LORD convulses the wilderness;
   the LORD convulses the wilderness of Kadesh;
   9the voice of the LORD causes hinds to calve,
   b-and strips forests bare;-b
   while in His temple all say "Glory!"
10The LORD sat enthroned at the Flood;
   the LORD sits enthroned, king forever.

11May the LORD grant strength to His people;
   may the LORD bestow on His people wellbeing.

30 A psalm of David. A song for the dedication of the House.a

2I extol You, O LORD,
   for You have lifted me up,
   and not let my enemies rejoice over me.
3O LORD, my God,
   I cried out to You,
   and You healed me.
4O LORD, You brought me up from Sheol,
   preserved me from going down into the Pit.

5O you faithful of the LORD, sing to Him,
   and praise His holy name.
6For He is angry but a moment,
   and when He is pleased there is life.
b-One may lie down weeping at nightfall;-b
   but at dawn there are shouts of joy.

7When I was untroubled,
   I thought, "I shall never be shaken,"
   8for You, O LORD, when You were pleased,

---

a-a *Lit. "He makes them skip like a calf, Lebanon and Sirion, etc."*
b-b *Or "brings ewes to early birth."*

a *I.e., the Temple.*
b-b *Or "Weeping may linger for the night."*

made [me]^c firm as a mighty mountain.
When You hid Your face,
    I was terrified.
⁹I called to You, O LORD;
    to my LORD I made appeal,
        ¹⁰"What is to be gained from my death,^d
    from my descent into the Pit?
Can dust praise You?
Can it declare Your faithfulness?
¹¹Hear, O LORD, and have mercy on me;
    O LORD, be my help!"

¹²You turned my lament into dancing,
    you undid my sackcloth and girded me with joy,
        ¹³that [my] whole being might sing hymns to You endlessly;
    O LORD my God, I will praise You forever.

31 For the leader. A psalm of David.

²I seek refuge in You, O LORD;
    may I never be disappointed;
    as You are righteous, rescue me.
³Incline Your ear to me;
    be quick to save me;
    be a rock, a stronghold for me,
    a citadel, for my deliverance.
⁴For You are my rock and my fortress;
    You lead me and guide me as befits Your name.
⁵You free me from the net laid for me,
    for You are my stronghold.
⁶Into Your hand I entrust my spirit;
    You redeem me, O LORD, faithful God.
⁷I detest those who rely on empty folly,
    but I trust in the LORD.
⁸Let me exult and rejoice in Your faithfulness
    when You notice my affliction,

---

c *Following Saadia, R. Isaiah of Trani; cf. Ibn Ezra.*
d *Lit. "blood."*

are mindful of my deep distress,
⁹and do not hand me over to my enemy,
but ^{a-}grant me relief.^{-a}

¹⁰Have mercy on me, O LORD,
for I am in distress;
my eyes are wasted by vexation,
^{b-}my substance and body too.^{-b}
¹¹My life is spent in sorrow,
my years in groaning;
my strength fails because of my iniquity,
my limbs waste away.
¹²Because of all my foes
I am the particular butt of my neighbors,
a horror to my friends;
those who see me on the street avoid me.
¹³I am put out of mind like the dead;
I am like an object given up for lost.
¹⁴I hear the whisperings of many,
intrigue^c on every side,
as they scheme together against me,
plotting to take my life.

¹⁵But I trust in You, O LORD;
I say, "You are my God!"
¹⁶My fate is in Your hand;
save me from the hand of my enemies and pursuers.
¹⁷Show favor to Your servant;
as You are faithful, deliver me.
¹⁸O LORD, let me not be disappointed when I call You;
let the wicked be disappointed;
let them be silenced in Sheol;
¹⁹let lying lips be stilled
that speak haughtily against the righteous
with arrogance and contempt.
²⁰How abundant is the good
that You have in store for those who fear You,
that You do in the full view of men

---

^{a-a} Lit. "make my feet stand in a broad place."
^{b-b} Meaning of Heb. uncertain.
^c Others "terror."

for those who take refuge in You.
21You grant them the protection of Your presence
b-against scheming men;-b
You shelter them in Your pavilion
from contentious tongues.
22Blessed is the LORD,
for He has been wondrously faithful to me,
a veritable bastion.
23Alarmed, I had thought,
"I am thrust out of Your sight";
yet You listened to my plea for mercy
when I cried out to You.
24So love the LORD, all you faithful;
the LORD guards the loyal,
and more than requites
him who acts arrogantly.
25Be strong and of good courage,
all you who wait for the LORD.

32 Of David. a-A *maskil.*-a

Happy is he whose transgression is forgiven,
whose sin is covered over.
2Happy the man whom the LORD does not hold guilty,
and in whose spirit there is no deceit.

3As long as I said nothing,
my limbs wasted away
from my anguished roaring all day long.
4For night and day
Your hand lay heavy on me;
my vigor waned
as in the summer drought.   *Selah.*
5Then I acknowledged my sin to You;
I did not cover up my guilt;
I resolved, "I will confess my transgressions to the LORD,"
and You forgave the guilt of my sin.   *Selah.*

a-a *Meaning of Heb. uncertain.*

[6]Therefore let every faithful man pray to You
   [b]upon discovering [his sin],[-b]
   that the rushing mighty waters
   not overtake him.
[7]You are my shelter;
   You preserve me from distress;
   You surround me with the joyous shouts of deliverance.

                                      Selah.

[8]Let me enlighten you
   and show you which way to go;
   let me offer counsel; my eye is on you.
[9]Be not like a senseless horse or mule
   [a]whose movement must be curbed by bit and bridle;[-a]
   [c]far be it from you![-c]
[10]Many are the torments of the wicked,
   but he who trusts in the LORD
   shall be surrounded with favor.
[11]Rejoice in the LORD and exult, O you righteous;
   shout for joy, all upright men!

33 Sing forth, O you righteous, to the LORD;
   it is fit that the upright acclaim Him.
[2]Praise the LORD with the lyre;
   with the ten-stringed harp sing to Him;
   [3]sing Him a new song;
   play sweetly with shouts of joy.
[4]For the word of the LORD is right;
   His every deed is faithful.
[5]He loves what is right and just;
   the earth is full of the LORD's faithful care.
[6]By the word of the LORD the heavens were made,
   by the breath of His mouth, all their host.
[7]He heaps up the ocean waters like a mound,
   stores the deep in vaults.

[8]Let all the earth fear the LORD;
   let all the inhabitants of the world dread Him.

[b-b] *Meaning of Heb. uncertain; others "in a time when You may be found."*
[c-c] *Meaning of Heb. uncertain; for this rendering cf. Ibn Ezra.*

⁹For He spoke, and it was;
  He commanded, and it endured.
¹⁰The LORD frustrates the plans of nations,
  brings to naught the designs of peoples.
¹¹What the LORD plans endures forever,
  what He designs, for ages on end.

¹²Happy the nation whose God is the LORD,
  the people He has chosen to be His own.
¹³The LORD looks down from heaven;
  He sees all mankind.
¹⁴From His dwelling-place He gazes
  on all the inhabitants of the earth—
    ¹⁵He who fashions the hearts of them all,
    who discerns all their doings.

¹⁶Kings are not delivered by a large force;
  warriors are not saved by great strength;
    ¹⁷horses are a false hope for deliverance;
    for all their great power they provide no escape.
¹⁸Truly the eye of the LORD is on those who fear Him,
  who wait for His faithful care
    ¹⁹to save them from death,
    to sustain them in famine.
²⁰We set our hope on the LORD,
  He is our help and shield;
    ²¹in Him our hearts rejoice,
    for in His holy name we trust.
²²May we enjoy, O LORD, Your faithful care,
  as we have put our hope in You.

34 Of David, ᵃwhen he feigned madness in the presence of Abimelech, who turned him out, and he left.⁻ᵃ

א　　²I bless the LORD at all times;
  praise of Him is ever in my mouth.
ב　　³I glory in the LORD;

ᵃ⁻ᵃ *Cf. 1 Sam. 21.14 ff.*

let the lowly hear it and rejoice.

ג   4Exalt the LORD with me;
let us extol His name together.

ד   5I turned to the LORD, and He answered me;
He saved me from all my terrors.

ה   6Men look to Him and are radiant;
let their faces not be downcast.

ו   7Here was a lowly man who called,
and the LORD listened,
and delivered him from all his troubles.

ח   8The angel of the LORD camps around those who fear Him
and rescues them.

ט   9Taste and see how good the LORD is;
happy the man who takes refuge in Him!

י   10Fear the LORD, you His consecrated ones,
for those who fear Him lack nothing.

כ   11Lions have been reduced to starvation,
but those who turn to the LORD shall not lack any good.

ל   12Come, my sons, listen to me;
I will teach you what it is to fear the LORD.

מ   13Who is the man who is eager for life,
who desires years of good fortune?

נ   14Guard your tongue from evil,
your lips from deceitful speech.

ס   15Shun evil and do good,
seek amity[b] and pursue it.

ע   16The eyes of the LORD are on the righteous,
His ears attentive to their cry.

פ   17The face of the LORD is set against evildoers,
to erase their names from the earth.

צ   18They[c] cry out, and the LORD hears,
and saves them from all their troubles.

ק   19The LORD is close to the brokenhearted;
those crushed in spirit He delivers.

ר   20Though the misfortunes of the righteous be many,
the LORD will save him from them all,

ש   21Keeping all his bones intact,
not one of them being broken.

b *Or "integrity."*
c *Viz., the righteous of v. 16.*

ח   22One misfortune is the deathblow of the wicked;
     the foes of the righteous shall be ruined.
23The LORD redeems the life of His servants;
     all who take refuge in Him shall not be ruined.

35 Of David.

O LORD, strive with my adversaries,
     give battle to my foes,
     2take up shield and buckler,
     and come to my defense;
     3ready the spear and javelin
     against my pursuers;
     tell me, "I am your deliverance."
4Let those who seek my life
     be frustrated and put to shame;
     let those who plan to harm me
     fall back in disgrace.
5Let them be as chaff in the wind,
     the LORD's angel driving them on.
6Let their path be dark and slippery,
     with the LORD's angel in pursuit.
7For without cause they hid a net to trap me;
     without cause they dug a pit[a] for me.
8Let disaster overtake them unawares;
     let the net they hid catch them;
     let them fall into it when disaster [strikes].
9Then shall I exult in the LORD,
     rejoice in His deliverance.
10All my bones shall say,
     "LORD, who is like You?
You save the poor from one stronger than he,
     the poor and needy from his despoiler."

11Malicious witnesses appear
     who question me about things I do not know.
12They repay me evil for good,

---

a Transferred from first clause for clarity.

[seeking] my bereavement.
¹³Yet, when they were ill,
my dress was sackcloth,
I kept a fast—
ᵇ‑may what I prayed for happen to me!‑ᵇ
¹⁴I walked about as though it were my friend or my brother;
I was bowed with gloom, like one mourning for his mother.
¹⁵But when I stumble, they gleefully gather;
wretches gather against me,
I know not why;
ᶜ‑they tear at me without end.
¹⁶With impious, mocking grimace‑ᶜ
they gnash their teeth at me.

¹⁷O Lord, how long will You look on?
Rescue me ᶜ‑from their attacks,‑ᶜ
my precious life, from the lions,
¹⁸that I may praise You in a great congregation,
acclaim You in a mighty throng.
¹⁹Let not my treacherous enemies rejoice over me,
or those who hate me without reason wink their eyes.
²⁰For they do not offer amity,
but devise fraudulent schemes against harmless folk.
²¹They open wide their mouths at me,
saying, "Aha, aha, we have seen it!"

²²You have seen it, O LORD;
do not hold aloof!
O Lord, be not far from me!
²³Wake, rouse Yourself for my cause,
for my claim, O my God and my Lord!
²⁴Take up my cause, O LORD my God, as You are beneficent,
and let them not rejoice over me.
²⁵Let them not think,
"Aha, just what we wished!"
Let them not say,
"We have destroyed him!"
²⁶May those who rejoice at my misfortune

ᵇ⁻ᵇ *Meaning of Heb. uncertain; lit. "my prayer returns upon my bosom."*
ᶜ⁻ᶜ *Meaning of Heb. uncertain.*

be frustrated and utterly disgraced;
may those who vaunt themselves over me
be clad in frustration and shame.
27May those who desire my vindication
sing forth joyously;
may they always say,
"Extolled be the LORD
who desires the well-being of His servant,"
28while my tongue shall recite Your beneficent acts,
Your praises all day long.

36

For the leader. Of the servant of the LORD, of David.

2a-I know-a what Transgression says to the wicked;
he has no sense of the dread of God,
3b-because its speech is seductive to him
till his iniquity be found out and he be hated.-b
4His words are evil and deceitful;
he will not consider doing good.
5In bed he plots mischief;
he is set on a path of no good,
he does not reject evil.

6O LORD, Your faithfulness reaches to heaven;
Your steadfastness to the sky;
7Your beneficence is like the high mountains;
Your justice like the great deep;
man and beast You deliver, O LORD.
8How precious is Your faithful care, O God!
Mankind shelters in the shadow of Your wings.
9They feast on the rich fare of Your house;
You let them drink at Your refreshing stream.
10With You is the fountain of life;
by Your light do we see light.
11Bestow Your faithful care on those devoted to You,
and Your beneficence on upright men.
12Let not the foot of the arrogant tread on me,
or the hand of the wicked drive me away.

a-a *Lit. "In my heart is."*
b-b *Meaning of Heb. uncertain.*

¹³There lie the evildoers, fallen,
    thrust down, unable to rise.

37 Of David.

א   Do not be vexed by evil men;
    do not be incensed by wrongdoers;
      ²for they soon wither like grass,
    like verdure fade away.

ב   ³Trust in the LORD and do good,
    abide in the land and remain loyal.
    ⁴Seek the favor of the LORD,
    and He will grant you the desires of your heart.

ג   ⁵Leave allᵃ to the LORD;
    trust in Him; He will do it.
    ⁶He will cause your vindication to shine forth like the light,
    the justice of your case, like the noonday sun.

ד   ⁷Be patient and wait for the LORD,
    do not be vexed by the prospering man
    who carries out his schemes.

ה   ⁸Give up anger, abandon fury,
    do not be vexed;
    it can only do harm.
    ⁹For evil men will be cut off,
    but those who look to the LORD—
    they shall inherit the land.

ו   ¹⁰A little longer and there will be no wicked man;
    you will look at where he was—
    he will be gone.
    ¹¹But the lowly shall inherit the land,
    and delight in abundant well-being.

ז   ¹²The wicked man schemes against the righteous,
    and gnashes his teeth at him.
    ¹³The Lord laughs at him,
    for He knows that his day will come.

ח   ¹⁴The wicked draw their swords, bend their bows,

ᵃ *Lit. "your way."*

to bring down the lowly and needy,
to slaughter b-upright men.-b
15Their swords shall pierce their own hearts,
and their bows shall be broken.

ט 16Better the little that the righteous man has
than the great abundance of the wicked.
17For the arms of the wicked shall be broken,
but the LORD is the support of the righteous.

י 18The LORD is concerned for the needsc of the blameless;
their portion lasts forever;
19they shall not come to grief in bad times;
in famine, they shall eat their fill.

כ 20But the wicked shall perish,
and the enemies of the LORD shall be consumed,
like meadow grassd consumed in smoke.

ל 21The wicked man borrows and does not repay;
the righteous is generous and keeps giving.
22Those blessed by Him shall inherit the land,
but those cursed by Him shall be cut off.

מ 23The steps of a man are made firm by the LORD,
when He delights in his way.
24Though he stumbles, he does not fall down,
for the LORD gives him support.

נ 25I have been young and am now old,
but I have never seen a righteous man abandoned,
or his children seeking bread.
26He is always generous, and lends,
and his children are held blessed.

ס 27Shun evil and do good,
and you shall abide forever.
28For the LORD loves what is right,
He does not abandon His faithful ones.
They are preserved forever,
while the children of the wicked will be cut off.
29The righteous shall inherit the land,
and abide forever in it.

פ 30The mouth of the righteous utters wisdom,
and his tongue speaks what is right.

b-b Lit. "those whose way is upright."
c Lit. "days."
d Meaning of Heb. uncertain.

1149

³¹The teaching of his God is in his heart;
  his feet do not slip.

צ ³²The wicked watches for the righteous,
  seeking to put him to death;
  ³³the LORD will not abandon him to his power;
  He will not let him be condemned in judgment.

ק ³⁴Look to the LORD and keep to His way,
  and He will raise you high that you may inherit the land;
  when the wicked are cut off, you shall see it.

ר ³⁵I saw a wicked man, powerful,
  well-rooted like a robust native tree.

³⁶Suddenly he vanished and was gone;
  I sought him, but he was not to be found.

ש ³⁷Mark the blameless, note the upright,
  for there is a future for the man of integrity.

³⁸But transgressors shall be utterly destroyed,
  the future of the wicked shall be cut off.

ת ³⁹The deliverance of the righteous comes from the LORD,
  their stronghold in time of trouble.

⁴⁰The LORD helps them and rescues them,
  rescues them from the wicked and delivers them,
  for they seek refuge in Him.

38 A psalm of David. *Lehazkir.*ᵃ

²O LORD, do not punish me in wrath;
  do not chastise me in fury.

³For Your arrows have struck me;
  Your blows have fallen upon me.

⁴There is no soundness in my flesh because of Your rage,
  no wholeness in my bones because of my sin.

⁵For my iniquities have ᵇ⁻overwhelmed me;⁻ᵇ
  they are like a heavy burden, more than I can bear.

⁶My wounds stink and fester
  because of my folly.

⁷I am all bent and bowed;
  I walk about in gloom all day long.

ᵃ *Meaning of Heb. uncertain.*
ᵇ⁻ᵇ *Lit. "passed over my head."*

8For my sinews are full of fever;
   there is no soundness in my flesh.
9I am all benumbed and crushed;
   I roar because of the turmoil in my mind.

10O Lord, You are aware of all my entreaties;
   my groaning is not hidden from You.
11My mind reels;
   my strength fails me;
   my eyes too have lost their luster.
12My friends and companions stand back from my affliction;
   my kinsmen stand far off.
13Those who seek my life lay traps;
   those who wish me harm speak malice;
   they utter deceit all the time.
14But I am like a deaf man, unhearing,
   like a dumb man who cannot speak up;
   15I am like one who does not hear,
   who has no retort on his lips.
16But I wait for You, O Lord;
   You will answer, O Lord, my God.
17For I fear they will rejoice over me;
   when my foot gives way they will vaunt themselves against
      me.
18For I am on the verge of collapse;
   my pain is always with me.
19I acknowledge my iniquity;
   I am fearful over my sin;
   20for my mortal enemies are numerous;
   my treacherous foes are many.
21Those who repay evil for good
   harass me for pursuing good.

22Do not abandon me, O Lord;
   my God, be not far from me;
   23hasten to my aid,
   O Lord, my deliverance.

39

For the leader; for *Jeduthun*. A psalm of David.

²I resolved I would watch my step
lest I offend by my speech;
I would keep my mouth muzzled
while the wicked man was in my presence.
³I was dumb, silent;
I was very[a] still
while my pain was intense.
⁴My mind was in a rage,
my thoughts were all aflame;
I spoke out:
⁵Tell me, O LORD, what my term is,
what is the measure of my days;
I would know how fleeting my life is.
⁶You have made my life just handbreadths long;
its span is as nothing in Your sight;
[b]no man endures any longer than a breath.[b]   Selah.
⁷Man walks about as a mere shadow;
mere futility is his hustle and bustle,
amassing and not knowing who will gather in.
⁸What, then, can I count on, O Lord?
In You my hope lies.
⁹Deliver me from all my transgressions;
make me not the butt of the benighted.
¹⁰I am dumb, I do not speak up,
for it is Your doing.
¹¹Take away Your plague from me;
I perish from Your blows.
¹²You chastise a man in punishment for his sin,
consuming like a moth what he treasures.
No man is more than a breath.   Selah.

¹³Hear my prayer, O LORD;
give ear to my cry;
do not disregard my tears;

ᵃ *Cf. use of* ṭwb *in Hos. 10.1; Jonah 4.4.*
ᵇ⁻ᵇ *Meaning of Heb. uncertain.*

for like all my forebears
I am an alien, resident with You.
14Look away from me, b-that I may recover,-b
before I pass away and am gone.

40 For the leader. A psalm of David.

2I put my hope in the LORD;
He inclined toward me,
and heeded my cry.
3He lifted me out of the miry pit,
the slimy clay,
and set my feet on a rock,
steadied my legs.
4He put a new song into my mouth,
a hymn to our God.
May many see it and stand in awe,
and trust in the LORD.
5Happy is the man who makes the LORD his trust,
who turns not to the arrogant or to followers of falsehood.
6 a-You, O LORD my God, have done many things;
the wonders You have devised for us
cannot be set out before You;-a
I would rehearse the tale of them,
but they are more than can be told.
7 b-You gave me to understand that-b
You do not desire sacrifice and meal offering;
You do not ask for burnt offering and sin offering.
8Then I said,
b-"See, I will bring a scroll recounting what befell me."-b
9To do what pleases You, my God, is my desire;
Your teaching is in my inmost parts.
10I proclaimed [Your] righteousness in a great congregation;
see, I did not withhold my words;
O LORD, You must know it.
11I did not keep Your beneficence to myself;

a-a Or "You, O LORD my God, have done many things—/the wonders You have devised for us;/
none can equal You."
b-b Meaning of Heb. uncertain.

I declared Your faithful deliverance;
   I did not fail to speak of Your steadfast love in a great
      congregation.
12O LORD, You will not withhold from me Your compassion;
   Your steadfast love will protect me always.

13For misfortunes without number envelop me;
   my iniquities have caught up with me;
   I cannot see;
   they are more than the hairs of my head;
   c-I am at my wits' end.-c
14 dO favor me, LORD, and save me;
   O LORD, hasten to my aid.
15Let those who seek to destroy my life
   be frustrated and disgraced;
   let those who wish me harm
   fall back in shame.
16Let those who say "Aha! Aha!" over me
   be desolate because of their frustration.
17But let all who seek You be glad and rejoice in You;
   let those who are eager for Your deliverance always say,
   "Extolled be the LORD!"
18But I am poor and needy;
   may the Lord devise [deliverance] for me.
   You are my help and my rescuer;
   my God, do not delay.

41 For the leader. A psalm of David.

2Happy is he who is thoughtful of the wretched;
   in bad times may the LORD keep him from harm.
3May the LORD guard him and preserve him;
   and may he be thought happy in the land.
Do not subject him to the will of his enemies.
4The LORD will sustain him on his sickbed;
   a-You shall wholly transform his bed of suffering.-a
5I said, "O LORD, have mercy on me,

c-c Or "my courage fails me."
d With vv. 14–18, cf. Ps. 70.

a-a Meaning of Heb. uncertain.

heal me, for I have sinned against You."
6My enemies speak evilly of me,
   "When will he die and his name perish?"
7If one comes to visit, he speaks falsely;
   his mind stores up evil thoughts;
   once outside, he speaks them.
8All my enemies whisper together against me,
   imagining the worst for me.
9"Something baneful has settled in him;
   he'll not rise from his bed again."
10My ally in whom I trusted,
   even he who shares my bread,
   a-has been utterly false to me.-a
11But You, O LORD, have mercy on me;
   let me rise again and repay them.
12Then shall I know that You are pleased with me:
   when my enemy cannot shout in triumph over me.
13You will support me because of my integrity,
   and let me abide in Your presence forever.

14Blessed is the LORD, God of Israel,
   from eternity to eternity.
   Amen and Amen.

BOOK TWO

42 For the leader. A *maskil* of the Korahites.

2Like a hind crying for water,a
   my soul cries for You, O God;
   3my soul thirsts for God, the living God;
   O when will I come to appear before God!
4My tears have been my food day and night;
   I am ever taunted with, "Where is your God?"
5When I think of this, I pour out my soul:

---

a Lit. *"watercourses."*

how I b-walked with the crowd, moved with them,-b
the festive throng, to the House of God
with joyous shouts of praise.
6Why so downcast, my soul,
why disquieted within me?
Have hope in God;
I will yet praise Him
c-for His saving presence.-c

7O my God, my soul is downcast;
therefore I think of You
in this land of Jordan and Hermon,
in Mount Mizar,
8where deep calls to deep
in the roar of b-Your cataracts;-b
all Your breakers and billows have swept over me.
9By day may the LORD vouchsafe His faithful care,
so that at night a song to Him may be with me,
a prayer to the God of my life.
10I say to God, my rock,
"Why have You forgotten me,
why must I walk in gloom,
oppressed by my enemy?"
11b-Crushing my bones,-b
my foes revile me,
taunting me always with, "Where is your God?"
12Why so downcast, my soul,
why disquieted within me?
Have hope in God;
I will yet praise Him,
my ever-present help, my God.

43 aVindicate me, O God,
champion my cause
against faithless people;
rescue me from the treacherous, dishonest man.

b-b *Meaning of Heb. uncertain.*
c-c *Several ancient versions and Heb. mss. connect the first word in v. 7 with the end of 6, reading* yeshu'ot panai we'Elohai, *"my ever-present help, my God," as in vv. 12 and Ps. 43.5.*
a *A continuation of Ps. 42.*

2For You are my God, my stronghold;
  why have You rejected me?
Why must I walk in gloom,
  oppressed by the enemy?
3Send forth Your light and Your truth;
  they will lead me;
  they will bring me to Your holy mountain,
  to Your dwelling-place,
  4that I may come to the altar of God,
  God, my delight, my joy;
  that I may praise You with the lyre,
  O God, my God.
5Why so downcast, my soul,
  why disquieted within me?
Have hope in God;
  I will yet praise Him,
  my ever-present help, my God.

44 For the leader. Of the Korahites. A *maskil.*

2We have heard, O God,
  our fathers have told us
  the deeds You performed in their time,
  in days of old.
3With Your hand You planted them,
  displacing nations;
  You brought misfortune on peoples,
  and drove them out.
4It was not by their sword that they took the land,
  their arm did not give them victory,
  but Your right hand, Your arm, and Your goodwill,
  for You favored them.
5You are my king, O God;
  decree victories for Jacob!
6Through You we gore our foes;
  by Your name we trample our adversaries;

⁷I do not trust in my bow;
  it is not my sword that gives me victory;
⁸You give us victory over our foes;
  You thwart those who hate us.
⁹In God we glory at all times,
  and praise Your name unceasingly.   *Selah.*

¹⁰Yet You have rejected and disgraced us;
  You do not go with our armies.
¹¹You make us retreat before our foe;
  our enemies plunder us at will.
¹²You let them devour us like sheep;
  You disperse us among the nations.
¹³You sell Your people for no fortune,
  You set no high price on them.
¹⁴You make us the butt of our neighbors,
  the scorn and derision of those around us.
¹⁵You make us a byword among the nations,
  a laughingstockª among the peoples.
¹⁶I am always aware of my disgrace;
  I am wholly covered with shame
    ¹⁷at the sound of taunting revilers,
  in the presence of the vengeful foe.

¹⁸All this has come upon us,
  yet we have not forgotten You,
  or been false to Your covenant.
¹⁹Our hearts have not gone astray,
  nor have our feet swerved from Your path,
    ²⁰though You cast us, crushed, to where the ᵇ-sea monster-ᵇ
      is,
  and covered us over with deepest darkness.
²¹If we forgot the name of our God
  and spread forth our hands to a foreign god,
    ²²God would surely search it out,
  for He knows the secrets of the heart.
²³It is for Your sake that we are slain all day long,
  that we are regarded as sheep to be slaughtered.

ª *Lit. "a wagging of the head."*
ᵇ-ᵇ*Heb.* tannim = tannin, *as in Ezek. 29.3 and 32.2.*

24Rouse Yourself; why do You sleep, O Lord?
Awaken, do not reject us forever!
25Why do You hide Your face,
ignoring our affliction and distress?
26We lie prostrate in the dust;
our body clings to the ground.
27Arise and help us,
redeem us, as befits Your faithfulness.

45

For the leader; a-on *shoshannim.*-a Of the Korahites. A *maskil.* A love song.

2My heart is astir with gracious words;
I speak my poem to a king;
my tongue is the pen of an expert scribe.

3You are fairer than all men;
your speech is endowed with grace;
rightly has God given you an eternal blessing.
4Gird your sword upon your thigh, O hero,
in your splendor and glory;
5a-in your glory, win success;
ride on in the cause of truth and meekness and right;
and let your right hand lead you to awesome deeds.-a
6Your arrows, sharpened,
b-[pierce] the breast of the king's enemies;
peoples fall at your feet.-b
7Your c-divine throne-c is everlasting;
your royal scepter is a scepter of equity.
8You love righteousness and hate wickedness;
rightly has God, your God, chosen to anoint you
with oil of gladness over all your peers.
9All your robes [are fragrant] with
myrrh and aloes and cassia;
from ivoried palaces
lutes entertain you.
10Royal princesses are your favorites;

a-a *Meaning of Heb. uncertain.*
b-b *Order of Heb. clauses inverted for clarity.*
c-c *Cf. 1 Chron. 29.23.*

the consort stands at your right hand,
　　decked in gold of Ophir.

11Take heed, lass, and note,
　　incline your ear:
　　forget your people and your father's house,
　　12and let the king be aroused by your beauty;
　　since he is your lord, bow to him.
13O Tyrian lass,
　　the wealthiest people will court your favor with gifts,
　　14a-goods of all sorts.

The royal princess,
　　her dress embroidered with golden mountings,
　　15is led inside to the king;-a
　　maidens in her train, her companions,
　　are presented to you.
16They are led in with joy and gladness;
　　they enter the palace of the king.
17Your sons will succeed your ancestors;
　　you will appoint them princes throughout the land.

18I commemorate your fame for all generations,
　　so peoples will praise you forever and ever.

46 For the leader. Of the Korahites; a-on *alamoth.*-a A song.

2God is our refuge and stronghold,
　　a help in trouble, very near.
3Therefore we are not afraid
　　though the earth reels,
　　though mountains topple into the sea—
　　4its waters rage and foam;
　　in its swell mountains quake.　　　　　　　　　　*Selah.*

5There is a river whose streams gladden God's city,
　　the holy dwelling-place of the Most High.

a-a *Meaning of Heb. uncertain.*

⁶God is in its midst, it will not be toppled;
　by daybreak God will come to its aid.
⁷Nations rage, kingdoms topple;
　at the sound of His thunder the earth dissolves.
⁸The Lord of hosts is with us;
　the God of Jacob is our haven.　　　　　　　*Selah.*

⁹Come and see what the Lord has done,
　how He has wrought desolation on the earth.
¹⁰He puts a stop to wars throughout the earth,
　breaking the bow, snapping the spear,
　consigning wagons to the flames.
¹¹"Desist! Realize that I am God!
　I dominate the nations;
　I dominate the earth."
¹²The Lord of hosts is with us;
　the God of Jacob is our haven.　　　　　　　*Selah.*

47 For the leader. Of the Korahites. A psalm.

²All you peoples, clap your hands,
　raise a joyous shout for God.
³For the Lord Most High is awesome,
　great king over all the earth;
⁴He subjects peoples to us,
　sets nations at our feet.
⁵He chose our heritage for us,
　the pride of Jacob whom He loved.　　　　　*Selah.*

⁶God ascends midst acclamation;
　the Lord, to the blasts of the horn.
⁷Sing, O sing to God;
　sing, O sing to our king;
⁸for God is king over all the earth;
　sing a hymn.ᵃ
⁹God reigns over the nations;
　God is seated on His holy throne.
¹⁰The great of the peoples are gathered together,

ᵃ *Heb.* maskil, *a musical term of uncertain meaning.*

the retinue of Abraham's God;
for the guardians of the earth belong to God;
He is greatly exalted.

48

A song. A psalm of the Korahites.

²The LORD is great and much acclaimed
in the city of our God,
His holy mountain—
³fair-crested, joy of all the earth,
Mount Zion, summit of Zaphon,ᵃ
city of the great king.
⁴Through its citadels, God has made Himself known as a haven.
⁵See, the kings joined forces;
they advanced together.
⁶At the mere sight of it they were stunned,
they were terrified, they panicked;
⁷they were seized there with a trembling,
like a woman in the throes of labor,
⁸as the Tarshish fleet was wrecked
in an easterly gale.ᵇ
⁹The likes of what we heard we have now witnessed
in the city of the LORD of hosts,
in the city of our God—
may God preserve it forever!   *Selah.*

¹⁰In Your temple, God,
we meditate upon Your faithful care.
¹¹The praise of You, God, like Your name,
reaches to the ends of the earth;
Your right hand is filled with beneficence.
¹²Let Mount Zion rejoice!
Let the townsᶜ of Judah exult,
because of Your judgments.

¹³Walk around Zion,
circle it;
count its towers,

ᵃ *A term for the divine abode.*
ᵇ *See 1 Kings 22.49.*
ᶜ *Or "women."*

¹⁴take note of its ramparts;
ᵈ⁻go through⁻ᵈ its citadels,
that you may recount it to a future age.
¹⁵For God—He is our God forever;
He will lead us ᵈ⁻evermore.⁻ᵈ

49

For the leader. Of the Korahites. A psalm.

²Hear this, all you peoples;
give ear, all inhabitants of the world,
³men of all estates,
rich and poor alike.
⁴My mouth utters wisdom,
my speechᵃ is full of insight.
⁵I will turn my attention to a theme,
set forth my lesson to the music of a lyre.

⁶In time of trouble, why should I fear
the encompassing evil of those who would supplant me—
⁷men who trust in their riches,
who glory in their great wealth?
⁸ᵇ⁻Ah, it⁻ᵇ cannot redeem a man,
or pay his ransom to God;
⁹the price of life is too high;
and so one ceases to be, forever.
¹⁰Shall he live eternally,
and never see the grave?
¹¹For one sees that the wise die,
that the foolish and ignorant both perish,
leaving their wealth to others.
¹²Their graveᶜ is their eternal home,
the dwelling-place for all generations
of those once famous on earth.
¹³Man does not abide in honor;
he is like the beasts that perish.

¹⁴Such is the fate of those who are self-confident,
ᵈ⁻the end of those pleased with their own talk.⁻ᵈ   *Selah.*

ᵈ⁻ᵈ *Meaning of Heb. uncertain.*

ᵃ *Lit. "utterance of my heart"; on* leb, *cf. Ps. 19.15.*
ᵇ⁻ᵇ *Or "A brother."*
ᶜ *Taken with ancient versions and medieval commentators as the equivalent of* qibram.
ᵈ⁻ᵈ *Meaning of Heb. uncertain.*

¹⁵Sheeplike they head for Sheol,
with Death as their shepherd.
The upright shall rule over them at daybreak,
ᵈ⁻and their form shall waste away in Sheol
till its nobility be gone.⁻ᵈ
¹⁶But God will redeem my life from the clutches of Sheol,
for He will take me.   *Selah.*

¹⁷Do not be afraid when a man becomes rich,
when his household goods increase;
¹⁸for when he dies he can take none of it along;
his goods cannot follow him down.
¹⁹Though he congratulates himself in his lifetime
—ᵈ⁻"They must admit that you did well by yourself"⁻ᵈ—
²⁰yet he must join the company of his ancestors,
who will never see daylight again.
²¹Man does not understand honor;
he is like the beasts that perish.

50 A psalm of Asaph.

ᵃ⁻God, the LORD Godᵃ spoke
and summoned the world from east to west.
²From Zion, perfect in beauty,
God appeared
³—let our God come and not fail to act!
Devouring fire preceded Him;
it stormed around Him fiercely.
⁴He summoned the heavens above,
and the earth, for the trial of His people.
⁵"Bring in My devotees,
who made a covenant with Me over sacrifice!"
⁶Then the heavens proclaimed His righteousness,
for He is a God who judges.   *Selah.*

⁷"Pay heed, My people, and I will speak,
O Israel, and I will arraign you.

ᵃ⁻ᵃ *Heb.* 'El 'Elohim YHWH.

1164

I am God, your God.
⁸I censure you not for your sacrifices,
and your burnt offerings, made to Me daily;
⁹I claim no bull from your estate,
no he-goats from your pens.
¹⁰For Mine is every animal of the forest,
the beasts on ᵇ⁻a thousand mountains.⁻ᵇ
¹¹I know every bird of the mountains,
the creatures of the field are subject to Me.
¹²Were I hungry, I would not tell you,
for Mine is the world and all it holds.
¹³Do I eat the flesh of bulls,
or drink the blood of he-goats?
¹⁴Sacrifice a thank offering to God,
and pay your vows to the Most High.
¹⁵Call upon Me in time of trouble;
I will rescue you, and you shall honor Me."

¹⁶And to the wicked, God said:
"Who are you to recite My laws,
and mouth the terms of My covenant,
¹⁷seeing that you spurn My discipline,
and brush My words aside?
¹⁸When you see a thief, you fall in with him,
and throw in your lot with adulterers;
¹⁹you devote your mouth to evil,
and yoke your tongue to deceit;
²⁰you are busy maligning your brother,
defaming the son of your mother.
²¹If I failed to act when you did these things,
you would fancy that I was like you;
so I censure you and confront you with charges.
²²Mark this, you who are unmindful of God,
lest I tear you apart and no one save you.

²³He who sacrifices a thank offering honors Me,
ᵇ⁻and to him who improves his way⁻ᵇ
I will show the salvation of God."

ᵇ⁻ᵇ *Meaning of Heb. uncertain.*

51
For the leader. A psalm of David, [2] when Nathan the prophet came to him after he had come to Bathsheba.[a]

[3]Have mercy upon me, O God,
as befits Your faithfulness;
in keeping with Your abundant compassion,
blot out my transgressions.
[4]Wash me thoroughly of my iniquity,
and purify me of my sin;
[5]for I recognize my transgressions,
and am ever conscious of my sin.
[6]Against You alone have I sinned,
and done what is evil in Your sight;
so You are just in Your sentence,
and right in Your judgment.
[7]Indeed I was born with iniquity;
with sin my mother conceived me.
[8] [b-]Indeed You desire truth about that which is hidden;
teach me wisdom about secret things.[-b]

[9]Purge me with hyssop till I am pure;
wash me till I am whiter than snow.
[10]Let me hear tidings of joy and gladness;
let the bones You have crushed exult.
[11]Hide Your face from my sins;
blot out all my iniquities.
[12]Fashion a pure heart for me, O God;
create in me a steadfast spirit.
[13]Do not cast me out of Your presence,
or take Your holy spirit away from me.
[14]Let me again rejoice in Your help;
let a vigorous spirit sustain me.
[15]I will teach transgressors Your ways,
that sinners may return to You.

[16]Save me from bloodguilt,
O God, God, my deliverer,

[a] *Cf. 2 Sam. 12.*
[b-b] *Meaning of Heb. uncertain.*

that I may sing forth Your beneficence.
¹⁷O LORD, open my lips,
and let my mouth declare Your praise.
¹⁸You do not want me to bring sacrifices;
You do not desire burnt offerings;
¹⁹True sacrifice to God is a contrite spirit;
God, You will not despise
a contrite and crushed heart.

²⁰May it please You to make Zion prosper;
rebuild the walls of Jerusalem.
²¹Then You will want sacrifices offered in righteousness,
burnt and whole offerings;
then bulls will be offered on Your altar.

52

For the leader. A *maskil* of David, ²when Doeg the Edomite came and informed Saul, telling him, "David came to Ahimelech's house."ᵃ

³Why do you boast of your evil, brave fellow?
God's faithfulness ᵇ⁻never ceases.⁻ᵇ
⁴Your tongue devises mischief,
like a sharpened razor that works treacherously.
⁵You prefer evil to good,
the lie, to speaking truthfully.   *Selah.*
⁶You love all pernicious words,
treacherous speech.
⁷So God will tear you down for good,
will break you and pluck you from your tent,
and root you out of the land of the living.   *Selah.*
⁸The righteous, seeing it, will be awestruck;
they will jibe at him, saying,
⁹"Here was a fellow who did not make God his refuge,
but trusted in his great wealth,
relied upon his mischief."

¹⁰But I am like a thriving olive tree in God's house;
I trust in the faithfulness of God forever and ever.

ᵃ *Cf. 1 Sam. 22.9 ff.*
ᵇ⁻ᵇ *Lit. "is all the day."*

¹¹I praise You forever, for You have acted;
 ^{c-}I declare that Your name is good^{-c}
 in the presence of Your faithful ones.

53

^aFor the leader; on *mahalath*.^b A *maskil* of David.

²The benighted man thinks,
 ^{c-}"God does not care."^{-c}
Man's wrongdoing is corrupt and loathsome;
 no one does good.
³God looks down from heaven on mankind
 to find a man of understanding,
 a man mindful of God.
⁴Everyone is dross,
 altogether foul;
 there is none who does good,
 not even one.
⁵Are they so witless, those evildoers,
 who devour my people as they devour food,
 and do not invoke God?
⁶There they will be seized with fright
 —^{d-}never was there such a fright—
 for God has scattered the bones of your besiegers;
 you have put them to shame,^{-d}
 for God has rejected them.

⁷O that the deliverance of Israel might come from Zion!
When God restores the fortunes of His people,
 Jacob will exult, Israel will rejoice.

54

For the leader; with instrumental music. A *maskil* of David, ²when
the Ziphites came and told Saul, "Know, David is in hiding among us."^a

³O God, deliver me by Your name;
 by Your power vindicate me.

---

^{c-c} *Meaning of Heb. uncertain; others "I will wait for Your name for it is good."*

^a *Cf. Ps. 14.*
^b *Meaning of Heb. unknown.*
^{c-c} *Lit. "There is no God"; cf. Ps. 10.4.*
^{d-d} *Meaning of Heb. uncertain.*

^a *Cf. 1 Sam. 23.19.*

⁴O God, hear my prayer;
  give ear to the words of my mouth.
⁵For strangers have risen against me,
  and ruthless men seek my life;
  they are unmindful of God. Selah.

⁶See, God is my helper;
  the LORD is my support.
⁷He will repay the evil of my watchful foes;
  by Your faithfulness, destroy them!
⁸Then I will offer You a freewill sacrifice;
  I will praise Your name, LORD, for it is good,
  ⁹for it has saved me from my foes,
  and let me gaze triumphant upon my enemies.

55

For the leader; with instrumental music. A *maskil* of David.

²Give ear, O God, to my prayer;
  do not ignore my plea;
  ³pay heed to me and answer me.
I am tossed about, complaining and moaning
  ⁴at the clamor of the enemy,
  because of the oppression of the wicked;
  for they bring evil upon me
  and furiously harass me.
⁵My heart is convulsed within me;
  terrors of death assail me.
⁶Fear and trembling invade me;
  I am clothed with horror.
⁷I said,
  "O that I had the wings of a dove!
  I would fly away and find rest;
  ⁸surely, I would flee far off;
  I would lodge in the wilderness; Selah.
  ⁹I would soon find me a refuge
  from the sweeping wind,
  from the tempest."

¹⁰O LORD, confound their speech, confuse it!
For I see lawlessness and strife in the city;
  ¹¹day and night they make their rounds on its walls;
  evil and mischief are inside it.
¹²Malice is within it;
  fraud and deceit never leave its square.

¹³It is not an enemy who reviles me
  —I could bear that;
  it is not my foe who vaunts himself against me
  —I could hide from him;
  ¹⁴but it is you, my equal,
  my companion, my friend;
  ¹⁵sweet was our fellowship;
  we walked together in God's house.
¹⁶Let Him incite death against them;
  may they go down alive into Sheol!
For where they dwell,
  there evil is.

¹⁷As for me, I call to God;
  the LORD will deliver me.
¹⁸Evening, morning, and noon,
  I complain and moan,
  and He hears my voice.
¹⁹He redeems me unharmed
  from the battle against me;
  ^ait is as though many are on my side.^{-a}
²⁰God who has reigned from the first,
  who will have no successor,
  hears and humbles those who have no fear of God.   *Selah.*

²¹He^b harmed his ally,
  he broke his pact;
  ²²his talk was smoother than butter,
  yet his mind was on war;
  his words were more soothing than oil,
  yet they were drawn swords.

---

a-a *Meaning of Heb. uncertain.*
b *I.e., the friend of v. 14.*

²³Cast your burden on the LORD and He will sustain you;
> He will never let the righteous man collapse.

²⁴For You, O God, will bring them down to the nethermost
> Pit—
> those murderous, treacherous men;
> they shall not live out half their days;
> but I trust in You.

56 For the leader; ª-on *jonath elem rehokim.*-ª Of David. A *michtam*;
when the Philistines seized him in Gath.

²Have mercy on me, O God,
> for men persecute me;
> all day long my adversary oppresses me.

³My watchful foes persecute me all day long;
> many are my adversaries, O Exalted One.

⁴When I am afraid, I trust in You,
> ⁵in God, whose word I praise,
> in God I trust;
> I am not afraid;
> what can mortals^b do to me?

⁶All day long ª-they cause me grief in my affairs,-ª
> they plan only evil against me.

⁷They plot, they lie in ambush;
> they watch my every move, hoping for my death.

⁸Cast them out for their evil;
> subdue peoples in Your anger, O God.

⁹ª-You keep count of my wanderings;
> put my tears into Your flask,
> into Your record.-ª

¹⁰Then my enemies will retreat when I call on You;
> this I know, that God is for me.

¹¹In God, whose word I praise,
> in the LORD, whose word I praise,
> ¹²in God I trust;
> I am not afraid;

ª-ª *Meaning of Heb. uncertain.*
b *Lit. "flesh."*

what can man do to me?
¹³I must pay my vows to You, O God;
   I will render thank offerings to You.
¹⁴For You have saved me from death,
   my foot from stumbling,
   that I may walk before God in the light of life.

57 For the leader; ᵃ-*al tashheth.*-ᵃ Of David. A *michtam*; when he fled from Saul into a cave.

²Have mercy on me, O God, have mercy on me,
   for I seek refuge in You,
   I seek refuge in the shadow of Your wings,
   until danger passes.
³I call to God Most High,
   to God who is good to me.
⁴He will reach down from heaven and deliver me:
   God will send down His steadfast love;
   my persecutor reviles.   *Selah.*

⁵As for me, I lie down among man-eating lions
   whose teeth are spears and arrows,
   whose tongue is a sharp sword.
⁶Exalt Yourself over the heavens, O God,
   let Your glory be over all the earth!
⁷They prepared a net for my feet ᵇ-to ensnare me;-ᵇ
   they dug a pit for me,
   but they fell into it.   *Selah.*

⁸ᶜMy heart is firm, O God;
   my heart is firm;
   I will sing, I will chant a hymn.
⁹Awake, O my soul!
   Awake, O harp and lyre!
   I will wake the dawn.
¹⁰I will praise You among the peoples, O LORD;
   I will sing a hymn to You among the nations;

ᵃ-ᵃ *Meaning of Heb. uncertain.*
ᵇ-ᵇ *Cf. Mishnaic Heb.* kefifah, *a wicker basket used in fishing.*
ᶜ *With vv. 8–12, cf. Ps. 108.2–6.*

¹¹for Your faithfulness is as high as heaven;
 Your steadfastness reaches to the sky.
¹²Exalt Yourself over the heavens, O God,
 let Your glory be over all the earth!

58 For the leader; *al tashheth*. Of David. A *michtam*.

²^{a-}O mighty ones,^{-a} do you really decree what is just?
Do you judge mankind with equity?
³In your minds you devise wrongdoing in the land;
 ^{a-}with your hands you deal out lawlessness.^{-a}
⁴The wicked are defiant from birth;
 the liars go astray from the womb.
⁵Their venom is like that of a snake,
 a deaf viper that stops its ears
 ⁶so as not to hear the voice of charmers
 or the expert mutterer of spells.

⁷O God, smash their teeth in their mouth;
 shatter the fangs of lions, O LORD;
 ⁸let them melt, let them vanish like water;
 let Him aim His arrows that they be cut down;
 ⁹^{a-}like a snail that melts away as it moves;^{-a}
 like a woman's stillbirth, may they never see the sun!
¹⁰Before ^{a-}the thorns grow into a bramble,
 may He whirl them away alive in fury.^{-a}

¹¹The righteous man will rejoice when he sees revenge;
 he will bathe his feet in the blood of the wicked.
¹²Men will say,
 "There is, then, a reward for the righteous;
 there is, indeed, divine justice on earth."

59 For the leader; *al tashheth*. Of David. A *michtam;* when Saul sent men to watch his house in order to put him to death.^a

^{a-a} *Meaning of Heb. uncertain.*
^a *Cf. 1 Sam. 19.11.*

²Save me from my enemies, O my God;
   secure me against my assailants.
³Save me from evildoers;
   deliver me from murderers.
⁴For see, they lie in wait for me;
   fierce men plot against me
   for no offense of mine,
   for no transgression, O LORD;
   ⁵for no guilt of mine
   do they rush to array themselves against me.
Look, rouse Yourself on my behalf!
⁶You, O LORD God of hosts,
   God of Israel,
   bestir Yourself to bring all nations to account;
   have no mercy on any treacherous villain.   *Selah.*

⁷They come each evening growling like dogs,
   roaming the city.
⁸They rave with their mouths,
   ᵇ⁻sharp words⁻ᵇ are on their lips;
   [they think,] "Who hears?"
⁹But You, O LORD, laugh at them;
   You mock all the nations.

¹⁰O myᶜ strength, I wait for You;
   for God is my haven.
¹¹My faithful God will come to aid me;
   God will let me gloat over my watchful foes.
¹²Do not kill them lest my people be unmindful;
   with Your power make wanderers of them;
   bring them low, O our shield, the Lord,
   ¹³because of their sinful mouths,
   the words on their lips.
Let them be trapped by their pride,
   and by the imprecations and lies they utter.
¹⁴In Your fury put an end to them;
   put an end to them that they be no more;
   that it may be known to the ends of the earth
   that God does rule over Jacob.   *Selah.*

ᵇ⁻ᵇ *Lit. "swords."*
ᶜ *With several mss.; cf. v. 18; lit. "His."*

¹⁵They come each evening growling like dogs,
    roaming the city.
¹⁶They wander in search of food;
    and whine if they are not satisfied.
¹⁷But I will sing of Your strength,
    extol each morning Your faithfulness;
    for You have been my haven,
    a refuge in time of trouble.

¹⁸O my strength, to You I sing hymns;
    for God is my haven, my faithful God.

60

For the leader; on ᵃ‑*shushan eduth*.⁻ᵃ A *michtam* of David (to be taught), ²when he fought with Aram-Naharaim and Aram-Zobah, and Joab returned and defeated Edom—[an army] of twelve thousand men— in the Valley of Salt.ᵇ

³O God, You have rejected us,
    You have made a breach in us;
    You have been angry;
    restore us!
⁴You have made the land quake;
    You have torn it open.
Mend its fissures,
    for it is collapsing.
⁵You have made Your people suffer hardship;
    ᶜ‑You have given us wine that makes us reel.⁻ᶜ
⁶ᵃ‑Give those who fear You because of Your truth
    a banner for rallying.⁻ᵃ   *Selah.*
⁷ᵈThat those whom You love might be rescued,
    deliver with Your right hand and answer me.

⁸God promised ᵉ‑in His sanctuary⁻ᵉ
    that I would exultingly divide up Shechem,
    and measure the Valley of Sukkoth;
⁹Gilead and Manasseh would be mine,
    Ephraim my chief stronghold,
    Judah my scepter;

ᵃ⁻ᵃ *Meaning of Heb. uncertain.*
ᵇ *Cf. 2 Sam. 8; 1 Chron. 18.*
ᶜ⁻ᶜ *Or "You have sated Your people with a bitter draft."*
ᵈ *Cf. Ps. 108.7–14.*
ᵉ⁻ᵉ *Or "by His holiness."*

¹⁰Moab would be my washbasin;
on Edom I would cast my shoe;
acclaim me, O Philistia!

¹¹Would that I were brought to the bastion!
Would that I were led to Edom!

¹²But You have rejected us, O God;
God, You do not march with our armies.
¹³Grant us Your aid against the foe,
for the help of man is worthless.
¹⁴With God we shall triumph;
He will trample our foes.

61 For the leader; with instrumental music. Of David.

²Hear my cry, O God,
heed my prayer.
³From the end of the earth I call to You;
when my heart is faint,
You lead me to a rock that is high above me.
⁴For You have been my refuge,
a tower of strength against the enemy.
⁵O that I might dwell in Your tent forever,
take refuge under Your protecting wings. *Selah.*

⁶O God, You have heard my vows;
grant the request[a] of those who fear Your name.
⁷Add days to the days of the king;
may his years extend through generations;
⁸may he dwell in God's presence forever;
appoint[b] steadfast love to guard him.
⁹So I will sing hymns to Your name forever,
as I fulfill my vows day after day.

---

a *Taking the noun* yršt *as an alternate form of* 'ršt; *cf. Ps. 21.3.*
b *Meaning of Heb. uncertain.*

62
For the leader; on *Jeduthun*. A psalm of David.

²Truly my soul waits quietly for God;
my deliverance comes from Him.
³Truly He is my rock and deliverance,
my haven; I shall never be shaken.
⁴How long will all of you attackᵃ a man,
to crushᵃ him, as though he were
a leaning wall, a tottering fence?
⁵They lay plans to topple him from his rank;
they delight in falsehood;
they bless with their mouths,
while inwardly they curse.   *Selah.*

⁶Truly, wait quietly for God, O my soul,
for my hope comes from Him.
⁷He is my rock and deliverance,
my haven; I shall not be shaken.
⁸I rely on God, my deliverance and glory,
my rock of strength;
in God is my refuge.
⁹Trust in Him at all times, O people;
pour out your hearts before Him;
God is our refuge.   *Selah.*

¹⁰Men are mere breath;
mortals, illusion;
placed on a scale all together,
they weigh even less than a breath.
¹¹Do not trust in violence,
or put false hopes in robbery;
if force bears fruit pay it no mind.
¹²One thing God has spoken;
two things have I heard:
that might belongs to God,
¹³and faithfulness is Yours, O Lord,
to reward each man according to his deeds.

ᵃ *Meaning of Heb. uncertain.*

63

A psalm of David, when he was in the Wilderness of Judah.

²God, You are my God;
I search for You,
my soul thirsts for You,
my body yearns for You,
as a parched and thirsty land that has no water.
³I shall behold You in the sanctuary,
and see Your might and glory,
⁴Truly Your faithfulness is better than life;
my lips declare Your praise.
⁵I bless You all my life;
I lift up my hands, invoking Your name.
⁶I am sated as with a ᵃ⁻rich feast,⁻ᵃ
I sing praises with joyful lips
⁷when I call You to mind upon my bed,
when I think of You in the watches of the night;
⁸for You are my help,
and in the shadow of Your wings
I shout for joy.
⁹My soul is attached to You;
Your right hand supports me.

¹⁰May those who seek to destroy my life
enter the depths of the earth.
¹¹May they be gutted by the sword;
may they be prey to jackals.
¹²But the king shall rejoice in God;
all who swear by Him shall exult,
when the mouth of liars is stopped.

64

For the leader. A psalm of David.

²Hear my voice, O God, when I plead;
guard my life from the enemy's terror.
³Hide me from a band of evil men,

ᵃ⁻ᵃ *Lit. "suet and fat."*

from a crowd of evildoers,
4who whet their tongues like swords;
they aim their arrows—cruel words—
5to shoot from hiding at the blameless man;
they shoot him suddenly and without fear.
6a-They arm themselves with an evil word;
when they speak, it is to conceal traps;-a
they think, "Who will see them?"
7bLet the wrongdoings they have concealed,c
each one inside him, his secret thoughts,
be wholly exposed.
8God shall shoot them with arrows;
they shall be struck down suddenly.
9Their tongue shall be their downfall;
all who see them shall recoil in horror;
10all men shall stand in awe;
they shall proclaim the work of God
and His deed which they perceived.
11The righteous shall rejoice in the LORD,
and take refuge in Him;
all the upright shall exult.

65 For the leader. A psalm of David. A song.

2Praise befits You in Zion, O God;
vows are paid to You;
3all mankinda comes to You,
You who hear prayer.
4When all manner of sins overwhelm me,
it is You who forgive our iniquities.
5Happy is the man You choose and bring near
to dwell in Your courts;
may we be sated with the blessings of Your house,
Your holy temple.

6Answer us with victory through awesome deeds,
O God, our deliverer,

---

a-a *Meaning of Heb. uncertain.*
b *Meaning of verse uncertain.*
c *Reading* tamnu *with some mss. (cf. Minhat Shai) and Rashi; most printed editions,* tamnu
traditionally rendered "they have accomplished."

a *Lit. "flesh."*

in whom all the ends of the earth
and the distant seas
put their trust;
⁷who by His power fixed the mountains firmly,
who is girded with might,
⁸who stills the raging seas,
the raging waves,
and tumultuous peoples.
⁹Those who live at the ends of the earth are awed by Your signs;
You make the lands of sunrise and sunset shout for joy.
¹⁰You take care of the earth and irrigate it;
You enrich it greatly,
with the channel of God full of water;
You provide grain for men;
for so do You prepare it.
¹¹Saturating its furrows,
leveling its ridges,
You soften it with showers,
You bless its growth.
¹²You crown the year with Your bounty;
fatness is distilled in Your paths;
¹³the pasturelands distill it;
the hills are girded with joy.
¹⁴The meadows are clothed with flocks,
the valleys mantled with grain;
they raise a shout, they break into song.

66 For the leader. A song. A psalm.

²Raise a shout for God, all the earth;
sing the glory of His name,
make glorious His praise.
³Say to God,
"How awesome are Your deeds,
Your enemies cower before Your great strength;
⁴all the earth bows to You,

and sings hymns to You;
all sing hymns to Your name." Selah.

5Come and see the works of God,
who is held in awe by men for His acts.
6He turned the sea into dry land;
they crossed the river on foot;
we therefore rejoice in Him.
7He rules forever in His might;
His eyes scan the nations;
let the rebellious not assert themselves. Selah.

8O peoples, bless our God,
celebrate His praises;
9who has granted us life,
and has not let our feet slip.

10You have tried us, O God,
refining us, as one refines silver.
11You have caught us in a net,
a-caught us in trammels.-a
12You have let men ride over us;
we have endured fire and water,
and You have brought us through to prosperity.

13I enter Your house with burnt offerings,
I pay my vows to You,
14[vows] that my lips pronounced,
that my mouth uttered in my distress.
15I offer up fatlings to You,
with the odor of burning rams;
I sacrifice bulls and he-goats. Selah.

16Come and hear, all God-fearing men,
as I tell what He did for me.
17I called aloud to Him,
glorification on my tongue.

a-a Lit. "put a trammel on our loins."

¹⁸Had I an evil thought in my mind,
the LORD would not have listened.
¹⁹But God did listen;
He paid heed to my prayer.
²⁰Blessed is God who has not turned away my prayer,
or His faithful care from me.

67

For the leader; with instrumental music. A psalm. A song.

²May God be gracious to us and bless us;
may He show us favor,   *Selah.*
³that Your way be known on earth,
Your deliverance among all nations.

⁴Peoples will praise You, O God;
all peoples will praise You.
⁵Nations will exult and shout for joy,
for You rule the peoples with equity,
You guide the nations of the earth.   *Selah.*
⁶The peoples will praise You, O God;
all peoples will praise You.

⁷May the earth yield its produce;
may God, our God, bless us.
⁸May God bless us,
and be revered to the ends of the earth.

68

^aFor the leader. Of David. A psalm. A song.

²God will arise,
His enemies shall be scattered,
His foes shall flee before Him.
³Disperse them as smoke is dispersed;
as wax melts at fire,
so the wicked shall perish before God.
⁴But the righteous shall rejoice;

---

^a *The coherence of this psalm and the meaning of many of its passages are uncertain.*

they shall exult in the presence of God;
    they shall be exceedingly joyful.

5Sing to God, chant hymns to His name;
    extol Him who rides the clouds;
    the LORD is His name.
Exult in His presence—
    6the father of orphans, the champion of widows,
    God, in His holy habitation.
7God restores the lonely to their homes,
    sets free the imprisoned, safe and sound,
    while the rebellious must live in a parched land.

8O God, when You went at the head of Your army,
    when You marched through the desert,   *Selah.*
    9the earth trembled, the sky rained because of God,
    yon Sinai, because of God, the God of Israel.
10You released a bountiful rain, O God;
    when Your own land languished, You sustained it.
11Your tribe dwells there;
    O God, in Your goodness You provide for the needy.

12The LORD gives a command;
    the women who bring the news are a great host:
    13"The kings and their armies are in headlong flight;
    housewives are sharing in the spoils;
    14even for those of you who lie among the sheepfolds
    there are wings of a dove sheathed in silver,
    its pinions in fine gold."
15When Shaddai scattered the kings,
    it seemed like a snowstorm in Zalmon.

16O majestic mountain, Mount Bashan;
    O jagged mountain, Mount Bashan;
    17why so hostile, O jagged mountains,
    toward the mountain God desired as His dwelling?
The LORD shall abide there forever.

¹⁸God's chariots are myriads upon myriads,
  thousands upon thousands;
  the Lord is among them as in Sinai in holiness.

¹⁹You went up to the heights, having taken captives,
  having received tribute of men,
  even of those who rebel
  against the LORD God's abiding there.

²⁰Blessed is the LORD.
Day by day He supports us,
  God, our deliverance.   *Selah.*
²¹God is for us a God of deliverance;
  GOD the Lord provides an escape from death.
²²God will smash the heads of His enemies,
  the hairy crown of him who walks about in his guilt.
²³The LORD said, "I will retrieve from Bashan,
  I will retrieve from the depths of the sea;
  ²⁴that your feet may wade through blood;
  that the tongue of your dogs may have its portion of your
  enemies."

²⁵Men see Your processions, O God,
  the processions of my God, my king,
  into the sanctuary.
²⁶First come singers, then musicians,
  amidst maidens playing timbrels.
²⁷In assemblies bless God,
  the LORD, O you who are from the fountain of Israel.
²⁸There is little Benjamin who rules them,
  the princes of Judah who command them,
  the princes of Zebulun and Naphtali.

²⁹Your God has ordained strength for you,
  the strength, O God,
  which You displayed for us
  ³⁰from Your temple above Jerusalem.
The kings bring You tribute.

³¹Blast the beast of the marsh,
   the herd of bulls among the peoples, the calves,
   till they come cringing with pieces of silver.
Scatter the peoples who delight in wars!
³²Tribute-bearers shall come from Egypt;
   Cush shall hasten its gifts to God.

³³O kingdoms of the earth,
   sing to God;
   chant hymns to the Lord,   *Selah.*
³⁴to Him who rides the ancient highest heavens,
   who thunders forth with His mighty voice.
³⁵Ascribe might to God,
   whose majesty is over Israel,
   whose might is in the skies.
³⁶You are awesome, O God, in Your holy places;
   it is the God of Israel who gives might and power to the
      people.
Blessed is God.

69 For the leader. On *shoshannim.*ᵃ Of David.

²Deliver me, O God,
   for the waters have reached my neck;
   ³I am sinking into the slimy deep
   and find no foothold;
   I have come into the watery depths;
   the flood sweeps me away.
⁴I am weary with calling;
   my throat is dry;
   my eyes fail
   while I wait for God.
⁵More numerous than the hairs of my head
   are those who hate me without reason;
   many are those who would destroy me,
   my treacherous enemies.
Must I restore what I have not stolen?

ᵃ *Meaning of Heb. uncertain.*

⁶God, You know my folly;
 my guilty deeds are not hidden from You.
⁷Let those who look to You,
  O LORD, God of hosts,
 not be disappointed on my account;
 let those who seek You,
  O God of Israel,
 not be shamed because of me.
⁸It is for Your sake that I have been reviled,
 that shame covers my face;
 ⁹I am a stranger to my brothers,
 an alien to my kin.
¹⁰My zeal for Your house has been my undoing;
 the reproaches of those who revile You have fallen upon me.
¹¹When I wept and fasted,
 I was reviled for it.
¹²I made sackcloth my garment;
 I became a byword among them.
¹³Those who sit in the gate talk about me;
 I am the taunt of drunkards.

¹⁴As for me, may my prayer come to You, O LORD,
 at a favorable moment;
 O God, in Your abundant faithfulness,
 answer me with Your sure deliverance.
¹⁵Rescue me from the mire;
 let me not sink;
 let me be rescued from my enemies,
 and from the watery depths.
¹⁶Let the floodwaters not sweep me away;
 let the deep not swallow me;
 let the mouth of the Pit not close over me.
¹⁷Answer me, O LORD,
 according to Your great steadfastness;
 in accordance with Your abundant mercy
 turn to me;
 ¹⁸do not hide Your face from Your servant,
 for I am in distress;

answer me quickly.
19Come near to me and redeem me;
    free me from my enemies.

20You know my reproach,
    my shame, my disgrace;
    You are aware of all my foes.
21Reproach breaks my heart,
    I am in despair;a
    I hope for consolation, but there is none,
    for comforters, but find none.
22They give me gall for food,
    vinegar to quench my thirst.
23May their table be a trap for them,
    a snare for their allies.
24May their eyes grow dim so that they cannot see;
    may their loins collapse continually.
25Pour out Your wrath on them;
    may Your blazing anger overtake them;
    26may their encampments be desolate;
    may their tents stand empty.
27For they persecute those You have struck;
    they talk about the pain of those You have felled.
28Add that to their guilt;
    let them have no share of Your beneficence;
    29may they be erased from the book of life,
    and not be inscribed with the righteous.

30But I am lowly and in pain;
    Your help, O God, keeps me safe.
31I will extol God's name with song,
    and exalt Him with praise.
32That will please the LORD more than oxen,
    than bulls with horns and hooves.
33The lowly will see and rejoice;
    you who are mindful of God, take heart!
34For the LORD listens to the needy,
    and does not spurn His captives.

35Heaven and earth shall extol Him,
the seas, and all that moves in them.
36For God will deliver Zion
and rebuild the cities of Judah;
they shall live there and inherit it;
37the offspring of His servants shall possess it;
those who cherish His name shall dwell there.

70 For the leader. Of David. *Lehazkir.*a

2bHasten, O God, to save me;
O LORD, to aid me!
3Let those who seek my life
be frustrated and disgraced;
let those who wish me harm,
fall back in shame.
4Let those who say, "Aha! Aha!"
turn back because of their frustration.

5But let all who seek You be glad and rejoice in You;
let those who are eager for Your deliverance always say,
"Extolled be God!"
6But I am poor and needy;
O God, hasten to me!
You are my help and my rescuer;
O LORD, do not delay.

71 I seek refuge in You, O LORD;
may I never be disappointed.
2As You are beneficent, save me and rescue me;
incline Your ear to me and deliver me.
3Be a sheltering rock for me to which I may always repair;
decree my deliverance,
for You are my rock and my fortress.
4My God, rescue me from the hand of the wicked,
from the grasp of the unjust and the lawless.

---

a *Meaning of Heb. uncertain.*
b *Cf. Ps. 40.14–18.*

⁵For You are my hope,
  O Lord GOD,
  my trust from my youth.
⁶While yet unborn, I depended on You;
  in the womb of my mother, You were my support;ᵃ
  I sing Your praises always.
⁷I have become an example for many,
  since You are my mighty refuge.
⁸My mouth is full of praise to You,
  glorifying You all day long.
⁹Do not cast me off in old age;
  when my strength fails, do not forsake me!

¹⁰For my enemies talk against me;
  those who wait for me are of one mind,
  ¹¹saying, "God has forsaken him;
  chase him and catch him,
  for no one will save him!"
¹²O God, be not far from me;
  my God, hasten to my aid!
¹³Let my accusers perish in frustration;
  let those who seek my ruin be clothed in reproach and
    disgrace!

¹⁴As for me, I will hope always,
  and add to the many praises of You.
¹⁵My mouth tells of Your beneficence,
  of Your deliverance all day long,
  though I know not how to tell it.
¹⁶I come with praise of Your mighty acts, O Lord GOD;
  I celebrate Your beneficence, Yours alone.
¹⁷You have let me experience it, God, from my youth;
  until now I have proclaimed Your wondrous deeds,
  ¹⁸and even in hoary old age do not forsake me, God,
  until I proclaim Your strength to the next generation,
  ¹⁹Your mighty acts, to all who are to come,
  Your beneficence, high as the heavens, O God,
  You who have done great things;

ᵃ *Meaning of Heb. uncertain.*

O God, who is Your peer!
20You who have made me undergo many troubles and
    misfortunes
    will revive me again,
    and raise me up from the depths of the earth.
21You will grant me much greatness,
    You will turn and comfort me.
22Then I will acclaim You to the music of the lyre
    for Your faithfulness, O my God;
    I will sing a hymn to You with a harp,
    O Holy One of Israel.
23My lips shall be jubilant, as I sing a hymn to You,
    my whole being, which You have redeemed.
24All day long my tongue shall recite Your beneficent acts,
    how those who sought my ruin were frustrated and
    disgraced.

72 Of Solomon.

O God, endow the king with Your judgments,
    the king's son with Your righteousness;
    2that he may judge Your people rightly,
    Your lowly ones, justly.
3Let the mountains produce well-being for the people,
    the hills, the reward of justice.
4Let him champion the lowly among the people,
    deliver the needy folk,
    and crush those who wrong them.
5Let them fear You as long as the sun shines,
    while the moon lasts, generations on end.
6Let him be like rain that falls on a mown field,
    like a downpour of rain on the ground,
    7that the righteous may flourish in his time,
    and well-being abound, till the moon is no more.
8Let him rule from sea to sea,
    from the river to the ends of the earth.

⁹Let desert-dwellers kneel before him,
and his enemies lick the dust.
¹⁰Let kings of Tarshish and the islands pay tribute,
kings of Sheba and Seba offer gifts.
¹¹Let all kings bow to him,
and all nations serve him.

¹²For he saves the needy who cry out,
the lowly who have no helper.
¹³He cares about the poor and the needy;
He brings the needy deliverance.
¹⁴He redeems them from fraud and lawlessness;
ᵃ⁻the shedding of their blood weighs heavily upon him.⁻ᵃ

¹⁵So let him live, and receive gold of Sheba;
let prayers for him be said always,
blessings on him invoked at all times.
¹⁶ᵇ⁻Let abundant grain be in the land, to the tops of the
mountains;
let his crops thrive like the forest of Lebanon;
and let men sprout up in towns like country grass.
¹⁷May his name be eternal;
while the sun lasts, may his name endure;⁻ᵇ
let men invoke his blessedness upon themselves;
let all nations count him happy.

¹⁸Blessed is the LORD God, God of Israel,
who alone does wondrous things;
¹⁹Blessed is His glorious name forever;
His glory fills the whole world.
Amen and Amen.

²⁰End of the prayers of David son of Jesse.

ᵃ⁻ᵃ *Or "their life is precious in his sight."*
ᵇ⁻ᵇ *Meaning of some Heb. phrases in these verses uncertain.*

BOOK THREE

73 A psalm of Asaph.

God is truly good to Israel,
    to those whose heart is pure.
²As for me, my feet had almost strayed,
    my steps were nearly led off course,
        ³for I envied the wanton;
    I saw the wicked at ease.
⁴Death has no pangs for them;
    their body is healthy.
⁵They have no part in the travail of men;
    they are not afflicted like the rest of mankind.
⁶So pride adorns their necks,
    lawlessness enwraps them as a mantle.
^{7a-}Fat shuts out their eyes;
    their fancies are extravagant.^{-a}
⁸They scoff and plan evil;
    from their eminence they plan wrongdoing.
⁹They set their mouths against heaven,
    and their tongues range over the earth.
^{10a-}So they pound His people again and again,
    until they are drained of their very last tear.^{-a}
¹¹Then they say, "How could God know?
    Is there knowledge with the Most High?"
¹²Such are the wicked;
    ever tranquil, they amass wealth.

¹³It was for nothing that I kept my heart pure
    and washed my hands in innocence,
        ¹⁴seeing that I have been constantly afflicted,
    that each morning brings new punishments.
¹⁵Had I decided to say these things,
    I should have been false to the circle of Your disciples.
¹⁶So I applied myself to understand this,
    but it seemed a hopeless task

---

^{a-a} Meaning of Heb. uncertain.

¹⁷till I entered God's sanctuary
and reflected on their fate.

¹⁸You surround them with flattery;
You make them fall through blandishments.
¹⁹How suddenly are they ruined,
wholly swept away by terrors.
²⁰ᵃ⁻When You are aroused You despise their image,
as one does a dream after waking, O LORD.⁻ᵃ

²¹My mind was stripped of its reason,
ᵇ⁻my feelings were numbed.⁻ᵇ
²²I was a dolt, without knowledge;
I was brutish toward You.

²³Yet I was always with You,
You held my right hand;
²⁴You guided me by Your counsel
ᶜ⁻and led me toward honor.⁻ᶜ
²⁵Whom else have I in heaven?
And having You, I want no one on earth.
²⁶My body and mind fail;
but God is the stayᵈ of my mind, my portion forever.
²⁷Those who keep far from You perish;
You annihilate all who are untrue to You.
²⁸As for me, nearness to God is good;
I have made the Lord GOD my refuge,
that I may recount all Your works.

74 A *maskil* of Asaph.

Why, O God, do You forever reject us,
do You fume in anger at the flock that You tend?
²Remember the community You made Yours long ago,
Your very own tribe that You redeemed,
Mount Zion, where You dwell.
³ᵃ⁻Bestir Yourself⁻ᵃ because of the ᵇ⁻perpetual tumult,⁻ᵇ

ᵇ⁻ᵇ *Lit. "I was pierced through in my kidneys."*
ᶜ⁻ᶜ *Meaning of Heb. uncertain; others "And afterward receive me with glory."*
ᵈ *Lit. "rock."*

ᵃ⁻ᵃ *Lit. "Lift up Your feet."*
ᵇ⁻ᵇ *Meaning of Heb. uncertain.*

all the outrages of the enemy in the sanctuary.
⁴Your foes roar inside Your meeting-place;
    they take their signs for true signs.
⁵ᵇ⁻It is like men wielding axes
    against a gnarled tree;
      ⁶with hatchet and pike
    they hacked away at its carved work.⁻ᵇ
⁷They made Your sanctuary go up in flames;
    they brought low in dishonor the dwelling-place of Your
      presence.
⁸They resolved, "Let us destroy them altogether!"
    They burned all God's tabernacles in the land.
⁹No signs appear for us;
    there is no longer any prophet;
    no one among us knows for how long.

¹⁰Till when, O God, will the foe blaspheme,
    will the enemy forever revile Your name?
¹¹Why do You hold back Your hand, Your right hand?
ᵇ⁻Draw it out of Your bosom!⁻ᵇ

¹²O God, my king from of old,
    who brings deliverance throughout the land;
      ¹³it was You who drove back the sea with Your might,
    who smashed the heads of the monsters in the waters;
      ¹⁴it was You who crushed the heads of Leviathan,
    who left him as food for ᶜ⁻the denizens of the desert;⁻ᶜ
      ¹⁵it was You who released springs and torrents,
    who made mighty rivers run dry;
      ¹⁶the day is Yours, the night also;
    it was You who set in place the orb of the sun;
      ¹⁷You fixed all the boundaries of the earth;
    summer and winter—You made them.

¹⁸Be mindful of how the enemy blasphemes the LORD,
    how base people revile Your name.
¹⁹Do not deliver Your dove to the wild beast;

ᶜ⁻ᶜ *Or "seafaring men"; meaning of Heb. uncertain.*

do not ignore forever the band of Your lowly ones.
20Look to the covenant!
For the dark places of the land are full of the haunts of
    lawlessness.
21Let not the downtrodden turn away disappointed;
    let the poor and needy praise Your name.
22Rise, O God, champion Your cause;
    be mindful that You are blasphemed by base men all day
        long.
23Do not ignore the shouts of Your foes,
    the din of Your adversaries that ascends all the time.

75 For the leader; *al tashheth.*
A psalm of Asaph, a song.

2We praise You, O God;
    we praise You;
    Your presence is near;
    men tell of Your wondrous deeds.

3"At the time I choose,
    I will give judgment equitably.
4Earth and all its inhabitants dissolve;
    it is I who keep its pillars firm.   *Selah.*
5To wanton men I say, 'Do not be wanton!'
    to the wicked, 'Do not lift up your horns!' "

6Do not lift your horns up high
    a-in vainglorious bluster.-a
7For what lifts a man comes not from the east
    or the west or the wilderness;b
    8for God it is who gives judgment;
    He brings down one man, He lifts up another.
9There is a cup in the LORD's hand
    with foaming wine fully mixed;
    from this He pours;

a-a *Lit. "with arrogant neck you speak."*
b *Reading* midbār *with many mss.*

all the wicked of the earth drink,
draining it to the very dregs.
¹⁰As for me, I will declare forever,
I will sing a hymn to the God of Jacob.

¹¹"All the horns of the wicked I will cut;
but the horns of the righteous shall be lifted up."

76 For the leader; with instrumental music.
A psalm of Asaph, a song.

²God has made Himself known in Judah,
His name is great in Israel;
³Salem became His abode;
Zion, His den.
⁴There He broke the fiery arrows of the bow,
the shield and the sword of war.   *Selah.*

⁵You were resplendent,
glorious, on the mountains of prey.
⁶The stout-hearted were despoiled;
they were in a stupor;
the bravest of men could not lift a hand.
⁷At Your blast, O God of Jacob,
horse and chariot lay stunned.
⁸O You! You are awesome!
Who can withstand You
when You are enraged?
⁹In heaven You pronounced sentence;
the earth was numbed with fright
¹⁰as God rose to execute judgment,
to deliver all the lowly of the earth.   *Selah.*

¹¹ᵃ⁻The fiercest of men shall acknowledge You,
when You gird on the last bit of fury.⁻ᵃ
¹²Make vows and pay them to the LORD your God;

ᵃ⁻ᵃ *Meaning of Heb. uncertain.*

a-all who are around Him shall bring tribute to
the Awesome One.-a
13He curbs the spirit of princes,
inspires awe in the kings of the earth.

77 For the leader; on *Jeduthun*. Of Asaph. A psalm.

2I cry aloud to God;
I cry to God that He may give ear to me.
3In my time of distress I turn to the Lord,
a-with my hand [uplifted];
[my eyes] flow all night without respite;-a
I will not be comforted.
4I call God to mind, I moan,
I complain, my spirit fails.   *Selah.*

5You have held my eyelids open;
I am overwrought, I cannot speak.
6My thoughts turn to days of old,
to years long past.
7I recall at night their jibes at me;
I commune with myself;
my spirit inquires,
8"Will the Lord reject forever
and never again show favor?
9Has His faithfulness disappeared forever?
Will His promise be unfulfilled for all time?
10Has God forgotten how to pity?
Has He in anger stifled His compassion?"   *Selah.*
11And I said, a-"It is my fault
that the right hand of the Most High has changed."-a

12I recall the deeds of the LORD;
yes, I recall Your wonders of old;
13I recount all Your works;

a-a *Meaning of Heb. uncertain.*

I speak of Your acts.
¹⁴O God, Your ways are holiness;
　what god is as great as God?
¹⁵You are the God who works wonders;
　You have manifested Your strength among the peoples.
¹⁶By Your arm You redeemed Your people,
　the children of Jacob and Joseph.　　　　　　　　　*Selah.*
¹⁷The waters saw You, O God,
　the waters saw You and were convulsed;
　the very deep quaked as well.
¹⁸Clouds streamed water;
　the heavens rumbled;
　Your arrows flew about;
　¹⁹Your thunder rumbled like wheels;
　lightning lit up the world;
　the earth quaked and trembled.
²⁰Your way was through the sea,
　Your path, through the mighty waters;
　Your tracks could not be seen.
²¹You led Your people like a flock
　in the care of Moses and Aaron.

78 A *maskil* of Asaph.

Give ear, my people, to my teaching,
　turn your ear to what I say.
²I will expound a theme,
　hold forth on the lessons of the past,
　³things we have heard and known,
　that our fathers have told us.
⁴We will not withhold them from their children,
　telling the coming generation
　the praises of the LORD and His might,
　and the wonders He performed.
⁵He established a decree in Jacob,
　ordained a teaching in Israel,
　charging our fathers

to make them known to their children,
⁶that a future generation might know
—children yet to be born—
and in turn tell their children
⁷that they might put their confidence in God,
and not forget God's great deeds,
but observe His commandments,
⁸and not be like their fathers,
a wayward and defiant generation,
a generation whose heart was inconstant,
whose spirit was not true to God.

⁹Like the Ephraimite bowmen
who played false in the day of battle,
¹⁰they did not keep God's covenant,
they refused to follow His instruction;
¹¹they forgot His deeds
and the wonders that He showed them.
¹²He performed marvels in the sight of their fathers,
in the land of Egypt, the plain of Zoan.
¹³He split the sea and took them through it;
He made the waters stand like a wall.
¹⁴He led them with a cloud by day,
and throughout the night by the light of fire.
¹⁵He split rocks in the wilderness
and gave them drink as if from the great deep.
¹⁶He brought forth streams from a rock
and made them flow down like a river.

¹⁷But they went on sinning against Him,
defying the Most High in the parched land.
¹⁸To test God was in their mind
when they demanded food for themselves.
¹⁹They spoke against God, saying,
"Can God spread a feast in the wilderness?
²⁰True, He struck the rock and waters flowed,
streams gushed forth;

but can He provide bread?
Can He supply His people with meat?"
21The Lord heard and He raged;
    fire broke out against Jacob,
    anger flared up at Israel,
    22because they did not put their trust in God,
    did not rely on His deliverance.
23So He commanded the skies above,
    He opened the doors of heaven
    24and rained manna upon them for food,
    giving them heavenly grain.
25Each man ate a hero's meal;
    He sent them provision in plenty.
26He set the east wind moving in heaven,
    and drove the south wind by His might.
27He rained meat on them like dust,
    winged birds like the sands of the sea,
    28making them come down inside His camp,
    around His dwelling-place.
29They ate till they were sated;
    He gave them what they craved.
30They had not yet wearied of what they craved,
    the food was still in their mouths
    31when God's anger flared up at them.
He slew their sturdiest,
    struck down the youth of Israel.
32Nonetheless, they went on sinning
    and had no faith in His wonders.
33He made their days end in futility,
    their years in sudden death.
34When He struck[a] them, they turned to Him
    and sought God once again.
35They remembered that God was their rock,
    God Most High, their Redeemer.
36Yet they deceived Him with their speech,
    lied to Him with their words;
37their hearts were inconstant toward Him;

[a] Lit. "killed."

they were untrue to His covenant.
38But He, being merciful, forgave iniquity
and would not destroy;
He restrained His wrath time and again
and did not give full vent to His fury;
39for He remembered that they were but flesh,
a passing breath that does not return.

40How often did they defy Him in the wilderness,
did they grieve Him in the wasteland!
41Again and again they tested God,
vexedb the Holy One of Israel.
42They did not remember His strength,
or the day He redeemed them from the foe;
43how He displayed His signs in Egypt,
His wonders in the plain of Zoan.
44He turned their rivers into blood;
He made their waters undrinkable.
45He inflicted upon them swarms of insects to devour them,
frogs to destroy them.
46He gave their crops over to grubs,
their produce to locusts.
47He killed their vines with hail,
their sycamores c-with frost.-c
48He gave their beasts over to hail,
their cattle to lightning bolts.
49He inflicted His burning anger upon them,
wrath, indignation, trouble,
a band of deadly messengers.
50He cleared a path for His anger;
He did not stop short of slaying them,
but gave them over to pestilence.
51He struck every first-born in Egypt,
the first fruits of their vigor in the tents of Ham.
52He set His people moving like sheep,
drove them like a flock in the wilderness.
53He led them in safety; they were unafraid;

b Or "set a limit to."
c-c Meaning of Heb. uncertain.

as for their enemies, the sea covered them.
⁵⁴He brought them to His holy realm,^d
the mountain His right hand had acquired.
⁵⁵He expelled nations before them,
^{e-}settled the tribes of Israel in their tents,
allotting them their portion by the line.^{-e}

⁵⁶Yet they defiantly tested God Most High,
and did not observe His decrees.
⁵⁷They fell away, disloyal like their fathers;
they played false like a treacherous bow.
⁵⁸They vexed Him with their high places;
they incensed Him with their idols.
⁵⁹God heard it and was enraged;
He utterly rejected Israel.
⁶⁰He forsook the tabernacle of Shiloh,
the tent He had set among men.
⁶¹He let His might^f go into captivity,
His glory into the hands of the foe.
⁶²He gave His people over to the sword;
He was enraged at His very own.
⁶³Fire consumed their young men,
and their maidens ^{g-}remained unwed.^{-g}
⁶⁴Their priests fell by the sword,
and their widows could not weep.

⁶⁵The Lord awoke as from sleep,
like a warrior ^{e-}shaking off^{-e} wine.
⁶⁶He beat back His foes,
dealing them lasting disgrace.
⁶⁷He rejected the clan of Joseph;
He did not choose the tribe of Ephraim.
⁶⁸He did choose the tribe of Judah,
Mount Zion, which He loved.
⁶⁹He built His Sanctuary like the heavens,
like the earth that He established forever.
⁷⁰He chose David, His servant,
and took him from the sheepfolds.

d *Or "hill" with Septuagint and Saadia.*
e-e *Inverted for clarity.*
f *I.e., the Ark; cf. Ps. 132.8.*
g-g *Lit. "had no nuptial song."*

71He brought him from minding the nursing ewes
   to tend His people Jacob, Israel, His very own.
72He tended them with blameless heart;
   with skillful hands he led them.

79 A psalm of Asaph.

O God, heathens have entered Your domain,
   defiled Your holy temple,
   and turned Jerusalem into ruins.
2They have left Your servants' corpses
   as food for the fowl of heaven,
   and the flesh of Your faithful for the wild beasts.
3Their blood was shed like water around Jerusalem,
   with none to bury them.
4We have become the butt of our neighbors,
   the scorn and derision of those around us.

5How long, O LORD, will You be angry forever,
   will Your indignation blaze like fire?
6Pour out Your fury on the nations that do not know You,
   upon the kingdoms that do not invoke Your name,
   7for they have devoured Jacob
   and desolated his home.
8Do not hold our former iniquities against us;
   let Your compassion come swiftly toward us,
   for we have sunk very low.
9Help us, O God, our deliverer,
   for the sake of the glory of Your name.
Save us and forgive our sin,
   for the sake of Your name.
10Let the nations not say, "Where is their God?"
Before our eyes let it be known among the nations
   that You avenge the spilled blood of Your servants.
11Let the groans of the prisoners reach You;
   reprieve those condemned to death,
   as befits Your great strength.

¹²Pay back our neighbors sevenfold
    for the abuse they have flung at You, O LORD.
¹³Then we, Your people,
    the flock You shepherd,
    shall glorify You forever;
    for all time we shall tell Your praises.

80 For the leader; on *shoshannim, eduth*. Of Asaph. A psalm.

²Give ear, O shepherd of Israel
    who leads Joseph like a flock!
Appear, You who are enthroned on the cherubim,
    ³at the head of Ephraim, Benjamin, and Manasseh!
Rouse Your might and come to our help!
⁴Restore us, O God;
    show Your favor that we may be delivered.

⁵O LORD, God of hosts,
    how long will You be wrathful
    toward the prayers of Your people?
⁶You have fed them tears as their daily bread,
    made them drink great measures of tears.
⁷You set us at strife with our neighbors;
    our enemies mock us at will.
⁸O God of hosts, restore us;
    show Your favor that we may be delivered.

⁹You plucked up a vine from Egypt;
    You expelled nations and planted it.
¹⁰You cleared a place for it;
    it took deep root and filled the land.
¹¹The mountains were covered by its shade,
    mighty cedars by its boughs.
¹²Its branches reached the sea,
    its shoots, the river.
¹³Why did You breach its wall
    so that every passerby plucks its fruit,

¹⁴wild boars gnaw at it,
and creatures of the field feed on it?

¹⁵O God of hosts, turn again,
look down from heaven and see;
take note of that vine,
¹⁶the stock planted by Your right hand,
the stemᵃ you have taken as Your own.
¹⁷For it is burned by fire and cut down,
perishing before Your angry blast.
¹⁸Grant Your helpᵇ to the man at Your right hand,
the one You have taken as Your own.
¹⁹We will not turn away from You;
preserve our life that we may invoke Your name.
²⁰O LORD, God of hosts, restore us;
show Your favor that we may be delivered.

81

For the leader; on the *gittith*. Of Asaph.

²Sing joyously to God, our strength;
raise a shout for the God of Jacob.
³Take up the song,
sound the timbrel,
the melodious lyre and harp.
⁴Blow the horn on the new moon,
on the full moon for our feast day.
⁵For it is a law for Israel,
a ruling of the God of Jacob;
⁶He imposed it as a decree upon Joseph
when ᵃ⁻he went forth from⁻ᵃ the land of Egypt;
I heard a language that I knew not.

⁷I relieved his shoulder of the burden,
his hands were freed from the basket.
⁸In distress you called and I rescued you;
I answered you from the ᵇ⁻secret place of thunder⁻ᵇ
I tested you at the waters of Meribah.   *Selah.*

ᵃ *Lit. "son."*
ᵇ *Lit. "hand."*

ᵃ⁻ᵃ *Or "He went forth against."*
ᵇ⁻ᵇ *Meaning of Heb. uncertain.*

⁹Hear, My people, and I will admonish you;
    Israel, if you would but listen to Me!
¹⁰You shall have no foreign god,
    you shall not bow to an alien god.
¹¹I the LORD am your God
    who brought you out of the land of Egypt;
    open your mouth wide and I will fill it.

¹²But My people would not listen to Me,
    Israel would not obey Me.
¹³So I let them go after their willful heart
    that they might follow their own devices.
¹⁴If only My people would listen to Me,
    if Israel would follow My paths,
    ¹⁵then would I subdue their enemies at once,
    strike their foes again and again.
¹⁶Those who hate the LORD shall cower before Him;
    their doom shall be eternal.
¹⁷He fed them*c* the finest wheat;
    I sated you with honey from the rock.

82A psalm of Asaph.

God stands in the divine assembly;
    among the divine beings He pronounces judgment.
²How long will you judge perversely,
    showing favor to the wicked?   *Selah.*
³Judge the wretched and the orphan,
    vindicate the lowly and the poor,
    ⁴rescue the wretched and the needy;
    save them from the hand of the wicked.

⁵They neither know nor understand,
    they go about in darkness;
    all the foundations of the earth totter.
⁶I had taken you for divine beings,
    sons of the Most High, all of you;

---

c *Lit. "him," i.e., Israel.*

⁷but you shall die as men do,
  fall like any prince.

⁸Arise, O God, judge the earth,
  for all the nations are Your possession.

83 A song, a psalm of Asaph.

²O God, do not be silent;
  do not hold aloof;
  do not be quiet, O God!
³For Your enemies rage,
  Your foes ᵃ⁻assert themselves.⁻ᵃ
⁴They plot craftily against Your people,
  take counsel against Your treasured ones.
⁵They say, "Let us wipe them out as a nation;
  Israel's name will be mentioned no more."
⁶Unanimous in their counsel
    they have made an alliance against You—
  ⁷the clans of Edom and the Ishmaelites,
  Moab and the Hagrites,
⁸Gebal, Ammon, and Amalek,
  Philistia with the inhabitants of Tyre;
⁹Assyria too joins forces with them;
  they give support to the sons of Lot.   *Selah.*

¹⁰Deal with them as You did with Midian,
  with Sisera, with Jabin,
  at the brook Kishon—
    ¹¹who were destroyed at En-dor,
  who became dung for the field.
¹²Treat their great men like Oreb and Zeeb,
  all their princes like Zebah and Zalmunna,
    ¹³who said, "Let us take the meadows of God
    as our possession."
¹⁴O my God, make them like thistledown,
  like stubble driven by the wind.

ᵃ⁻ᵃ *Lit. "lift up the head."*

¹⁵As a fire burns a forest,
    as flames scorch the hills,
¹⁶pursue them with Your tempest,
    terrify them with Your storm.
¹⁷Coverᵇ their faces with shame
    so that they seek Your name, O LORD.
¹⁸May they be frustrated and terrified,
    disgraced and doomed forever.
¹⁹May they know
    that Your name, Yours alone, is the LORD,
    supreme over all the earth.

84

For the leader; on the *gittith*. Of the Korahites. A psalm.

²How lovely is Your dwelling-place,
    O LORD of hosts.
³I long, I yearn for the courts of the LORD;
    my body and soul shout for joy to the living God.
⁴Even the sparrow has found a home,
    and the swallow a nest for herself
    in which to set her young,
    near Your altar, O LORD of hosts,
    my king and my God.
⁵Happy are those who dwell in Your house;
    they forever praise You.   *Selah.*

⁶Happy is the man who finds refuge in You,
    whose mind is on the [pilgrim] highways.
⁷They pass through the Valley of Baca,
    ᵃregarding it as a place of springs,
    as if the early rain had covered it with blessing.⁻ᵃ
⁸They go from ᵇrampart to rampart,⁻ᵇ
    appearing before God in Zion.
⁹O LORD, God of hosts,
    hear my prayer;
    give ear, O God of Jacob.   *Selah.*

ᵇ *Lit. "Fill."*

ᵃ⁻ᵃ *Meaning of Heb. uncertain.*
ᵇ⁻ᵇ *Others "strength to strength."*

¹⁰O God, behold our shield,
 look upon the face of Your anointed.

¹¹Better one day in Your courts than a thousand [anywhere
  else];
 I would rather stand at the threshold of God's house
 than dwell in the tents of the wicked.
¹²For the LORD God is sunᶜ and shield;
 the LORD bestows grace and glory;
 He does not withhold His bounty from those who live
  without blame.
¹³O LORD of hosts,
 happy is the man who trusts in You.

85 For the leader. Of the Korahites. A psalm.

²O LORD, You ᵃ⁻will favor⁻ᵃ Your land,
 restoreᵇ Jacob's fortune;
  ³You ᶜ⁻will forgive⁻ᶜ Your people's iniquity,
  pardonᵈ all their sins;   *Selah.*
  ⁴You ᵉ⁻will withdraw⁻ᵉ all Your anger,
  turnᶠ away from Your rage.
⁵Turn again, O God, our helper,
 revoke Your displeasure with us.
⁶Will You be angry with us forever,
 prolong Your wrath for all generations?
⁷Surely You will revive us again,
 so that Your people may rejoice in You.
⁸Show us, O LORD, Your faithfulness;
 grant us Your deliverance.

⁹Let me hear what God, the LORD, will speak;
 He will promise well-being to His people, His faithful ones;
 may they not turn to folly.
¹⁰His help is very near those who fear Him,
 to make His glory dwell in our land.

ᶜ Or *"bulwark,"* with *Targum; cf. Isa. 54.12.*

ᵃ⁻ᵃ Or *"have favored."*
ᵇ Or *"have restored."*
ᶜ⁻ᶜ Or *"have forgiven."*
ᵈ Or *"have pardoned."*
ᵉ⁻ᵉ Or *"have withdrawn."*
ᶠ Or *"have turned."*

¹¹Faithfulness and truth meet;
    justice and well-being kiss.
¹²Truth springs up from the earth;
    justice looks down from heaven.
¹³The LORD also bestows His bounty;
    our land yields its produce.
¹⁴Justice goes before Him
    as He sets out on His way.

86 A prayer of David.

Incline Your ear, O LORD,
    answer me,
    for I am poor and needy.
²Preserve my life, for I am steadfast;
    O You, my God,
    deliver Your servant who trusts in You.
³Have mercy on me, O LORD,
    for I call to You all day long;
⁴bring joy to Your servant's life,
    for on You, LORD, I set my hope.
⁵For You, LORD, are good and forgiving,
    abounding in steadfast love to all who call on You.
⁶Give ear, O LORD, to my prayer;
    heed my plea for mercy.
⁷In my time of trouble I call You,
    for You will answer me.

⁸There is none like You among the gods, O LORD,
    and there are no deeds like Yours.
⁹All the nations You have made
    will come to bow down before You, O LORD,
    and they will pay honor to Your name.
¹⁰For You are great and perform wonders;
    You alone are God.

11Teach me Your way, O LORD;
    I will walk in Your truth;
    let my heart be undivided in reverence for Your name.
12I will praise You, O LORD, my God, with all my heart
    and pay honor to Your name forever.
13For Your steadfast love toward me is great;
    You have saved me from the depths of Sheol.

14O God, arrogant men have risen against me;
    a band of ruthless men seek my life;
    they are not mindful of You.
15But You, O LORD, are a God
    compassionate and merciful,
    slow to anger, abounding in steadfast love and faithfulness.
16Turn to me and have mercy on me;
    grant Your strength to Your servant
    and deliver the son of Your maidservant.
17Show me a sign of Your favor,
    that my enemies may see and be frustrated
    because You, O LORD, have given me aid and comfort.

87

a1-2Of the Korahites. A psalm. A song.

b-The LORD loves the gates of Zion,
    His foundation on the holy mountains,-b
    more than all the dwellings of Jacob.
3Glorious things are spoken of you,
    O city of God.   *Selah.*
4I mention Rahabc and Babylon among those who acknowledge
    Me;
    Philistia, and Tyre, and Cush—each was born there.
5Indeed, it shall be said of Zion,
    "Every man was born there."
d-He, the Most High, will preserve it.-d
6The LORD will inscribe in the register of peoples
    that each was born there.   *Selah.*

---

a *The meaning of many passages in this psalm is uncertain.*
b-b *Order of lines inverted for clarity.*
c *A primeval monster; here, a poetic term for Egypt; cf. Isa. 30.7.*
d-d *Or "He will preserve it supreme."*

⁷Singers and dancers alike [will say]:
"All my rootsᶜ are in You."

88

A song. A psalm of the Korahites. For the leader; ᵃ⁻on *mahalath leannoth.*⁻ᵃ A *maskil* of Heman the Ezrahite.

²O LORD, God of my deliverance,
ᵇ⁻when I cry out in the night⁻ᵇ before You,
³let my prayer reach You;
incline Your ear to my cry.
⁴For I am sated with misfortune;
I am at the brink of Sheol.
⁵I am numbered with those who go down to the Pit;
I am a helpless man
⁶abandonedᶜ among the dead,
like bodies lying in the grave
of whom You are mindful no more,
and who are cut off from Your care.
⁷You have put me at the bottom of the Pit,
in the darkest places, in the depths.
⁸Your fury lies heavy upon me;
You afflict me with all Your breakers.   *Selah.*
⁹You make my companions shun me;
You make me abhorrent to them;
I am shut in and do not go out.
¹⁰My eyes pine away from affliction;
I call to You, O LORD, each day;
I stretch out my hands to You.

¹¹Do You work wonders for the dead?
Do the shades rise to praise You?   *Selah.*
¹²Is Your faithful care recounted in the grave,
Your constancy in the place of perdition?
¹³Are Your wonders made known in the netherworld,ᵈ
Your beneficent deeds in the land of oblivion?

¹⁴As for me, I cry out to You, O LORD;
each morning my prayer greets You.

ᶜ *Lit. "sources."*

ᵃ⁻ᵃ *Meaning of Heb. uncertain.*
ᵇ⁻ᵇ *Or "by day I cry out [and] by night."*
ᶜ *Lit. "released."*
ᵈ *Lit. "darkness."*

¹⁵Why, O LORD, do You reject me,
do You hide Your face from me?
¹⁶From my youth I have been afflicted
and near death;
I suffer Your terrors ᶜ⁻wherever I turn.⁻ᶜ
¹⁷Your fury overwhelms me;
Your terrors destroy me.
¹⁸They swirl about me like water all day long;
they encircle me on every side.
¹⁹You have put friend and neighbor far from me
and my companions out of my sight.ᶠ

89 A *maskil* of Ethan the Ezrahite.

²I will sing of the LORD's steadfast love forever;
to all generations I will proclaim Your faithfulness with my
mouth.
³I declare, "Your steadfast love is confirmed forever;
there in the heavens You establish Your faithfulness."

⁴"I have made a covenant with My chosen one;
I have sworn to My servant David:
⁵I will establish your offspring forever,
I will confirm your throne for all generations." *Selah.*

⁶Your wonders, O LORD, are praised by the heavens,
Your faithfulness, too, in the assembly of holy beings.
⁷For who in the skies can equal the LORD,
can compare with the LORD among the divine beings,
⁸a God greatly dreaded in the council of holy beings,
held in awe by all around Him?
⁹O LORD, God of hosts,
who is mighty like You, O LORD?
Your faithfulness surrounds You;
¹⁰You rule the swelling of the sea;
when its waves surge, You still them.
¹¹You crushed Rahab; he was like a corpse;
with Your powerful arm You scattered Your enemies.
¹²The heaven is Yours,

ᶜ⁻ᶜ *Following Saadia; meaning of Heb. uncertain.*
ᶠ *Lit. "into darkness."*

the earth too;
the world and all it holds—
You established them.
13North and south—
You created them;
Tabor and Hermon sing forth Your name.
14Yours is an arm endowed with might;
Your hand is strong;
Your right hand, exalted.
15Righteousness and justice are the base of Your throne;
steadfast love and faithfulness stand before You.

16Happy is the people who know the joyful shout;
O LORD, they walk in the light of Your presence.
17They rejoice in Your name all day long;
they are exalted through Your righteousness.
18For You are their strength in which they glory;
our horn is exalted through Your favor.
19Truly our shield is of the LORD,
our king, of the Holy One of Israel.

20Then[a] You spoke to Your faithful ones in a vision
and said, "I have conferred power upon a warrior;
I have exalted one chosen out of the people.
21I have found David, My servant;
anointed him with My sacred oil.
22My hand shall be constantly with him,
and My arm shall strengthen him.
23No enemy shall [b]oppress him,[b]
no vile man afflict him.
24I will crush his adversaries before him;
I will strike down those who hate him.
25My faithfulness and steadfast love shall be with him;
his horn shall be exalted through My name.
26I will set his hand upon the sea,
his right hand upon the rivers.
27He shall say to Me,

---

a Referring to vv. 4–5; cf. 2 Sam. 7.1–17.
b-b Meaning of Heb. uncertain.

'You are my father, my God, the rock of my deliverance.'
28I will appoint him first-born,
   highest of the kings of the earth.
29I will maintain My steadfast love for him always;
   My covenant with him shall endure.
30I will establish his line forever,
   his throne, as long as the heavens last.
31If his sons forsake My Teaching
   and do not live by My rules;
      32if they violate My laws,
   and do not observe My commands,
      33I will punish their transgression with the rod,
   their iniquity with plagues.
34But I will not take away My steadfast love from him;
   I will not betray My faithfulness.
35I will not violate My covenant,
   or change what I have uttered.
36I have sworn by My holiness, once and for all;
   I will not be false to David.
37His line shall continue forever,
   his throne, as the sun before Me,
      38as the moon, established forever,
   an enduring witness in the sky."   *Selah.*

39Yet You have rejected, spurned,
   and become enraged at Your anointed.
40You have repudiated the covenant with Your servant;
   You have dragged his dignity in the dust.
41You have breached all his defenses,
   shattered his strongholds.
42All who pass by plunder him;
   he has become the butt of his neighbors.
43You have exalted the right hand of his adversaries,
   and made all his enemies rejoice.
44You have turned back the blade of his sword,
   and have not sustained him in battle.
45You have brought b-his splendor-b to an end

and have hurled his throne to the ground.
⁴⁶You have cut short the days of his youth;
You have covered him with shame. *Selah.*
⁴⁷How long, O Lord; will You forever hide Your face,
will Your fury blaze like fire?
⁴⁸O remember ᵇ⁻how short my life is;⁻ᵇ
why should You have created every man in vain?
⁴⁹What man can live and not see death,
can save himself from the clutches of Sheol? *Selah.*
⁵⁰O Lord, where is Your steadfast love of old
which You swore to David in Your faithfulness?
⁵¹Remember, O Lord, the abuse flung at Your servants
ᵇ⁻that I have borne in my bosom [from] many peoples,⁻ᵇ
⁵²how Your enemies, O Lord, have flung abuse,
abuse at Your anointed at every step.

⁵³Blessed is the Lord forever;
Amen and Amen.

BOOK FOUR

90
A prayer of Moses, the man of God.

O Lord, You have been our refuge in every generation.
²Before the mountains came into being,
before You brought forth the earth and the world,
from eternity to eternity You are God.

³You return man to dust;ᵃ
You decreed, "Return you mortals!"
⁴ᵇ⁻For in Your sight a thousand years
are like yesterday that has past,
like a watch of the night.
⁵You engulf men in sleep;⁻ᵇ
at daybreak they are like grass that renews itself;
⁶at daybreak it flourishes anew;

ᵃ *Or "contrition."*
ᵇ⁻ᵇ *Meaning of Heb. uncertain.*

by dusk it withers and dries up.
7So we are consumed by Your anger,
    terror-struck by Your fury.
8You have set our iniquities before You,
    our hidden sins in the light of Your face.
9All our days pass away in Your wrath;
    we spend our years like a sigh.
10The span of our life is seventy years,
    or, given the strength, eighty years;
    but the b-best of them-b are trouble and sorrow.
They pass by speedily, and we c-are in darkness.-c
11Who can know Your furious anger?
Your wrath matches the fear of You.
12Teach us to count our days rightly,
    that we may obtain a wise heart.

13Turn, O LORD!
How long?
Show mercy to Your servants.
14Satisfy us at daybreak with Your steadfast love
    that we may sing for joy all our days.
15Give us joy for as long as You have afflicted us,
    for the years we have suffered misfortune.
16Let Your deeds be seen by Your servants,
    Your glory by their children.
17May the favor of the LORD, our God, be upon us;
    let the work of our hands prosper,
    O prosper the work of our hands!

91 O you who dwell in the shelter of the Most High
    and abide in the protection of Shaddai—
    2I say of the LORD, my refuge and stronghold,
    my God in whom I trust,
    3that He will save you from the fowler's trap,
    from the destructive plague.
4He will cover you with His pinions;
    you will find refuge under His wings;

c-c Or "fly away."

His fidelity is an encircling shield.
⁵You need not fear the terror by night,
    or the arrow that flies by day,
      ⁶the plague that stalks in the darkness,
    or the scourge that ravages at noon.
⁷A thousand may fall at your left side,
    ten thousand at your right,
    but it shall not reach you.
⁸You will see it with your eyes,
    you will witness the punishment of the wicked.
⁹Because you took the LORD—my refuge,
    the Most High—as your haven,
      ¹⁰no harm will befall you,
    no disease touch your tent.
¹¹For He will order His angels
    to guard you wherever you go.
¹²They will carry you in their hands
    lest you hurt your foot on a stone.
¹³You will tread on cubs and vipers;
    you will trample lions and asps.

¹⁴"Because he is devoted to Me I will deliver him;
    I will keep him safe, for he knows My name.
¹⁵When he calls on Me, I will answer him;
    I will be with him in distress;
    I will rescue him and make him honored;
      ¹⁶I will let him live to a ripe old age,
    and show him My salvation."

92 A psalm. A song; for the sabbath day.

²It is good to praise the LORD,
    to sing hymns to Your name, O Most High,
³To proclaim Your steadfast love at daybreak,
    Your faithfulness each night
⁴With a ten-stringed harp,
    with voice and lyre together.

5You have gladdened me by Your deeds, O LORD;
  I shout for joy at Your handiwork.
6How great are Your works, O LORD,
  how very subtle[a] Your designs!
7A brutish man cannot know,
  a fool cannot understand this:
    8though the wicked sprout like grass,
    though all evildoers blossom,
    it is only that they may be destroyed forever.

9But You are exalted, O LORD, for all time.

10Surely, Your enemies, O LORD,
  surely, Your enemies perish;
  all evildoers are scattered.
11You raise my horn high like that of a wild ox;
  I am soaked in freshening oil.
12I shall see the defeat of my watchful foes,
  hear of the downfall of the wicked who beset me.
13The righteous bloom like a date-palm;
  they thrive like a cedar in Lebanon;
    14planted in the house of the LORD,
    they flourish in the courts of our God.
15In old age they still produce fruit;
  they are full of sap and freshness,
    16attesting that the LORD is upright,
    my rock, in whom there is no wrong.

93

The LORD is king,
  He is robed in grandeur;
  the LORD is robed,
  He is girded with strength.
The world stands firm;
  it cannot be shaken.
2Your throne stands firm from of old;
  from eternity You have existed.
3The ocean sounds, O LORD,

---

a Or "profound."

the ocean sounds its thunder,
the ocean sounds its pounding.
4Above the thunder of the mighty waters,
more majestic than the breakers of the sea
is the LORD, majestic on high.
5Your decrees are indeed enduring;
holiness befits Your house,
O LORD, for all times.

94God of retribution, LORD,
God of retribution, appear!
2Rise up, judge of the earth,
give the arrogant their deserts!
3How long shall the wicked, O LORD,
how long shall the wicked exult,
4shall they utter insolent speech,
shall all evildoers vaunt themselves?
5They crush Your people, O LORD,
they afflict Your very own;
6they kill the widow and the stranger;
they murder the fatherless,
7thinking, "The LORD does not see it,
the God of Jacob does not pay heed."

8Take heed, you most brutish people;
fools, when will you get wisdom?
9Shall He who implants the ear not hear,
He who forms the eye not see?
10Shall He who disciplines nations not punish,
He who instructs men in knowledge?
11The LORD knows the designs of men to be futile.

12Happy is the man whom You discipline, O LORD,
the man You instruct in Your teaching,
13to give him tranquillity in times of misfortune,
until a pit be dug for the wicked.
14For the LORD will not forsake His people;

He will not abandon His very own.
15Judgment shall again accord with justice
   and all the upright shall rally to it.

16Who will take my part against evil men?
Who will stand up for me against wrongdoers?
17Were not the LORD my help,
   I should soon dwell in silence.
18When I think my foot has given way,
   Your faithfulness, O LORD, supports me.
19When I am filled with cares,
   Your assurance soothes my soul.

20Shall the seat of injustice be Your partner,
   that frames mischief by statute?
21They band together to do away with the righteous;
   they condemn the innocent to death.
22But the LORD is my haven;
   my God is my sheltering rock.
23He will make their evil recoil upon them,
   annihilate them through their own wickedness;
   the LORD our God will annihilate them.

95 Come, let us sing joyously to the LORD,
   raise a shout for our rock and deliverer;
   2let us come into His presence with praise;
   let us raise a shout for Him in song!
3For the LORD is a great God,
   the great king of all divine beings.
4In His hand are the depths of the earth;
   the peaks of the mountains are His.
5His is the sea, He made it;
   and the land, which His hands fashioned.

6Come, let us bow down and kneel,
   bend the knee before the LORD our maker,
   7for He is our God,

and we are the people He tends, the flock in His care.
O, if you would but heed His charge this day:
⁸Do not be stubborn as at Meribah,
  as on the day of Massah, in the wilderness,
⁹when your fathers put Me to the test,
  tried Me, though they had seen My deeds.
¹⁰Forty years I was provoked by that generation;
I thought, "They are a senseless people;
  they would not know My ways."
¹¹Concerning them I swore in anger,
  "They shall never come to My resting-place!"

96

ᵃSing to the LORD a new song,
  sing to the LORD, all the earth.
²Sing to the LORD, bless His name,
  proclaim His victory day after day.
³Tell of His glory among the nations,
  His wondrous deeds, among all peoples.
⁴For the LORD is great and much acclaimed,
  He is held in awe by all divine beings.
⁵All the gods of the peoples are mere idols,
  but the LORD made the heavens.
⁶Glory and majesty are before Him;
  strength and splendor are in His temple.

⁷Ascribe to the LORD, O families of the peoples,
  ascribe to the LORD glory and strength.
⁸Ascribe to the LORD the glory of His name,
  bring tribute and enter His courts.
⁹Bow down to the LORD majestic in holiness;
  tremble in His presence, all the earth!
¹⁰Declare among the nations, "The LORD is king!"
  the world stands firm; it cannot be shaken;
  He judges the peoples with equity.
¹¹Let the heavens rejoice and the earth exult;
  let the sea and all within it thunder,
  ¹²the fields and everything in them exult;

ᵃ *Cf. 1 Chron. 16.23–33.*

then shall all the trees of the forest shout for joy
13at the presence of the LORD, for He is coming,
for He is coming to rule the earth;
He will rule the world justly,
and its peoples in faithfulness.

97

The LORD is king!
Let the earth exult,
    the many islands rejoice!
2Dense clouds are around Him,
    righteousness and justice are the base of His throne.
3Fire is His vanguard,
    burning His foes on every side.
4His lightnings light up the world;
    the earth is convulsed at the sight;
    5mountains melt like wax at the LORD's presence,
    at the presence of the Lord of all the earth.
6The heavens proclaim His righteousness
    and all peoples see His glory.
7All who worship images,
    who vaunt their idols,
    are dismayed;
    all divine beings bow down to Him.
8Zion, hearing it, rejoices,
    the towns[a] of Judah exult,
    because of Your judgments, O LORD.
9For You, LORD, are supreme over all the earth;
    You are exalted high above all divine beings.

10O you who love the LORD, hate evil!
He guards the lives of His loyal ones,
    saving them from the hand of the wicked.
11Light is sown for the righteous,
    radiance[b] for the upright.
12O you righteous, rejoice in the LORD
    and acclaim His holy name!

a *Or "women."*
b *Others "joy."*

98
A psalm.

Sing to the LORD a new song,
   for He has worked wonders;
   His right hand, His holy arm,
   has won Him victory.
²The LORD has manifested His victory,
   has displayed His triumph in the sight of the nations.
³He was mindful of His steadfast love and faithfulness
     toward the house of Israel;
   all the ends of the earth beheld the victory of our God.
⁴Raise a shout to the LORD, all the earth,
   break into joyous songs of praise!
⁵Sing praise to the LORD with the lyre,
   with the lyre and melodious song.
⁶With trumpets and the blast of the horn
   raise a shout before the LORD, the king.
⁷Let the sea and all within it thunder,
   the world and its inhabitants;
⁸let the rivers clap their hands,
   the mountains sing joyously together
⁹at the presence of the LORD,
   for He is coming to rule the earth;
   He will rule the world justly,
   and its peoples with equity.

99
ᵃ⁻The LORD, enthroned on cherubim, is king,
   peoples tremble, the earth quakes.⁻ᵃ
²The LORD is great in Zion,
   and exalted above all peoples.
³They praise Your name as great and awesome;
   He is holy!

⁴ᵇ⁻Mighty king⁻ᵇ who loves justice,
   it was You who established equity,

ᵃ⁻ᵃ *Clauses transposed for clarity.*
ᵇ⁻ᵇ *Meaning of Heb. uncertain.*

You who worked righteous judgment in Jacob.
⁵Exalt the LORD our God
and bow down to His footstool;
He is holy!

⁶Moses and Aaron among His priests,
Samuel, among those who call on His name—
when they called to the LORD,
He answered them.
⁷He spoke to them in a pillar of cloud;
they obeyed His decrees,
the law He gave them.
⁸O LORD our God, You answered them;
You were a forgiving God for them,
but You exacted retribution for their misdeeds.

⁹Exalt the LORD our God,
and bow toward His holy hill,
for the LORD our God is holy.

100 A psalm ᵃ⁻for praise.⁻ᵃ

Raise a shout for the LORD, all the earth;
²worship the LORD in gladness;
come into His presence with shouts of joy.
³Acknowledge that the LORD is God;
He made us and ᵇ⁻we are His,⁻ᵇ
His people, the flock He tends.
⁴Enter His gates with praise,
His courts with acclamation.
Praise Him!
Bless His name!
⁵For the LORD is good;
His steadfast love is eternal;
His faithfulness is for all generations.

ᵃ⁻ᵃ Traditionally "for the thanksgiving offering."
ᵇ⁻ᵇ So qere; kethib and some ancient versions "not we ourselves."

101 Of David. A psalm.

I will sing of faithfulness and justice;
   I will chant a hymn to You, O LORD.
²I will study the way of the blameless;
   when shall I attain it?
I will live without blame within my house.
³I will not set before my eyes anything base;
   I hate crooked dealing;
   I will have none of it.
⁴Perverse thoughts will be far from me;
   I will know nothing of evil.
⁵He who slanders his friend in secret I will destroy;
   I cannot endure the haughty and proud man.
⁶My eyes are on the trusty men of the land,
   to have them at my side.
He who follows the way of the blameless
   shall be in my service.
⁷He who deals deceitfully
   shall not live in my house;
   he who speaks untruth
   shall not stand before my eyes.
⁸Each morning I will destroy
   all the wicked of the land,
   to rid the city of the LORD
   of all evildoers.

102 A prayer of the lowly man when he is faint and pours forth his plea before the LORD.

²O LORD, hear my prayer;
   let my cry come before You.
³Do not hide Your face from me
   in my time of trouble;
   turn Your ear to me;
   when I cry, answer me speedily.

4For my days have vanished like smoke
and my bones are charred like a hearth.
5My body is stricken and withered like grass;
a-too wasted-a to eat my food;
6on account of my vehement groaning
my bones b-show through my skin.-b
7I am like a great owl in the wilderness,
an owl among the ruins.
8I lie awake; I am like
a lone bird upon a roof.
9All day long my enemies revile me;
my deriders use my name to curse.
10For I have eaten ashes like bread
and mixed my drink with tears,
11because of Your wrath and Your fury;
for You have cast me far away.
12My days are like a lengthening shadow;
I wither like grass.

13But You, O LORD, are enthroned forever;
Your fame endures throughout the ages.
14You will surely arise and take pity on Zion,
for it is time to be gracious to her;
the appointed time has come.
15Your servants take delight in its stones,
and cherish its dust.
16The nations will fear the name of the LORD,
all the kings of the earth, Your glory.
17For the LORD has built Zion;
He has appeared in all His glory.
18He has turned to the prayer c-of the destitute-c
and has not spurned their prayer.
19May this be written down for a coming generation,
that people yet to be created may praise the LORD.
20For He looks down from His holy height;
the LORD beholds the earth from heaven
21to hear the groans of the prisoner,
to release those condemned to death;

a-a Others "I forget."
b-b Lit. "cling to my flesh."
c-c Meaning of Heb. uncertain.

²²that the fame of the L<small>ORD</small> may be recounted in Zion,
His praises in Jerusalem,
²³when the nations gather together,
the kingdoms, to serve the L<small>ORD</small>.

²⁴He drained my strength in mid-course,
He shortened my days.
²⁵I say, "O my God, do not take me away
in the midst of my days,
You whose years go on for generations on end.
²⁶Of old You established the earth;
the heavens are the work of Your hands.
²⁷They shall perish, but You shall endure;
they shall all wear out like a garment;
You change them like clothing and they pass away.
²⁸But You are the same, and Your years never end.
²⁹May the children of Your servants dwell securely
and their offspring endure in Your presence."

103 Of David.

Bless the L<small>ORD</small>, O my soul,
all my being, His holy name.
²Bless the L<small>ORD</small>, O my soul
and do not forget all His bounties.
³He forgives all your sins,
heals all your diseases.
⁴He redeems your life from the Pit,
surrounds you with steadfast love and mercy.
⁵He satisfies you with good things in ^{a-}the prime of life,^{-a}
so that your youth is renewed like the eagle's.

⁶The L<small>ORD</small> executes righteous acts
and judgments for all who are wronged.
⁷He made known His ways to Moses,
His deeds to the children of Israel.
⁸The L<small>ORD</small> is compassionate and gracious,

a-a *Meaning of Heb. uncertain.*

slow to anger, abounding in steadfast love.
9He will not contend forever,
   or nurse His anger for all time.
10He has not dealt with us according to our sins,
   nor has He requited us according to our iniquities.
11For as the heavens are high above the earth,
   so great is His steadfast love toward those who fear Him.
12As east is far from west,
   so far has He removed our sins from us.
13As a father has compassion for his children,
   so the LORD has compassion for those who fear Him.
14For He knows how we are formed;
   He is mindful that we are dust.

15Man, his days are like those of grass;
   he blooms like a flower of the field;
      16a wind passes by and it is no more,
   its own place no longer knows it.
17But the LORD's steadfast love is for all eternity
   toward those who fear Him,
   and His beneficence is for the children's children
      18of those who keep His covenant
   and remember to observe His precepts.
19The LORD has established His throne in heaven,
   and His sovereign rule is over all.

20Bless the LORD, O His angels,
   mighty creatures who do His bidding,
   ever obedient to His bidding;
      21bless the LORD, all His hosts,
   His servants who do His will;
      22bless the LORD, all His works,
   through the length and breadth of His realm;
   bless the LORD, O my soul.

104 Bless the LORD, O my soul;
   O LORD, my God, You are very great;

You are clothed in glory and majesty,
²wrapped in a robe of light;
You spread the heavens like a tent cloth.
³He sets the rafters of His lofts in the waters,
makes the clouds His chariot,
moves on the wings of the wind.
⁴He makes the winds His messengers,
fiery flames His servants.
⁵He established the earth on its foundations,
so that it shall never totter.
⁶You made the deep cover it as a garment;
the waters stood above the mountains.
⁷They fled at Your blast,
rushed away at the sound of Your thunder,
⁸—mountains rising, valleys sinking—
to the place You established for them.
⁹You set bounds they must not pass
so that they never again cover the earth.

¹⁰You make springs gush forth in torrents;
they make their way between the hills,
¹¹giving drink to all the wild beasts;
the wild asses slake their thirst.
¹²The birds of the sky dwell beside them
and sing among the foliage.
¹³You water the mountains from Yourᵃ lofts;
the earth is sated from the fruit of Your work.
¹⁴You make the grass grow for the cattle,
and herbage for man's labor
that he may get food out of the earth—
¹⁵wine that cheers the hearts of men
ᵇ⁻oil that makes the face shine,⁻ᵇ
and bread that sustains man's life.
¹⁶The trees of the LORD drink their fill,
the cedars of Lebanon, His own planting,
¹⁷where birds make their nests;
the stork has her home in the junipers.

ᵃ *Lit. "His."*
ᵇ⁻ᵇ *Lit. "to make the face shine from oil."*

18The high mountains are for wild goats;
  the crags are a refuge for rock-badgers.

19He made the moon to mark the seasons;
  the sun knows when to set.
20You bring on darkness and it is night,
  when all the beasts of the forests stir.
21The lions roar for prey,
  seeking their food from God.
22When the sun rises, they come home
  and couch in their dens.
23Man then goes out to his work,
  to his labor until the evening.

24How many are the things You have made, O LORD;
  You have made them all with wisdom;
  the earth is full of Your creations.
25There is the sea, vast and wide,
  with its creatures beyond number,
  living things, small and great.
26There go the ships,
  and Leviathan that You formed to sport with.
27All of them look to You
  to give them their food when it is due.
28Give it to them, they gather it up;
  open Your hand, they are well satisfied;
  29hide Your face, they are terrified;
  take away their breath, they perish
  and turn again into dust;
  30send back Your breath, they are created,
  and You renew the face of the earth.

31May the glory of the LORD endure forever;
  may the LORD rejoice in His works!
32He looks at the earth and it trembles;
  He touches the mountains and they smoke.

³³I will sing to the LORD as long as I live;
all my life I will chant hymns to my God.
³⁴May my prayer be pleasing to Him;
I will rejoice in the LORD.
³⁵May sinners disappear from the earth,
and the wicked be no more.
Bless the LORD, O my soul.
Hallelujah.

105 Praise the LORD;
call on His name;
proclaim His deeds among the peoples.
²Sing praises to Him;
speak of all His wondrous acts.
³Exult in His holy name;
let all who seek the LORD rejoice.
⁴Turn to the LORD, to His might;^a
seek His presence constantly.
⁵Remember the wonders He has done,
His portents and the judgments He has pronounced,
⁶O offspring of Abraham, His servant,
O descendants of Jacob, His chosen ones.

⁷He is the LORD our God;
His judgments are throughout the earth.
⁸He is ever mindful of His covenant,
the promise He gave for a thousand generations,
⁹that He made with Abraham,
swore to Isaac,
¹⁰and confirmed in a decree for Jacob,
for Israel, as an eternal covenant,
¹¹saying, "To you I will give the land of Canaan
as your allotted heritage."

¹²They were then few in number,
a mere handful, sojourning there,
¹³wandering from nation to nation,

---

^a I.e., the Ark; cf. Ps. 78.61; 132.8.

from one kingdom to another.
14He allowed no one to oppress them;
   He reproved kings on their account,
   15"Do not touch My anointed ones;
   do not harm My prophets."

16He called down a famine on the land,
   destroyed every staff of bread.
17He sent ahead of them a man,
   Joseph, sold into slavery.
18His feet were subjected to fetters;
   an iron collar was put on his neck.
19Until his prediction came true
   the decree of the LORD purged him.
20The king sent to have him freed;
   the ruler of nations released him.
21He made him the lord of his household,
   empowered him over all his possessions,
   22to discipline his princes at will,
   to teach his elders wisdom.
23Then Israel came to Egypt;
   Jacob sojourned in the land of Ham.

24He made His people very fruitful,
   more numerous than their foes.
25b-He changed their heart-b to hate His people,
   to plot against His servants.
26He sent His servant Moses,
   and Aaron, whom He had chosen.
27They performed His signs among them,
   His wonders, against the land of Ham.
28He sent darkness; it was very dark;
   c-did they not defy His word?-c
29He turned their waters into blood
   and killed their fish.
30Their land teemed with frogs,
   even the rooms of their king.
31Swarms of insects came at His command,

b-b *Or "Their heart changed."*
c-c *Meaning of Heb. uncertain.*

lice, throughout their country.
32He gave them hail for rain,
and flaming fire in their land.
33He struck their vines and fig trees,
broke down the trees of their country.
34Locusts came at His command,
grasshoppers without number.
35They devoured every green thing in the land;
they consumed the produce of the soil.
36He struck down every first-born in the land,
the first fruit of their vigor.
37He led Israeld out with silver and gold;
none among their tribes faltered.
38Egypt rejoiced when they left,
for dread of Israeld had fallen upon them.

39He spread a cloud for a cover,
and fire to light up the night.
40They asked and He brought them quail,
and satisfied them with food from heaven.
41He opened a rock so that water gushed forth;
it flowed as a stream in the parched land.
42Mindful of His sacred promise
to His servant Abraham,
43He led His people out in gladness,
His chosen ones with joyous song.
44He gave them the lands of nations;
they inherited the wealth of peoples,
45that they might keep His laws
and observe His teachings.
Hallelujah.

106 Hallelujah.
Praise the LORD for He is good;
His steadfast love is eternal.

d Lit. "them."

²Who can tell the mighty acts of the LORD,
  proclaim all His praises?

³Happy are those who act justly,
  who do right at all times.
⁴Be mindful of me, O LORD, when You favor Your people;
  take note of me when You deliver them,
  ⁵that I may enjoy the prosperity of Your chosen ones,
  share the joy of Your nation,
  glory in Your very own people.

⁶We have sinned like our forefathers;
  we have gone astray, done evil.
⁷Our forefathers in Egypt did not perceive Your wonders;
  they did not remember Your abundant love,
  but rebelled at the sea, at the Sea of Reeds.
⁸Yet He saved them, as befits His name,
  to make known His might.
⁹He sent His blast against the Sea of Reeds;
  it became dry;
  He led them through the deep as through a wilderness.
¹⁰He delivered them from the foe,
  redeemed them from the enemy.
¹¹Water covered their adversaries;
  not one of them was left.
¹²Then they believed His promise,
  and sang His praises.
¹³But they soon forgot His deeds;
  they would not wait to learn His plan.
¹⁴They were seized with craving in the wilderness,
  and put God to the test in the wasteland.
¹⁵He gave them what they asked for,
  then made them waste away.
¹⁶There was envy of Moses in the camp,
  and of Aaron, the holy one of the LORD.
¹⁷The earth opened up and swallowed Dathan,
  closed over the party of Abiram.

¹⁸A fire blazed among their party,
a flame that consumed the wicked.
¹⁹They made a calf at Horeb
and bowed down to a molten image.
²⁰They exchanged their glory
for the image of a bull that feeds on grass.
²¹They forgot God who saved them,
who performed great deeds in Egypt,
²²wondrous deeds in the land of Ham,
awesome deeds at the Sea of Reeds.
²³He would have destroyed them
had not Moses His chosen one
confronted Him in the breach
to avert His destructive wrath.
²⁴They rejected the desirable land,
and put no faith in His promise.
²⁵They grumbled in their tents
and disobeyed the LORD.
²⁶So He raised His hand in oath
to make them fall in the wilderness,
²⁷to disperse[a] their offspring among the nations
and scatter them through the lands.
²⁸They attached themselves to Baal Peor,
ate sacrifices offered to the dead.
²⁹They provoked anger by their deeds,
and a plague broke out among them.
³⁰Phinehas stepped forth and intervened,
and the plague ceased.
³¹It was reckoned to his merit
for all generations, to eternity.
³²They provoked wrath at the waters of Meribah
and Moses suffered on their account,
³³because they rebelled against Him
and he spoke rashly.

³⁴They did not destroy the nations
as the LORD had commanded them,

[a] *Cf. Targum, Kimhi.*

35but mingled with the nations
and learned their ways.
36They worshiped their idols,
which became a snare for them.
37Their own sons and daughters
they sacrificed to demons.
38They shed innocent blood,
the blood of their sons and daughters,
whom they sacrificed to the idols of Canaan;
so the land was polluted with bloodguilt.
39Thus they became defiled by their acts,
debauched through their deeds.
40The LORD was angry with His people
and He abhorred His inheritance.
41He handed them over to the nations;
their foes ruled them.
42Their enemies oppressed them
and they were subject to their power.
43He saved them time and again,
but they were deliberately rebellious,
and so they were brought low by their iniquity.
44When He saw that they were in distress,
when He heard their cry,
45He was mindful of His covenant
and in His great faithfulness relented.
46He made all their captors kindly disposed toward them.

47Deliver us, O LORD our God,
and gather us from among the nations,
to acclaim Your holy name,
to glory in Your praise.

48Blessed is the LORD, God of Israel,
From eternity to eternity.
Let all the people say, "Amen."
Hallelujah.

BOOK FIVE

107 "Praise the LORD, for He is good;
His steadfast love is eternal!"
²Thus let the redeemed of the LORD say,
those He redeemed from adversity,
³whom He gathered in from the lands,
from east and west,
from the north and from the sea.

⁴Some lost their way in the wilderness,
in the wasteland;
they found no settled place.
⁵Hungry and thirsty,
their spirit failed.
⁶In their adversity they cried to the LORD,
and He rescued them from their troubles.
⁷He showed them a direct way
to reach a settled place.
⁸Let them praise the LORD for His steadfast love,
His wondrous deeds for mankind;
⁹for He has satisfied the thirsty,
filled the hungry with all good things.

¹⁰Some lived in deepest darkness,
bound in cruel irons,
¹¹because they defied the word of God,
spurned the counsel of the Most High.
¹²He humbled their hearts through suffering;
they stumbled with no one to help.
¹³In their adversity they cried to the LORD,
and He rescued them from their troubles.
¹⁴He brought them out of deepest darkness,
broke their bonds asunder.
¹⁵Let them praise the LORD for His steadfast love,
His wondrous deeds for mankind,
¹⁶For He shattered gates of bronze,
He broke their iron bars.

17There were fools who suffered for their sinful way,
and for their iniquities.
18All food was loathsome to them;
they reached the gates of death.
19In their adversity they cried to the LORD
and He saved them from their troubles.
20He gave an order and healed them;
He delivered them from the pits.ᵃ
21Let them praise the LORD for His steadfast love,
His wondrous deeds for mankind.
22Let them offer thanksgiving sacrifices,
and tell His deeds in joyful song.

23Others go down to the sea in ships,
ply their trade in the mighty waters;
24they have seen the works of the LORD
and His wonders in the deep.
25By His word He raised a storm wind
that made the waves surge.
26Mounting up to the heaven,
plunging down to the depths,
disgorging in their misery,
27they reeled and staggered like a drunken man,
all their skill to no avail.
28In their adversity they cried to the LORD,
and He saved them from their troubles.
29He reduced the storm to a whisper;
the waves were stilled.
30They rejoiced when all was quiet,
and He brought them to the port they desired.
31Let them praise the LORD for His steadfast love,
His wondrous deeds for mankind.
32Let them exalt Him in the congregation of the people,
acclaim Him in the assembly of the elders.

33He turns the rivers into a wilderness,
springs of water into thirsty land,
34fruitful land into a salt marsh,
because of the wickedness of its inhabitants.

ᵃ *Viz., of death.*

³⁵He turns the wilderness into pools,
  parched land into springs of water.
³⁶There He settles the hungry;
  they build a place to settle in.
³⁷They sow fields and plant vineyards
  that yield a fruitful harvest.
³⁸He blesses them and they increase greatly;
  and He does not let their cattle decrease,
  ³⁹after they had been few and crushed
  by oppression, misery, and sorrow.
⁴⁰He pours contempt on great men
  and makes them lose their way in trackless deserts;
  ⁴¹but the needy He secures from suffering,
  and increases their families like flocks.

⁴²The upright see it and rejoice;
  the mouth of all wrongdoers is stopped.
⁴³The wise man will take note of these things;
  he will consider the steadfast love of the LORD.

108 A song. A psalm of David.

²ᵃMy heart is firm, O God;
  I will sing and chant a hymn with all my soul.
³Awake, O harp and lyre!
  I will wake the dawn.
⁴I will praise You among the peoples, O LORD,
  sing a hymn to You among the nations;
  ⁵for Your faithfulness is higher than the heavens;
  Your steadfastness reaches to the sky.
⁶Exalt Yourself over the heavens, O God;
  let Your glory be over all the earth!
⁷ᵇThat those whom You love may be rescued,
  deliver with Your right hand and answer me.

⁸God promised ᶜ⁻in His sanctuary⁻ᶜ
  that I would exultingly divide up Shechem,

ᵃ *With vv. 2–6, cf. Ps. 57.8–12.*
ᵇ *With vv. 7–14, cf. Ps. 60.7–14.*
ᶜ⁻ᶜ *Or "by His holiness."*

and measure the Valley of Sukkoth;
⁹Gilead and Manasseh would be mine,
Ephraim my chief stronghold,
Judah my scepter;
¹⁰Moab would be my washbasin;
on Edom I would cast my shoe;
I would raise a shout over Philistia.
¹¹Would that I were brought to the bastion!
Would that I were led to Edom!

¹²But You have rejected us, O God;
God, You do not march with our armies.
¹³Grant us Your aid against the foe,
for the help of man is worthless.
¹⁴With God we shall triumph;
He will trample our foes.

109 For the leader. Of David. A psalm.

O God of my praise,
do not keep aloof,
²for the wicked and the deceitful
open their mouth against me;
they speak to me with lying tongue.
³They encircle me with words of hate;
they attack me without cause.
⁴They answer my love with accusation
ᵃ⁻and I must stand judgment.⁻ᵃ
⁵They repay me with evil for good,
with hatred for my love.

⁶Appoint a wicked man over him;
may an accuser stand at his right side;
⁷may he be tried and convicted;
may he be judged and found guilty.
⁸May his days be few;
may another take over ᵇ⁻his position.⁻ᵇ

ᵃ⁻ᵃ *Or "but I am all prayer"; meaning of Heb. uncertain, but see v. 7.*
ᵇ⁻ᵇ *Meaning of Heb. uncertain.*

⁹May his children be orphans,
  his wife a widow.
¹⁰May his children wander from their hovels,
  begging in search of [bread].
¹¹May his creditor seize all his possessions;
  may strangers plunder his wealth.
¹²May no one show him mercy;
  may none pity his orphans;
  ¹³may his posterity be cut off;
  may their names be blotted out in the next generation.
¹⁴May God be ever mindful of his father's iniquity,
  and may the sin of his mother not be blotted out.
¹⁵May the LORD be aware of them always
  and cause their names to be cut off from the earth,
  ¹⁶because he was not minded to act kindly,
  and hounded to death the poor and needy man,
  one crushed in spirit.
¹⁷He loved to curse—may a curse come upon him!
He would not bless—may blessing be far from him!
¹⁸May he be clothed in a curse like a garment,
  may it enter his body like water,
  his bones like oil.
¹⁹Let it be like the cloak he wraps around him,
  like the belt he always wears.
²⁰May the LORD thus repay my accusers,
  all those who speak evil against me.

²¹Now You, O God, my Lord,
  act on my behalf as befits Your name.
Good and faithful as You are, save me.
²²For I am poor and needy,
  and my heart is pierced within me.
²³I fade away like a lengthening shadow;
  I am shaken off like locusts.
²⁴My knees give way from fasting;
  my flesh is lean, has lost its fat.
²⁵I am the object of their scorn;
  when they see me, they shake their head.

26Help me, O LORD, my God;
 save me in accord with Your faithfulness,
  27that men may know that it is Your hand,
 that You, O LORD, have done it.
28Let them curse, but You bless;
 let them rise up, but come to grief,
 while Your servant rejoices.
29My accusers shall be clothed in shame,
 wrapped in their disgrace as in a robe.

30My mouth shall sing much praise to the LORD;
 I will acclaim Him in the midst of a throng,
  31because He stands at the right hand of the needy,
 to save him from those who would condemn him.

110 Of David. A psalm.

The LORD said to my lord,
 "Sit at My right hand
 while I make your enemies your footstool."

2The LORD will stretch forth from Zion your mighty scepter;
 hold sway over your enemies!
3a-Your people come forward willingly on your day of battle.
In majestic holiness, from the womb,
 from the dawn, yours was the dew of youth.-a

4The LORD has sworn and will not relent,
 "You are a priest forever, b-a rightful king by My decree."-b
5The Lord is at your right hand.
He crushes kings in the day of His anger.

6He works judgment upon the nations,
 heaping up bodies,
 crushing heads far and wide.
7He drinks from the stream on his way;
 therefore he holds his head high.

a-a *Meaning of Heb. uncertain.*
b-b *Or "after the manner of Melchizedek."*

111 Hallelujah.

א I praise the LORD with all my heart
ב   in the assembled congregation of the upright.
ג ²The works of the LORD are great,
ד   ᵃ-within reach of all who desire them.-ᵃ
ה ³His deeds are splendid and glorious;
ו   His beneficence is everlasting;
ז   ⁴He has won renown for His wonders.
ח The LORD is gracious and compassionate;
ט   ⁵He gives food to those who fear Him;
י   He is ever mindful of His covenant.
כ ⁶He revealed to His people His powerful works,
ל   in giving them the heritage of nations.
מ ⁷His handiwork is truth and justice;
נ   all His precepts are enduring,
ס   ⁸well-founded for all eternity,
ע   wrought of truth and equity.
פ ⁹He sent redemption to His people;
צ   He ordained His covenant for all time;
ק   His name is holy and awesome.
ר ¹⁰The beginningᵇ of wisdom is the fear of the LORD;
ש   all who practice it gain sound understanding.
ת Praise of Him is everlasting.

112 Hallelujah.

א Happy is the man who fears the LORD,
ב   who is ardently devoted to His commandments.
ג ²His descendants will be mighty in the land,
ד   a blessed generation of upright men.
ה ³Wealth and riches are in his house,
ו   and his beneficence lasts forever.
ז ⁴ᵃ-A light shines-ᵃ for the upright in the darkness;
ח   he is gracious, compassionate, and beneficent.
ט ⁵All goes well with the man who lends generously,
י   who conducts his affairs with equity.
כ ⁶He shall never be shaken;

ᵃ⁻ᵃ *Meaning of Heb. uncertain.*
ᵇ *Or "chief part."*
ᵃ⁻ᵃ *Or "He shines as a light."*

ל	the beneficent man will be remembered forever.
מ	7He is not afraid of evil tidings;
נ	his heart is firm, he trusts in the LORD.
ס	8His heart is resolute, he is unafraid;
ע	in the end he will see the fall of his foes.
פ	9He gives freely to the poor;
צ	his beneficence lasts forever;
ק	his horn is exalted in honor.
ר	10The wicked man shall see it and be vexed;
ש	he shall gnash his teeth; his courage shall fail.
ת	The desire of the wicked shall come to nothing.

113 Hallelujah.

O servants of the LORD, give praise;
  praise the name of the LORD.
2Let the name of the LORD be blessed
  now and forever.
3From east to west
  the name of the LORD is praised.
4The LORD is exalted above all nations;
  His glory is above the heavens.
5Who is like the LORD our God,
  who, enthroned on high,
6sees what is below,
  in heaven and on earth?
7He raises the poor from the dust,
  lifts up the needy from the refuse heap
8to set them with the great,
  with the great men of His people.
9He sets the childless woman among her household
  as a happy mother of children.
  Hallelujah.

114 When Israel went forth from Egypt,
  the house of Jacob from a people of strange speech,
  2Judah became His a-holy one,-a

a-a Or "sanctuary."

Israel, His dominion.
³The sea saw them and fled,
   Jordan ran backward,
   ⁴mountains skipped like rams,
   hills like sheep.
⁵What alarmed you, O sea, that you fled,
   Jordan, that you ran backward,
   ⁶mountains, that you skipped like rams,
   hills, like sheep?
⁷Tremble, O earth, at the presence of the LORD,
   at the presence of the God of Jacob,
   ⁸who turned the rock into a pool of water,
   the flinty rock into a fountain.

115 Not to us, O LORD, not to us
   but to Your name bring glory
   for the sake of Your love and Your faithfulness.
²Let the nations not say,
   "Where, now, is their God?"
   ³when our God is in heaven
   and all that He wills He accomplishes.
⁴ᵃTheir idols are silver and gold,
   the work of men's hands.
⁵They have mouths, but cannot speak,
   eyes, but cannot see;
   ⁶they have ears, but cannot hear,
   noses, but cannot smell;
   ⁷they have hands, but cannot touch,
   feet, but cannot walk;
   they can make no sound in their throats.
⁸Those who fashion them,
   all who trust in them,
   shall become like them.
⁹O Israel, trust in the LORD!
He is their help and shield.
¹⁰O house of Aaron, trust in the LORD!
He is their help and shield.

ᵃ *With vv. 4–11, cf. Ps. 135.15–20.*

¹¹O you who fear the Lord, trust in the Lord!
He is their help and shield.

¹²The Lord is mindful of us.
He will bless us;
    He will bless the house of Israel;
    He will bless the house of Aaron;
    ¹³He will bless those who fear the Lord,
    small and great alike.

¹⁴May the Lord increase your numbers,
    yours and your children's also.
¹⁵May you be blessed by the Lord,
    Maker of heaven and earth.
¹⁶The heavens belong to the Lord,
    but the earth He gave over to man.
¹⁷The dead cannot praise the Lord,
    nor any who go down into silence.
¹⁸But we will bless the Lord
    now and forever.
    Hallelujah.

116

^{a-}I love the Lord
    for He hears^{-a} my voice, my pleas;
    ²for He turns His ear to me
    whenever I call.
³The bonds of death encompassed me;
    the torments of Sheol overtook me.
I came upon trouble and sorrow
    ⁴and I invoked the name of the Lord,
    "O Lord, save my life!"

⁵The Lord is gracious and beneficent;
    our God is compassionate.
⁶The Lord protects the simple;
    I was brought low and He saved me.
⁷Be at rest, once again, O my soul,

---

^{a-a} *Heb. transposed for clarity; others "I would love that the* Lord *hear," etc.*

for the LORD has been good to you.
⁸You^b have delivered me from death,
   my eyes from tears,
   my feet from stumbling.
⁹I shall walk before the LORD
   in the lands of the living.
¹⁰ᶜ-I trust [in the LORD];
   out of great suffering I spoke-ᶜ
   ¹¹and said rashly,
   "All men are false."

¹²How can I repay the LORD
   for all His bounties to me?
¹³I raise the cup of deliverance
   and invoke the name of the LORD.
¹⁴I will pay my vows to the LORD
   in the presence of all His people.
¹⁵The death of His faithful ones
   is grievous in the LORD's sight.

¹⁶O LORD,
   I am Your servant,
   Your servant, the son of Your maidservant;
   You have undone the cords that bound me.
¹⁷I will sacrifice a thank offering to You
   and invoke the name of the LORD.
¹⁸I will pay my vows to the LORD
   in the presence of all His people,
   ¹⁹in the courts of the house of the LORD,
   in the midst of^d Jerusalem.
   Hallelujah.

117

Praise the LORD, all you nations;
   extol Him, all you peoples,
   ²for great is His steadfast love toward us;
   the faithfulness of the LORD endures forever.
   Hallelujah.

ᵇ *I.e., God.*
ᶜ⁻ᶜ *Meaning of Heb. uncertain.*
ᵈ *Others "of you."*

118 Praise the Lord, for He is good,
His steadfast love is eternal.
²Let Israel declare,
"His steadfast love is eternal."
³Let the house of Aaron declare,
"His steadfast love is eternal."
⁴Let those who fear the Lord declare,
"His steadfast love is eternal."

⁵In distress I called on the Lord;
the Lord answered me and brought me relief.
⁶The Lord is on my side,
I have no fear;
what can man do to me?
⁷With the Lord on my side as my helper,
I will see the downfall of my foes.

⁸It is better to take refuge in the Lord
than to trust in mortals;
⁹it is better to take refuge in the Lord
than to trust in the great.

¹⁰All nations have beset me;
by the name of the Lord I will surely a-cut them down.-a
¹¹They beset me, they surround me;
by the name of the Lord I will surely cut them down.
¹²They have beset me like bees;
they shall be extinguished like burning thorns;
by the name of the Lord I will surely cut them down.

¹³Youᵇ pressed me hard,
I nearly fell;
but the Lord helped me.
¹⁴The Lord is my strength and might;ᶜ
He has become my deliverance.
¹⁵The tents of the victoriousᵈ resound with joyous shouts of
deliverance,

---

a-a Meaning of 'amilam in this and the following two verses uncertain.
ᵇ I.e., the enemy.
ᶜ Others "song."
ᵈ Or "righteous."

"The right hand of the LORD is triumphant!
16The right hand of the LORD is exalted!
The right hand of the LORD is triumphant!"

17I shall not die but live
and proclaim the works of the LORD.
18The LORD punished me severely,
but did not hand me over to death.

19Open the gates of victory^e for me
that I may enter them and praise the LORD.
20This is the gateway to the LORD—
the victorious^d shall enter through it.

21I praise You, for You have answered me,
and have become my deliverance.
22The stone that the builders rejected
has become the chief cornerstone.
23This is the LORD's doing;
it is marvelous in our sight.
24This is the day that the LORD has made—
let us exult and rejoice on it.

25O LORD, deliver us!
O LORD, let us prosper!

26May he who enters be blessed in the name of the LORD;
we bless you from the House of the LORD.
27The LORD is God;
He has given us light;
f-bind the festal offering to the horns of the altar with cords.-f
28You are my God and I will praise You;
You are my God and I will extol You.
29Praise the LORD for He is good,
His steadfast love is eternal.

e *Or "righteousness."*
f-f *Meaning of Heb. uncertain.*

119

א Happy are those whose way is blameless,
who follow the teaching of the LORD.
2Happy are those who observe His decrees,
who turn to Him wholeheartedly.
3They have done no wrong,
but have followed His ways.
4You have commanded that Your precepts
be kept diligently.
5Would that my ways were firm
in keeping Your laws;
6then I would not be ashamed
when I regard all Your commandments.
7I will praise You with a sincere heart
as I learn Your just rules.
8I will keep Your laws;
do not utterly forsake me.

ב 9How can a young man keep his way pure?—
by holding to Your word.
10I have turned to You with all my heart;
do not let me stray from Your commandments.
11In my heart I treasure Your promise;
therefore I do not sin against You.
12Blessed are You, O LORD;
train me in Your laws.
13With my lips I rehearse
all the rules You proclaimed.
14I rejoice over the way of Your decrees
as over all riches.
15I study Your precepts;
I regard Your ways;
16I take delight in Your laws;
I will not neglect Your word.

ג 17Deal kindly with Your servant,
that I may live to keep Your word.

¹⁸Open my eyes, that I may perceive
the wonders of Your teaching.
¹⁹I am only a sojourner in the land;
do not hide Your commandments from me.
²⁰My soul is consumed with longing
for Your rules at all times.
²¹You blast the accursed insolent ones
who stray from Your commandments.
²²Take away from me taunt and abuse,
because I observe Your decrees.
²³Though princes meet and speak against me,
Your servant studies Your laws.
²⁴For Your decrees are my delight,
my intimate companions.

ד

²⁵My soul clings to the dust;
revive me in accordance with Your word.
²⁶I have declared my way, and You have answered me;
train me in Your laws.
²⁷Make me understand the way of Your precepts,
that I may study Your wondrous acts.
²⁸I am racked with grief;
sustain me in accordance with Your word.
²⁹Remove all false ways from me;
favor me with Your teaching.
³⁰I have chosen the way of faithfulness;
I have set Your rules before me.
³¹I cling to Your decrees;
O LORD, do not put me to shame.
³²I eagerly pursue Your commandments,
for You broaden my understanding.

ה

³³Teach me, O LORD, the way of Your laws;
I will observe them ^a-to the utmost.^{-a}
³⁴Give me understanding, that I may observe Your teaching
and keep it wholeheartedly.
³⁵Lead me in the path of Your commandments,
for that is my concern.

^{a-a} *Meaning of Heb. uncertain.*

³⁶Turn my heart to Your decrees
   and not to love of gain.
³⁷Avert my eyes from seeing falsehood;
   by Your ways preserve me.
³⁸Fulfill Your promise to Your servant,
   which is for those who worship You.
³⁹Remove the taunt that I dread,
   for Your rules are good.
⁴⁰See, I have longed for Your precepts;
   by Your righteousness preserve me.

ו ⁴¹May Your steadfast love reach me, O LORD,
   Your deliverance, as You have promised.
⁴²I shall have an answer for those who taunt me,
   for I have put my trust in Your word.
⁴³Do not utterly take the truth away from my mouth,
   for I have put my hope in Your rules.
⁴⁴I will always obey Your teaching,
   forever and ever.
⁴⁵I will walk about at ease,
   for I have turned to Your precepts.
⁴⁶I will speak of Your decrees,
   and not be ashamed in the presence of kings.
⁴⁷I will delight in Your commandments,
   which I love.
⁴⁸I reach out for Your commandments, which I love;
   I study Your laws.

ז ⁴⁹Remember Your word to Your servant
   through which You have given me hope.
⁵⁰This is my comfort in my affliction,
   that Your promise has preserved me.
⁵¹Though the arrogant have cruelly mocked me,
   I have not swerved from Your teaching.
⁵²I remember Your rules of old, O LORD,
   and find comfort in them.
⁵³I am seized with rage
   because of the wicked who forsake Your teaching.

⁵⁴Your laws are ^{b-}a source of strength to me^{-b}
  wherever I may dwell.
⁵⁵I remember Your name at night, O LORD,
  and obey Your teaching.
⁵⁶This has been my lot,
  for I have observed Your precepts.

ח   ⁵⁷The LORD is my portion;
  I have resolved to keep Your words.
⁵⁸I have implored You with all my heart;
  have mercy on me, in accordance with Your promise.
⁵⁹I have considered my ways,
  and have turned back to Your decrees.
⁶⁰I have hurried and not delayed
  to keep Your commandments.
⁶¹Though the bonds of the wicked are coiled round me,
  I have not neglected Your teaching.
⁶²I arise at midnight to praise You
  for Your just rules.
⁶³I am a companion to all who fear You,
  to those who keep Your precepts.
⁶⁴Your steadfast love, O LORD, fills the earth;
  teach me Your laws.

ט   ⁶⁵You have treated Your servant well,
  according to Your word, O LORD.
⁶⁶Teach me good sense and knowledge,
  for I have put my trust in Your commandments.
⁶⁷Before I was humbled I went astray,
  but now I keep Your word.
⁶⁸You are good and beneficent;
  teach me Your laws.
⁶⁹Though the arrogant have accused me falsely,
  I observe Your precepts wholeheartedly.
⁷⁰Their minds are thick like fat;
  as for me, Your teaching is my delight.
⁷¹It was good for me that I was humbled,

b-b *Or "songs for me."*

so that I might learn Your laws.
⁷²I prefer the teaching You proclaimed
to thousands of gold and silver pieces.

י ⁷³Your hands made me and fashioned me;
give me understanding that I may learn Your
commandments.
⁷⁴Those who fear You will see me and rejoice,
for I have put my hope in Your word.
⁷⁵I know, O LORD, that Your rulings are just;
rightly have You humbled me.
⁷⁶May Your steadfast love comfort me
in accordance with Your promise to Your servant.
⁷⁷May Your mercy reach me, that I might live,
for Your teaching is my delight.
⁷⁸Let the insolent be dismayed, for they have
wronged me without cause;
I will study Your precepts.
⁷⁹May those who fear You,
those who know Your decrees,
turn again to me.
⁸⁰May I wholeheartedly follow Your laws
so that I do not come to grief.

כ ⁸¹I long for Your deliverance;
I hope for Your word.
⁸²My eyes pine away for Your promise;
I say, "When will You comfort me?"
⁸³Though I have become like a water-skin dried in smoke,
I have not neglected Your laws.
⁸⁴How long has Your servant to live?
when will You bring my persecutors to judgment?
⁸⁵The insolent have dug pits for me,
flouting Your teaching.
⁸⁶All Your commandments are enduring;
I am persecuted without cause; help me!
⁸⁷Though they almost wiped me off the earth,

I did not abandon Your precepts.
88As befits Your steadfast love, preserve me,
so that I may keep the decree You proclaimed.

ל 89The LORD exists forever;
Your word stands firm in heaven.
90Your faithfulness is for all generations;
You have established the earth, and it stands.
91They stand this day to [carry out] Your rulings,
for all are Your servants.
92Were not Your teaching my delight
I would have perished in my affliction.
93I will never neglect Your precepts,
for You have preserved my life through them.
94I am Yours; save me!
For I have turned to Your precepts.
95The wicked hope to destroy me,
but I ponder Your decrees.
96I have seen that all things have their limit,
but Your commandment is broad beyond measure.

מ 97O how I love Your teaching!
It is my study all day long.
98Your commandments make me wiser than my enemies;
they always stand by me.
99I have gained more insight than all my teachers,
for Your decrees are my study.
100I have gained more understanding than my elders,
for I observe Your precepts.
101I have avoided every evil way
so that I may keep Your word.
102I have not departed from Your rules,
for You have instructed me.
103How pleasing is Your word to my palate,
sweeter than honey.
104I ponder Your precepts;
therefore I hate every false way.

נ 105Your word is a lamp to my feet,
a light for my path.
106I have firmly sworn
to keep Your just rules.
107I am very much afflicted;
O LORD, preserve me in accordance with Your word.
108Accept, O LORD, my freewill offerings;
teach me Your rules.
109Though my life is always in danger,
I do not neglect Your teaching.
110Though the wicked have set a trap for me,
I have not strayed from Your precepts.
111Your decrees are my eternal heritage;
they are my heart's delight.
112I am resolved to follow Your laws
a-to the utmost-a forever.

ס 113I hate men of divided heart,
but I love Your teaching.
114You are my protection and my shield;
I hope for Your word.
115Keep away from me, you evildoers,
that I may observe the commandments of my God.
116Support me as You promised, so that I may live;
do not thwart my expectation.
117Sustain me that I may be saved,
and I will always muse upon Your laws.
118You reject all who stray from Your laws,
for they are false and deceitful.
119You do away with the wicked as if they were dross;
rightly do I love Your decrees.
120My flesh creeps from fear of You;
I am in awe of Your rulings.

ע 121I have done what is just and right;
do not abandon me to those who would wrong me.
122Guarantee Your servant's well-being;
do not let the arrogant wrong me.

¹²³My eyes pine away for Your deliverance,
for Your promise of victory.
¹²⁴Deal with Your servant as befits Your steadfast love;
teach me Your laws.
¹²⁵I am Your servant;
give me understanding,
that I might know Your decrees.
¹²⁶It is a time to act for the LORD,
for they have violated Your teaching.
¹²⁷Rightly do I love Your commandments
more than gold, even fine gold.
¹²⁸Truly ^{c-}by all [Your] precepts I walk straight;^{-c}
I hate every false way.

פ ¹²⁹Your decrees are wondrous;
rightly do I observe them.
¹³⁰^{d-}The words You inscribed give^{-d} light,
and grant understanding to the simple.
¹³¹I open my mouth wide, I pant,
longing for Your commandments.
¹³²Turn to me and be gracious to me,
as is Your rule with those who love Your name.
¹³³Make my feet firm through Your promise;
do not let iniquity dominate me.
¹³⁴Redeem me from being wronged by man,
that I may keep Your precepts.
¹³⁵Show favor to Your servant,
and teach me Your laws.
¹³⁶My eyes shed streams of water
because men do not obey Your teaching.

צ ¹³⁷You are righteous, O LORD;
Your rulings are just.
¹³⁸You have ordained righteous decrees;
they are firmly enduring.
¹³⁹I am consumed with rage
over my foes' neglect of Your words.
¹⁴⁰Your word is exceedingly pure,

c-c *Or "I declare all [Your] precepts to be just."*
d-d *With Targum; or "The exposition of Your words gives"; meaning of Heb. uncertain.*

and Your servant loves it.

¹⁴¹Though I am belittled and despised,
    I have not neglected Your precepts.
¹⁴²Your righteousness is eternal;
    Your teaching is true.
¹⁴³Though anguish and distress come upon me,
    Your commandments are my delight.
¹⁴⁴Your righteous decrees are eternal;
    give me understanding, that I might live.

ק

¹⁴⁵I call with all my heart;
    answer me, O LORD,
    that I may observe Your laws.
¹⁴⁶I call upon You; save me,
    that I may keep Your decrees.
¹⁴⁷I rise before dawn and cry for help;
    I hope for Your word.
¹⁴⁸My eyes greet each watch of the night,
    as I meditate on Your promise.
¹⁴⁹Hear my voice as befits Your steadfast love;
    O LORD, preserve me, as is Your rule.
¹⁵⁰Those who pursue intrigue draw near;
    they are far from Your teaching.
¹⁵¹You, O LORD, are near,
    and all Your commandments are true.
¹⁵²I know from Your decrees of old
    that You have established them forever.

ר

¹⁵³See my affliction and rescue me,
    for I have not neglected Your teaching.
¹⁵⁴Champion my cause and redeem me;
    preserve me according to Your promise.
¹⁵⁵Deliverance is far from the wicked,
    for they have not turned to Your laws.
¹⁵⁶Your mercies are great, O LORD;
    as is Your rule, preserve me.
¹⁵⁷Many are my persecutors and foes;
    I have not swerved from Your decrees.

¹⁵⁸I have seen traitors and loathed^c them,
    because they did not keep Your word in mind.
¹⁵⁹See that I have loved Your precepts;
    O LORD, preserve me, as befits Your steadfast love.
¹⁶⁰Truth is the essence of Your word;
    Your just rules are eternal.

ש ¹⁶¹Princes have persecuted me without reason;
    my heart thrills at Your word.
¹⁶²I rejoice over Your promise
    as one who obtains great spoil.
¹⁶³I hate and abhor falsehood;
    I love Your teaching.
¹⁶⁴I praise You seven times each day
    for Your just rules.
¹⁶⁵Those who love Your teaching enjoy well-being;
    they encounter no adversity.
¹⁶⁶I hope for Your deliverance, O LORD;
    I observe Your commandments.
¹⁶⁷I obey Your decrees
    and love them greatly.
¹⁶⁸I obey Your precepts and decrees;
    all my ways are before You.

ת ¹⁶⁹May my plea reach You, O LORD;
    grant me understanding according to Your word.
¹⁷⁰May my petition come before You;
    save me in accordance with Your promise.
¹⁷¹My lips shall pour forth praise,
    for You teach me Your laws.
¹⁷²My tongue shall declare Your promise,
    for all Your commandments are just.
¹⁷³Lend Your hand to help me,
    for I have chosen Your precepts.
¹⁷⁴I have longed for Your deliverance, O LORD;
    Your teaching is my delight.
¹⁷⁵Let me live, that I may praise You;
    may Your rules be my help;

---

c *Or "have contended with."*

176I have strayed like a lost sheep;
　　search for Your servant,
　　for I have not neglected Your commandments.

120 A song of ascents.ᵃ

In my distress I called to the LORD
　　and He answered me.
2O LORD, save me from treacherous lips,
　　from a deceitful tongue!
3What can you profit,
　　what can you gain,
　　O deceitful tongue?
4A warrior's sharp arrows,
　　with hot coals of broom-wood.

5Woe is me, that I live with Meshech,
　　that I dwell among the clans of Kedar.
6Too long have I dwelt with those who hate peace.
7I am all peace;
　　but when I speak,
　　they are for war.

121 A song for ascents.

I turn my eyes to the mountains;
　　from where will my help come?
2My help comes from the LORD,
　　maker of heaven and earth.
3He will not let your foot give way;
　　your guardian will not slumber;
4See, the guardian of Israel
　　neither slumbers nor sleeps!
5The LORD is your guardian,
　　the LORD is your protection
　　at your right hand.

ᵃ *A term of uncertain meaning.*

⁶By day the sun will not strike you,
  nor the moon by night.
⁷The LORD will guard you from all harm;
  He will guard your life.
⁸The LORD will guard your going and coming
  now and forever.

122 A song of ascents. Of David.

I rejoiced when they said to me,
  "We are going to the House of the LORD."
²Our feet stood inside your gates, O Jerusalem,
  ³Jerusalem built up, a city knit together,
  ⁴to which tribes would make pilgrimage,
  the tribes of the LORD,
  —as was enjoined upon Israel—
  to praise the name of the LORD.
⁵There the thrones of judgment stood,
  thrones of the house of David.
⁶Pray for the well-being of Jerusalem;
  "May those who love you be at peace.
⁷May there be well-being within your ramparts,
  peace in your citadels."
⁸For the sake of my kin and friends,
  I pray for your well-being;
  ⁹for the sake of the house of the LORD our God,
  I seek your good.

123 A song of ascents.

To You, enthroned in heaven,
  I turn my eyes.
²As the eyes of slaves follow their master's hand,
  as the eyes of a slave-girl follow the hand of her mistress,
  so our eyes are toward the LORD our God,
  awaiting His favor.

³Show us favor, O LORD,
    show us favor!
We have had more than enough of contempt.
⁴Long enough have we endured
    the scorn of the complacent,
    the contempt of the haughty.

124 A song of ascents. Of David.

Were it not for the LORD, who was on our side,
    let Israel now declare,
    ²were it not for the LORD, who was on our side
    when men assailed us,
    ³they would have swallowed us alive
    in their burning rage against us;
    ⁴the waters would have carried us off,
    the torrent would have swept over us;
    ⁵over us would have swept
    the seething waters.
⁶Blessed is the LORD, who did not let us
    be ripped apart by their teeth.
⁷We are like a bird escaped from the fowler's trap;
    the trap broke and we escaped.
⁸Our help is the name of the LORD,
    maker of heaven and earth.

125 A song of ascents.

Those who trust in the LORD
    are like Mount Zion
    that cannot be moved,
    enduring forever.
²Jerusalem, hills enfold it,
    and the LORD enfolds His people
    now and forever.
    ³ᵃ⁻The scepter of the wicked shall never rest

ᵃ⁻ᵃ *Meaning of Heb. uncertain.*

upon the land allotted to the righteous,
   that the righteous not set their hand to wrongdoing.-a
4Do good, O LORD, to the good,
   to the upright in heart.
5a-But those who in their crookedness act corruptly,-a
   let the LORD make them go the way of evildoers.
May it be well with Israel!

126 A song of ascents.

When the LORD restores the fortunes of Zion
   —a-we see it as in a dream-a—
   2our mouths shall be filled with laughter,
   our tongues, with songs of joy.
Then shall they say among the nations,
   "The LORD has done great things for them!"
3The LORD will do great things for us
   and we shall rejoice.

4Restore our fortunes, O LORD,
   like watercourses in the Negeb.
5They who sow in tears
   shall reap with songs of joy.
6Though he goes along weeping,
   carrying the seed-bag,
   he shall come back with songs of joy,
   carrying his sheaves.

127 A song of ascents. Of Solomon.

Unless the LORD builds the house,
   its builders labor in vain on it;
   unless the LORD watches over the city,
   the watchman keeps vigil in vain.
2In vain do you rise early

---

a-a Lit. "we are veritable dreamers."

and stay up late,
   you who toil for the bread you eat;
   a-He provides as much for His loved ones while they sleep.-a

3Sons are the provisionb of the LORD;
   the fruit of the womb, His reward.
4Like arrows in the hand of a warrior
   are sons born to a man in his youth.
5Happy is the man who fills his quiver with them;
   they shall not be put to shame
   when they contend with the enemy in the gate.

128 A song of ascents.

Happy are all who fear the LORD,
   who follow His ways.
2You shall enjoy the fruit of your labors;
   you shall be happy and you shall prosper.
3Your wife shall be like a fruitful vine within your house;
   your sons, like olive saplings around your table.
4So shall the man who fears the LORD be blessed.

5May the LORD bless you from Zion;
   may you share the prosperity of Jerusalem
   all the days of your life,
      6and live to see your children's children.
May all be well with Israel!

129 A song of ascents.

Since my youth they have often assailed me,
   let Israel now declare,
      2since my youth they have often assailed me,
   but they have never overcome me.
3Plowmen plowed across my back;

a-a *Meaning of Heb. uncertain.*
b *Lit. "heritage."*

they made long furrows.
⁴The LORD, the righteous one,
    has snapped the cords of the wicked.

⁵Let all who hate Zion
    fall back in disgrace.
⁶Let them be like grass on roofs
    that fades before it can be pulled up,
    ⁷that affords no handful for the reaper,
    no armful for the gatherer of sheaves,
    ⁸no exchange with passersby:
    "The blessing of the LORD be upon you."
"We bless you by the name of the LORD."

130 A song of ascents.

Out of the depths I call You, O LORD.
²O Lord, listen to my cry;
    let Your ears be attentive
    to my plea for mercy.
³If You keep account of sins, O LORD,
    Lord, who will survive?
⁴Yours is the power to forgive
    so that You may be held in awe.

⁵I look to the LORD;
    I look to Him;
    I await His word.
⁶I am more eager for the Lord
    than watchmen for the morning,
    watchmen for the morning.

⁷O Israel, wait for the LORD;
    for with the LORD is steadfast love
    and great power to redeem.
⁸It is He who will redeem Israel from all their iniquities.

131 A song of ascents. Of David.

O LORD, my heart is not proud
    nor my look haughty;
    I do not aspire to great things
    or to what is beyond me;
    2a-but I have taught myself to be contented
    like a weaned child with its mother;
    like a weaned child am I in my mind.-a
3O Israel, wait for the LORD
    now and forever.

132 A song of ascents.

O LORD, remember in David's favor
    his extreme self-denial,
    2how he swore to the LORD,
    vowed to the Mighty One of Jacob,
    3"I will not enter my house,
    nor will I mount my bed,
    4I will not give sleep to my eyes,
    or slumber to my eyelidsa
    5until I find a place for the LORD,
    an abode for the Mighty One of Jacob."

6We heard it was in Ephrath;
    we came upon it in the region of Jaar.b
7Let us enter His abode,
    bow at His footstool.
8Advance, O LORD, to Your resting-place,
    You and Your mighty Ark!
9Your priests are clothed in triumph;
    Your loyal ones sing for joy.
10For the sake of Your servant David
    do not reject Your anointed one.

a-a *Meaning of Heb. uncertain.*

a *Lit. "eyes."*
b *Cf. 1 Sam. 7.1–2; 1 Chron. 13.5–6.*

11The LORD swore to David
a firm oath that He will not renounce,
"One of your own issue I will set upon your throne.
12If your sons keep My covenant
and My decrees that I teach them,
then their sons also,
to the end of time,
shall sit upon your throne."
13For the LORD has chosen Zion;
He has desired it for His seat.
14"This is my resting-place for all time;
here I will dwell, for I desire it.
15I will amply bless its store of food,
give its needy their fill of bread.
16I will clothe its priests in victory,
its loyal ones shall sing for joy.
17There I will make a horn sprout for David;
I have prepared a lamp for My anointed one.
18I will clothe his enemies in disgrace,
while on him his crown shall sparkle."

133 A song of ascents. Of David.

How good and how pleasant it is
that brothers dwell together.
2It is like fine oil on the head
running down onto the beard,
the beard of Aaron,
that comes down over the collar of his robe;
3like the dew of Hermon
that falls upon the mountains of Zion.
There the LORD ordained blessing,
everlasting life.

134 A song of ascents.

Now bless the LORD,
　　all you servants of the LORD
　　who stand nightly
　　in the house of the LORD.
2Lift your hands toward the sanctuary
　　and bless the LORD.
3May the LORD,
　　maker of heaven and earth,
　　bless you from Zion.

135 Hallelujah.

Praise the name of the LORD;
　　give praise, you servants of the LORD
　2who stand in the house of the LORD,
　　in the courts of the house of our God.
3Praise the LORD, for the LORD is good;
　　sing hymns to His name, for it is pleasant.
4For the LORD has chosen Jacob for Himself,
　　Israel, as His treasured possession.

5For I know that the LORD is great,
　　that our LORD is greater than all gods.
6Whatever the LORD desires He does
　　in heaven and earth,
　　in the seas and all the depths.
7He makes clouds rise from the end of the earth;
　　He makes lightning for the rain;
　　He releases the wind from His vaults.
8He struck down the first-born of Egypt,
　　man and beast alike;
　9He sent signs and portents against^a Egypt,
　　against Pharaoh and all his servants;
　10He struck down many nations
　　and slew numerous kings—

ᵃ Others "against you."

¹¹Sihon, king of the Amorites,
Og, king of Bashan,
and all the royalty of Canaan—
¹²and gave their lands as a heritage,
as a heritage to His people Israel.

¹³O LORD, Your name endures forever,
Your fame, O LORD, through all generations;
¹⁴for the LORD will champion His people,
and obtain satisfaction for His servants.

^{15b}The idols of the nations are silver and gold,
the work of men's hands.
¹⁶They have mouths, but cannot speak;
they have eyes, but cannot see;
¹⁷they have ears, but cannot hear,
nor is there breath in their mouths.
¹⁸Those who fashion them,
all who trust in them,
shall become like them.

¹⁹O house of Israel, bless the LORD;
O house of Aaron, bless the LORD;
²⁰O house of Levi, bless the LORD;
you who fear the LORD, bless the LORD.
²¹Blessed is the LORD from Zion,
He who dwells in Jerusalem.
Hallelujah.

136

Praise the LORD; for He is good,
His steadfast love is eternal.
²Praise the God of gods,
His steadfast love is eternal.
³Praise the Lord of lords,
His steadfast love is eternal;
⁴Who alone works great marvels,
His steadfast love is eternal;

---

b *With vv. 15–20, cf. Ps. 115.4–11.*

5Who made the heavens with wisdom,
His steadfast love is eternal;
6Who spread the earth over the water,
His steadfast love is eternal;
7Who made the great lights,
His steadfast love is eternal;
8the sun to dominate the day,
His steadfast love is eternal;
9the moon and the stars to dominate the night,
His steadfast love is eternal;
10Who struck Egypt through their first-born,
His steadfast love is eternal;
11and brought Israel out of their midst,
His steadfast love is eternal;
12with a strong hand and outstretched arm,
His steadfast love is eternal;
13Who split apart the Sea of Reeds,
His steadfast love is eternal;
14and made Israel pass through it,
His steadfast love is eternal;
15Who hurled Pharaoh and his army into the Sea of Reeds,
His steadfast love is eternal;
16Who led His people through the wilderness,
His steadfast love is eternal;
17Who struck down great kings,
His steadfast love is eternal;
18and slew mighty kings—
His steadfast love is eternal;
19Sihon, king of the Amorites,
His steadfast love is eternal;
20Og, king of Bashan—
His steadfast love is eternal;
21and gave their land as a heritage,
His steadfast love is eternal;
22a heritage to His servant Israel,
His steadfast love is eternal;
23Who took note of us in our degradation,
His steadfast love is eternal;

24and rescued us from our enemies,
   His steadfast love is eternal;
25Who gives food to all flesh,
   His steadfast love is eternal.
26Praise the God of heaven,
   His steadfast love is eternal.

137

By the rivers of Babylon,
   there we sat,
   sat and wept,
   as we thought of Zion.
2There on the poplars
   we hung up our lyres,
   3for our captors asked us there for songs,
   our tormentors,a for amusement,
   "Sing us one of the songs of Zion."
4How can we sing a song of the LORD
   on alien soil?
5If I forget you, O Jerusalem,
   let my right hand wither;b
   6let my tongue stick to my palate
   if I cease to think of you,
   if I do not keep Jerusalem in memory
   even at my happiest hour.

7Remember, O LORD, against the Edomites
   the day of Jerusalem's fall;
   how they cried, "Strip her, strip her
   to her very foundations!"
8Fair Babylon, you predator,c
   a blessing on him who repays you in kind
   what you have inflicted on us;
   9a blessing on him who seizes your babies
   and dashes them against the rocks!

---

a Meaning of Heb. uncertain.
b Others "forget its cunning."
c With Targum; others "who are to be destroyed."

138 Of David.

I praise You with all my heart,
    sing a hymn to You before the divine beings;
²I bow toward Your holy temple
    and praise Your name for Your steadfast love and
        faithfulness,
    because You have exalted ᵃ⁻Your name, Your word,
        above all.⁻ᵃ
³When I called, You answered me,
    ᵃ⁻You inspired me with courage.⁻ᵃ
⁴All the kings of the earth shall praise You, O LORD,
    for they have heard the words You spoke.
⁵They shall sing of the ways of the LORD,
    "Great is the majesty of the LORD!"
⁶High though the LORD is, He sees the lowly;
    lofty, He perceives from afar.
⁷Though I walk among enemies,
    You preserve me in the face of my foes;
    You extend Your hand;
    with Your right hand You deliver me.
⁸The LORD will settle accounts for me.
O LORD, Your steadfast love is eternal;
    do not forsake the work of Your hands.

139 For the leader. Of David. A psalm.

O LORD, You have examined me and know me.
²When I sit down or stand up You know it;
    You discern my thoughts from afar.
³ᵃ⁻You observe⁻ᵃ my walking and reclining,
    and are familiar with all my ways.
⁴There is not a word on my tongue
    but that You, O LORD, know it well.
⁵You hedge me before and behind;
    You lay Your hand upon me.

ᵃ⁻ᵃ *Meaning of Heb. uncertain.*

ᵃ⁻ᵃ *Meaning of Heb. uncertain.*

⁶It is beyond my knowledge;
   it is a mystery; I cannot fathom it.
⁷Where can I escape from Your spirit?
Where can I flee from Your presence?
⁸If I ascend to heaven, You are there;
   if I descend to Sheol, You are there too.
⁹If I take wing with the dawn
   to come to rest on the western horizon,
   ¹⁰even there Your hand will be guiding me,
   Your right hand will be holding me fast.
¹¹If I say, "Surely darkness ᵇ⁻will conceal me,
   night will provide me with cover,"⁻ᵇ
   ¹²darkness is not dark for You;
   night is as light as day;
   darkness and light are the same.
¹³It was You who created my conscience;ᶜ
   You fashioned me in my mother's womb.
¹⁴I praise You,
   for I am awesomely, wondrously made;
   Your work is wonderful;
   I know it very well.
¹⁵My frame was not concealed from You
   when I was shaped in a hidden place,
   knit together in the recesses of the earth.
¹⁶Your eyes saw my unformed limbs;
   they were all recorded in Your book;
   in due time they were formed,
   ᵃ⁻to the very last one of them.⁻ᵃ
¹⁷How weighty Your thoughts seem to me, O God,
   how great their number!
¹⁸I count them—they exceed the grains of sand;
   I end—but am still with You.

¹⁹O God, if You would only slay the wicked—
   you murderers, away from me!—
   ²⁰ᵃ⁻who invoke You for intrigue,
   Your enemies who swear by You falsely.⁻ᵃ
²¹O LORD, You know I hate those who hate You,

ᵇ⁻ᵇ *Cf. Rashi, Ibn Ezra; meaning of Heb. uncertain.*
ᶜ *Lit. "kidneys."*

and loathe Your adversaries.
²²I feel a perfect hatred toward them;
    I count them my enemies.

²³Examine me, O God, and know my mind;
    probe me and know my thoughts.
²⁴See if I have vexatious ways,
    and guide me in ways everlasting.

140 For the leader. A psalm of David.

²Rescue me, O LORD, from evil men;
    save me from the lawless,
    ³whose minds are full of evil schemes,
    who plot war every day.
⁴They sharpen their tongues like serpents;
    spiders' poison is on their lips.   *Selah.*

⁵O LORD, keep me out of the clutches of the wicked;
    save me from lawless men
    who scheme to ᵃ⁻make me fall.⁻ᵃ
⁶Arrogant men laid traps with ropes for me;
    they spread out a net along the way;
    they set snares for me.   *Selah.*

⁷I said to the LORD: You are my God;
    give ear, O LORD, to my pleas for mercy.
⁸O GOD, my Lord, the strength of my deliverance,
    You protected my head on the day of battle.ᵇ
⁹O LORD, do not grant the desires of the wicked;
    do not let their plan succeed,
    ᶜ⁻else they be exalted.   *Selah.*

¹⁰May the heads of those who beset me
    be covered with the mischief of their lips.⁻ᶜ
¹¹may coals of fire drop down upon them,
    and they be cast into pits, never to rise again.

ᵃ⁻ᵃ *Lit. "push my feet."*
ᵇ *Lit. "arms."*
ᶜ⁻ᶜ *Meaning of Heb. uncertain.*

¹²Let slanderers have no place in the land;
  let the evil of the lawless man drive him into corrals.
¹³I know that the LORD will champion
  the cause of the poor, the right of the needy.
¹⁴Righteous men shall surely praise Your name;
  the upright shall dwell in Your presence.

141 A psalm of David.

I call You, O LORD, hasten to me;
  give ear to my cry when I call You.
²Take my prayer as an offering of incense,
  my upraised hands as an evening sacrifice.
³O LORD, set a guard over my mouth,
  a watch at the door of my lips;
  ⁴let my mind not turn to an evil thing,
  to practice deeds of wickedness
  with men who are evildoers;
  let me not feast on their dainties.
^{5a}Let the righteous man strike me in loyalty,
  let him reprove me;
  let my head not refuse such choice oil.
My prayers are still against their^b evil deeds.
⁶May their judges slip on the rock,
  but let my words be heard, for they are sweet.
⁷As when the earth is cleft and broken up
  our bones are scattered at the mouth of Sheol.
⁸My eyes are fixed upon You, O GOD my Lord;
  I seek refuge in You, do not put me in jeopardy.
⁹Keep me from the trap laid for me,
  and from the snares of evildoers.
¹⁰Let the wicked fall into their nets
  while I alone come through.

---

^a *Meaning of vv. 5–7 uncertain.*
^b *I.e., the evildoers of v. 4.*

142 A *maskil* of David, while he was in the cave.[a] A prayer.

2I cry aloud to the LORD;
  I appeal to the LORD loudly for mercy.
3I pour out my complaint before Him;
  I lay my trouble before Him
    4when my spirit fails within me.
You know my course;
  they have laid a trap in the path I walk.
5Look at my right and see—
  I have no friend;
    there is nowhere I can flee,
    no one cares about me.
6So I cry to You, O LORD;
  I say, "You are my refuge,
    all I have in the land of the living."
7Listen to my cry, for I have been brought very low;
  save me from my pursuers,
  for they are too strong for me.
8Free me from prison,
  that I may praise Your name.
The righteous [b-shall glory in me-b]
  for Your gracious dealings with me.

143 A psalm of David.

O LORD, hear my prayer;
  give ear to my plea, as You are faithful;
  answer me, as You are beneficent.
2Do not enter into judgment with Your servant,
  for before You no creature is in the right.

3My foe hounded me;
  he crushed me to the ground;
  he made me dwell in darkness
  like those long dead.

a Cf. 1 Sam. 24.3–4.
b-b *Meaning of Heb. uncertain.*

⁴My spirit failed within me;
    my mind was numbed with horror.
⁵Then I thought of the days of old;
    I rehearsed all Your deeds,
    recounted the work of Your hands.
⁶I stretched out my hands to You,
    longing for You like thirsty earth.   *Selah.*

⁷Answer me quickly, O LORD;
    my spirit can endure no more.
Do not hide Your face from me,
    or I shall become like those who descend into the Pit.
⁸Let me learn of Your faithfulness by daybreak,
    for in You I trust;
    let me know the road I must take,
    for on You I have set my hope.
⁹Save me from my foes, O LORD;
    ᵃ⁻to You I look for cover.⁻ᵃ
¹⁰Teach me to do Your will,
    for You are my God.
Let Your gracious spirit lead me
    on level ground.
¹¹For the sake of Your name, O LORD, preserve me;
    as You are beneficent, free me from distress.
¹²As You are faithful, put an end to my foes;
    destroy all my mortal enemies,
    for I am Your servant.

144 Of David.

Blessed is the LORD, my rock,
    who trains my hands for battle,
    my fingers for warfare;
    ²my faithful one, my fortress,
    my haven and my deliverer,
    my shield, in whom I take shelter,

ᵃ⁻ᵃ *Meaning of Heb. uncertain.*

who makes peoples[a] subject to me.

3O LORD, what is man that You should care about him,
    mortal man, that You should think of him?
4Man is like a breath;
    his days are like a passing shadow.
5O LORD, bend Your sky and come down;
    touch the mountains and they will smoke.
6Make lightning flash and scatter them;
    shoot Your arrows and rout them.
7Reach Your hand down from on high;
    rescue me, save me from the mighty waters,
    from the hands of foreigners,
8whose mouths speak lies,
    and whose oaths[b] are false.

9O God, I will sing You a new song,
    sing a hymn to You with a ten-stringed harp,
10to You who give victory to kings,
    who rescue His servant David from the deadly sword.
11Rescue me, save me from the hands of foreigners,
    whose mouths speak lies,
    and whose oaths[b] are false.

12cFor our sons are like saplings,
    well-tended in their youth;
    our daughters are like cornerstones
    trimmed to give shape to a palace.
13Our storehouses are full,
    supplying produce of all kinds;
    our flocks number thousands,
    even myriads, in our fields;
    14our cattle are well cared for.
There is no breaching and no sortie,
    and no wailing in our streets.

15Happy the people who have it so;
    happy the people whose God is the LORD.

a *So Targum, Saadia; others "my people."*
b *With Rashi; lit. "right hand."*
c *The meaning of several phrases in vv. 12–14 is uncertain.*

145 A song of praise. Of David.

א   I will extol You, my God and king,
     and bless Your name forever and ever.

ב   2Every day will I bless You
     and praise Your name forever and ever.

ג   3Great is the LORD and much acclaimed;
     His greatness cannot be fathomed.

ד   4One generation shall laud Your works to another
     and declare Your mighty acts.

ה   5The glorious majesty of Your splendor
     a-and Your wondrous acts-a will I recite.

ו   6Men shall talk of the might of Your awesome deeds,
     and I will recount Your greatness.

ז   7They shall celebrate Your abundant goodness,
     and sing joyously of Your beneficence.

ח   8The LORD is gracious and compassionate,
     slow to anger and abounding in kindness.

ט   9The LORD is good to all,
     and His mercy is upon all His works.

י   10All Your works shall praise You, O LORD,
     and Your faithful ones shall bless You.

כ   11They shall talk of the majesty of Your kingship,
     and speak of Your might,

ל   12to make His mighty acts known among men
     and the majestic glory of His kingship.

מ   13Your kingship is an eternal kingship;
     Your dominion is for all generations.

ס   14The LORD supports all who stumble,
     and makes all who are bent stand straight.

ע   15The eyes of all look to You expectantly,
     and You give them their food when it is due.

פ   16You give it openhandedly,
     feeding every creature to its heart's content.

צ   17The LORD is beneficent in all His ways
     and faithful in all His works.

ק   18The LORD is near to all who call Him,

---

a-a *A Qumran Pss. scroll reads: "they will speak of, and Your wonders."*

to all who call Him with sincerity.

ר ¹⁹He fulfills the wishes of those who fear Him;
    He hears their cry and delivers them.

ש ²⁰The LORD watches over all who love Him,
    but all the wicked He will destroy.

ת ²¹My mouth shall utter the praise of the LORD,
    and all creaturesᵇ shall bless His holy name forever and ever.

146 Hallelujah.

Praise the LORD, O my soul!
²I will praise the LORD all my life,
    sing hymns to my God while I exist.

³Put not your trust in the great,
    in mortal man who cannot save.
⁴His breath departs;
    he returns to the dust;
    on that day his plans come to nothing.

⁵Happy is he who has the God of Jacob for his help,
    whose hope is in the LORD his God,
    ⁶maker of heaven and earth,
    the sea and all that is in them;
    who keeps faith forever;
    ⁷who secures justice for those who are wronged,
    gives food to the hungry.
The LORD sets prisoners free;
    ⁸The LORD restores sight to the blind;
    the LORD makes those who are bent stand straight;
    the LORD loves the righteous;
    ⁹The LORD watches over the stranger;
    He gives courage to the orphan and widow,
    but makes the path of the wicked tortuous.

¹⁰The LORD shall reign forever,
    your God, O Zion, for all generations.
    Hallelujah.

ᵇ Lit. "flesh."

147 Hallelujah.

It is good to chant hymns to our God;
    it is pleasant to sing glorious praise.

²The LORD rebuilds Jerusalem;
    He gathers in the exiles of Israel.
³He heals their broken hearts,
    and binds up their wounds.
⁴He reckoned the number of the stars;
    to each He gave its name.
⁵Great is our LORD and full of power;
    His wisdom is beyond reckoning.
⁶The LORD gives courage to the lowly,
    and brings the wicked down to the dust.

⁷Sing to the LORD a song of praise,
    chant a hymn with a lyre to our God,
⁸who covers the heavens with clouds,
    provides rain for the earth,
    makes mountains put forth grass;
⁹who gives the beasts their food,
    to the raven's brood what they cry for.
¹⁰He does not prize the strength of horses,
    nor value the fleetness[a] of men;
¹¹but the LORD values those who fear Him,
    those who depend on His faithful care.

¹²O Jerusalem, glorify the LORD;
    praise your God, O Zion!
¹³For He made the bars of your gates strong,
    and blessed your children within you.
¹⁴He endows your realm with well-being,
    and satisfies you with choice wheat.

¹⁵He sends forth His word to the earth;
    His command runs swiftly.
¹⁶He lays down snow like fleece,
    scatters frost like ashes.
¹⁷He tosses down hail like crumbs—

---

a Lit. "thighs."

who can endure His icy cold?
¹⁸He issues a command—it melts them;
    He breathes—the waters flow.
¹⁹He issued His commands to Jacob,
    His statutes and rules to Israel.
²⁰He did not do so for any other nation;
    of such rules they know nothing.
    Hallelujah.

148 Hallelujah.

Praise the LORD from the heavens;
    praise Him on high.
²Praise Him, all His angels,
    praise Him, all His hosts.
³Praise Him, sun and moon,
    praise Him, all bright stars.
⁴Praise Him, highest heavens,
    and you waters that are above the heavens.
⁵Let them praise the name of the LORD,
    for it was He who commanded that they be created.
⁶He made them endure forever,
    establishing an order that shall never change.
⁷Praise the LORD, O you who are on earth,
    all sea monsters and ocean depths,
    ⁸fire and hail, snow and smoke,
    storm wind that executes His command,
    ⁹all mountains and hills,
    all fruit trees and cedars,
    ¹⁰all wild and tamed beasts,
    creeping things and winged birds,
    ¹¹all kings and peoples of the earth,
    all princes of the earth and its judges,
    ¹²youths and maidens alike,
    old and young together.
¹³Let them praise the name of the LORD,
    for His name, His alone, is sublime;
    His splendor covers heaven and earth.
¹⁴He has exalted the horn of His people
    for the glory of all His faithful ones,

Israel, the people close to Him.
Hallelujah.

149 Hallelujah.
Sing to the LORD a new song,
His praises in the congregation of the faithful.
²Let Israel rejoice in its maker;
let the children of Zion exult in their king.
³Let them praise His name in dance;
with timbrel and lyre let them chant His praises.
⁴For the LORD delights in His people;
He adorns the lowly with victory.
⁵Let the faithful exult in glory;
let them shout for joy upon their couches,
⁶with paeans to God in their throats
and two-edged swords in their hands,
⁷to impose retribution upon the nations,
punishment upon the peoples,
⁸binding their kings with shackles,
their nobles with chains of iron,
⁹executing the doom decreed against them.
This is the glory of all His faithful.
Hallelujah.

150 Hallelujah.
Praise God in His sanctuary;
praise Him in the sky, His stronghold.
²Praise Him for His mighty acts;
praise Him for[a] His exceeding greatness.
³Praise Him with blasts of the horn;
praise Him with harp and lyre.
⁴Praise Him with timbrel and dance;
praise Him with lute and pipe.
⁵Praise Him with resounding cymbals;
praise Him with loud-clashing cymbals.
⁶Let all that breathes praise the LORD.
Hallelujah.

---

a *Or "as befits."*

PROVERBS

1 The proverbs of Solomon son of David, king of Israel:

²For learning wisdom and discipline;
For understanding words of discernment;
³For acquiring the discipline for success,
Righteousness, justice, and equity;
⁴For endowing the simple with shrewdness,
The young with knowledge and foresight.
⁵—The wise man, hearing them, will gain more wisdom;
The discerning man will learn to be adroit;
⁶For understanding proverb and epigram,
The words of the wise and their riddles.

⁷The fear of the LORD is the beginning[a] of knowledge;
Fools despise wisdom and discipline.

⁸My son, heed the discipline of your father,
And do not forsake the instruction of your mother;
⁹For they are a graceful wreath upon your head,
A necklace about your throat.

¹⁰My son, if sinners entice you, do not yield;
¹¹If they say, "Come with us,
Let us set an ambush to shed blood,
Let us lie in wait for the innocent
(Without cause!)
¹²Like Sheol, let us swallow them alive;
Whole, like those who go down into the Pit.
¹³We shall obtain every precious treasure;

a Or "best part."

We shall fill our homes with loot.
¹⁴Throw in your lot with us;
We shall all have a common purse."
¹⁵My son, do not set out with them;
Keep your feet from their path.
¹⁶For their feet run to evil;
They hurry to shed blood.
¹⁷In the eyes of every winged creature
The outspread net means nothing.
¹⁸But they lie in ambush for their own blood;
They lie in wait for their own lives.
¹⁹Such is the fate of all who pursue unjust gain;
It takes the life of its possessor.

²⁰Wisdomᵇ cries aloud in the streets,
Raises her voice in the squares.
²¹At the head of the busy streets she calls;
At the entrance of the gates, in the city, she speaks out:
²²"How long will you simple ones love simplicity,
You scoffers be eager to scoff,
You dullards hate knowledge?
²³You are indifferent to my rebuke;
I will now speak my mind to you,
And let you know my thoughts.
²⁴Since you refused me when I called,
And paid no heed when I extended my hand,
²⁵You spurned all my advice,
And would not hear my rebuke,
²⁶I will laugh at your calamity,
And mock when terror comes upon you,
²⁷When terror comes like a disaster,
And calamity arrives like a whirlwind,
When trouble and distress come upon you.
²⁸Then they shall call me but I will not answer;
They shall seek me but not find me.
²⁹Because they hated knowledge,
And did not choose fear of the LORD;
³⁰They refused my advice,

ᵇ *In Proverbs, wisdom is personified as a woman.*

And disdained all my rebukes,
31They shall eat the fruit of their ways,
And have their fill of their own counsels.
32The tranquillity of the simple will kill them,
And the complacency of dullards will destroy them.
33But he who listens to me will dwell in safety,
Untroubled by the terror of misfortune."

2 My son, if you accept my words
And treasure up my commandments;
2If you make your ear attentive to wisdom
And your mind open to discernment;
3If you call to understanding
And cry aloud to discernment,
4If you seek it as you do silver
And search for it as for treasures,
5Then you will understand the fear of the LORD
And attain knowledge of God.
6For the LORD grants wisdom;
Knowledge and discernment are by His decree.
7He reserves ability for the upright
And is a shield for those who live blamelessly,
8Guarding the paths of justice,
Protecting the way of those loyal to Him.
9You will then understand what is right, just,
And equitable—every good course.
10For wisdom will enter your mind
And knowledge will delight you.
11Foresight will protect you,
And discernment will guard you.
12It will save you from the way of evil men,
From men who speak duplicity,
13Who leave the paths of rectitude
To follow the ways of darkness,
14Who rejoice in doing evil
And exult in the duplicity of evil men,
15Men whose paths are crooked

And who are devious in their course.
¹⁶It will save you from the forbiddenª woman,
From the alien woman whose talk is smooth,
¹⁷Who forsakes the companion of her youth
And disregards the covenant of her God.
¹⁸Her house sinks down to Death,
And her course leads to the shades.
¹⁹All who go to her cannot return
And find again the paths of life.

²⁰So follow the way of the good
And keep to the paths of the just.
²¹For the upright will inhabit the earth,
The blameless will remain in it.
²²While the wicked will vanish from the land
And the treacherous will be rooted out of it.

3 My son, do not forget my teaching,
But let your mind retain my commandments;
²For they will bestow on you length of days,
Years of life and well-being.
³Let fidelity and steadfastness not leave you;
Bind them about your throat,
Write them on the tablet of your mind,
⁴And you will find favor and approbation
In the eyes of God and man.
⁵Trust in the LORD with all your heart,
And do not rely on your own understanding.
⁶In all your ways acknowledge Him,
And He will make your paths smooth.
⁷Do not be wise in your own eyes;
Fear the LORD and shun evil.
⁸It will be a cure for your body,ª
A tonic for your bones.
⁹Honor the LORD with your wealth,
With the best of all your income,
¹⁰And your barns will be filled with grain,

ª Lit. *"strange."*
ª Lit. *"navel."*

Your vats will burst with new wine.
11Do not reject the discipline of the LORD, my son;
Do not abhor His rebuke.
12For whom the LORD loves, He rebukes,
As a father the son whom he favors.

13Happy is the man who finds wisdom,
The man who attains understanding.
14Her value in trade is better than silver,
Her yield, greater than gold.
15She is more precious than rubies;
All of your goods cannot equal her.
16In her right hand is length of days,
In her left, riches and honor.
17Her ways are pleasant ways,
And all her paths, peaceful.
18She is a tree of life to those who grasp her,
And whoever holds on to her is happy.

19The LORD founded the earth by wisdom;
He established the heavens by understanding;
20By His knowledge the depths burst apart,
And the skies distilled dew.
21My son, do not lose sight of them;
Hold on to resourcefulness and foresight.
22They will give life to your spirit
And grace to your throat.
23Then you will go your way safely
And not injure your feet.
24When you lie down you will be unafraid;
You will lie down and your sleep will be sweet.
25You will not fear sudden terror
Or the disaster that comes upon the wicked,
26For the LORD will be your trust;
He will keep your feet from being caught.

27Do not withhold good from one who deserves it
When you have the power to do it [for him].
28Do not say to your fellow, "Come back again;

I'll give it to you tomorrow," when you have it with you.
29Do not devise harm against your fellow
Who lives trustfully with you.
30Do not quarrel with a man for no cause,
When he has done you no harm.
31Do not envy a lawless man,
Or choose any of his ways;
32For the devious man is an abomination to the LORD,
But He is intimate with the straightforward.
33The curse of the LORD is on the house of the wicked,
But He blesses the abode of the righteous.
34At scoffers He scoffs,
But to the lowly He shows grace.
35The wise shall obtain honor,
But dullards get disgrace as their portion.

4 Sons, heed the discipline of a father;
Listen and learn discernment,
2For I give you good instruction;
Do not forsake my teaching.

3Once I was a son to my father,
The tender darling of my mother.
4He instructed me and said to me,
"Let your mind hold on to my words;
Keep my commandments and you will live.
5Acquire wisdom, acquire discernment;
Do not forget and do not swerve from my words.
6Do not forsake her and she will guard you;
Love her and she will protect you.
7The beginninga of wisdom is—acquire wisdom;
With all your acquisitions, acquire discernment.
8Hug her to you and she will exalt you;
She will bring you honor if you embrace her.
9She will adorn your head with a graceful wreath;
Crown you with a glorious diadem."

a Or "best part."

¹⁰My son, heed and take in my words,
And you will have many years of life.
¹¹I instruct you in the way of wisdom;
I guide you in straight courses.
¹²You will walk without breaking stride;
When you run, you will not stumble.
¹³Hold fast to discipline; do not let go;
Keep it; it is your life.
¹⁴Do not enter on the path of the wicked;
Do not walk on the way of evil men.
¹⁵Avoid it; do not pass through it;
Turn away from it; pass it by.
¹⁶For they cannot sleep unless they have done evil;
Unless they make someone fall they are robbed of sleep.
¹⁷They eat the bread of wickedness
And drink the wine of lawlessness.
¹⁸The path of the righteous is like radiant sunlight,
Ever brightening until noon.
¹⁹The way of the wicked is all darkness;
They do not know what will make them stumble.

²⁰My son, listen to my speech;
Incline your ear to my words.
²¹Do not lose sight of them;
Keep them in your mind.
²²They are life to him who finds them,
Healing for his whole body.
²³More than all that you guard, guard your mind,
For it is the source of life.
²⁴Put crooked speech away from you;
Keep devious talk far from you.
²⁵Let your eyes look forward,
Your gaze be straight ahead.
²⁶Survey the course you take,
And all your ways will prosper.
²⁷Do not swerve to the right or the left;
Keep your feet from evil.

5 My son, listen to my wisdom;
Incline your ear to my insight,
²That you may have foresight,
While your lips hold fast to knowledge.
³For the lips of a forbiddenᵃ woman drip honey;
Her mouth is smoother than oil;
⁴But in the end she is as bitter as wormwood,
Sharp as a two-edged sword.
⁵Her feet go down to Death;
Her steps take hold of Sheol.
⁶She does not chart a path of life;
Her course meanders for lack of knowledge.
⁷So now, sons, pay heed to me,
And do not swerve from the words of my mouth.
⁸Keep yourself far away from her;
Do not come near the doorway of her house
⁹Lest you give up your vigor to others,
Your years to a ruthless one;
¹⁰Lest strangers eat their fill of your strength,
And your toil be for the house of another;
¹¹And in the end you roar,
When your flesh and body are consumed,
¹²And say,
"O how I hated discipline,
And heartily spurned rebuke.
¹³I did not pay heed to my teachers,
Or incline my ear to my instructors.
¹⁴Soon I was in dire trouble
Amidst the assembled congregation."
¹⁵Drink water from your own cistern,
Running water from your own well.
¹⁶Your springs will gush forth
In streams in the public squares.
¹⁷They will be yours alone,
Others having no part with you.
¹⁸Let your fountain be blessed;

ᵃ Lit. *"strange."*

Find joy in the wife of your youth—
¹⁹A loving doe, a graceful mountain goat.
Let her breasts satisfy you at all times;
Be infatuated with love of her always.
²⁰Why be infatuated, my son, with a forbiddenᵃ woman?
Why clasp the bosom of an alien woman?
²¹For a man's ways are before the eyes of God;
He surveys his entire course.
²²The wicked man will be trapped in his iniquities;
He will be caught up in the ropes of his sin.
²³He will die for lack of discipline,
Infatuated by his great folly.

6 My son, if you have stood surety for your fellow,
Given your hand for another,ᵃ
²You have been trapped by the words of your mouth,
Snared by the words of your mouth.
³Do this, then, my son, to extricate yourself,
For you have come into the power of your fellow:
Go grovel—and badger your fellow;
⁴Give your eyes no sleep,
Your pupils no slumber.
⁵Save yourself like a deer out of the hand [of a hunter],
Like a bird out of the hand of a fowler.

⁶Lazybones, go to the ant;
Study its ways and learn.
⁷Without leaders, officers, or rulers,
⁸It lays up its stores during the summer,
Gathers in its food at the harvest.
⁹How long will you lie there, lazybones;
When will you wake from your sleep?
¹⁰A bit more sleep, a bit more slumber,
A bit more hugging yourself in bed,
¹¹And poverty will come ᵇ⁻calling upon you,⁻ᵇ
And want, like a man with a shield.

ᵃ Or "a stranger."
ᵇ⁻ᵇ Meaning of Heb. uncertain.

¹²A scoundrel, an evil man
Lives by crooked speech,
¹³Winking his eyes,
Shuffling his feet,
Pointing his finger.
¹⁴Duplicity is in his heart;
He plots evil all the time;
He incites quarrels.
¹⁵Therefore calamity will come upon him without warning;
Suddenly he will be broken beyond repair.

¹⁶Six things the LORD hates;
Seven are an abomination to Him:
¹⁷A haughty bearing,
A lying tongue,
Hands that shed innocent blood,
¹⁸A mind that hatches evil plots,
Feet quick to run to evil,
¹⁹A false witness testifying lies,
And one who incites brothers to quarrel.

²⁰My son, keep your father's commandment;
Do not forsake your mother's teaching.
²¹Tie them over your heart always;
Bind them around your throat.
²²When you walk it will lead you;
When you lie down it will watch over you;
And when you are awake it will talk with you.
²³For the commandment is a lamp,
The teaching is a light,
And the way to life is the rebuke that disciplines.
²⁴It will keep you from an evil woman,
From the smooth tongue of a forbiddenᶜ woman.
²⁵Do not lust for her beauty
Or let her captivate you with her eyes.
²⁶The last loaf of bread will go for a harlot;
A married woman will snare a person of honor.
²⁷Can a man rake embers into his bosom

ᶜ Lit. "alien."

Without burning his clothes?
28Can a man walk on live coals
Without scorching his feet?
29It is the same with one who sleeps with his fellow's wife;
None who touches her will go unpunished.
30A thief is not held in contempt
For stealing to appease his hunger;
31Yet if caught he must pay sevenfold;
He must give up all he owns.
32He who commits adultery is devoid of sense;
Only one who would destroy himself does such a thing.
33He will meet with disease and disgrace;
His reproach will never be expunged.
34The fury of the husband will be passionate;
He will show no pity on his day of vengeance.
35He will not have regard for any ransom;
He will refuse your bribe, however great.

7 My son, heed my words;
And store up my commandments with you.
2Keep my commandments and live,
My teaching, as the apple of your eye.
3Bind them on your fingers;
Write them on the tablet of your mind.
4Say to Wisdom, "You are my sister,"
And call Understanding a kinswoman.
5She will guard you from a forbiddena woman;
From an alien woman whose talk is smooth.

6From the window of my house,
Through my lattice, I looked out
7And saw among the simple,
Noticed among the youths,
A lad devoid of sense.
8He was crossing the street near her corner,
Walking toward her house
9In the dusk of evening,

---

a Lit. "strange."

In the dark hours of night.
10A woman comes toward him
b-Dressed like a harlot, with set purpose.-b
11She is bustling and restive;
She is never at home.
12Now in the street, now in the square,
She lurks at every corner.
13She lays hold of him and kisses him;
Brazenly she says to him,
14"I had to make a sacrifice of well-being;
Today I fulfilled my vows.
15Therefore I have come out to you,
Seeking you, and have found you.
16I have decked my couch with covers
Of dyed Egyptian linen;
17I have sprinkled my bed
With myrrh, aloes, and cinnamon.
18Let us drink our fill of love till morning;
Let us delight in amorous embrace.
19For the man of the house is away;
He is off on a distant journey.
20He took his bag of money with him
And will return only at mid-month."

21She sways him with her eloquence,
Turns him aside with her smooth talk.
22Thoughtlessly he follows her,
Like an ox going to the slaughter,
b-Like a fool to the stocks for punishment-b—
23Until the arrow pierces his liver.
He is like a bird rushing into a trap,
Not knowing his life is at stake.
24Now, sons, listen to me;
Pay attention to my words;
25Let your mind not wander down her ways;
Do not stray onto her paths.
26For many are those she has struck dead,
And numerous are her victims.

b-b *Meaning of Heb. uncertain.*

²⁷Her house is a highway to Sheol
Leading down to Death's inner chambers.

8 It is Wisdom calling,
Understanding raising her voice.
²She takes her stand at the topmost heights,
By the wayside, at the crossroads,
³Near the gates at the city entrance;
At the entryways, she shouts,
⁴"O men, I call to you;
My cry is to all mankind.
⁵O simple ones, learn shrewdness;
O dullards, instruct your minds.
⁶Listen, for I speak noble things;
Uprightness comes from my lips;
⁷My mouth utters truth;
Wickedness is abhorrent to my lips.
⁸All my words are just,
None of them perverse or crooked;
⁹All are straightforward to the intelligent man,
And right to those who have attained knowledge.
¹⁰Accept my discipline rather than silver,
Knowledge rather than choice gold.
¹¹For wisdom is better than rubies;
No goods can equal her.

¹²"I, Wisdom, live with Prudence;
I attain knowledge and foresight.
¹³To fear the LORD is to hate evil;
I hate pride, arrogance, the evil way,
And duplicity in speech.
¹⁴Mine are counsel and resourcefulness;
I am understanding; courage is mine.
¹⁵Through me kings reign
And rulers decree just laws;
¹⁶Through me princes rule,
Great men and all the ªrighteous judges.⁻ª

ª⁻ª *According to some Heb. mss. and printed editions, "judges of the earth."*

17Those who love me I love,
And those who seek me will find me.
18Riches and honor belong to me,
Enduring wealth and success.
19My fruit is better than gold, fine gold,
And my produce better than choice silver.
20I walk on the way of righteousness,
On the paths of justice.
21I endow those who love me with substance;
I will fill their treasuries.

22"The LORD created me at the beginning of His course
As the first of His works of old.
23In the distant past I was fashioned,
At the beginning, at the origin of earth.
24There was still no deep when I was brought forth,
No springs rich in water;
25Before [the foundation of] the mountains were sunk,
Before the hills I was born.
26He had not yet made earth and fields,
Or the world's first clumps of clay.
27I was there when He set the heavens into place;
When He fixed the horizon upon the deep;
28When He made the heavens above firm,
And the fountains of the deep gushed forth;
29When He assigned the sea its limits,
So that its waters never transgress His command;
When He fixed the foundations of the earth,
30I was with Him as a confidant,
A source of delight every day,
Rejoicing before Him at all times,
31Rejoicing in His inhabited world,
Finding delight with mankind.
32Now, sons, listen to me;
Happy are they who keep my ways.
33Heed discipline and become wise;
Do not spurn it.
34Happy is the man who listens to me,

Coming early to my gates each day,
Waiting outside my doors.
35For he who finds me finds life
And obtains favor from the LORD.
36But he who misses me destroys himself;
All who hate me love death."

9 Wisdom has built her house,
She has hewn her seven pillars.
2She has prepared the feast,
Mixed the wine,
And also set the table.
3She has sent out her maids to announce
On the heights of the town,
4"Let the simple enter here";
To those devoid of sense she says,
5"Come, eat my food
And drink the wine that I have mixed;
6Give up simpleness and live,
Walk in the way of understanding."

7To correct a scoffer,
a-Or rebuke a wicked man for his blemish,
Is to call down abuse on oneself.-a
8Do not rebuke a scoffer, for he will hate you;
Reprove a wise man, and he will love you.
9Instruct a wise man, and he will grow wiser;
Teach a righteous man, and he will gain in learning.
10The beginning of wisdom is fear of the LORD,
And knowledge of the Holy One is understanding.
11For through me your days will increase,
And years be added to your life.
12If you are wise, you are wise for yourself;
If you are a scoffer, you bear it alone.
13The stupid woman bustles about;
She is simple and knows nothing.
14She sits in the doorway of her house,

a-a Clauses transposed for clarity.

Or on a chair at the heights of the town,
15Calling to all the wayfarers
Who go about their own affairs,
16"Let the simple enter here";
And to those devoid of sense she says,
17"Stolen waters are sweet,
And bread eaten furtively is tasty."
18He does not know that the shades are there,
That her guests are in the depths of Sheol.

10 The proverbs of Solomon:

A wise son brings joy to his father;
A dull son is his mother's sorrow.
2Ill-gotten wealth is of no avail,
But righteousness saves from death.
3The LORD will not let the righteous go hungry,
But He denies the wicked what they crave.
4Negligent hands cause poverty,
But diligent hands enrich.
5He who lays in stores during the summer is a capable son,
But he who sleeps during the harvest is an incompetent.
6Blessings light upon the head of the righteous,
But lawlessness covers the mouth of the wicked.
7The name of the righteous is invoked in blessing,
But the fame of the wicked rots.
8He whose heart is wise accepts commands,
But he whose speech is foolish comes to grief.
9He who lives blamelessly lives safely,
But he who walks a crooked path will be found out.
10He who winks his eye causes sorrow;
He whose speech is foolish comes to grief.
11The mouth of the righteous is a fountain of life,
But lawlessness covers the mouth of the wicked.
12Hatred stirs up strife,
But love covers up all faults.
13Wisdom is to be found on the lips of the intelligent,

But a rod is ready for the back of the senseless.
14The wise store up knowledge;
The mouth of the fool is an imminent ruin.
15The wealth of a rich man is his fortress;
The poverty of the poor is his ruin.
16The labor of the righteous man makes for life;
The produce of the wicked man makes for want.
17He who follows discipline shows the way to life,
But he who ignores reproof leads astray.
18He who conceals hatred has lying lips,
While he who speaks forth slander is a dullard.
19Where there is much talking, there is no lack of transgressing,
But he who curbs his tongue^a shows sense.
20The tongue of a righteous man is choice silver,
But the mind of the wicked is of little worth.
21The lips of the righteous sustain many,
But fools die for lack of sense.
22It is the blessing of the LORD that enriches,
And no toil can increase it.
23As mischief is sport for the dullard,
So is wisdom for the man of understanding.
24What the wicked man plots overtakes him;
What the righteous desire is granted.
25When the storm passes the wicked man is gone,
But the righteous is an everlasting foundation.
26Like vinegar to the teeth,
Like smoke to the eyes,
Is a lazy man to those who send him on a mission.
27The fear of the LORD prolongs life,
While the years of the wicked will be shortened.
28The righteous can look forward to joy,
But the hope of the wicked is doomed.
29The way of the LORD is a stronghold for the blameless,
But a ruin for evildoers.
30The righteous will never be shaken;
The wicked will not inhabit the earth.
31The mouth of the righteous produces wisdom,
But the treacherous tongue shall be cut off.

a Lit. "lips."

³²The lips of the righteous know what is pleasing;
The mouth of the wicked [knows] duplicity.

11 False scales are an abomination to the LORD;
An honest^a weight pleases Him.
²When arrogance appears, disgrace follows,
But wisdom is with those who are unassuming.
³The integrity of the upright guides them;
The deviousness of the treacherous leads them to ruin.
⁴Wealth is of no avail on the day of wrath,
But righteousness saves from death.
⁵The righteousness of the blameless man smooths his way,
But the wicked man is felled by his wickedness.
⁶The righteousness of the upright saves them,
But the treacherous are trapped by their malice.
⁷At death the hopes of a wicked man are doomed,
And the ambition of evil men comes to nothing.
⁸The righteous man is rescued from trouble
And the wicked man takes his place.
⁹The impious man destroys his neighbor through speech,
But through their knowledge the righteous are rescued.
¹⁰When the righteous prosper the city exults;
When the wicked perish there are shouts of joy.
¹¹A city is built up by the blessing of the upright,
But it is torn down by the speech of the wicked.
¹²He who speaks contemptuously of his fellowman is devoid of sense;
A prudent man keeps his peace.
¹³A base fellow gives away secrets,
But a trustworthy soul keeps a confidence.
¹⁴For want of strategy an army falls,
But victory comes with much planning.
¹⁵Harm awaits him who stands surety for another;^b
He who spurns pledging shall be secure.
¹⁶A graceful woman obtains honor;
Ruthless men obtain wealth.
¹⁷A kindly man benefits himself;

---

^a Lit. "whole."
^b Or "a stranger."

A cruel man makes trouble for himself.
18The wicked man earns illusory wages,
But he who sows righteousness has a true reward.
19Righteousness is a prop of life,
But to pursue evil leads to death.
20Men of crooked mind are an abomination to the LORD,
But those whose way is blameless please Him.
21Assuredly,ᶜ the evil man will not escape,
But the offspring of the righteous will be safe.
22Like a gold ring in the snout of a pig
Is a beautiful woman bereft of sense.
23What the righteous desire can only be good;
What the wicked hope for [stirs] wrath.
24One man gives generously and ends with more;
Another stints on doing the right thing and incurs a loss.
25A generous person enjoys prosperity;
He who satisfies others shall himself be sated.
26He who withholds grain earns the curses of the people,
But blessings are on the head of the one who dispenses it.
27He who earnestly seeks what is good pursues what is pleasing;
He who is bent on evil, upon him it shall come.
28He who trusts in his wealth shall fall,
But the righteous shall flourish like foliage.
29He who makes trouble for his household shall inherit the
    wind;
A fool is a slave to the wise-hearted.
30The fruit of the righteous is a tree of life;
A wise man captivates people.
31If the righteous on earth get their deserts,
How much more the wicked man and the sinner.

12 He who loves discipline loves knowledge;
He who spurns reproof is a brutish man.
2A good man earns the favor of the LORD,
A man of intrigues, His condemnation.
3A man cannot be established in wickedness,
But the root of the righteous will not be shaken loose.

ᶜ Lit. "Hand to hand"; meaning of Heb. uncertain.

⁴A capable wife is a crown for her husband,
But an incompetent one is like rot in his bones.
⁵The purposes of the righteous are justice,
The schemes of the wicked are deceit.
⁶The words of the wicked are a deadly ambush,
But the speech of the upright saves them.
⁷Overturn the wicked and they are gone,
But the house of the righteous will endure.
⁸A man is commended according to his intelligence;
A twisted mind is held up to contempt.
⁹Better to be lightly esteemed and have a servant
Than to put on airs and have no food.
¹⁰A righteous man knows the needs of his beast,
But the compassion of the wicked is cruelty.
¹¹He who tills his land shall have food in plenty,
But he who pursues vanities is devoid of sense.
¹²ᵃ⁻The wicked covet the catch of evil men;
The root of the righteous yields [fruit].⁻ᵃ
¹³Sinful speech is a trap for the evil man,
But the righteous escapes from trouble.
¹⁴A man gets his fill of good from the fruit of his speech;
One is repaid in kind for one's deeds.
¹⁵The way of a fool is right in his own eyes;
But the wise man accepts advice.
¹⁶A fool's vexation is known at once,
But a clever man conceals his humiliation.
¹⁷He who testifies faithfully tells the truth,
But a false witness, deceit.
¹⁸There is blunt talk like sword-thrusts,
But the speech of the wise is healing.
¹⁹Truthful speech abides forever,
A lying tongue for but a moment.
²⁰Deceit is in the minds of those who plot evil;
For those who plan good there is joy.
²¹No harm befalls the righteous,
But the wicked have their fill of misfortune.
²²Lying speech is an abomination to the LORD,
But those who act faithfully please Him.

ᵃ⁻ᵃ *Meaning of Heb. uncertain.*

23A clever man conceals what he knows,
But the mind of a dullard cries out folly.
24The hand of the diligent wields authority;
The negligent are held in subjection.
25If there is anxiety in a man's mind let him quash it,
And turn it into joy with a good word.
26A righteous man a-gives his friend direction,-a
But the way of the wicked leads astray.
27A negligent man never has game to roast;
a-A diligent man has precious wealth.-a
28The road of righteousness leads to life;
By way of its path there is no death.

13 A wise son—it is through the discipline of his father;
A scoffer—he never heard reproof.
2A man enjoys good from the fruit of his speech;
But out of the throat of the treacherous comes lawlessness.
3He who guards his tonguea preserves his life;
He who opens wide his lips, it is his ruin.
4A lazy man craves, but has nothing;
The diligent shall feast on rich fare.
5A righteous man hates lies;
The wicked man is vile and disgraceful.
6Righteousness protects him whose way is blameless;
Wickedness subverts the sinner.
7One man pretends to be rich and has nothing;
Another professes to be poor and has much wealth.
8Riches are ransom for a man's life,
The poor never heard a reproof.
9The light of the righteous is radiant;
The lamp of the wicked is extinguished.
10b-Arrogance yields nothing but strife;-b
Wisdom belongs to those who seek advice.
11Wealth may dwindle to less than nothing,
But he who gathers little by little increases it.
12Hope deferred sickens the heart,
But desire realized is a tree of life.

a Lit. "mouth."
b-b Meaning of Heb. uncertain.

¹³He who disdains a precept will be injured thereby;
He who respects a command will be rewarded.
¹⁴The instruction of a wise man is a fountain of life,
Enabling one to avoid deadly snares.
¹⁵Good sense wins favor;
The way of treacherous men is unchanging.ᶜ
¹⁶Every clever man acts knowledgeably,
But a dullard exposes his stupidity.
¹⁷Harm befalls a wicked messenger;
A faithful courier brings healing.
¹⁸Poverty and humiliation are for him who spurns discipline;
But he who takes reproof to heart gets honor.
¹⁹Desire realized is sweet to the soul;
To turn away from evil is abhorrent to the stupid.
²⁰He who keeps company with the wise becomes wise,
But he who consorts with dullards comes to grief.
²¹Misfortune pursues sinners,
But the righteous are well rewarded.
²²A good man has what to bequeath to his grandchildren,
For the wealth of sinners is stored up for the righteous.
²³The tillage of the poor yields much food;
But substance is swept away for lack of moderation.
²⁴He who spares the rod hates his son,
But he who loves him disciplines him early.
²⁵The righteous man eats to his heart's content,
But the belly of the wicked is empty.

14 The wisest of women builds her house,
But folly tears it down with its own hands.
²He who maintains his integrity fears the LORD;
A man of devious ways scorns Him.
³In the mouth of a fool is a rod of haughtiness,
But the lips of the wise protect them.
⁴If there are no oxen the crib is clean,
But a rich harvest comes through the strength of the ox.
⁵An honest witness will not lie;
A false witness testifies lies.

ᶜ Or "harsh."

⁶A scoffer seeks wisdom in vain,
But knowledge comes easily to the intelligent man.
⁷Keep your distance from a dullard,
For you will not learn wise speech.
⁸It is the wisdom of a clever man to understand his course;
But the stupidity of the dullard is delusion.
⁹Reparations mediate between fools,
Between the upright, good will.
¹⁰The heart alone knows its bitterness,
And no outsider can share in its joy.
¹¹The house of the wicked will be demolished,
But the tent of the upright will flourish.
¹²A road may seem right to a man,
But in the end it is a road to death.
¹³The heart may ache even in laughter,
And joy may end in grief.
¹⁴An unprincipled man reaps the fruits of his ways;
ᵃ⁻A good man, of his deeds.⁻ᵃ
¹⁵A simple person believes anything;
A clever man ponders his course.
¹⁶A wise man is diffident and shuns evil,
But a dullard rushes in confidently.
¹⁷An impatient man commits folly;
A man of intrigues will be hated.
¹⁸Folly is the lot of the simple,
But clever men ᵇ⁻glory in knowledge.⁻ᵇ
¹⁹Evil men are brought low before the good,
So are the wicked at the gates of the righteous.
²⁰A pauper is despised even by his peers,
But a rich man has many friends.
²¹He who despises his fellow is wrong;
He who shows pity for the lowly is happy.
²²Surely those who plan evil go astray,
While those who plan good earn steadfast love.
²³From all toil there is some gain,
But idle chatter is pure loss.
²⁴The ornament of the wise is their wealth;
The stupidity of dullards is stupidity.

ᵃ⁻ᵃ *Taking* ʿal *as from* ʾll; *cf. Hos. 12.3.*
ᵇ⁻ᵇ*Meaning of Heb. uncertain.*

²⁵A truthful witness saves lives;
He who testifies lies [spreads] deceit.
²⁶Fear of the LORD is a stronghold,
A refuge for a man's children.
²⁷Fear of the LORD is a fountain of life,
Enabling one to avoid deadly snares.
²⁸A numerous people is the glory of a king;
Without a nation a ruler is ruined.
²⁹Patience results in much understanding;
Impatience gets folly as its portion.
³⁰A calm disposition gives bodily health;
Passion is rot to the bones.
³¹He who withholds what is due to the poor affronts his Maker;
He who shows pity for the needy honors Him.
³²The wicked man is felled by his own evil;
The righteous man finds security in his death.
³³Wisdom rests quietly in the mind of a prudent man,
But among dullards it makes itself known.
³⁴Righteousness exalts a nation;
Sin is a reproach to any people.
³⁵The king favors a capable servant;
He rages at an incompetent one.

15 A gentle response allays wrath;
A harsh word provokes anger.
²The tongue of the wise produces much knowledge,
But the mouth of dullards pours out folly.
³The eyes of the LORD are everywhere,
Observing the bad and the good.
⁴A healing tongue is a tree of life,
But a devious one makes for a broken spirit.
⁵A fool spurns the discipline of his father,
But one who heeds reproof becomes clever.
⁶In the house of the righteous there is much treasure,
But in the harvest of the wicked there is trouble.
⁷The lips of the wise disseminate knowledge;
Not so the minds of dullards.

⁸The sacrifice of the wicked is an abomination to the LORD,
But the prayer of the upright pleases Him.
⁹The way of the wicked is an abomination to the LORD,
But He loves him who pursues righteousness.
¹⁰Discipline seems bad to him who forsakes the way;
He who spurns reproof will die.
¹¹Sheol and Abaddon lie exposed to the LORD,
How much more the minds of men!
¹²The scoffer dislikes being reproved;
He will not resort to the wise.
¹³A joyful heart makes a cheerful face;
A sad heart makes a despondent mood.
¹⁴The mind of a prudent man seeks knowledge;
The mouth of the dullard pursues folly.
¹⁵All the days of a poor man are wretched,
But contentment is a feast without end.
¹⁶Better a little with fear of the LORD
Than great wealth with confusion.
¹⁷Better a meal of vegetables where there is love
Than a fattened ox where there is hate.
¹⁸A hot-tempered man provokes a quarrel;
A patient man calms strife.
¹⁹The way of a lazy man is like a hedge of thorns,
But the path of the upright is paved.
²⁰A wise son makes his father happy;
A fool of a man humiliates his mother.
²¹Folly is joy to one devoid of sense;
A prudent man walks a straight path.
²²Plans are foiled for want of counsel,
But they succeed through many advisers.
²³A ready response is a joy to a man,
And how good is a word rightly timed!
²⁴For an intelligent man the path of life leads upward,
In order to avoid Sheol below.
²⁵The LORD will tear down the house of the proud,
But He will establish the homestead of the widow.
²⁶Evil thoughts are an abomination to the LORD,
But pleasant words are pure.

²⁷He who pursues ill-gotten gain makes trouble for his
household;
He who spurns gifts will live long.
²⁸The heart^a of the righteous man rehearses his answer,
But the mouth of the wicked blurts out evil things.
²⁹The LORD is far from the wicked,
But He hears the prayer of the righteous.
³⁰What brightens the eye gladdens the heart;
Good news puts fat on the bones.
³¹He whose ear heeds the discipline of life
Lodges among the wise.
³²He who spurns discipline hates himself;
He who heeds reproof gains understanding.
³³The fear of the LORD is the discipline of wisdom;
Humility precedes honor.

16
A man may arrange his thoughts,
But what he says depends on the LORD.
²All the ways of a man seem right to him,
But the LORD probes motives.
³Entrust your affairs to the LORD,
And your plans will succeed.
⁴The LORD made everything for a purpose,
Even the wicked for an evil day.
⁵Every haughty person is an abomination to the LORD;
Assuredly,^a he will not go unpunished.
⁶Iniquity is expiated by loyalty and faithfulness,
And evil is avoided through fear of the LORD.
⁷When the LORD is pleased with a man's conduct,
He may turn even his enemies into allies.
⁸Better a little with righteousness
Than a large income with injustice.
⁹A man may plot out his course,
But it is the LORD who directs his steps.

¹⁰There is magic on the lips of the king;
He cannot err in judgment.

---

^a For leb *as a source of speech, see note to Eccl. 5.1.*

^a *Lit. "Hand to hand"; meaning of Heb. uncertain.*

¹¹Honest scales and balances are the LORD's;
All the weights in the bag are His work.
¹²Wicked deeds are an abomination to kings,
For the throne is established by righteousness.
¹³Truthful speech wins the favor of kings;
They love those who speak honestly.
¹⁴The king's wrath is a messenger of death,
But a wise man can appease it.
¹⁵The king's smile means life;
His favor is like a rain cloud in spring.

¹⁶How much better to acquire wisdom than gold;
To acquire understanding is preferable to silver.
¹⁷The highway of the upright avoids evil;
He who would preserve his life watches his way.
¹⁸Pride goes before ruin,
Arrogance, before failure.
¹⁹Better to be humble and among the lowly
Than to share spoils with the proud.
²⁰He who is adept in a matter will attain success;
Happy is he who trusts in the LORD.
²¹The wise-hearted is called discerning;
One whose speech is pleasing gains wisdom.
²²Good sense is a fountain of life to those who have it,
And folly is the punishment of fools.
²³The mind of the wise man makes his speech effective
And increases the wisdom on his lips.
²⁴Pleasant words are like a honeycomb,
Sweet to the palate and a cure for the body.
²⁵A road may seem right to a man,
But in the end it is a road to death.
²⁶The appetite of a laborer labors for him,
Because his hunger^b ^cforces him on.^{-c}

²⁷A scoundrel plots^c evil;
What is on his lips is like a scorching fire.
²⁸A shifty man stirs up strife,
And a querulous one alienates his friend.

---

b *Lit. "mouth."*
c-c *Meaning of Heb. uncertain.*

²⁹A lawless man misleads his friend,
Making him take the wrong way.
³⁰He closes his eyes while meditating deception;
He purses his lips while deciding upon evil.

³¹Gray hair is a crown of glory;
It is attained by the way of righteousness.
³²Better to be forbearing than mighty,
To have self-control than to conquer a city.
³³Lots are cast into the lap;
The decision depends on the LORD.

17 Better a dry crust with peace
Than a house full of feasting with strife.
²A capable servant will dominate an incompetent son
And share the inheritance with the brothers.
³For silver—the crucible;
For gold—the furnace,
And the LORD tests the mind.
⁴An evildoer listens to mischievous talk;
A liar gives ear to malicious words.
⁵He who mocks the poor affronts his Maker;
He who rejoices over another's misfortune will not go unpunished.
⁶Grandchildren are the crown of their elders,
And the glory of children is their parents.
⁷Lofty words are not fitting for a villain;
Much less lying words for a great man.
⁸A bribe seems like a charm to him who uses it;
He succeeds at every turn.
⁹He who seeks love overlooks faults,
But he who harps on a matter alienates his friend.
¹⁰A rebuke works on an intelligent man
More than one hundred blows on a fool.
¹¹An evil man seeks only to rebel;
A ruthless messenger will be sent against him.
¹²Sooner meet a bereaved she-bear
Than a fool with his nonsense.

¹³Evil will never depart from the house
Of him who repays good with evil.
¹⁴To start a quarrel is to open a sluice;
Before a dispute ᵃ⁻flares up,⁻ᵃ drop it.
¹⁵To acquit the guilty and convict the innocent—
Both are an abomination to the LORD.
¹⁶What good is money in the hand of a fool
To purchase wisdom, when he has no mind?
¹⁷A friend is devoted at all times;
A brother is born to share adversity.
¹⁸Devoid of sense is he who gives his hand
To stand surety for his fellow.
¹⁹He who loves transgression loves strife;
He who builds a high threshold invites broken bones.
²⁰Man of crooked mind comes to no good,
And he who speaks duplicity falls into trouble.
²¹One begets a dullard to one's own grief;
The father of a villain has no joy.
²²A joyful heart makes for ᵇ⁻good health;⁻ᵇ
Despondency dries up the bones.
²³The wicked man draws a bribe out of his bosom
To pervert the course of justice.
²⁴Wisdom lies before the intelligent man;
The eyes of the dullard range to the ends of the earth.
²⁵A stupid son is vexation for his father
And a heartache for the woman who bore him.
²⁶To punish the innocent is surely not right,
Or to flog the great for their uprightness.
²⁷A knowledgeable man is sparing with his words;
A man of understanding is reticent.
²⁸Even a fool, if he keeps silent, is deemed wise;
Intelligent, if he seals his lips.

18 ᵃ⁻He who isolates himself pursues his desires;
He disdains all competence.⁻ᵃ
²The fool does not desire understanding,
But only to air his thoughts.

ᵃ⁻ᵃ *Meaning of Heb. uncertain.*
ᵇ⁻ᵇ *Or "a cheerful face"; meaning of Heb. uncertain.*
ᵃ⁻ᵃ *Meaning of Heb. uncertain.*

³Comes the wicked man comes derision,
And with the rogue, contempt.
⁴The words a man speaks are deep waters,
A flowing stream, a fountain of wisdom.
⁵It is not right to be partial to the guilty
And subvert the innocent in judgment.
⁶The words of a fool lead to strife;
His speech invites blows.
⁷The fool's speech is his ruin;
His words are a trap for him.
⁸The words of a querulous man are bruising;ᵃ
They penetrate one's inmost parts.
⁹One who is slack in his work
Is a brother to a vandal.
¹⁰The name of the LORD is a tower of strength
To which the righteous man runs and is safe.
¹¹The wealth of a rich man is his fortress;
ᵃ⁻In his fancyᵃ it is a protective wall.
¹²Before ruin a man's heart is proud;
Humility goes before honor.
¹³To answer a man before hearing him out
Is foolish and disgraceful.
¹⁴A man's spirit can sustain him through illness;
But low spirits—who can bear them?
¹⁵The mind of an intelligent man acquires knowledge;
The ears of the wise seek out knowledge.
¹⁶A man's gift eases his way
And gives him access to the great.
¹⁷The first to plead his case seems right
Till the other party examines him.
¹⁸The lot puts an end to strife
And separates those locked in dispute.
¹⁹A brother offended is more formidable than a stronghold;
Such strife is like the bars of a fortress.
²⁰A man's belly is filled by the fruit of his mouth;
He will be filled by the produce of his lips.
²¹Death and life are in the power of the tongue;
Those who love it will eat its fruit.

22He who finds a wife has found happiness
And has won the favor of the LORD.
23The poor man speaks beseechingly;
The rich man's answer is harsh.
24There are companions to keep one company,
And there is a friend more devoted than a brother.

19Better a poor man who lives blamelessly
Than one who speaks perversely and is a dullard.
2A person without knowledge is surely not good;
He who moves hurriedly blunders.
3A man's folly subverts his way,
And his heart rages against the LORD.
4Wealth makes many friends,
But a poor man loses his last friend.
5A false witness will not go unpunished;
He who testifies lies will not escape.
6Many court the favor of a great man,
And all are the friends of a dispenser of gifts.
7All the brothers of a poor man despise him;
How much more is he shunned by his friends!
a-He who pursues words—they are of no avail.-a
8He who acquires wisdom is his own best friend;
He preserves understanding and attains happiness.
9A false witness will not go unpunished;
He who testifies falsely is doomed.
10Luxury is not fitting for a dullard,
Much less that a servant rule over princes.
11A man shows intelligence by his forebearance;
It is his glory when he overlooks an offense.
12The rage of a king is like the roar of a lion;
His favor is like dew upon the grass.
13A stupid son is a calamity to his father;
The nagging of a wife is like the endless dripping of water.
14Property and riches are bequeathed by fathers,
But an efficient wife comes from the LORD.
15Laziness induces sleep,

a-a *Meaning of Heb. uncertain.*

And a negligent person will go hungry.

16He who has regard for his life pays regard to commandments;

He who is heedless of his ways will die.

17He who is generous to the poor makes a loan to the LORD;

He will repay him his due.

18Discipline your son while there is still hope,

Andb do not c-set your heart on his destruction.-c

19A hot-tempered man incurs punishment;

a-If you try to save him you will only make it worse.-a

20Listen to advice and accept discipline

In order that you may be wise in the end.

21Many designs are in a man's mind,

But it is the LORD's plan that is accomplished.

22a-Greed is a reproach to a man;-a

Better be poor than a liar.

23He who fears the LORD earns life;

a-He shall abide in contentment,-a

Free from misfortune.

24The lazy man buries his hand in the bowl;

He will not even bring it to his mouth.

25Beat the scoffer and the simple will become clever;

Reprove an intelligent man and he gains knowledge.

26A son who causes shame and disgrace

Plunders his father, puts his mother to flight.

27My son, cease to stray from words of knowledge

And receive discipline.

28A malicious witness scoffs at justice,

And the speech of the wicked conceals mischief.

29Punishments are in store for scoffers

And blows for the backs of dullards.

20 Wine is a scoffer, strong drink a roisterer;

He who is muddled by them will not grow wise.

2The terror of a king is like the roar of a lion;

He who provokes his anger risks his life.

3It is honorable for a man to desist from strife,

But every fool a-becomes embroiled.-a

b Or "But."

c-c Or "pay attention to his moaning."

a-a Meaning of Heb. uncertain.

⁴In winter the lazy man does not plow;
At harvesttime he seeks, and finds nothing.
⁵The designs in a man's mind are deep waters,
But a man of understanding can draw them out.
⁶He calls many a man his loyal friend,
But who can find a faithful man?
⁷The righteous man lives blamelessly;
Happy are his children who come after him.
⁸The king seated on the throne of judgment
Can winnow out all evil by his glance.
⁹Who can say, "I have cleansed my heart,
I am purged of my sin"?
¹⁰False weights and false measures,
Both are an abomination to the LORD.
¹¹A child may be dissembling in his behavior
Even though his actions are blameless and proper.
¹²The ear that hears, the eye that sees—
The LORD made them both.
¹³Do not love sleep lest you be impoverished;
Keep your eyes open and you will have plenty of food.
¹⁴"Bad, bad," says the buyer,
But having moved off, he congratulates himself.
¹⁵Gold is plentiful, jewels abundant,
But wise speech is a precious object.
¹⁶Seize his garment, for he stood surety for another;ᵇ
Take it as a pledge, [for he stood surety] for an unfamiliar woman.
¹⁷Bread gained by fraud may be tasty to a man,
But later his mouth will be filled with gravel.
¹⁸Plans laid in council will succeed;
Wage war with stratagems.
¹⁹He who gives away secrets is a base fellow;
Do not take up with a garrulous man.
²⁰One who reviles his father or mother,
Light will fail him when darkness comes.
²¹An estate acquired in haste at the outset
Will not be blessed in the end.
²²Do not say, "I will requite evil";
Put your hope in the LORD and He will deliver you.

ᵇ Or "a stranger."

²³False weights are an abomination to the LORD;
Dishonest scales are not right.
²⁴A man's steps are decided by the LORD;
What does a man know about his own way?
²⁵It is a snare for a man ᵃ⁻to pledge a sacred gift rashly⁻ᵃ
And to give thought to his vows only after they have been made.
²⁶A wise king winnows out the wicked,
And turns the wheel upon them.
²⁷The lifebreath of man is the lamp of the LORD
Revealing all his inmost parts.
²⁸Faithfulness and loyalty protect the king;
He maintains his throne by faithfulness.
²⁹The glory of youths is their strength;
The majesty of old men is their gray hair.
³⁰Bruises and wounds are repaymentᵃ for evil,
Striking at one's inmost parts.

21 Like channeled water is the mind of the king in the LORD's hand;
He directs it to whatever He wishes.
²All the ways of a man seem right to him,
But the LORD probes the mind.
³To do what is right and just
Is more desired by the LORD than sacrifice.
⁴Haughty looks, a proud heart—
The tillage of the wicked is sinful.
⁵The plans of the diligent make only for gain;
All rash haste makes only for loss.
⁶Treasures acquired by a lying tongue
ᵃ⁻Are like driven vapor, heading for extinction.⁻ᵃ
⁷The violence of the wicked sweeps them away,
For they refuse to act justly.
⁸The way of a man may be tortuous and strange,
Though his actions are blameless and proper.
⁹Dwelling in the corner of a roof is better
Than a contentious wife in a ᵃ⁻spacious house.⁻ᵃ
¹⁰The desire of the wicked is set upon evil;
His fellowman finds no favor in his eyes.

ᵃ⁻ᵃ *Meaning of Heb. uncertain.*

11When a scoffer is punished, the simple man is edified;
When a wise man is taught, he gains insight.
12The Righteous One observes the house of the wicked man;
He subverts the wicked to their ruin.
13Who stops his ears at the cry of the wretched,
He too will call and not be answered.
14A gift in secret subdues anger,
A present in private, fierce rage.
15Justice done is a joy to the righteous,
To evildoers, ruination.
16A man who strays from the path of prudence
Will rest in the company of ghosts.
17He who loves pleasure comes to want;
He who loves wine and oil does not grow rich.
18The wicked are the ransom of the righteous;
The traitor comes in place of the upright.
19It is better to live in the desert
Than with a contentious, vexatious wife.
20Precious treasure and oil are in the house of the wise man,
And a fool of a man will run through them.
21He who strives to do good and kind deeds
Attains life, success, and honor.
22One wise man prevailed over a city of warriors
And brought down its mighty stronghold.
23He who guards his mouth and tongue
Guards himself from trouble.
24The proud, insolent man, scoffer is his name,
Acts in a frenzy of insolence.
25The craving of a lazy man kills him,
For his hands refuse to work.
26All day long he is seized with craving
While the righteous man gives without stint.
27The sacrifice of the wicked man is an abomination,
The more so as he offers it in depravity.
28A false witness is doomed,
But one who really heard will testify with success.
29The wicked man is brazen-faced;
The upright man discerns his course.

³⁰No wisdom, no prudence, and no counsel
Can prevail against the LORD.
³¹The horse is readied for the day of battle,
But victory comes from the LORD.

22 Repute is preferable to great wealth,
Grace is better than silver and gold.
²Rich man and poor man meet;
The LORD made them both.
³The shrewd man saw trouble and took cover;
The simple kept going and paid the penalty.
⁴The effect of humility is fear of the LORD,
Wealth, honor, and life.
⁵Thorns and snares are in the path of the crooked;
He who values his life will keep far from them.
⁶Train a lad in the way he ought to go;
He will not swerve from it even in old age.
⁷The rich rule the poor,
And the borrower is a slave to the lender.
⁸He who sows injustice shall reap misfortune;
His rod of wrath shall fail.
⁹The generous man is blessed,
For he gives of his bread to the poor.
¹⁰Expel the scoffer and contention departs,
Quarrel and contumely cease.
¹¹A pure-hearted friend,
His speech is gracious;
He has the king for his companion.
¹²The eyes of the LORD watch the wise man;
He subverts the words of the treacherous.
¹³The lazy man says, "There's a lion in the street;
I shall be killed ᵃ⁻if I step outside."⁻ᵃ
¹⁴The mouth of a forbiddenᵇ woman is a deep pit;
He who is doomed by the LORD falls into it.
¹⁵If folly settles in the heart of a lad,
The rod of discipline will remove it.

ᵃ⁻ᵃ *Lit. "in the square."*
ᵇ *Lit. "strange."*

¹⁶To profit by withholding what is due to the poor
Is like making gifts to the rich—pure loss.

¹⁷Incline your ear and listen to the words of the sages;
Pay attention to my wisdom.
¹⁸It is good that you store them inside you,
And that all of them be constantly on your lips,
¹⁹That you may put your trust in the LORD.
I let you know today—yes, you—
²⁰Indeed, I wrote down for you ^{c-}a threefold lore,^{-c}
Wise counsel,
²¹To let you know truly reliable words,
That you may give a faithful reply to him who sent you.
²²Do not rob the wretched because he is wretched;
Do not crush the poor man in the gate;
²³For the LORD will take up their cause
And despoil those who despoil them of life.
²⁴Do not associate with an irascible man,
Or go about with one who is hot-tempered,
²⁵Lest you learn his ways
And find yourself ensnared.
²⁶Do not be one of those who give their hand,
Who stand surety for debts,
²⁷Lest your bed be taken from under you
When you have no money to pay.
²⁸Do not remove the ancient boundary stone
That your ancestors set up.
²⁹See a man skilled at his work—
He shall attend upon kings;
He shall not attend upon ^{c-}obscure men.^{-c}

23 When you sit down to dine with a ruler,
Consider well who is before you.
²Thrust a knife into your gullet
If you have a large appetite.

^{c-c} *Meaning of Heb. uncertain.*

³Do not crave for his dainties,
For they are counterfeit food.

⁴Do not toil to gain wealth;
Have the sense to desist.
⁵You see it, then it is gone;
It grows wings and flies away,
Like an eagle, heavenward.

⁶Do not eat of a stingy man's food;
Do not crave for his dainties;
⁷He is like one keeping accounts;
"Eat and drink," he says to you,
But he does not really mean it.
⁸The morsel you eat you will vomit;
You will waste your courteous words.

⁹Do not speak to a dullard,
For he will disdain your sensible words.
¹⁰Do not remove ancient boundary stones;
Do not encroach upon the field of orphans,
¹¹For they have a mighty Kinsman,
And He will surely take up their cause with you.

¹²Apply your mind to discipline
And your ears to wise sayings.
¹³Do not withhold discipline from a child;
If you beat him with a rod he will not die.
¹⁴Beat him with a rod
And you will save him from the grave.

¹⁵My son, if your mind gets wisdom,
My mind, too, will be gladdened.
¹⁶I shall rejoice with all my heartª
When your lips speak right things.
¹⁷Do not envy sinners in your heart,
But only God-fearing men, at all times,

ª *Lit. "kidneys."*

¹⁸For then you will have a future,
And your hope will never fail.

¹⁹Listen, my son, and get wisdom;
Lead your mind in a [proper] path.
²⁰Do not be of those who guzzle wine,
Or glut themselves on meat;
²¹For guzzlers and gluttons will be impoverished,
And drowsing will clothe you in tatters.

²²Listen to your father who begot you;
Do not disdain your mother when she is old.
²³Buy truth and never sell it,
And wisdom, discipline, and understanding.
²⁴The father of a righteous man will exult;
He who begets a wise son will rejoice in him.
²⁵Your father and mother will rejoice;
She who bore you will exult.
²⁶Give your mind to me, my son;
Let your eyes watch my ways.
²⁷A harlot is a deep pit;
A forbidden^b woman is a narrow well.
²⁸She too lies in wait as if for prey,
And destroys the unfaithful among men.

²⁹Who cries, "Woe!" who, "Alas!";
Who has quarrels, who complaints;
Who has wounds without cause;
Who has bleary eyes?
³⁰Those whom wine keeps till the small hours,
Those who gather to drain the cups.
³¹Do not ogle that red wine
As it lends its color to the cup,
As it flows on smoothly;
³²In the end, it bites like a snake;
It spits like a basilisk.
³³Your eyes will see strange sights;

b *Lit. "alien."*

Your heart[c] will speak distorted things.
34You will be like one lying in bed on high seas,
Like one lying [d]on top of the rigging.[-d]
35"They struck me, but I felt no hurt;
They beat me, but I was unaware;
As often as I wake,
I go after it again."

24 Do not envy evil men;
Do not desire to be with them;
2For their hearts[a] talk violence,
And their lips speak mischief.

3A house is built by wisdom,
And is established by understanding;
4By knowledge are its rooms filled
With all precious and beautiful things.

5A wise man is strength;
A knowledgeable man exerts power;
6For by stratagems you wage war,
And victory comes with much planning.

7Wisdom is too lofty for a fool;
He does not open his mouth in the gate.
8He who lays plans to do harm
Is called by men a schemer.
9The schemes of folly are sin,
And a scoffer is an abomination to men.

10If you showed yourself slack in time of trouble,
Wanting in power,
11If you refrained from rescuing those taken off to death,
Those condemned to slaughter—
12If you say, "We knew nothing of it,"
Surely He who fathoms hearts will discern [the truth],
He who watches over your life will know it,
And He will pay each man as he deserves.

---

[c] *See note to 15.28.*
[d-d] *Meaning of Heb. uncertain.*

[a] *See note to 15.28.*

13My son, eat honey, for it is good;
Let its sweet drops be on your palate.
14Know: such is wisdom for your soul;
If you attain it, there is a future;
Your hope will not be cut off.

15Wicked man! Do not lurk by the home of the righteous man;
Do no violence to his dwelling.
16Seven times the righteous man falls and gets up,
While the wicked are tripped by one misfortune.

17If your enemy falls, do not exult;
If he trips, let your heart not rejoice,
18Lest the LORD see it and be displeased,
And avert His wrath from him.

19Do not be vexed by evildoers;
Do not be incensed by the wicked;
20For there is no future for the evil man;
The lamp of the wicked goes out.

21Fear the LORD, my son, and the king,
And do not mix with dissenters,
22For disaster comes from them suddenly;
The doom both decree who can foreknow?

23These also are by the sages:

It is not right to be partial in judgment.
24He who says to the guilty, "You are innocent,"
Shall be cursed by peoples,
Damned by nations;
25But it shall go well with them who decide justly;
Blessings of good things will light upon them.

26Giving a straightforward reply
Is like giving a kiss.
27Put your external affairs in order,

Get ready what you have in the field,
Then build yourself a home.
28Do not be a witness against your fellow without good cause;
Would you mislead with your speech?
29Do not say, "I will do to him what he did to me;
I will pay the man what he deserves."

30I passed by the field of a lazy man,
By the vineyard of a man lacking sense.
31It was all overgrown with thorns;
Its surface was covered with chickweed,
And its stone fence lay in ruins.
32I observed and took it to heart;
I saw it and learned a lesson.
33A bit more sleep, a bit more slumber,
A bit more hugging yourself in bed,
34And poverty will come b-calling upon you,-b
And want, like a man with a shield.

25 These too are proverbs of Solomon, which the men of King Hezekiah of Judah copied:

2It is the glory of God to conceal a matter,
And the glory of a king to plumb a matter.
3Like the heavens in their height, like the earth in its depth,
Is the mind of kings—unfathomable.
4The dross having been separated from the silver,
A vessel emerged for the smith.
5Remove the wicked from the king's presence,
And his throne will be established in justice.
6Do not exalt yourself in the king's presence;
Do not stand in the place of nobles.
7For it is better to be told, "Step up here,"
Than to be degraded in the presence of the great.

Do not let what your eyes have seen
8Be vented rashly in a quarrel;

b-b *Meaning of Heb. uncertain.*

Think[a] of what it will effect in the end,
When your fellow puts you to shame.
9Defend your right against your fellow,
But do not give away the secrets of another,
10Lest he who hears it reproach you,
And your bad repute never end.

11Like golden apples in silver showpieces[b]
Is a phrase well turned.
12Like a ring of gold, a golden ornament,
Is a wise man's reproof in a receptive ear.
13Like the coldness of snow at harvesttime
Is a trusty messenger to those who send him;
He lifts his master's spirits.
14Like clouds, wind—but no rain—
Is one who boasts of gifts not given.
15Through forbearance a ruler may be won over;
A gentle tongue can break bones.
16If you find honey, eat only what you need,
Lest, surfeiting yourself, you throw it up.
17Visit your neighbor sparingly,
Lest he have his surfeit of you and loathe you.
18Like a club, a sword, a sharpened arrow,
Is a man who testifies falsely against his fellow.
19Like a loose tooth and an unsteady leg,
Is a treacherous support in time of trouble.
20Disrobing on a chilly day,
Like vinegar on natron,
Is one who sings songs to a sorrowful soul.

21If your enemy is hungry, give him bread to eat;
If he is thirsty, give him water to drink.
22You will be heaping live coals on his head,
And the LORD will reward you.

23A north wind produces rain,
And whispered words, a glowering face.

a Lit. "Lest."
b Meaning of Heb. uncertain.

24Dwelling in the corner of a roof is better
Than a contentious woman in b-a spacious house.-b
25Like cold water to a parched throat
Is good news from a distant land.
26Like a muddied spring, a ruined fountain,
Is a righteous man fallen before a wicked one.
27It is not good to eat much honey,
b-Nor is it honorable to search for honor.-b
28Like an open city without walls
Is a man whose temper is uncurbed.

26

Like snow in summer and rain at harvesttime,
So honor is not fitting for a dullard.
2As a sparrow must flit and a swallow fly,
So a gratuitous curse must backfire.a
3A whip for a horse and a bridle for a donkey,
And a rod for the back of dullards.
4Do not answer a dullard in accord with his folly,
Else you will become like him.
5Answer a dullard in accord with his folly,
Else he will think himself wise.
6He who sends a message by a dullard
Will wear out legs and b-must put up with-b lawlessness.
7As legs hang limp on a cripple,
So is a proverb in the mouth of dullards.
8Like a pebble in a sling,
So is paying honor to a dullard.
9As a thorn comes to the hand of a drunkard,
So a proverb to the mouth of a dullard.
10c-A master can produce anything,-c
But he who hires a dullard is as one who hires transients.c
11As a dog returns to his vomit,
So a dullard repeats his folly.
12If you see a man who thinks himself wise,
There is more hope for a dullard than for him.

13A lazy man says,

---

a Kethib, *"fail."*
b-b Lit. *"drink."*
c-c *Meaning of Heb. uncertain.*

"There's a cub on the road, a lion in the squares."
14The door turns on its hinge,
And the lazy man on his bed.
15The lazy man buries his hand in the bowl;
He will not even bring it to his mouth.
16The lazy man thinks himself wiser
Than seven men who give good advice.

17A passerby who gets embroiled in someone else's quarrel
Is like one who seizes a dog by its ears.
18Like a madmanᶜ scattering deadly firebrands, arrows,
19Is one who cheats his fellow and says, "I was only joking."

20For lack of wood a fire goes out,
And without a querulous man contention is stilled.
21Charcoal for embers and wood for a fire
And a contentious man for kindling strife.
22The words of a querulous man are bruising;ᶜ
They penetrate one's inmost parts.

23Base silver laid over earthenware
Are ardent lips with an evil mind.
24An enemy dissembles with his speech,
Inwardly he harbors deceit.
25Though he be fair-spoken do not trust him,
For seven abominations are in his mind.
26His hatred may be concealed by dissimulation,
But his evil will be exposed to public view.

27He who digs a pit will fall in it,
And whoever rolls a stone, it will roll back on him.
28A lying tongue hates ᶜthose crushed by it;ᶜ
Smooth speech throws one down.

27

Do not boast of tomorrow,
For you do not know what the day will bring.
²Let the mouth of another praise you, not yours,
The lips of a stranger, not your own.
³A stone has weight, sand is heavy,
But a fool's vexation outweighs them both.
⁴There is the cruelty of fury, the overflowing of anger,
But who can withstand jealousy?
⁵Open reproof is better than concealed love.
⁶Wounds by a loved one are long lasting;
The kisses of an enemy are profuse.
⁷A sated person disdains honey,
But to a hungry man anything bitter seems sweet.
⁸Like a sparrow wandering from its nest
Is a man who wanders from his home.
⁹Oil and incense gladden the heart,
And the sweetness of a friend is better than one's own counsel.
¹⁰Do not desert your friend and your father's friend;
Do not enter your brother's house in your time of misfortune;
A close neighbor is better than a distant brother.
¹¹Get wisdom, my son, and gladden my heart,
That I may have what to answer those who taunt me.
¹²The shrewd man saw trouble and took cover;
The simple kept going and paid the penalty.
¹³Seize his garment, for he stood surety for another;ᵃ
Take it as a pledge, [for he stood surety] for an unfamiliar woman.
¹⁴He who greets his fellow loudly early in the morning
Shall have it reckoned to him as a curse.
¹⁵An endless dripping on a rainy day
And a contentious wife are alike;
¹⁶As soon repress her as repress the wind,
Or declare one's right hand to be oil.
¹⁷As iron sharpens iron
So a man sharpens the witᵇ of his friend.
¹⁸He who tends a fig tree will enjoy its fruit,
And he who cares for his master will be honored.
¹⁹As face answers to face in water,

ᵃ Or "a stranger."
ᵇ Lit. "face."

So does one man's heart to another.
20Sheol and Abaddon cannot be satisfied,
Nor can the eyes of man be satisfied.
21For silver—the crucible, for gold—the furnace,
And a man is tested by his praise.
22Even if you pound the fool in a mortar
With a pestle along with grain,
His folly will not leave him.

23Mind well the looks of your flock;
Pay attention to your herds;
24For property does not last forever,
Or a crown for all generations.
25Grass vanishes, new grass appears,
And the herbage of the hills is gathered in.
26The lambs will provide you with clothing,
The he-goats, the price of a field.
27The goats' milk will suffice for your food,
The food of your household,
And the maintenance of your maids.

28 The wicked flee though no one gives chase,
But the righteous are as confident as a lion.
2When there is rebellion in the land, many are its rulers;
a-But with a man who has understanding and knowledge, stability
will last.-a
3A poor man who withholds what is due to the wretched
Is like a destructive rain that leaves no food.
4Those who forsake instruction praise the wicked,
But those who heed instruction fight them.
5Evil men cannot discern judgment,
But those who seek the LORD discern all things.
6Better is a poor man who lives blamelessly
Than a rich man whose ways are crooked.
7An intelligent son heeds instruction,
But he who keeps company with gluttons disgraces his father.
8He who increases his wealth by loans at discount or interest

a-a Meaning of Heb. uncertain.

Amasses it for one who is generous to the poor.
⁹He who turns a deaf ear to instruction—
His prayer is an abomination.
¹⁰He who misleads the upright into an evil course
Will fall into his own pit,
But the blameless will prosper.
¹¹A rich man is clever in his own eyes,
But a perceptive poor man can see through him.
¹²When the righteous exult there is great glory,
But when the wicked rise up men make themselves scarce.
¹³He who covers up his faults will not succeed;
He who confesses and gives them up will find mercy.
¹⁴Happy is the man who is anxious always,
But he who hardens his heart falls into misfortune.
¹⁵A roaring lion and a prowling bear
Is a wicked man ruling a helpless people.
¹⁶A prince who lacks understanding is very oppressive;
He who spurns ill-gotten gains will live long.
¹⁷A man oppressed by bloodguilt will flee to a pit;
Let none give him support.
¹⁸He who lives blamelessly will be delivered,
But he who is crooked in his ways will fall all at once.
¹⁹He who tills his land will have food in plenty,
But he who pursues vanities will have poverty in plenty.
²⁰A dependable man will receive many blessings,
But one in a hurry to get rich will not go unpunished.
²¹To be partial is not right;
A man may do wrong for a piece of bread.
²²A miserly man runs after wealth;
He does not realize that loss will overtake it.
²³He who reproves a man will in the end
Find more favor than he who flatters him.
²⁴He who robs his father and mother and says, "It is no
  offense,"
Is a companion to vandals.
²⁵A greedy man provokes quarrels,
But he who trusts the LORD shall enjoy prosperity.
²⁶He who trusts his own instinct is a dullard,

But he who lives by wisdom shall escape.
27He who gives to the poor will not be in want,
But he who shuts his eyes will be roundly cursed.
28When the wicked rise up, men go into hiding,
But when they perish the righteous increase.

29 One oft reproved may become stiff-necked,
But he will be suddenly broken beyond repair.
2When the righteous become great the people rejoice,
But when the wicked dominate the people groan.
3A man who loves wisdom brings joy to his father,
But he who keeps company with harlots will lose his wealth.
4By justice a king sustains the land,
But a fraudulent man tears it down.
5A man who flatters his fellow
Spreads a net for his feet.
6An evil man's offenses are a trap for himself,
But the righteous sing out joyously.
7A righteous man is concerned with the cause of the wretched;
A wicked man cannot understand such concern.
8Scoffers inflame a city,
But the wise allay anger.
9When a wise man enters into litigation with a fool
There is ranting and ridicule, but no satisfaction.
10Bloodthirsty men detest the blameless,
But the upright seek them out.
11A dullard vents all his rage,
But a wise man calms it down.
12A ruler who listens to lies,
All his ministers will be wicked.
13A poor man and a fraudulent man meet;
The LORD gives luster to the eyes of both.
14A king who judges the wretched honestly,
His throne will be established forever.
15Rod and reproof produce wisdom,
But a lad out of control is a disgrace to his mother.
16When the wicked increase, offenses increase,

But the righteous will see their downfall.
¹⁷Discipline your son and he will give you peace;
He will gratify you with dainties.
¹⁸For lack of vision a people lose restraint,
But happy is he who heeds instruction.
¹⁹A slave cannot be disciplined by words;
Though he may comprehend, he does not respond.
²⁰If you see a man hasty in speech,
There is more hope for a fool than for him.
²¹A slave pampered from youth
^a-Will come to a bad end.^{-a}
²²An angry man provokes a quarrel;
A hot-tempered man commits many offenses.
²³A man's pride will humiliate him,
But a humble man will obtain honor.
²⁴He who shares with a thief is his own enemy;
He hears the imprecation and does not tell.^b
²⁵A man's fears become a trap for him,
But he who trusts in the LORD shall be safeguarded.
²⁶Many seek audience with a ruler,
But it is from the LORD that a man gets justice.
²⁷The unjust man is an abomination to the righteous,
And he whose way is straight is an abomination to the wicked.

30

The words of Agur son of Jakeh, [man of] Massa; The speech of the man to Ithiel, to Ithiel and Ucal:

²I am brutish, less than a man;
I lack common sense.
³I have not learned wisdom,
Nor do I possess knowledge of the Holy One.
⁴Who has ascended heaven and come down?
Who has gathered up the wind in the hollow of his hand?
Who has wrapped the waters in his garment?
Who has established all the extremities of the earth?
What is his name or his son's name, if you know it?

---

^{a-a} *Meaning of Heb. uncertain.*
^b *Cf. Lev. 5.1.*

⁵Every word of God is pure,
A shield to those who take refuge in Him.
⁶Do not add to His words,
Lest He indict you and you be proved a liar.

⁷Two things I ask of you; do not deny them to me before I die:
⁸Keep lies and false words far from me;
Give me neither poverty nor riches,
But provide me with my daily bread,
⁹Lest, being sated, I renounce, saying,
"Who is the Lord?"
Or, being impoverished, I take to theft
And profaneᵃ the name of my God.
¹⁰Do not inform on a slave to his master,
Lest he curse you and you incur guilt.

¹¹There is a breed of men that brings a curse on its fathers
And brings no blessing to its mothers,
¹²A breed that thinks itself pure,
Though it is not washed of its filth;
¹³A breed so haughty of bearing, so supercilious;
¹⁴A breed whose teeth are swords,
Whose jaws are knives,
Ready to devour the poor of the land,
The needy among men.

¹⁵The leech has two daughters, "Give!" and "Give!"
Three things are insatiable;
Four never say, "Enough!":
¹⁶Sheol, a barren womb,
Earth that cannot get enough water,
And fire which never says, "Enough!"

¹⁷The eye that mocks a father
And disdains the homage due a mother—
The ravens of the brook will gouge it out,
Young eagles will devour it.

ᵃ *Meaning of Heb. uncertain.*

¹⁸Three things are beyond me;
Four I cannot fathom:
¹⁹How an eagle makes its way over the sky;
How a snake makes its way over a rock;
How a ship makes its way through the high seas;
How a man has his way with a maiden.
²⁰Such is the way of an adulteress:
She eats, wipes her mouth,
And says, "I have done no wrong."

²¹The earth shudders at three things,
At four which it cannot bear:
²²A slave who becomes king;
A scoundrel sated with food;
²³A loathsome woman who gets married;
A slave-girl who supplants her mistress.

²⁴Four are among the tiniest on earth,
Yet they are the wisest of the wise:
²⁵Ants are a folk without power,
Yet they prepare food for themselves in summer;
²⁶The badger is a folk without strength,
Yet it makes its home in the rock;
²⁷The locusts have no king,
Yet they all march forth in formation;
²⁸You can catch the lizard[b] in your hand,
Yet it is found in royal palaces.

²⁹There are three that are stately of stride,
Four that carry themselves well:
³⁰The lion is mightiest among the beasts,
And recoils before none;
^{31a-}The greyhound, the he-goat,
The king whom none dares resist.^{-a}

³²If you have been scandalously arrogant,
If you have been a schemer,
Then clap your hand to your mouth.

b *Or "spider."*

³³As milk under pressure produces butter,
And a nose under pressure produces blood,
So patience under pressure produces strife.

31 The words of Lemuel, king of Massa, with which his mother admonished him:

²No, my son!
No, O son of my womb!
No, O son of my vows!
³Do not give your strength to women,
Your vigor,ᵃ ᵇ⁻to those who destroy kings.⁻ᵇ
⁴Wine is not for kings, O Lemuel;
Not for kings to drink,
Nor any strong drink for princes,
⁵Lest they drink and forget what has been ordained,
And infringe on the rights of the poor.
⁶Give strong drink to the hapless
And wine to the embittered.
⁷Let them drink and forget their poverty,
And put their troubles out of mind.
⁸Speak up for the dumb,
For the rights of all the unfortunate.
⁹Speak up, judge righteously,
Champion the poor and the needy.

א ¹⁰What a rare find is a capable wife!
Her worth is far beyond that of rubies.

ב ¹¹Her husband puts his confidence in her,
And lacks no good thing.

ג ¹²She is good to him, never bad,
All the days of her life.

ד ¹³She looks for wool and flax,
And sets her hand to them with a will.

ה ¹⁴She is like a merchant fleet,
Bringing her food from afar.

ᵃ *Lit. "ways."*
ᵇ⁻ᵇ *Meaning of Heb. uncertain.*

ו   ¹⁵She rises while it is still night,
And supplies provisions for her household,
The daily fare of her maids.

ז   ¹⁶She sets her mind on an estate and acquires it;
She plants a vineyard by her own labors.

ח   ¹⁷She girds herself with strength,
c-And performs her tasks with vigor.-c

ט   ¹⁸She seesᵈ that her business thrives;
Her lamp never goes out at night.

י   ¹⁹She sets her hand to the distaff;
Her fingers work the spindle.

כ   ²⁰She gives generously to the poor;
Her hands are stretched out to the needy.

ל   ²¹She is not worried for her household because of snow,
For her whole household is dressed in crimson.

מ   ²²She makes covers for herself;
Her clothing is linen and purple.

נ   ²³Her husband is prominent in the gates,
As he sits among the elders of the land.

ס   ²⁴She makes cloth and sells it,
And offers a girdle to the merchant.

ע   ²⁵She is clothed with strength and splendor;
She looks to the future cheerfully.

פ   ²⁶Her mouth is full of wisdom,
Her tongue with kindly teaching.

צ   ²⁷She oversees the activities of her household
And never eats the bread of idleness.

ק   ²⁸Her children declare her happy;
Her husband praises her,

ר   ²⁹"Many women have done well,
But you surpass them all."

ש   ³⁰Grace is deceptive,
Beauty is illusory;
It is for her fear of the LORD
That a woman is to be praised.

ת   ³¹Extol her for the fruit of her hand,
And let her works praise her in the gates.

c-c *Lit. "And exerts her arms."*
d *Lit. "tastes."*

JOB

1 There was a man in the land of Uz named Job. That man was blameless and upright; he feared God and shunned evil. ²Seven sons and three daughters were born to him; ³his possessions were seven thousand sheep, three thousand camels, five hundred yoke of oxen and five hundred she-asses, and a very large household. That man was wealthier than anyone in the East.

⁴It was the custom of his sons to hold feasts, each on his set day in his own home. They would invite their three sisters to eat and drink with them. ⁵When a round of feast days was over, Job would send word to them to sanctify themselves, and, rising early in the morning, he would make burnt offerings, one for each of them; for Job thought, "Perhaps my children have sinned and blasphemed God in their thoughts." This is what Job always used to do.

⁶One day the divine beings presented themselves before the LORD, ᵃ⁻and the Adversary⁻ᵃ came along with them. ⁷The LORD said to the Adversary, "Where have you been?" The Adversary answered the LORD, "I have been roaming all over the earth." ⁸The LORD said to the Adversary, "Have you noticed My servant Job? There is no one like him on earth, a blameless and upright man who fears God and shuns evil!" ⁹The Adversary answered the LORD, "Does Job not have good reason to fear God? ¹⁰Why, it is You who have fenced him round, him and his household and all that he has. You have blessed his efforts so that his possessions spread out in the land. ¹¹But lay Your hand upon all that he has and he will surely blaspheme You to Your face." ¹²The LORD replied to the Adversary, "See, all that he has is in your power; only do not lay a hand on him." The Adversary departed from the presence of the LORD.

¹³One day, as his sons and daughters were eating and drinking wine in the house of their eldest brother, ¹⁴a messenger came to Job and said, "The oxen were plowing and the she-asses were grazing alongside them

ᵃ⁻ᵃ *Heb.* ha-ṣatan.

15when Sabeans attacked them and carried them off, and put the boys to the sword; I alone have escaped to tell you." 16This one was still speaking when another came and said, "God's fire fell from heaven, took hold of the sheep and the boys, and burned them up; I alone have escaped to tell you." 17This one was still speaking when another came and said, "A Chaldean formation of three columns made a raid on the camels and carried them off and put the boys to the sword; I alone have escaped to tell you." 18This one was still speaking when another came and said, "Your sons and daughters were eating and drinking wine in the house of their eldest brother 19when suddenly a mighty wind came from the wilderness. It struck the four corners of the house so that it collapsed upon the young people and they died; I alone have escaped to tell you."

20Then Job arose, tore his robe, cut off his hair, and threw himself on the ground and worshiped. 21He said, "Naked came I out of my mother's womb, and naked shall I return there; the LORD has given, and the LORD has taken away; blessed be the name of the LORD."

22For all that, Job did not sin nor did he cast reproach on God.

2 One day the divine beings presented themselves before the LORD. The Adversary came along with them to present himself before the LORD. 2The LORD said to the Adversary, "Where have you been?" The Adversary answered the LORD, "I have been roaming all over the earth." 3The LORD said to the Adversary, "Have you noticed My servant Job? There is no one like him on earth, a blameless and upright man who fears God and shuns evil. He still keeps his integrity; so you have incited Me against him to destroy him for no good reason." 4The Adversary answered the LORD, a-"Skin for skin-a—all that a man has he will give up for his life. 5But lay a hand on his bones and his flesh, and he will surely blaspheme You to Your face." 6So the LORD said to the Adversary, "See, he is in your power; only spare his life." 7The Adversary departed from the presence of the LORD and inflicted a severe inflammation on Job from the sole of his foot to the crown of his head. 8He took a potsherd to scratch himself as he sat in ashes. 9His wife said to him, "You still keep your integrity! Blaspheme God and die!" 10But he said to her, "You talk as any shameless woman might talk! Should we accept only good from God and not accept evil?" For all that, Job said nothing sinful.

a-a *Apparently a proverb whose meaning is uncertain.*

11When Job's three friends heard about all these calamities that had befallen him, each came from his home—Eliphaz the Temanite, Bildad the Shuhite, and Zophar the Naamathite. They met together to go and console and comfort him. 12When they saw him from a distance, they could not recognize him, and they broke into loud weeping; each one tore his robe and threw dust into the air onto his head. 13They sat with him on the ground seven days and seven nights. None spoke a word to him for they saw how very great was his suffering.

3 aAfterward, Job began to speak and cursed the day of his birth. 2Job spoke up and said:

> 3Perish the day on which I was born,
> And the night it was announced,
> "A male has been conceived!"
> 4May that day be darkness;
> May God above have no concern for it;
> May light not shine on it;
> 5May darkness and deep gloom reclaim it;
> May a pall lie over it;
> May b-what blackens-b the day terrify it.
> 6May obscurity carry off that night;
> May it not be counted among the days of the year;
> May it not appear in any of its months;
> 7May that night be desolate;
> May no sound of joy be heard in it;
> 8May those who cast spells upon the dayc damn it,
> Those prepared to disable Leviathan;
> 9May its twilight stars remain dark;
> May it hope for light and have none;
> May it not see the glimmerings of the dawn—
> 10Because it did not block my mother's womb,
> And hide trouble from my eyes.
>
> 11Why did I not die at birth,
> Expire as I came forth from the womb?

---

a There are many difficulties in the poetry of Job, making the interpretation of words, verses, and even chapters uncertain. The rubric "Meaning of Heb. uncertain" in this book indicates only some of the extreme instances.

b-b Meaning of Heb. uncertain.

c Or "sea," taking Heb. yom as equivalent of yam; compare the combination of sea with Leviathan in Ps. 74.13, 14 and with Dragon in Job 7.12; cf. also Isa. 27.1.

¹²Why were there knees to receive me,
Or breasts for me to suck?
¹³For now would I be lying in repose, asleep and at rest,
¹⁴With the world's kings and counselors who rebuild ruins for
themselves,
¹⁵Or with nobles who possess gold and who fill their houses
with silver.
¹⁶Or why was I not like a buried stillbirth,
Like babies who never saw the light?
¹⁷There the wicked cease from troubling;
There rest those whose strength is spent.
¹⁸Prisoners are wholly at ease;
They do not hear the taskmaster's voice.
¹⁹Small and great alike are there,
And the slave is free of his master.

²⁰Why does He give light to the sufferer
And life to the bitter in spirit;
²¹To those who wait for death but it does not come,
Who search for it more than for treasure,
²²Who rejoice to exultation,
And are glad to reach the grave;
²³To the man who has lost his way,
Whom God has hedged about?

²⁴My groaning serves as my bread;
My roaring pours forth as water.
²⁵For what I feared has overtaken me;
What I dreaded has come upon me.
²⁶I had no repose, no quiet, no rest,
And trouble came.

4 Then Eliphaz the Temanite said in reply:

²If one ventures a word with you, will it be too much?
But who can hold back his words?

3See, you have encouraged many;
You have strengthened failing hands.
4Your words have kept him who stumbled from falling;
You have braced knees that gave way.
5But now that it overtakes you, it is too much;
It reaches you, and you are unnerved.
6Is not your piety your confidence,
Your integrity your hope?
7Think now, what innocent man ever perished?
Where have the upright been destroyed?
8As I have seen, those who plow evil
And sow mischief reap them.
9They perish by a blast from God,
Are gone at the breath of His nostrils.
10The lion may roar, the cub may howl,
But the teeth of the king of beasts a-are broken.-a
11The lion perishes for lack of prey,
And its whelps are scattered.

12A word came to me in stealth;
My ear caught a whisper of it.
13In thought-filled visions of the night,
When deep sleep falls on men,
14Fear and trembling came upon me,
Causing all my bones to quake with fright.
15A wind passed by me,
Making the hair of my flesh bristle.
16It halted; its appearance was strange to me;
A form loomed before my eyes;
I heard a murmur, a voice,
17"Can mortals be acquitted by God?
Can man be cleared by his Maker?
18If He cannot trust His own servants,
And casts reproacha on His angels,
19How much less those who dwell in houses of clay,
Whose origin is dust,
Who are crushed like the moth,

---

a-a *Meaning of Heb. uncertain.*

²⁰Shattered between daybreak and evening,
Perishing forever, unnoticed.
²¹Their cord is pulled up
And they die, and not with wisdom."

5 Call now! Will anyone answer you?
To whom among the holy beings will you turn?
²Vexation kills the fool;
Passion slays the simpleton.
³I myself saw a fool who had struck roots;
Impulsively, I cursed his home:
⁴May his children be far from success;
May they be oppressed in the gate with none to deliver them;
⁵May the hungry devour his harvest,
^{a-}Carrying it off in baskets;
May the thirsty swallow their wealth.^{-a}
⁶Evil does not grow out of the soil,
Nor does mischief spring from the ground;
⁷For man is born to [do] mischief,
Just as sparks fly upward.

⁸But I would resort to God;
I would lay my case before God,
⁹Who performs great deeds which cannot be fathomed,
Wondrous things without number;
¹⁰Who gives rain to the earth,
And sends water over the fields;
¹¹Who raises the lowly up high,
So that the dejected are secure in victory;
¹²Who thwarts the designs of the crafty,
So that their hands cannot gain success;
¹³Who traps the clever in their own wiles;
The plans of the crafty go awry.
¹⁴By day they encounter darkness,
At noon they grope as in the night.
¹⁵But He saves the needy from the sword of their mouth,
From the clutches of the strong.

^{a-a} *Meaning of Heb. uncertain.*

¹⁶So there is hope for the wretched;
The mouth of wrongdoing is stopped.

¹⁷See how happy is the man whom God reproves;
Do not reject the discipline of the Almighty.
¹⁸He injures, but He binds up;
He wounds, but His hands heal.
¹⁹He will deliver you from six troubles;
In seven no harm will reach you:
²⁰In famine He will redeem you from death,
In war, from the sword.
²¹You will be sheltered from the scourging tongue;
You will have no fear when violence comes.
²²You will laugh at violence and starvation,
And have no fear of wild beasts.
²³For you will have a pact with the rocks in the field,
And the beasts of the field will be your allies.
²⁴You will know that all is well in your tent;
When you visit your wife^b you will never fail.
²⁵You will see that your offspring are many,
Your descendants like the grass of the earth.
²⁶You will come to the grave ^a-in ripe old age,-^a
As shocks of grain are taken away in their season.
²⁷See, we have inquired into this and it is so;
Hear it and accept it.

6 Then Job said in reply:

²If my anguish were weighed,
My full calamity laid on the scales,
³It would be heavier than the sand of the sea;
That is why I spoke recklessly.^a
⁴For the arrows of the Almighty are in me;
My spirit absorbs their poison;
God's terrors are arrayed against me.
⁵Does a wild ass bray when he has grass?
Does a bull bellow over his fodder?

^b *Lit. "home."*

^a *Meaning of Heb. uncertain.*

⁶Can what is tasteless be eaten without salt?
Does ᵃ⁻mallow juice⁻ᵃ have any flavor?
⁷I refuse to touch them;
They are like food when I am sick.

⁸Would that my request were granted,
That God gave me what I wished for;
⁹Would that God consented to crush me,
Loosed His hand and cut me off.
¹⁰Then this would be my consolation,
ᵃ⁻As I writhed in unsparing⁻ᵃ pains:
That I did not ᵇ⁻suppress my words against the Holy One.⁻ᵇ
¹¹What strength have I, that I should endure?
How long have I to live, that I should be patient?
¹²Is my strength the strength of rock?
Is my flesh bronze?
¹³Truly, I cannot help myself;
I have been deprived of resourcefulness.

¹⁴ᵃ⁻A friend owes loyalty to one who fails,
Though he forsakes the fear of the Almighty;⁻ᵃ
¹⁵My comrades are fickle, like a wadi,
Like a bed on which streams once ran.
¹⁶ᵃ⁻They are dark with ice;
Snow obscures them;⁻ᵃ
¹⁷But when they thaw, they vanish;
In the heat, they disappear where they are.
¹⁸Their course twists and turns;
They run into the desert and perish.
¹⁹Caravans from Tema look to them;
Processions from Sheba count on them.
²⁰They are disappointed in their hopes;
When they reach the place, they stand aghast.
²¹So you are as nothing:ᶜ
At the sight of misfortune, you take fright.
²²Did I say to you, "I need your gift;
Pay a bribe for me out of your wealth;
²³Deliver me from the clutches of my enemy;

ᵇ⁻ᵇ *Meaning of Heb. uncertain; others "deny the words of the Holy One."*
ᶜ *Following* kethib, *with Targum; meaning of Heb. uncertain.*

Redeem me from violent men"?
24Teach me; I shall be silent;
Tell me where I am wrong.
25a-How trenchant honest words are;-a
But what sort of reproof comes from you?
26Do you devise words of reproof,
But count a hopeless man's words as wind?
27You would even cast lots over an orphan,
Or barter away your friend.
28Now be so good as to face me;
I will not lie to your face.
29Relent! Let there not be injustice;
Relent! I am still in the right.
30Is injustice on my tongue?
Can my palate not discern evil?

7 Truly man has a term of service on earth;
His days are like those of a hireling—
2Like a slave who longs for [evening's] shadows,
Like a hireling who waits for his wage.
3So have I been allotted months of futility;
Nights of misery have been apportioned to me.
4When I lie down, I think,
"When shall I rise?"
Night a-drags on,-a
And I am sated with tossings till morning twilight.
5My flesh is covered with maggots and clods of earth;
My skin is broken and festering.
6My days fly faster than a weaver's shuttle,
And come to their end b-without hope.-b
7Consider that my life is but wind;
I shall never see happiness again.
8The eye that gazes on me will not see me;
Your eye will seek me, but I shall be gone.
9As a cloud fades away,
So whoever goes down to Sheol does not come up;

a-a *Meaning of Heb. uncertain.*
b-b *Or "when the thread runs out."*

¹⁰He returns no more to his home;
His place does not know him.

¹¹On my part, I will not speak with restraint;
I will give voice to the anguish of my spirit;
I will complain in the bitterness of my soul.
¹²Am I the sea or the Dragon,ᶜ
That You have set a watch over me?
¹³When I think, "My bed will comfort me,
My couch will share my sorrow,"
¹⁴You frighten me with dreams,
And terrify me with visions,
¹⁵Till I prefer strangulation,
Death, to my wasted frame.
¹⁶I am sick of it.
I shall not live forever;
Let me be, for my days are a breath.

¹⁷What is man, that You make much of him,
That You fix Your attention upon him?
¹⁸You inspect him every morning,
Examine him every minute.
¹⁹Will You not look away from me for a while,
Let me be, till I swallow my spittle?
²⁰If I have sinned, what have I done to You,
Watcher of men?
Why make of me Your target,
And a burden to myself?
²¹Why do You not pardon my transgression
And forgive my iniquity?
For soon I shall lie down in the dust;
When You seek me, I shall be gone.

8 Bildad the Shuhite said in reply:

²How long will you speak such things?
Your utterances are a mighty wind!

ᶜ *See note at 3.8.*

³Will God pervert the right?
Will the Almighty pervert justice?
⁴If your sons sinned against Him,
He dispatched them for their transgression.
⁵But if you seek God
And supplicate the Almighty,
⁶If you are blameless and upright,
He will protect you,
And grant well-being to your righteous home.
⁷Though your beginning be small,
In the end you will grow very great.

⁸Ask the generation past,
Study what their fathers have searched out
⁹—For we are of yesterday and know nothing;
Our days on earth are a shadow—
¹⁰Surely they will teach you and tell you,
Speaking out of their understanding.
¹¹Can papyrus thrive without marsh?
Can rushes grow without water?
¹²While still tender, not yet plucked,
They would wither before any other grass.
¹³Such is the fate of all who forget God;
The hope of the impious man comes to naught—
¹⁴Whose confidence is a ⁻ᵃthread of gossamer,⁻ᵃ
Whose trust is a spider's web.
¹⁵He leans on his house—it will not stand;
He seizes hold of it, but it will not hold.
¹⁶He stays fresh even in the sun;
His shoots spring up in his garden;
¹⁷ᵃ⁻His roots are twined around a heap,
They take hold of a house of stones.⁻ᵃ
¹⁸When he is uprooted from his place,
It denies him, [saying,]
"I never saw you."
¹⁹Such is his happy lot;
And from the earth others will grow.
²⁰Surely God does not despise the blameless;

ᵃ⁻ᵃ *Meaning of Heb. uncertain.*

He gives no support to evildoers.
21He will yet fill your mouth with laughter,
And your lips with shouts of joy.
22Your enemies will be clothed in disgrace;
The tent of the wicked will vanish.

9 Job said in reply:

2Indeed I know that it is so:
Man cannot win a suit against God.
3If he insisted on a trial with Him,
He would not answer one charge in a thousand.
4Wise of heart and mighty in power—
Who ever challenged Him and came out whole?—
5Him who moves mountains without their knowing it,
Who overturns them in His anger;
6Who shakes the earth from its place,
Till its pillars quake;
7Who commands the sun not to shine;
Who seals up the stars;
8Who by Himself spread out the heavens,
And trod on the back of the sea;
9Who made the Bear[a] and Orion,
Pleiades, and the chambers of the south wind;
10Who performs great deeds which cannot be fathomed,
And wondrous things without number.
11He passes me by—I do not see Him;
He goes by me, but I do not perceive Him.
12He snatches away—who can stop Him?
Who can say to Him, "What are You doing?"
13God does not restrain His anger;
Under Him Rahab's[b] helpers sink down.
14How then can I answer Him,
Or choose my arguments against Him?
15Though I were in the right, I could not speak out,
But I would plead for mercy with my judge.
16If I summoned Him and He responded,

a Meaning of Heb. uncertain.
b A primeval monster.

I do not believe He would lend me His ear.
17For He crushes me c-for a hair;-c
He wounds me much for no cause.
18He does not let me catch my breath,
But sates me with bitterness.
19If a trial of strength—He is the strong one;
If a trial in court—who will summon Him for me?
20Though I were innocent,
My mouth would condemn me;
Though I were blameless, He would prove me crooked.
21I am blameless—I am distraught;
I am sick of life.
22It is all one; therefore I say,
"He destroys the blameless and the guilty."
23When suddenly a scourge brings death,
He mocks as the innocent fail.
24The earth is handed over to the wicked one;
He covers the eyes of its judges.
If it is not He, then who?

25My days fly swifter than a runner;
They flee without seeing happiness;
26They pass like reed-boats,
Like an eagle swooping onto its prey.
27If I say, "I will forget my complaint;
Abandon my sorrowd and be diverted,"
28I remain in dread of all my suffering;
I know that You will not acquit me.
29It will be I who am in the wrong;
Why then should I waste effort?
30If I washed with soap,
Cleansed my hands with lye,
31You would dip me in muck
Till my clothes would abhor me.
32He is not a man, like me, that I can answer Him,
That we can go to law together.
33No arbiter is between us
To lay his hand on us both.

c-c *With Targum and Peshitta; or "with a storm."*
d *Lit. "face."*

³⁴If He would only take His rod away from me
And not let His terror frighten me,
³⁵Then I would speak out without fear of Him;
For I know myself not to be so.

10

I am disgusted with life;
I will give rein to my complaint,
Speak in the bitterness of my soul.
²I say to God, "Do not condemn me;
Let me know what You charge me with.
³Does it benefit You to defraud,
To despise the toil of Your hands,
While smiling on the counsel of the wicked?
⁴Do You have the eyes of flesh?
Is Your vision that of mere men?
⁵Are Your days the days of a mortal,
Are Your years the years of a man,
⁶That You seek my iniquity
And search out my sin?
⁷You know that I am not guilty,
And that there is none to deliver from Your hand.

⁸"Your hands shaped and fashioned me,
Then destroyed every part of me.
⁹Consider that You fashioned me like clay;
Will You then turn me back into dust?
¹⁰You poured me out like milk,
Congealed me like cheese;
¹¹You clothed me with skin and flesh
And wove me of bones and sinews;
¹²You bestowed on me life and care;
Your providence watched over my spirit.
¹³Yet these things You hid in Your heart;
I know that You had this in mind:
¹⁴To watch me when I sinned
And not clear me of my iniquity;

¹⁵Should I be guilty—the worse for me!
And even when innocent, I cannot lift my head;
So sated am I with shame,
And drenched in my misery.
¹⁶ᵃ⁻It is something to be proud of⁻ᵃ to hunt me like a lion,
To ᵇ⁻show Yourself wondrous through⁻ᵇ me time and again!
¹⁷You keep sending fresh witnesses against me,
Letting Your vexation with me grow.
ᵃ⁻I serve my term and am my own replacement.⁻ᵃ

¹⁸"Why did You let me come out of the womb?
Better had I expired before any eye saw me,
¹⁹Had I been as though I never was,
Had I been carried from the womb to the grave.
²⁰My days are few, so desist!
Leave me alone, let me be diverted a while
²¹Before I depart—never to return—
For the land of deepest gloom;
²²A land whose light is darkness,
All gloom and disarray,
Whose light is like darkness."

11 Then Zophar the Naamathite said in reply:

²Is a multitude of words unanswerable?
Must a loquacious person be right?
³Your prattle may silence men;
You may mock without being rebuked,
⁴And say, "My doctrine is pure,
And I have been innocent in Your sight."
⁵But would that God might speak,
And talk to you Himself.
⁶He would tell you the secrets of wisdom,
ᵃ⁻For there are many sides to sagacity;
And know that God has overlooked for you some of your
 iniquity.⁻ᵃ

ᵃ⁻ᵃ *Meaning of Heb. uncertain.*
ᵇ⁻ᵇ *Or "make sport of"; cf. Pal. Aram. 'afli.*

ᵃ⁻ᵃ *Meaning of Heb. uncertain.*

7Would you discover the mystery of God?
Would you discover the limit of the Almighty?
8Higher than heaven—what can you do?
Deeper than Sheol—what can you know?
9Its measure is longer than the earth
And broader than the sea.
10a-Should He pass by, or confine,
Or call an assembly, who can stop Him?-a
11For He knows deceitful men;
When He sees iniquity, does He not discern it?
12a-A hollow man will get understanding,
When a wild ass is born a man.-a

13But if you direct your mind,
And spread forth your hands toward Him—
14If there is iniquity with you, remove it,
And do not let injustice reside in your tent—
15Then, free of blemish, you will hold your head high,
And, b-when in straits,-b be unafraid.
16You will then put your misery out of mind,
Consider it as water that has flowed past.
17a-Life will be brighter than noon;-a
You will shine, you will be like the morning.
18You will be secure, for there is hope,
a-And, entrenched,-a you will rest secure;
19You will lie down undisturbed;
The great will court your favor.
20But the eyes of the wicked pine away;
Escape is cut off from them;
They have only their last breath to look forward to.

12 Then Job said in reply:

2Indeed, you are the [voice of] the people,
And wisdom will die with you.
3But I, like you, have a mind,

b-b *Heb.* muṣaq; *other Heb. editions* muṣṣaq, *"you will be firm."*

And am not less than you.
Who does not know such things?
⁴I have become a laughingstock to my friend—
"One who calls to God and is answered,
Blamelessly innocent"—a laughingstock.
⁵ᵃ⁻In the thought of the complacent there is contempt for
   calamity;
It is ready for those whose foot slips.⁻ᵃ
⁶Robbers live untroubled in their tents,
And those who provoke God are secure,
ᵃ⁻Those whom God's hands have produced.⁻ᵃ

⁷But ask the beasts, and they will teach you;
The birds of the sky, they will tell you,
⁸Or speak to the earth, it will teach you;
The fish of the sea, they will inform you.
⁹Who among all these does not know
That the hand of the LORD has done this?
¹⁰In His hand is every living soul
And the breath of all mankind.
¹¹Truly, the ear tests arguments
As the palate tastes foods.
¹²Is wisdom in the aged
And understanding in the long-lived?
¹³With Him are wisdom and courage;
His are counsel and understanding.
¹⁴Whatever He tears down cannot be rebuilt;
Whomever He imprisons cannot be set free.
¹⁵When He holds back the waters, they dry up;
When He lets them loose, they tear up the land.
¹⁶With Him are strength and resourcefulness;
Erring and causing to err are from Him.
¹⁷He makes counselors go about naked[b]
And causes judges to go mad.
¹⁸He undoes the belts of kings,
And fastens loincloths on them.
¹⁹He makes priests go about naked,[b]
And leads temple-servants[c] astray.

ᵃ⁻ᵃ *Meaning of Heb. uncertain.*
ᵇ *A sign of madness.*
ᶜ *Cf. Ugaritic ytnm, a class of temple servants; others "the mighty."*

²⁰He deprives trusty men of speech,
And takes away the reason of elders.
²¹He pours disgrace upon great men,
And loosens the belt of the mighty.
²²He draws mysteries out of the darkness,
And brings obscurities to light.
²³He exalts nations, then destroys them;
He expands nations, then leads them away.
²⁴He deranges the leaders of the people,
And makes them wander in a trackless waste.
²⁵They grope without light in the darkness;
He makes them wander as if drunk.

13 My eye has seen all this;
My ear has heard and understood it.
²What you know, I know also;
I am not less than you.
³Indeed, I would speak to the Almighty;
I insist on arguing with God.
⁴But you invent lies;
All of you are quacks.
⁵If you would only keep quiet
It would be considered wisdom on your part.
⁶Hear now my arguments,
Listen to my pleading.
⁷Will you speak unjustly on God's behalf?
Will you speak deceitfully for Him?
⁸Will you be partial toward Him?
Will you plead God's cause?
⁹Will it go well when He examines you?
Will you fool Him as one fools men?
¹⁰He will surely reprove you
If in ᵃ⁻your heartᵃ you are partial toward Him.
¹¹His threat will terrify you,
And His fear will seize you.
¹²Your briefs are emptyᵇ platitudes;
Your responses are unsubstantial.ᶜ

ᵃ⁻ᵃ *Lit. "secret."*
ᵇ *Lit. "ashen."*
ᶜ *Lit. "clayey."*

¹³Keep quiet; I will have my say,
Come what may upon me.
¹⁴How long! I will take my flesh in my teeth;
I will take my life in my hands.
¹⁵ᵈ⁻He may well slay me; I may have no hope;⁻ᵈ
Yet I will argue my case before Him.
¹⁶In this too is my salvation:
That no impious man can come into His presence.

¹⁷Listen closely to my words;
Give ear to my discourse.
¹⁸See now, I have prepared a case;
I know that I will win it.
¹⁹For who is it that would challenge me?
I should then keep silent and expire.
²⁰But two things do not do to me,
So that I need not hide from You:
²¹Remove Your hand from me,
And let not Your terror frighten me.
²²Then summon me and I will respond,
Or I will speak and You reply to me.
²³How many are my iniquities and sins?
Advise me of my transgression and sin.
²⁴Why do You hide Your face,
And treat me like an enemy?
²⁵Will You harass a driven leaf,
Will You pursue dried-up straw,
²⁶That You decree for me bitter things
And make me ᵉ⁻answer for⁻ᵉ the iniquities of my youth,
²⁷That You put my feet in the stocks
And watch all my ways,
ᶠ⁻Hemming in my footsteps?⁻ᶠ
²⁸Man wastes away like a rotten thing,
Like a garment eaten by moths.

14 Man born of woman is short-lived and sated with trouble.
²He blossoms like a flower and withers;

ᵈ⁻ᵈ *So with kethib; others with qere "Though He slay me, yet will I trust in Him."*
ᵉ⁻ᵉ *Lit. "inherit."*
ᶠ⁻ᶠ *Meaning of Heb. uncertain.*

He vanishes like a shadow and does not endure.
³Do You fix Your gaze on such a one?
Will You go to law with me?
⁴ᵃ⁻Who can produce a clean thing out of an unclean one? No
　　one!⁻ᵃ
⁵His days are determined;
You know the number of his months;
You have set him limits that he cannot pass.
⁶Turn away from him, that he may be at ease
Until, like a hireling, he finishes out his day.

⁷There is hope for a tree;
If it is cut down it will renew itself;
Its shoots will not cease.
⁸If its roots are old in the earth,
And its stump dies in the ground,
⁹At the scent of water it will bud
And produce branches like a sapling.
¹⁰But mortals languish and die;
Man expires; where is he?
¹¹The waters of the sea fail,
And the river dries up and is parched.
¹²So man lies down never to rise;
He will awake only when the heavens are no more,
Only then be aroused from his sleep.
¹³O that You would hide me in Sheol,
Conceal me until Your anger passes,
Set me a fixed time to attend to me.
¹⁴If a man dies, can he live again?
All the time of my service I wait
Until my replacement comes.
¹⁵You would call and I would answer You;
You would set Your heart on Your handiwork.
¹⁶Then You would not count my steps,
Or keep watch over my sin.
¹⁷My transgression would be sealed up in a pouch;
You would coat over my iniquity.

ᵃ⁻ᵃ *Meaning of Heb. uncertain.*

¹⁸Mountains collapse and crumble;
Rocks are dislodged from their place.
¹⁹Water wears away stone;
Torrents wash away earth;
So you destroy man's hope,
²⁰You overpower him forever and he perishes;
You alter his visage and dispatch him.
²¹His sons attain honor and he does not know it;
They are humbled and he is not aware of it.
²²He feels only the pain of his flesh,
And his spirit mourns in him.

15 Eliphaz the Temanite said in reply:

²Does a wise man answer with windy opinions,
And fill his belly with the east wind?
³Should he argue with useless talk,
With words that are of no worth?
⁴You subvert piety
And restrain prayer to God.
⁵Your sinfulness dictates your speech,
So you choose crafty language.
⁶Your own mouth condemns you—not I;
Your lips testify against you.

⁷Were you the first man born?
Were you created before the hills?
⁸Have you listened in on the council of God?
Have you sole possession of wisdom?
⁹What do you know that we do not know,
Or understand that we do not?
¹⁰Among us are gray-haired old men,
Older by far than your father.
¹¹Are God's consolations not enough for you,
And His gentle words to you?
¹²How your heart has carried you away,

How your eyes ^{a-}have failed^{-a} you,
¹³That you could vent your anger on God,
And let such words out of your mouth!
¹⁴What is man that he can be cleared of guilt,
One born of woman, that he be in the right?
¹⁵He puts no trust in His holy ones;
The heavens are not guiltless in His sight;
¹⁶What then of one loathsome and foul,
Man, who drinks wrongdoing like water!

¹⁷I will hold forth; listen to me;
What I have seen, I will declare—
¹⁸That which wise men have transmitted from their fathers,
And have not withheld,
¹⁹To whom alone the land was given,
No stranger passing among them:
²⁰The wicked man writhes in torment all his days;
Few years are reserved for the ruthless.
²¹Frightening sounds fill his ears;
When he is at ease a robber falls upon him.
²²He is never sure he will come back from the dark;
A sword stares him in the face.
²³He wanders about for bread—where is it?
He knows that the day of darkness has been readied for him.
²⁴Troubles terrify him, anxiety overpowers him,
Like a king ^{a-}expecting a siege.^{-a}
²⁵For he has raised his arm against God
And played the hero against the Almighty.
²⁶He runs at Him defiantly^b
^{a-}With his thickly bossed shield.
²⁷His face is covered with fat
And his loins with blubber.^{-a}
²⁸He dwells in cities doomed to ruin,
In houses that shall not be lived in,
That are destined to become heaps of rubble.
²⁹He will not be rich;
His wealth will not endure;
^{a-}His produce shall not bend to the earth.^{-a}

---

^{a-a} *Meaning of Heb. uncertain.*
^b *Lit. "with neck."*

30He will never get away from the darkness;
Flames will sear his shoots;
ᵃ⁻He will pass away by the breath of His mouth.
31He will not be trusted;
He will be misled by falsehood,
And falsehood will be his recompense.⁻ᵃ
32He will wither before his time,
His boughs never having flourished.
33He will drop his unripe grapes like a vine;
He will shed his blossoms like an olive tree.
34For the company of the impious is desolate;
Fire consumes the tents of the briber;
35For they have conceived mischief, given birth to evil,
And their womb has produced deceit.

16 Job said in reply:

2I have often heard such things;
You are all mischievous comforters.
3Have windy words no limit?
What afflicts you that you speak on?
4Iwould also talk like you
If you were in my place;
I would barrage you with words,
I would wag my head over you.
5I would encourage you with words,ᵃ
My moving lips would bring relief.
6If I speak, my pain will not be relieved,
And if I do not—what have I lost?
7Now He has truly worn me out;
You have destroyed my whole community.
8You have shriveled me;
My gauntness serves as a witness,
And testifies against me.
9In His anger He tears and persecutes me;
He gnashes His teeth at me;
My foe stabs me with his eyes.

ᵃ Lit. "my mouth."

¹⁰They open wide their mouths at me;
Reviling me, they strike my cheeks;
They inflame themselves against me.
¹¹God hands me over to an evil man,
Thrusts me into the clutches of the wicked.
¹²I had been untroubled, and He broke me in pieces;
He took me by the scruff and shattered me;
He set me up as His target;
¹³His bowmen surrounded me;
He pierced my kidneys; He showed no mercy;
He spilled my bile onto the ground.
¹⁴He breached me, breach after breach;
He rushed at me like a warrior.
¹⁵I sewed sackcloth over my skin;
I ᵇ-buried my glory-ᵇ in the dust.
¹⁶My face is red with weeping;
Darkness covers my eyes
¹⁷ᶜ-For no injustice on my part
And for the purity of my prayer!-ᶜ

¹⁸Earth, do not cover my blood;
Let there be no resting place for my outcry!
¹⁹Surely now my witness is in heaven;
He who can testify for me is on high.
²⁰O my advocates, my fellows,
Before God my eyes shed tears;
²¹Let Him arbitrate between a man and God
As between a man and his fellow.
²²For a few more years will pass,
And I shall go the way of no return.

17 ¹My spirit is crushed, my days run out;
The graveyard waits for me.

²Surely mocking men keep me company,
And with their provocations I close my eyes.
³Come now, stand surety for me!
Who will give his hand on my behalf?
⁴You have hidden understanding from their minds;

ᵇ-ᵇ *Lit. "made my horn enter into."*
ᶜ-ᶜ *Or "Though I did no injustice, / And my prayer was pure."*

Therefore You must not exalt [them].
⁵He informs on his friends for a share [of their property],
And his children's eyes pine away.

⁶He made me a byword among people;
I have become like Tophetᵃ of old.
⁷My eyes fail from vexation;
All shapes seem to me like shadows.
⁸The upright are amazed at this;
The pure are aroused against the impious.
⁹The righteous man holds to his way;
He whose hands are clean grows stronger.
¹⁰But all of you, come back now;
I shall not find a wise man among you.
¹¹My days are done, my tendons severed,
The strings of my heart.
¹²They say that night is day,
That light is here—in the face of darkness.
¹³If I must look forward to Sheol as my home,
And make my bed in the dark place,
¹⁴Say to the Pit, "You are my father,"
To the maggots, "Mother," "Sister"—
¹⁵Where, then, is my hope?
Who can see hope for me?
¹⁶Will it descend to Sheol?
Shall we go down together to the dust?

18 Then Bildad the Shuhite said in reply:

²How long? Put an end to talk!
Consider, and then we shall speak.
³Why are we thought of as brutes,
Regarded by you as stupid?
⁴You who tear yourself to pieces in anger—
Will ᵃ-earth's order be disruptedᵃ for your sake?
Will rocks be dislodged from their place?

ᵃ *That consumed children; cf. Jer. 7.31.*

ᵃ⁻ᵃ *Lit. "the earth be abandoned."*

⁵Indeed, the light of the wicked fails;
The flame of his fire does not shine.
⁶The light in his tent darkens;
His lamp fails him.
⁷His iniquitous strides are hobbled;
His schemes overthrow him.
⁸He is led by his feet into the net;
He walks onto the toils.
⁹The trap seizes his heel;
The noose tightens on him.
¹⁰The rope for him lies hidden on the ground;
His snare, on the path.
¹¹Terrors assault him on all sides
And send his feet flying.
¹²His progeny hunger;
Disaster awaits his wife.ᵇ
¹³The tendons under his skin are consumed;
Death's first-born consumes his tendons.
¹⁴He is torn from the safety of his tent;
Terror marches him to the king.ᶜ
¹⁵It lodges in his desolate tent;
Sulfur is strewn upon his home.
¹⁶His roots below dry up,
And above, his branches wither.
¹⁷All mention of him vanishes from the earth;
He has no name abroad.
¹⁸He is thrust from light to darkness,
Driven from the world.
¹⁹He has no seed or breed among his people,
No survivor where he once lived.
²⁰Generations to come will be appalled at his fate,
As the previous ones are seized with horror.
²¹"These were the haunts of the wicked;
Here was the place of him who knew not God."

ᵇ *Lit. "rib" (cf. Gen. 2.22); or "stumbling."*
ᶜ *Viz., of the netherworld.*

19 Job said in reply:

2How long will you grieve my spirit,
And crush me with words?
3a-Time and again-a you humiliate me,
And are not ashamed to abuse me.
4If indeed I have erred,
My error remains with me.
5Though you are overbearing toward me,
Reproaching me with my disgrace,
6Yet know that God has wronged me;
He has thrown up siege works around me.
7I cry, "Violence!" but am not answered;
I shout, but can get no justice.
8He has barred my way; I cannot pass;
He has laid darkness upon my path.
9He has stripped me of my glory,
Removed the crown from my head.
10He tears down every part of me; I perish;
He uproots my hope like a tree.
11He kindles His anger against me;
He regards me as one of His foes.
12His troops advance together;
They build their road toward me
And encamp around my tent.
13He alienated my kin from me;
My acquaintances disown me.
14My relatives are gone;
My friends have forgotten me.
15My dependents and maidservants regard me as a stranger;
I am an outsider to them.
16I summon my servant but he does not respond;
I must myself entreat him.
17My odor is repulsive to my wife;
I am loathsome to my children.
18Even youngsters disdain me;

a-a Lit. "Ten times."

When I rise, they speak against me.
¹⁹All my bosom friends detest me;
Those I love have turned against me.
²⁰My bones stick to my skin and flesh;
I escape with the skin of my teeth.

²¹Pity me, pity me! You are my friends;
For the hand of God has struck me!
²²Why do you pursue me like God,
ᵇ⁻Maligning me insatiably?⁻ᵇ
²³O that my words were written down;
Would they were inscribed in a record,
²⁴Incised on a rock forever
With iron stylus and lead!
²⁵But I know that my Vindicator lives;
In the end He will testify on earth—
²⁶This, after my skin will have been peeled off.
But I would behold God while still in my flesh,
²⁷I myself, not another, would behold Him;
Would see with my own eyes:
My heartᶜ pines within me.
²⁸You say, "How do we persecute him?
The root of the matter is in him."ᵈ
²⁹Be in fear of the sword,
For [your] fury is iniquity worthy of the sword;
Know there is a judgment!

20 Zophar the Naamathite said in reply:

²In truth, my thoughts urge me to answer
(It is because of my feelings
³When I hear reproof that insults me);
A spirit out of my understanding makes me reply:
⁴Do you not know this, that from time immemorial,
Since man was set on earth,
⁵The joy of the wicked has been brief,
The happiness of the impious, fleeting?

ᵇ⁻ᵇ *Lit. "You are not satisfied with my flesh."*
ᶜ *Lit. "kidneys."*
ᵈ *With many mss. and versions; printed editions, "me."*

6Though he grows as high as the sky,
His head reaching the clouds,
7He perishes forever, like his dung;
Those who saw him will say, "Where is he?"
8He flies away like a dream and cannot be found;
He is banished like a night vision.
9Eyes that glimpsed him do so no more;
They cannot see him in his place any longer.
10His sons ingratiate themselves with the poor;
His own hands must give back his wealth.
11His bones, still full of vigor,
Lie down in the dust with him.
12Though evil is sweet to his taste,
And he conceals it under his tongue;
13Though he saves it, does not let it go,
Holds it inside his mouth,
14His food in his bowels turns
Into asps' venom within him.
15The riches he swallows he vomits;
God empties it out of his stomach.
16He sucks the poison of asps;
The tongue of the viper kills him.
17Let him not enjoy the streams,
The rivers of honey, the brooks of cream.
18He will give back the goods unswallowed;
The value of the riches, undigested.
19Because he crushed and tortured the poor,
He will not build up the house he took by force.
20He will not see his children tranquil;
He will not preserve one of his dear ones.ᵃ
21With no survivor to enjoy it,
His fortune will not prosper.
22When he has all he wants, trouble will come;
Misfortunes of all kinds will batter him.
23Let that fill his belly;
Let Him loose His burning anger at him,
And rain down His weapons upon him.
24Fleeing from iron arrows,

ᵃ *For this meaning of* beṭen *and* ḥamud, *cf. Hos. 9.16.*

He is shot through from a bow of bronze.
25Brandished and run through his body,
The blade, through his gall,
Strikes terror into him.
26Utter darkness waits for his treasured ones;
A fire fanned by no man will consume him;
Who survives in his tent will be crushed.
27Heaven will expose his iniquity;
Earth will rise up against him.
28His household will be cast forth by a flood,
Spilled out on the day of His wrath.
29This is the wicked man's portion from God,
The lot God has ordained for him.

21 Job said in reply:

2Listen well to what I say,
And let that be your consolation.
3Bear with me while I speak,
And after I have spoken, you may mock.
4Is my complaint directed toward a man?
Why should I not lose my patience?
5Look at me and be appalled,
And clap your hand to your mouth.
6When I think of it I am terrified;
My body is seized with shuddering.

7Why do the wicked live on,
Prosper and grow wealthy?
8Their children are with them always,
And they see their children's children.
9Their homes are secure, without fear;
They do not feel the rod of God.
10Their bull breeds and does not fail;
Their cow calves and never miscarries;
11They let their infants run loose like sheep,
And their children skip about.

¹²They sing to the music of timbrel and lute,
And revel to the tune of the pipe;
¹³They spend their days in happiness,
And go down to Sheol in peace.
¹⁴They say to God, "Leave us alone,
We do not want to learn Your ways;
¹⁵What is Shaddai that we should serve Him?
What will we gain by praying to Him?"
¹⁶Their happiness is not their own doing.
(The thoughts of the wicked are beyond me!)
¹⁷How seldom does the lamp of the wicked fail,
Does the calamity they deserve befall them,
Does He apportion [their] lot in anger!
¹⁸Let them become like straw in the wind,
Like chaff carried off by a storm.
¹⁹[You say,] "God is reserving his punishment for his sons";
Let it be paid back to him that he may feel it,
²⁰Let his eyes see his ruin,
And let him drink the wrath of Shaddai!
²¹For what does he care about the fate of his family,
When his number of months runs out?
²²Can God be instructed in knowledge,
He who judges from such heights?
²³One man dies in robust health,
All tranquil and untroubled;
²⁴His pails are full of milk;
The marrow of his bones is juicy.
²⁵Another dies embittered,
Never having tasted happiness.
²⁶They both lie in the dust
And are covered with worms.

²⁷Oh, I know your thoughts,
And the tactics you will devise against me.
²⁸You will say, "Where is the house of the great man—
And where the tent in which the wicked dwelled?"
²⁹You must have consulted the wayfarers;
You cannot deny their evidence.

³⁰For the evil man is spared on the day of calamity,
On the day when wrath is led forth.
³¹Who will upbraid him to his face?
Who will requite him for what he has done?
³²He is brought to the grave,
While a watch is kept at his tomb.
³³The clods of the wadi are sweet to him,
Everyone follows behind him,
Innumerable are those who precede him.
³⁴Why then do you offer me empty consolation?
Of your replies only the perfidy remains.

22 Eliphaz the Temanite said in reply:

²Can a man be of use to God,
A wise man benefit Him?
³Does Shaddai gain if you are righteous?
Does He profit if your conduct is blameless?
⁴Is it because of your piety that He arraigns you,
And enters into judgment with you?
⁵You know that your wickedness is great,
And that your iniquities have no limit.
⁶You exact pledges from your fellows without reason,
And leave them naked, stripped of their clothes;
⁷You do not give the thirsty water to drink;
You deny bread to the hungry.
⁸The land belongs to the strong;
The privileged occupy it.
⁹You have sent away widows empty-handed;
The strength of the fatherless is broken.
¹⁰Therefore snares are all around you,
And sudden terrors frighten you,
¹¹Or darkness, so you cannot see;
A flood of waters covers you.

¹²God is in the heavenly heights;
See the highest stars, how lofty!

¹³You say, "What can God know?
Can He govern through the dense cloud?
¹⁴The clouds screen Him so He cannot see
As He moves about the circuit of heaven."
¹⁵Have you observed the immemorial path
That evil men have trodden;
¹⁶How they were shriveled up before their time
And their foundation poured out like a river?
¹⁷They said to God, "Leave us alone;
What can Shaddai do about it?"
¹⁸But it was He who filled their houses with good things.
(The thoughts of the wicked are beyond me!)
¹⁹The righteous, seeing it,^a rejoiced;
The innocent laughed with scorn.
²⁰Surely their substance was destroyed,
And their remnant consumed by fire.

²¹Be close to Him and wholehearted;
Good things will come to you thereby.
²²Accept instruction from His mouth;
Lay up His words in your heart.
²³If you return to Shaddai you will be restored,
If you banish iniquity from your tent;
²⁴If you regard treasure as dirt,
Ophir-gold as stones of the wadi,
²⁵And Shaddai be your treasure
And precious silver for you,
²⁶When you seek the favor of Shaddai,
And lift up your face to God,
²⁷You will pray to Him, and He will listen to you,
And you will pay your vows.
²⁸You will decree and it will be fulfilled,
And light will shine upon your affairs.
²⁹When others sink low, you will say it is pride;
For He saves the humble.
³⁰He will deliver the guilty;
He will be delivered through the cleanness of your hands.

---

^a *Referring to v. 16.*

23

Job said in reply:

²Today again my complaint is bitter;
^{a-}My strength is spent^{-a} on account of my groaning.
³Would that I knew how to reach Him,
How to get to His dwelling-place.
⁴I would set out my case before Him
And fill my mouth with arguments.
⁵I would learn what answers He had for me
And know how He would reply to me.
⁶Would He contend with me overbearingly?
Surely He would not accuse me!
⁷There the upright would be cleared by Him,
And I would escape forever from my judge.

⁸But if I go East—He is not there;
West—I still do not perceive Him;
⁹North—since He is concealed, I do not behold Him;
South—He is hidden, and I cannot see Him.
¹⁰But He knows the way I take;
Would He assay me, I should emerge pure as gold.
¹¹I have followed in His tracks,
Kept His way without swerving,
¹²I have not deviated from what His lips commanded;
I have treasured His words more than my daily bread.
¹³He is one; who can dissuade Him?
Whatever He desires, He does.
¹⁴For He will bring my term to an end,
But He has many more such at His disposal.
¹⁵Therefore I am terrified at His presence;
When I consider, I dread Him.
¹⁶God has made me fainthearted;
Shaddai has terrified me.
¹⁷Yet I am not cut off by the darkness;
He has concealed the thick gloom from me.

a-a *Lit. "My hand is heavy."*

24 Why are times for judgment not reserved by Shaddai?
Even those close to Him cannot foresee His actions.[a]
²People remove boundary-stones;
They carry off flocks and pasture them;
³They lead away the donkeys of the fatherless,
And seize the widow's bull as a pledge;
⁴They chase the needy off the roads;
All the poor of the land are forced into hiding.
⁵Like the wild asses of the wilderness,
They go about their tasks, seeking food;
The wilderness provides each with food for his lads;
⁶They harvest fodder in the field,
And glean the late grapes in the vineyards of the wicked.
⁷They pass the night naked for lack of clothing,
They have no covering against the cold;
⁸They are drenched by the mountain rains,
And huddle against the rock for lack of shelter.
⁹[b]They snatch the fatherless infant from the breast,
And seize the child of the poor as a pledge.
¹⁰They go about naked for lack of clothing,
And, hungry, carry sheaves;
¹¹Between rows [of olive trees] they make oil,
And, thirsty, they tread the winepresses.
¹²Men groan in the city;
The souls of the dying cry out;
Yet God does not regard it as a reproach.

¹³They are rebels against the light;
They are strangers to its ways,
And do not stay in its path.
¹⁴The murderer arises [c]in the evening[c]
To kill the poor and needy,
And at night he acts the thief.
¹⁵The eyes of the adulterer watch for twilight,
Thinking, "No one will glimpse me then."
He masks his face.

[a] Lit. "days."
[b] This verse belongs to the description of the wicked in vv. 2–4a.
[c-c] Cf. Mishnaic Heb. 'or, Aramaic 'orta, "evening"; others "with the light."

¹⁶In the dark they break into houses;
By day they shut themselves in;
They do not know the light.
¹⁷For all of them morning is darkness;
It is then that they discern the terror of darkness.
¹⁸ᵈMay they be flotsam on the face of the water;
May their portion in the land be cursed;
May none turn aside by way of their vineyards.
¹⁹May drought and heat snatch away their snow waters,
And Sheol, those who have sinned.
²⁰May the womb forget him;
May he be sweet to the worms;
May he be no longer remembered;
May wrongdoers be broken like a tree.
²¹May he consort with a barren woman who bears no child,
Leave his widow deprived of good.
²²Though he has the strength to seize bulls,
May he live with no assurance of survival.
²³Yet [God] gives him the security on which he relies,
And keeps watch over his affairs.
²⁴Exalted for a while, let them be gone;
Be brought low, and shrivel like mallows,
And wither like the heads of grain.

²⁵Surely no one can confute me,
Or prove that I am wrong.

25 Bildad the Shuhite said in reply:

²Dominion and dread are His;
He imposes peace in His heights.
³Can His troops be numbered?
On whom does His light not shine?
⁴How can man be in the right before God?
How can one born of woman be cleared of guilt?

ᵈ *From here to the end of the chapter the translation is largely conjectural.*

⁵Even the moon is not bright,
And the stars are not pure in His sight.
⁶How much less man, a worm,
The son-of-man, a maggot.

26 Then Job said in reply:

²You would help without having the strength;
You would deliver with arms that have no power.
³Without having the wisdom, you offer advice
And freely give your counsel.
⁴To whom have you addressed words?
Whose breath issued from you?

⁵The shades tremble
Beneath the waters and their denizens.
⁶Sheol is naked before Him;
Abaddon has no cover.
⁷He it is who stretched out Zaphonᵃ over chaos,
Who suspended earth over emptiness.
⁸He wrapped up the waters in His clouds;
Yet no cloud burst under their weight.
⁹ᵇ⁻He shuts off the view of His throne,
Spreading His cloud over it.⁻ᵇ
¹⁰He drew a boundary on the surface of the waters,
At the extreme where light and darkness meet.
¹¹The pillars of heaven tremble,
Astounded at His blast.
¹²By His power He stilled the sea;
By His skill He struck down Rahab.
¹³By His wind the heavens were calmed;
His hand pierced the ᶜ⁻Elusive Serpent.⁻ᶜ
¹⁴These are but glimpses of His rule,
The mere whisper that we perceive of Him;
Who can absorb the thunder of His mighty deeds?

ᵃ Used for heaven; cf. Isa. 14.13; Ps. 48.3.
ᵇ⁻ᵇ Meaning of Heb. uncertain.
ᶜ⁻ᶜ Cf. Isa. 27.1.

27

Job again took up his theme and said:

2By God who has deprived me of justice!
By Shaddai who has embittered my life!
3As long as there is life in me,
And God's breath is in my nostrils,
4My lips will speak no wrong,
Nor my tongue utter deceit.
5Far be it from me to say you are right;
Until I die I will maintain my integrity.
6I persist in my righteousness and will not yield;
a-I shall be free of reproach-a as long as I live.

7May my enemy be as the wicked;
My assailant, as the wrongdoer.
8For what hope has the impious man when he is cut down,
When God takes away his life?
9Will God hear his cry
When trouble comes upon him,
10When he seeks the favor of Shaddai,
Calls upon God at all times?
11I will teach you what is in God's power,
And what is with Shaddai I will not conceal.
12All of you have seen it,
So why talk nonsense?
13This is the evil man's portion from God,
The lot that the ruthless receive from Shaddai:
14Should he have many sons—they are marked for the sword;
His descendants will never have their fill of bread;
15Those who survive him will be buried in a plague,
And their widows will not weep;
16Should he pile up silver like dust,
Lay up clothing like dirt—
17He may lay it up, but the righteous will wear it,
And the innocent will share the silver.
18The house he built is like a bird's nest,

a-a *Meaning of Heb. uncertain.*

Like the booth a watchman makes.
¹⁹He lies down, a rich man, with [his wealth] intact;
When he opens his eyes it is gone.
²⁰Terror overtakes him like a flood;
A storm wind makes off with him by night.
²¹The east wind carries him far away, and he is gone;
It sweeps him from his place.
²²Then it hurls itself at him without mercy;
He tries to escape from its force.
²³It claps its hands at him,
And whistles at him from its place.

28

There is a mine for silver,
And a place where gold is refined.
²Iron is taken out of the earth,
And copper smelted from rock.
³He sets bounds for darkness;
To every limit man probes,
To rocks in deepest darkness.
⁴ᵃ⁻They open up a shaft far from where men live,
[In places] forgotten by wayfarers,
Destitute of men, far removed.⁻ᵃ
⁵Earth, out of which food grows,
Is changed below as if into fire.
⁶Its rocks are a source of sapphires;
It contains gold dust too.
⁷No bird of prey knows the path to it;
The falcon's eye has not gazed upon it.
⁸The proud beasts have not reached it;
The lion has not crossed it.
⁹Man sets his hand against the flinty rock
And overturns mountains by the roots.
¹⁰He carves out channels through rock;
His eyes behold every precious thing.
¹¹He dams up the sources of the streams
So that hidden things may be brought to light.

ᵃ⁻ᵃ *Meaning of Heb. uncertain.*

¹²But where can wisdom be found;
Where is the source of understanding?
¹³No man can set a value on it;
It cannot be found in the land of the living.
¹⁴The deep says, "It is not in me";
The sea says, "I do not have it."
¹⁵It cannot be bartered for gold;
Silver cannot be paid out as its price.
¹⁶The finest gold of Ophir cannot be weighed against it,
Nor precious onyx, nor sapphire.
¹⁷Gold or glass cannot match its value,
Nor vessels of fine gold be exchanged for it.
¹⁸Coral and crystal cannot be mentioned with it;
A pouch of wisdom is better than rubies.
¹⁹Topaz from Nubia cannot match its value;
Pure gold cannot be weighed against it.

²⁰But whence does wisdom come?
Where is the source of understanding?
²¹It is hidden from the eyes of all living,
Concealed from the fowl of heaven.
²²Abaddon and Death say,
"We have only a report of it."
²³God understands the way to it;
He knows its source;
²⁴For He sees to the ends of the earth,
Observes all that is beneath the heavens.
²⁵When He fixed the weight of the winds,
Set the measure of the waters;
²⁶When He made a rule for the rain
And a course for the thunderstorms,
²⁷Then He saw it and gauged it;
He measured it and probed it.
²⁸He said to man,
"See! Fear of the Lord is wisdom;
To shun evil is understanding."

29

Job again took up his theme and said:

²O that I were as in months gone by,
In the days when God watched over me,
³When His lamp shone over my head,
When I walked in the dark by its light,
⁴When I was in my prime,
When God's company graced my tent,
⁵When Shaddai was still with me,
When my lads surrounded me,
⁶When my feet were bathed in cream,
And rocks poured out streams of oil for me.
⁷When I passed through the city gates
To take my seat in the square,
⁸Young men saw me and hid,
Elders rose and stood;
⁹Nobles held back their words;
They clapped their hands to their mouths.
¹⁰The voices of princes were hushed;
Their tongues stuck to their palates.
¹¹The ear that heard me acclaimed me;
The eye that saw, commended me.
¹²For I saved the poor man who cried out,
The orphan who had none to help him.
¹³I received the blessing of the lost;
I gladdened the heart of the widow.
¹⁴I clothed myself in righteousness and it robed me;
Justice was my cloak and turban.
¹⁵I was eyes to the blind
And feet to the lame.
¹⁶I was a father to the needy,
And I looked into the case of the stranger.
¹⁷I broke the jaws of the wrongdoer,
And I wrested prey from his teeth.
¹⁸I thought I would end my days with my family,ᵃ
And ᵇ⁻be as long-lived as the phoenix,⁻ᵇ

ᵃ *Lit. "nest."*
ᵇ⁻ᵇ *Others "multiply days like sand."*

¹⁹My roots reaching water,
And dew lying on my branches;
²⁰My vigor refreshed,
My bow ever new in my hand.
²¹Men would listen to me expectantly,
And wait for my counsel.
²²After I spoke they had nothing to say;
My words were as drops [of dew] upon them.
²³They waited for me as for rain,
For the late rain, their mouths open wide.
²⁴When I smiled at them, they would not believe it;
They never expected^c a sign of my favor.
²⁵I decided their course and presided over them;
I lived like a king among his troops,
Like one who consoles mourners.

30 But now those younger than I deride me,
[Men] whose fathers I would have disdained to put among my
   sheep dogs.
²Of what use to me is the strength of their hands?
All their vigor^a is gone.
³Wasted from want and starvation,
They flee to a parched land,
To the gloom of desolate wasteland.
⁴They pluck saltwort and wormwood;
The roots of broom are their food.
⁵Driven out ^{a-}from society,^{-a}
They are cried at like a thief.
⁶They live in the gullies of wadis,
In holes in the ground, and in rocks,
⁷Braying among the bushes,
Huddling among the nettles,
⁸Scoundrels, nobodies,
Stricken from the earth.

⁹Now I am the butt of their gibes;
I have become a byword to them.

---

^c *Taking* yappilun *as from* pll; *cf. Gen. 48.11.*
^a *Meaning of Heb. uncertain.*

¹⁰They abhor me; they keep their distance from me;
They do not withhold spittle from my face.
¹¹Because God[b] has disarmed[c] and humbled me,
They have thrown off restraint in my presence.
¹²Mere striplings assail me at my right hand;
They put me to flight;
They build their roads for my ruin.
¹³They tear up my path;
They promote my fall,
Although it does them no good.
¹⁴They come as through a wide breach;
They roll in [a-]like raging billows.[-a]
¹⁵Terror tumbles upon me;
It sweeps away my honor like the wind;
My dignity[d] vanishes like a cloud.
¹⁶So now my life runs out;
Days of misery have taken hold of me.
¹⁷By night my bones feel gnawed;
My sinews never rest.
¹⁸[a-]With great effort I change clothing;
The neck of my tunic fits my waist.[-a]
¹⁹He regarded me as clay,
I have become like dust and ashes.

²⁰I cry out to You, but You do not answer me;
I wait, but You do [not] consider me.
²¹You have become cruel to me;
With Your powerful hand You harass me.
²²You lift me up and mount me on the wind;
You make my courage melt.
²³I know You will bring me to death,
The house assigned for all the living.
²⁴[a-]Surely He would not strike at a ruin
If, in calamity, one cried out to Him.[-a]
²⁵Did I not weep for the unfortunate?
Did I not grieve for the needy?
²⁶I looked forward to good fortune, but evil came;
I hoped for light, but darkness came.

b *Lit. "He."*
c *Lit. "loosened my [bow] string."*
d *Heb.* yeshuʿathi *taken as related to* shoaʿ, *"noble."*

²⁷My bowels are in turmoil without respite;
Days of misery confront me.
²⁸I walk about in sunless gloom;
I rise in the assembly and cry out.
²⁹I have become a brother to jackals,
A companion to ostriches.
³⁰My skin, blackened, is peeling off me;
My bones are charred by the heat.
³¹So my lyre is given over to mourning,
My pipe, to accompany weepers.

31 I have covenanted with my eyes
Not to gaze on a maiden.
²What fate is decreed by God above?
What lot, by Shaddai in the heights?
³Calamity is surely for the iniquitous;
Misfortune, for the worker of mischief.
⁴Surely He observes my ways,
Takes account of my every step.

⁵Have I walked with worthless men,
Or my feet hurried to deceit?
⁶Let Him weigh me on the scale of righteousness;
Let God ascertain my integrity.
⁷If my feet have strayed from their course,
My heart followed after my eyes,
And a stain sullied my hands,
⁸May I sow, but another reap,
May the growth of my field be uprooted!
⁹If my heart was ravished by the wife of my neighbor,
And I lay in wait at his door,
¹⁰May my wife grind for another,
May others kneel over her!
¹¹For that would have been debauchery,
A criminal offense,
¹²A fire burning down to Abaddon,
Consuming the roots of all my increase.

¹³Did I ever brush aside the case of my servants, man or maid,
When they made a complaint against me?
¹⁴What then should I do when God arises;
When He calls me to account, what should I answer Him?
¹⁵Did not He who made me in my mother's belly make him?
Did not One form us both in the womb?
¹⁶Did I deny the poor their needs,
Or let aᵃ widow pine away,
¹⁷By eating my food alone,
The fatherless not eating of it also?
¹⁸Why, from my youth he grew up with me as though I were
his father;
Since I left my mother's womb I was herᵇ guide.
¹⁹I never saw an unclad wretch,
A needy man without clothing,
²⁰Whose loins did not bless me
As he warmed himself with the shearings of my sheep.
²¹If I raised my hand against the fatherless,
Looking to my supporters in the gate,
²²May my arm drop off my shoulder;
My forearm break off ᶜ⁻at the elbow.⁻ᶜ
²³For I am in dread of God-sent calamity;
I cannot bear His threat.
²⁴Did I put my reliance on gold,
Or regard fine gold as my bulwark?
²⁵Did I rejoice in my great wealth,
In having attained plenty?
²⁶If ever I saw the light shining,
The moon on its course in full glory,
²⁷And I secretly succumbed,
And my hand touched my mouth in a kiss,
²⁸That, too, would have been a criminal offense,
For I would have denied God above.
²⁹Did I rejoice over my enemy's misfortune?
Did I thrill because evil befell him?
³⁰I never let my mouthᵈ sin
By wishing his death in a curse.
³¹(Indeed, the men of my clan said,

ᵃ Lit. "the eyes of a."
ᵇ Viz., the widow's.
ᶜ⁻ᶜ Lit. "from its shaft," i.e., the humerus.
ᵈ Lit. "palate."

"We would consume his flesh insatiably!")
³²No sojourner spent the night in the open;
I opened my doors to the road.
³³Did I hide my transgressions like Adam,
Bury my wrongdoing in my bosom,
³⁴That I should [now] fear the great multitude,
And am shattered by the contempt of families,
So that I keep silent and do not step outdoors?

³⁵O that I had someone to give me a hearing;
O that Shaddai would reply to my writ,
Or my accuser draw up a true bill!
³⁶I would carry it on my shoulder;
Tie it around me for a wreath.
³⁷I would give him an account of my steps,
Offer it as to a commander.

³⁸If my land cries out against me,
Its furrows weep together;
³⁹If I have eaten its produce without payment,
And made its [rightful] owners despair,
⁴⁰May nettles grow there instead of wheat;
Instead of barley, stinkweed!

The words of Job are at an end.

32 These three men ceased replying to Job, for he considered himself right. ²Then Elihu son of Barachel the Buzite, of the family of Ram, was angry—angry at Job because he thought himself right against God. ³He was angry as well at his three friends, because they found no reply, but merely condemned Job. ⁴Elihu waited out Job's speech, for they were all older than he. ⁵But when Elihu saw that the three men had nothing to reply, he was angry.

⁶Then Elihu son of Barachel the Buzite said in reply:

I have but few years, while you are old;
Therefore I was too awestruck and fearful
To hold forth among you.
7I thought, "Let age speak;
Let advanced years declare wise things."
8But truly it is the spirit in men,
The breath of Shaddai, that gives them understanding.
9It is not the aged who are wise,
The elders, who understand how to judge.
10Therefore I say, "Listen to me;
I too would hold forth."
11Here I have waited out your speeches,
I have given ear to your insights,
While you probed the issues;
12But as I attended to you,
I saw that none of you could argue with Job,
Or offer replies to his statements.
13I fear you will say, "We have found the wise course;
God will defeat him, not man."
14He did not set out his case against me,
Nor shall I use your reasons to reply to him.
15They have been broken and can no longer reply;
Words fail them.
16I have waited till they stopped speaking,
Till they ended and no longer replied.
17Now I also would have my say;
I too would like to hold forth,
18For I am full of words;
The wind in my belly presses me.
19My belly is like wine not yet opened,
Like jugs of new wine ready to burst.
20Let me speak, then, and get relief;
Let me open my lips and reply.
21I would not show regard for any man,
Or temper my speech for anyone's sake;
22For I do not know how to temper my speech—
My Maker would soon carry me off!

33 But now, Job, listen to my words,
Give ear to all that I say.
²Now I open my lips;
My tongue forms words in my mouth.
³My words bespeak the uprightness of my heart;
My lips utter insight honestly.
⁴The spirit of God formed me;
The breath of Shaddai sustains me.
⁵If you can, answer me;
Argue against me, take your stand.
⁶You and I are the same before God;
I too was nipped from clay.
⁷You are not overwhelmed by fear of me;
My pressure does not weigh heavily on you.

⁸Indeed, you have stated in my hearing,
I heard the words spoken,
⁹"I am guiltless, free from transgression;
I am innocent, without iniquity.
¹⁰But He finds reasons to oppose me,
Considers me His enemy.
¹¹He puts my feet in stocks,
Watches all my ways."

¹²In this you are not right;
I will answer you: God is greater than any man.
¹³Why do you complain against Him
That He does not reply to any of man's charges?
¹⁴For God speaks ᵃ-time and again-ᵃ
—Though man does not perceive it—
¹⁵In a dream, a night vision,
When deep sleep falls on men,
While they slumber on their beds.
¹⁶Then He opens men's understanding,
And by disciplining them leaves His signature
¹⁷To turn man away from an action,
To suppress pride in man.

ᵃ-ᵃ Lit. "once . . . twice."

¹⁸He spares him from the Pit,
His person, from perishing by the sword.
¹⁹He is reproved by pains on his bed,
And the trembling in his bones is constant.
²⁰He detests food;
Fine food [is repulsive] to him.
²¹His flesh wastes away till it cannot be seen,
And his bones are rubbed away till they are invisible.
²²He comes close to the Pit,
His life [verges] on death.
²³If he has a representative,
One advocate against a thousand
To declare the man's uprightness,
²⁴Then He has mercy on him and decrees,
"Redeem him from descending to the Pit,
For I have obtained his ransom;
²⁵Let his flesh be healthier^b than in his youth;
Let him return to his younger days."
²⁶He prays to God and is accepted by Him;
He enters His presence with shouts of joy,
For He requites a man for his righteousness.
²⁷He^c declares^b to men,
"I have sinned; I have perverted what was right;
But I was not paid back for it."
²⁸He redeemed ^{d-}him from passing into the Pit;
He-^d will enjoy the light.
²⁹Truly, God does all these things
Two or three times to a man,
³⁰To bring him back from the Pit,
That he may bask in the light of life.

³¹Pay heed, Job, and hear me;
Be still, and I will speak;
³²If you have what to say, answer me;
Speak, for I am eager to vindicate you.
³³But if not, you listen to me;
Be still, and I will teach you wisdom.

---

^b *Meaning of Heb. uncertain.*
^c *I.e., the contrite man.*
^{d-d} *Or with* kethib, *"me . . . I."*

34 Elihu said in reply:

²Listen, O wise men, to my words;
You who have knowledge, give ear to me.
³For the ear tests arguments
As the palate tastes food.
⁴Let us decide for ourselves what is just;
Let us know among ourselves what is good.
⁵For Job has said, "I am right;
God has deprived me of justice.
⁶I declare the judgment against me false;
My arrow-wound is deadly, though I am free from
  transgression."
⁷What man is like Job,
Who drinks mockery like water;
⁸Who makes common cause with evildoers,
And goes with wicked men?
⁹For he says, "Man gains nothing
When he is in God's favor."

¹⁰Therefore, men of understanding, listen to me;
Wickedness be far from God,
Wrongdoing, from Shaddai!
¹¹For He pays a man according to his actions,
And provides for him according to his conduct;
¹²For God surely does not act wickedly;
Shaddai does not pervert justice.
¹³Who placed the earth in His charge?
Who ordered the entire world?
¹⁴If He but intends it,
He can call back His spirit and breath;
¹⁵All flesh would at once expire,
And mankind return to dust.

¹⁶If you would understand, listen to this;
Give ear to what I say.
¹⁷Would one who hates justice govern?
Would you condemn the Just Mighty One?

18Would you call a king a scoundrel,
Great men, wicked?
19He is not partial to princes;
The noble are not preferred to the wretched;
For all of them are the work of His hands.
20Some die suddenly in the middle of the night;
People are in turmoil and pass on;
Even great men are removed—not by human hands.
21For His eyes are upon a man's ways;
He observes his every step.
22Neither darkness nor gloom offers
A hiding-place for evildoers.
23He has no set time for man
To appear before God in judgment.
24He shatters mighty men without number
And sets others in their place.
25Truly, He knows their deeds;
Night is over, and they are crushed.
26He strikes them down with the wicked
Where people can see,
27Because they have been disloyal to Him
And have not understood any of His ways;
28Thus He lets the cry of the poor come before Him;
He listens to the cry of the needy.
29When He is silent, who will condemn?
If He hides His face, who will see Him,
Be it nation or man?
30The impious man rule no more,
Nor do those who ensnare the people.
31Has he said to God,
"I will bear [my punishment] and offend no more.
32What I cannot see You teach me.
If I have done iniquity, I shall not do so again"?
33Should He requite as you see fit?
But you have despised [Him]!
You must decide, not I;
Speak what you know.
34Men of understanding say to me,

Wise men who hear me,
35"Job does not speak with knowledge;
His words lack understanding."
36Would that Job were tried to the limit
For answers which befit sinful men.
37He adds to his sin;
He increases his transgression among us;
He multiplies his statements against God.

35 Elihu said in reply:

2Do you think it just
To say, "I am right against God"?
3If you ask how it benefits you,
"What have I gained from not sinning?"
4I shall give you a reply,
You, along with your friends.
5Behold the heavens and see;
Look at the skies high above you.
6If you sin, what do you do to Him?
If your transgressions are many,
How do you affect Him?
7If you are righteous,
What do you give Him;
What does He receive from your hand?
8Your wickedness affects men like yourself;
Your righteousness, mortals.

9Because of contention the oppressed cry out;
They shout because of the power of the great.
10But none says, "Where is my God, my Maker,
Who gives strength in the night;
11Who gives us more knowledge than the beasts of the earth,
Makes us wiser than the birds of the sky?"
12Then they cry out, but He does not respond
Because of the arrogance of evil men.
13Surely it is false that God does not listen,

That Shaddai does not take note of it.
¹⁴Though you say, "You do not take note of it,"
The case is before Him;
So wait for Him.
¹⁵ᵃ⁻But since now it does not seem so,
He vents his anger;
He does not realize that it may be long drawn out.⁻ᵃ
¹⁶Hence Job mouths empty words,
And piles up words without knowledge.

36 Then Elihu spoke once more.

²Wait a little and let me hold forth;
There is still more to say for God.
³I will make my opinions widely known;
I will justify my Maker.
⁴In truth, my words are not false;
A man of sound opinions is before you.

⁵See, God is mighty; He is not contemptuous;
He is mighty in strength and mind.
⁶He does not let the wicked live;
He grants justice to the lowly.
⁷He does not withdraw His eyes from the righteous;
With kings on thrones
He seats them forever, and they are exalted.
⁸If they are bound in shackles
And caught in trammels of affliction,
⁹He declares to them what they have done,
And that their transgressions are excessive;
¹⁰He opens their understanding by discipline,
And orders them back from mischief.
¹¹If they will serve obediently,
They shall spend their days in happiness,
Their years in delight.
¹²But if they are not obedient,
They shall perish by the sword,

ᵃ⁻ᵃ *Meaning of Heb. uncertain.*

Die for lack of understanding.
¹³But the impious in heart become enraged;
They do not cry for help when He afflicts them.
¹⁴They die in their youth;
[Expire] among the depraved.
¹⁵He rescues the lowly from their affliction,
And opens their understanding through distress.
¹⁶Indeed, He draws you away from the brink of distress
To a broad place where there is no constraint;
Your table is laid out with rich food.
¹⁷You are obsessed with the case of the wicked man,
But the justice of the case will be upheld.
¹⁸Let anger at his affluence not mislead you;
Let much bribery not turn you aside.
¹⁹ᵃ⁻Will your limitless wealth avail you,⁻ᵃ
All your powerful efforts?
²⁰Do not long for the night
When peoples vanish where they are.
²¹Beware! Do not turn to mischief;
Because of that you have been tried by affliction.
²²See, God is beyond reach in His power;
Who governs like Him?
²³Who ever reproached Him for His conduct?
Who ever said, "You have done wrong"?
²⁴Remember, then, to magnify His work,
Of which men have sung,
²⁵Which all men have beheld,
Men have seen, from a distance.
²⁶See, God is greater than we can know;
The number of His years cannot be counted.
²⁷He forms the droplets of water,
Which cluster into rain, from His mist.
²⁸The skies rain;
They pour down on all mankind.
²⁹Can one, indeed, contemplate the expanse of clouds,
The thunderings from His pavilion?
³⁰See, He spreads His lightning over it;

ᵃ⁻ᵃ *Meaning of Heb. uncertain.*

It fills the bed of the sea.
³¹By these things He controls peoples;
He gives food in abundance.
³²Lightning fills His hands;
He orders it to hit the mark.
³³Its noise tells of Him.
ᵃ⁻The kindling of anger against iniquity.⁻ᵃ

37 Because of this, too, my heart quakes,
And leaps from its place.
²Just listen to the noise of His rumbling,
To the sound that comes out of His mouth.
³He lets it loose beneath the entire heavens—
His lightning, to the ends of the earth.
⁴After it, He lets out a roar;
He thunders in His majestic voice.
No one can find a trace of it by the time His voice is heard.
⁵God thunders marvelously with His voice;
He works wonders that we cannot understand.
⁶He commands the snow, "Fall to the ground!"
And the downpour of rain, His mighty downpour of rain,
⁷Is as a sign on every man's hand,
That all men may know His doings.
⁸Then the beast enters its lair,
And remains in its den.
⁹The storm wind comes from its chamber,
And the cold from the constellations.
¹⁰By the breath of God ice is formed,
And the expanse of water becomes solid.
¹¹He also loads the clouds with moisture
And scatters His lightning-clouds.
¹²ᵃ⁻He keeps turning events by His stratagems,⁻ᵃ
That they might accomplish all that He commands them
Throughout the inhabited earth,
¹³Causing each of them to happen to His land,
Whether as a scourge or as a blessing.

ᵃ⁻ᵃ *Meaning of Heb. uncertain.*

¹⁴Give ear to this, Job;
Stop to consider the marvels of God.
¹⁵Do you know what charge God lays upon them
When His lightning-clouds shine?
¹⁶Do you know the marvels worked upon the expanse of clouds
By Him whose understanding is perfect,
¹⁷ᵃ-Why your clothes become hot-ᵃ
When the land is becalmed by the south wind?
¹⁸Can you help him stretch out the heavens,
Firm as a mirror of cast metal?
¹⁹Inform us, then, what we may say to Him;
We cannot argue because [we are in] darkness.
²⁰Is anything conveyed to Him when I speak?
Can a man say anything when he is confused?
²¹Now, then, one cannot see the sun,
Though it be bright in the heavens,
Until the wind comes and clears them [of clouds].
²²By the north wind the golden rays emerge;
The splendor about God is awesome.
²³Shaddai—we cannot attain to Him;
He is great in power and justice
And abundant in righteousness; He does not torment.
²⁴Therefore, men are in awe of Him
Whom none of the wise can perceive.

38

Then the LORD replied to Job out of the tempest and said:

²Who is this who darkens counsel,
Speaking without knowledge?
³Gird your loins like a man;
I will ask and you will inform Me.

⁴Where were you when I laid the earth's foundations?
Speak if you have understanding.
⁵Do you know who fixed its dimensions
Or who measured it with a line?
⁶Onto what were its bases sunk?

Who set its cornerstone
⁷When the morning stars sang together
And all the divine beings shouted for joy?

⁸Who closed the sea behind doors
When it gushed forth out of the womb,
⁹When I clothed it in clouds,
Swaddled it in dense clouds,
¹⁰When I made breakers My limit for it,
And set up its bar and doors,
¹¹And said, "You may come so far and no farther;
Here your surging waves will stop"?

¹²Have you ever commanded the day to break,
Assigned the dawn its place,
¹³So that it seizes the corners of the earth
And shakes the wicked out of it?
¹⁴It changes like clay under the seal
Till [its hues] are fixed like those of a garment.
¹⁵Their light is withheld from the wicked,
And the upraised arm is broken.

¹⁶Have you penetrated to the sources of the sea,
Or walked in the recesses of the deep?
¹⁷Have the gates of death been disclosed to you?
Have you seen the gates of deep darkness?
¹⁸Have you surveyed the expanses of the earth?
If you know of these—tell Me.

¹⁹Which path leads to where light dwells,
And where is the place of darkness,
²⁰That you may take it to its domain
And know the way to its home?
²¹Surely you know, for you were born then,
And the number of your years is many!

²²Have you penetrated the vaults of snow,
Seen the vaults of hail,

23Which I have put aside for a time of adversity,
For a day of war and battle?
24By what path is the west winda dispersed,
The east wind scattered over the earth?
25Who cut a channel for the torrents
And a path for the thunderstorms,
26To rain down on uninhabited land,
On the wilderness where no man is,
27To saturate the desolate wasteland,
And make the crop of grass sprout forth?
28Does the rain have a father?
Who begot the dewdrops?
29From whose belly came forth the ice?
Who gave birth to the frost of heaven?
30Water congeals like stone,
And the surface of the deep compacts.

31Can you tie cords to Pleiades
Or undo the reins of Orion?
32Can you lead out Mazzarothb in its season,
Conduct the Bear with her sons?
33Do you know the laws of heaven
Or impose its authority on earth?

34Can you send up an order to the clouds
For an abundance of water to cover you?
35Can you dispatch the lightning on a mission
And have it answer you, "I am ready"?
36Who put wisdom in the hidden parts?
Who gave understanding to the mind?c
37Who is wise enough to give an account of the heavens?
Who can tilt the bottles of the sky,
38Whereupon the earth melts into a mass,
And its clods stick together.

39Can you hunt prey for the lion,
And satisfy the appetite of the king of beasts?

---

a As Aramaic 'urya.
b Evidently a constellation.
c Or "rooster"; meaning of Heb. uncertain.

⁴⁰They crouch in their dens,
Lie in ambush in their lairs.
⁴¹Who provides food for the raven
When his young cry out to God
And wander about without food?

39 Do you know the season when the mountain goats give birth?
Can you mark the time when the hinds calve?
²Can you count the months they must complete?
Do you know the season they give birth,
³When they couch to bring forth their offspring,
To deliver their young?
⁴Their young are healthy; they grow up in the open;
They leave and return no more.

⁵Who sets the wild ass free?
Who loosens the bonds of the onager,
⁶Whose home I have made the wilderness,
The salt land his dwelling-place?
⁷He scoffs at the tumult of the city,
Does not hear the shouts of the driver.
⁸He roams the hills for his pasture;
He searches for any green thing.

⁹Would the wild ox agree to serve you?
Would he spend the night at your crib?
¹⁰Can you hold the wild ox by ropes to the furrow?
Would he plow up the valleys behind you?
¹¹Would you rely on his great strength
And leave your toil to him?
¹²Would you trust him to bring in the seed
And gather it in from your threshing floor?

¹³The wing of the ostrich beats joyously;
Are her pinions and plumage like the stork's?
¹⁴She leaves her eggs on the ground,

Letting them warm in the dirt,
¹⁵Forgetting they may be crushed underfoot,
Or trampled by a wild beast.
¹⁶Her young are cruelly abandoned as if they were not hers;
Her labor is in vain for lack of concern.
¹⁷For God deprived her of wisdom,
Gave her no share of understanding,
¹⁸Else she would soar on high,
Scoffing at the horse and its rider.

¹⁹Do you give the horse his strength?
Do you clothe his neck with a mane?
²⁰Do you make him quiver like locusts,
His majestic snorting [spreading] terror?
²¹He^a paws with force, he runs with vigor,
Charging into battle.
²²He scoffs at fear; he cannot be frightened;
He does not recoil from the sword.
²³A quiverful of arrows whizzes by him,
And the flashing spear and the javelin.
²⁴Trembling with excitement, he swallows^b the land;
He does not turn aside at the blast of the trumpet.
²⁵As the trumpet sounds, he says, "Aha!"
From afar he smells the battle,
The roaring and shouting of the officers.

²⁶Is it by your wisdom that the hawk grows pinions,
Spreads his wings to the south?
²⁷Does the eagle soar at your command,
Building his nest high,
²⁸Dwelling in the rock,
Lodging upon the fastness of a jutting rock?
²⁹From there he spies out his food;
From afar his eyes see it.
³⁰His young gulp blood;
Where the slain are, there is he.

---

^a *Lit. "They . . ."*
^b *Or "digs up."*

40
The LORD said in reply to Job.

2a-Shall one who should be disciplined complain against
  Shaddai?-a
He who arraigns God must respond.

3Job said in reply to the LORD:

4See, I am of small worth; what can I answer You?
I clap my hand to my mouth.
5I have spoken once, and will not reply;
Twice, and will do so no more.

6Then the LORD replied to Job out of the tempest and said:

7Gird your loins like a man;
I will ask, and you will inform Me.
8Would you impugn My justice?
Would you condemn Me that you may be right?
9Have you an arm like God's?
Can you thunder with a voice like His?
10Deck yourself now with grandeur and eminence;
Clothe yourself in glory and majesty.
11Scatter wide your raging anger;
See every proud man and bring him low.
12See every proud man and humble him,
And bring them down where they stand.
13Bury them all in the earth;
Hide their faces in obscurity.
14Then even I would praise you
For the triumph your right hand won you.

15Take now behemoth, whom I made as I did you;
He eats grass, like the cattle.
16His strength is in his loins,
His might in the muscles of his belly.

a-a Meaning of Heb. uncertain.

17ᵃ⁻He makes his tail stand up⁻ᵃ like a cedar;
The sinews of his thighs are knit together.
18His bones are like tubes of bronze,
His limbs like iron rods.
19He is the first of God's works;
Only his Maker can draw the sword against him.
20The mountains yield him produce,
Where all the beasts of the field play.
21He lies down beneath the lotuses,
In the cover of the swamp reeds.
22The lotuses embower him with shade;
The willows of the brook surround him.
23He can restrain the river from its rushing;
He is confident the streamᵇ will gush at his command.
24Can he be taken by his eyes?
Can his nose be pierced by hooks?
25Can you draw out Leviathan by a fishhook?
Can you press down his tongue by a rope?
26Can you put a ring through his nose,
Or pierce his jaw with a barb?
27Will he plead with you at length?
Will he speak soft words to you?
28Will he make an agreement with you
To be taken as your lifelong slave?
29Will you play with him like a bird,
And tie him down for your girls?
30ᵃ⁻Shall traders traffic in him?⁻ᵃ
Will he be divided up among merchants?
31Can you fill his skin with darts
Or his head with fish-spears?
32Lay a hand on him,
And you will never think of battle again.

41 See, any hope [of capturing] him must be disappointed;
One is prostrated by the very sight of him.
2There is no one so fierce as to rouse him;
Who then can stand up to Me?

ᵇ *Lit. "Jordan."*

3Whoever confronts Me I will requite,
For everything under the heavens is Mine.
4a-I will not be silent concerning him
Or the praise of his martial exploits.-a
5Who can uncover his outer garment?
Who can penetrate the folds of his jowls?
6Who can pry open the doors of his face?
His bared teeth strike terror.
7His protective scales are his pride,
Locked with a binding seal.
8One scale touches the other;
Not even a breath can enter between them.
9Each clings to each;
They are interlocked so they cannot be parted.
10His sneezings flash lightning,
And his eyes are like the glimmerings of dawn.
11Firebrands stream from his mouth;
Fiery sparks escape.
12Out of his nostrils comes smoke
As from a steaming, boiling cauldron.
13His breath ignites coals;
Flames blaze from his mouth.
14Strength resides in his neck;
Power leaps before him.
15The layers of his flesh stick together;
He is as though cast hard; he does not totter.
16His heart is cast hard as a stone,
Hard as the nether millstone.
17Divine beings are in dread as he rears up;
As he crashes down, they cringe.
18No sword that overtakes him can prevail,
Nor spear, nor missile, nor lance.
19He regards iron as straw,
Bronze, as rotted wood.
20No arrow can put him to flight;
Slingstones turn into stubble for him.
21Clubsa are regarded as stubble;
He scoffs at the quivering javelin.

a-a *Meaning of Heb. uncertain.*

²²His underpart is jagged shards;
It spreads a threshing-sledge on the mud.
²³He makes the depths seethe like a cauldron;
He makes the sea [boil] like an ointment-pot.
²⁴His wake is a luminous path;
He makes the deep seem white-haired.
²⁵There is no one on land who can dominate him,
Made as he is without fear.
²⁶He sees all that is haughty;
He is king over all proud beasts.

42 Job said in reply to the LORD:

²I know that You can do everything,
That nothing you propose is impossible for You.
³Who is this who obscures counsel without knowledge?
Indeed, I spoke without understanding
Of things beyond me, which I did not know.
⁴Hear now, and I will speak;
I will ask, and You will inform me.
⁵I had heard You with my ears,
But now I see You with my eyes;
⁶Therefore, I recant and relent,
Being but dust and ashes.

⁷After the LORD had spoken these words to Job, the LORD said to Eliphaz the Temanite, "I am incensed at you and your two friends, for you have not spoken the truth about Me as did My servant Job. ⁸Now take seven bulls and seven rams and go to My servant Job and sacrifice a burnt offering for yourselves. And let Job, My servant, pray for you; for to him I will show favor and not treat you vilely, since you have not spoken the truth about Me as did My servant Job." ⁹Eliphaz the Temanite and Bildad the Shuhite and Zophar the Naamathite went and did as the LORD had told them, and the LORD showed favor to Job. ¹⁰The LORD restored Job's fortunes when he prayed on behalf of his friends, and the LORD gave Job twice what he had before.

¹¹All his brothers and sisters and all his former friends came to him and

had a meal with him in his house. They consoled and comforted him for all the misfortune that the LORD had brought upon him. Each gave him one *kesitah*ᵃ and each one gold ring. ¹²Thus the LORD blessed the latter years of Job's life more than the former. He had fourteen thousand sheep, six thousand camels, one thousand yoke of oxen, and one thousand she-asses. ¹³He also had seven sons and three daughters. ¹⁴The first he named Jemimah, the second Keziah, and the third Keren-happuch. ¹⁵Nowhere in the land were women as beautiful as Job's daughters to be found. Their father gave them estates together with their brothers. ¹⁶Afterward, Job lived one hundred and forty years to see four generations of sons and grandsons. ¹⁷So Job died old and contented.

ᵃ *A unit of unknown value.*

שִׁיר הַשִּׁירִים

THE SONG OF SONGS

1 The Song of Songs, by[a] Solomon.

2 [b-]Oh, give me of the kisses of your mouth,[-b]
For your love is more delightful than wine.
3 Your ointments yield a sweet fragrance,
Your name is like finest[c] oil—
Therefore do maidens love you.
4 Draw me after you, let us run!
[d-]The king has brought me to his chambers.[-d]
Let us delight and rejoice in your love,
Savoring it more than wine—
[e-]Like new wine[-e] they love you!

5 I am dark, but comely,
O daughters of Jerusalem—
Like the tents of Kedar,
Like the pavilions of Solomon.
6 Don't stare at me because I am swarthy,
Because the sun has gazed upon me.
My mother's sons quarreled with me,
They made me guard the vineyards;
My own vineyard I did not guard.

7 Tell me, you whom I love so well;
Where do you pasture your sheep?
Where do you rest them at noon?
Let me not be [c-]as one who strays[-c]
Beside the flocks of your fellows.
8 If you do not know, O fairest of women,

---

a Or "concerning."
b-b Heb. "Let him give me of the kisses of his mouth!"
c Meaning of Heb. uncertain.
d-d Emendation yields "Bring me, O king, to your chambers."
e-e Understanding mesharim as related to tirosh; cf. Aramaic merath.

Go follow the tracks of the sheep,
And graze your kids[f]
By the tents of the shepherds.

[9]I have likened you, my darling,
To a mare in Pharaoh's chariots:
[10]Your cheeks are comely with plaited wreaths,
Your neck with strings of jewels.
[11]We will add wreaths of gold
To your spangles of silver.

[12]While the king was on his couch,
My nard gave forth its fragrance.
[13]My beloved to me is a bag of myrrh
Lodged between my breasts.
[14]My beloved to me is a spray of henna blooms
From the vineyards of En-gedi.

[15]Ah, you are fair, my darling,
Ah, you are fair,
With your dove-like eyes!
[16]And you, my beloved, are handsome,
Beautiful indeed!
Our couch is in a bower;
[17]Cedars are the beams of our house,
Cypresses the rafters.

2

I am a rose[a] of Sharon,
A lily of the valleys.

[2]Like a lily among thorns,
So is my darling among the maidens.

[3]Like an apple tree among trees of the forest,
So is my beloved among the youths.
I delight to sit in his shade,
And his fruit is sweet to my mouth.

[f] *As a pretext for coming.*
[a] *Lit. "crocus."*

⁴He brought me to the banquet room
ᵇ⁻And his banner of love was over me.⁻ᵇ
⁵"Sustain me with raisin cakes,
Refresh me with apples,
For I am faint with love."
⁶His left hand was under my head,
His right arm embraced me.
⁷I adjure you, O maidens of Jerusalem,
By gazelles or by hinds of the field:
Do not wake or rouse
Love until it please!

⁸Hark! My beloved!
There he comes,
Leaping over mountains,
Bounding over hills.
⁹My beloved is like a gazelle
Or like a young stag.
There he stands behind our wall,
Gazing through the window,
Peering through the lattice.
¹⁰My beloved spoke thus to me,
"Arise, my darling;
My fair one, come away!
¹¹For now the winter is past,
The rains are over and gone.
¹²The blossoms have appeared in the land,
The time of pruningᶜ has come;
The song of the turtledove
Is heard in our land.
¹³The green figs form on the fig tree,
The vines in blossom give off fragrance.
Arise, my darling;
My fair one, come away!

¹⁴"O my dove, in the cranny of the rocks,
Hidden by the cliff,
Let me see your face,

ᵇ⁻ᵇ *Meaning of Heb. uncertain.*
ᶜ *Or "singing."*

Let me hear your voice;
For your voice is sweet
And your face is comely."
15Catch us the foxes,
The little foxes
That ruin the vineyards—
For our vineyard is in blossom.

16My beloved is mine
And I am his
Who browses among the lilies.
17When the day d-blows gently-d
And the shadows flee,e
Set out, my beloved,
Swift as a gazelle
Or a young stag,
For the hills of spices!f

3 Upon my couch at nighta
I sought the one I love—
I sought, but found him not.
2"I must rise and roam the town,
Through the streets and through the squares;
I must seek the one I love."
I sought but found him not.
3b-I met the watchmen-b
Who patrol the town.
"Have you seen the one I love?"
4Scarcely had I passed them
When I found the one I love.
I held him fast, I would not let him go
Till I brought him to my mother's house,
To the chamber of her who conceived me
5I adjure you, O maidens of Jerusalem,
By gazelles or by hinds of the field:
Do not wake or rouse
Love until it please!

d-d *Emendation yields "declines"; cf. Jer. 6.4.*
e *Septuagint reads "lengthen"; cf. Jer. 6.4.*
f *Heb.* bather *of uncertain meaning;* 8.14 *reads* besamim, *"spices."*
a *I.e., in a dream.*
b-b *Lit. "The watchmen met me."*

⁶Who is she that comes up from the desert
Like columns of smoke,
In clouds of myrrh and frankincense,
Of all the powders of the merchant?
⁷There is Solomon's couch,
Encircled by sixty warriors
Of the warriors of Israel,
⁸All of them trained^c in warfare,
Skilled in battle,
Each with sword on thigh
Because of terror by night.

⁹King Solomon made him a palanquin
Of wood from Lebanon.
¹⁰He made its posts of silver,
Its back^d of gold,
Its seat of purple wool.
Within, it was decked with ᶜ⁻love
By the maidens of Jerusalem.⁻ᶜ
¹¹O maidens of Zion, go forth
And gaze upon King Solomon
Wearing the crown that his mother
Gave him on his wedding day,
On his day of bliss.

4 Ah, you are fair, my darling,
Ah, you are fair.
Your eyes are like doves
Behind your veil.
Your hair is like a flock of goats
Streaming down Mount Gilead.
²Your teeth are like a flock of ewes^a
Climbing up from the washing pool;
All of them bear twins,
And not one loses her young.
³Your lips are like a crimson thread,
Your mouth is lovely.

ᶜ *Cf. Akkadian aḥāzu, "to learn."*
ᵈ *Meaning of Heb. uncertain.*
ᵉ⁻ᵉ *Emendation yields "ebony, / O maidens of Jerusalem!"*

ᵃ *Cf. 6.6; exact nuance of* qesuboth *uncertain, perhaps "shorn ones."*

Your brow behind your veil
[Gleams] like a pomegranate split open.
4Your neck is like the Tower of David,
Built b-to hold weapons,-b
Hung with a thousand shields—
All the quivers of warriors.
5Your breasts are like two fawns,
Twins of a gazelle,
Browsing among the lilies.
6cWhen the day blows gently
And the shadows flee,
I will betake me to the mount of myrrh,
To the hill of frankincense.
7Every part of you is fair, my darling,
There is no blemish in you
8From Lebanon come with me;
From Lebanon, my bride, with me!
Trip down from Amana's peak,
From the peak of Senird and Hermon,
From the dens of lions,
From the hillse of leopards.

9You have captured my heart,
My own,f my bride,
You have captured my heart
With one [glance] of your eyes,
With one coil of your necklace.
10How sweet is your love,
My own, my bride!
How much more delightful your love than wine,
Your ointments more fragrant
Than any spice!
11Sweetness drops
From your lips, O bride;
Honey and milk
Are under your tongue;
And the scent of your robes
Is like the scent of Lebanon.

b-b *Apparently a poetic figure for jewelry; meaning of Heb. uncertain.*
c *See notes at 2.17.*
d *Cf. Deut. 3.9.*
e *Emendation yields "lairs"; cf. Nah. 2.13.*
f *Lit. "sister"; and so frequently below.*

¹²A garden locked
Is my own, my bride,
A fountain locked,
A sealed-up spring.
¹³Your limbs are an orchard of pomegranates
And of all luscious fruits,
Of henna and of nard—
¹⁴Nard and saffron,
Fragrant reed and cinnamon,
With all aromatic woods,
Myrrh and aloes—
All the choice perfumes.
¹⁵ᵍ-[You are] a garden spring,
A well of fresh water,⁻ᵍ
A rill of Lebanon.

¹⁶Awake, O north wind,
Come, O south wind!
Blow upon my garden,
That its perfume may spread.
Let my beloved come to his garden
And enjoy its luscious fruits!

5 I have come to my garden,
My own, my bride;
I have plucked my myrrh and spice,
Eaten my honey and honeycomb,
Drunk my wine and my milk.

Eat, lovers, and drink:
Drink deep of love!

²ᵃI was asleep,
But my heart was wakeful.
Hark, my beloved knocks!
"Let me in, my own,
My darling, my faultless dove!

ᵍ⁻ᵍ *Emendation yields "The spring in my garden / Is a well of fresh water."*
ᵃ *In vv. 2–8 the maiden relates a dream.*

For my head is drenched with dew,
My locks with the damp of night."
³I had taken off my robe—
Was I to don it again?
I had bathed my feet—
Was I to soil them again?
⁴My beloved ᵇ⁻took his hand off the latch,⁻ᵇ
And my heart was stirred ᶜ⁻for him.⁻ᶜ
⁵I rose to let in my beloved;
My hands dripped myrrh—
My fingers, flowing myrrh—
Upon the handles of the bolt.
⁶I opened the door for my beloved,
But my beloved had turned and gone.
I was faint ᵈ⁻because of what he said.⁻ᵈ
I sought, but found him not;
I called, but he did not answer.
⁷I met the watchmenᵉ
Who patrol the town;
They struck me, they bruised me.
The guards of the walls
Stripped me of my mantle.
⁸I adjure you, O maidens of Jerusalem!
If you meet my beloved, tell him this:
That I am faint with love.

⁹How is your beloved better than another,ᶠ
O fairest of women?
How is your beloved better than anotherᶠ
That you adjure us so?

¹⁰My beloved is clear-skinned and ruddy,
Preeminent among ten thousand.
¹¹His head is finest gold,
His locks are curled
And black as a raven.
¹²His eyes are like doves
By watercourses,

ᵇ⁻ᵇ *Meaning of Heb. uncertain.*
ᶜ⁻ᶜ *Many manuscripts and editions read "within me"* ('alai).
ᵈ⁻ᵈ *Change of vocalization yields "because of him."*
ᵉ *See note at 3.3.*
ᶠ *Or "What sort of beloved is your beloved?"*

Bathed in milk,
b-Set by a brimming pool.-b
13His cheeks are like beds of spices,
g-Banks of -g perfume
His lips are like lilies;
They drip flowing myrrh.
14His hands are rods of gold,
Studded with beryl;
His belly a tablet of ivory,
Adorned with sapphires.
15His legs are like marble pillars
Set in sockets of fine gold.
He is majestic as Lebanon,
Stately as the cedars.
16His mouth is delicious
And all of him is delightful.
Such is my beloved,
Such is my darling,
O maidens of Jerusalem!

6 "Whither has your beloved gone,
O fairest of women?
Whither has your beloved turned?
Let us seek him with you."
2My beloved has gone down to his garden,
To the beds of spices,
To browse in the gardens
And to pick lilies.
3I am my beloved's
And my beloved is mine;
He browses among the lilies.

4You are beautiful, my darling, as Tirzah,
Comely as Jerusalem,
a-Awesome as bannered hosts.-a
5Turn your eyes away from me,
For they overwhelm me!

g-g Septuagint vocalizes as participle, "producing."
a-a Meaning of Heb. uncertain.

Your hair is like a flock of goats
Streaming down from Gilead.
6Your teeth are like a flock of ewes
Climbing up from the washing pool;
All of them bear twins,
And not one loses her young.
7Your brow behind your veil
[Gleams] like a pomegranate split open.
8There are sixty queens,
And eighty concubines,
And damsels without number.
9Only one is my dove,
My perfect one,
The only one of her mother,
The delight of her who bore her.
Maidens see and acclaim her;
Queens and concubines, and praise her.

10Who is she that shines through like the dawn,
Beautiful as the moon,
Radiant as the sun
a-Awesome as bannered hosts?-a

11I went down to the nut grove
To see the budding of the vale;
To see if the vines had blossomed,
If the pomegranates were in bloom.
12a-Before I knew it,
My desire set me
Mid the chariots of Ammi-nadib.-a

7 Turn back, turn back,
O maid of Shulem!
Turn back, turn back,
That we may gaze upon you.
"Why will you gaze at the Shulammite
Ina the Mahanaim dance?"

---

a With many manuscripts and editions; others read "like." Meaning of entire line uncertain.

²How lovely are your feet in sandals,
O daughter of nobles!
Your rounded thighs are like jewels,
The work of a master's hand.
³Your navel is like a round goblet—
Let mixed wine not be lacking!—
Your belly like a heap of wheat
Hedged about with lilies.
⁴Your breasts are like two fawns,
Twins of a gazelle.
⁵Your neck is like a tower of ivory,
Your eyes like pools in Heshbon
By the gate of Bath-rabbim,
Your nose like the Lebanon tower
That faces toward Damascus.
⁶The head upon you is like ᵇ⁻crimson wool,⁻ᵇ
The locks of your head are like purple—
ᶜ⁻A king is held captive in the tresses.⁻ᶜ
⁷How fair you are, how beautiful!
O Love, with all its rapture!
⁸Your stately form is like the palm,
Your breasts are like clusters.
⁹I say: Let me climb the palm,
Let me take hold of its branches;
Let your breasts be like clusters of grapes,
Your breath like the fragrance of apples,
¹⁰And your mouth like choicest wine.
"Let it flow to my beloved as new wineᵈ
ᶜ⁻Gliding over the lips of sleepers."⁻ᶜ

¹¹I am my beloved's,
And his desire is for me.
¹²Come, my beloved,
Let us go into the open;
Let us lodge ᵉ⁻among the henna shrubs.⁻ᵉ
¹³Let us go early to the vineyards;
Let us see if the vine has flowered,
If its blossoms have opened,

ᵇ⁻ᵇ *So Ibn Janah and Ibn Ezra, taking* karmil *as a by-form of* karmil: *cf. 2 Chron. 2.6, 13; 3.14.*
ᶜ⁻ᶜ *Meaning of Heb. uncertain.*
ᵈ *See note at 1.4 end.*
ᵉ⁻ᵉ *Or "in the villages."*

If the pomegranates are in bloom.
There I will give my love to you.
14The mandrakes yield their fragrance,
At our doors are all choice fruits;
Both freshly picked and long-stored
Have I kept, my beloved, for you.

8 If only it could be as with a brother,
As if you had nursed at my mother's breast:
Then I could kiss you
When I met you in the street,
And no one would despise me.
2I would lead you, I would bring you
To the house of my mother,
Of her who taughta me—
I would let you drink of the spiced wine,
Of my pomegranate juice.

3His left hand was under my head,
His right hand caressed me.
4I adjure you, O maidens of Jerusalem:
Do not wake or rouse
Love until it please!

5Who is she that comes up from the desert,
Leaning upon her beloved?

Under the apple tree I roused you;
It was there your mother conceived you,
There she who bore you conceived you.

6Let me be a seal upon your heart,
Like the seal upon your hand.b
For love is fierce as death,
Passion is mighty as Sheol;
Its darts are darts of fire,
A blazing flame.

a Emendation yields "bore"; cf. 6.9; 8.5.
b Lit. "arm."

7Vast floods cannot quench love,
Nor rivers drown it.
If a man offered all his wealth for love,
He would be laughed to scorn.

8"We have a little sister,
Whose breasts are not yet formed.
What shall we do for our sister
When she is spoken for?
9If she be a wall,
We will build upon it a silver battlement;
If she be a door,
We will panel it in cedar."
10I am a wall,
My breasts are like towers.
So I became in his eyes
As one who finds favor.

11Solomon had a vineyard
In Baal-hamon.
He had to post guards in the vineyard:
A man would give for its fruit
A thousand pieces of silver.
12I have my very own vineyard:
You may have the thousand, O Solomon,
And the guards of the fruit two hundred!

13O you who linger in the garden,c
A loverc is listening;
Let me hear your voice.
14"Hurry, my beloved,
Swift as a gazelle or a young stag,
To the hills of spices!"

c Heb. plural. Meaning of verse uncertain.

RUTH

1 In the days when the chieftains[a] ruled, there was a famine in the land; and a man of Bethlehem in Judah, with his wife and two sons, went to reside in the country of Moab. [2]The man's name was Elimelech, his wife's name was Naomi, and his two sons were named Mahlon and Chilion— Ephrathites of Bethlehem in Judah. They came to the country of Moab and remained there.

[3]Elimelech, Naomi's husband, died; and she was left with her two sons. [4]They married Moabite women, one named Orpah and the other Ruth, and they lived there about ten years. [5]Then those two—Mahlon and Chilion—also died; so the woman was left without her two sons and without her husband.

[6]She started out with her daughters-in-law to return from the country of Moab; for in the country of Moab she had heard that the LORD had taken note of His people and given them food. [7]Accompanied by her two daughters-in-law, she left the place where she had been living; and they set out on the road back to the land of Judah.

[8]But Naomi said to her two daughters-in-law, "Turn back, each of you to her mother's house. May the LORD deal kindly with you, as you have dealt with the dead and with me! [9]May the LORD grant that each of you find security in the house of a husband!" And she kissed them farewell. They broke into weeping [10]and said to her, "No, we will return with you to your people."

[11]But Naomi replied, "Turn back, my daughters! Why should you go with me? Have I any more sons in my body who might be husbands for you? [12]Turn back, my daughters, for I am too old to be married. Even if I thought there was hope for me, even if I were married tonight and I also bore sons, [13]should you wait for them to grow up? Should you on their account debar yourselves from marriage? Oh no, my daughters! My lot is far more bitter than yours, for the hand of the LORD has struck out against me."

---

[a] I.e., the leaders who arose in the period before the monarchy; others "judges."

¹⁴They broke into weeping again, and Orpah kissed her mother-in-law farewell. But Ruth clung to her. ¹⁵So she said, "See, your sister-in-law has returned to her people and her gods. Go follow your sister-in-law." ¹⁶But Ruth replied, "Do not urge me to leave you, to turn back and not follow you. For wherever you go, I will go; wherever you lodge, I will lodge; your people shall be my people, and your God my God. ¹⁷Where you die, I will die, and there I will be buried. ᵇ⁻Thus and more may the LORD do to me⁻ᵇ if anything but death parts me from you." ¹⁸When [Naomi] saw how determined she was to go with her, she ceased to argue with her; ¹⁹and the two went on until they reached Bethlehem.

When they arrived in Bethlehem, the whole city buzzed with excitement over them. The women said, "Can this be Naomi?" ²⁰"Do not call me Naomi,"ᶜ she replied. "Call me Mara,ᵈ for Shaddaiᵉ has made my lot very bitter. ²¹I went away full, and the LORD has brought me back empty. How can you call me Naomi, when the LORD has ᶠ⁻dealt harshly with⁻ᶠ me, when Shaddai has brought misfortune upon me!"

²²Thus Naomi returned from the country of Moab; she returned with her daughter-in-law Ruth the Moabite. They arrived in Bethlehem at the beginning of the barley harvest.

2 Now Naomi had a kinsman on her husband's side, a man of substance, of the family of Elimelech, whose name was Boaz.

²Ruth the Moabite said to Naomi, "I would like to go to the fields and glean among the ears of grain, behind someone who may show me kindness." "Yes, daughter, go," she replied; ³and off she went. She came and gleaned in a field, behind the reapers; and, as luck would have it, it was the piece of land belonging to Boaz, who was of Elimelech's family.

⁴Presently Boaz arrived from Bethlehem. He greeted the reapers, "The LORD be with you!" And they responded, "The LORD bless you!" ⁵Boaz said to the servant who was in charge of the reapers, "Whose girl is that?" ⁶The servant in charge of the reapers replied, "She is a Moabite girl who came back with Naomi from the country of Moab. ⁷She said, 'Please let me glean and gather among the sheaves behind the reapers.' She has been on her feet ever since she came this morning. ᵃ⁻She has rested but little in the hut."⁻ᵃ

ᵇ⁻ᵇ *A formula of imprecation.*
ᶜ *I.e., "Pleasantness."*
ᵈ *I.e., "Bitterness."*
ᵉ *Usually rendered "the Almighty."*
ᶠ⁻ᶠ *Others "testified against."*

ᵃ⁻ᵃ *Meaning of Heb. uncertain.*

⁸Boaz said to Ruth, ᵇ⁻"Listen to me, daughter.⁻ᵇ Don't go to glean in another field. Don't go elsewhere, but stay here close to my girls. ⁹Keep your eyes on the field they are reaping, and follow them. I have ordered the men not to molest you. And when you are thirsty, go to the jars and drink some of [the water] that the men have drawn."

¹⁰She prostrated herself with her face to the ground, and said to him, "Why are you so kind as to single me out, when I am a foreigner?"

¹¹Boaz said in reply, "I have been told of all that you did for your mother-in-law after the death of your husband, how you left your father and mother and the land of your birth and came to a people you had not known before. ¹²May the LORD reward your deeds. May you have a full recompense from the LORD, the God of Israel, under whose wings you have sought refuge!"

¹³She answered, "You are most kind, my lord, to comfort me and to speak gently to your maidservant—though I am not so much as one of your maidservants."

¹⁴At mealtime, Boaz said to her, "Come over here and partake of the meal, and dip your morsel in the vinegar." So she sat down beside the reapers. He handed her roasted grain, and she ate her fill and had some left over.

¹⁵When she got up again to glean, Boaz gave orders to his workers, "You are not only to let her glean among the sheaves, without interference, ¹⁶but you must also pull some [stalks] out of the heaps and leave them for her to glean, and not scold her."

¹⁷She gleaned in the field until evening. Then she beat out what she had gleaned—it was about an *ephah* of barley—¹⁸and carried it back with her to the town. When her mother-in-law saw what she had gleaned, and when she also took out and gave her what she had left over after eating her fill, ¹⁹her mother-in-law asked her, "Where did you glean today? Where did you work? Blessed be he who took such generous notice of you!" So she told her mother-in-law whom she had worked with, saying, "The name of the man with whom I worked today is Boaz."

²⁰Naomi said to her daughter-in-law, "Blessed be he of the LORD, who has not failed in His kindness to the living or to the dead! For," Naomi explained to her daughter-in-law, "the man is related to us; he is one of our redeeming kinsmen."ᶜ ²¹Ruth the Moabite said, "He even told me,

---

ᵇ⁻ᵇ *Lit. "Have you not heard, daughter?"*
ᶜ *Cf. Lev. 25.25 and note and Deut. 25.5–6. The fact that Boaz was a kinsman of Ruth's dead husband opened up the possibility of providing an heir for the latter.*

'Stay close by my workers until all my harvest is finished.' " 22And Naomi answered her daughter-in-law Ruth, "It is best, daughter, that you go out with his girls, and not be annoyed in some other field." 23So she stayed close to the maidservants of Boaz, and gleaned until the barley harvest and the wheat harvest were finished. Then she stayed at home with her mother-in-law.

3 Naomi, her mother-in-law, said to her, "Daughter, I must seek a home for you, where you may be happy. 2Now there is our kinsman Boaz, whose girls you were close to. He will be winnowing barley on the threshing floor tonight. 3So bathe, anoint yourself, dress up, and go down to the threshing floor. But do not disclose yourself to the man until he has finished eating and drinking. 4When he lies down, note the place where he lies down, and go over and uncover his feet and lie down. He will tell you what you are to do." 5She replied, "I will do everything you tell me."

6She went down to the threshing floor and did just as her mother-in-law had instructed her. 7Boaz ate and drank, and in a cheerful mood went to lie down beside the grainpile. Then she went over stealthily and uncovered his feet and lay down. 8In the middle of the night, the man gave a start and pulled back—there was a woman lying at his feet!

9"Who are you?" he asked. And she replied, "I am your handmaid Ruth. a-Spread your robe over your handmaid,-a for you are a redeeming kinsman."

10He exclaimed, "Be blessed of the LORD, daughter! Your latest deed of loyalty is greater than the first, in that you have not turned to younger men, whether poor or rich.b 11And now, daughter, have no fear. I will do in your behalf whatever you ask, for all the c-elders of my town-c know what a fine woman you are. 12But while it is true I am a redeeming kinsman, there is another redeemer closer than I. 13Stay for the night. Then in the morning, if he will act as a redeemer, good! let him redeem. But if he does not want to act as redeemer for you, I will do so myself, as the LORD lives! Lie down until morning."

14So she lay at his feet until dawn. She rose before one person could distinguish another, for he thought, "Let it not be known that the woman came to the threshing floor." 15And he said, "Hold out the shawl you are

---

a-a *A formal act of espousal; cf. Ezek. 16.8.*

b *I.e., she sought out a kinsman of her dead husband; see note at 2.20 above. Her first act of loyalty had been to return with Naomi.*

c-c *Lit. "gate of my people."*

wearing." She held it while he measured out six measures of barley, and he put it on her back.

When she[d] got back to the town, [16]she came to her mother-in-law, who asked, "How is it with you, daughter?" She told her all that the man had done for her; [17]and she added, "He gave me these six measures of barley, saying to me, 'Do not go back to your mother-in-law empty-handed.' " [18]And Naomi said, "Stay here, daughter, till you learn how the matter turns out. For the man will not rest, but will settle the matter today."

4 Meanwhile, Boaz had gone to the gate and sat down there. And now the redeemer whom Boaz had mentioned passed by. He called, "Come over and sit down here, So-and-so!" And he came over and sat down. [2]Then [Boaz] took ten elders of the town and said, "Be seated here"; and they sat down.

[3]He said to the redeemer, "Naomi, now returned from the country of Moab, must sell the piece of land which belonged to our kinsman Elimelech. [4]I thought I should disclose the matter to you and say: Acquire it in the presence of those seated here and in the presence of the elders of my people. If you are willing to redeem it, redeem! But if you[a] will not redeem, tell me, that I may know. For there is no one to redeem but you, and I come after you." "I am willing to redeem it," he replied. [5]Boaz continued, "When you acquire the property from Naomi [b-]and from Ruth the Moabite, you must also acquire the wife of the deceased,[-b] so as to perpetuate the name of the deceased upon his estate." [6]The redeemer replied, "Then I cannot redeem it for myself, lest I impair my own estate.[c] You take over my right of redemption, for I am unable to exercise it."

[7]Now this was formerly done in Israel in cases of redemption or exchange: to validate any transaction, one man would take off his sandal and hand it to the other. Such was the practice[d] in Israel. [8]So when the redeemer said to Boaz, "Acquire for yourself," he drew off his sandal. [9]And Boaz said to the elders and to the rest of the people, "You are witnesses today that I am acquiring from Naomi all that belonged to Elimelech and all that belonged to Chilion and Mahlon. [10]I am also acquiring Ruth the Moabite, the wife of Mahlon, as my wife, so as to

---

d *So in many Heb. mss; most mss. read "he."*

a *So many Heb. mss., Septuagint, and Targum; most mss. read "he."*

b-b *Emendation yields "you must also acquire Ruth the Moabite, the wife of the deceased"; cf. v. 10.*

c *I.e., by expending capital for property which will go to the son legally regarded as Mahlon's; see Deut. 25.5–6.*

d *Understanding Heb.* te 'udah *in the sense of the Arabic* 'ādah *and Syriac* 'yādā. *Cf. Ibn Ezra.*

perpetuate the name of the deceased upon his estate, that the name of the deceased may not disappear from among his kinsmen and from the gate of his home town. You are witnesses today."

[11]All the people at the gate and the elders answered, "We are. May the LORD make the woman who is coming into your house like Rachel and Leah, both of whom built up the House of Israel! Prosper in Ephrathah[c] and perpetuate your name in Bethlehem! [12]And may your house be like the house of Perez whom Tamar bore to Judah—through the offspring which the LORD will give you by this young woman."

[13]So Boaz married Ruth; she became his wife, and he cohabited with her. The LORD let her conceive, and she bore a son. [14]And the women said to Naomi, "Blessed be the LORD, who has not withheld a redeemer from you today! May his name be perpetuated in Israel! [15]He will renew your life and sustain your old age; for he is born of your daughter-in-law, who loves you and is better to you than seven sons."

[16]Naomi took the child and held it to her bosom. She became its foster mother, [17]and the women neighbors gave him a name, saying, "A son is born to Naomi!" They named him Obed; he was the father of Jesse, father of David.

[18]This is the line of Perez: Perez begot Hezron, [19]Hezron begot Ram, Ram begot Amminadab, [20]Amminadab begot Nahshon, Nahshon begot Salmon,[f] [21]Salmon begot Boaz, Boaz begot Obed, [22]Obed begot Jesse, and Jesse begot David.

---

[c] *Ephrathah is another name applied to Bethlehem; cf. 1.2; Gen. 35.16, 19; 48.7; Mic. 5.1.*
[f] *Heb. "Salmah."*

LAMENTATIONS

איכה

1 א aAlas!
  Lonely sits the city
  Once great with people!
  She that was great among nations
  Is become like a widow;
  The princess among states
  Is become a thrall.
ב 2Bitterly she weeps in the night,
  Her cheek wet with tears.
  There is none to comfort her
  Of all her friends.
  All her allies have betrayed her;
  They have become her foes.
ג 3Judah has gone into exile
  Because of misery and harsh oppression;
  When she settled among the nations,
  She found no rest;
  All her pursuers overtook her
  b-In the narrow places.-b
ד 4Zion's roads are in mourning,
  Empty of festival pilgrims;
  All her gates are deserted.
  Her priests sigh,
  Her maidens are unhappy—
  She is utterly disconsolate!
ה 5Her enemies are now the masters,
  Her foes are at ease,
  Because the LORD has afflicted her
  For her many transgressions;

---

a *Chaps. 1–4 are alphabetical acrostics, i.e., the verses begin with the successive letters of the Heb.
alphabet. Chap. 3 is a triple acrostic. In chaps. 2–4 the letter pe precedes the ʿayin.*
b-b *Meaning of Heb. uncertain.*

Her infants have gone into captivity
Before the enemy.
ו 6Gone from Fair Zion are all
That were her glory;
Her leaders were like stags
That found no pasture;
They could only walk feebly
Before the pursuer.

ז 7All the precious things she had
In the days of old
Jerusalem recalled
In her days of woe and sorrow,
When her people fell by enemy hands
With none to help her;
When enemies looked on and gloated
Over her downfall.
ח 8Jerusalem has greatly sinned,
Therefore she is become a mockery.
All who admired her despise her,
For they have seen her disgraced;
And she can only sigh
And shrink back.
ט 9Her uncleanness clings to her skirts.
She gave no thought to her future;
She has sunk appallingly,
With none to comfort her.—
See, O LORD, my misery;
How the enemy jeers!
י 10The foe has laid hands
On everything dear to her.
She has seen her Sanctuary
Invaded by nations
Which You have denied admission
Into Your community.
כ 11All her inhabitants sigh
As they search for bread;
They have bartered their treasures for food,
To keep themselves alive.—

See, O LORD, and behold,
c-How abject-c I have become!

ל 12b-May it never befall you,-b
All who pass along the road—
Look about and see:
Is there any agony like mine,
Which was dealt out to me
When the LORD afflicted me
On His day of wrath?

מ 13From above He sent a fire
Down into my bones.
He spread a net for my feet,
He hurled me backward;
He has left me forlorn,
In constant misery.

נ 14dThe yoke of my offenses is bound fast,
Lashed tight by His hand;
Imposed upon my neck,
It saps my strength;
The Lord has delivered me into the hands
Of those I cannot withstand.

ס 15The Lord in my midst has rejected
All my heroes;
He has proclaimed a set time against me
To crush my young men.
As in a press the Lord has trodden
Fair Maiden Judah.

ע 16For these things do I weep,
My eyes flow with tears:
Far from me is any comforter
Who might revive my spirit;
My children are forlorn,
For the foe has prevailed.

פ 17Zion spreads out her hands,
She has no one to comfort her;
The LORD has summoned against Jacob
His enemies all about him;

c-c Or (ironically) "What a glutton"; cf. Prov. 23.20–21.
d Meaning of parts of vv. 14 and 15 uncertain.

Jerusalem has become among them
A thing unclean.

צ ¹⁸The LORD is in the right,
For I have disobeyed Him.
Hear, all you peoples,
And behold my agony:
My maidens and my youths
Have gone into captivity!
ק ¹⁹I cried out to my friends,
But they played me false.
My priests and my elders
Have perished in the city
As they searched for food
To keep themselves alive.
ר ²⁰See, O LORD, the distress I am in!
My heart is in anguish,
ᵉ⁻I know how wrong I wasᵉ
To disobey.
Outside the sword deals death;
Indoors, the plague.
ש ²¹When they heard how I was sighing,
There was none to comfort me;
All my foes heard of my plight and exulted.
For it is Your doing:
ᶠ⁻You have brought on the day that You threatened.
Oh, let them become like me!ᶠ
ת ²²Let all their wrongdoing come before You,
And deal with them
As You have dealt with me
For all my transgressions.
For my sighs are many,
And my heart is sick.

2

א Alas!
The Lord in His wrath
Has shamedᵃ Fair Zion,

ᵉ⁻ᵉ *Lit. "My heart has turned over within me"; cf. Exod. 14.5; Hos. 11.8.*
ᶠ⁻ᶠ *Emendation yields "Oh, bring on them what befell me, / And let them become like me!"*

ᵃ *Meaning of Heb. uncertain.*

Has cast down from heaven to earth
The majesty of Israel.
He did not remember His Footstool[b]
On His day of wrath.

ב   2The Lord has laid waste without pity
All the habitations of Jacob;
He has razed in His anger
Fair Judah's strongholds.
He has brought low in dishonor
The kingdom and its leaders.

ג   3In blazing anger He has cut down
All the might of Israel;
He has withdrawn His right hand
In the presence of the foe;
He has ravaged Jacob like flaming fire,
Consuming on all sides.

ד   4He bent His bow like an enemy,
Poised His right hand like a foe;
He slew all who delighted the eye.
He poured out His wrath like fire
In the Tent of Fair Zion.

ה   5The Lord has acted like a foe,
He has laid waste Israel,
Laid waste all her citadels,
Destroyed her strongholds.
He has increased within Fair Judah
Mourning and moaning.

ו   6He has stripped His Booth[b] like a garden,
He has destroyed His Tabernacle;[c]
The LORD has ended in Zion
Festival and sabbath;
In His raging anger He has spurned
King and priest.

ז   7The Lord has rejected His altar,
Disdained His Sanctuary.
He has handed over to the foe
The walls of its citadels;
They raised a shout in the House of the LORD

b *I.e., the Temple.*
c *Lit. "(Tent of) Meeting."*

As on a festival day.

ח ⁸The LORD resolved to destroy
The wall of Fair Zion;
ᵈ⁻He measured with a line,⁻ᵈ refráined not
From bringing destruction.
He has made wall and rampart to mourn,
Together they languish.

ט ⁹Her gates have sunk into the ground,
He has smashed her bars to bits;
Her king and her leaders are ᵉ⁻in exile,⁻ᵉ
Instructionᶠ is no more;
Her prophets, too, receive
No vision from the LORD.

י ¹⁰Silent sit on the ground
The elders of Fair Zion;
They have strewn dust on their heads
And girded themselves with sackcloth;
The maidens of Jerusalem have bowed
Their heads to the ground.

כ ¹¹My eyes are spent with tears,
My heart is in tumult,
ᵍ⁻My being melts away⁻ᵍ
Over the ruin of ʰ⁻my poor people,⁻ʰ
As babes and sucklings languish
In the squares of the city.

ל ¹²They keep asking their mothers,
"Where is bread and wine?"
As they languish like battle-wounded
In the squares of the town,
As their life runs out
In their mothers' bosoms.

מ ¹³What can I ⁱ⁻take as witness⁻ⁱ or liken
To you, O Fair Jerusalem?
What can I match with you to console you,
O Fair Maiden Zion?
For your ruin is vast as the sea:
Who can heal you?

ᵈ⁻ᵈ *I.e., He made His plans.*
ᵉ⁻ᵉ *Lit. "among the nations."*
ᶠ *Heb. torah, here priestly instruction; cf. Jer. 18.18; Hag. 2.11; Mal. 2.6.*
ᵍ⁻ᵍ *Lit. "My liver spills on the ground."*
ʰ⁻ʰ *Lit. "the daughter of my people"; so elsewhere in poetry.*
ⁱ⁻ⁱ *Emendation yields "compare."*

נ 14Your seers prophesied to you
Delusion and folly.
They did not expose your iniquity
So as to restore your fortunes,
But prophesied to you oracles
Of delusion and deception.

ס 15All who pass your way
Clap their hands at you;
They hiss and wag their head
At Fair Jerusalem:ʲ
"Is this the city that was called
Perfect in Beauty,
Joy of All the Earth?"

פ 16All your enemies
Jeer at you;
They hiss and gnash their teeth,
And cry: "We've ruined her!
Ah, this is the day we hoped for;
ᵏ⁻We have lived to see it!"⁻ᵏ

ע 17The LORD has done what He purposed,
Has carried out the decree
That He ordained long ago;
He has torn down without pity.
He has let the foe rejoice over you,
Has exalted the might of your enemies.

צ 18ˡ⁻Their heart cried out⁻ˡ to the Lord.
O wall of Fair Zion,
Shed tears like a torrent
Day and night!
Give yourself no respite,
Your eyes no rest.

ק 19Arise, cry out in the night
At the beginning of the watches,
Pour out your heart like water
In the presence of the Lord!
Lift up your hands to Him

ⁱ *These gestures were intended to ward off the calamity from the viewer; cf., e.g., Jer. 18.16 and note; Job 27.23.*
ᵏ⁻ᵏ *Lit. "We have attained, we have seen."*
ˡ⁻ˡ *Emendation yields "Cry aloud."*

For the life of your infants,
Who faint for hunger
At every street corner,

ר   ²⁰See, O LORD, and behold,
To whom You have done this!
Alas, women eat their own fruit,
Their new-bornᵐ babes!
Alas, priest and prophet are slain
In the Sanctuary of the Lord!

ש   ²¹Prostrate in the streets lie
Both young and old.
My maidens and youths
Are fallen by the sword;
You slew them on Your day of wrath,
You slaughtered without pity.

ת   ²²You summoned, as on a festival,
My neighbors from roundabout.
On the day of the wrath of the LORD,
None survived or escaped;
Those whom I boreᵐ and reared
My foe has consumed.

3

א   I am the man ᵃ⁻who has known affliction
Underᵃ the rod of His wrath;
²Me He drove on and on
In unrelieved darkness;
³On none but me He brings down His hand
Again and again, without cease.

ב   ⁴He has worn away my flesh and skin;
He has shattered my bones.
⁵All around me He has built
Miseryᵇ and hardship;
⁶He has made me dwell in darkness,
Like those long dead.

ג   ⁷He has walled me in and I cannot break out;
He has weighed me down with chains.

ᵐ *The root has this meaning in Arabic; others "dandled."*

ᵃ⁻ᵃ *Emendation yields "whom the Lord has shepherded with."*
ᵇ *Taking* rosh *as equivalent to* resh.

⁸And when I cry and plead,
He shuts out my prayer;
⁹He has walled in my ways with hewn blocks,
He has made my paths a maze.

ד   ¹⁰He is a lurking bear to me,
A lion in hiding;
¹¹ᶜ⁻He has forced me off my way⁻ᶜ and mangled me,
He has left me numb.
¹²He has bent His bow and made me
The target of His arrows:
ה   ¹³He has shot into my vitals
The shafts of His quiver.
¹⁴I have become a laughingstock to all people,
The butt of their gibes all day long.
¹⁵He has filled me with bitterness,
Sated me with wormwood.

ו   ¹⁶He has broken my teeth on gravel,
Has ground me into the dust.
¹⁷My life was bereft of peace,
I forgot what happiness was.
¹⁸I thought my strength and hope
Had perished before the LORD.
ז   ¹⁹To recall my distress and my misery
Was wormwood and poison;
²⁰Whenever I thought of them,
I was bowed low.

²¹But this do I call to mind,
Therefore I have hope:
ח   ²²The kindness of the LORD has not ended,
His mercies are not spent.
²³They are renewed every morning—
Ample is Your grace!
²⁴"The LORD is my portion," I say with full heart;
Therefore will I hope in Him.
ט   ²⁵The LORD is good to those who trust in Him,

ᶜ⁻ᶜ *Meaning of Heb. uncertain.*

To the one who seeks Him;
²⁶It is good to wait patiently
Till rescue comes from the LORD.
²⁷It is good for a man, when young,
To bear a yoke;

י   ²⁸Let him sit alone and be patient,
When He has laid it upon him.
²⁹Let him put his mouth to the dust—
There may yet be hope.
³⁰Let him offer his cheek to the smiter;
Let him be surfeited with mockery.

כ   ³¹For the Lord does not
Reject forever,
³²But first afflicts, then pardons
In His abundant kindness.
³³For He does not willfully bring grief
Or affliction to man,

ל   ³⁴Crushing under His feet
All the prisoners of the earth.
³⁵To deny a man his rights
In the presence of the Most High,
³⁶To wrong a man in his cause—
This the Lord does not choose.

מ   ³⁷Whose decree was ever fulfilled,
Unless the Lord willed it?
³⁸Is it not at the word of the Most High,
That weal and woe befall?
³⁹Of what shall a living man complain?
Each one of his own sins!

נ   ⁴⁰Let us search and examine our ways,
And turn back to the LORD;
⁴¹Let us lift up our hearts with^d our hands
To God in heaven:
⁴²We have transgressed and rebelled,
And You have not forgiven.

ס   ⁴³You have clothed Yourself in anger and pursued us,
You have slain without pity.

---

^d *Lit. "to"; emendation yields "rather than"; cf. Joel 2.13.*

44You have screened Yourself off with a cloud,
That no prayer may pass through.
45You have made us filth and refuse
In the midst of the peoples.

פ 46All our enemies loudly
Rail against us.
47Panic and pitfall are our lot,
Death and destruction.
48My eyes shed streams of water
Over the ruin of my poor^e people.

ע 49My eyes shall flow without cease,
Without respite,
50f-Until the LORD looks down
And beholds from heaven.
51My eyes have brought me grief-f
Over all the maidens of my city.

צ 52My foes have snared me like a bird,
Without any cause.
53They have ended my life in a pit
And cast stones at me.
54Waters flowed over my head;
I said: I am lost!

ק 55I have called on Your name, O LORD,
From the depths of the Pit.
56Hear my plea;
Do not shut Your ear
To my groan, to my cry!
57You have ever drawn nigh when I called You;
You have said, "Do not fear!"

ר 58You championed my cause, O Lord,
You have redeemed my life.
59You have seen, O LORD, the wrong done me;
Oh, vindicate my right!
60You have seen all their malice,
All their designs against me;

ש 61You have heard, O LORD, their taunts,
All their designs against me,

---

^e Lit. "the daughter of my"; so frequently in poetry.
^{f-f} Emendation yields:
50"Until the LORD looks down from heaven
And beholds
51   my affliction.
     The LORD has brought me grief."

⁶²The mouthings and pratings of my adversaries
Against me all day long.
⁶³See how, at their ease or at work,
I am the butt of their gibes.

ת ⁶⁴Give them, O LORD, their deserts
According to their deeds.
⁶⁵Give them anguishᶜ of heart;
Your curse be upon them!
⁶⁶Oh, pursue them in wrath and destroy them
From under the heavens of the LORD!

4

א Alas!
The gold is dulled,ᵃ
Debased the finest gold!
The sacredᵇ gems are spilled
At every street corner.

ב ²The precious children of Zion;
Once valued as gold—
Alas, they are accounted as earthen pots,
Work of a potter's hands!

ג ³Even jackals offer the breast
And suckle their young;
But my poor people has turned cruel,
Like ostriches of the desert.

ד ⁴The tongue of the suckling cleaves
To its palate for thirst.
Little children beg for bread;
None gives them a morsel.

ה ⁵Those who feasted on dainties
Lie famished in the streets;
Those who were reared in purple
Have embraced refuse heaps.

ו ⁶The guiltᶜ of my poorᵈ people
Exceeded the iniquityᶜ of Sodom,
Which was overthrown in a moment,
Without a hand striking it.

ז ⁷Her elect were purer than snow,

ᵃ Meaning of Heb. uncertain.
ᵇ Emendation yields "precious."
ᶜ I.e., punishment.
ᵈ See note at 3.48.

Whiter than milk;
Their limbs were ruddier than coral,
Their bodies^a were like sapphire.

ח   ⁸Now their faces are blacker than soot,
They are not recognized in the streets;
Their skin has shriveled on their bones,
It has become dry as wood.

ט   ⁹Better off were the slain of the sword
Than those slain by famine,
^{a-}Who pined away, [as though] wounded,
For lack of^{-a} the fruits of the field.

י   ¹⁰With their own hands, tenderhearted women
Have cooked their children;
Such became their fare,
In the disaster of my poor^d people.

כ   ¹¹The Lord vented all His fury,
Poured out His blazing wrath;
He kindled a fire in Zion
Which consumed its foundations.

ל   ¹²The kings of the earth did not believe,
Nor any of the inhabitants of the world,
That foe or adversary could enter
The gates of Jerusalem.

מ   ¹³It was for the sins of her prophets,
The iniquities of her priests,
Who had shed in her midst
The blood of the just.

נ   ¹⁴They wandered blindly through the streets,
Defiled with blood,
So that no one was able
To touch their garments.

ס   ¹⁵"Away! Unclean!" people shouted at them,
"Away! Away! Touch not!"
So they wandered and wandered again;
For the nations had resolved:
"They shall stay here no longer."

פ   ^{16e}The Lord's countenance has turned away from them,

---

^e *Meaning of line uncertain.*

He will look on them no more.
They showed no regard for priests,
No favor to elders.

ע 17Even now our eyes pine away
In vain for deliverance.
As we waited, still we wait
For a nation that cannot help.

צ 18Our steps were checked,
We could not walk f-in our squares.-f
Our doom is near, our days are done—
Alas, our doom has come!

ק 19Our pursuers were swifter
Than the eagles in the sky;
They chased us in the mountains,
Lay in wait for us in the wilderness.

ר 20The breath of our life, the LORD's anointed,
Was captured in their traps—
He in whose shade we had thought
To live among the nations.

ש 21Rejoice and exult, Fair Edom,
Who dwell in the land of Uz!
To you, too, the cup shall pass,
You shall get drunk and expose your nakedness.

ת 22Your iniquity, Fair Zion, is expiated;
He will exile you no longer.
Your iniquity, Fair Edom, He will note;
He will uncover your sins.

5

Remember, O LORD, what has befallen us;
Behold, and see our disgrace!
2Our heritage has passed to aliens,
Our homes to strangers.
3We have become orphans, fatherless;
Our mothers are like widows.
4We must pay to drink our own water,

f-f Or "With long strides."

Obtain our own kindling at a price.
⁵We are hotlyᵃ pursued;
Exhausted, we are given no rest.
⁶We hold out a hand to Egypt;
To Assyria, for our fill of bread.
⁷Our fathers sinned and are no more;
And we must bear their guilt.
⁸Slaves are ruling over us,
With none to rescue us from them.
⁹We get our bread at the peril of our lives,
Because of the ᵇ⁻sword of the wilderness.⁻ᵇ
¹⁰Our skin glows like an oven,
With the fever of famine.
¹¹Theyᶜ have ravished women in Zion,
Maidens in the towns of Judah.
¹²Princes have been hanged by them;ᶜ
No respect has been shown to elders.
¹³Young men must carry millstones,
And youths stagger under loads of wood.
¹⁴The old men are gone from the gate,
The young men from their music.
¹⁵Gone is the joy of our hearts;
Our dancing is turned into mourning.
¹⁶The crown has fallen from our head;
Woe to us that we have sinned!

¹⁷Because of this our hearts are sick,
Because of these our eyes are dimmed:
¹⁸Because of Mount Zion, which lies desolate;
Jackals prowl over it.

¹⁹But You, O LORD, are enthroned forever,
Your throne endures through the ages.
²⁰Why have You forgotten us utterly,
Forsaken us for all time?
²¹Take us back, O LORD, to Yourself,

ᵃ Lit. "on our neck"; meaning of Heb. uncertain.
ᵇ⁻ᵇ Or "heat (cf. Deut. 28.22) of the wilderness"; meaning of Heb. uncertain.
ᶜ I.e., the slaves of v. 8.

And let us come back;
Renew our days as of old!
22For truly, You have rejected us,
Bitterly raged against us.

Take us back, O LORD, to Yourself,
And let us come back;
Renew our days as of old!

ECCLESIASTES

1 The words of Koheleth[a] son of David, king in Jerusalem.

> [2]Utter futility!—said Koheleth—
> Utter futility! All is futile!
> [3]What real value is there for a man
> In all the gains[b] he makes beneath the sun?

> [4]One generation goes, another comes,
> But the earth remains the same forever.
> [5]The sun rises, and the sun sets—
> And glides[c] back to where it rises.
> [6]Southward blowing,
> Turning northward,
> Ever turning blows the wind;
> On its rounds the wind returns.
> [7]All streams flow into the sea,
> Yet the sea is never full;
> To the place [from] which they flow
> The streams flow back again.[d]
> [8]All such things are wearisome:
> No man can ever state them;
> The eye never has enough of seeing,
> Nor the ear enough of hearing.
> [9]Only that shall happen
> Which has happened,
> Only that occur

---

a *Probably "the Assembler," i.e., of hearers or of sayings; cf. 12.9–11.*
b *So Rashbam. Heb. 'amal usually has this sense in Ecclesiastes; cf. Ps. 105.44.*
c *So Targum; cf. Bereshith Rabbah on Gen. 1.17.*
d *According to popular belief, through tunnels; so Targum and Rashi.*

Which has occurred;
There is nothing new
Beneath the sun!

10Sometimes there is a phenomenon of which they say, "Look, this one is new!"—it occurred long since, in ages that went by before us. 11The earlier ones are not remembered; so too those that will occur later ᵉ-will no more be remembered than-ᵉ those that will occur at the very end.

12I, Koheleth, was king in Jerusalem over Israel. 13I set my mind to study and to probe with wisdom all that happens under the sun.—An unhappy business, that, which God gave men to be concerned with! 14I observed all the happenings beneath the sun, and I found that all is futile and pursuitᶠ of wind:

15A twisted thing that cannot be made straight,

A lack that cannot be made good.

16I said to myself: "Here I have grown richer and wiser than any that ruled before me over Jerusalem, and my mind has zealously absorbed wisdom and learning." 17And so I set my mind to appraise wisdom and to appraise madness and folly. And I learned—that this too was pursuit of wind:

18For as wisdom grows, vexation grows;

To increase learning is to increase heartache.

2 I said to myself, "Come, I will treat you to merriment. Taste mirth!" That too, I found, was futile.

2Of revelry I said, "It's mad!"

Of merriment, "What good is that?"

3I ventured to tempt my flesh with wine, and to grasp folly, while letting my mind direct with wisdom, to the end that I might learn which of the two was better for men to practice in their few days of life under heaven. 4I multiplied my possessions. I built myself houses and I planted vineyards. 5I laid out gardens and groves, in which I planted every kind of fruit tree. 6I constructed pools of water, enough to irrigate a forest shooting up with trees. 7I bought male and female slaves, and I acquired stewards. I also acquired more cattle, both herds and flocks, than all who were

ᵉ⁻ᵉ Lit. "will not be remembered like. . ." For ʻim meaning "like," cf. 2.16; 7.11; Job 9.26.
ᶠ Lit. "tending," from root raʻah, "to shepherd."

before me in Jerusalem. ⁸I further amassed silver and gold and treasures of kings and provinces; and I got myself male and female singers, as well as the luxuries of commoners—coffers^a and coffers of them. ⁹Thus, I gained more wealth than anyone before me in Jerusalem. In addition, my wisdom remained with me: ¹⁰I withheld from my eyes nothing they asked for, and denied myself no enjoyment; rather, I got enjoyment out of^b all my wealth. And that was all I got out of my wealth.

¹¹Then my thoughts turned to all the fortune my hands had built up, to the wealth I had acquired and won—and oh, it was all futile and pursuit of wind; there was no real value under the sun! ¹²^cFor what will the man be like who will succeed ^{d-}the one who is ruling-^d over what was built up long ago?

My thoughts also turned to appraising wisdom and madness and folly. ¹³I found that

> Wisdom is superior to folly
> As light is superior to darkness;
> ¹⁴A wise man has his eyes in his head,
> Whereas a fool walks in darkness.

But I also realized that the same fate awaits them both. ¹⁵So I reflected: "The fate of the fool is also destined for me; to what advantage, then, have I been wise?" And I came to the conclusion that that too was futile, ¹⁶because the wise man, just like^e the fool, is not remembered forever; for, as the succeeding days roll by, both are forgotten. Alas, the wise man dies, just like^e the fool!

¹⁷And so I loathed life. For I was distressed by all that goes on under the sun, because everything is futile and pursuit of wind.

¹⁸So, too, I loathed all the wealth that I was gaining under the sun. For I shall leave it to the man who will succeed me—¹⁹and who knows whether he will be wise or foolish?—and he will control all the wealth that I gained by toil and wisdom under the sun. That too is futile. ²⁰And so I came to view with despair all the gains I had made under the sun. ²¹For sometimes a person whose fortune was made with wisdom, knowledge, and skill must hand it on to be the portion of somebody who did not toil for it. That too is futile, and a grave evil. ²²For what does a man get for all the toiling and worrying he does under the sun? ²³All his days his thoughts are grief and heartache, and even at night his mind has no respite. That too is futile!

²⁴There is nothing worthwhile for a man but to eat and drink and afford

---

^a *The Heb.* shiddah *occurs only here in the Bible; in the Mishnah it designates a kind of chest.*
^b *Septuagint and a few Heb. manuscripts have "(in exchange) for"; cf. 2.24; 3.13, 22; 5.17.*
^c *The order of the two sentences in this verse is reversed in the translation for clarity.*
^{d-d} *Change of vocalization yields "me, and who is to rule"; cf. vv. 18–19.*
^e *See note on 1.11.*

himself enjoyment with his means. And even that, I noted, comes from God. 25For who eats and who enjoys but myself?[f] 26To the man, namely, who pleases Him He has given g-the wisdom and shrewdness to enjoy himself;-g and to him who displeases, He has given the urge to gather and amass—only for handing on to one who is pleasing to God. That too is futile and pursuit of wind.

3

A season is set for everything, a time for every experience under heaven:[a]

2A time for b-being born-b and a time for dying,
A time for planting and a time for uprooting the planted;
3A time for c-slaying and a time for healing,-c
A time for tearing down and a time for building up;
4A time for weeping and a time for laughing,
A time for wailing and a time for dancing;
5A time for throwing stones and a time for gathering stones,
A time for embracing and a time for shunning embraces;
6A time for seeking and a time for losing,
A time for keeping and a time for discarding;
7A time for ripping and a time for sewing,
A time for silence and a time for speaking;
8A time for loving and a time for hating;
A time for war and a time for peace.

9What value, then, can the man of affairs get from what he earns? 10I have observed the business that God gave man to be concerned with: 11He brings everything to pass precisely at its time; He also puts eternity in their mind,[d] but without man ever guessing, from first to last, all the things that God brings to pass. 12Thus I realized that the only worthwhile thing there is for them is to enjoy themselves and do what is good[e] in their lifetime; 13also, that whenever a man does eat and drink and get enjoyment out of all his wealth, it is a gift of God.

14I realized, too, that whatever God has brought to pass will recur evermore:

Nothing can be added to it
And nothing taken from it—

and God has brought to pass that men revere Him.

[f] Some mss. and ancient versions read mimmennu, "by His doing."
g-g Lit. "wisdom and knowledge and enjoyment."

[a] I.e., all human experiences are preordained by God; see v. 11.
b-b Lit. "giving birth."
c-c Emendation yields "wrecking . . . repairing"; cf. 1 Kings 18.30.
[d] I.e., He preoccupies man with the attempt to discover the times of future events; cf. 8.17.
[e] I.e., what the author has already concluded (2.24) is good.

15fWhat is occurring occurred long since,

And what is to occur occurred long since:

and God seeks the pursued. 16And, indeed, I have observed under the sun:

Alongside justice there is wickedness,

Alongside righteousness there is wickedness.

17I mused: "God will doom both righteous and wicked, for g-there is-g a time for every experience and for every happening." 18fSo I decided, as regards men, to dissociate them [from] the divine beings and to face the fact that they are beasts.h 19For in respect of the fate of man and the fate of beast, they have one and the same fate: as the one dies so dies the other, and both have the same lifebreath; man has no superiority over beast, since both amount to nothing. 20Both go to the same place; both came from dust and both return to dust. 21Who knows if a man's lifebreath does rise upward and if a beast's breath does sink down into the earth?

22I saw that there is nothing better for man than to enjoy his possessions, since that is his portion. For who can enable him to see what will happen afterward?

4 I further observeda all the oppression that goes on under the sun: the tears of the oppressed, with none to comfort them; and the power of their oppressors—with none to comfort them. 2Then I accounted those who died long since more fortunate than those who are still living; 3and happier than either are those who have not yet come into being and have never witnessed the miseries that go on under the sun.

4I have also noted that all labor and skillful enterprise come from men's envy of each other—another futility and pursuit of wind!

5[True,]

The fool folds his hands togetherb

And has to eat his own flesh.

6[But no less truly,]

Better is a handful of gratification

Than two fistfuls of labor which is pursuit of wind.

7And I have noted this further futility under the sun: 8the case of the man who is alone, with no companion, who has neither son nor brother;

---

f Meaning of parts of verse uncertain.
g-g Shift of a diacritical point yields "He has set."
h Contrast Ps. 8.5–6.

a Cf. 3.16.
b I.e., does not work; cf. Prov. 6.10; 24.33.

yet he amasses wealth without limit, and his eye is never sated with riches. For whom, now, c-is he amassing it while denying himself-c enjoyment? That too is a futility and an unhappy business.

9d Two are better off than one, in that they have greater e-benefit from-e their earnings. 10For should they fall, one can raise the other; but woe betide him who is alone and falls with no companion to raise him! 11Further, when two lie together they are warm; but how can he who is alone get warm? 12Also, if one attacks, two can stand up to him. A threefold cord is not readily broken!

13Better a poor but wise youth than an old but foolish king who no longer has the sense to heed warnings. 14For the former can emerge from a dungeon to become king; while the latter, even if born to kingship, can become a pauper.f 15[However,] I reflected about g-all the living who walk under the sun with-g that youthful successor who steps into his place. 16Unnumbered are the multitudes of all those who preceded them;h and later generations will not acclaim him either.i For thatj too is futile and pursuit of wind.

17k-Be not overeager to go-k to the House of God: more acceptable is obedience than the offering of fools, for they know nothing [but] to do wrong.

5 Keep your mouth from being rash, and let not your throata be quick to bring forth speech before God. For God is in heaven and you are on earth; that is why your words should be few. 2Just as dreams come with much brooding, so does foolish utterance come with much speech. 3When you make a vow to God, do not delay to fulfill it. For He has no pleasure in fools; what you vow, fulfill. 4It is better not to vow at all than to vow and not fulfill. 5Don't let your mouth bring you into disfavor, and don't plead before the messengerb that it was an error, c-but fear God;-c

---

c-c Lit. "am I amassing . . . myself."
d 4.9–5.8 consists of a series of observations, each of which is introduced by some slight association with what precedes. The theme of 4.4–8 is not resumed until 5.9.
e-e Emendation yields "hope for"; cf. 2.20.
f Taking rash as a verb; cf. Ps. 34.11.
g-g I.e., "the contemporaries of."
h And so never heard of the gifted youth.
i For despite his wisdom, he too will be forgotten; cf. 2.16.
j I.e., the advantage of wisdom over folly.
k-k Lit. "Guard your foot when it [or, you] would go."

a Heb. leb, lit. "heart," sometimes designates the organ of speech; cf. Isa. 33.18; 59.13; Ps. 19.15; 49.4; Job 8.10.
b Some ancient versions read "God."
c-c Moved up from v. 6 for clarity.

else God may be angered by your talk and destroy your possessions. ⁶ᵈFor much dreaming leads to futility and to superfluous talk.

⁷If you see in a province oppression of the poor and suppression of right and justice, don't wonder at the fact; for one high official is protected by a higher one, and both of them by still higher ones. ⁸Thus the greatest advantage in all the land is his: he controls a field that is cultivated.ᵉ

⁹A lover of money never has his fill of money, nor a lover of wealth his fill of income. That too is futile. ¹⁰As his substance increases, so do those who consume it; what, then, does the success of its owner amount to but feasting his eyes? ¹¹A worker'sᶠ sleep is sweet, whether he has much or little to eat; but the rich man's abundance doesn't let him sleep.

¹²Here is a grave evil I have observed under the sun: riches hoarded by their owner to his misfortune, ¹³in that those riches are lost in some unlucky venture; and if he begets a son, he has nothing in hand.

¹⁴ᵍ-Another grave evil is this: He must depart just as he came.⁻ᵍ As he came out of his mother's womb, so must he depart at last, naked as he came. He can take nothing of his wealth to carry with him. ¹⁵So what is the good of his toiling for the wind? ¹⁶Besides, all his days ʰ-he eats in darkness,⁻ʰ with much vexation and grief and anger.

¹⁷Only this, I have found, is a real good: that one should eat and drink and get pleasure with all the gains he makes under the sun, during the numbered days of life that God has given him; for that is his portion. ¹⁸Also, whenever a man is given riches and property by God, and is also permitted by Him to enjoy them and to take his portion and get pleasure for his gains—that is a gift of God. ¹⁹For [such a man] will not brood much over the days of his life,ⁱ because God keeps him busy enjoying himself.

6 There is an evil I have observed under the sun, and a grave one it is for man: ²that God sometimes grants a man riches, property, and wealth, so that he does not want for anything his appetite may crave, but God does not permit him to enjoy it; instead, a stranger will enjoy it. That is futility and a grievous ill. ³Even if a man should beget a hundred children and live many years—no matter how many the days of his years may come to, if his gullet is not sated through his wealth, I say: The stillbirth, though

---

ᵈ *Meaning of verse uncertain. Emendation yields "Much brooding results in dreams; and much talk in futilities"; cf. v. 2.*
ᵉ *I.e., the high official profits from the labor of others; but meaning of verse uncertain.*
ᶠ *Some ancient versions have "slave's."*
ᵍ⁻ᵍ *Moved up from v. 15 for clarity.*
ʰ⁻ʰ *Septuagint reads "are [spent] in darkness and mourning."*
ⁱ *The thought of which is depressing; see v. 16.*

it was not even accorded a burial,[a] is more fortunate than he. [4]Though it comes into futility and departs into darkness, and its very name is covered with darkness, [5]though it has never seen or experienced the sun, it is better off than he—[6]yes, even if the other lived a thousand years twice over but never had his fill of enjoyment! For are not both of them bound for the same place? [7b]All of man's earning is for the sake of his mouth, [c-]yet his gullet is not sated. [8]What advantage then has the wise man over the fool, what advantage has the pauper who knows how to get on in life?[-c] [9d]Is the feasting of the eyes more important than the pursuit of desire? That, too, is futility and pursuit of wind.

[10]Whatever happens, it was designated long ago and it was known that it would happen; as for man, he cannot contend with what is stronger than he. [11]Often, much talk means much futility. How does it benefit a man? [12]Who can possibly know what is best for a man to do in life—the few days of his fleeting life? For[e] who can tell him what the future holds for him under the sun?

7 [a]A good name is better than fragrant oil, and the day of death than the day of birth.[b]

[2]It is better to go to a house of mourning than to a house of feasting; for that is the end of every man, and a living one should take it to heart.

[3]Vexation is better than revelry;[c] for though the face be sad, the heart may be glad. [4]Wise men are drawn to a house of mourning, and fools to a house of merrymaking.

[5]It is better to listen to a wise man's reproof than to listen to the praise of fools. [6]For the levity[d] of the fool is like the crackling of nettles under a kettle. [c]But that too is illusory; [7]for cheating[f] may rob the wise man of reason and destroy the prudence of the cautious.[g]

[8]The end of a matter is better than the beginning of it.

Better a patient spirit than a haughty spirit.

---

a *Stillbirths were cast into pits or hidden in the ground in no recognizable graves; cf. v. 4 end.*
b *Cf. Prov. 16.26.*
c-c *Meaning of Heb. uncertain; emendation yields "And if the gullet is not sated, [8]what advantage has the wise man over the fool, he who knows how to get on in life over the pauper?"*
d *Meaning of first half of verse uncertain.*
e *Lit. "according to the shadow that"; cf. Qumran Aramaic betel and Syriac mettol; and see 8.13.*

a *The author now offers a number of practical maxims, which, however, he concludes (vv. 23–24) are of limited value.*
b *Until a man dies, there is always danger that he may forfeit his good name.*
c *For empty revelry precludes real happiness; cf. 2.2.*
d *Emendation yields "praise" (shbh).*
e *This section, to end of verse 7, is apparently a continuation of the thought in vv. 11–12 and 19.*
f *Emendation yields "riches."*
g *Lit. "caution"; cf. postbiblical mathun, "cautious."*

9Don't let your spirit be quickly vexed, for vexation abides in the breasts of fools.

10Don't say, "How has it happened that former times were better than these?" For it is not wise of you to ask that question.

11Wisdom is as good as a patrimony, and even better, for those who behold the sun. 12For to be in the shelter of wisdom is to be also in the shelter of money,h and the advantage of intelligence is that wisdom preserves the life of him who possesses it.

13iConsider God's doing! Who can straighten what He has twisted? 14So in a time of good fortune enjoy the good fortune; and in a time of misfortune, reflect: The one no less than the other was God's doing; consequently, man may find no fault with Him.j

15In my own brief span of life, I have seen both these things: sometimes a good man perishes in spite of his goodness, and sometimes a wicked one endures in spite of his wickedness. 16So don't overdo goodness and don't act the wise man to excess, or you may be dumfounded. 17Don't overdo wickedness and don't be a fool, or you may die before your time. 18It is best that you grasp the one without letting go of the other, for one who fears God will do his dutyk by both.

19Wisdom is more of a stronghold to a wise man than l-ten magnates-l that a city may contain.

20mFor there is not one good man on earth who does what is bestn and doesn't err.

21Finally, don't pay attention to everything that is said, so that you may not hear your slave reviling you; 22for well you remembero the many times that you yourself have reviled others.

23All this I tested with wisdom. I thought I could fathom it,n but it eludes me. 24[The secret of] what happens is elusive and deep, deep down; who can discover it? 25I put my mind to studying, exploring, and seeking wisdom and the reason of things, and to studying wickedness, stupidity, madness, and folly. 26Now, I find woman more bitter than death; she is all traps, her hands are fetters and her heart is snares. He who is pleasing to God escapes her, and he who is displeasing is caught by her. 27See, this is what I found, said Koheleth, item by item in my search for the reason of things. 28As for what I sought further but did not find, I found only one human being in a thousand, and the one I found among so

h Emendation yields "For the possessor of wisdom becomes a possessor of money."
i Vv. 13–14 continue the thought of v. 10.
j So Rashi; cf. the same thought in Job 1.22; 2.10.
k Cf. postbiblical yaṣa yede.
l-l Emendation yields "the riches of the magnates"; cf. Prov. 18.11.
m Apparently continuing the thought of v. 16.
n Refers back to 6.12.
o The same idiom occurs again in 8.5.

many was never a woman. 29But, see, this I did find: God made men plain, but they have engaged in too much reasoning.

8

a-Who is like the wise man,-a and who knows the meaning of the adage:

> "A man's wisdom lights up his face,
> So that his deep discontentb is dissembled"?

2I do! "Obey the king's orders—and c-don't rush-c into uttering an oath by God."d 3e-Leave his presence; do not tarry-e in a dangerous situation, for he can do anything he pleases; 4inasmuch as a king's command is authoritative, and none can say to him, "What are you doing?" 5One who obeys orders will not suffer from the dangerous situation.

A wise man, however, will bear in mindf that there is a time of doom.g 6For there is a time for every experience, including the doom; for a man's calamityh overwhelms him. 7Indeed, he does not know what is to happen; even when it is on the point of happening, who can tell him? 8No man has authority over the lifebreath—to hold back the lifebreath;i there is no authority over the day of death. There is no mustering out from that war; wickednessj is powerless to save its owner.

9All these things I observed; I noted all that went on under the sun, while men still had authority over men to treat them unjustly. 10And then I saw scoundrels k-coming from the Holy Site and being brought to burial,-k while such as had acted righteously were forgotten in the city.

And here is another frustration: 11the fact that the sentence imposed for evil deeds is not executed swiftly, which is why men are emboldened to do evil—12the fact that a sinner may do evil a hundred times and his [punishment] still be delayed. For although I am aware that "It will be well with those who revere God since they revere Him, 13and it will not be well with the scoundrel, and he will not live long, becausel he does

---

a-a Some ancient versions read "Who here is wise."
b Lit. "face"; cf. 1 Sam. 1.18; Job 9.27.
c-c Moved up from v. 3 for English word order.
d The answer to the inquiry about the implications of the proverb in v. 1 is given in the form of another proverb, of which only the first half is relevant and is enlarged upon.
e-e Or "Give ground before him; do not resist."
f The same idiom as in 7.22.
g Lit. "time and doom"; cf. the synonymous "time of misfortune," lit. "time and misfortune," 9.11.
h Still another term for death; cf. "the time of calamity" for "the hour of death," 9.12.
i From leaving the body when the time comes; see 12.7; cf. Ps. 104.29; 146.4.
j Emendation yields "riches."
k-k Meaning uncertain; emendation yields "approaching [to minister]. They would come and profane the Holy Site."
l See note on 6.12.

not revere God"—[14]here is a frustration that occurs in the world: sometimes an upright man is requited according to the conduct of the scoundrel; and sometimes the scoundrel is requited according to the conduct of the upright. I say all that is frustration.

[15]I therefore praised enjoyment. For the only good a man can have under the sun is to eat and drink and enjoy himself. That much can accompany him, in exchange for his wealth, through the days of life that God has granted him under the sun.

[16]For I have set my mind to learn wisdom and to observe the business that goes on in the world—even to the extent of going without sleep day and night—[17]and I have observed all that God brings to pass. Indeed, man cannot guess the events that occur under the sun. For man tries strenuously, but fails to guess them; and even if a sage should think to discover them he would not be able to guess them.

9 For all this I noted, and I ascertained[a] all this: that the actions of even the righteous and the wise are determined by God. [b-]Even love! Even hate! Man knows none of these in advance[2]—none![-b] For the same fate is in store for all: for the righteous, and for the wicked; for the good and pure,[c] and for the impure; for him who sacrifices, and for him who does not;[d] for him who is pleasing,[e] and for him who is displeasing; and for him who swears, and for him who shuns oaths.[f] [3]That is the sad thing about all that goes on under the sun: that the same fate is in store for all. (Not only that, but men's hearts are full of sadness, and their minds of madness, while they live; and then—to the dead!) [4]For he who is [g-]reckoned among[-g] the living has something to look forward to—even a live dog is better than a dead lion—[5]since the living know they will die. But the dead know nothing; they have no more recompense,[h] for even the memory of them has died. [6]Their loves, their hates, their jealousies have long since perished; and they have no more share till the end of time in all that goes on under the sun.

[7]Go, eat your bread in gladness, and drink your wine in joy; for your action was long ago approved by God.[i] [8]Let your clothes always be freshly

---

[a] *Meaning of verb uncertain; construction as in Hos. 12.3; Ezra 3.12.*
[b-b] *Emendation yields "Even love, even hate, no man can know in advance. All [2]are insignificant."*
[c] *I.e., those who observe the laws of ritual purity.*
[d] *Cf. 4.17.*
[e] *I.e., to God; cf. 2.26; 7.26.*
[f] *Cf. 8.2.*
[g-g] *Lit. "joined to all."*
[h] *Emendation yields "hope."*
[i] *Cf. 2.24–25; 3.13; 5.18.*

washed, and your head never lack ointment. [9]Enjoy happiness with a woman you love all the fleeting days of life that have been granted to you under the sun—all your fleeting days. For that alone is what you can get out of life and out of the means you acquire under the sun. [10]Whatever it is in your power to do, do with all your might. For there is no action, no reasoning, no learning, no wisdom in Sheol, where you are going.

[11]I have further observed under the sun that

The race is not won by the swift,
Nor the battle by the valiant;
Nor is bread won by the wise,
Nor wealth by the intelligent,
Nor favor by the learned.

For the time of mischance[j] comes to all.[k] [12]And a man cannot even know his time. As fishes are enmeshed in a fatal net, and as birds are trapped in a snare, so men are caught at the time of calamity,[j] when it comes upon them without warning.

[13]This thing too I observed under the sun about wisdom, and it affected me profoundly. [14]There was a little city, with few men in it; and to it came a great king, who invested it and built mighty siege works against it. [15]Present in the city was a poor wise man [l]who might have saved[-l] it with his wisdom, but nobody thought of that poor man. [16]So I observed: Wisdom is better than valor; but

A poor man's wisdom is scorned,
And his words are not heeded.

[17m]Words spoken softly by wise men are heeded [n]sooner than those shouted by a lord in folly.[-n]

[18]Wisdom is more valuable than [o]weapons of war,[-o] but a single error destroys much of value.

10

Dead flies turn the perfumer's ointment fetid and putrid;[a] so a little folly outweighs massive wisdom.

[2]A wise man's mind tends toward the right hand, a fool's toward the left.[b] [3]A fool's mind is also wanting when he travels, and he lets everybody know he is a fool.

---

[j] *Euphemism for death.*
[k] *I.e., the insignificant duration of life renders all successes illusory; cf. 4.15–16.*
[l-l] *Others "who saved."*
[m] *Verses 9.17–10.19 constitute a group of loosely connected aphorisms.*
[n-n] *Lit. "than the scream of a lord in [the manner of] the fools."*
[o-o] *Emendation yields "everything precious."*

[a] *Meaning of Heb. uncertain.*
[b] *I.e., a wise man's mind brings him good luck; a fool's brings him bad luck.*

4If the wrath of a lord flares up against you, don't give up your post;c for d-when wrath abates, grave offenses are pardoned.-d

5Here is an evil I have seen under the sun as great as an error committed by a ruler: 6Folly was placed on lofty heights, while rich men sat in low estate. 7I have seen slaves on horseback, and nobles walking on the ground like slaves.

8He who digs a pit will fall into it; he who breaches a stone fence will be bitten by a snake. 9He who quarries stones will e-be hurt by them; he who splits wood will be harmed by-e it. 10fIf the ax has become dull and he has not whetted the edge, he must exert more strength. Thus the advantage of a skill [depends on the exercise of] prudence. 11If the snake bites because no spell was uttered, no advantage is gained by the trained charmer.

12A wise man's talk brings him favor, but a fool's lips are his undoing. 13His talk begins as silliness and ends as disastrous madness. 14Yet the fool talks and talks!

gA man cannot know what will happen; who can tell him what the future holds?

15hA fool's exertions tire him out, for he doesn't know how to get to a town.

16Alas for you, O land whose king is a lackey and whose ministers dine in the morning! 17Happy are you, O land whose king is a master and whose ministers dine at the proper time—with restraint, not with guzzling!

18Through slothfulness the ceiling sags,
Through lazy hands the house caves in.

19Theyi make a banquet for revelry; wine makes life merry, and money answers every need.

20Don't revile a king even among your intimates.j
Don't revile a rich man even in your bedchamber;
For a bird of the air may carry the utterance,
And a winged creature may report the word.

---

c Emendation yields "hope."
d-d Lit. "abatement (2 Chron. 36.16) remits grave offenses." For hinniaḥ, "to remit," cf. Abodah Zarah 13a; cf. hanaḥah, "remission of taxes," Esth. 2.18.
e-e Emendation yields "profit . . . shall make use of."
f Meaning of verse uncertain.
g The thought of this sentence is resumed at v. 20.
h This verse continues the thought of v. 3.
i I.e., the ministers of v. 16.
j Others "thoughts"; meaning of Heb. uncertain.

11 Send your bread forth upon the waters; for after many days you will find it. ²Distribute portions to seven or even to eight, for you cannot know what misfortune may occur on earth.

³If the clouds are filled, they will pour down rain on the earth; and a-if a tree falls to the south or to the north, the tree will stay where it falls.-a ⁴If one watches the wind, he will never sow; and if one observes the clouds, he will never reap. ⁵Just as you do not know how the lifebreath passes intoᵇ the limbs within the womb of the pregnant woman, so you cannot foresee the actions of God, who causes all things to happen. ⁶Sow your seed in the morning, and don't hold back your hand in the evening, since you don't know which is going to succeed, the one or the other, or if both are equally good.

⁷How sweet is the light, what a delight for the eyes to behold the sun! ⁸Even if a man lives many years, let him enjoy himself in all of them, remembering how many the days of darkness are going to be. The only future is nothingness!

⁹O youth, enjoy yourself while you are young! Let your heart lead you to enjoyment in the days of your youth. Follow the desires of your heart and the glances of your eyes—but know well that God will call you to account for all such things—¹⁰and banish care from your mind, and pluck sorrow out of your flesh! For youth and black hair are fleeting.

12 So appreciate your vigorᵃ in the days of your youth, before those days of sorrow come and those years arrive of which you will say, "I have no pleasure in them"; ²before sun and light and moon and stars grow dark, and the clouds come back again after the rain:

³When the guards of the houseᵇ become shaky,
And the men of valorᶜ are bent,
And the maids that grind,ᵈ grown few, are idle,
And the ladies that peer through the windowsᵉ grow dim,

---

a-a Emendation yields, "if a thunderbolt (lit. arrow, cf., e.g., 2 Sam. 22.15) falls . . . where the thunderbolt falls, only there will it strike."
ᵇ So many mss. and Targum; most mss. read "like."

ᵃ Cf. postbiblical bori; others "Remember thy Creator."
ᵇ I.e., the arms.
ᶜ I.e., the legs.
ᵈ I.e., the teeth.
ᵉ I.e., the eyes.

⁴And the doors to the street[f] are shut—
With the noise of the hand mill growing fainter,
And the song of the bird g‑growing feebler,‑g
And all the strains of music dying down;[h]
⁵When one is afraid of heights
And there is terror on the road.—
For the almond tree may blossom,
i‑The grasshopper be burdened,‑i
And the caper bush may bud again;[j]
But man sets out for his eternal abode,
With mourners all around in the street.—
⁶Before the silver cord snaps
And the golden bowl crashes,
The jar is shattered at the spring,
And the jug[k] is smashed at the cistern.[l]
⁷And the dust returns to the ground
As it was,
And the lifebreath returns to God
Who bestowed it.
⁸Utter futility—said Koheleth—
All is futile!

⁹A further word: Because Koheleth was a sage, he continued to instruct the people. He listened to and tested the soundness[m] of many maxims. ¹⁰Koheleth sought to discover useful sayings and recorded[n] genuinely truthful sayings. ¹¹The sayings of the wise are like goads, like nails fixed o‑in prodding sticks.‑o p‑They were given by one Shepherd.‑p

[f] *I.e., the ears.*
g-g *Exact meaning of Heb. uncertain.*
[h] *Cf. 2 Sam. 19.36.*
i-i *Emendation yields "The squill (postbiblical Heb. ḥaṣab) resume its burden," i.e., its blossom-stalk and its leaves.*
[j] *These plants, after seeming dead for part of the year, revive, unlike man; cf. Job 14.7–10.*
[k] *So in Punic; others "wheel."*
[l] *Poetic figure for the end of life.*
[m] *A noun, like* dibber *(Jer. 5.13), which occurs in such postbiblical phrases as* shanim kethiq(qe)nan, *"normal years" (lit. "years according to their propriety").*
[n] Wekhathub *is equivalent to* wekhathob, *an infinitive employed as in Esth. 9.16 and elsewhere.*
o-o *Meaning of Heb. uncertain. Others "are those that are composed in collections."*
p-p *Meaning of Heb. uncertain. Emendation yields "They are accounted as a sharp ox goad" (postbiblical* mardeaʻ).

¹²A further word: ⁹⁻Against them,⁻⁹ my son, be warned!

The making of many books is without limit

And much study[r] is a wearying of the flesh.

¹³The sum of the matter, when all is said and done: Revere God and observe His commandments! For this applies to all mankind: ¹⁴that God will call every creature to account for ˢ⁻everything unknown,⁻ˢ be it good or bad.

The sum of the matter, when all is said and done: Revere God and observe His commandments! For this applies to all mankind.

---

⁹⁻⁹ *Emendation yields "Slow, there!" Cf. Arabic* mah *and* mah mah; *so also* mah (meh) *in Prov. 31.2.*

ʳ *Meaning of Heb. uncertain.*

ˢ⁻ˢ *Emendation yields "all their conduct."*

ESTHER

1 It happened in the days of Ahasuerus—that Ahasuerus who reigned over a hundred and twenty-seven provinces from India to Ethiopia. ²In those days, when King Ahasuerus occupied the royal throne in the for-tress^a Shushan, ³in the third year of his reign, he gave a banquet for all the officials and courtiers—the administration of Persia and Media, the nobles and the governors of the provinces in his service. ⁴For no fewer than a hundred and eighty days he displayed the vast riches of his kingdom and the splendid glory of his majesty. ⁵At the end of this period, the king gave a banquet for seven days in the court of the king's palace garden for all the people who lived in the fortress Shushan, high and low alike. ⁶ᵇ[There were hangings of] white cotton and blue wool, caught up by cords of fine linen and purple wool to silver rods and alabaster columns; and there were couches of gold and silver on a pavement of marble, alabaster, mother-of-pearl, and mosaics. ⁷Royal wine was served in abundance, as befits a king, in golden beakers, beakers of varied design. ⁸And the rule for the drinking was, "No restrictions!" For the king had given orders to every palace steward to comply with each man's wishes. ⁹In addition, Queen Vashti gave a banquet for women, in the royal palace of King Ahasuerus.

¹⁰On the seventh day, when the king was merry with wine, he ordered Mehuman, Bizzetha, Harbona, Bigtha, Abagtha, Zethar, and Carcas, the seven eunuchs in attendance on King Ahasuerus, ¹¹to bring Queen Vashti before the king wearing a royal diadem, to display her beauty to the peoples and the officials; for she was a beautiful woman. ¹²But Queen Vashti refused to come at the king's command conveyed by the eunuchs. The king was greatly incensed, and his fury burned within him.

¹³Then the king consulted the sages learned in procedure.^c (For it was the royal practice [to turn] to all who were versed in law and precedent. ¹⁴His closest advisers were Carshena, Shethar, Admatha, Tarshish, Meres, Marsena, and Memucan, the seven ministers of Persia and Media who

---

^a I.e., the fortified city.
^b Meaning of part of this verse uncertain.
^c Lit. "the times."

had access to the royal presence and occupied the first place in the kingdom.) 15"What," [he asked,] "shall be done, according to law, to Queen Vashti for failing to obey the command of King Ahasuerus conveyed by the eunuchs?"

16Thereupon Memucan declared in the presence of the king and the ministers: "Queen Vashti has committed an offense not only against Your Majesty but also against all the officials and against all the peoples in all the provinces of King Ahasuerus. 17For the queen's behavior will make all wives despise their husbands, as they reflect that King Ahasuerus himself ordered Queen Vashti to be brought before him, but she would not come. 18This very day the ladies of Persia and Media, who have heard of the queen's behavior, will cite it to all Your Majesty's officials, and there will be no end of scorn and provocation!

19"If it please Your Majesty, let a royal edict be issued by you, and let it be written into the laws of Persia and Media, so that it cannot be abrogated, that Vashti shall never enter the presence of King Ahasuerus. And let Your Majesty bestow her royal state upon another who is more worthy than she. 20Then will the judgment executed by Your Majesty resound throughout your realm, vast though it is; and all wives will treat their husbands with respect, high and low alike."

21The proposal was approved by the king and the ministers, and the king did as Memucan proposed. 22Dispatches were sent to all the provinces of the king, to every province in its own script and to every nation in its own language, that every man should wield authority in his home and speak the language of his own people.

2 Some time afterward, when the anger of King Ahasuerus subsided, he thought of Vashti and what she had done and what had been decreed against her. 2The king's servants who attended him said, "Let beautiful young virgins be sought out for Your Majesty. 3Let Your Majesty appoint officers in every province of your realm to assemble all the beautiful young virgins at the fortress Shushan, in the harem under the supervision of Hege, the king's eunuch, guardian of the women. Let them be provided with their cosmetics. 4And let the maiden who pleases Your Majesty be queen instead of Vashti." The proposal pleased the king, and he acted upon it.

⁵In the fortress Shushan lived a Jew by the name of Mordecai, son of Jair son of Shimei son of Kish, a Benjaminite. ⁶[Kish] had been exiled from Jerusalem in the group that was carried into exile along with King Jeconiah of Judah, which had been driven into exile by King Nebuchadnezzar of Babylon.—⁷He was foster father to Hadassah—that is, Esther—his uncle's daughter, for she had neither father nor mother. The maiden was shapely and beautiful; and when her father and mother died, Mordecai adopted her as his own daughter.

⁸When the king's order and edict was proclaimed, and when many girls were assembled in the fortress Shushan under the supervision of Hegai,ᵃ Esther too was taken into the king's palace under the supervision of Hegai, guardian of the women. ⁹The girl pleased him and won his favor, and he hastened to furnish her with her cosmetics and her rations, as well as with the seven maids who were her due from the king's palace; and he treated her and her maids with special kindness in the harem. ¹⁰Esther did not reveal her people or her kindred, for Mordecai had told her not to reveal it. ¹¹Every single day Mordecai would walk about in front of the court of the harem, to learn how Esther was faring and what was happening to her.

¹²When each girl's turn came to go to King Ahasuerus at the end of the twelve months' treatment prescribed for women (for that was the period spent on beautifying them: six months with oil of myrrh and six months with perfumes and women's cosmetics, ¹³and it was after that that the girl would go to the king), whatever she asked for would be given her to take with her from the harem to the king's palace. ¹⁴She would go in the evening and leave in the morning for a second harem in charge of Shaashgaz, the king's eunuch, guardian of the concubines. She would not go again to the king unless the king wanted her, when she would be summoned by name. ¹⁵When the turn came for Esther daughter of Abihail—the uncle of Mordecai, who had adopted her as his own daughter—to go to the king, she did not ask for anything but what Hegai, the king's eunuch, guardian of the women, advised. Yet Esther won the admiration of all who saw her.

¹⁶Esther was taken to King Ahasuerus, in his royal palace, in the tenth month, which is the month of Tebeth, in the seventh year of his reign. ¹⁷The king loved Esther more than all the other women, and she won his grace and favor more than all the virgins. So he set a royal diadem on

ᵃ Identical with Hege in v. 3.

her head and made her queen instead of Vashti. ¹⁸The king gave a great banquet for all his officials and courtiers, "the banquet of Esther." He proclaimed a remission of taxes[b] for the provinces and distributed gifts as befits a king.

¹⁹[c]When the virgins were assembled a second time, Mordecai sat in the palace gate. ²⁰But Esther still did not reveal her kindred or her people, as Mordecai had instructed her; for Esther obeyed Mordecai's bidding, as she had done when she was under his tutelage.

²¹At that time, when Mordecai was sitting in the palace gate, Bigthan and Teresh, two of the king's eunuchs who guarded the threshold, became angry, and plotted to do away with King Ahasuerus. ²²Mordecai learned of it and told it to Queen Esther, and Esther reported it to the king in Mordecai's name. ²³The matter was investigated and found to be so, and the two were impaled on stakes. This was recorded in the book of annals at the instance of the king.

3 Some time afterward, King Ahasuerus promoted Haman son of Hammedatha the Agagite; he advanced him and seated him higher than any of his fellow officials. ²All the king's courtiers in the palace gate knelt and bowed low to Haman, for such was the king's order concerning him; but Mordecai would not kneel or bow low. ³Then the king's courtiers who were in the palace gate said to Mordecai, "Why do you disobey the king's order?" ⁴When they spoke to him day after day and he would not listen to them, they told Haman, in order to see whether Mordecai's resolve would prevail; for he had explained to them that he was a Jew.[a] ⁵When Haman saw that Mordecai would not kneel or bow low to him, Haman was filled with rage. ⁶But he disdained to lay hands on Mordecai alone; having been told who Mordecai's people were, Haman plotted to do away with all the Jews, Mordecai's people, throughout the kingdom of Ahasuerus.

⁷In the first month, that is, the month of Nisan, in the twelfth year of King Ahasuerus, *pur*—which means "the lot"—was cast before Haman concerning every day and every month, [until it fell on] the twelfth month, that is, the month of Adar. ⁸Haman then said to King Ahasuerus, "There is a certain people, scattered and dispersed among the other peoples in all the provinces of your realm, whose laws are different from those of any other people and who do not obey the king's laws; and it is not in Your

---

[b] *Or "an amnesty."*
[c] *Meaning of verse uncertain.*

[a] *I.e., that as a Jew he could not bow to a descendant of Agag, the Amalekite king; see 1 Sam. 15, and cf. Exod. 17.14–16; Deut. 25.17–19.*

Majesty's interest to tolerate them. ⁹If it please Your Majesty, let an edict be drawn for their destruction, and I will pay ten thousand talents of silver to the stewards for deposit in the royal treasury." ¹⁰Thereupon the king removed his signet ring from his hand and gave it to Haman son of Hammedatha the Agagite, the foe of the Jews. ¹¹And the king said, "The money and the people are yours to do with as you see fit."

¹²On the thirteenth day of the first month, the king's scribes were summoned and a decree was issued, as Haman directed, to the king's satraps, to the governors of every province, and to the officials of every people, to every province in its own script and to every people in its own language. The orders were issued in the name of King Ahasuerus and sealed with the king's signet. ¹³Accordingly, written instructions were dispatched by couriers to all the king's provinces to destroy, massacre, and exterminate all the Jews, young and old, children and women, on a single day, on the thirteenth day of the twelfth month—that is, the month of Adar—and to plunder their possessions. ¹⁴The text of the document was to the effect that a law should be proclaimed in every single province; it was to be publicly displayed to all the peoples, so that they might be ready for that day.

¹⁵The couriers went out posthaste on the royal mission, and the decree was proclaimed in the fortress Shushan. The king and Haman sat down to feast, but the city of Shushan was dumfounded.

4 When Mordecai learned all that had happened, Mordecai tore his clothes and put on sackcloth and ashes. He went through the city, crying out loudly and bitterly, ²until he came in front of the palace gate; for one could not enter the palace gate wearing sackcloth.—³Also, in every province that the king's command and decree reached, there was great mourning among the Jews, with fasting, weeping, and wailing, and everybody lay in sackcloth and ashes.—⁴When Esther's maidens and eunuchs came and informed her, the queen was greatly agitated. She sent clothing for Mordecai to wear, so that he might take off his sackcloth; but he refused. ⁵Thereupon Esther summoned Hathach, one of the eunuchs whom the king had appointed to serve her, and sent him to Mordecai to learn the why and wherefore of it all. ⁶Hathach went out to Mordecai in the city square in front of the palace gate; ⁷and Mordecai told him all that had happened to him, and all about the money that Haman had offered to pay into the royal treasury for the destruction of the Jews. ⁸He also gave him the written text of the law that had been proclaimed in Shushan for their destruction. [He bade him] show it to Esther and inform her, and charge her to go to the king and to appeal to him and to plead with him for her people. ⁹When Hathach came and delivered Mordecai's message to Esther, ¹⁰Esther told Hathach to take back to Mordecai the following reply: ¹¹"All the king's courtiers and the people of the king's provinces know that if any person, man or woman, enters the king's presence in the inner court without having been summoned, there is but one law for him—that he be put to death. Only if the king extends the golden scepter to him may he live. Now I have not been summoned to visit the king for the last thirty days."

¹²When Mordecai was told what Esther had said, ¹³Mordecai had this message delivered to Esther: "Do not imagine that you, of all the Jews, will escape with your life by being in the king's palace. ¹⁴On the contrary, if you keep silent in this crisis, relief and deliverance will come to the Jews from another quarter, while you and your father's house will perish. And who knows, perhaps you have attained to royal position for just such a crisis." ¹⁵Then Esther sent back this answer to Mordecai: ¹⁶"Go, assemble all the Jews who live in Shushan, and fast in my behalf; do not eat or drink for three days, night or day. I and my maidens will observe the same fast. Then I shall go to the king, though it is contrary to the law; and if I am to perish, I shall perish!" ¹⁷So Mordecai went about [the city] and did just as Esther had commanded him.

5 On the third day, Esther put on royal apparel and stood in the inner court of the king's palace, facing the king's palace, while the king was sitting on his royal throne in the throne room facing the entrance of the palace. ²As soon as the king saw Queen Esther standing in the court, she won his favor. The king extended to Esther the golden scepter which he had in his hand, and Esther approached and touched the tip of the scepter. ³"What troubles you, Queen Esther?" the king asked her. "And what is your request? Even to half the kingdom, it shall be granted you." ⁴"If it please Your Majesty," Esther replied, "let Your Majesty and Haman come today to the feast that I have prepared for him." ⁵The king commanded, "Tell Haman to hurry and do Esther's bidding." So the king and Haman came to the feast that Esther had prepared.

⁶At the wine feast, the king asked Esther, "What is your wish? It shall be granted you. And what is your request? Even to half the kingdom, it shall be fulfilled." ⁷"My wish," replied Esther, "my request—⁸if Your Majesty will do me the favor, if it please Your Majesty to grant my wish and accede to my request—let Your Majesty and Haman come to the feast which I will prepare for them; and tomorrow I will do Your Majesty's bidding."

⁹That day Haman went out happy and lighthearted. But when Haman saw Mordecai in the palace gate, and Mordecai did not rise or even stir on his account, Haman was filled with rage at him. ¹⁰Nevertheless, Haman controlled himself and went home. He sent for his friends and his wife Zeresh, ¹¹and Haman told them about his great wealth and his many sons, and all about how the king had promoted him and advanced him above the officials and the king's courtiers. ¹²"What is more," said Haman, "Queen Esther gave a feast, and besides the king she did not have anyone but me. And tomorrow too I am invited by her along with the king. ¹³Yet all this means nothing to me every time I see that Jew Mordecai sitting in the palace gate." ¹⁴Then his wife Zeresh and all his friends said to him, "Let a stake be put up, fifty cubits high, and in the morning ask the king to have Mordecai impaled on it. Then you can go gaily with the king to the feast." The proposal pleased Haman, and he had the stake put up.

6 That night, sleep deserted the king, and he ordered the book of records, the annals, to be brought; and it was read to the king. ²There it was found written that Mordecai had denounced Bigthana and Teresh, two of the king's eunuchs who guarded the threshold, who had plotted to do away with King Ahasuerus. ³"What honor or advancement has been conferred on Mordecai for this?" the king inquired. "Nothing at all has been done for him," replied the king's servants who were in attendance on him. ⁴"Who is in the court?" the king asked. For Haman had just entered the outer court of the royal palace, to speak to the king about having Mordecai impaled on the stake he had prepared for him. ⁵"It is Haman standing in the court," the king's servants answered him. "Let him enter," said the king. ⁶Haman entered, and the king asked him, "What should be done for a man whom the king desires to honor?" Haman said to himself, "Whom would the king desire to honor more than me?" ⁷So Haman said to the king, "For the man whom the king desires to honor,

⁸let royal garb which the king has worn be brought, and a horse on which the king has ridden and on whose head a royal diadem has been set; ⁹and let the attire and the horse be put in the charge of one of the king's noble courtiers. And let the man whom the king desires to honor be attired and paraded on the horse through the city square, while they proclaim before him: This is what is for the man whom the king desires to honor!" ¹⁰"Quick, then!" said the king to Haman. "Get the garb and the horse, as you have said, and do this to Mordecai the Jew, who sits in the king's gate. Omit nothing of all you have proposed." ¹¹So Haman took the garb and the horse and arrayed Mordecai and paraded him through the city square; and he proclaimed before him: This is what is done for the man whom the king desires to honor!

¹²Then Mordecai returned to the king's gate, while Haman hurried home, his head covered in mourning. ¹³There Haman told his wife Zeresh and all his friends everything that had befallen him. His advisers and his wife Zeresh said to him, "If Mordecai, before whom you have begun to fall, is of Jewish stock, you will not overcome him; you will fall before him to your ruin."

¹⁴While they were still speaking with him, the king's eunuchs arrived and hurriedly brought Haman to the banquet which Esther had prepared.

7 So the king and Haman came to feast with Queen Esther. ²On the second day, the king again asked Esther at the wine feast, "What is your wish, Queen Esther? It shall be granted you. And what is your request? Even to half the kingdom, it shall be fulfilled." ³Queen Esther replied: "If Your Majesty will do me the favor, and if it pleases Your Majesty, let my life be granted me as my wish, and my people as my request. ⁴For we have been sold, my people and I, to be destroyed, massacred, and exterminated. Had we only been sold as bondmen and bondwomen, I would have kept silent; for ᵃ-the adversary-ᵃ is not worthy of the king's trouble."

⁵Thereupon King Ahasuerus demanded of Queen Esther, "Who is he and where is he who dared to do this?" ⁶"The adversary and enemy," replied Esther, "is this evil Haman!" And Haman cringed in terror before the king and the queen. ⁷The king, in his fury, left the wine feast for the palace garden, while Haman remained to plead with Queen Esther for his life; for he saw that the king had resolved to destroy him. ⁸When the king returned from the palace garden to the banquet room, Haman was

---

ᵃ⁻ᵃ *Emendation yields "a trifle"* (ḥiṣṣar), *lit. "little finger."*

lying prostrate on the couch on which Esther reclined. "Does he mean," cried the king, "to ravish the queen in my own palace?" No sooner did these words leave the king's lips than Haman's face b-was covered.-b 9Then Harbonah, one of the eunuchs in attendance on the king, said, "What is more, a stake is standing at Haman's house, fifty cubits high, which Haman made for Mordecai—the man whose words saved the king." "Impale him on it!" the king ordered. 10So they impaled Haman on the stake which he had put up for Mordecai, and the king's fury abated.

8 That very day King Ahasuerus gave the property of Haman, the enemy of the Jews, to Queen Esther. Mordecai presented himself to the king, for Esther had revealed how he was related to her. 2The king slipped off his ring, which he had taken back from Haman, and gave it to Mordecai; and Esther put Mordecai in charge of Haman's property.

3Esther spoke to the king again, falling at his feet and weeping, and beseeching him to avert the evil plotted by Haman the Agagite against the Jews. 4The king extended the golden scepter to Esther, and Esther arose and stood before the king. 5"If it please Your Majesty," she said, "and if I have won your favor and the proposal seems right to Your Majesty, and if I am pleasing to you—let dispatches be written countermanding those which were written by Haman son of Hammedatha the Agagite, embodying his plot to annihilate the Jews throughout the king's provinces. 6For how can I bear to see the disaster which will befall my people! And how can I bear to see the destruction of my kindred!"

7Then King Ahasuerus said to Queen Esther and Mordecai the Jew, "I have given Haman's property to Esther, and he has been impaled on the stake for scheming against the Jews. 8And you may further write with regard to the Jews as you see fit. [Write it] in the king's name and seal it with the king's signet, for an edict that has been written in the king's name and sealed with the king's signet may not be revoked."

9So the king's scribes were summoned at that time, on the twenty-third day of the third month, that is, the month of Sivan; and letters were written, at Mordecai's dictation, to the Jews and to the satraps, the governors and the officials of the one hundred and twenty-seven provinces from India to Ethiopia: to every province in its own script and to every people in its own language, and to the Jews in their own script and language. 10He had them written in the name of King Ahasuerus and

b-b *Meaning of Heb. uncertain. Emendation yields "blanched"; cf. Ps. 34.6.*

sealed with the king's signet. Letters were dispatched by mounted couriers, riding steeds ᵃ⁻used in the king's service, bred of the royal stud,⁻ᵃ ¹¹to this effect: The king has permitted the Jews of every city to assemble and fight for their lives; if any people or province attacks them, they may destroy, massacre, and exterminate its armed force together with women and children, and plunder their possessions—¹²on a single day in all the provinces of King Ahasuerus, namely, on the thirteenth day of the twelfth month, that is, the month of Adar. ¹³The text of the document was to be issued as a law in every single province: it was to be publicly displayed to all the peoples, so that the Jews should be ready for that day to avenge themselves on their enemies. ¹⁴The couriers, mounted on royal steeds, went out in urgent haste at the king's command; and the decree was proclaimed in the fortress Shushan.

¹⁵Mordecai left the king's presence in royal robes of blue and white, with a magnificent crown of gold and a mantle of fine linen and purple wool. And the city of Shushan rang with joyous cries. ¹⁶The Jews enjoyed light and gladness, happiness and honor. ¹⁷And in every province and in every city, when the king's command and decree arrived, there was gladness and joy among the Jews, a feast and a holiday. And many of the people of the land professed to be Jews, for the fear of the Jews had fallen upon them.

9 And so, on the thirteenth day of the twelfth month—that is, the month of Adar—when the king's command and decree were to be executed, the very day on which the enemies of the Jews had expected to get them in their power, the opposite happened, and the Jews got their enemies in their power. ²Throughout the provinces of King Ahasuerus, the Jews mustered in their cities to attack those who sought their hurt; and no one could withstand them, for the fear of them had fallen upon all the peoples. ³Indeed, all the officials of the provinces—the satraps, the governors, and the king's stewards—showed deference to the Jews, because the fear of Mordecai had fallen upon them. ⁴For Mordecai was now powerful in the royal palace, and his fame was spreading through all the provinces; the man Mordecai was growing ever more powerful. ⁵So the Jews struck at their enemies with the sword, slaying and destroying; they wreaked their will upon their enemies.

ᵃ⁻ᵃ *Meaning of Heb. uncertain.*

⁶In the fortress Shushan the Jews killed a total of five hundred men. ⁷They also killedᵃ Parshandatha, Dalphon, Aspatha, ⁸Poratha, Adalia, Aridatha, ⁹Parmashta, Arisai, Aridai, and Vaizatha, ¹⁰the ten sons of Haman son of Hammedatha, the foe of the Jews. But they did not lay hands on the spoil. ¹¹When the number of those slain in the fortress Shushan was reported on that same day to the king, ¹²the king said to Queen Esther, "In the fortress Shushan alone the Jews have killed a total of five hundred men, as well as the ten sons of Haman. What then must they have done in the provinces of the realm! What is your wish now? It shall be granted you. And what else is your request? It shall be fulfilled." ¹³"If it please Your Majesty," Esther replied, "let the Jews in Shushan be permitted to act tomorrow also as they did today; and let Haman's ten sons be impaled on the stake." ¹⁴The king ordered that this should be done, and the decree was proclaimed in Shushan. Haman's ten sons were impaled: ¹⁵and the Jews in Shushan mustered again on the fourteenth day of Adar and slew three hundred men in Shushan. But they did not lay hands on the spoil.

¹⁶The rest of the Jews, those in the king's provinces, likewise mustered and fought for their lives. They disposed of their enemies, killing seventy-five thousand of their foes; but they did not lay hands on the spoil. ¹⁷That was on the thirteenth day of the month of Adar; and they rested on the fourteenth day and made it a day of feasting and merrymaking. (¹⁸But the Jews in Shushan mustered on both the thirteenth and fourteenth days, and so rested on the fifteenth, and made it a day of feasting and merrymaking.) ¹⁹That is why village Jews, who live in unwalled towns, observe the fourteenth day of the month of Adar and make it a day of merrymaking and feasting, and as a holiday and an occasion for sending gifts to one another.

²⁰Mordecai recorded these events. And he sent dispatches to all the Jews throughout the provinces of King Ahasuerus, near and far, ²¹charging them to observe the fourteenth and fifteenth days of Adar, every year— ²²the same days on which the Jews enjoyed relief from their foes and the same month which had been transformed for them from one of grief and mourning to one of festive joy. They were to observe them as days of feasting and merrymaking, and as an occasion for sending gifts to one another and presents to the poor. ²³The Jews accordingly assumed as an obligation that which they had begun to practice and which Mordecai prescribed for them.

ᵃ *Moved up from v. 10 for greater clarity.*

24For Haman son of Hammedatha the Agagite, the foe of all the Jews, had plotted to destroy the Jews, and had cast *pur*—that is, the lot—with intent to crush and exterminate them. 25But when [Esther] came before the king, he commanded: b-"With the promulgation of this decree,-b let the evil plot, which he devised against the Jews, recoil on his own head!" So they impaled him and his sons on the stake. 26For that reason these days were named Purim, after *pur*.

In view, then, of all the instructions in the said letter and of what they had experienced in that matter and what had befallen them, 27the Jews undertook and irrevocably obligated themselves and their descendants, and all who might join them, to observe these two days in the manner prescribed and at the proper time each year. 28Consequently, these days are recalled and observed in every generation: by every family, every province, and every city. And these days of Purim shall never cease among the Jews, and the memory of them shall never perish among their descendants.

29cThen Queen Esther daughter of Abihail wrote a second letter of Purim for the purpose of confirming with full authority the aforementioned one of Mordecai the Jew. 30Dispatches were sent to all the Jews in the hundred and twenty-seven provinces of the realm of Ahasuerus with an ordinance of "equity and honesty:"d 31These days of Purim shall be observed at their proper time, as Mordecai the Jew—and now Queen Esther—has obligated them to do, and just as they have assumed for themselves and their descendants the obligation of the fasts with their lamentations.e

32And Esther's ordinance validating these observances of Purim was recorded in a scroll.

10 King Ahasuerus imposed tribute on the mainland and the islands. 2All his mighty and powerful acts, and a full account of the greatness to which the king advanced Mordecai, are recorded in the Annals of the Kings of Media and Persia. 3For Mordecai the Jew ranked next to King Ahasuerus and was highly regarded by the Jews and popular with the multitude of his brethren; he sought the good of his people and interceded for the welfare of all his kindred.

b-b *Meaning of Heb. uncertain.*
c *Force of vv. 29–31 uncertain in part. Verse 29 reads literally, "Then Queen Esther, daughter of Abihail, and Mordecai the Jew, wrote with full authority to confirm this second letter of Purim."*
d *I.e., of new holidays, the instituting of which is linked to love of equity and honesty in Zech. 8.19.*
e *The Jews had long been observing fast days in commemoration of national calamities; see Zech. 7.5; 8.19.*

DANIEL

1 In the third year of the reign of King Jehoiakim of Judah, King Nebuchadnezzar of Babylon came to Jerusalem and laid siege to it. ²The Lord delivered King Jehoiakim of Judah into his power, together with some of the vessels of the House of God, and he brought them to the land of Shinar to the house of his god; he deposited the vessels in the treasury of his god. ³Then the king ordered Ashpenaz, his chief officer, to bring some Israelites of royal descent and of the nobility—⁴youths without blemish, handsome, proficient in all wisdom, knowledgeable and intelligent, and capable of serving in the royal palace—and teach them the writings and the language of the Chaldeans. ⁵The king allotted daily rations to them from the king's food and from the wine he drank. They were to be educated for three years, ᵃ-at the end of which they-ᵃ were to enter the king's service.

⁶Among them were the Judahites Daniel, Hananiah, Mishael and Azariah. ⁷The chief officer gave them new names; he named Daniel Belteshazzar, Hananiah Shadrach, Mishael Meshach, and Azariah Abed-nego. ⁸Daniel resolved not to defile himself with the king's food or the wine he drank, so he sought permission of the chief officer not to defile himself, ⁹and God disposed the chief officer to be kind and compassionate toward Daniel. ¹⁰The chief officer said to Daniel, "I fear that my lord the king, who allotted food and drink to you, will notice that you look out of sorts, unlike the other youths of your age—and you will put my lifeᵇ in jeopardy with the king." ¹¹Daniel replied to the guard whom the chief officer had put in charge of Daniel, Hananiah, Mishael and Azariah, ¹²"Please test your servants for ten days, giving us legumes to eat and water to drink. ¹³Then compare our appearance with that of the youths who eat of the king's food, and do with your servants as you see fit." ¹⁴He agreed to this plan of theirs, and tested them for ten days. ¹⁵When the ten days were

---

ᵃ⁻ᵃ *Or "and some of them."*
ᵇ *Lit. "head."*

over, they looked better and healthier than all the youths who were eating of the king's food. [16]So the guard kept on removing their food, and the wine they were supposed to drink, and gave them legumes. [17]God made all four of these young men intelligent and proficient in all writings and wisdom, and Daniel had understanding of visions and dreams of all kinds.[18]When the time the king had set for their presentation had come, the chief officer presented them to Nebuchadnezzar. [19]The king spoke with them, and of them all none was equal to Daniel, Hananiah, Mishael and Azariah; so these entered the king's service. [20]Whenever the king put a question to them requiring wisdom and understanding, he found them to be ten times better than all the magicians and exorcists throughout his realm. [21]Daniel was there until the first year of King Cyrus.

2 In the second year of the reign of Nebuchadnezzar, Nebuchadnezzar had a dream; his spirit was agitated, yet he [a-]was overcome by[-a] sleep. [2]The king ordered the magicians, exorcists, sorcerers, and Chaldeans to be summoned in order to tell the king what he had dreamed. They came and stood before the king, [3]and the king said to them, "I have had a dream and [b-]I am full of anxiety[-b] to know what I have dreamed." [4]The Chaldeans spoke to the king in Aramaic, "O king, live forever! Relate the dream to your servants, and we will tell its meaning." [5]The king said in reply to the Chaldeans, "I hereby decree: If you will not make the dream and its meaning known to me, you shall be torn limb from limb and your houses confiscated.[c] [6]But if you tell the dream and its meaning, you shall receive from me gifts, presents, and great honor; therefore, tell me the dream and its meaning." [7]Once again they answered, "Let the king relate the dream to his servants, and we will tell its meaning." [8]The king said in reply, "It is clear to me that you are playing for time, since you see that I have decreed [9]that if you do not make the dream known to me, there is but one verdict for you. You have conspired to tell me something false and fraudulent until circumstances change; so relate the dream to me, and I will then know that you can tell its meaning." [10]The Chaldeans said in reply to the king, "There is no one on earth who can [d-]satisfy the king's demand,[-d] for great king or ruler—none has ever asked such a thing of any magician, exorcist, or Chaldean. [11]The thing asked by the king is difficult; there is no one who can tell it to the king except the gods whose

---

a-a *Meaning of Heb. uncertain; others "could not."*
b-b *Meaning uncertain; or "turned into ruins."*
c *Lit. "tell the king's matter."*
d-d *Lit. "flesh."*

abode is not among mortals."ᵉ ¹²Whereupon the king flew into a violent rage, and gave an order to do away with all the wise men of Babylon.

¹³The decree condemning the wise men to death was issued. Daniel and his companions were about to be put to death ¹⁴when Daniel remonstrated with Arioch, the captain of the royal guard who had set out to put the wise men of Babylon to death. ¹⁵He spoke up and said to Arioch, the royal officer, "Why is the decree of the king so urgent?" Thereupon Arioch informed Daniel of the matter. ¹⁶So Daniel went to ask the king for time, that he might tell the meaning to the king. ¹⁷Then Daniel went to his house and informed his companions, Hananiah, Mishael, and Azariah, of the matter, ¹⁸that they might implore the God of Heaven for help regarding this mystery, so that Daniel and his colleagues would not be put to death together with the other wise men of Babylon.

¹⁹The mystery was revealed to Daniel in a night vision; then Daniel blessed the God of Heaven. ²⁰Daniel spoke up and said:

"Let the name of God be blessed forever and ever,
For wisdom and power are His.
²¹He changes times and seasons,
Removes kings and installs kings;
He gives the wise their wisdom
And knowledge to those who know.
²²He reveals deep and hidden things,
Knows what is in the darkness,
And light dwells with Him.
²³I acknowledge and praise You,
O God of my fathers,
You who have given me wisdom and power,
For now You have let me know what we asked of You;
You have let us know what concerns the king."

²⁴Thereupon Daniel went to Arioch, whom the king had appointed to do away with the wise men of Babylon; he came and said to him as follows, "Do not do away with the wise men of Babylon; bring me to the king and I will tell the king the meaning!" ²⁵So Arioch rushed Daniel into the king's presence and said to him, "I have found among the exiles of Judah a man who can make the meaning known to the king!" ²⁶The king said in reply to Daniel (who was called Belteshazzar), "Can you really make known to me the dream that I saw and its meaning?" ²⁷Daniel

ᵉ *Meaning uncertain.*

answered the king and said, "The mystery about which the king has inquired—wise men, exorcists, magicians, and diviners cannot tell to the king. 28But there is a God in heaven who reveals mysteries, and He has made known to King Nebuchadnezzar what is to be at the end of days. This is your dream and the vision that entered your mind in bed: 29O king, the thoughts that came to your mind in your bed are about future events; He who reveals mysteries has let you know what is to happen. 30Not because my wisdom is greater than that of other creatures has this mystery been revealed to me, but in order that the meaning should be made known to the king, and that you may know the thoughts of your mind.

31"O king, as you looked on, there appeared a great statue. This statue, which was huge and its brightness surpassing, stood before you, and its appearance was awesome. 32The head of that statue was of fine gold; its breast and arms were of silver; its belly and thighs, of bronze; 33its legs were of iron, and its feet part iron and part clay. 34As you looked on, a stone was hewn out, not by hands, and struck the statue on its feet of iron and clay and crushed them. 35All at once, the iron, clay, bronze, silver, and gold were crushed, and became like chaff of the threshing floors of summer; a wind carried them off until no trace of them was left. But the stone that struck the statue became a great mountain and filled the whole earth.

36"Such was the dream, and we will now tell the king its meaning. 37You, O king—king of kings, to whom the God of Heaven has given kingdom, power, might, and glory; 38into whose hands He has given men, wild beasts, and the fowl of heaven, wherever they may dwell; and to whom He has given dominion over them all—you are the head of gold. 39But another kingdom will arise after you, inferior to yours; then yet a third kingdom, of bronze, which will rule over the whole earth. 40But the fourth kingdom will be as strong as iron; just as iron crushes and shatters everything—and like iron that smashes—so will it crush and smash all these. 41You saw the feet and the toes, part potter's clay and part iron; that means it will be a divided kingdom; it will have only some of the stability of iron, inasmuch as you saw iron mixed with common clay. 42And the toes were part iron and part clay; that [means] the kingdom will be in part strong and in part brittle. 43You saw iron mixed with common clay; that means: e-they shall intermingle with the offspring of men,-e but shall not hold together, just as iron does not mix with clay.

44And in the time of those kings, the God of Heaven will establish a kingdom that shall never be destroyed, a kingdom that shall not be transferred to another people. It will crush and wipe out all these kingdoms, but shall itself last forever—45just as you saw how a stone was hewn from the mountain, not by hands, and crushed the iron, bronze, clay, silver, and gold. The great God has made known to the king what will happen in the future. The dream is sure and its interpretation reliable."

46Then King Nebuchadnezzar prostrated himself and paid homage to Daniel and ordered that a meal offering and pleasing offerings be made to him. 47The king said in reply to Daniel, "Truly your God must be the God of gods and Lord of kings and the revealer of mysteries to have enabled you to reveal this mystery." 48The king then elevated Daniel and gave him very many gifts, and made him governor of the whole province of Babylon and chief prefect of all the wise men of Babylon. 49At Daniel's request, the king appointed Shadrach, Meshach, and Abed-nego to administer the province of Babylon; while Daniel himself was at the king's court.

3 King Nebuchadnezzar made a statue of gold sixty cubits high and six cubits broad. He set it up in the plain of Dura in the province of Babylon. 2King Nebuchadnezzar then sent word to gather the satraps, prefects, governors, counselors, treasurers, judges, officers, and all the provincial officials to attend the dedication of the statue that King Nebuchadnezzar had set up. 3So the satraps, prefects, governors, counselors, treasurers, judges, officers, and all the provincial officials assembled for the dedication of the statue that King Nebuchadnezzar had set up, and stood before the statue that Nebuchadnezzar had set up. 4The herald proclaimed in a loud voice, "You are commanded, O peoples and nations of every language, 5when you hear the sound of the horn, pipe, zither, lyre, psaltery, bagpipe, and all other types of instruments, to fall down and worship the statue of gold that King Nebuchadnezzar has set up. 6Whoever will not fall down and worship shall at once be thrown into a burning fiery furnace." 7And so, as soon as all the peoples heard the sound of the horn, pipe, zither, lyre, psaltery, and all other types of instruments, all peoples and nations of every language fell down and worshiped the statue of gold that King Nebuchadnezzar had set up.

8Seizing the occasion, certain Chaldeans came forward to slander the

Jews. 9They spoke up and said to King Nebuchadnezzar, "O king, live forever! 10You, O king, gave an order that everyone who hears the horn, pipe, zither, lyre, psaltery, bagpipe, and all types of instruments must fall down and worship the golden statue, 11and whoever does not fall down and worship shall be thrown into a burning fiery furnace. 12There are certain Jews whom you appointed to administer the province of Babylon, Shadrach, Meshach, and Abed-nego; those men pay no heed to you, O king; they do not serve your god or worship the statue of gold that you have set up."

13Then Nebuchadnezzar, in raging fury, ordered Shadrach, Meshach, and Abed-nego to be brought; so those men were brought before the king. 14Nebuchadnezzar spoke to them and said, "Is it true, Shadrach, Meshach, and Abed-nego, that you do not serve my god or worship the statue of gold that I have set up? 15Now if you are ready to fall down and worship the statue that I have made when you hear the sound of the horn, pipe, zither, lyre, psaltery, and bagpipe, and all other types of instruments, [well and good]; but if you will not worship, you shall at once be thrown into a burning fiery furnace, and what god is there that can save you from my power?" 16Shadrach, Meshach, and Abed-nego said in reply to the king, "O Nebuchadnezzar, we have no need to answer you in this matter, 17for if so it must be, our God whom we serve is able to save us from the burning fiery furnace, and He will save us from your power, O king. 18But even if He does not, be it known to you, O king, that we will not serve your god or worship the statue of gold that you have set up."

19Nebuchadnezzar was so filled with rage at Shadrach, Meshach, and Abed-nego that his visage was distorted, and he gave an order to heat up the furnace to seven times its usual heat. 20He commanded some of the strongest men of his army to bind Shadrach, Meshach, and Abed-nego, and to throw them into the burning fiery furnace. 21So these men, in their shirts, trousers, hats, and other garments, were bound and thrown into the burning fiery furnace. 22Because the king's order was urgent, and the furnace was heated to excess, a tongue of flame killed the men who carried up Shadrach, Meshach, and Abed-nego. 23But those three men, Shadrach, Meshach, and Abed-nego, dropped, bound, into the burning fiery furnace.

24Then King Nebuchadnezzar was astonished and, rising in haste, addressed his companions, saying, "Did we not throw three men, bound, into the fire?" They spoke in reply, "Surely, O king." 25He answered, "But

I see four men walking about unbound and unharmed in the fire and the fourth looks like a divine being." 26Nebuchadnezzar then approached the hatch of the burning fiery furnace and called, "Shadrach, Meshach, Abed-nego, servants of the Most High God, come out!" So Shadrach, Meshach, and Abed-nego came out of the fire. 27The satraps, the prefects, the governors, and the royal companions gathered around to look at those men, on whose bodies the fire had had no effect, the hair of whose heads had not been singed, whose shirts looked no different, to whom not even the odor of fire clung. 28Nebuchadnezzar spoke up and said, "Blessed be the God of Shadrach, Meshach, and Abed-nego, who sent His angel to save His servants who, trusting in Him, flouted the king's decree at the risk of their lives rather than serve or worship any god but their own God. 29I hereby give an order that [anyone of] any people or nation of whatever language who blasphemes the God of Shadrach, Meshach, and Abed-nego shall be torn limb from limb, and his house confiscated, for there is no other God who is able to save in this way."

30Thereupon the king promoted Shadrach, Meshach, and Abed-nego in the province of Babylon.

31"King Nebuchadnezzar to all people and nations of every language that inhabit the whole earth: May your well-being abound! 32The signs and wonders that the Most High God has worked for me I am pleased to relate. 33How great are His signs; how mighty His wonders! His kingdom is an everlasting kingdom, and His dominion endures throughout the generations."

4 I, Nebuchadnezzar, was living serenely in my house, flourishing in my palace. 2I had a dream that frightened me, and my thoughts in bed and the vision of my mind alarmed me. 3I gave an order to bring all the wise men of Babylon before me to let me know the meaning of the dream. 4The magicians, exorcists, Chaldeans, and diviners came, and I related the dream to them, but they could not make its meaning known to me. 5Finally, Daniel, called Belteshazzar after the name of my god, in whom the spirit of the holy gods was, came to me, and I related the dream to him, [saying], 6"Belteshazzar, chief magician, in whom I know the spirit of the holy gods to be, and whom no mystery baffles, tell me the meaning of my dream vision that I have seen. 7In the visions of my mind in bed

I saw a tree of great height in the midst of the earth;
⁸The tree grew and became mighty;
Its top reached heaven,
⁹And it was visible to the ends of the earth.
Its foliage was beautiful
And its fruit abundant;
There was food for all in it.
Beneath it the beasts of the field found shade,
And the birds of the sky dwelt on its branches;
All creatures fed on it.

¹⁰In the vision of my mind in bed, I looked and saw a holy Watcher coming down from heaven. ¹¹He called loudly and said:

'Hew down the tree, lop off its branches,
Strip off its foliage, scatter its fruit.
Let the beasts of the field flee from beneath it
And the birds from its branches,
¹²But leave the stump with its roots in the ground.
In fetters of iron and bronze
In the grass of the field,
Let him be drenched with the dew of heaven,
And share earth's verdure with the beasts.
¹³Let his mind be altered from that of a man,
And let him be given the mind of a beast,
And let seven seasons pass over him.
¹⁴This sentence is decreed by the Watchers;
This verdict is commanded by the Holy Ones
So that all creatures may know
That the Most High is sovereign over the realm of man,
And He gives it to whom He wishes
And He may set over it even the lowest of men.'

¹⁵"I, King Nebuchadnezzar, had this dream; now you, Belteshazzar, tell me its meaning, since all the wise men of my kingdom are not able to make its meaning known to me, but you are able, for the spirit of the holy gods is in you."

¹⁶Then Daniel, called Belteshazzar, was perplexed for a while, and alarmed by his thoughts. The king addressed him, "Let the dream and its meaning not alarm you." Belteshazzar replied, "My lord, would that the dream were for your enemy and its meaning for your foe! ¹⁷The tree that you

saw grow and become mighty, whose top reached heaven, which was visible throughout the earth,[18]whose foliage was beautiful, whose fruit was so abundant that there was food for all in it, beneath which the beasts of the field dwelt, and in whose branches the birds of the sky lodged—[19]it is you, O king, you who have grown and become mighty, whose greatness has grown to reach heaven, and whose dominion is to the end of the earth. [20]The holy Watcher whom the king saw descend from heaven and say,

> Hew down the tree and destroy it,
> But leave the stump with its roots in the ground.
> In fetters of iron and bronze
> In the grass of the field,
> Let him be drenched with the dew of heaven,
> And share the lot of the beasts of the field
> Until seven seasons pass over him—

[21]this is its meaning, O king; it is the decree of the Most High which has overtaken my lord the king. [22]You will be driven away from men and have your habitation with the beasts of the field. You will be fed grass like cattle, and be drenched with the dew of heaven; seven seasons will pass over you until you come to know that the Most High is sovereign over the realm of man, and He gives it to whom He wishes. [23]And the meaning of the command to leave the stump of the tree with its roots is that the kingdom will remain yours from the time you come to know that Heaven is sovereign. [24]Therefore, O king, may my advice be acceptable to you: Redeem your sins by beneficence and your iniquities by generosity to the poor; then your serenity may be extended."

[25]All this befell King Nebuchadnezzar. [26]Twelve months later, as he was walking on the roof of the royal palace at Babylon, [27]the king exclaimed, "There is great Babylon, which I have built by my vast power to be a royal residence for the glory of my majesty!" [28]The words were still on the king's lips, when a voice fell from heaven, "It has been decreed for you, O King Nebuchadnezzar: The kingdom has passed out of your hands. [29]You are being driven away from men, and your habitation is to be with the beasts of the field. You are to be fed grass like cattle, and seven seasons will pass over you until you come to know that the Most High is sovereign over the realm of man and He gives it to whom He wishes." [30]There and then the sentence was carried out upon Nebuchadnezzar. He was driven away from men, he ate grass like cattle, and his

body was drenched with the dew of heaven until his hair grew like eagle's [feathers] and his nails like [the talons of] birds.

³¹"When the time had passed, I, Nebuchadnezzar, lifted my eyes to heaven, and my reason was restored to me. I blessed the Most High, and praised and glorified the Ever-Living One,

Whose dominion is an everlasting dominion
And whose kingdom endures throughout the generations.
³²All the inhabitants of the earth are of no account.
He does as He wishes with the host of heaven,
And with the inhabitants of the earth.
There is none to stay His hand
Or say to Him, 'What have You done?'

³³There and then my reason was restored to me, and my majesty and splendor were restored to me for the glory of my kingdom. My companions and nobles sought me out, and I was reestablished over my kingdom, and added greatness was given me. ³⁴So now I, Nebuchadnezzar, praise, exalt, and glorify the King of Heaven, all of whose works are just and whose ways are right, and who is able to humble those who behave arrogantly."

5 King Belshazzar gave a great banquet for his thousand nobles, and in the presence of the thousand he drank wine. ²Under the influence of the wine, Belshazzar ordered the gold and silver vessels that his father Nebuchadnezzar had taken out of the temple at Jerusalem to be brought so that the king and his nobles, his consorts, and his concubines could drink from them. ³The golden vessels that had been taken out of the sanctuary of the House of God in Jerusalem were then brought, and the king, his nobles, his consorts, and his concubines drank from them. ⁴They drank wine and praised the gods of gold and silver, bronze, iron, wood, and stone. ⁵Just then, the fingers of a human hand appeared and wrote on the plaster of the wall of the king's palace opposite the lampstand, so that the king could see the hand as it wrote. ⁶The king's face darkened, and his thoughts alarmed him; the joints of his loins were loosened and his knees knocked together. ⁷The king called loudly for the exorcists, Chaldeans, and diviners to be brought. The king addressed the wise men of Babylon, "Whoever can read this writing and tell me its meaning shall be clothed

in purple and wear a golden chain on his neck, and shall rule as a-one of three-a in the kingdom."

8Then all the king's wise men came, but they could not read the writing or make known its meaning to the king. 9King Belshazzar grew exceedingly alarmed and his face darkened, and his nobles were dismayed. 10Because of the state of the king and his nobles, the queen came to the banquet hall. The queen spoke up and said, "O king, live forever! Let your thoughts not alarm you or your face darken. 11There is a man in your kingdom who has the spirit of the holy gods in him; in your father's time, illumination, understanding, and wisdom like that of the gods were to be found in him, and your father, King Nebuchadnezzar, appointed him chief of the magicians, exorcists, Chaldeans, and diviners. 12Seeing that there is to be found in Daniel (whom the king called Belteshazzar) extraordinary spirit, knowledge, and understanding to interpret dreams, to explain riddles and solve problems, let Daniel now be called to tell the meaning [of the writing]."

13Daniel was then brought before the king. The king addressed Daniel, "You are Daniel, one of the exiles of Judah whom my father, the king, brought from Judah. 14I have heard about you that you have the spirit of the gods in you, and that illumination, knowledge, and extraordinary wisdom are to be found in you. 15Now the wise men and exorcists have been brought before me to read this writing and to make known its meaning to me. But they could not tell what it meant. 16I have heard about you, that you can give interpretations and solve problems. Now if you can read the writing and make known its meaning to me, you shall be clothed in purple and wear a golden chain on your neck and rule as one of three in the kingdom."

17Then Daniel said in reply to the king, "You may keep your gifts for yourself, and give your presents to others. But I will read the writing for the king, and make its meaning known to him. 18O king, the Most High God bestowed kingship, grandeur, glory, and majesty upon your father Nebuchadnezzar. 19And because of the grandeur that He bestowed upon him, all the peoples and nations of every language trembled in fear of him. He put to death whom he wished, and whom he wished he let live; he raised high whom he wished and whom he wished he brought low. 20But when he grew haughty and willfully presumptuous, he was deposed from his royal throne and his glory was removed from him. 21He was driven away from men, and his mind made like that of a beast, and his

a-a Cf. Dan. 6.3; or "third in rank."

habitation was with wild asses. He was fed grass like cattle, and his body was drenched with the dew of heaven until he came to know that the Most High God is sovereign over the realm of man, and sets over it whom He wishes. ²²But you, Belshazzar his son, did not humble yourself although you knew all this. ²³You exalted yourself against the Lord of Heaven, and had the vessels of His temple brought to you. You and your nobles, your consorts, and your concubines drank wine from them and praised the gods of silver and gold, bronze and iron, wood and stone, which do not see, hear, or understand; but the God who controls your lifebreath and every move you make—Him you did not glorify! ²⁴He therefore made the hand appear, and caused the writing to be inscribed. ²⁵This is the writing that is inscribed: MENE MENE TEKEL UPHARSIN. ²⁶And this is its meaning: MENE—God has numbered[b] [the days of] your kingdom and brought it to an end; ²⁷TEKEL—[c]you have been weighed[c] in the balance and found wanting; ²⁸PERES—your kingdom [d]has been divided[d] and given to the Medes and the Persians." ²⁹Then, at Belshazzar's command, they clothed Daniel in purple, placed a golden chain on his neck, and proclaimed that he should rule as one of three in the kingdom.

³⁰That very night, Belshazzar, the Chaldean king, was killed, 6 ¹and Darius the Mede received the kingdom, being about sixty-two years old. ²It pleased Darius to appoint over the kingdom one hundred and twenty satraps to be in charge of the whole kingdom; ³over them were three ministers, one of them Daniel, to whom these satraps reported, in order that the king not be troubled. ⁴This man Daniel surpassed the other ministers and satraps by virtue of his extraordinary spirit, and the king considered setting him over the whole kingdom. ⁵The ministers and satraps looked for some fault in Daniel's conduct in matters of state, but they could find neither fault nor corruption, inasmuch as he was trustworthy, and no negligence or corruption was to be found in him. ⁶Those men then said, "We are not going to find any fault with this Daniel, unless we find something against him in connection with the laws of his God." ⁷Then these ministers and satraps came thronging in to the king and said to him, "O King Darius, live forever! ⁸All the ministers of the kingdom, the prefects, satraps, companions, and governors are in agreement that a royal ban should be issued under sanction of an oath that whoever shall address a petition to any god or man, besides you, O king, during the next thirty days shall be thrown into a lions' den. ⁹So issue the ban, O

---

b *Aramaic* mena.
c-c *Aramaic* tekilta.
d-d *Aramaic* perisat.

king, and put it in writing so that it be unalterable as a law of the Medes and Persians that may not be abrogated." ¹⁰Thereupon King Darius put the ban in writing.

¹¹When Daniel learned that it had been put in writing, he went to his house, in whose upper chamber he had had windows made facing Jerusalem, and three times a day he knelt down, prayed, and made confession to his God, as he had always done. ¹²Then those men came thronging in and found Daniel petitioning his God in supplication. ¹³They then approached the king and reminded him of the royal ban: "Did you not put in writing a ban that whoever addresses a petition to any god or man besides you, O king, during the next thirty days, shall be thrown into a lions' den?" The king said in reply, "The order stands firm, as a law of the Medes and Persians that may not be abrogated." ¹⁴Thereupon they said to the king, "Daniel, one of the exiles of Judah, pays no heed to you, O king, or to the ban that you put in writing; three times a day he offers his petitions [to his God]." ¹⁵Upon hearing that, the king was very disturbed, and he set his heart upon saving Daniel, and until the sun set made every effort to rescue him. ¹⁶Then those men came thronging in to the king and said to the king, "Know, O king, that it is a law of the Medes and Persians that any ban that the king issues under sanction of oath is unalterable." ¹⁷By the king's order, Daniel was then brought and thrown into the lions' den. The king spoke to Daniel and said, "Your God, whom you serve so regularly, will deliver you." ¹⁸A rock was brought and placed over the mouth of the den; the king sealed it with his signet and with the signet of his nobles, so that nothing might be altered concerning Daniel.

¹⁹The king then went to his palace and spent the night fasting; no diversions were brought to him, and his sleep fled from him. ²⁰Then, at the first light of dawn, the king arose and rushed to the lions' den. ²¹As he approached the den, he cried to Daniel in a mournful voice; the king said to Daniel, "Daniel, servant of the living God, was the God whom you served so regularly able to deliver you from the lions?" ²²Daniel then talked with the king, "O king, live forever! ²³My God sent His angel, who shut the mouths of the lions so that they did not injure me, inasmuch as I was found innocent by Him, nor have I, O king, done you any injury." ²⁴The king was very glad, and ordered Daniel to be brought up out of the den. Daniel was brought up out of the den, and no injury was found on him, for he had trusted in his God. ²⁵Then, by order of the king, those

men who had slandered Daniel were brought and, together with their children and wives, were thrown into the lions' den. They had hardly reached the bottom of the den when the lions overpowered them and crushed all their bones.

²⁶Then King Darius wrote to all peoples and nations of every language that inhabit the earth, "May your well-being abound! ²⁷I have hereby given an order that throughout my royal domain men must tremble in fear before the God of Daniel, for He is the living God who endures forever; His kingdom is indestructible, and His dominion is to the end of time; ²⁸He delivers and saves, and performs signs and wonders in heaven and on earth, for He delivered Daniel from the power of the lions." ²⁹Thus Daniel prospered during the reign of Darius and during the reign of Cyrus the Persian.

7 In the first year of King Belshazzar of Babylon, Daniel saw a dream and a vision of his mind in bed; afterward he wrote down the dream. Beginning the account, ²Daniel related the following:

"In my vision at night, I saw the four winds of heaven stirring up the great sea. ³Four mighty beasts different from each other emerged from the sea. ⁴The first was like a lion but had eagles' wings. As I looked on, its wings were plucked off, and it was lifted off the ground and set on its feet like a man and given the mind of a man. ⁵Then I saw a second, different beast, which was like a bear but raised on one side, and with three fangs in its mouth among its teeth; it was told, 'Arise, eat much meat!' ⁶After that, as I looked on, there was another one, like a leopard, and it had on its back four wings like those of a bird; the beast had four heads, and dominion was given to it. ⁷After that, as I looked on in the night vision, there was a fourth beast—fearsome, dreadful, and very powerful, with great iron teeth—that devoured and crushed, and stamped the remains with its feet. It was different from all the other beasts which had gone before it; and it had ten horns. ⁸While I was gazing upon these horns, a new little horn sprouted up among them; three of the older horns were uprooted to make room for it. There were eyes in this horn like those of a man, and a mouth that spoke arrogantly. ⁹As I looked on,

Thrones were set in place,
And the Ancient of Days took His seat.
His garment was like white snow,

And the hair of His head was like lamb's[a] wool.

His throne was tongues of flame;

Its wheels were blazing fire.

¹⁰A river of fire streamed forth before Him;

Thousands upon thousands served Him;

Myriads upon myriads attended Him;

The court sat and the books were opened.

¹¹I looked on. Then, because of the arrogant words that the horn spoke, the beast was killed as I looked on; its body was destroyed and it was consigned to the flames. ¹²The dominion of the other beasts was taken away, but an extension of life was given to them for a time and season. ¹³As I looked on, in the night vision,

One like a human being

Came with the clouds of heaven;

He reached the Ancient of Days

And was presented to Him.

¹⁴Dominion, glory, and kingship were given to him;

All peoples and nations of every language must serve him.

His dominion is an everlasting dominion that shall not pass

away,

And his kingship, one that shall not be destroyed.

¹⁵As for me, Daniel, my spirit was disturbed within me and the vision of my mind alarmed me. ¹⁶I approached one of the attendants and asked him the true meaning of all this. He gave me this interpretation of the matter: ¹⁷'These great beasts, four in number [mean] four kingdoms[b] will arise out of the earth; ¹⁸then holy ones of the Most High will receive the kingdom, and will possess the kingdom forever—forever and ever.' ¹⁹Then I wanted to ascertain the true meaning of the fourth beast, which was different from them all, very fearsome, with teeth of iron, claws of bronze, that devoured and crushed, and stamped the remains; ²⁰and of the ten horns on its head; and of the new one that sprouted, to make room for which three fell—the horn that had eyes, and a mouth that spoke arrogantly, and which was more conspicuous than its fellows. ²¹(I looked on as that horn made war with the holy ones and overcame them, ²²until the Ancient of Days came and judgment was rendered in favor of the holy ones of the Most High, for the time had come, and the holy ones took possession of the kingdom.) ²³This is what he said: 'The fourth beast [means]—there will be a fourth kingdom upon the earth which will be

---

a *Or "clean."*
b *Lit. "kings."*

different from all the kingdoms; it will devour the whole earth, tread it down, and crush it. 24And the ten horns [mean]—from that kingdom, ten kings will arise, and after them another will arise. He will be different from the former ones, and will bring low three kings. 25He will speak words against the Most High, and will harass the holy ones of the Most High. He will think of changing times and laws, and they will be delivered into his power for a ᶜ‑time, times, and half a time.‑ᶜ 26Then the court will sit and his dominion will be taken away, to be destroyed and abolished for all time. 27The kingship and dominion and grandeur belonging to all the kingdoms under Heaven will be given to the people of the holy ones of the Most High. Their kingdom shall be an everlasting kingdom, and all dominions shall serve and obey them.' " 28Here the account ends.

I, Daniel, was very alarmed by my thoughts, and my face darkened; and I could not put the matter out of my mind.

8 In the third year of the reign of King Belshazzar, a vision appeared to me, to me, Daniel, after the one that had appeared to me earlier. 2I saw in the vision—at the time I saw it I was in the fortress of Shushan, in the province of Elam—I saw in the vision that I was beside the Ulai River. 3I looked and saw a ram standing between me and the river; he had two horns; the horns were high, with one higher than the other, and the higher sprouting last. 4I saw the ram butting westward, northward, and southward. No beast could withstand him, and there was none to deliver from his power. He did as he pleased and grew great. 5As I looked on, a he-goat came from the west, passing over the entire earth without touching the ground. The goat had a conspicuous horn on its forehead. 6He came up to the two-horned ram that I had seen standing between me and the river and charged at him with furious force. 7I saw him reach the ram and rage at him; he struck the ram and broke its two horns, and the ram was powerless to withstand him. He threw him to the ground and trampled him, and there was none to deliver the ram from his power. 8Then the he-goat grew very great, but at the peak of his power his big horn was broken. In its place, four conspicuous horns sprouted toward the four winds of heaven. 9From one of them emerged a small horn, which extended itself greatly toward the south, toward the east, and to-

ᶜᶜ *I.e., a year, two years, and a half a year.*

ward the beautiful land. 10It grew as high as the host of heaven and it hurled some stars of the [heavenly] host to the ground and trampled them. 11It vaunted itself against the very chief of the host; on its account the regular offering was suspended, and His holy place was abandoned. 12a-An army was arrayed iniquitously against the regular offering;-a it hurled truth to the ground and prospered in what it did.

13Then I heard a holy being speaking, and another holy being said to whoever it was who was speaking, "How long will [what was seen in] the vision last—a-the regular offering be forsaken because of transgression; the sanctuary be surrendered and the [heavenly] host be trampled?"-a 14He answered me,b "For twenty-three hundred evenings and mornings; then the sanctuary shall be cleansed." 15While I, Daniel, was seeing the vision, and trying to understand it, there appeared before me one who looked like a man. 16I heard a human voice from the middle of Ulai calling out, "Gabriel, make that man understand the vision." 17He came near to where I was standing, and as he came I was terrified, and fell prostrate. He said to me, "Understand, O man, that the vision refers to the time of the end." 18When he spoke with me, I was overcome by a deep sleep as I lay prostrate on the ground. Then he touched me and made me stand up, 19and said, "I am going to inform you of what will happen when wrath is at an end, for [it refers] to the time appointed for the end.

20"The two-horned ram that you saw [signifies] the kings of Media and Persia; 21and the buck, the he-goat—the king of Greece; and the large horn on his forehead, that is the first king. 22One was broken and four came in its stead—that [means]: four kingdoms will arise out of a nation, but without its power. 23When their kingdoms are at an end, when the measure of transgressionc has been filled, then a king will arise, impudent and versed in intrigue. 24He will have great strength, but not through his own strength. He will be extraordinarily destructive; he will prosper in what he does, and destroy the mighty and the people of holy ones. 25By his cunning, he will use deceit successfully. He will make great plans, will destroy many, taking them unawares, and will rise up against the chief of chiefs, but will be broken, not by [human] hands. 26What was said in the vision about evenings and mornings is true. Now you keep the vision a secret, for it pertains to far-off days." 27So I, Daniel, was stricken,a and languished many days. Then I arose and attended to the king's business, but I was dismayed by the vision and no one could explain it.

a-a *Meaning of Heb. uncertain.*
b *Several ancient versions "him."*
c *Lit. "transgressors."*

9 In the first year of Darius son of Ahasuerus, of Median descent, who was made king over the kingdom of the Chaldeans—²in the first year of his reign, I, Daniel, consulted the books concerning the number of years that, according to the word of the LORD that had come to Jeremiah the prophet, were to be the term of Jerusalem's desolation—seventy years. ³I turned my face to the Lord God, devoting myself to prayer and supplication, in fasting, in sackcloth and ashes. ⁴I prayed to the LORD my God, making confession thus: "O Lord, great and awesome God, who stays faithful to His covenant with those who love Him and keep His commandments! ⁵We have sinned; we have gone astray; we have acted wickedly; we have been rebellious and have deviated from Your commandments and Your rules, ⁶and have not obeyed Your servants the prophets who spoke in Your name to our kings, our officers, our fathers, and all the people of the land. ⁷With You, O Lord, is the right, and the shame is on us to this very day, on the men of Judah and the inhabitants of Jerusalem, all Israel, near and far, in all the lands where You have banished them, for the trespass they committed against You. ⁸The shame, O LORD, is on us, on our kings, our officers, and our fathers, because we have sinned against You. ⁹To the Lord our God belong mercy and forgiveness, for we rebelled against Him, ¹⁰and did not obey the LORD our God by following His teachings that He set before us through His servants the prophets. ¹¹All Israel has violated Your teaching and gone astray, disobeying You; so the curse and the oath written in the Teaching of Moses, the servant of God, have been poured down upon us, for we have sinned against Him. ¹²He carried out the threat that He made against us, and against our rulers who ruled us, to bring upon us great misfortune; under the whole heaven there has never been done the like of what was done to Jerusalem. ¹³All that calamity, just as is written in the Teaching of Moses, came upon us, yet we did not supplicate the LORD our God, did not repent of our iniquity or become wise through Your truth. ¹⁴Hence the LORD was intent upon bringing calamity upon us, for the LORD our God is in the right in all that He has done, but we have not obeyed Him.

¹⁵"Now, O Lord our God—You who brought Your people out of the land of Egypt with a mighty hand, winning fame for Yourself to this very day—we have sinned, we have acted wickedly. ¹⁶O Lord, as befits Your abundant benevolence, let Your wrathful fury turn back from Your city Jerusalem, Your holy mountain; for because of our sins and the iniquities

of our fathers, Jerusalem and Your people have become a mockery among all who are around us. 17"O our God, hear now the prayer of Your servant and his plea, and show Your favor to Your desolate sanctuary, for the Lord's sake. 18Incline Your ear, O my God, and hear; open Your eyes and see our desolation and the city to which Your name is attached. Not because of any merit of ours do we lay our plea before You but because of Your abundant mercies. 19O Lord, hear! O Lord, forgive! O Lord, listen, and act without delay for Your own sake, O my God; for Your name is attached to Your city and Your people!"

20While I was speaking, praying, and confessing my sin and the sin of my people Israel, and laying my supplication before the LORD my God on behalf of the holy mountain of my God—21while I was uttering my prayer, the man Gabriel, whom I had previously seen in the vision, was sent forth in flight and reached me about the time of the evening offering. 22He made me understand by speaking to me and saying, "Daniel, I have just come forth to give you understanding. 23A word went forth as you began your plea, and I have come to tell it, for you are precious; so mark the word and understand the vision.

24"Seventy weeks[a] have been decreed for your people and your holy city until the measure of transgression is filled and that of sin complete, until iniquity is expiated, and eternal righteousness ushered in; and prophetic vision ratified,[b] and the Holy of Holies anointed. 25You must know and understand: From the issuance of the word to restore and rebuild Jerusalem until the [time of the] anointed leader is seven weeks; and for sixty-two weeks it will be rebuilt, square and moat, but in a time of distress. 26And after those sixty-two weeks, the anointed one will disappear and vanish.[c] The army of a leader who is to come will destroy the city and the sanctuary, but its end will come through a flood. Desolation is decreed until the end of war. 27During one week he will make a firm covenant with many. For half a week he will put a stop to the sacrifice and the meal offering. At the [c-corner [of the altar]-c] will be an appalling abomination until the decreed destruction will be poured down upon the appalling thing."

10

In the third year of King Cyrus of Persia, an oracle was revealed to Daniel, who was called Belteshazzar. That oracle was true, [a-but it was]

---

a *Viz., of years.*
b *Lit. "sealed."*
c *Meaning of Heb. uncertain.*
a-a *Meaning of Heb. uncertain.*

a great task to understand the prophecy; understanding came to him through the vision.⁻ᵃ

²At that time, I, Daniel, kept three full weeks of mourning. ³I ate no tasty food, nor did any meat or wine enter my mouth. I did not anoint myself until the three weeks were over. ⁴It was on the twenty-fourth day of the first month, when I was on the bank of the great river—the Tigris— ⁵that I looked and saw a man dressed in linen, his loins girt in ᵇ⁻fine gold.⁻ᵇ ⁶His body was like beryl, his face had the appearance of lightning, his eyes were like flaming torches, his arms and legs had the color of burnished bronze, and the sound of his speech was like the noise of a multitude.

⁷I, Daniel, alone saw the vision; the men who were with me did not see the vision, yet they were seized with a great terror and fled into hiding. ⁸So I was left alone to see this great vision. I was drained of strength, my vigor was destroyed, and I could not summon up strength. ⁹I heard him speaking; and when I heard him speaking, overcome by a deep sleep, I lay prostrate on the ground. ¹⁰Then a hand touched me, and shook me onto my hands and knees. ¹¹He said to me, "O Daniel, precious man, mark what I say to you and stand up, for I have been sent to you." After he said this to me, I stood up, trembling. ¹²He then said to me, "Have no fear, Daniel, for from the first day that you set your mind to get understanding, practicing abstinence before your God, your prayer was heard, and I have come because of your prayer. ¹³However, the prince of the Persian kingdom opposed me for twenty-one days; now Michael, a prince of the first rank, has come to my aid, after I was detained there with the kings of Persia. ¹⁴So I have come to make you understand what is to befall your people in the days to come, for there is yet a vision for those days."

¹⁵While he was saying these things to me, I looked down and kept silent. ¹⁶Then one who looked like a man touched my lips, and I opened my mouth and spoke, saying to him who stood before me, "My lord, because of the vision, I have been seized with pangs and cannot summon strength. ¹⁷How can this servant of my lord speak with my lord, seeing that my strength has failed and no spirit is left in me?" ¹⁸He who looked like a man touched me again, and strengthened me. ¹⁹He said, "Have no fear, precious man, all will be well with you; be strong, be strong!" As he spoke with me, I was strengthened, and said, "Speak on, my lord, for you have strengthened me!" ²⁰Then he said, "Do you know why I have

b-b Or "gold of Uphaz."

come to you? Now I must go back to fight the prince of Persia. When I go off, the prince of Greece will come in. 21c-No one is helping me against them except your prince, Michael. However, I will tell you what is recorded in the book of truth.-c

11 "In the first year of Darius the Mede, I took my stand to strengthen and fortify him. 2And now I will tell you the truth: Persia will have three more kings, and the fourth will be wealthier than them all; by the power he obtains through his wealth, he will stir everyone up against the kingdom of Greece. 3Then a warrior king will appear who will have an extensive dominion and do as he pleases. 4But after his appearance, his kingdom will be broken up and scattered to the four winds of heaven, but not for any of his posterity, nor with dominion like that which he had; for his kingdom will be uprooted and belong to others beside these.

5"The king of the south will grow powerful; however, one of his officers will overpower him and rule, having an extensive dominion. 6After some years, an alliance will be made, and the daughter of the king of the south will come to the king of the north to effect the agreement, but she will not maintain her strength, nor will his strength endure. She will be surrendered together with those who escorted her and the one who begot her and helped her during those times. 7A shoot from her stock will appear in his place, will come against the army and enter the fortress of the king of the north; he will fight and overpower them. 8He will also take their gods with their molten images and their precious vessels of silver and gold back to Egypt as booty. For some years he will leave the king of the north alone, 9who will [later] invade the realm of the king of the south, but will go back to his land.

10"His sons will wage war, collecting a multitude of great armies; he will advance and sweep through as a flood, and will again wage war as far as his stronghold. 11Then the king of the south, in a rage, will go out to do battle with him, with the king of the north. He will muster a great multitude, but the multitude will be delivered into his [foe's] power. 12But when the multitude is carried off, he will grow arrogant; he will cause myriads to perish, but will not prevail. 13Then the king of the north will again muster a multitude even greater than the first. After a time, a matter of years, he will advance with a great army and much baggage. 14In those times, many will resist the king of the south, and the lawless sons of your people will assert themselves to confirm the vision, but they will fail. 15The king of the north will advance and throw up siege ramps and capture a

c-c *Order of clauses inverted for clarity.*

fortress city, and the forces of the south will not hold out; even the elite of his army will be powerless to resist. 16His opponent will do as he pleases, for none will hold out against him; he will install himself in the beautiful land with destruction within his reach. 17He will set his mind upon invading the strongholds throughout his [foe's] kingdom, but in order to destroy it he will effect an agreement with him and give him a daughter in marriage; he will not succeed at it and it will not come about. 18He will turn to the coastlands and capture many; but a consul will put an end to his insults, nay pay him back for his insults. 19He will head back to the strongholds of his own land, but will stumble, and fall, and vanish. 20His place will be taken by one who will dispatch an officer to exact tribute for royal glory, but he will be broken in a few days, not by wrath or by war. 21His place will be taken by a contemptible man, on whom royal majesty was not conferred; he will come in unawares and seize the kingdom through trickery. 22The forces of the flood will be overwhelmed by him and will be broken, and so too the covenant leader. 23And, from the time an alliance is made with him, he will practice deceit; and he will rise to power with a small band. 24He will invade the richest of provinces unawares, and will do what his father and forefathers never did, lavishing on thema spoil, booty, and wealth; he will have designs upon strongholds, but only for a time.

25"He will muster his strength and courage against the king of the south with a great army. The king of the south will wage war with a very great and powerful army but will not stand fast, for they will devise plans against him. 26Those who eat of his food will ruin him. His army will be overwhelmed, and many will fall slain. 27The minds of both kings will be bent on evil; while sitting at the table together, they will lie to each other, but to no avail, for there is yet an appointed term. 28He will return to his land with great wealth, his mind set against the holy covenant. Having done his pleasure, he will return to his land. 29At the appointed time, he will again invade the south, but the second time will not be like the first. 30Ships from Kittim will come against him. He will be checked, and will turn back, raging against the holy covenant. Having done his pleasure, he will then attend to those who forsake the holy covenant. 31Forces will be levied by him; they will desecrate the temple, the fortress; they will abolish the regular offering and set up the appalling abomination. 32He will flatter with smooth words those who act wickedly toward the cove-

---

a I.e., his followers.

nant, but the people devoted to their God will stand firm. ³³The knowledgeable among the people will make the many understand; and for a while they shall fall by sword and flame, suffer captivity and spoliation. ³⁴In defeat, they will receive a little help, and many will join them insincerely. ³⁵Some of the knowledgeable will fall, that they may be refined and purged and whitened until the time of the end, for an interval still remains until the appointed time.

³⁶"The king will do as he pleases; he will exalt and magnify himself above every god, and he will speak awful things against the God of gods. He will prosper until wrath is spent, and what has been decreed is accomplished. ³⁷He will not have regard for the god of his ancestors or for the one dear to women; he will not have regard for any god, but will magnify himself above all. ³⁸He will honor the god of fortresses on his stand; he will honor with gold and silver, with precious stones and costly things, a god that his ancestors never knew. ³⁹He will deal with fortified strongholds with the help of an alien god. He will heap honor on those who acknowledge him, and will make them master over many; he will distribute land for a price. ⁴⁰At the time of the end, the king of the south will lock horns with him, but the king of the north will attack him with chariots and riders and many ships. He will invade lands, sweeping through them like a flood; ⁴¹he will invade the beautiful land, too, and many will fall, but these will escape his clutches: Edom, Moab, and the chief part of the Ammonites. ⁴²He will lay his hands on lands; not even the land of Egypt will escape. ⁴³He will gain control over treasures of gold and silver and over all the precious things of Egypt, and the Libyans and Cushites will follow at his heel. ⁴⁴But reports from east and north will alarm him, and he will march forth in a great fury to destroy and annihilate many. ⁴⁵He will pitch his royal pavilion between the sea and the beautiful holy mountain, and he will meet his doom with no one to help him.

12 "At that time, the great prince, Michael, who stands beside the sons of your people, will appear. It will be a time of trouble, the like of which has never been since the nation came into being. At that time, your people will be rescued, all who are found inscribed in the book. ²Many of those that sleep in the dust of the earth will awake, some to eternal life, others to reproaches, to everlasting abhorrence. ³And the knowledgeable will be radiant like the bright expanse of sky, and those who lead the many to righteousness will be like the stars forever and ever.

4"But you, Daniel, keep the words secret, and seal the book until the time of the end. Many will range far and wide and knowledge will increase."

5Then I, Daniel, looked and saw two others standing, one on one bank of the river, the other on the other bank of the river. 6One said to the man clothed in linen, who was above the water of the river, "How long until the end of these awful things?" 7Then I heard the man dressed in linen, who was above the water of the river, swear by the Ever-Living One as he lifted his right hand and his left hand to heaven: "For a ᵃ-time, times, and half a time;-ᵃ and when the breaking of the power of the holy people comes to an end, then shall all these things be fulfilled."

8I heard and did not understand, so I said, "My lord, what will be the outcome of these things?" 9He said, "Go, Daniel, for these words are secret and sealed to the time of the end. 10Many will be purified and purged and refined; the wicked will act wickedly and none of the wicked will understand; but the knowledgeable will understand. (11From the time the regular offering is abolished, and an appalling abomination is set up— it will be a thousand two hundred and ninety days. Happy the one who waits and reaches one thousand three hundred and thirty-five days.) 12But you, go on to the end; you shall rest, and arise to your destiny at the end of the days."

a-a *See note at 7.25.*

EZRA

1 In the first year of King Cyrus of Persia, when the word of the LORD spoken by Jeremiah was fulfilled,[a] the LORD roused the spirit of King Cyrus of Persia to issue a proclamation throughout his realm by word of mouth and in writing as follows:

2"Thus said King Cyrus of Persia: The LORD God of Heaven has given me all the kingdoms of the earth and has charged me with building Him a house in Jerusalem, which is in Judah. 3Anyone of you of all His people—may his God be with him, and let him go up to Jerusalem that is in Judah and build the House of the LORD God of Israel, the God that is in Jerusalem; 4and all who stay behind, wherever he may be living, let the people of his place assist him with silver, gold, goods, and livestock, besides the freewill offering to the House of God that is in Jerusalem."

5So the chiefs of the clans of Judah and Benjamin, and the priests and Levites, all whose spirit had been roused by God, got ready to go up to build the House of the LORD that is in Jerusalem. 6All their neighbors supported them with silver vessels, with gold, with goods, with livestock, and with precious objects, besides what had been given as a freewill offering. 7King Cyrus of Persia released the vessels of the LORD's house which Nebuchadnezzar had taken away from Jerusalem and had put in the house of his god. 8These King Cyrus of Persia released through the office of Mithredath the treasurer, who gave an inventory of them to Sheshbazzar the prince of Judah. 9This is the inventory: 30 gold basins, 1,000 silver basins, 29 knives, 1030 gold bowls, 410 silver [b-double bowls,-b] 1,000 other vessels; 11in all, 5,400 gold and silver vessels. Sheshbazzar brought all these back when the exiles came back from Babylon to Jerusalem.

---

[a] Cf. Jer. 29.10.
[b-b] Meaning of Heb. uncertain.

2 ᵃThese are the people of the province who came up from among the captive exiles whom King Nebuchadnezzar of Babylon had carried into exile to Babylon, who returned to Jerusalem and Judah, each to his own city, ²who came with Zerubbabel, Jeshua, Nehemiah, Seraiah, Reelaiah, Mordecai, Bilshan, Mispar, Bigvai, Rehum, Baanah:

The list of the men of the people of Israel: ³the sons of Parosh—2,172; ⁴the sons of Shephatiah—372; ⁵the sons of Arah—775; ⁶the sons of Pahath-moab: the sons of Jeshua and Joab—2,812; ⁷the sons of Elam—1,254; ⁸the sons of Zattu—945; ⁹the sons of Zaccai—760; ¹⁰the sons of Bani—642; ¹¹the sons of Bebai—623; ¹²the sons of Azgad—1,222; ¹³the sons of Adonikam—666; ¹⁴the sons of Bigvai—2,056; ¹⁵the sons of Adin—454; ¹⁶the sons of Ater: Hezekiah—98; ¹⁷the sons of Bezai—323; ¹⁸the sons of Jorah—112; ¹⁹the sons of Hashum—223; ²⁰the sons of Gibbar—95; ²¹the sons of Bethlehem—123; ²²the sons of Netophah—56; ²³the sons of Anathoth—128; ²⁴the sons of Azmaveth—42; ²⁵the sons of Kiriath-arim: Chephirah and Beeroth—743; ²⁶the sons of Ramah and Geba—621; ²⁷the men of Michmas—122; ²⁸the men of Beth-el and Ai—223; ²⁹the men of Nebo—52; ³⁰the sons of Magbish—156; ³¹the sons of the other Elam—1,254; ³²the sons of Harim—320; ³³the sons of Lod, Hadid, and Ono—725; ³⁴the sons of Jericho—345; ³⁵the sons of Senaah—3,630.

³⁶The priests: the sons of Jedaiah: the house of Jeshua—973; ³⁷the sons of Immer—1,052; ³⁸the sons of Pashhur—1,247; ³⁹the sons of Harim—1,017.

⁴⁰The Levites: the sons of Jeshua and Kadmiel: the sons of Hodaviah—74.

⁴¹The singers: the sons of Asaph—128.

⁴²The gatekeepers: the sons of Shallum, the sons of Ater, the sons of Talmon, the sons of Akkub, the sons of Hatita, the sons of Shobai, all told—139.

⁴³The temple servants: the sons of Ziha, the sons of Hasupha, the sons of Tabbaoth, ⁴⁴the sons of Keros, the sons of Siaha, the sons of Padon, ⁴⁵the sons of Lebanah, the sons of Hagabah, the sons of Akkub, ⁴⁶the sons of Hagab, the sons of Salmai, the sons of Hanan, ⁴⁷the sons of Giddel, the sons of Gahar, the sons of Reaiah, ⁴⁸the sons of Rezin, the sons of Nekoda, the sons of Gazzam, ⁴⁹the sons of Uzza, the sons of Paseah, the sons of Besai, ⁵⁰the sons of Asnah, the sons of Meunim, the sons of Nephusim, ⁵¹the sons of Bakbuk, the sons of Hakupha, the sons

---

ᵃ *This chapter appears as Neh. 7.6–73 with variations in the names and numbers.*

of Harhur, 52the sons of Bazluth, the sons of Mehida, the sons of Harsha, 53the sons of Barkos, the sons of Sisera, the sons of Temah, 54the sons of Neziah, the sons of Hatipha.

55The sons of Solomon's servants: the sons of Sotai, the sons of Hassophereth, the sons of Peruda, 56the sons of Jaalah, the sons of Darkon, the sons of Giddel, 57the sons of Shephatiah, the sons of Hattil, the sons of Pochereth-hazzebaim, the sons of Ami.

58The total of temple servants and the sons of Solomon's servants— 392.

59The following were those who came up from Tel-melah, Tel-harsha, Cherub, Addan, and Immer—they were unable to tell whether their father's house and descent were Israelite: 60the sons of Delaiah, the sons of Tobiah, the sons of Nekoda—652.

61Of the sons of the priests, the sons of Habaiah, the sons of Hakkoz, the sons of Barzillai who had married a daughter of Barzillai and had taken hisb name—62these searched for their genealogical records, but they could not be found, so they were disqualified for the priesthood. 63The Tirshathac ordered them not to eat of the most holy things until a priest with Urim and Thummim should appear.

64The sum of the entire community was 42,360, 65not counting their male and female servants, those being 7,337; they also had 200 male and female singers. 66Their horses—736; their mules—245; 67their camels— 435; their asses—6,720.

68Some of the chiefs of the clans, on arriving at the House of the LORD in Jerusalem, gave a freewill offering to erect the House of God on its site. 69In accord with their means, they donated to the treasury of the work: gold—6,100 drachmas, silver—5,000 minas, and priestly robes— 100.

70The priests, the Levites and some of the people, and the singers, gatekeepers, and the temple servants took up residence in their towns and all Israel in their towns.

3 When the seventh month arrived—the Israelites being settled in their towns—the entire people assembled as one man in Jerusalem. 2Then Jeshua son of Jozadak and his brother priests, and Zerubbabel son of Shealtiel and his brothers set to and built the altar of the God of Israel to offer burnt offerings upon it as is written in the Teaching of Moses, the man

b Lit. "their."
c A Persian title.

of God. ³They set up the altar on its site because they were in fear of the peoples of the land, and they offered burnt offerings on it to the LORD, burnt offerings each morning and evening. ⁴Then they celebrated the festival of Tabernacles as is written, with its daily burnt offerings in the proper quantities, on each day as is prescribed for it, ⁵followed by the regular burnt offering and the offerings for the new moons and for all the sacred fixed times of the LORD, and whatever freewill offerings were made to the LORD. ⁶From the first day of the seventh month they began to make burnt offerings to the LORD, though the foundation of the Temple of the LORD had not been laid. ⁷They paid the hewers and craftsmen with money, and the Sidonians and Tyrians with food, drink, and oil to bring cedarwood from Lebanon by sea to Joppa, in accord with the authorization granted them by King Cyrus of Persia.

⁸In the second year after their arrival at the House of God, at Jerusalem, in the second month, Zerubbabel son of Shealtiel and Jeshua son of Jozadak, and the rest of their brother priests and Levites, and all who had come from the captivity to Jerusalem, as their first step appointed Levites from the age of twenty and upward to supervise the work of the House of the LORD. ⁹Jeshua, his sons and brothers, Kadmiel and his sons, ª⁻the sons of Judah,⁻ª together were appointed in charge of those who did the work in the House of God; also the sons of Henadad, their sons and brother Levites.

¹⁰When the builders had laid the foundation of the Temple of the LORD, priests in their vestments with trumpets, and Levites sons of Asaph with cymbals were stationed to give praise to the LORD, as King David of Israel had ordained. ¹¹They sang songs extolling and praising the LORD, ᵇ⁻"For He is good, His steadfast love for Israel is eternal."⁻ᵇ All the people raised a great shout extolling the LORD because the foundation of the House of the LORD had been laid. ¹²Many of the priests and Levites and the chiefs of the clans, the old men who had seen the first house, wept loudly at the sight of the founding of this house. Many others shouted joyously at the top of their voices. ¹³The people could not distinguish the shouts of joy from the people's weeping, for the people raised a great shout, the sound of which could be heard from afar.

4 When the adversaries of Judah and Benjamin heard that the returned exiles were building a temple to the LORD God of Israel, ²they approached Zerubbabel and the chiefs of the clans and said to them, "Let us build

---

ª⁻ª *I.e., Hodaviah of 2.40.*
ᵇ⁻ᵇ *Cf. Pss. 106.1; 136.*

with you, since we too worship your God, having offered sacrifices to Him since the time of King Esarhaddon of Assyria, who brought us here." ³Zerubbabel, Jeshua, and the rest of the chiefs of the clans of Israel answered them, "It is not for you and us to build a House to our God, but we alone will build it to the LORD God of Israel, in accord with the charge that the king, King Cyrus of Persia, laid upon us." ⁴Thereupon the people of the land undermined the resolve of the people of Judah, and made them afraid to build. ⁵They bribed ministers in order to thwart their plans all the years of King Cyrus of Persia and until the reign of King Darius of Persia.

⁶And in the reign of Ahasuerus, at the start of his reign, they drew up an accusation against the inhabitants of Judah and Jerusalem.

⁷And in the time of Artaxerxes, Bishlam, Mithredath, Tabeel, and the rest of their colleagues wrote to King Artaxerxes of Persia, a letter written in Aramaic and translated.ᵃ

Aramaic:ᵇ ⁸Rehum the commissioner and Shimshai the scribe wrote a letter concerning Jerusalem to King Artaxerxes as follows: (⁹ᶜThen Rehum the commissioner and Shimshai the scribe, and the rest of their colleagues, the judges, officials, officers, and overseers, the men of Erech, and of Babylon, and of Susa—that is the Elamites—¹⁰and other peoples whom the great and glorious Osnappar deported and settled in the city of Samaria and the rest of the province Beyond the River [wrote]—and now ¹¹this is the text of the letter which they sent to him:)—"To King Artaxerxes [from] your servants, men of the province Beyond the River. And now ¹²be it known to the king that the Jews who came up from you to us have reached Jerusalem and are rebuilding that rebellious and wicked city; they are completing the walls and repairing the foundation. ¹³Now be it known to the king that if this city is rebuilt and the walls completed, they will not pay tribute, poll-tax, or land-tax, and in the end it will harm the kingdom. ¹⁴Now since we eat the salt of the palace, and it is not right that we should see the king dishonored, we have written to advise the king [of this] ¹⁵so that you may search the records of your fathers and find in the records and know that this city is a rebellious city, harmful to kings and states. Sedition has been rife in it from early times; on that account this city was destroyed. ¹⁶We advise the king that if this city is rebuilt and its walls are completed, you will no longer have any portion in the province Beyond the River."

ᵃ Cf. below v. 18 and note d.
ᵇ A note indicating that what follows is in the Aramaic language.
ᶜ Vv. 9–11 amplify v. 8.

17The king sent back the following message: "To Rehum the commissioner and Shimshai the scribe, and the rest of their colleagues, who dwell in Samaria and in the rest of the province of Beyond the River, greetings. 18Now the letter that you wrote me has been read to me in translation.d 19At my order a search has been made, and it has been found that this city has from earliest times risen against kings, and that rebellion and sedition have been rife in it. 20Powerful kings have ruled over Jerusalem and exercised authority over the whole province of Beyond the River, and tribute, poll-tax, and land-tax were paid to them. 21Now issue an order to stop these men; this city is not to be rebuilt until I so order. 22Take care not to be lax in this matter or there will be much damage and harm to the kingdom."

23When the text of the letter of King Artaxerxes was read before Rehum and Shimshai the scribe and their colleagues, they hurried to Jerusalem, to the Jews, and stopped them by main force. 24At that time, work on the House of God in Jerusalem stopped and remained in abeyance until the second year of the reign of King Darius of Persia.

5 Then the prophets, Haggai the prophet and Zechariah son of Iddo, prophesied to the Jews in Judah and Jerusalem, a-inspired by the God of Israel.-a 2Thereupon Zerubbabel son of Shealtiel and Jeshua son of Jozadak began rebuilding the House of God in Jerusalem, with the full support of the prophets of God. 3At once Tattenai, governor of the province of Beyond the River, Shethar-bozenai, and their colleagues descended upon them and said this to them, "Who issued orders to you to rebuild this house and complete its furnishing?" 4Then web said to them, "What are the names of the men who are engaged in the building?" 5But God watched over the elders of the Jews and they were not stopped while a report went to Darius and a letter was sent back in reply to it.

6This is the text of the letter that Tattenai, governor of the province of Beyond the River, and Shethar-bozenai and his colleagues, the officials of Beyond the River, sent to King Darius. 7They sent a message to him and this is what was written in it: "To King Darius, greetings, and so forth. 8Be it known to the king, that we went to the province of Judah, to the house of the great God. It is being rebuilt of hewn stone, and wood is being laid in the walls. The work is being done with dispatch and is going well. 9Thereupon we directed this question to these elders, 'Who issued orders to you to rebuild this house and to complete its furnishings?' 10We

---

d *I.e., from Aramaic to Persian.*

a-a *Lit. "with the name of the God of Israel upon them."*
b *The officials of v. 3; cf. v. 10. Greek and Syriac read "they."*

also asked their names so that we could write down the names of their leaders for your information. ¹¹This is what they answered us: 'We are the servants of the God of heaven and earth; we are rebuilding the house that was originally built many years ago; a great king of Israel built it and completed it. ¹²But because our fathers angered the God of Heaven, He handed them over to Nebuchadnezzar the Chaldean, king of Babylon, who demolished this house and exiled the people to Babylon. ¹³But in the first year of King Cyrus of Babylon, King Cyrus issued an order to rebuild this House of God. ¹⁴Also the silver and gold vessels of the House of God that Nebuchadnezzar had taken away from the temple in Jerusalem and brought to the temple in Babylon—King Cyrus released them from the temple in Babylon to be given to the one called Sheshbazzar whom he had appointed governor. ¹⁵He said to him, "Take these vessels, go, deposit them in the temple in Jerusalem, and let the House of God be rebuilt on its original site." ¹⁶That same Sheshbazzar then came and laid the foundations for the House of God in Jerusalem; and ever since then it has been under construction, but is not yet finished.' ¹⁷And now, if it please the king, let the royal archives there in Babylon be searched to see whether indeed an order had been issued by King Cyrus to rebuild this House of God in Jerusalem. May the king convey to us his pleasure in this matter."

6 Thereupon, at the order of King Darius, they searched the archives where the treasures were stored in Babylon. ²But it was in the citadel of Ecbatana, in the province of Media, that a scroll was found in which the following was written: "Memorandum: ³In the first year of King Cyrus, King Cyrus issued an order concerning the House of God in Jerusalem: 'Let the house be rebuilt, a place for offering sacrifices, with a base built up high. Let it be sixty cubits high and sixty cubits wide, ⁴with a course of unused timber for each three courses of hewn stone. The expenses shall be paid by the palace. ⁵And the gold and silver vessels of the House of God which Nebuchadnezzar had taken away from the temple in Jerusalem and transported to Babylon shall be returned, and let each go back to the temple in Jerusalem where it belongs; you shall deposit it in the House of God.'

⁶"Nowª you, Tattenai, governor of the province of Beyond the River, Shethar-bozenai and colleagues, the officials of the province of Beyond

---

ª This introduces the text of the reply of Darius that doubtless contained the preceding narrative (vv. 1–5) as a preliminary.

the River, stay away from that place. ⁷Allow the work of this House of God to go on; let the governor of the Jews and the elders of the Jews rebuild this House of God on its site. ⁸And I hereby issue an order concerning what you must do to help these elders of the Jews rebuild this House of God: the expenses are to be paid to these men with dispatch out of the resources of the king, derived from the taxes of the province of Beyond the River, so that the work not be stopped. ⁹They are to be given daily, without fail, whatever they need of young bulls, rams, or lambs as burnt offerings for the God of Heaven, and wheat, salt, wine, and oil, at the order of the priests in Jerusalem, ¹⁰so that they may offer pleasing sacrifices to the God of Heaven and pray for the life of the king and his sons. ¹¹I also issue an order that whoever alters this decree shall have a beam removed from his house, and he shall be impaled on it and his house confiscated.ᵇ ¹²And may the God who established His name there cause the downfall of any king or nation that undertakes to alter or damage that House of God in Jerusalem. I, Darius, have issued the decree; let it be carried out with dispatch."

¹³Then Tattenai, governor of the province of Beyond the River, Shethar-bozenai, and their colleagues carried out with dispatch what King Darius had written. ¹⁴So the elders of the Jews progressed in the building, urged on by the prophesying of Haggai the prophet and Zechariah son of Iddo, and they brought the building to completion under the aegis of the God of Israel and by the order of Cyrus and Darius and King Artaxerxes of Persia. ¹⁵The house was finished on the third of the month of Adar in the sixth year of the reign of King Darius. ¹⁶The Israelites, the priests, and the Levites, and all the other exiles celebrated the dedication of the House of God with joy. ¹⁷And they sacrificed for the dedication of this House of God one hundred bulls, two hundred rams, four hundred lambs, and twelve goats as a purification offering for all of Israel, according to the number of the tribes of Israel. ¹⁸They appointed the priests in their courses and the Levites in their divisions for the service of God in Jerusalem, according to the prescription in the Book of Moses.

¹⁹ᶜThe returned exiles celebrated the Passover on the fourteenth day of the first month, ²⁰for the priests and Levites had purified themselves to a man; they were all pure. They slaughtered the passover offering for all the returned exiles, and for their brother priests and for themselves. ²¹The children of Israel who had returned from the exile, together with all who

ᵇ *Meaning uncertain; or "turned into ruins."*
ᶜ *Hebrew resumes here.*

joined them in separating themselves from the uncleanliness of the nations of the lands to worship the LORD God of Israel, ate of it. ²²They joyfully celebrated the Feast of Unleavened Bread for seven days, for the LORD had given them cause for joy by inclining the heart of the Assyrian king toward them so as to give them support in the work of the House of God, the God of Israel.

7 After these events, during the reign of King Artaxerxes of Persia, Ezra son of Seraiah son of Azariah son of Hilkiah ²son of Shallum son of Zadok son of Ahitub ³son of Amariah son of Azariah son of Meraioth ⁴son of Zerahiah son of Uzzi son of Bukki ⁵son of Abishua son of Phinehas son of Eleazar son of Aaron the chief priest—⁶that Ezra came up from Babylon, a scribe expert in the Teaching of Moses which the LORD God of Israel had given, whose request the king had granted in its entirety, thanks to the benevolence of the LORD toward him.

(⁷Some of the Israelites, the priests and Levites, the singers, the gatekeepers, and the temple servants set out for Jerusalem in the seventh year of King Artaxerxes, ⁸arriving in Jerusalem in the fifth month in the seventh year of the king.) ⁹On the first day of the first month the journey up from Babylon was started, and on the first day of the fifth month he arrived in Jerusalem, thanks to the benevolent care of his God for him. ¹⁰For Ezra had dedicated himself to study the Teaching of the LORD so as to observe it, and to teach laws and rules to Israel.

¹¹The following is the text of the letter which King Artaxerxes gave Ezra the priest-scribe, a scholar in matters concerning the commandments of the LORD and His laws to Israel:

¹²ᵃ"Artaxerxes king of kings, to Ezra the priest, scholar in the law of the God of heaven, ᵇ⁻and so forth.⁻ᵇ And now, ¹³I hereby issue an order that anyone in my kingdom who is of the people of Israel and its priests and Levites who feels impelled to go to Jerusalem may go with you. ¹⁴For you are commissioned by the king and his seven advisers to regulate Judah and Jerusalem according to the law of your God, which is in your care, ¹⁵and to bring the freewill offering of silver and gold, which the king and his advisers made to the God of Israel, whose dwelling is in Jerusalem, ¹⁶and whatever silver and gold that you find throughout the province of Babylon, together with the freewill offerings that the people and the priests will give for the House of their God, which is in Jerusalem. ¹⁷You

---

ᵃ *Aramaic resumes here through v. 26.*
ᵇ⁻ᵇ *Meaning uncertain.*

shall, therefore, with dispatch acquire with this money bulls, rams, and lambs, with their meal offerings and libations, and offer them on the altar of the House of your God in Jerusalem. [18]And whatever you wish to do with the leftover silver and gold, you and your kinsmen may do, in accord with the will of your God. [19]The vessels for the service of the House of your God that are given to you, deliver to God in Jerusalem, [20]and any other needs of the House of your God that it falls to you to supply, do so from the royal treasury. [21]I, King Artaxerxes, for my part, hereby issue an order to all the treasurers in the province of Beyond the River that whatever request Ezra the priest, scholar in the law of the God of Heaven, makes of you is to be fulfilled with dispatch [22]up to the sum of one hundred talents of silver, one hundred *kor* of wheat, one hundred *bath* of wine, one hundred *bath* of oil, and salt without limit. [23]Whatever is by order of the God of Heaven must be carried out diligently for the House of the God of Heaven, else wrath will come upon the king and his sons. [24]We further advise you that it is not permissible to impose tribute, poll tax, or land tax on any priest, Levite, singer, gatekeeper, temple servant, or other servant of this House of God. [25]And you, Ezra, by the divine wisdom you possess, appoint magistrates and judges to judge all the people in the province of Beyond the River who know the laws of your God, and to teach those who do not know them. [26]Let anyone who does not obey the law of your God and the law of the king be punished with dispatch, whether by death, corporal punishment, confiscation of possessions, or imprisonment."

[27c]Blessed is the LORD God of our fathers, who put it into the mind of the king to glorify the House of the LORD in Jerusalem, [28]and who inclined the king and his counselors and the king's military officers to be favorably disposed toward me. For my part, thanks to the care of the LORD for me, I summoned up courage and assembled leading men in Israel to go with me.

8 These are the chiefs of the clans and the register of the genealogy of those who came up with me from Babylon in the reign of King Artaxerxes: [2]Of the sons of Phinehas, Gershom; of the sons of Ithamar, Daniel; of the sons of David, Hattush. [3]Of the sons of Shecaniah: of the sons of Parosh, Zechariah; through him the genealogy of 150 males was registered. [4]Eliehoenai son of Zerahiah, of the sons of Pahath-moab, and with him 200 males. [5]Of the sons of Shecaniah son of Jahaziel; and with

c *Hebrew resumes here.*

him 300 males. 6And of the sons of Adin, Ebed son of Jonathan; and with him 50 males. 7And of the sons of Elam, Jeshaiah son of Athaliah; and with him 70 males. 8And of the sons of Shephatiah, Zebadiah son of Michael; and with him 80 males. 9Of the sons of Joab, Obadiah son of Jehiel; and with him 218 males. 10And of the sons of Shelomith, the son of Josiphiah; and with him 160 males. 11And of the sons of Bebai, Zechariah son of Bebai; and with him 28 males. 12And of the sons of Azgad, Johanan son of Hakkatan; and with him 110 males. 13And of the sons of Adonikam, who were the last; and these are their names: Eliphelet, Jeiel, and Shemaiah; and with them 60 males. 14And of the sons of Bigvai, Uthai and Zaccur; and with them 70 males.

15These I assembled by the river that enters Ahava, and we encamped there for three days. I reviewed the people and the priests, but I did not find any Levites there. 16I sent for Eliezer, Ariel, Shemaiah, Elnathan, Jarib, Elnathan, Nathan, Zechariah, and Meshullam, the leading men, and also for Joiarib and Elnathan, the instructors, 17and I gave them an order for Iddo, the leader at the place [called] Casiphia. I gave them a message to convey to Iddo [and] his brother, temple-servants at the place [called] Casiphia, that they should bring us attendants for the House of our God. 18Thanks to the benevolent care of our God for us, they brought us a capable man of the family of Mahli son of Levi son of Israel, and Sherebiah and his sons and brothers, 18 in all, 19and Hashabiah, and with him Jeshaiah of the family of Merari, his brothers and their sons, 20 in all; 20and of the temple servants whom David and the officers had appointed for the service of the Levites—220 temple servants, all of them listed by name.

21I proclaimed a fast there by the Ahava River to afflict ourselves before our God to beseech Him for a smooth journey for us and for our children and for all our possessions; 22for I was ashamed to ask the king for soldiers and horsemen to protect us against any enemy on the way, since we had told the king, "The benevolent care of our God is for all who seek Him, while His fierce anger is against all who forsake Him." 23So we fasted and besought our God for this, and He responded to our plea. 24Then I selected twelve of the chiefs of the priests, namely Sherebiah and Hashabiah with ten of their brothers, 25and I weighed out to them the silver, the gold, and the vessels, the contribution to the House of our God which the king, his counselors and officers, and all Israel who were present had made. 26I entrusted to their safekeeping the weight of six hundred and fifty talents of silver, one hundred silver vessels of one talent each, one hundred talents of gold; ²⁷also, twenty gold bowls worth one thousand *darics* and two vessels of good, shining bronze, as precious as gold. ²⁸I said to them, "You are consecrated to the LORD, and the vessels are consecrated, and the silver and gold are a freewill offering to the LORD God of your fathers. ²⁹Guard them diligently until such time as you weigh them out in the presence of the officers of the priests and the Levites and the officers of the clans of Israel in Jerusalem in the chambers of the House of the LORD."

³⁰So the priests and the Levites received the cargo of silver and gold and vessels by weight, to bring them to Jerusalem to the House of our God. ³¹We set out for Jerusalem from the Ahava River on the twelfth of the first month. We enjoyed the care of our God, who saved us from enemy ambush on the journey.

³²We arrived in Jerusalem and stayed there three days. ³³On the fourth day the silver, gold, and vessels were weighed out in the House of our God into the keeping of Meremoth son of Uriah the priest, with whom was Eleazar son of Phinehas. Jozabad son of Jeshua, and Noadiah son of Binnui, the Levites, were with them. ³⁴Everything accorded as to number and weight, the entire cargo being recorded at that time.

³⁵The returning exiles who arrived from captivity made burnt offerings to the God of Israel: twelve bulls for all Israel, ninety-six rams, seventy-seven lambs and twelve he-goats as a purification offering, all this a burnt offering to the LORD. ³⁶They handed the royal orders to the king's satraps and the governors of the province of Beyond the River who gave support to the people and the House of God.

9 When this was over, the officers approached me, saying, "The people of Israel and the priests and Levites have not separated themselves from the peoples of the land whose abhorrent practices are like those of the Canaanites, the Hittites, the Perizzites, the Jebusites, the Ammonites, the Moabites, the Egyptians, and the Amorites. ²They have taken their daughters as wives for themselves and for their sons, so that the holy seed has become intermingled with the peoples of the land; and it is the officers and prefects who have taken the lead in this trespass."

³When I heard this, I rent my garment and robe, I tore hair out of my

head and beard, and I sat desolate. ⁴Around me gathered all who were concerned over the words of the God of Israel because of the returning exiles' trespass, while I sat desolate until the evening offering. ⁵At the time of the evening offering I ended my self-affliction; still in my torn garment and robe, I got down on my knees and spread out my hands to the LORD my God, ⁶and said, "O my God, I am too ashamed and mortified to lift my face to You, O my God, for our iniquities ^{a-}are overwhelming^{-a} and our guilt has grown high as heaven. ⁷From the time of our fathers to this very day we have been deep in guilt. Because of our iniquities, we, our kings, and our priests have been handed over to foreign kings, to the sword, to captivity, to pillage, and to humiliation, as is now the case.

⁸"But now, for a short while, there has been a reprieve from the LORD our God, who has granted us a surviving remnant and given us a stake in His holy place; our God has restored the luster to our eyes and furnished us with a little sustenance in our bondage. ⁹For bondsmen we are, though even in our bondage God has not forsaken us, but has disposed the king of Persia favorably toward us, to furnish us with sustenance and to raise again the House of our God, repairing its ruins and giving us a hold^b in Judah and Jerusalem.

¹⁰"Now, what can we say in the face of this, O our God, for we have forsaken Your commandments, ¹¹which You gave us through Your servants the prophets when You said, 'The land that you are about to possess is a land unclean through the uncleanness of the peoples of the land, through their abhorrent practices with which they, in their impurity, have filled it from one end to the other. ¹²Now then, do not give your daughters in marriage to their sons or let their daughters marry your sons; do nothing for their well-being or advantage, then you will be strong and enjoy the bounty of the land and bequeath it to your children forever.' ¹³After all that has happened to us because of our evil deeds and our deep guilt—though You, our God, have been forbearing, [punishing us] less than our iniquity [deserves] in that You have granted us such a remnant as this—¹⁴shall we once again violate Your commandments by intermarrying with these peoples who follow such abhorrent practices? Will You not rage against us till we are destroyed without remnant or survivor? ¹⁵O LORD, God of Israel, You are benevolent,^c for we have survived as a remnant, as is now the case. We stand before You in all our guilt, for we cannot face You on this account."

^{a-a} Lit. "are numerous above the head."
^b Lit. "fence."
^c Or "in the right."

10 While Ezra was praying and making confession, weeping and prostrating himself before the House of God, a very great crowd of Israelites gathered about him, men, women, and children; the people were weeping bitterly. ²Then Shecaniah son of Jehiel of the family of Elam spoke up and said to Ezra, "We have trespassed against our God by bringing into our homes foreign women from the peoples of the land; ᵃ⁻but there is still hope for Israel despite this.⁻ᵃ ³Now then, let us make a covenant with our God to expel all these women and those who have been born to them, in accordance with the bidding of the LORD and of all who are concerned over the commandment of our God, and let the Teaching be obeyed. ⁴Take action, for the responsibility is yours and we are with you. Act with resolve!"

⁵So Ezra at once put the officers of the priests and the Levites and all Israel under oath to act accordingly, and they took the oath. ⁶Then Ezra rose from his place in front of the House of God and went into the chamber of Jehohanan son of Eliashib; there, he ate no bread and drank no water, for he was in mourning over the trespass of those who had returned from exile. ⁷Then a proclamation was issued in Judah and Jerusalem that all who had returned from the exile should assemble in Jerusalem, ⁸and that anyone who did not come in three days would, by decision of the officers and elders, have his property confiscated and himself excluded from the congregation of the returning exiles.

⁹All the men of Judah and Benjamin assembled in Jerusalem in three days; it was the ninth month, the twentieth of the month. All the people sat in the square of the House of God, trembling on account of the event and because of the rains. ¹⁰Then Ezra the priest got up and said to them, "You have trespassed by bringing home foreign women, thus aggravating the guilt of Israel. ¹¹So now, make confession to the LORD, God of your fathers, and do His will, and separate yourselves from the peoples of the land and from the foreign women."

¹²The entire congregation responded in a loud voice, "We must surely do just as you say. ¹³However, many people are involved, and it is the rainy season; it is not possible to remain out in the open, nor is this the work of a day or two, because we have transgressed extensively in this matter. ¹⁴Let our officers remain on behalf of the entire congregation, and all our townspeople who have brought home foreign women shall appear before them at scheduled times, together with the elders and judges

---

ᵃ⁻ᵃ *Or "Is there. . . ?"*

of each town, in order to avert the burning anger of our God from us on this account." ¹⁵Only Jonathan son of Asahel and Jahzeiah son of Tikvah remained for this purpose, assisted by Meshullam and Shabbethai, the Levites. ¹⁶The returning exiles did so. Ezra the priest and the men who were the chiefs of the ancestral clans—all listed by name—sequestered themselves on the first day of the tenth month to study the matter. ¹⁷By the first day of the first month they were done with all the men who had brought home foreign women. ¹⁸Among the priestly families who were found to have brought foreign women were Jeshua son of Jozadak and his brothers Maaseiah, Eliezer, Jarib, and Gedaliah. ¹⁹They gave their word[b] to expel their wives and, acknowledging their guilt, offered a ram from the flock to expiate it. ²⁰Of the sons of Immer: Hanani and Zebadiah; ²¹of the sons of Harim: Maaseiah, Elijah, Shemaiah, Jehiel, and Uzziah; ²²of the sons of Pashhur: Elioenai, Maaseiah, Ishmael, Nethanel, Jozabad, and Elasah; ²³of the Levites: Jozabad, Shimei, Kelaiah who is Kelita, Pethahiah, Judah, and Eliezer. ²⁴Of the singers: Eliashib. Of the gatekeepers: Shallum, Telem, and Uri. ²⁵Of the Israelites: of the sons of Parosh: Ramiah, Izziah, Malchijah, Mijamin, Eleazar, Malchijah, and Benaiah; ²⁶of the sons of Elam: Mattaniah, Zechariah, Jehiel, Abdi, Jeremoth, and Elijah; ²⁷of the sons of Zattu: Elioenai, Eliashib, Mattaniah, Jeremoth, Zabad, and Aziza; ²⁸of the sons of Bebai: Jehohanan, Hananiah, Zabbai, and Athlai; ²⁹of the sons of Bani: Meshullam, Malluch, Adaiah, Jashub, Sheal, and Ramoth; ³⁰of the sons of Pahath-moab: Adna, Chelal, Benaiah, Maaseiah, Mattaniah, Bezalel, Binnui, and Manasseh; ³¹of the sons of Harim: Eliezer, Isshijah, Malchijah, Shemaiah, and Shimeon; ³²also Benjamin, Malluch, and Shemariah; ³³of the sons of Hashum: Mattenai, Mattattah, Zabad, Eliphelet, Jeremai, Manasseh, and Shimei; ³⁴of the sons of Bani: Maadai, Amram, and Uel; ³⁵also Benaiah, Bedeiah, Cheluhu, ³⁶Vaniah, Meremoth, Eliashib, ³⁷Mattaniah, Mattenai, Jaasai, ³⁸Bani, Binnui, Shimei, ³⁹Shelemiah, Nathan, Adaiah, ⁴⁰Machnadebai, Shashai, Sharai, ⁴¹Azarel, Shelemiah, Shemariah, ⁴²Shallum, Amariah, and Joseph; ⁴³of the sons of Nebo: Jeiel, Mattithiah, Zabad, Zebina, Jaddai, Joel, and Benaiah.

⁴⁴All these had married foreign women, among whom were some women [c-]who had borne children.[-c]

---

b *Lit. "hand."*
c-c *Meaning of Heb. uncertain.*

NEHEMIAH

1 The narrative of Nehemiah son of Hacaliah:

In the month of Kislev of the twentieth year,[a] when I was in the fortress of Shushan, [2]Hanani, one of my brothers, together with some men of Judah, arrived, and I asked them about the Jews, the remnant who had survived the captivity, and about Jerusalem. [3]They replied, "The survivors who have survived the captivity there in the province are in dire trouble and disgrace; Jerusalem's wall is full of breaches, and its gates have been destroyed by fire."

[4]When I heard that, I sat and wept, and was in mourning for days, fasting and praying to the God of Heaven. [5]I said, "O LORD, God of Heaven, great and awesome God, who stays faithful to His covenant with those who love Him and keep His commandments! [6]Let Your ear be attentive and Your eyes open to receive the prayer of Your servant that I am praying to You now, day and night, on behalf of the Israelites, Your servants, confessing the sins that we Israelites have committed against You, sins that I and my father's house have committed. [7]We have offended You by not keeping the commandments, the laws, and the rules that You gave to Your servant Moses. [8]Be mindful of the promise You gave to Your servant Moses: 'If you are unfaithful, I will scatter you among the peoples; [9]but if you turn back to Me, faithfully keep My commandments, even if your dispersed are at the ends of the earth,[b] I will gather them from there and bring them to the place where I have chosen to establish My name.' [10]For they are Your servants and Your people whom You redeemed by Your great power and Your mighty hand. [11]O Lord! Let Your ear be attentive to the prayer of Your servant, and to the prayer of Your servants who desire to hold Your name in awe. Grant Your servant success today, and dispose that man to be compassionate toward him!"

I was the king's cupbearer at the time.

---

[a] I.e., of King Artaxerxes; cf. 2.1.
[b] Lit. "sky."

2 In the month of Nisan, in the twentieth year of King Artaxerxes, wine was set before him; I took the wine and gave it to the king—I had never been out of sorts in his presence. ²The king said to me, "How is it that you look bad, though you are not ill? It must be bad thoughts." I was very frightened, ³but I answered the king, "May the king live forever! How should I not look bad when the city of the graveyard of my ancestors lies in ruins, and its gates have been consumed by fire?" ⁴The king said to me, "What is your request?" With a prayer to the God of Heaven, ⁵I answered the king, "If it please the king, and if your servant has found favor with you, send me to Judah, to the city of my ancestors' graves, to rebuild it." ⁶With the consort seated at his side, the king said to me, "How long will you be gone and when will you return?" So it was agreeable to the king to send me, and I gave him a date. ⁷Then I said to the king, "If it please the king, let me have letters to the governors of the province of Beyond the River, directing them to grant me passage until I reach Judah; ⁸likewise, a letter to Asaph, the keeper of the King's Park, directing him to give me timber for roofing the gatehouses of the temple fortress and the city walls and for the house I shall occupy." The king gave me these, thanks to my God's benevolent care for me. ⁹When I came to the governors of the province of Beyond the River I gave them the king's letters. The king also sent army officers and cavalry with me.

¹⁰When Sanballat the Horonite and Tobiah the Ammonite servant heard, it displeased them greatly that someone had come, intent on improving the condition of the Israelites.

¹¹I arrived in Jerusalem. After I was there three days ¹²I got up at night, I and a few men with me, and telling no one what my God had put into my mind to do for Jerusalem, and taking no other beast than the one on which I was riding, ¹³I went out by the Valley Gate, at night, toward the Jackals' Spring and the Dung Gate; and I surveyed the walls of Jerusalem that were breached, and its gates, consumed by fire. ¹⁴I proceeded to the Fountain Gate and to the King's Pool, where there was no room for the beast under me to continue. ¹⁵So I went up the wadi by night, surveying the wall, and, entering again by the Valley Gate, I returned. ¹⁶The prefects knew nothing of where I had gone or what I had done, since I had not yet divulged it to the Jews—the priests, the nobles, the prefects, or the rest of the officials.

¹⁷Then I said to them, "You see the bad state we are in—Jerusalem lying in ruins and its gates destroyed by fire. Come, let us rebuild the wall of Jerusalem and suffer no more disgrace." ¹⁸I told them of my God's benevolent care for me, also of the things that the king had said to me, and they said, "Let us start building!" They were encouraged by [His] benevolence.

¹⁹When Sanballat the Horonite and Tobiah the Ammonite servant and Geshem the Arab heard, they mocked us and held us in contempt and said, "What is this that you are doing? Are you rebelling against the king?" ²⁰I said to them in reply, "The God of Heaven will grant us success, and we, His servants, will start building. But you have no share or claim or stakeᵃ in Jerusalem!"

3 Then Eliashib the high priest and his fellow priests set to and rebuilt the Sheep Gate; they consecrated it and set up its doors, consecrating it as far as the Hundred's Tower, as far as the Tower of Hananel. ²Next to him, the men of Jericho built. Next to them,ᵃ Zaccur son of Imri. ³The sons of Hassenaah rebuilt the Fish Gate; they roofed it and set up its doors, locks, and bars. ⁴Next to them, Meremoth son of Uriah son of Hakkoz repaired; and next to him,ᵇ Meshullam son of Berechiah son of Meshezabel. Next to him,ᵇ Zadok son of Baana repaired. ⁵Next to him,ᵇ the Tekoites repaired, though their nobles would not ᶜ⁻take upon their shoulders⁻ᶜ the work of their lord. ⁶Joiada son of Paseah and Meshullam son of Besodeiah repaired the Jeshanah Gate; they roofed it and set up its doors, locks, and bars. ⁷Next to them, Melatiah the Gibeonite and Jadon the Meronothite repaired, [with] the men of Gibeon and Mizpah, ᵈ⁻under the jurisdiction⁻ᵈ of the governor of the province of Beyond the River. ⁸Next to them,ᵃ Uzziel son of Harhaiah, [of the] smiths, repaired. Next to him, Hananiah, ofᵉ the perfumers. They restored Jerusalem as far as the Broad Wall. ⁹Next to them, Rephaiah son of Hur, chief of half the district of Jerusalem, repaired. ¹⁰Next to him,ᵇ Jedaiah son of Harumaph repaired in front of his house. Next to him, Hattush son of Hashabneiah repaired. ¹¹Malchijah son of Harim and Hasshub son of Pahathmoab repaired a second stretch, including the Tower of Ovens. ¹²Next to

---

ᵃ Lit. "record."

ᵃ Lit. "him."
ᵇ Lit. "them."
ᶜ⁻ᶜ Lit. "bring their neck into."
ᵈ⁻ᵈ Lit. "of the throne"; meaning of Heb. uncertain.
ᵉ Lit. "son of," i.e., member of the guild of.

them,[a] Shallum son of Hallohesh,[f] chief of half the district of Jerusalem, repaired—he and his daughters. 13Hanun and the inhabitants of Zanoah repaired the Valley Gate; they rebuilt it and set up its doors, locks, and bars. And [they also repaired] a thousand cubits of wall to the Dung Gate. 14Malchijah son of Rechab, chief of the district of Beth-haccherem, repaired the Dung Gate; he rebuilt it and set up its doors, locks, and bars. 15Shallun son of Col-hozeh, chief of the district of Mizpah, repaired the Fountain Gate; he rebuilt it and covered it, and set up its doors, locks, and bars, as well as the wall of the irrigation[g] pool of the King's Garden as far as the steps going down from the City of David. 16After him, Nehemiah son of Azbuk, chief of half the district of Beth-zur, repaired, from in front of the graves of David as far as the artificial pool, and as far as the House of the Warriors. 17After him, the Levites repaired: Rehum son of Bani. Next to him, Hashabiah, chief of half the district of Keilah, repaired for his district. 18After him, their brothers repaired: Bavvai son of Henadad, chief of half the district of Keilah. 19Next to him, Ezer son of Jeshua, the chief of Mizpah, repaired a second stretch, from in front of the ascent to the armory [at] the angle [of the wall]. 20After him, Baruch son of Zaccai zealously repaired a second stretch, from the angle to the entrance to the house of Eliashib, the high priest. 21After him, Meremoth son of Uriah son of Hakkoz repaired a second stretch, from the entrance to Eliashib's house to the end of Eliashib's house. 22After him, the priests, inhabitants of the plain, repaired. 23After them,[a] Benjamin and Hasshub repaired in front of their houses. After them,[a] Azariah son of Maaseiah son of Ananiah repaired beside his house. 24After him, Binnui son of Henadad repaired a second stretch, from the house of Azariah to the angle, to the corner. 25Palal son of Uzai—from in front of the angle and the tower that juts out of the house of the king, the upper [tower] of the prison compound. After him, Pedaiah son of Parosh. (26The temple servants were living on the Ophel, as far as a point in front of the Water Gate in the east, and the jutting tower.) 27After him, the Tekoites repaired a second stretch, from in front of the great jutting tower to the wall of the Ophel. 28Above the Horse Gate, the priests repaired, each in front of his house. 29After them,[a] Zadok son of Immer repaired in front of his house. After him, Shemaiah son of Shechaniah, keeper of the East Gate, repaired. 30After him, Hananiah son of Shelemiah and Hanun, the sixth son of Zalaph, repaired a second stretch. After them,[a] Meshullam son of Berechiah repaired in front of his chamber.

---

f *I.e., the charmer.*
g *Following Kimhi; cf. Mishnaic Heb.* bet hashelaḥin, *irrigated field.*

31After him, Malchijah of the smiths repaired as far as the house of the temple servants and the merchants, [from] in front of the Muster Gate to the corner loft. 32And between the corner loft to the Sheep Gate the smiths and the merchants repaired.

33When Sanballat heard that we were rebuilding the wall, it angered him, and he was extremely vexed. He mocked the Jews, 34saying in the presence of his brothers and the Samarian force, "What are the miserable Jews doing? Will they restore, offer sacrifice, and finish one day? Can they revive those stones out of the dust heaps, burned as they are?" 35Tobiah the Ammonite, alongside him, said, "That stone wall they are building— if a fox climbed it he would breach it!"

36Hear, our God, how we have become a mockery, and return their taunts upon their heads! Let them be taken as spoil to a land of captivity! 37Do not cover up their iniquity or let their sin be blotted out before You, for they hurled provocations at the builders.

38We rebuilt the wall till it was continuous all around to half its height; for the people's heart was in the work.

4 When Sanballat and Tobiah, and the Arabs, the Ammonites, and the Ashdodites heard that healing had come to the walls of Jerusalem, that the breached parts had begun to be filled, it angered them very much, 2and they all conspired together to come and fight against Jerusalem and to throw it into confusion. 3Because of them we prayed to our God, and set up a watch over them^a day and night.

4Judah was saying,

"The strength of the basket-carrier has failed,
And there is so much rubble;
We are not able ourselves
To rebuild the wall."

5And our foes were saying, "Before they know or see it, we shall be in among them and kill them, and put a stop to the work." 6When the Jews living near them^b would arrive, they would tell us ^{c-}time and again^{-c} ^{d-}". . . from all the places where . . . you shall come back to us. . . ."^{-d} 7I stationed, on the lower levels of the place, behind the walls, on the bare rock—I stationed the people by families with their swords, their lances, and their bows. 8Then I decided to exhort the nobles, the prefects, and

---

^a I.e., the workers on the walls.
^b I.e., the foes.
^{c-c} Lit. "ten times."
^{d-d} Heb. seems to be abbreviated; a possible restoration of the sentence, with the missing elements enclosed in brackets, is: [of their evil plan; and we would say to them,] "From all the places where [you get such information] you shall come back to us [and convey it]."

the rest of the people, "Do not be afraid of them! Think of the great and awesome Lord, and fight for your brothers, your sons and daughters, your wives and homes!"

⁹When our enemies learned that it had become known to us, since God had thus frustrated their plan, we could all return to the wall, each to his work. ¹⁰From that day on, half my servants did work and half held lances and shields, bows and armor. And the officers stood behind the whole house of Judah ¹¹who were rebuilding the wall. The basket-carriers were burdened, doing work with one hand while the other held a weapon. ¹²As for the builders, each had his sword girded at his side as he was building. The trumpeter stood beside me. ¹³I said to the nobles, the prefects, and the rest of the people, "There is much work and it is spread out; we are scattered over the wall, far from one another. ¹⁴When you hear a trumpet call, gather yourselves to me at that place; our God will fight for us!" ¹⁵And so we worked on, while half were holding lances, from the break of day until the stars appeared.

¹⁶I further said to the people at that time, "Let every man with his servant lodge in Jerusalem, that we may use the night to stand guard and the day to work." ¹⁷Nor did I, my brothers, my servants, or the guards following me ever take off our clothes, ᶜ⁻[or] each his weapon, even at the water.⁻ᶜ

5 There was a great outcry by the common folk and their wives against their brother Jews. ²Some said, "Our sons and daughters are numerous; we must get grain to eat in order that we may live!" ³Others said, "We must pawn our fields, our vineyards, and our homes to get grain to stave off hunger." ⁴Yet others said, "We have borrowed money against our fields and vineyards to pay the king's tax. ⁵Now ᵃ⁻we are as good as⁻ᵃ our brothers, and our children as good as theirs; yet here we are subjecting our sons and daughters to slavery—some of our daughters are already subjected—and we are powerless, while our fields and vineyards belong to others."

⁶It angered me very much to hear their outcry and these complaints. ⁷After pondering the matter carefully, I censured the nobles and the prefects, saying, "Are you pressing claims on loans made to your brothers?" Then I raised a large crowd against them ⁸and said to them, "We have done our best to buy back our Jewish brothers who were sold to the

---

ᶜ⁻ᶜ *Meaning of Heb. uncertain.*

ᵃ⁻ᵃ *Lit. "our flesh is as good as the flesh of."*

nations; will you now sell your brothers so that they must be sold [back] to us?" They kept silent, for they found nothing to answer. 9So I continued, "What you are doing is not right. You ought to act in a God-fearing way so as not to give our enemies, the nations, room to reproach us. 10I, my brothers, and my servants also have claims of money and grain against them; let us now abandon those claims! 11Give back at once their fields, their vineyards, their olive trees, and their homes, and [abandon] the claims for the hundred pieces of silver, the grain, the wine, and the oil that you have been pressing against them!" 12They replied, "We shall give them back, and not demand anything of them; we shall do just as you say." Summoning the priests, I put them under oath to keep this promise. 13I also shook out the bosom of my garment and said, "So may God shake free of his household and property any man who fails to keep this promise; may he be thus shaken out and stripped." All the assembled answered, "Amen," and praised the LORD.

The people kept this promise.

14Furthermore, from the day I was commissioned to be governor in the land of Judah—from the twentieth year of King Artaxerxes until his thirty-second year, twelve years in all—neither I nor my brothers ever ate of the governor's food allowance. 15The former governors who preceded me laid heavy burdens on the people, and took from them for bread and wine more than[b] forty shekels of silver. Their servants also tyrannized over the people. But I, out of the fear of God, did not do so. 16I also supported the work on this wall; we did not buy any land, and all my servants were gathered there at the work. 17Although there were at my table, between Jews and prefects, one hundred and fifty men in all, beside those who came to us from surrounding nations; 18and although what was prepared for each day came to one ox, six select sheep, and fowl, all prepared for me, and at ten-day intervals all sorts of wine in abundance— yet I did not resort to the governor's food allowance, for the [king's] service lay heavily on the people.

19O my God, remember to my credit all that I have done for this people!

6 When word reached Sanballat, Tobiah, Geshem the Arab, and the rest of our enemies that I had rebuilt the wall and not a breach remained in it—though at that time I had not yet set up doors in the gateways— 2Sanballat and Geshem sent a message to me, saying, "Come, let us get

b *Lit. "after"; meaning of Heb. uncertain.*

together in Kephirim in the Ono valley"; they planned to do me harm. ³I sent them messengers, saying, "I am engaged in a great work and cannot come down, for the work will stop if I leave it in order to come down to you." ⁴They sent me the same message four times, and I gave them the same answer. ⁵Sanballat sent me the same message a fifth time by his servant, who had an open letter with him. ⁶Its text was: "Word has reached the nations, and Geshemᵃ too says that you and the Jews are planning to rebel—for which reason you are building the wall—and that you are to be their king. ᵇ⁻Such is the word.⁻ᵇ ⁷You have also set up prophets in Jerusalem to proclaim about you, 'There is a king in Judah!' Word of these things will surely reach the king; so come, let us confer together."

⁸I sent back a message to him, saying, "None of these things you mention has occurred; they are figments of your imagination"—⁹for they all wished to intimidate us, thinking, "They will desist from the work, and it will not get done." Now strengthen my hands!

¹⁰Then I visited Shemaiah son of Delaiah son of Mehetabel when he was housebound, and he said,

"Let us meet in the House of God, inside the sanctuary,
And let us shut the doors of the sanctuary, for they are coming
    to kill you,
By night they are coming to kill you."

¹¹I replied, "Will a man like me take flight? Besides, who such as I can go into the sanctuary and live? I will not go in." ¹²Then I realized that it was not God who sent him, but that he uttered that prophecy about me—Tobiah and Sanballat having hired him—¹³because he was a hireling, that I might be intimidated and act thus and commit a sin, and so provide them a scandal with which to reproach me.

¹⁴"O my God, remember against Tobiah and Sanballat these deeds of theirs,ᶜ and against Noadiah the prophetess, and against the other prophets that they wished to intimidate me!"

¹⁵The wall was finished on the twenty-fifth of Elul, after fifty-two days. ¹⁶When all our enemies heard it, all the nations round about us were intimidated, and fell very low in their own estimation; they realized that this work had been accomplished by the help of our God.

¹⁷Also in those days, the nobles of Judah kept up a brisk correspondence with Tobiah, and Tobiah with them. ¹⁸Many in Judah were his confederates, for he was a son-in-law of Shecaniah son of Arah, and his son Jehohanan had married the daughter of Meshullam son of Berechiah.

ᵃ *Heb.* Gashmu.
ᵇ⁻ᵇ *Meaning of Heb. uncertain.*
ᶜ *Lit. "his."*

¹⁹They would also speak well of him to me, and would divulge my affairs to him. Tobiah sent letters to intimidate me.

7 When the wall was rebuilt and I had set up the doors, tasks were assigned to the gatekeepers, the singers, and the Levites. ²I put Hanani my brother and Hananiah, the captain of the fortress, in charge of Jerusalem, for he was a more trustworthy and God-fearing man than most. ³I said to them, "The gates of Jerusalem are not to be opened until the heat of the day,ᵃ and ᵇ⁻before you leave your posts⁻ᵇ let the doors be closed and barred. And assign the inhabitants of Jerusalem to watches, each man to his watch, and each in front of his own house."

⁴The city was broad and large, the people in it were few, and houses were not yet built. ⁵My God put it into my mind to assemble the nobles, the prefects, and the people, in order to register them by families. I found the genealogical register of those who were the first to come up, and there I found written:

⁶ᶜThese are the people of the province who came up from among the captive exiles that Nebuchadnezzar, king of Babylon, had deported, and who returned to Jerusalem and to Judah, each to his own city, ⁷who came with Zerubbabel, Jeshua, Nehemiah, Azariah, Raamiah, Nahamani, Mordecai, Bilshan, Mispereth, Bigvai, Nehum, Baanah.

The number of the men of the people of Israel: ⁸the sons of Parosh—2,172; ⁹the sons of Shephatiah—372; ¹⁰the sons of Arah—652; ¹¹the sons of Pahath-moab: the sons of Jeshua and Joab—2,818; ¹²the sons of Elam—1,254; ¹³the sons of Zattu—845; ¹⁴the sons of Zaccai—760; ¹⁵the sons of Binnui—648; ¹⁶the sons of Bebai—628; ¹⁷the sons of Azgad—2,322; ¹⁸the sons of Adonikam—667; ¹⁹the sons of Bigvai—2,067; ²⁰the sons of Adin—655; ²¹the sons of Ater: Hezekiah—98; ²²the sons of Hashum—328; ²³the sons of Bezai—324; ²⁴the sons of Hariph—112; ²⁵the sons of Gibeon—95; ²⁶the men of Bethlehem and Netophah—188; ²⁷the men of Anathoth—128; ²⁸the men of Beth-azmaveth—42; ²⁹the men of Kiriath-jearim, Chephirah, and Beeroth—743; ³⁰the men of Ramah and Geba—621; ³¹the men of Michmas—122; ³²the men of Bethel and Ai—123; ³³the men of the other Nebo—52; ³⁴the sons of the other Elam—1,254; ³⁵the sons of Harim—320; ³⁶the sons of Jericho—345; ³⁷the sons of Lod, Hadid, and Ono—721; ³⁸the sons of Senaah—3,930.

ᵃ Lit. "sun."
ᵇ⁻ᵇ Lit. "while they are still standing."
ᶜ Vv. 6–43 appear as Ezra 2 with variations in the names and numbers.

³⁹The priests: the sons of Jedaiah: the house of Jeshua—973; ⁴⁰the sons of Immer—1,052; ⁴¹the sons of Pashhur—1,247; ⁴²the sons of Harim—1,017.

⁴³The Levites: the sons of Jeshua: Kadmiel, the sons of Hodeiah—74.

⁴⁴The singers: the sons of Asaph—148.

⁴⁵The gatekeepers: the sons of Shallum, the sons of Ater, the sons of Talmon, the sons of Akkub, the sons of Hatita, the sons of Shobai—138.

⁴⁶The temple servants: the sons of Ziha, the sons of Hasupha, the sons of Tabbaoth, ⁴⁷the sons of Keros, the sons of Siah, the sons of Padon, ⁴⁸the sons of Lebanah, the sons of Hagabah, the sons of Shalmai, ⁴⁹the sons of Hanan, the sons of Giddel, the sons of Gahar, ⁵⁰the sons of Reaiah, the sons of Rezin, the sons of Nekoda, ⁵¹the sons of Gazzam, the sons of Uzza, the sons of Paseah, ⁵²the sons of Besai, the sons of Meunim, the sons of Nephishesim, ⁵³the sons of Bakbuk, the sons of Hakupha, the sons of Harhur, ⁵⁴the sons of Bazlith, the sons of Mehida, the sons of Harsha, ⁵⁵the sons of Barkos, the sons of Sisera, the sons of Temah, ⁵⁶the sons of Neziah, the sons of Hatipha.

⁵⁷The sons of Solomon's servants: the sons of Sotai, the sons of Sophereth, the sons of Perida, ⁵⁸the sons of Jala, the sons of Darkon, the sons of Giddel, ⁵⁹the sons of Shephatiah, the sons of Hattil, the sons of Pochereth-hazzebaim, the sons of Amon.

⁶⁰The total of temple servants and the sons of Solomon's servants—392.

⁶¹The following were those who came up from Tel-melah, Tel-harsha, Cherub, Addon, and Immer—they were unable to tell whether their father's house and descent were Israelite: ⁶²the sons of Delaiah, the sons of Tobiah, the sons of Nekoda—642.

⁶³Of the priests: the sons of Habaiah, the sons of Hakkoz, the sons of Barzillai who had married a daughter of Barzillai the Gileadite and had taken his^d name—⁶⁴these searched for their genealogical records, but they could not be found, so they were disqualified for the priesthood. ⁶⁵The Tirshatha^e ordered them not to eat of the most holy things until a priest with Urim and Thummim should appear.

⁶⁶The sum of the entire community was 42,360, ⁶⁷not counting their male and female servants, these being 7,337; they also had 245 male and

---

^d *Lit. "their."*
^e *A Persian title.*

female singers. 68f-[Their horses—736, their mules—245,]-f camels—435, asses—6,720.

69Some of the heads of the clans made donations for the work. The Tirshatha donated to the treasury: gold—1,000 drachmas, basins—50, priestly robes—530.

70Some of the heads of the clans donated to the work treasury: gold—20,000 drachmas, and silver—2,200 minas.

71The rest of the people donated: gold—20,000 drachmas, silver—2,000, and priestly robes—67.

72The priests, the Levites, the gatekeepers, the singers, some of the people, the temple servants, and all Israel took up residence in their towns.

8 When the seventh month arrived—the Israelites being [settled] in their towns—1the entire people assembled as one man in the square before the Water Gate, and they asked Ezra the scribe to bring the scroll of the Teaching of Moses with which the LORD had charged Israel. 2On the first day of the seventh month, Ezra the priest brought the Teaching before the congregation, men and women and all who could listen with understanding. 3He read from it, facing the square before the Water Gate, from the first light until midday, to the men and the women and those who could understand; the ears of all the people were given to the scroll of the Teaching.

4Ezra the scribe stood upon a wooden tower made for the purpose, and beside him stood Mattithiah, Shema, Anaiah, Uriah, Hilkiah, and Maaseiah at his right, and at his left Pedaiah, Mishael, Malchijah, Hashum, Hashbaddanah, Zechariah, Meshullam. 5Ezra opened the scroll in the sight of all the people, for he was above all the people; as he opened it, all the people stood up. 6Ezra blessed the LORD, the great God, and all the people answered, "Amen, Amen," with hands upraised. Then they bowed their heads and prostrated themselves before the LORD with their faces to the ground. 7Jeshua, Bani, Sherebiah, Jamin, Akkub, Shabbethai, Hodiah, Maaseiah, Kelita, Azariah, Jozabad, Hanan, Pelaiah, and the Levites explained the Teaching to the people, while the people stood in their places. 8They read from the scroll of the Teaching of God, translating it and giving the sense; so they understood the reading.

9Nehemiah the Tirshatha, Ezra the priest and scribe, and the Levites who were explaining to the people said to all the people, "This day is holy to the LORD your God: you must not mourn or weep," for all the people were weeping as they listened to the words of the Teaching. 10He

f-f *These words are missing in some mss. and editions; but cf. Ezra 2.66.*

further said to them, "Go, eat choice foods and drink sweet drinks and send portions to whoever has nothing prepared, for the day is holy to our Lord. Do not be sad, for your rejoicing in the LORD is the source of your strength." ¹¹The Levites were quieting the people, saying, "Hush, for the day is holy; do not be sad." ¹²Then all the people went to eat and drink and send portions and make great merriment, for they understood the things they were told.

¹³On the second day, the heads of the clans of all the people and the priests and Levites gathered to Ezra the scribe to study the words of the Teaching. ¹⁴They found written in the Teaching that the LORD had commanded Moses that the Israelites must dwell in booths during the festival of the seventh month, ¹⁵and that they must announce and proclaim throughout all their towns and Jerusalem as follows, "Go out to the mountains and bring leafy branches of olive trees, pine[a] trees, myrtles, palms and [other] leafy[a] trees to make booths, as it is written." ¹⁶So the people went out and brought them, and made themselves booths on their roofs, in their courtyards, in the courtyards of the House of God, in the square of the Water Gate and in the square of the Ephraim Gate. ¹⁷The whole community that returned from the captivity made booths and dwelt in the booths—the Israelites had not done so from the days of Joshua[b] son of Nun to that day—and there was very great rejoicing. ¹⁸He read from the scroll of the Teaching of God each day, from the first to the last day. They celebrated the festival seven days, and there was a solemn gathering on the eighth, as prescribed.

9 On the twenty-fourth day of this month, the Israelites assembled, fasting, in sackcloth, and with earth upon them. ²Those of the stock of Israel separated themselves from all foreigners, and stood and confessed their sins and the iniquities of their fathers. ³Standing in their places, they read from the scroll of the Teaching of the LORD their God for one-fourth of the day, and for another fourth they confessed and prostrated themselves before the LORD their God. ⁴On the raised platform of the Levites stood Jeshua and Bani, Kadmiel, Shebaniah, Bunni, Sherebiah, Bani, and Chenani, and cried in a loud voice to the LORD their God. ⁵The Levites Jeshua, Kadmiel, Bani, Hashabniah, Sherebiah, Hodiah, and Pethahiah said, "Rise, bless the LORD your God who is from eternity to

---

[a] Meaning of Heb. uncertain.
[b] Heb. Jeshua.

eternity: 'May Your glorious name be blessed, exalted though it is above every blessing and praise!' 6"You alone are the LORD. You made the heavens, the highest[a] heavens, and all their host, the earth and everything upon it, the seas and everything in them. You keep them all alive, and the host of heaven prostrate themselves before You. 7You are the LORD God, who chose Abram, who brought him out of Ur of the Chaldeans and changed his name to Abraham. 8Finding his heart true to You, You made a covenant with him to give the land of the Canaanite, the Hittite, the Amorite, the Perizzite, the Jebusite, and the Girgashite—to give it to his descendants. And You kept Your word, for You are righteous. 9You took note of our fathers' affliction in Egypt, and heard their cry at the Sea of Reeds. 10You performed signs and wonders against Pharaoh, all his servants, and all the people of his land, for You knew that they acted presumptuously toward them. You made a name for Yourself that endures to this day. 11You split the sea before them; they passed through the sea on dry land, but You threw their pursuers into the depths, like a stone into the raging waters.

12"You led them by day with a pillar of cloud, and by night with a pillar of fire, to give them light in the way they were to go. 13You came down on Mount Sinai and spoke to them from heaven; You gave them right rules and true teachings, good laws and commandments. 14You made known to them Your holy sabbath, and You ordained for them laws, commandments and Teaching, through Moses Your servant. 15You gave them bread from heaven when they were hungry, and produced water from a rock when they were thirsty. You told them to go and possess the land that You swore to give them. 16But they—our fathers— acted presumptuously; they stiffened their necks and did not obey Your commandments. 17Refusing to obey, unmindful of Your wonders that You did for them, they stiffened their necks, and in their defiance resolved to return to their slavery. But You, being a forgiving God, gracious and compassionate, long-suffering and abounding in faithfulness, did not abandon them. 18Even though they made themselves a molten calf and said, 'This is your God who brought you out of Egypt,' thus committing great impieties, 19You, in Your abundant compassion, did not abandon them in the wilderness. The pillar of cloud did not depart from them to lead them on the way by day, nor the pillar of fire by night to give them light in the way they were to go. 20You endowed them with Your good spirit to instruct them. You did not withhold Your manna from their

---

[a] Lit. "the heavens of the."

mouth; You gave them water when they were thirsty. ²¹Forty years You sustained them in the wilderness so that they lacked nothing; their clothes did not wear out, and their feet did not swell.

²²"You gave them kingdoms and peoples, and ^{b-}allotted them territory.^{-b} They took possession of the land of Sihon, the land of the king of Heshbon, and the land of Og, king of Bashan. ²³You made their children as numerous as the stars of heaven, and brought them to the land which You told their fathers to go and possess. ²⁴The sons came and took possession of the land: You subdued the Canaanite inhabitants of the land before them; You delivered them into their power, both their kings and the peoples of the land, to do with them as they pleased. ²⁵They captured fortified cities and rich lands; they took possession of houses filled with every good thing, of hewn cisterns, vineyards, olive trees, and fruit trees in abundance. They ate, they were filled, they grew fat; they luxuriated in Your great bounty. ²⁶Then, defying You, they rebelled; they cast Your Teaching behind their back. They killed Your prophets who admonished them to turn them back to You; they committed great impieties.

²⁷"You delivered them into the power of their adversaries who oppressed them. In their time of trouble they cried to You; You in heaven heard them, and in Your abundant compassion gave them saviors who saved them from the power of their adversaries. ²⁸But when they had relief, they again did what was evil in Your sight, so You abandoned them to the power of their enemies, who subjugated them. Again they cried to You, and You in heaven heard and rescued them in Your compassion, time after time. ²⁹You admonished them in order to turn them back to Your Teaching, but they acted presumptuously and disobeyed Your commandments, and sinned against Your rules, by following which a man shall live. They turned a defiant shoulder, stiffened their neck, and would not obey. ³⁰You bore with them for many years, admonished them by Your spirit through Your prophets, but they would not give ear, so You delivered them into the power of the peoples of the lands. ³¹Still, in Your great compassion You did not make an end of them or abandon them, for You are a gracious and compassionate God.

³²"And now, our God, great, mighty, and awesome God, who stays faithful to His covenant, do not treat lightly all the suffering that has overtaken us—our kings, our officers, our priests, our prophets, our fathers, and all Your people—from the time of the Assyrian kings to this day.

^{b-b} *Meaning of Heb. uncertain.*

³³Surely You are in the right with respect to all that has come upon us, for You have acted faithfully, and we have been wicked. ³⁴Our kings, officers, priests, and fathers did not follow Your Teaching, and did not listen to Your commandments or to the warnings that You gave them. ³⁵When they had their own kings and enjoyed the good that You lavished upon them, and the broad and rich land that You put at their disposal, they would not serve You, and did not turn from their wicked deeds. ³⁶Today we are slaves, and the land that You gave our fathers to enjoy its fruit and bounty—here we are slaves on it! ³⁷On account of our sins it yields its abundant crops to kings whom You have set over us. They rule over our bodies and our beasts as they please, and we are in great distress.

10

"In view of all this, we make this pledge and put it in writing; and on the sealed copy [are subscribed] our officials, our Levites, and our priests.

²"On the sealed copyᵃ [are subscribed]: Nehemiah the Tirshatha son of Hacaliah and Zedekiah, ³Seraiah, Azariah, Jeremiah, ⁴Pashhur, Amariah, Malchijah, ⁵Hattush, Shebaniah, Malluch, ⁶Harim, Meremoth, Obadiah, ⁷Daniel, Ginnethon, Baruch, ⁸Meshullam, Abijah, Mijamin, ⁹Maaziah, Bilgai, Shemaiah; these are the priests.

¹⁰"And the Levites: Jeshua son of Azaniah, Binnui of the sons of Henadad, and Kadmiel. ¹¹And their brothers: Shebaniah, Hodiah, Kelita, Pelaiah, Hanan, ¹²Mica, Rehob, Hashabiah, ¹³Zaccur, Sherebiah, Shebaniah, ¹⁴Hodiah, Bani, and Beninu.

¹⁵"The heads of the people: Parosh, Pahath-moab, Elam, Zattu, Bani, ¹⁶Bunni, Azgad, Bebai, ¹⁷Adonijah, Bigvai, Adin, ¹⁸Ater, Hezekiah, Azzur, ¹⁹Hodiah, Hashum, Bezai, ²⁰Hariph, Anathoth, Nebai, ²¹Magpiash, Meshullam, Hezir, ²²Meshezabel, Zadok, Jaddua, ²³Pelatiah, Hanan, Anaiah, ²⁴Hoshea, Hananiah, Hasshub, ²⁵Hallohesh, Pilha, Shobek, ²⁶Rehum, Hashabnah, Maaseiah,²⁷and Ahiah, Hanan, Anan, ²⁸Malluch, Harim, Baanah.

²⁹"And the rest of the people, the priests, the Levites, the gatekeepers, the singers, the temple servants, and all who separated themselves from the peoples of the lands to [follow] the Teaching of God, their wives, sons and daughters, all who know enough to understand, ³⁰join with their

---

ᵃ *Heb. plural.*

noble brothers, and take an oath with sanctions to follow the Teaching of God, given through Moses the servant of God, and to observe carefully all the commandments of the LORD our Lord, His rules and laws.

31"Namely: We will not give our daughters in marriage to the peoples of the land, or take their daughters for our sons.

32"The peoples of the land who bring their wares and all sorts of foodstuff for sale on the sabbath day—we will not buy from them on the sabbath or a holy day.

"We will forgo [the produce of] the seventh year, and every outstanding debt.

33"We have laid upon ourselves obligations: To charge ourselves one-third of a shekel yearly for the service of the House of our God—34for the rows of bread, for the regular meal offering and for the regular burnt offering, [for those of the] sabbaths, new moons, festivals, for consecrations, for sin offerings to atone for Israel, and for all the work in the House of our God.

35"We have cast lots [among] the priests, the Levites, and the people, to bring the wood offering to the House of our God by clans annually at set times in order to provide fuel for the altar of the LORD our God, as is written in the Teaching.

36"And [we undertake] to bring to the House of the LORD annually the first fruits of our soil, and of every fruit of every tree; 37also, the firstborn of our sons and our beasts, as is written in the Teaching; and to bring the firstlings of our cattle and flocks to the House of our God for the priests who minister in the House of our God.

38"We will bring to the storerooms of the House of our God the first part of our dough, and our gifts [of grain], and of the fruit of every tree, wine and oil for the priests, and the tithes of our land for the Levites— the Levites who collect the tithe in all our towns b-subject to royal service.-b 39An Aaronite priest must be with the Levites when they collect the tithe, and the Levites must bring up a tithe of the tithe to the House of our God, to the storerooms of the treasury. 40For it is to the storerooms that the Israelites and the Levites must bring the gifts of grain, wine, and oil. The equipment of the sanctuary and of the ministering priests and the gatekeepers and the singers is also there.

"We will not neglect the House of our God."

b-b *For this sense of* 'abodah, *"service," cf. 5.18.*

11 The officers of the people settled in Jerusalem; the rest of the people cast lots for one out of ten to come and settle in the holy city of Jerusalem, and the other nine-tenths to stay in the towns. ²The people gave their blessing to all the men who willingly settled in Jerusalem.

³These are the heads of the province who lived in Jerusalem—in the countryside[a] of Judah, the people lived in their towns, each on his own property, Israelites, priests, Levites, temple servants, and the sons of Solomon's servants, ⁴while in Jerusalem some of the Judahites and some of the Benjaminites lived:

Of the Judahites: Athaiah son of Uzziah son of Zechariah son of Amariah son of Shephatiah son of Mahalalel, of the clan of Periz, ⁵and Maaseiah son of Baruch son of Col-hozeh son of Hazaiah son of Adaiah son of Joiarib son of Zechariah son of the Shilohite. ⁶All the clan of Periz who were living in Jerusalem—468 valorous men.

⁷These are the Benjaminites: Sallu son of Meshullam son of Joed son of Pedaiah son of Kolaiah son of Maaseiah son of Ithiel son of Jesaiah. ⁸After him, Gabbai and Sallai—928.

⁹Joel son of Zichri was the official in charge of them, and Judah son of Hassenuah was the second-in-command of the city.

¹⁰Of the priests: Jedaiah son of Joiarib, Jachin, ¹¹Seraiah son of Hilkiah son of Meshullam son of Zadok son of Meraioth son of Ahitub, chief officer of the House of God, ¹²and their brothers, who did the work of the House—822; and Adaiah son of Jeroham son of Pelaliah son of Amzi son of Zechariah son of Pashhur son of Malchijah, ¹³and his brothers, heads of clans—242; and Amashsai son of Azarel son of Ahzai son of Meshillemoth son of Immer, ¹⁴and their brothers, valorous warriors— 128. Zabdiel son of Haggedolim was the official in charge of them.

¹⁵Of the Levites: Shemaiah son of Hasshub son of Azrikam son of Hashabiah son of Bunni, ¹⁶and Shabbethai and Jozabad of the heads of the Levites were in charge of the external work of the House of God. ¹⁷Mattaniah son of Micha son of Zabdi son of Asaph was the head; at prayer, he would lead off with praise; and Bakbukiah, one of his brothers, was his second-in-command; and Abda son of Shammua son of Galal son of Jeduthun. ¹⁸All the Levites in the holy city—284.

¹⁹And the gatekeepers: Akkub, Talmon, and their brothers, who stood watch at the gates—172.

ᵃ Lit. "towns."

20And the rest of the Israelites, the priests, and the Levites in all the towns of Judah [lived] each on his estate.

21The temple servants lived on the Ophel; Ziha and Gishpa were in charge of the temple servants.

22The overseer of the Levites in Jerusalem was Uzzi son of Bani son of Hashabiah son of Mattaniah son of Micha, of the Asaphite singers, over the work of the House of God. 23There was a royal order concerning them, a stipulation concerning the daily duties of the singers.

24Petahiah son of Meshezabel, of the sons of Zerah son of Judah, advised the king concerning all the affairs of the people.

25As concerns the villages with their fields: Some of the Judahites lived in Kiriath-arba and its outlying hamlets, in Dibon and its outlying hamlets, and in Jekabzeel and its villages; 26in Jeshua, in Moladah, and in Beth-pelet; 27in Hazar-shual, in Beer-sheba and its outlying hamlets; 28and in Ziklag and in Meconah and its outlying hamlets; 29in En-rimmon, in Zorah and in Jarmuth; 30Zanoah, Adullam, and their villages; Lachish and its fields; Azekah and its outlying hamlets. They settled from Beer-sheba to the Valley of Hinnom.

31The Benjaminites: from Geba, Michmash, Aija, and Bethel and its outlying hamlets; 32Anathoth, Nob, Ananiah, 33Hazor, Ramah, Gittaim, 34Hadid, Zeboim, Neballat, 35Lod, Ono, Ge-harashim. 36Some of the Judahite divisions of Levites were [shifted] to Benjamin.

12 These are the priests and the Levites who came up with Zerubbabel son of Shealtiel and Jeshua:

Seraiah, Jeremiah, Ezra, 2Amariah, Malluch, Hattush, 3Shecaniah, Rehum, Meramoth, 4Iddo, Ginnethoi, Abijah, 5Mijamin, Maadiah, Bilgah, 6Shemaiah, Joiarib, Jedaiah, 7Sallu, Amok, Hilkiah, Jedaiah. These were the heads of the priests and their brothers in the time of Jeshua.

8The Levites: Jeshua, Binnui, Kadmiel, Sherebiah, Judah, and Mattaniah, in charge of thanksgiving songs,a he and his brothers; 9and Bakbukiah and Unni [and] their brothers served opposite them by shifts.

10Jeshua begot Joiakim; Joiakim begot Eliashib; Eliashib begot Joiada; 11Joiada begot Jonathan; Jonathan begot Jaddua.

12In the time of Joiakim, the heads of the priestly clans were: Meriaiah—of the Seraiah clan; Hananiah—of the Jeremiah clan; 13Meshullam—

a Meaning of Heb. uncertain.

of the Ezra clan; Jehohanan—of the Amariah clan; ¹⁴Jonathan—of the Melicu clan; Joseph—of the Shebaniah clan; ¹⁵Adna—of the Harim clan; Helkai—of the Meraioth clan; ¹⁶Zechariah—of the Iddo clan; Meshullam—of the Ginnethon clan; ¹⁷Zichri—of the Abijah clan . . . of the Miniamin clan; Piltai—of the Moadiah clan; ¹⁸Shammua—of the Bilgah clan; Jehonathan—of the Shemaiah clan; ¹⁹Mattenai—of the Joiarib clan; Uzzi—of the Jedaiah clan; ²⁰Kallai—of the Sallai clan; Eber—of the Amok clan; ²¹Hashabiah—of the Hilkiah clan; Nethanel—of the Jedaiah clan.

²²The Levites and the priests were listed by heads of clans in the days of Eliashib, Joiada, Johanan, and Jaddua, down to the reign of Darius the Persian. ²³But the Levite heads of clans are listed in the book of the chronicles to the time of Johanan son of Eliashib.

²⁴The heads of the Levites: Hashabiah, Sherebiah, Jeshua son of Kadmiel, and their brothers served opposite them, singing praise and thanksgiving hymns by the ordinance of David the man of God—served opposite them in shifts; ²⁵Mattaniah, Bakbukiah, Obadiah, Meshullam, Talmon, and Akkub, guarding as gatekeepers by shifts at the vestibules of the gates.

²⁶These were in the time of Joiakim son of Jeshua son of Jozadak, and in the time of Nehemiah the governor, and of Ezra the priest, the scribe.

²⁷At the dedication of the wall of Jerusalem, the Levites, wherever they lived, were sought out and brought to Jerusalem to celebrate a joyful dedication with thanksgiving and with song, accompanied by cymbals, harps, and lyres. ²⁸The companies of singers assembled from the [Jordan] plain, the environs of Jerusalem, and from the Netophathite villages; ²⁹from Beth-hagilgal, from the countryside of Geba and Azmaveth, for the singers built themselves villages in the environs of Jerusalem.

³⁰The priests and Levites purified themselves; then they purified the people, and the gates, and the wall.

³¹I had the officers of Judah go up onto the wall, and I appointed two large thanksgiving [choirs] and processions. [One marched] south on the wall, to the Dung Gate; ³²behind them were Hoshaiah and half the officers of Judah, ³³and Azariah, Ezra, Meshullam, ³⁴Judah, Benjamin, Shemaiah, and Jeremiah, ³⁵and some of the young priests, with trumpets; Zechariah son of Jonathan son of Shemaiah son of Mattaniah son of Micaiah son of Zaccur son of Asaph, ³⁶and his brothers Shemaiah, and Azarel, Milalai, Gilalai, Maai, Nethanel, Judah, and Hanani, with the musical instruments of David, the man of God; and Ezra the scribe went ahead of them. ³⁷From there to the Fountain Gate, where they ascended the steps of the

City of David directly before them, by the ascent on the wall, above the house of David, [and onward] to the Water Gate on the east.

38The other thanksgiving [choir] marched on the wall in the opposite direction, with me and half the people behind it, above the Tower of Ovens to the Broad Wall; 39and above the Gate of Ephraim, the Jeshanah Gate, the Fish Gate, the Tower of Hananel, the Tower of the Hundred, to the Sheep Gate; and they halted at the Gate of the Prison Compound. 40Both thanksgiving choirs halted at the House of God, and I and half the prefects with me, 41and the priests Eliakim, Maaseiah, Miniamin, Micaiah, Elioenai, Zechariah, Hananiah, with trumpets, 42and Maaseiah and Shemaiah, Eleazar, Uzzi, Jehohanan, Malchijah, Elam, and Ezer. Then the singers sounded forth, with Jezrahiah in charge.

43On that day, they offered great sacrifices and rejoiced, for God made them rejoice greatly; the women and children also rejoiced, and the rejoicing in Jerusalem could be heard from afar.

44At that time men were appointed over the chambers that served as treasuries for the gifts, the first fruits, and the tithes, into which the portions prescribed by the Teaching for the priests and Levites were gathered from the fields of the towns; for the people of Judah were grateful to the priests and Levites who were in attendance, 45who kept the charge of their God and the charge of purity, as well as to the singers and gatekeepers [serving] in accord with the ordinance of David and Solomon his son—46for the chiefs of the singers and songs of praise and thanksgiving to God already existed in the time of David and Asaph. 47And in the time of Zerubbabel, and in the time of Nehemiah, all Israel contributed the daily portions of the singers and the gatekeepers, and made sacred contributions for the Levites, and the Levites made sacred contributions for the Aaronites.

13 At that time they read to the people from the Book of Moses, and it was found written that no Ammonite or Moabite might ever enter the congregation of God, 2since they did not meet Israel with bread and water, and hired Balaam against them to curse them; but our God turned the curse into a blessing. 3When they heard the Teaching, they separated all the alien admixture from Israel.

4Earlier, the priest Eliashib, a relative of Tobiah, who had been appointed over the rooms in the House of our God, 5had assigned to hima

---

a I.e., Tobiah.

a large room where they used to store the meal offering, the frankincense, the equipment, the tithes of grain, wine, and oil, the dues of the Levites, singers and gatekeepers, and the gifts for the priests. 6During all this time, I was not in Jerusalem, for in the thirty-second year of King Artaxerxes of Babylon, I went to the king, and only after a while did I ask leave of the king [to return]. 7When I arrived in Jerusalem, I learned of the outrage perpetrated by Eliashib on behalf of Tobiah in assigning him a room in the courts of the House of God. 8I was greatly displeased, and had all the household gear of Tobiah thrown out of the room; 9I gave orders to purify the rooms, and had the equipment of the House of God and the meal offering and the frankincense put back.

10I then discovered that the portions of the Levites had not been contributed, and that the Levites and the singers who performed the [temple] service had made off, each to his fields. 11I censured the prefects, saying, "How is it that the House of God has been neglected?" Then I recalled [the Levites] and installed them again in their posts; 12and all Judah brought the tithes of grain, wine, and oil into the treasuries. 13I put the treasuries in the charge of the priest Shelemiah, the scribe Zadok, and Pedaiah of the Levites; and assisting them was Hanan son of Zaccur son of Mattaniah—for they were regarded as trustworthy persons, and it was their duty to distribute the portions to their brothers.

14O my God, remember me favorably for this, and do not blot out the devotion I showed toward the House of my God and its attendants.

15At that time I saw men in Judah treading winepresses on the sabbath, and others bringing heaps of grain and loading them onto asses, also wine, grapes, figs, and all sorts of goods, and bringing them into Jerusalem on the sabbath. I admonished them there and then for selling provisions. 16Tyrians who lived there brought fish and all sorts of wares and sold them on the sabbath to the Judahites in Jerusalem. 17I censured the nobles of Judah, saying to them, "What evil thing is this that you are doing, profaning the sabbath day! 18This is just what your ancestors did, and for it God brought all this misfortune on this city; and now you give cause for further wrath against Israel by profaning the sabbath!"

19When shadows filled the gateways of Jerusalem at the approach of the sabbath, I gave orders that the doors be closed, and ordered them not to be opened until after the sabbath. I stationed some of my servants at the gates, so that no goods should enter on the sabbath. 20Once or twice the merchants and the vendors of all sorts of wares spent the night outside

Jerusalem, 21but I warned them, saying, "What do you mean by spending the night alongside the wall? If you do so again, I will lay hands upon you!" From then on they did not come on the sabbath. 22I gave orders to the Levites to purify themselves and come and guard the gates, to preserve the sanctity of the sabbath.

This too, O my God, remember to my credit, and spare me in accord with your abundant faithfulness.

23Also at that time, I saw that Jews had married Ashdodite, Ammonite, and Moabite women; 24a good number of their children spoke the language of Ashdod and the language of those various peoples, and did not know how to speak Judean. 25I censured them, cursed them, flogged them, tore out their hair, and adjured them by God, saying, "You shall not give your daughters in marriage to their sons, or take any of their daughters for your sons or yourselves. 26It was just in such things that King Solomon of Israel sinned! Among the many nations there was not a king like him, and so well loved was he by his God that God made him king of all Israel, yet foreign wives caused even him to sin. 27How, then, can we acquiesce in your doing this great wrong, breaking faith with our God by marrying foreign women?" 28One of the sons of Joiada son of the high priest Eliashib was a son-in-law of Sanballat the Horonite; I drove him away from me.

29Remember to their discredit, O my God, how they polluted the priesthood, the covenant of the priests and Levites. 30I purged them of every foreign element, and arranged for the priests and the Levites to work each at his task by shifts, 31and for the wood offering [to be brought] at fixed times and for the first fruits.

O my God, remember it to my credit!

דִּבְרֵי הַיָּמִים א

I CHRONICLES

1 Adam, Seth, Enosh; ²Kenan, Mahalalel, Jared; ³Enoch, Methuselah, Lamech; ⁴Noah, Shem, Ham, and Japheth.

⁵ᵃThe sons of Japheth: Gomer, Magog, Madai, Javan, Tubal, Meshech, and Tiras. ⁶The sons of Gomer: Ashkenaz, Diphath, and Togarmah. ⁷The sons of Javan: Elishah, Tarshish, Kittim, and Rodanim.

⁸The sons of Ham: Cush, Mizraim, Put, and Canaan. ⁹The sons of Cush: Seba, Havilah, Sabta, Raama, and Sabteca. The sons of Raamah: Sheba and Dedan. ¹⁰Cush begot Nimrod; he was the first mighty one on earth.

¹¹Mizraim begot the Ludim, the Anamim, the Lehabim, the Naphtuhim, ¹²the Pathrusim, the Casluhim (whence the Philistines came forth), and the Caphtorim.

¹³Canaan begot Sidon his first-born, and Heth, ¹⁴and the Jebusites, the Amorites, the Girgashites, ¹⁵the Hivites, the Arkites, the Sinites, ¹⁶the Arvadites, the Zemarites, and the Hamathites.

¹⁷The sons of Shem: Elam, Asshur, Arpachshad, Lud, Aram, Uz, Hul, Gether, and Meshech. ¹⁸Arpachshad begot Shelah; and Shelah begot Eber. ¹⁹Two sons were born to Eber: the name of the one was Peleg (for in his days the earth was divided), and the name of his brother Joktan. ²⁰Joktan begot Almodad, Sheleph, Hazarmaveth, Jerah, ²¹Hadoram, Uzal, Diklah, ²²Ebal, Abimael, Sheba, ²³Ophir, Havilah, and Jobab; all these were the sons of Joktan.

²⁴Shem, Arpachshad, Shelah; ²⁵Eber, Peleg, Reu; ²⁶Serug, Nahor, Terah; ²⁷Abram, that is, Abraham.

²⁸ᵇThe sons of Abraham: Isaac and Ishmael. ²⁹This is their line: The first-born of Ishmael, Nebaioth; and Kedar, Abdeel, Mibsam, ³⁰Mishma, Dumah, Massa, Hadad, Tema, ³¹Jetur, Naphish, and Kedmah. These are

---

ᵃ *With vv. 5–23, cf. Gen. 10.1–30.*
ᵇ *With vv. 28–33, cf. Gen. 25.1–16.*

the sons of Ishmael. ³²The sons of Keturah, Abraham's concubine: she bore Zimran, Jokshan, Medan, Midian, Ishbak, and Shuah. The sons of Jokshan: Sheba and Dedan. ³³The sons of Midian: Ephah, Epher, Enoch, Abida, and Eldaah. All these were the descendants of Keturah.

³⁴Abraham begot Isaac. The sons of Isaac: Esau and Israel. ³⁵The sons of Esau: Eliphaz, Reuel, Jeush, Jalam, and Korah. ³⁶The sons of Eliphaz: Teman, Omar, Zephi, Gatam, Kenaz, Timna, and Amalek. ³⁷The sons of Reuel: Nahath, Zerah, Shammah, and Mizzah.

³⁸The sons of Seir: Lotan, Shobal, Zibeon, Anah, Dishon, Ezer, and Dishan. ³⁹The sons of Lotan: Hori and Homam; and Lotan's sister was Timna. ⁴⁰The sons of Shobal: Alian, Manahath, Ebal, Shephi, and Onam. The sons of Zibeon: Aiah and Anah. ⁴¹The sons of Anah: Dishon. The sons of Dishon: Hamran, Eshban, Ithran, and Cheran. ⁴²The sons of Ezer: Bilhan, Zaavan, and Jaakan. The sons of Dishan: Uz and Aran.

^{43c}These are the kings who reigned in the land of Edom before any king reigned over the Israelites: Bela son of Beor, and the name of his city was Dinhabah. ⁴⁴When Bela died, Jobab son of Zerah from Bozrah succeeded him as king. ⁴⁵When Jobab died, Husham of the land of the Temanites succeeded him as king. ⁴⁶When Husham died, Hadad son of Bedad, who defeated the Midianites in the country of Moab, succeeded him as king, and the name of his city was Avith. ⁴⁷When Hadad died, Samlah of Masrekah succeeded him as king. ⁴⁸When Samlah died, Saul of Rehoboth-on-the-River succeeded him as king. ⁴⁹When Saul died, Baal-hanan son of Achbor succeeded him as king. ⁵⁰When Baal-hanan died, Hadad succeeded him as king; and the name of his city was Pai, and his wife's name Mehetabel daughter of Matred daughter of Me-zahab. ⁵¹And Hadad died.

The clans of Edom were the clans of Timna, Alvah, Jetheth, ⁵²Oholibamah, Elah, Pinon, ⁵³Kenaz, Teman, Mibzar, ⁵⁴Magdiel, and Iram; these are the clans of Edom.

2

These are the sons of Israel: Reuben, Simeon, Levi, Judah, Issachar, Zebulun, ²Dan, Joseph, Benjamin, Naphtali, Gad, and Asher. ³The sons of Judah: Er, Onan, and Shelah; these three, Bath-shua the Canaanite woman bore to him. But Er, Judah's first-born, was displeasing to the LORD, and He took his life. ⁴His daughter-in-law Tamar also bore him Perez and Zerah. Judah's sons were five in all.

c *With vv. 43–50, cf. Gen. 36.31–43.*

⁵The sons of Perez: Hezron and Hamul. ⁶The sons of Zerah: Zimri, Ethan, Heman, Calcol, and Dara, five in all. ⁷The sons of Carmi: Achar, the troubler of Israel, who committed a trespass against the proscribed thing; ⁸and Ethan's son was Azariah.

⁹The sons of Hezron that were born to him: Jerahmeel, Ram, and Chelubai. ¹⁰Ram begot Amminadab, and Amminadab begot Nahshon, prince of the sons of Judah. ¹¹Nahshon was the father of Salma, Salma of Boaz, ¹²Boaz of Obed, Obed of Jesse. ¹³Jesse begot Eliab his first-born, Abinadab the second, Shimea the third, ¹⁴Nethanel the fourth, Raddai the fifth, ¹⁵Ozem the sixth, David the seventh; ¹⁶their sisters were Zeruiah and Abigail. The sons of Zeruiah: Abishai, Joab, and Asahel, three. ¹⁷Abigail bore Amasa, and the father of Amasa was Jether the Ishmaelite.

¹⁸Caleb son of Hezron had children by his wife Azubah, and by Jerioth; these were her sons: Jesher, Shobab, and Ardon. ¹⁹When Azubah died, Caleb married Ephrath, who bore him Hur. ²⁰Hur begot Uri, and Uri begot Bezalel.

²¹Afterward Hezron had relations with the daughter of Machir father of Gilead—he had married her when he was sixty years old—and she bore him Segub; ²²and Segub begot Jair; he had twenty-three cities in the land of Gilead. ²³But Geshur and Aram took from them Havvoth-jair, Kenath and its dependencies, sixty towns. All these were the sons of Machir, the father of Gilead. ²⁴After the death of Hezron, in Caleb-ephrathah, Abijah, wife of Hezron, bore Ashhur, the father of Tekoa.

²⁵The sons of Jerahmeel the first-born of Hezron: Ram his first-born, Bunah, Oren, Ozem, and Ahijah. ²⁶Jerahmeel had another wife, whose name was Atarah; she was the mother of Onam. ²⁷The sons of Ram the first-born of Jerahmeel: Maaz, Jamin, and Eker. ²⁸The sons of Onam: Shammai and Jada. The sons of Shammai: Nadab and Abishur. ²⁹The name of Abishur's wife was Abihail, and she bore him Ahban and Molid. ³⁰The sons of Nadab: Seled and Appaim; Seled died childless. ³¹The sons of Appaim: Ishi. The sons of Ishi: Sheshan. The sons of Sheshan: Ahlai. ³²The sons of Jada, Shammai's brother: Jether and Jonathan; Jether died childless. ³³The sons of Jonathan: Peleth and Zaza. These were the descendants of Jerahmeel. ³⁴Sheshan had no sons, only daughters; Sheshan had an Egyptian slave, whose name was Jarha. ³⁵So Sheshan gave his daughter in marriage to Jarha his slave; and she bore him Attai. ³⁶Attai begot Nathan and Nathan begot Zabad. ³⁷Zabad begot Ephlal, and Ephlal begot Obed. ³⁸Obed begot Jehu, and Jehu begot Azariah. ³⁹Azariah begot

Helez, and Helez begot Eleasah. ⁴⁰Eleasah begot Sisamai, and Sisamai begot Shallum. ⁴¹Shallum begot Jekamiah, and Jekamiah begot Elishama.

⁴²The sons of Caleb brother of Jerahmeel: Meshah his first-born, who was the father of Ziph. The sons of Mareshah father of·Hebron. ⁴³The sons of Hebron: Korah, Tappuah, Rekem, and Shema. ⁴⁴Shema begot Raham the father of Jorkeam, and Rekem begot Shammai. ⁴⁵The son of Shammai: Maon, and Maon begot Bethzur. ⁴⁶Ephah, Caleb's concubine, bore Haran, Moza, and Gazez; Haran begot Gazez. ⁴⁷The sons of Jahdai: Regem, Jotham, Geshan, Pelet, Ephah, and Shaaph. ⁴⁸Maacah, Caleb's concubine, bore Sheber and Tirhanah. ⁴⁹She also bore Shaaph father of Madmannah, Sheva father of Machbenah and father of Gibea; the daughter of Caleb was Achsah. ⁵⁰These were the descendants of Caleb.

The sons of Hur the first-born of Ephrathah: Shobal father of Kiriath-jearim, ⁵¹Salma father of Bethlehem, Hareph father of Beth-gader. ⁵²Shobal father of Kiriath-jearim had sons: Haroeh, half of the Menuhoth. ⁵³And the families of Kiriath-jearim: the Ithrites, the Puthites, the Shumathites, and the Mishraites; from these came the Zorathites and the Eshtaolites. ⁵⁴The sons of Salma: Bethlehem, the Netophathites, Atroth-beth-joab, and half of the Manahathites, the Zorites. ⁵⁵The families of the scribes that dwelt at Jabez: the Tirathites, the Shimeathites, the Sucathites; these are the Kenites who came from Hammath, father of the house of Rechab.

3 These are the sons of David who were born to him in Hebron: the first-born Amnon, by Ahinoam the Jezreelite; the second Daniel, by Abigail the Carmelite; ²the third Absalom, son of Maacah daughter of King Talmai of Geshur; the fourth Adonijah, son of Haggith; ³the fifth Shephatiah, by Abital; the sixth Ithream, by his wife Eglah; ⁴six were born to him in Hebron. He reigned there seven years and six months, and in Jerusalem he reigned thirty-three years. ⁵These were born to him in Jerusalem: Shimea, Shobab, Nathan, and Solomon, four by Bath-shua daughter of Ammiel; ⁶then Ibhar, Elishama, Eliphelet, ⁷Nogah, Nepheg, Japhia, ⁸Elishama, Eliada, and Eliphelet—nine. ⁹All were David's sons, besides the sons of the concubines; and Tamar was their sister.

¹⁰The son of Solomon: Rehoboam; his son Abijah, his son Asa, his son Jehoshaphat, ¹¹his son Joram, his son Ahaziah, his son Joash, ¹²his son Amaziah, his son Azariah, his son Jotham,¹³his son Ahaz, his son Hezekiah, his son Manasseh, ¹⁴his son Amon, and his son Josiah. ¹⁵The

sons of Josiah: Johanan the first-born, the second Jehoiakim, the third Zedekiah, the fourth Shallum. ¹⁶The descendants of Jehoiakim: his son Jeconiah, his son Zedekiah; ¹⁷and the sons of Jeconiah, the captive: Sheal-tiel his son, ¹⁸Malchiram, Pedaiah, Shenazzar, Jekamiah, Hoshama, and Nedabiah; ¹⁹the sons of Pedaiah: Zerubbabel and Shimei; the sons of Zerubbabel: Meshullam and Hananiah, and Shelomith was their sister; ²⁰Hashubah, Ohel, Berechiah, Hasadiah, and Jushab-hesed—five. ²¹And the sons of Hananiah: Pelatiah and Jeshaiah; the sons of [Jeshaiah]: Re-phaiah; the sons of [Rephaiah]: Arnan; the sons of [Arnan]: Obadiah; the sons of [Obadiah]: Shecaniah. ²²And the sons of Shecaniah: She-maiah; and the sons of Shemaiah: Hattush, and Igal, and Bariah, and Neariah, and Shaphat—six. ²³And the sons of Neariah: Elioenai, and Hizkiah, and Azrikam—three. ²⁴And the sons of Elioenai: Hodaviah, and Eliashib, and Pelaiah, and Akkub, and Johanan, and Delaiah, and Anani—seven.

4 The sons of Judah: Perez, Hezron, Carmi, Hur, and Shobal. ²Reaiah son of Shobal begot Jahath, and Jahath begot Ahumai and Lahad. These were the families of the Zorathites. ³These were [the sons of] the father of Etam: Jezreel, Ishma, and Idbash; and the name of their sister was Hazlelponi, ⁴and Penuel was the father of Gedor, and Ezer the father of Hushah. These were the sons of Hur, the first-born of Ephrathah, the father of Bethlehem. ⁵Ashhur the father of Tekoa had two wives, Helah and Naarah; ⁶Naarah bore him Ahuzam, Hepher, Temeni, and Ahashtari. These were the sons of Naarah. ⁷The sons of Helah: Zereth, Zohar, and Ethnan. ⁸Koz was the father of Anub, Zobebah, and the families of Ahar-hel son of Harum. ⁹Jabez was more esteemed than his brothers; and his mother named him Jabez, "Because," she said, "I bore him in pain."ᵃ ¹⁰Jabez invoked the God of Israel, saying, "Oh, bless me, enlarge my territory, stand by me, and make me not suffer pain from misfortune!" And God granted what he asked. ¹¹Chelub the brother of Shuhah begot Mehir, who was the father of Eshton. ¹²Eshton begot Bethrapha, Paseah, and Tehinnah father of Ir-nahash. These were the men of Recah. ¹³The sons of Kenaz: Othniel and Seraiah; and the sons of Othniel: ¹⁴Hathath and Meonothai. He begot Ophrah. Seraiah begot Joab father of Ge-harashim,ᵇ so-called because they were craftsmen. ¹⁵The sons of Caleb son of Jephunneh: Iru, Elah, and Naam; and the sons of Elah: Kenaz.

ᵃ *Heb. 'oṣeb, connected with "Jabez."*
ᵇ *Lit. "the valley of the craftsmen."*

16The sons of Jehallelel: Ziph, Ziphah, Tiria, and Asarel. 17The sons of Ezrah: Jether, Mered, Epher, and Jalon. She[c] conceived and bore Miriam, Shammai, and Ishbah father of Eshtemoa. 18And his Judahite wife bore Jered father of Gedor, Heber father of Soco, and Jekuthiel father of Zanoah. These were the sons of Bithiah daughter of Pharaoh, whom Mered married. 19The sons of the wife of Hodiah sister of Naham were the fathers of Keilah the Garmite and Eshtemoa the Maacathite. 20The sons of Shimon: Amnon, Rinnah, Ben-hanan, and Tilon. The sons of Ishi: Zoheth and Ben-zoheth. 21The sons of Shelah son of Judah: Er father of Lecah, Laadah father of Mareshah, and the families of the linen factory at Beth-ashbea; 22and Jokim, and the men of Cozeba and Joash, and Saraph, who married into Moab and Jashubi Lehem (the records are ancient). 23These were the potters who dwelt at Netaim and Gederah; they dwelt there in the king's service.

24The sons of Simeon: Nemuel, Jamin, Jarib, Zerah, Shaul; 25his son Shallum, his son Mibsam, his son Mishma. 26The sons of Mishma: his son Hammuel, his son Zaccur, his son Shimei. 27Shimei had sixteen sons and six daughters; but his brothers had not many children; in all, their families were not as prolific as the Judahites. 28They dwelt in Beersheba, Moladah, Hazar-shual, 29Bilhah, Ezem, Tolad, 30Bethuel, Hormah, Ziklag, 31Beth-marcaboth, Hazar-susim, Beth-biri, and Shaaraim. These were their towns until David became king, 32together with their villages, Etam, Ain, Rimmon, Tochen, and Ashan—five towns, 33along with all their villages that were around these towns as far as Baal; such were their settlements.

Registered in their genealogy were: 34Meshobab, Jamlech, Joshah son of Amaziah, 35Joel, Jehu son of Joshibiah son of Seraiah son of Asiel. 36Elioenai, Jaakobah, Jeshohaiah, Asaiah, Adiel, Jesimiel, Benaiah, 37Ziza son of Shiphi son of Allon son of Jedaiah son of Shimri son of Shemaiah— 38these mentioned by name were chiefs in their families, and their clans increased greatly. 39They went to the approaches to Gedor, to the eastern side of the valley, in search of pasture for their flocks. 40They found rich, good pasture, and the land was ample, quiet, and peaceful. The former inhabitants were of Ham; 41those recorded by name came in the days of King Hezekiah of Judah, and attacked their encampments and the Meunim who were found there, and wiped them out forever, and settled in their place, because there was pasture there for their flocks. 42And some of them, five hundred of the Simeonites, went to Mount Seir, with Pe-

---

[c] *Apparently Bithiah; cf. v. 18.*

latiah, Neariah, Rephaiah, and Uzziel, sons of Ishi, at their head, ⁴³and they destroyed the last surviving Amalekites, and they live there to this day.

5 The sons of Reuben the first-born of Israel. (He was the first-born; but when he defiled his father's bed, his birthright was given to the sons of Joseph son of Israel, so he is not reckoned as first-born in the genealogy; ²though Judah became more powerful than his brothers and a leader came from him, yet the birthright belonged to Joseph.) ³The sons of Reuben, the first-born of Israel: Enoch, Pallu, Hezron, and Carmi. ⁴The sons of Joel: his son Shemaiah, his son Gog, his son Shimei, ⁵his son Micah, his son Reaiah, his son Baal, ⁶his son Beerah—whom King Tillegath-pilneser of Assyria exiled—was chieftain of the Reubenites. ⁷And his kinsmen, by their families, according to their lines in the genealogy: the head, Jeiel, and Zechariah, ⁸and Bela son of Azaz son of Shema son of Joel; he dwelt in Aroer as far as Nebo and Baal-meon. ⁹He also dwelt to the east as far as the fringe of the wilderness this side of the Euphrates, because their cattle had increased in the land of Gilead. ¹⁰And in the days of Saul they made war on the Hagrites, who fell by their hand; and they occupied their tents throughout all the region east of Gilead.

¹¹The sons of Gad dwelt facing them in the land of Bashan as far as Salcah: ¹²Joel the chief, Shapham the second, Janai, and Shaphat in Bashan. ¹³And by clans: Michael, Meshullam, Sheba, Jorai, Jacan, Zia, and Eber—seven. ¹⁴These were the sons of Abihail son of Huri son of Jaroah son of Gilead son of Michael son of Jeshishai son of Jahdo son of Buz; ¹⁵Ahi son of Abdiel son of Guni was chief of their clan, ¹⁶and they dwelt in Gilead, in Bashan, and in its dependencies, and in all the pasturelands of Sharon, to their limits. ¹⁷All of them were registered by genealogies in the days of King Jotham of Judah, and in the days of King Jeroboam of Israel.

¹⁸The Reubenites, the Gadites, and the half-tribe of Manasseh had warriors who carried shield and sword, drew the bow, and were experienced at war—44,760, ready for service. ¹⁹They made war on the Hagrites—Jetur, Naphish, and Nodab. ²⁰They prevailed against them; the Hagrites and all who were with them were delivered into their hands, for they cried to God in the battle, and He responded to their entreaty because they trusted in Him. ²¹They carried off their livestock: 50,000 of their

camels, 250,000 sheep, 2,000 asses, and 100,000 people. ²²For many fell slain, because it was God's battle. And they dwelt in their place until the exile.

²³The members of the half-tribe of Manasseh dwelt in the land; they were very numerous from Bashan to Baal-hermon, Senir, and Mount Hermon. ²⁴These were the chiefs of their clans: Epher, Ishi, Eliel, Azriel, Jeremiah, Hodaviah, and Jahdiel, men of substance, famous men, chiefs of their clans. ²⁵But they trespassed against the God of their fathers by going astray after the gods of the peoples of the land, whom God had destroyed before them. ²⁶So the God of Israel roused the spirit of King Pul of Assyria—the spirit of King Tillegath-pilneser of Assyria—and he carried them away, namely, the Reubenites, the Gadites, and the half-tribe of Manasseh, and brought them to Halah, Habor, Hara, and the river Gozan, to this day.

^{27a}The sons of Levi: Gershom, Kohath, and Merari. ²⁸The sons of Kohath: Amram, Izhar, Hebron, and Uzziel. ²⁹The children of Amram: Aaron, Moses, and Miriam. The sons of Aaron: Nadab, Abihu, Eleazar, and Ithamar. ³⁰Eleazar begot Phinehas, Phinehas begot Abishua, ³¹Abishua begot Bukki, Bukki begot Uzzi, ³²Uzzi begot Zerahiah, Zerahiah begot Meraioth, ³³Meraioth begot Amariah, Amariah begot Ahitub, ³⁴Ahitub begot Zadok, Zadok begot Ahimaaz, ³⁵Ahimaaz begot Azariah, Azariah begot Johanan, ³⁶and Johanan begot Azariah (it was he who served as priest in the House that Solomon built in Jerusalem). ³⁷Azariah begot Amariah, Amariah begot Ahitub, ³⁸Ahitub begot Zadok, Zadok begot Shallum, ³⁹Shallum begot Hilkiah, Hilkiah begot Azariah, ⁴⁰Azariah begot Seraiah, Seraiah begot Jehozadak; ⁴¹and Jehozadak went into exile when the LORD exiled Judah and Jerusalem by the hand of Nebuchadnezzar.

6

The sons of Levi: Gershom, Kohath, and Merari. ²And these are the names of the sons of Gershom: Libni and Shimei. ³The sons of Kohath: Amram, Izhar, Hebron, and Uzziel. ⁴The sons of Merari: Mahli and Mushi. These were the families of the Levites according to their clans. ⁵Of Gershom: his son Libni, his son Jahath, his son Zimmah, ⁶his son Joah, his son Iddo, his son Zerah, his son Jeatherai. ⁷The sons of Kohath: his son Amminadab, his son Korah, his son Assir, ⁸his son Elkanah, his son Ebiasaph, his son Assir, ⁹his son Tahath, his son Uriel, his son Uzziah,

---

^a *In some editions, chap. 6 begins here.*

and his son Shaul. ¹⁰The sons of Elkanah: Amasai and Ahimoth, ¹¹his son Elkanah, his son Zophai, his son Nahath, ¹²his son Eliab, his son Jeroham, his son Elkanah. ¹³The sons of Samuel: his first-born ^{a-}Vashni, and^{-a} Abijah. ¹⁴The sons of Merari: Mahli, his son Libni, his son Shimei, his son Uzzah, ¹⁵his son Shimea, his son Haggiah, and his son Asaiah.

¹⁶These were appointed by David to be in charge of song in the House of the LORD, from the time the Ark came to rest. ¹⁷They served at the Tabernacle of the Tent of Meeting with song until Solomon built the House of the LORD in Jerusalem; and they carried out their duties as prescribed for them. ¹⁸Those were the appointed men; and their sons were: the Kohathites: Heman the singer, son of Joel son of Samuel ¹⁹son of Elkanah son of Jeroham son of Eliel son of Toah ²⁰son of Zuph son of Elkanah son of Mahath son of Amasai ²¹son of Elkanah son of Joel son of Azariah son of Zephaniah ²²son of Tahath son of Assir son of Ebiasaph son of Korah ²³son of Izhar son of Kohath son of Levi son of Israel; ²⁴and his kinsman Asaph, who stood on his right, namely, Asaph son of Berechiah son of Shimea ²⁵son of Michael son of Baaseiah son of Malchijah ²⁶son of Ethni son of Zerah son of Adaiah ²⁷son of Ethan son of Zimmah son of Shimei ²⁸son of Jahath son of Gershom son of Levi. ²⁹On the left were their kinsmen: the sons of Merari: Ethan son of Kishi son of Abdi son of Malluch ³⁰son of Hashabiah son of Amaziah son of Hilkiah ³¹son of Amzi son of Bani son of Shemer ³²son of Mahli son of Mushi son of Merari son of Levi; ³³and their kinsmen the Levites were appointed for all the service of the Tabernacle of the House of God.

³⁴But Aaron and his sons made offerings upon the altar of burnt offering and upon the altar of incense, performing all the tasks of the most holy place, to make atonement for Israel, according to all that Moses the servant of God had commanded. ³⁵These are the sons of Aaron: his son Eleazar, his son Phinehas, his son Abishua, ³⁶his son Bukki, his son Uzzi, his son Zerahiah, ³⁷his son Meraioth, his son Amariah, his son Ahitub, ³⁸his son Zadok, his son Ahimaaz. ^{39b}These are their dwelling-places according to their settlements within their borders: to the sons of Aaron of the families of Kohathites, for theirs was the [first] lot; ⁴⁰they gave them Hebron in the land of Judah and its surrounding pasturelands, ⁴¹but the fields of the city and its villages they gave to Caleb son of Jephunneh.⁴²To the sons of Aaron they gave the cities^c of refuge: Hebron and Libnah with its pasturelands, Jattir and Eshtemoa with its pasturelands, ⁴³Hilen with its pasturelands, Debir with its pasturelands, ⁴⁴Ashan with

^{a-a} Some ancient vv. read "Joel, and the second"; cf. 1 Sam. 8.2.
^b With vv. 24–51, cf. Josh. 21.3–42.
^c Josh. 21.13, "city."

its pasturelands, and Beth-shemesh with its pasturelands. ⁴⁵From the tribe of Benjamin, Geba with its pasturelands, Alemeth with its pasturelands, and Anathoth with its pasturelands. All their cities throughout their families were thirteen.

⁴⁶To the remaining Kohathites were given by lot out of the family of the tribe, out of the half-tribe, the half of Manasseh, ten cities. ⁴⁷To the Gershomites according to their families were allotted thirteen cities out of the tribes of Issachar, Asher, Naphtali, and Manasseh in Bashan. ⁴⁸To the Merarites according to their families were allotted twelve cities out of the tribes of Reuben, Gad, and Zebulun. ⁴⁹So the people of Israel gave the Levites the cities with their pasturelands. ⁵⁰They gave them by lot out of the tribe of the Judahites these cities that are mentioned by name, and out of the tribe of the Simeonites, and out of the tribe of the Benjaminites.

⁵¹And some of the families of the sons of Kohath had cities of their territory out of the tribe of Ephraim. ⁵²They gave them the cities of refuge: Shechem with its pasturelands in the hill country of Ephraim, Gezer with its pasturelands, ⁵³Jokmeam with its pasturelands, Beth-horon with its pasturelands, ⁵⁴Aijalon with its pasturelands, Gath-rimmon with its pasturelands; ⁵⁵and out of the half-tribe of Manasseh: Aner with its pasturelands, and Bileam with its pasturelands, for the rest of the families of the Kohathites.

⁵⁶To the Gershomites; out of the half-tribe of Manasseh: Golan in Bashan with its pasturelands and Ashtaroth with its pasturelands; ⁵⁷and out of the tribe of Issachar: Kedesh with its pasturelands, Dobrath with its pasturelands, ⁵⁸Ramoth with its pasturelands, and Anem with its pasturelands; ⁵⁹out of the tribe of Asher: Mashal with its pasturelands, Abdon with its pasturelands, ⁶⁰Hukok with its pasturelands, and Rehob with its pasturelands; ⁶¹and out of the tribe of Naphtali: Kedesh in Galilee with its pasturelands; Hammon with its pasturelands, and Kiriathaim with its pasturelands. ⁶²To the rest of the Merarites, out of the tribe of Zebulun: Rimmono with its pasturelands, Tabor with its pasturelands; ⁶³and beyond the Jordan at Jericho, on the east side of the Jordan, out of the tribe of Reuben: Bezer in the wilderness with its pasturelands, Jahaz with its pasturelands, ⁶⁴Kedemoth with its pasturelands, and Mephaath with its pasturelands; ⁶⁵and out of the tribe of Gad: Ramoth in Gilead with its pasturelands, Mahanaim with its pasturelands, ⁶⁶Heshbon with its pasturelands, and Jazer with its pasturelands.

7 The sons of Issachar: Tola, Puah, Jashub, and Shimron—four. ²The sons of Tola: Uzzi, Rephaiah, Jeriel, Jahmai, Ibsam, Shemuel, chiefs of their clans, men of substance according to their lines; their number in the days of David was 22,600. ³The sons of Uzzi: Izrahiah. And the sons of Izrahiah: Michael, Obadiah, Joel, and Isshiah—five. All of them were chiefs. ⁴And together with them, by their lines, according to their clans, were units of the fighting force, 36,000, for they had many wives and sons. ⁵Their kinsmen belonging to all the families of Issachar were in all 87,000 men of substance; they were all registered by genealogy.

⁶[The sons of] Benjamin: Bela, Becher, and Jediael—three. ⁷The sons of Bela: Ezbon, Uzzi, Uzziel, Jerimoth, and Iri—five, chiefs of clans, men of substance, registered by genealogy—22,034. ⁸The sons of Becher: Zemirah, Joash, Eliezer, Elioenai, Omri, Jeremoth, Abijah, Anathoth, and Alemeth. All these were the sons of Becher; ⁹and they were registered by genealogy according to their lines, as chiefs of their clans, men of substance—20,200. ¹⁰The sons of Jediael: Bilhan. And the sons of Bilhan: Jeush, Benjamin, Ehud, Chenaanah, Zethan, Tarshish, and Ahishahar. ¹¹All these were the sons of Jediael, chiefs of the clans, men of substance—17,200, who made up the fighting force. ¹²And Shuppim and Huppim were the sons of Ir; Hushim the sons of Aher.

¹³The sons of Naphtali: Jahziel, Guni, Jezer, and Shallum, the descendants of Bilhah.

¹⁴The sons of Manasseh: Asriel, whom his Aramean concubine bore; she bore Machir the father of Gilead. ¹⁵And Machir took wives for Huppim and for Shuppim. The name of his sister was Maacah. And the name of the second was Zelophehad; and Zelophehad had daughters. ¹⁶And Maacah the wife of Machir bore a son, and she named him Peresh; and the name of his brother was Sheresh; and his sons were Ulam and Rekem. ¹⁷The sons of Ulam: Bedan. These were the sons of Gilead son of Machir son of Manasseh. ¹⁸And his sister Hammolecheth bore Ishhod, Abiezer, and Mahlah. ¹⁹The sons of Shemida were Ahian, Shechem, Likhi, and Aniam.

²⁰The sons of Ephraim: Shuthelah, his son Bered, his son Tahath, his son Eleadah, his son Tahath, ²¹his son Zabad, his son Shuthelah, also Ezer and Elead. The men of Gath, born in the land, killed them because they had gone down to take their cattle. ²²And Ephraim their father mourned many days, and his brothers came to comfort him. ²³He cohab-

ited with his wife, who conceived and bore a son; and she named him Beriah, because it occurred when there was misfortune[a] in his house. 24His daughter was Sheerah, who built both Lower and Upper Beth-horon, and Uzzen-sheerah. 25His son Rephah, his son Resheph, his son Telah, his son Tahan, 26his son Ladan, his son Ammihud, his son Elishama, 27his son Non, his son Joshua. 28Their possessions and settlements were Bethel and its dependencies, and on the east Naaran, and on the west Gezer and its dependencies, Shechem and its dependencies, and Aiah and its dependencies; 29also along the borders of the Manassites, Beth-shean and its dependencies, Taanach and its dependencies, Megiddo and its dependencies, Dor and its dependencies. In these dwelt the sons of Joseph son of Israel.

30The sons of Asher: Imnah, Ishvah, Ishvi, Beriah, and their sister Serah. 31The sons of Beriah: Heber and Malchiel, who was the father of Birzaith. 32Heber begot Japhlet, Shomer, Hotham, and their sister, Shua. 33The sons of Japhlet: Pasach, Bimhal, and Ashvath. These were the sons of Japhlet. 34The sons of Shemer: Ahi, Rohgah, Hubbah, and Aram. 35The sons of Helem his brother: Zophah, Imna, Shelesh, and Amal. 36The sons of Zophah: Suah, Harnepher, Shual, Beri, Imrah, 37Bezer, Hod, Shamma, Shilshah, Ithran, and Beera. 38The sons of Jether: Jephunneh, Pispa, and Ara. 39The sons of Ulla: Arah, Hanniel, and Rizia. 40All of these men of Asher, chiefs of the clans, select men, men of substance, heads of the chieftains. And they were registered by genealogy according to fighting force; the number of the men was 26,000 men.

8 Benjamin begot Bela his first-born, Ashbel the second, Aharah the third, 2Nohah the fourth, and Rapha the fifth. 3And Bela had sons: Addar, Gera, Abihud, 4Abishua, Naaman, Ahoah, 5Gera, Shephuphan, and Huram. 6These were the sons of Ehud—they were chiefs of clans of the inhabitants of Geba, and they were exiled to Manahath: 7Naaman, Ahijah, and Gera— he exiled them and begot Uzza and Ahihud. 8And Shaharaim had sons in the country of Moab after he had sent away Hushim and Baara his wives. 9He had sons by Hodesh his wife: Jobab, Zibia, Mesha, Malcam, 10Jeuz, Sachiah, and Mirmah. These were his sons, chiefs of clans. 11He also begot by Hushim: Abitub and Elpaal. 12The sons of Elpaal: Eber, Misham, and Shemed, who built Ono and Lod with its dependencies, 13and Beriah and Shema—they were chiefs of clans of the inhabitants of

[a] *Heb.* bera‘ah.

Aijalon, who put to flight the inhabitants of Gath; ¹⁴and Ahio, Shashak, and Jeremoth. ¹⁵Zebadiah, Arad, Eder, ¹⁶Michael, Ishpah, and Joha were sons of Beriah. ¹⁷Zebadiah, Meshullam, Hizki, Heber, ¹⁸Ishmerai, Izliah, and Jobab were the sons of Elpaal. ¹⁹Jakim, Zichri, Zabdi, ²⁰Elienai, Zillethai, Eliel, ²¹Adaiah, Beraiah, and Shimrath were the sons of Shimei. ²²Ishpan, Eber, Eliel, ²³Abdon, Zichri, Hanan, ²⁴Hananiah, Elam, Anthothiah, ²⁵Iphdeiah, and Penuel were the sons of Shashak. ²⁶Shamsherai, Shehariah, Athaliah, ²⁷Jaareshiah, Elijah, and Zichri were the sons of Jeroham. ²⁸These were the chiefs of the clans, according to their lines. These chiefs dwelt in Jerusalem.

²⁹The father of Gibeon dwelt in Gibeon, and the name of his wife was Maacah. ³⁰His first-born son: Abdon; then Zur, Kish, Baal, Nadab, ³¹Gedor, Ahio, Zecher. ³²Mikloth begot Shimeah. And they dwelt in Jerusalem opposite their kinsmen, with their kinsmen. ³³Ner begot Kish, Kish begot Saul, Saul begot Jonathan, Malchi-shua, Abinadab, and Eshbaal; ³⁴and the son of Jonathan was Merib-baal; and Merib-baal begot Micah. ³⁵The sons of Micah: Pithon, Melech, Taarea, and Ahaz. ³⁶Ahaz begot Jehoaddah; and Jehoaddah begot Alemeth, Azmaveth, and Zimri; Zimri begot Moza. ³⁷Moza begot Binea; his son Raphah; his son Eleasah, his son Azel. ³⁸Azel had six sons, and these are their names: Azrikam, Bocheru, Ishmael, Sheariah, Obadiah, and Hanan. All these were the sons of Azel. ³⁹The sons of Eshek his brother: Ulam his first-born, Jeush the second, and Eliphelet the third. ⁴⁰The descendants of Ulam—men of substance, who drew the bow, had many children and grandchildren—one hundred and fifty; all these were Benjaminites.

9

All Israel was registered by genealogies; and these are in the book of the kings of Israel. And Judah was taken into exile in Babylon because of their trespass. ²ᵃThe first to settle in their towns, on their property, were Israelites, priests, Levites, and temple servants, ³while some of the Judahites and some of the Benjaminites and some of the Ephraimites and Manassehites settled in Jerusalem; ⁴Uthai son of Ammihud son of Omri son of Imri son of Bani, from the sons of Perez son of Judah; ⁵and of the Shilonites: Asaiah the first-born and his sons. ⁶Of the sons of Zerah: Jeuel and their kinsmen—690. ⁷Of the Benjaminites: Sallu son of Meshullam son of Hodaviah son of Hassenuah, ⁸Ibneiah son of Jeroham, Elah son of Uzzi son of Michri, and Meshullam son of Shephatiah son of Reuel

ᵃ *With vv. 2–17, cf. Neh. 11.3–19.*

son of Ibneiah; 9and their kinsmen, according to their lines—956. All these were chiefs of their ancestral clans.

10Of the priests: Jedaiah, Jehoiarib, Jachin, 11and Azariah son of Hilkiah son of Meshullam son of Zadok son of Meraioth son of Ahitub, chief officer of the House of God; 12and Adaiah son of Jeroham son of Pashhur son of Malchijah, and Maasai son of Adiel son of Jahzerah son of Meshullam son of Meshillemith son of Immer, 13together with their kinsmen, chiefs of their clans—1,760, men of substance for the work of the service of the House of God.

14Of the Levites: Shemaiah son of Hasshub son of Azrikam son of Hashabiah, of the sons of Merari; 15and Bakbakkar, Heresh, Galal, and Mattaniah son of Mica son of Zichri son of Asaph; 16and Obadiah son of Shemaiah son of Galal son of Jeduthun, and Berechiah son of Asa son of Elkanah, who dwelt in the villages of the Netophathites.

17The gatekeepers were: Shallum, Akkub, Talmon, Ahiman; and their kinsman Shallum was the chief 18hitherto in the King's Gate on the east. They were the keepers belonging to the Levite camp. 19Shallum son of Kore son of Ebiasaph son of Korah, and his kinsmen of his clan, the Korahites, were in charge of the work of the service, guards of the threshold of the Tent; their fathers had been guards of the entrance to the camp of the LORD. 20And Phinehas son of Eleazar was the chief officer over them in time past; the LORD was with him. 21Zechariah the son of Meshelemiah was gatekeeper at the entrance of the Tent of Meeting. 22All these, who were selected as gatekeepers at the thresholds, were 212. They were selected by genealogies in their villages. David and Samuel the seer established them in their office of trust. 23They and their descendants were in charge of the gates of the House of the LORD, that is, the House of the Tent, as guards. 24The gatekeepers were on the four sides, east, west, north, and south; 25and their kinsmen in their villages were obliged to join them every seven days, according to a fixed schedule. 26The four chief gatekeepers, who were Levites, were entrusted to be over the chambers and the treasuries of the House of God. 27They spent the night near the House of God; for they had to do guard duty, and they were in charge of opening it every morning.

28Some of them had charge of the service vessels, for they were counted when they were brought back and taken out. 29Some of them were in charge of the vessels and all the holy vessels, and of the flour, wine, oil, incense, and spices. 30Some of the priests blended the compound of spices.

³¹Mattithiah, one of the Levites, the first-born of Shallum the Korahite, was entrusted with making the flat cakes. ³²Also some of their Kohathite kinsmen had charge of the rows of bread, to prepare them for each sabbath.

³³Now these are the singers, the chiefs of Levitical clans who remained in the chambers free of other service, for they were on duty day and night. ³⁴These were chiefs of Levitical clans, according to their lines; these chiefs lived in Jerusalem.

³⁵The father of Gibeon, Jeiel, lived in Gibeon, and the name of his wife was Maacah. ³⁶His first-born son, Abdon; then Zur, Kish, Baal, Ner, Nadab, ³⁷Gedor, Ahio, Zechariah, and Mikloth; ³⁸Mikloth begot Shimeam; and they lived in Jerusalem opposite their kinsmen, with their kinsmen. ³⁹Ner begot Kish, Kish begot Saul, Saul begot Jonathan, Malchishua, Abinadab, and Eshbaal; ⁴⁰and the son of Jonathan was Merib-baal; and Merib-baal begot Micah.⁴¹The sons of Micah: Pithon, Melech, Taharea; ⁴²Ahaz begot Jarah, and Jarah begot Alemeth, Azmaveth, and Zimri; Zimri begot Moza. ⁴³Moza begot Binea; his son was Rephaiah, his son Eleasah, his son Azel. ⁴⁴Azel had six sons and these were their names: Azrikam, Bocheru, Ishmael, Sheariah, Obadiah, and Hanan. These were the sons of Azel.

10

ᵃThe Philistines attacked Israel, and the men of Israel fled before the Philistines and [many] fell on Mount Gilboa. ²The Philistines pursued Saul and his sons, and the Philistines struck down Jonathan, Abinadab, and Malchi-shua, sons of Saul. ³The battle raged around Saul, and the archers hit him, and he ᵇ⁻was wounded⁻ᵇ by the archers. ⁴Saul said to his arms-bearer, "Draw your sword and run me through, so that these uncircumcised may not come and make sport of me." But his arms-bearer, out of great awe, refused; whereupon Saul grasped the sword and fell upon it. ⁵When the arms-bearer saw that Saul was dead, he too fell on his sword and died. ⁶Thus Saul and his three sons and his entire house died together. ⁷And when all the men of Israel who were in the valley saw that theyᶜ had fled and that Saul and his sons were dead, they abandoned their towns and fled; the Philistines then came and occupied them.

⁸The next day the Philistines came to strip the slain, and they found Saul and his sons lying on Mount Gilboa. ⁹They stripped him, and carried off his head and his armor, and sent them throughout the land of the

---

ᵃ With vv. 1–12, cf. 1 Sam. 31.1–13.
ᵇ⁻ᵇ Meaning of Heb. uncertain.
ᶜ I.e., Israel.

Philistines to spread the news to their idols and among the people. ¹⁰They placed his armor in the temple of their god, and they impaled his head in the temple of Dagan. ¹¹When all Jabesh-gilead heard everything that the Philistines had done to Saul, ¹²all their stalwart men set out, removed the bodies of Saul and his sons, and brought them to Jabesh. They buried the bones under the oak tree in Jabesh, and they fasted for seven days. ¹³Saul died for the trespass that he had committed against the LORD in not having fulfilled the command of the LORD; moreover, he had consulted a ghost to seek advice, ¹⁴and did not seek advice of the LORD; so He had him slain and the kingdom transferred to David son of Jesse.

11 ᵃAll Israel gathered to David at Hebron and said, "We are your own flesh and blood. ²Long before now, even when Saul was king, you were the leader of Israel; and the LORD your God said to you: You shall shepherd My people Israel; you shall be ruler of My people Israel." ³All the elders of Israel came to the king at Hebron, and David made a pact with them in Hebron before the LORD. And they anointed David king over Israel, according to the word of the LORD through Samuel.

⁴David and all Israel set out for Jerusalem, that is Jebus, where the Jebusite inhabitants of the land lived. ⁵David was told by the inhabitants of Jebus, "You will never get in here!" But David captured the stronghold of Zion; it is now the City of David. ⁶David said, "Whoever attacks the Jebusites first will be the chief officer"; Joab son of Zeruiah attacked first, and became the chief.

⁷David occupied the stronghold; therefore it was renamed the City of David. ⁸David also fortified the surrounding area, from the Millo roundabout, and Joab rebuilt the rest of the city. ⁹David kept growing stronger, for the LORD of Hosts was with him.

¹⁰And these were David's chief warriors who strongly supported him in his kingdom, together with all Israel, to make him king, according to the word of the LORD concerning Israel.

¹¹This is the list of David's warriors: Jashobeam son of Hachmoni, the chief officer; he wielded his spear against three hundred and slew them all on one occasion. ¹²Next to him was Eleazar son of Dodo, the Ahohite; he was one of the three warriors. ¹³He was with David at Pas Dammim when the Philistines gathered there for battle. There was a plot of ground full of barley there; the troops had fled from the Philistines, ¹⁴but they

---

ᵃ With vv. 1–9, cf. 2 Sam. 5.1–10, and with vv. 11–41, cf. 2 Sam. 23.8–39.

took their stand in the middle of the plot and defended it, and they routed the Philistines. Thus the LORD wrought a great victory.

¹⁵Three of the thirty chiefs went down to the rock to David, at the cave of Adullam, while a force of Philistines was encamped in the Valley of Rephaim. ¹⁶David was then in the stronghold, and a Philistine garrison was then at Bethlehem. ¹⁷David felt a craving and said, "If only I could get a drink of water from the cistern which is by the gate of Bethlehem!" ¹⁸So the three got through the Philistine camp, and drew water from the cistern which is by the gate of Bethlehem, and they carried it back to David. But David would not drink it, and he poured it out as a libation to the LORD. ¹⁹For he said, "God forbid that I should do this! Can I drink the blood of these men who risked their lives?"—for they had brought it at the risk of their lives, and he would not drink it. Such were the exploits of the three warriors.

²⁰Abshai, the brother of Joab, was head of another three. He once wielded his spear against three hundred and slew them. He won a name among the three; ²¹among the three he was more highly regarded than the other two, and so he became their commander. However, he did not attain to the other three.

²²Benaiah son of Jehoiada from Kabzeel was a brave soldier who performed great deeds. He killed the two [sons] of Ariel of Moab. Once, on a snowy day, he went down into a pit and killed a lion. ²³He also killed an Egyptian, a giant of a man five cubits tall. The Egyptian had a spear in his hand, like a weaver's beam, yet [Benaiah] went down against him with a club, wrenched the spear out of the Egyptian's hand, and killed him with his own spear. ²⁴Such were the exploits of Benaiah son of Jehoiada; and he won a name among the three warriors. ²⁵He was highly regarded among the thirty, but he did not attain to the three. David put him in charge of his bodyguard.ᵇ

²⁶The valiant warriors: Asahel brother of Joab, Elhanan son of Dodo from Bethlehem, ²⁷Shammoth the Harorite, Helez the Pelonite, ²⁸Ira son of Ikkesh from Tekoa, Abiezer of Anathoth, ²⁹Sibbecai the Hushathite, Ilai the Ahohite, ³⁰Mahrai the Netophathite, Heled son of Baanah the Netophathite, ³¹Ittai son of Ribai from Gibeah of the Benjaminites, Benaiah of Pirathon, ³²Hurai of Nahale-gaash, Abiel the Arbathite, ³³Azmaveth the Bahrumite, Eliahba of Shaalbon, ³⁴the sons of Hashem the Gizonite, Jonathan son of Shageh the Hararite, ³⁵Ahiam son of Sacar the Hararite, Eliphal son of Ur, ³⁶Hepher the Mecherathite, Ahijah the Pelonite, ³⁷Hezro

ᵇ *Meaning of Heb. uncertain.*

the Carmelite, Naarai son of Ezbai, [38]Joel brother of Nathan, Mibhar son of Hagri, [39]Zelek the Ammonite, Naharai the Berothite—the arms-bearer of Joab son of Zeruiah—[40]Ira the Ithrite, Gareb the Ithrite, [41]Uriah the Hittite, Zabad son of Ahlai. [42]Adina son of Shiza the Reubenite, a chief of the Reubenites, and thirty with him; [43]Hanan son of Maacah, and Joshaphat the Mithnite; [44]Uzziah the Ashterathite, Shama and Jeiel sons of Hotham the Aroerite; [45]Jedaiael son of Shimri, and Joha his brother, the Tizite; [46]Eliel the Mahavite, and Jeribai and Joshaviah sons of Elnaam, and Ithmah the Moabite; [47]Eliel, Obed, and Jaassiel the Mezobaite.

12 The following joined David at Ziklag while he was still in hiding from Saul son of Kish; these were the warriors who gave support in battle; [2]they were armed with the bow and could use both right hand and left hand to sling stones or shoot arrows with the bow; they were kinsmen of Saul from Benjamin. [3]At the head were Ahiezer and Joash, sons of Shemaah of Gibeah; and Jeziel and Pelet, sons of Azmaveth; and Beracah and Jehu of Anathoth; [4]Ishmaiah of Gibeon, a warrior among the thirty, leading the thirty; [5]Jeremiah, Jahaziel, Johanan, and Jozabad of Gederah; [6]Eluzai, Jerimoth, Bealiah, Shemariah, and Shephatiah the Hariphite; [7]Elkanah, Isshiah, Azarel, Joezer, and Jashobeam the Korahites; [8]Joelah and Zebadiah, sons of Jeroham of Gedor.[a] [9]Of the Gadites, there withdrew to follow David to the wilderness stronghold valiant men, fighters fit for battle, armed with shield and spear; they had the appearance of lions, and were as swift as gazelles upon the mountains: [10]Ezer the chief, Obadiah the second, Eliab the third, [11]Mashmannah the fourth, Jeremiah the fifth, [12]Attai the sixth, Eliel the seventh, [13]Johanan the eighth, Elzabad the ninth, [14]Jeremiah the tenth, Machbannai the eleventh. [15]Those were the Gadites, heads of the army. The least was equal to a hundred, the greatest to a thousand. [16]These were the ones who crossed the Jordan in the first month, when it was at its crest, and they put to flight all the lowlanders to the east and west. [17]Some of the Benjaminites and Judahites came to the stronghold to David, [18]and David went out to meet them, saying to them, "If you come on a peaceful errand, to support me, then I will make common cause with you, but if to betray me to my foes, for no injustice on my part, then let the God of our fathers take notice and give judgment." [19]Then the spirit seized Amasai, chief of the captains:

---

[a] Or, "the troop," reading Heb. gedud with several mss.

"We are yours, David,
  On your side, son of Jesse;
  At peace, at peace with you,
  And at peace with him who supports you,
  For your God supports you."
So David accepted them, and placed them at the head of his band.

20Some Manassites went over to David's side when he came with the Philistines to make war against Saul, but they were of no help to them, because the lords of the Philistines in council dismissed him, saying, "He will go over to the side of his lord, Saul, and it will cost us our heads"; 21when he went to Ziklag, these Manassites went over to his side—Adnah, Jozabad, Jediael, Michael, Jozabad, Elihu, and Zillethai, chiefs of the clans of Manasseh.

22It was they who gave support to David against the band,b for all were valiant men; and they were officers of the force.

23Day in day out, people came to David to give him support, until there was an army as vast as the army of God.

24These are the numbers of the [men of the] armed bands who joined David at Hebron to transfer Saul's kingdom to him, in accordance with the word of the LORD:

25Judahites, equipped with shield and spear—6,800 armed men; 26Simeonites, valiant men, fighting troops—7,100; 27of the Levites—4,600; 28Jehoiada, chief officer of the Aaronides; with him, 3,700; 29Zadok, a young valiant man, with his clan—22 officers; 30of the Benjaminites, kinsmen of Saul, 3,000 in their great numbers, hitherto protecting the interests of the house of Saul; 31of the Ephraimites, 20,800 valiant men, famous in their clans; 32of the half-tribe of Manasseh, 18,000, who were designated by name to come and make David king; 33of the Issacharites, men who knew how to interpret the signs of the times, to determine how Israel should act; their chiefs were 200, and all their kinsmen followed them; 34of Zebulun, those ready for service, able to man a battle line with all kinds of weapons, 50,000, giving support wholeheartedly; 35of Naphtali, 1,000 chieftains with their shields and lances—37,000; 36Of the Danites, able to man the battle line—28,600; 37of Asher, those ready for service to man the battle line—40,000; 38from beyond the Jordan, of the Reubenites, the Gadites, and the half-tribe of Manasseh, together with all kinds of military weapons—120,000.

b _I.e., the band of Amalekite raiders; cf. 1 Sam. 30.8, 15._

³⁹All these, fighting men, manning the battle line with whole heart, came to Hebron to make David king over all Israel. Likewise, all the rest of Israel was of one mind to make David king.

⁴⁰They were there with David three days, eating and drinking, for their kinsmen had provided for them.

⁴¹And also, their relatives as far away as Issachar, Zebulun, and Naphtali brought food by ass, camel, mule, and ox—provisions of flour, cakes of figs, raisin cakes, wine, oil, cattle, and sheep in abundance, for there was joy in Israel.

13 Then David consulted with the officers of the thousands and the hundreds, with every chief officer. ²David said to the entire assembly of Israel, "If you approve, and if the LORD our God concurs,^a let us send far and wide to our remaining kinsmen throughout the territories of Israel, including the priests and Levites in the towns where they have pasture-lands, that they should gather together to us ³in order to transfer the Ark of our God to us, for throughout the days of Saul we paid no regard to it." ⁴The entire assembly agreed to do so, for the proposal pleased all the people. ⁵David then assembled all Israel from Shihor of Egypt to Lebo-hamath, in order to bring the Ark of God from Kiriath-jearim. ^{6b}David and all Israel went up to Baalah, Kiriath-jearim of Judah, to bring up from there the Ark of God, the LORD, Enthroned on the Cherubim, to which the Name was attached. ⁷They transported the Ark of God on a new cart from the house of Abinadab; Uzza and Ahio guided the cart, ⁸and David and all Israel danced before God with all their might—with songs, lyres, harps, timbrels, cymbals, and trumpets. ⁹But when they came to the threshing floor of Chidon, Uzza put out his hand to hold the Ark of God because the oxen had stumbled.^a ¹⁰The LORD was incensed at Uzza, and struck him down, because he laid a hand on the Ark; and so he died there before God. ¹¹David was distressed because the LORD ^chad burst out^c against Uzza; and that place was named Perez-uzzah, as it is still called.

¹²David was afraid of God that day; he said, "How can I bring the Ark of God here?" ¹³So David did not remove the Ark to his place in the City of David; instead, he diverted it to the house of Obed-edom the Gittite. ¹⁴The Ark of God remained in the house of Obed-edom, in its own abode,

^a *Meaning of Heb. uncertain.*
^b *With vv. 6–14, cf. 2 Sam. 6.2–11.*
^{c-c} *Heb.* paraṣ . . . pereṣ.

three months, and the LORD blessed the house of Obed-edom and all he had.

14 ᵃKing Hiram of Tyre sent envoys to David with cedar logs, stone-masons, and carpenters to build a palace for him. ²Thus David knew that the LORD had established him as king over Israel, and that his kingship was highly exalted for the sake of His people Israel.

³David took more wives in Jerusalem, and David begot more sons and daughters. ⁴These are the names of the children born to him in Jerusalem:ᵇ Shammua, Shobab, Nathan, and Solomon; ⁵Ibhar, Elishua, and Elpelet; ⁶Nogah, Nepheg, and Japhia; ⁷Elishama, Beeliada, and Eliphelet.

⁸When the Philistines heard that David had been anointed king over all Israel, all the Philistines went up in search of David; but David heard of it, and he went out to them. ⁹The Philistines came and raided the Valley of Rephaim. ¹⁰David inquired of God, "Shall I go up against the Philistines? Will You deliver them into my hands?" And the LORD answered him, "Go up, and I will deliver them into your hands." ¹¹Thereupon David ascended Baal-perazim, and David defeated them there. David said, "God ᶜ⁻burst out⁻ᶜ against my enemies by my hands as waters burst out." That is why that place was named Baal-perazim. ¹²They abandoned their gods there, and David ordered these to be burned.

¹³Once again the Philistines raided the valley. ¹⁴David inquired of God once more, and God answered, "Do not go up after them, but circle around them and confront them at the *baca*ᵈ trees. ¹⁵And when you hear the sound of marching in the tops of the *baca* trees, then go out to battle, for God will be going in front of you to attack the Philistine forces." ¹⁶David did as God had commanded him; and they routed the Philistines from Gibeon all the way to Gezer. ¹⁷David became famous throughout the lands, and the LORD put the fear of him in all the nations.

15 He had houses made for himself in the City of David, and he prepared a place for the Ark of God, and pitched a tent for it. ²Then David gave orders that none but the Levites were to carry the Ark of God, for the LORD had chosen them to carry the Ark of the LORD and to minister to Him forever. ³David assembled all Israel in Jerusalem to

ᵃ *With vv. 1–16, cf. 2 Sam. 5.11–25.*
ᵇ *With the list in vv. 4–7, cf. also 1 Chron. 3.5–8.*
ᶜ⁻ᶜ *Heb.* paraṣ . . . pereṣ.
ᵈ *Meaning of Heb. uncertain.*

bring up the Ark of the LORD to its place, which he had prepared for it. ⁴Then David gathered together the Aaronides and the Levites: ⁵the sons of Kohath: Uriel the officer and his kinsmen—120; ⁶the sons of Merari: Asaiah the officer and his kinsmen—220; ⁷the sons of Gershom: Joel the officer and his kinsmen—130; ⁸the sons of Elizaphan: Shemaiah the officer and his kinsmen—200; ⁹the sons of Hebron: Eliel the officer and his kinsmen—80; ¹⁰the sons of Uzziel: Amminadab the officer and his kinsmen—112.

¹¹David sent for Zadok and Abiathar the priests, and for the Levites: Uriel, Asaiah, Joel, Shemaiah, Eliel, and Amminadab. ¹²He said to them, "You are the heads of the clans of the Levites; sanctify yourselves, you and your kinsmen, and bring up the Ark of the LORD God of Israel to [the place] I have prepared for it. ¹³ᵃ⁻Because you were not there the first time,⁻ᵃ the LORD our God burst out against us, for we did not show due regard for Him."

¹⁴The priests and Levites sanctified themselves in order to bring up the Ark of the LORD God of Israel. ¹⁵The Levites carried the Ark of God by means of poles on their shoulders, as Moses had commanded in accordance with the word of the LORD. ¹⁶David ordered the officers of the Levites to install their kinsmen, the singers, with musical instruments, harps, lyres, and cymbals, joyfully making their voices heard. ¹⁷So the Levites installed Heman son of Joel and, of his kinsmen, Asaph son of Berechiah; and, of the sons of Merari their kinsmen, Ethan son of Kushaiah. ¹⁸Together with them were their kinsmen of second rank, Zechariah, Ben, Jaaziel, Shemiramoth, Jehiel, Unni, Eliab, Benaiah, Maaseiah, Mattithiah, Eliphalehu, Mikneiah, Obed-edom and Jeiel the gatekeepers. ¹⁹Also the singers Heman, Asaph, and Ethan to sound the bronze cymbals, ²⁰and Zechariah, Aziel, Shemiramoth, Jehiel, Unni, Eliab, Maaseiah, and Benaiah with harps ᵃ⁻on *alamoth;*⁻ᵃ ²¹also Mattithiah, Eliphalehu, Mikneiah, Obed-edom, Jeiel, and Azaziah, with lyres to lead ᵃ⁻on the *sheminith;*⁻ᵃ ²²also Chenaniah, officer of the Levites in song;ᵃ he was in charge of the songᵃ because he was a master. ²³Berechiah and Elkanah were gatekeepers for the Ark. ²⁴Shebaniah, Joshaphat, Nethanel, Amasai, Zechariah, Benaiah, and Eliezer the priests sounded the trumpets before the Ark of God, and Obed-edom and Jehiah were gatekeepers for the Ark. ²⁵ᵇThen David and the elders of Israel and the officers of the thousands who were going to bring up the Ark of the Covenant of the LORD from the house of Obed-edom were joyful. ²⁶Since God helped the Levites

---

ᵃ⁻ᵃ *Meaning of Heb. uncertain.*
ᵇ *Vv. 25–29 are found also in 2 Sam. 6.12–16.*

who were carrying the Ark of the Covenant of the LORD, they sacrificed seven bulls and seven rams. 27Now David and all the Levites who were carrying the Ark, and the singers and Chenaniah, officer of song of the singers, a-were wrapped-a in robes of fine linen, and David wore a linen ephod. 28All Israel brought up the Ark of the Covenant of the LORD with shouts and with blasts of the horn, with trumpets and cymbals, playing on harps and lyres. 29As the Ark of the Covenant of the LORD arrived at the City of David, Michal daughter of Saul looked out of the window and saw King David leaping and dancing, and she despised him for it.

16

aThey brought in the Ark of God and set it up inside the tent that David had pitched for it, and they sacrificed burnt offerings and offerings of well-being before God. 2When David finished sacrificing the burnt offerings and the offerings of well-being, he blessed the people in the name of the LORD. 3And he distributed to every person in Israel—man and woman alike—to each a loaf of bread, b-a cake made in a pan, and a raisin cake.-b 4He appointed Levites to minister before the Ark of the LORD, to invoke, to praise, and to extol the LORD God of Israel: 5Asaph the chief, Zechariah second in rank, Jeiel, Shemiramoth, Jehiel, Mattithiah, Eliab, Benaiah, Obed-edom, and Jeiel, with harps and lyres, and Asaph sounding the cymbals, 6and Benaiah and Jahaziel the priests, with trumpets, regularly before the Ark of the Covenant of God. 7Then, on that day, David first commissioned Asaph and his kinsmen to give praise to the LORD:

> 8c"Praise the LORD;
> call on His name;
> proclaim His deeds among the peoples.
> 9Sing praises unto Him;
> speak of all His wondrous acts.
> 10Exult in His holy name;
> let all who seek the LORD rejoice.
> 11Turn to the LORD, to His might;d
> seek His presence constantly.
> 12Remember the wonders He has done;
> His portents and the judgments He has pronounced,
> 13O offspring of Israel, His servant,
> O descendants of Jacob, His chosen ones.

---

a *With vv. 1–3, cf. 2 Sam. 6.17–19.*
b-b *Meaning of Heb. uncertain.*
c *With vv. 8–22, cf. Ps. 105.1–15.*
d *I.e., the Ark; cf. Pss. 78.61; 132.8.*

¹⁴He is the LORD our God;
His judgments are throughout the earth.
¹⁵Be ever mindful of His covenant,
the promise He gave for a thousand generations,
¹⁶that He made with Abraham,
swore to Isaac,
¹⁷and confirmed in a decree for Jacob,
for Israel, as an eternal covenant,
¹⁸saying, 'To you I will give the land of Canaan
as your allotted heritage.'
¹⁹You were then few in number,
a handful, merely sojourning there,
²⁰wandering from nation to nation,
from one kingdom to another.
²¹He allowed no one to oppress them;
He reproved kings on their account,
²²'Do not touch My anointed ones;
do not harm My prophets.'

^{23c}"Sing to the LORD, all the earth.
proclaim His victory day after day.
²⁴Tell of His glory among the nations,
His wondrous deeds among all peoples.
²⁵For the LORD is great and much acclaimed,
He is held in awe by all divine beings.
²⁶All the gods of the peoples are mere idols,
but the LORD made the heavens.
²⁷Glory and majesty are before Him;
strength and joy are in His place.

²⁸"Ascribe to the LORD, O families of the peoples,
ascribe to the LORD glory and strength.
²⁹Ascribe to the LORD the glory of His name,
bring tribute and enter before Him,
bow down to the LORD majestic in holiness.
³⁰Tremble in His presence, all the earth!
The world stands firm; it cannot be shaken.

c *With vv. 23–33, cf. Ps. 96.1–13.*

31Let the heavens rejoice and the earth exult;
let them declare among the nations, "The LORD is King!"
32Let the sea and all within it thunder,
the fields and everything in them exult;
33then shall all the trees of the forest shout for joy
at the presence of the LORD,
for He is coming to rule the earth.
34Praise the LORD for He is good;
His steadfast love is eternal.
35f-Declare:
Deliver us, O God, our deliverer,
and gather us and save us from the nations,
to acclaim Your holy name,
to glory in Your praise.

36Blessed is the LORD, God of Israel, from eternity to eternity." And all the people said, "Amen" and "Praise the LORD."-f

37He left Asaph and his kinsmen there before the Ark of the Covenant of the LORD to minister before the Ark regularly as each day required, 38as well as Obed-edom with their kinsmen—68; also Obed-edom son of Jedithun and Hosah as gatekeepers; 39also Zadok the priest and his fellow priests before the Tabernacle of the LORD at the shrine which was in Gibeon; 40to sacrifice burnt offerings to the LORD on the altar of the burnt offering regularly, morning and evening, in accordance with what was prescribed in the Teaching of the LORD with which He charged Israel. 41With them were Heman and Jeduthun and the other selected men designated by name to give praise to the LORD, "For His steadfast love is eternal." 42Heman and Jeduthun had with them trumpets and cymbals to sound, and instruments for the songs of God; and the sons of Jeduthun were to be at the gate. 43Then all the people went every one to his home, and David returned to greet his household.

17

aWhen David settled in his palace, David said to the prophet Nathan, "Here I am dwelling in a house of cedar, while the Ark of the Covenant of the LORD is under tent-cloths." 2Nathan said to David, "Do whatever you have in mind, for God is with you."

3But that same night the word of God came to Nathan: 4"Go and say

---

f-f Cf. Ps. 106.47–48.
a With this chapter, cf. 2 Sam. 7.

to My servant David: Thus said the LORD: You are not the one to build a house for Me to dwell in. ⁵From the day that I brought out Israel to this day, I have not dwelt in a house, but have [gone] from tent to tent and from one Tabernacle [to another]. ⁶As I moved about wherever Israel went, did I ever reproach any of the judges of Israel whom I appointed to care for My people Israel: Why have you not built Me a house of cedar?

⁷"Further, say thus to My servant David: Thus said the LORD of Hosts: I took you from the pasture, from following the flock, to be ruler of My people Israel, ⁸and I have been with you wherever you went, and have cut down all your enemies before you. Moreover, I will give you renown like that of the greatest men on earth. ⁹I will establish a home for My people Israel and will plant them firm, so that they shall dwell secure and shall tremble no more. Evil men shall not wear them down anymore as in the past, ¹⁰ever since I appointed judges over My people Israel. I will subdue all your enemies.

And I declare to you: The LORD will build a houseᵇ for you. ¹¹When your days are done and you follow your fathers, I will raise up your offspring after you, one of your own sons, and I will establish his kingship. ¹²He shall build a house for Me, and I will establish his throne forever. ¹³I will be a father to him, and he shall be a son to Me, but I will never withdraw My favor from him as I withdrew it from your predecessor. ¹⁴I will install him in My house and in My kingship forever, and his throne shall be established forever."

¹⁵Nathan spoke to David in accordance with all these words and all this prophecy. ¹⁶Then King David came and sat before the LORD, and he said, "What am I, O LORD God, and what is my family, that You have brought me thus far? ¹⁷Yet even this, O God, has seemed too little to You; for You have spoken of Your servant's house for the future. ᶜYou regard me as a man of distinction,ᶜ O LORD God. ¹⁸What more can David add regarding the honoring of Your servant? You know Your servant. ¹⁹O LORD, ᶜfor Your servant's sake, and of Your own accord,ᶜ You have wrought this great thing, and made known all these great things. ²⁰O LORD, there is none like You, and there is no other God but You, as we have always heard. ²¹And who is like Your people Israel, a unique nation on earth, whom God went and redeemed as His people, winning renown for Yourself for great and marvelous deeds, driving out nations before Your people whom You redeemed from Egypt. ²²You have established Your people Israel as Your very own people forever; and You, O LORD, have become their God.

ᵇ I.e., a dynasty; play on "house" (i.e., Temple) in v. 4.
ᶜ⁻ᶜ Meaning of Heb. uncertain.

23"And now, O LORD, let Your promise concerning Your servant and his house be fulfilled forever; and do as You have promised. 24Let it be fulfilled that Your name be glorified forever, in that men will say, 'The LORD of Hosts, God of Israel, is Israel's God'; and may the house of Your servant David be established before You. 25Because You, my God, have revealed to Your servant that You will build a house for him, Your servant has ventured to pray to You. 26And now, O LORD, You are God and You have made this gracious promise to Your servant. 27Now, it has pleased You to bless Your servant's house, that it abide before You forever; for You, O LORD, have blessed and are blessed forever."

18 aSometime afterward, David attacked the Philistines and subdued them; and David took Gath and its dependencies from the Philistines. 2He also defeated the Moabites; the Moabites became tributary vassals of David.

3David defeated Hadadezer, king of Zobah-hamath, who was on his way to set up his monument at the Euphrates River. 4David captured 1,000 chariots and 7,000 horsemen and 20,000 foot soldiers of his force; and David hamstrung all the chariot horses except for 100, which he retained. 5And when the Arameans of Damascus came to the aid of King Hadadezer of Zobah-hamath, David struck down 22,000 of the Arameans. 6David stationed [garrisons] in Aram of Damascus, and the Arameans became tributary vassals of David. The LORD gave David victory wherever he went. 7David took the gold shieldsb carried by Hadadezer's retine and brought them to Jerusalem; 8and from Tibbath and Cun, towns of Hadadezer, David took a vast amount of copper, from which Solomon made the bronze tank, the columns, and the bronze vessels.

9When King Tou of Hamath heard that David had defeated the entire army of King Hadadezer of Zobah, 10he sent his son Hadoram to King David to greet him and to congratulate him on his military victory over Hadadezer—for Hadadezer had been at war with Tou; [he brought with him] all manner of gold, silver, and copper objects. 11King David dedicated these to the LORD, along with the other silver and gold that he had taken from all the nations: from Edom, Moab, and Ammon; from the Philistines and the Amalekites.

12Abshai son of Zeruiah struck down Edom in the Valley of Salt, 18,000

---

a *With this chapter, cf. 2 Sam. 8.*
b *Or "quivers."*

in all. 13He stationed garrisons in Edom, and all the Edomites became vassals of David. The LORD gave David victory wherever he went.

14David reigned over all Israel, and David executed true justice among all his people. 15Joab son of Zeruiah was commander of the army; Jehoshaphat son of Ahilud was recorder; 16Zadok son of Ahitub and Abimelech son of Abiathar were priests; Shavsha was scribe; 17Benaiah son of Jehoiada was commander of the Cherethites and the Pelethites; and David's sons were first ministers of the king.

19

aSometime afterward, Nahash the king of the Ammonites died, and his son succeeded him as king. 2David said, "I will keep faith with Hanun son of Nahash, since his father kept faith with me." David sent messengers with condolences to him over his father. But when David's courtiers came to the land of Ammon to Hanun, with condolences, 3the Ammonite officials said to Hanun, "Do you think David is really honoring your father just because he sent you men with condolences? Why, it is to explore, to subvert, and to spy out the land that his courtiers have come to you." 4So Hanun seized David's courtiers, shaved them, and cut away half of their garments up to the buttocks, and sent them off. 5When David was told about the men, he dispatched others to meet them, for the men were greatly embarrassed. And the king gave orders, "Stay in Jericho until your beards grow back; then you can return."

6The Ammonites realized that they had incurred the wrath of David; so Hanun and the Ammonites sent 1,000 silver talents to hire chariots and horsemen from Aram-naharaim, Aram-maacah, and Zobah. 7They hired 32,000 chariots, the king of Maacah, and his army, who came and encamped before Medeba. The Ammonites were mobilized from their cities and came to do battle.

8On learning this, David sent out Joab and the whole army, [including] the professional fighters. 9The Ammonites marched out and took up their battle position at the entrance of the city, while the kings who came [took their stand] separately in the open. 10Joab saw that there was a battle line against him both front and rear. So he made a selection from all the picked men of Israel and arrayed them against the Arameans, 11and the rest of the troops he put under the command of his brother Abishai and arrayed them against the Ammonites. 12Joab said, "If the Arameans prove too strong for me, you come to my aid; and if the Ammonites prove too

a With this chapter, cf. 2 Sam. 10.

strong for you, I will come to your aid. ¹³Let us be strong and resolute for the sake of our people and the towns of our God; and the LORD will do what He deems right."

¹⁴Joab and the troops with him marched into battle against the Arameans, who fled before him. ¹⁵And when the Ammonites saw that the Arameans had fled, they too fled before his brother Abishai, and withdrew into the city. So Joab went to Jerusalem.

¹⁶When the Arameans saw that they had been routed by Israel, they sent messengers to bring out the Arameans from across the Euphrates; Shophach, Hadadezer's army commander, led them. ¹⁷David was informed of it; he assembled all Israel, crossed the Jordan, and came and took up positions against them. David drew up his forces against Aram; and they fought with him. ¹⁸But the Arameans were put to flight by Israel. David killed 7,000 Aramean charioteers and 40,000 footmen; he also killed Shophach, the army commander. ¹⁹And when all the vassals of Hadadezer saw that they had been routed by Israel, they submitted to David and became his vassals. And the Arameans would not help the Ammonites anymore.

20 ᵃAt the turn of the year, the season when kings go out [to battle], Joab led out the army force and devastated the land of Ammon, and then besieged Rabbah, while David remained in Jerusalem; Joab reduced Rabbah and left it in ruins. ²David took the crown from the head of their king; he found that it weighed a talent of gold, and in it were precious stones. It was placed on David's head. He also carried off a vast amount of booty from the city. ³He led out the people who lived there and ᵇ⁻he hacked them⁻ᵇ with saws and iron threshing boards and axes;ᶜ David did thus to all the towns of Ammon. Then David and all the troops returned to Jerusalem. ⁴After this, fighting broke out with the Philistines at Gezer; that was when Sibbecai the Hushathite killed Sippai, a descendant of the Rephaim, and they were humbled.

⁵Again there was fighting with the Philistines, and Elhanan son of Jair killed Lahmi, the brother of Goliath the Gittite; his spear had a shaft like a weaver's beam. ⁶Once again there was fighting at Gath. There was a giant of a man who had twenty-four fingers [and toes], six [on each hand] and six [on each foot]; he too was descended from the Raphah. ⁷When he taunted Israel, Jonathan son of David's brother Shimea killed him.

ᵃ *With vv. 1–3, cf. 2 Sam. 11.1; 12.30–31.*
ᵇ⁻ᵇ *Meaning of Heb. uncertain. 2 Sam. 12.31 has "set them to work."*
ᶜ *Heb. megeroth; cf. 2 Sam. 12.31 magzeroth, "axes."*

⁸These were descended from the Raphah in Gath, and they fell by the hands of David and his men.

21 ᵃSatan arose against Israel and incited David to number Israel. ²David said to Joab and to the commanders of the army, "Go and count Israel from Beer-sheba to Dan and bring me information as to their number." ³Joab answered, "May the LORD increase His people a hundredfold; my lord king, are they not all subjects of my lord? Why should my lord require this? Why should it be a cause of guilt for Israel?"

⁴However, the king's command to Joab remained firm, so Joab set out and traversed all Israel; he then came to Jerusalem. ⁵Joab reported to David the number of the people that had been recorded. All Israel comprised 1,100,000 ready to draw the sword, while in Judah there were 470,000 men ready to draw the sword. ⁶He did not record among them Levi and Benjamin, because the king's command had become repugnant to Joab. ⁷God was displeased about this matter and He struck Israel.

⁸David said to God, "I have sinned grievously in having done this thing; please remit the guilt of Your servant, for I have acted foolishly." ⁹The LORD ordered Gad, David's seer: ¹⁰"Go and tell David: Thus said the LORD: I offer you three things; choose one of them and I will bring it upon you." ¹¹Gad came to David and told him, "Thus said the LORD: Select for yourself ¹²a three-year famine; or that you be swept away three months before your adversaries with the sword of your enemies overtaking you; or three days of the sword of the LORD, pestilence in the land, the angel of the LORD wreaking destruction throughout the territory of Israel. Now consider what reply I shall take back to Him who sent me." ¹³David said to Gad, "I am in great distress. Let me fall into the hands of the LORD, for His compassion is very great; and let me not fall into the hands of men."

¹⁴The LORD sent a pestilence upon Israel, and 70,000 men fell in Israel. ¹⁵God sent an angel to Jerusalem to destroy it, but as he was about to wreak destruction, the LORD saw and renounced further punishment and said to the destroying angel, "Enough! Stay your hand!" The angel of the LORD was then standing by the threshing floor of Ornan the Jebusite. ¹⁶David looked up and saw the angel of the LORD standing between heaven and earth, with a drawn sword in his hand directed against Jerusalem. David and the elders, covered in sackcloth, threw themselves on

---

ᵃ With vv. 1–26, cf. 2 Sam. 24.

their faces. ¹⁷David said to God, "Was it not I alone who ordered the numbering of the people? I alone am guilty, and have caused severe harm; but these sheep, what have they done? O LORD my God, let Your hand fall upon me and my father's house, and let not Your people be plagued!" ¹⁸The angel of the LORD told Gad to inform David that David should go and set up an altar to the LORD on the threshing floor of Ornan the Jebusite. ¹⁹David went up, following Gad's instructions, which he had delivered in the name of the LORD. ²⁰Ornan too saw the angel; his four sons who were with him hid themselves while Ornan kept on threshing wheat. ²¹David came to Ornan; when Ornan looked up, he saw David and came off the threshing floor and bowed low to David, with his face to the ground. ²²David said to Ornan, "Sell me the site of the threshing floor, that I may build on it an altar to the LORD. Sell it to me at the full price, that the plague against the people will be checked." ²³Ornan said to David, "Take it and let my lord the king do whatever he sees fit. See, I donate oxen for burnt offerings, and the threshing boards for wood, as well as wheat for a meal offering—I donate all of it." ²⁴But King David replied to Ornan, "No, I will buy them at the full price. I cannot make a present to the LORD of what belongs to you, or sacrifice a burnt offering that has cost me nothing." ²⁵So David paid Ornan for the site 600 shekels' worth of gold. ²⁶And David built there an altar to the LORD and sacrificed burnt offerings and offerings of well-being. He invoked the LORD, who answered him with fire from heaven on the altar of burnt offerings. ²⁷The LORD ordered the angel to return his sword to its sheath. ²⁸At that time, when David saw that the LORD answered him at the threshing floor of Ornan the Jebusite, then he sacrificed there—²⁹for the Tabernacle of the LORD, which Moses had made in the wilderness, and the altar of burnt offerings, were at that time in the shrine at Gibeon, ³⁰and David was unable to go to it to worship the LORD because he was terrified by the sword of the angel of the LORD. ¹David said, "Here will be the House of the LORD and here the altar of burnt offerings for Israel."

22 ²David gave orders to assemble the aliens living in the land of Israel, and assigned them to be hewers, to quarry and dress stones for building the House of God. ³Much iron for nails for the doors of the gates and for clasps did David lay aside, and so much copper it could not be weighed, ⁴and cedar logs without number—for the Sidonians and the Tyrians brought many cedar logs to David.

⁵For David thought, "My son Solomon is an untried youth, and the

House to be built for the LORD is to be made exceedingly great to win fame and glory throughout all the lands; let me then lay aside material for him." So David laid aside much material before he died. ⁶Then he summoned his son Solomon and charged him with building the House for the LORD God of Israel.

⁷David said to Solomon, "My son, I wanted to build a House for the name of the LORD my God. ⁸But the word of the LORD came to me, saying, 'You have shed much blood and fought great battles; you shall not build a House for My name for you have shed much blood on the earth in My sight. ⁹But you will have a son who will be a man at rest, for I will give him rest from all his enemies on all sides; Solomonᵃ will be his name and I shall confer peaceᵇ and quiet on Israel in his time. ¹⁰He will build a House for My name; he shall be a son to Me and I to him a father, and I will establish his throne of kingship over Israel forever.' ¹¹Now, my son, may the LORD be with you, and may you succeed in building the House of the LORD your God as He promised you would. ¹²Only let God give you sense and understanding and put you in charge of Israel and the observance of the Teaching of the LORD your God. ¹³Then you shall succeed, if you observantly carry out the laws and the rules that the LORD charged Moses to lay upon Israel. Be strong and of good courage; do not be afraid or dismayed. ¹⁴See, ᶜ-by denying my-self,-ᶜ I have laid aside for the House of the LORD one hundred thousand talents of gold and one million talents of silver, and so much copper and iron it cannot be weighed; I have also laid aside wood and stone, and you shall add to them. ¹⁵An abundance of workmen is at your disposal— hewers, workers in stone and wood, and every kind of craftsman in every kind of material—¹⁶gold, silver, copper, and iron without limit. Go and do it, and may the LORD be with you."

¹⁷David charged all the officers of Israel to support his son Solomon, ¹⁸"See, the LORD your God is with you, and He will give you rest on every side, for He delivered the inhabitants of the land into my hand so that the land lies conquered before the LORD and before His people. ¹⁹Now, set your minds and hearts on worshiping the LORD your God, and go build the Sanctuary of the LORD your God so that you may bring the Ark of the Covenant of the LORD and the holy vessels of God to the house that is built for the name of the LORD."

ᵃ *Heb*. Shelomoh.
ᵇ *Heb*. shalom.
ᶜ⁻ᶜ *With Targum; or "in my poverty."*

23 When David reached a ripe old age, he made his son Solomon king over Israel. [2]Then David assembled all the officers of Israel and the priests and the Levites. [3]The Levites, from the age of thirty and upward, were counted; the head-count of their males was 38,000: [4]of these there were 24,000 in charge of the work of the House of the LORD, 6,000 officers and magistrates, [5]4,000 gatekeepers, and 4,000 for praising the LORD "with instruments I devised for singing praises." [6]David formed them into divisions:

The sons of Levi: Gershon, Kohath, and Merari. [7]The Gershonites: Ladan and Shimei. [8]The sons of Ladan: Jehiel the chief, Zetham, and Joel—3. [9]The sons of Shimei: Shelomith, Haziel, and Haran—3. These were the chiefs of the clans of the Ladanites. [10]And the sons of Shimei: Jahath, Zina, Jeush, and Beriah; these were the sons of Shimei—4. [11]Jahath was the chief and Zizah the second, but Jeush and Beriah did not have many children, so they were enrolled together as a single clan. [12]The sons of Kohath: Amram, Izhar, Hebron, and Uzziel—4. [13]The sons of Amram: Aaron and Moses. Aaron was set apart, he and his sons, forever, to be consecrated as most holy, to make burnt offerings to the LORD and serve Him and pronounce blessings in His name forever. [14]As for Moses, the man of God, his sons were named after the tribe of Levi. [15]The sons of Moses: Gershom and Eliezer. [16]The sons of Gershom: Shebuel the chief. [17]And the sons of Eliezer were: Rehabiah the chief. Eliezer had no other sons, but the sons of Rehabiah were very numerous. [18]The sons of Izhar: Shelomith the chief. [19]The sons of Hebron: Jeriah the chief, Amariah the second, Jahaziel the third, and Jekameam the fourth. [20]The sons of Uzziel: Micah the chief and Isshiah the second. [21]The sons of Merari: Mahli and Mushi. The sons of Mahli: Eleazar and Kish. [22]Eleazar died having no sons but only daughters; the sons of Kish, their kinsmen, married them. [23]The sons of Mushi: Mahli, Eder, and Jeremoth—3.

[24]These are the sons of Levi by clans, with their clan chiefs as they were enrolled, with a list of their names by heads, who did the work of the service of the House of the LORD from the age of twenty and upward. [25]For David said, "The LORD God of Israel has given rest to His people and made His dwelling in Jerusalem forever. [26]Therefore the Levites need not carry the Tabernacle and all its various service vessels." [27]Among the last acts of David was the counting of the Levites from the age of twenty

and upward. ²⁸For their appointment was alongside the Aaronites for the service of the House of the LORD, to look after the courts and the chambers, and the purity of all the holy things, and the performance of the service of the House of God, ²⁹and the rows of bread, and the fine flour for the meal offering, and the unleavened wafers, and the cakes made on the griddle and soaked, and every measure of capacity and length; ³⁰and to be present every morning to praise and extol the LORD, and at evening too, ³¹and whenever offerings were made to the LORD, according to the quantities prescribed for them, on sabbaths, new moons and holidays, regularly, before the LORD; ³²and so to keep watch over the Tent of Meeting, over the holy things, and over the Aaronites their kinsmen, for the service of the House of the LORD.

24 The divisions of the Aaronites were: The sons of Aaron: Nadab and Abihu, Eleazar and Ithamar. ²Nadab and Abihu died in the lifetime of their father, and they had no children, so Eleazar and Ithamar served as priests.

³David, Zadok of the sons of Eleazar, and Ahimelech of the sons of Ithamar divided them into offices by their tasks. ⁴The sons of Eleazar turned out to be more numerous by male heads than the sons of Ithamar, so they divided the sons of Eleazar into sixteen chiefs of clans and the sons of Ithamar into eight clans. ⁵They divided them by lot, both on an equal footing, since they were all sanctuary officers and officers of God— the sons of Eleazar and the sons of Ithamar. ⁶Shemaiah son of Nathanel, the scribe, who was of the Levites, registered them under the eye of the king, the officers, and Zadok the priest, and Ahimelech son of Abiathar, and the chiefs of clans of the priests and Levites—ᵃ⁻one clan more taken for Eleazar for each one taken of Ithamar.⁻ᵃ

⁷The first lot fell on Jehoiarib; the second on Jedaiah; ⁸the third on Harim; the fourth on Seorim; ⁹the fifth on Malchijah; the sixth on Mijamin; ¹⁰the seventh on Hakkoz; the eighth on Abijah; ¹¹the ninth on Jeshua; the tenth on Shecaniah; ¹²the eleventh on Eliashib; the twelfth on Jakim; ¹³the thirteenth on Huppah; the fourteenth on Jeshebeab; ¹⁴the fifteenth on Bilgah; the sixteenth on Immer; ¹⁵the seventeenth on Hezir; the eighteenth on Happizzez; ¹⁶the nineteenth on Pethahiah; the twentieth on Jehezkel; ¹⁷the twenty-first on Jachin; the twenty-second on Gamul; ¹⁸the twenty-third on Delaiah; the twenty-fourth on Maaziah.

ᵃ⁻ᵃ *Meaning of Heb. uncertain.*

19 According to this allocation of offices by tasks, they were to enter the House of the LORD as was laid down for them by Aaron their father, as the LORD God of Israel had commanded him.

20 The remaining Levites: the sons of Amram: Shubael; the sons of Shubael: Jehdeiah; 21 Rehabiah. The sons of Rehabiah: Isshiah, the chief. 22 Izharites: Shelomoth. The sons of Shelomoth: Jahath 23 and Benai, Jeriah; the second, Amariah; the third, Jahaziel; the fourth, Jekameam. 24 The sons of Uzziel: Micah. The sons of Micah: Shamir. 25 The brother of Micah: Isshiah. The sons of Isshiah: Zechariah. 26 The sons of Merari: Mahli and Mushi. The sons of Jaazaiah, his son 27 —the sons of Merari by Jaazaiah his son: Shoham, Zakkur, and Ibri. 28 Mahli: Eleazar; he had no sons. 29 Kish: the sons of Kish: Jerahmeel. 30 The sons of Mushi: Mahli, Eder, and Jerimoth. These were the sons of the Levites by their clans.

31 These too cast lots corresponding to their kinsmen, the sons of Aaron, under the eye of King David and Zadok and Ahimelech and the chiefs of the clans of the priests and Levites, on the principle of "chief and youngest brother alike."

25 David and the officers of the army set apart for service the sons of Asaph, of Heman, and of Jeduthun, who prophesied to the accompaniment of lyres, harps, and cymbals. The list of men who performed this work, according to their service, was:

2 Sons of Asaph: Zaccur, Joseph, Nethaniah, and Asarelah—sons of Asaph under the charge of Asaph, who prophesied by order of the king. 3 Jeduthun—the sons of Jeduthun: Gedaliah, Zeri, Jeshaiah, Hashabiah, Mattithiah—6, under the charge of their father Jeduthun, who, accompanied on the harp, prophesied, praising and extolling the LORD. 4 Heman— the sons of Heman: Bukkiah, Mattaniah, Uzziel, Shebuel, Jerimoth, Hananiah, Hanani, Eliathah, Giddalti, Romamti-ezer, Joshbekashah, Mallothi, Hothir, and Mahazioth; 5 all these were sons of Heman, the seer of the king, [who uttered] prophecies of God for His greater glory. God gave Heman fourteen sons and three daughters; 6 all these were under the charge of their father for the singing in the House of the LORD, to the accompaniment of cymbals, harps, and lyres, for the service of the House of God by order of the king. Asaph, Jeduthun, and Heman—7 their total number with their kinsmen, trained singers of the LORD—all the masters, 288.

⁸They cast lots for shifts on the principle of "small and great alike, like master like apprentice."

⁹The first lot fell to Asaph—to Joseph; the second, to Gedaliah, he and his brothers and his sons—12; ¹⁰the third, to Zaccur: his sons and his brothers—12; ¹¹the fourth, to Izri: his sons and his brothers—12; ¹²the fifth, to Nethaniah: his sons and his brothers—12; ¹³the sixth, to Bukkiah: his sons and his brothers—12; ¹⁴the seventh, to Jesarelah: his sons and his brothers—12; ¹⁵the eighth, to Jeshaiah: his sons and his brothers— 12; ¹⁶the ninth, to Mattaniah: his sons and his brothers—12; ¹⁷the tenth, to Shimei: his sons and his brothers—12; ¹⁸the eleventh to Azarel: his sons and his brothers—12; ¹⁹the twelfth, to Hashabiah: his sons and his brothers—12; ²⁰the thirteenth, to Shubael: his sons and his brothers— 12; ²¹the fourteenth, to Mattithiah: his sons and his brothers—12; ²²the fifteenth, to Jeremoth: his sons and his brothers—12; ²³the sixteenth, to Hananiah: his sons and his brothers—12; ²⁴the seventeenth, to Joshbe-kashah: his sons and his brothers—12; ²⁵the eighteenth, to Hanani: his sons and his brothers—12; ²⁶the nineteenth, to Mallothi: his sons and his brothers—12; ²⁷the twentieth, to Eliathah: his sons and his brothers— 12; ²⁸the twenty-first, to Hothir: his sons and his brothers—12; ²⁹the twenty-second, to Giddalti: his sons and his brothers—12; ³⁰the twenty-third, to Mahazioth: his sons and his brothers—12; ³¹the twenty-fourth, to Romamti-ezer: his sons and his brothers—12.

26 The divisions of the gatekeepers: Korahites: Meshelemiah son of Kore, of the sons of Asaph. ²Sons of Meshelemiah: Zechariah the first-born, Jediael the second, Zebadiah the third, Jathniel the fourth, ³Elam the fifth, Jehohanan the sixth, Eliehoenai the seventh. ⁴Sons of Obed-edom: Shemaiah the first-born, Jehozabad the second, Joah the third, Sacar the fourth, Nethanel the fifth, ⁵Ammiel the sixth, Issachar the seventh, Peullethai the eighth—for God had blessed him. ⁶To his son She-maiah were born sons who exercised authority in their clans because they were men of substance. ⁷The sons of Shemaiah: Othni, Rephael, Obed, Elzabad—his brothers, men of ability, were Elihu and Semachiah. ⁸All these, sons of Obed-edom; they and their sons and brothers, strong and able men for the service—62 of Obed-edom. ⁹Meshelemiah had sons and brothers, able men—18. ¹⁰Hosah of the Merarites had sons: Shimri the chief (he was not the first-born, but his father designated him chief),

¹¹Hilkiah the second, Tebaliah the third, Zechariah the fourth. All the sons and brothers of Hosah—13.

¹²These are the divisions of the gatekeepers, by their chief men, [who worked in] shifts corresponding to their kinsmen, ministering in the House of the LORD. ¹³They cast lots, small and great alike, by clans, for each gate.

¹⁴The lot for the east [gate] fell to Shelemiah. Then they cast lots [for] Zechariah his son, a prudent counselor, and his lot came out to be the north [gate]. ¹⁵For Obed-edom, the south [gate], and for his sons, the vestibule. ¹⁶For Shuppim and for Hosah, the west [gate], with the Shallecheth gate on the ascending highway. Watch corresponded to watch: ¹⁷At the east—six Levites; at the north—four daily; at the south—four daily; at the vestibule—two by two; ¹⁸at the colonnade on the west—four at the causeway and two at the colonnade. ¹⁹These were the divisions of the gatekeepers of the sons of Korah and the sons of Merari.

²⁰And the Levites: Ahijah over the treasuries of the House of God and the treasuries of the dedicated things. ²¹The sons of Ladan: the sons of the Gershonites belonging to Ladan; the chiefs of the clans of Ladan, the Gershonite—Jehieli. ²²The sons of Jehieli: Zetham and Joel; his brother was over the treasuries of the House of the LORD.

²³Of the Amramites, the Izharites, the Hebronites, the Uzzielites: ²⁴Shebuel son of Gershom son of Moses was the chief officer over the treasuries. ²⁵And his brothers: Eliezer, his son Rehabiah, his son Jeshaiah, his son Joram, his son Zichri, his son Shelomith—²⁶that Shelomith and his brothers were over all the treasuries of dedicated things that were dedicated by King David and the chiefs of the clans, and the officers of thousands and hundreds and the other army officers; ²⁷they dedicated some of the booty of the wars to maintain the House of the LORD. ²⁸All that Samuel the seer had dedicated, and Saul son of Kish, and Abner son of Ner, and Joab son of Zeruiah—or [what] any other man had dedicated, was under the charge of Shelomith and his brothers.

²⁹The Izharites: Chenaniah and his sons were over Israel as clerks and magistrates for affairs outside [the sanctuary]. ³⁰The Hebronites: Hashabiah and his brothers, capable men, 1,700, supervising Israel on the west side of the Jordan in all matters of the LORD and the service of the king. ³¹The Hebronites: Jeriah, the chief of the Hebronites—they were investigated in the fortieth year of David's reign by clans of all their lines, and men of substance were found among them in Jazer-gilead. ³²His

brothers, able men, 2,700, chiefs of clans—David put them in charge of the Reubenites, the Gadites, and the half-tribe of Manasseh in all matters of God and matters of the king.

27 The number of Israelites—chiefs of clans, officers of thousands and hundreds and their clerks, who served the king in all matters of the divisions, who worked in monthly shifts during all the months of the year— each division, 24,000. ²Over the first division for the first month—Jashobeam son of Zabdiel; his division had 24,000. ³Of the sons of Perez, he, the chief of all the officers of the army, [served] for the first month. ⁴Over the division of the second month—Dodai the Ahohite; Mikloth was chief officer of his division; his division had 24,000. ⁵The third army officer for the third month—Benaiah son of Jehoiada, the chief priest; his division had 24,000. ⁶That was Benaiah, one of the warriors of the thirty and over the thirty; and [over] his division was Ammizabad his son. ⁷The fourth, for the fourth month, Asahel brother of Joab, and his son Zebadiah after him; his division had 24,000. ⁸The fifth, for the fifth month, the officer Shamhut the Izrahite; his division had 24,000. ⁹The sixth, for the sixth month, Ira son of Ikkesh the Tekoite; his division had 24,000. ¹⁰The seventh, for the seventh month, Helez the Pelonite, of the Ephraimites; his division had 24,000. ¹¹The eighth, for the eighth month, Sibbecai the Hushathite, of Zerah; his division had 24,000. ¹²The ninth, for the ninth month, Abiezer the Anathothite, of Benjamin; his division had 24,000. ¹³The tenth, for the tenth month, Mahrai the Netophathite, of Zerah; his division had 24,000. ¹⁴The eleventh, for the eleventh month, Benaiah the Pirathonite, of the Ephraimites; his division had 24,000. ¹⁵The twelfth, for the twelfth month, Heldai the Netophathite, of Othniel; his division had 24,000.

¹⁶Over the tribes of Israel: Reuben: the chief officer, Eliezer son of Zichri. Simeon: Shephatiah son of Maaca. ¹⁷Levi: Hashabiah son of Kemuel. Aaron: Zadok. ¹⁸Judah: Elihu, of the brothers of David. Issachar: Omri son of Michael. ¹⁹Zebulun: Ishmaiah son of Obadiah. Naphtali: Jerimoth son of Azriel. ²⁰Ephraimites: Hoshea son of Azaziah. The halftribe of Manasseh: Joel son of Pedaiah. ²¹Half Manasseh in Gilead: Iddo son of Zechariah. Benjamin: Jaasiel son of Abner. ²²Dan: Azarel son of Jeroham. These were the officers of the tribes of Israel.

²³David did not take a census of those under twenty years of age, for

the LORD had promised to make Israel as numerous as the stars of heaven. ²⁴Joab son of Zeruiah did begin to count them, but he did not finish; wrath struck Israel on account of this, and the census was not entered into the account of the chronicles of King David.

²⁵Over the royal treasuries: Azmaveth son of Adiel. Over the treasuries in the country—in the towns, the hamlets, and the citadels: Jonathan son of Uzziah. ²⁶Over the field laborers in agricultural work: Ezri son of Chelub. ²⁷Over the vineyards: Shimei the Ramathite. And over the produce in the vineyards for wine cellars: Zabdi the Shiphmite. ²⁸Over the olive trees and the sycamores in the Shephelah: Baal-hanan the Gederite. Over the oil-stores: Joash. ²⁹Over the cattle pasturing in Sharon: Shirtai the Sharonite. And over the cattle in the valleys: Shaphat son of Adlai. ³⁰Over the camels: Obil the Ishmaelite. And over the she-asses: Jehdeiah the Meronothite. ³¹Over the flocks: Jaziz the Hagrite. All these were stewards of the property of King David. ³²Jonathan, David's uncle, was a counselor, a master, and a scribe: Jehiel son of Hachmoni was with the king's sons. ³³Ahitophel was a counselor to the king. Hushai the Archite was the king's friend. ³⁴After Ahitophel were Jehoiada son of Benaiah and Abiathar. The commander of the king's army was Joab.

28 David assembled all the officers of Israel—the tribal officers, the divisional officers who served the king, the captains of thousands and the captains of hundreds, and the stewards of all the property and cattle of the king and his sons, with the eunuchs and the warriors, all the men of substance—to Jerusalem. ²King David rose to his feet and said, "Hear me, my brothers, my people! I wanted to build a resting-place for the Ark of the Covenant of the LORD, for the footstool of our God, and I laid aside material for building. ³But God said to me, 'You will not build a house for My name, for you are a man of battles and have shed blood.' ⁴The LORD God of Israel chose me of all my father's house to be king over Israel forever. For He chose Judah to be ruler, and of the family of Judah, my father's house; and of my father's sons, He preferred to make me king over all Israel; ⁵and of all my sons—for many are the sons the LORD gave me—He chose my son Solomon to sit on the throne of the kingdom of the LORD over Israel. ⁶He said to me, 'It will be your son Solomon who will build My House and My courts, for I have chosen him to be a son to Me, and I will be a father to him. ⁷I will establish his kingdom forever, if he keeps firmly to the observance of My commandments and rules as he does now.' [8]And now, in the sight of all Israel, the congregation of the LORD, and in the hearing of our God, [I say:] Observe and apply yourselves to all the commandments of the LORD your God in order that you may possess this good land and bequeath it to your children after you forever.

[9]"And you, my son Solomon, know the God of your father, and serve Him with single mind and fervent heart, for the LORD searches all minds and discerns the design of every thought; if you seek Him He will be available to you, but if you forsake Him He will abandon you forever. [10]See then, the LORD chose you to build a house as the sanctuary; be strong and do it."

[11]David gave his son Solomon the plan of the porch and its houses, its storerooms and its upper chambers and inner chambers; and of the place of the Ark-cover; [12]and the plan of all that he had by the spirit: of the courts of the House of the LORD and all its surrounding chambers, and of the treasuries of the House of God and of the treasuries of the holy things; [13]the divisions of priests and Levites for all the work of the service of the House of the LORD and all the vessels of the service of the House of the LORD; [14]and gold, the weight of gold for vessels of every sort of use; silver for all the vessels of silver by weight, for all the vessels of every kind of service; [15]the weight of the gold lampstands and their gold lamps, and the weight of the silver lampstands, each lampstand and its silver lamps, according to the use of every lampstand; [16]and the weight of gold for the tables of the rows of bread, for each table, and of silver for the silver tables; [17]and of the pure gold for the forks and the basins and the jars; and the weight of the gold bowls, every bowl; and the weight of the silver bowls, each and every bowl; [18]the weight of refined gold for the incense altar and the gold for the figure of the chariot—the cherubs—those with outspread wings screening the Ark of the Covenant of the LORD. [19]"All this that the LORD made me understand by His hand on me, I give you in writing—the plan of all the works."

[20]David said to his son Solomon, "Be strong and of good courage and do it; do not be afraid or dismayed, for the LORD God my God is with you; He will not fail you or forsake you till all the work on the House of the LORD is done. [21]Here are the divisions of the priests and Levites for all kinds of service of the House of God, and with you in all the work

are willing men, skilled in all sorts of tasks; also the officers and all the people are at your command."

29 King David said to the entire assemblage, "God has chosen my son Solomon alone, an untried lad, although the work to be done is vast—for the temple[a] is not for a man but for the LORD God. [2]I have spared no effort to lay up for the House of my God gold for golden objects, silver for silver, copper for copper, iron for iron, wood for wooden, onyx-stone and inlay-stone, stone of antimony and variegated colors—every kind of precious stone and much marble. [3]Besides, out of my solicitude for the House of my God, I gave over my private hoard of gold and silver to the House of my God—in addition to all that I laid aside for the holy House: [4]3,000 gold talents of Ophir gold, and 7,000 talents of refined silver for covering the walls of the houses [5](gold for golden objects, silver for silver for all the work)—into the hands of craftsmen. Now who is going to make a freewill offering and devote himself today to the LORD?"

[6]The officers of the clans and the officers of the tribes of Israel and the captains of thousands and hundreds and the supervisors of the king's work made freewill offerings, [7]giving for the work of the House of God: 5,000 talents of gold, 10,000 darics, 10,000 talents of silver, 18,000 talents of copper, 100,000 talents of iron. [8]Whoever had stones in his possession gave them to the treasury of the House of the LORD in the charge of Jehiel the Gershonite. [9]The people rejoiced over the freewill offerings they made, for with a whole heart they made freewill offerings to the LORD; King David also rejoiced very much.

[10]David blessed the LORD in front of all the assemblage; David said, "Blessed are You, LORD, God of Israel our father, from eternity to eternity. [11]Yours, LORD, are greatness, might, splendor, triumph, and majesty—yes, all that is in heaven and on earth; to You, LORD, belong kingship and preeminence above all. [12]Riches and honor are Yours to dispense; You have dominion over all; with You are strength and might, and it is in Your power to make anyone great and strong. [13]Now, God, we praise You and extol Your glorious name. [14]Who am I and who are my people, that we should have the means to make such a freewill offering; but all is from You, and it is Your gift that we have given to You. [15]For we are sojourners with You, mere transients like our fathers; our days on earth

---

[a] Lit. "fortress."

are like a shadow, with nothing in prospect. ¹⁶O LORD our God, all this great mass that we have laid aside to build You a House for Your holy name is from You, and it is all Yours. ¹⁷I know, God, that You search the heart and desire uprightness; I, with upright heart, freely offered all these things; now Your people, who are present here—I saw them joyously making freewill offerings. ¹⁸O LORD God of Abraham, Isaac, and Israel, our fathers, remember this to the eternal credit of the thoughts of Your people's hearts, and make their hearts constant toward You. ¹⁹As to my son Solomon, give him a whole heart to observe Your commandments, Your admonitions, and Your laws, and to fulfill them all, and to build this temple^a for which I have made provision."

²⁰David said to the whole assemblage, "Now bless the LORD your God." All the assemblage blessed the LORD God of their fathers, and bowed their heads low to the LORD and the king. ²¹They offered sacrifices to the LORD and made burnt offerings to the LORD on the morrow of that day: 1,000 bulls, 1,000 rams, 1,000 lambs, with their libations; [they made] sacrifices in great number for all Israel, ²²and they ate and drank in the presence of the LORD on that day with great joy. They again proclaimed Solomon son of David king, and they anointed him as ruler before the LORD, and Zadok as high priest. ²³Solomon successfully took over the throne of the LORD as king instead of his father David, and all went well with him. All Israel accepted him; ²⁴all the officials and the warriors, and the sons of King David as well, gave their hand in support of King Solomon. ²⁵The LORD made Solomon exceedingly great in the eyes of all Israel, and endowed him with a regal majesty that no king of Israel before him ever had.

²⁶Thus David son of Jesse reigned over all Israel; ²⁷the length of his reign over Israel was forty years: he reigned seven years in Hebron and thirty-three years in Jerusalem. ²⁸He died at a ripe old age, having enjoyed long life, riches and honor, and his son Solomon reigned in his stead. ²⁹The acts of King David, early and late, are recorded in the history of Samuel the seer, the history of Nathan the prophet, and the history of Gad the seer, ³⁰together with all the mighty deeds of his kingship and the events that befell him and Israel and all the kingdoms of the earth.

דברי הימים ב

II CHRONICLES

1 ^aSolomon son of David took firm hold of his kingdom, for the LORD his God was with him and made him exceedingly great. ²Solomon summoned all Israel—the officers of thousands and of hundreds, and the judges, and all the chiefs of all Israel, the heads of the clans. ³Then Solomon, and all the assemblage with him, went to the shrine at Gibeon, for the Tent of Meeting, which Moses the servant of the LORD had made in the wilderness, was there. (⁴But the Ark of God David had brought up from Kiriath-jearim to the place which David had prepared for it; for he had pitched a tent for it in Jerusalem.) ⁵The bronze altar, which Bezalel son of Uri son of Hur had made, was also there before the Tabernacle of the LORD, and Solomon and the assemblage resorted to it. ⁶There Solomon ascended the bronze altar before the LORD, which was at the Tent of Meeting, and on it sacrificed a thousand burnt offerings.

⁷That night, the LORD appeared to Solomon and said to him, "Ask, what shall I grant you?" ⁸Solomon said to God, "You dealt most graciously with my father David, and now You have made me king in his stead. ⁹Now, O LORD God, let Your promise to my father David be fulfilled; for You have made me king over a people as numerous as the dust of the earth. ¹⁰Grant me then the wisdom and the knowledge ^{b-}to lead this people,^{-b} for who can govern Your great people?" ¹¹God said to Solomon, "Because you want this, and have not asked for wealth, property, and glory, nor have you asked for the life of your enemy, or long life for yourself, but you have asked for the wisdom and the knowledge to be able to govern My people over whom I have made you king, ¹²wisdom and knowledge are granted to you, and I grant you also wealth, property, and glory, the like of which no king before you has had, nor shall any

---

^a *With vv. 3–13, cf. 1 Kings 3. 4–15; with vv. 14–17, cf. 1 Kings 10.26–29.*
^{b-b} *Lit. "that I may go out before this people and come in."*

after you have." 13From the shrine at Gibeon, from the Tent of Meeting, Solomon went to Jerusalem and reigned over Israel.

14Solomon assembled chariots and horsemen; he had 1,400 chariots and 12,000 horses that he stationed in the chariot towns and with the king in Jerusalem. 15The king made silver and gold as plentiful in Jerusalem as stones, and cedars as plentiful as the sycamores in the Shephelah. 16Solomon's horses were imported from Egypt and from Que; the king's traders would buy them from Que at the market price. 17A chariot imported from Egypt cost 600 shekels of silver, and a horse 150. These in turn were exported by them^c to all the kings of the Hittites and the kings of the Arameans.

18Then Solomon resolved to build a House for the name of the LORD **2** and a royal palace for himself. ^aSolomon mustered 70,000 basket carriers and 80,000 quarriers in the hills, with 3,600 men supervising them. 2Solomon sent this message to King Huram of Tyre, "In view of what you did for my father David in sending him cedars to build a palace for his residence—3see, I intend to build a House for the name of the LORD my God; I will dedicate it to Him for making incense offering of sweet spices in His honor, for the regular rows of bread, and for the morning and evening burnt offerings on sabbaths, new moons, and festivals, as is Israel's eternal duty. 4The House that I intend to build will be great, inasmuch as our God is greater than all gods. 5Who indeed is capable of building a House for Him! Even the heavens to their uttermost reaches cannot contain Him, and who am I that I should build Him a House—except as a place for making burnt offerings to Him? 6Now send me a craftsman to work in gold, silver, bronze, and iron, and in purple, crimson, and blue yarn, and who knows how to engrave, alongside the craftsmen I have here in Judah and in Jerusalem, whom my father David provided. 7 Send me cedars, cypress, and algum wood from the Lebanon, for I know that your servants are skilled at cutting the trees of Lebanon. My servants will work with yours 8to provide me with a great stock of timber; for the House that I intend to build will be singularly great. 9I have allocated for your servants, the wood-cutters who fell the trees, 20,000 *kor* of crushed wheat and 20,000 *kor* of barley, 20,000 *bath* of wine and 20,000 *bath* of oil."

10Huram, king of Tyre, sent Solomon this written message in reply,

---

^c *That is, Solomon's dealers.*

^a *Cf. 1 Kings 5.*

"Because the LORD loved His people, He made you king over them."

11Huram continued, "Blessed is the LORD, God of Israel, who made the heavens and the earth, who gave King David a wise son, endowed with intelligence and understanding, to build a House for the LORD and a royal palace for himself. 12Now I am sending you a skillful and intelligent man, my master[b] Huram,13 the son of a Danite woman, his father a Tyrian. He is skilled at working in gold, silver, bronze, iron, precious stones, and wood; in purple, blue, and crimson yarn and in fine linen; and at engraving and designing whatever will be required of him, alongside your craftsmen and the craftsmen of my lord, your father David. 14As to the wheat, barley, oil, and wine which my lord mentioned, let him send them to his servants. 15We undertake to cut down as many trees of Lebanon as you need, and deliver them to you as rafts by sea to Jaffa; you will transport them to Jerusalem."

16Solomon took a census of all the aliens who were in the land of Israel, besides the census taken by his father David, and they were found to be 153,600. 17 He made 70,000 of them basket carriers, and 80,000 of them quarriers, with 3,600 supervisors to see that the people worked.

3

aThen Solomon began to build the House of the LORD in Jerusalem on Mount Moriah, where [the LORD] had appeared to his father David, at the place which David had designated, at the threshing floor of Ornan the Jebusite. 2He began to build on the second day of the second month of the fourth year of his reign. 3These were the dimensions Solomon established for building the House of God: its length in cubits, by the former measure, was 60, and its breadth was 20. 4The length of the porch in front [was equal] to the breadth of the House—20 cubits, and its height was 120. Inside he overlaid it with pure gold. 5The House itself he paneled with cypress wood. He overlaid it with fine gold and embossed on it palms and chains. 6He studded the House with precious stones for decoration; the gold was from Parvaim. 7 He overlaid the House with gold—the beams, the thresholds, its walls and doors; he carved cherubim on the walls. 8He made the Holy of Holies: its length was [equal to] the breadth of the house—20 cubits, and its breadth was 20 cubits. He overlaid it with 600 talents of fine gold. 9 The weight of the nails was 50 shekels of gold; the upper chambers he overlaid with gold. 10He made two sculp-

b Lit. "my father."
a With vv. 2–17, cf. 1 Kings 6; 7.1–22.

tured cherubim in the Holy of Holies, and they were overlaid with gold. [11]The outspread wings of the cherubim were 20 cubits across: one wing 5 cubits long touching one wall of the House, and the other wing 5 cubits long touching the wing of the other cherub; [12]one wing of the other [cherub] 5 cubits long extending to the other wall of the House, and its other wing 5 cubits long touching the wing of the first cherub. [13]The wingspread of these cherubim was thus 20 cubits across, and they were standing up facing the House. [14]He made the curtain of blue, purple, and crimson yarn and fine linen, and he worked cherubim into it. [15]At the front of the House he made two columns 35 cubits high; the capitals[b] on top of them were 5 cubits high. [16]He made chainwork in the inner Sanctuary and set it on the top of the columns; he made a hundred pomegranates and set them into the chainwork. [17]He erected the columns in front of the Great Hall, one to its right and one to its left; the one to the right was called Jachin, and the one to the left, Boaz.

4 [a]He made an altar of bronze 20 cubits long, 20 cubits wide, and 10 cubits high.

[2]He made the sea[b] of cast metal 10 cubits across from brim to brim, perfectly round; it was 5 cubits high, and its circumference was 30 cubits. [3]Beneath were figures of oxen set all around it, of 10 cubits, encircling the sea; the oxen were in two rows, cast in one piece with it. [4]It stood upon twelve oxen: three faced north, three faced west, three faced south, and three faced east, with the sea resting upon them; their haunches were all turned inward. [5]It was a handbreadth thick, and its brim was made like that of a cup, like the petals of a lily. It held 3,000 *bath*.

[6]He made ten bronze lavers for washing; he set five on the right and five on the left; they would rinse off in them the parts of the burnt offering; but the sea served the priests for washing. [7]He made ten lampstands of gold as prescribed, and placed them in the Great Hall, five on the right and five on the left. [8]He made ten tables and placed them in the Great Hall, five on the right and five on the left. He made one hundred gold basins. [9]He built the court of the priests and the great court, and doors for the great court; he overlaid the doors with bronze. [10]He set the sea on the right side, at the southeast corner.

[11]Huram made the pails, the shovels, and the basins. With that Huram completed the work he had undertaken for King Solomon in the House

---

[b] *Meaning of Heb. uncertain.*

[a] *Cf. 1 Kings 7.23–50.*
[b] *I.e., a large basin.*

of God: 12the two columns, the globes, and the two capitals on top of the columns; and the two pieces of network to cover the two globes of the capitals on top of the columns; 13the four hundred pomegranates for the two pieces of network, two rows of pomegranates for each network, to cover the two globes of the capitals on top of the columns; 14he made the stands and the lavers upon the stands; 15one sea with the twelve oxen beneath it; 16the pails, the shovels, and the bowls.c And all the vessels made for King Solomon for the House of the LORD by Huram his master were of burnished bronze. 17The king had them cast in molds dug out of the earth, in the plain of the Jordan between Succoth and Zeredah. 18Solomon made a very large number of vessels; the weight of the bronze used could not be reckoned. 19And Solomon made all the furnishings that were in the House of God: the altar of gold; the tables for the bread of display; 20the lampstands and their lamps, to burn as prescribed in front of the inner Sanctuary, of solid gold; 21and the petals, lamps, and tongs, of purest gold; 22the snuffers, basins, ladles, and fire pans, of solid gold; and the entrance to the House: the doors of the innermost part of the House, the Holy of Holies, and the doors of the Great Hall of the House, of gold.

5

aWhen all the work that King Solomon undertook for the House of the LORD was completed, Solomon brought the things that his father David had consecrated—the silver, the gold, and the utensils—and deposited them in the treasury of the House of God.

2Then Solomon convoked the elders of Israel—all the heads of the tribes and the ancestral chiefs of the Israelites—in Jerusalem, to bring up the Ark of the Covenant of the LORD from the City of David, that is, Zion.

3All the men of Israel assembled before the king at the Feast,b in the seventh month. 4When all the elders of Israel had come, the Levites carried the Ark. 5They brought up the Ark and the Tent of Meeting and all the holy vessels that were in the Tent—the Levite priests brought them up. 6Meanwhile, King Solomon and the whole community of Israel, who had gathered to him before the Ark, were sacrificing sheep and oxen in such abundance that they could not be numbered or counted.

7The priests brought the Ark of the LORD's Covenant to its place in the inner Sanctuary of the House, in the Holy of Holies, beneath the wings of the cherubim; 8for the cherubim had their wings spread out over

---

c Or "forks."

a Cf. 1 Kings 7.51–8.11.
b I.e., of Tabernacles.

the place of the Ark so that the cherubim covered the Ark and its poles from above. ⁹The poles projected beyond the Ark and the ends of the poles were visible from the front of the inner Sanctuary, but they could not be seen from the outside; and there they remain to this day. ¹⁰There was nothing inside the Ark but the two tablets that Moses placed [there] at Horeb, when the LORD made [a Covenant] with the Israelites after their departure from Egypt. ¹¹When the priests came out of the Sanctuary—all the priests present had sanctified themselves, without keeping to the set divisions—¹²all the Levite singers, Asaph, Heman, Jeduthun, their sons and their brothers, dressed in fine linen, holding cymbals, harps, and lyres, were standing to the east of the altar, and with them were 120 priests who blew trumpets. ¹³The trumpeters and the singers joined in unison to praise and extol the LORD; and as the sound of the trumpets, cymbals, and other musical instruments, and the praise of the LORD, "For He is good, for His steadfast love is eternal," grew louder, the House, the House of the LORD, was filled with a cloud. ¹⁴The priests could not stay and perform the service because of the cloud, for the glory of the LORD filled the House of God.

6 ªThen Solomon declared:
"The LORD has chosen
To abide in a thick cloud;
²I have built for You
A stately House,
And a place where You
May dwell forever."

³Then, as the whole congregation of Israel stood, the king turned and blessed the whole congregation of Israel. ⁴He said, "Blessed is the LORD God of Israel, ᵇ⁻who made a promise to my father David and fulfilled it.⁻ᵇ For He said, ⁵'From the time I brought My people out of the land of Egypt, I never chose a city from among all the tribes of Israel to build a House where My name might abide; nor did I choose anyone to be the leader of my people Israel. ⁶But then I chose Jerusalem for My name to abide there, and I chose David to rule My people Israel.'

⁷"Now my father David had wanted to build a House for the name of the LORD God of Israel. ⁸But the LORD said to my father David, 'As for your wanting to build a House for My name, you do well to want that.

ª Cf. 1 Kings 8.12–53.
ᵇ⁻ᵇ Lit. "who spoke with His own mouth a promise to my father David and has fulfilled with His own hands."

⁹However, you shall not build the House; your son, the issue of your loins, he shall build the House for My name.' ¹⁰Now the LORD has fulfilled the promise that He made. I have succeeded[c] my father David and have ascended the throne of Israel, as the LORD promised. I have built the House for the name of the LORD God of Israel, ¹¹and there I have set the Ark containing the Covenant that the LORD made with the Israelites."

¹²Then, standing before the altar of the LORD in front of the whole congregation of Israel, he spread forth his hands. ¹³Solomon had made a bronze platform[d] and placed it in the midst of the Great Court; it was 5 cubits long and 5 cubits wide and 3 cubits high. He stood on it; then, kneeling in front of the whole congregation of Israel, he spread forth his hands to heaven ¹⁴and said, "O LORD God of Israel, there is no god like You in the heavens and on the earth, You who steadfastly maintain the Covenant with Your servants who walk before You with all their heart; ¹⁵You who have kept the promises You made to Your servant, my father David; You made a promise and have fulfilled it—as is now the case. ¹⁶And now, O LORD God of Israel, keep that promise that You made to Your servant, my father David, 'You shall never lack a descendant in My sight sitting on the throne of Israel if only your children will look to their way and walk in the [path] of My teachings as you have walked before Me.' ¹⁷Now, therefore, O God of Israel, let the promise that You made to Your servant, my father David, be confirmed.

¹⁸"Does God really dwell with man on earth? Even the heavens to their uttermost reaches cannot contain You; how much less this House that I have built! ¹⁹Yet turn, O LORD my God, to the prayer and supplication of Your servant, and hear the cry and the prayer that Your servant offers to You. ²⁰May Your eyes be open day and night toward this House, toward the place where You have resolved to make Your name abide; may You heed the prayers that Your servant offers toward this place. ²¹And when You hear the supplications that Your servant and Your people Israel offer toward this place, give heed in Your heavenly abode—give heed and pardon.

²²"If a man commits an offense against his fellow, and an oath is exacted from him, causing him to utter an imprecation against himself, and he comes with his imprecation before Your altar in this House, ²³may You hear in heaven and take action to judge Your servants, requiting him who is in the wrong by bringing down the punishment of his conduct on his

---

c Lit. "risen in place of."
d Meaning of Heb. uncertain.

head, vindicating him who is in the right by rewarding him according to his righteousness.

24"Should Your people Israel be defeated by an enemy because they have sinned against You, and then once again acknowledge Your name and offer prayer and supplication to You in this House, 25may You hear in heaven and pardon the sin of Your people Israel, and restore them to the land that You gave to them and to their fathers.

26"Should the heavens be shut up and there be no rain because they have sinned against You, and then they pray toward this place and acknowledge Your name and repent of their sins, because You humbled them, 27may You hear in heaven and pardon the sin of Your servants, Your people Israel, when You have shown them the proper way in which they are to walk, and send down rain upon the land that You gave to Your people as their heritage. 28So, too, if there is a famine in the land, if there is pestilence, blight, mildew, locusts, or caterpillars, or if an enemy oppresses them in any of the settlements of their land.

"In any plague and in any disease, 29any prayer or supplication offered by any person among all Your people Israel—each of whom knows his affliction and his pain—when he spreads forth his hands toward this House, 30may You hear in Your heavenly abode, and pardon. Deal with each man according to his ways as You know his heart to be—for You alone know the hearts of all men—31so that they may revere You all the days that they live on the land that You gave to our fathers.

32"Or if a foreigner who is not of Your people Israel comes from a distant land for the sake of Your great name, Your mighty hand, and Your outstretched arm, if he comes to pray toward this House, 33may You hear in Your heavenly abode and grant whatever the foreigner appeals to You for. Thus all the peoples of the earth will know Your name and revere You, as does Your people Israel; and they will recognize that Your name is attached to this House that I have built.

34"When Your people take the field against their enemies in a campaign on which You send them, and they pray to You in the direction of the city which You have chosen and the House which I have built to Your name, 35may You hear in heaven their prayer and supplication and uphold their cause.

36"When they sin against You—for there is no person who does not sin—and You are angry with them and deliver them to the enemy, and their captors carry them off to an enemy land, near or far; [37]and they take it to heart in the land to which they have been carried off, and repent and make supplication to You in the land of their captivity, saying, 'We have sinned, we have acted perversely, we have acted wickedly,' [38]and they turn back to You with all their heart and soul, in the land of their captivity where they were carried off, and pray in the direction of their land which You gave to their fathers and the city which You have chosen, and toward the House which I have built for Your name—[39]may You hear their prayer and supplication in Your heavenly abode, uphold their cause, and pardon Your people who have sinned against You. [40]Now My God, may Your eyes be open and Your ears attentive to prayer from this place, and now,

[41]Advance, O LORD God, to your resting-place,
You and Your mighty Ark.
Your priests, O LORD God, are clothed in triumph;
Your loyal ones will rejoice in [Your] goodness.
[42]O LORD God,
do not reject Your anointed one;
remember the loyalty of Your servant David."

7 [a]When Solomon finished praying, fire descended from heaven and consumed the burnt offering and the sacrifices, and the glory of the LORD filled the House. [2]The priests could not enter the House of the LORD, for the glory of the LORD filled the House of the LORD. [3]All the Israelites witnessed the descent of the fire and the glory of the LORD on the House; they knelt with their faces to the ground and prostrated themselves, praising the LORD, "For He is good, for His steadfast love is eternal."

[4]Then the king and all the people offered sacrifices before the LORD. [5]King Solomon offered as sacrifices 22,000 oxen and 120,000 sheep; thus the king and all the people dedicated the House of God. [6]The priests stood at their watches; the Levites with the instruments for the LORD's music that King David had made to praise the LORD, "For His steadfast love is eternal," by means of the psalms of David that they knew. The priests opposite them blew trumpets while all Israel were standing.

[7]Solomon consecrated the center of the court in front of the House of the LORD, because he presented there the burnt offerings and the fat parts

---

[a] Cf. 1 Kings 8.54–9.9.

of the offerings of well-being, since the bronze altar that Solomon had made was not able to hold the burnt offerings, the meal offerings, and the fat parts. 8At that time Solomon kept the Feast for seven days—all Israel with him—a great assemblage from Lebo-hamath to the Wadi of Egypt.

9On the eighth day they held a solemn gathering; they observed the dedication of the altar seven days, and the Feast seven days. 10On the twenty-third day of the seventh month he dismissed the people to their homes, rejoicing and in good spirits over the goodness that the LORD had shown to David and Solomon and His people Israel.

11Thus Solomon finished building the House of the LORD and the royal palace; Solomon succeeded in everything he had set his heart on accomplishing with regard to the House of the LORD and his palace. 12The LORD appeared to Solomon at night and said to him, "I have heard your prayer and have chosen this site as My House of sacrifice. 13If I shut up the heavens and there is no rain; if I command the locusts to ravage the land; or if I let loose pestilence against My people, 14when My people, who bear My name, humble themselves, pray, and seek My favor and turn from their evil ways, I will hear in My heavenly abode and forgive their sins and heal their land. 15Now My eyes will be open and My ears attentive to the prayers from this place. 16And now I have chosen and consecrated this House that My name be there forever. My eyes and My heart shall always be there. 17As for you, if you walk before Me as your father David walked before Me, doing all that I have commanded you, keeping My laws and rules, 18then I will establish your royal throne over Israel forever, in accordance with the Covenant I made with your father David, saying, 'You shall never lack a descendant ruling over Israel.' 19But if you turn away from Me and forsake My laws and commandments that I set before you, and go and serve other gods and worship them, 20then I will uproot themᵇ from My land that I gave them, and this House that I consecrated to My name I shall cast out of my sight, and make it a proverb and a byword among all peoples. 21And as for this House, once so exalted, everyone passing by it shall be appalled and say, 'Why did the LORD do thus to this land and to this House?' 22And the reply will be, 'It is because they forsook the LORD God of their fathers who freed them from the land of Egypt, and adopted other gods and worshiped them and served them; therefore He brought all this calamity upon them.' "

---

b *I.e., Israel; cf. 1 Kings 9.7.*

8 [a]At the end of twenty years, during which Solomon constructed the House of the LORD and his palace—[2]Solomon also rebuilt the cities that Huram had given to him,[b] and settled Israelites in them—[3]Solomon marched against Hamath-zobah and overpowered it. [4]He built Tadmor in the desert and all the garrison towns that he built in Hamath. [5]He built Upper Beth-horon and Lower Beth-horon as fortified cities with walls, gates, and bars, [6]as well as Baalath and all of Solomon's garrison towns, chariot towns, and cavalry towns—everything that Solomon desired to build in Jerusalem and in the Lebanon, and throughout the territory that he ruled. [7]All the people that were left of the Hittites, Amorites, Perizzites, Hivites, and Jebusites, none of whom were of Israelite stock—[8]those of their descendants who were left after them in the land, whom the Israelites had not annihilated—these Solomon subjected to forced labor, as is still the case. [9]But the Israelites, none of whom Solomon enslaved for his works, served as soldiers and as his chief officers, and as commanders of his chariotry and cavalry. [10]These were King Solomon's prefects—250 foremen over the people. [11]Solomon brought up Pharaoh's daughter from the City of David to the palace that he had built for her, for he said, "No wife of mine shall dwell in a palace of King David of Israel, for [the area] is sacred since the Ark of the LORD has entered it."

[12]At that time, Solomon offered burnt offerings on the altar that he had built in front of the porch. [13]What was due for each day he sacrificed according to the commandment of Moses for the sabbaths, the new moons, and the thrice-yearly festivals—the Feast of Unleavened Bread, the Feast of Weeks, and the Feast of Booths. [14]Following the prescription of his father David, he set up the divisions of the priests for their duties, and the Levites for their watches, to praise and to serve alongside the priests, according to each day's requirement, and the gatekeepers in their watches, gate by gate, for such was the commandment of David, the man of God. [15]They did not depart from the commandment of the king relating to the priests and the Levites in all these matters and also relating to the treasuries. [16]And all of Solomon's work was well executed from the day the House of the LORD was founded until the House of the LORD was completed to perfection.

[17]At that time Solomon went to Ezion-geber and to Eloth on the seacoast of the land of Edom. [18]Huram sent him, under the charge of servants, a fleet with a crew of expert seamen; they went with Solomon's

---

[a] Cf. 1 Kings 9.10–28.
[b] Lit. "Solomon."

men to Ophir, and obtained gold there in the amount of 450 talents, which they brought to King Solomon.

9 [a]The queen of Sheba heard of Solomon's fame, and came to Jerusalem to test Solomon with hard questions, accompanied by a very large retinue, including camels bearing spices, a great quantity of gold, and precious stones. When she came to Solomon, she spoke to him of all that she had on her mind. 2Solomon had answers for all her questions; there was nothing that Solomon did not know, nothing to which he could not give her an answer.

3When the queen of Sheba saw how wise Solomon was and the palace he had built, 4the fare of his table, the seating of his courtiers, the service and attire of his attendants, his butlers and their attire, and the procession with which he went up to the House of the LORD, it took her breath away. 5She said to the king, "What I heard in my own land about you and your wisdom was true. 6I did not believe what they said until I came and saw with my own eyes that not even the half of your great wisdom had been described to me; you surpass the report that I heard. 7How fortunate are your men and how fortunate are these courtiers of yours who are always in attendance on you and can hear your wisdom! 8Blessed is the LORD your God, who favored you and set you on His throne as a king before the LORD. It is because of your God's love for Israel and in order to establish them forever that He made you king over them to execute righteous justice."

9She presented the king with 120 talents of gold, and a vast quantity of spices and precious stones. There were no such spices as those which the queen of Sheba gave to King Solomon—10also, the servants of Huram and Solomon who brought gold from Ophir brought algum-wood and precious stones. 11The king made of the algum-wood ramps for the House of the LORD and for the royal palace, and lyres and harps for the musicians, whose like had never before been seen in the land of Judah—12King Solomon, in turn, gave the queen of Sheba everything she expressed a desire for, exceeding a return for what she had brought to the king. Then she and her courtiers left and returned to her own land.

13The gold that Solomon received every year weighed 666 gold talents, 14besides what traders and merchants brought, and the gold and silver

---

[a] Cf. 1 Kings 10; 11.41–43.

that all the kings of Arabia and governors of the regions brought to Solomon. ¹⁵King Solomon made 200 shields of beaten gold—600 shekels of beaten gold for each shield, ¹⁶and 300 bucklers of beaten gold—300 [shekels] of gold for each buckler. The king placed them in the Lebanon Forest House. ¹⁷The king also made a large throne of ivory, overlaid with pure gold. ¹⁸Six steps led up to the throne; and the throne had a golden footstool attached to it, and arms on either side of the seat. Two lions stood beside the arms, ¹⁹and twelve lions stood on the six steps, six on either side. None such was ever made for any other kingdom. ²⁰All of King Solomon's drinking vessels were of gold, and all the utensils of the Lebanon Forest House were of pure gold; silver counted for nothing in Solomon's days. ²¹The king's fleet traveled to Tarshish with Huram's servants. Once every three years, the Tarshish fleet came in, bearing gold and silver, ivory, apes, and peacocks.

²²King Solomon surpassed all the kings of the earth in wealth and wisdom. ²³All the kings of the earth came to pay homage to Solomon and to listen to the wisdom with which God had endowed him. ²⁴Each brought his tribute—silver and gold objects, robes, weapons, and spices, horses and mules—in the amount due each year. ²⁵Solomon had 4,000 stalls for horses and chariots, and 12,000 horsemen, which he stationed in the chariot towns and with the king in Jerusalem. ²⁶He ruled over all the kings from the Euphrates to the land of the Philistines and to the border of Egypt. ²⁷The king made silver as plentiful in Jerusalem as stones, and cedars as plentiful as sycamores in the Shephelah. ²⁸Horses were brought for Solomon from Egypt and all the lands. ²⁹The other events of Solomon's reign, early and late, are recorded in the chronicle of the prophet Nathan and in the prophecies of Ahijah the Shilonite and in the visions of Jedo the seer concerning Jeroboam son of Nebat. ³⁰Solomon reigned forty years over all Israel in Jerusalem. ³¹Solomon slept with his fathers and was buried in the city of his father David; his son Rehoboam succeeded him as king.

10

ªRehoboam went to Shechem, for all Israel had come to Shechem to acclaim him king. ²Jeroboam son of Nebat learned of it while he was in Egypt where he had fled from King Solomon, and Jeroboam returned from Egypt. ³They sent for him; and Jeroboam and all Israel came and

---

ª *Cf. 1 Kings 12.1–19.*

spoke to Rehoboam as follows: 4"Your father made our yoke heavy. Now lighten the harsh labor and the heavy yoke that your father laid on us, and we will serve you." 5He answered them, "Come back to me in three days." So the people went away.

6King Rehoboam took counsel with the elders who had served during the lifetime of his father Solomon. He said, "What answer do you counsel to give these people?" 7They answered him, "If you will be good to these people and appease them and speak to them with kind words, they will be your servants always." 8But he ignored the counsel that the elders gave him, and took counsel with the young men who had grown up with him and were serving him. 9"What," he asked, "do you counsel that we reply to these people who said to me, 'Lighten the yoke that your father laid on us'?" 10And the young men who had grown up with him answered, "Speak thus to the people who said to you, 'Your father made our yoke heavy, now you make it lighter for us.' Say to them, 'My little finger is thicker than my father's loins. 11My father imposed a heavy yoke on you, and I will add to your yoke; my father flogged you with whips, but I [will do so] with scorpions.' "

12Jeroboam and all the people came to Rehoboam on the third day, since the king had told them, "Come back on the third day." 13The king answered them harshly; thus King Rehoboam ignored the elders' counsel. 14He spoke to them in accordance with the counsel of the young men, and said, b-"I will make-b your yoke heavy, and I will add to it; my father flogged you with whips, but I [will do so] with scorpions." 15The king did not listen to the people, for God had brought it about in order that the LORD might fulfill the promise that He had made through Ahijah the Shilonite to Jeroboam son of Nebat. 16When all Israel [saw] that the king had not listened to them, the people answered the king:

> "We have no portion in David,
> No share in Jesse's son!
> To your tents, O Israel!
> Now look to your own house, O David."

So all Israel returned to their homes.c 17But Rehoboam continued to reign over the Israelites who lived in the towns of Judah. 18King Rehoboam sent out Hadoram, who was in charge of the forced labor, but the Israelites pelted him to death with stones. Thereupon, King Rehoboam hurriedly mounted his chariot and fled to Jerusalem. 19Israel has been in revolt against the house of David to this day.

b-b *Some mss. and printed editions read "my father made"; cf. 1 Kings 12.14.*
c *Lit. "tents."*

11 ªWhen Rehoboam arrived in Jerusalem, he mustered the house of Judah and Benjamin, 180,000 picked fighting men, to make war with Israel in order to restore the kingdom to Rehoboam. ²But the word of the LORD came to Shemaiah, the man of God: ³"Say to Rehoboam son of Solomon king of Judah, and to all Israel in Judah and Benjamin: ⁴Thus said the LORD: You shall not set out to make war on your kinsmen. Let every man return to his home, for this thing has been brought about by Me." They heeded the words of the LORD and refrained from marching against Jeroboam. ⁵Rehoboam dwelt in Jerusalem and built fortified towns in Judah. ⁶He built up Bethlehem, and Etam, and Tekoa, ⁷and Beth-zur, and Soco, and Adullam, ⁸and Gath, and Mareshah, and Ziph, ⁹and Adoraim, and Lachish, and Azekah, ¹⁰and Zorah, and Aijalon, and Hebron, which are in Judah and in Benjamin, as fortified towns. ¹¹He strengthened the fortified towns and put commanders in them, along with stores of food, oil, and wine, ¹²and shields and spears in every town. He strengthened them exceedingly; thus Judah and Benjamin were his.

¹³The priests and the Levites, from all their territories throughout Israel, presented themselves to him. ¹⁴The Levites had left their pasturelands and their holdings and had set out for Judah and Jerusalem, for Jeroboam and his sons had prevented them from serving the LORD, ¹⁵having appointed his own priests for the shrines, goat-demons, and calves which he had made. ¹⁶From all the tribes of Israel, those intent on seeking the LORD God of Israel followed them to Jerusalem, to sacrifice to the LORD God of their fathers. ¹⁷They strengthened the kingdom of Judah, and supported Rehoboam son of Solomon for three years, for they followed the ways of David and Solomon for three years.

¹⁸Rehoboam married Mahalath daughter of Jerimoth son of David, and Abihail daughter of Eliab son of Jesse. ¹⁹She bore him sons: Jeush, Shemariah, and Zaham. ²⁰He then took Maacah daughter of Absalom; she bore him Abijah, Attai, Ziza, and Shelomith. ²¹Rehoboam loved Maacah daughter of Absalom more than his other wives and concubines—for he took eighteen wives and sixty concubines; he begot twenty-eight sons and sixty daughters. ²²Rehoboam designated Abijah son of Maacah as chief and leader among his brothers, for he intended him to be his successor. ²³He prudently distributed all his sons throughout the regions of Judah and Benjamin and throughout the fortified towns; he provided them with abundant food, and he sought many wives for them.

ª *With 11.1–4, cf. 1 Kings 12.21–24.*

12 When the kingship of Rehoboam was firmly established, and he grew strong, he abandoned the Teaching of the LORD, he and all Israel with him.

²In the fifth year of King Rehoboam, King Shishak of Egypt marched against Jerusalem—for they had trespassed against the LORD—³with 1,200 chariots, 60,000 horsemen and innumerable troops who came with him from Egypt: Lybians, Sukkites, and Kushites. ⁴He took the fortified towns of Judah and advanced on Jerusalem. ⁵The prophet Shemaiah came to Rehoboam and the officers of Judah, who had assembled in Jerusalem because of Shishak, and said to them, "Thus said the LORD: You have abandoned Me, so I am abandoning you to Shishak." ⁶Then the officers of Israel and the king humbled themselves and declared, "The LORD is in the right." ⁷When the LORD saw that they had submitted, the word of the LORD came to Shemaiah, saying, "Since they have humbled themselves, I will not destroy them but will grant them some measure of deliverance, and My wrath will not be poured out on Jerusalem through Shishak. ⁸They will be subject to him, and they will know the difference between serving Me and serving the kingdoms of the earth." King Shishak of Egypt marched against Jerusalem. ⁹ᵃHe took away the treasures of the House of the LORD and the treasures of the royal palace; he took away everything; he took away the golden shields that Solomon had made. ¹⁰King Rehoboam had bronze shields made in their place, and entrusted them to the officers of the guardᵇ who guarded the entrance to the royal palace. ¹¹Whenever the king entered the House of the LORD, the guards would carry them and then bring them back to the armory of the guards. ¹²After he had humbled himself, the anger of the LORD was averted and He did not destroy him entirely; in Judah, too, good things were found.

¹³King Rehoboam grew strong in Jerusalem and exercised kingship. Rehoboam was forty-one years old when he became king, and he reigned seventeen years in Jerusalem—the city the LORD had chosen out of all the tribes of Israel to establish His name there. His mother's name was Naamah the Ammonitess. ¹⁴He did what was wrong, for he had not set his heart to seek the LORD. ¹⁵The deeds of Rehoboam, early and late, are recorded in the chronicles of the prophet Shemaiah and Iddo the seer, in the manner of genealogy. There was continuous war between Rehoboam and Jeroboam. ¹⁶Rehoboam slept with his fathers and was buried in the City of David. His son Abijah succeeded him as king.

ᵃ *With vv. 9–16, cf. 1 Kings 14.26–31.*
ᵇ *Lit. "runners."*

13

In the eighteenth year of King Jeroboam, Abijah became king over Judah. ²He reigned three years in Jerusalem; his mother's name was Micaiah daughter of Uriel of Gibeah. There was war between Abijah and Jeroboam. ³Abijah joined battle with a force of warriors, 400,000 picked men. Jeroboam arrayed for battle against him 800,000 picked men, warriors. ⁴Abijah stood on top of Mount Zemaraim in the hill country of Ephraim and said, "Listen to me, Jeroboam and all Israel. ⁵Surely you know that the LORD God of Israel gave David kingship over Israel forever—to him and his sons—by a covenant of salt. ⁶Jeroboam son of Nebat had been in the service of Solomon son of David, but he rose up and rebelled against his master. ⁷Riffraff and scoundrels gathered around him and pressed hard upon Rehoboam son of Solomon. Rehoboam was inexperienced and fainthearted and could not stand up to them. ⁸Now you are bent on opposing the kingdom of the LORD, which is in the charge of the sons of David, because you are a great multitude and possess the golden calves that Jeroboam made for you as gods. ⁹Did you not banish the priests of the LORD, the sons of Aaron and the Levites, and, like the peoples of the land, appoint your own priests? Anyone who offered himself for ordination with a young bull of the herd and seven rams became a priest of no-gods! ¹⁰As for us, the LORD is our God, and we have not forsaken Him. The priests who minister to the LORD are the sons of Aaron, and the Levites are at their tasks. ¹¹They offer burnt offerings in smoke each morning and each evening, and the aromatic incense, the rows of bread on the pure table; they kindle the golden lampstand with its lamps burning each evening, for we keep the charge of the LORD our God, while you have forsaken it. ¹²See, God is with us as our chief, and His priests have the trumpets for sounding blasts against you. O children of Israel, do not fight the LORD God of your fathers, because you will not succeed." ¹³Jeroboam, however, had directed the ambush to go around and come from the rear, thus ᵃ⁻the main body was⁻ᵃ in front of Judah, while the ambush was behind them. ¹⁴When Judah turned around and saw that the fighting was before and behind them, they cried out to the LORD, and the priests blew the trumpets. ¹⁵The men of Judah raised a shout; and when the men of Judah raised a shout, God routed Jeroboam and all Israel before Abijah and Judah. ¹⁶The Israelites fled before Judah, and God delivered them into their hands. ¹⁷Abijah and his army inflicted a severe defeat on them; 500,000 men of Israel fell slain. ¹⁸The Israelites

---

ᵃ⁻ᵃ Lit. "they were."

were crushed at that time, while the people of Judah triumphed because they relied on the LORD God of their fathers. 19Abijah pursued Jeroboam and captured some of his cities—Bethel with its dependencies, Jeshanah with its dependencies, and Ephrain with its dependencies. 20Jeroboam could not muster strength again during the days of Abijah. The LORD struck him down and he died. 21But Abijah grew powerful; he married fourteen wives and begat twenty-two sons and sixteen daughters.

22The other events of Abijah's reign, his conduct and his acts, are recorded in the story of the prophet Iddo. 23Abijah slept with his fathers and was buried in the City of David; his son Asa succeeded him as king. The land was untroubled for ten years.

14 Asa did what was good and pleasing to the LORD his God. 2He abolished the alien altars and shrines; he smashed the pillars and cut down the sacred posts. 3He ordered Judah to turn to the LORD God of their fathers and to observe the Teaching and the Commandment. 4He abolished the shrines and the incense stands throughout the cities of Judah, and the kingdom was untroubled under him. 5He built fortified towns in Judah, since the land was untroubled and he was not engaged in warfare during those years, for the LORD had granted him respite. 6He said to Judah, "Let us build up these cities and surround them with walls and towers, gates and bars, while the land is at our disposal because we turned to the LORD our God—we turned [to Him] and He gave us respite on all sides." They were successful in their building.

7Asa had an army of 300,000 men from Judah bearing shields and spears, and 280,000 from Benjamin bearing bucklers and drawing the bow; all these were valiant men. 8Zerah the Cushite marched out against them with an army of a thousand thousand and 300 chariots. When he reached Mareshah 9Asa confronted him, and the battle lines were drawn in the valley of Zephat by Mareshah. 10Asa called to the LORD his God, and said, "O LORD, it is all the same to You to help the numerous and the powerless. Help us, O LORD our God, for we rely on You, and in Your name we have come against this great multitude. You are the LORD our God. Let no mortal hinder You." 11So the LORD routed the Cushites before Asa and Judah, and the Cushites fled. 12Asa and the army with him pursued them as far as Gerar. Many of the Cushites fell wounded beyond recovery, for they broke before the LORD and His camp. Very much spoil was taken. ¹³All the cities in the vicinity of Gerar were ravaged, for a terror of the LORD seized them. All the cities were plundered, and they yielded much booty. ¹⁴They also ravaged the encampment of herdsmen, capturing much sheep and camels. Then they returned to Jerusalem.

15 The spirit of God came upon Azariah son of Oded. ²He came to Asa and said to him, "Listen to me, Asa and all Judah and Benjamin; the LORD is with you as long as you are with Him. If you turn to Him, He will respond to you, but if you forsake Him, He will forsake you. ³Israel has gone many days without the true God, without a priest to give instruction and without Teaching. ⁴But in distress it returned to the LORD God of Israel, and sought Him, and He responded to them. ⁵At those times, ᵃ⁻no wayfarer⁻ᵃ was safe, for there was much tumult among all the inhabitants of the lands. ⁶Nation was crushed by nation and city by city, for God threw them into panic with every kind of trouble. ⁷As for you, be strong, do not be disheartened, for there is reward for your labor."

⁸When Asa heard these words, the prophecy of Oded the prophet, he took courage and removed the abominations from the entire land of Judah and Benjamin and from the cities that he had captured in the hill country of Ephraim. He restored the altar of the LORD in front of the porch of the LORD. ⁹He assembled all the people of Judah and Benjamin and those people of Ephraim, Manasseh, and Simeon who sojourned among them, for many in Israel had thrown in their lot with him when they saw that the LORD his God was with him. ¹⁰They were assembled in Jerusalem in the third month of the fifteenth year of the reign of Asa. ¹¹They brought sacrifices to the LORD on that day; they brought 700 oxen and 7,000 sheep of the spoil. ¹²They entered into a covenant to worship the LORD God of their fathers with all their heart and with all their soul. ¹³Whoever would not worship the LORD God of Israel would be put to death, whether small or great, whether man or woman. ¹⁴So they took an oath to the LORD in a loud voice and with shouts, with trumpeting and blasts of the horn. ¹⁵All Judah rejoiced over the oath, for they swore with all their heart and sought Him with all their will. He responded to them and gave them respite on every side.

¹⁶ᵇHeᶜ also deposed Maacah mother of King Asa from the rank of queen mother, because she had made an abominable thing for [the goddess] Asherah. Asa cut down her abominable thing, reduced it to dust,

---

ᵃ⁻ᵃ *Lit. "one who goes out and one who comes in."*
ᵇ *With vv. 16–19, cf. 1 Kings 15.13–16.*
ᶜ *I.e., Asa.*

and burned it in the Wadi Kidron. ¹⁷The shrines, indeed, were not abolished in Israel; however, Asa was wholehearted [with the LORD] all his life. ¹⁸He brought into the House of God the things that he and his father had consecrated—silver, gold, and utensils. ¹⁹There was no war until the thirty-fifth year of the reign of Asa.

16 ᵃIn the thirty-sixth year of the reign of Asa, King Baasha of Israel marched against Judah and built up Ramah to block ᵇ⁻all movement⁻ᵇ of King Asa of Judah. ²Asa took all the silver and gold from the treasuries of the House of the LORD and the royal palace, and sent them to King Ben-hadad of Aram, who resided in Damascus, with this message: ³"There is a pact between me and you, as there was between my father and your father. I herewith send you silver and gold; go and break your pact with King Baasha of Israel so that he may withdraw from me." ⁴Ben-hadad acceded to King Asa's request; he sent his army commanders against the towns of Israel and ravaged Ijon, Dan, Abel-maim, and all the garrison towns of Naphtali. ⁵When Baasha heard about it, he stopped building up Ramah and put an end to the work on it. ⁶Then King Asa mustered all Judah, and they carried away the stones and timber with which Baasha had built up Ramah; with these King Asa built up Geba and Mizpah.

⁷At that time, Hanani the seer came to King Asa of Judah and said to him, "Because you relied on the king of Aram and did not rely on the LORD your God, therefore the army of the king of Aram has slipped out of your hands. ⁸The Cushites and Lybians were a mighty army with chariots and horsemen in very great numbers, yet because you relied on the LORD He delivered them into your hands. ⁹For the eyes of the LORD range over the entire earth, to give support to those who are wholeheartedly with Him. You have acted foolishly in this matter, and henceforth you will be beset by wars." ¹⁰Asa was vexed at the seer and put him into the stocks,ᶜ for he was furious with him because of that. Asa inflicted cruelties on some of the people at that time.

¹¹The acts of Asa, early and late, are recorded in the annals of the kings of Judah and Israel. ¹²In the thirty-ninth year of his reign, Asa suffered from an acute foot ailment; but ill as he was, he still did not turn to the LORD but to physicians. ¹³Asa slept with his fathers. He died in the forty-first year of his reign ¹⁴and was buried in the grave that he had made for himself in the City of David. He was laid in his resting-place, which was

---

ᵃ Cf. 1 Kings 15.17–24.
ᵇ⁻ᵇ Lit. "one who goes out and one who comes in."
ᶜ Meaning of Heb. uncertain.

filled with spices of all kinds, expertly blended; a very great fire was made in his honor.

17 His son Jehoshaphat succeeded him as king, and took firm hold of Israel. ²He stationed troops in all the fortified towns of Judah, and stationed garrisons throughout the land of Judah and the cities of Ephraim which his father Asa had captured. ³The LORD was with Jehoshaphat because he followed the earlier ways of his father David, and did not worship the Baalim, ⁴but worshiped the God of his father and followed His commandments—unlike the behavior of Israel. ⁵So the LORD established the kingdom in his hands, and all Judah gave presents to Jehoshaphat. He had wealth and glory in abundance. ⁶His mind was elevated in the ways of the LORD. Moreover, he abolished the shrines and the sacred posts from Judah.

⁷In the third year of his reign he sent his officers Ben-hail, Obadiah, Zechariah, Nethanel, and Micaiah throughout the cities of Judah to offer instruction. ⁸With them were the Levites, Shemaiah, Nethaniah, Zebadiah, Asahel, Shemiramoth, Jehonathan, Adonijah, Tobijah and Tobadonijah the Levites; with them were Elishama and Jehoram the priests. ⁹They offered instruction throughout Judah, having with them the Book of the Teaching of the LORD. They made the rounds of all the cities of the LORD and instructed the people. ¹⁰A terror of the LORD seized all the kingdoms of the lands around Judah, and they did not go to war with Jehoshaphat. ¹¹From Philistia a load of silver was brought to Jehoshaphat as tribute. The Arabs, too, brought him flocks: 7,700 rams and 7,700 he-goats. ¹²Jehoshaphat grew greater and greater, and he built up fortresses and garrison towns in Judah. ¹³He carried out extensive works in the towns of Judah, and had soldiers, valiant men, in Jerusalem. ¹⁴They were enrolled according to their clans. Judah: chiefs of thousands, Adnah the chief, who had 300,000 valiant men; ¹⁵next to him was Jehohanan the captain, who had 280,000; ¹⁶next to him was Amasiah son of Zichri, who made a freewill offering to the LORD. He had 200,000 valiant men. ¹⁷Benjamin: Eliada, a valiant man, who had 200,000 men armed with bow and buckler; ¹⁸next to him was Jehozabad, who had 180,000 armed men. ¹⁹These served the king, besides those whom the king assigned to the fortified towns throughout Judah.

18

¹ᵃSo Jehoshaphat had wealth and honor in abundance, and he allied himself by marriage to Ahab. ²After some years had passed, he came to visit Ahab at Samaria. Ahab slaughtered sheep and oxen in abundance for him and for the people with him, and persuaded him to march against Ramoth-gilead. ³King Ahab of Israel said to King Jehoshaphat of Judah, "Will you accompany me to Ramoth-gilead?" He answered him, "I will do what you do; my troops shall be your troops and shall accompany you in battle." ⁴Jehoshaphat then said to the king of Israel, "But first inquire for the word of the LORD."

⁵So the king of Israel gathered the prophets, four hundred men, and asked them, "Shall I march upon Ramoth-gilead for battle, or shall I not?" "March," they said, "and God will deliver it into the king's hands." ⁶Then Jehoshaphat asked, "Is there not another prophet of the LORD here through whom we can inquire?" ⁷And the king of Israel answered Jehoshaphat, "There is one more man through whom we can inquire of the LORD; but I hate him, because he never prophesies anything good for me but always misfortune. He is Micaiah son of Imlah." Jehoshaphat replied, "Let the king not say such a thing." ⁸So the king of Israel summoned an officer and said, "Bring Micaiah son of Imlah at once."

⁹The king of Israel and King Jehoshaphat of Judah, wearing their robes, were seated on their thrones situated in the threshing floor at the entrance of the gate of Samaria; and all the prophets were prophesying before them. ¹⁰Zedekiah son of Chenaanah had provided himself with iron horns; and he said, "Thus said the LORD: With these you shall gore the Arameans till you make an end of them." ¹¹All the other prophets were prophesying similarly, "March against Ramoth-gilead and be victorious! The LORD will deliver it into Your Majesty's hands."

¹²The messenger who had gone to summon Micaiah said to him, "Look, the words of the prophets are unanimously favorable to the king. Let your word be like that of the rest of them; speak a favorable word." ¹³"By the life of the LORD," Micaiah answered, "I will speak only what my God tells me." ¹⁴When he came before the king, the king said to him, "Micah,ᵇ shall we march against Ramoth-gilead for battle or shall we not?" He answered him, "March and be victorious! They will be delivered into your hands." ¹⁵The king said to him, "How many times must I adjure you to tell me nothing but the truth in the name of the LORD?" ¹⁶Then he said,

---

ᵃ *Cf. 1 Kings 22.*
ᵇ *A shortened form of Micaiah.*

"I saw all Israel scattered over the hills like sheep without a shepherd; and the LORD said, 'These have no master; let everyone return to his home in safety.' " 17The king of Israel said to Jehoshaphat, "Did I not tell you that he would not prophesy good fortune for me, but only misfortune?"

18Then [Micaiah] said, "Indeed, hear now the word of the LORD! I saw the LORD seated upon His throne, with all the host of heaven standing in attendance to the right and to the left of Him. 19The LORD asked, 'Who will entice King Ahab of Israel so that he will march and fall at Ramoth-gilead?' Then one said this and another said that, 20until a certain spirit came forward and stood before the LORD and said, 'I will entice him.' 'How?' said the LORD to him. 21And he replied, 'I will go forth and become a lying spirit in the mouth of all his prophets.' Then He said, 'You will entice with success. Go forth and do it.' 22Thus the LORD has put a lying spirit in the mouth of all these prophets of yours; for the LORD has decreed misfortune for you."

23Thereupon Zedekiah son of Chenaanah came up and struck Micaiah on the cheek, and exclaimed, "However did the spirit of the LORD pass from me to speak with you!" 24Micaiah replied, "You will see on the day when you try to hide in the innermost room." 25Then the king of Israel said, "Take Micaiah and turn him over to Amon, the governor of the city, and to Prince Joash, 26and say, 'The king's orders are: Put this fellow in prison, and let his fare be scant bread and scant water until I come home safe.' " 27To which Micaiah retorted, "If you ever come home safe, the LORD has not spoken through me." He said further, c-"Listen, all you peoples!"-c

28The king of Israel and King Jehoshaphat of Judah marched against Ramoth-gilead. 29The king of Israel said to Jehoshaphat, d-"I will disguise myself and go-d into the battle, but you, wear your robes." So the king of Israel disguised himself, and they went into the battle. 30The king of Aram had given these instructions to his chariot officers: "Do not attack anyone, small or great, except the king of Israel." 31When the chariot officers saw Jehoshaphat, whom they took for the king of Israel, they wheeled around to attack him, and Jehoshaphat cried out and the LORD helped him, and God diverted them from him. 32And when the chariot officers realized that he was not the king of Israel, they gave up the pursuit. 33Then a man drew his bow at random and hit the king of Israel between the e-plates of the-e armor and he said to his charioteer, "Turn around

c-c Cf. Mic. 1.2.
d-d Infinitives used for finite verb; cf. note at 1 Kings 22.30.
e-e Meaning of Heb. uncertain.

and get me behind the lines; I am wounded." ³⁴The battle ᶜ⁻raged all day long,⁻ᶜ and the king remained propped up in the chariot facing Aram until dusk; he died as the sun was setting.

19 King Jehoshaphat of Judah returned safely to his palace, to Jerusalem. ²Jehu son of Hanani the seer went out to meet King Jehoshaphat and said to him, "Should one give aid to the wicked and befriend those who hate the LORD? For this, wrath is upon you from the LORD. ³However, there is some good in you, for you have purged the land of the sacred posts and have dedicated yourself to worship God."

⁴Jehoshaphat remained in Jerusalem a while and then went out among the people from Beer-sheba to the hill country of Ephraim; he brought them back to the LORD God of their fathers. ⁵He appointed judges in the land in all the fortified towns of Judah, in each and every town. ⁶He charged the judges: "Consider what you are doing, for you judge not on behalf of man, but on behalf of the LORD, and He is with you when you pass judgment. ⁷Now let the dread of the LORD be upon you; act with care, for there is no injustice or favoritism or bribe-taking with the LORD our God." ⁸Jehoshaphat also appointed in Jerusalem some Levites and priests and heads of the clans of Israelites for rendering judgment in matters of the LORD, and for disputes. Then they returned to Jerusalem. ⁹He charged them, "This is how you shall act: in fear of the LORD, with fidelity, and with whole heart. ¹⁰When a dispute comes before you from your brothers living in their towns, whether about homicide, or about ritual, or laws or rules, you must instruct them so that they do not incur guilt before the LORD and wrath be upon you and your brothers. Act so and you will not incur guilt. ¹¹See, Amariah the chief priest is over you in all cases concerning the LORD, and Zebadiah son of Ishmael is the commander of the house of Judah in all cases concerning the king; the Levitical officials are at your disposal; act with resolve and the LORD be with the good."

20 After that, Moabites, Ammonites, together with some Ammonim,ᵃ came against Jehoshaphat to wage war. ²The report was brought to Jehoshaphat: "A great multitude is coming against you from beyond the sea, from Aram, and is now in Hazazon-tamar"—that is, Ein-gedi.

ᵃ *Probably for* mʻnym *"Meunites" (1 Chron. 4.41); cf. Kimhi.*

³Jehoshaphat was afraid; he decided to resort to the LORD and proclaimed a fast for all Judah. ⁴Judah assembled to beseech the LORD. They also came from all the towns of Judah to seek the LORD.

⁵Jehoshaphat stood in the congregation of Judah and Jerusalem in the House of the LORD at the front of the new court. ⁶He said, "LORD God of our fathers, truly You are the God in heaven and You rule over the kingdoms of the nations; power and strength are Yours; none can oppose You. ⁷O our God, you dispossessed the inhabitants of this land before Your people Israel, and You gave it to the descendants of Your friend Abraham forever. ⁸They settled in it and in it built for You a House for Your name. They said, ⁹'Should misfortune befall us—the punishing sword, pestilence, or famine, we shall stand before this House and before You—for Your name is in this House—and we shall cry out to You in our distress, and You will listen and deliver us.' ¹⁰Now the people of Ammon, Moab, and the hill country of Seir, into whose [land] You did not let Israel come when they came from Egypt, but they turned aside from them and did not wipe them out, ¹¹these now repay us by coming to expel us from Your possession which You gave us as ours. ¹²O our God, surely You will punish them, for we are powerless before this great multitude that has come against us, and do not know what to do, but our eyes are on You." ¹³All Judah stood before the LORD with their little ones, their womenfolk, and their children.

¹⁴Then in the midst of the congregation the spirit of the LORD came upon Jahaziel son of Zechariah son of Benaiah son of Jeiel son of Mattaniah the Levite, of the sons of Asaph, ¹⁵and he said, "Give heed, all Judah and the inhabitants of Jerusalem and King Jehoshaphat; thus said the LORD to you, 'Do not fear or be dismayed by this great multitude, for the battle is God's, not yours. ¹⁶March down against them tomorrow as they come up by the Ascent of Ziz; you will find them at the end of the wadi in the direction of the wilderness of Jeruel. ¹⁷It is not for you to fight this battle; stand by, wait, and witness your deliverance by the LORD, O Judah and Jerusalem; do not fear or be dismayed; go forth to meet them tomorrow and the LORD will be with you.' " ¹⁸Jehoshaphat bowed low with his face to the ground, and all Judah and the inhabitants of Jerusalem threw themselves down before the LORD to worship the LORD. ¹⁹Levites of the sons of Kohath and of the sons of Korah got up to extol the LORD God of Israel at the top of their voices.

²⁰Early the next morning they arose and went forth to the wilderness

of Tekoa. As they went forth, Jehoshaphat stood and said, "Listen to me, O Judah and inhabitants of Jerusalem: Trust firmly in the LORD your God and you will stand firm; trust firmly in His prophets and you will succeed." 21After taking counsel with the people, he stationed singers to the LORD extolling the One majestic in holiness as they went forth ahead of the vanguard, saying, "Praise the LORD, for His steadfast love is eternal." 22As they began their joyous shouts and hymns, the LORD set ambushes for the men of Amon, Moab, and the hill country of Seir, who were marching against Judah, and they were routed. 23The Ammonites and Moabites turned against the men of the hill country of Seir to exterminate and annihilate them. When they had made an end of the men of Seir, each helped to destroy his fellow.

24When Judah reached the lookout in the wilderness and looked for the multitude, they saw them lying on the ground as corpses; not one had survived. 25Jehoshaphat and his army came to take the booty, and found an abundance of goods, corpses, and precious objects, which they pillaged, more than they could carry off. For three days they were taking booty, there was so much of it. 26On the fourth day they assembled in the Valley of Blessing—for there they blessed the LORD; that is why that place is called the Valley of Blessing to this day. 27All the men of Judah and Jerusalem with Jehoshaphat at their head returned joyfully to Jerusalem, for the LORD had given them cause for rejoicing over their enemies. 28They came to Jerusalem to the House of the LORD, to the accompaniment of harps, lyres, and trumpets. 29The terror of God seized all the kingdoms of the lands when they heard that the LORD had fought the enemies of Israel. 30The kingdom of Jehoshaphat was untroubled, and his God granted him respite on all sides.

31bJehoshaphat reigned over Judah. He was thirty-five years old when he became king, and he reigned in Jerusalem for twenty-five years. His mother's name was Azubah daughter of Shilhi. 32He followed the course of his father Asa and did not deviate from it, doing what was pleasing to the LORD. 33However, the shrines did not cease; the people still did not direct their heart toward the God of their fathers. 34As for the other events of Jehoshaphat's reign, early and late, they are recorded in the annals of Jehu son of Hanani, which were included in the book of the kings of Israel.

35Afterward, King Jehoshaphat of Judah entered into a partnership with King Ahaziah of Israel, thereby acting wickedly. 36He joined with him in

b *With vv. 31–37, cf. 1 Kings 22.41–49.*

constructing ships to go to Tarshish; the ships were constructed in Ezion-geber. [37]Eliezer son of Dodavahu of Mareshah prophesied against Jehosh-aphat, "As you have made a partnership with Ahaziah, the LORD will break up your work." The ships were wrecked and were unable to go to Tarshish.

21 [a]Jehoshaphat slept with his fathers and was buried with his fathers in the City of David; his son Jehoram succeeded him as king. [2]He had brothers, sons of Jehoshaphat: Azariah, Jehiel, Zechariah, Azariahu, Mi-chael, and Shephatiah; all these were sons of King Jehoshaphat of Israel. [3]Their father gave them many gifts of silver, gold, and [other] presents, as well as fortified towns in Judah, but he gave the kingdom to Jehoram because he was the first-born.

[4]Jehoram proceeded to take firm hold of his father's kingdom and put to the sword all his brothers, as well as some of the officers of Israel. [5]Jehoram was thirty-two years old when he became king, and he reigned in Jerusalem eight years. [6]He followed the practices of the kings of Israel doing what the House of Ahab had done, for he married a daughter of Ahab; he did what was displeasing to the LORD. [7]However, the LORD refrained from destroying the House of David for the sake of the covenant he had made with David, and in accordance with his promise to maintain a lamp for him and his descendants for all time. [8]During his reign, the Edomites rebelled against Judah's rule and set up a king of their own. [9]Jehoram advanced [against them] with his officers and all his chariotry. He arose by night and attacked the Edomites, who surrounded him and the chariot commanders. [10]Edom has been in rebellion against Judah, to this day; Libnah also rebelled against him at that time, because he had forsaken the LORD God of his fathers. [11]Moreover, he built shrines in the hill country of Judah; he led astray the inhabitants of Jerusalem and made Judah wayward.

[12]A letter from Elijah the prophet came to him which read, "Thus says the LORD God of your father David: Since you have not followed the practices of your father Jehoshaphat and the practices of King Asa of Judah, [13]but have followed the practices of the kings of Israel, leading astray Judah and the inhabitants of Jerusalem as the House of Ahab led them astray, and have also killed your brothers of your father's house, who were better than you, [14]therefore, the LORD will inflict a great blow

a Cf. 2 Kings 8.17–24.

upon your people, your sons, and your wives and all your possessions. [15]As for you, you will be severely stricken with a disorder of the bowels year after year until your bowels drop out."

[16]The LORD stirred up the spirit of the Philistines and the Arabs who were neighbors of the Cushites against Jehoram. [17]They marched against Judah, breached its defenses, and carried off all the property that was found in the king's palace, as well as his sons and his wives. The only son who remained was Jehoahaz, his youngest. [18]After this, the LORD afflicted him with an incurable disease of the bowels. [19]Some years later, when a period of two years had elapsed, his bowels dropped out because of his disease, and he died a gruesome death. His people did not make a fire for him like the fire for his fathers. [20]He was thirty-two years old when he became king, and he reigned in Jerusalem eight years. He departed unpraised,[b] and was buried in the City of David, but not in the tombs of the kings.

22 [a]The inhabitants of Jerusalem made Ahaziah, his youngest son, king in his stead, because all the older ones had been killed by the troops that penetrated the camp with the Arabs. Ahaziah son of Jehoram reigned as king of Judah. [2]Ahaziah was forty-two years old when he became king, and he reigned in Jerusalem one year; his mother's name was Athaliah daughter of Omri. [3]He too followed the practices of the house of Ahab, for his mother counseled him to do evil. [4]He did what was displeasing to the LORD, like the house of Ahab, for they became his counselors after his father's death, to his ruination. [5]Moreover, he followed their counsel and marched with Jehoram son of King Ahab of Israel to battle against King Hazael of Aram at Ramoth-gilead, where the Arameans wounded Joram. [6]He returned to Jezreel to recover from the wounds inflicted on him at Ramah when he fought against King Hazael of Aram. King Azariah son of Jehoram of Judah went down to Jezreel to visit Jehoram son of Ahab while he was ill. [7]The LORD caused the downfall of Ahaziah because he visited Joram. During his visit he went out with Jehoram to Jehu son of Nimshi, whom the LORD had anointed to cut off the house of Ahab. [8]In the course of bringing the house of Ahab to judgment, Jehu came upon the officers of Judah and the nephews of Ahaziah, ministers of Ahaziah, and killed them. [9]He sent in search of Ahaziah, who was caught hiding in Samaria, was brought to Jehu, and put to death. He was

---

[b] Following Septuagint; cf. Arabic ḥamada, "praise."

[a] With vv. 1–6, cf. 2 Kings 8.25–29; with vv. 8–9, cf. 2 Kings 9.27–28; with vv. 10–12, cf. 2 Kings 11.1–3.

given a burial, because it was said, "He is the son of Jehoshaphat who worshiped the LORD wholeheartedly." So the house of Ahaziah could not muster the strength to rule.

10When Athaliah, Ahaziah's mother, learned that her son was dead, she promptly did away with all who were of the royal stock of the house of Judah. 11But Jehoshabeath, daughter of the king, spirited away Ahaziah's son Joash from among the princes who were being slain, and put him and his nurse in a bedroom. Jehoshabeath, daughter of King Jehoram, wife of the priest Jehoiada—she was the sister of Ahaziah—kept him hidden from Athaliah so that he was not put to death. 12He stayed with them for six years, hidden in the House of God, while Athaliah reigned over the land.

23 aIn the seventh year, Jehoiada took courage and brought the chiefs of the hundreds, Azariah son of Jeroham, Ishmael son of Jehohanan, Azariah son of Obed, Maaseiah son of Adaiah, and Elishaphat son of Zichri, into a compact with him. 2They went through Judah and assembled the Levites from all the towns of Judah, and the chiefs of the clans of Israel. They came to Jerusalem 3and the entire assembly made a covenant with the king in the House of God. Heb said to them, "The son of the king shall be king according to the promise the LORD made concerning the sons of David. 4This is what you must do: One third of you, priests and Levites, who are on duty for the week, shall be gatekeepers at the thresholds; 5another third shall be stationed in the royal palace, and the other third at the Foundation Gate. All the people shall be in the courts of the House of the LORD. 6Let no one enter the House of the LORD except the priests and the ministering Levites. They may enter because they are sanctified, but all the people shall obey the proscription of the LORD. 7The Levites shall surround the king on every side, every man with his weapons at the ready; and whoever enters the House shall be killed. Stay close to the king in his comings and goings." 8The Levites and all Judah did just as Jehoiada the priest ordered: each took his men— those who were on duty that week and those who were off duty that week, for Jehoiada the priest had not dismissed the divisions. 9Jehoiada the priest gave the chiefs of the hundreds King David's spears and shields and quivers that were kept in the House of God. 10He stationed the entire force, each man with his weapons at the ready, from the south end of the

---

a *Cf. 2 Kings 11.4–20.*
b *I.e., Jehoiada.*

House to the north end of the House, at the altar and the House, to guard the king on every side. [11]Then they brought out the king's son, and placed upon him the crown and the insignia. They proclaimed him king, and Jehoiada and his sons anointed him and shouted, "Long live the king!"

[12]When Athaliah heard the shouting of the people and the guards and the acclamation of the king, she came out to the people, to the House of the LORD. [13]She looked about and saw the king standing by his pillar at the entrance, the chiefs with their trumpets beside the king, and all the people of the land rejoicing and blowing trumpets, and the singers with musical instruments leading the hymns. Athaliah rent her garments and cried out, "Treason, treason!" [14]Then the priest Jehoiada ordered out the army officers, the chiefs of hundreds, and said to them, "Take her out between the ranks, and if anyone follows her, put him to the sword." For the priest thought, "Let her not be put to death in the House of the LORD." [15]They cleared a passage for her and she came to the entrance of the Horse Gate to the royal palace; there she was put to death.

[16]Then Jehoiada solemnized a covenant between himself and the people and the king that they should be the people of the LORD. [17]All the people then went to the temple of Baal; they tore it down and smashed its altars and images to bits, and they slew Mattan, the priest of Baal, in front of the altars. [18]Jehoiada put the officers of the House of the LORD in the charge of Levite priests whom David had assigned over the House of the LORD to offer up burnt offerings, as is prescribed in the Teaching of Moses, accompanied by joyful song as ordained by David. [19]He stationed the gatekeepers at the gates of the House of the LORD to prevent the entry of anyone unclean for any reason. [20]He took the chiefs of hundreds, the nobles, and the rulers of the people and all the people of the land, and they escorted the king down from the House of the LORD into the royal palace by the upper gate, and seated the king on the royal throne. [21]All the people of the land rejoiced, and the city was quiet. As for Athaliah, she had been put to the sword.

24

[a]Jehoash was seven years old when he became king, and he reigned in Jerusalem forty years. His mother's name was Zibiah of Beer-sheba. [2]All the days of the priest Jehoiada, Jehoash did what was pleasing to the

---

[a] Cf. 2 Kings 12.1–22.

LORD. ³Jehoiada took two wives for him, by whom he had sons and daughters.

⁴Afterward, Joash decided to renovate the House of the LORD. ⁵He assembled the priests and the Levites and charged them as follows: "Go out to the towns of Judah and collect money from all Israel for the annual repair of the House of your God. Do it quickly." But the Levites did not act quickly. ⁶The king summoned Jehoiada the chief and said to him, "Why have you not seen to it that the Levites brought the tax imposed by Moses, the servant of the LORD, and the congregation of Israel from Judah and Jerusalem to the Tent of the Pact?" ⁷For the children of the wicked Athaliah had violated the House of God and had even used the sacred things of the House of the LORD for the Baals. ⁸The king ordered that a chest be made and placed on the outside of the gate of the House of the LORD. ⁹A proclamation was issued in Judah and Jerusalem to bring the tax imposed on Israel in the wilderness by Moses, the servant of God. ¹⁰All the officers and all the people gladly brought it and threw it into the chest till it was full. ¹¹Whenever the chest was brought to the royal officers by the Levites, and they saw that it contained much money, the royal scribe and the agent of the chief priest came and emptied out the chest and carried it back to its place. They did this day by day, and much money was collected. ¹²The king and Jehoiada delivered the money to those who oversaw the tasks connected with the work of the House of the LORD. They hired masons and carpenters to renovate the House of the LORD, as well as craftsmen in iron and bronze to repair the House of the LORD. ¹³The overseers did their work; under them the work went well and they restored the House of God to its original form and repaired it. ¹⁴When they had finished, they brought the money that was left over to the king and Jehoiada; it was made into utensils for the House of the LORD, service vessels: buckets and ladles, golden and silver vessels. Burnt offerings were offered up regularly in the House of the LORD all the days of Jehoiada. ¹⁵Jehoiada reached a ripe old age and died; he was one hundred and thirty years old at his death. ¹⁶They buried him in the City of David together with the kings, because he had done good in Israel, and on behalf of God and His House.

¹⁷But after the death of Jehoiada, the officers of Judah came, bowing low to the king; and the king listened to them. ¹⁸They forsook the House of the LORD God of their fathers to serve the sacred posts and idols; and

there was wrath upon Judah and Jerusalem because of this guilt of theirs. [19]The LORD sent prophets among them to bring them back to Him; they admonished them but they would not pay heed. [20]Then the spirit of God enveloped Zechariah son of Jehoiada the priest; he stood above the people and said to them, "Thus God said: Why do you transgress the commandments of the LORD when you cannot succeed? Since you have forsaken the LORD, He has forsaken you." [21]They conspired against him and pelted him with stones in the court of the House of the LORD, by order of the king. [22]King Joash disregarded the loyalty that his father Jehoiada had shown to him, and killed his son. As he was dying, he said, "May the LORD see and requite it."

[23]At the turn of the year, the army of Aram marched against him; they invaded Judah and Jerusalem, and wiped out all the officers of the people from among the people, and sent all the booty they took to the king of Damascus. [24]The invading army of Aram had come with but a few men, but the LORD delivered a very large army into their hands, because they had forsaken the LORD God of their fathers. They inflicted punishments on Joash. [25]When they withdrew, having left him with many wounds, his courtiers plotted against him because of the murder[b] of the sons of Jehoiada the priest, and they killed him in bed. He died and was buried in the City of David; he was not buried in the tombs of the kings. [26]These were the men who conspired against him: Zabad son of Shimeath the Ammonitess, and Jehozabad son of Shimrith the Moabitess. [27]As to his sons, and the many pronouncements against him, and his rebuilding of the House of God, they are recorded in the story in the book of the kings. His son Amaziah succeeded him as king.

25 [a]Amaziah was twenty-five years old when he became king, and he reigned twenty-nine years in Jerusalem; his mother's name was Jehoaddan of Jerusalem. [2]He did what was pleasing to the LORD, but not with a whole heart. [3]Once he had the kingdom firmly under control, he executed the courtiers who had assassinated his father the king. [4]But he did not put their children to death for [he acted] in accordance with what is written in the Teaching, in the Book of Moses, where the LORD commanded, [b]-"Parents shall not die for children, nor shall children die for parents, but every person shall die only for his own crime."-[b]

[5]Amaziah assembled the men of Judah, and he put all the men of Judah

---

[b] Lit. "blood."

[a] Cf. 2 Kings 14.
[b-b] Cf. Deut. 24.16.

and Benjamin under officers of thousands and officers of hundreds, by clans. He mustered them from the age of twenty upward, and found them to be 300,000 picked men fit for service, able to bear spear and shield. 6He hired 100,000 warriors from Israel for 100 talents of silver. 7Then a man of God came to him and said, "O king! Do not let the army of Israel go with you, for the LORD is not with Israel—all these Ephraimites. 8But go by yourself and do it; take courage for battle, [else] God will make you fall before the enemy. For in God there is power to help one or make one fall!" 9Amaziah said to the man of God, "And what am I to do about the 100 talents I gave for the Israelite force?" The man of God replied, "The LORD has the means to give you much more than that." 10So Amaziah detached the force that came to him from Ephraim, [ordering them] to go back to their place. They were greatly enraged against Judah and returned to their place in a rage.

11Amaziah took courage and, leading his army, he marched to the Valley of Salt. He slew 10,000 men of Seir; 12another 10,000 the men of Judah captured alive and brought to the top of Sela. They threw them down from the top of Sela and every one of them was burst open. 13The men of the force that Amaziah had sent back so they would not go with him into battle made forays against the towns of Judah from Samaria to Beth-horon. They slew 3,000 of them, and took much booty.

14After Amaziah returned from defeating the Edomites, he had the gods of the men of Seir brought, and installed them as his gods; he prostrated himself before them, and to them he made sacrifice. 15The LORD was enraged at Amaziah, and sent a prophet to him who said to him, "Why are you worshiping the gods of a people who could not save their people from you?" 16As he spoke to him, [Amaziah] said to him, "Have we appointed you a counselor to the king? Stop, else you will be killed!" The prophet stopped, saying, "I see God has counseled that you be destroyed, since you act this way and disregard my counsel."

17Then King Amaziah of Judah took counsel and sent this message to Joash son of Jehoahaz son of Jehu, king of Israel, "Come, let us confront each other!" 18King Joash of Israel sent back this message to King Amaziah of Judah, "The thistle in Lebanon sent this message to the cedar in Lebanon, 'Give your daughter to my son in marriage.' But a wild beast in Lebanon passed by and trampled the thistle. 19You boast that you have defeated the Edomites and you are ambitious to get more glory. Now stay at home, lest, provoking disaster you fall, dragging Judah down with you." 20But Amaziah paid no heed—it was God's doing, in order to deliver them up because they worshiped the gods of Edom. 21King Joash of Israel marched up, and he and King Amaziah of Judah confronted each other at Beth-shemesh in Judah. 22The men of Judah were routed by Israel, and they all fled to their homes. 23King Joash of Israel captured Amaziah son of Joash son of Jehoahaz, king of Judah, in Beth-shemesh. He brought him to Jerusalem and made a breach of 400 cubits in the wall of Jerusalem, from the Ephraim Gate to the Corner Gate. 24Then, with all the gold and silver and all the utensils that were to be found in the House of God in the custody of Obed-edom, and with the treasuries of the royal palace, and with the hostages, he returned to Samaria.

25King Amaziah son of Joash of Judah lived fifteen years after the death of King Joash son of Jehoahaz of Israel. 26The other events of Amaziah's reign, early and late, are recorded in the book of the kings of Judah and Israel. 27From the time that Amaziah turned from following the LORD, a conspiracy was formed against him in Jerusalem, and he fled to Lachish; but they sent men after him to Lachish and they put him to death there. 28They brought his body back on horses and buried him with his fathers in the city of Judah.

26 Then all the people of Judah took Uzziah, who was sixteen years old, and proclaimed him king to succeed his father Amaziah. 2It was he who rebuilt Eloth and restored it to Judah after King [Amaziah] slept with his fathers.

3Uzziah was sixteen years old when he became king, and he reigned fifty-two years in Jerusalem; his mother's name was Jecoliah of Jerusalem. 4He did what was pleasing to the LORD just as his father Amaziah had done. 5He applied himself to the worship of God during the time of Zechariah, instructor in the visionsª of God; during the time he worshiped the LORD, God made him prosper. 6He went forth to fight the Philistines, and breached the wall of Gath and the wall of Jabneh and the wall of Ashdod; he built towns in [the region of] Ashdod and among the Philistines. 7God helped him against the Philistines, against the Arabs who lived in Gur-baal, and the Meunites. 8The Ammonites paid tribute to Uzziah, and his fame spread to the approaches of Egypt, for he grew exceedingly strong. 9Uzziah built towers in Jerusalem on the Corner Gate and the Valley Gate and on the Angle, and fortified them. 10He built

---

ª Some Heb. mss. read byr't; compare ancient versions, "fear."

towers in the wilderness and hewed out many cisterns, for he had much cattle, and farmers in the foothills and on the plain, and vine dressers in the mountains and on the fertile lands, for he loved the soil.

¹¹Uzziah had an army of warriors, a battle-ready force who were mustered by Jeiel the scribe and Maaseiah the adjutant under Hananiah, one of the king's officers. ¹²The clan chiefs, valiants, totaled 2,600; ¹³under them was the trained army of 307,500, who made war with might and power to aid the king against the enemy. ¹⁴Uzziah provided them—the whole army—with shields and spears, and helmets and mail, and bows and slingstones. ¹⁵He made clever devices in Jerusalem, set on the towers and the corners, for shooting arrows and large stones. His fame spread far, for he was helped wonderfully, and he became strong.

¹⁶When he was strong, he grew so arrogant he acted corruptly: he trespassed against his God by entering the Temple of the LORD to offer incense on the incense altar. ¹⁷The priest Azariah, with eighty other brave priests of the LORD, followed him in ¹⁸and, confronting King Uzziah, said to him, "It is not for you, Uzziah, to offer incense to the LORD, but for the Aaronite priests, who have been consecrated, to offer incense. Get out of the Sanctuary, for you have trespassed; there will be no glory in it for you from the LORD God." ¹⁹Uzziah, holding the censer and ready to burn incense, got angry; but as he got angry with the priests, leprosy broke out on his forehead in front of the priests in the House of the LORD beside the incense altar. ²⁰When the chief priest Azariah and all the other priests looked at him, his forehead was leprous, so they rushed him out of there; he too made haste to get out, for the LORD had struck him with a plague. ²¹King Uzziah was a leper until the day of his death. He lived in ᵇ⁻isolated quarters⁻ᵇ as a leper, for he was cut off from the House of the LORD—while Jotham his son was in charge of the king's house and governed the people of the land.

²²The other events of Uzziah's reign, early and late, were recorded by the prophet Isaiah son of Amoz. ²³Uzziah slept with his fathers in the burial field of the kings, because, they said, he was a leper; his son Jotham succeeded him as king.

27

Jotham was twenty-five years old when he became king, and he reigned sixteen years in Jerusalem; his mother's name was Jerushah daughter of Zadok. ²He did what was pleasing to the LORD just as his father

---

ᵇ⁻ᵇ *Meaning of Heb. uncertain.*

Uzziah had done, but he did not enter the Temple of the LORD; however, the people still acted corruptly. 3It was he who built the Upper Gate of the House of the LORD; he also built extensively on the wall of Ophel. 4He built towns in the hill country of Judah, and in the woods he built fortresses and towers. 5Moreover, he fought with the king of the Ammonites and overcame them; the Ammonites gave him that year 100 talents of silver and 10,000 *kor* of wheat and another 10,000 of barley; that is what the Ammonites paid him, and [likewise] in the second and third years. 6Jotham was strong because he maintained a faithful course before the LORD his God.

7The other events of Jotham's reign, and all his battles and his conduct, are recorded in the book of the kings of Israel and Judah. 8He was twenty-five years old when he became king, and he reigned sixteen years in Jerusalem. 9Jotham slept with his fathers, and was buried in the City of David; his son Ahaz succeeded him as king.

28

Ahaz was twenty years old when he became king, and he reigned sixteen years in Jerusalem. He did not do what was pleasing to the LORD as his father David had done, 2but followed the ways of the kings of Israel; he even made molten images for the Baals. 3He made offerings in the Valley of Ben-hinnom and burned his sons in fire, in the abhorrent fashion of the nations which the LORD had dispossessed before the Israelites. 4He sacrificed and made offerings at the shrines, on the hills, and under every leafy tree. 5The LORD his God delivered him over to the king of Aram, who defeated him and took many of his men captive, and brought them to Damascus. He was also delivered over to the king of Israel, who inflicted a great defeat on him. 6Pekah son of Remaliah killed 120,000 in Judah—all brave men—in one day, because they had forsaken the LORD God of their fathers. 7Zichri, the champion of Ephraim, killed Maaseiah the king's son, and Azrikam chief of the palace, and Elkanah, the second to the king. 8The Israelites captured 200,000 of their kinsmen, women, boys, and girls; they also took a large amount of booty from them and brought the booty to Samaria.

9A prophet of the LORD by the name of Oded was there, who went out to meet the army on its return to Samaria. He said to them, "Because of the fury of the LORD God of your fathers against Judah, He delivered them over to you, and you killed them in a rage that reached heaven.

¹⁰Do you now intend to subjugate the men and women of Judah and Jerusalem to be your slaves? As it is, you have nothing but offenses against the LORD your God. ¹¹Now then, listen to me, and send back the captives you have taken from your kinsmen, for the wrath of the LORD is upon you!" ¹²Some of the chief men of the Ephraimites—Azariah son of Jehohanan, Berechiah son of Meshillemoth, Jehizkiah son of Shallum, and Amasa son of Hadlai—confronted those returning from the campaign ¹³and said to them, "Do not bring these captives here, for it would mean our offending the LORD, adding to our sins and our offenses; for our offense is grave enough, and there is already wrath upon Israel." ¹⁴So the soldiers released the captives and the booty in the presence of the officers and all the congregation. ¹⁵Then the men named above proceeded to take the captives in hand, and with the booty they clothed all the naked among them—they clothed them and shod them and gave them to eat and drink and anointed them and provided donkeys for all who were failing and brought them to Jericho, the city of palms, back to their kinsmen. Then they returned to Samaria.

¹⁶At that time, King Ahaz sent to the king of Assyria for help. ¹⁷Again the Edomites came and inflicted a defeat on Judah and took captives. ¹⁸And the Philistines made forays against the cities of the Shephelah and the Negeb of Judah; they seized Beth-shemesh and Aijalon and Gederoth, and Soco with its villages, and Timnah with its villages, and Gimzo with its villages; and they settled there. ¹⁹Thus the LORD brought Judah low on account of King Ahaz of Israel,ᵃ for he threw off restraint in Judah and trespassed against the LORD. ²⁰Tillegath-pilneser, king of Assyria, marched against him and gave him trouble, instead of supporting him. ²¹For Ahaz plundered the House of the LORD and the house of the king and the officers, and made a gift to the king of Assyria—to no avail.

²²In his time of trouble, this King Ahaz trespassed even more against the LORD, ²³sacrificing to the gods of Damascus which had defeated him, for he thought, "The gods of the kings of Aram help them; I shall sacrifice to them and they will help me"; but they were his ruin and that of all Israel. ²⁴Ahaz collected the utensils of the House of God, and cut the utensils of the House of God to pieces. He shut the doors of the House of the LORD and made himself altars in every corner of Jerusalem. ²⁵In every town in Judah he set up shrines to make offerings to other gods, vexing the LORD God of his fathers.

²⁶The other events of his reign and all his conduct, early and late, are

---

ᵃ Some mss. and ancient versions read "Judah."

recorded in the book of the kings of Judah and Israel. ²⁷Ahaz slept with his fathers and was buried in the city, in Jerusalem; his body was not brought to the tombs of the kings of Israel. His son Hezekiah succeeded him as king.

29 Hezekiah became king at the age of twenty-five, and he reigned twenty-nine years in Jerusalem; his mother's name was Abijah daughter of Zechariah. ²He did what was pleasing to the LORD, just as his father David had done.

³He, in the first month of the first year of his reign, opened the doors of the House of the LORD and repaired them. ⁴He summoned the priests and the Levites and assembled them in the east square. ⁵He said to them, "Listen to me, Levites! Sanctify yourselves and sanctify the House of the LORD God of your fathers, and take the abhorrent things out of the holy place. ⁶For our fathers trespassed and did what displeased the LORD our God; they forsook Him and turned their faces away from the dwelling-place of the LORD, turning their backs on it. ⁷They also shut the doors of the porch and put out the lights; they did not offer incense and did not make burnt offerings in the holy place to the God of Israel. ⁸The wrath of the LORD was upon Judah and Jerusalem; He made them an object of horror, amazement, and hissing^a as you see with your own eyes. ⁹Our fathers died by the sword, and our sons and daughters and wives are in captivity on account of this. ¹⁰Now I wish to make a covenant with the LORD God of Israel, so that His rage may be withdrawn from us. ¹¹Now, my sons, do not be slack, for the LORD chose you to attend upon Him, to serve Him, to be His ministers and to make offerings to Him."

¹²So the Levites set to—Mahath son of Amasai and Joel son of Azariah of the sons of Kohath; and of the sons of Merari, Kish son of Abdi and Azariah son of Jehallelel; and of the Gershonites, Joah son of Zimmah and Eden son of Joah; ¹³and of the sons of Elizaphan, Shimri and Jeiel; and of the sons of Asaph, Zechariah and Mattaniah; ¹⁴and of the sons of Heman, Jehiel and Shimei; and of the sons of Jeduthun, Shemaiah and Uzziel—¹⁵and, gathering their brothers, they sanctified themselves and came, by a command of the king concerning the LORD's ordinances, to purify the House of the LORD. ¹⁶The priests went into the House of the LORD to purify it, and brought all the unclean things they found in the Temple of the LORD out into the court of the House of the LORD; [there]

ᵃ *See note at Jer. 18.16.*

the Levites received them, to take them outside to Wadi Kidron. [17]They began the sanctification on the first day of the first month; on the eighth day of the month they reached the porch of the LORD. They sanctified the House of the LORD for eight days, and on the sixteenth day of the first month they finished. [18]Then they went into the palace of King Hezekiah and said, "We have purified the whole House of the LORD and the altar of burnt offering and all its utensils, and the table of the bread of display and all its utensils; [19]and all the utensils that King Ahaz had befouled during his reign, when he trespassed, we have made ready and sanctified. They are standing in front of the altar of the LORD."

[20]King Hezekiah rose early, gathered the officers of the city, and went up to the House of the LORD. [21]They brought seven bulls and seven rams and seven lambs and seven he-goats as a sin offering for the kingdom and for the Sanctuary and for Judah. He ordered the Aaronite priests to offer them on the altar of the LORD. [22]The cattle were slaughtered, and the priests received the blood and dashed it against the altar; the rams were slaughtered and the blood was dashed against the altar; the lambs were slaughtered and the blood was dashed against the altar. [23]The he-goats for the sin offering were presented to the king and the congregation, who laid their hands upon them. [24]The priests slaughtered them and performed the purgation rite with the blood against the altar, to expiate for all Israel, for the king had designated the burnt offering and the sin offering to be for all Israel. [25]He stationed the Levites in the House of the LORD with cymbals and harps and lyres, as David and Gad the king's seer and Nathan the prophet had ordained, for the ordinance was by the LORD through His prophets.

[26]When the Levites were in place with the instruments of David, and the priests with their trumpets, [27]Hezekiah gave the order to offer the burnt offering on the altar. When the burnt offering began, the song of the LORD and the trumpets began also, together with the instruments of King David of Israel. [28]All the congregation prostrated themselves, the song was sung and the trumpets were blown—all this until the end of the burnt offering. [29]When the offering was finished, the king and all who were there with him knelt and prostrated themselves. [30]King Hezekiah and the officers ordered the Levites to praise the LORD in the words of David and Asaph the seer; so they praised rapturously, and they bowed and prostrated themselves.

[31]Then Hezekiah said, "Now you have consecrated yourselves to the

LORD; come, bring sacrifices and thanksgiving to the House of the LORD." The congregation brought sacrifices of well-being and thanksgiving, and all who felt so moved brought burnt offerings. 32The number of burnt offerings that the congregation brought was 70 cattle, 100 rams, 200 lambs—all these for burnt offerings to the LORD. 33The sacred offerings were 600 large cattle and 3,000 small cattle. 34The priests were too few to be able to flay all the burnt offerings, so their kinsmen, the Levites, reinforced them till the end of the work, and till the [rest of the] priests sanctified themselves. (The Levites were more conscientious about sanctifying themselves than the priests.) 35For beside the large number of burnt offerings, there were the fat parts of the sacrifices of well-being and the libations for the burnt offerings; so the service of the House of the LORD was properly accomplished. 36Hezekiah and all the people rejoiced over what God had enabled the people to accomplish, because it had happened so suddenly.

30 Hezekiah sent word to all Israel and Judah; he also wrote letters to Ephraim and Manasseh to come to the House of the LORD in Jerusalem to keep the Passover for the LORD God of Israel. 2The king and his officers and the congregation in Jerusalem had agreed to keep the Passover in the second month, 3for at the time, they were unable to keep it,a for not enough priests had sanctified themselves, nor had the people assembled in Jerusalem. 4The king and the whole congregation thought it proper 5to issue a decree and proclaim throughout all Israel from Beer-sheba to Dan that they come and keep the Passover for the LORD God of Israel in Jerusalem—not often did they act in accord with what was written. 6The couriers went out with the letters from the king and his officers through all Israel and Judah, by order of the king, proclaiming, "O you Israelites! Return to the LORD God of your fathers, Abraham, Isaac, and Israel, and He will return to the remnant of you who escaped from the hand of the kings of Assyria. 7Do not be like your fathers and brothers who trespassed against the LORD God of their fathers and He turned them into a horror, as you see. 8Now do not be stiffnecked like your fathers; submit yourselves to the LORD and come to His sanctuary, which He consecrated forever, and serve the LORD your God so that His anger may turn back from you. 9If you return to the LORD, your brothers and children will be regarded with compassion by their captors, and will return

---

a *I.e., on its proper date; cf. Num. 9.1–14.*

to this land; for the LORD your God is gracious and merciful; He will not turn His face from you if you return to Him."

¹⁰As the couriers passed from town to town in the land of Ephraim and Manasseh till they reached Zebulun, they were laughed at and mocked. ¹¹Some of the people of Asher and Manasseh and Zebulun, however, were contrite, and came to Jerusalem. ¹²The hand of God was on Judah, too, making them of a single mind to carry out the command of the king and officers concerning the ordinance of the LORD. ¹³A great crowd assembled at Jerusalem to keep the Feast of Unleavened Bread in the second month, a very great congregation. ¹⁴They set to and removed the altars that were in Jerusalem, and they removed all the incense stands and threw them into Wadi Kidron. ¹⁵They slaughtered the paschal sacrifice on the fourteenth of the second month. The priests and Levites were ashamed, and they sanctified themselves and brought burnt offerings to the House of the LORD. ¹⁶They took their stations, as was their rule according to the Teaching of Moses, man of God. The priests dashed the blood [which they received] from the Levites. ¹⁷Since many in the congregation had not sanctified themselves, the Levites were in charge of slaughtering the paschal sacrifice for everyone who was not clean, so as to consecrate them to the LORD. ¹⁸For most of the people—many from Ephraim and Manasseh, Issachar and Zebulun—had not purified themselves, yet they ate the paschal sacrifice in violation of what was written. Hezekiah prayed for them, saying, "The good LORD will provide atonement for ¹⁹everyone who set his mind on worshiping God, the LORD God of his fathers, even if he is not purified for the sanctuary." ²⁰The LORD heard Hezekiah and healed the people.

²¹The Israelites who were in Jerusalem kept the Feast of Unleavened Bread seven days, with great rejoicing, the Levites and the priests praising the LORD daily with powerful instruments for the LORD. ²²Hezekiah persuaded all the Levites who performed skillfully for the LORD to spend the seven days of the festival making offerings of well-being, and confessing to the LORD God of their fathers. ²³All the congregation resolved to keep seven more days, so they kept seven more days of rejoicing. ²⁴King Hezekiah of Judah contributed to the congregation 1,000 bulls and 7,000 sheep. And the officers contributed to the congregation 1,000 bulls and 10,000 sheep. And the priests sanctified themselves in large numbers. ²⁵All the congregation of Judah and the priests and the Levites and all the congregation that came from Israel, and the resident aliens who came

from the land of Israel and who lived in Judah, rejoiced. [26]There was great rejoicing in Jerusalem, for since the time of King Solomon son of David of Israel nothing like it had happened in Jerusalem. [27]The Levite priests rose and blessed the people, and their voice was heard, and their prayer went up to His holy abode, to heaven.

31

When all this was finished, all Israel who were present went out into the towns of Judah and smashed the pillars, cut down the sacred posts, demolished the shrines and altars throughout Judah and Benjamin, and throughout Ephraim and Manasseh, to the very last one. Then all the Israelites returned to their towns, each to his possession.

[2]Hezekiah reconstituted the divisions of the priests and Levites, each man of the priests and Levites according to his office, for the burnt offerings, the offerings of well-being, to minister, and to sing hymns and praises in the gates of the courts of the LORD; [3]also the king's portion, from his property, for the burnt offerings—the morning and evening burnt offering, and the burnt offerings for sabbaths, and new moons, and festivals, as prescribed in the Teaching of the LORD.

[4]He ordered the people, the inhabitants of Jerusalem, to deliver the portions of the priests and the Levites, so that they might devote themselves to the Teaching of the LORD. [5]When the word spread, the Israelites brought large quantities of grain, wine, oil, honey, and all kinds of agricultural produce, and tithes of all, in large amounts. [6]The men of Israel and Judah living in the towns of Judah—they too brought tithes of cattle and sheep and tithes of sacred things consecrated to the LORD their God, piling them in heaps. [7]In the third month the heaps began to accumulate, and were finished in the seventh month. [8]When Hezekiah and the officers came and saw the heaps, they blessed the LORD and his people Israel. [9]Hezekiah asked the priests and Levites about the heaps. [10]The chief priest Azariah, of the house of Zadok, replied to him, saying, "Ever since the gifts began to be brought to the House of the LORD, people have been eating to satiety and leaving over in great amounts, for the LORD has blessed His people; this huge amount is left over!" [11]Hezekiah then gave orders to prepare store-chambers in the House of the LORD; and they were prepared. [12]They brought in the gifts and the tithes and the sacred things faithfully. Their supervisor was Conaniah the Levite, and Shimei his brother was second in rank. [13]Jehiel and Azariah and Nahath

and Asahel and Jerimoth and Jozabad and Eliel and Ismachiah and Mahath and Benaiah were commissioners under Conaniah and Shimei his brother by appointment of King Hezekiah; Azariah was supervisor of the House of God. ¹⁴Kore son of Imnah the Levite, the keeper of the East Gate, was in charge of the freewill offerings to God, of the allocation of gifts to the LORD, and the most sacred things. ¹⁵Under him were Eden, Miniamin, Jeshua, Shemaiah, Amariah, and Shecaniah, in offices of trust in the priestly towns, making allocation to their brothers by divisions, to great and small alike; ¹⁶besides allocating their daily rations to those males registered by families from three years old and up, all who entered the House of the LORD according to their service and their shift by division; ¹⁷and in charge of the registry of priests by clans, and of the Levites, from twenty years old and up, by shifts, in their divisions; ¹⁸and the registry of the dependents of their whole company—wives, sons, and daughters— for, relying upon them, they sanctified themselves in holiness. ¹⁹And for the Aaronite priests, in each and every one of their towns with adjoining fields, the above-named men were to allocate portions to every male of the priests and to every registered Levite. ²⁰Hezekiah did this throughout Judah. He acted in a way that was good, upright, and faithful before the LORD his God. ²¹Every work he undertook in the service of the House of God or in the Teaching and the Commandment, to worship his God, he did with all his heart; and he prospered.

32

ᵃAfter these faithful deeds, King Sennacherib of Assyria invaded Judah and encamped against its fortified towns with the aim of taking them over. ²When Hezekiah saw that Sennacherib had come, intent on making war against Jerusalem, ³he consulted with his officers and warriors about stopping the flow of the springs outside the city, and they supported him. ⁴A large force was assembled to stop up all the springs and the wadi that flowed through the land, for otherwise, they thought, the king of Assyria would come and find water in abundance. ⁵He acted with vigor, rebuilding the whole breached wall, raising towers on it, and building another wall outside it. He fortified the Millo of the City of David, and made a great quantity of arms and shields. ⁶He appointed battle officers over the people; then, gathering them to him in the square of the city gate, he rallied them, saying, ⁷"Be strong and of good courage; do not be frightened or dismayed by the king of Assyria or by the horde that is

ᵃ *Cf. 2 Kings 18–20; Isa. 36–39.*

with him, for we have more with us than he has with him. ⁸With him is an arm of flesh, but with us is the LORD our God, to help us and to fight our battles." The people were encouraged by the speech of King Hezekiah of Judah.

⁹Afterward, King Sennacherib of Assyria sent his officers to Jerusalem—he and all his staff being at Lachish—with this message to King Hezekiah of Judah and to all the people of Judah who were in Jerusalem: ¹⁰"Thus said King Sennacherib of Assyria: On what do you trust to enable you to endure a siege in Jerusalem? ¹¹Hezekiah is seducing you to a death of hunger and thirst, saying, 'The LORD our God will save us from the king of Assyria.' ¹²But is not Hezekiah the one who removed His shrines and His altars and commanded the people of Judah and Jerusalem saying, 'Before this one altar you shall prostrate yourselves, and upon it make your burnt offerings'? ¹³Surely you know what I and my fathers have done to the peoples of the lands? Were the gods of the nations of the lands able to save their lands from me? ¹⁴Which of all the gods of any of those nations whom my fathers destroyed was able to save his people from me, that your God should be able to save you from me? ¹⁵Now then, do not let Hezekiah delude you; do not let him seduce you in this way; do not believe him. For no god of any nation or kingdom has been able to save his people from me or from my fathers—much less your God, to save you from me!" ¹⁶His officers said still more things against the LORD God and against His servant Hezekiah. ¹⁷He also wrote letters reviling the LORD God of Israel, saying of Him, "Just as the gods of the other nations of the earth did not save their people from me, so the God of Hezekiah will not save his people from me." ¹⁸They called loudly in the language of Judah to the people of Jerusalem who were on the wall, to frighten them into panic, so as to capture the city. ¹⁹They spoke of the God of Jerusalem as though He were like the gods of the other peoples of the earth, made by human hands. ²⁰Then King Hezekiah and the prophet Isaiah son of Amoz prayed about this, and cried out to heaven.

²¹The LORD sent an angel who annihilated every mighty warrior, commander, and officer in the army of the king of Assyria, and he returned in disgrace to his land. He entered the house of his god, and there some of his own offspring struck him down by the sword. ²²Thus the LORD delivered Hezekiah and the inhabitants of Jerusalem from King Sennacherib of Assyria, and from everyone; He provided for them on all sides.

23Many brought tribute to the LORD to Jerusalem, and gifts to King Hezekiah of Judah; thereafter he was exalted in the eyes of all the nations. 24At that time, Hezekiah fell deathly sick. He prayed to the LORD, who responded to him and gave him a sign. 25Hezekiah made no return for what had been bestowed upon him, for he grew arrogant; so wrath was decreed for him and for Judah and Jerusalem. 26Then Hezekiah humbled himself where he had been arrogant, he and the inhabitants of Jerusalem, and no wrath of the LORD came on them during the reign of Hezekiah. 27Hezekiah enjoyed riches and glory in abundance; he filled treasuries with silver and gold, precious stones, spices, shields, and all lovely objects; 28and store-cities with the produce of grain, wine, and oil, and stalls for all kinds of beasts, and flocks for sheepfolds. 29And he acquired towns, and flocks of small and large cattle in great number, for God endowed him with very many possessions. 30It was Hezekiah who stopped up the spring of water of Upper Gihon, leading it downward west of the City of David; Hezekiah prospered in all that he did. 31So too in the matter of the ambassadors of the princes of Babylon, who were sent to him to inquire about the sign that was in the land, when God forsook him in order to test him, to learn all that was in his mind.

32The other events of Hezekiah's reign, and his faithful acts, are recorded in the visions of the prophet Isaiah son of Amoz and in the book of the kings of Judah and Israel. 33Hezekiah slept with his fathers, and was buried on the upper part of the tombs of the sons of David. When he died, all the people of Judah and the inhabitants of Jerusalem accorded him much honor. Manasseh, his son, succeeded him.

33 aManasseh was twelve years old when he became king, and he reigned fifty-five years in Jerusalem. 2He did what was displeasing to the LORD, following the abhorrent practices of the nations that the LORD had dispossessed before the Israelites. 3He rebuilt the shrines that his father Hezekiah had demolished; he erected altars for the Baals and made sacred posts. He bowed down to all the host of heaven and worshiped them, 4and he built altars [to them] in the House of the LORD, of which the LORD had said, "My name will be in Jerusalem forever." 5He built altars for all the host of heaven in the two courts of the House of the LORD. 6He consigned his sons to the fire in the Valley of Ben-hinnom,

a Cf. 2 Kings 21.

and he practiced soothsaying, divination, and sorcery, and consulted ghosts and familiar spirits; he did much that was displeasing to the LORD in order to vex Him. 7He placed a sculptured image that he made in the House of God, of which God had said to David and to his son Solomon, "In this House and in Jerusalem, which I chose out of all the tribes of Israel, I will establish My name forever. 8And I will never again remove the feet of Israel from the land that I assigned to their fathers, if only they observe faithfully all that I have commanded them—all the teaching and the laws and the rules given by Moses." 9Manasseh led Judah and the inhabitants of Jerusalem astray into evil greater than that done by the nations that the LORD had destroyed before the Israelites.

10The LORD spoke to Manasseh and his people, but they would not pay heed, 11so the LORD brought against them the officers of the army of the king of Assyria, who took Manasseh captive in manacles, bound him in fetters, and led him off to Babylon. 12In his distress, he entreated the LORD his God and humbled himself greatly before the God of his fathers. 13He prayed to Him, and He granted his prayer, heard his plea, and returned him to Jerusalem to his kingdom. Then Manasseh knew that the LORD alone was God. 14Afterward he built the outer wall of the City of David west of Gihon in the wadi on the way to the Fish Gate, and it encircled Ophel; he raised it very high. He also placed army officers in all the fortified towns of Judah. 15He removed the foreign gods and the image from the House of the LORD, as well as all the altars that he had built on the Mount of the House of the LORD and in Jerusalem, and dumped them outside the city. 16He rebuilt the altar of the LORD and offered on it sacrifices of well-being and thanksgiving, and commanded the people of Judah to worship the LORD God of Israel. 17To be sure, the people continued sacrificing at the shrines, but only to the LORD their God.

18The other events of Manasseh's reign, and his prayer to his God, and the words of the seers who spoke to him in the name of the LORD God of Israel are found in the chronicles of the kings of Israel. 19His prayer and how it was granted to him, the whole account of his sin and trespass, and the places in which he built shrines and installed sacred posts and images before he humbled himself are recorded in the words of Hozai.b 20Manasseh slept with his fathers and was buried on his palace grounds; his son Amon succeeded him as king.

21Amon was twenty-two years old when he became king, and he reigned

b Or "seers."

two years in Jerusalem. ²²He did what was displeasing to the LORD, as his father Manasseh had done. Amon sacrificed to all the idols that his father Manasseh had made and worshiped them. ²³He did not humble himself before the LORD, as his father Manasseh had humbled himself; instead, Amon incurred much guilt. ²⁴His courtiers conspired against him and killed him in his palace. ²⁵But the people of the land struck down all who had conspired against King Amon; and the people of the land made his son Josiah king in his stead.

34
ªJosiah was eight years old when he became king, and he reigned thirty-one years in Jerusalem. ²He did what was pleasing to the LORD, following the ways of his father David without deviating to the right or to the left. ³In the eighth year of his reign, while he was still young, he began to seek the God of his father David, and in the twelfth year he began to purge Judah and Jerusalem of the shrines, the sacred posts, the idols, and the molten images. ⁴At his bidding, they demolished the altars of the Baals, and he had the incense stands above them cut down; he smashed the sacred posts, the idols, and the images, ground them into dust, and strewed it onto the graves of those who had sacrificed to them. ⁵He burned the bones of priests on their altars and purged Judah and Jerusalem. ⁶In the towns of Manasseh and Ephraim and Simeon, as far as Naphtali, [lying] in ruins on every side, ⁷he demolished the altars and the sacred posts and smashed the idols and ground them into dust; and he hewed down all the incense stands throughout the land of Israel. Then he returned to Jerusalem.

⁸In the eighteenth year of his reign, after purging the land and the House, he commissioned Shaphan son of Azaliah, Maaseiah the governor of the city, and Joah son of Joahaz the recorder to repair the House of the LORD his God. ⁹They came to the high priest Hilkiah and delivered to him the silver brought to the House of God, which the Levites, the guards of the threshold, had collected from Manasseh and Ephraim and from all the remnant of Israel and from all Judah and Benjamin and ᵇ⁻the inhabitants of Jerusalem.⁻ᵇ ¹⁰They delivered it into the custody of the overseers who were in charge at the House of the LORD, and the overseers who worked in the House of the LORD spent it on examining and repairing the House. ¹¹They paid it out to the artisans and the masons to buy quarried stone and wood for the couplings and for making roof-

---

ª Cf. 2 Kings 22; 23.1–20.
ᵇ⁻ᵇ With kethib and ancient versions; qere, "they returned to Jerusalem."

beams for the buildings that the kings of Judah had allowed to fall into ruin. 12The men did the work honestly; over them were appointed the Levites Jahath and Obadiah, of the sons of Merari, and Zechariah and Meshullam, of the sons of Kohath, to supervise; while other Levites, all the master musicians, 13were over the porters, supervising all who worked at each and every task; some of the Levites were scribes and officials and gatekeepers.

14As they took out the silver that had been brought to the House of the LORD, the priest Hilkiah found a scroll of the LORD's Teaching given by Moses. 15Hilkiah spoke up and said to the scribe Shaphan, "I have found a scroll of the Teaching in the House of the LORD"; and Hilkiah gave the scroll to Shaphan. 16Shaphan brought the scroll to the king and also reported to the king, "All that was entrusted to your servants is being done; 17they have melted down the silver that was found in the House of the LORD and delivered it to those who were in charge, to the overseers." 18The scribe Shaphan also told the king, "The priest Hilkiah has given me a scroll"; and Shaphan read from it to the king. 19When the king heard the words of the Teaching, he tore his clothes. 20The king gave orders to Hilkiah, and Ahikam son of Shaphan, and Abdon son of Micah, and the scribe Shaphan, and Asaiah the king's minister, saying, 21"Go, inquire of the LORD on my behalf and on behalf of those who remain in Israel and Judah concerning the words of the scroll that has been found, for great indeed must be the wrath of the LORD that has been poured down upon us because our fathers did not obey the word of the LORD and do all that is written in this scroll."

22Hilkiah and those whom the king [had ordered] went to the prophetess Huldah, wife of Shallum son of Tokhath son of Hasrah, keeper of the wardrobe, who was living in Jerusalem in the Mishneh,c and spoke to her accordingly. 23She responded to them: "Thus said the LORD God of Israel: Say to the man who sent you to Me, 24'Thus said the LORD: I am going to bring disaster upon this place and its inhabitants—all the curses that are written in the scroll that was read to the king of Judah— 25because they forsook Me and made offerings to other gods in order to vex Me with all the works of their hands; My wrath shall be poured out against this place and not be quenched.' 26But say this to the king of Judah who sent you to inquire of the LORD: 'Thus said the LORD God of Israel: As for the words which you have heard, 27since your heart was softened and you humbled yourself before God when you heard His

c A quarter in Jerusalem; cf. Zeph. 1.10.

1620

words concerning this place and its inhabitants, and you humbled yourself before Me and tore your clothes and wept before Me, I for My part have listened, declares the LORD. [28] Assuredly, I will gather you to your fathers, and you will be laid in your grave in peace; your eyes shall see nothing of the disaster that I will bring upon this place and its inhabitants.' " They reported this back to the king.

[29] Then the king sent word and assembled all the elders of Judah and Jerusalem. [30] The king went up to the House of the LORD with all the men of Judah and the inhabitants of Jerusalem and the priests and the Levites—all the people, young and old—and he read to them the entire text of the covenant scroll that was found in the House of the LORD. [31] The king stood in his place and solemnized the covenant before the LORD: to follow the LORD and observe His commandments, His injunctions, and His laws with all his heart and soul, to fulfill all the terms of the covenant written in this scroll. [32] He obligated all the men of Jerusalem and Benjamin who were present; and the inhabitants of Jerusalem acted in accord with the Covenant of God, God of their fathers. [33] Josiah removed all the abominations from the whole territory of the Israelites and obliged all who were in Israel to worship the LORD their God. Throughout his reign they did not deviate from following the LORD God of their fathers.

35

[a] Josiah kept the Passover for the LORD in Jerusalem; the passover sacrifice was slaughtered on the fourteenth day of the first month. [2] He reinstated the priests in their shifts and rallied them to the service of the House of the LORD. [3] He said to the Levites, consecrated to the LORD, who taught all Israel, "Put the Holy Ark in the House that Solomon son of David, king of Israel, built; as you no longer carry it on your shoulders, see now to the service of the LORD your God and His people Israel, [4] and dispose yourselves by clans according to your divisions, as prescribed in the writing of King David of Israel and in the document of his son Solomon, [5] and attend in the Sanctuary, by clan divisions, on your kinsmen, the people—by clan divisions of the Levites. [6] Having sanctified yourselves, slaughter the passover sacrifice and prepare it for your kinsmen, according to the word of God given by Moses." [7] Josiah donated to the people small cattle—lambs and goats, all for passover sacrifices for all present—to the sum of 30,000, and large cattle, 3,000—these from the

a *Cf. 2 Kings 23.21–30.*

property of the king. 8His officers gave a freewill offering to the people, to the priests, and to the Levites. Hilkiah and Zechariah and Jehiel, the chiefs of the House of God, donated to the priests for passover sacrifices 2,600 [small cattle] and 300 large cattle. 9Conaniah, Shemaiah, and Nethanel, his brothers, and Hashabiah and Jeiel and Jozabad, officers of the Levites, donated 5,000 [small cattle] and 500 large cattle to the Levites for passover sacrifices.

10The service was arranged well: the priests stood at their posts and the Levites in their divisions, by the king's command. 11They slaughtered the passover sacrifice and the priests [received its blood] from them and dashed it, while the Levites flayed the animals. 12They removed the parts to be burnt, distributing them to divisions of the people by clans, and making the sacrifices to the LORD, as prescribed in the scroll of Moses; they did the same for the cattle. 13They roasted the passover sacrifice in fire, as prescribed, while the sacred offerings they cooked in pots, cauldrons, and pans, and conveyed them with dispatch to all the people. 14Afterward they provided for themselves and the priests, for the Aaronite priests were busy offering the burnt offerings and the fatty parts until nightfall, so the Levites provided both for themselves and for the Aaronite priests. 15The Asaphite singers were at their stations, by command of David and Asaph and Heman and Jeduthun, the seer of the king; and the gatekeepers were at each and every gate. They did not have to leave their tasks, because their Levite brothers provided for them. 16The entire service of the LORD was arranged well that day, to keep the Passover and to make the burnt offerings on the altar of the LORD, according to the command of King Josiah. 17All the Israelites present kept the Passover at that time, and the Feast of Unleavened Bread for seven days. 18Since the time of the prophet Samuel, no Passover like that one had ever been kept in Israel; none of the kings of Israel had kept a Passover like the one kept by Josiah and the priests and the Levites and all Judah and Israel there present and the inhabitants of Jerusalem. 19That Passover was kept in the eighteenth year of the reign of Josiah.

20After all this furbishing of the Temple by Josiah, King Necho of Egypt came up to fight at Carchemish on the Euphrates, and Josiah went out against him. 21[Necho] sent messengers to him, saying, "What have I to do with you, king of Judah? I do not march against you this day but against the kingdom that wars with me, and it is God's will that I hurry. Refrain, then, from interfering with God who is with me, that He not destroy you." ²²But Josiah would not let him alone; instead, ᵇ⁻he donned [his armor]⁻ᵇ to fight him, heedless of Necho's words from the mouth of God; and he came to fight in the plain of Megiddo. ²³Archers shot King Josiah, and the king said to his servants, "Get me away from here, for I am badly wounded." ²⁴His servants carried him out of his chariot and put him in the wagon of his second-in-command, and conveyed him to Jerusalem. There he died, and was buried in the grave of his fathers, and all Judah and Jerusalem went into mourning over Josiah. ²⁵Jeremiah composed laments for Josiah which all the singers, male and female, recited in their laments for Josiah, as is done to this day; they became customary in Israel and were incorporated into the laments. ²⁶The other events of Josiah's reign and his faithful deeds, in accord with the Teaching of the LORD, ²⁷and his acts, early and late, are recorded in the book of the kings of Israel and Judah.

36

ᵃThe people of the land took Jehoahaz son of Josiah and made him king instead of his father in Jerusalem. ²Jehoahaz was twenty-three years old when he became king and he reigned three months in Jerusalem. ³The king of Egypt deposed him in Jerusalem and laid a fine on the land of 100 silver talents and one gold talent. ⁴The king of Egypt made his brother Eliakim king over Judah and Jerusalem, and changed his name to Jehoiakim; Necho took his brother Joahaz and brought him to Egypt.

⁵Jehoiakim was twenty-five years old when he became king, and he reigned eleven years in Jerusalem; he did what was displeasing to the LORD his God. ⁶King Nebuchadnezzar of Babylon marched against him; he bound him in fetters to convey him to Babylon. ⁷Nebuchadnezzar also brought some vessels of the House of the LORD to Babylon, and set them in his palace in Babylon. ⁸The other events of Jehoiakim's reign, and the abominable things he did, and what was found against him, are recorded in the book of the kings of Israel and Judah. His son Jehoiachin succeeded him as king.

⁹Jehoiachin was eight years old when he became king, and he reigned three months and ten days in Jerusalem; he did what was displeasing to the LORD. ¹⁰At the turn of the year, King Nebuchadnezzar sent to have him brought to Babylon with the precious vessels of the House of the LORD, and he made his kinsman Zedekiah king over Judah and Jerusalem.

¹¹Zedekiah was twenty-one years old when he became king, and he

ᵇ⁻ᵇ *With Targum.*

ᵃ *With vv. 1–13, cf. 2 Kings 23.28–37; 24.1–20.*

reigned eleven years in Jerusalem. 12He did what was displeasing to the LORD his God; he did not humble himself before the prophet Jeremiah, who spoke for the LORD. 13He also rebelled against Nebuchadnezzar, who made him take an oathᵇ by God; he stiffened his neck and hardened his heart so as not to turn to the LORD God of Israel. 14All the officers of the priests and the people committed many trespasses, following all the abominable practices of the nations. They polluted the House of the LORD, which He had consecrated in Jerusalem. 15The LORD God of their fathers had sent word to them through His messengers daily without fail, for He had pity on His people and His dwelling-place. 16But they mocked the messengers of God and disdained His words and taunted His prophets until the wrath of the LORD against His people grew beyond remedy. 17He therefore brought the king of the Chaldeans upon them, who killed their youths by the sword in their sanctuary; He did not spare youth, maiden, elder, or graybeard, but delivered all into his hands. 18All the vessels of the House of God, large and small, and the treasures of the House of the LORD and the treasures of the king and his officers were all brought to Babylon. 19They burned the House of God and tore down the wall of Jerusalem, burned down all its mansions, and consigned all its precious objects to destruction. 20Those who survived the sword he exiled to Babylon, and they became his and his sons' servants till the rise of the Persian kingdom, 21in fulfillment of the word of the LORD spoken by Jeremiah, until the land paid back its sabbaths; as long as it lay desolate it kept sabbath, till seventy years were completed.

22And in the first year of King Cyrus of Persia, when the word of the LORD spoken by Jeremiah was fulfilled, the LORD roused the spirit of King Cyrus of Persia to issue a proclamation throughout his realm by word of mouth and in writing, as follows: 23"Thus said King Cyrus of Persia: The LORD God of Heaven has given me all the kingdoms of the earth, and has charged me with building Him a House in Jerusalem, which is in Judah. Any one of you of all His people, the LORD his God be with him and let him go up."

ᵇ *Viz., a vassal oath.*